Street by Street

WEST MID  S

PLUS BROMSGROVE, CANNOCK, KIDDERMINSTER, LICHFIELD, NUNEATON, REDDITCH, ROYAL LEAMINGTON SPA, RUGBY, TAMWORTH, WARWICK

Enlarged Areas Birmingham, Coventry, Walsall, Wolverhampton

2nd edition November 2003
© Automobile Association Developments Limited 2003

Original edition printed May 2001

Ordnance Survey® This product includes map data licensed from Ordnance Survey ® with the permission of the Controller of Her Majesty's Stationery Office.
© Crown copyright 2003.
All rights reserved. Licence number 399221.

Published by AA Publishing (a trading name of Automobile Association Developments Limited, whose registered office is Millstream, Maidenhead Road, Windsor, Berkshire SL4 5GD. Registered number 1878835).

Mapping produced by the Cartography Department of The Automobile Association. (A01723)

A CIP Catalogue record for this book is available from the British Library.

Printed in Italy by Printer Trento srl.

The contents of this atlas are believed to be correct at the time of the latest revision. However, the publishers cannot be held responsible for loss occasioned to any person acting or refraining from action as a result of any material in this atlas, nor for any errors, omissions or changes in such material. This does not affect your statutory rights. The publishers would welcome information to correct any errors or omissions and to keep this atlas up to date. Please write to Publishing, The Automobile Association, Fanum House (FH17), Basing View, Basingstoke, Hampshire, RG21 4EA.

Ref: MX035z

Key to map pages	ii-iii
Key to map symbols	iv–1
Enlarged map pages	2-9
Main map pages	10-207
Index – towns & villages	208–209
Index – streets	210-262
Index – featured places	262-272
Acknowledgements	272

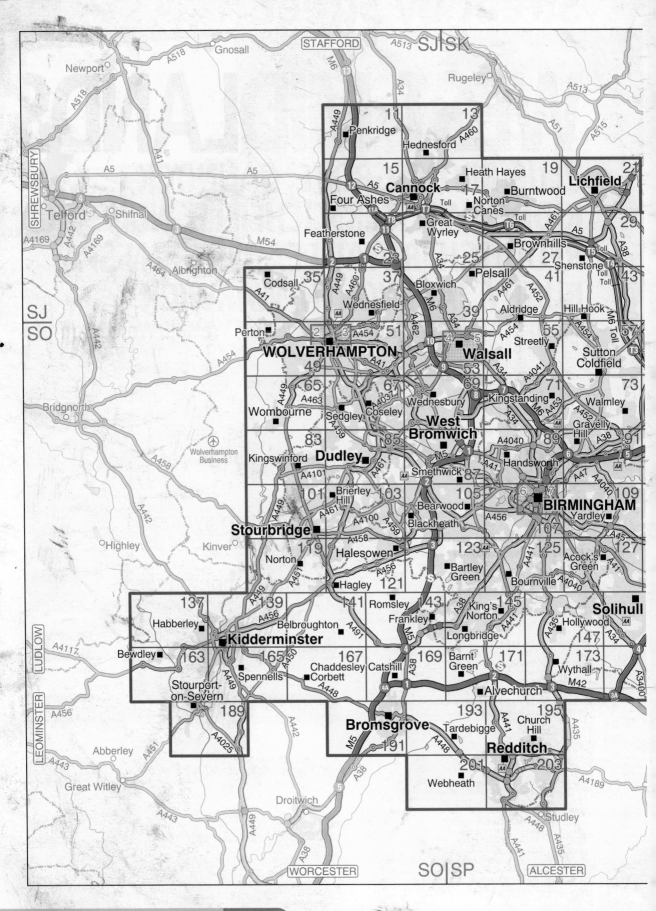

Scale of enlarged map pages **1:10,000** 6.3 inches to 1 mile

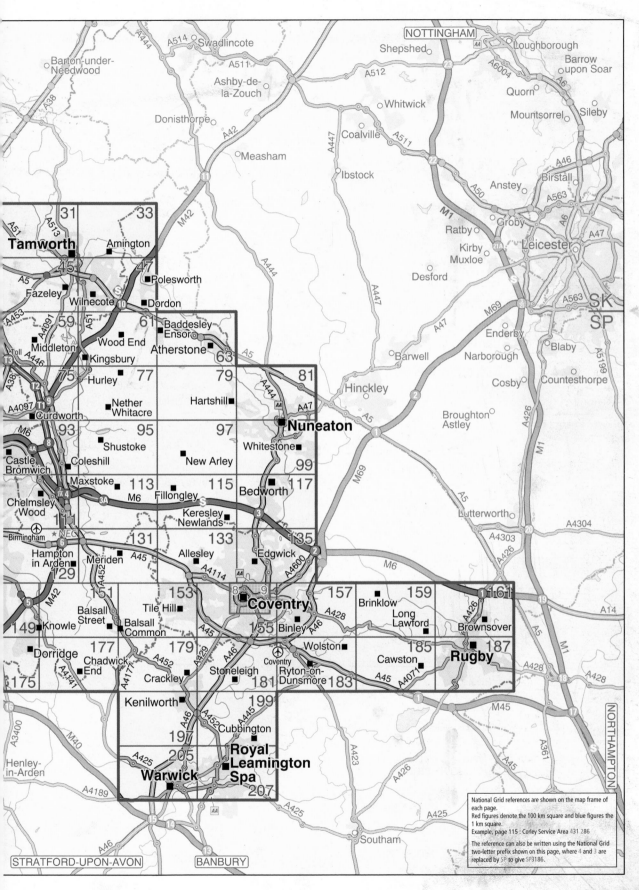

National Grid references are shown on the map frame of each page.
Red figures denote the 100 km square and blue figures the 1 km square.
Example, page 115 : Corley Service Area 431 286

The reference can also be written using the National Grid two-letter prefix shown on this page, where 4 and 3 are replaced by SP to give SP3186.

3.6 inches to 1 mile   **Scale of main map pages 1:17,500**

	Motorway/Toll Motorway		Light railway & station
Junction 9	Motorway junction	++++++++++	Preserved private railway
Services	Motorway service area	LC	Level crossing
	Primary road single/dual carriageway	•—•—•—•—	Tramway
Services	Primary road service area	- - - - - - -	Ferry route
	A road single/dual carriageway	....	Airport runway
	B road single/dual carriageway	— · — · — · —	County, administrative boundary
	Other road single/dual carriageway	ꜰꜰꜰꜰꜰꜰꜰ	Mounds
	Minor/private road, access may be restricted	93	Page continuation 1:17,500
← ←	One-way street	7	Page continuation to enlarged scale 1:10,000
	Pedestrian area		River/canal, lake
- - - - - - -	Track or footpath		Aqueduct, lock, weir
▮▮▮▮▮▮	Road under construction	465 ▲ Winter Hill	Peak (with height in metres)
⌐ - - - = ⌐	Road tunnel		Beach
AA	AA Service Centre		Woodland
P	Parking		Park
P+🚃	Park & Ride		Cemetery
🚌	Bus/coach station		Built-up area
	Railway & main railway station		Featured building
	Railway & minor railway station	ꞁꞁꞁꞁꞁ	City wall
⊖	Underground station		

A&E   Hospital with 24-hour A&E department

PO   Post Office

Public library

Tourist Information Centre

Seasonal Tourist Information Centre

Petrol station, 24 hour
Major suppliers only

Church/chapel

Public toilets

Toilet with disabled facilities

PH   Public house
AA recommended

Restaurant
AA inspected

Madeira Hotel   Hotel
AA inspected

Theatre or performing arts centre

Cinema

Golf course

Camping
AA inspected

Caravan site
AA inspected

Camping & caravan site
AA inspected

Theme park

Abbey, cathedral or priory

Castle

Historic house or building

Wakehurst Place NT   National Trust property

Museum or art gallery

Roman antiquity

Ancient site, battlefield or monument

Industrial interest

Garden

Garden Centre
Garden Centre Association Member

Garden Centre
Wyevale Garden Centre

Arboretum

Farm or animal centre

Zoological or wildlife collection

Bird collection

Nature reserve

Aquarium

Visitor or heritage centre

Country park

Cave

Windmill

Distillery, brewery or vineyard

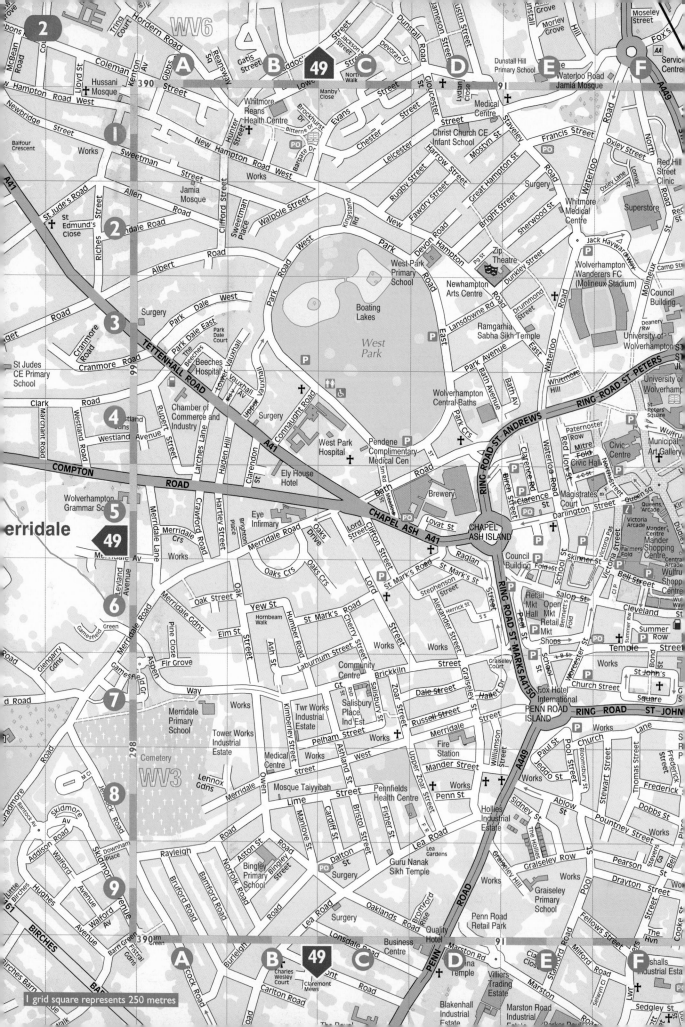

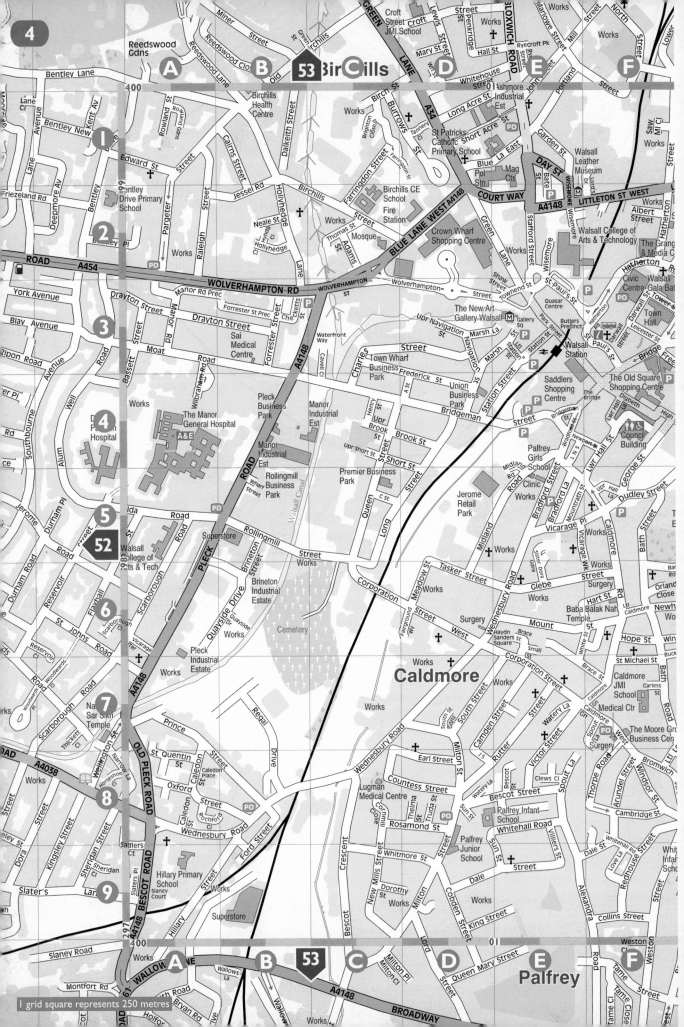

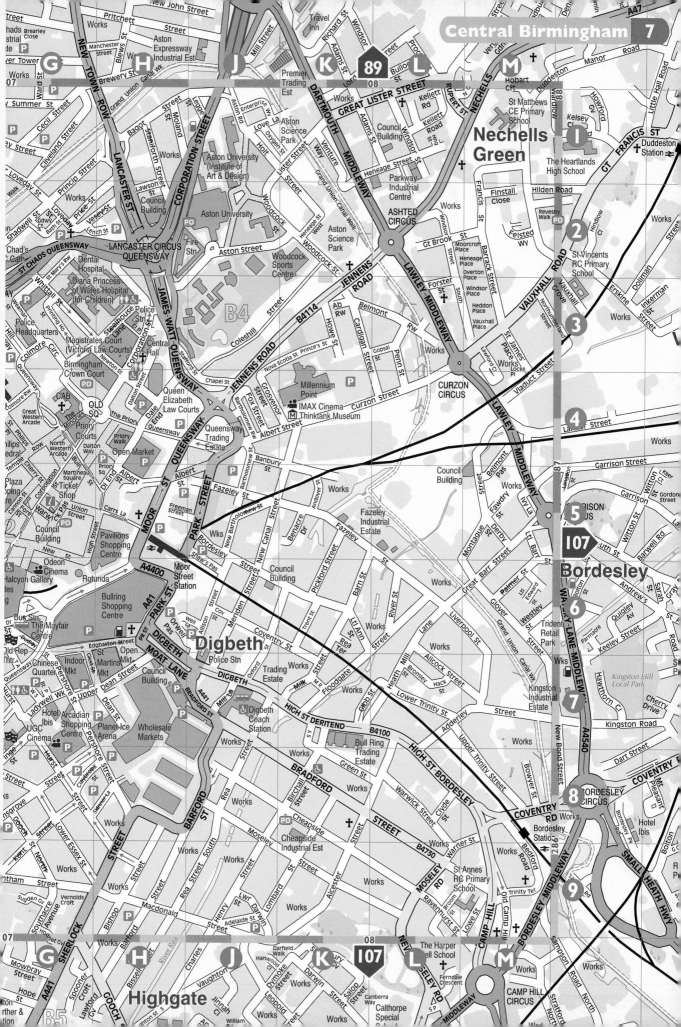

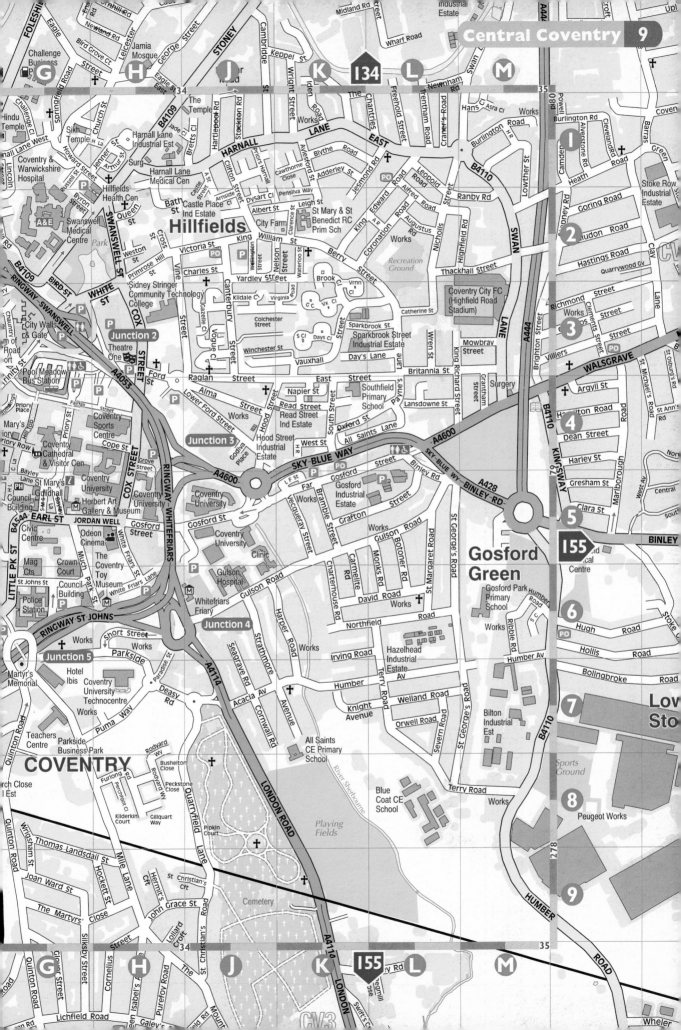

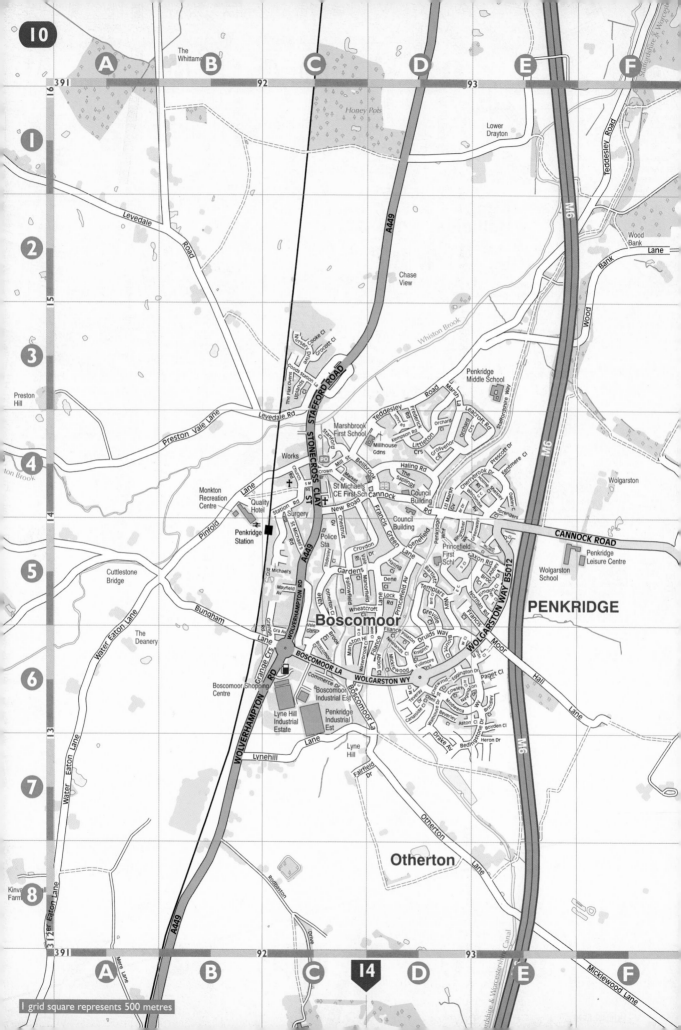

G H J K L M

Staffordshire

Teddesley Home Farm

Teddesley Park

Teddesley Park

Coppice Farm

Pottal Valley

Keepers Lodge

Bangley Park

Newtown

Yewtree Farm

Pottal Pool Road

A34

Quarry Heath

CANNOCK ROAD

Newlands Wood

Littleton Dr

Business Park

B5012

Pillaton

Industrial Estate

Gravel La

Gravel La

Mansty Farm

Mansty Wood

B5012

Horsemoor Wood

Cocksparrow Lane

G H J **15** K L M

G   H   J   I1   K   L   M

95   96   97

I

2

CA

3

NEW PENKRIDG

4

16

5

6

7

8

Horsemoor
Wood

Micklewood
Micklewood Lane

Fullmoor
Wood

Fullmoor
Lodge

Cocksparrow Lane

Parkside Lane

B5012

Parkside Lane

Church Road

Hatherton

Hatherton

Gorsey

Chaseley Av
Pasture Ga
Rowen Rd
Downesway
Bel
Orchard Rd
Shield
Cft
Chaseley
Cft

The
Kilmore

Holder Drive
Dursley
Dr
Shoal Hill Cl
Adamson
Cl
Gowland
Dr
Hatherton
Cft
Sherbrook
Cl
Foxholt
Crs

Boyden Cl

Sandy
Lane

Hatton Rd
Sunfield Rd
Sunfield Rd
Waverley
Gv
Alton
Gv

Dorchester Rd
Br Grn
Barnwood
Rd

Meriden
Close
Exeter
Road
Hazlemere
Grove
Kendal
Cl
Bideford Way
Reading
Place
Surger

Berwick
Dr
Filey
Close
Whitby
Wy
Lo
Pri
Sc
Birch

Langford

Leamington Drive

ASCOT
Ullesmere
Rd Gv
Redcar
Cl
Spurlings
Carlisle Rd
Cl
Skipton
Pl
Langdale
Skipton
Dr
PR
Oaks Dr
Elms
Dr
Surger

Wellington
Conway Rd

Four Crosses

Oak
Farm

Poplar
Lane

Church Lane

A5

Calley Lea Lane

Oak Lane

Oak Lane

Catsbridge Lane

Four Crosses Lane

Lane

Wood Lane

Great Saredon

Works

House
Lane

M6

Saredon
Hall Farm

WATLING STREET

A5

Travel Inn

Roman Way
Hotel

AVON ROAD

Avon
Busine
Park

4601

Wolverhampton Road

AA
Service
Centre

Linkway
Retail
Park

WATLIN

Wedge's
Mills

Hall
Meadow

Woodhaven

WOLVERHAMPTON ROAD

A460

60

308

Junction 11A

95   96   97

Windy
Arbour
Lane

**Middle
Hill**

M6 TOLL

South S
Busine

Windy Arbour
Lane

G H J K L M

13 14 15

WS13

Curborough

Curborough House

Business Park

Wellington Crescent

Wood End Lane

Lancaster

A38

Bears Farm

Watery Lane

Norwich Close

Ringway Industrial Estate

Trent Valley Trading Estate

Lincoln Close

Shepherd Cl

Charnwood County Primary Sch

Samuel Close

York Close

Chester Rd

Brownsfields Farm

Nether Stowe

Streethay

Netherstowe Lane

Spring Rd

Walkers Croft

Netherstowe

Stowecroft

Verdi Court

Gilbert Road

Fecknam Way

Johnson Close

Hermes Works Road

A38

Stowe

EASTERN AVENUE A5192

Brownsfield Road

Scotch Orchard

Furnival Rd

Vulcan Road

Lichfield Business Centre

Scotch Orchard County Primary School

BURTON ROAD

Burton Old Road

Hill Farm

Cemetery

St Chad's Road

Wissage Croft

Wissage Road

Benson Cl

Covey Close

Mallicot Close

Wissage Lane

Manley Rd

Hob's Road

TRENT VALLEY RD

A5127

Works

Cross Keys

Rd

0

10

Stowe Pool

Partridge Cft

Lime Gr School

Drake Croft

Smithfield

Mallard Croft

St Michael Road

Wissage Road

Rocklands Special Sch

St Chads CE (VC) Primary School

Valley Lane

Ash

Rwen Cl

Crossfield Industrial Est

Lichfield Trent Valley Station

Burton Old Rd

Britannia Way

Frank Halfpenny Hall

Works

Lime Grove

Enterprise Industrial Park

Europa Way

Europa

Greenhill Mews

CHURCH ST

Health Cen

Laurel

Wissage Court

Bich Rd

Burton

Old Road West

The Crossings

Burton Cl

Saddlers

Gorsty Bk

CAPPERS

LANE

Werherbridge

Prospect Drive

Coppice Grove

The Pines

09

Capper's Lane

Levetts

CAB

Stations Rd

Rotten Rw

Deans Crt

St Michaels CE Primary School

Sturgeon's

Hndrs Cl

Hawkesmoor Drive

Bluebird

SpearHill

Yew Tree Av

Lewis Close

Cornfield Dr

Austin

Cote La

Maple Grove

Cedar Close

Walnut Grove

Amb Stn

Mesnes Green Industrial Est

St Josephs RC Primary School

Oakhurst

Orchard

Roman

Way Vale Cl

Boley

Epsom Gr

Ascot Cl

Hatherford Av

Bloomsbury

Lawford Av

Birchwood Road

Curlew

Willowtree

Superstore

PO

Boley Park

Cherry

Elm

Cdne

Hazel Grove

Manor Rise

Broad

Filton

Richmond

Baskeyfield Cl

Coltman Close

Haymoor

Warren Close

Boley Cottage La

Heritage Court

Sheriffs

Gable Croft

Tudor Cl

Beech Gdns

Saxon Hill Special School

The Brambles

Terrance Cl

Mawgan Drive

Pentire Road

Honiwell Rise

Cross

Tregon

Heritage

Balmoral

Darnford Lane

The Spires

Freeford Gdns

Darnford Moors

King Edward VI County School

King's Hill Road

Grosvenor Close

Minors

Hunter Cl

Bracken

Wightman Rd

Elias

Ashmole

Gorse Lane

Darnford

King Edward VI Leisure Centre

Hillside

Hills Lane

Spooner

Borrowcop

Hills Lane

Quarry

Wentworth Drive

Woodfields

Lichfield RUFC

Ellfield House

Darnford Lane

The

TAMWORTH ROAD A51

Long Bridge Road

Cromwells Meadow

A38

Marsh Lane

Common

B3082

LONDON ROAD

Cricket

Whittington

Heart of England Way

A52

G H J ▼29 K L M

13 14 15

Freeford

Pipehill

G H J **19** K L M

07 08 09 08

Oaklands
Academy of Theatre Dance

Noose Lane

Pingle Lane

Burntwood Road

Mansion Dr

Overton Lane

Hammerwich

PO

Blackroot Close

Meerash Lane

Mill Lane

Church Lane

Hall Lane

Station Road

Hammerwich Lane

Lion's Den

Hall Lane

Coppice Lane

Bridge Farm

Pipe Place

Moat Bank

I

2

3

Muckley Corner

The Olde Corner House Hotel

A5

B4155

LICHFIELD ROAD

M6 Toll

Summerhill

Barracks Lane

WALSALL ROAD

Boat Lane

Bullmoor Lane

Cranebrook Lane

Hilton

28

4

5

Barracks Lane

A461

LICHFIELD ROAD

Springhill

Whitacre Lane

Whitacre Farm

Pouk Lane

Cranebrook Lane

Thornyhurst Lane

Owletts Hall Farm

Raikes Lane

6

7

8

Cattersfield Lane

Lynn Lane

Lynn

Lynn Lane

Mill Lane

Heath Close

Heath Lane

06 05 04

G H J **41** K L M

Stonnall

Main Street

Garnet Close

Westwick Close

Thornes Cl

St Peter's Cl

Wallheath Crs

Berryfields

St Peters CE Primary School

Church Lane

Mill Lane

Lower Stonnall

Footherley

Fisherwick

A 415 08 16 **B** **C** Whittington **D** 17 **E** Had**F** more

Ennfield House

Church Street

Lane

Church Lane

Babbington Cl

Windmilhill

Beechwood

Cloister Wk

Green

Falcon Dr

Osprey Close

Fisherwick Road

L.C.

Birmingham & Fazeley Canal

I Sandy Lane

Whittington Primary School

Golf Course

2 A51 Whittington Heath Golf Club

Worcester Rd

Heath Avenue

PO

Stafford Crescent

Derby Rd

Chester Road

Nottingham Road

Common Lane

Whittington Heath

Tamhorn House Bridge

3 TAMWORTH ROAD

Staffordshire Regiment Museum, Whittington

Tamhorn Park

4 Levett Road

Jerry's Lane

Packington Hall

29 06

5 Heart of England Wy

Hopwas Hays Wood

6 Knox's Grave Lane

Knox's Grave Lane

05

Hopwas

The Woodhouse

Thomas Barnes CP School

Lichfield Crescent

School Lane

Daintr

Church Drive

PO

A51 Hopwas Hill

Nursery Lane

Hints Lane

7 304 England Wy

Packington Lane

Packington Farm

Hopwas House Farm

Hints Lane

Lane

8 The Devil's Dressing Room

Hints Lane

PLAN N

ck's Head

A 415 16 **B** **C** 44 **D** 17 **E** **F**

The Bodnets

32

A   B   C   D   E   F

421   22   23

1

Wigginton
Fields

Gorse Farm

Statfold
Farm

Syerscote
Manor

B79

2

Syerscote Lane

3

Statfold
Hall

St Leonards
CE Primary
School

Syerscote
Barn

Main Street

Walrand Cl

Arkall Farm

4

31

Browns La

Mildenhall

Benson Ww

Manston Ww

Ashlands
Farm

Amington
Hall

5

Cemetery

Mildenhall

Lakenheath

Ashcroft
County
Infants
Sch

ASHBY ROAD

River Anker

Amington Hall
Farm

Chestnut Av

Flax Hill
Junior
School

Borough Rd

B5493

Tavistock Cl

Belvedere

6

Wigginton Rd

Windsor

Burton Cl

Hampton Cl

Admands

Norton

Perrycrofts

Kingston Cl

Henley Cl

Farm Cl

Close

**Perry
Crofts**

Moor
Farm

Queen
Elizabeth's
Mercian School

TAMWORTH

7

UPPER GUNGATE

Croft St

Tamworth &
Lichfield College

Tamworth Station

Moor
Lane

Tom Hartley
Park Homes

Shuttington

Tamworth
Road

Bracklesham Wy

Caister

Hodge La

8

OFFA DRIVE

Youth
Cen

Surgery

Police
Stn

Council
Building

Albert Rd

SAXON DRIVE

Stationfields

Jason Cl

Marlow

Bridgewater
Street

Dormer Av

Rene Road

Whitley Av

Selker Way

Emberton Wy

Duriston Dr

Brancaster

By Pass Rd

Primary
School

Chandlers Dr

Mercian

Surgery

Woodhouse Lane

Ridgewood

Florendine St

Sharpe Street

Tilia Rd

Cem

Gleneagles

Moor Lane

Leedham Av

Ashdale

Riverfield

Goostry Cl

June

Crs

Ankermoor
Primary
School

Talland Avenue

Whitesands

Waterside
Court

Wemc

Tamworth
Road

Florendine
Primary
School

Ingram Pit La

Amington

Bolehall

421   22   46   23

A   B   C   D   E   F

Summerfield

Rosewood Cl

Thomas Street

Amington Road

Longfield Cl

Torc Av

Warwick Rd

Bartow

Treasure Cl

Anchor

Canning

St George's Way

Scott Rd

Hanbury

Davis La

Highlands Lane

Woodhouse High School &
Community Sports Centre

Playing
Field

Hareholt

Greenheart

Greenholm

Surg

Juniper

Kernal

Woodland Rd

Madrona

Car

Sorrel Wy

1 grid square represents 500 metres

G H J K L M

Lonkhills Farm

Staffordshire County
Warwickshire County

B5493

Newton Lane

Seck

Seckington

The Gn

B5493

Main Road

The Poplars

Hangman's Lane

New Road

Statfold Barn Farm

The Decoy

Shuttington Fields Farm

PO

Pear Tree Cl

Shuttington

Crnt Crs

School Lane

Milner Drive

Church La

Shuttington Bridge

Road

Alvecote

Coventry Canal

M42

Bramcote Hall

rnberry
lytham

oustle

Potford Bridge

G H J 47 K L M

Golf Course

Robey's Lane

Tamworth Municipal Golf Club

Anker

I 2 3 4 5 6 7 8

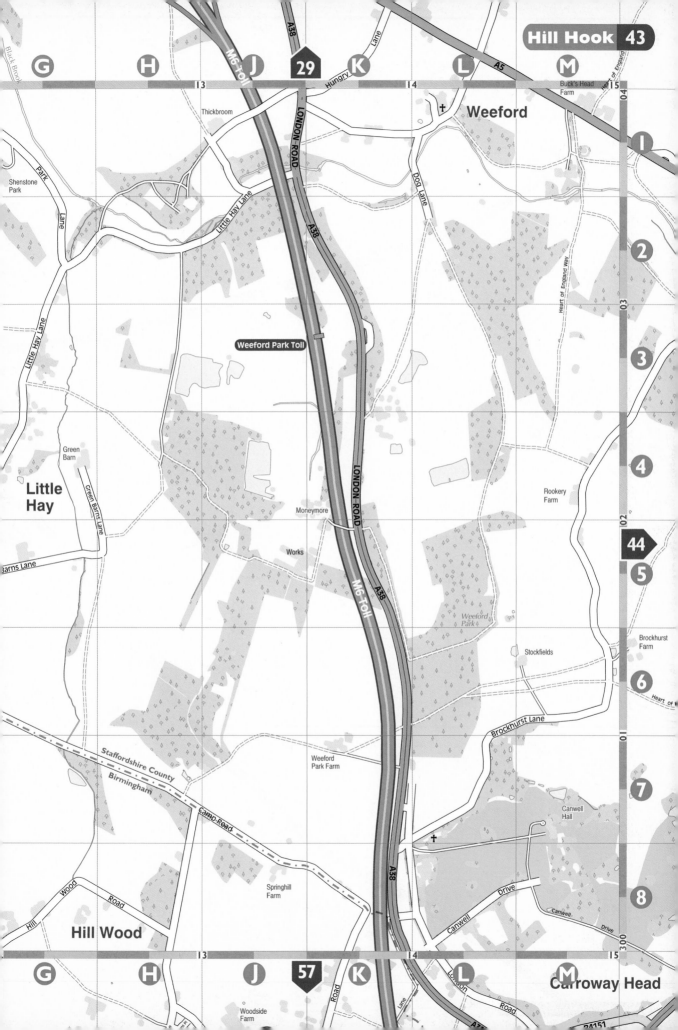

Drayton
Bassett

45

Old Mnr Cl

Ed Cl

PO

Manor Sch

Drayton Lane

Moat Drive

Rectory Cl

Salts La

A4091

Heart of England Way

River Tame

Portleys Lane

Brook
Farm

Brook End
Farm

Gallows Brook

Maxstoke Cl

Slade Lane

MWORTH ROAD

ton

Church Lane

Crowberry

Lane

Middleton
Pool

Middleton
Hall

New House
Farm

B78

Birmingham & Fazeley Canal

Heart of England Way

Tame View
Caravan Site

Cliff Hall La

River Tame

60

Mar
Farm

Lane

**Hunts
Green**

A4091

Wishaw Lane

Brick Kiln Lane

Bodymoor

Heath

Road

Lower
Farm

Heart of England Way

Broomey
Croft Farm

M42

Brace

Middleton House
Farm

**Bodymoor
Heath**

Boymr Hth La

Kingsbury
Water Park

Works

Centenary Wy

North
Wood

A4091

75

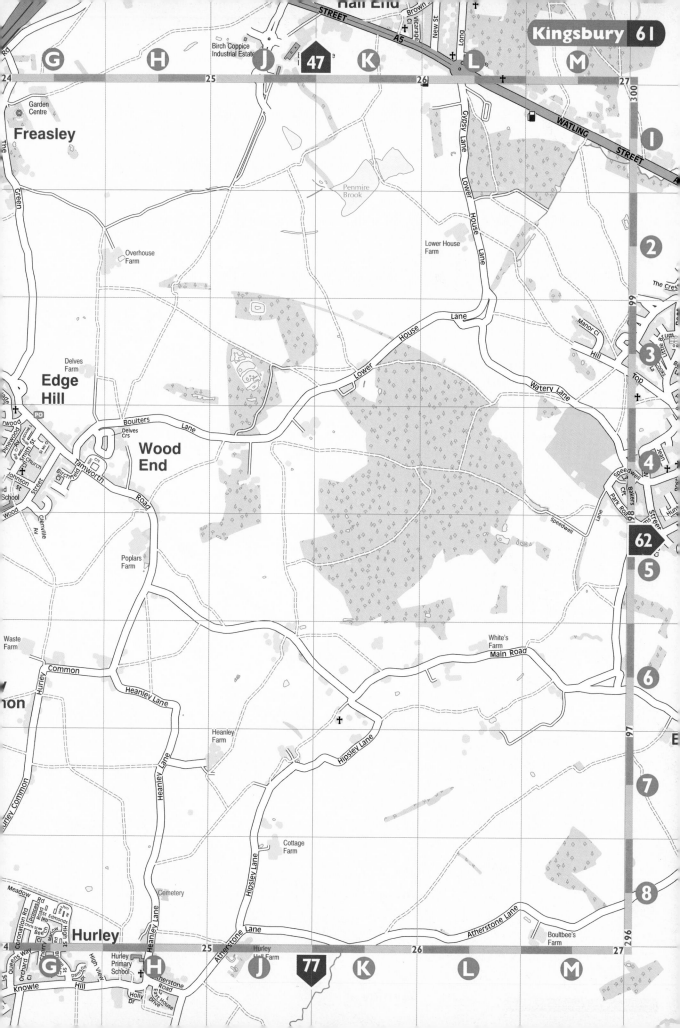

Hall End

STREET A5

Brown
Vicarage
Cl

New St

Long

WATLING STREET

G 24 H 25 J **47** K 26 L M 27 300

Garden
Centre

Freasley

Birch Coppice
Industrial Estate

Gypsy Lane

Lower House Lane

Watling

Street

The Crest

I

2

99

Overhouse
Farm

Penmire
Brook

Lower House
Farm

Manor Cl

Hill

Top

3

Delves
Farm

**Edge
Hill**

Lower

House

Lane

Watery Lane

Boulters Lane

Delves
Crs

**Wood
End**

Tamworth Road

Speedwell

4

Speedwell

Park Road

Bakers

Jean St

Little Brum

62

Glenville
Av

Poplars
Farm

5

Waste
Farm

White's
Farm

Main Road

6

Common

Hurley

Heanley Lane

97

Heanley
Farm

Heanley Lane

Hipsley Lane

E

7

Hurley Common

Cottage
Farm

8

Cemetery

Hipsley Lane

Atherstone Lane

Boultbee's
Farm

296

Meadow

Coronation Rd

Princes

St Edmonds

Hurley

High View

Hurley
Primary
School

Atherstone
Road

East House Drive

Atherstone Lane

Hurley
Hall Farm

G 24 H 25 J **77** K 26 L M 27

Meadow
Rd
Cemetery
Hipsley La
Atherstone Lane
Boultbee's Farm

G Hurley
H
J
61
K
L
M
25
Atherstone
26
Atherstone Lane
27
96

Coronation Rd
Princes
Queens Way
Orchard Cl
Cherry
Bridge St
Ely Cl
Knowle
High View
Hill
Hurley Primary School
Atherstone Road
East House
Holly Dr
Drive
Hurley Hall Farm

I

Kimberley Hall Farm

2

Foul End
Brook End
Brook End Farm
Nightingale's Farm
95

3

Manor House Farm

B4116
94

4

Whitacre Hall

78

Gospel Oak

5

B4116
Hoar Park

6
93

Botts Green
Centenary Way

7

New House Farm
Holt Hall Farm
Hoar Park Farm

Botts Green Lane
Hurley Lane
Whitacre Fields
ATHERSTONE ROAD
Centenary Way

8
92

G
H
J
95
K
L
M
25
Pound Lane
26
Hoar Hall
27
NUNEATON Rd

B4098

Monwode

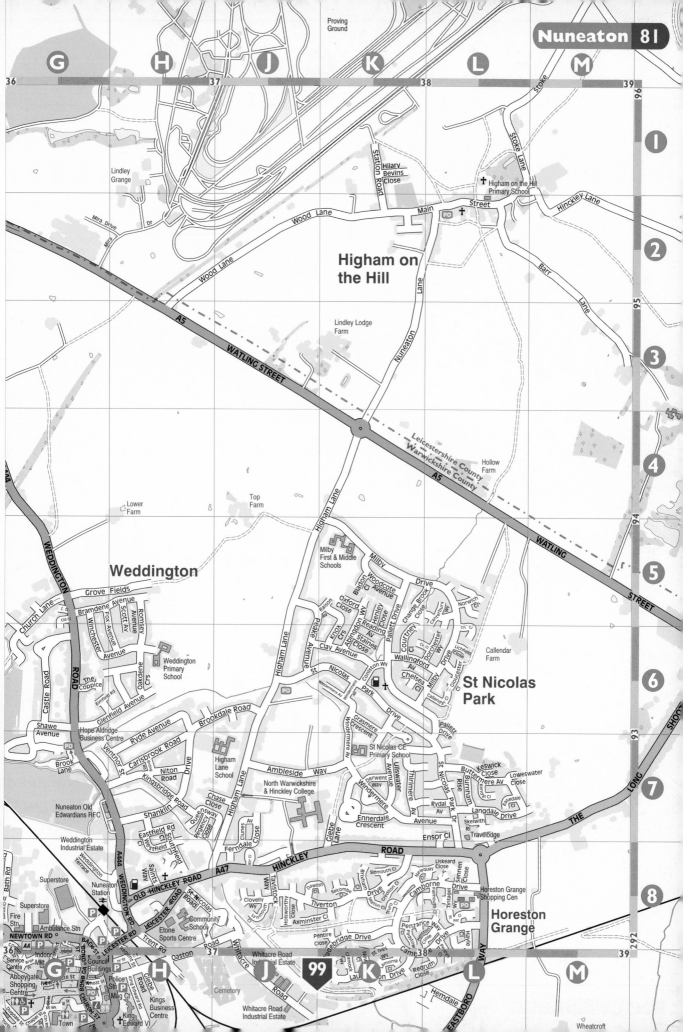

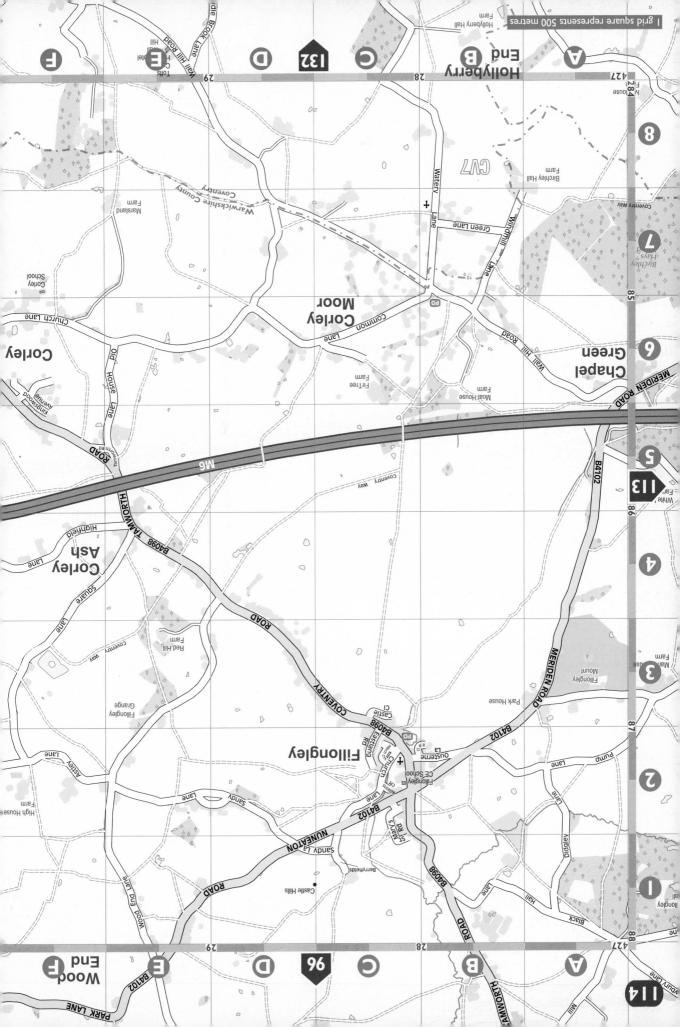

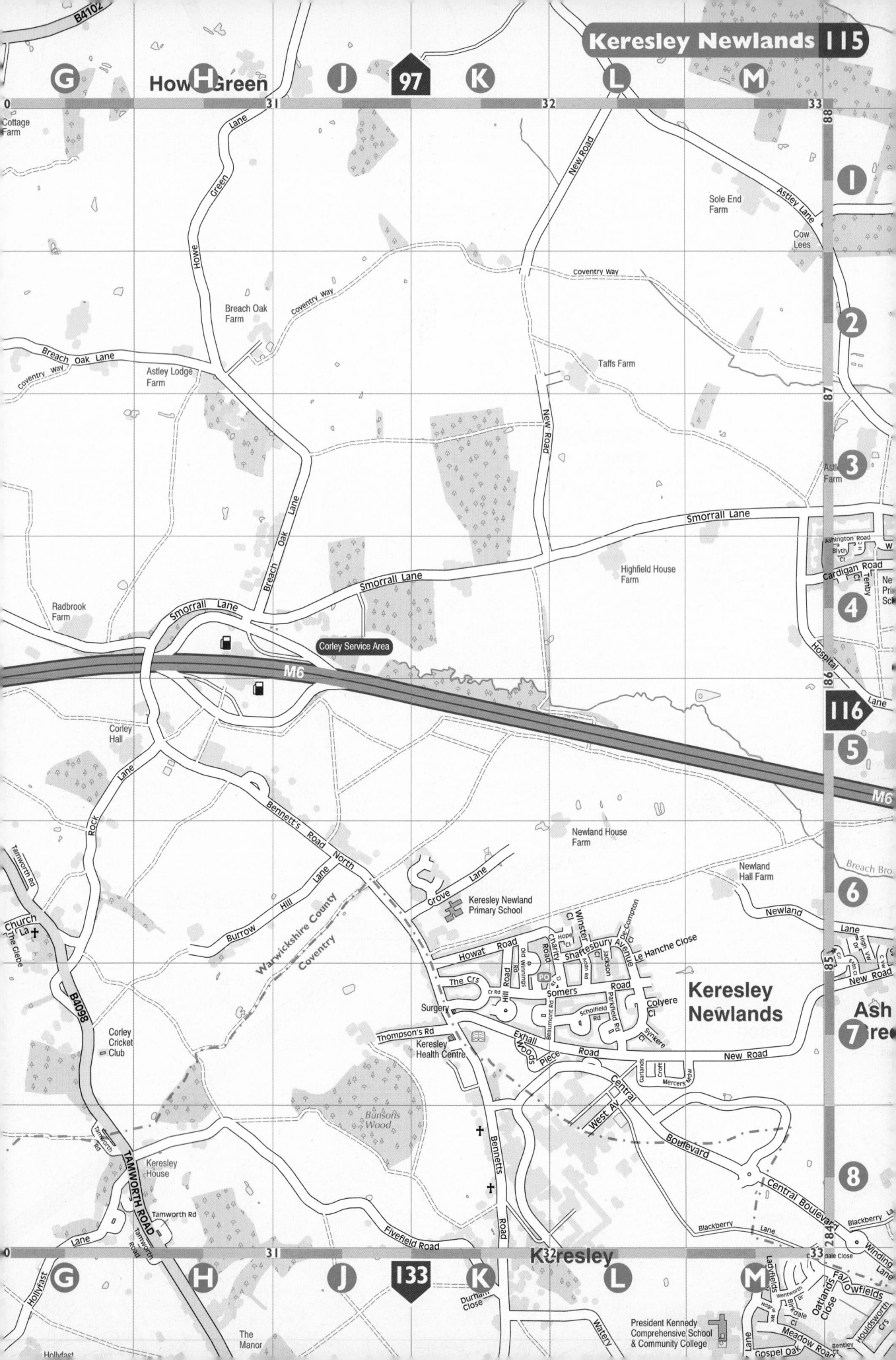

B40

G   H   J   III   K   L   M

18   19   20   21

Bickenhill
Plantations

Est

Natic
Exhibi
Centre

Northway

North
Av

Park Farm

Warwickshire County

Solihull

Exhibition Way

Perimeter

The Underpass

Pendigo Wy

Pendigo-Wy

E Car Pk Rd

CHESTER ROAD

Novotel

Comet Rd

Trident Rd

B4438

Ramp

Harbet Dr

Pendigo Way

Middle Bickenhill Lane

I

Birmingham
National Airport

Vanguard Rd

Concorde Rd

Birmingham International Stn

Perimeter Wy

Perimeter Rd

Perimeter Rd

Pendigo
Wy

S Car
Pk Rd

Pendigo
Wy

East Way

**Middle
Bickenhill**

2

Hermes rd

Airport
Way

Airport Way

Airport Way

Trinity
Business Park

S Car Pk Rd

Pendigo
Rd

South Way

S Car
Pk Rd

S Car
Pk Rd

East Way

Coventry Road

COVENTRY R

84

83

Arden Hotel &
Leisure Club

A45

A45

Clock Lane

B4438
LANE

Pirt La

Church
Lane

Junction 6

M42

National
Motorcycle
Museum

Stonebridge

Pasture Farm

3

Welsh
RFC

Works

Bickenhill

BARNES

St. Peters Lane

The Grove

4

82

130

B92

DE

Shadowbrook
Lane

M42

Fiddlers
Green

MERIDEN

5

CATHERINE

Corberts
Close

Lap Wing

Nesfield
Grove

Drive

6

81

Barber's
Coppice

Hampton
Lane Farm

Hampton in Arden

HIGH STREET

Fentham
Road

Hampton in Arden
Station

The
Crescent

Hampton Manor
Homes

George Fentham
J&I School

Meadow
Drive

Fentham

Elm
Tree Rd

Peel Close

7

Barbers

M42

SOLIHULL

ROAD

B4102

PO

Surgery

Bells Vue

Eastcote
Lane

Belle Vue

Bellemere Road

Marsh Lane

280

Walford
Hall Farm

**Hook
End**

8

Friday
Lane

Eastcote Lane

Butler's End

G · 24 · H · 25 · J · **113** · K · 26 · L · M · 27 · Ivy House

High Ash Farm

I

White Stitch

Lodge Green

Lodge Green Lane North

Lodge Green Lane

B4102

FILLONGLEY ROAD

Shaft Lane

Becks Lane

2

Meriden Shafts

Lane · Old Hall Farm

Warwickshire County · Solihull

Walsh Lane

Eaves Green

Heart of England Way

3 · 83

Alspath Hall

Meriden CE Primary School

B4102

B4104

FILLONGLEY ROAD

Highfield · Alspath Road · Arden Cl · Leymere Close

Meriden

Leys Lane

Farnfield Rd · The Croft · Glovers Cl · Waterfall · W A · Cottage

PO

Innkeepers Lodge Hotel

MAIN · ROAD

B4104

Old · Road

Surgery

Manor Hotel

Meriden House

Eaves Green Lane

Showell Lane

Solihull Coventry

4 · 82

Meriden Green Business Park

132

Church Lane

Berkswell Road

†

Millison's Wood

Albert Road

BIRMINGHAM · ROAD

B4104

Grace Road

Daytona Dr · Bonneville Cl · Olympus · James Davidson Dr · Ar Dr · Thebes Cl · Close · Luxor La

Copse · Close

Entry Court

5

Barkers Butts RFC

Pickford Grange

6 · 81

Heart of England Way

Greenways Farm

7

Uppe East Gree

Coventry Solihull

† Church

8 · 280

Four Oaks

Meriden Road

Back Lane

Shirley Lane

Flint's Green

andrews nfant School

End Lane

Ho R

G · 24 · H · 25 · Blind Hall Farm · J · **152** · K · 26 · L · M · 27 · **Hockley**

Coventry Way

Hill House Farm

Broad Lane

Broad La Tradin

1 grid square represents 500 metres

Bark Hill

Newton

DY12

Forest Lodge

Flitterhill Coppice

Town Coppice

Lodge Hill Farm

Chamberline Wood

Dowles

DOWLES

Dry

B4194

Whitpbed Wood

Northwood House

NORTHWOOD Lane

Crundalls Lane

North Wood

LG

Skeys Wood

Hawkbatch Valleys

Mill

Hawkbatch Farm

Seckley Wood

Woodhouse Farm

Hill Farm

NORTHWOOD Lane

River Severn

Mary Moors

Severn Valley Railway

Holbeache

Trimpley Reservoir

Trimpley Works

Victoria Bridge

The Meadows

Eymore Wood

Huntsfield Farm

Worcestershire Way

Oak Tree Farm

Chestnut Tree Farm

Arley Station

Upper Arley

Upper Arley

Arley

Cottage

Upper Arley CE First School

PO

Works

Severn Valley Railway

ROAD

Severn Valley Railway

Works

Green

Grey

Nurseries

Riverside

Woodbury Lane

NORTHWOOD Lane

376

276

8

7

6

5

4

3

2

1

77

78

79

77

78

A B C D E F

Five ways

Austcliffe
House Farm

G H J **118** K L M

I

Churc

2

Whitehouse
Farm

Ismere
House

ROAD A449

Axborough Lane

STOURBRIDGE ROAD

A451

A451

STO

Churchill Lane

Churchill Lane

The
Croft

Talbotshill La

Orchard Road

Pemberton
Crs

Roseberry
Gdns

New Rd

Clifton Rd

Castle

Woodland

Drive

Grove

The Alexander Patterson
Special School

Waggon Lane

Waggon Lane

Golf Course

Churchill &
Blakedown
Golf Club

Scuthorpe Road

Wheatmill
Cl

Brookside Way

Mill Lane

Mill Cl

Elm Dr

Station

Drive

Blakedown
Fm

The Av

Royal Cl

BIRMINGHAM

Bla

3

Blakedown
First Scho

ROAD

A451

Woodhouse
Farm

Kennels

Lynwood

Wannerton Road

Swan Cl

PO

4

Hurcott
Wood

Wannerton
Farm

A456

Forge Lane

Halfshire Lane

Hurcott Lane

Hurcott

Park
Hall

New Wood Lane

140

5

Sandy Lane

A456

Deansford Lane

BIRMINGHAM ROAD

6

Husum Way

arrie Av

Drive

Munro Cl

Rosetti
Cl

Dunbar Way

yson

Rusd
Av

Chaucer
Crs

Nashe
Cl

Prior Cl

Elmdale

Silver Birch

Dr

Ashdene
Close

Offmore Farm
Close

Offmore
Farm

Little Dunclent
Farm

Bissell
Wood

Bellington
Farm

7

Mount
Segg

Mearse
Farm

Bar

8

Deansford Lane

Dunclent

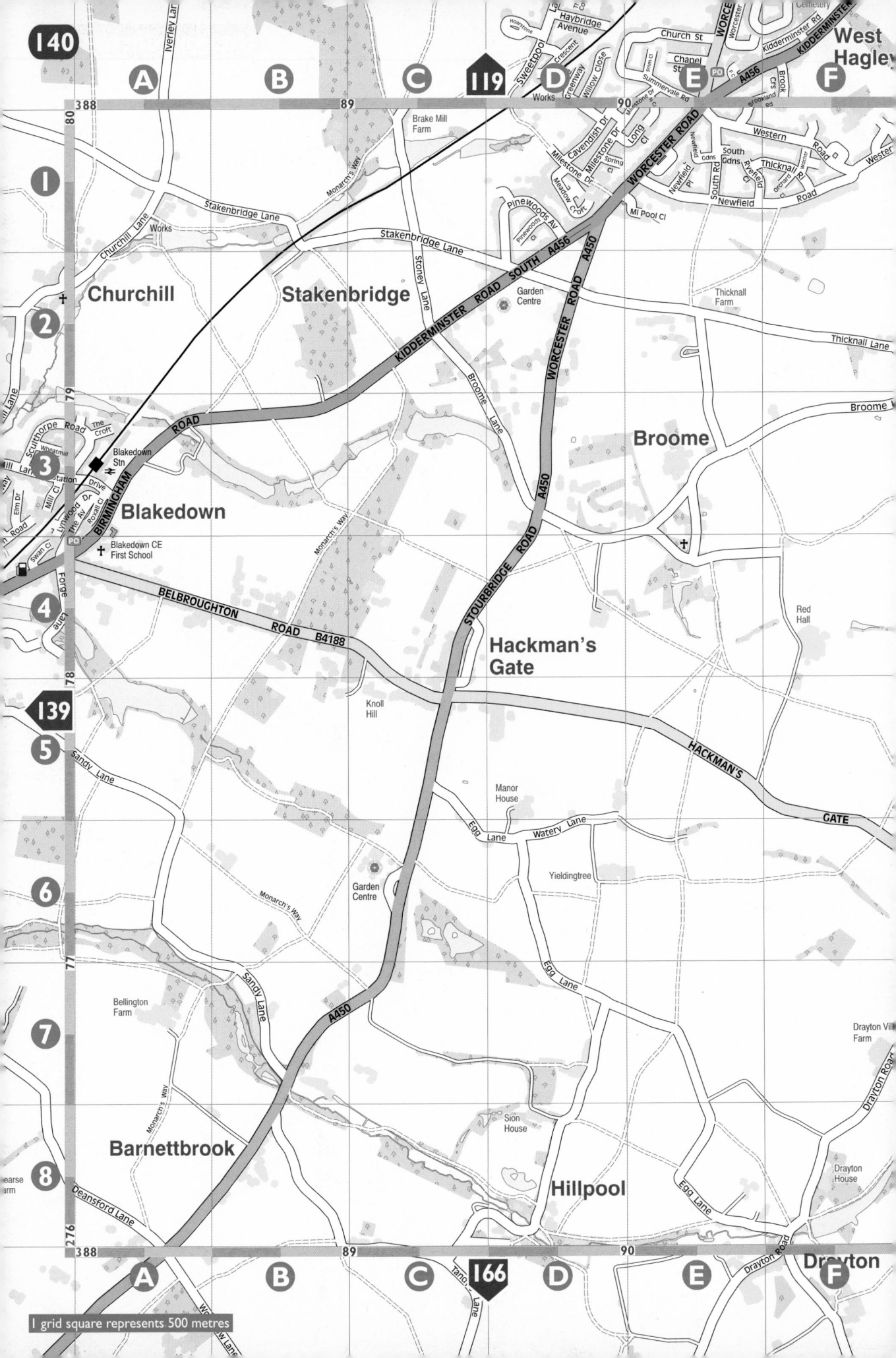

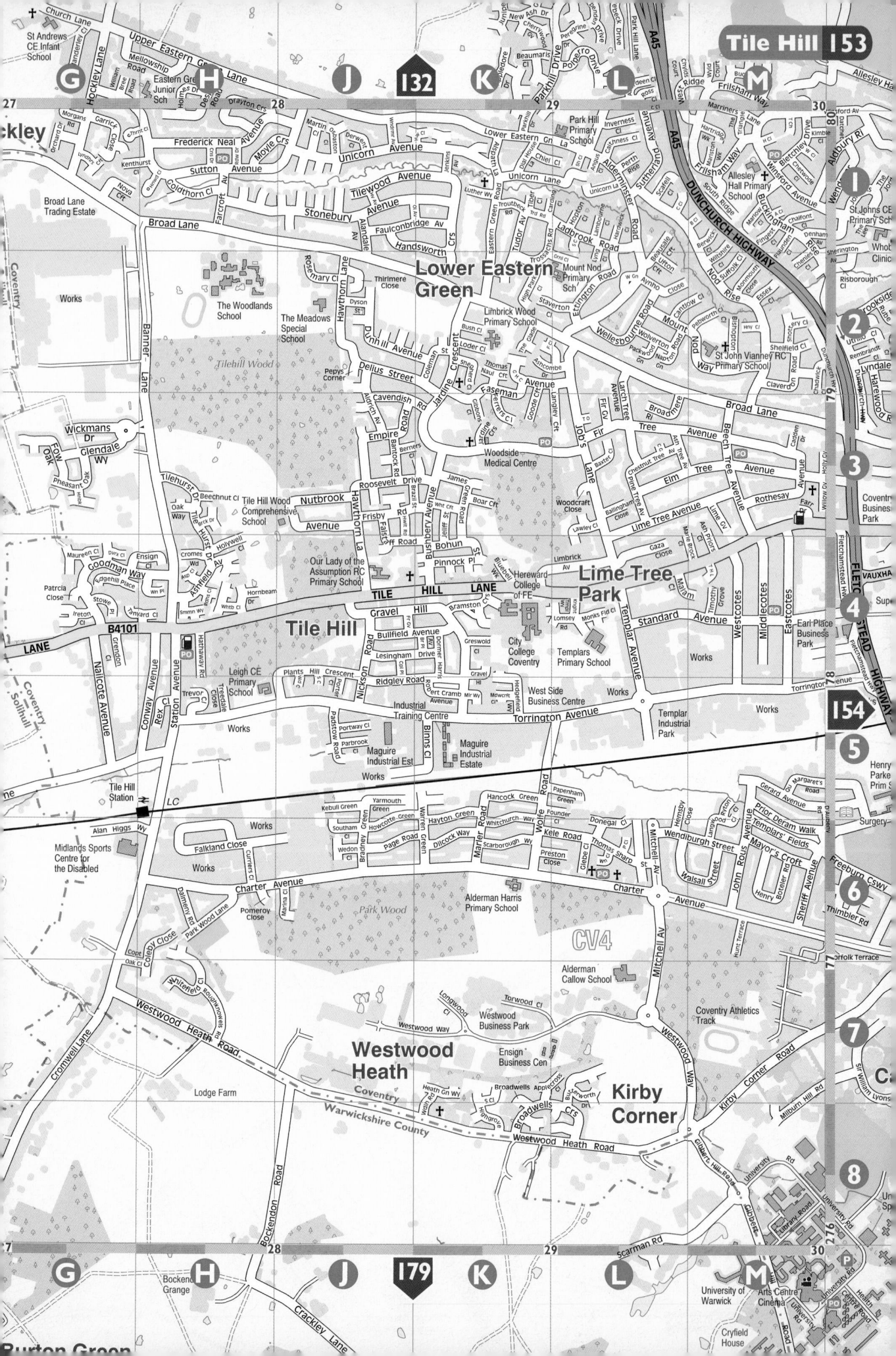

156

A · B · C **135** · D · E · F

Church End

Stoke

Stoke Aldermoor

155

CV3

Willenhall

Tollbar End

A · B · C **182** · D · E · F

1 grid square represents 500 metres

The Priory
Brandon Grange Farm
River Avon
Binklow Heath
Birchley Wood
Birchley Farm
Woodhill Farm
Wood Hill

St Margarets Cemetery
St Peters Churchyard
Erdene Close
Main Meadow
Police Station (Wd Ed Ex Ston)
Hawthorne Close
Wolston Business Park
The Priory
Prory Road

RUGBY ROAD
Brandon
Brandon Station
Avondale Crescent
Hallams Cl
King Cl
The Brandon Hall Hotel
Works

Speedway Lane
Centenary Way
Cossell Lane

Binley Woods Primary School
Combe Drive
Ashda
Friars Close
Saxon Cl
Craven Av
Craven Rd
Craven Rd
Court Leet
Abbey Craven Cl
Fenndale Rd
Avenue
Woodlands Road
Heather Road
Monks Road
Birchwood Road
Abbots Way
Pinewood Dr
Elm Cl
Greenway
Oakdale Road
Norman Ashman Coppice
Binley Woods

RUGBY ROAD
A428
Works
PO

New Close Wood
Old Lodge Farm
B4027
B4027

The Woodlands
Combe Abbey Country Park
Coombe Pool

City of Coventry-Brandon Wood Golf Club
Brandon Lane
Brandon Wood Farm
Brandon Wood
Golf Course

Marst

Smithbrook Way
Combe Field
Twelve o'clock

183
158

42 41 40 39
77 78 79 80

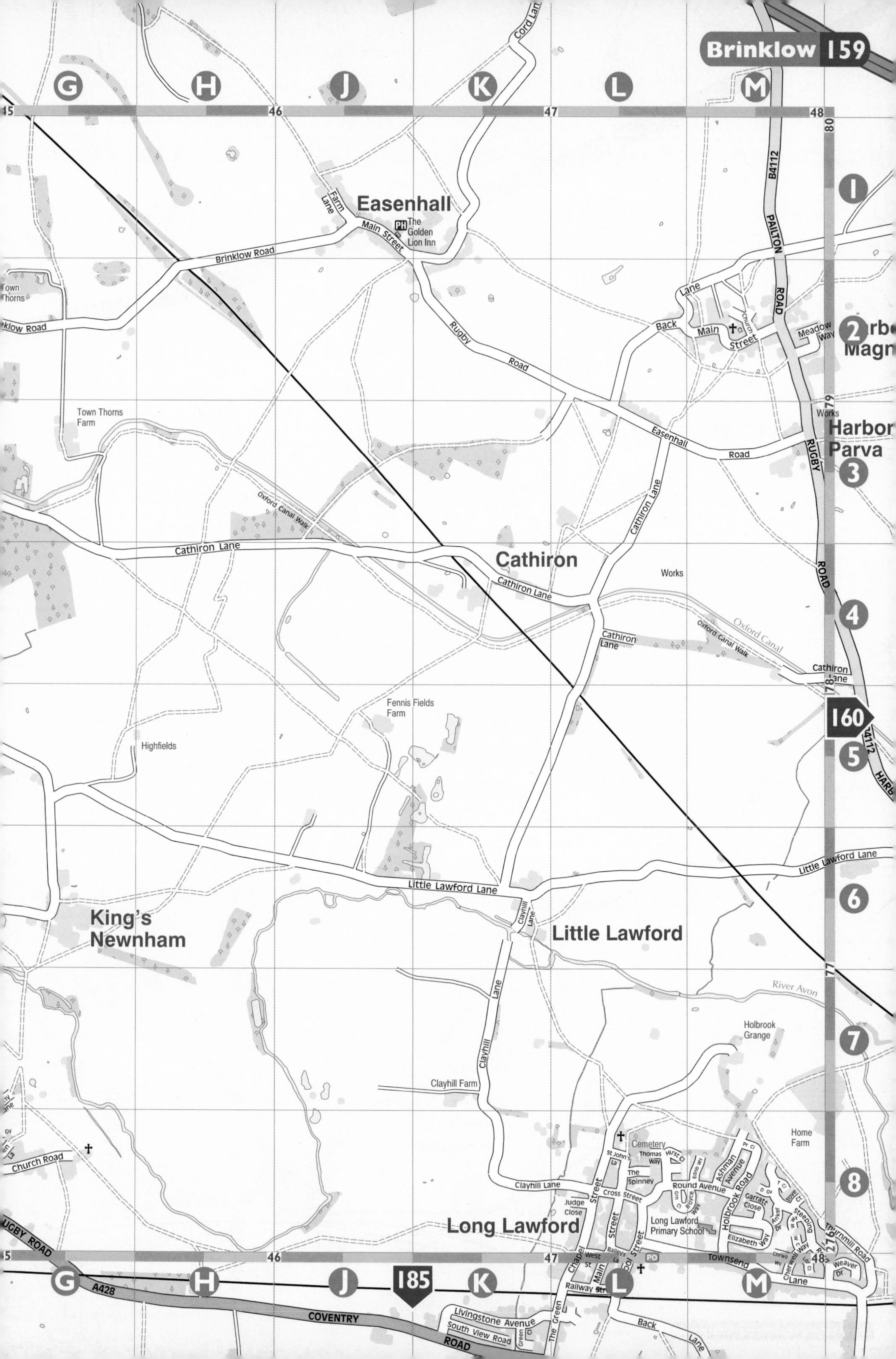

G H J K L M

45 46 47 48 **80**

I

Easenhall

Farm Lane

Main Street

PH The Golden Lion Inn

Brinklow Road

own horns

nklow Road

Rugby Road

Back Lane

Main Street

Meadow Way

PAILTON ROAD

B4112

2 rbo Magn

Town Thorns Farm

Easenhall Road

Works

Harbor Parva

RUGBY ROAD

3

Cathiron Lane

Oxford Canal Walk

Cathiron Lane

Cathiron

Cathiron Lane

Works

Oxford Canal

4

78

Cathiron Lane

Cathiron Lane

Oxford Canal Walk

160

B4112

HARB

5

Highfields

Fennis Fields Farm

King's Newnham

Little Lawford Lane

Little Lawford Lane

Little Lawford

Clayhill Lane

6

Clayhill Lane

River Avon

77

Holbrook Grange

Holbrook Road

7

Clayhill Farm

Home Farm

† Church Road

†

Cemetery

Thomas Way

St John St

Hu St Cl

The Spinney

Round Avenue

Ashman Avenue

Garratt Close

8

Clayhill Lane

Cross Street

Judge Close

Long Lawford Primary School

Elizabeth Way

Steeping

Thornhill Road

Long Lawford

West

Bailey's La

School Street

Main Street

Sol Street

PO

Townsend

48

Weaver Dr

Chapel West

Railway Str

The Green

Back Lane

COVENTRY ROAD

Livingstone Avenue

South View Road

Green Lane

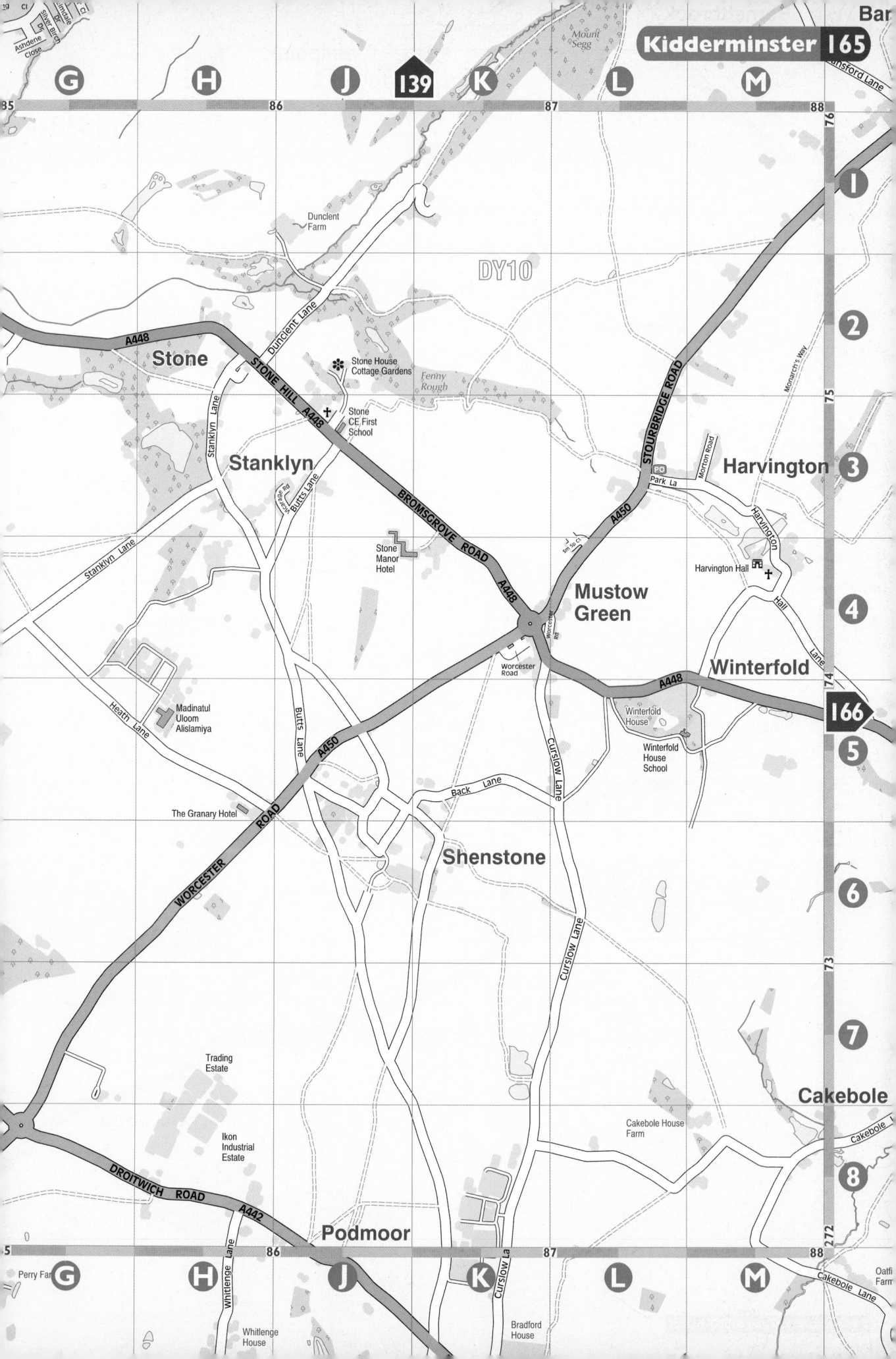

G   H   J   **141**   K   L   M

Bradford Lane
Bradford House
Mearse Farm

I

Waystone Lane

Hockley Brook Lane

Dordale Road

Hurst Farm

2

Broom Hill

Woodlands Farm

Pepper Wood

Monarch's Way

3

Bournes Green

Hockley Brook

Hockley Brook Lane

Dordale

4

Dordale Road

Insetton House

Royal Content Farm

Monarch's Way

168

Yarnold Lane Fm

5

Santery Hill Wood

Woodcote Lane

Works

Warbage Lane

Yarnold Lane

6

Nature Reserve

Nutnells Wood

Woodland Road

Church Road

Road

Warbage Lane

Priory Road

Nibletts Hill

Victoria Road

Whinfield Road

Monarch's Way

Alfreds

7 ed's Well

Randan Wood

Dodford

Priory Road

B61

8

Woodcote Green

Woodcote Lane

Woodcote Manor House

Dodford First School

Fockbury Road

Monarch's Way

Fockbury Rd

Fockbur Farm

KIDDERMINSTER ROAD

G   H   J   **190**   K   L   Park Farm   M

Monarch's Way

KIDDER

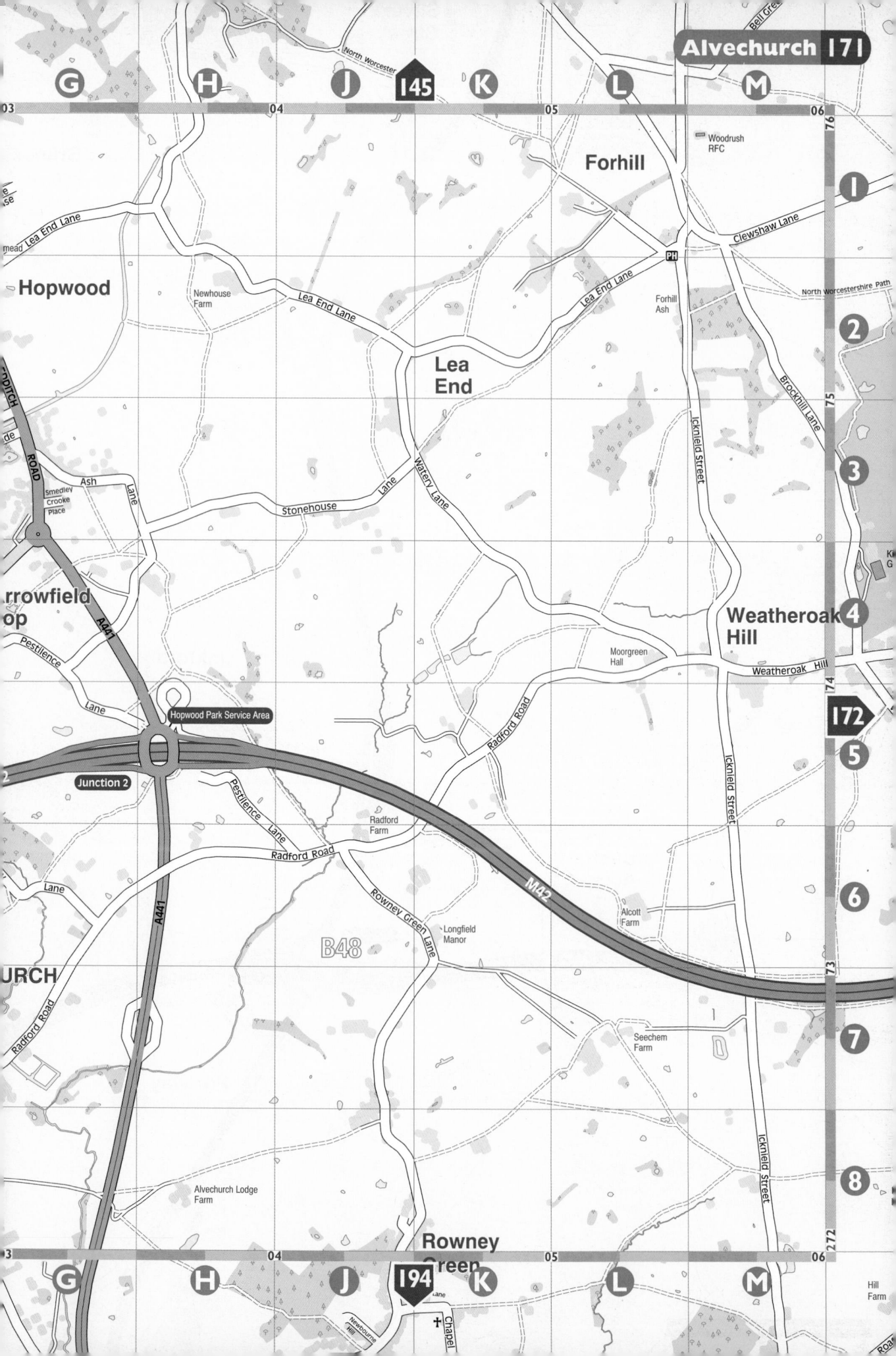

215

A B C D E F

172

146

Silver Street
Grimes Hill

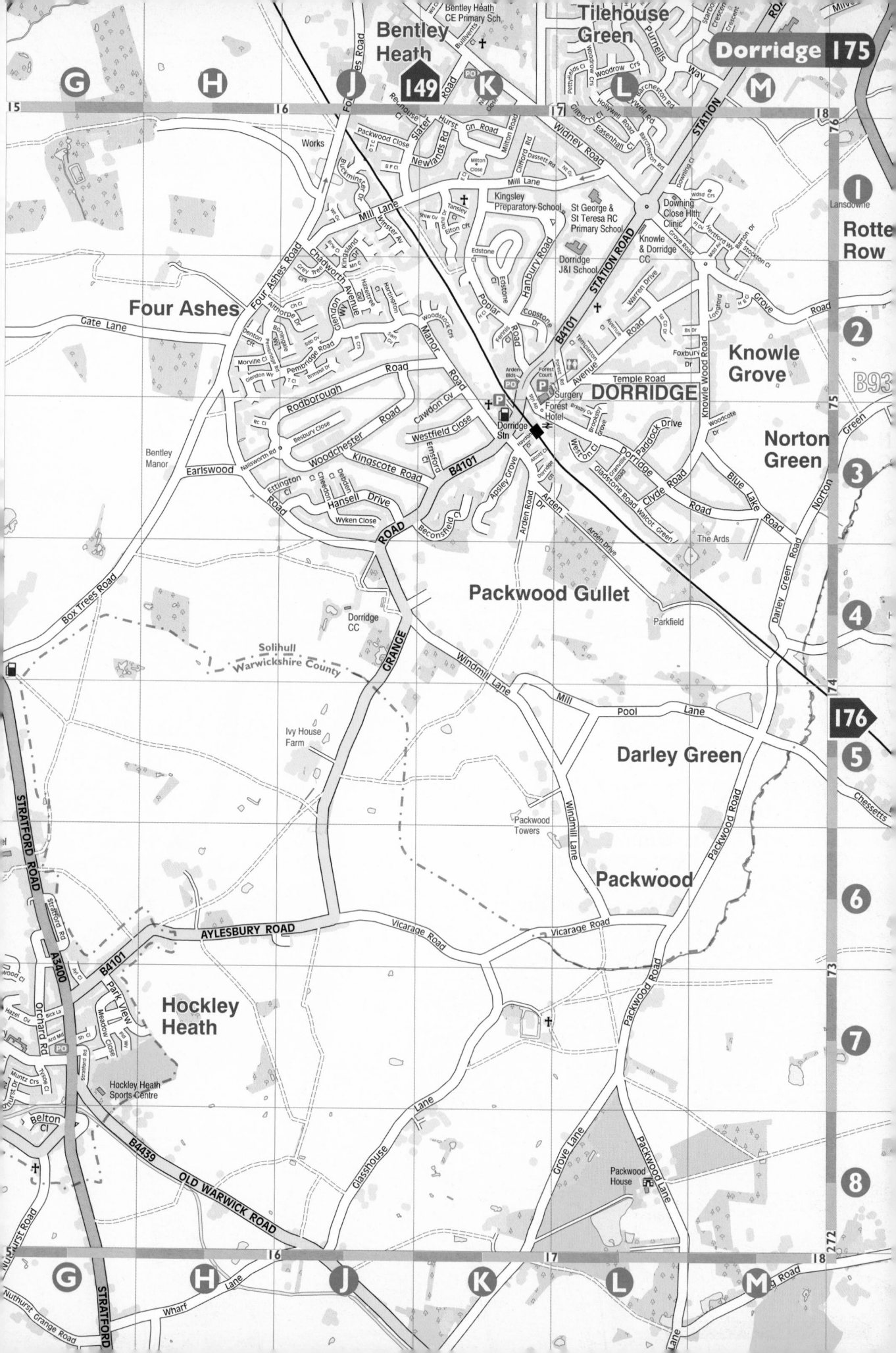

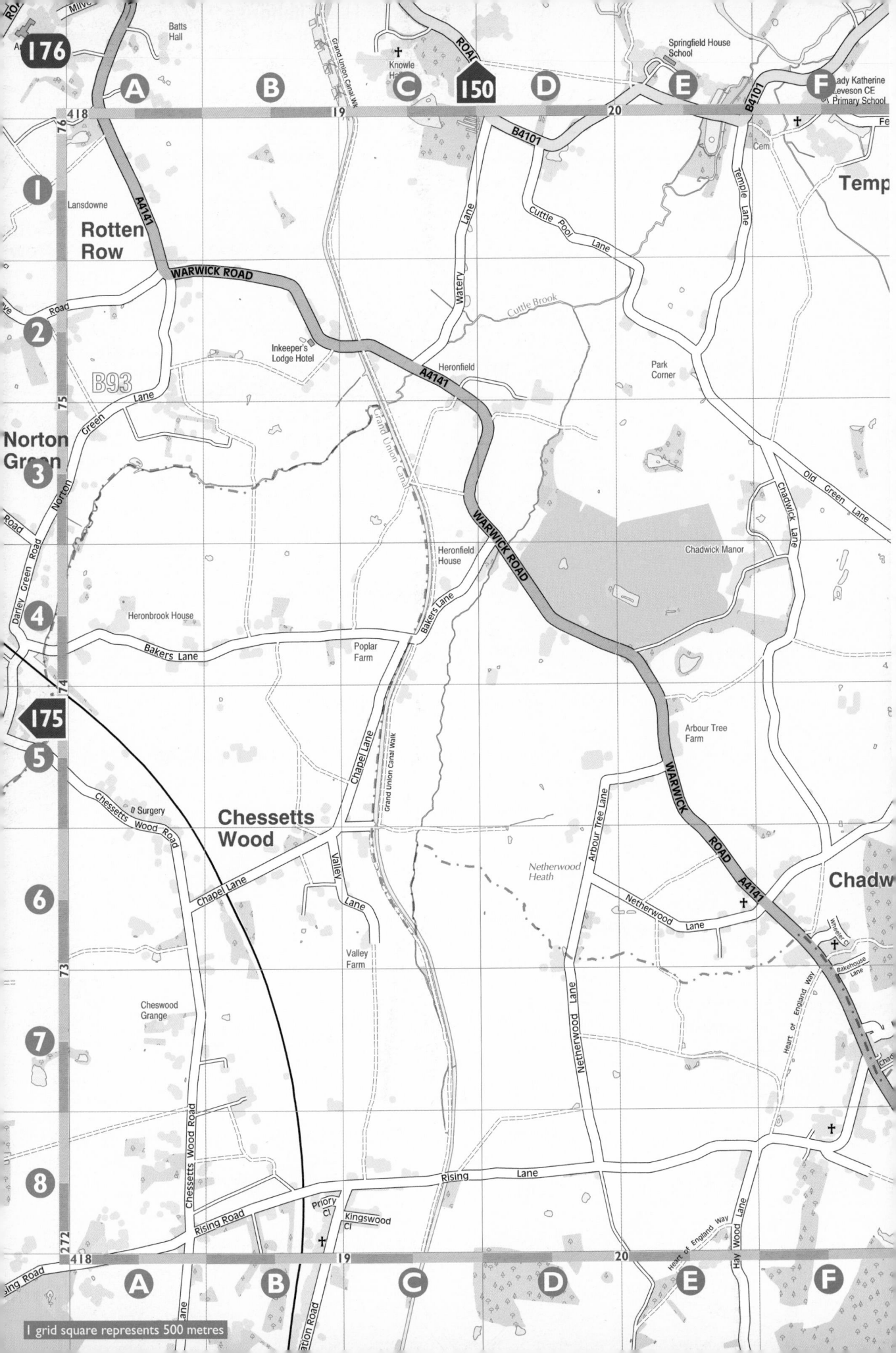

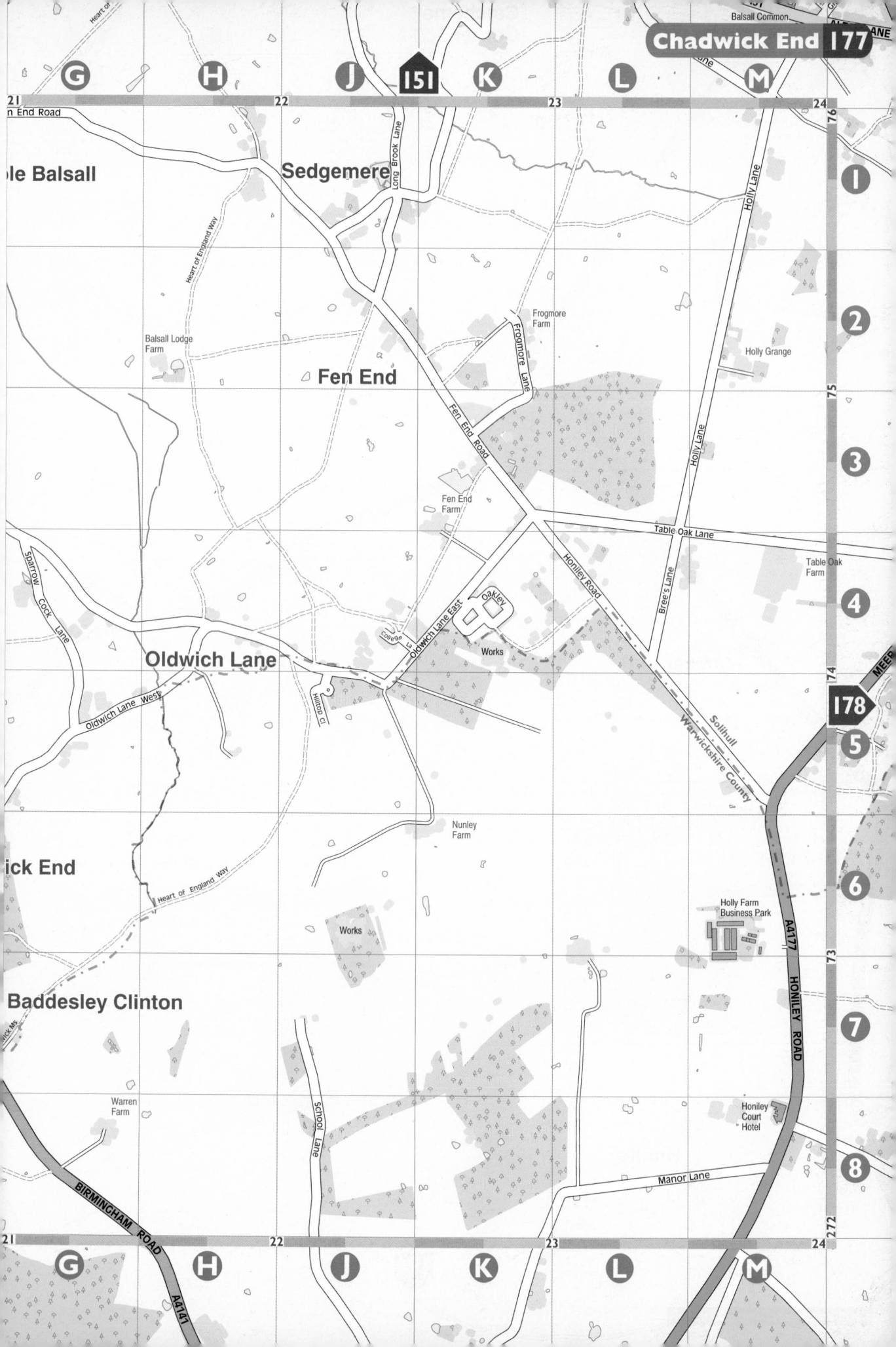

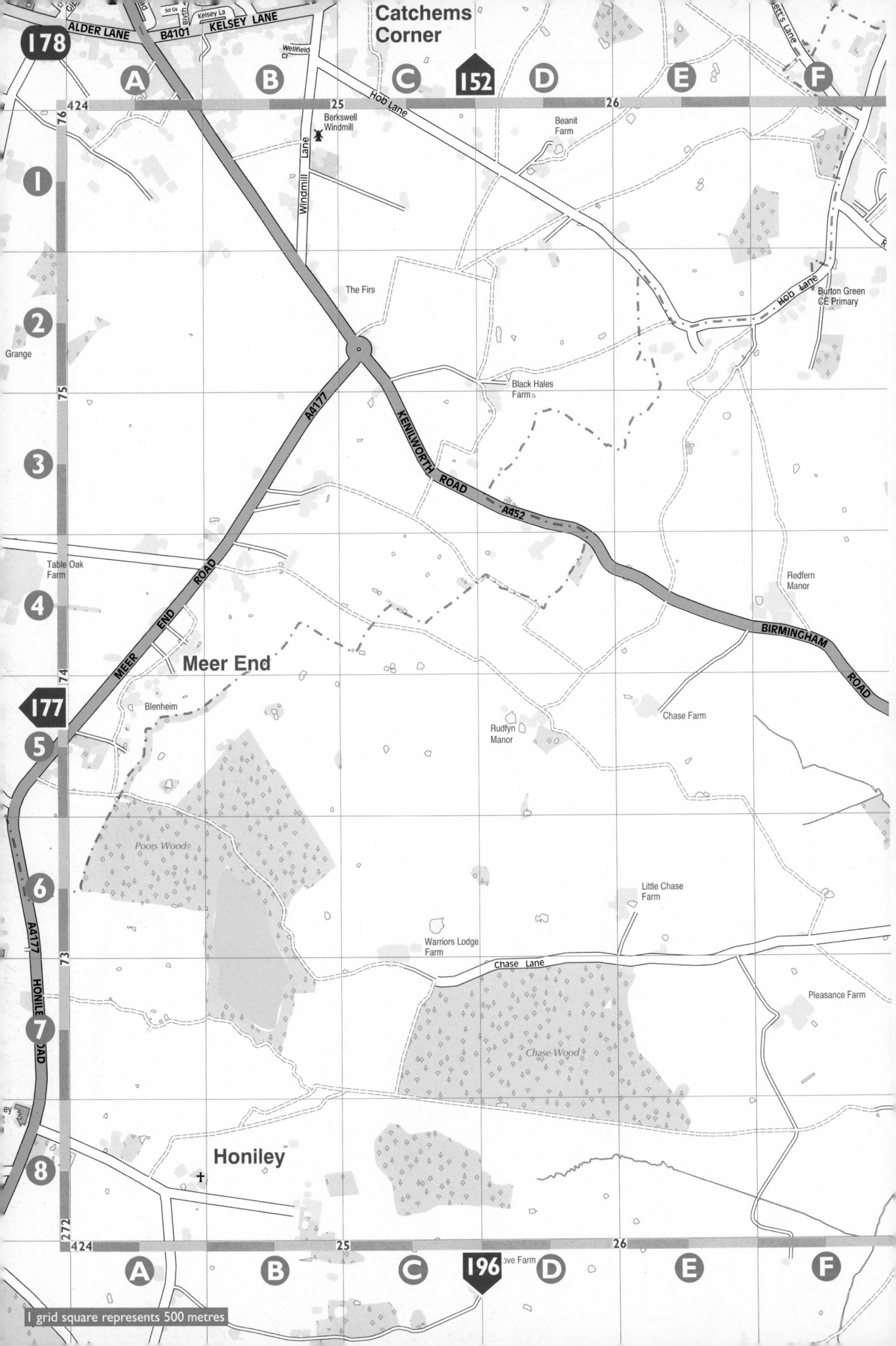

Catchems Corner

ALDER LANE B4101 KELSEY LANE

Sd Gv
Kelsey La

Wellfield
Cl

152

Ⓐ Ⓑ Ⓒ Ⓓ Ⓔ Ⓕ

424 25 Hob Lane 26

76

Berkswell
Windmill

Windmill Lane

Beanit
Farm

1

75

2

Grange

The Firs

Black Hales
Farm

Hob Lane

Burton Green
CE Primary

A4177

KENILWORTH ROAD

3

A452

74

Table Oak
Farm

MEER END ROAD

Redfern
Manor

4

Meer End

177

Blenheim

BIRMINGHAM ROAD

Chase Farm

73

5

Rudfyn
Manor

A4177

Poors Wood

6

Little Chase
Farm

HONILEY ROAD

Warriors Lodge
Farm

Chase Lane

7

Pleasance Farm

Chase Wood

8

Honiley

272

424 25 **196** ve Farm 26

Ⓐ Ⓑ Ⓒ Ⓓ Ⓔ Ⓕ

I grid square represents 500 metres

G   H   J   153   K   L   M

27   28   29   30   76

Burton Green

Westwood Heath Road

University of Warwick

Arts Centre Cinema

Cryfield House

Bockendon Grange

Crackley Lane

Scarman Rd

University Rd

1

PO

Hurst Farm

South Hurst Farm

2

75

Long Meadow Barn Farm

Rye Meadow

Cryfield Grange

3

Crackley Wood

4

74

Centenary Way

Dunns Pitts Farm

A452

Red Lane

Hollis Lane

Camp Farm

180

5

Princes Drive Industrial Estate

Princes Dr

Crackley

Woodland Rd

Common Lane

6

Chase Lane

A452 BEEHIVE HILL

St Augustines RC Primary School

The Spring

COVENTRY ROAD A429

Ladyes Hill

St Josephs School

Centenary Way

73

East Chase Farm

Priors Field CP School

B4103

CLINTON LANE

Phorsfield Road

Woodcote

Cobbs Rd

Malthouse Lane

Grange Av

De Montfort Road

Quarry Rd

Rose Croft

Amherst Road

Fernhill Close

Bromley

Berkeley Road

FIELDGATE LANE

Upper Spring Lane

NEW STREET A429

Tainters Cl

Manor Road

Hawkesworth Dr

Alpine Ct

Lower Ladyes Hills

Windmill Hills

Woodmill Mdw

Mill End

7

Park Hill Junior School

Avenue Rd

Clinton Av

Denton Close

Elizabeth Way

Castle Green

High Street

Elmbank Road

PO

PH

Clarendon House Hotel

Pears Cl

Abbotsford School

School Lane

Hyde Road

Albion Street

Henry Street

Arthur Street

Park Road

Parkfield Drive

Keeling Road

8

Whitemoor

Purlieu Lane

Works

Kenilworth Castle

CASTLE ROAD

Castle Hill

Abbey Fields Swimming Pool

Finham Brook

ROSEMARY HILL

ABBEY HILL

A452 PRIORY ROAD

St Nicholas CE Combined School

Priory Thtr

Piper's Lane

272

Kenilworth School

G   H   J   197   K   L   M

27   28   B4103   29   30

Grounds Farm

Police Stn

Welfare

Montfort

Council

Surgery

Station Rd

Playbox Theatre

Thorns County Infant

University of Warwick Centre

Cannon Park Primary School

KENPAS HWY

A45

Bishop Ullathorne RC Comprehensive School

Finham Park School

Finham Primary School

Finham

PO

The Leasowes

Coventry Warwickshire County

King's Hill

A

B

C

D

E

F

Arts Centre Cinema

I

PO

The University of Warwick

P

2

Gibbet Hill Rd

Wainbody Wood Special School

Gibbet Hill

King's Hill Lane

3

Cryfield Grange

KENILWORTH ROAD

A429

Cryfield Grange Road

Stoneleigh Road

Wainbody Wood Farm

A46

King's Hill Lane

4

Millburn Grange

Finham Brook

Westley Bridge

Manor Fields Farm

B4115

179

5

rackley

CV8

Dalehouse Lane

Finham Brook

6

Common Lane Industrial Est

Highland Road

Inchbrook Road

Kingswood Farm

Centenary Wy

Dalehouse Lane Ind Est

Dalehouse Lane

Birmingham Road

B4115

Centenary Way

Walkers Orchard

7

Knowle

Golf Course

Vicarage Road

Kenilworth Golf Club

Crew Lane

A46

8

Park Hill Junior School

Park Hill

Leyes Lane

Kenilworth School

Crewe Farm

Crew Lane

B4115

Sowe Mouth

A

B

C

D

E

F

Tulip Inn Hotel

1 grid square represents 500 metres

G   H   **157**   J   K   L   M

40   41   42

76

I

City of Coventry-Brandon
Wood Golf Club

Brandon Wood
Farm

Brandon Lane

Brandon
Hall Hotel

Wolston
Business
Park

Main Street

Meadow Close

Priory Road

The Priory

Coalpit Lane

Police
Station

St Margarets
CE Primary
School

Elmdene
Close

Larchfields

School Street

Surgery

Wolston

2

Golf Course

Wolston Fields
Farm

Coventry Way

Paddocks

Manor Estate

Warwick Road

Wolston Lane

Mill Wy

Manor Est

Brook Street

John
Simpson
Close

Dyer's Lane

Cemetery

75

Works

Centenary Way

Stretton Road

Dyer's Lane

Fosse Farm

3

Grounds Farm

Ryton Gardens

4

Wolston Lane

A445   **LONDON ROAD**   A45

Grange Farm

B4455

74

184 ▶

5

Stretton Road

Lane

Frog
Hall

6

Freeboard Lane

Knightlow CE (Aided)
Primary School

School Lane

A45   **LONDON ROA**

73

Ryton
Heath Farm

Plott Lane

Squires Rd

Roberts
Close

Moor
Farm
Close

Meadow Close

FOSSE WAY

7

Rugby

Orchard
Way

Manor
House

Surgery

Brookside

Knob Hill

Rugby Lane

Church Hill

PO

**Stretton-
on-Dunsmore**

8

Oxford Rd

Stretton Lodge
Farm

Fineacre Lane

Frankton Lane

272

40   41   42

G   H   J   K   L   M

OXFORD ROA

Park
Farm

Asylum
Farm

Astley CE Primary School

Astley Hall

Astley Farm

Aconda Farm

Pool House

Syntley Farm

Woodhampton House

Weatherlane Farm

Hampstall Lane

Seedgreen Lane

Scots Lane

Winnall

Win...

The Bull

F

D

C

B

A

81

80

379

268

8

7

69

DY13

Larford Farm

Works

Longmore Hill

Longmore Hill Farm

Abbey Gdns

B4196

Ridgley Cross

Sych Cottages

Oakhampton

A451

6

Dunley Hall

Astley Cross

Areley Common

PEARL LANE

Cherry Tree Wk

Apple Cl

Elm Gv

Maw La

Oak Cl

Red House La

Chiltern Cl

Cleeve Av

Cheviot Cl

Abberley Av

Witley Wy

Burnthorne Lane

Dunley

Dunley Hall

5

Redstone Rock

Windsor Drive

Marlborough Close

Woodhampton Close

Redstone Lane

Berkeley Crs

Barnfield Rd

William Coley Pl

Queen's Rd

Linden Av

Wesley Av

Beach Av

Jackson Cr

Waverley Cl

Swiss The Tts

The Windmill First Sch

Areley Common First Sch

Cheshire Cl

Chesshire W

Martley Rd

Callow Cl Bowpatch Rd

Oakhampton La

Hillside

Abberley Cl

Wrekin Wk

Alderdine

B4194

Cotswold Avenue

DUNLEY ROAD

Areley Kings

4

Sandy Indust Est

Nelson Rd

Sandy Rd

Broach Rd

Heath Rd

The Grinnall Business Cen

Lower Heath

Ind Est

Hemingway

Lavamon Walk

The Walshes

Hartstone Rd

Windmill Rd

Beach Av

ARELEY COMMON

Ankerdine Av

Heightington Av

DUNLEY ROAD

A451

Dunley Rd

Areley Av

RIBBESFORD RD

Areley Wood

3

Power Station Rd

Holden Hill Dr

The Heathlands The Birc...

Worcester Rd

Riverside Business Centre

Severnside Business Park

Cheapside

Stourport Sports Centre

The Bridge Medical Cen

Maltworks

Severn La

Lavamon Walk

Church Wk

Bower Hill Dr St Brittm's Rd

Areley Cl

Surgery

Rectory Lane

Areley Ct

A451

2

B4193

Works

WORCESTER RD

GILGAL

Vale Bus Pk

York House Medical Cen

Bell Row

Engine La

New St

Moorhall

Areley Lane

Bridge St

Lion Hl

VALE RD

MITTON ST

HIGH ST

YORK ST

Council Building

STOURPORT-ON-SEVERN

River Severn

Severn Way

B4194

Church Wk Bank

Cedar Cl

1

Mill Rd

Mill Lane

Holly Rd

Orchard Gr

Baldwin Road

Sumberland Rd

Mill Rd

Mitton Gdns

Stourport on Severn First Sch

Church La

Lichfield Middle School

Stourport Tennis Club

B4195

Dorsett Av

Park Av

Olive Gr

Lichfill

Harlem Wy

Vernon Road

Moor La

Ian Lane

Lembrands Wy

Cromwell Rd

Lickhill Road

New Way

Lime Cross

Lime La

Moseley Rd

Snowberry Cl

Bromyard

Lichfill First School

Astley Wk

A

F

E

D

C

B

188

Longboat Lane

Prospect Road

Bullus Road

Manor Rd

Brindley Street

Derwent St

St John's Rd

Windermere Way

Baldwin Rd North

LICKHILL ROAD

WOODBURY RD

Works

163

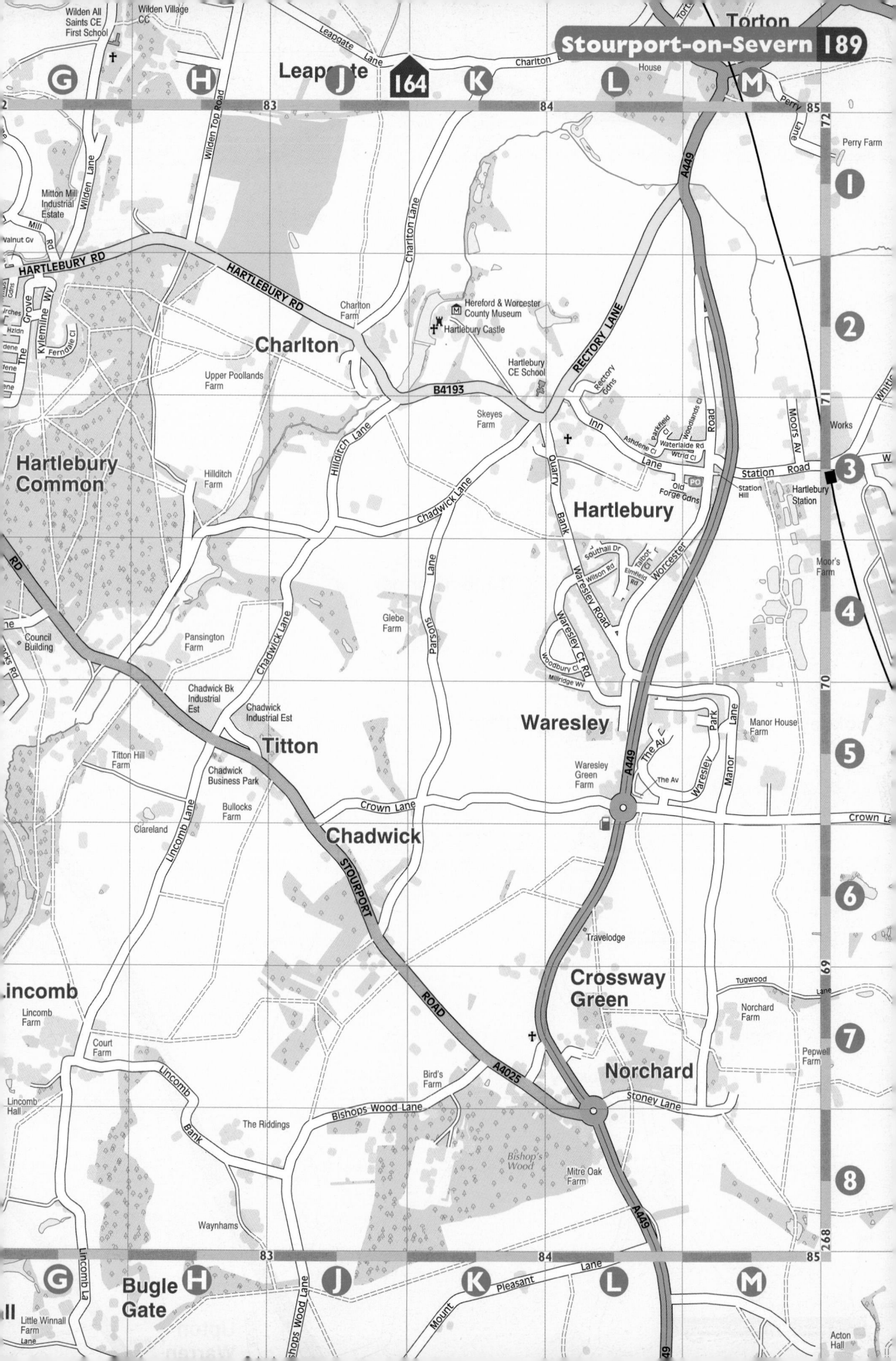

190

167

A B C D E F

I

Fockbury Rd

Dodford First School

Monarch Way

Fockbury Road

Park Farm

KIDDERMINSTER ROAD A448

Park Gate

2

Durrance Farm

Bungay Lake Lane

Bungay Lake Farm

Warridge Lodge Farm

Monsieurs Hall Lane

3

Risingbridge

Berry Lane

4

Timberhonger

Timberhonger Lane

70

5

Cooksey Green

Green Lane

Cooksey

Newhouse Lane

Cobbler's Coppice

M5

6

Berrylane Farm

Berry Lane

Foxwalks Farm

Grafton Mar House

7

Dog Lane

West Lodge Farm

8

Cooksey Lodge Farm

Cooksey Corner

Crutch Lane

Swan Lane

Rectory Lane

...ESTER ROAD

Upton Warren

Works

1 grid square represents 500 metres

A B C D E F

A B C **171** D E F

Rowney Green

Alvechurch Lodge Farm

Rockwell Lane

Newbourne Mill

Lye Bridge Farm

Rowney Green Lane

Gravel Pit Lane

Chapel Lane

Storrage House

The Holloway

Storrage Lane

Grange Farm

A441

Redditch Road

Bordesley Hall

Lower Park Farm

River Arrow

BIRMINGHAM ROAD A441

Bordesley Park Farm

DAGNELL END ROAD B410

Weights Farm

The Abbey Hotel Golf & Country Club

Golf Course

Weights Lane

Hither Green Lane

Weights Lane

Marshfield Cl

Stoke Lane

Radway Cl Rulings Preston Cl Parkfield Cl

Rush Lane Snowshill Cl

PAPER MILL

Wordsley Cl

Lowan's Hill Farm

Abbey Stadium

Works

Bordesley La

Cemetery Council Building

River Arrow

Riverside

Bordesley Abbey (remains of)

Bordesley La

Dolphin Road

Offenham Cl

Church Hill

Aldermans La

Birley's Lane

BIRMINGHAM ROAD

ALVECHURCH HWY

Council Building

MDDLHS LA

Superstore

Abbey Trading Centre

Abbey Works

Needle Mill La

P

Bordesley Abbey Visitors Centre

Forge Mill Needle Museum

Forge Mill Road

St Stephens CE First School

Park Way

Brooklands Lane

Marshfield La

Northern Cl

DRIVE

B4184 HEWELL RD

WINDSOR ROAD

B4184

Enfield Industrial Est

Enfield

Works

Hewell Road Est

Enfield Industrial Est

Hewell Road Swimming Pool

Fishing Line Rd

Millrace Rd

Meadow Crs

Meadow Cr

Meadownhill Road

St Stephens St

Neville Cl

Vernon Cl

Sand Cl

Lygon Cl

Stanley Close

Terry's Cl

Coppins Cl

Dale Road

Hayford Cl

Sedgley Close

COVENTRY HIGHWAY

Works

Hazel Tree Road

Lime Tree Crs

Cedar Vw

Bowood

Birchensale Middle School

Holyoakes Field First School

Cedar Road

Bridge st

Melen St

Mill St

Health Centre

Surg

202

Redditch Mosque

Archer Rd

Grove St

Prospect Hi

NE Worcestershire College

High School 6th Form College

A441

ARROW

Prospect Hill N

Prospect

A4023

Brook Street

Lakeside Trading Cen

HOLLOWAY

PROCTORS

Batchley United FC

The Business Centre

Redditch Stn

Redditch Co Court

Surgery

Peakmans St

St

Clive Works Albert St

Business Park Albert St

LYDHAM CL

ALVECHURCH HIGHWAY

Dale Road

Church Rd

PO

PO

A B **202** D E F

Honiley

A   B   C   **178**   D   E   F

424   25   26

72

1

71

Grove Farm

2

Inchford Brook

3

Beausale

Butlers End   Barracks La

Rouncil Lane

Fernwood Farm

Fernhill Farm

70

Elmwood Farm

4

Kites Nest Lane

Roundshill Farm

5

Haseley Green

Beausale Ho

Beausale Lane

Bannerhill Farm

6

Waste Green

69

Bulloak Farm

Deer Park Farm

7

Kingstanding Farm

Larch Cove

Old Man Farm

8

Kites Nest Lane

268

Haseley Business Centre

424   25   26

Haseley Manor

A   B   C   **204**   D   E   F

ale Lane

Prospe

1 grid square represents 500 metres

Stoneleigh Deer Park Golf Club

Cloud Bridge

River Avon

Golf Course

181

STONELEIGH ROAD

Centenary Way

Way

Centenary

LEAMINGTON ROAD

Stoneleigh Deer Park
Business Village

Waverley
Farm

Stareton

Waverley
Wood

Stone House
Farm

LEICESTER LANE

A445

Furzenhill
Farm

LEICESTER LANE A445

LEICESTER

A445

Cubbington Heath
Farm

Coventry Road

North
Cubbington
Wood

B4453

RUGBY ROAD

**Weston
Wether**

St Mic
Close

Kenilworth Road

Cubbington

Cotton M Thorn Stile
Close
Spinney

Three

Cornered

Wk Close

South
Cubbington
Wood

Beaufort Avenue

Girvan
Grove

Dunblane Drive

West
View
Road

Telford
Infant
School

High View Rd

South View
Road

Our Lady &
St Teresas RC
Combined School

Windmill Hill

Stonehouse
Close

Ledbrook
Road

Queen St

North
Brookfield
Rd

Broadway

Boddington
Close

Church Lane

Pinehurst

Church Wk

High Street

New Street

Ladycroft

Price Rd

Crest

Penns

Knightley

Cubbington CE
Primary School

Mill
Lane

207

Hill
Farm

Works

New Manor
Farm

B4453

Leighton
Close

Oldbridge Rd

Parklands Avenue

Sherwood Wk

Meadow

Gambolds

A   B   C   192   D   E   F

Patchetts Farm

397 98 99

68

Worcester & Birmingham Canal

1

Upper Gambolds Lane

Sheltwood Lane

Copyholt Lane

Cur Lane

Tardebigge Farm

2

67

Coalash Lane

Monarch's Way

Sheltwood Farm

Bank's Green

Copyholt Lane

Bentley House

Banks Green

3

Hatchetts Farm

Black Lake Lane

Middle Road

Woodgate

4

66

Woodgate Road

Bentley Lane

Lower Lane

The Thrift

Manor Road

Angel Street

Upper Bentley

Bentley Lane

Pumphouse Lane

Lower Bentley

5

Elms Lane

Keys Farm

Upper Bentley Farm

6

65

Fosters Green

High Lane

Foster's Green

7

Hill Lane

Leasowes Farm

8

264

Forest Farm

Forest Lane

Forest Lane

Wallhouse Lane

Wallhouse Farm

Ditchford Bank

397 98 99

A   B   C   D   E   F

I grid square represents 500 metres

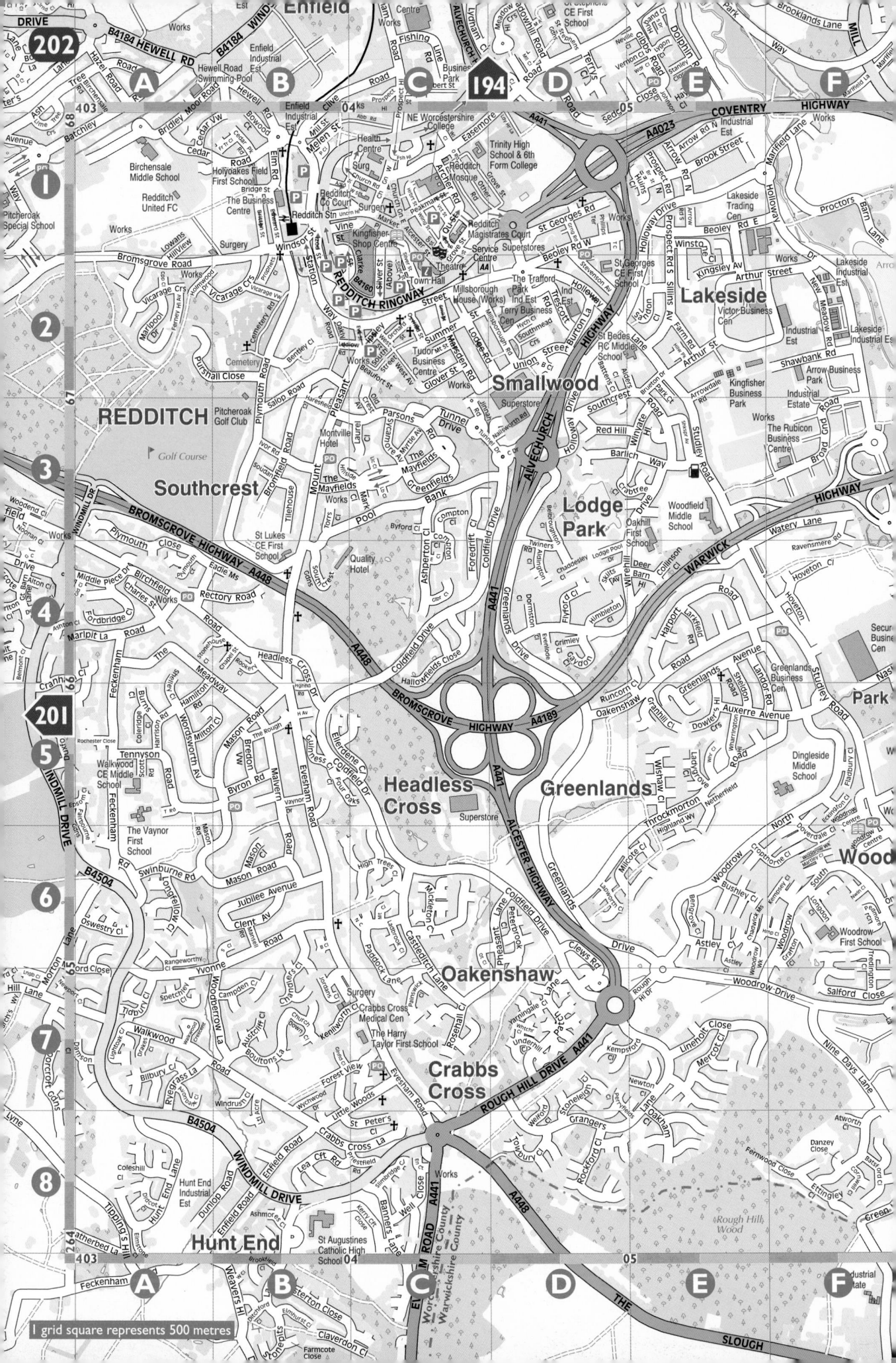

199

Offchurch

Radford Semele

Sydenham

Campion Hills

Lillington

SOUTHAM ROAD A425

A425 ROAD

West Road

Offchurch Road

Grand Union Canal Walk

Grand Union Canal

River Leam

Newbold Comyn Park

Golf Course

Newbold Comyn Lf Club

Leasowe Farm

Ham Farm

Ford Farm

Redhouse Farm

Glebe Farm

New Manor Farm

Lower Grange

School Hill

School Lane

Church End

Welsh Road

Offchurch Lane

The Greswoldes

Radford Semele CE Primary School

St Nicholas St

Valley Rd

The Valley

Campion School

St Anthony's RC Infant School

Gainsborough

Cubbington CE Primary School

St Teresa's RC Combined School

Our Lady & St Teresa's RC Primary School

661

Acock's Green 126 E2
Aggborough 164 C2
Alcester Lane's End 125 H7
Alderman's Green 135 G1
Aldershawe 28 C2
The Alders 31 J7
Aldridge 40 E5
Alfred's Well 168 A7
Allen End 58 D7
Allesley 132 F5
Alum Rock 108 E2
Alvechurch 170 F7
Alvecote 33 H7
Amblecote 101 K6
Amington 32 E8
Ansley 96 F1
Ansley Common 79 K6
Apes Dale 169 K7
Areley Kings 188 A4
Arrowfield Top 170 F4
Ash Green 116 A7
Ashmore Lake 51 M1
Ashmore Park 37 K4
Ashow 198 C4
Ashwood 82 C8
Astley 97 H6
Astley Cross 188 C5
Aston 89 K7
Aston Fields 191 L5
Atherstone 63 J3
Attleborough 99 G3
Bacon's End 111 G1
Baddesley Clinton 177 G7
Baddesley Ensor 79 M1
Baginton 181 K3
Ballard's Green 96 B2
Balls Hill 68 E4
Balsall Common 152 A6
Balsall Heath 107 J8
Balsall Street 151 K8
Bank's Green 200 E2
Banners Gate 71 L1
Baptist End 85 G7
Bark Hill 162 D1
Barnacle 117 M7
Barnettbrook 140 A8
Barnt Green 170 B4
Barr Common 55 G2
Barston 150 F5
Bartley Green 123 H5
Batchley 201 L2
Bateman's Green 146 D6
Baxterley 62 A7
Baylis Green 195 M4
Bearwood 105 L3
Beausale 196 A3
Bedworth 116 F5
Bedworth Heath 116 B3
Beech Lanes 105 J6
Beechwood 152 D7
Belbroughton 141 J6
Belgrave 46 C4
Bell End 141 M6
Belle Vale 103 K8
Bellevue 169 G3
Bell Green 134 F5
Bell Heath 142 B5
Bentley 78 B1
Bentley Common 62 B8
Bentley Heath 149 J8
Benton Green 152 C3
Beoley 195 H6
Berkswell 152 B2
Bermuda 98 E5
Bescot 53 G7
Bewdley 162 F3
Bickenhill 129 H4
Bilbrook 35 C1
Billesley 125 H4
Billesley Common 125 L6
Bilston 51 G6
Bilton 186 A6
Bilton Fields 186 D7
Binley 156 C5
Binley Woods 157 G6
Birch Acre 172 B6
Birchen Coppice 163 M4
Birch End 69 K6
Birches Green 90 E2
Birchfield 89 H4
Birchills 53 H2
Birchley Heath 78 C4
Birchmoor 47 J6
Birmingham 6 C7
Bitterscote 45 L2
Black Bank 116 E4
Blackdown 198 D8
Blackfords 16 D2
Blackheath 103 M3
Black Lake 68 E6
Blackstone 163 H4
Blackwell 169 L8
Blakebrook 138 K7
Blakedown 140 A3
Blakeley 64 E8
Blakenall Heath 39 G4
Blakenhall 49 M6
Bloomfield 67 K7
Blossomfield 148 C3
Bloxwich 38 E4
Bluntington 166 C4
Blyth End 94 A3
Bodymoor Heath 59 L8
Boldmere 72 E4
Bolehall 46 A1
Boley Park 21 K6
Bonehill 45 J4
Boney Hay 18 F4
Bordesley Green 108 C4
Borough Park 31 M6
Boscomoor 10 C5
Botts Green 77 H8
Bournbrook 124 E4
Bournes Green 167 G3
Bourne Vale 54 B2
Bournheath 168 B5
Bournville 124 D6
Bowling Green 103 H2
Box Trees 174 F4
Brades Village 86 B4
Bradley 67 H2
Bradmore 49 J5
Bradnock's Marsh 151 H2
Bramford 66 E6
Brandon 157 K8
Brandwood End 146 B1
Branson's Cross 195 L3
The Bratch 64 D5
Bretford 158 C6
Bridge End 205 L2
Bridgetown 16 B6
Brierley Hill 102 A3
Brinklow 158 C2
Brinsford 22 B6
Bristnall Fields 104 F2
Broad Green 192 E3
Broadwaters 138 C4
Brockencote 166 B5

Brockmoor 101 M1
Bromford 91 J4
Bromley 83 L8
Bromsgrove 191 M3
Broome 140 F3
Broom Hill 167 H2
Brownhills 26 E5
Brown's Green 88 D1
Brownshill Green 133 G4
Brownsover 161 G6
Bubbenhall 182 B7
Buckland End 91 L6
Buckpool 101 K3
Budbrooke 204 C6
Burcot 192 C1
Burlish Park 163 K6
Burnt Tree 85 K3
Burntwood 18 E6
Burntwood Green 19 H7
Burton Green 179 G1
Bushbury 36 C2
Caldecote 165 M7
Caldecote 80 C3
Caldmore 4 C7
Calf Heath 14 D7
California 123 K3
Camp Hill 80 C8
Campion Hills 207 G4
Canley 154 A7
Cannock 16 A2
The Cape 205 H4
Carol Green 152 D5
Carpenter's Hill 195 K5
Carroway Head 57 M1
Castle Bromwich 92 A5
Castlecroft 48 C5
Castle Vale 91 L2
Catchems Corner 152 C8
Catchems End 137 H8
Catherine-de-Barnes 128 E8
Cathiron 159 K4
Catshill 26 E7
Catshill 168 E5
Caunsall 118 A6
Causeway Green 104 D2
Cawston 185 L6
Chaddesley Corbett 166 C5
Chadsmoor 16 C1
Chad Valley 106 D6
Chadwick 189 J6
Chadwick End 176 F6
Chapel End 79 M5
Chapel Fields 154 C3
Chapel Green 114 A6
Chapman's Hill 142 F4
Charford 191 J5
Charlemont 69 H6
Charlton 189 H2
Chase Terrace 18 C5
Chasetown 18 D7
Chattle Hill 93 J3
Chelmsley Wood 111 G4
Cheslyn Hay 24 B2
Chessetts Wood 176 B5
Chesterfield 28 C5
Cheswick Green 174 C1
Cheylesmore 155 J6
Chilvers Coton 98 E4
Chorley 19 L8
The Chuckery 5 K4
Churchbridge 16 B1
Church End 78 E7
Church End 95 G3
Church End 156 A2
Churchfield 69 J8
Church Hill 13 H8
Church Hill 68 E1
Church Hill 194 E8
Church Hill 10 A2
Church Lawford 158 F8
Cinder Hill 66 D4
Claregate 35 H7
Clayhanger 26 B7
Clent 141 L2
Cliff 59 M5
Clifton upon Dunsmore 161 L8
Coalpit Field 117 H4
Coal Pool 39 K8
Cobley Hill 193 J1
Codsall 34 D1
Cofton Common 144 D7
Cofton Hackett 170 B2
Cole End 93 K5
Colehall 91 M8
Coleshill 93 L7
Collycroft 116 F1
Colton Hills 65 L2
Comberford 31 H2
Comberton 138 E7
Compton 49 H3
Cooksey Corner 190 B7
Coombeswood 104 A7
Copt Heath 149 L4
Corley 114 F6
Corley Ash 114 F4
Corley Moor 114 C6
Coseley 67 G4
Cosford 160 D2
Coton 31 G7
Cotteridge 124 C3
Coundon 133 J6
Court House Green 134 E5
Coven Heath 22 A7
Coventry 9 C8
Crabbs Cross 202 C7
Crackley 179 M6
Cradley 103 G7
Cradley Heath 103 G5
Creswell Green 19 J3
Cross Green 22 B4
Crossway Green 189 L7
Cubbington 199 H7
Curdworth 74 E7
Dam Mill 34 F4
Darby End 103 H1
Darby's Hill 85 M6
Darlaston 52 A6
Darlaston Green 52 A5
Darley Green 175 L5
Darnford 21 K7
Daw End 39 M8
Dayhouse Bank 142 F3
Deepfields 66 F4
The Delves 69 L1
Dennis 39 K6
Dennis Heath 147 L8
Devitts Green 96 A4
Dickens Heath 147 L8
Digbeth 7 J6
Dodford 167 K7
Doe Bank 58 B7
Dogingtree Estate 12 B5
Dordale 167 K8
Dordon 47 K7
Dorridge 175 L2
Dosthill 45 M8
Dowles 136 D7
Drakes Cross 146 E7
Drayton 166 F1
Drayton Bassett 45 H8
Druids Heath 41 G4

Dudley 85 H3
Dudley Port 86 A1
Dudley's Fields 38 C5
Dudley Wood 103 G3
Duke End 112 C1
Dunsley 118 A1
Dunstall Hill 35 M8
Eachway 143 K7
Earlsdon 8 A8
Earlswood 173 L4
Easenhall 159 J1
Eastcote 150 C2
Eaves Green 131 K3
Edgbaston 106 D7
Edge Hill 61 G3
Edgwick 134 C5
Edial 19 J7
Elcock's Brook 201 H7
Elmdon 128 E2
Elmdon Heath 128 C6
Emscote 205 L5
Enfield 194 B8
Erdington 90 E2
Essington 37 K2
Ettingshall 50 D8
Ettingshall Park 66 B2
Eve Hill 84 E3
Exhall 116 F6
Fairfield 137 M2
Fairfield 168 A7
Falcon Lodge 57 M7
Fallings Heath 52 C8
Farewell 19 L1
Fazeley 45 L4
Featherstone 23 G6
Fen End 177 J2
Fillongley 114 C2
Finham 180 F2
Finstall 192 C4
Fishley 39 G1
Five Ways 118 E8
Flint's Green 131 K8
Foleshill 134 D5
Foley Park 164 A2
Footherley 42 C5
Fordbridge 110 E2
Fordhouses 35 M2
Forhill 171 L1
Forshaw Heath 173 G6
Foster's Green 200 A6
Foul End 77 G3
Four Ashes 14 A3
Four Ashes 175 G2
Four Crosses 15 H6
Four Oaks 56 C2
Four Oaks 131 H8
Four Oaks Park 56 D5
Foxford 134 D1
Foxlydiate 137 M4
Franche 137 K1
Frankley 122 F8
Frankley 143 K3
Frankley Green 122 E8
Frankley Hill 143 K2
Freasley 61 G1
Friar Park 69 H2
Furnace End 95 J2
Gailey Wharf 14 D3
Galley Common 79 L8
Garrets Green 109 L4
Gentleshaw 18 E1
Gibbet Hill 180 C3
Gib Heath 88 E6
Giggetty 64 C3
Gilbertstone 109 K7
Gillway 31 K3
Gilson 93 J4
Glascote 46 A2
Glebe Farm 109 K1
Golds Green 68 C5
Goldthorn Park 66 B1
Goodyers End 116 A4
Gornalwood 84 A3
Gorstey Ley 19 G6
Goscote 39 K5
Gosford Green 9 K5
Gospel End Village 65 K5
Gothersley 100 C3
Gravelly Hill 90 D3
Great Barr 70 D3
Great Bridge 68 D3
Great Heath 134 C6
Great Saredon 15 M7
Great Wyrley 24 E2
Green End 113 J4
Green Heath 12 E6
Greenhill 138 E6
Greenlands 202 D5
Green Lane 154 E8
Green Lane 203 H7
Greensforge 82 B7
Grendon 61 B1
Grendon Common 62 A3
Griff 98 F7
Griffin's Hill 124 B6
Grimes Hill 172 F1
Grove End 74 D2
Grove Vale 70 A4
Gun Hill 96 D6
Guns Village 86 E1
The Gutter 142 C6
Guy's Cliffe 205 K3
Habberley 137 L7
Hackman's Gate 140 D4
Haden Cross 103 L5
Hagley 120 B7
Halesowen 122 A1
Hales Park 162 C2
Hall End 47 K8
Hall Flat 169 G6
Hall Green 69 C5
Hall Green 126 E6
Hall Green 134 F2
Hammerwich 27 H1
Hampton in Arden 129 K6
Hampton Magna 204 D7
Hampton on the Hill 204 C8
Hamstead 70 C5
Handsworth 88 C3
Handsworth Wood 88 F2
Harborne 105 L7
Harborough Magna 160 A2
Harborough Parva 160 A3
Harden 39 K6
Hardwick 55 K3
Hartle 141 K7
Hartlebury 189 G3
Hartlebury Common 189 G3
Hartshill 79 M4
Hart's Hill 84 C8
Hartshill Green 79 L3
Harvest Hill 132 K3
Harvills Hawthorn 68 K3
Harvington 165 M3
Hasbury 121 J2
Hasluck's Green 147 J3
Hateley Heath 69 G7
Hatherton 15 K4
Hatton 204 A2

Hawkes End 132 E3
Hawkesley 145 J5
Hawks Green 16 K4
Hawne 103 L8
Hayfield Hill 18 D1
Hayley Green 121 G4
Hay Mills 108 F7
Hazelslade 13 L7
Headless Cross 202 C5
Heaskey Heath 146 A6
Heath End 39 K4
Heath Green 195 J2
Heath Hayes 17 K4
Heath Town 50 E1
Hednesford 12 E8
Henley Green 135 H5
Higham on the Hill 81 K2
Highbridge 25 L7
Highbury Park 125 H4
Highgate 107 K5
High Heath 40 A3
High Heath 37 M5
Highter's Heath 146 F3
High Town 12 D8
Hill 56 E1
Hillfield 148 E6
Hillfields 9 H2
Hill Hook 42 C7
Hillmorton 187 K5
Hillpool 140 D8
Hill Top 68 E5
Hill Top 96 E4
Hill Top 69 G4
Hill Wood 43 G8
Hill Wootton 198 A7
Hilton 27 L5
Himley 82 F2
Hinksford 82 D5
Hints 44 B3
Hobble End 25 G6
Hockley 46 C8
Hockley 152 F1
Hockley Heath 175 H7
Hodgehill 91 H8
Hoggrill's End 93 M8
Holbeache 136 E2
Holbeach 134 A2
Holly Bank 40 F2
Hollyberry End 132 B1
Hollyhurst 117 J3
Hollywood 146 F5
Holt End 195 K6
Holy Cross 141 J3
Honiley 178 B8
Hoobrook 164 A8
Hook End 129 M8
Hopwas 30 E6
Hopwood 171 G2
Horeston Grange 81 L8
Horseley Heath 68 A8
Howe Green 97 H8
Hunnington 121 M6
Hunt End 202 A8
Huntington 12 B7
Hunts Green 59 G6
Hurcott 139 G5
Hurley 77 J2
Hurley Common 60 F6
Hurst Green 104 D5
Hurst Hill 66 D5
Illey 122 C5
Illshaw Heath 174 B5
Inkford 172 E4
Ipsley 203 G4
Iverley 119 H5
Kates Hill 85 J4
Kendal End 170 B1
Kenilworth 197 J2
Keresley 133 K1
Keresley Newlands 115 M7
Kettlebrook 45 M2
Kidderminster 164 A1
Kineton Green 127 H5
Kingsbury 60 B7
King's Heath 125 J6
King's Hill 68 D2
Kings Hill 180 F3
Kingshurst 92 E6
King's Newnham 159 D6
King's Norton 145 J3
Kingstanding 71 M7
Kingswinford 82 F7
Kinwalsey 113 K6
Kirby Corner 153 L7
Kitt's Green 110 A1
Kitwell 122 E6
Knowle 150 A7
Knowle Grove 175 M2
The Knowle 85 L8
The Laches 22 D2
Ladies Hill 179 L2
Ladywood 106 D4
Lakeside 202 E2
The Lakes 162 C1
Lambert's End 86 E2
Landywood 24 C3
Lane Green 35 G2
Lane Head 38 A7
Lanesfield 66 E1
Laney Green 23 L3
Langley 86 D8
Langley Green 104 F1
Lapal 122 A2
Lawford Heath 185 H6
Lawns Wood 100 F2
Lea End 171 K2
Lea Hall 109 L3
Lea Marston 75 L6
Leamore 38 E7
Leapgate 164 C8
Lee Bank 6 C9
Leek Wootton 197 L2
Leighswood 40 C6
Leomansley 20 C5
Leyfields 31 K7
Ley Hill 56 E4
The Leys 31 L8
Lichfield 20 D5
Lickey 169 L2
Lickey End 169 H7
Lickhill 163 J8
Lifford 145 K1
Lillington 207 H2
Lime Tree Park 153 L4
Lincomb 189 C2
Linthurst 169 M7
Little Aston 42 E6
Little Bloxwich 39 H2
Little Bromwich 108 A3
Little Hay 43 G4
Little Heath 134 D4
Little Lawford 159 L6
Little Norton 25 K3
Little Packington 111 M7
Little Saredon 23 H2
Littlewood 24 D2
Littleworth 17 K1
Littleworth End 58 A5
Little Wyrley 25 H5

Lode Heath 128 A7
Lodge Green 131 H2
Lodge Hill 123 M3
Lodge Park 202 D3
Londonderry 105 G1
London Fields 84 C3
Long Bank 162 A4
Longbridge 144 B5
Longford 134 D1
Long Lawford 159 K8
Lower Bentley 200 B5
Lower Bradley 67 K1
Lower Clent 141 H1
Lower Eastern Green 153 J2
Lower Gornal 84 C1
Lower Heath 188 F4
Lower Illey 122 C6
Lower Penn 48 D8
Lower Stoke 155 L4
Lower Stonnall 41 L1
Low Habberley 137 K5
Low Hill 36 B6
Lozells 89 G5
The Lunt 51 L6
Lutley 120 F3
Lydiate Ash 169 G2
Lye 102 C7
Lyndon Green 109 K6
Lynn 27 K8
Madeley Heath 142 C6
Major's Green 147 H5
Mancetter 79 J4
Maney 72 F1
Manor House 135 G3
Mapplehorough Green 203 L5
Marlbrook 169 H4
Marston 75 L3
Marston 158 A8
Marston Green 110 E5
Marston Jabbett 99 K8
Matchborough 203 J5
Maw Green 53 M7
Maxstoke 93 J2
Mayer's Green 86 F2
Meer End 178 A4
Mere Green 56 F2
Meriden 131 H4
Merridale 49 J3
Merry Hill 49 J5
Merry Hill 102 D2
Mesty Croft 68 E3
Middle Bickenhill 129 L2
Middle Hill 23 L1
Middle Stoke 155 L2
Middleton 58 F4
Mill Green 18 A3
Mill Green 41 L6
Milverton 206 B2
Minworth 74 A8
Monkspath 148 E8
Monmore Green 50 E5
Monwode Lea 95 J2
Moon's Moat 195 K8
Moor Hall 57 H4
Moseley 50 E4
Moseley 125 K5
Mount Pleasant 18 C7
Mount Pleasant 201 G8
Moxley 67 M1
Muckley Corner 27 L3
Mushroom Green 102 F4
Mustow Green 165 L4
Myton 206 A6
Neal's Green 116 B7
Nechells 90 B5
Nechells Green 7 M1
Nechells Green 107 M1
Nether Stowe 21 H3
Netherton 84 F8
Nether Whitacre 76 E7
New Arley 96 F5
New Bilton 186 C3
Newbold on Avon 160 C8
Newbolds 36 E7
Newbridge 49 H2
Newhall Green 113 M4
New Invention 38 A5
New Oscott 72 B3
Newton 70 A5
Newton 161 L4
Newtown 89 G7
Newtown 26 F3
New Town 86 B1
Newtown 89 G8
Norchard 189 L7
Northfield 144 F1
Norton 119 J3
Norton Canes 17 J8
Norton East 17 L7
Norton Green 18 A1
Norton Green 175 M3
Nuneaton 98 D2
Oaken 34 A3
Oakenshaw 202 C7
Oakham 85 K6
Ocker Hill 68 A4
Old Arley 96 D3
Oldbury 79 J3
Oldbury 86 E8
Old Fallings 36 D6
Oldfallow 16 A2
Old Hill 103 L4
Old Milverton 205 L2
Old Perton 48 A2
Old Swinford 119 L2
Oldwich Lane 177 H4
Olton 127 L3
Orton 64 D2
Orton Hill 64 E3
Otherton 10 D8
Ounsdale 64 D7
Outwood 166 F8
Outwoods 103 J7
Overend 74 D4
Over Green 74 D4
Overslade 186 C4
Over Whitacre 95 J2
Oxbarn 49 J6
Oxley 35 M5
Packmores 205 J5
Packwood 175 L6
Packwood Gullet 175 K4
Palfrey 53 H7
Palmers Cross 34 F5
Park End 162 B5
Park Farm 202 F5
Parkfield 50 D8
Park Gate 190 E2
Park Hill 180 A8
Park Village 36 D8
Pedmore 120 B5
Pelsall 39 M2
Pelsall Wood 25 K8
Pendeford 35 J3
Penkridge 10 F3
Penn 48 F6
Pennett 83 M6
Perry Barr 70 F8
Perry Beeches 70 F6

Perry Common 71 M5
Perry Crofts 32 A6
Perryfields 191 H1
Perton 48 C1
Pheasey 71 G1
Piccadilly 60 D5
Pickford 132 C5
Pickford Green 132 B6
Pillaton 11 G6
Pinkett's Booth 132 B5
Pink Green 195 M5
Pinley 155 L6
Pipehill 19 M8
Pleck 52 F7
Plough Hill 79 L6
Podmoor 165 J8
Polesworth 47 L4
Portobello 51 J3
Portway 86 A7
Portway 172 E7
Potter's Green 135 K4
Prestwood 100 C4
Priestfield 50 F7
Primrose Hill 103 H1
Princes End 67 J4
Prospect Village 17 M1
Pye Green 12 D4
Pype Hayes 73 H8
Quarry Bank 102 D5
Quarry Heath 11 G5
Quarry Hill 46 E7
Queslett 71 G3
Quinton 104 E7
Radford 134 A7
Radford Semele 207 K8
Ratcliffe Culey 63 M1
Rawnsley 13 M8
Reddicap Heath 73 L1
Redditch 202 A3
Rednal 144 A8
Reeves Green 152 E5
Ribbesford 162 F4
Ridgacre 105 G7
Ridge Lane 78 E3
Riverside 194 C7
Robinson's End 97 J2
Rodbaston 14 B1
Romsley 142 E1
Romsley Hill 142 E3
Rood End 87 G7
Roseville 66 E5
Rotten Row 176 A1
Rotton Park 106 C1
Roughley 57 G2
Round Oak 102 C1
Round's Green 86 C5
Rowley Regis 85 M8
Rowley's Green 134 C1
Rowney Green 171 K8
Royal Leamington Spa 206 F4
Rubery 143 L6
Rugby 186 C3
Ruiton 84 B1
Rumbow Cottages 142 B2
Rumbush 173 J2
Rumer Hill 16 C5
Rushall 40 A6

Russell's Hall 84 C5
Ryton-on-Dunsmore 182 F3
St Godwalds 192 A6
St Helena 47 K4
St Johns 197 K3
St Nicolas Park 81 L6
Salter Street 174 A3
Saltley 108 C1
Sandfields 20 F8
Sandwell 87 L7
Scotlands 36 E5
Seckington 33 L2
Sedgemere 177 J1
Sedgley 66 C5
Selly Oak 124 B4
Selly Park 124 E4
Shard End 92 B8
Shareshill 23 H3
Sharmans Cross 148 C1
Sheldon 109 M8
Shelfield 40 A5
Shenley Fields 123 J6
Shenstone 28 D8
Shenstone Woodend 42 E4
Shire Oak 26 D7
Shire Oak Hill 26 F8
Shirley 148 A2
Shirley Heath 148 A4
Short Cross 121 L1
Short Heath 38 C7
Short Heath 72 D7
Shustoke 94 D5
Shuttington 33 J6
Sidemoor 191 K1
Silver End 101 M4
Silver Street 146 C8
Slade Heath 22 C3
Slideslow 192 A3
Small Heath 108 A5
Smallwood 202 D2
Smestow 82 A1
Smethwick 87 J8
Soho 88 A7
Solihull 151 K7
Solihull Lodge 147 C3
Southcrest 202 A3
South Yardley 109 H7
Sparkbrook 107 M6
Sparkhill 126 A2
Spennells 164 E4
Spon End 8 B5
Springfield 3 K2
Springfield 85 K8
Springfield 126 A4
Springhill 24 B8
Springhill 27 H6
Spring Hill 65 C1
The Spring 179 K6
Stakenbridge 140 B2
Stambermill 102 A8
Standeford 22 A1
Stanklyn 165 H3
Staple Hill 169 G5
Stareton 199 H2
Stechford 109 J2
Stirchley 124 E6

Stivichall 155 G8
Stockfield 127 G1
Stockingford 97 M3
Stockland Green 90 A1
Stockwell End 35 G8
Stoke 156 A3
Stoke Aldermoor 156 A5
Stoke End 58 D6
Stoke Heath 134 E7
Stoke Heath 191 H8
Stone 165 H2
Stonebridge 129 M3
Stone Cross 69 H4
Stoneleigh 181 G7
Stoneydelph 46 F4
Stoney Hill 191 L4
Stonnall 41 H1
Stourbridge 119 H1
Stourport-on-Severn 188 C2
Stourton 100 D6
Stowe 21 G4
Stow Lawn 51 H5
The Straits 85 M8
Streethay 21 L3
Streetly 55 M4
Stretton-on-Dunsmore 183 L8
Stubber's Green 40 C5
Summerfield 164 E6
Summerhill 27 J4
Summer Hill 67 L4
Summerhill 137 L8
Sutton Coldfield 57 H8
Swan Village 86 D1
Swindon 82 D3
Sydenham 207 G8
Tamworth 31 M7
Tanner's Green 172 F3
Tansley Hill 85 K6
Tanwood 166 E3
Tardebigge 192 E6
Tat Bank 86 E6
Temple Balsall 176 F1
Ten Acres 124 F5
Terry's Green 173 K6
Tettenhall 35 G8
Tettenhall Wood 73 L4
Thimble End 58 C1
Thornes 41 J2
Three Maypoles 147 M6
Tidbury Green 173 J1
Tile Cross 110 C3
Tile Hill 153 J4
Tilehouse Green 149 L8
Timberhonger 190 C4
Tipper's Hill 96 C7
Tipton 67 L6
Tipton Green 57 H7
Titton 189 H5
Tividale 85 M4
Tollbar End 156 B8
Toll End 67 M7
Torton 164 F8
Tower Hill 70 E7
Trescott 48 A7
Triangle 26 F1
Trimpley 136 F4
Trueman's Heath 147 G6

Trysull 64 A4
Tudor Hill 56 E7
Turves Green 144 E4
Tutnall 192 E4
Two Gates 46 A5
Tyburn 91 J2
Tyseley 108 E8
Ulverley Green 127 J5
Upper Bentley 200 F4
Upper Catshill 168 F4
Upper Eastern Green 105 H4
Upper Gambolds 192 A8
Upper Gornal 66 C7
Upper Landywood 24 C6
Upper Stoke 134 F8
Upper Witton 72 A7
Vauxhall 107 M2
Vigo 40 D3
The Village 83 J6
Wake Green 125 L4
Walker's Heath 145 M4
Walkwood 201 L7
Wall 28 B3
Wallbrook 67 G6
Wall Heath 82 F5
Wallington Heath 38 E2
Walmley 73 K5
Walmley Ash 73 M6
Walsal End 150 E2
Walsall 5 G7
Walsall Wood 40 D1
Walsgrave on Sowe 135 M6
The Walshes 188 D4
Walton Pool 141 L3
Ward End 90 E8
Waresley 189 K5
Waring's Green 174 A4
Warley Woods 105 J4
Warstock 147 G2
Warstone 23 M5
Warwick 205 L7
Washford 203 J5
Washwood Heath 90 C7
Waste Green 196 A6
Water Orton 92 F2
Watford Gap 42 D6
Weatheroak Hill 171 M4
Webheath 201 J4
Weddington 81 G5
Wednesbury 68 B3
Wednesbury Oak 67 K4
Wednesfield 37 H7
Weeford 43 L1
Weoley Castle 123 K4
Wergs 34 D7
West Bromwich 86 F4
West Chadsmoor 12 D7
Westcroft 36 F2
West Hagley 119 M8
West Heath 145 G6
West Hill 12 E7
Weston in Arden 117 M1
Westwood Heath 153 J7
Whateley 60 C2
Whitacre Heath 76 A7
Whiteheath Gate 104 C1
Whitehouse Common 57 K7

Whitemoor 179 L8
Whitestone 99 K5
Whitley 155 K7
Whitlock's End 147 J7
Whitmore Park 133 M4
Whittington 63 G2
Whittington 118 A3
Whoberley 154 A3
Wigginton 31 M3
Wightwick 48 D4
Wilden 164 B7
Wildmoor 168 D2
Willenhall 51 M2
Willenhall 156 A7
Wilnecote 46 D6
Wimblebury 17 K2
Windy Arbour 197 L2
Winson Green 88 C8
Winterfold 165 M4
Winyates 203 J2
Winyates Green 203 K1
Wishaw 74 E5
Witherley 63 M6
Withybed Green 170 C7
Withymoor Village 102 C4
Witton 89 J2
Wollaston 101 J7
Wollescote 120 C1
Wolston 183 M2
Wolverhampton 3 J4
Wolverley 138 C1
Wombourne 64 B7
Woodcock Hill 123 J5
Woodcote 19 J6
Woodcote Green 167 G7
Wood End 37 G6
Wood End 61 H4
Wood End 96 F8
Wood End 135 G3
Woodgate 122 D4
Woodgate Valley 123 G2
Wood Green 52 E8
Wood Hayes 36 F4
Woodhouses 157 M1
Woodloes Park 205 H4
Woodrow 166 B2
Woodrow 202 F6
Woods Bank 52 B8
Woodsetton 66 C6
Woodside 84 D7
The Woods 69 G1
Woodway Park 135 J5
Wootton Green 151 K4
Wordsley 101 J2
Worlds End 127 L6
Worms Ash 168 B7
Wribbenhall 163 C1
Wyken 135 H8
Wylde Green 73 H4
Wythall 172 C3
Yardley 109 H5
Yardley Wood 147 J1
Yew Tree 69 M2

USING THE STREET INDEX

Street names are listed alphabetically. Each street name is followed by its postal town or area locality, the Postcode District, the page number, and the reference to the square in which the name is found.

Standard index entries are shown as follows:

Abberley Av *STRPT* DY13 ....**188** B5

Street names and selected addresses not shown on the map due to scale restrictions are shown in the index with an asterisk:

Abbey Cottages *COVS* CV3 * **156** D6

GENERAL ABBREVIATIONS

ACC	ACCESS	CTYD	COURTYARD	HLS	HILLS	MWY	MOTORWAY
ALY	ALLEY	CUTT	CUTTINGS	HO	HOUSE	N	NORTH
AP	APPROACH	CV	COVE	HOL	HOLLOW	NE	NORTH EAST
AR	ARCADE	CYN	CANYON	HOSP	HOSPITAL	NW	NORTH WEST
ASS	ASSOCIATION	DEPT	DEPARTMENT	HRB	HARBOUR	O/P	OVERPASS
AV	AVENUE	DL	DALE	HTH	HEATH	OFF	OFFICE
BCH	BEACH	DM	DAM	HTS	HEIGHTS	ORCH	ORCHARD
BLDS	BUILDINGS	DR	DRIVE	HVN	HAVEN	OV	OVAL
BND	BEND	DRO	DROVE	HWY	HIGHWAY	PAL	PALACE
BNK	BANK	DRY	DRIVEWAY	IMP	IMPERIAL	PAS	PASSAGE
BR	BRIDGE	DWGS	DWELLINGS	IN	INLET	PAV	PAVILION
BRK	BROOK	E	EAST	IND EST	INDUSTRIAL ESTATE	PDE	PARADE
BTM	BOTTOM	EMB	EMBANKMENT	INF	INFIRMARY	PH	PUBLIC HOUSE
BUS	BUSINESS	EMBY	EMBASSY	INFO	INFORMATION	PK	PARK
BVD	BOULEVARD	ESP	ESPLANADE	INT	INTERCHANGE	PKWY	PARKWAY
BY	BYPASS	EST	ESTATE	IS	ISLAND	PL	PLACE
CATH	CATHEDRAL	EX	EXCHANGE	JCT	JUNCTION	PLN	PLAIN
CEM	CEMETERY	EXPY	EXPRESSWAY	JTY	JETTY	PLNS	PLAINS
CEN	CENTRE	EXT	EXTENSION	KG	KING	PLZ	PLAZA
CFT	CROFT	F/O	FLYOVER	KNL	KNOLL	POL	POLICE STATION
CH	CHURCH	FC	FOOTBALL CLUB	L	LAKE	PR	PRINCE
CHA	CHASE	FK	FORK	LA	LANE	PREC	PRECINCT
CHYD	CHURCHYARD	FLD	FIELD	LDG	LODGE	PREP	PREPARATORY
CIR	CIRCLE	FLDS	FIELDS	LGT	LIGHT	PRIM	PRIMARY
CIRC	CIRCUS	FLS	FALLS	LK	LOCK	PROM	PROMENADE
CL	CLOSE	FLS	FLATS	LKS	LAKES	PRS	PRINCESS
CLFS	CLIFFS	FM	FARM	LNDG	LANDING	PRT	PORT
CMP	CAMP	FT	FORT	LTL	LITTLE	PT	POINT
CNR	CORNER	FWY	FREEWAY	LWR	LOWER	PTH	PATH
CO	COUNTY	FY	FERRY	MAG	MAGISTRATE	PZ	PIAZZA
COLL	COLLEGE	GA	GATE	MAN	MANSIONS	QD	QUADRANT
COM	COMMON	GAL	GALLERY	MD	MEAD	QU	QUEEN
COMM	COMMISSION	GDN	GARDEN	MDW	MEADOWS	QY	QUAY
CON	CONVENT	GDNS	GARDENS	MEM	MEMORIAL	R	RIVER
COT	COTTAGE	GLD	GLADE	MKT	MARKET	RBT	ROUNDABOUT
COTS	COTTAGES	GLN	GLEN	MKTS	MARKETS	RD	ROAD
CP	CAPE	GN	GREEN	ML	MALL	RDG	RIDGE
CPS	COPSE	GND	GROUND	ML	MILL	REP	REPUBLIC
CR	CREEK	GRA	GRANGE	MNR	MANOR	RES	RESERVOIR
CREM	CREMATORIUM	GRG	GARAGE	MS	MEWS	RFC	RUGBY FOOTBALL CLUB
CRS	CRESCENT	GT	GREAT	MSN	MISSION	RI	RISE
CSWY	CAUSEWAY	GTWY	GATEWAY	MT	MOUNT	RP	RAMP
CT	COURT	GV	GROVE	MTN	MOUNTAIN	RW	ROW
CTRL	CENTRAL	HGR	HIGHER	MTS	MOUNTAINS	S	SOUTH
CTS	COURTS	HL	HILL	MUS	MUSEUM	SCH	SCHOOL

SE	SOUTH EAST
SER	SERVICE AREA
SH	SHORE
SHOP	SHOPPING
SKWY	SKYWAY
SMT	SUMMIT
SOC	SOCIETY
SP	SPUR
SPR	SPRING
SQ	SQUARE
ST	STREET
STN	STATION
STR	STREAM
STRD	STRAND
SW	SOUTH WEST
TDG	TRADING
TER	TERRACE
THWY	THROUGHWAY
TNL	TUNNEL
TOLL	TOLLWAY
TPK	TURNPIKE
TR	TRACK
TRL	TRAIL
TWR	TOWER
U/P	UNDERPASS
UNI	UNIVERSITY
UPR	UPPER
V	VALE
VA	VALLEY
VIAD	VIADUCT
VIL	VILLA
VIS	VISTA
VLG	VILLAGE
VLS	VILLAS
VW	VIEW
W	WEST
WD	WOOD
WHF	WHARF
WK	WALK
WKS	WALKS
WLS	WELLS
WY	WAY
YD	YARD
YHA	YOUTH HOSTEL

POSTCODE TOWNS AND AREA ABBREVIATIONS

ACGN.................................Acock's Green
ALDR...Aldridge
ALE/KHTH/YWD ...Alcester Lane's End/
King's Heath/Yardley Wood
ALVE......................................Alvechurch
AST/WIT..........................Aston/Witton
ATHST....................................Atherstone
BDMR/CCFT....Bradmore/Castlecroft
BDWTH....................................Bedworth
BEWD..Bewdley
BFLD/HDSWWD ....Birchfield/
Handsworth Wood
BHAMNEC........Birmingham N.E.C.
BHTH/HG ....Balsall Heath/Highgate
BILS/COS....................Bilston/Coseley
BKDE/SHDE....Buckland End/Shard End
BKHL/PFLD........Blakenhall/Priestfield
BLKHTH/ROWR ....Blackheath/
Rowley Regis
BLOX/PEL ....Bloxwich/Pelsall
BNTWD....................................Burntwood
BORD..Bordesley
BRGRVE..........................Bromsgrove east
BRGRVW........................Bromsgrove west
BRLYHL................................Brierley Hill
BRWNH..................................Brownhills
BTACH/HAR ....Bishop's Tachbrook/
Harbury
BVILLE....................................Bournville
CBHAM................Central Birmingham
CBHAMNE ....Central Birmingham
northeast
CBHAMNW ....Central Birmingham
northwest

CBHAMW ....Central Birmingham west
CBROM................Castle Bromwich
CDSL..Codsall
CDYHTH..............................Cradley Heath
CHWD/FDBR/MGN ....Chelmsley Wood/
Fordbridge/Marston Green
CNCK/NC ....Cannock/Norton Canes
COV..Coventry
COVE............................Coventry east
COVEN..Coven
COVN............................Coventry north
COVS............................Coventry south
COVW............................Coventry west
CRTAM............Central & Rural Tamworth
CSCFLD/WYGN ....Central Sutton
Coldfield/Wylde Green
CSHL/WTROR ....Coleshill/Water Orton
CVALE......................................Castle Vale
DARL/WED ....Darlaston/Wednesbury
DIG/EDG............Digbeth/Edgbaston
DOR/KN ....Dorridge/Knowle
DROIT......................................Droitwich
DSYBK/YTR ......Daisy Bank/Yew Tree
DUDN................................Dudley north
DUDS................................Dudley south
DUNHL/THL/PER ....Dunstall Hill/
Tettenhall/Perton
EDG......................................Edgbaston
ERDE/BCHGN ....Erdington east/
Birches Green
ERDW/GRVHL ....Erdington west/
Gravelly Hill
ETTPK/GDPK/PENN ....Ettingshall Park/
Goldthorn Park/Penn

FOAKS/STRLY..........Four Oaks/Streetly
GTB/HAM..........Great Barr/Hamstead
GTWY................................Great Wyrley
HAG/WOL..........Hagley/Wollescote
HALE......................................Halesowen
HDSW................................Handsworth
HEDN....................................Hednesford
HHTH/SAND ....Hateley Heath/Sandwell
HIA/OLT......Hampton in Arden/Olton
HLGN/YWD ....Hall Green/Yardley Wood
HLYWD....................................Hollywood
HOCK/TIA ....Hockley Heath/
Tanworth-in-Arden
HRBN....................................Harborne
HWK/WKHTH..................Hawkesley/
Walker's Heath
KGSTG..............................Kingstanding
KGSWFD............................Kingswinford
KIDD................................Kidderminster
KIDDW ....Kidderminster west
KINVER....................................Kinver
KNWTH ....Kenilworth
LDYWD/EDGR ....Ladywood/
Edgbaston Reservoir
LGLYGN/QTN ....Langley Green/Quinton
LGN/SDN/BHAMAIR ....Lyndon Green/
Sheldon/
Birmingham Airport
LICH..Lichfield
LICHS........................Lichfield south
LOZ/NWT ....Lozells/Newtown
LUTT....................................Lutterworth
MGN/WHC ....Mere Green/
Whitehouse Common

MKTBOS/BARL/STKG...Market Bosworth/
Barlestone/Stoke Golding
MOS/BIL ....Moseley/Billesley
NFLD/LBR........Northfield/Longbridge
NUN..Nuneaton
NUNW/HART ....Nuneaton west/
Hartshill
OLDBY......................................Oldbury
PBAR/PBCH ....Perry Bar/Perry Beeches
PENK....................................Penkridge
POL/KGSB/FAZ..........Polesworth/
Kingsbury/Fazeley
RBRY..Rubery
RCOVN/BALC/EX ......Rural Coventry
north/Balsall Common/Exhall
REDE................................Redditch east
REDW................................Redditch west
RIDG/WDGT ....Ridgacre/Woodgate
RLSN............Royal Leamington Spa north
RLSS............Royal Leamington Spa south
RMSLY......................................Romsley
RRUGBY ....Rural Rugby
RSTAF ....Rural Stafford
RUGBYN/HIL ....Rugby north/
Hillmorton
RUGBYS/DCH ....Rugby south/
Dunchurch
RUGE..Rugeley
RUSH/SHEL..........Rushall/Shelfield
RWWCK/WEL ....Rural Warwick/
Wellesbourne
SCFLD/BOLD..............Sutton Coldfield/
Boldmere
SEDG..Sedgley

SHHTH................................Short Heath
SHLY..Shirley
SLYOAK..................................Selly Oak
SMTH..................................Small Heath
SMTHWK..............................Smethwick
SMTHWKW ....Smethwick west
SOLH..Solihull
SPARK............Sparkhill/Sparkbrook
STAFS..........................Stafford south
STETCH..................................Stetchford
STRBR..................................Stourbridge
STRPT ....Stourport-on-Severn
STUD..Studley
TAM/AM/WIL ....Tamworth/
Amington/Wilnecote
TLHL/CAN ....Tile Hill/Canley
TPTN/OCK ......Tipton/Ocker Hill
VAUX/NECH..............Vauxhall/Nechells
WALM/CURD ....Walmley/Curdworth
WASH/WDE ....Washwood Heath/
Ward End
WBROM..........................West Bromwich
WLNHL....................................Willenhall
WMBN..............................Wombourne
WNSFLD............................Wednesfield
WOLV............................Wolverhampton
WOLVN ....Wolverhampton north
WSL..Walsall
WSLW................................Walsall west
WSNGN ....Winson Green
WWCK..Warwick
YDLY..Yardley

Index - streets

Aar - Alf

A

Aaron Manby Ct
TPTN/OCK DY4 * 67 K5
Abberley Av *STRPT* DY13 ....188 B6
Abberley Cl *HALE* B63 ....121 K3
REDE B98 ....195 G8
Abberley Rd *LGLYGN/QTN* B68 ....104 F5
SEDG DY3 ....84 A1
Abberley St *DUDS* DY2 ....85 G5
SMTHWK B66 ....88 B8
Abberton Cl *BRGRVE* B60 ......191 M3
Abberton Gv *SOLH* B91 ....148 F6
Abberton Wy *TLHL/CAN* DY4 ..180 B2
Abbess Gv *YDLY* B25 ....109 J4
Abbey Cl *BRGRVE* B60 ....191 M3
PENK ST19 ....10 E5
Abbey Cottages *COVS* CV3 * ..156 D6
Abbey Crs *HALE* B63 ....121 H1
LGLYGN/QTN B68 ....105 H3
Abbey Cft *POL/KGSB/FAZ* B78....47 L3
Abbeydale Cl *COVS* CV3 ....156 D2
Abbeydale Rd *NFLD/LBR* B31 ..144 E3
Abbey Dr *BLOX/PEL* WS3 ....25 L8
Abbey End *KNWTH* CV8 ....197 K1
Abbeyfield Rd *ERDW/GRVHL* B23..72 C5
WOLVN WV10 ....36 C1
Abbeyfields Dr *STUD* B80 ......203 J6
Abbeygate *NUN* CV11 * 99 C1
Abbey Gn *NUN* CV11 * 80 F8
Abbey Green Ct
POL/KGSB/FAZ B78 ....47 L4
Abbey Hl *KNWTH* CV8 ....197 K1
Abbey Rd *COVS* CV3 ....155 K7
DUDS DY2 ....85 H7
ERDW/GRVHL B23 ....90 B3
HALE B63 ....121 G1
HRBN B17 ....106 D8
KIDDW DY11 ....137 L7
REDW B97 ....202 C1
SEDG DY3 ....84 A2
SMTHWK B67 ....105 H4
TAM/AM/WIL B77 ....46 B2
Abbey Sq *BLOX/PEL* WS3 ....38 C3
Abbey St *HEDN* WS12 ....12 F6
NUN CV11 ....80 F8
RUGBY/HIL CV21 ....187 G1
SEDG DY3 ....84 A2
WSNGN B18 ....88 B8
Abbey St North *WSNGN* B18 ....88 B8
Abbey Vw *POL/KGSB/FAZ* B78 ..47 M5
Abbey Vw *COVS* CV3 ....155 K7
Abbot Rd *HALE* B63 ....121 G1
Abbotsbury Cl *COVE* CV2 ......156 E1
Abbotsbury Wy *NUN* CV11 ......99 J6
Abbots Cl *DOR/KN* B93 ....149 L6
RUSH/SHEL WS4 ....40 A7
Abbotsfield Av *GTB/HAM* B43 ..70 A1
Abbotsford Dr *DUDN* DY1 ....84 C6
Abbotsford Rd *LICHS* WS14 ....21 H6
NUN CV11 ....99 J4
SPARK B11 ....108 A7
Abbots Ms *BRLYHL* DY5 ....102 B4
Abbots Rd *ALE/KHTH/YWD* B14 ..125 J4
WSNGN B18 ....88 F7
Abbots Wy *BDMR/CCFT* WV3 ..49 J4
WBROM B70 ....86 E2
WSLW WS2 ....4 C2
Abbots Wood Cl *REDE* B98 ....203 L2
Abbotts Cl *STRPT* DY13 ....164 F7
Abbotts La *COV* CV1 ....8 D3
Abbotts Pl *BLOX/PEL* WS3 ......39 H4
Abbotts Rd *ERDE/BCHGN* B24 ..90 A4
Abbotts St *BLOX/PEL* WS3 ......39 H3
RLSS CV31 ....206 D6
Abbotts Wk *COVS* CV3 ....157 C6
Abdon Av *SLYOAK* B29 ....123 M6
Abeles Wy *ATHST* CV9 ....63 K7
Abelia *TAM/AM/WIL* B77 ....46 D2
Abercorn Rd *COVW* CV6 ....154 D3
Aberdeen Cl *COVW* CV5 ....132 E8
Aberdeen Rd *NUN* CV11 ....99 J4
Aberdeen St *WSNGN* B18 ......106 C1
Aberford Cl *SHHTH* WV12 ....52 D1
Abergavenny Wk *COVS* CV3 ..156 D4
Abigails Cl
LGN/SDN/BHAMAIR B26 ....109 M6
Abingdon Cl *WOLV* WV1 ....50 F3
Abingdon Rd *BLOX/PEL* WS3 ..38 D3
DUDS DY2 ....103 H2
ERDW/GRVHL B23 ....71 M7
WOLV WV1 ....50 F3
Abingdon Wy *BLOX/PEL* WS3 ..38 D3
CVALE B35 ....91 L2
NUN CV11 ....81 K6
Ablewell St *WSL* WS1 ....5 G4

Ablon Ct *PENK* ST19 ....10 D6
Ablow St *BKHL/PFLD* WV2 ....2 E8
Abnalls Cft *LICH* WS13 ....20 D4
Abnalls La *LICH* WS13 ....20 A5
Ab Rw *CBHAMNE* B4 ....7 J2
Aboyne Cl *DIG/EDG* B5 ....107 H7
Acacia Av *BEWD* DY12 ....163 G2
CHWD/FDBR/MGN B37 ....92 D7
COV CV1 ....9 J7
DSYBK/YTR WS5 ....69 L1
Acacia Cl *CHWD/FDBR/MGN* B37 ..92 D7
DUDN DY1 ....84 E2
OLDBY B69 ....85 M3
Acacia Crs *BDWTH* CV12 ......117 H2
CDSL WV8 ....34 F2
Acacia Dr *BILS/COS* WV14 ......66 E6
Acacia Gv *BLOX/PEL* WS12 ....117 M2
RUGBY/HIL CV21 ....186 E1
Acacia Rd *BVILLE* B30 ....124 C5
NUNW/HART CV10 ....80 C8
RLSN CV32 ....206 B4
Acanthus Rd *REDE* B98 ....195 K7
Acfold Rd *BFLD/HDSWWD* B20 ..70 C8
Achal Cl *COVN* CV6 ....133 L5
Acheson Rd *HLGN/YWD* B28 ..147 K2
Achilees Cl *WSN* WV6 ....24 A7
Achilles Rd *COVN* CV6 ....134 E7
Ackleton Gdns *BDMR/CCFT* WV3 ..49 K6
Ackleton Gv *SLYOAK* B29 ......123 K5
Acorn Cl *ACGN* B27 * 108 F9
BDWTH CV12 ....116 A5
BNTWD WS7 ....18 E4
BVILLE B30 ....124 C5
CNCK/NC WS11 ....17 G3
GTWY WS6 ....24 C4
KNWTH CV8 ....180 F6
WBROM B70 ....86 F3
Acorn Dr *RUGBYS/DCH* CV22 ..185 M4
Acorn Gdns *SLYOAK* B29 ......124 C5
Acorn Gv *CBHAMW* B1 ....6 A4
CDSL WV8 ....34 C3
STRBR DY8 ....101 J4
Acorn Rd *BRGRVW* B61 ....168 F5
RMSLY B62 ....104 A5
WNSFLD WV11 ....37 L4
The Acorns *BRGRVW* B61 ......168 E5
Acorn St *COVS* CV3 ....155 M5
WLNHL WV13 ....52 A3
Acre La *REDW* B97 ....201 J3
Acre Ri *SHHTH* WV12 ....51 M2
Acre Rd *BRLYHL* DY5 ....102 C5
Acton Cl *REDE* B98 ....195 H8
Acton Dr *SEDG* DY3 ....83 M2
Acton Gv *BILS/COS* WV14 ....66 F1
KGSTG B44 ....71 L3
Ada Lewis Ct *GTB/HAM* B43 * ..70 A2
Adam Rd *COVN* CV6 ....134 C6
Adams Brook Dr
RIDG/WDGT B32 ....122 F4
Adams Ct *KIDD* DY10 ....138 E6
Adam's Hl *HAG/WOL* DY9 ......141 J1
Adams Rd *BDMR/CCFT* WV3 ..49 G6
RIDG/WDGT B32 ....122 F4
Adams Rd *CNCK/NC* WS11 ......15 M6
Adams Rd *RUGBY/HIL* CV21 ..186 C2
BRWNH WS8 ....26 E8
Adams St *RUGBY/HIL* CV21 ..186 C2
VAUX/NECH B7 ....7 K1
WBROM B70 ....86 E2
WSLW WS2 ....4 C2
Adam St *KIDDW* DY11 ....138 A8
Adare Dr *COVS* CV3 ....8 D9
Ada Rd *SMTHWK* B66 ....105 M2
YDLY B25 ....108 F7
Ada Wrighton Cl *SHHTH* WV12 ..38 A6
Adcock Dr *KNWTH* CV8 ....179 M8
Addenbrooke Crs *KIDDW* DY11 ..163 L4
Addenbrooke Dr
SCFLD/BOLD B73 ....72 F3
Addenbrooke Rd
RCOVN/BALC/EX CV7 ....115 L6
SMTHWK B67 ....105 H6
Addenbrooke St *BLOX/PEL* WS3 ..39 G6
DARL/WED WS10 ....68 B2
Addenbrook Wy *TPTN/OCK* DY4 ..68 B5
Adderley Park Cl
WASH/WDE B8 * 108 C1
Adderley Rd *WASH/WDE* B8 ..108 A2
Adderley Rd South
WASH/WDE B8 ....108 A2
Adderley St *BORD* B9 ....7 L7
COV CV1 ....9 K1
Addingham Cl *WWCK* CV34 ....205 J4
Addison Cl *CNCK/NC* WS11 ......17 H4
DARL/WED WS10 ....69 J3
NUNW/HART CV10 ....80 A4
Addison Cft *SEDG* DY3 ....65 L8
Addison Gv *WNSFLD* WV11 ......36 F4

Addison Pl *BILS/COS* WV14 ......51 K6
CSHL/WTROR B46 ....92 F2
Addison Rd
ALE/KHTH/YWD B14 ....125 K6
BDMR/CCFT WV3 ....49 K5
BRLYHL DY5 ....91 M3
COVN CV6 ....133 L5
DARL/WED WS10 ....69 J3
RUGBYS/DCH CV22 ....186 A3
VAUX/NECH B7 ....90 A5
Addison St *DARL/WED* WS10 ..68 D3
Addison Ter *DARL/WED* WS10 * ..68 D3
Adelaide Av *WBROM* B70 ....68 E6
Adelaide Dr *HEDN* WS12 ....17 K2
Adelaide Rd *RLSN* CV32 ....206 C5
Adelaide St *BHTH/HG* B12 ....7 J9
BRLYHL DY5 ....102 B2
COV CV1 ....9 J1
REDW B97 ....202 B1
Adey Rd *WNSFLD* WV11 ....37 K5
Adkins Cft *RCOVN/BALC/EX* CV7 ..114 C2
Adkins La *SMTHWKW* B67 ......105 K4
Admington Dr
RWWCK/WEL CV35 ....204 C3
Admington Rd *STETCH* B33 ..110 A5
Admiral Gdns *KNWTH* CV8 ......180 A7
Admiral Parker Dr *LICHS* WS14 ..28 D8
Admiral Pl *MOS/BIL* B13 ....125 K1
Admirals Wy
BLKHTH/ROWR B65 ....103 M3
Adonis Cl *CRTAM* B79 ....32 A7
Adrian Cft *MOS/BIL* B13 ....126 A4
Adrians' Cl *ATHST* CV9 ....63 K7
Adria Rd *SPARK* B11 ....125 M1
Adshead Rd *DUDS* DY2 ....85 G6
Adstone Gv *NFLD/LBR* B31 ....144 D4
Adwalton Rd
DUNHL/THL/PER WV6 ....48 D2
Affleck Av *POL/KGSB/FAZ* B78 ..45 H4
Agenoria Dr *STRBR* DY8 ....101 K8
Aggborough Crs *KIDD* DY10 ..164 C1
Agincourt Rd *COVS* CV3 ....155 J6
Agmore La *BRGRVE* B60 ....192 F2
Agmore Rd *BRGRVE* B60 ......192 E1
Ainsbury Rd *COVW* CV5 ....154 C5
Ainsdale Cl *COVE* CV2 ....134 F1
STRBR DY8 ....119 K3
Ainsdale Gdns *HALE* B63 ......121 H3
Ainsworth Rd *WOLVN* WV10 ....36 B1
Aintree Cl *BDWTH* CV12 ....116 F1
BRGRVW B61 ....168 E4
COVN CV6 ....134 C8
HEDN WS12 ....13 J2
KIDDW DY11 ....138 B5
Aintree Dr *RLSN* CV32 ....207 G2
Aintree Gv *BKDE/SHDE* B34 ....92 B7
Aintree Rd *WOLVN* WV10 ....36 B1
Aintree Wy *DUDN* DY1 ....84 C3
Aire Cft *NFLD/LBR* B31 ....144 F4
Airfield Dr *ALDR* WS9 ....54 C2
Airport Wy *HIA/OLT* B92 ....129 H2
Aitken Cl *POL/KGSB/FAZ* B78 ..45 H4
Ajax Cl *GTWY* WS6 ....24 D4
RUGBY/HIL CV21 ....160 F7
Akdene Cl *CNCK/NC* WS11 ......24 E3
Akrill Cl *WBROM* B70 * 86 D2
Alamein Rd *WLNHL* WV13 ....51 J3
Alandale Av *COVW* CV5 ....153 J1
Alan Higgs Wy *TLHL/CAN* CV4 ..153 G6
Albany Cl *KIDD* DY10 ....138 F7
Albany Crs *BILS/COS* WV14 ....51 G2
Albany Dr *HEDN* WS12 ....17 J2
Albany Gdns *SOLH* B91 ....149 H1
Albany Gv *KGSWFD* DY6 ....83 J6
SHHTH WV12 ....38 A4
Albany Rd *COVW* CV5 ....8 B3
HRBN B17 ....106 A7
Albany Ter *RLSN* CV32 ....206 C4
Albemarle Rd *STRBR* DY8 ......119 K3
Albermarle Rd *KGSWFD* DY6 ..83 J6
Albert Av *BHTH/HG* B12 ....107 L7
Albert Clarke Dr *SHHTH* WV12 ..38 A6
Albert Cl *CDSL* WV8 ....34 C1
Albert Crs *COVN* CV6 ....133 M2
Albert Davie Dr *HEDN* WS12 ....17 J1
Albert Dr *HALE* B63 ....121 K3
SEDG DY3 ....82 C3
Albert Fearn Gdns *COVN* CV6 ..134 D4
Albert Rd *ALE/KHTH/YWD* B14 ..125 K6
AST/WIT B6 ....89 J6
BRGRVW B61 ....191 J5
COVW CV5 ....131 L5
CRTAM B79 ....31 M8
ERDW/GRVHL B23 ....90 B2
HALE B63 ....121 K3
HDSW B21 ....88 C4
HRBN B17 ....105 M8
KIDD DY10 ....138 D7
LGLYGN/QTN B68 ....105 G5
POL/KGSB/FAZ B78 ....45 L5

Alderminster Gv
RWWCK/WEL CV35 ....204 C3
Alderminster Rd *COVW* CV5 ..153 L1
SOLH B91 ....148 F4
Aldermoor La *COVS* CV6 ....133 L8
Aldermore Dr *MGN/WHC* B75 *..57 K7
Alderney Cl *COVN* CV6 ....133 M3
Alderney Gdns
HWK/WKHTH B38 ....145 H4
Alder Park Rd *SOLH* B91 ......148 D2
Alderpits Rd *BKDE/SHDE* B34 ..92 B7
Alder Rd *BHTH/HG* B12 ....125 L1
COVN CV6 ....134 E3
DARL/WED WS10 ....68 D2
KGSWFD DY6 ....83 L8
Alders Cl *REDE* B98 ....202 D2
Alders Dr *REDE* B98 ....203 K1
Aldersea Dr *AST/WIT* B6 ....89 K6
Aldersgate *POL/KGSB/FAZ* B78 ..60 B6
Aldershaw Rd
LGN/SDN/BHAMAIR B26 ....109 J8
Aldershaws *SHLY* B90 ....147 L8
Alders La *CRTAM* B79 ....31 J8
NUNW/HART CV10 ....79 L6
Aldersley Av
DUNHL/THL/PER WV6 ....35 J6
Aldersley Cl
DUNHL/THL/PER WV6 ....35 K6
Aldersley Rd
DUNHL/THL/PER WV6 ....35 J6
Aldermead Rd *NFLD/LBR* B31 ..145 G4
Alderson Rd *WASH/WDE* B8 ..108 D1
The Alders *BDWTH* CV12 ......116 C3
RMSLY B62 ....142 D1
Alderton Cl *SOLH* B91 ....148 F4
Alderton Dr *BDMR/CCFT* WV3 ..49 J5
Alderton Ms *RLSS* CV31 ....207 G7
Alder Wy *BRGRVE* B60 ....191 M3
FOAKS/STRLY B74 ....55 J5
HEDN WS12 ....13 L7
Alderwood Pl *SOLH* B91 ....148 F2
Alderwood Ri *SEDG* DY3 ....66 B8
Aldgate Dr *BRLYHL* DY5 ....102 A6
Aldgate Gv *LOZ/NWT* B19 ......89 H8
Aldin Cl *POL/KGSB/FAZ* B78 ....45 J3
Aldington Cl *REDE* B98 ....202 E4
Aldis Cl *HLGN/YWD* B28 ......126 C4
WSLW WS2 * 52 E6
Aldis Rd *WSLW* WS2 ....52 E6
Aldrich Av *TLHL/CAN* CV4 ......153 J3
Aldridge By-Pass *ALDR* WS9 ..40 E7
POL/KGSB/FAZ B78 ....47 K5
STRBR DY8 ....101 J3
Aldridge Rd *FOAKS/STRLY* B74 ..41 L8
FOAKS/STRLY B74 ....55 H5
LGLYGN/QTN B68 ....104 F3
PBAR/PBCH B42 ....70 D5
RUSH/SHEL WS4 ....53 M2
Aldridge St *DARL/WED* WS10 ..52 B4
Aldrin Wy *TLHL/CAN* CV4 ......154 B8
Aldwick Cl *RLSN* CV32 ....206 E1
Aldwych Cl *ALDR* WS9 ....40 F5
Aldwych Dr *BRLYHL* DY5 ....48 E5
Alesmore Meadow *LICH* WS13 ..20 D7
Alexander Cl *BRGRVW* B61 ....168 E4
Alexander Gdns *PBAR/PBCH* B42 ..89 K2
Alexander Hl *BRLYHL* DY5 ....102 D5
Alexander Rd *ACGN* B27 ....126 F1
BDWTH CV12 ....117 G2
CDSL WV8 ....35 G2
SMTHWK B67 ....105 J3
WSLW WS2 ....52 D3
Alexander St *BDMR/CCFT* WV3 ..2 D6
Alexander Ter *SMTHWKW* B67 * ..87 K7
Alexandra Av *HDSW* B21 ....88 B6
Alexandra Crs *HHTH/SAND* B71 ..69 J5
Alexandra Ms *CRTAM* B79 ......32 A8
Alexandra Pl *BILS/COS* WV14 ..51 H7
Alexandra Rd *BVILLE* B30 ......124 C6
COV CV1 ....9 L2
DARL/WED WS10 ....107 J7
DIG/EDG B5 ....107 J7
ETTPK/GDPK/PENN WV4 ....49 L8
HALE B63 ....121 K2
HDSW B21 ....88 B6
RLSS CV31 ....206 E7
RUGBY/HIL CV21 ....186 F1
TPTN/OCK DY4 ....67 L8
WSL WS1 ....4 E9
Alexandra St *DUDN* DY1 ....84 F4
NUN CV11 ....98 F1
Alexandra Wy *ALDR* WS9 ......40 F8
TPTN/OCK DY4 ....67 L8
Alex Grierson Cl *COVS* CV3 ..156 C6
Alfall Rd *COVE* CV2 ....134 E4
Alford Cl *RBRY* B45 ....144 D5
Alfreda Av *HLYWD* B47 ....146 D5
Alfred Green Cl
RUGBYS/DCH CV22 ....186 E3
Alfred Rd *COV* CV1 ....133 L8

HDSW B21 ....88 C5
SPARK B11 ....107 M8
Alfred St *ALE/KHTH/YWD* B14 ...115 A5
AST/WIT B6............................
BHTH/HG B12 ....107 M8
BLOX/PEL WS3 ....38 F4
CRTAM B79 ....31 L8
DARL/WED WS10 ....52 A8
RUGBYN/HIL CV21 ....186 D3
SMTHWK B66 ....87 M6
WBROM B70 ....87 H1
Alfreds Well *BRGRVW* B61 ....168 A1
Alfriston Rd *COVS* CV3 ....181 G1
Algernon Rd *LDYWD/EDGR* B16 ...106 B1
Algernon St *RLSS* CV31 ....192 A4
Alhambra Rd *BRGRVE* B60 ....192 A4
Alice Cl *BDWTH* CV12 ....116 D4
Alice St *BILS/COS* WV14 ....51 H7
Alicia Cl *RUGBYS/DCH* CV22 ....185 L6
Alison Cl *TPTN/OCK* DY4 ....67 L3
Alison Rd *RMSLY* B62 ....122 C2
Alison Sq *COVE* CV2 ....134 F1
Allan Cl *STRBR* DY8 ....101 K4
Allan Rd *COVN* CV6 ....154 D1
Allans La *RRUGBY* CV23 ....161 L8
Allans La *RRUGBY* CV23 ....161 L8
Allard *TAM/AM/WIL* B77 ....46 C3
Allard Wy *COVS* CV3 ....156 A6
Allbut St *CDYHTH* B64 ....103 H4
Allcock St *DIG/EDG* B9 ....7 J7
TPTN/OCK DY4 ....68 A5
Allcroft Rd *SPARK* B11 ....126 D3
Allenby Cl *KGSWFD* DY6 ....83 L8
Allen Cl *GTB/HAM* B43 ....70 C6
Allen St *WBROM* B70 ....86 E7
Allendale Gv *GTB/HAM* B43 ....70 C5
Allendale Rd *WALM/CURD* B76 ......73 J5
YDLY B25 ....
Allen Dr *DARL/WED* WS10 ....52 A7
WBROM B70 ....87 K4
Allen Rd *DARL/WED* WS10 ....52 D8
DUNHL/THL/PER WV6 ....49 L2
TPTN/OCK DY4 ....67 K4
Allens Av *WSNGN* B18 * 88 D7
Allens Cl *ATHST* CV9 ....62 A5
SHHTH WV12 ....37 M8
Allens Croft Rd
ALE/KHTH/YWD B14 ....124 F8
Allens Farm Rd *NFLD/LBR* B31 ...144 B2
Allens La *BLOX/PEL* WS3 ....39 K3
Allensmead *TAM/AM/WIL* B77 ....46 A3
Allensmore Cl *REDE* B98 ....203 K3
Allens Rd *WSNGN* B18 ....88 D7
Allerdale Rd *BRWNH* WS8 ....26 C7
Allerton Cl *COVE* CV2 ....156 C7
Allerton La *HHTH/SAND* B71 ....108 F6
Allesley Cl *MGN/WHC* B75 ....57 C6
Allesley Cft *COVW* CV5 ....132 E7
Allesley Hall Dr *COVW* CV5 ....133 C8
Allesley Old Rd *COVW* CV5 133
COVW CV5 ....133 G8
Allesley Rd *HIA/OLT* B92 ....127 H5
RUGBYN/HIL CV21 ....160 D7
Allesley St *AST/WIT* B6 ....89 J8
Alleston Rd *WOLVN* WV10 ....36 B4
Alleyne Gv *ERDE/BCHGN* B24 ....90 E4
Alleyne Rd *ERDE/BCHGN* B24 ....90 E4
The Alley *SEDG* DY3 ....83 M2
Alliance Cl *NUN* CV11 ....99 K2
Alliance Wy *COVE* CV2 ....134 E1
Allied Cl *COVN* CV6 ....134 B5
Allingham Gv *GTB/HAM* B43 ....71 H1
Allington Cl *RUSH/SHEL* WS4 ......54 B5
Allison St *DIG/EDG* B5 ....7 J6
Allitt Gv *KNWTH* CV8 ....179 M8
Allman Rd *ERDE/BCHGN* B24 ....90 F1
Allmyn Dr *FOAKS/STRLY* B74 ....55 L7
Allport Rd *CNCK/NC* WS11 ....16 C4
Allport St *CNCK/NC* WS11 ....16 C4
All Saints Av *BEWD* DY12 ....163 G1
All Saints Wy *HHTH/SAND* B71 ......87 J8
Allsops Cl *BLKHTH/ROWR* B65 .....103 K1
Allton Av *POL/KGSB/FAZ* B78 ......45 H4
Allton St *TAM/AM/WIL* B77 ....46 C2
Allwell Dr *ALE/KHTH/YWD* B14 ....146 D2
Allwood Gdns *RIDG/WDGT* B32 ....122 E3
Alma Av *TPTN/OCK* DY4 ....67 L6
Alma Crs *VAUX/NECH* B7 ....107 M1
Alma Pl *DUDS* DY2 ....85 J2
Alma St *COV* CV1 ....9 J4
DARL/WED WS10 ....52 A7
DARL/WED WS10 ....68 F7
HALE B63 ....103 G8
LOZ/NWT B19 ....89 J7
SMTHWK B66 ....88 A7
WLNHL WV13 ....51 M3
WOLVN WV10 ....36 F8
WSLW WS2 ....53 H1
Alma Wy *LOZ/NWT* B19 ....89 H6
Almond Av *DSYBK/YTR* WS5 ....69 L1
KIDDW DY11 ....137 L5
NUNW/HART CV10 ....80 A7
RLSS CV32 ....206 D2
WSLW WS2 ....53 J2
Almond Cl *BLOX/PEL* WS3 ....39 K3
CNCK/NC WS11 ....17 G3
SLYOAK B29 ....123 L7
Almond Cft *PBAR/PBCH* B42 ....70 D1
Almond Gv
DUNHL/THL/PER WV6 ....50 A1
RUGBYN/HIL CV21 ....160 C6
WWCK CV34 ....205 L4
Almond Rd *HEDN* WS12 ....12 B5
KGSWFD DY6 ....83 J5
Almond Tree Av *COVE* CV2 ....135 G5
Almond Wy *STRPT* DY13 ....188 B1
Alnwick Cl *HEDN* WS12 ....11 J1
Alnwick Rd *BLOX/PEL* WS3 ....38 E1
Alperton Dr *HAG/WOL* DY9 ....120 C3
Alpha Cl *BHTH/HG* B12 ....107 J7
Alpha Wy *GTWY* WS6 ....24 C5
Alpine Cl *KNWTH* CV8 ....179 L7
Alpine Dr *DUDS* DY2 ....102 F1
HEDN WS12 ....17 H1
Alpine Ri *COVS* CV3 ....154 E8
Alpine Wy *BDMR/CCFT* WV3 ....49 G3
Alport Cft *BORD* B9 ....107 M3
Alspath La *COVW* CV5 ....153 K1
Alspath Rd
RCOVN/BALC/EX CV7 ....131 G4
Alston Cl *FOAKS/STRLY* B74 ....56 A1
SOLH B91 ....128 B7
Alston Gv *BORD* B9 ....108 F2
Alston Rd *BORD* B9 ....108 F2
OLDBY B69 ....86 C6
SOLH B91 ....128 B7

Alston St *LDYWD/EDGR* B16 ....106 D3
Althorpe Dr *DOR/KN* B93 ....175 H2
Althorpe St *RLSS* CV31 ....192 A5
Alton Av *SHHTH* WV12 ....37 M8
Alton Cl *COVE* CV2 ....135 H3
REDW B97 ....201 M4
WOLVN WV10 ....36 M2
Alton Cottages
ETTPK/GDPK/PENN WV4 * 65 K4
Alton Gv *CNCK/NC* WS11 ....15 M4
DUDS DY2 ....85 J4
HHTH/SAND B71 ....69 J6
Alton Rd *SLYOAK* B29 ....124 D2
Alum Cl *COVN* CV6 ....134 E5
Alum Dr *BORD* B9 ....108 E2
Alumhurst Av *WASH/WDE* B8 ......108 F1
Alum Rock Rd *WASH/WDE* B8 ....90 B8
Alumwell Cl *WSLW* WS2 * 52 A4
Alum Well Rd *WSLW* WS2 ....52 A4
Alvaston Cl *BLOX/PEL* WS3 ....39 G2
DOR/KN B93 ....149 M6
Alvechurch Hwy *BRGRVE* B60 .....169 G2
REDE B98 ....194 C8
Alvechurch Rd *HALE* B63 ....121 K3
NFLD/LBR B31 ....144 F6
Alverley Cl *KGSWFD* DY6 ....83 G8
Alverley Rd *COVN* CV6 ....134 A7
Alverstoke Cl *COVEN* WV9 ....35 K3
Alverstone Rd *COVE* CV2 ....155 L1
Alverton Cl *TAM/AM/WIL* B77 * 60 A1
Alveston Cl *REDE* B98 ....203 F3
Alveston Gv *BORD* B9 ....108 F3
DOR/KN B93 ....149 M6
Alveston Rd *HLYWD* B47 ....146 E6
Alvin Cl *COVS* CV3 ....156 D4
Alvis Cl *CRTAM* B79 ....31 J8
Alwen St *STRBR* DY8 ....101 K4
Alwin Rd *BLKHTH/ROWR* B65 .....103 M3
Alwold Rd *SLYOAK* B29 ....123 L3
Alwyn *TAM/AM/WIL* B77 ....46 A3
Alwyn Cl *GTWY* WS6 ....24 D2
Alwyn Freeman Ct
RCOVN/BALC/EX CV7 * 115 L3
Alwyn Rd *RUGBYS/DCH* CV22 .....186 A6
Amanda Av
ETTPK/GDPK/PENN WV4 ....65 K1
Amanda Dr
LGN/SDN/BHAMAIR B26 ....109 K4
Ambassador Rd
CHWD/FDBR/MGN B37 ....129 G1
Amber Cl *TAM/AM/WIL* B77 ....46 A2
Amber Dr *OLDBY* B69 ....86 E8
Ambergate Cl *BLOX/PEL* WS3 ....39 G2
Ambergate Dr *KGSWFD* DY6 ....83 C5
Amber Gv *CNCK/NC* WS11 ....17 G3
Amberley Gn *GTB/HAM* B43 ....70 C7
Amberley Rd *AST/WIT* B6 ....89 L2
Amberley Rd *HIA/OLT* B92 ....127 H4
Amberley Wy *FOAKS/STRLY* B74 ...55 L4
Amber Wy *RMSLY* B62 ....105 M7
Amberwood Cl *SHHTH* WV12 ....52 B2
Ambien Rd *ATHST* CV9 ....63 H6
Amblecote Av *ALE/KHTH/YWD* B14 124 E1
Amblecote Rd *BRLYHL* DY5 ....102 F5
KIDD DY10 ....138 F8
Ambler Gv *COVE* CV2 ....156 A2
Ambleside *COVE* CV2 ....135 J3
RIDG/WDGT B32 ....123 G4
Ambleside Cl *BILS/COS* WV14 ......51 H5
Ambleside Dr *BRLYHL* DY5 ....102 A5
Ambleside Gv *SHHTH* WV12 ....37 M4
Ambleside Rd *BDWTH* CV12 ....116 B5
Ambleside Wy *BRGRVW* B61 ....191 M4
KGSWFD DY6 ....83 G7
NUN CV11 ....81 J7
Ambrose Cl *RUGBYN/HIL* CV21 ...161 G2
WLNHL WV13 ....51 J3
Ambrose Crs *KGSWFD* DY6 ....83 H5
Amelas Cl *STRBR* DY8 ....101 L1
Amersham Cl *COVW* CV5 ....133 M1
RIDG/WDGT B32 ....105 J8
Amesbury Rd *MOS/BIL* B13 ....125 J4
Ames Rd *DARL/WED* WS10 ....52 A7
Amherst Av *BFLD/HDSWWD* B20 ...88 E2
Amherst Rd *KNWTH* CV8 ....179 J7
Amicombe *TAM/AM/WIL* B77 ....47 G4
Amington Cl *MGN/WHC* B75 ....57 H2
Amington Rd *SHLY* B90 ....147 L5
TAM/AM/WIL B77 ....46 E7
YDLY B25 ....108 F7
Amiss Gdns *SMHTH* B10 ....108 A5
Amity Cl *SMTHWK* B66 ....87 M8
Amos Av *NUNW/HART* CV10 ....98 B5
Amos Cl *WNSFLD* WV11 ....37 G7
Amos Jacques Rd *BDWTH* CV12 ..116 E1
Amos La *WNSFLD* WV11 ....37 G7
Amos Rd *HAG/WOL* DY9 ....120 D3
Amphlett Cft *TPTN/OCK* DY4 ....67 L4
Amphletts Cl *DUDS* DY2 ....103 J2
Ampton Rd *EDG* B15 ....6 D7
Amroth Cl *RBRY* B45 ....143 H6
Amroth Ms *RLSS* CV31 ....207 G1
Amwell Gv *ALE/KHTH/YWD* B14 ...146 D2
Amy Cl *COVN* CV6 ....134 D1
Anchorage Rd *ERDW/GRVHL* B23 ...90 B2
FOAKS/STRLY B74 ....56 F7
Anchor Cl *LDYWD/EDGR* B16 ......106 C4
TAM/AM/WIL B77 ....46 C1
Anchorfields *KIDD* DY10 ....138 D7
Anchor La *BILS/COS* WV14 ....66 E5
Anchor Rd *ALDR* WS9 ....40 F7
BILS/COS WV14 ....67 G3
Anchorway Rd *COVS* CV3 ....180 F1
Anders *CRTAM* B79 ....31 J7
Andersleigh Dr *BILS/COS* WV14 ....67 L4
Anderson Av
RUGBYS/DCH CV22 ....186 E5
Anderson Crs *GTB/HAM* B43 ....70 C3
Anderson Rd *ERDW/GRVHL* B23 ...72 C7
SMTHWK B66 ....105 L4
TPTN/OCK DY4 ....67 L8
Anderton Cl *FOAKS/STRLY* B74 ....56 A1
Anderton Park Rd *MOS/BIL* B13 ..125 L2
Anderton Rd *BDWTH* CV12 ....116 A4
COVN CV6 ....134 A5
SPARK B11 ....108 A7
Anderton St *BHAMNW* B1 ....6 A4
Andover Crs *KGSWFD* DY6 ....101 K1
Andover Pl *CNCK/NC* WS11 ....16 E1
Andover St *DIG/EDG* B5 ....7 J5
Andressy Ms *BRGRVW* B61 ....168 B4
Andrew Cl *SHHTH* WV12 ....38 B7
Andrew Dr *SHHTH* WV12 ....38 B7
Andrew Gdns *HDSW* B21 ....88 C4
Andrew Rd *BRLYHL* DY5 ....102 C5
HHTH/SAND B71 ....69 K3
TPTN/OCK DY4 ....67 L4
Andrews Cl *BRLYHL* DY5 ....102 C5
Andrews Rd *ALDR* WS9 ....40 F1
Anerley Gv *KGSTG* B44 ....71 L1
Anerley Rd *KGSTG* B44 ....71 L1
Angela Av *BLKHTH/ROWR* B65 ....104 A4
Angela Cl *COVE* CV2 ....135 K1
Angela Pl *BILS/COS* WV14 ....51 H7
Angel Cft *BNTWD* WS7 ....18 C4

Angelica *TAM/AM/WIL* B77 ....46 D2
Angelica Cl *DSYBK/YTR* WS5 ....69 L2
Angelina St *BHTH/HG* B12 ....107 J8
Angel Pas *STRBR* DY8 ....101 L8
Angel St *DUDN* DY1 ....84 F5
Angel Wy *REDW* B97 ....200 F4
Anglesey Av *CBROM* B36 ....92 F7
Anglesey Cl *BNTWD* WS7 ....26 D1
COVW CV5 ....132 E6
Anglesey Crs *BRWNH* WS8 ....26 D5
HEDN WS12 ....13 G8
Anglesey Rd *BRWNH* WS8 ....26 D3
LICH WS13 ....20 F3
Anglesey St *HEDN* WS12 ....12 F8
LOZ/NWT B19 ....89 G6
Angless Wy *KNWTH* CV8 ....197 K2
Anglian Rd *ALDR* WS9 ....40 B7
Anglia Rd *CNCK/NC* WS11 ....16 B2
Angorfa Cl *LICH* WS13 ....20 D6
Angus Cl *COVW* CV5 ....153 L1
HHTH/SAND B71 ....69 G7
Anita Av *TPTN/OCK* DY4 ....85 L3
Anita Cft *ERDW/GRVHL* B23 ....90 C3
Ankadine Rd *STRBR* DY8 ....101 M7
Anker Cl *BNTWD* WS7 ....19 H7
Ankerdine Av *STRPT* DY13 ....188 B4
Ankerdine Ct *HALE* B63 ....121 L2
Ankerdrive *CRTAM* B79 ....89 C6
Anker Dr *RRUGBY* CV23 ....159 M8
Ankermoor Cl *BKDE/SHDE* B34 ....91 M1
Ankerside *POL/KGSB/FAZ* B78 ......47 L2
Anker St *NUN* CV11 ....99 H2
Anker Vw *POL/KGSB/FAZ* B78 ....47 L1
TAM/AM/WIL B77 ....46 A2
Annan Av *WOLVN* WV10 ....36 F3
Ann Crs *CNCK/NC* WS11 ....9 H1
Ann Cft *LGN/SDN/BHAMAIR* B26 ..128 B1
Anne Cl *WBROM* B70 ....86 C2
Anne Ct *COVS* CV3 ....156 A6
Anne Gv *TPTN/OCK* DY4 ....67 M4
ETTPK/GDPK/PENN WV4 ....49 M8
SMTHWK B66 ....88 A6
Ann Rd *HLYWD* B47 ....172 E2
Annscroft *HWK/WKHTH* B38 ....145 H3
Ansbro Cl *WSNGN* B18 ....88 D3
Anscuff Rd *STRBR* DY8 ....101 M4
Ansell Dr *COVN* CV6 ....116 E8
Ansell Rd *ERDE/BCHGN* B24 ....90 D4
SPARK B11 ....108 A7
WWCK CV34 ....205 H6
Ansley Cl *REDE* B98 ....203 K4
Ansley Common
NUNW/HART CV10 ....79 L6
Ansley La *RCOVN/BALC/EX* CV7 ....96 D6
Ansley Rd *NUNW/HART* CV10 ....97 H2
NUNW/HART CV10 ....98 A3
Anslow Gdns *WNSFLD* WV11 ....37 K4
Anslow Rd *ERDW/GRVHL* B23 ....72 A8
Anson Cl *LICH* WS13 ....20 E5
Anson Ct *BNTWD* WS7 ....19 G6
DUNHL/THL/PER WV6 ....34 C8
GTWY WS6 ....24 D4
RUGBYS/DCH CV22 ....186 A3
Anson Gv *ACGN* B27 ....127 H3
Anson Rd *GTWY* WS6 ....24 D4
WBROM B70 ....68 C5
WSLW WS2 ....52 C3
Anson Wy *COVE* CV2 ....135 K5
Anstey Cft
CHWD/FDBR/MGN B37 * 110 E1
Anstey Gv *ACGN* B27 ....126 F4
Anstey Rd *KGSTG* B44 ....71 J7
Anston Wy *WNSFLD* WV11 ....37 J3
Anstree Cl *GTWY* WS6 ....24 B4
Anstruther Rd *EDG* B15 ....106 C3
Ansty Dr *HEDN* WS12 ....17 H3
Ansty Rd *COVE* CV2 ....135 K7
COVE CV2 ....156 A1
Antelope Gdns *WWCK* CV34 ....205 K8
Anthony Rd *WASH/WDE* B8 ....108 C2
Anthony Wy *COVE* CV2 ....156 A3
Anton Cl *BEWD* DY12 ....137 H8
Anton Dr *WALM/CURD* B76 ....73 J7
Antony Rd *SHLY* B90 ....147 M4
Antrim Cl *COVW* CV5 ....132 E6
Antringham Gdns *EDG* B15 ....106 B5
Antrobus Rd *HDSW* B21 ....88 C4
SCFLD/BOLD B73 ....72 C4
Anvil Crs *BILS/COS* WV14 ....67 G3
Anvil Dr *OLDBY* B69 ....86 E7
Apex Rd *BRWNH* WS8 ....26 B8
Apley Rd *STRBR* DY8 ....101 J6
Apollo *CRTAM* B79 ....31 K7
Apollo Cl *CNCK/NC* WS11 ....12 E8
Apollo Cft *ERDE/BCHGN* B24 ....91 H2
Apollo Rd *HAG/WOL* DY9 ....102 A8
LGLGYN/QTN B68 ....87 G7
Apollo Wy *BFLD/HDSWWD* B20 ....89 G4
WWCK CV34 ....206 C3
Apperley Wy *HALE* B63 ....102 F6
Appian Cl *ALE/KHTH/YWD* B14 ....125 J8
TAM/AM/WIL B77 ....46 A6
Appian Wy *SHLY* B90 ....174 B1
Appleby Cl
ALE/KHTH/YWD B14 ....125 H8
Appleby Gdns *WNSFLD* WV11 ....38 A3
Appleby Gv *SHLY* B90 ....148 F7
Applecross *FOAKS/STRLY* B74 .....56 A4
Applecross Cl *TLHL/CAN* CV4 .....153 K7
HEDN WS12 ....17 J2
Appledore Dr *COVW* CV5 ....132 D6
Appledore Rd *DSYBK/YTR* WS5 ....54 F8
Appledorne Gdns
BKDE/SHDE B34 ....91 M7
Apple Cl *RUGBYS/DCH* CV22 ......185 M3
Apple Pie La *NUNW/HART* CV10 ...79 M2
Applesham Ct *SPARK* B11 ....108 B7
Appleton Av *GTB/HAM* B43 ....70 C5
STRBR DY8 ....119 J3
Appleton Cl *BVILLE* B30 ....124 C5
Appleton Crs
ETTPK/GDPK/PENN WV4 ....49 L8
Apple Tree Cl *ERDW/GRVHL* B23 ...89 M1
KIDD DY10 ....138 D7
Appletree Cl *NFLD/LBR* B31 ....144 C4
Appletree Gv *ALDR* WS9 ....40 A8
Appletree La *REDW* B97 ....193 M8
Appletrees Crs *BRGRVW* B61 .....168 B7
Apple Wk *CNCK/NC* WS11 ....17 G3
Applewood Gv *CDYHTH* B64 ......103 J4
The Approach *RLSS* CV31 ....206 D3
April Cft *MOS/BIL* B13 ....125 M3
Apse Cl *WMBN* WV5 ....64 D6
Apsley Cl *LGLGYN/QTN* B68 ......104 C1
Apsley Gv *DOR/KN* B93 ....175 K3
ERDE/BCHGN B24 ....90 C2
Apsley Rd *LGLGYN/QTN* B68 ......104 E6
Aqueduct La *ALDR* WS9 ....41 G6
Aqueduct Rd *SHLY* B90 ....147 J3
Aragon Dr *RLSS* CV31 ....206 F1
SCFLD/BOLD B73 ....56 F7
Arbor Cl *TAM/AM/WIL* B77 ....46 B1
Arboretum Rd *WSL* WS1 ....5 J1
The Arboretum *TLHL/CAN* CV4 ...180 D2
Arbor Ga *ALDR* WS9 ....40 F1

Arbor Wy
CHWD/FDBR/MGN B37 ....111 G4
Arbour Cl *KNWTH* CV8 ....197 M2
RUGBYS/DCH CV22 ....186 B7
Arbour Ms *CNCK/NC* WS11 ....17 K7
Arbour Tree La *DOR/KN* B93 ......176 D6
Arbury Av *BDWTH* CV12 ....116 E3
COVN CV6 ....134 C3
Arbury Cl *RLSN* CV32 ....206 E2
Arbury Dr *STRBR* DY8 ....101 K2
Arbury Garth
NUNW/HART CV10 ....98 A2
Arbury Hall Rd *SHLY* B90 ....148 B5
Arbury Rd *NUNW/HART* CV10 ....98 B3
Arcal St *SEDG* DY3 ....66 C6
Archer Cl *DARL/WED* WS10 ....68 C2
LGLGYN/QTN B68 * 104 F1
Archer Rd *COVE* CV2 ....135 J8
Archer Rd *ALE/KHTH/YWD* B14 ...147 G1
BLOX/PEL WS3 ....39 J7
KNWTH CV8 ....197 J2
REDE B98 ....202 C1
Archers Spinney
RUGBYN/HIL CV21 ....187 M5
Archery Flds *WWCK* CV34 ....205 K8
Archery Rd
RCOVN/BALC/EX CV7 ....130 F4
RLSS CV31 ....206 C5
Arches La *RUGBYN/HIL* CV21 ......161 G8
Arch Hill St *DUDS* DY2 ....85 J5
Archibald Rd *LOZ/NWT* B19 ....89 G5
Arch Rd *COVE* CV2 ....135 J8
Arcot Rd *HLGN/YWD* B28 ....126 D3
Ardarth Rd *HWK/WKHTH* B38 .....145 L3
Ardav Rd *WBROM* B70 ....68 D5
Arden Av *ATHST* CV9 ....63 G5
Arden Bldgs *DOR/KN* B93 * 175 K2
RCOVN/BALC/EX CV7 ....151 G4
RLSS CV31 ....206 F8
RUGBYS/DCH CV22 ....186 B8
Ardencote Rd *ALE/KHTH/YWD* B14 147 H1
Arden Ct *HIA/OLT* B92 * 129 L6
Arden Dr *CSHL/WTROR* B46 ....93 K4
HIA/OLT B92 ....128 A1
Arden Dr *DOR/KN* B93 ....175 K3
LGN/SDN/BHAMAIR B26 ....109 K6
MGN/WHC B75 ....57 M8
SCFLD/BOLD B73 ....72 F5
Arden Forest Est
NUNW/HART CV10 ....78 D3
Arden Gv *LDYWD/EDGR* B16 ......106 E4
OLDBY B69 ....86 E8
Arden Meads *HOCK/TIA* B94 ....175 G7
Arden Oak Rd
LGN/SDN/BHAMAIR B26 ....110 B8
Arden Pl *DARL/WED* WS10 ....67 M1
Arden Rd *ACGN* B27 ....126 F1
AST/WIT B6 ....89 H5
DOR/KN B93 ....175 K3
HLYWD B47 ....146 E7
KNWTH CV8 ....197 M2
NUN CV11 ....99 L4
RBRY B45 ....143 L4
SMTHWKW B67 ....105 L1
TAM/AM/WIL B77 ....46 D8
Arden St *COV* CV1 * 108 A2
WASH/WDE B8 ....108 A2
Ardens Cl *REDE* B98 ....203 L3
Arden St *ATHST* CV9 ....63 G5
COVW CV5 ....154 D4
Arderne Dr
CHWD/FDBR/MGN B37 ....110 E4
Ardgay Dr *HEDN* WS12 ....12 D6
Ardingley Wk *BRLYHL* DY5 ....101 M6
Ardley Cl *DUDS* DY2 ....85 H5
Ardley Rd *ALE/KHTH/YWD* B14 ...147 G1
Arena Wy *NUN* CV11 ....98 B3
Aretha Cl *KGSWFD* DY6 ....83 L7
Argil Cl *WNSFLD* WV11 ....37 H5
Argus Cl *WALM/CURD* B76 ....73 L4
Argyle Av *TAM/AM/WIL* B77 ....46 B1
Argyle Cl *RUSH/SHEL* WS4 ....54 B5
STRBR DY8 ....101 J4
WOLVN WV10 ....35 M3
Argyle Rd *BKHL/PFLD* WV2 ....49 M7
RUSH/SHEL WS4 ....54 B5
Argyle St *RUGBYN/HIL* CV21 ......187 G2
VAUX/NECH B7 ....107 M1
Argyll St *COVE* CV2 ....155 L2
Ariane *CRTAM* B79 ....31 K6
Ariel Wy *RUGBYS/DCH* CV22 ......186 B7
Arion Cl *TAM/AM/WIL* B77 ....32 B8
Arkall Cl *CRTAM* B79 ....32 A6
Arkle *TAM/AM/WIL* B77 ....60 B1
Arkle Cft *BLKHTH/ROWR* B65 ....65 K7
CBROM B36 ....92 C1
Arkley Dr *COVE* CV2 ....135 K6
Arklet Cl *NUNW/HART* CV10 ....80 A4
Arkley Gv *HLGN/YWD* B28 ....126 F6
Arkley Rd *HLGN/YWD* B28 ....126 F6
Arkwright Rd *RIDG/WDGT* B32 ....105 G8
WSLW WS2 ....38 D7
Arlen Dr *GTB/HAM* B43 ....70 B4
Arlescote Cl *MGN/WHC* B75 ....57 M8
Arlescote Rd *HIA/OLT* B92 ....128 A3
Arleston Wy *SHLY* B90 ....148 B5
Arley Cl *KIDDW* DY11 ....163 L3
OLDBY B69 ....86 B8
Arley Dr *STRBR* DY8 ....119 J2
Arley Gv
ETTPK/GDPK/PENN WV4 ....49 H8
Arley La *NUNW/HART* CV10 ....97 H3
Arley Ms *RLSN* CV32 ....206 D1
Arley Rd *SLYOAK* B29 ....124 D2
SOLH B91 ....148 E1
WASH/WDE B8 ....90 B7
Arlidge Cl *BILS/COS* WV14 ....67 H1
Arlidge Crs *KNWTH* CV8 ....180 A8
Arlington Av *RLSN* CV32 ....206 D3
Arlington Cl *KGSWFD* DY6 ....101 K1
Arlington Ct *STRBR* DY8 ....119 J1
Arlington Gdns *STRBR* DY8 ....119 J1
Arlington Gv
ALE/KHTH/YWD B14 ....146 F2
HHTH/SAND B71 ....69 J1
Arlington Ms *RLSN* CV32 ....206 D3
Arlington Rd
ALE/KHTH/YWD B14 ....146 F2
WBROM B70 ....68 B4
Arlon Av *NUNW/HART* CV10 ....80 B4
Armada Cl *ERDW/GRVHL* B23 ......72 B8
Armarna Dr *COVE* CV2 ....135 K5
Armfield St *COVN* CV6 ....134 C1
Armorial Rd *COVS* CV3 ....154 B8
Armour Cl *GTWY* WS6 ....24 B3
Armoury Rd *SPARK* B11 ....108 B6
Armscote Gv
RWWCK/WEL CV35 ....204 B1
Armscott Rd *COVE* CV2 ....135 G8
Armside Cl *BLOX/PEL* WS3 ....39 L1

Armson Rd
RCOVN/BALC/EX CV7 ....116 E4
Armstead Rd *COVEN* WV9 ....35 L2
Armstrong *CRTAM* B79 ....31 K7
Armstrong Av *COVS* CV3 ....155 L4
Armstrong Cl
RUGBYS/DCH CV22 ....186 A5
STRBR DY8 ....101 M7
Armstrong Dr *CBROM* B36 ....92 D4
DUNHL/THL/PER WV6 ....35 L7
WSLW WS2 ....52 E1
Armstrong Wy *WLNHL* WV13 ....51 M5
Arncliffe Cl *NUN* CV11 ....99 L3
Arncliffe Wy *WWCK* CV34 ....205 K4
Arne Rd *COVE* CV2 ....135 L7
Arnhem Cl *WNSFLD* WV11 ....36 F5
Arnhem Cnr *COVS* CV3 ....156 B7
Arnhem Rd *WLNHL* WV13 ....51 J5
Arnhem Wy *TPTN/OCK* DY4 ....68 A2
Arnold Av *COVS* CV3 ....155 G8
Arnold Cl *CRTAM* B79 ....31 L7
WSLW WS2 ....52 D2
Arnold Gv *BVILLE* B30 ....145 H1
SHLY B90 ....147 H5
Arnold Rd *SHLY* B90 ....148 A1
Arnolds La *CSHL/WTROR* B46 .....112 D2
Arnotdale Dr *HEDN* WS12 ....12 D6
Arnside Cl *COVS* CV3 * 9 J2
Arnwood Cl *WSLW* WS2 ....52 D3
Arosa Dr *HRBN* B17 ....123 H2
Arps Rd *CDSL* WV8 ....34 D2
Arran Cl *CNCK/NC* WS11 ....16 E2
GTB/HAM B43 ....70 C2
NUNW/HART CV10 ....98 D2
Arran Dr *TAM/AM/WIL* B77 ....46 D6
Arran Rd *CBROM* B36 ....92 C1
Arras Bvd *RWWCK/WEL* CV35 ....204 E7
Arras Rd *DUDS* DY2 ....85 J3
Arrow Cl *DOR/KN* B93 ....149 L7
Arrowdale Rd *REDE* B98 ....202 E3
Arrowfield Gn
HWK/WKHTH B38 ....145 H6
Arrowfield Top *ALVE* B48 * 170 F4
Arrow Rd *BLOX/PEL* WS3 ....39 J7
Arrow Rd North *REDE* B98 ....202 E1
Arrow Rd South *REDE* B98 ....202 E1
Arsenal St *BORD* B9 ....108 A4
Arthingworth Cl *COVS* CV3 ....156 C4
Arthur Dr *KIDDW* DY11 ....164 C4
Arthur Gunby Cl
MGN/WHC B75 * 57 K6
Arthur Harris Cl *SMTHWK* B66 ...105 M2
Arthur Pl *CBHAMW* B1 ....6 E4
Arthur Rd *EDG* B15 ....106 F1
ERDE/BCHGN B24 ....90 F1
HDSW B21 ....88 D5
TPTN/OCK DY4 ....67 J4
YDLY B25 ....108 E7
Arthur St *BILS/COS* WV14 * 51 H7
BKHL/PFLD WV2 ....50 B7
CNCK/NC WS11 ....16 D1
COV CV1 ....9 H1
HEDN WS12 ....17 J2
KNWTH CV8 ....179 L8
REDE B98 ....202 E2
SMHTH B10 ....107 M4
WBROM B70 ....87 H4
Artillery St *BORD* B9 ....107 M3
Arundel *TAM/AM/WIL* B77 ....46 D8
Arundel Av *DARL/WED* WS10 ....68 D2
Arundel Cl *WWCK* CV34 ....205 K5
Arundel Dr *OLDBY* B69 ....85 K5
Arundel Gv
DUNHL/THL/PER WV6 ....48 E2
Arundel Pl *SPARK* B11 ....107 L7
Arundel Rd *ALE/KHTH/YWD* B14 ...146 E4
BRGRVE B60 ....191 M4
COVS CV3 ....155 H7
SHHTH WV12 ....38 C2
STRBR DY8 ....101 C5
WOLVN WV10 ....35 M3
Arundel St *WSL* WS1 4
Arun Wy *WALM/CURD* B76 ....73 L4
Asbury Rd *DARL/WED* WS10 ....69 G3
RCOVN/BALC/EX CV7 ....151 M8
Ascot Cl *BDWTH* CV12 ....116 A7
COVS CV3 ....156 A7
LDYWD/EDGR B16 ....106 D3
LICHS WS14 ....21 H6
OLDBY B69 ....86 C7
Ascot Dr *CNCK/NC* WS11 ....15 M5
DUDN DY1 ....84 D3
ETTPK/GDPK/PENN WV4 ....65 L1
TAM/AM/WIL B77 ....60 B2
Ascot Gdns *STRBR* DY8 ....101 H3
Ascot Ride *RLSN* CV32 ....207 G2
Ascot Rd *MOS/BIL* B13 ....125 J4
Ascot Wy *BRGRVW* B61 ....168 F4
Ash Av *BHTH/HG* B12 ....107 J8
Ashborough Dr *SOLH* B91 ....149 G6
Ashbourne Cl *CNCK/NC* WS11 ....
Ashbourne Cl *AST/WIT* B6 * 89 J5
Ashbourne Rdg *HALE* B63 ....103 H8
Ashbourne Rd *BLOX/PEL* WS3 .....39 G2
ETTPK/GDPK/PENN WV4 ....66 C2
LDYWD/EDGR B16 ....106 B2
WOLV WV1 ....50 D2
Ashbourne Wy *SHLY* B90 ....148 B5
Ashbridge Rd *COVW* CV5 ....154 A1
Ashbrook Crs *SOLH* B91 ....149 J4
Ashbrook Dr *RBRY* B45 ....143 M5
Ashbrook Gv *BVILLE* B30 ....125 G5
Ashbrook Ri *NUNW/HART* CV10 ....79 M3
Ashbrook Rd *BVILLE* B30 ....125 G5
Ashburn Gv *WLNHL* WV13 ....52 A3
Ashburton Cl
ALE/KHTH/YWD B14 ....125 H8
COVE CV2 ....135 K6
Ashbury Covert *BVILLE* B30 ......146 A2
Ashby Cl *CBROM* B36 ....91 G7
COVS CV3 ....156 D5
Ashby Ct *NUN* CV11 ....99 H3
SOLH B91 ....149 G4
Ashby Rd *CRTAM* B79 ....31 M8
Ash Cl *CDSL* WV8 ....34 C2
Ashcombe Av
BFLD/HDSWWD B20 ....88 C2
Ashcombe Dr *TLHL/CAN* CV4 .....153 K2
Ashcombe Gdns
ERDE/BCHGN B24 ....91 H2
Ashcott Cl *HWK/WKHTH* B38 ......145 H3
Ash Crs *CHWD/FDBR/MGN* B37 ....92 D1
KGSWFD DY6 ....83 J7
Ashcroft *HEDN* WS12 ....13 K8
Ashcroft Cl *COVE* CV2 ....135 L3
Ashcroft Gv *BFLD/HDSWWD* B20 ...89 H3
Ashcroft La *LICHS* WS14 ....28 C5
Ashcroft Wy
RCOVN/BALC/EX CV7 ....135 M5
Ashdale Cl *COVS* CV3 ....157 A6
HEDN WS12 ....12 A6
KGSWFD DY6 ....83 H5

Ashdale Dr ALE/KHTH/YWD B14 146 E4
Ashdale Gv
LGN/SDN/BHAMAIR B26 109 L5
Ashdale Rd TAM/AM/WIL B77 32 B8
Ashdene Cl KIDD DY10 139 G8
KIDDW DY11 189 L3
SCFLD/BOLD B73 72 E2
Ashdene Gdns KNWTH CV8 197 M1
STRBR DY8 101 G3
Ashdown Cl COVS CV3 156 B5
MOS/BIL B13 125 L4
RBRY B45 143 L3
Ashdown Dr NUNW/HART CV10 98 D3
STRBR DY8 101 J2
Ash Dr BRGRVW B61 168 E4
HHTH/SAND B71 69 G7
KNWTH CV8 197 L1
NUNW/HART CV10 79 L5
Ashen Cl
ETTPK/GDPK/PENN WV4 66 A2
Ashenden Ri BDMR/CCFT WV3 48 E4
Ashenhurst Rd DUDN DY1 84 D5
Ashe Rd NUNW/HART CV10 97 M2
Ashes Rd OLDBY B69 104 D1
Ashfern Dr WALM/CURD B76 73 K6
Ashfield Av ALE/KHTH/YWD B14 125 K4
TLHL/CAN CV4 153 H4
Ashfield Cl BLOX/PEL WS3 53 J1
Ashfield Crs DUDS DY2 103 G2
HAG/WOL DY9 120 D2
Ashfield Gv HALE B63 121 J3
WOLVN WV10 36 A2
Ashfield Rd
ALE/KHTH/YWD B14 125 K4
BDMR/CCFT WV3 49 H3
BILS/COS WV14 67 L2
KNWTH CV8 197 M2
WOLVN WV10 36 A2
Ashford Dr BDWTH CV12 116 E2
SEDG DY3 66 C6
WALM/CURD B76 73 J8
Ashford La HOCK/TIA B94 174 E6
Ashfurlong Cl
RCOVN/BALC/EX CV7 151 M7
Ashfurlong Crs MGN/WHC B75 57 J6
Ash Gn DUDN DY1 66 E8
Ash Green La
RCOVN/BALC/EX CV7 116 A7
Ashgrove BNTWD WS7 18 D8
Ash Gv BHTH/HG B12 107 M8
BORD B9 * 107 M3
CNCK/NC WS11 16 D1
HAG/WOL DY9 120 B2
KIDDW DY11 137 M6
LICH WS13 21 J5
POL/KGSB/FAZ B78 60 B6
RCOVN/BALC/EX CV7 96 C3
RCOVN/BALC/EX CV7 116 A6
SEDG DY3 84 A3
STRPT DY13 188 C1
TAM/AM/WIL B77 46 D8
Ashgrove Cl BRGRVE B60 169 H4
Ashgrove Rd KGSTG B44 71 G3
Ash Hl BDMR/CCFT WV3 49 H4
Ashill Rd RBRY B45 143 M6
Ashington Gv COVS CV3 155 L8
Ashington Rd BDWTH CV12 116 A4
Ashlands Cl CRTAM B79 32 A6
Ashland St BDMR/CCFT WV3 2 C7
Ash La ALVE B48 171 G3
GTWY WS6 24 E2
Ashlawn Crs SOLH B91 127 H8
Ashlawn Rd RUGBYN/HIL CV21 187 K5
RUGBYS/DCH CV22 186 C8
RUGBYS/DCH CV22 186 F7
Ashlea POL/KGSB/FAZ B78 47 K8
Ashleigh Dr BFLD/HDSWWD B20 88 F3
NUN CV11 99 K4
TAM/AM/WIL B77 46 C5
Ashleigh Gv MOS/BIL B13 125 M4
Ashleigh Rd OLDBY B69 86 A5
SOLH B91 148 F1
Ashley Cl EDG B15 107 G6
KGSWFD DY6 101 G1
STRBR DY8 119 H3
Ashley Ct RBRY B45 169 L4
Ashley Crs WWCK CV34 205 M7
Ashley Gdns CDSL WV8 34 D1
WASH/WDE B8 108 B1
Ashley Mt DUNHL/THL/PER WV6 35 H8
Ashley Rd BLOX/PEL WS3 38 D4
BNTWD WS7 18 B4
ERDW/GRVHL B23 90 C2
ETTPK/GDPK/PENN WV4 49 J8
KIDD DY10 138 F4
Ashley St BILS/COS WV14 51 J7
BLKHTH/ROWR B65 104 A4
Ashley Ter SLYOAK B29 * 124 C4
Ashley Wy RCOVN/BALC/EX CV7 151 M6
Ashmall BNTWD WS7 27 H1
Ashman Av RRUGBY CV23 159 M8
Ashmead Dr RBRY B45 170 A1
Ashmead Gv ERDE/BCHGN B24 90 E3
Ashmead Ri RBRY B45 170 A1
Ashmead Rd BNTWD WS7 18 E5
Ash Ms ACGN B27 109 G8
Ashmole Av BNTWD WS7 19 K5
Ashmole Cl LICHS WS14 21 J7
Ashmole Rd WBROM B70 68 D6
Ashmore Av WNSFLD WV11 37 L4
Ashmore Lake Rd SHHTH WV12 51 M1
Ashmore Lake Wy SHHTH WV12 51 M1
Ashmore Rd BVILLE B30 124 D8
COVN CV6 8 C1
Ashmores Cl REDW B97 202 B8
Ashold Farm Rd
ERDE/BCHGN B24 91 G3
Asholme Cl CBROM B36 91 G6
Ashorne Cl ACGN B27 126 F6
COVE CV2 135 G3
REDE B98 203 H5
Ashover Gv WSNGN B18 106 C1
Ashow Cl KNWTH CV8 197 M1
Ashperton Cl REDE B98 202 C4
Ash Priors Cl TLHL/CAN CV4 153 M3
Ashridge Cl NUN CV11 99 K5
Ash Rd DARL/WED WS10 52 D8
DUDN DY1 84 F2
TPTN/OCK DY4 85 J1
WASH/WDE B8 108 B1
Ashstead Cl WALM/CURD B76 73 M7
Ash St BDMR/CCFT WV3 2 B6
BILS/COS WV14 67 J2
BLOX/PEL WS3 39 H4
CDYHTH B64 103 J3
Ashted Circ VAUX/NECH B7 7 L2
Ash Ter OLDBY B69 85 M4
Ashton Cl REDW B97 201 M4
Ashton Cft LDYWD/EDGR B16 106 E3
SOLH B91 148 E4
Ashton Dr RUSH/SHEL WS4 40 A2
Ashton Park Dr BRLYHL DY5 102 A4
Ashton Rd YDLY B25 108 F6
Ash Tree Av TLHL/CAN CV4 153 L3
Ashtree Cl STRBR DY8 101 L5
Ash Tree Dr
LGN/SDN/BHAMAIR B26 109 H6
Ashtree Gv BILS/COS WV14 67 M2
Ash Tree La LICH WS13 21 L4
Ash Tree Rd BVILLE B30 124 E7
REDW B97 201 M1
Ashtree Rd BLOX/PEL WS3 39 L2
CDYHTH B64 103 K3
OLDBY B69 86 B5
Ashurst Cl COVN CV6 116 F8
Ashurst Rd WALM/CURD B76 73 K7
Ash Vw HEDN WS12 12 B5
Ashville Av BKDE/SHDE B34 91 K6
Ashville Dr HALE B63 103 L8
Ashwater Dr
ALE/KHTH/YWD B14 146 B3
Ash Wy ERDW/GRVHL B23 72 A5
SPARK B11 107 M8
Ashwell Dr SHLY B90 148 B1
Ashwells Gv COVEN WV9 35 K3
Ashwin Rd HDSW B21 88 D6
Ashwood Av COVN CV6 133 K8
STRBR DY8 101 G3
Ashwood Cl FOAKS/STRLY B74 55 J5
Ashwood Ct
RUGBYN/HIL CV21 * 186 D1
Ashwood Dr
CHWD/FDBR/MGN B37 111 H2
Ashwood Gv
ETTPK/GDPK/PENN WV4 49 L8
Ashwood Lower La
KGSWFD DY6 * 82 C8
Ashwood Rd NUNW/HART CV10 80 C7
Ashworth Rd PBAR/PBCH B42 70 F4
Askew Bridge Rd SEDG DY3 * 83 M2
Askew Cl SEDG DY3 66 C8
Aspbury Cft CBROM B36 92 B4
Aspen Cl ACGN B27 126 F2
TLHL/CAN CV4 153 H4
WALM/CURD B76 73 K3
Aspen Ct HEDN WS12 13 L7
Aspen Dr
CHWD/FDBR/MGN B37 111 G5
COVN CV6 117 G7
Aspen Gdns BFLD/HDSWWD B20 88 F4
Aspen Gv BNTWD WS7 18 D5
BORD B9 108 E2
HLYWD B47 146 F8
SHHTH WV12 38 C6
The Aspens POL/KGSB/FAZ B78 60 A6
Aspens Wy BRGRVW B61 168 E7
Aspen Wk STRPT DY13 163 J8
Aspen Wy BDMR/CCFT WV3 2 A7
Asplen Ct KNWTH CV8 198 A1
Aspley Cl WOLVN WV10 14 C8
Aspley La WOLVN WV10 22 B2
Asquith Dr CNCK/NC WS11 17 G3
OLDBY B69 86 B3
Asquith Rd WASH/WDE B8 90 F8
Asra Cl COVE CV2 9 M1
SMTHWK B66 87 L5
Assheton Cl RUGBYS/DCH CV22 186 A5
Astbury Av SMTHWKW B67 105 K2
Astbury Cl BLOX/PEL WS3 38 E1
WOLV WV1 50 E4
Aster Av KIDDW DY11 138 B4
Aster Cl NUN CV11 99 L4
Aster Wk COVEN WV9 35 L2
Asthill Cft COVS CV3 8 E8
Asthill Gv COVS CV3 8 E9
Astley Av COVN CV6 134 C3
RMSLY B62 104 D7
Astley Cl REDE B98 202 E6
RLSN CV32 206 B3
TPTN/OCK DY4 68 B7
Astley Ct STRPT DY13 * 188 C5
Astley Gdns STRPT DY13 188 C7
Astley La NUNW/HART CV10 97 K7
NUNW/HART CV10 97 M4
RCOVN/BALC/EX CV7 114 F2
Astley Pl RUGBYN/HIL CV21 187 M6
Astley Rd BRGRVE B60 192 A4
HDSW B21 88 B4
Aston Brook Gn AST/WIT B6 * 89 K8
Aston Brook St AST/WIT B6 89 J7
Aston Brook St East AST/WIT B6 89 K8
Aston Bury EDG B15 106 B5
Aston Church Rd VAUX/NECH B7 90 A6
Aston Cl BILS/COS WV14 67 L1
LICHS WS14 28 D7
PENK ST19 10 D6
Aston Expressway AST/WIT B6 89 L5
Aston Hall Rd AST/WIT B6 89 L5
Aston La BFLD/HDSWWD B20 89 J3
Aston Manor Cl
BFLD/HDSWWD B20 89 J3
Aston Rd AST/WIT B6 7 J1
BRGRVE B60 191 K7
COVW CV5 154 D4
NUN CV11 80 F8
OLDBY B69 85 L4
WLNHL WV13 51 J3
Aston Rd North AST/WIT B6 89 K7
Astons Cl BRLYHL DY5 102 B6
Astons Fold BRLYHL DY5 102 B6
Aston St BDMR/CCFT WV3 2 B9
CBHAMNE B4 7 J2
TPTN/OCK DY4 68 A7
Astor Dr MOS/BIL B13 126 A4
Astoria Cl SHHTH WV12 38 B4
Astor Rd FOAKS/STRLY B74 55 L4
KGSWFD DY6 83 K8
Atcham Cl REDE B98 203 K2
Athelney Ct BLOX/PEL WS3 * 39 L2
Athelstan Cl PENK ST19 10 E5
Athelstan Gv
DUNHL/THL/PER WV6 34 C8
Athelstan Wy CRTAM B79 31 K6
Athena Dr RLSS CV31 206 B8
Atherstone Cl REDE B98 203 K4
SHLY B90 147 J3
Atherstone La ATHST CV9 77 J1
Atherstone Rd ATHST CV9 63 H1
ATHST CV9 63 L3
ATHST CV9 77 H1
CSHL/WTROR B46 77 K8
NUNW/HART CV10 79 M3
WOLV WV1 50 F3
Atherstone St
POL/KGSB/FAZ B78 45 M5
Atherston Pl TLHL/CAN CV4 154 B7
Athlone Rd DSYBK/YTR WS5 54 A5
Athol Cl RIDG/WDGT B32 123 H5
Athole St BHTH/HG B12 107 L6
Atholl Crs NUNW/HART CV10 98 C3
Athol Rd COVE CV2 135 L7
Atlantic Rd KGSTG B44 71 K5
Atlantic Wy DARL/WED WS10 68 C4
Atlas Cft WOLVN WV10 36 A7
Atlas Est AST/WIT B6 * 89 L3
Atlas Gv WBROM B70 86 D2
Attenborough Cl LOZ/NWT B19 89 H8
Atterton La ATHST CV9 63 M5
Attingham Dr CNCK/NC WS11 16 F4
GTB/HAM B43 70 B3
Attleborough La
CSHL/WTROR B46 92 E4
Attleborough Rd NUN CV11 99 H3
Attlee Cl OLDBY B69 86 B3
Attlee Crs BILS/COS WV14 67 J3
Attlee Gv CNCK/NC WS11 17 G3
Attlee Rd WSLW WS2 52 C2
Attoxhall Rd COVE CV2 156 C1
Attwell Pk BDMR/CCFT WV3 49 H6
Attwell Rd TPTN/OCK DY4 67 K4
Attwood Cl WASH/WDE B8 90 C7
Attwood Crs COVE CV2 135 G7
Attwood Gdns
ETTPK/GDPK/PENN WV4 50 C8
Attwood Rd BNTWD WS7 18 A6
Attwood St HAG/WOL DY9 102 D8
HALE B63 103 K8
Atworth Cl REDE B98 202 F8
Aubrey Rd RIDG/WDGT B32 105 J6
SMHTH B10 108 D6
Auchinleck Dr LICH WS13 21 G4
Auchinleck Sq EDG B15 6 A8
Auckland Dr CBROM B36 92 D5
Auckland Rd KGSWFD DY6 101 J1
SMTHWKW B67 87 J8
SPARK B11 107 L6
Auden Cl NUNW/HART CV10 97 K1
Auden Ct DUNHL/THL/PER WV6 48 D1
Audley Dr KIDDW DY11 137 L5
Audley Rd STETCH B33 109 J1
Audnam STRBR DY8 101 J4
Augusta Pl RLSN CV32 206 D5
Augusta Rd ACGN B27 109 G8
MOS/BIL B13 125 J1
Augusta Rd East MOS/BIL B13 125 K1
Augusta St WSNGN B18 6 C1
Augustine Gv FOAKS/STRLY B74 42 D8
WSNGN B18 88 D7
Augustus Cl CSHL/WTROR B46 93 K4
Augustus Ct EDG B15 106 D5
Augustus Rd COV CV1 9 L2
EDG B15 106 C5
Augustus St WSLW WS2 4 D4
Aulton Rd MGN/WHC B75 57 J3
Ault St WBROM B70 87 H4
Austcliff Cl REDW B97 202 B7
Austcliff Dr SOLH B91 149 G5
Austen Cl NUNW/HART CV10 79 K8
Austen Pl EDG B15 106 F5
Austin Cl ACGN B27 127 H1
ATHST CV9 63 H6
DUDN DY1 84 D3
Austin Cote La LICHS WS14 21 J6
Austin Cft CBROM B36 92 C4
Austin Dr COVN CV6 134 E6
Austin Edwards Dr WWCK CV34 205 M5
Austin Ri NFLD/LBR B31 144 D6
Austin Rd BRGRVE B60 191 J5
HDSW B21 88 A4
Austin St DUNHL/THL/PER WV6 49 M1
Austin Wy PBAR/PBCH B42 70 E8
Austrey Cl DOR/KN B93 149 L7
Austrey Gv SLYOAK B29 * 123 L5
Austrey Rd KGSWFD DY6 83 L8
Austwick Cl WWCK CV34 205 J4
Austy Cl CBROM B36 91 J5
Autherley Jct COVEN WV9 * 35 L4
Autumn Berry Gv SEDG DY3 66 C7
Autumn Cl RUSH/SHEL WS4 40 A3
Autumn Dr LICH WS13 21 H3
RUSH/SHEL WS4 40 A3
SEDG DY3 84 B2
Autumn Gv LOZ/NWT B19 89 G7
Auxerre Av REDE B98 202 E5
Avalon Cl ERDE/BCHGN B24 90 F1
Avalon Rd BRGRVE B60 192 A3
Avebury Cl NUN CV11 99 K3
Avebury Gv BVILLE B30 125 G6
Avebury Rd BVILLE B30 125 G5
Ave Maria Cl CDYHTH B64 103 J4
Avenbury Cl REDE B98 203 K4
Avenbury Dr SOLH B91 149 J1
Aventine Wy RUGBYN/HIL CV21 160 D6
Avenue Cl DOR/KN B93 175 L2
VAUX/NECH B7 89 L8
Avenue Perry WOLVN WV10 36 D5
Avenue Rd ALE/KHTH/YWD B14 125 H5
AST/WIT B6 89 L7
BDMR/CCFT WV3 49 J3
BILS/COS WV14 67 G5
BLKHTH/ROWR B65 104 B4
DARL/WED WS10 52 B7
DOR/KN B93 175 L2
DUDS DY2 84 C7
ERDW/GRVHL B23 90 D1
HDSW B21 88 B3
HEDN WS12 17 J3
KNWTH CV8 179 H7
NUN CV11 99 H3
RLSS CV31 206 D6
RUGBYN/HIL CV21 186 C1
Avenue Station Ap RLSS CV31 * 206 D6
The Avenue ACGN B27 127 H2
BDMR/CCFT WV3 48 F5
BLKHTH/ROWR B65 103 L2
BRGRVE B60 169 K7
COVS CV3 155 L7
ETTPK/GDPK/PENN WV4 65 J1
KIDD DY10 139 M3
KIDDW DY11 164 D5
KIDDW DY11 189 L5
LOZ/NWT B19 89 G5
RBRY B45 143 J6
WALM/CURD B76 73 J4
Averill Rd
LGN/SDN/BHAMAIR B26 109 L5
Avern Cl TPTN/OCK DY4 67 M7
Aversley Rd HWK/WKHTH B38 145 H5
Avery Cft CVALE B35 91 K3
Avery Dell BVILLE B30 * 124 F8
Avery Dr ACGN B27 127 G1
Avery Myers Cl LGLYGN/QTN B68 86 F8
Avery Rd SCFLD/BOLD B73 72 A3
SMTHWK B66 88 B7
Aviemore Cl NUNW/HART CV10 98 E3
Aviemore Crs GTB/HAM B43 70 F1
Avill TAM/AM/WIL B77 46 E8
Avill Gv KIDDW DY11 138 A6
Avington Cl SEDG DY3 66 B6
Avion Cl WSL WS1 5 G8
Avocet Cl COVN CV6 134 F3
STETCH B33 109 J2
Avocet Dr KIDD DY10 164 E3
STRPT DY13 188 F3
Avon TAM/AM/WIL B77 46 E8
Avonbank Cl REDW B97 202 A7
Avon Cl BDWTH CV12 99 M7
BRGRVE B60 191 K7
BRLYHL DY5 83 M6
DUNHL/THL/PER WV6 48 D2
Avon Crs BLOX/PEL WS3 39 L4
Avoncroft Rd BRGRVE B60 191 H8
Avondale Cl KGSWFD DY6 83 J5
Avondale Rd COVW CV5 8 A9
DUNHL/THL/PER WV6 49 K2
KNWTH CV8 157 K8
RLSN CV32 206 F1
SPARK B11 126 B1
Avon Dr CBROM B36 92 D6
HLYWD B47 172 C3
MOS/BIL B13 125 M3
WLNHL WV13 52 A3
Avon Gv DSYBK/YTR WS5 69 L2
Avonlea Ri RLSN CV32 206 A3
Avonmere RUGBYN/HIL CV21 160 C7
Avon Ms STRBR DY8 * 101 G3
Avon Rd BLOX/PEL WS3 39 J4
BNTWD WS7 18 D8
CNCK/NC WS11 15 M6
CNCK/NC WS11 16 B6
HALE B63 102 F8
KIDDW DY11 163 M2
KNWTH CV8 197 J2
SHLY B90 148 B5
STRBR DY8 119 K2
Avon St COVE CV2 134 F8
RRUGBY CV23 187 J1
RUGBYN/HIL CV21 186 E1
SPARK B11 108 A8
WWCK CV34 205 L6
Awbridge Br WMBN WV5 64 C3
Awbridge Rd DUDS DY2 103 G2
Awefields Crs SMTHWKW B67 105 H1
Awlmakers Gv BLOX/PEL WS3 39 G6
Awson St COVN CV6 134 D7
Axborough La KIDD DY10 139 G1
Axholme Rd COVE CV2 156 C1
Axletree Wy DARL/WED WS10 52 F8
Axminster Cl NUN CV11 81 J8
Ayala Cft CBROM B36 91 J5
Aylesbury Cl HOCK/TIA B94 175 G7
Aylesbury Crs KGSTG B44 71 L5
Aylesbury Rd HOCK/TIA B94 175 H6
Aylesford Cl SEDG DY3 65 M3
Aylesford Dr
CHWD/FDBR/MGN B37 110 E6
FOAKS/STRLY B74 42 C8
Aylesford Rd HDSW B21 88 B4
Aylesford St COV CV1 9 K1
RLSS CV31 206 E7
Aylesmore Cl HIA/OLT B92 127 J5
RIDG/WDGT B32 123 G4
Aynho Cl COVW CV5 153 L2
Ayre Rd ERDE/BCHGN B24 90 F1
Ayrshire Cl CBROM B36 91 H5
Ayrton Cl DUNHL/THL/PER WV6 48 E1
Aysgarth Cl NUN CV11 99 L3
Azalea Cl CDSL WV8 34 F2
Azalea Gv BORD B9 108 D3
Aziz Isaac Cl LGLYGN/QTN B68 * 87 G7

B

Babbacombe Rd COVS CV3 155 H8
Babington Rd HDSW B21 88 C6
Bablake Cl COVN CV6 133 K5
Bablake Cft HIA/OLT B92 127 L4
Babors Fld BILS/COS WV14 66 E2
Babworth Cl COVEN WV9 35 L3
Baccabox La HLYWD B47 146 C6
Bacchus Rd WSNGN B18 88 D7
Bachelors Bench ATHST CV9 63 H6
Bache St WBROM B70 87 G4
Bach Mill Dr
ALE/KHTH/YWD B14 147 H2
Backcester La LICH WS13 20 F5
Backcrofts CNCK/NC WS11 16 C4
Backhouse La WNSFLD WV11 51 G1
Back La ALDR WS9 41 K6
CSHL/WTROR B46 94 D3
KIDD DY10 165 K5
LICHS WS14 42 B4
RCOVN/BALC/EX CV7 131 H8
RRUGBY CV23 159 L2
RRUGBY CV23 185 L1
SHLY B90 147 L8
WWCK CV34 205 J7
Back Rd HWK/WKHTH B38 145 K3
KGSWFD DY6 83 H6
Back St NUN CV11 81 G8
Badby Leys RUGBYS/DCH CV22 186 D6
Baddesley Cl RLSS CV31 207 H8
Baddesley Rd HIA/OLT B92 127 J3
Bader Rd DUNHL/THL/PER WV6 48 B2
WSLW WS2 52 D3
Bader Wk CVALE B35 91 K3
Badger Cl HEDN WS12 12 A7
REDE B98 203 H2
SHLY B90 174 B1
Badger Dr WOLVN WV10 3 H1
Badger Rd COVS CV3 156 B5
Badgers Bank Rd
FOAKS/STRLY B74 42 D8
Badgers Cl BLOX/PEL WS3 25 L8
Badgers Cft RMSLY B62 103 M6
The Badgers RBRY B45 169 L3
Badger St HAG/WOL DY9 102 C7
SEDG DY3 66 C8
Badgers Wk STRPT DY13 * 188 E1
Badgers Wy HEDN WS12 17 H4
Badger Wy BRGRVE B60 169 M8
Badland Av KIDD DY10 138 D4
Badminton Cl DUDN DY1 84 D2
Badsey Cl NFLD/LBR B31 145 G1
Badsey Rd OLDBY B69 86 B8
Baffin Cl RUGBYS/DCH CV22 186 C4
Baggeridge Cl SEDG DY3 65 L5
Baggott St BKHL/PFLD WV2 50 A6
Baginton Cl SOLH B91 127 M8
Baginton Rd COVS CV3 154 F7
CVALE B35 91 M1
Bagley St HAG/WOL DY9 102 A7
Bagnall Cl
LGN/SDN/BHAMAIR B26 109 H7
Bagnall Rd BILS/COS WV14 51 G7
Bagnall St BLOX/PEL WS3 39 G6
TPTN/OCK DY4 68 A4
WBROM B70 87 J3
Bagnall Wk BRLYHL DY5 102 B4
Bagnell Rd ALE/KHTH/YWD B14 125 K6
Bagot St CBHAMNE B4 7 H1
Bagridge Cl BDMR/CCFT WV3 48 F5
Bagridge Rd BDMR/CCFT WV3 48 F5
Bagshaw Cl KNWTH CV8 182 E4
Bagshawe Cft ERDW/GRVHL B23 72 B6
Bagshaw Rd STETCH B33 109 J2
Bailey Av TAM/AM/WIL B77 46 D8
Bailey Cl CNCK/NC WS11 16 E1
Bailey Rd BILS/COS WV14 50 F6
Bailey's La RRUGBY CV23 159 L8
Bailey St WBROM B70 86 E1
WOLVN WV10 3 J4
Bakehouse La CSHL/WTROR B46 76 C7
DOR/KN B93 176 F7
RUGBYN/HIL CV21 186 D2
Baker Av BILS/COS WV14 66 D3
RLSS CV31 206 D7
Baker Cl BNTWD WS7 18 D7
Baker House Gv GTB/HAM B43 70 B6
Baker Rd BILS/COS WV14 67 J2
Bakers Cft ATHST CV9 62 A4
Bakers Gdns CDSL WV8 34 C1
Baker's La ALDR WS9 40 F7
COVW CV5 154 C3
DOR/KN B93 176 A4
FOAKS/STRLY B74 55 K8
Bakers Ms DOR/KN B93 * 176 F7
Baker St BNTWD WS7 18 D7
BORD B9 108 B4
COVN CV6 116 F7
HDSW B21 88 D5
SPARK B11 126 A1
TPTN/OCK DY4 85 J1
WBROM B70 86 F2
Bakers Wy CDSL WV8 34 C1
Bakewell Cl BLOX/PEL WS3 39 G2
COVS CV3 156 D5
Balaams Dr NFLD/LBR B31 143 M4
Balaclava Rd
ALE/KHTH/YWD B14 125 J5
Bala Cl STRPT DY13 163 K8
Balcaskie Cl EDG B15 106 C6
Balcombe Rd
RUGBYS/DCH CV22 187 H5
Balden Rd RIDG/WDGT B32 105 J6
Baldmoor Lake Rd
ERDW/GRVHL B23 72 D6
Bald's La HAG/WOL DY9 102 D8
Baldwin Cl OLDBY B69 86 B3
Baldwin Cft COVN CV6 134 F4
Baldwin Gv CNCK/NC WS11 17 G3
Baldwin Rd BEWD DY12 162 D1
BVILLE B30 145 L2
KIDD DY10 138 F5
STRPT DY13 188 F1
Baldwins La HLGN/YWD B28 147 K1
Baldwin St BILS/COS WV14 67 K1
SMTHWK B66 87 M7
Baldwin Wy SEDG DY3 82 C3
Balfour CRTAM B79 45 L1
Balfour Dr OLDBY B69 86 B3
Balfour Rd KGSWFD DY6 83 J5
Balfour St BHTH/HG B12 107 J7
Balham Gv KGSTG B44 71 L3
Balking Cl BILS/COS WV14 66 F2
Ballantine Rd COVN CV6 133 M7
Ballarat Wk STRBR DY8 101 K8
Ballard Crs DUDS DY2 85 H8
Ballard Rd DUDS DY2 85 H8
Ballard Wk
CHWD/FDBR/MGN B37 92 E7
Ball Flds TPTN/OCK DY4 68 A8
Ballingham Cl TLHL/CAN CV4 153 L3
Balliol Rd COVE CV2 155 M1
Ball La COVEN WV9 22 A7
Ballot St SMTHWK B66 87 M8
Balls Hl WSL WS1 5 H3
Balls St WSL WS1 5 H3
Balmain Crs WNSFLD WV11 36 F5
Balmoral Cl COVE CV2 135 J7
CRTAM B79 31 M6
LICHS WS14 21 H7
RMSLY B62 103 M6
RUSH/SHEL WS4 40 B6
Balmoral Dr HEDN WS12 12 D6
SHHTH WV12 37 M6
WMBN WV5 64 E4
Balmoral Rd CBROM B36 92 E6
ERDW/GRVHL B23 72 D8
ETTPK/GDPK/PENN WV4 49 L8
FOAKS/STRLY B74 42 D8
RIDG/WDGT B32 122 F6
STRBR DY8 101 G3
Balmoral Vw DUDN DY1 84 C3
Balmoral Wy
BLKHTH/ROWR B65 104 B1
RLSN CV32 199 G7
WSLW WS2 52 E1
Balsall Heath Rd DIG/EDG B5 107 J6
Balsall St RCOVN/BALC/EX CV7 151 G7
Balsall St East
RCOVN/BALC/EX CV7 151 L8
Baltic Cl CNCK/NC WS11 16 C3
Baltimore Rd PBAR/PBCH B42 70 E8
Balvenie Wy DUDN DY1 84 D2
Bamber Cl BDMR/CCFT WV3 49 J5
Bamburgh TAM/AM/WIL B77 46 A6
Bamburgh Gv RLSN CV32 206 C2
Bamford Cl BLOX/PEL WS3 39 G2
Bamford Rd BDMR/CCFT WV3 2 A9
BLOX/PEL WS3 39 G2
Bamford St TAM/AM/WIL B77 46 B2
Bampfylde Pl PBAR/PBCH B42 * 71 G6
Bampton Av BNTWD WS7 18 E5
Bamville Rd WASH/WDE B8 90 E8
Banbery Dr WMBN WV5 82 D1
Banbrook Cl HIA/OLT B92 128 B5
Banbury Cl SEDG DY3 66 C7
Banbury Cft
CHWD/FDBR/MGN B37 110 D3
Banbury Rd CNCK/NC WS11 15 M5
WWCK CV34 205 L8
Banbury St DIG/EDG B5 7 J4
Bancroft TAM/AM/WIL B77 46 D2
Bancroft Cl BILS/COS WV14 66 F6
Bandywood Rd KGSTG B44 71 J1
Baneberry Dr WOLVN WV10 22 F6
Banfield Av DARL/WED WS10 52 A6
Banfield Rd DARL/WED WS10 68 A1
Banford Rd WASH/WDE B8 108 E1
Bangham Pit Rd NFLD/LBR B31 123 J6
Bangley La POL/KGSB/FAZ B78 44 C7
Bangor Rd BORD B9 108 B3
Bangor Vls DARL/WED WS10 * 52 D7
Bank Crs BNTWD WS7 18 D8
Bank Cft RLSS CV31 207 G8
Bankdale Rd WASH/WDE B8 108 F1
Bankes Rd SMHTH B10 108 C4
Bank Farm Cl HAG/WOL DY9 120 A4
Bankfield Dr RLSN CV32 206 A4
Bankfield Rd BILS/COS WV14 51 H8
TPTN/OCK DY4 68 A5
Banklands Rd DUDS DY2 85 J7
Bank Rd ATHST CV9 63 J5
DUDS DY2 85 H7
SEDG DY3 84 A2
Banks Gn REDW B97 200 E2
Bankside GTB/HAM B43 70 C6
MOS/BIL B13 126 B3
WMBN WV5 64 D6
Bankside Cl COVS CV3 155 K7
Bankside Crs FOAKS/STRLY B74 55 K6
Bankside Wy ALDR WS9 40 F3
Banks Rd COVN CV6 133 L8
Banks St WLNHL WV13 51 L3
Bank St ALE/KHTH/YWD B14 125 J5
BILS/COS WV14 67 G5
BILS/COS WV14 67 J1
BRLYHL DY5 102 B1
CDYHTH B64 103 G4
HEDN WS12 17 J4
HHTH/SAND B71 69 G7
RUGBYN/HIL CV21 * 186 E2
WOLVN WV10 36 C8
WSL WS1 5 H4
Bankwell St BRLYHL DY5 102 B1
Banner La TLHL/CAN CV4 153 H2
Bannerlea Rd
CHWD/FDBR/MGN B37 92 D8
Bannerley Rd STETCH B33 110 A3
Banners Ct SCFLD/BOLD B73 * 71 M2
Banners Gate Rd
SCFLD/BOLD B73 71 M2
Banners Gv ERDW/GRVHL B23 72 E7
Banners La HALE B63 103 H7
REDW B97 202 C8
Banners St HALE B63 103 H7
Banners Wk KGSTG B44 71 M3
Bannister Rd DARL/WED WS10 68 B3
Bannister St CDYHTH B64 103 H3

Banstead Cl BKHL/PFLD WV2 50 C6
Bantam Gv COVN CV6 133 L2
Bantams Cl STETCH B33 110 A3
Bant Mill Rd BRGRVE B60 191 L4
Bantock Av BDMR/CCFT WV3 49 K5
Bantock Gdns BDMR/CCFT WV3 49 J4
Bantock Rd TLHL/CAN CV4 153 J3
The Bantocks WBROM B70 68 E7
Bantock Wy HRBN B17 124 A1
Banton Cl ERDW/GRVHL B23 72 B5
Bantry Cl
LGN/SDN/BHAMAIR B26 128 A1
Baptist End Rd DUDS DY2 85 G8
Barbara Rd HLGN/YWD B28 147 J2
Barbara St CRTAM B79 31 L8
Barbel Dr WOLV WV1 50 F1
Barber Cl HEDN WS12 17 J3
Barbers La HIA/OLT B92 129 G7
Barbican Ri COVE CV2 156 C3
Barbourne Cl SOLH B91 148 F6
Barbridge Rd BDWTH CV12 117 M3
Barbrook Dr BRLYHL DY5 101 M6
Barby La RUGBYN/HIL CV21 187 K6
Barby Rd RUGBYS/DCH CV22 186 E4
Barcheston Dr
RWWCK/WEL CV35 204 B3
Barcheston Rd DOR/KN B93 149 L8
SLYOAK B29 123 L4
Barclay Rd SMTHWKW B67 105 J4
Barcliff Av TAM/AM/WIL B77 46 C2
Barcroft WLNHL WV13 51 M2
Bardell Cl LICH WS13 20 C7
Bardfield Cl PBAR/PBCH B42 70 D5
Bardley Dr COVN CV6 134 A7
Bardon Dr SHLY B90 148 B3
Bardon View Rd
POL/KGSB/FAZ B78 47 L6
Bard St SPARK B11 108 A8
Bardwell Cl CDSL WV8 35 K5
Barford Cl COVS CV3 156 B5
DARL/WED WS10 52 A5
REDE B98 203 K4
WALM/CURD B76 73 K1
Barford Crs
ALE/KHTH/YWD B14 146 A3
Barford Rd KNWTH CV8 197 M2
SHLY B90 148 B3
WSNGN B18 106 C1
Barford St DIG/EDG B5 107 J5
Bargate Dr DUNHL/THL/PER WV6 2 B1
Bargery Rd WNSFLD WV11 37 L4
Barham Cl SHLY B90 148 E8
Barker Rd FOAKS/STRLY B74 56 F6
Barker's Butts La COVN CV6 8 B1
Barkers La HLYWD B47 172 D4
Barker St LGLYGN/QTN B68 87 G8
LOZ/NWT B19 88 F6
Bark Piece RIDG/WDGT B32 123 G2
Barlands Cft BKDE/SHDE B34 91 M7
Barle Gv CBROM B36 92 D6
Barley Cl ALDR WS9 55 J3
CDSL WV8 35 J4
RUGBYN/HIL CV21 187 L5
SEDG DY3 * 66 D6
Barley Ct RLSN CV32 * 206 D3
Barley Cft BRGRVE B60 191 H6
DUNHL/THL/PER WV6 48 B2
Barleyfield Ri KGSWFD DY6 82 E5
Barleyfield Rw WSL WS1 4 F6
The Barley Lea COVS CV3 155 M5
Barley Mow La BRGRVW B61 168 E5
Barley Pl COVS CV3 * 155 M5
Barlich Wy REDE B98 202 D3
Barling Wy NUNW/HART CV10 98 F4
Barlow Cl LGLYGN/QTN B68 104 E2
RBRY B45 143 J3
TAM/AM/WIL B77 46 C1
Barlow Ct POL/KGSB/FAZ B78 60 B7
Barlow Dr WBROM B70 87 K4
Barlow Rd COVE CV2 135 H2
DARL/WED WS10 52 E8
Barlows Rd EDG B15 106 B8
Barmouth Cl SHHTH WV12 38 A7
Barnabas Rd ERDW/GRVHL B23 90 D1
Barnaby Sq WOLVN WV10 36 D1
Barnack Av COVS CV3 154 F8
Barnack Dr WWCK CV34 205 J4
Barnard Cl
CHWD/FDBR/MGN B37 111 H4
RLSN CV32 207 G2
Barnard Pl BKHL/PFLD WV2 50 C7
Barnard Rd MGN/WHC B75 57 J6
WNSFLD WV11 37 K4
Barnard Wy CNCK/NC WS11 16 D3
Barn Av SEDG DY3 66 A6
Barnbridge TAM/AM/WIL B77 46 A3
Barnbrook Rd DOR/KN B93 149 L6
Barn Cl BRGRVE B60 191 J7
BVILLE B30 124 F7
CDYHTH B64 103 J7
HAG/WOL DY9 120 A1
HALE B63 121 J3
LICH WS13 20 F2
POL/KGSB/FAZ B78 47 K7
Barn Cft BNTWD WS7 26 E1
GTWY WS6 24 E2
RIDG/WDGT B32 123 J4
Barncroft Rd OLDBY B69 85 L5
Barncroft St WBROM B70 68 E5
Barne Cl NUN CV11 99 M6
Barnes Cl STETCH B33 110 C3
Barnes Hl SLYOAK B29 123 K3
Barnes Rd LICHS WS14 28 E7
Barnesville Cl SMHTH B10 108 E5
Barnet Rd ERDW/GRVHL B23 72 B8
Barnett Cl BILS/COS WV14 67 H1
KGSWFD DY6 101 H1
Barnett Gn KGSWFD DY6 101 H1
Barnett La KGSWFD DY6 83 H8
Barnett Rd WLNHL WV13 51 J4
Barnetts Cl KIDD DY10 164 E1
Barnetts Gv KIDD DY10 164 E1
Barnetts La BRWNH WS8 26 D5
KIDD DY10 164 E1
Barnett St STRBR DY8 101 H2
TPTN/OCK DY4 85 L1
Barney Cl TPTN/OCK DY4 85 K2
Barn Farm Cl BILS/COS WV14 51 L6
Barnfield Av COVW CV5 132 F6
Barnfield Cl LICHS WS14 20 F7
Barnfield Dr HIA/OLT B92 128 D7
Barnfield Gv BFLD/HDSWWD B20 70 C8
Barnfield Rd BRGRVW B61 191 J4
RMSLY B62 104 B6
STRPT DY13 188 D4
TPTN/OCK DY4 67 J6
WOLV WV1 50 E3
Barnfield Wy HEDN WS12 13 L7
Barnford Cl SMHTH B10 * 108 A4
Barnford Crs LGLYGN/QTN B68 104 E2
Barnfordhill Cl
LGLYGN/QTN B68 104 F1
Barn Gn BDMR/CCFT WV3 49 K6
Barnhurst La CDSL WV8 35 H2
Barn La HDSW B21 88 C6
HIA/OLT B92 127 J1
MOS/BIL B13 125 L6
Barn Meadow YDLY B25 109 H4
Barnmoor Ri SOLH B91 128 A6
Barn Owl Cl KIDD DY10 164 E3
Barn Owl Dr BLOX/PEL WS3 39 K1
Barnpark Covert
ALE/KHTH/YWD B14 146 A3
Barn Piece RIDG/WDGT B32 122 F1
Barnsbury Av CSCFLD/WYGN B72 73 G7
Barns Cl ALDR WS9 40 D1
Barns Cft FOAKS/STRLY B74 55 M2
Barnsdale Crs NFLD/LBR B31 144 C1
Barns La RUSH/SHEL WS4 40 A5
Barnsley Cl ATHST CV9 63 H6
Barnsley Hall Rd BRGRVW B61 168 D7
Barnsley Rd BRGRVW B61 191 L1
HRBN B17 105 L4
Barnstaple Cl COVW CV5 * 132 D8
Barnstaple Rd SMTHWK B66 87 M8
Barn St DIG/EDG B5 7 K6
Barnswood Cl CNCK/NC WS11 15 M5
HALE B63 103 G8
Barnt Green Rd RBRY B45 170 A2
Barnwood Cl REDE B98 195 H8
Barnwood Rd CDSL WV8 35 J4
RIDG/WDGT B32 123 K1
Baron Cl BNTWD WS7 18 C4
Baron Leigh Dr TLHL/CAN CV4 * 153 H7
Barons Cl HRBN B17 105 M7
Baron's Cft COVS CV3 155 J6
NUNW/HART CV10 98 A1
Baron's Field Rd COVS CV3 155 H6
Barpool Rd NUNW/HART CV10 98 D1
Barrack Cl MGN/WHC B75 57 L7
Barrack La HALE B63 102 F7
Barracks Cl BLOX/PEL WS3 39 J5
Barracks La BLOX/PEL WS3 39 H5
BRWNH WS8 27 G4
RWWCK/WEL CV35 196 A3
Barracks Rd STRPT DY13 189 G4
Barrack St VAUX/NECH B7 7 M2
WBROM B70 68 E5
WWCK CV34 205 J6
Barracks Wy COV CV1 * 8 F5
Barra Cft CVALE B35 91 M1
Barrar Cl STRBR DY8 101 J5
Barras Gn COVE CV2 155 L1
Barras La COV CV1 8 C4
Barratts Cl BEWD DY12 162 E2
Barratts Cft BRLYHL DY5 84 A4
Barratts Rd HWK/WKHTH B38 145 L5
Barratts Stile La BEWD DY12 162 E2
Barr Common Cl ALDR WS9 54 F2
Barr Common Rd ALDR WS9 54 F2
Barrett Cl KIDD DY10 138 F7
Barretts La
RCOVN/BALC/EX CV7 152 A7
Barrhill Cl GTB/HAM B43 70 C3
Barrie Av KIDD DY10 139 G6
Barrington Cl DSYBK/YTR WS5 69 L2
WOLVN WV10 36 A4
Barrington Rd HIA/OLT B92 127 J3
RBRY B45 143 J6
RUGBYS/DCH CV22 186 A3
Barr Lakes La DSYBK/YTR WS5 54 C6
Barr La
MKTBOS/BARL/STKG CV13 81 M2
RRUGBY CV23 158 C1
Barron Rd NFLD/LBR B31 144 F2
Barrow Cl COVE CV2 135 M7
REDE B98 203 K2
Barrowfield La KNWTH CV8 197 K1
Barrow Hill Rd BRLYHL DY5 84 A4
Barrow Rd KNWTH CV8 197 K1
Barrows La
LGN/SDN/BHAMAIR B26 109 J5
Barrows Rd SPARK B11 108 A7
Barrow Wk DIG/EDG B5 107 J6
Barrs Crs CDYHTH B64 103 K5
Barrs Rd CDYHTH B64 103 J6
Barrs St LGLYGN/QTN B68 104 E1
Barr St LOZ/NWT B19 89 G8
SEDG DY3 84 A2
Barry Rd DSYBK/YTR WS5 54 A6
Barsby Cl ATHST CV9 63 H6
Barsham Cl DIG/EDG B5 107 G7
Barsham Dr BRLYHL DY5 102 A5
Barston Cl COVN CV6 134 E2
Barston La HIA/OLT B92 150 D3
RCOVN/BALC/EX CV7 151 H5
SOLH B91 149 M3
Bartestree Cl REDE B98 203 K4
Bartholemews La BRGRVW B61 168 D8
Bartholomew Ct COVS CV3 * 155 L7
Bartholomew Rw CBHAMNE B4 7 J4
Bartholomew St DIG/EDG B5 7 J5
Bartic Av KGSWFD DY6 101 K1
Bartleet Rd REDE B98 203 H6
SMTHWKW B67 87 H8
Bartlett Cl COVN CV6 134 C3
PENK ST19 10 D5
TPTN/OCK DY4 67 M4
Bartley Cl HIA/OLT B92 127 K3
Bartley Dr NFLD/LBR B31 123 J5
Bartley Woods RIDG/WDGT B32 122 F3
Barton Crs RLSS CV31 207 G7
Barton Cft HLGN/YWD B28 147 K1
Barton Dr DOR/KN B93 175 M1
Barton La KGSWFD DY6 83 G5
Barton Lodge Rd
HLGN/YWD B28 147 J1
Barton Rd BDWTH CV12 116 F1
COVN CV6 134 D3
ETTPK/GDPK/PENN WV4 66 D1
NUNW/HART CV10 99 G4
RUGBYS/DCH CV22 186 B5
Bartons Bank LOZ/NWT B19 89 J6
Bartons Ct COVE CV2 * 155 L1
Barton's Meadow COVE CV2 134 F8
Barton St WBROM B70 86 F3
Bar Wk ALDR WS9 41 G4
Barwell Cl DOR/KN B93 175 J1
RLSN CV32 206 D2
Barwell Rd BORD B9 107 M3
Barwick St CBHAMNW B3 6 F4
Basalt Cl WSLW WS2 52 E1
Basant Cl WWCK CV34 205 L6
Bascote Cl REDW B97 201 M4
Basford Brook Dr COVN CV6 116 D8
Basil Gv NFLD/LBR B31 144 C1
Basil Rd NFLD/LBR B31 144 C1
Basin La TAM/AM/WIL B77 46 B2
Baskerville Rd KIDD DY10 138 D4
Baskeyfield Cl LICHS WS14 21 H6
Basley Wy COVN CV6 134 B1
Baslow Cl BLOX/PEL WS3 38 F2
STETCH B33 109 J1
Baslow Rd BLOX/PEL WS3 38 F2
Basons La LGLYGN/QTN B68 87 G8
Bassano Rd BLKHTH/ROWR B65 104 A4
Bassenthwaite Ct KGSWFD DY6 83 H7
Bassett Cl
ETTPK/GDPK/PENN WV4 49 G7
SHHTH WV12 52 B1
WALM/CURD B76 73 J1
Bassett Cft SMHTH B10 107 M5
Bassett Rd COVN CV6 133 L8
DARL/WED WS10 69 G3
HALE B63 102 E7
Bassetts Gv
CHWD/FDBR/MGN B37 92 C8
Bassett St WSLW WS2 4 A4
Bassnage Rd HALE B63 121 J3
Batchcroft BILS/COS WV14 51 H8
DARL/WED WS10 52 B5
Batchelor Cl STRBR DY8 101 K5
Batchley Rd REDW B97 201 M1
Bateman Dr SCFLD/BOLD B73 72 F4
Bateman Rd CSHL/WTROR B46 93 K4
Bateman's Acre South COVN CV6 8 A1
Batemans La HLYWD B47 146 C8
Bates Cl WALM/CURD B76 73 L6
Bates Gv WNSFLD WV11 36 E8
Bates Hl REDW B97 * 202 B1
Bates Rd COVW CV5 154 C6
Bate St ETTPK/GDPK/PENN WV4 66 E2
WSLW WS2 4 E1
Batham Rd KIDD DY10 138 E5
Bath Av WOLV WV1 2 E4
Batheaston Cl
HWK/WKHTH B38 145 H6
Bath Meadow HALE B63 103 J8
Bath Pas DIG/EDG B5 7 G7
Bath Pl RLSS CV31 206 D6
Bath Rd ATHST CV9 63 J6
BRLYHL DY5 102 E3
CNCK/NC WS11 12 C8
NUN CV11 81 G8
STRBR DY8 101 K7
TPTN/OCK DY4 67 L8
WOLV WV1 2 C5
WSL WS1 4 F7
Bath Rw EDG B15 6 D8
OLDBY B69 86 B5
Bath St BILS/COS WV14 51 J8
CBHAMNE B4 7 G2
COV CV1 9 H2
DUDS DY2 85 G5
RLSS CV31 206 D6
RUGBYN/HIL CV21 186 F2
SEDG DY3 66 C4
WLNHL WV13 51 M4
WOLV WV1 * 3 J6
WSL WS1 4 F5
Bathurst Cl RUGBYS/DCH CV22 186 C5
Bathurst Rd COVN CV6 133 L7
Bath Wk BHTH/HG B12 107 J8
Bathway Rd COVS CV3 180 E1
Batmans Hill Rd BILS/COS WV14 67 J3
Batsford Cl REDE B98 202 F8
Batsford Rd COVN CV6 154 D1
Batson Ri STRBR DY8 101 L5
Battalion Ct COVN CV6 133 L4
Battenhall Rd HRBN B17 105 L8
Battens Cl REDE B98 202 D2
Battens Dr REDE B98 203 H1
Battery Wy SPARK B11 126 C1
Battlefield Hl WMBN WV5 64 F6
Battlefield La WMBN WV5 64 F7
Baulk La RCOVN/BALC/EX CV7 152 B5
Bavaro Gdns BRLYHL DY5 102 E3
Baverstock Rd
ALE/KHTH/YWD B14 146 D3
Bawnmore Ct
RUGBYS/DCH CV22 186 B5
Bawnmore Pk
RUGBYS/DCH CV22 186 C6
Bawnmore Rd
RUGBYS/DCH CV22 186 B5
Baxter Av KIDD DY10 138 C6
Baxter Cl TLHL/CAN CV4 153 L3
Baxter Ct RLSS CV31 206 E6
Baxter Gdns KIDD DY10 138 D6
Baxterley Gn SOLH B91 148 B1
WALM/CURD B76 73 K4
Baxter Rd BRLYHL DY5 102 A3
Baxters Rd SHLY B90 147 M5
Bayer St BILS/COS WV14 67 G5
Bayford Av
LGN/SDN/BHAMAIR B26 128 A1
NFLD/LBR B31 144 C7
Bayley Crs DARL/WED WS10 52 A5
Bayley La COV CV1 9 G5
Bayleys La TPTN/OCK DY4 68 A6
Baylie St STRBR DY8 119 K1
Baylis Av WNSFLD WV11 37 K5
Bayliss Av COVN CV6 134 E1
ETTPK/GDPK/PENN WV4 66 E3
Bayliss Cl BILS/COS WV14 51 G6
NFLD/LBR B31 123 M8
Baynton Rd SHHTH WV12 38 A6
Bayston Av BDMR/CCFT WV3 49 J5
Bayston Rd
ALE/KHTH/YWD B14 146 C1
Bayswater Rd
BFLD/HDSWWD B20 89 H4
SEDG DY3 84 B3
Bayton Rd RCOVN/BALC/EX CV7 116 F5
Bayton Wy
RCOVN/BALC/EX CV7 117 G6
Baytree Cl BLOX/PEL WS3 38 E3
Bay Tree Cl COVE CV2 135 H4
HWK/WKHTH B38 145 H5
Baytree Rd BLOX/PEL WS3 38 E3
Baywell Cl SHLY B90 148 E6
Beach Av BHTH/HG B12 107 M8
ETTPK/GDPK/PENN WV4 66 E3
Beach Brook Cl SPARK B11 107 M8
Beachburn Wy
BFLD/HDSWWD B20 88 E2
Beach Cl NFLD/LBR B31 145 G4
Beachcroft Rd KGSWFD DY6 83 G4
Beach Dr HALE B63 103 L8
Beach Rd BILS/COS WV14 51 H6
SPARK B11 107 M8
STRPT DY13 188 C4
Beach St HALE B63 103 L8
Beachwood Av KGSWFD DY6 83 G4
Beacon Cl GTB/HAM B43 70 D4
RBRY B45 143 K7
SMTHWK B66 87 L6
Beacon Dr WSL WS1 5 K7
Beaconfields LICH WS13 20 E5
Beacon Gdns LICH WS13 20 E4
Beacon Hl ALDR WS9 55 G4
AST/WIT B6 89 J5
RBRY B45 143 J8
Beacon La BRGRVE B60 169 H2
SEDG DY3 66 C4
Beacon Ri ALDR WS9 54 F2
HAG/WOL DY9 120 B1
SEDG DY3 66 C4
Beacon Rd ALDR WS9 54 F6
COVN CV6 134 B2
DSYBK/YTR WS5 54 B8
GTB/HAM B43 71 G2
KGSTG B44 71 L1
SCFLD/BOLD B73 72 E4
SHHTH WV12 38 A5
Beaconsfield Av
ETTPK/GDPK/PENN WV4 50 B8
RUGBYS/DCH CV22 186 E4
Beaconsfield Ct WSL WS1 5 L6
Beaconsfield Crs
BHTH/HG B12 * 107 J8
Beaconsfield Dr
ETTPK/GDPK/PENN WV4 50 B8
Beaconsfield Rd BHTH/HG B12 125 J1
COVE CV2 155 M3
FOAKS/STRLY B74 56 F6
Beaconsfield St HHTH/SAND B71 69 H8
RLSS CV31 206 F5
Beacon St BILS/COS WV14 66 D4
LICH WS13 20 E5
WSL WS1 5 K5
Beacon Vw RBRY B45 143 K7
Beacon View Dr KGSTG B44 71 K1
Beacon View Rd
HHTH/SAND B71 69 K4
Beacon Wy ALDR WS9 40 E2
HEDN WS12 17 K2
RUSH/SHEL WS4 53 M1
Beadborough Wk ALDR WS9 40 F4
Beake Av COVN CV6 133 M7
Beakes Rd SMTHWKW B67 105 K2
Beaks Farm Gdns
LDYWD/EDGR B16 106 B3
Beaks Hill Rd HWK/WKHTH B38 145 J4
Beak St CBHAMW B1 6 F6
Beale Cl CVALE B35 91 L3
Beales St AST/WIT B6 89 M5
Beale St STRBR DY8 101 K8
Bealeys Av WNSFLD WV11 37 G5
Bealeys La BLOX/PEL WS3 38 E3
Beamans Cl HIA/OLT B92 127 L1
Beaminster Rd SOLH B91 148 D1
Beamish Cl COVE CV2 135 L7
Bean Cft RIDG/WDGT B32 123 G3
Beanfield Av COVS CV3 180 D1
Bean Rd DUDS DY2 85 H5
TPTN/OCK DY4 67 H7
Beardmore Rd
CSCFLD/WYGN B72 73 G5
Bear Hl ALVE B48 170 F8
Bearhill Dr ALVE B48 170 F7
Bear Lane Cl POL/KGSB/FAZ B78 47 L3
Bearley Cft SHLY B90 148 A5
Bearmore Rd CDYHTH B64 103 J4
Bearnett Dr
ETTPK/GDPK/PENN WV4 65 G3
Bearnett La WMBN WV5 64 F4
Bearwood Rd SMTHWK B66 105 L3
Beasley Gv PBAR/PBCH B42 70 F4
Beaton Cl WLNHL WV13 51 J3
Beaton Rd FOAKS/STRLY B74 56 E2
Beatrice St BLOX/PEL WS3 39 G7
Beatrice Wk TPTN/OCK DY4 85 L3
Beatty Dr RUGBYS/DCH CV22 186 B3
Beaubrook Gdns STRBR DY8 101 H2
Beauchamp Av
BFLD/HDSWWD B20 70 D8
KIDDW DY11 164 A2
RLSN CV32 206 D4
Beauchamp Cl
CHWD/FDBR/MGN B37 110 F3
WALM/CURD B76 73 M6
Beauchamp Gdns WWCK CV34 205 M7
Beauchamp Hl RLSN CV32 206 C4
Beauchamp Ms RLSN CV32 * 206 D4
Beauchamp Rd KNWTH CV8 197 J3
MOS/BIL B13 125 M8
RLSN CV32 206 D4
SOLH B91 127 L8
TAM/AM/WIL B77 46 D8
WWCK CV34 205 M5
Beau Ct CNCK/NC WS11 16 C4
Beaudesert BNTWD WS7 18 E4
Beaudesert Cl HLYWD B47 146 E7
Beaudesert Rd
BFLD/HDSWWD B20 88 F5
COVW CV5 8 A7
HLYWD B47 146 E7
Beaudesert Vw HEDN WS12 13 L8
Beaufell Cl WWCK CV34 205 J4
Beaufort Av CBROM B36 91 H7
KIDDW DY11 137 L6
RLSN CV32 199 G8
Beaufort Dr COVS CV3 156 D6
Beaufort Rd LDYWD/EDGR B16 106 D4
Beaufort St REDW B97 202 C2
Beaufort Wy ALDR WS9 54 F1
Beaulieu Av KGSWFD DY6 101 K1
Beaulieu Cl KIDDW DY11 138 A5
Beaulieu Pk RLSS CV31 207 H7
Beaumaris Cl COVW CV5 132 D8
DUDN DY1 84 D2
Beaumont Cl GTWY WS6 24 D3
TPTN/OCK DY4 67 J7
Beaumont Crs COVN CV6 8 A1
Beaumont Dr BRLYHL DY5 101 M6
HRBN B17 123 M1
Beaumont Gdns WSNGN B18 88 D7
Beaumont Gv SOLH B91 127 K8
Beaumont Lawns BRGRVE B60 169 G4
Beaumont Pl NUNW/HART CV10 98 D1
Beaumont Rd BVILLE B30 124 C7
DARL/WED WS10 68 D1
GTWY WS6 24 D3
NUN CV11 98 D1
RCOVN/BALC/EX CV7 115 L7
RMSLY B62 104 C5
Beaumont Wy CNCK/NC WS11 17 L8
Beaurevoir Wy WWCK CV34 205 L5
Beausale Cft COVW CV5 153 L2
Beausale Dr DOR/KN B93 149 M6
Beausale La RWWCK/WEL CV35 196 A5
Beauty Bank CDYHTH B64 103 K5
Beauty Bank Crs STRBR DY8 101 J7
Beaver Cl WNSFLD WV11 37 K8
Bebington Cl COVEN WV9 35 K4
Beccles Dr WLNHL WV13 51 K5
Beckbury Av
ETTPK/GDPK/PENN WV4 49 G8
Beckbury Rd COVE CV2 135 K7
SLYOAK B29 123 L4
Beck Cl SMTHWK B66 105 L1
Beckenham Av KGSTG B44 71 L4
Beckensall Cl DUDN DY1 84 F4
Becket Cl MGN/WHC B75 42 D7
Beckett Cl REDE B98 194 D8
Beckett St BILS/COS WV14 51 J7
Beckfield Cl
ALE/KHTH/YWD B14 146 C3
RUSH/SHEL WS4 40 A5
Beckfoot Cl RUGBYN/HIL CV21 161 H5
Beckfoot Dr COVE CV2 135 K4
Beckford Cft DOR/KN B93 * 175 K2
Beckman Rd HAG/WOL DY9 120 A3
Beckminster Rd
BDMR/CCFT WV3 49 K6
Becks La RCOVN/BALC/EX CV7 113 L8
Beconsfield Cl DOR/KN B93 175 K3
Becton Gv PBAR/PBCH B42 71 H6
Bedcote Pl STRBR DY8 101 M8
Beddoe Cl TPTN/OCK DY4 68 B8
Beddow Av BILS/COS WV14 67 G6
Beddows Rd BLOX/PEL WS3 39 J8
Bede Rd BDWTH CV12 116 E1
COVN CV6 133 M8
NUNW/HART CV10 98 B1
Bede Village BDWTH CV12 * 116 A5
Bedford Dr MGN/WHC B75 57 J7
Bedford Pl HEDN WS12 16 F1
RLSN CV32 206 D5
Bedford Rd HHTH/SAND B71 68 F6
MGN/WHC B75 57 J6
SPARK B11 7 M9
Bedford St COV CV1 8 B6
RLSN CV32 206 D4
TPTN/OCK DY4 67 M8
WOLV WV1 50 E6
Bedford Ter LOZ/NWT B19 * 89 H5
Bedingstone Dr PENK ST19 10 D7
Bedlam La COVN CV6 134 C3
Bedlam Wood Rd
NFLD/LBR B31 144 A4
Bedworth Cl BDWTH CV12 117 M3
Bedworth Cft TPTN/OCK DY4 85 M1
Bedworth Gv BORD B9 108 F3
Bedworth La BDWTH CV12 116 A1
Bedworth Rd BDWTH CV12 117 L3
COVN CV6 116 E8
Beebee Rd DARL/WED WS10 52 D8
Beecham Cl ALDR WS9 40 E5
Beech Av BHTH/HG B12 107 L8
CHWD/FDBR/MGN B37 110 F4
RIDG/WDGT B32 105 H7
RMSLY B62 104 A5
TAM/AM/WIL B77 46 C2
Beech Cliffe WWCK CV34 205 K5
Beech Cl ATHST CV9 61 G8
MGN/WHC B75 56 E1
NUNW/HART CV10 79 L5
POL/KGSB/FAZ B78 60 A6
SEDG DY3 66 C4
WOLVN WV10 35 M5
Beechcote Av KIDDW DY11 138 B3
Beech Ct GTWY WS6 * 24 E1
HEDN WS12 * 12 F6
SMTHWK B66 87 G6
WSL WS1 5 J6
Beech Crs BNTWD WS7 18 D7
DARL/WED WS10 52 D8
TPTN/OCK DY4 68 A5
Beechcroft BDWTH CV12 116 D4
Beechcroft Av HLGN/YWD B28 126 D7
Beechcroft Crs
FOAKS/STRLY B74 55 H4
Beechcroft Dr BRGRVE B60 191 M1
Beechcroft Est HALE B63 103 G7
Beechcroft Pl WOLVN WV10 36 A7
Beechcroft Rd CBROM B36 91 M5
CDYHTH B64 103 J4
KIDDW DY11 137 L5
Beechdale Av KGSTG B44 71 J3
Beechdale Rd BLOX/PEL WS3 38 D5
Beech Dene Gv
ERDW/GRVHL B23 72 C8
Beech Dr KNWTH CV8 179 M8
RUGBYS/DCH CV22 186 A4
Beechen Gv BNTWD WS7 18 D5
Beecher Pl HALE B63 103 H8
Beecher Rd HALE B63 103 H8
Beecher Rd East HALE B63 103 H8
Beecher St HALE B63 103 G8
Beeches Av ACGN B27 127 G1
Beeches Cl KGSWFD DY6 83 H8
RBRY B45 143 H6
Beeches Dr ERDE/BCHGN B24 91 G1
Beeches Farm Dr
NFLD/LBR B31 144 E6
Beeches Pl BLOX/PEL WS3 39 H6
Beeches Rd BLKHTH/ROWR B65 103 M4
BLOX/PEL WS3 39 H7
HHTH/SAND B71 87 J2
KIDDW DY11 138 A4
LGLYGN/QTN B68 105 G2
PBAR/PBCH B42 71 G6
The Beeches BDWTH CV12 116 C3
POL/KGSB/FAZ B78 47 L5
WBROM B70 87 J3
WOLV WV1 2 A3
Beeches View Av HALE B63 121 G1
Beeches Wk SCFLD/BOLD B73 72 F2
Beeches Wy NFLD/LBR B31 144 E6
Beechey Cl GTB/HAM B43 55 H8
Beech Farm Cft NFLD/LBR B31 144 E2
Beechfield Cl RMSLY B62 104 A5
Beechfield Dr KIDDW DY11 138 A4
Beechfield Gv BILS/COS WV14 66 F6
Beechfield Ri LICH WS13 21 H5
Beechfield Rd SMTHWKW B67 105 K1
SPARK B11 107 M7
Beech Gdns CDSL WV8 34 D4
LICHS WS14 21 G7
Beech Ga FOAKS/STRLY B74 41 M8
Beechglade BFLD/HDSWWD B20 88 D1
Beech Gn DUDN DY1 66 E8
Beech Gv ALE/KHTH/YWD B14 125 L8
HEDN WS12 12 B5
RCOVN/BALC/EX CV7 96 C3
WWCK CV34 205 M4
Beech Hill Rd CSCFLD/WYGN B72 73 G6
Beech Hurst HWK/WKHTH B38 145 J5
Beechlawn Dr KINVER DY7 100 C6
Beechmore Rd
LGN/SDN/BHAMAIR B26 109 K8
Beechmount Dr
ERDW/GRVHL B23 72 E7
Beechnut Cl SOLH B91 128 B8
TLHL/CAN CV4 153 H3
Beechnut La SOLH B91 128 C8
Beech Park Dr RBRY B45 170 A5
Beech Pine Cl HEDN WS12 12 E5
Beech Rd BRGRVW B61 191 K1
BVILLE B30 124 C6
COVN CV6 133 M8
CRTAM B79 31 L5
DARL/WED WS10 52 D8
DUDN DY1 85 G1
ERDW/GRVHL B23 72 D6
HLYWD B47 146 F7
KGSWFD DY6 83 H8
OLDBY B69 85 L5
STRBR DY8 119 J2
WLNHL WV13 51 J3
WOLVN WV10 35 M5
Beech Tree Av COVW CV5 153 M3
WNSFLD WV11 37 G5
Beech Tree Cl KGSWFD DY6 83 J5
REDW B97 201 L1
Beech Tree La CNCK/NC WS11 16 B5
Beechtree La KIDD DY10 118 D7
Beechtree Rd ALDR WS9 40 D2
Beech Wk HWK/WKHTH B38 145 K5
Beech Wy SMTHWK B66 87 M8
Beechwood Av COVW CV5 154 C4
WNSFLD WV11 36 F5
Beechwood Cl BLOX/PEL WS3 38 F2
SHLY B90 174 B1
Beechwood Ct
DUNHL/THL/PER WV6 * 49 G2
RUGBYN/HIL CV21 * 186 D1
Beechwood Crs
TAM/AM/WIL B77 32 D8
Beechwood Cft
FOAKS/STRLY B74 42 B8
KNWTH CV8 197 K3
Beechwood Dr
DUNHL/THL/PER WV6 48 E3
Beechwood Park Rd SOLH B91 127 J8
Beechwood Rd
ALE/KHTH/YWD B14 125 K8
BDWTH CV12 117 G1
DUDS DY2 85 J4
GTB/HAM B43 70 D4
NUNW/HART CV10 80 B7
SMTHWKW B67 105 J5
WBROM B70 86 F2

Beecroft Av *LICH* WS13 ....20 F4
Beecroft Rd *CNCK/NC* WS11 ....16 C4
Beehive Ct *BRGRVW* B61 ....168 E4
Beehive Hl *KNWTH* CV8 ....179 H6
Beehive La *WOLVN* WV10 ....36 B2
Beeston Cl *AST/WIT* B6 ....89 L6
  BRLYHL DY5 ....102 A5
  COVS CV3 ....156 D5
Beeton Rd *WSNGN* B18 ....88 B3
Beet St *BLKHTH/ROWR* B65 .....104 A4
Beever Rd *TPTN/OCK* DY4 ....68 B6
Beggars Bush La *WMBN* WV5 ....64 F4
Beighton Cl *FOAKS/STRLY* B74 ..42 C7
Beilby Rd *BVILLE* B30 ....124 F7
Belbroughton Cl *REDE* B98 ......202 D3
Belbroughton Rd
  HAG/WOL DY9 ....141 J4
  HALE B63 ....121 K3
  KIDD DY10 ....140 A4
  STRBR DY8 ....119 J2
Belchers La *BORD* B9 ....108 E3
Beldray Pk *BILS/COS* WV14 ....51 J7
Beldray Rd *BILS/COS* WV14 ....51 J7
Belfry Cl *BLOX/PEL* WS3 ....38 E2
Belfry Dr *STRBR* DY8 ....101 J7
The Belfry *DUNHL/THL/PER* WV6 ..48 B1
Belgrade Av *WOLVN* WV10 ....35 M3
Belgrade Sq *COV* CV1 * 8 E4
Belgrave Ct *KGSWFD* DY6 ....101 K1
Belgrave Dr *RUGBYN/HIL* CV21 ..161 H7
Belgrave Int *DIG/EDG* B5 ....107 H6
Belgrave Middleway
  DIG/EDG B5 ....107 J3
  BHTH/HG B12 ....107 K7
  COVE CV2 ....156 C1
  RMSLY B62 ....104 B5
  TAM/AM/WIL B77 ....46 C5
Belgrave Sq *COVE* CV2 ....156 C1
Belgrave Ter *HDSW* B21 ....88 E6
Belgrave Wk *WSLW* WS2 ....52 F2
Belgrove Cl *EDG* B15 ....106 C7
Belinda Cl *WLNHL* WV13 ....51 K2
Bellairs Av *BDMR* CCFT WV3 .....116 C4
Bellamy Cl *SHLY* B90 ....148 B4
Bellamy Farm Rd *SHLY* B90 .....148 B4
Bellamy La *WNSFLD* WV11 ....37 H6
Bell Barn Rd *EDG* B15 ....6 D9
Bellbrook Penk ST19 ....10 C4
Bellbrooke Cl *COVE* CV2 ....134 F4
Bell Cl *BORD* B9 ....108 C2
  CBROM B36 ....92 F7
  DARL/WED WS10 ....52 B6
  LICH WS13 ....20 D4
Bell Ct *RLSN* CV32 * 206 D3
Bellcroft *LDYWD/EDGR* B16 ....6 A4
Bell Dr *DSYBK/YTR* WS5 ....53 L8
  HEDN WS12 ....13 G6
  RCOVN/BALC/EX CV7 ....116 C1
  WASH/WDE B8 ....108 D2
Bellefield Av *WSNGN* B18 ....106 C1
Bellefield Rd *WSNGN* B18 ....106 C1
Belle Isle *BRLYHL* DY5 ....102 A2
Bellemere Rd *HIA/OLT* B92 ....129 M8
Bellencroft Gdns
  BDMR/CCFT WV3 ....48 F6
Bell End *BLKHTH/ROWR* B65 .....104 A4
Belle Orch *KIDDW* DY11 ....137 M8
Belle V *HALE* B63 ....103 J8
Belle Vue *DIG/EDG* B5 ....107 H6
Belle Vue Cl *BRGRVE* B60 ....169 G5
Belle Vue Dr *RMSLY* B62 ....104 B7
Belle Vue Gdns
  BLKHTH/ROWR B65 * 104 A2
Bellevue Av *LDYWD/EDGR* B16 * ..106 B1
Belle Vue Cl *BRGRVE* B60 ....169 G5
Bellevue Rd *BILS/COS* WV14 ....67 K3
  LGN/SDN/BHAMAIR B26 ....109 L6
Bellevue St *BILS/COS* WV14 ....66 D3
Belle Vue Ter *HIA/OLT* B92 ....129 L7
Belfarm Ms *WOLVN* WV10 ....22 E6
Bellflower Cl *WNSFLD* WV11 ....37 G7
Bell Fold *LGLYGN/QTN* B68 ....67 L1
Bell Green La *HWK/WKHTH* B38 ..145 M8
Bell Green Rd *COVN* CV6 ....134 C5
Bell Heather Rd *BRWNH* WS8 ......26 B7
Bell Hl *NFLD/LBR* B31 ....123 L1
Bell Holloway *NFLD/LBR* B31 .....123 K8
Bellington Cft *SHLY* B90 ....148 E7
Bellis St *LDYWD/EDGR* B16 ....106 C4
Bell La *BLOX/PEL* WS3 ....38 F4
  DSYBK/YTR WS5 ....69 L1
  NFLD/LBR B31 ....144 E1
  STETCH B33 ....110 C4
Bellman Cl *DARL/WED* WS10 ....52 B6
Bell Meadow *HAG/WOL* DY9 ......119 M5
Bell Meadow Wy
  ALE/KHTH/YWD B14 ....146 B3
Bell Pl *BKHL/PFLD* WV2 * 2 F7
Bell Rd *DSYBK/YTR* WS5 ....54 B7
  DUDS DY2 ....85 G8
  WMBN WV5 ....64 A4
Bells Rw *STRPT* DY13 ....188 E2
Bells Farm Cl
  ALE/KHTH/YWD B14 ....146 A3
Belsize Cl *CNCK/NC* WS11 ....17 K8
Bells La *BNTWD* WS7 ....18 D4
  HWK/WKHTH B38 ....146 A3
  STRBR DY8 ....101 H4
Bell Rw At South *BRLYHL* DY5 .....102 B3
Bell Tower Ms *RLSN* CV32 ....206 D1
Bellview Wy *COVN* CV6 ....134 C4
Bell Vue Rd *BLKHTH/ROWR* B65 ..104 A3
Bell Wk *RUGBYN/HIL* CV21 ....187 L5
Bellwood Rd *NFLD/LBR* B31 ......144 D1
Belmont Av *CNCK/NC* WS11 ....16 A3
Belmont Cl *ALDR* WS9 ....24 E1
  CTWY WS6 ....24 E1
  REDW B97 ....201 M4
  TPTN/OCK DY4 ....67 K7
Belmont Covert *NFLD/LBR* B31 ..123 M7
Belmont Dr *RLSN* CV32 ....206 E1
Belmont Gdns *BILS/COS* WV14 * ..67 L1
Belmont Ms *RLSN* CV32 * 206 D1
Belmont Pas *CBHAMNE* B4 ....7 M5
Belmont Rd *BRLYHL* DY5 ....84 B7
  COVN CV6 ....134 D6
  ETTPK/GDPK/PENN WV4 ....49 L3
  HDSW B21 ....120 C1
  RBRY B45 ....143 K7
  RUGBYS/DCH CV22 ....186 E5
  SMTHWK B66 ....105 L3
  TAM/AM/WIL B77 ....46 C5
Belmont Rd East *HDSW* B21 ....88 A5

Belmont Rw *CBHAMNE* B4 ....7 K3
Belmont St *BILS/COS* WV14 ....67 L1
Belper *DUDN* DY1 ....84 F4
Belper Rd *BLOX/PEL* WS3 ....39 G2
  WBROM B70 ....86 D2
Belper Rw *DUDS* DY2 ....103 J1
Belsize *TAM/AM/WIL* B77 ....46 A6
Belstone Cl *ALE/KHTH/YWD* B14 ..125 H8
Belton Av *WNSFLD* WV11 ....36 F4
Belton Cl *HOCK/TIA* B94 ....175 G8
Belton Gv *RBRY* B45 ....144 A5
Belt Rd *WS12 ....12 E8
Belvedere Av
  ETTPK/GDPK/PENN WV4 ....49 M8
Belvedere Cl *BNTWD* WS7 ....18 D3
  KGSWFD DY6 ....101 K1
  KIDD DY10 ....138 E8
Belvedere Ct *BS BEWD* DY12 .....137 G8
Belvedere Rd *BRGRVW* B61 ....191 L1
Belvedere Gdns
  DUNHL/THL/PER WV6 ....35 H6
  ERDE/BCHGN B24 ....90 E3
Belvide Gdns *CDSL* WV8 ....34 D1
Belvide Gv *SLYOAK* B29 ....123 M5
Belvidere Gdns *SPARK* B11 ......125 M1
Belvior Cl *DUDN* DY1 ....84 C3
Belvoir *TAM/AM/WIL* B77 ....46 A4
Belvoir Cl *DUDN* DY1 ....84 C3
Belvoir Rd *BRGRVE* B60 ....192 A5
Belwell Dr *FOAKS/STRLY* B74 ......56 E3
Belwell La *FOAKS/STRLY* B74 ......56 E3
Bembridge Cl *SHHTH* WV12 ....37 M5
Benacre Dr *DIG/EDG* B5 ....7 K5
Benbeck Gv *TPTN/OCK* DY4 ....67 J3
Benches Cl *BNTWD* WS7 ....18 B7
Bendall Rd *KGSTG* B44 ....71 M3
Benedictine Rd *COVS* CV3 ....155 G6
Benedon Rd
  LGN/SDN/BHAMAIR B26 ....109 L6
Bengrove Cl *REDE* B98 ....202 E6
Benion Rd *CNCK/NC* WS11 ....16 D1
Benmore Av *DIG/EDG* B5 ....107 H7
Bennett Av *DUDN* DY1 ....66 F7
Bennett Cl *KNWTH* CV8 * 183 K2
Bennett Dr *WWCK* CV34 ....205 M6
Bennett Rd *FOAKS/STRLY* B74 .....56 B2
Bennett's Fold *BKHL/PFLD* WV2 * ..2 E6
Bennett's Hl *CBHAMNW* B3 ....6 F5
  DUDS DY2 ....85 J5
Bennett's Rd
  RCOVN/BALC/EX CV7 ....115 K3
  WASH/WDE B8 ....90 B7
Bennett's Rd North
  RCOVN/BALC/EX CV7 ....115 H5
Bennetts Rd South
  RCOVN/BALC/EX CV7 ....133 K2
  LOZ/NWT B19 ....89 A7
  RUGBYN/HIL CV21 ....186 D2
Ben Nevis Wy *STRBR* DY8 ....101 L7
Bennfield Rd *RUGBY/HIL* CV21 ...186 E2
Benn Rd *BDWTH* CV12 ....117 M3
Benn St *RUGBYS/DCH* CV22 .....187 G3
Benson Av
  ETTPK/GDPK/PENN WV4 ....50 A8
Benson Cl *DUNHL/THL/PER* WV6 ..35 H4
  LICH WS13 ....21 H4
Benson Rd *ALE/KHTH/YWD* B14 ..146 F4
  COVN CV6 ....133 L4
  WSNGN B18 ....88 D7
Benson Vw *CRTAM* B79 ....32 A5
Bent Av *RIDG/WDGT* B32 ....105 H7
Benthall Rd *COVN* CV6 ....134 D3
Bentham Ct *NFLD/LBR* B31 ....123 K8
Bentley Bridge Pk
  WLNHL WV13 * 50 F1
Bentleybridge Wy *WLNHL* WV13 ..51 G1
Bentley Brook La *HEDN* WS12 ......13 L7
Bentley Cl *REDW* B97 ....202 B2
  RLSN CV32 ....206 F2
Bentley Ct *COVN* CV6 ....134 A1
  CDSL WV8 ....34 D1
  WSLW WS2 ....52 E3
Bentley Farm Cl *DOR/KN* B93 ....175 J1
Bentley Gv *SLYOAK* B29 ....123 K5
Bentley La *RCOVN/BALC/EX* CV7 ..113 C3
  REDW B97 ....200 F5
  SHHTH WV12 ....38 B8
  WSLW WS2 ....52 E1
Bentley Mill Cl *WSLW* WS2 ....52 D4
Bentley Mill La *WSLW* WS2 ....52 D4
Bentley Mill Wy *WSLW* WS2 ....52 C4
Bentley New Dr *WSLW* WS2 ....52 F2
Bentley Pl *WSLW* WS2 ....52 E1
  NUN CV11 ....98 B6
  RCOVN/BALC/EX CV7 ....116 E4
  WOLVN WV10 ....36 C3
Bentley Rd North *WSLW* WS2 ......52 C4
Bentley Rd South
  DARL/WED WS10 ....52 B5
Bentley Wy *CRTAM* B79 ....31 K6
Bentmead Gv *HWK/WKHTH* B38 ..145 L4
Benton Av *SPARK* B11 ....108 A7
Benton Cl *SHHTH* WV12 ....52 B1
Benton Crs *BLOX/PEL* WS3 ....38 F3
Benton Green La
  RCOVN/BALC/EX CV7 ....152 D3
Benton Rd *SPARK* B11 ....108 A7
Benton's Ct *KIDDW* DY11 ....138 A7
Benton's La *CTWY* WS6 ....24 E4
Bentons Mill Cft *VAUX/NECH* B7 ..90 A5
The Bentree *COVS* CV3 ....155 M5
Bent St *BRLYHL* DY5 ....102 B1
Ben Willetts Wk
  BLKHTH/ROWR B65 ....104 A4
Beoley Cl *CSCFLD/WYGN* B72 .....73 G4
Beoley Gv *RBRY* B45 ....143 L6
Beoley La *REDE* B98 ....195 L4
Beoley Rd East *REDE* B98 ....202 E1
Beoley Rd West *REDE* B98 ....202 D1
Berberry Cl *BVILLE* B30 ....124 B7
Berenska Dr *RLSN* CV32 ....206 E3
Beresford Crs *WBROM* B70 ....86 F2
Beresford Dr *SCFLD/BOLD* B73 ...73 L2
Beresford Rd *BLOX/PEL* WS3 ......39 J5
  OLDBY B69 ....87 G6
The Berets *MGN/WHC* B75 ....57 H7
Bericote Cft *ACGN* B27 ....127 H2
Bericote Rd *RLSN* CV32 ....198 C5
Berkeley Cl
  DUNHL/THL/PER WV6 ....48 D1
  NUNW/HART CV10 ....98 D1
  REDE B98 ....202 C3
  WSLW WS2 ....52 D2
Berkeley Dr *KGSWFD* DY6 ....83 G6
Berkeley Rd *KNWTH* CV8 ....179 J7
  SHLY B90 ....147 K2
Berkeley Rd East *YDLY* B25 ......108 F6
Berkeley Rd North *COVW* CV5 ......8 A8
Berkeley St *WSLW* WS2 ....52 D2
Berkeswell Cl *REDE* B98 ....194 F6
Berkett Rd *COVN* CV6 ....115 J7
Berkley Cl *BRGRVE* B60 ....191 M5

Berkley Crs *MOS/BIL* B13 ....126 A4
Berkley St *CBHAMNE* B1 ....6 C6
Berkshire Cl *HHTH/SAND* B71 ....69 G1
  NUNW/HART CV10 ....98 C2
Berkshire Crs *DARL/WED* WS10 ...69 G1
The Berkshire *BLOX/PEL* WS3 * ...38 E2
Berkswell Cl *DUDN* DY1 ....84 C1
  FOAKS/STRLY B74 ....42 A7
  HIA/OLT B92 ....127 M5
Berkswell Rd *COVN* CV6 ....134 E3
  ERDE/BCHGN B24 ....90 F1
  RCOVN/BALC/EX CV7 ....131 C5
Bermuda Cl *DUDN* DY1 ....66 F7
Bermuda Pk *NUNW/HART* CV10 ..98 C7
Bermuda Rd *NUNW/HART* CV10 ..98 C5
Bernard Pl *WSNGN* B18 * 88 D8
Bernard Rd *HHTH/SAND* B71 ......87 C1
  WSL WS1 ....5 J6
Berners Cl *LOZ/NWT* B19 ....89 C6
Berners St *LOZ/NWT* B19 ....89 C6
Bernhard Dr *HDSW* B21 ....88 C5
Bernie Crossland Wk
  KIDD DY10 ....164 D2
Bernwall Cl *STRBR* DY8 ....119 K1
Berrandale Rd *CBROM* B36 ....91 K5
Berrington Cl *REDE* B98 ....203 E3
Berrington Dr *BILS/COS* WV14 ....66 F5
Berrington Rd
  NUNW/HART CV10 ....80 B6
  RLSS CV31 ....206 F7
Berrington Wk *DIG/EDG* B5 ....107 J6
Berrow Dr *EDG* B15 ....106 A6
Berrow Hill Rd *KIDDW* DY11 ......137 M4
Berrowside Rd *BKDE/SHDE* B34 ..92 C7
Berrow Vw *BRGRVE* B60 ....191 H6
Berry Av *DARL/WED* WS10 ....68 C6
Berrybush Gdns *SEDG* DY3 ....66 E6
Berry Cl *LOZ/NWT* B19 ....89 H7
Berry Crs *DSYBK/YTR* WS5 ....70 A1
Berry Dr *DR ALDR* WS9 ....40 E5
  RBRY B45 ....169 L4
  SMTHWK B66 ....87 L7
Berryfield Rd
  LGN/SDN/BHAMAIR B26 ....110 B8
Berryfields *ALDR* WS9 ....27 J8
  ALDR WS9 ....40 C8
  RCOVN/BALC/EX CV7 ....114 C1
Berryfields Rd *WALM/CURD* B76 ..73 K2
Berry Hall La *SOLH* B91 ....149 L1
Berry Hl *HEDN* WS12 ....17 C1
Berry La *BRGRVW* B61 ....190 A4
Berry Rd *DUDN* DY1 ....67 C8
  WASH/WDE B8 ....90 C8
Berry St *COV* CV1 ....9 K2
  WOLV WV1 ....3 C5
  WSNGN B18 ....88 D7
Bertha Rd *SPARK* B11 ....108 B8
Bertie Ct *KNWTH* CV8 * 197 L1
Bertie Rd *KNWTH* CV8 * 197 K1
Bertie Ter *RLSN* CV32 * 206 C4
Bertram Cl *TPTN/OCK* DY4 ....68 A4
Bertram Rd *BORD* B9 ....108 B4
  SMTHWK B66 ....87 J3
Berwick Cl *COVW* CV5 ....153 M1
  WWCK CV34 ....205 J3
Berwick Dr *GTB/HAM* B43 ....70 F1
  NFLD/LBR B31 ....144 B2
Berwicks La
  CHWD/FDBR/MGN B37 ....110 F4
Berwood Farm Rd
  CSCFLD/WYGN B72 ....73 G7
Berwood Gdns
  ERDE/BCHGN B24 ....73 G7
Berwood Gv *HIA/OLT* B92 ....127 M4
Berwood La *ERDE/BCHGN* B24 ...91 J2
Berwood Pk *CVALE* B35 ....91 L3
Berwood Rd *WALM/CURD* B76 ....73 J7
Berwyn Av *COVN* CV6 ....133 L4
Berwyn Gv *GTWY* WS6 ....24 D2
Berwyn Wy *NUNW/HART* CV10 ....98 A1
Besant Gv *ACGN* B27 ....126 E3
Besbury Cl *DOR/KN* B93 ....175 J3
Bescot Crs *WSL* WS1 ....4 C9
Bescot Cft *PBAR/PBCH* B42 ....70 F6
Bescot Dr *WSLW* WS2 ....52 F7
Bescot Rd *WSLW* WS2 ....4 B4
Bescot St *CDYHTH* B64 ....103 K3
Beswick Gdns
  RUGBYS/DCH CV22 ....186 B6
Beswick Gv *STETCH* B33 ....109 L1
Beta Gv *ALE/KHTH/YWD* B14 ....147 G1
Betjeman Cl *KIDD* DY10 ....138 F8
Betjeman Pl *WOLVN* WV10 ....36 E4
Betley Gv *STETCH* B33 ....109 L1
Betony *DSYBK/YTR* WS5 ....69 L2
Betsham Cl *KGSTG* B44 ....71 M4
Bettany Gld *WOLVN* WV10 ....36 C1
Betteridge Dr *WALM/CURD* B76 ..73 J7
Bettina Cl *NUNW/HART* CV10 ......80 F3
Bettman Cl *COVS* CV3 ....155 J7
Bett Rd *BFLD/HDSWWD* B20 ....88 C2
Betty's La *CNCK/NC* WS11 ....25 C1
Bevan Av
  ETTPK/GDPK/PENN WV4 ....66 C1
Bevan Cl *BILS/COS* WV14 ....51 K7
  RUSH/SHEL WS4 ....40 C4
Bevan Lee Rd *CNCK/NC* WS11 ....16 B2
Bevan Rd *BRLYHL* DY5 ....101 L3
  TPTN/OCK DY4 ....85 M1
Bevan Wy *SMTHWK* B66 ....87 K5
Beverley Av *NUNW/HART* CV10 ...79 M7
Beverley Cl *CSCFLD/WYGN* B72 ..73 G6
  KIDDW DY11 * 137 K7
  PENK ST19 ....10 D1
  RCOVN/BALC/EX CV7 ....152 A1
Beverley Court Rd
  RIDG/WDGT B32 ....104 F7
Beverley Crs
  ETTPK/GDPK/PENN WV4 ....66 D1
Beverley Cft *ERDW/GRVHL* B23 ..90 B4
Beverley Dr *KGSWFD* DY6 ....83 G6
Beverley Gv
  LGN/SDN/BHAMAIR B26 ....109 M8
Beverley Hl *HEDN* WS12 ....13 H1
Beverley Rd *HHTH/SAND* B71 ......69 H4
  RBRY B45 ....143 K7
  RLSN CV32 ....206 B4
Beverly Dr *TLHL/CAN* CV4 ....180 B3
Beverston Rd
  DUNHL/THL/PER WV6 ....48 E1
  TPTN/OCK DY4 ....67 M7
Bevington Crs *COVN* CV6 ....133 J8
Bevington Rd *AST/WIT* B6 ....89 K5
Bevin Rd *WSLW* WS2 ....52 C2
Bewdley Dr *WOLV* WV1 ....50 F1
Bewdley Hl *HALE* B63 ....137 L8
Bewdley Rd *BVILLE* B30 ....124 F5
  KIDDW DY11 ....138 A3
  STRPT DY13 ....163 K8

Bewdley Rd North *STRPT* DY13 ..163 J7
Bewdley Vls *WSNGN* B18 * 106 B1
Bewell Head *BRGRVW* B61 ....191 K1
Bewlay Dr *BRLYHL* DY5 ....101 M6
Bewley Rd *SHHTH* WV12 ....52 B1
Bewlys Av *BFLD/HDSWWD* B20 ...88 C1
Bexfield Cl *COVW* CV5 ....132 C7
Bexhill Gv *EDG* B15 ....6 A8
Bexley Gv *HHTH/SAND* B71 ....69 J6
Bexley Rd *KGSTG* B44 ....71 M5
Bexmore Dr *LICH* WS13 ....21 H1
Beyer Rd *TAM/AM/WIL* B77 ....46 E3
Bhylls Crs *BDMR/CCFT* WV3 ....49 G6
Bhylls La *BDMR/CCFT* WV3 ....48 F6
Biart Pl *RUGBYN/HIL* CV21 ......187 H2
Bibbey's Gn *WOLVN* WV10 ....36 D1
Bibsworth Av *MOS/BIL* B13 ......126 A5
Bibury Rd *HLGN/YWD* B28 ....126 C6
Bicester Sq *CVALE* B35 ....91 M1
Bickenhill La
  CHWD/FDBR/MGN B37 ....111 H7
Bickenhill Park Rd *HIA/OLT* B92 ..127 H4
Bickenhill Pkwy
  CHWD/FDBR/MGN B37 ....111 H7
Bickenhill Rd
  CHWD/FDBR/MGN B37 ....110 F6
Bickford Rd *COVN* CV6 ....114 B7
  WOLVN WV10 ....36 D8
Bickington Rd *RIDG/WDGT* B32 ..123 H4
Bickley Av *FOAKS/STRLY* B74 .....42 C8
  SPARK B11 * 108 A7
Bickley Gv
  LGN/SDN/BHAMAIR B26 ....109 M8
Bickley Rd *BILS/COS* WV14 ....51 L7
  RUSH/SHEL WS4 ....40 A4
Bicknell Cft
  ALE/KHTH/YWD B14 ....146 C3
Bickton Cl *ERDE/BCHGN* B24 .....73 C7
Biddings La *BILS/COS* WV14 ....66 F3
Biddle St *KNWTH* CV8 * 197 L1
Biddlestone Pl *DARL/WED* WS10 ..51 M5
Biddlestone Gv *DSYBK/YTR* WS5 ..70 A1
Biddulph Pk *MGN/WHC* B75 * 18 B4
Bideford Dr *SLYOAK* B29 ....124 A4
Bideford Rd *COVE* CV2 ....135 C6
  SMTHWK B66 ....87 L3
Bideford Wy *CNCK/NC* WS11 ......15 M5
Bidford Cl *SHLY* B90 ....148 B3
Bidford Rd *NFLD/LBR* B31 ....144 C2
Bierton Rd *YDLY* B25 ....109 C5
Bigbury Cl *COVS* CV3 ....155 H6
Bigbury La *STRPT* DY13 ....164 B7
Biggin Cl *CVALE* B35 ....91 M1
Biggin Hall Crs *COVS* CV3 ....155 H3
The Big Peg *WSNGN* B18 * 6 C2
Bigwood Dr *MGN/WHC* B75 ....57 L7
  RIDG/WDGT B32 ....123 G4
Bilberry Cl *STRPT* DY13 ....163 C8
Bilberry Crs *HEDN* WS12 ....12 E8
  WALM/CURD B76 ....73 J2
Bilberry Dr *RBRY* B45 ....190 A4
Bilberry Rd *ALE/KHTH/YWD* B14 ..125 C7
  COVE CV2 ....135 H3
Biboe Rd *BILS/COS* WV14 ....67 K2
Bilbrook Cl *CDSL* WV8 ....34 F2
Bilbrook Gv *CDSL* WV8 ....34 F2
  SLYOAK B29 ....123 K3
Bilbrook Rd *CDSL* WV8 ....34 E1
Bilbury Cl *REDW* B97 ....202 B1
Bilhay La *WBROM* B70 ....68 E8
Bilhay St *WBROM* B70 ....68 E8
Billau Rd *BILS/COS* WV14 ....67 H3
Billesley La *HALE* B48 ....172 C7
Billesden Cl *COVS* CV3 ....155 M8
Billesley La *MOS/BIL* B13 ....125 L5
Billingham Cl *SOLH* B91 ....148 F5
Billing Rd *COVW* CV5 ....154 B3
Billingsley Rd
  LGN/SDN/BHAMAIR B26 ....109 L5
Billinton Cl *COVE* CV2 ....156 C1
Bills La *SHLY* B90 ....147 K5
Billsmore Gn *HIA/OLT* B92 ....128 C3
Bills St *DARL/WED* WS10 ....52 C7
Billy Buns La *WMBN* WV5 ....64 E5
Billy La *BRGRVE* B60 ....169 L6
Billy Wright Ct
  ETTPK/GDPK/PENN WV4 ....49 H7
Bilport La *DARL/WED* WS10 ....68 D5
Bilston La *WLNHL* WV13 ....51 M5
Bilston Rd *BKHL/PFLD* WV2 * 3 J7
  TPTN/OCK DY4 ....67 M3
  WLNHL WV13 ....51 L6
  WOLV WV1 ....3 L4
Bilston Street Island *WOLV* WV1 ..3 H6
Bilton Grange Rd
  LGN/SDN/BHAMAIR B26 ....109 K6
Bilton La *RRUGBY* CV23 ....185 M3
Bilton Rd *RUGBYS/DCH* CV22 ...186 B4
Binbrook Rd *SHHTH* WV12 ....52 B1
Bincomb Av
  LGN/SDN/BHAMAIR B26 ....109 M7
Binfield St *TPTN/OCK* DY4 ....85 L1
Bingley Av *WASH/WDE* B8 ....108 F1
Bingley St *BDMR/CCFT* WV3 ....2 B4
Biney Av *COVS* CV3 ....156 D6
Binley Cl
  LGN/SDN/BHAMAIR B26 ....109 H7
  SHLY B90 ....147 L5
Binley Gv *COVS* CV3 ....156 D6
Binley Rd *COV* CV1 ....9 L4
Binns Cl *TLHL/CAN* CV4 ....153 K5
Binstead Rd *KGSTG* B44 ....71 L3
Binswood Av *RLSN* CV32 ....206 D3
Binswood Cl *COVE* CV2 ....135 K3
Binswood Rd *RLSN* CV32 ....206 C3
Binton Cl *REDE* B98 ....203 A4
Binton Cft *MOS/BIL* B13 ....125 C4
Binton Rd *COVE* CV2 ....135 K3
  SHLY B90 ....147 K4
Birbeck Pl *BRLYHL* DY5 ....83 M7
Birchall St *BHTH/HG* B12 ....7 K8
Birch Av *BNTWD* WS7 ....18 D4
  BRLYHL DY5 ....102 E3
  BRWNH WS8 ....26 C5
  CNCK/NC WS11 ....16 C1
  NFLD/LBR B31 ....144 A4
  RCOVN/BALC/EX CV7 ....131 M5
Birch Brook La *LICHS WS14 ....29 L4
Birch Cl *BDWTH* CV12 ....117 H1
  BVILLE B30 ....124 C7
  COVW CV5 ....132 C7
  POL/KGSB/FAZ B78 ....73 J7
  WALM/CURD B76 ....73 K3
Birch Coppice *BRLYHL* DY5 ......102 E4
  WMBN WV5 ....64 A6
Birchcoppice Gdns *SHHTH* WV12 ..52 C1
Birch Crs *OLDBY* B69 ....85 M4
Birch Cft *ALDR* WS9 ....41 C5
  CHWD/FDBR/MGN B37 ....111 G4
Birchcroft *COVEN* WV9 ....22 A1
Birch Cft *ERDE/BCHGN* B24 ....91 H8
Birchcroft *SMTHWK* B66 * 88 A4
Birch Croft *MGN/WHC* B75 ....57 H6
Birchdale *BILS/COS* WV14 ....51 H6

Birchdale Av *ERDW/GRVHL* B23 ..90 C2
Birchdale Rd *ERDW/GRVHL* B23 ..72 B8
Birch Dr *FOAKS/STRLY* B74 ....42 B8
  MGN/WHC B75 ....57 K6
  RMSLY B62 ....104 C4
  RUGBYS/DCH CV22 ....102 C8
Birch End *WWCK* CV34 ....205 M5
Birchensale Rd *REDW* B97 ....194 A8
Birches Av *CDSL* WV8 ....35 C4
Birches Barn Rd
  BDMR/CCFT WV3 ....49 K6
Birches Barn Rd
  BDMR/CCFT WV3 ....49 K5
Birches Cl *MOS/BIL* B13 ....125 K4
Birches Green Rd
  ERDE/BCHGN B24 ....90 F3
Birches La *ALVE* B48 ....170 D2
  KNWTH CV8 ....197 L2
Birches Park Rd *CDSL* WV8 ....34 E3
Birches Ri *WLNHL* WV13 ....51 K4
Birches Rd *CDSL* WV8 ....34 F3
The Birches *BDWTH* CV12 ....117 M1
  STRPT DY13 ....188 F2
Birchfield Av
  DUNHL/THL/PER WV6 ....34 F7
Birchfield Cl *ATHST* CV9 ....61 C4
  HALE B63 ....121 J3
Birchfield Crs *HAG/WOL* DY9 ....120 D2
Birchfield Dr *STRPT* DY13 ....163 J8
Birchfield Gdns *AST/WIT* B6 * 89 H5
Birchfield La *OLDBY* B69 ....104 C1
Birchfield Rd *COVN* CV6 ....120 K6
  HAG/WOL DY9 ....120 D2
  KIDDW DY11 ....137 M8
  PBAR/PBCH B42 ....89 H2
  REDW B97 ....201 K2
  REDW B97 ....201 M3
Birchfield Wy *DSYBK/YTR* WS5 ...69 M1
Birchgate *HAG/WOL* DY9 ....120 D1
Birchglade *BDMR/CCFT* WV3 ......49 H4
Birch Gv *LGLYGN/QTN* B68 ......105 H6
  LICH WS13 ....21 H5
  POL/KGSB/FAZ B78 ....47 H6
Birch Hill Av *WMBN* WV5 ....64 A6
Birch Hollow *EDG* B15 ....106 D7
Birchill Pl *WMBN* WV5 ....64 D6
Birchills St *WSLW* WS2 ....52 A3
Birch La *ALDR* WS9 ....41 H4
  LGLYGN/QTN B68 ....105 H4
  RUSH/SHEL WS4 ....40 A4
Birchley Heath Rd
  NUNW/HART CV10 ....78 D5
Birchley Park Av *OLDBY* B69 ......86 C7
Birchley Ri *HIA/OLT* B92 ....109 K3
Birchmoor Cl *HLGN/YWD* B28 ...126 C6
Birchmoor Rd
  POL/KGSB/FAZ B78 ....47 J5
Birchover Rd *WSLW* WS2 ....52 E1
Birch Rd *AST/WIT* B6 ....89 L3
  LGLYGN/QTN B68 ....105 H4
  RBRY B45 ....143 J7
  SEDG DY3 ....67 H1
  WNSFLD WV11 ....37 K4
Birch Rd East *AST/WIT* B6 ....89 L3
Birch St *LGLYGN/QTN* B68 ....87 C7
  TPTN/OCK DY4 ....85 H1
  WOLV WV1 ....2 E5
  WSLW WS2 ....4 C1
Birch Ter *BNTWD* WS7 ....18 D3
  DUDS DY2 ....103 G1
Birch Tree Gdns *ALDR* WS9 ....40 F8
Birchtree Gdns *BRLYHL* DY5 .....102 E4
Birch Tree Gv *SOLH* B91 ....148 C1
Birchtree Hollow *SHHTH* WV12 ...38 B8
Birch Tree Rd *BEWD* DY12 ....162 D2
Birchtree Rd *NUNW/HART* CV10 ..80 A7
The Birches *BDWTH* CV12 ....117 M1
Birchtrees *ERDE/BCHGN* B24 * ..91 H8
Birchtrees Cft
  LGN/SDN/BHAMAIR B26 ....109 H8
Birchtrees Dr *STETCH* B33 ....110 B2
Birch Wk *LGLYGN/QTN* B68 ......105 H4
Birchway Cl *RLSN* CV32 ....206 A4
Birchwood Av
  POL/KGSB/FAZ B78 ....47 K6
Birchwood Cl *KIDDW* DY11 ....137 L6
  WNSFLD WV11 ....37 J4
Birchwood Crs *BHTH/HG* B12 ...125 L1
Birchwood Rd *BHTH/HG* B12 ....125 L1
  COVS CV3 ....157 C6
  ETTPK/GDPK/PENN WV4 ....49 J8
  LICHS WS13 ....8 B5
Birchwoods *RIDG/WDGT* B32 ....122 F3
Birchy Cl *SHLY* B90 ....147 K7
Birchy Leasowes La *SHLY* B90 ..147 K8
Birchbrook Rd *KGSTG* B44 ....71 J5
Bird End *HHTH/SAND* B71 ....69 K5
Bird Grove Ct *COV* CV1 ....134 B8
Birdie Cl *HWK/WKHTH* B38 ......145 H4
Birdlip Gv *RIDG/WDGT* B32 ......104 E4
Birds Bush Rd *TAM/AM/WIL* B77 ..46 C5
Birds Meadow *BRLYHL* DY5 ....83 M6
Bird St *COV* CV1 ....9 J3
  LICH WS13 ....20 F5
  DUDS DY2 ....103 G1
Birdwell Cft *MOS/BIL* B13 ....125 K7
Birkdale Av *BRGRVE* B60 ....169 L8
  SLYOAK B29 ....124 D4
Birkdale Cl *COVN* CV6 ....133 M1
  NUN CV11 ....99 L4
  STRBR DY8 ....119 K4
  WOLV WV1 ....50 F1
Birkdale Gv *SLYOAK* B29 ....124 E5
Birkdale Rd *BLOX/PEL* WS3 ....38 E1
Birkenshaw Rd *KGSTG* B44 ....71 J5
Birley Gv *HALE* B63 ....121 C5
Birmingham New Rd *DUDN* DY1 ..67 G7
  ETTPK/GDPK/PENN WV4 ....66 C1
Birmingham Rd *ALDR* WS9 ....54 E1
  ALVE B48 ....170 C7
  BKHL/PFLD WV2 * 3 G9
  BLKHTH/ROWR B65 ....104 A3
  BRGRVE B60 ....191 L2
  CBROM B36 ....91 L5
  COVS CV3 ....132 D6
  CSCFLD/WYGN B72 ....72 F5
  CSHL/WTROR B46 ....92 D3
  DSYBK/YTR WS5 ....5 M9
  DUDN DY1 ....67 C1
  GTB/HAM B43 ....70 C1
  GTB/HAM B43 ....91 L5
  HAG/WOL DY9 ....120 B7
  HALE B63 ....121 M2
  KIDD DY10 ....139 G6
  KIDD DY10 ....158 D2
  KNWTH CV8 ....197 K7
  LICH WS13 ....4 F6
  LICH WS13 ....20 B1
  NUNW/HART CV10 ....78 E6
  OLDBY B69 ....86 B3
  RCOVN/BALC/EX CV7 ....130 B2
  RCOVN/BALC/EX CV7 ....131 L5
  REDW B97 ....194 B5
  RWWCK/WEL CV35 ....177 C8
  RWWCK/WEL CV35 ....204 D4

Bradley Thursfield Ct KIDD DW11 ...138 A6
Bradmore Cl SOLH B91 ...138 A6
Bradmore Gv SLYOAK B29 ...123 L5
Bradney Gn TLHL/CAN CV4 ...153 J6
Bradnick Pl TLHL/CAN CV4 ...153 J6
Bradnock Pl MOS/BIL B13 ...126 A6
Bradnock's Marsh La HIA/OLT B92 ...151 J3
Bradshaw Av DARL/WED WS10 ...51 M8
HWK/WKHTH B38 ...145 H4
Bradshaw Cl TPTN/OCK DY4 ...85 L2
Bradshawe Cft ALE/KHTH/YWD B14 ...147 H2
Bradshaw St WOLV WV1 * ...5 H5
Bradstock Cft MGN/WHC B75 ...146 A2
Bradwell Cft MGN/WHC B75 ...146 A1
Braeburn Cl LICH WS13 ...21 H4
Braemar Av STRBR DY8 ...101 L4
Braemar Cl COVE CV2 ...135 L7
SEDG DY3 ...66 A4
SHHTH WV12 ...37 L7
Braemar Dr ERDW/GRVHL B23 ...71 M8
Braemar Gdns HEDN WS12 ...12 D6
Braemar Rd CNCK/NC WS11 ...25 L1
HIA/OLT B92 ...127 J4
RLSN CV32 ...206 F1
SCFLD/BOLD B73 ...72 D3
Braemar Wy NUNW/HART CV10 ...98 E3
Braeside Cft CHWD/FDBR/MGN B37 ...111 H3
Braeside Wy BLOX/PEL WS3 ...39 K2
Brafield Leys RUGBYS/DCH CV22 ...186 F1
Bragg Rd BFLD/HDSWWD B20 ...89 H3
Braggs Farm La SHLY B90 ...173 L1
Braham CRTAM B79 ...31 H7
Braid Cl HWK/WKHTH B38 ...145 H4
Braids Cl RRUGBY CV21 ...187 H1
Brailes Cl HIA/OLT B92 ...128 C6
Brailes Dr WALM/CURD B76 ...73 H7
Brailes Gv BORD B9 ...108 F4
Brailsford Cl WNSFLD WV11 ...37 L1
Brailsford Dr SMTHWK B66 ...87 L8
Brain St TAM/AM/WIL B77 ...46 E3
Braithwaite Cl KGSWFD DY6 ...83 H7
Braithwaite Rd SPARK B11 ...107 L6
Brake La STRBR DY8 ...119 J7
Brakesmead RLSS CV31 ...206 D3
Bramah Wy TPTN/OCK DY4 ...68 A7
Bramber Dr WMBN WV5 ...64 D7
Bramber Wy STRBR DY8 ...119 K3
Bramble Cl AST/WIT B6 ...89 J7
BRWNH WS8 ...26 C6
CDYHTH B64 ...103 K1
CSHL/WTROR B46 ...93 L4
NFLD/LBR B31 ...123 K8
NUN CV11 ...99 K3
SHHTH WV12 ...38 A6
Bramble Dell BORD B9 ...108 C2
Bramble Dr HALE B63 ...13 G6
LGN/SDN/BHAMAIR B26 ...109 J7
Bramble Gn DUDN DY1 ...66 D8
Bramble La BNTWD WS7 ...18 F5
Brambleside STRBR DY8 ...18 L8
The Brambles CNCK/NC WS11 ...17 L8
HAG/WOL DY9 ...120 B2
LICHS WS14 ...21 H1
WALM/CURD B76 ...73 L5
Bramble St COV CV1 ...9 K5
Bramblewood WMBN WV5 ...64 D7
Bramblewood Dr BDMR/CCFT WV3 ...49 J5
Bramblewoods BKDE/SHDE B34 ...92 A8
Brambling TAM/AM/WIL B77 ...46 E6
Brambling Cl RRUGBY CV23 ...161 G4
Brambling Rd EDC B15 ...164 F4
Brambling Wk EDC B15 ...107 G6
Bramcote Dr HIA/OLT B92 ...128 A6
Bramcote Ri FOAKS/STRLY B74 ...57 G6
Bramcote Rd RIDG/WDGT B32 ...105 G8
Bramdean Dr PENK ST19 ...10 C7
Bramdene Av NUNW/HART CV10 ...81 G5
Bramerton Dr WNSFLD WV11 ...36 E3
Bramford Dr DUDN DY1 ...66 F7
Bramley Cl DSYBK/YTR WS5 ...54 B5
GTB/HAM B43 ...59 G3
Bramley Cft SHLY B90 ...148 A3
Bramley Dr BFLD/HDSWWD B20 ...88 F2
HLYWD B47 ...146 F7
Bramley Mews Ct ACGN B27 ...127 G1
Bramley Rd ACGN B27 ...109 G8
DSYBK/YTR WS5 ...69 M1
Bramley Wy BEWD DY12 ...162 C2
Brampton Av HLGN/YWD B28 ...126 F7
Brampton Cl KIDD DY10 ...138 F1
Brampton Crs HIA/OLT B92 ...126 F1
Brampton Dr HEDN WS12 ...17 J3
Brampton Wy BDWTH CV12 ...117 M2
Bramshall Dr DOR/KN B93 ...175 J2
Bramshaw Cl ALE/KHTH/YWD B14 ...146 A3
Bramstead Av DUNHL/THL/PER WV6 ...48 B1
Bramston Crs TLHL/CAN CV4 ...153 J6
Bramwell Dr GTWY WS6 ...24 B5
Bramwell Gdns RCOVN/BALC/EX CV7 ...116 D8
Brancaster Cl TAM/AM/WIL B77 ...32 E7
Branchal Rd ALDR WS9 ...41 G4
Branches Cl BEWD DY12 ...163 G3
Branch Rd HWK/WKHTH B38 ...145 H5
Branden Rd ALVE B48 ...170 C6
Brandfield Rd COVS CV6 ...133 K5
Brandhall Rd LGLYGN/QTN B68 ...104 F1
Brandhall Ri LGLYGN/QTN B68 ...104 F4
SEDG DY3 ...66 C6
WBROM B70 ...86 D5
Brandon Gv NFLD/LBR B31 ...144 D6
Brandon La KNWTH CV8 ...180 B7
KNWTH CV8 ...182 B1
Brandon Pde RLSN CV32 ...206 E5
Brandon Pk BDMR/CCFT WV3 ...49 J6
Brandon Rd BKDE/SHDE B34 ...92 B6
COVS CV6 ...156 F5
HLGN/YWD B28 ...126 C3
KNWTH CV8 ...158 A7
RMSLY B62 ...104 C4
SOLH B91 ...148 C3
Brandon Wy BRLYHL DY5 ...102 C5
WBROM B70 ...86 B3
Brandwood Gv ALE/KHTH/YWD B14 ...125 H8
Brandwood Park Rd ALE/KHTH/YWD B14 ...146 A1
Brandwood Rd ALE/KHTH/YWD B14 ...125 H8
Branfield Cl BILS/COS WV14 ...67 J3
Branksome Av HDSW B21 ...88 D5
Branksome Rd COVN CV6 ...133 L7
Branscombe Cl ALE/KHTH/YWD B14 ...125 H8
Bransdale Av COVN CV6 ...134 B2
Bransdale Cl DUNHL/THL/PER WV6 ...35 L8
Bransdale Rd BRWNH WS8 ...26 C6

Bransford Av TLHL/CAN CV4 ...154 B8
Bransford Ri SOLH B91 ...128 F8
Branstree Dr COVN CV6 ...134 B3
Brantford Av YDLY B25 ...109 G5
Branthill Cft SOLH B91 ...148 F4
Brantley Av BDMR/CCFT WV3 ...49 G4
Brantley Rd AST/WIT B6 ...89 L3
Branton Hill La ALDR WS9 ...41 G8
Brantwood Av BNTWD WS7 ...18 E8
Brasshouse La SMTHWK B66 ...87 K7
Brassie Cl HWK/WKHTH B38 ...145 H4
Brassington Av SCFLD/BOLD B73 ...56 F8
Bratch Cl DUDS DY2 ...103 G2
Bratch Common Rd WMBN WV5 ...64 C6
Bratch La WMBN WV5 ...64 C5
Bratch Hollow WMBN WV5 ...64 C5
Bratch Pk WMBN WV5 ...64 C5
Brathay Cl COVS CV3 ...155 H7
Bratt St WBROM B70 ...87 G1
Braunston Cl WALM/CURD B76 ...73 L3
Braunston Pl RUGBYS/DCH CV22 ...187 H5
Bray Bank CSHL/WTROR B46 ...95 H2
Brayford Av BRLYHL DY5 ...101 M6
COVS CV3 ...155 G7
Braymoor Rd STECH B33 ...110 C4
Brays Cl RRUGBY CV23 ...158 C2
Bray's La COVE CV2 ...155 L2
Brays Rd LGN/SDN/BHAMAIR B26 ...109 L7
Bray St WLNHL WV13 ...51 M3
Braytoft Cl COVN CV6 ...134 A3
Brazil St TLHL/CAN CV4 ...153 J3
Breaches La REDE B98 ...203 H5
Breach Oak La RCOVN/BALC/EX CV7 ...115 G2
RCOVN/BALC/EX CV7 ...115 G3
Breakback Rd BRGRVW B61 ...191 H5
Bream TAM/AM/WIL B77 ...46 E6
Bream Cl CHWD/FDBR/MGN B37 ...111 J3
WOLV WV1 ...50 F1
Breamore Crs DUDN DY1 ...84 D2
Brean Av LGN/SDN/BHAMAIR B26 ...109 K8
Brearley Cl LOZ/NWT B19 ...89 H7
Brearley St HDSW B21 ...88 B5
LOZ/NWT B19 ...89 H7
Brecknell Rd KIDD DY10 ...138 D5
Brecknock Rd HHTH/SAND B71 ...68 C7
Brecon Av STRBR DY8 ...101 M7
Brecon Dr STRBR DY8 ...101 M7
Brecon Rd BFLD/HDSWWD B20 ...88 F5
Brecon Av COVS CV3 ...156 D6
HAG/WOL DY9 ...102 A3
KIDD DY11 ...163 L4
Bredon Cl HALE B63 ...121 L2
Bredon Cft BNTWD WS18 ...18 A4
Bredon Rd BRGRVE B60 ...191 H6
OLDBY B69 ...86 B8
STRBR DY8 ...101 L7
Bredon Vw REDW B97 ...202 B5
Bredon Wy STRPT DY13 ...188 B4
Breech Cl FOAKS/STRLY B74 ...55 J6
Bree Cl COVW CV5 ...132 A1
Breeden Dr WALM/CURD B76 ...74 A7
Breedon Rd BVILLE B30 ...124 E2
Breedon Ter WSNGN B18 * ...88 B7
Breen Rydding Dr BILS/COS WV14 ...66 F4
Bree's La KNWTH CV8 ...177 L4
Breeze Av CNCK/NC WS11 ...17 M8
Brelades Cl DUDN DY1 ...84 C2
Brendan Cl CSHL/WTROR B46 ...93 L8
Brendon TAM/AM/WIL B77 ...46 B6
Brendon Wy NUNW/HART CV10 ...97 J3
Brennand Rd LGLYGN/QTN B68 ...104 F4
Brent TAM/AM/WIL B77 ...46 C6
Brentford Rd ALE/KHTH/YWD B14 ...125 K8
SOLH B91 ...148 C2
Brentmill Cl WOLVN WV10 ...36 D1
Brentnall Dr MGN/WHC B75 ...56 F2
Brenton Rd ETTPK/GDPK/PENN WV4 ...65 K1
Brent Rd BVILLE B30 ...125 G5
Brentwood Av COVS CV3 ...181 G2
Brentwood Cl SOLH B91 ...148 C2
Brentwood Gv KGSTG B44 ...71 J3
Brenwood Cl KGSWFD DY6 ...82 F6
Brereton Cl DUDS DY2 ...85 J4
Brereton Rd SHHTH WV12 ...38 A6
Brese Av WWCK CV34 ...205 H4
Bretby Gv ERDW/GRVHL B23 ...72 C7
Bretford Rd COVE CV2 ...135 G4
Bretshall Cl SHLY B90 ...148 D8
Brett Dr RIDG/WDGT B32 ...123 G5
Brettell La STRBR DY8 ...101 L4
Brettell St DUDS DY2 ...84 F6
Bretton Rd ACGN B27 ...127 H3
Bretts Cl COV CV1 ...9 J1
Bretts Hall Est NUNW/HART CV10 ...79 K6
Brett St HHTH/SAND B71 ...68 B7
Brett Young Cl KIDD DY10 ...138 F8
Brevitt Rd BKHL/PFLD WV2 ...50 B7
Brewer Cl COVS CV3 ...156 E4
Brewers Dr BLOX/PEL WS3 ...39 L4
Brewer St WSLW WS2 ...53 J1
Brewery St AST/WIT B6 ...5
DUDS DY2 ...85 J4
SMTHWKW B67 ...87 K7
TPTN/OCK DY4 ...85 K1
Brewhouse La LICH WS13 * ...20 D7
Brewins Wy BRLYHL DY5 ...102 D1
Brewood Rd WOLVN WV10 ...22 A1
Brewster Cl COVE CV2 ...156 C3
POL/KGSB/FAZ B78 ...45 J4
Breydon Cv WLNHL WV13 ...51 K5
Brian Rd SMTHWK B67 ...87 J7
Briansway COVN CV6 ...134 C2
Briar TAM/AM/WIL B77 ...46 A6
Briar Av FOAKS/STRLY B74 ...55 L4
Briarbeck RUSH/SHEL WS4 ...40 A5
Briar Cl BRGRVE B60 ...169 G7
ERDE/BCHGN B24 ...90 E1
HEDN WS12 ...12 E5
RLSN CV32 ...206 F1
Briardene Av BDWTH CV12 ...116 F4
Briarfield Rd SPARK B11 ...126 D2
Briar Hl KIDD DY10 ...166 C5
Briars Cl BRLYHL DY5 ...101 M4
COVE CV2 ...156 A3
NUN CV11 ...81 J8
RRUGBY CV23 ...185 M1
The Briars ERDW/GRVHL B23 ...72 B7
Briars Wy HEDN WS12 ...18 A1
Briar Wy STRPT DY13 ...188 B4
Briar Wood Cl BKHL/PFLD WV2 ...50 B6
Briarwood Cl SHLY B90 ...174 A1
Brickbridge La WMBN WV5 ...64 B7
Brickheath Rd WOLV WV1 ...50 C1
Brickhill Dr CHWD/FDBR/MGN B37 ...110 D3
Brick Hill La COVW CV5 ...132 B5
Brickhouse La WBROM B70 ...68 D7

Brickhouse La South TPTN/OCK DY4 ...68 B7
Brickhouse Rd BLKHTH/ROWR B65 ...103 L1
Bricklin St BRWNH WS8 ...26 D6
Bricklin St ATHST CV9 ...76 F1
Brick Kiln La HLYWD B47 ...172 D1
KGSTG B44 ...71 J6
POL/KGSB/FAZ B78 ...59 G7
SOLH B91 ...148 B5
Brick Kiln St BRLYHL DY5 ...84 C8
BRLYHL DY5 ...102 E5
TPTN/OCK DY4 ...67 J7
Bridgeacre Gdns COVS CV3 ...156 D3
Bridge Av GTWY WS6 ...16 C8
Bridge Bk BHTH/HG B12 ...107 J1
Bridge Cross Rd BNTWD WS7 ...18 E6
Bridge End WWCK CV34 ...205 K8
Bridgeford Rd BKDE/SHDE B34 ...91 M7
Bridgelands Wy BFLD/HDSWWD B20 ...89 H4
Bridge La ATHST CV9 ...63 L6
Bridgeman Cft CBROM B36 ...92 A6
Bridgeman St WSLW WS2 ...4 D1
Bridgemary Cl WOLVN WV10 ...36 D1
Bridge Meadow Dr DOR/KN B93 ...149 K8
Bridgend Cft BRLYHL DY5 ...83 M7
Bridge Piece NFLD/LBR B31 ...144 F3
Bridge Rd RUSH/SHEL WS4 ...39 M4
TPTN/OCK DY4 ...68 A6
WASH/WDE B8 ...108 C2
Bridges Crs CNCK/NC WS11 ...17 G3
Bridgeside TAM/AM/WIL B77 ...46 A3
Bridges Rd CNCK/NC WS11 ...17 G3
Bridge St ATHST CV9 ...77 G1
BILS/COS WV14 ...51 J8
BILS/COS WV14 ...67 G5
BRWNH WS8 ...26 C7
CBHAMW B1 ...6 C5
CNCK/NC WS11 ...16 C5
COVN CV6 ...134 D6
DARL/WED WS10 ...68 D3
HALE B63 ...103 G6
KIDD DY10 ...138 C8
NUN CV11 ...99 J5
OLDBY B69 ...86 A5
POL/KGSB/FAZ B78 ...47 L4
REDW B97 ...202 B1
RUGBY/HIL CV21 ...187 G2
STRBR DY8 ...101 J4
STRPT DY13 ...188 D2
TAM/AM/WIL B77 ...32 C8
WBROM B70 ...68 B3
WLNHL WV13 ...51 K4
WOLVN WV10 ...36 C8
WSL WS1 ...4 F3
WWCK CV34 ...205 H4
Bridge St North SMTHWK B66 ...87 M7
Bridge St South SMTHWK B66 ...87 M7
Bridge St West LOZ/NWT B19 ...89 H7
The Bridge WSL WS1 ...4 E4
Bridget St RUGBY/HIL CV21 ...186 D2
Bridge Vw CSHL/WTROR B46 ...93 K6
KNWTH CV8 ...181 K2
Bridge Wk ACGN B27 * ...127 H2
Bridgewater Av OLDBY B69 ...104 F1
Bridgewater Crs DUDS DY2 ...85 M8
Bridgewater Dr BILS/COS WV14 ...67 G3
WMBN WV5 ...82 D1
Bridgnorth Av WMBN WV5 ...82 D1
Bridgnorth Gv SHHTH WV12 ...37 M7
Bridgnorth Rd DUNHL/THL/PER WV6 ...49 G3
KIDD DY11 ...137 K2
KINVER DY7 ...101 L2
SEDG DY3 ...64 A8
STRBR DY8 ...101 L7
WMBN WV5 ...82 C8
Bridge Wy BRWNH WS8 ...26 C7
Bridle Brook La COVW CV5 ...132 D1
Bridle Gv HHTH/SAND B71 ...69 K5
Bridle La FOAKS/STRLY B74 ...55 H7
Bridle Rd HIA/OLT B92 ...101 M7
Bridlewood FOAKS/STRLY B74 ...55 K5
Bridley Moor Rd REDW B97 ...202 A4
Bridport Cl COVE CV2 ...156 E1
Brierley Hill Rd STRBR DY8 ...101 J3
Brierley Hill La RUGE WS15 ...18 F1
Briertey La BILS/COS WV14 ...67 J3
Briery Cl CDYHTH B64 ...103 K3
Briery Rd HALE B63 ...121 J2
Brigfield Crs MOS/BIL B13 ...125 M8
Brigfield Rd MOS/BIL B13 ...125 M8
Bright Crs TAM/AM/WIL B77 ...46 A3
Brighton Cl WSLW WS2 ...4 C1
Brighton Pl BDMR/CCFT WV3 ...2 B5
Brighton Rd BHTH/HG B12 ...107 K8
Brighton St COVE CV2 ...9 M3
Bright Rd LGLYGN/QTN B68 ...86 F8
Brightstone Cl WOLVN WV10 ...36 D1
Brightstone Rd RBRY B45 ...144 L3
Bright St COVN CV6 ...134 C7
DARL/WED WS10 ...52 B8
STRBR DY8 ...101 H8
WOLV WV1 ...2 D1
Brightwalton Rd COVS CV3 ...155 H6
Brightwell Crs DOR/KN B93 ...175 J2
Brill Cl TLHL/CAN CV4 ...153 K7
Brimfield Pl DUNHL/THL/PER WV6 * ...49 K1
Brimstone La BRGRVW B61 ...168 A6
Brindle Cl LGN/SDN/BHAMAIR B26 ...109 J8
Brindlefields Wy TPTN/OCK DY4 ...85 G5
Brindle Rd DSYBK/YTR WS5 ...70 A1
Brindley Av WNSFLD WV11 ...37 L2
Brindley Brae KINVER DY7 ...118 A3
Brindley Cl ATHST CV9 ...63 J1
PENK ST19 ...10 E6
STRBR DY8 ...84 B7
WMBN WV5 ...64 B7
Brindley Ct LGLYGN/QTN B68 * ...104 F6
TPTN/OCK DY4 ...67 J8
Brindley Dr CBHAMW B1 ...6 C5
Brindley Dr HEDN WS12 ...13 G6
Brindley Heath Rd HEDN WS12 ...13 G2
Brindley Paddocks COV CV1 ...8 F2

Broadwas Cl REDE B98 ...195 C8
Broadwater COVW CV5 ...154 E5
Broadwaters Av DARL/WED WS10 ...68 A1
Broadwaters Dr KIDD DY10 ...138 C5
Broadwaters Rd DARL/WED WS10 ...68 A1
Broad Wy RUSH/SHEL WS4 ...40 A3
CDSL WV8 ...34 C2
COVW WV8 ...8 B8
HEDN WS12 ...12 D7
LGLYGN/QTN B68 ...105 G5
RLSN CV32 ...199 J7
SHLY B90 ...147 M1
WOLV WV1 ...36
WSL WS1 ...5 K2
Broadway Av BORD B9 ...108 E3
HALE B63 ...120 E3
Broadway Cft LGLYGN/QTN B68 ...105 G4
LGN/SDN/BHAMAIR B26 ...109 L7
Broadway Man COVW CV5 * ...8 B8
Broadway North WSL WS1 ...5 K2
The Broadway BFLD/HDSWWD B20 ...89 H3
DUDN DY1 ...84 E2
HHTH/SAND B71 ...68 C3
STRBR DY8 ...119 H3
WMBN WV5 ...64 E8
Broadway West WSL WS1 ...53 H1
Broadwell Rd HIA/OLT B92 ...127 L3
OLDBY B69 ...86 B5
Broadwells Ct TLHL/CAN CV4 * ...153 K7
Broadwells Crs TLHL/CAN CV4 ...153 K8
Broadyates Gv YDLY B25 ...109 G7
Broadyates Rd YDLY B25 ...109 G7
Brobury Cft SHLY B90 ...148 B1
Broc Cl PENK ST19 ...10 E5
Brockenhurst Wy COVN CV6 ...116 F7
Brockeridge Cl SHHTH WV12 ...38 A1
Brocket Cl STRPT DY13 ...163 J7
Brockhall Gv CHWD/FDBR/MGN B37 ...92 D8
Brockhill Dr REDW B97 ...193 M8
Brockhill La ALVE B48 ...171 M2
BRGRVE B60 ...193 G4
REDE B98 ...195 G2
REDW B97 ...193 L7
Brockhurst Crs DSYBK/YTR WS5 ...53 H8
Brockhurst Dr DUNHL/THL/PER WV6 ...2 B1
HLGN/YWD B28 ...126 E8
TLHL/CAN CV4 ...153 H5
Brockhurst La MGN/WHC B75 ...43 L7
SHLY B90 ...147 M8
Brockhurst Pl DSYBK/YTR WS5 ...53 K8
Brockhurst Rd CBROM B36 ...91 G7
MGN/WHC B75 ...57 H4
Brockhurst St DSYBK/YTR DY5 ...102 D8
Brockley Cl BRLYHL DY5 ...102 B3
Brockley Gv MOS/BIL B13 ...125 G4
Brockley Pl VAUX/NECH B7 ...90 A4
Brockmoor Cl HAG/WOL DY9 ...120 A3
Brock Rd TPTN/OCK DY4 ...85 M1
Brockwell Gv KGSTG B44 ...71 J1
Brockwell Rd KGSTG B44 ...71 J1
Brockworth Rd ALE/KHTH/YWD B14 ...146 A3
Brocton Cl BILS/COS WV14 ...66 C2
Brodick Wy NUNW/HART CV10 ...98 A3
Brogden Cl HHTH/SAND B71 ...69 K5
Bromage Av POL/KGSB/FAZ B78 ...60 A7
Bromfield Cl AST/WIT B6 ...89 J6
Bromfield Ct DUNHL/THL/PER WV6 * ...48 F2
Bromfields Crs DARL/WED WS10 ...69 G2
Bromfield Rd REDW B97 ...202 B3
Bromford Cl ERDW/GRVHL B23 ...71 L5
ERDE/BCHGN B24 ...90 C7
Bromford Dl DUNHL/THL/PER WV6 * ...49 K2
Bromford Dell NFLD/LBR B31 ...145 G1
Bromford Dr CBROM B36 ...91 G5
Bromford Hl BFLD/HDSWWD B20 ...89 G2
Bromford La ERDE/BCHGN B24 ...90 C7
OLDBY B69 ...86 E5
Bromford Ri BDMR/CCFT WV3 ...90 C7
Bromford Rd CBROM B36 ...90 F7
DUDS DY2 ...84 E7
WBROM B70 ...86 A6
Bromleigh Dr COVE CV2 ...156 A3
Bromleigh Vis DARL/WED WS10 * ...52 A7
Bromley BRLYHL DY5 ...83 M4
Bromley Cl HEDN WS12 ...13 G6
KNWTH CV8 ...179 J7
Bromley Gdns CDSL WV8 ...34 E1
Bromley La KGSWFD DY6 ...101 J3
Bromley Pl ETTPK/GDPK/PENN WV4 ...49 L8
Bromley St BKHL/PFLD WV2 ...50 B7
BORD B9 ...108 E3
HAG/WOL DY9 ...102 A3
Brompton Dr BRLYHL DY5 ...101 M6
Brompton Lawns DUNHL/THL/PER WV6 ...48 E2
Brompton Pool Rd HLGN/YWD B28 ...147 J2
Brompton Rd KGSTG B44 ...71 J2
Bromsgrove Hwy BRGRVE B60 ...192 B4
REDE B98 ...202 C5
REDW B97 ...201 J2
Bromsgrove Rd BRGRVW B61 ...168 B7
HAG/WOL DY9 ...141 J2
KIDD DY10 ...165 J3
REDW B97 ...201 G2
RMSLY B62 ...121 M4
Bromsgrove St DIG/EDG B5 ...6 F8
Bromwall Rd MOS/BIL B13 ...125 M7
Bromwich Cl COVS CV3 ...156 D5
Bromwich Dr MGN/WHC B75 ...57 G6
Bromwich La HAG/WOL DY9 ...119 M6
Bromwynd Cl RUGBYN/HIL CV21 ...187 K4
Bromwich Rd RUGBYN/HIL CV21 ...187 K4
Bromyard Av WALM/CURD B76 ...73 L5
Bromyard Rd SPARK B11 ...126 C2
Bronte Cl DSYBK/YTR WS5 ...53 K8
SHLY B90 ...148 A3
Bronte Ct CRTAM B79 ...31 L7
Bronte Dr CNCK/NC WS11 ...17 G5
KIDD DY10 ...138 F7
Bronte Farm Rd SHLY B90 ...148 B4
Bronte Rd BKHL/PFLD WV2 ...50 D7
Bronte Wk COVE CV2 ...156 E1
Bronwen Rd BILS/COS WV14 ...67 G6
Bronwen Vis DARL/WED WS10 * ...52 A7
Bronze Cl NUN CV11 ...99 J5
Brook Av TAM/AM/WIL B77 ...46 E6
Brook Av BKDE/SHDE B34 ...92 B7
Brookbank Gdns SEDG DY3 ...83 M3
Brookbank Rd SEDG DY3 ...83 M3
Brook Cl ALDR WS9 ...40 E2
COV CV1 ...9 M4
LGN/SDN/BHAMAIR B26 ...109 G8
LICH WS13 ...20 E4
PENK ST19 ...10 C7

POL/KGSB/FAZ B78 ....76 B1
SHLY B90 ....147 K4
STETCH B33 ....109 J1
Brook Crs HAG/WOL DY9 ....119 M8
HAG/WOL DY9 ....120 D2
KGSWFD DY6 ....83 G6
Brook Cft
CHWD/FDBR/MGN B37 ....110 F6
LGN/SDN/BHAMAIR B26 ....109 M6
Brookdale KIDD DY10 ....138 D5
SEDG DY3 ....84 A2
Brookdale Cl RBRY B45 ....143 K4
Brookdale Dr
ETTPK/GDPK/PENN WV4 ....65 H7
Brookdale Rd NUNW/HART CV10 ....81 H6
Brook Dr RIDG/WDGT B32 ....123 H4
Brookend Dr RBRY B45 ....143 K6
POL/KGSB/FAZ B78 ....45 L5
Brooke End BNTWD WS7 ....26 E1
Brooke Rd HEDN WS12 ....12 D7
KNWTH CV8 ....197 M1
Brookes Cl OLDBY B69 ....85 G5
Brooke St DUDS DY2 ....85 G5
Brook Farm Cl CNCK/NC WS11 ....16 C6
Brookfield Cl ALDR WS9 ....40 E3
Brookfield Dr CNCK/NC WS11 ....16 C6
Brookfield Rd ALDR WS9 ....40 E4
CDSL WV8 ....34 F2
RLSN CV32 ....199 J8
WSNGN B18 ....88 D3
Brookfields Cl
LGLYGN/QTN B68 ....105 G1
Brookfield Wy HIA/OLT B92 ....127 H6
TPTN/OCK DY4 ....67 L7
Brookford Av COVN CV6 ....133 L2
Brook Green La ALE/KHTH/YWD B14 ....150 E4
Brookhill Cl WNSFLD WV11 ....38 A4
Brook Hill Rd WASH/WDE B8 ....108 E1
Brook Holloway HAG/WOL DY9 ....120 C2
Brookhouse La WOLVN WV10 ....22 F7
Brookhouse La WOLVN WV10 ....22 E7
Brookhouse Rd BRGRVE B60 ....169 K5
DSYBK/YTR WS5 ....5 L8
Brookhus Farm Rd
WALM/CURD B76 ....73 L5
Brooking Cl GTB/HAM B43 ....71 H1
Brookland Gv ALDR WS9 ....40 D3
Brookland Rd ALDR WS9 ....40 D3
HAG/WOL DY9 ....119 L8
Brooklands STRBR DY8 ....101 K4
Brooklands Av CLTWT WS6 ....24 D1
Brooklands Cl HLGN/YWD B28 ....126 D4
Brooklands Dr
ALE/KHTH/YWD B14 ....125 J8
KIDDM DY11 ....138 B4
Brooklands Gv ALDR WS9 ....40 D3
Brooklands La REDE B98 ....194 F8
Brooklands Pde WOLV WV1 ....50 F3
Brooklands Rd CNCK/NC WS11 ....16 C6
HLGN/YWD B28 ....126 D4
The Brooklands SEDG DY3 ....82 C4
Brooklands Wy
CHWD/FDBR/MGN B37 ....110 F5
Brook La ALDR WS9 ....40 E2
ALE/KHTH/YWD B14 ....125 K5
CDYHTH B64 ....24 E2
GTWY WS6 ....24 E2
HIA/OLT B92 ....127 H5
NUNW/HART CV10 ....81 K7
RIDG/WDGT B32 ....105 K8
Brooklea BDWTH CV12 ....116 D3
Brooklea Gv HWK/WKHTH B38 ....145 L4
Brooklime Dr RRUGBY CV23 ....161 J5
Brooklyn Av AST/WIT B6 ....89 K6
Brooklyn Gv BILS/COS WV14 ....67 K5
KGSWFD DY6 ....82 F5
Brooklyn Rd BNTWD WS7 ....19 J8
COV CV1 * 13 B2
HEDN WS12 ....17 H4
Brookmans Rd RIDG/WDGT B32 ....123 H1
Brookmeadow Ct
HLGN/YWD B28 ....126 B7
Brook Meadow Rd
BKDE/SHDE B34 ....91 L2
RUSH/SHEL WS4 ....40 E1
Brook Rd BRGRVE B61 ....168 A3
EDG B15 ....106 C5
GTWY WS6 ....24 C1
LGLYGN/QTN B68 ....104 C3
RBRY B45 ....143 J6
STRBR DY8 ....119 M2
WLNHL WV13 ....51 J4
WMBN WV5 ....64 D7
Brooksbank Dr CDYHTH B64 ....103 K1
Brooksby Gv DOR/KN B93 ....175 J5
Brooks Cft CVALE B35 ....91 L3
Brookshaw Wy COVE CV2 ....135 K5
Brookside DARL/WED WS10 ....68 F2
GTB/HAM B43 ....70 B7
NFLD/LBR B31 ....123 K8
RRUGBY CV23 ....183 K7
SEDG DY3 ....84 B3
Brookside Av COVW CV5 ....154 A2
KNWTH CV8 ....197 J1
MOS/BIL B13 ....125 M6
Brookside Cl ALVE B48 ....170 C1
ERDW/GRVHL B23 ....72 A6
HALE B63 ....121 H3
RUGBYS/DCH CV22 ....186 C4
WMBN WV5 ....64 D7
Brookside Dr BRGRVE B61 ....168 D5
Brookside Rd POL/KGSB/FAZ B78 ....45 H4
KIDD DY10 ....139 M3
TAM/AM/WIL B77 ....46 D3
Brooks Rd CSCFLD/WYGN B72 ....73 G4
Brook St BDWTH CV12 ....98 F4
BILS/COS WV14 ....51 J8
BRLYHL DY5 ....102 E5
CBHAMW B3 ....6 D4
HAG/WOL DY9 ....102 D8
KGSWFD DY6 ....82 F4
KIDDW DY11 ....138 A7
KNWTH CV8 ....183 L7
REDE B98 ....202 E6
SEDG DY3 ....66 E6
SEDG DY3 ....84 A2
SMTHWK B66 ....87 M7
STRBR DY8 ....101 J8
STRBR DY8 ....101 K4
TPTN/OCK DY4 ....67 J7
WSLW WS2 ....4 C4
WSLW WS2 ....205 J1
Brook Ter BILS/COS WV14 ....51 J8
Brookthorpe Dr SHHTH WV12 ....52 A1
Brook V BEWD DY12 ....163 G4
Brookvale Av COVS CV3 ....156 C1
Brookvale Gv BRGRVE B60 ....191 M4
Brookvale Gv HIA/OLT B92 ....127 H4
Brookvale Ms SLYOAK B29 ....124 F3
Brookvale Park Rd
ERDW/GRVHL B23 ....71 M8

Brookvale Rd AST/WIT B6 ....89 L2
HIA/OLT B92 ....127 H4
Brookview SMTHWKW B67 * 105 K2
Brook View Cl LOZ/NWT B19 ....89 G7
Brook Wk ATHST CV9 ....63 K7
RIDG/WDGT B32 ....123 H3
Brookwillow Rd HALE B63 ....121 H3
Brookwood Av HLGN/YWD B28 ....126 D6
Broom Cl BRGRVE B60 ....191 M3
RUGBYS/DCH CV22 ....186 C6
Broom Crs KIDD DY10 ....138 E7
Broom Covert Rd LICHS WS14 ....29 J5
Broomcroft Rd
CHWD/FDBR/MGN B37 ....92 D8
Broomdene Av BKDE/SHDE B34 ....91 L6
Broom Dr ALE/KHTH/YWD B14 ....146 C1
Broome Av GTB/HAM B43 ....70 A6
Broome Cl HALE B63 ....121 L2
Broome Cft COVN CV6 ....133 M2
Broome Gdns MGN/WHC B75 ....57 G8
Broomehill Cl KIDDW DY11 ....137 M6
Broomehill Cl KIDD DY11 ....137 M6
Broome La HAG/WOL DY9 ....140 C2
Broome Rd WOLVN WV10 ....36 B6
Broomfield SMTHWKW B67 ....87 K8
Broomfield Cl KIDDW DY11 ....137 M6
Broomfield Gn KIDDW DY11 ....137 M6
Broomfield Ri NUNW/HART CV10 ....98 D3
Broomfield Rd COVW CV5 ....154 D4
DARL/WED WS10 ....69 G2
ERDW/GRVHL B23 ....90 D3
KIDDW DY11
Broomfields Cl SOLH B91 ....128 B8
Broomhall Av WNSFLD WV11 ....37 H7
Broom Hall Crs ACGN B27 ....126 F6
Broom Hall Gv ACGN B27 ....126 C1
Broomhill Bank CNCK/NC WS11 ....16 C1
Broomhill Cl CNCK/NC WS11 ....16 C1
GTB/HAM B43 ....70 B5
Broomhill La GTB/HAM B43 ....70 B5
Broomhill Rd ERDW/GRVHL B23 ....71 M6
Broomhurst EDG B15 ....106 C5
Broomie La MGN/WHC B75 ....73 H1
Broomlea La SHLY B90 ....147 L7
Broomlea Cl FOAKS/STRLY B74 ....55 J5
Broom Rd DSYBK/YTR WS5 ....69 M2
DUDN DY1 ....84 E1
Broom St BHTH/HG B12 ....7 L9
Broomybank KNWTH CV8 ....179 M7
Broomy Cl STETCH B33 ....91 H8
STRPT DY13 ....163 H8
Broseley Av NFLD/LBR B31 ....144 E5
Broseley Brook Cl BORD B9 ....89 H6
Brosil Av BFLD/HDSWWD B20 ....88 C2
Brotherton Av REDE B98 ....201 K3
Brougham St LOZ/NWT B19 ....88 F6
Brough Cl
ETTPK/GDPK/PENN WV4 ....66 D2
VAUX/NECH B7 ....89 M7
Broughton Crs NFLD/LBR B31 ....144 A6
Broughton Rd BDMR/CCFT WV3 ....49 G4
BFLD/HDSWWD B20 ....88 E5
HAG/WOL DY9 ....120 B2
Browett Rd COVN CV6 ....133 K8
Brown Av TAM/AM/WIL B77 ....46 A5
Brownfield Rd BKDE/SHDE B34 ....92 A7
Brownhills Rd BRWNH WS8 ....26 D8
CNCK/NC WS11 ....17 M8
Browning Av WWCK CV34 ....205 G8
Browning Cl CRTAM B79 ....31 J5
KIDD DY10 ....138 F7
NUNW/HART CV10 ....79 L8
SHHTH WV12 ....38 C6
Browning Crs WOLVN WV10 ....36 A3
Browning Gv
DUNHL/THL/PER WV6 ....48 C1
Browning Rd BNTWD WS7 ....19 G6
COVE CV2 ....135 G2
RUGBY/HIL CV21 ....187 M5
Browning St CBHAMW B1 ....6 C5
Brownley Rd SHLY B90 ....148 C6
Brown Lion St TPTN/OCK DY4 ....67 J4
Brownlow St RLSN CV32 ....206 E3
Brown Rd DARL/WED WS10 ....52 B6
Brownsea Cl RBRY B45 ....143 J4
Brownsea Dr CBHAMW B1 ....6 C8
Brownsfield Rd LICH WS13 ....21 H4
Browns Gn BFLD/HDSWWD B20 ....88 D2
Brownshill Ct COVN CV6 ....133 J4
Brownshore La WNSFLD WV11 ....37 L2
Brown's La COVW CV5 ....132 F5
CRTAM B79 ....32 A5
DOR/KN B93 ....149 J7
POL/KGSB/FAZ B78 ....47 K8
Brownsover La RUGBYN/HIL CV21 ....160 F6
Brownsover Rd
RUGBYN/HIL CV21 ....160 C6
Brown St BKHL/PFLD WV2 ....50 B6
Brownswall Rd SEDG DY3 ....65 M8
Browsholme CRTAM B79 ....31 H7
Broxell Cl WWCK CV34 ....205 G1
Broxwood Pk
DUNHL/THL/PER WV6 ....48 F2
Bruce Rd COVN CV6 ....133 L5
KIDD DY10 ....138 F6
RCOV/BALC/EX CV7 ....116 D6
Bruce Williams Wy
RUGBYS/DCH CV22 ....186 C5
Brudenell Cl RUGBYS/DCH CV22 ....185 L5
Brueton Av BRGRVE B60 ....191 L5
SOLH B91 ....148 H2
Brueton Dr ERDE/BCHGN B24 ....90 F2
REDE B98 ....202 E2
Brueton Rd BILS/COS WV14 ....51 L6
Bruford Rd BDMR/CCFT WV3 ....2 F4
Brunel Cl BHTH/HG B12 ....107 L8
BNTWD WS7 ....18 F5
COVE CV2 * 9 L4
CRTAM B79 ....31 L7
STRPT DY13 ....163 L8
Brunel Gv BILS/COS WV14 ....67 J5
Brunel Rd TPTN/OCK DY4 ....67 H6
Brunel St CBHAM B2 ....6 D6
Brunel Wk DARL/WED WS10 * 52 B6
Brunel Wy BKHL/PFLD WV2 ....47 L2
Brunslow Cl WLNHL WV13 ....52 A4
WOLVN WV10 ....36 A4
Brunswick Park Rd
DARL/WED WS10 ....68 D2
CNCK/NC WS11 ....16 C3
COV CV1 ....188 B2
Brunswick St CBHAMW B1 ....6 B6

RLSS CV31 ....206 F2
WSLW WS2 * 4 B9
Brunswick Ter DARL/WED WS10 ....68 D2
Bruntingthorpe Wy COVS CV3 ....156 C5
Brunton Cl COVE CV2 ....156 D6
Brunton Rd SMHTH B10 ....108 D6
Brushfield Rd PBAR/PBCH B42 ....71 H5
Brutus Dr CSHL/WTROR B46 ....93 J4
Bryan Av
ETTPK/GDPK/PENN WV4 ....65 H1
Bryan Rd WSLW WS2 ....52 B1
Bryanston Cl COVE CV2 ....156 E1
Bryanston Ct SOLH B91 * 127 K6
Bryanston Rd SOLH B91 ....127 K7
Bryans Wy HEDN WS12 ....17 H1
Bryant St WSNGN B18 ....88 C8
Bryce Rd BRLYHL DY5 ....83 M8
Brylan Cft KGSTG B44 ....71 K7
Brympton Rd COVS CV3 ....156 A3
Bryn Arden Rd
LGN/SDN/BHAMAIR B26 ....109 J3
HIA/OLT B92 ....127 L2
Bryn Jones Cl COVS CV3 ....156 D6
Brynmawr Rd
ETTPK/GDPK/PENN WV4 ....66 D2
Bryn Rd COVN CV6 ....134 D6
Brynside Cl ALE/KHTH/YWD B14 ....146 B3
Bryony Cl BDWTH CV12 ....116 C4
Bryony Gdns DARL/WED WS10 ....52 B6
Bryony Rd SLYOAK B29 ....123 M6
Buchanan Rd
RUGBYS/DCH CV22 ....186 C4
RUSH/SHEL WS4 ....53 L2
Buchanan View RUSH/SHEL WS4 ....53 L2
Buchan Cl CNCK/NC WS11 ....12 B8
Buckbury Cl HAG/WOL DY9 ....120 B4
Buckbury Cft SHLY B90 ....148 F7
Buckden TAM/AM/WIL B77 ....47 G4
Buckden Cl WWCK CV34 ....205 K4
Buckfast Cl BRGRVE B61 ....191 H4
COVS CV3 ....155 J8
Buckhold Dr COVW CV5 ....132 F8
Buckingham Cl DARL/WED WS10 ....69 G1
NUNW/HART CV10 ....81 H8
Buckingham Dr SHHTH WV12 ....37 M6
Buckingham Gdns LICHS WS14 * 20 F7
Buckingham Gv KGSWFD DY6 ....82 G6
Buckingham Ms
SCFLD/BOLD B73 ....72 E3
Buckingham Pl HEDN WS12 ....17 J4
Buckingham Ri COVW CV5 ....153 M1
DUDN DY1 ....84 C3
Buckingham Rd
BLKHTH/ROWR B65 ....104 B1
CBROM B36 ....92 D6
CRTAM B79 ....31 J6
ETTPK/GDPK/PENN WV4 ....65 L1
Buckingham St LOZ/NWT B19 ....6 E1
Buckland Cl HEDN WS12 ....17 H4
Buckland End BKDE/SHDE B34 ....91 L7
Bucklands End La
BKDE/SHDE B34 ....91 K7
Buckle Cl WSL WS1 ....4 F7
Buckley Rd
ETTPK/GDPK/PENN WV4 ....49 H8
WOLV WV1 ....50 E2
The Buckleys ALVE B48 ....170 E7
Buckminster Dr DOR/KN B93 ....175 J1
Bucknall Rd WNSFLD WV11 ....37 L4
Bucknell Cl SOLH B91 ....128 A8
Bucknill Crs RUGBYN/HIL CV21 ....187 M5
Buckridge Cl HWK/WKHTH B38 ....145 H6
Buckridge La SHLY B90 ....147 L8
Bucks Head Cottages
LICHS WS14 ....30 A7
Bucks Hl NUNW/HART CV10 ....79 M6
Buckton Cl HEDN WS12 ....12 C5
Buckton Cl MGN/WHC B75 ....57 J3
Buckwell La RRUGBY CV23 ....161 L7
Budbrooke Cl COVE CV2 ....135 J3
Budbrooke Gv BKDE/SHDE B34 ....92 C7
Budden Rd TPTN/OCK DY4 ....67 K6
Bude Rd DSYBK/YTR WS5 ....54 B6
Buffery Rd DUDS DY2 ....85 H6
Bufferys Cl SOLH B91 ....148 F5
Buildwas Cl BLOX/PEL WS3 ....38 D3
Bulford Cl ALE/KHTH/YWD B14 ....146 D3
Bulger Rd BILS/COS WV14 ....51 J6
Bulkington La NUN CV11 ....99 L5
Bulkington Rd BDWTH CV12 ....117 H3
Bullace Cft EDG B15 ....124 B2
Bulldog La LICH WS13 ....20 F4
Buller St
ETTPK/GDPK/PENN WV4 ....50 C8
Bullfield Av TLHL/CAN CV4 ....153 J4
Bullfields Cl BLKHTH/ROWR B65 ....85 K8
Bullfinch Cl DUDN DY1 ....84 C5
Bullimore Gv KNWTH CV8 ....196 D7
Bullivents Cl DOR/KN B93 ....149 K8
Bull La BILS/COS WV14 ....68 D1
WBROM B70 ....86 E2
WMBN WV5 ....64 F6
Bullmeadow La WMBN WV5 ....64 E6
Bullmoor La LICHS WS14 ....27 L4
Bullock's Rw WSL WS1 ....5 G4
Bullock St VAUX/NECH B7 ....89 J8
WBROM B70 ....87 H5
Bullows Rd BRWNH WS8 ....26 A7
Bull Ring HALE B63 ....121 M2
WBROM B70 ....138 C7
Bull's Head La COVS CV3 ....155 L4
Bull's La WALM/CURD B76 ....74 A3
Bull St BRLYHL DY5 ....101 M4
CBHAM B2 ....7 G4
DARL/WED WS10 ....52 C7
DUDN DY1 ....84 E5
HRBN B17 ....106 B7
NUN CV11 ....99 H3
SEDG DY3 ....84 A3
WBROM B70 ....87 H4
Bullus Rd STRPT DY13 ....188 A3
Bull Yd COV CV1 ....8 E5
Bulrush Cl BRWNH WS8 ....26 C6
Bulwell Cl AST/WIT B6 ....89 L6
Bulwer Rd COVN CV6 ....133 L6
Bulwick Cl COVS CV3 ....156 F4
Bumble Hole La BRGRVE B61 ....168 B4
Bumblehole Mdw WMBN WV5 ....64 D6
Bunbury Gdns NFLD/LBR B31 ....145 L1
Bunbury Rd NFLD/LBR B31 ....145 L1
Bundle HI HALE B63 ....121 L2
Bungalow Est CGN WV6 ....134 D1
Bungalows GTWY WS6 * 24 E2
The Bungalows WBROM B70 * 86 E2
Bungay Lake La BRGRVE B61 ....190 D3
Bungham La PENK ST19 ....10 B5
Bunker's Hill La BILS/COS WV14 ....51 J5
Bunn's La DUDS DY2 ....85 K4
Buntsford HI BRGRVE B60 ....191 J8
Buntsford Park Rd
BRGRVE B60 ....191 K8
Bunyan Pl CNCK/NC WS11 ....16 C1

Burbage Cl WOLVN WV10 ....36 C7
Burbages La COVN CV6 ....116 B8
Burberry Gv
RCOV/BALC/EX CV7 ....151 L7
Burbidge Rd BORD B9 ....108 B2
Burbury Cl BDWTH CV12 ....117 C1
RLSN CV32 ....207 G3
Burbury Ct WWCK CV34 ....205 K8
Burbury St LOZ/NWT B19 ....89 G7
Burbury St South
LOZ/NWT B19 * 89 G7
Burcot Av BRGRVE B60 ....191 M1
WOLV WV1 ....50 E2
Burcote Rd ERDE/BCHGN B24 ....90 F3
Burcot La BRGRVE B60 ....191 M2
Burdock Cl CNCK/NC WS11 ....16 C2
DSYBK/YTR WS5 ....69 J2
Burdock Rd SLYOAK B29 ....123 L7
Burdons Cl STETCH B33 ....91 H8
Bure Gv WLNHL WV13 ....52 B4
Burfield Rd HALE B63 ....103 J3
Burford Cl HIA/OLT B92 ....127 L2
Burford Rd HLYWD B47 ....175 J2
KGSTG B44 ....71 K6
Burgage Pl NUN CV11 ....99 G3
Burges COV CV1 ....8 F3
Burges Gv WWCK CV34 ....205 K4
Burgess Cft HIA/OLT B92 ....128 C2
Burghley Cl NUN CV11 ....99 K3
Burghley Dr HHTH/SAND B71 ....69 K3
KIDDW DY11 ....137 M8
Burghley Wk BRLYHL DY5 ....101 K5
Burgh Wy WSLW WS2 ....52 E1
Burgoyne St CNCK/NC WS11 ....12 B8
Burhill Wy
CHWD/FDBR/MGN B37 ....110 F1
Burke Av MOS/BIL B13 ....126 B4
Burkitt Dr TPTN/OCK DY4 ....68 A5
Burland Av
DUNHL/THL/PER WV6 ....35 J6
COVS CV3 ....155 J8
Burleigh Cft BNTWD WS7 ....26 E1
Burleigh Rd BDMR/CCFT WV3 ....49 C6
SHHTH WV12 ....37 M7
Burleigh St WSL WS1 ....5 J5
Burleton Rd STETCH B33 ....110 C3
Burley Cl SHLY B90 ....147 K3
Burlington Av COVE CV2 ....9 M1
NUNW/HART CV10 ....98 F4
SMHTH B10 ....108 D4
WBROM B70 ....87 H4
Burlington St AST/WIT B6 ....89 J7
Burlish Av HIA/OLT B92 ....127 K4
Burlish Cl STRPT DY13 ....163 K7
Burlish Crossing STRPT DY13 ....163 J7
Buttons Ter BEWD DY12 * 162 F2
Burman Cl SHLY B90 ....147 L3
Burman Dr CSHL/WTROR B46 ....93 K8
Burmese Wy BLKHTH/ROWR B65 ....85 K7
Burnaby Cl NUNW/HART CV10 ....79 M8
Burnaby Rd COVN CV6 ....134 A4
Burnaston Crs SHLY B90 ....149 G6
Burnaston Rd HLGN/YWD B28 ....126 C5
Burnbank Gv ERDE/BCHGN B24 ....90 F1
Burncross Wy WOLVN WV10 ....36 D7
Burnel Rd SLYOAK B29 ....123 L3
Burnell Gdns BDMR/CCFT WV3 ....49 K4
Burnett Rd FOAKS/STRLY B74 ....55 H5
Burney La WASH/WDE B8 ....91 G8
Burnfields Cl ALDR WS9 ....40 E4
Burnham Av WOLVN WV10 ....36 A5
YDLY B25 ....109 G7
Burnham Cl KGSWFD DY6 ....101 K1
Burnham Gn CNCK/NC WS11 ....15 M5
Burnham Meadow
HLGN/YWD B28 ....126 E7
Burnham Ri NUN CV11 ....81 L7
Burnham Rd COVS CV3 ....155 L2
KGSTG B44 ....71 J3
Burnhill Gv SLYOAK B29 ....123 J5
Burnlea Gv NFLD/LBR B31 ....145 L4
Burnsall Cl
CHWD/FDBR/MGN B37 ....110 D3
COVEN WV12 ....35 L2
Burnsall Gv COVW CV5 ....154 B5
Burnsall Rd COVW CV5 ....154 B5
Burns Av TPTN/OCK DY4 ....67 L6
WOLVN WV10 ....36 A2
WWCK CV34 ....205 G8
Burns Cl KIDD DY10 ....138 F7
LICHS WS14 ....20 E7
REDW B97 ....202 A5
STRBR DY8 ....101 L5
Burns Dr BNTWD WS7 ....19 G6
Burnside COVS CV3 ....156 E3
RUGBYS/DCH CV22 ....186 C3
Burnside Gdns DSYBK/YTR WS5 ....54 B7
Burns Pl DARL/WED WS10 ....51 L8
Burns Rd COVE CV2 ....155 M2
CRTAM B79 ....31 J2
DARL/WED WS10 ....51 L8
RLSN CV32 ....206 F1
Burns St CNCK/NC WS11 ....16 C1
Burns Wk BDWTH CV12 ....117 C4
Burnthorne La STRPT DY13 ....188 A3
Burnthurst Crs SOLH B91 ....148 E6
Burnt Meadow Rd REDE B98 ....195 J8
Burnt Oak Dr STRBR DY8 ....101 K5
Burnt Tree TPTN/OCK DY4 ....85 K3
Burntwood Rd BNTWD WS7 ....27 H1
CNCK/NC WS11 ....17 H7
Burrington Rd RIDG/WDGT B32 ....122 F7
Burrowes St WSLW WS2 ....4 F2
Burrow Hill Cl CBROM B36 ....92 A3
Burrow Hill La
RCOV/BALC/EX CV7 ....115 H3
Burrows Rd KGSWFD DY6 ....101 K1
Burrows St WSLW WS2 ....4 C1
Burslem Cl BLOX/PEL WS3 ....38 C1
Burstips Rd WNSFLD WV11 ....38 A1
Burton Av RUSH/SHEL WS4 ....53 K2
Burton Cl COVW CV5 ....133 G4
CRTAM B79 ....32 A4
Burton Crs WOLVN WV10 ....3 J3
Burton Farm Rd
RUSH/SHEL WS4 ....53 M2
Burton La REDE B98 ....202 D3
Burton Old Rd LICH WS13 ....21 M1
Burton Old Rd East LICHS WS14 ....21 L1
Burton Old Rd West LICH WS13 ....21 H1
Burton Rd DUDN DY1 ....84 D1
LICH WS13 ....21 K2
Burton Wood Dr
BFLD/HDSWWD B20 ....89 H3
Buryfield Rd SOLH B91 ....127 L4
Bury Hill Rd OLDBY B69 ....86 B6
Bury Rd RLSS CV31 ....206 E5
Busby Cl COVS CV3 ....156 D6
Bush Av SMTHWK B66 ....88 D4
Bushbery Av TLHL/CAN CV4 ....153 K4

Bushbury Cft
CHWD/FDBR/MGN B37 ....111 G2
Bushbury La WOLVN WV10 ....36 D3
Bushbury Rd STETCH B33 ....91 L8
WOLVN WV10 ....36 E7
Bush Cl TLHL/CAN CV4 ....153 K2
Bushell Dr SOLH B91 ....149 H1
Bushelton Cl COV CV1 ....9 H8
Bushey Cl FOAKS/STRLY B74 ....55 K3
Bushey Fields Rd DUDN DY1 ....84 C6
Bush Gv BLOX/PEL WS3 ....39 L3
HDSW B21 ....88 A4
Bushley Cl REDE B98 ....202 E6
Bushley Cft SOLH B91 ....148 F5
Bushman Wy BKDE/SHDE B34 ....92 C3
Bushmore Rd HLGN/YWD B28 ....126 C6
Bush Rd DUDS DY2 ....103 C3
TPTN/OCK DY4 ....85 J1
Bush St DARL/WED WS10 ....52 B6
Bushway Cl BRLYHL DY5 ....101 L3
Bushwood Dr DOR/KN B93 ....175 L2
Bushwood Rd SLYOAK B29 ....123 K4
Bustleholme Av HHTH/SAND B71 ....69 K4
Bustleholme Crs
HHTH/SAND B71 ....69 K3
Bustleholme La HHTH/SAND B71 ....69 K3
Butcher's La RRUGBY CV23 ....158 D2
Butcher's La COVW CV5 ....133 G7
HALE B63 ....103 C6
Butchers Rd HIA/OLT B92 ....129 L7
Butcroft Gdns DARL/WED WS10 ....52 C7
Bute Cl RBRY B45 ....143 J4
SHHTH WV12 ....37 M7
Butler Cl KNWTH CV8 ....180 A6
Butler Rd HIA/OLT B92 ....127 K2
Butlers Cl BFLD/HDSWWD B20 ....88 C2
ERDW/GRVHL B23 ....72 B4
Butlers Dr
RCOV/BALC/EX CV7 ....116 E4
Butlers End RWWCK/WEL CV35 ....196 A3
Butlers La ATHST CV9 ....62 A3
FOAKS/STRLY B74 ....56 D2
Butlers Leap RUGBYN/HIL CV21 ....161 H8
Butlers Precinct WSL WS1 ....4 E3
Butler's Rd BFLD/HDSWWD B20 ....88 C2
Butler St WBROM B70 ....86 E6
Butlin Rd COVN CV6 ....134 A1
RUGBYN/HIL CV21 ....187 H2
Butlin St VAUX/NECH B7 ....90 A6
Buttercup Cl DSYBK/YTR WS5 ....69 L2
KIDDW DY11 ....138 C5
Buttercup Dr BRGRVE B60 ....169 G2
Butterfield Cl
DUNHL/THL/PER WV6 ....48 B2
Butterfield Rd BRLYHL DY5 ....83 M6
TAM/AM/WIL B77 ....46 F5
Buttermere RUGBYN/HIL CV21 ....161 H7
Buttermere Cl BRLYHL DY5 ....101 K6
CNCK/NC WS11 ....16 C2
COVS CV3 ....156 D6
DUNHL/THL/PER WV6 ....35 H7
Buttermere Ct
DUNHL/THL/PER WV6 ....48 D1
WNSFLD WV11 ....37 M4
Buttermere Dr RIDG/WDGT B32 ....123 K2
Buttermere Gv SHHTH WV12 ....37 M4
Butterworth Cl BILS/COS WV14 ....66 L4
Butterworth Dr TLHL/CAN CV4 ....153 L7
Butterworth Rd SMTHWKW B67 ....87 J7
Butt La COVW CV5 ....132 F4
Buttons Farm Rd
ETTPK/GDPK/PENN WV4 ....65 H2
Buttress Wy SMTHWK B66 ....87 L7
Butts COV CV1 ....8 B5
Butts La CNCK/NC WS11 ....25 J1
KIDD DY10 ....165 J5
Butts Rd COV CV1 ....8 B5
ETTPK/GDPK/PENN WV4 ....65 K1
RUSH/SHEL WS4 ....53 K2
Butts St RUSH/SHEL WS4 ....53 K2
Buxton Av POL/KGSB/FAZ B78 ....45 M5
Buxton Cl BLOX/PEL WS3 ....39 L1
Buxton Rd BLOX/PEL WS3 ....39 L2
DUDS DY2 ....84 E7
ERDW/GRVHL B23 ....71 M7
SCFLD/BOLD B73 ....72 C4
Byfield Cl STETCH B33 ....110 C4
Byfield Rd COVN CV6 ....133 J8
Byfleet Cl
ETTPK/GDPK/PENN WV4 ....66 D2
Byford St REDE B98 ....202 C3
Byford St NUNW/HART CV10 ....98 D1
Byford Wy
CHWD/FDBR/MGN B37 ....110 F5
Byland TAM/AM/WIL B77 ....46 F6
Bylands Cl BRGRVE B60 ....191 J4
Byland Wy BLOX/PEL WS3 ....38 E3
By Pass Rd TAM/AM/WIL B77 ....32 C8
Byrchen Moor Gdns BRLYHL DY5 ....83 M6
Byrne Rd BKHL/PFLD WV2 ....50 D6
Byron Av BDWTH CV12 ....117 H3
WWCK CV34 ....205 M2
Byron Cl BNTWD WS7 ....19 G6
KIDD DY10 ....138 F7
SMHTH B10 ....108 D6
Byron Crs DUDN DY1 ....66 F2
Byron Cft FOAKS/STRLY B74 ....42 D7
SEDG DY3 ....83 L1
Byron Pl CNCK/NC WS11 ....16 C1
Byron Rd CRTAM B79 ....31 L6
REDW B97 ....202 A5
SHHTH WV12 ....37 M7
WOLVN WV10 ....36 A3
Byron St BRLYHL DY5 ....84 B6
COV CV1 ....9 K1
HHTH/SAND B71 ....68 F3
Byron Wy BRGRVW B61 ....168 E5
Bywater Cl COVS CV3 ....154 F5
Byways BLOX/PEL WS3 ....39 G2

C

Caban Cl NFLD/LBR B31 ....123 J8
Cable Dr WSLW WS2 ....53 G1
Cable St BKHL/PFLD WV2 ....5 K9
Cabot Gv DUNHL/THL/PER WV6 ....48 C1
Cadbury Dr CVALE B35 ....91 K4
Cadbury Rd MOS/BIL B13 ....125 M1
Cadbury Wy HRBN B17 ....105 M8
Cadden Dr COVW CV5 ....153 M5
Caddick Crs HHTH/SAND B71 ....69 H6
Caddick Rd PBAR/PBCH B42 ....70 F4
Caddick St BILS/COS WV14 ....66 E5
Cadet Dr SHLY B90 ....148 E5
Cadgwith Gdns BILS/COS WV14 ....67 L3
Cadine Gdns MOS/BIL B13 ....125 G4

Cadle Rd WOLVN WV10 ....36 B6
Cadman Cl BDWTH CV12 ...117 G2
Cadman Crs WOLVN WV10 ...36 C7
Cadman's La GTWY WS6 ....25 C5
Cadnam Cl HRBN B17 .....124 A2
  WLNHL WV13 ....51 M5
Cadogan Rd DSYBK/YTR WS5 ..69 L1
Caen Cl RWWCK/WEL CV35 ...204 E6
Caernarfon Cl NUN CV11 ...99 H2
Caernarfon Dr SHHTH WV12 ..38 A2
Caernarvon Wy DUDN DY1 ...84 B4
Caesar Rd KNWTH CV8 ....197 J2
Caesar Wy CSHL/WTROR B46 ..93 J4
Cairndhu Dr KIDD DY10 ...138 E6
Cairn Dr WSLW WS2 ......52 D3
Cairns St WSLW WS2 ......4 B1
Caister TAM/AM/WIL B77 ...32 C1
Caister Dr WLNHL WV13 ...51 K5
Caistor Cl POL/KGSB/FAZ B78 ..44 F5
Caithness Cl COVS CV3 ...153 L1
Cakemore Rd RMSLY B62 ..104 C3
Cala Dr EDG B15 ....106 F6
Calcot Dr DUNHL/THL/PER WV6 ..147 J7
Caldecote Cl NUNW/HART CV10 ..81 L5
Caldecote Gv BORD B9 ...109 G4
Caldecott Pl RUGBYN/HIL CV21 .197 J2
Caldecott St RUGBYN/HIL CV21 .187 J5
Caldeford Av SHLY B90 ..148 E6
Calder TAM/AM/WIL B77 ...46 F3
Calder Av WSL WS1 ....5 J3
  COVS CV3 ....
Calder Cl BDWTH CV12 ...117 M3
Calderfields Cl RUSH/SHEL WS4 ..53 L2
Calder Gv BFLD/HDSWWD B20 ..88 D3
Calder Ri DUDN DY1 .....84 F3
Calder Rd STRPT DY13 ...163 J6
Calder Wk RLSS CV31 ....207 G8
Caldmore Gn WSL WS1 .....4 F7
Caldmore Rd WSL WS1 .....4 F7
Caldwall Crs KIDDW DY11 .138 B8
Caldwell Gv SOLH B91 ...128 A8
Caldwell Rd BORD B9 ....108 F2
  NUN CV11 ....99 H4
Caldwell St HHTH/SAND B71 ..69 H5
Caldy Wk STRPT DY13 ....163 J7
Cale Cl TAM/AM/WIL B77 ...46 A3
Caledonia BRLYHL DY5 ...102 B6
Caledonian TAM/AM/WIL B77 ..46 D3
Caledonia Rd BILS/COS WV14 ..51 J7
Caledon Pl WSLW WS2 .....4 A8
Caledon St WSLW WS2 .....4 A8
Calewood Rd BRLYHL DY5 .102 B6
Californian Gv BNTWD WS7 ..18 D5
California Rd OLDBY B69 ..85 L4
California Wy RIDG/WDGT B32 .123 G2
Callaghan Dr CNCK/NC WS11 ..17 G3
Callcott Dr BRLYHL DY5 ..102 B6
Callear Rd DARL/WED WS10 ..68 B4
Callendar Cl NUN CV11 ...81 L6
Calley Cl TPTN/OCK DY4 ...85 K2
Callowbridge Rd RBRY B45 .143 K6
Callowbrook La RBRY B45 .143 K6
Callow Cl STRPT DY13 ...188 B4
Callow Hill La REDW B97 .200 K7
Callow Hill Rd ALVE B48 .170 D6
Callows La KIDD DY10 ...138 E6
Calmere Cl COVE CV2 ....135 K5
Calshot Rd PBAR/PBCH B42 ..70 F7
Calstock Rd SHHTH WV12 ..52 B1
Calthorpe Rd
  BFLD/HDSWWD B20 .....89 G3
  DSYBK/YTR WS5 ....54 B7
  EDG B15 ....107 G6
Caludon Park Av COVE CV2 .135 J8
Caludon Rd COVE CV2 ....155 L1
Calver Crs WNSFLD WV11 ...37 K8
Calver Gv KGSTG B44 ....71 H2
Calvert Cl COVS CV3 ....155 H7
Calverley Rd HWK/WKHTH B38 .145 L4
Calverton Gv GTB/HAM B43 ..70 C5
Calves Cft WLNHL WV13 ...51 L2
Calvestone Pl
  RUGBYS/DCH CV22 * ..185 L6
Calvestone Rd
  RUGBYS/DCH CV22 ...185 L6
Calvestone Sq
  RUGBYS/DCH CV22 * ..185 M5
Calvin Cl WMBN WV5 .....64 D8
  WOLVN WV10 ....36 B3
Calving Hl CNCK/NC WS11 ..16 C3
Camberley Crs
  ETTPK/GDPK/PENN WV4 ...
Camberley Dr
  ETTPK/GDPK/PENN WV4 ..65 L1
Camberley Gv
  ERDW/GRVHL B23 ......72 C7
Camberley Rd KGSWFD DY6 .101 L1
Camberwell Ter RLSS CV31 .206 E6
Camborne Cl AST/WIT B6 ..89 J1
Camborne Dr NUN CV11 ...81 K8
Camborne Rd DSYBK/YTR WS5 .54 B6
Cambourne Rd
  BLKHTH/ROWR B65 ....104 A2
Cambrai Dr HLGN/YWD B28 .126 C3
Cambria Cl SHLY B90 ...147 H6
Cambria St CNCK/NC WS11 ..16 B3
Cambridge Av SCFLD/BOLD B73 .72 F5
  SOLH B91 ....148 C2
Cambridge Dr
  CHWD/FDBR/MGN B37 ..110 D4
  NUNW/HART CV10 ......98 B2
Cambridge Gdns RLSN CV32 .206 E4
Cambridge Rd DUDS DY2 ...84 E6
  MOS/BIL B13 ....125 K4
  SMTHWK B66 ....87 L6
Cambridge St CBHAMNE B1 ..6 D5
  COV CV1 ....134 C8
  RUGBYN/HIL CV21 ....187 G3
  WBROM B70 ....86 F3
  WOLVN WV10 ....3 H1
  WSL WS1 ....4 F8
Cambridge Wy ACGN B27 ..127 H1
Camden Cl CBROM B36 ....91 L5
  DSYBK/YTR WS5 * 69 L1
Camden Dr CBHAMNW B1 ....6 A2
  TAM/AM/WIL B77 ......46 D3
Camden St ALDR WS9 .....40 C1
  CBHAMNW B1 ....6 B3
  COVE CV2 ....155 L1
  WSL WS1 ....4 D7
Camden Wy KGSWFD DY6 ...83 G4
Camelia Gdns COVW WV9 ...35 H5
Camellia Rd COVE CV2 ...135 K5
Camelot Cl CNCK/NC WS11 ..16 D1
Camelot Wy SMHTH B10 ...108 A5
Cameo Dr STRBR DY8 ....101 A5
Cameo Dr COVW CV5 .....132 E6
  RLSN CV32 ....206 E1
Cameron Rd RUSH/SHEL WS4 ..5 K1

Camford Gv
  ALE/KHTH/YWD B14 ...146 D2
Cam Gdns BRLYHL DY5 ....83 M6
Camhouses TAM/AM/WIL B77 .46 F4
Camino Rd RIDG/WDGT B32 .121 K2
Camomile Cl DSYBK/YTR WS5 .69 L2
Campbell Cl CRTAM B79 ...31 K5
  NUNW/HART CV10 ......81 L1
  RUSH/SHEL WS4 ....53 L2
Campbell Pl DARL/WED WS10 .52 B7
Campbells Dr
  LGN/SDN/BHAMAIR B26 .109 M8
Campbell St BRLYHL DY5 .102 A1
  RUGBYN/HIL CV21 ....186 C2
Campden Cl REDW B97 ...202 B7
Campden Gn HIA/OLT B92 .127 L2
Campden Gv
  RWWCK/WEL CV35 .....204 C3
Camp Hl BHTH/HG B12 ...107 L5
Camp Hill Circ BHTH/HG B12 .107 L5
Camp Hill Dr NUNW/HART CV10 .80 B7
Camphill La DARL/WED WS10 .52 A8
Camp Hill Rd NUNW/HART CV10 .80 A6
Campian's Av GTWY WS6 ..24 D3
Campion Cl COVS CV3 ...155 H7
  DSYBK/YTR WS5 ....69 L2
  WMBN WV5 ....64 A7
Campion Dr TAM/AM/WIL B77 .46 A2
  WOLVN WV10 ....22 E6
Campion Gn RLSN CV32 ..206 E3
Campion Gv HALE B63 ...121 H2
Campion Rd RLSN CV32 ..206 E4
Campion Ter RLSN CV32 .206 E4
Campion Wy BEWD DY12 ..137 H6
  RRUGBY CV23 ....161 H5
  SHLY B90 ....147 L8
Camp La HDSW B21 ......87 M3
  HWK/WKHTH B38 ......145 K2
Camplea Cft
  CHWD/FDBR/MGN B37 ..110 E3
Camplin Crs BFLD/HDSWWD B20 .70 C8
Campling Cl BDWTH CV12 .117 M3
Campriano Dr WWCK CV34 .205 L4
Camp Rd MGN/WHC B75 ...43 H7
  BORD B9 ....108 A4
Camp St DARL/WED WS10 ..68 D3
  BNTWD WS7 ....19 J5
  WOLV WV1 ....2 D1
Campville Crs HHTH/SAND B71 .69 J4
Campville Gv
  CHWD/FDBR/MGN B37 ..92 D8
Camp Wood Cl SLYOAK B29 .124 C5
Camrose Cft BHTH/HG B12 .107 J7
  BKDE/SHDE B34 ....
Camrose Gdns COVEN WV9 ..35 L2
Camsey La BNTWD WS7 ....19 J5
Camville COVS CV3 .....156 E3
Canal Rd COVN CV6 .....134 C5
  RWWCK/WEL CV35 .....204 A3
Canal Side ALVE B48 ...170 F3
  BVILLE B30 * 145 L1
Canalside DUDS DY2 ....103 J1
Canalside BLOX/PEL WS3 ..39 J4
  HHTH/SAND B71 ....69 J3
  PENK ST19 ....10 D6
Canal St BRLYHL DY5 ....84 C8
  OLDBY B69 ....86 D6
  STOUR 111 K7
Canary Gv LOZ/NWT B19 ..89 G5
Canberra Rd COVE CV2 ...135 G1
  DSYBK/YTR WS5 ....54 A8
Canberra Wy BHTH/HG B12 * .107 K5
Canford Cl BHTH/HG B12 .107 K6
  COVS CV3 ....181 G2
Canford Crs CDSL WV8 ...34 C2
Canford Pl CNCK/NC WS11 * .16 D4
Canley Ford COVW CV5 ..154 C2
Canley Rd COVW CV5 ....154 C2
Cannas Ct TLHL/CAN CV4 * .154 B7
Cannel Rd BNTWD WS7 ....18 F4
Canning Cl DSYBK/YTR WS5 .54 B7
Canning Gdns WSNGN B18 .106 C1
Canning Rd DSYBK/YTR WS5 .54 B7
  TAM/AM/WIL B77 ......46 C1
Cannock Rd ATHST CV9 ...63 K5
  CNCK/NC WS11 ....16 E1
  HEDN WS12 ....
  SHHTH WV12 ....38 A6
  WOLVN WV10 ....36 D5
  WOLVN WV10 ....3 H1
  WOLVN WV10 ....35 E5
Cannocks La TLHL/CAN CV4 .154 B7
Cannock Wood Rd HEDN WS12 .13 M8
Cannock Wood St HEDN WS12 .13 L7
Cannon Cl TLHL/CAN CV4 .154 C7
Cannon Dr BILS/COS WV14 ..67 G3
Cannon Hill Gv BHTH/HG B12 .107 J8
Cannon Hill Pl BHTH/HG B12 * .107 J8
Cannon Hill Rd BHTH/HG B12 .107 H8
  TLHL/CAN CV4 ....154 B7
Cannon Park Rd TLHL/CAN CV4 .154 C8
Cannon St CBHAM B2 .....7 G5
  WLNHL WV13 ....51 M3
  WSLW WS2 ....53 J1
Cannon St North WSLW WS2 .53 J1
Canon Dr RCOVN/BALC/EX CV7 .116 B8
Canon Hudson Cl COVS CV3 .156 A7
Canterbury Av WLNHL WV13 .52 B1
Canterbury Cl
  BLKHTH/ROWR B65 ....104 C1
  BLOX/PEL WS3 ....25 L8
  HHTH/SAND B71 ....69 J4
  TAM/AM/WIL B77 ......46 A2
Canterbury Dr BNTWD WS7 ..19 H6
  CHWD/FDBR/MGN B37 ..110 E6
  DUNHL/THL/PER WV6 ...48 B7
Canterbury Rd
  BFLD/HDSWWD B20 .....89 H4
  ETTPK/GDPK/PENN WV4 .49 H8
  HHTH/SAND B71 ....69 H6
  KIDDW DY11 ....137 K6
Canterbury St COV CV1 ...9 J2
Canterbury Wy CNCK/NC WS11 .16 F1
  NUN CV11 ....81 L5
Cantlow Cl COVW CV5 ...153 G1
Cantlow Rd MOS/BIL B13 .125 L7
Canton La WALM/CURD B76 .75 L3
Canute Cl WSL WS1 .....5 H6
Canvey Cl RBRY B45 ....143 L4
Canwell Av
  CHWD/FDBR/MGN B37 ..92 D8
Canwell Dr MGN/WHC B75 .43 M8
Canwell Gdns BILS/COS WV14 .66 F1
Canwell La MGN/WHC B75 ..57 J1
Capcroft Rd MOS/BIL B13 .125 M7
Cape Hl SMTHWK B66 ....105 M1
Capener Rd GTB/HAM B43 ..70 E8
Capern Gv RIDG/WDGT B32 .105 K8
Cape St WBROM B70 .....86 C1
  WSNGN B18 ....106 B1
Capethorn Rd SMTHWK B66 .105 L2
Capilano Rd ERDW/GRVHL B23 .72 A6
Capmartin Rd COVN CV6 .133 M6
Cappers La LICHS WS14 ..21 J5
Capponfield Cl BILS/COS WV14 .66 F2
Capstone Av WOLVN WV10 .35 M5

  WSNGN B18 ....106 E1
Captain's Cl BDMR/CCFT WV3 .49 H3
Captains Pool Rd KIDD DY10 .164 E4
Capulet Cl COVS CV3 ...156 A2
  RUGBYS/DCH CV22 ....186 C2
Caradoc TAM/AM/WIL B77 ..46 F3
Caradoc Cl COVE CV2 ...135 H6
Carcroft Rd YDLY B25 ...109 G5
Cardale Cft BLKHTH/ROWR B65 .104 D3
Cardale St BRLYHL DY5 ..84 D7
Carden Crs BILS/COS WV14 .51 H7
Carder Dr BRLYHL DY5 ..102 A3
Cardiff St BDMR/CCFT WV3 .2 C7
Cardigan Cl HHTH/SAND B71 .69 G6
Cardigan Dr SHHTH WV12 .37 M7
Cardigan Pl HEDN WS12 ..13 G8
Cardigan Rd BDWTH CV12 .116 A4
Cardigan St CBHAMNE B4 ..7 K3
Cardinal Crs BRGRVW B61 .191 H6
Cardinal Dr KIDD DY10 ..164 D2
Cardinal Wy CNCK/NC WS11 .16 E3
Cardinal Cl COVS CV3 ...155 J8
Cardington Av PBAR/PBCH B42 .70 F4
Cardoness Pl DUDN DY1 ..84 D3
Cardy Cl REDW B97 ....201 L1
Careless Av HAG/WOL DY9 .120 D1
Carey TAM/AM/WIL B77 ...46 F4
Carey St COVN CV6 .....134 F4
Carfax CNCK/NC WS11 ...16 C5
Cargill Cl COVN CV6 ...116 D8
Carhampton Rd MGN/WHC B75 .57 L7
Carillon Gdns
  BLKHTH/ROWR B65 ....104 A2
Carisbrooke TAM/AM/WIL B77 .46 E3
Carisbrooke Av
  CHWD/FDBR/MGN B37 ..111 G3
Carisbrooke Cl DARL/WED WS10 .69 J3
Carisbrooke Ct
  DUNHL/THL/PER WV6 ...48 F2
Carisbrooke Crs
  DARL/WED WS10 ....69 J2
Carisbrooke Dr RMSLY B62 .122 B3
Carisbrooke Gdns WOLVN WV10 .36 C2
Carisbrooke Rd
  NUNW/HART CV10 ......81 H7
  DUNHL/THL/PER WV6 ...48 F2
  HRBN B17 ....105 M4
  WOLVN WV10 ....36 C2
Carisbrook Rd
  NUNW/HART CV10 ......81 H7
Carlcroft TAM/AM/WIL B77 .46 F3
Carless Av HRBN B17 ...105 M6
Carless St WSL WS1 ....4 F7
Carlisle Rd CNCK/NC WS11 .15 M4
Carlisle St WSNGN B18 ..88 C8
Carl St WSLW WS2 .....39 H4
Carlton Av BILS/COS WV14 .51 K6
  FOAKS/STRLY B74 .....57 J3
  HAG/WOL DY9 ....120 C2
  HDSW B21 ....88 C4
  WNSFLD WV11 ....36 E7
Carlton Cl BDWTH CV12 ..117 M2
  DUDN DY1 ....67 G7
  HEDN WS12 ....17 H4
  KIDDW DY11 ....137 J5
  MGN/WHC B75 ....57 M4
  REDW B97 ....201 M4
Carlton Crs BNTWD WS7 ..18 E5
  CRTAM B79 ....31 L3
Carlton Cft FOAKS/STRLY B74 .55 L5
Carlton Gdns COVW CV5 * .154 E5
Carlton Ms RUGBYN/HIL CV21 .186 F2
Carlton Rd BDMR/CCFT WV3 .49 L6
  BORD B9 ....108 B2
  COVN CV6 ....134 D4
  RUGBYS/DCH CV22 ....186 B4
  SMTHWK B66 ....87 L5
Carlyon Rd ATHST CV9 ...63 K5
Carmel Cl HEDN WS12 ...13 G8
Carmel Gv RIDG/WDGT B32 .122 F4
Carmelite Rd COV CV1 ...9 K5
Carmichael Cl LICHS WS14 .21 L6
Carmodale Av PBAR/PBCH B42 .70 F7
Carmbroe Av COVS CV3 ..156 D6
Carnegie Av TPTN/OCK DY4 .85 L1
Carnegie Cl COVS CV3 ..155 M8
Carnegie Dr DARL/WED WS10 .68 C2
Carnegie Rd
  BLKHTH/ROWR B65 ....103 M3
Carnford Rd
  LGN/SDN/BHAMAIR B26 .109 M7
Carnforth Cl KGSWFD DY6 ..82 F3
Carnforth Rd BRGRVW B61 .191 M4
Carnoustie TAM/AM/WIL B77 .32 F2
Carnoustie Cl BLOX/PEL WS3 .25 L8
  BRGRVW B61 ....191 H5
  MGN/WHC B75 ....57 H5
Carnwath Rd SCFLD/BOLD B73 .72 C2
Carol Av BRGRVW B61 ...191 H6
Carol Crs HALE B63 ....103 K8
  WNSFLD WV11 ....37 J7
Carol Gdns STRBR DY8 ..101 K5
Caroline Cl NUN CV11 ...99 H6
Caroline Rd MOS/BIL B13 .125 K1
Caroline St CBHAMNW B1 ..6 C2
  DUDS DY2 ....85 J6
  WBROM B70 ....70 F8
Carpenter Gld HALE B63 .103 H6
Carpenter Rd EDG B15 ..106 F6
Carpenters Ct BHTH/HG B12 * .107 J5
Carpenter's Rd LOZ/NWT B19 .89 G6
Carpet Trades Wy KIDD DY10 * .138 D6
Carrick Cl BLOX/PEL WS3 .25 L8
Carriers Cl WSLW WS2 ...52 D4
Carriers Fold WMBN WV5 * .64 F6
Carrington Rd DARL/WED WS10 .69 H3
Carrisbrooke Av
  WALM/CURD B76 ......69 H3
Carroway Head Hl
  MGN/WHC B75 ....58 A1
Carrs La CBHAMNE B4 ...7 H5
Carsal Ct RCOVN/BALC/EX CV7 .116 B8
Carshalton Gv KGSTG B44 .71 L3
Cartbridge Crs BLOX/PEL WS3 .39 L8
Cartbridge La BLOX/PEL WS3 .39 L8
Cartbridge La South
  RUSH/SHEL WS4 ....39 L8
Carter Av COVS CV3 ....155 L5
Carter Rd COVS CV3 ....155 L5
  DUNHL/THL/PER WV6 ...35 M8
  GTB/HAM B43 ....70 D2
Carters Cl BRGRVE B60 ..191 M6
  WALM/CURD B76 ......73 J3
Carters Gn WBROM B70 ..86 F1
Carters Hurst STETCH B33 .109 M4
Carter's La RMSLY B62 ..104 A8
Carthorse La REDW B97 .193 M8
Carthusian Rd COVS CV3 .155 G5
Cartland Rd BVILLE B30 .124 F6

  SPARK B11 ....108 A6
Cartmel Cl COVW CV5 ...153 L1
Cart's La ATHST CV9 ....62 A3
The Cartway
  DUNHL/THL/PER WV6 ...48 B1
Cartwright Gdns OLDBY B69 .86 A3
Cartwright Rd MGN/WHC B75 .57 G2
Cartwright St BKHL/PFLD WV2 .3 G9
Carvell Cl COVW CV5 ...132 F4
Carver Cl COVE CV2 ....135 K5
Carver Ct TPTN/OCK DY4 * .67 L4
Carver Gdns STRBR DY8 .119 J5
Carver St WSNGN B18 ...6 A2
Cascade Cl COVS CV3 ...155 L7
Casern Vw MGN/WHC B75 .57 L7
Casewell Rd KGSWFD DY6 ..83 G5
Casey Av ERDW/GRVHL B23 .72 B5
Cash Joynson Av
  DARL/WED WS10 ....52 A5
Cashmore Av RLSS CV31 .206 D8
Cashmore Rd BDWTH CV12 .116 A4
  KNWTH CV8 ....198 A1
Casia Gv KNWTH CV8 ...198 A1
Caslon Crs STRBR DY8 ..119 H1
Caslon Rd HALE B63 ....103 G7
Caspian Wy COVE CV2 ...135 L5
Cassandra Cl BRLYHL DY5 .84 A4
  TLHL/CAN CV4 ....180 B2
Cassowary Rd
  BFLD/HDSWWD B20 .....88 D2
Castello Dr CBROM B36 ..92 B4
The Castings BILS/COS WV14 .67 H3
Castlebridge Rd WNSFLD WV11 .37 L6
Castle Cl BRWNH WS8 ...26 D3
  CDYHTH B64 ....103 M4
  COVS CV3 ....155 M4
  HIA/OLT B92 ....127 M4
  RCOVN/BALC/EX CV7 ..114 C3
  TAM/AM/WIL B77 ......46 C1
  WWCK CV34 ....205 H1
Castle Crs CBROM B36 ...92 A5
Castlecroft CNCK/NC WS11 .17 J8
Castle Cft LGLYGN/QTN B68 .105 J8
Castlecroft Av BDMR/CCFT WV3 .48 C1
Castlecroft Gdns
  BDMR/CCFT WV3 ......48 D5
Castlecroft La BDMR/CCFT WV3 .48 D5
Castlecroft Rd BDMR/CCFT WV3 .48 C5
Castle Dr CSHL/WTROR B46 .93 H7
  NUNW/HART CV10 ......97 J6
  SHHTH WV12 ....37 M8
Castle Dyke LICH WS13 ..20 F6
Castleford Gv SPARK B11 * .126 A1
Castleford Rd SPARK B11 .126 A1
Castlegate Rd ALDR WS9 .40 E2
Castlegate Dr DUDN DY1 ..85 J3
Castlegate Wy DUDN DY1 ..85 J3
Castle Gn KNWTH CV8 ...179 H8
Castle Grounds DUDN DY1 * .85 J3
Castlehall TAM/AM/WIL B77 .46 E3
Castle Hl DUDN DY1 ....85 J3
  KNWTH CV8 ....179 H8
Castle Hts CDYHTH B64 * .103 M4
Castle La BEWD DY12 ...163 G2
  CSHL/WTROR B46 .....94 D5
  HIA/OLT B92 ....127 L4
  WWCK CV34 ....205 J7
Castle Mill Rd DUDN DY1 .85 G1
Castle Ms RUGBYN/HIL CV21 .186 F2
Castle Mound Wy
  RRUGBY CV23 ....161 H3
Castle Pl COV CV1 * 9 J1
Castle Rd ALDR WS9 ....40 E8
  BVILLE B30 ....145 K1
  KIDD DY10 ....138 E1
  KIDDW DY11 ....138 E1
  KNWTH CV8 ....179 H8
  NUNW/HART CV10 ......79 M4
  TPTN/OCK DY4 ....67 J8
  WLNHL WV13 ....51 J3
Castle Rd East LGLYGN/QTN B68 .105 J8
Castle Rd West
  LGLYGN/QTN B68 .....105 G5
Castle St BILS/COS WV14 .67 G5
  COV CV1 ....9 J2
  DARL/WED WS10 ....52 B5
  DUDS DY2 ....85 H4
  RUGBYN/HIL CV21 ....186 F2
  TPTN/OCK DY4 ....67 J8
  WBROM B70 ....86 B7
  WOLV WV1 ....3 G5
Castleton Rd BLOX/PEL WS3 .39 G2
  KGSTG B44 ....71 J2
Castleton Vw DUDS DY2 ..85 G8
Castle Vw DUDN DY1 ....85 J3
  NUNW/HART CV10 ......79 M4
Castle View Cl DARL/WED WS10 .67 L1
Castle View Rd DARL/WED WS10 .67 L1
Caswell Rd RLSS CV31 ..206 F7
Cat & Kittens La WOLVN WV10 .22 C7
Cater Dr WALM/CURD B76 .73 K3
Caterham Dr STRBR DY8 .101 J2
Catesby Dr KGSWFD DY6 ..83 H5
Catesby Rd COVN CV6 ...133 M5
  RUGBYS/DCH CV22 ....187 H4
  SHLY B90 ....147 H4
Cateswell Rd HLGN/YWD B28 .126 D3
Cathcart Rd STRBR DY8 ..101 J8
Cathedral Av KIDDW DY11 .137 L7
Cathedral Rd LICH WS13 ..20 D3
Cathel Dr PBAR/PBCH B42 ..70 E6
Catherine De Barnes La
  HIA/OLT B92 ....129 G7
Catherine Dr SCFLD/BOLD B73 .56 F2
Catherine Rd BILS/COS WV14 .66 E4
Catherine St AST/WIT B6 .89 L6
  COV CV1 ....9 L1
Catherton Cl TPTN/OCK DY4 .68 A3
Cathiron La RRUGBY CV23 .158 D2
Catholic La SEDG DY3 ...66 A6
Catisfield Crs CDSL WV8 ..34 C2
Cat La BKDE/SHDE B34 ...92 A6
Caton Gv HLGN/YWD B28 .126 C6
Cato St North VAUX/NECH B7 .90 A1
Cato St VAUX/NECH B7 ...90 M1
Catshill Rd BRWNH WS8 ..26 E6
Catterall Dr MGN/WHC B75 .57 L7
Cattell Dr BORD B9 ....108 A4
  WWCK CV34 ....205 J7
Cattells Gv VAUX/NECH B7 .90 A7
Cattermole Gv GTB/HAM B43 .71 G2
Cattock Hurst Dr
  CSCFLD/WYGN B72 .....73 H6

Causeway BLKHTH/ROWR B65 .104 A3
Causeway Green Rd
  LGLYGN/QTN B68 .....104 F2
Causeway Rd BILS/COS WV14 .67 H5
The Causeway YDLY B25 .109 H6
Causey Farm Rd HALE B63 .121 G5
Cavalier Circ NUN CV11 .99 G1
Cavandale Av KGSTG B44 .71 J4
Cavan's Cl CNCK/NC WS11 .16 C1
Cavans Wy COVS CV3 ...156 E5
Cave Cl RUGBYS/DCH CV22 .185 L5
Cavell Closet WSLW WS2 .4 C3
Cavell Rd BNTWD WS7 ...19 J5
  DUDS DY2 ....85 K4
Cavendish CRTAM B79 ...31 J1
Cavendish Cl BRGRVE B60 .169 G4
  HWK/WKHTH B38 ......145 M4
  KGSWFD DY6 ....101 H1
Cavendish Gdns WSLW WS2 .52 E1
Cavendish Rd
  HAG/WOL DY9 ....140 D1
  TLHL/CAN CV4 ....153 D1
  WOLV WV1 ....50 F4
  WSLW WS2 ....38 D3
Cavendish Wy ALDR WS9 ..41 L8
Caversham Cl NUN CV11 ..81 K6
Caversham Rd KGSTG B44 .71 J3
Cawdon Gv DOR/KN B93 ..175 J3
Cawdor Crs LDYWD/EDGR B16 .106 C4
Cawnpore Rd COVN CV6 ..133 M3
Cawston La RUGBYS/DCH CV22 .185 L6
Cawston Wy
  RUGBYS/DCH CV22 ....186 A5
Cawthorne Cl COV CV1 ..9 K2
Caxton Gv KGSTG B44 ...72 A4
Caxton St CNCK/NC WS11 .16 C4
Caynham Cl REDE B98 ..203 H1
Caynham Rd RIDG/WDGT B32 .122 F5
Cayton Gv ERDW/GRVHL B23 .72 D7
Cecil Dr OLDBY B69 ....86 B5
Cecil Rd ERDE/BCHGN B24 .90 D2
  SLYOAK B29 ....125 G4
Cecil St CBHAMNE B4 ...7 G1
  CNCK/NC WS11 ....17 G1
  RUSH/SHEL WS4 ......53 K2
  STRBR DY8 ....101 K8
Cecily Rd COVS CV3 ....155 H6
Cedar Av BILS/COS WV14 .66 E6
  BRWNH WS8 ....26 E7
  CBROM B36 ....92 A6
  WWCK CV34 ....182 F4
Cedar Bridge Cft
  FOAKS/STRLY B74 ....56 E5
Cedar Cl BNTWD WS7 ....18 E7
  BVILLE B30 ....124 F7
  DSYBK/YTR WS5 ......69 M1
  HEDN WS12 ....12 E4
  LGLYGN/QTN B68 .....105 K8
  LICHS WS14 ....21 K6
  POL/KGSB/FAZ B78 ...45 L2
  RLSN CV32 ....206 E1
  STRBR DY8 ....119 G3
  STRPT DY13 ....119 G3
Cedar Crs KIDDW DY11 ..138 A7
Cedar Dr BRGRVE B60 ...191 L4
  CRTAM B79 ....31 L5
  ERDE/BCHGN B24 .....73 G8
  FOAKS/STRLY B74 ....55 J4
  KIDDW DY11 ....138 A7
  NFLD/LBR B31 ....144 F6
Cedar Gv BDMR/CCFT WV3 .49 K6
  CDSL WV8 ....34 F2
  GTWY WS6 ....25 J4
  WWCK CV34 ....205 L4
Cedarhill Dr CNCK/NC WS11 .16 D3
Cedarhurst RIDG/WDGT B32 .105 J8
  SOLH B91 ....148 A1
Cedar Park Rd REDW B97 .202 B1
  SHHTH WV12 ....38 A6
Cedar Ri STRPT DY13 ...188 C1
Cedar Rd BNTWD WS7 ...18 E7
  BVILLE B30 ....124 F7
  DARL/WED WS10 ......68 D2
  DUDN DY1 ....84 D7
  NUNW/HART CV10 .....80 B7
  REDW B97 ....202 A1
  TPTN/OCK DY4 ....67 H8
  WLNHL WV13 ....51 J3
Cedars Av ACGN B27 ...127 G1
  COVN CV6 ....114 B8
  KGSWFD DY6 ....101 H1
  WMBN WV5 ....64 E8
Cedars Rd RCOVN/BALC/EX CV7 .116 F4
The Cedars
  DUNHL/THL/PER WV6 * .35 H4
  DUNHL/THL/PER WV6 ...49 K2
  YDLY B25 ....109 J4
Cedar Ter BRGRVE B60 ..191 L4
Cedar Wy NFLD/LBR B31 .144 D4
  WNSFLD WV11 ....37 G6
Cedarwood FOAKS/STRLY B74 .56 F5
Cedarwood Cft PBAR/PBCH B42 .70 D5
Cedar Wood Dr
  RCOVN/BALC/EX CV7 ..151 M2
Cedar Wood Rd SEDG DY3 .84 A1
Cedric Cl COVS CV3 ....156 A8
Celandine RRUGBY CV23 .161 H5
  TAM/AM/WIL B77 .....46 A2
Celandine Cl STRBR DY8 .101 G1
Celandine Rd COVE CV2 .135 K5
  DUDN DY1 ....84 E1
The Celandines WMBN WV5 .64 C2
Celandine Wy BDWTH CV12 .116 C3
Celbury Wy GTB/HAM B43 .70 D5
Celeste Rd BRGRVE B60 .192 A4
Celtic Rd CNCK/NC WS11 .16 C2
Celts Cl BLKHTH/ROWR B65 .104 A2
Cemetery La NUNW/HART CV10 .79 M4
  WSNGN B18 ....88 F8
Cemetery Rd CNCK/NC WS11 .16 B1
  HAG/WOL DY9 ....102 B8
  LGLYGN/QTN B68 .....87 G7
  REDW B97 ....202 B2
  SMTHWKW B67 ....105 L1
  WLNHL WV13 ....51 L2
  WSLW WS2 ....52 D5
Cemetery St BILS/COS WV14 .51 G6
  GTWY WS6 ....25 G6
Cemetery Wy BLOX/PEL WS3 .38 F4
Centaur Rd COVW CV5 ...154 D3
Centenary Cl NFLD/LBR B31 .144 E4
Centenary Dr HDSW B21 ..88 C4
Centenary Rd TLHL/CAN CV4 .154 B6
Centenary Sq CBHAMNW B1 .6 D5
Centenary Wy COVS CV3 .157 J3
Central Ar WOLV WV1 ...2 E3

Central Av BILS/COS WV14 .....51 J6
BLKHTH/ROWR B65 .....104 A3
CDYHTH B64 .....103 H6
CNCK/NC WS11 .....12 D8
COVE CV2 .....155 L3
HAG/WOL DY9 .....120 C2
NFLD/LBR B31 .....144 D5
NUN CV11 .....98 D4
RLSS CV31 .....206 D7
TPTN/OCK DY4 .....67 K7
Central Bvd HOCK/TIA B94 .....174 D5
RCOVN/BALC/EX CV7 .....115 M8
Central Cl BLOX/PEL WS3 .....38 E4
Central Dr BILS/COS WV14 .....67 H6
BLOX/PEL WS3 .....38 E4
SEDG DY3 .....84 B3
Central Gv ACGN B27 .....127 G3
Central Pk DUDS DY2 * 103 J2
Central Park Dr RUGBY CV23 .....161 H5
WNSGN B18 .....88 D8
Central Rd BRGRVE B60 .....191 L4
Central Sq ERDE/BCHGN B24 * 90 E1
Central Wy BRLYHL DY5 .....102 D2
Centre La HALE B63 .....121 M2
The Centreway
ALE/KHTH/YWD B14 .....147 H1
Centurion Cl CSHL/WTROR B46 .....93 J4
Centurion Wy TAM/AM/WIL B77 .....46 F7
Century Pk BORD B9 .....108 A3
Century Rd OLDBY B69 .....86 E5
Ceolmund Crs
CHWD/FDBR/MGN B37 .....110 D2
Chace Av COVS CV3 .....155 M8
Chaceley Cl COVN CV6 .....135 L5
Chaceley Gv ERDW/GRVHL B23 * 72 B6
Chadbury Cft CDSL WV8 .....148 F5
Chadbury Rd HALE B63 .....122 A4
Chadcote Wy BRGRVW B61 .....168 D4
Chaddersley Cl RBRY B45 .....143 K5
Chaddesley Cl OLDBY B69 .....86 B8
REDE B98 .....202 D4
Chaddesley Dr HAG/WOL DY9 .....119 M4
Chaddesley Rd HALE B63 .....121 K3
HWK/WKHTH B38 .....145 H4
KIDD DY10 .....138 E8
Chadley Cl SOLH B91 .....127 L7
Chad Rd BILS/COS WV14 .....66 F6
EDG B15 .....106 D5
Chad's Ditch HEDN WS12 .....12 C3
Chadsmoor Ter VAUX/NECH B7 .....89 M7
Chadstone Cl SHLY B90 .....148 F7
Chadswell Hts LICH WS13 .....21 J4
Chad Valley Cl HRBN B17 .....106 B3
Chadwell Dr HIA/OLT B92 .....126 F7
Chadwell Gdns CDSL WV8 .....34 C1
Chadwich La HAG/WOL DY9 .....142 C7
Chadwick Av RBRY B45 .....143 M7
Chadwick Cl COVW CV5 .....153 M3
ETTPK/GDPK/PENN WV4 * 49 L7
Chadwick La DOR/KN B93 .....176 F3
STRPT DY13 .....189 H4
Chadwick Mnr DOR/KN B93 * 176 E4
Chadwick Ms DOR/KN B93 .....176 E4
Chadwick Rd MGN/WHC B75 .....57 K8
Chadwick Ms REDE B98 .....202 E6
Chadworth Av DOR/KN B93 .....175 J7
Chaffcombe Rd
LGN/SDN/BHAMAIR B26 .....110 A7
Chaffinch Cl HEDN WS12 .....16 F2
SEDG DY3 .....66 B4
Chaffinch Dr CBROM B36 .....92 F6
KIDD DY10 .....164 D5
Chaffinch Rd HAG/WOL DY9 .....120 A2
Chain Wk LOZ/NWT B19 .....89 H5
Chalcot Dr HEDN WS12 .....12 D6
Chalcot Gv BFLD/HDSWWD B20 .....70 D4
Chaldon Cl COVEN WV9 .....35 L3
Chale Gv ALE/KHTH/YWD B14 .....146 D1
Chalfield CRTAM B79 .....31 H7
Chalfont Av CNCK/NC WS11 .....16 A3
Chalfont Cl BDWTH CV12 .....116 C1
COVW CV5 .....153 M1
Chalfont Pl HAG/WOL DY9 .....120 C3
Chalford Rd ERDW/GRVHL B23 .....72 A5
Chalford Wy SHLY B90 .....148 A5
Chalgrove Av HWK/WKHTH B38 .....145 J4
Chalgrove Crs SOLH B91 .....148 F4
Challenge Cl COV CV1 .....9 G1
Challenor Av WOLVN WV10 .....36 C2
Challenor Av WMLVN WV13 .....51 H3
Chalybeate Cl RBRY B45 .....143 L5
Chamberlain Cl OLDBY B69 .....86 B5
RLSN CV32 .....199 J8
Chamberlain Crs SHLY B90 .....147 L3
Chamberlaine St BDWTH CV12 .....116 F1
RUGBYN/HIL CV21 .....187 M5
Chamberlain's La
ETTPK/GDPK/PENN WV4 .....65 J2
Chamberlain Sq CBHAMNW B3 .....6 E5
Chamberlain Wk
CSHL/WTROR B46 * 93 K6
SMTHWK B66 * 87 L7
Chance Cft ETTPK/GDPK/PENN WV4 .....104 F5
Chance Flds RLSS CV31 .....207 K7
Chancellor's Cl EDG B15 .....106 C5
TLHL/CAN CV4 .....180 B1
Chancel Wy RMSLY B62 .....104 A8
Chancery La NUN CV11 .....79 M6
Chancery La BRLYHL DY5 .....102 D2
Chanders Rd WWCK CV34 .....205 H4
Chandler Dr
ETTPK/GDPK/PENN WV4 .....65 H2
Chandlers Cl COVEN WV9 .....35 L4
REDW B97 .....202 B7
WNSGN B18 .....88 D8
Chandlers Dr TAM/AM/WIL B77 .....32 F8
Chandlers Keep BRWNH WS8 .....26 D7
Chandos St COVE CV2 .....155 L2
NUN CV11 .....98 C1
RLSN CV32 .....206 D1
Change Brook Cl NUN CV11 .....81 K5
Channon Dr BRLYHL DY5 .....102 B5
Chanston Av
ALE/KHTH/YWD B14 .....146 C1
Chanterelle Gdns
ETTPK/GDPK/PENN WV4 .....65 L1
Chantrey Crs BILS/COS WV14 .....51 K6
GTB/HAM B43 .....71 H1
The Chantries COV CV1 .....9 K1
Chantry Av BLOX/PEL WS3 .....39 H5
Chantry Cl HLYWD B47 .....146 F5
Chantry Dr RMSLY B62 .....104 B7
Chantry Heath Crs DOR/KN B93 .....149 M5
Chantry Rd HDSW B21 .....88 D5
MOS/BIL B13 .....107 L2
The Chantry WWCK CV34 .....205 L6
Chapel Ash WOLV WV1 .....2 C5
Chapel Ash Island WOLV WV1 .....2 C5
Chapel Av BRWNH WS8 .....26 C3
Chapel Cl CDYHTH B64 .....103 H6
WMBN WV5 .....64 D8

Chapel Ct KIDD DY10 .....138 E4
RLSN CV32 * 206 E5
Chapel Dr BRWNH WS8 .....26 C3
HLYWD B47 .....172 D2
RCOVN/BALC/EX CV7 .....151 M5
Chapel Farm Cl COVS CV3 .....156 A7
Chapelfield Ms RBRY B45 .....143 K7
Chapel Fields Rd HIA/OLT B92 .....127 K3
Chapel Gn WLNHL WV13 .....51 M3
Chapel Hl KIDD DY10 .....138 E4
Chapel House La HALE B63 .....103 G8
Chapelhouse Rd
CHWD/FDBR/MGN B37 .....110 D3
Chapel House St BHTH/HG B12 * 7 K7
Chapel La ALVE B48 .....194 D1
CDSL WV8 .....34 D2
DUDN DY1 .....84 F8
HAG/WOL DY9 .....142 B6
HLYWD B47 .....172 C3
HOCK/TIA B94 .....176 A6
KNWTH CV8 .....182 E3
LICHS WS14 .....20 F7
RCOVN/BALC/EX CV7 .....117 M7
REDE B98 .....195 K5
RMSLY B62 .....121 G7
RUGE WS15 .....18 E1
SEDG DY3 .....82 A1
SLYOAK B29 .....124 C3
STRPT DY13 .....188 C5
Chapelon TAM/AM/WIL B77 .....46 E3
Chapel Rw WWCK CV34 .....205 J6
Chapel Sq GTWY WS6 .....24 B2
Chapel St BDWTH CV12 .....116 F2
BILS/COS WV14 .....67 K1
BKHL/PFLD WV2 .....50 B6
BLOX/PEL WS3 .....39 H5
BNTWD WS7 .....18 B3
BRGRVE B60 .....191 L3
BRLYHL DY5 .....84 A6
BRLYHL DY5 .....102 B3
BRWNH WS8 .....26 C3
CBHAMNE B4 .....7 J4
COV CV1 .....8 E3
DARL/WED WS10 .....68 C2
DUDS DY2 .....103 H1
HAG/WOL DY9 .....102 D3
HAG/WOL DY9 .....119 L8
HALE B63 .....121 L2
HDSW B21 .....88 B6
HEDN WS12 .....17 J4
KGSWFD DY6 .....82 F5
KIDD DY11 .....138 B7
NUN CV11 .....99 G1
OLDBY B69 .....86 C5
REDW B97 .....202 B4
RLSS CV31 .....206 E6
RRUGBY CV23 .....185 L1
RUGBYN/HIL CV21 .....186 E2
STRBR DY8 .....101 H2
STRBR DY8 .....119 L1
TPTN/OCK DY4 .....67 J8
WBROM B70 .....68 F8
WMBN WV5 .....64 D8
WWCK CV34 .....205 J6
Chapel Vw SMTHWK B67 .....105 K1
Chapel Wk BRGRVW B60 .....191 L3
BVILLE B30 .....145 L2
SEDG DY3 .....84 A3
Chapelwood Gv
PBAR/PBCH B42 * 71 H8
Chapel Yd COVE CV2 * 117 M8
Chaplain Rd HEDN WS12 .....17 J3
Chapman Cl RLSS CV31 .....207 J8
Chapman Rd SMITH B10 .....108 A5
Chapman's Hi BRGRVW B61 .....142 F5
Chapmans Pas CBHAMW B1 * 6 C7
Chapman St WBROM B70 .....86 F2
Chapter House WBROM B70 * 68 F2
Chard Rd COVS CV3 .....156 B5
Charfield Cl BVILLE B30 .....124 B6
Charford Rd BRGRVE B60 .....191 K5
Charingworth Dr
RWWCK/WEL CV35 .....204 C3
Charingworth Rd HIA/OLT B92 .....128 A2
Chariot Wy RUGBYN/HIL CV21 .....160 E6
Charity Rd RCOVN/BALC/EX CV7 .....115 K6
Charlbury Av
CHWD/FDBR/MGN B37 .....110 D3
Charlbury Crs
LGN/SDN/BHAMAIR B26 .....109 K5
Charlbury Ms RLSS CV31 .....207 J2
Charlecote Cft SHLY B90 .....148 A5
Charlecote Dr DUDN DY1 .....84 C2
ERDW/GRVHL B23 .....72 C6
Charlecote Gdns RLSS CV31 .....207 H3
SCFLD/BOLD B73 .....72 E5
Charlecote Ri WLNHL WV13 .....51 K4
Charlecote Rd COVN CV6 .....133 L3
Charlecote Wk NUN CV11 .....99 K5
Charlecott Cl MOS/BIL B13 .....126 B6
Charlemont Av HHTH/SAND B71 .....68 E1
Charlemont Cl DSYBK/YTR WS5 .....54 A7
Charlemont Crs HHTH/SAND B71 .....68 F1
Charlemonte Cl HEDN WS12 .....17 H2
Charlemont Gdns
DSYBK/YTR WS5 .....53 M7
Charlemont Rd DSYBK/YTR WS5 .....53 M7
HHTH/SAND B71 .....68 F1
Charles Av BLKHTH/ROWR B65 .....104 A1
ETTPK/GDPK/PENN WV4 .....49 M8
KIDD DY10 .....138 E4
WNSFLD WV11 .....37 K1
Charles Crs BLOX/PEL WS3 .....25 L8
Charlesdale Dr ALDR WS9 .....54 F1
Charles Dr VAUX/NECH B7 .....89 M7
Charles Eaton Rd BDWTH CV12 .....116 F2
Charles Edward Rd
LGN/SDN/BHAMAIR B26 .....109 H7
Charlesfield Rd
RUGBYS/DCH CV22 .....186 E5
Charles Foster St
DARL/WED WS10 .....52 A1
Charles Gardner Rd RLSS CV31 .....207 G3
Charles Henry St DIG/EDG B5 .....107 J5
Charles Holland St WLNHL WV13 .....51 M3
Charles Rd AST/WIT B6 .....89 L4
ATHST CV9 .....63 K6
BFLD/HDSWWD B20 .....88 G4
BRLYHL DY5 .....102 E3
HALE B63 .....121 K1
SMITH B10 .....108 C5
SOLH B91 .....148 D3
STRBR DY8 .....119 L5
Charlton Pl COV CV1 .....9 G3
Charles St ATHST CV9 .....61 G8
COV CV1 .....9 J2
KIDD DY10 .....138 D7
NUN CV11 .....98 E5
RCOVN/BALC/EX CV7 .....96 E5
REDW B97 .....202 A4
RUGBYS/DCH CV22 .....186 D3
SMTHWK B66 .....88 A6
WBROM B70 .....68 E2
WLNHL WV13 .....52 A3

WSLW WS2 .....4 C3
WWCK CV34 .....205 L6
Charles Wk BLKHTH/ROWR B65 .....86 A3
Charles Warren Cl
RUGBYN/HIL CV21 .....186 F2
Charles Wesley Ct
BDMR/CCFT WV3 * 49 L6
Charlesworth Av SHLY B90 .....148 F7
Charleville Rd LOZ/NWT B19 .....89 H1
Charlewood Rd COVN CV6 .....133 M5
Charlock Dr CNCK/NC WS11 .....17 G2
Charlotte Cl TPTN/OCK DY4 .....85 L3
Charlotte Rd BVILLE B30 .....124 E7
DARL/WED WS10 .....68 A4
EDG B15 .....107 G5
Charlotte St CBHAMNW B3 .....6 C4
DUDN DY1 .....84 F5
RLSS CV31 .....206 D7
RUGBYN/HIL CV21 .....186 F2
Charlton Dr CDYHTH B64 .....103 H6
Charlton La KIDD DY11 .....138 A6
Charlton Rd KGSTG B44 .....71 L6
Charlton St BRLYHL DY5 .....101 L2
DUDN DY1 .....84 F4
Charminster Av YDLY B25 .....109 H5
Charminster Dr COVS CV3 .....181 H1
Charnley Dr MGN/WHC B75 .....57 J3
Charnwood Av
NUNW/HART CV10 .....98 A3
Charnwood Cl BILS/COS WV14 .....67 M2
BRLYHL DY5 .....101 M6
HEDN WS12 .....17 G1
LICH WS13 .....21 G4
RBRY B45 .....143 M2
Charnwood Ct HAG/WOL DY9 .....120 C3
Charnwood Dr
NUNW/HART CV10 .....79 L3
Charnwood Rd BILS/COS WV14 .....67 M2
PBAR/PBCH B42 .....70 D2
Charnwood Wy RLSN CV32 .....207 G2
Charter Ap WWCK CV34 .....205 H7
Charter Av TLHL/CAN CV4 .....153 H6
Charter Cl CNCK/NC WS11 .....25 J1
Charter Crs CDYHTH B64 .....103 M5
Charterfield Dr HEDN WS12 .....17 G4
KGSWFD DY6 .....83 H5
Charterhouse Dr SOLH B91 .....148 F4
Charterhouse Rd COV CV1 .....9 K5
Charter Rd RUGBYS/DCH CV22 .....187 J5
TPTN/OCK DY4 .....68 A4
Charters Av CDSL WV8 .....34 F4
The Charters LICH WS13 .....20 F7
Charter St BRLYHL DY5 .....84 C8
Chartist Rd WASH/WDE B8 .....90 B7
Chartley Cl DUNHL/THL/PER WV6 .....48 D1
Chartley Rd ERDW/GRVHL B23 .....90 A4
HHTH/SAND B71 .....69 H7
The Chartway BLOX/PEL WS3 .....39 M1
Chartwell CRTAM B79 .....31 H6
Chartwell Cl DUDN DY1 .....66 F7
NUN CV11 .....99 K4
Chartwell Dr FOAKS/STRLY B74 .....56 F1
SHLY B90 .....148 B8
WMBN WV5 .....64 D8
WOLVN WV10 .....36 C4
Charwelton Dr
RUGBYN/HIL CV21 .....161 J7
Chase Av GTWY WS6 .....24 C2
Chase Cl NUNW/HART CV10 .....81 H7
Chase Gv ERDE/BCHGN B24 .....73 H7
Chaselands KNWTH CV8 .....18 B6
Chase La KNWTH CV8 .....178 D7
Chase Rd CNCK/NC WS11 .....16 A3
Chaseley Av CNCK/NC WS11 .....16 A3
Chaseley Gdns BNTWD WS7 .....19 C6
Chaseley Rd BNTWD WS7 .....19 C6
The Chase Link WNSB8 * 26 E4
Chasepool Rd SEDG DY3 .....82 A6
Chase Rd BLOX/PEL WS3 .....38 E5
BNTWD WS7 .....18 B4
BRWNH WS8 .....26 E4
SEDG DY3 .....83 M4
Chaseside Dr HEDN WS12 .....16 F2
The Chase DUNHL/THL/PER WV6 .....35 M7
WMBN WV5 .....64 D8
WOLVN WV10 .....36 C4
Chase Vw
ETTPK/GDPK/PENN WV4 .....66 C3
Chasewater Wy CNCK/NC WS11 .....17 K8
Chater Dr WALM/CURD B76 .....73 L4
Chaters Cl TPTN/OCK DY4 .....67 J8
Chatham Cl COVS CV3 * 156 A5
Chatham Rd NFLD/LBR B31 .....144 E2
Chatsworth CSCFLD/WYGN B72 .....73 H6
SHHTH WV12 .....37 M8
SHLY B90 .....148 B8
Chatsworth Crs
RUSH/SHEL WS4 .....40 B6
Chatsworth Dr NUN CV11 .....99 K3
Chatsworth Gdns RLSS CV31 .....207 H1
Chatsworth Gv KNWTH CV8 .....180 A8
RLSS CV31 .....207 H1
Chatsworth Ms STRBR DY8 * 101 J8
Chatsworth Ri COVS CV3 .....155 J8
Chatsworth Rd BDWTH CV12 .....116 B4
Chattaway Dr
RCOVN/BALC/EX CV7 .....151 M7
Chattaway St VAUX/NECH B7 .....90 A6
Chatterton Av LICH WS13 .....20 C7
Chattle Hl CSHL/WTROR B46 .....93 J3
Chattock Av SOLH B91 .....149 J1
Chattock Cl CBROM B36 .....92 C5
Chatwell Gv SLYOAK B29 .....123 M3
Chatwin Pl BILS/COS WV14 .....67 J2
Chatwin St SMTHWK B66 .....87 K6
Chatwins Whf TPTN/OCK DY4 * 67 M5
Chaucer Av SEDG DY3 .....65 L8
SHHTH WV12 .....38 C5
TPTN/OCK DY4 .....67 M5
Chaucer Cl BILS/COS WV14 .....67 M1
CRTAM B79 .....31 L7
ERDW/GRVHL B23 .....89 M2
LICHS WS14 .....30 E4
STRBR DY8 .....101 L5
Chaucer Dr BNTWD WS7 .....18 E4
NUNW/HART CV10 .....97 L1
Chaucer Gv ACGN B27 .....126 F4
Chaucer Rd BLOX/PEL WS3 .....38 F5
BRGRVE B60 .....191 M1
RUGBYS/DCH CV22 .....186 D2
Chauntry Pl COV CV1 .....9 G3
Chauson Gv SOLH B91 .....148 E5
Chavasse Rd CSCFLD/WYGN B72 .....73 G2
Chawner Cl BNTWD WS7 .....18 C4
Chawn Hl HAG/WOL DY9 .....120 A2
Chawn Hill Cl HAG/WOL DY9 .....120 A2
Chawn Park Dr HAG/WOL DY9 .....120 A2
Chaynes Gv STECH B33 .....110 B3
Chaytor Rd POL/KGSB/FAZ B78 .....47 L5
Cheadle Dr ERDW/GRVHL B23 .....72 B3
Cheadle Dr COVN CV6 .....134 C1
PENK ST19 .....10 D1
Cheam Cl COVN CV6 .....134 E4

Cheam Gdns
DUNHL/THL/PER WV6 .....35 J5
Cheapside BHTH/HG B12 .....7 K8
STRPT DY13 .....188 D5
WSLW WS2 .....51 L4
Cheatham St VAUX/NECH B7 .....90 A7
Checketts St WSLW WS2 * 4 B5
Checkley Cl SHLY B90 .....147 L1
Checkley Cft WALM/CURD B76 .....73 K5
Cheddar Rd BHTH/HG B12 .....107 J7
Chedworth Cl REDE B98 .....195 G8
SLYOAK B29 .....123 M6
Cheedon Dr DOR/KN B93 .....175 J3
Chelford Cl PENK ST19 .....10 E4
Chelford Crs KGSWFD DY6 .....101 J3
Chell Cl PENK ST19 .....10 D6
Chells Gv MOS/BIL B13 .....125 M8
Chelmar Cl CBROM B36 .....92 D5
Chelmar Dr BRLYHL DY5 .....83 J7
Chelmarsh COVN CV6 .....134 C1
Chelmarsh Av BDMR/CCFT WV3 .....48 C5
Chelmarsh Cl REDE B98 .....195 G8
Chelmorton Rd PBAR/PBCH B42 .....71 G5
Chelmscote Rd SOLH B91 .....127 K4
Chelmsley Cir
CHWD/FDBR/MGN B37 .....110 D3
Chelmsley Gv STECH B33 .....110 B3
Chelmsley La
CHWD/FDBR/MGN B37 .....110 D5
Chelmsley Rd
CHWD/FDBR/MGN B37 .....110 C3
Chelney Wk COVS CV3 .....156 E4
Chelsea Cl NUN CV11 .....81 K6
RIDG/WDGT B32 .....123 K1
Chelsea Wy KGSWFD DY6 .....83 G7
Chelsey Rd COVE CV2 .....135 J3
Chelston Dr
DUNHL/THL/PER WV6 .....49 H7
Chelston Rd NFLD/LBR B31 .....144 D3
Chelveston Crs SOLH B91 .....148 F4
Chelveston Rd COVN CV6 .....133 J4
Chelwood Gdns
ETTPK/GDPK/PENN WV4 .....50 C3
Chelwood Gv COVE CV2 .....135 J2
Chelworth Rd HWK/WKHTH B38 .....145 M3
Chem Rd BILS/COS WV14 .....50 F8
Chenet Wy CNCK/NC WS11 .....16 E3
Chenies Cl COVW CV5 .....153 M2
Cheniston Rd SHHTH WV12 .....38 A7
Chepstow Cl COVS CV3 .....156 A4
DUNHL/THL/PER WV6 .....48 D1
Chepstow Dr BRGRVW B61 .....168 D4
Chepstow Gv RBRY B45 .....143 M7
Chepstow Rd BLOX/PEL WS3 .....38 D7
WOLVN WV10 .....22 B8
Chepstow Vls BHTH/HG B12 * 107 H8
Chequerfield Dr
BDMR/CCFT WV3 .....49 L7
Chequers Av WMBN WV5 .....64 E3
Chequers Cl STRPT DY13 .....188 C5
Chequers Ct CNCK/NC WS11 .....17 L8
The Chequers LICH WS13 * 21 G5
Chequer St BDMR/CCFT WV3 * 49 L7
Cherhill Covert
ALE/KHTH/YWD B14 .....146 D1
Cherington Cl REDE B98 .....203 K4
Cherington Rd SLYOAK B29 .....124 C5
Cheriton Cl COVW CV5 .....154 D1
Cheriton Gv
DUNHL/THL/PER WV6 .....48 C2
Cherrington Dr GTWY WS6 .....24 D3
Cherrington Gdns
DUNHL/THL/PER WV6 .....48 C2
HAG/WOL DY9 .....120 A2
Cherrington Wy SOLH B91 .....148 F4
Cherry Bank HEDN WS12 .....13 G5
Cherrybrook Dr PENK ST19 .....10 D4
Cherrybrook Wy COVE CV2 .....135 G2
Cherry Cl ATHST CV9 .....77 G1
BEWD DY12 .....162 D5
BNTWD WS7 .....18 C4
COVN CV6 .....134 B3
Cherry Crs BRGRVW B61 .....191 M1
ERDE/BCHGN B24 .....90 D2
Cherry Dr BORD B9 .....107 M4
Cherryfield Cl NUNW/HART CV10 .....79 M3
Cherry Gn DUDN DY1 .....84 B3
Cherry Gv RUGBYS/DCH CV22 .....186 C5
SMTHWK B66 .....88 B3
STRBR DY8 .....119 J1
Cherry Hill Av RBRY B45 .....170 A5
Cherry Hill Dr RBRY B45 .....170 A5
Cherry Hill Rd RBRY B45 .....170 A5
Cherry La DARL/WED WS10 .....68 A4
RWWCK/WEL CV35 .....204 D1
SCFLD/BOLD B73 .....72 E5
SEDG DY3 .....82 F2
Cherry Lea BKDE/SHDE B34 .....91 M7
Cherry Orch CDYHTH B64 .....103 K4
KIDD DY10 .....138 D8
KNWTH CV8 .....179 L8
LICHS WS14 .....21 G6
Cherry Orchard Av HALE B63 .....103 K8
Cherry Orchard Crs HALE B63 .....103 K8
Cherry Orchard Dr
BRGRVW B61 .....191 J2
Cherry Orchard Rd
BFLD/HDSWWD B20 .....70 D8
Cherry Pit La REDE B98 .....195 L4
Cherry St BDMR/CCFT WV3 .....2 C7
CBHAM B2 .....7 G5
CRTAM B79 .....31 M8
STRBR DY8 .....119 J1
WWCK CV34 .....205 K6
Cherry Tree Av NUN CV11 .....80 C7
Cherry Tree Ct DSYBK/YTR WS5 .....54 F6
Cherry Tree Cft ACGN B27 .....126 F1
Cherrytree Ct HAG/WOL DY9 .....120 C2
Cherry Tree Gdns CDSL WV8 .....34 C1
Cherry Tree La CDSL WV8 .....34 C1
HALE B63 .....121 H4
Cherry Tree Rd CNCK/NC WS11 .....25 M1
HEDN WS12 .....12 D5
KGSWFD DY6 .....83 J5
REDW B97 .....202 C7
STRPT DY13 .....188 C5
Cherry Tree Wk CRTAM B79 .....31 L5
Cherry Wk HLYWD B47 .....146 F5
Cherry Wy KNWTH CV8 .....179 L8
Cherrywood Cl BILS/COS WV14 .....67 L6
Cherrywood Crs SOLH B91 .....148 E6
Cherrywood Gn BILS/COS WV14 .....51 L5
Cherrywood Rd BORD B9 .....108 B3
Cherrywood Rd
FOAKS/STRLY B74 .....56 B1
Cherwell TAM/AM/WIL B77 .....46 E1
Cherwell Cl PBAR/PBCH B42 .....71 G6
Cherwell Ri WOLVN WV10 .....3 L2

Cherwell Dr BRWNH WS8 .....25 M3
CBROM B36 .....92 D5
Cherwell Gdns AST/WIT B6 * 89 L2
Cherwell Wy RRUGBY CV23 .....185 M1
Chesford Crs COVN CV6 .....134 F3
WWCK CV34 .....205 M4
Chesham St RLSS CV31 .....206 F6
Cheshire Av SHLY B90 .....147 L2
Cheshire Cl RUGBYS/DCH CV22 .....186 A5
STRBR DY8 .....101 H5
Cheshire Gv
DUNHL/THL/PER WV6 .....48 C1
KIDD DY11 .....137 L6
Cheshire Rd AST/WIT B6 .....89 L2
SMTHWKW B67 .....105 L1
WSLW WS2 .....52 D3
Chesholme Rd COVN CV6 .....133 M2
Cheshunt Pl
ALE/KHTH/YWD B14 * 125 J5
Cheslyn Dr GTWY WS6 .....24 D3
Chessetts Gv MOS/BIL B13 .....125 L7
Chessetts Wood Rd
HOCK/TIA B94 .....176 A5
Chesshire Av STRPT DY13 .....188 C5
Chesshire Cl STRPT DY13 .....188 C5
Chester Av
DUNHL/THL/PER WV6 .....36 E3
KIDDW DY11 .....137 L6
LICH WS13 .....21 G2
SLYOAK B29 .....123 L3
Chester Cl
CHWD/FDBR/MGN B37 .....110 E3
CNCK/NC WS11 .....16 F4
LICH WS13 .....21 G2
WLNHL WV13 .....52 B3
Chesterfield Cl NFLD/LBR B31 .....144 F3
Chesterfield Ct ALDR WS9 * 40 D1
Chester Gdns SCFLD/BOLD B73 .....72 A3
Chester Ms LICHS WS14 .....21 G5
Chester Gdns SCFLD/BOLD B73 .....72 E5
Chester PI WSLW WS2 .....52 F4
Chester Ri BEWD DY12 * 137 H8
Chester Rd ALDR WS9 .....41 J4
BRWNH WS8 .....26 F8
CDYHTH B64 .....103 G5
CHWD/FDBR/MGN B37 .....110 F4
CSHL/WTROR B46 .....111 J4
CVALE B35 .....91 K2
FOAKS/STRLY B74 .....55 K2
HHTH/SAND B71 .....68 F4
LICHS WS14 .....30 F1
RCOVN/BALC/EX CV7 .....129 K1
SCFLD/BOLD B73 .....72 B4
Chester Rd North BRWNH WS8 .....26 F4
FOAKS/STRLY B74 .....55 L7
KIDD DY10 .....138 E5
Chester Rd South KIDD DY10 .....164 D2
Chester St AST/WIT B6 * 6 C1
COV CV1 .....8 C1
DUNHL/THL/PER WV6 .....2 D3
RUGBYN/HIL CV21 .....187 G5
Chester Ter BEWD DY12 * 137 H8
Chesterton Cl SOLH B91 .....127 J8
Chesterton Dr
NUNW/HART CV10 .....97 K1
RLSS CV31 .....206 F8
Chesterton Rd BHTH/HG B12 * 107 L8
COVN CV6 .....133 G5
WOLVN WV10 .....36 E5
Chesterton Wy CRTAM B79 .....31 L7
Chesterwood ALDR WS9 .....55 J3
HLYWD B47 .....146 E7
Chesterwood Gdns
BFLD/HDSWWD B20 .....89 H3
Chesterwood Rd MOS/BIL B13 .....125 K7
Chestnut Av CRTAM B79 .....31 M6
DUDN DY1 .....85 G2
KNWTH CV8 .....197 G2
TPTN/OCK DY4 .....67 K6
Chestnut Cl CDSL WV8 .....34 D3
CNCK/NC WS11 .....17 G3
FOAKS/STRLY B74 .....55 L3
HIA/OLT B92 .....127 K5
POL/KGSB/FAZ B78 .....47 H6
STRBR DY8 .....119 G2
Chestnut Ct CBROM B36 .....92 C8
DARL/WED WS10 .....68 B3
Chestnut Dr CBROM B36 .....91 L5
ERDE/BCHGN B24 .....90 C1
GTWY WS6 .....24 B2
LICHS WS14 .....28 D8
RBRY B45 .....170 A1
RUSH/SHEL WS4 .....39 M5
WMBN WV5 .....64 E3
Chestnut Fld RUGBYN/HIL CV21 .....186 E2
Chestnut Gv CSHL/WTROR B46 .....93 J3
HRBN B17 .....106 C3
KGSWFD DY6 .....83 K7
KIDDW DY11 .....137 M5
KNWTH CV8 .....183 L2
MOS/BIL B13 .....125 K5
SLYOAK B29 .....153 L5
Chestnut Pl BLOX/PEL WS3 .....39 H7
Chestnut Rd BDWTH CV12 .....117 H1
BLOX/PEL WS3 .....39 J7
BRGRVW B61 .....191 K1
DARL/WED WS10 .....68 B3
LGLYGN/QTN B68 .....105 G3
MOS/BIL B13 .....125 L1
Chestnuts Av
LGN/SDN/BHAMAIR B26 .....109 M6
The chestnuts BDWTH CV12 .....116 C3
Chestnut Tree Av
TLHL/CAN CV4 .....153 L3
Chestom Rd BILS/COS WV14 .....67 G3
Cheston Rd VAUX/NECH B7 .....89 L7
Cheswell Cl
DUNHL/THL/PER WV6 .....48 F3
Cheswick Cl COVN CV6 * 134 D2
REDE B98 .....203 J1
Cheswick Wy SHLY B90 .....174 B2
Cheswood Dr WALM/CURD B76 .....73 K7
Chesworth Rd BRGRVE B60 .....191 M4
Chetland Cft HIA/OLT B92 .....128 D6
Chettle Rd BILS/COS WV14 .....67 L4
Chetton Av COVN CV6 .....134 A3
Chetton Gn WOLVN WV10 .....35 M1
Chetwode Cl COVW CV5 .....153 M1
Chetwood Cl
DUNHL/THL/PER WV6 .....48 L8
Chetwynd Av POL/KGSB/FAZ B78 .....47 L5
Chetwynd Cl WSLW WS2 .....52 A2
Chetwynd Gdns
WASH/WDE B8 .....90 B1
Chetwynd Pk HEDN WS12 .....13 L8
Chetwynd Rd BKHL/PFLD WV2 .....49 M7
WASH/WDE B8 .....90 B1
Cheveley Av RBRY B45 .....143 M6
Chevening Cl SEDG DY3 .....66 C5
Cheverel Pl COV CV1 .....8 B5
Cheverel Rd BDWTH CV12 .....116 E1
Cheverel St NUN CV11 .....98 E3
Cheveridge Cl SOLH B91 .....148 E4

Cheverton Rd NFLD/LBR B31 ......144 C2
Cheviot TAM/AM/WIL B77 ....47 G4
Cheviot Cl NUNW/HART CV10 ....97 M2
STRPT DY13 ....188 B5
Cheviot Ri HEDN WS12 ....17 G1
RLSN CV32 ....207 G2
Cheviot Rd BKHL/PFLD WV2 ....50 D6
STRBR DY8 ....101 L7
Cheviot Wy HALE B63 ....121 H2
Cheylesmore COV CV1 ....8 F6
Cheylesmore Cl SCFLD/BOLD B73..72 F1
Cheyne Gdns HLGN/YWD B28 ......147 J2
Cheyne Wk BRLYHL DY5................102 A6
Cheyney Cl
DUNHL/THL/PER WV6 ....35 L8
Chichester Av DUDS DY2 ....85 H8
KIDDW DY11 ....138 A4
Chichester Cl NUN CV11 ....81 L6
Chichester Ct SCFLD/BOLD B73 * ..56 F8
Chichester Dr CNCK/NC WS11 ....17 G4
RIDG/WDGT B32......................104 E8
Chichester Gv
CHWD/FDBR/MGN B37 ....110 F4
Chichester La
RWWCK/WEL CV35 ....204 C7
Chicory Dr RRUGBY CV23...............161 H5
Chideock Hl COVS CV3 ....154 E7
Chiel Cl COVW CV5.......................153 K1
Chigwell Cl CVALE B35 ....91 L2
Chilcote Cl HLGN/YWD B28 ....147 K1
Childs Av BILS/COS WV14..............66 E3
Childs Oak Cl
RCOVN/BALC/EX CV7 ....151 L7
Chilgrove Gdns
DUNHL/THL/PER WV6...................35 G8
Chilham Dr
CHWD/FDBR/MGN B37 ....111 G3
Chillaton Rd COVN CV6..................133 M3
Chillingham TAM/AM/WIL B77 ....46 A6
Chillinghome Rd CBROM B36.........91 H5
Chillington Cl GTWY WS6 ....24 C4
Chillington Dr CDSL WV8 ....34 D1
DUDN DY1...............................84 D2
Chillington Flds WOLV WV1 ....50 E4
Chillington Pl BILS/COS WV14.........51 G8
Chillington Rd TPTN/OCK DY4.........68 A4
Chillington St WOLV WV1..................3 L8
Chiltern Cl GTWY WS6...................24 B4
HALE B63 ....121 G3
SEDG DY3 ....84 B2
STRPT DY13 ....188 B5
Chiltern Dr WLNHL WV13 ....51 H4
Chiltern Leys COVN CV6....................8 A1
Chiltern Rd STRBR DY8..................101 M7
TAM/AM/WIL B77 ....47 G4
The Chilterns COVW CV5 ....153 M1
Chilton Rd ALE/KHTH/YWD B14 ..147 H1
Chilwell Cl SOLH B91.....................148 F4
Chilwell Cft LOZ/NWT B19 ....89 J7
Chilworth Av WNSFLD WV11 ....37 K6
Chilworth Cl AST/WIT B6 ....89 K7
NUN CV11.................................99 J5
Chimes Cl STETCH B33 ....110 C4
Chimney Rd TPTN/OCK DY4.............68 B6
The Chines NUNW/HART CV10 * 81 H6
Chingford Cl STRBR DY8 ....101 G1
Chingford Rd COVN CV6 ....134 E1
KGSTG B44................................71 L5
Chinley Gv KGSTG B44 ....72 A4
Chinn Brook Rd MOS/BIL B13........125 M8
Chip Cl HWK/WKHTH B38 ....145 H3
Chipperfield Rd CBROM B36...........91 J5
Chipstead Rd ERDW/GRVHL B23.....72 B6
Chipstone Cl SOLH B91..................149 G5
Chirbury Gv NFLD/LBR B31 ....144 F4
Chirk Cl KIDDW DY11....................164 C3
Chirton Gv ALE/KHTH/YWD B14 ..125 H7
Chiseldon Cft
ALE/KHTH/YWD B14 ....146 E2
Chisholm Gv ACGN B27.................127 G5
Chiswell Rd WSNGN B18...............106 C1
Chivington Cl SHLY B90 ....148 F7
Chorley Av BKDE/SHDE B34 ....91 K6
Chorley Gdns BILS/COS WV14 ....50 F8
Chorley Rd BNTWD WS7..................18 D4
Choyce Cl ATHST CV9 ....63 H5
Christchurch Cl EDG B15 ....106 C5
NUNW/HART CV10.......................98 D4
Christ Church Gdns LICH WS13......20 D6
Christ Church Gv WSL WS1 *...........5 K9
Christchurch La LICH WS13.............20 D6
Christchurch Rd COVN CV6 ....133 K7
Christine Cl DARL/WED WS10 ....68 A3
Christine Ledger Sq
RLSS CV31 * 206 E7
Christopher Rd BKHL/PFLD WV2 ....3 J9
RMSLY B62 ....122 C2
SLYOAK B29 ....124 A3
Chub TAM/AM/WIL B77 ....46 B6
Chubb St WOLV WV1.......................3 H4
Chuckery Rd WSL WS1 ....5 J4
Chudleigh Gv GTB/HAM B43 ....70 B5
Chudleigh Rd ERDW/GRVHL B23 ..90 C1
Church Av BFLD/HDSWWD B20 * ..89 G4
HAG/WOL DY9 ....141 J3
MOS/BIL B13 *.........................125 K2
STRBR DY8 ....101 L6
STRPT DY13 ....188 E1
Churchbridge OLDBY B69 ....86 D7
Churchbridge Pk
CNCK/NC WS11 * 16 C8
Church Cl ATHST CV9 ....61 G4
CHWD/FDBR/MGN B37 ....92 E7
HLYWD B47..............................172 D2
KNWTH CV8 ....182 F3
LICHS WS14..............................28 D8
NUNW/HART CV10.......................79 M5
POL/KGSB/FAZ B78 ....45 J8
RCOVN/BALC/EX CV7 ....96 C3
RRUGBY CV23..........................159 M2
Church Cft HALE B63 ....121 L1
HRBN B17 ....123 M1
Church Cross Vw BRLYHL DY5 ......84 B5
Churchdale Cl NUNW/HART CV10..98 A1
Churchdale Rd KGSTG B44..............71 H2
Church Down Cl REDW B97............202 B7
Church Dr BVILLE B30....................124 F6
POL/KGSB/FAZ B78 ....30 F6
STRPT DY13 ....188 E1
Church End RLSS CV31 ....207 J7
Churchfield Av TPTN/OCK DY4 ......67 K5
Churchfield Cl COVEN WV9 ....22 A3
VAUX/NECH B7 ....90 A7
Churchfield Rd WOLVN WV10 ....35 M5
Churchfields BRGRVW B61 ....191 K3
KIDD DY10...............................138 C6
Churchfields Cl BRGRVW B61 ....191 K2
Churchfields Gdns
BRGRVW B61 ....191 K2
Churchfields Rd BRGRVW B61 ......191 K2
DARL/WED WS10 ....68 D2
Churchfield St DUDS DY2...............85 G5
Church Gdns SMTHWKW B67 * 105 L2
WOLVN WV10 ....50 E1
Church Gn BFLD/HDSWWD B20 ....88 D3
BILS/COS WV14 ....51 G5
Church Gn East REDW B97 ....202 C1
Church Gn West REDW B97..........202 C1
Church Gv BFLD/HDSWWD B20 * ..88 F4
MOS/BIL B13 ....126 A8
Church Hl BRLYHL DY5 ....102 B3
CSHL/WTROR B46 ....93 L6
DARL/WED WS10 ....68 D2
ETTPK/GDPK/PENN WV4 ....65 J1
HAG/WOL DY9 ....141 H7
HEDN WS12 ....13 G8
NFLD/LBR B31 ....144 E2
REDE B98 ....195 G5
RIDG/WDGT B32........................122 E8
RLSN CV32 ....199 J8
RLSN CV32 ....206 C5
RRUGBY CV23..........................183 K8
WSL WS1....................................5 G4
Church Hill Cl SOLH B91 ....149 G3
Church Hill Rd
BFLD/HDSWWD B20 ....88 F4
DUNHL/THL/PER WV6..................35 H7
SOLH B91 ....149 G3
Church Hill St SMTHWKW B67 ....87 K7
Church Hill Wy REDE B98 ....195 G8
Churchill Av COVN CV6 ....134 C4
KNWTH CV8 ....179 L7
Churchill Cl OLDBY B69..................86 A3
Churchill Dr BLKHTH/ROWR B65..103 M3
STRBR DY8 ....101 L6
Churchill Gdns SEDG DY3..............66 A6
Churchill La KIDD DY10................139 M3
Churchill Pl STETCH B33 ....109 M4
Churchill Rd BORD B9 ....108 D3
BRGRVW B61 ....168 E4
HALE B63 ....121 K3
LICHS WS14...............................28 E8
MGN/WHC B75............................57 L8
RUGBYS/DCH CV22 ....186 E4
SCFLD/BOLD B73 ....72 A3
WSLW WS2 ....52 C2
Church La ALDR WS9......................41 J1
AST/WIT B6...............................89 L5
ATHST CV9 ....63 M1
BFLD/HDSWWD B20 ....88 D3
BKHL/PFLD WV2 ....2 E7
BNTWD WS7 ....27 H1
BRGRVW B61 ....191 K3
CDSL WV8..................................34 D1
CNCK/NC WS11...........................15 K5
COVE CV2 ....155 M2
COVEN WV9...............................22 A3
COVW CV5...............................132 A8
CRTAM B79 ....31 M8
CRTAM B79 ....33 J6
CSHL/WTROR B46 ....112 E1
HALE B63 ....121 M1
HHTH/SAND B71 ....68 F8
HIA/OLT B92 ....129 H4
KNWTH CV8 ....180 F7
NUNW/HART CV10.......................81 G6
NUNW/HART CV10.......................97 H4
POL/KGSB/FAZ B78 ....59 G4
POL/KGSB/FAZ B78 ....60 A8
RCOVN/BALC/EX CV7 ....96 D3
RCOVN/BALC/EX CV7 ....114 C2
RCOVN/BALC/EX CV7 ....114 F6
RCOVN/BALC/EX CV7 ....115 G6
RCOVN/BALC/EX CV7 ....116 C6
RCOVN/BALC/EX CV7 ....131 J5
RCOVN/BALC/EX CV7 ....152 A2
RLSN CV32 ....199 J7
RLSN CV32 ....206 E2
STETCH B33 ....109 K2
WALM/CURD B76 ....74 D4
WALM/CURD B76 ....74 F7
WALM/CURD B76 ....75 L7
Church Ms
RCOVN/BALC/EX CV7 * 96 C3
Church Moat Wy BLOX/PEL WS3 ..38 F5
Churchover Cl WALM/CURD B76 ..73 H7
Church Park Cl COVN CV6 ....133 K4
Church Pth RWWCK/WEL CV35....204 D7
Church Pl BLOX/PEL WS3................39 H5
Church Rd ALDR WS9 ....41 J2
AST/WIT B6...............................89 L5
ATHST CV9 ....63 M6
BDMR/CCFT WV3.........................49 J6
BILS/COS WV14 ....67 H4
BLKHTH/ROWR B65 ....104 A2
BLOX/PEL WS3............................39 L2
BNTWD WS7...............................19 H6
BRGRVW B61 ....167 L6
BRGRVW B61 ....168 D5
BRGRVW B61 ....191 K2
BRWNH WS8...............................26 D6
CDSL WV8..................................34 D1
CNCK/NC WS11...........................15 L4
CNCK/NC WS11...........................25 J1
CSHL/WTROR B46 ....94 E3
DUDS DY2 ....84 F8
DUNHL/THL/PER WV6...................35 J8
DUNHL/THL/PER WV6...................48 C1
DUNHL/THL/PER WV6...................48 F2
EDG B15.................................106 E6
ERDE/BCHGN B24........................90 E1
HAG/WOL DY9 ....102 C8
HAG/WOL DY9 ....141 H6
HALE B63 ....103 G6
KNWTH CV8 ....181 K3
KNWTH CV8 ....182 A7
KNWTH CV8 ....182 F3
LGN/SDN/BHAMAIR B26 ....109 H7
LGN/SDN/BHAMAIR B26 ....109 J5
LGN/SDN/BHAMAIR B26 ....110 A8
LICHS WS14...............................28 D8
MOS/BIL B13 ....125 L2
NFLD/LBR B31 ....144 E2
NUNW/HART CV10.......................79 M5
NUNW/HART CV10.......................98 A2
PBAR/PBCH B42 ....71 H8
PENK ST19..................................10 C4
POL/KGSB/FAZ B78 ....47 L8
REDW B97...............................201 K3
REDW B97...............................202 C1
RRUGBY CV23..........................159 G8
SCFLD/BOLD B73 ....72 D5
SCFLD/BOLD B73 ....72 F2
SEDG DY3 ....82 C3
SHHTH WV12 ....38 B7
SHLY B90................................147 M3
SMTHWKW B67 ....105 K1
STETCH B33 ....109 K3
STRBR DY8 ....101 H3
STRBR DY8 ....119 M2
TAM/AM/WIL B77 ....60 A1
WMBN WV5.................................64 F6
WOLVN WV10 ....23 G3
WOLVN WV10 ....36 A4
YDLY B25................................109 J5
Church Rw ATHST CV9 *................62 A4
Churchside Vw ALDR WS9 ....40 F3
Church Sq OLDBY B69 ....86 E6
Churchstone Cl BRGRVW B61 ....168 D5
Church St ATHST CV9 ....63 H5
BILS/COS WV14 ....51 H8
BKHL/PFLD WV2 ....2 E7
BLOX/PEL WS3............................38 F5
BLOX/PEL WS3............................39 G5
BNTWD WS7...............................18 C8
BRGRVW B61 ....191 K3
BRLYHL DY5 ....84 B6
BRLYHL DY5 ....102 A3
BRLYHL DY5 ....102 D4
BRWNH WS8...............................26 C8
CBHAMNW B3 ....6 F4
CDYHTH B64 ....103 J4
CNCK/NC WS11...........................16 B7
CNCK/NC WS11...........................16 C4
CNCK/NC WS11...........................16 E1
COV CV1 ....9 H1
CRTAM B79 ....31 M8
DARL/WED WS10 ....52 B7
DARL/WED WS10 ....67 M1
DUDS DY2 ....85 G5
HAG/WOL DY9 ....119 L8
KIDD DY10...............................138 C7
LICH WS13................................21 G5
LOZ/NWT B19 ....89 G6
NUN CV11.................................99 H1
OLDBY B69 ....86 E5
RLSS CV31 ....206 E6
RMSLY B62 ....104 B4
RRUGBY CV23..........................161 L8
RUGBYN/HIL CV21 ....186 E2
SEDG DY3 ....84 B2
STRBR DY8 ....101 L8
TPTN/OCK DY4 ....85 L3
WBROM B70 ....87 G1
WLNHL WV13 ....51 M3
WOLVN WV10 ....50 E1
WSL WS1....................................5 G5
WWCK CV34.............................205 J7
Church Ter MGN/WHC B75 * 57 G2
RLSS CV31 ....206 E6
STETCH B33 * 109 J4
Church V BFLD/HDSWWD B20.........88 F4
CNCK/NC WS11...........................25 J1
HHTH/SAND B71 ....69 H7
Church Vw ALDR WS9......................40 D2
BEWD DY12 ....162 E2
KNWTH CV8 * 182 F4
SPARK B11 ....108 A7
Church View Cl BLOX/PEL WS3 .....39 G5
Church View Dr CDYHTH B64 ......103 K4
Church Vls HDSW B21 * 88 C3
Church Wk ATHST CV9 ....63 K6
BDMR/CCFT WV3.........................49 K6
COVW CV5...............................133 G7
DUNHL/THL/PER WV6...................35 J8
KIDDW DY11 ....138 A7
RLSS CV31 ....206 D6
RUGBYN/HIL CV21 ....186 F2
RUGBYS/DCH CV22 ....186 B5
STRPT DY13 ....188 C3
WASH/WDE B8 ....90 E7
Churchward Cl STRBR DY8 ....101 M7
Churchward Gv WMBN WV5 ....64 E5
Church Wy BDWTH CV12 ....116 F2
RUSH/SHEL WS4 ....39 M3
Churchyard Rd TPTN/OCK DY4 ......67 M8
Churnet Gv
DUNHL/THL/PER WV6...................48 D1
Churn Hill Rd ALDR WS9.................54 E1
Churns Hill La SEDG DY3 ....82 F2
Churston Cl BLOX/PEL WS3 ....38 E2
Chylds Ct COVW CV5....................132 E8
Cider Av BRLYHL DY5 ....102 C5
Cinder Bank DUDS DY2 ....85 G7
Cinder Rd BNTWD WS7 ....18 C6
SEDG DY3 ....83 M4
Cinder Wy DARL/WED WS10 ....68 C2
Cinquefoil Leasow
TPTN/OCK DY4 ....68 A7
The Circle NUNW/HART CV10 ....98 C1
Circuit Cl WLNHL WV13..................51 M2
Circular Rd ACGN B27...................127 G4
Circus Av
CHWD/FDBR/MGN B37 ....111 G3
Cirencester Cl BRGRVE B60 ....191 M3
City Ar LICH WS13 * 20 F6
City Plaza CBHAM B2 *....................7 G5
City Rd LDYWD/EDGR B16 ....106 A3
OLDBY B69 ....85 M6
City Vw WASH/WDE B8 ....108 B1
Civic Cl CBHAMW B1 ....6 C5
Claerwen Av STRPT DY13..............163 J6
Claerwen Gv NFLD/LBR B31 ....123 J8
Claines Crs KIDD DY10 ....138 F7
Claines Rd HALE B63.....................103 H8
NFLD/LBR B31 ....145 G1
Clandon Cl ALE/KHTH/YWD B14 ..145 M3
Clanfield Av WNSFLD WV11 ....37 K5
Clapgate Gdns
ETTPK/GDPK/PENN WV4 ....66 E2
Clap Gate Gv WMBN WV5 ....64 C7
Clapgate La RIDG/WDGT B32 ....123 G3
Clap Gate Rd WMBN WV5 ....64 C6
Clapham Sq RLSS CV31 ....206 F6
Clapham St RLSS CV31 ....206 F7
Clapham Ter RLSS CV31 ....206 F6
Clapton Gv KGSTG B44 ....71 M4
Clara St COVE CV2 ....155 L3
Clare Av WNSFLD WV11 ....37 K4
Clare Cl RLSN CV32......................207 G3
Clare Ct RUGBYN/HIL CV21 ....186 D2
Clare Crs
ETTPK/GDPK/PENN WV4 ....66 D3
Clare Dr EDG B15.........................106 D5
Clarel Av WASH/WDE B8...............108 A2
Claremont Cl BDWTH CV12 ....117 M1
Claremont Ms BDMR/CCFT WV3.....49 L6
Claremont Pl WSNGN B18 * 88 E8
Claremont Rd BDMR/CCFT WV3 ....49 L6
CRTAM B79 ....31 K5
RLSS CV31 ....206 E7
RUGBYN/HIL CV21 ....187 G2
SEDG DY3 ....66 C5
SMTHWK B66 ....105 M1
SPARK B11 ....107 M6
WSNGN B18 ....88 E7
Claremont St BILS/COS WV14 ....51 G7
CDYHTH B64 ....103 J4
Claremont Wk COVW CV5 ....133 G7
Claremont Wy HALE B63 ....121 L2
Clarence Av HDSW B21 * 88 A5
Clarence Gdns FOAKS/STRLY B74 ..56 D3
Clarence Rd BILS/COS WV14 ....51 J6
DUDS DY2 ....85 H7
ERDW/GRVHL B23 ....90 B2
FOAKS/STRLY B74 ....42 C8
HDSW B21 ....88 A5
HRBN B17 ....106 B7
MOS/BIL B13 ....125 L5
RUGBYN/HIL CV21 ....186 C2
SPARK B11 ....126 A1
WOLV WV1...................................2 E4
Clarence St COV CV1 ....9 K2
KIDD DY10...............................138 D7
NUN CV11.................................98 F1
RLSS CV31 ....206 E7
SEDG DY3 ....66 C8
WOLV WV1...................................2 E5
Clarence Ter RLSN CV32 * 206 D4
Clarence Wy BEWD DY12 ....162 F1
Clarenden Pl HRBN B17 ....106 A8
Clarendon Av RLSN CV32 ....206 D4
Clarendon Cl REDW B97 ....193 M8
Clarendon Ct RLSN CV32 * 206 D4
Clarendon Crs RLSN CV32 ....206 C4
Clarendon Dr TPTN/OCK DY4 ....68 B5
Clarendon Pl BLOX/PEL WS3 ....39 K1
RLSN CV32 ....206 C4
RMSLY B62 ....104 D7
Clarendon Rd KNWTH CV8............197 L2
LDYWD/EDGR B16 ....106 C4
MGN/WHC B75............................57 G2
RUSH/SHEL WS4 ....40 A3
SMTHWKW B67 ....105 K1
Clarendon Sq RLSN CV32 ....206 D4
Clarendon St BDMR/CCFT WV3 ....2 B5
BLOX/PEL WS3............................38 F4
COVW CV5...............................154 D4
RLSN CV32 ....206 E4
Clare Rd BLOX/PEL WS3 ....39 K7
WOLVN WV10 ....36 C6
Clare's Ct KIDDW DY11 ....138 A7
Clarewell Av SOLH B91 ....148 E4
Clarion Wy CNCK/NC WS11 ....12 C8
Clarke's Av HEDN WS12 ....12 E4
KNWTH CV8 ....197 L2
Clarkes Gv TPTN/OCK DY4 ....68 A7
Clarke's La HHTH/SAND B71 ....69 G6
WLNHL WV13 ....52 A3
Clarke St REDW B97 ....202 C1
Clark Rd BDMR/CCFT WV3 ....49 K3
Clarkson Rd DARL/WED WS10 ....68 E2
Clark St COVN CV6 ....134 E4
LDYWD/EDGR B16 ....106 D3
STRBR DY8 ....101 J8
Clarry Dr FOAKS/STRLY B74 ....56 D5
Clary Gv DSYBK/YTR WS5 ....69 L2
Clatterbach La HAG/WOL DY9........141 L1
Clattercut La DROIT WR9 ....166 D8
Claughton Ct KIDDW DY11............138 A8
Claughton Rd DUDS DY2 ....85 H4
Claughton Rd North DUDS DY2 ......85 H4
Claughton St KIDDW DY11............138 A8
Clausen Cl GTB/HAM B43 ....71 J1
Clavedon Cl NFLD/LBR B31 ....123 J6
Claverdon Cl BRWNH WS8 ....26 E5
SOLH B91 ....148 C1
Claverdon Dr FOAKS/STRLY B74 ....55 M1
GTB/HAM B43 ....70 B5
Claverdon Gdns ACGN B27 ....108 F8
Claverdon Rd COVW CV5 ....153 M2
Claverley Dr
ETTPK/GDPK/PENN WV4 ....49 H8
Clay Av NUN CV11 ....81 K6
Claybrook Dr STUD B80 ....203 K6
Claybrook St DIG/EDG B5 ....7 G8
Claycroft Ter DUDN DY1 ....66 F7
Claydon Gv ALE/KHTH/YWD B14..146 E2
RWWCK/WEL CV35 ....204 C2
Claydon Rd KGSWFD DY6................83 G4
Clay Dr RIDG/WDGT B32..............104 E8
Claygate Rd HEDN WS12 ....17 J2
Clayhanger La BRWNH WS8 ....26 B7
Clayhanger Rd BRWNH WS8 ....26 D7
Clayhill La RRUGBY CV23 ....159 K6
Clay La COVE CV2 ....155 L1
COVW CV5...............................132 C1
LGN/SDN/BHAMAIR B26 ....127 J1
OLDBY B69 ....104 E1
Claymore TAM/AM/WIL B77 ....46 B7
Claypit Cl WBROM B70 ....86 E2
Claypit La BRGRVW B61 ....168 C4
Clay Pit La LICHS WS14..................28 D1
SHLY B90................................147 L8
Claypit La WBROM B70...................86 E2
Clay St PENK ST19 ....10 C4
Clayton Cl BKHL/PFLD WV2 ....50 A6
Clayton Dr BRGRVE B60 ....191 M6
CBROM B36 ....92 A5
Clayton Rd BILS/COS WV14 ....66 F6
COVN CV6 ....133 J8
WASH/WDE B8 ....90 B8
Clear Vw KGSWFD DY6....................82 F7
Clearwell Gdns DUDN DY1..............84 D2
Cleasby TAM/AM/WIL B77...............47 G4
Clee Av KIDDW DY11 ....164 A3
Clee Hill Dr BDMR/CCFT WV3..........48 D4
Clee Hill Rd SEDG DY3 ....84 A1
Clee Rd DUDS DY2 ....84 E6
LGLYGN/QTN B68 ....105 G1
NFLD/LBR B31 ....144 E5
STRBR DY8 ....101 L7
Cleeton St HEDN WS12 ....17 H4
Cleeve TAM/AM/WIL B77 ....46 B2
Cleeve Cl REDE B98......................195 H8
STRPT DY13 ....188 B5
Cleeve Dr FOAKS/STRLY B74 ....42 D7
Cleeve Rd ALE/KHTH/YWD B14 ....147 G1
BLOX/PEL WS3............................38 D2
Cleeves Av RLSS CV31 ....206 B7
Cleeve Wy BLOX/PEL WS3..............38 D3
Clee View Meadow SEDG DY3 ....66 B3
Clee View Rd WMBN WV5 ....64 C8
Clematis TAM/AM/WIL B77 ....46 D2
Clematis Dr COVEN WV9..................35 K2
Clemens St RLSS CV31 ....206 E6
Clement Pl BILS/COS WV14 * 51 H6
Clement Rd BILS/COS WV14 ....51 H6
RMSLY B62 ....104 B4
Clements Cl OLDBY B69 ....104 D1
Clements Rd YDLY B25.................109 H5
Clements St COVE CV2 ....155 L2
Clement St CBHAMW B1 ....6 B4
NUN CV11.................................98 F2
WSLW WS2 ....4 C5
Clement Wy RUGBYS/DCH CV22 ..185 L5
Clemson St WLNHL WV13................51 L3
Clennon Ri COVE CV2 ....135 H5
Clensmore St KIDD DY10 ....138 B6
Clent Av KIDDW DY11 ....163 M4
REDW B97...............................202 B6
Clent Dr HAG/WOL DY9.................120 A7
NUNW/HART CV10.......................97 M2
Clent Hill Dr BLKHTH/ROWR B65.....85 L8
Clent Rd HDSW B21........................88 B4
LGLYGN/QTN B68 ....105 G5
RBRY B45 ....143 J5
STRBR DY8 ....101 L7
Clent View Rd HALE B63 ....121 G1
RIDG/WDGT B32........................122 E4
STRBR DY8 ....119 G3
Clent Vls BHTH/HG B12 * 125 M1
Clent Wy RIDG/WDGT B32 ....122 D5
Cleobury Cl REDW B97 ....193 M8
Cleobury La HOCK/TIA B94 ....173 L2
Cleobury Rd BEWD DY12 ....162 C3
Cleton St TPTN/OCK DY4 ....85 M2
Clevedon Av CBROM B36.................92 C4
Clevedon Rd BHTH/HG B12............107 J7
Cleveland Cl WLNHL WV13..............51 H4
WNSFLD WV11 ....37 K4
Cleveland Dr CNCK/NC WS11 ....16 F1
RBRY B45 ....169 L3
Cleveland Pas BKHL/PFLD WV2 ....2 F6
Cleveland Rd BDWTH CV12 ....117 M2
BKHL/PFLD WV2 ....3 H7
COVE CV2 ....155 L1
Cleveland St BKHL/PFLD WV2 ....2 F6
DUDN DY1.................................84 F4
STRBR DY8 ....119 J1
Cleveley Dr NUNW/HART CV10 ......80 B6
Cleves Crs GTWY WS6 ....24 B4
Cleves Dr RBRY B45 ....143 J6
Cleves Rd RBRY B45 ....143 J5
Clewley Dr COVEN WV9 ....35 L2
Clewley Gv RIDG/WDGT B32 ....104 F8
Clews Cl WSL WS1..........................4 E8
Clewshaw La HWK/WKHTH B38 ..171 M1
Clews Rd REDE B98......................202 D6
Cley Cl DIG/EDG B5 ....107 H7
Clifden Gv KNWTH CV8.................180 A7
Cliffe Dr STETCH B33 ....109 M2
Cliffe Rd RLSN CV32 ....206 B4
Cliffe Wy WWCK CV34..................205 L5
Cliff Hall La POL/KGSB/FAZ B78......59 M5
Clifford Bridge Rd COVE CV2 ....156 D1
COVS CV3 ....156 D3
Clifford Rd DOR/KN B93...............175 K1
SMTHWKW B67 ....105 K4
WBROM B70 ....86 E3
Clifford St DUDN DY1 ....84 F5
DUNHL/THL/PER WV6.....................2 A2
LOZ/NWT B19 ....89 H6
TAM/AM/WIL B77 ....46 C2
Clifford Wk LOZ/NWT B19 ....89 H6
Cliff Rock Rd RBRY B45 ....143 M6
Clift Av SHHTH WV12 ....38 B6
Clift Cl SHHTH WV12 ....38 A7
Clifton Av ALDR WS9 ....41 G5
BRWNH WS8...............................26 B7
CNCK/NC WS11...........................16 A6
CRTAM B79 ....31 K6
Clifton Cl AST/WIT B6 ....89 K6
OLDBY B69 ....104 D1
REDE B98 ....203 H4
Clifton Crs SHLY B90 ....148 D4
Clifton Gdns CDSL WV8 ....35 G2
Clifton Gn HLGN/YWD B28 ....126 E8
Clifton La CRTAM B79 ....32 F2
HHTH/SAND B71 ....69 J5
Clifton Rd AST/WIT B6 ....89 K6
BHTH/HG B12...........................107 L8
CBROM B36 ....92 C5
DUNHL/THL/PER WV6...................35 H8
KIDD DY10...............................139 G2
KIDDW DY11 ....163 L4
NUNW/HART CV10.......................98 D1
RMSLY B62 ....104 B5
RUGBYN/HIL CV21 ....186 F2
RUGBYN/HIL CV21 ....187 H2
SCFLD/BOLD B73 ....72 E1
SMTHWKW B67 ....105 K1
Clifton St BDMR/CCFT WV3 ....2 C5
BILS/COS WV14 ....66 D4
CDYHTH B64 ....103 K4
COV CV1 ....9 J1
STRBR DY8 ....119 K1
Clifton Ter ERDW/GRVHL B23 * 90 D1
Clinic Dr HAG/WOL DY9 ....102 C8
NUN CV11.................................99 G2
Clinton Av KNWTH CV8.................179 H7
RWWCK/WEL CV35 ....204 E6
Clinton Crs BNTWD WS7 ....18 F5
Clinton Gv SHLY B90 ....148 B4
Clinton La KNWTH CV8 ....179 H7
Clinton Rd BILS/COS WV14 ....51 L6
COVN CV6 ....134 D3
CSHL/WTROR B46 ....93 K7
SHLY B90................................148 C5
Clinton St RLSS CV31 ....206 E6
WSNGN B18 ....88 C8
Clipper Vw LDYWD/EDGR B16........106 C4
Clipstone Rd COVN CV6 ....133 J7
Clipston Rd WASH/WDE B8 ....90 D8
Clissold Cl BHTH/HG B12 ....107 J6
Clissold Pas WSNGN B18 ....106 E1
Clissold St WSNGN B18 ....106 E1
Clive Cl MGN/WHC B75 ....57 H3
Cliveden Av ALDR WS9 ....40 F4
PBAR/PBCH B42 ....89 G1
Cliveden Coppice
FOAKS/STRLY B74 ....56 D4
Cliveden Wk NUN CV11 ....99 J5
Clivedon Wy CDYHTH B64 ....103 L6
Cliveland St CBHAMNE B4 ....7 G1
Clive Rd BNTWD WS7 ....18 E6
BRGRVE B60 ....191 M5
RCOVN/BALC/EX CV7 ....152 A8
REDW B97...............................194 B8
RIDG/WDGT B32........................105 H6
Clive St HHTH/SAND B71 ....69 G8
Clockfields Dr STRBR DY8 ....101 L4
Clock La HIA/OLT B92 ....129 H3
Clockmill Av BLOX/PEL WS3 ....39 J2
Clockmill Pl BLOX/PEL WS3 ....39 K2
Clockmill Rd BLOX/PEL WS3 ....39 J2
Clodeshall Rd WASH/WDE B8 ......108 C1
Cloister Cft COVE CV2 ....135 K7
Cloister Crofts RLSN CV32 ....206 D2
Cloister Dr RMSLY B62 ....122 B2
The Cloisters RUSH/SHEL WS4 ....5 G1
Cloister Wy RLSN CV32 ....206 D2
Clonmel Rd BVILLE B30 ....124 E7
Clopton Crs
CHWD/FDBR/MGN B37 ....111 G1
Clopton Rd STETCH B33 ....110 A5
The Close DARL/WED WS10............68 C2
HALE B63 ....103 H7
HIA/OLT B92 ....127 K5
HLYWD B47..............................146 E8
HRBN B17 ....105 K6
KNWTH CV8 ....157 K8
LICH WS13................................20 F5
RLSS CV31 ....206 E7
RMSLY B62 ....121 L6
SEDG DY3 ....82 C3
SEDG DY3 ....84 A1
SLYOAK B29 * 124 B5
Clothier Gdns WLNHL WV13.............51 L2
Clothier St WLNHL WV13 ....51 L2
Cloud Br KNWTH CV8 ....181 J8
Cloudbridge Dr HIA/OLT B92 ....128 D6
Cloud Gn TLHL/CAN CV4...............154 B8
Cloudsley Gv HIA/OLT B92 ....127 K2
Clovelly Gdns COVE CV2...............135 G8
Clovelly Rd COVE CV2...................134 F8
Clovelly Wy NUN CV11 ....81 J8
Clover Av
CHWD/FDBR/MGN B37 ....111 H3
Clover Cl RRUGBY CV23 ....161 H5
Cloverdale DUNHL/THL/PER WV6..48 B1
Cloverdale Cl
RCOVN/BALC/EX CV7 ....133 M1
Clover Dr RIDG/WDGT B32 ....123 G3
Clover Hl DSYBK/YTR WS5 ....54 C5
Clover La KGSWFD DY6 ....82 E6
Clover Lea Sq WASH/WDE B8 ....90 E7
Clover Ley WOLVN WV10 ....3 L3
Clover Mdw HEDN WS12 ....17 G4
Clover Piece TPTN/OCK DY4 ....68 A7
Clover Rdg GTWY WS6 ....24 A2
Clover Rd SLYOAK B29 ....123 L6
Clowesswood La HOCK/TIA B94 ...173 K5
Club La WOLVN WV10 ....22 A7
Club Rw SEDG DY3 ....66 C8
Club Vw HWK/WKHTH B38.............145 H3
Clunbury Cft BKDE/SHDE B34..........91 M8
Clunbury Rd NFLD/LBR B31 ....144 E5
Clun Cl DUDS DY2 ....85 K4
Clunes Av NUN CV11 ....81 J7
Clun Rd NFLD/LBR B31 ....123 K7
Clyde Av RMSLY B62 ....104 C5
Clyde Ms BRLYHL DY5 ....83 M7
Clyde Rd BDWTH CV12 ....117 L2
DOR/KN B93 ....175 L3

Clydesdale
LGN/SDN/BHAMAIR B26 ....109 L8
Clydesdale Rd *RIDG/WDGT B32* ..104 F7
Clyde St *BHTH/HG B12* 7 J4
CDYHTH B64 ....103 J4
Coalash La *BRGRVE B60* 200 C6
Coalbourne Gdns *HALE B63* 63 G8
Coalbourn La *STRBR DY8* 101 K6
Coalheath La *RUSH/SHEL WS4* 40 H5
Coalpit Fields Rd *BDWTH CV12* 117 G3
Coalpit La *KNWTH CV8* 184 A1
Coal Pool La *BLOX/PEL WS3* 39 K6
Coalport Rd *WOLV WV1* 50 E4
Coalway Av *BDMR/CCFT WV3* 49 L7
LGN/SDN/BHAMAIR B26 ....128 A1
Coalway Gdns *BDMR/CCFT WV3* ...49 H7
BLOX/PEL WS3 ....38 E5
Coates Rd *KIDD DY10* 138 F6
Coat of Arms Bridge Rd
COVS CV3 ....154 E7
Cobbett Rd *BNTWD WS7* 7 H6
The Cobbles *CSCFLD/WYGN B72* ..73 C6
Cobble Wk *WSNGN B18 ** 8 E8
Cobbs Rd *KNWTH CV8* 179 H7
Cobden Av *RLSS CV31* 207 G6
Cobden Cl *DARL/WED WS10* 52 D7
HEDN WS12 ....13 G6
TPTN/OCK DY4 ....67 K5
Cobden Gdns *BHTH/HG B12* 107 J8
Cobden St *COVN CV6* 134 C8
DARL/WED WS10 ....52 D7
KIDD DY11 ....138 A7
STRBR DY8 ....101 H7
*WSL WS1 ** 4 D9
Cobham Cl *BRGRVE B60* 191 K6
CVALE B35 ....91 K2
Cobham Court Ms
HAG DY9 ....120 B7
Cobham Crs *BEWD DY12* 162 E2
Cobham Rd *BORD B9* 108 B3
DARL/WED WS10 ....69 J3
HALE B63 ....121 M1
KIDD DY11 ....164 C1
STRBR DY8 ....119 L3
Cobia *TAM/AM/WIL B77* 86 B6
Cob La *NFLD/LBR B31* 124 A6
Cobnall Rd *BRGRVW B61* 168 E3
Cobs Fld *BVILLE B30* 124 A7
Coburg Cft *TPTN/OCK DY4 ** 68 A7
Coburn Dr *MGN/WHC B75* 57 H3
Cochrane Cl *HAG/WOL DY9* 120 A5
*TPTN/OCK DY4 ** 68 A7
Cochrane's Meadow
RUGBYN/HIL CV21 ....187 L5
Cockermouth Cl *RLSS CV32* 206 B3
Cock Hill La *RBRY B45* 143 K5
Cockshut Hl
LGN/SDN/BHAMAIR B26 ....109 G6
Cockshutt La *BKHL/PFLD WV2 ** 50 B6
BRGRVW B61 ....168 B7
Cockshutts La *BKHL/PFLD WV2* 50 B6
Cocksmead Cft
ALE/KHTH/YWD B14 ....125 H8
Cocksparrow La *CNCK/NC WS11* 15 J1
Cocksparrow St *WWCK CV34* 205 H6
Cockspur St *POL/KGSB/FAZ B78* ...47 J6
Cockthorpe Cl *HRBN B17* 105 K6
Cocton Cl *DUNHL/THL/PER WV6* ...34 C8
Codsall Gdns *CDSL WV8* 34 C1
Codsall Rd *CDSL WV8* 35 C3
CDYHTH B64 ....103 J5
DUNHL/THL/PER WV6 ....35 J6
Cofield Rd *SCFLD/BOLD B73* 72 D4
Cofton Church La *RBRY B45* 170 E3
Cofton Cl *REDW B97* 195 M8
Cofton Ct *RBRY B45* 144 C6
Cofton Gv *NFLD/LBR B31* 144 C7
Cofton Lake Rd *RBRY B45* 170 A2
Cofton Rd *NFLD/LBR B31* 144 F6
Cokeland Pl *CDYHTH B64* 103 H5
Colaton Cl *WOLVN WV10* 50 C1
Colbek Ct *NUNW/HART CV10* 97 J1
Colbourne Grove Dr
*RLSS CV32 ** 206 B3
Colbourne Rd
POL/KGSB/FAZ B78 ....45 L3
TPTN/OCK DY4 ....85 L1
Colbrand Gv *EDG B15* 107 H5
Colchester St *COV CV1 ** 9 J5
Coldbath Rd *MOS/BIL B13* 125 H5
Coldfield Dr *REDE B98* 202 D3
Coldridge Cl *COVEN WV9* 35 K4
Coldstream Dr *STRBR DY8* 81 J2
Coldstream Rd *WALM/CURD B76* ...73 J3
Cole Bank Rd *HLGN/YWD B28* 126 C5
Colebridge Crs *CSHL/WTROR B46* ..93 K5
Colebrook Cl *COVS CV3* 156 D5
Colebrook Rd *SHLY B90* 147 K3
SPARK B11 ....108 B8
Coleby Cl *TLHL/CAN CV4* 153 H7
Coleford Cl *CHWD/FDBR/MGN B37* 110 E3
REDW B97 ....201 L3
STRBR DY8 ....101 G3
Coleford Dr
CHWD/FDBR/MGN B37 ....110 E3
Cole Gn *SHLY B90* 147 J3
Cole Hall La *BKDE/SHDE B34* 91 L7
Colehill *CRTAM B79* 31 M8
Colehurst Cft *SHLY B90* 148 D7
Coleman Rd *DARL/WED WS10* 52 E8
Coleman St
DUNHL/THL/PER WV6 ....49 K1
TLHL/CAN CV4 ....153 K2
Colemeadow Rd
CSHL/WTROR B46 ....93 K6
MOS/BIL B13 ....125 M8
REDE B98 ....195 K7
Colenso Rd *SMTHWK B66* 106 A4
Coleraine Rd *PBAR/PBCH B42* 70 E7
Coleridge Cl *BLOX/PEL WS3 ** 25 L8
CRTAM B79 ....31 L7
REDW B97 ....202 A5
SHHTH WV12 ....38 C6
Coleridge Dr
DUNHL/THL/PER WV6 ....48 C1
Coleridge Pas *CBHAMNE B4 ** 7 H3
Coleridge Ri *SEDG DY3* 83 C1
Coleridge Rd *COVE CV2* 156 A1
GTB/HAM B43 ....70 C6
Colesbourne Av
ALE/KHTH/YWD B14 ....146 A3
Colesbourne Rd *HIA/OLT B92* 127 M2
Coleshill Cl *REDW B97* 202 A8
Coleshill Heath Rd
CHWD/FDBR/MGN B37 ....111 G7
Coleshill Rd *ATHST CV9* 62 D7
ATHST CV9 ....78 B2
BKDE/SHDE B34 ....91 K6
CHWD/FDBR/MGN B37 ....110 G6
CSHL/WTROR B46 ....92 F3
CSHL/WTROR B46 ....94 D3
CSHL/WTROR B46 ....94 C8
MGN/WHC B75 ....57 H8

POL/KGSB/FAZ B78 ....45 L6
WALM/CURD B76 ....75 C8
Coleshill St *CBHAMNE B4* 7 J3
MGN/WHC B75 ....57 C8
Coleside Av *MOS/BIL B13* 126 B6
Coles La *CSCFLD/WYGN B72* 73 C2
HHTH/SAND B71 ....68 E6
The Colesleys *CSHL/WTROR B46* ...93 L7
Cole St *DUDS DY2* 103 J1
Coleview Crs *STETCH B33* 110 C2
Coleville Rd *WALM/CURD B76* 73 M7
Coleys La *NFLD/LBR B31* 144 E3
Colgreave Av *MOS/BIL B13* 126 B3
Colina Cl *COVS CV3* 156 A8
Colindale Rd *KGSTG B44* 71 L2
Colinwood Cl *GTWY WS6* 24 C4
Colledge Cl *RRUGBY CV23* 158 B2
Colledge Rd *COVN CV6* 134 D4
Colleen Av *BVILLE B30* 145 M2
College Cl *DARL/WED WS10* 68 E3
College Ct *BFLD/HDSWWD B20* 88 C2
RLSW CV32 ....206 D3
College Farm Dr
ERDW/GRVHL B23 ....72 B5
College Gv *BFLD/HDSWWD B20 ** ...88 F9
College La *CRTAM B79* 31 M8
KNWTH CV8 ....177 J4
College Rd *BFLD/HDSWWD B20* 88 C3
BRGRVE B60 ....191 J3
DUNHL/THL/PER WV6 ....49 H1
KGSTG B44 ....71 J8
KIDD DY10 ....164 C1
MOS/BIL B13 ....126 A3
RMSLY B62 ....104 E7
SCFLD/BOLD B73 ....72 B4
STRBR DY8 ....119 L1
WASH/WDE B8 ....108 C2
College St *NUNW/HART CV10* 98 F3
WSNGN B18 ....106 E1
College Vw
DUNHL/THL/PER WV6 ....49 H2
College Wk *BRGRVE B60* 191 L3
Collet Rd *CDSL WV8* 34 C8
Colletts Brook *MGN/WHC B75* 57 L5
Collett *TAM/AM/WIL B77* 46 E4
Collett Cl *STRBR DY8* 101 L7
Colletts Gv
CHWD/FDBR/MGN B37 ....110 D1
Collett Wk *COV CV1 ** 9 L2
KNWTH CV8 ....197 K1
Colley Av *WOLVN WV10* 36 D5
Colley Ga *HALE B63* 103 G7
Colley La *HALE B63* 103 G7
Colley Orch *HALE B63* 103 G7
Colley St *WBROM B70* 87 H1
Collier Cl *BRWNH WS8* 26 A6
GTWY WS6 ....24 B3
Colliers Cl *SHHTH WV12* 37 M7
Colliery Dr *BLOX/PEL WS3* 38 D2
Colliery La *RCOVN/BALC/EX CV7* ..116 F4
Colliery Rd *HHTH/SAND B71* 87 L4
WOLV WV1 ....3 M5
Collindale Ct *KGSWFD DY6* 83 H4
Collingbourne Av *CBROM B36* 91 H6
Collingdon Av
LGN/SDN/BHAMAIR B26 ....110 A7
Colling Wk
CHWD/FDBR/MGN B37 ....92 E8
Collingwood Av
RUGBYS/DCH CV22 ....186 A4
Collingwood Dr *GTB/HAM B43* 71 H2
Collingwood Rd *COVW CV5* 8 A6
WOLVN WV10 ....36 C3
Collins Cl *RIDG/WDGT B32* 104 C8
Collins Gv *TLHL/CAN CV4* 154 B8
Collins Hl *LICH WS13* 20 E3
Collins Rd *REDE B98* 202 E4
Collins Rd *BRWNH WS8* 26 B3
DARL/WED WS10 ....68 F2
WWCK CV34 ....206 B8
Collins St *WBROM B70* 86 C2
WSL WS1 ....4 F7
Collis Cl *BRGRVE B60* 191 J7
Collis St *STRBR DY8* 101 L5
Collister Cl *SHLY B90* 126 F8
Columbine Cl *DSYBK/YTR WS5* 69 K2
Colly Cft *CHWD/FDBR/MGN B37* 92 E8
Collycroft Pl *ACGN B27* 108 F8
Colman Av *WNSFLD WV11* 37 K7
Colman Crs *LGLYGN/QTN B68* 105 C3
Colman Hl *HALE B63* 103 H7
Colman Hill Av *HALE B63* 103 H7
Colmers Wk *HAG/WOL DY9* 102 C8
Colmore Av
ALE/KHTH/YWD B14 ....125 H6
Colmore Circus Queensway
CBHAMNE B4 ....7 C3
Colmore Crs *MOS/BIL B13* 125 M4
Colmore Dr *MGN/WHC B75* 57 L8
Colmore Flats *LOZ/NWT B19 ** 6 F1
Colmore Rd
ALE/KHTH/YWD B14 ....125 H6
Colmore Rw *CBHAMNW B3* 6 F4
Coln Cl *NFLD/LBR B31* 123 K7
Colonial Rd *BORD B9* 108 D3
Colshaw Rd *STRBR DY8* 119 J1
Colston Rd *ERDE/BCHGN B24* 90 F2
Colt Cl *FOAKS/STRLY B74* 55 J6
Coltham Rd *SHHTH WV12* 38 B7
Coltishall Cft *CVALE B35* 91 J5
Coltman Cl *LICHS WS14* 21 H6
Coltsfoot Cl *WNSFLD WV11* 37 K7
Coltsfoot Vw *GTWY WS6* 24 C3
Colts La *REDE B98* 203 H2
Columbia Cl *DIG/EDG B5* 107 H7
Columbia Gdns *BDWTH CV12* 117 H3
Columbian Crs *CNCK/NC WS11* 18 D5
Columbian Dr *CNCK/NC WS11* 16 D2
Columbian Wy *CNCK/NC WS11* 16 D2
Columbine Wy *BDWTH CV12* 116 C4
Colville Cl *TPTN/OCK DY4* 68 A8
Colville Rd *BHTH/HG B12* 107 M8
Colville Wk *BHTH/HG B12* 107 M8
Colwall Rd *SEDG DY3* 84 B1
Colwall Wk *ACGN B27* 127 H1
Colworth Rd *NFLD/LBR B31* 144 C1
Colyere Cl *RCOVN/BALC/EX CV7* ..115 L7
Colyns Gv *STETCH B33* 91 K8
Comber Cft *MOS/BIL B13* 125 K5
Comber Dr *BRLYHL DY5* 83 M7
Comberford Ct
*DARL/WED WS10 ** 68 E2
Comberford Dr *DARL/WED WS10* 69 H1
Comberford La *CRTAM B79* 31 L3
Comberford Rd *CRTAM B79* 31 L5
Comberton Av *KIDD DY10* 138 E7
Comberton Hl *KIDD DY10* 138 D6
Comberton Park Rd *KIDD DY10* 164 F1
Comberton Pl *KIDD DY10* 138 D7
Comberton Rd *KIDD DY10* 138 D6
LGN/SDN/BHAMAIR B26 ....109 M6
Comberton Ter *KIDD DY10* 138 D7
Combine *MGN/WHC B75* 57 H2
Combroke Gv
RWWCK/WEL CV35 ....204 C3
Comet Rd
LGN/SDN/BHAMAIR B26 ....129 G1

Commainge Cl *WWCK CV34* 205 H6
Commerce Dr *PENK ST19* 10 C6
Commercial Rd *WOLV WV1* 3 K6
WSLW WS2 ....38 E6
Commercial St *CBHAMW B1* 6 E6
The Coleys La *KIDD DY10* 118 D9
Commonfield Cft *WASH/WDE B8* 90 B8
Common La *CNCK/NC WS11* 16 C2
KNWTH CV8 ....179 M6
LGN/SDN/BHAMAIR B26 ....109 J8
LICHS WS14 ....30 E2
POL/KGSB/FAZ B78 ....47 L5
RCOVN/BALC/EX CV7 ....183 M7
STUD B80 ....203 M2
WASH/WDE B8 ....90 D7
Common Rd *WMBN WV5* 82 D1
Commonside *BLOX/PEL WS3* 39 L5
BRLYHL DY5 ....84 A7
Common Side *BRWNH WS8* 26 A8
RUGE WS15 ....18 E2
The Common *ATHST CV9* 62 A4
Common Vw *BNTWD WS7* 18 E4
HEDN WS12 ....12 F6
Common Wy *COVE CV2* 134 C7
Communication Rw *EDG B15* 6 C8
Compton Cl *REDE B98* 202 C3
RLSN CV32 ....207 G3
SOLH B91 ....148 B1
Compton Cft
CHWD/FDBR/MGN B37 ....111 H4
Compton Dr *DUDS DY2* 85 K5
FOAKS/STRLY B74 ....55 J6
KGSWFD DY6 ....83 H8
Compton Gv *HALE B63* 121 C1
KGSWFD DY6 ....83 H8
Compton Hill Dr
BDMR/CCFT WV3 ....49 H3
Compton Rd *BDMR/CCFT WV3* 49 K3
CDYHTH B64 ....103 G4
COVN CV6 ....134 B3
CRTAM B79 ....31 J4
ERDE/BCHGN B24 ....90 C4
HAG/WOL DY9 ....120 B4
RMSLY B62 ....104 D8
Compton Rd West
BDMR/CCFT WV3 ....49 H3
Comrie Cl *COVE CV2* 135 K7
Comsey Rd *GTB/HAM B43* 70 D2
Comwall Cl *BLOX/PEL WS3* 39 C6
Comyn St *RLSN CV32* 206 F1
Conchar Cl *CSCFLD/WYGN B72* 73 C8
Conchar Rd *CSCFLD/WYGN B72* 73 C8
Concorde Rd
LGN/SDN/BHAMAIR B26 ....129 G1
Condor Gv *CNCK/NC WS11* 17 C4
Condover Cl *WSLW WS2* 52 B2
Condover Rd *NFLD/LBR B31* 144 F5
Conduit Rd *CNCK/NC WS11* 25 L1
Coneyford Rd *BKDE/SHDE B34* 92 A7
Coney Gn *STRBR DY8* 101 M8
Coney Green Dr *NFLD/LBR B31* 144 D5
Coneygree Rd *TPTN/OCK DY4* 85 L2
Congleton Cl *COVN CV6* 134 C3
Congreve St *WWCK CV34* 205 K3
Conifer Cl *BDWTH CV12* 117 C6
BRLYHL DY5 ....102 A5
HEDN WS12 ....12 E6
Conifer Ct *MOS/BIL B13* 125 J3
Conifer Dr *HDSW B21* 88 C6
NFLD/LBR B31 ....88 E3
Conifer Gv *BRGRVW B61* 191 K2
RLSS CV31 ....206 E2
Conifer Paddock *COVS CV3* 156 A4
RMSLY B62 ....104 D4
Conifer Rd *FOAKS/STRLY B74* 55 J5
Coningsby Cl *RLSS CV31* 207 C8
Coningsby Dr *KIDD DY11* 137 L5
Conington Gv *HRBN B17* 105 H4
Coniston Av *HIA/OLT B92* 127 K1
Coniston Cl *BRGRVE B60* 191 M4
HLGN/YWD B28 ....126 D6
RUGBYN/HIL CV21 ....70 D6
Coniston Crs *GTB/HAM B43* 70 F6
Coniston Dr *COVW CV5* 153 H1
KGSWFD DY6 ....82 F6
Coniston Rd *COVW CV5* 154 D4
DUNHL/THL/PER WV6 ....35 H1
ERDW/GRVHL B23 ....72 B8
FOAKS/STRLY B74 ....55 J3
RLSN CV32 ....206 D4
Coniston Wy *BEWD DY12* 162 C6
CNCK/NC WS11 ....16 C4
NUN CV11 ....159 H1
Connaught Av *DARL/WED WS10* 69 G2
KIDD DY11 ....164 A2
Connaught Cl *DSYBK/YTR WS5* 54 A6
Connaught Dr *WMBN WV5* 64 E4
Connaught Rd *BILS/COS WV14* 51 L6
BRGRVE B60 ....192 A4
WOLV WV1 ....2 B4
Connops Wy *HAG/WOL DY9* 102 C8
Connor Rd *HHTH/SAND B71* 69 J5
Conolly Dr *RBRY B45* 143 M5
Conrad Cl *BHTH/HG B12* 107 L6
RUGBYS/DCH CV22 ....186 D5
Conrad Rd *COVN CV6* 133 L6
Consort Crs *BRLYHL DY5* 84 A6
Consort Dr *DARL/WED WS10* 52 A5
Consort Rd *BVILLE B30* 145 L2
Constable Cl *BDWTH CV12* 98 E8
GTB/HAM B43 ....71 C2
Constable Rd
RUGBYN/HIL CV21 ....187 M4
The Constables
LGLYGN/QTN B68 ....104 F3
Constance Av *WBROM B70* 87 H4
Constance Cl
RCOVN/BALC/EX CV7 ....116 D5
Constance Rd *DIG/EDG B5* 107 H3
Constantine La
CSHL/WTROR B46 ....93 K4
Constantine Wy *BILS/COS WV14* 67 L4
Constitution Hl *DUDS DY2* 85 H5
LOZ/NWT B19 ....6 E1
Consul Rd *RUGBYN/HIL CV21* 160 D7
Containerbase
*PBAR/PBCH B42 ** 71 K8
Convent Cl *ATHST CV9* 63 K6
BKHL/PFLD WV2 ....3 G1
CNCK/NC WS11 ....16 D5
KNWTH CV8 ....179 M6
Convent La *ATHST CV9* 63 J6
Conway Av *NUN CV11* 99 M6
NFLD/LBR B31 ....123 L6
Conway Crs *SHHTH WV12* 38 A6
Conway Gv *GTB/HAM B43* 70 B6
Conway Rd *BRGRVE B60* 191 M6
CHWD/FDBR/MGN B37 ....110 G2
CNCK/NC WS11 ....15 M5
DUNHL/THL/PER WV6 ....48 D2
RLSN CV32 ....206 B1
SHLY B90 ....148 B4

SPARK B11 ....108 A7
Conwy Cl *NUN CV11* 99 H3
Conyere St *BHTH/HG B12* 107 K6
Conyworth Cl *ACGN B27* 127 H1
Cook Cl *COVN CV6* 134 E1
DOR/KN B93 ....150 A7
DUNHL/THL/PER WV6 ....48 C1
RUGBYN/HIL CV21 ....161 C6
Cooke Cl *PENK ST19* 10 C3
WWCK CV34 ....205 H3
Cooke St *NFLD/LBR B31* 145 C5
Cookesley Cl *GTB/HAM B43* 71 H1
Cooke St *BKHL/PFLD WV2* 50 A6
Cookley Cl *HALE B63* 121 K3
Cooknell Dr *STRBR DY8* 101 H5
Cook Rd *BLOX/PEL WS3* 39 H1
Cooks Cl *ATHST CV9* 63 H5
Cooksey La *KGSTG B44* 71 K1
Cooksey Rd *SMHTH B10* 107 M5
Cooks La *ATHST CV9* 62 A3
STETCH B33 ....110 C2
Cook St *COVN CV1* 9 C7
DARL/WED WS10 ....68 D7
VAUX/NECH B7 ....90 A6
Cooper Av *BRLYHL DY5* 101 L3
Cooper Cl *BRGRVE B60* 191 L3
Cooper St *NUN CV11* 99 H1
WBROM B70 ....87 H2
WOLV WV1 ....3 M9
Coopers Wk *KNWTH CV8* 182 A7
Coopers Coppice *HEDN WS12 ** 17 K1
Coopers Hl *ALVE B48* 170 C1
Coopers La *SMTHWK B66* 87 L8
Coopers Rd *BFLD/HDSWWD B20* 88 C2
Cooper St *NUN CV11* 99 H1
WBROM B70 ....87 H2
WOLV WV1 ....3 M9
Cophall St *TPTN/OCK DY4* 68 D8
Cophams Cl *HIA/OLT B92* 128 A3
Copland Pl *TLHL/CAN CV4* 153 J2
Cope Arnolds Cl *COVN CV6* 134 D1
Copeland *RUGBYN/HIL CV21* 161 C6
Copeley Hl *AST/WIT B6* 89 M4
Copes Crs *WOLVN WV10* 36 E7
Cope's Dr *CRTAM B79* 31 L6
Cope St *BLOX/PEL WS3* 39 C7
COV CV1 ....8 C3
DARL/WED WS10 ....52 C7
VAUX/NECH B7 ....90 A6
Cophall Rd *HDSW B21* 88 A3
Copley Hl *AST/WIT B6* 89 M4
Coplow Cottages
*LDYWD/EDGR B16 ** 106 D2
Coplow St *LDYWD/EDGR B16* 106 D2
Coplow Ter *LDYWD/EDGR B16* 106 D2
Copnor Gv
LGN/SDN/BHAMAIR B26 ....109 J7
Coppenhall Gv *STETCH B33* 109 L2
Copperas St *COVE CV2* 134 F1
Copperbeech Cl
RIDG/WDGT B32 ....105 K8
Copperbeech Dr
*BHTH/HG B12 ** 107 L8
Copper Beech Dr *KGSWFD DY6* 83 H4
Copper Beech Gdns
BFLD/HDSWWD B20 ....88 D3
Copperfield Cl *COVE CV2* 155 M2
Copperfields *LICHS WS14* 21 H6
Copperkins Rd *HEDN WS12* 12 C3
Coppermill Rd *HEDN WS12* 12 C1
Coppice Av *HAG/WOL DY9* 120 D2
Coppice Cl *BNTWD WS7* 18 C5
ERDE/BCHGN B24 ....90 D2
GTWY WS6 ....24 B1
RBRY B45 ....143 K6
REDW B97 ....202 A2
SHLY B90 ....174 A1
*SOLH B91 ** 149 J1
WNSFLD WV11 ....37 L1
Coppice Ct *CNCK/NC WS11 ** 15 M6
Coppice Crs *BRWNH WS8* 26 B6
Coppice Dr *ACGN B27* 126 F3
POL/KGSB/FAZ B78 ....58 A3
Coppice Farm Wy *SHHTH WV12* 37 M6
Coppice Gv *LICHS WS14* 21 K6
Coppice Hts *KIDD DY11* 163 M4
Coppice Hollow
RIDG/WDGT B32 ....122 F4
Coppice La *ALDR WS9* 40 D1
BNTWD WS7 ....27 L2
BRLYHL DY5 ....102 A4
BRWNH WS8 ....26 B8
CNCK/NC WS11 ....24 B1
DUNHL/THL/PER WV6 ....34 C8
POL/KGSB/FAZ B78 ....58 A3
Coppice Ri *BRLYHL DY5* 102 B3
Coppice Rd
BDMR/CCFT WV3 ....40 D1
BILS/COS WV14 ....66 C5
CDYHTH B64 ....103 J6
HIA/OLT B92 ....128 C3
MOS/BIL B13 ....125 J2
Coppice Side *BRWNH WS8* 26 B6
Coppice St *TPTN/OCK DY4* 67 J7
WBROM B70 ....86 D1
The Coppice *ATHST CV9* 63 J6
BFLD/HDSWWD B20 ....88 C3
COVS CV3 ....155 M5
HEDN WS12 ....17 J4
NUNW/HART CV10 ....81 K6
SHHTH WV12 ....38 A7
STRBR DY8 ....119 K8
TPTN/OCK DY4 ....68 C5
Coppice View Rd
SCFLD/BOLD B73 ....71 L1
Coppice Wk *SHLY B90* 174 A1
Copplestone Cl *BKDE/SHDE B34* 91 M7
Copps Rd *RLSN CV32* 206 B5
Coppstone Dr *DOR/KN B93* 175 C2
Copston Gv *SLYOAK B29* 123 M5
Copthall Rd *HDSW B21* 88 A3

Copt Heath Cft *DOR/KN B93* 149 M5
Copt Heath Dr *DOR/KN B93* 149 L6
Copthorne Av *BNTWD WS7* 26 C8
Copthorne Rd *BDMR/CCFT WV3* 49 L6
COVN CV6 ....133 K5
KGSTG B44 ....71 J2
Copt Oak Cl *TLHL/CAN CV4* 153 G6
Copyholt La *BRGRVE B60* 200 A1
Coral Cl *COVW CV5* 154 A3
Coralin Cl
CHWD/FDBR/MGN B37 ....110 F3
Corbett Cl *BRGRVE B60* 191 M5
Corbett Crs *STRBR DY8* 101 L6
Corbett Rd *BRLYHL DY5* 102 C4
HLYWD B47 ....146 E6
KIDD DY11 ....137 L5
Corbetts Cl *HIA/OLT B92* 129 M6
Corbett St *RUSH/SHEL WS4* 40 C4
SMTHWK B66 ....105 M1
Corbin Rd *POL/KGSB/FAZ B78* 47 J6
Corbison Cl *WWCK CV34* 205 H4
Corbridge Av *KGSTG B44* 71 J3
Corbridge Rd *SCFLD/BOLD B73* 72 D3
Corbyn Rd *BORD B9* 108 C2
DUDN DY1 ....84 D5
Corbyns Cl *BRLYHL DY5* 83 M6
Corbyns Hall La *BRLYHL DY5* 83 M6
Corbyns Hall Rd *BRLYHL DY5* 83 M6
Cordelia Wy *RUGBYS/DCH CV22* ..186 C5
Cordley St *WBROM B70* 86 F1
Corfe Cl *COVE CV2* 135 K8
DUNHL/THL/PER WV6 ....48 C2
RIDG/WDGT B32 ....105 K8
Corfe Dr *OLDBY B69* 85 H5
Corfe Rd *BILS/COS WV14* 69 G5
Crofton Dr *DUNHL/THL/PER WV6* 49 C2
Coriander Cl *NFLD/LBR B31* 143 K6
Corinne Cl
CHWD/FDBR/MGN B37 ....110 E1
Corinthian Pl *COVE CV2* 135 H6
Corisande Rd *SLYOAK B29* 124 A3
Corley Av *NFLD/LBR B31* 147 J4
Corley St *SHLY B90* 147 J4
Corley Vw *RCOVN/BALC/EX CV7* ..116 A6
Cornbrook Rd *SLYOAK B29* 123 L2
Cornbury Gv *SHLY B90* 148 B1
Corncrake Cl *CSCFLD/WYGN B72* ...73 H3
Corncrake Dr *CBROM B36* 92 E5
Corncrake Rd *DUDN DY1* 84 B8
Corndon Cl *KIDD DY11* 163 M3
Cornel *TAM/AM/WIL B77* 46 D1
Cornel Cl
CHWD/FDBR/MGN B37 ....111 G5
Cornelius St *COVS CV3* 155 H5
Corner La *REDW B97* 202 A5
Cornerway *HWK/WKHTH B38* 145 K6
Corners End La
RCOVN/BALC/EX CV7 ....130 C6
Cornfield *CDSL WV8* 35 K3
Cornfield Av *BRGRVE B60* 191 H7
Cornfield Cl *KGSWFD DY6* 82 E5
Cornfield Cft
CHWD/FDBR/MGN B37 ....111 H2
WALM/CURD B76 ....73 K4
Cornfield Dr *LICHS WS14* 21 J6
Cornfield Rd
BLKHTH/ROWR B65 ....103 K1
NFLD/LBR B31 ....144 F1
The Cornfield *COVS CV3* 156 A4
Cornflower Cl *WOLVN WV10* 22 E6
Cornflower Crs *DUDS DY2* 85 L6
Cornflower Dr *RRUGBY CV23* 158 B2
Cornflower Rd *BRWNH WS8* 26 B7
Cornforth Cl
*POL/KGSB/FAZ B78 ** 60 B7
Corngreaves Rd *CDYHTH B64* 103 J6
The Corngreaves
BKDE/SHDE B34 ....92 A7
Corngreaves Wk *CDYHTH B64* 103 J6
Cornhampton Cl *REDW B97* 193 M8
Cornhill *CNCK/NC WS11* 12 C8
WOLV WV1 ....3 H5
Cornhill Gv *BVILLE B30* 125 C7
KNWTH CV8 ....179 G8
Cornish Cl *NUNW/HART CV10* 79 K5
Cornish Crs *NUNW/HART CV10* 98 E3
Corn Mdw *BDWTH CV12* 117 C3
Corn Mill Cl *RIDG/WDGT B32* 123 J4
WALM/CURD B76 ....73 K4
Cornmill Cl *WSL WS1 ** 4 C8
Cornmill Gdns *BRGRVE B60* 169 L8
Cornmill Gv
DUNHL/THL/PER WV6 ....48 B2
Cornovian Cl
DUNHL/THL/PER WV6 ....48 C8
Corns Gv *WMBN WV5* 64 C8
Cornwall Av *LGLYGN/QTN B68* 104 F5
POL/KGSB/FAZ B78 ....45 L4
Cornwall Cl *ALDR WS9* 40 H2
DARL/WED WS10 ....69 H2
KGSWFD DY6 ....83 H4
WWCK CV34 ....205 K4
Cornwall Ga *SHHTH WV12* 37 M3
Cornwallis Rd
RUGBYS/DCH CV22 ....186 D4
WBROM B70 ....86 C4
Cornwall Pl *RLSN CV32* 206 C2
WSLW WS2 ....52 C2
Cornwall Rd *BFLD/HDSWWD B20* ...88 C7
CNCK/NC WS11 ....9 J7
DSYBK/YTR WS5 ....55 M8
DUNHL/THL/PER WV6 ....12 F8
HEDN WS12 ....12 F8
RBRY B45 ....143 J3
*SMTHWK B66 ** 87 M6
STRBR DY8 ....101 H5
Cornwall St *CBHAMNW B3* 6 E4
Cornwell Cl *REDE B98* 67 L8
TPTN/OCK DY4 ....67 L8
Cornyx La *SOLH B91* 148 C2
Coronation Av
POL/KGSB/FAZ B78 ....45 H4
POL/KGSB/FAZ B78 ....58 B3
WLNH WV13 ....52 B3
Coronation Crs *CRTAM B79* 31 K7
Coronation Rd *ALDR WS9* 40 D2
ATHST CV9 ....51 G7
BILS/COS WV14 ....51 L5
COV CV1 ....9 L2
DARL/WED WS10 ....69 G2
GTB/HAM B43 ....70 C7
RRUGBY CV23 ....158 F9
SLYOAK B29 ....124 C3
TPTN/OCK DY4 ....67 M5
WASH/WDE B8 ....90 D7
WNSFLD WV11 ....36 E8
Coronation St *CRTAM B79* 31 L8
Coronation Ter *BRGRVE B60* 191 M6
Coronation Wy *KIDD DY10* 138 E7
Coronel Av *COVN CV6* 134 C1
Corporation Rd *DUDS DY2* 85 K4
Corporation St *CBHAMNE B4 ** 7 J2
COV CV1 ....8 E5

CRTAM B79 ....31 M8
DARL/WED WS10 ....68 E3
KIDD DY10 ....138 C8
NUN CV11 ....80 F3
NUN CV11 ....81 L8
RUGBYN/HIL CV21 ....186 C2
WOLV WV1 ....2 E5
WSL WS1 ....4 E7
Corporation St West WSLW WS2 ...4 E7
Correen TAM/AM/WIL B77 ......47 G4
Corrie Cft
 LGN/SDN/BHAMAIR B26 ...109 M6
 RIDG/WDGT B32 ....122 F6
Corrin Gv KGSWFD DY6 ....83 C5
Corron HI HALE B63 * 121 M1
Corser St DUDS DY1 ....84 D3
 STRBR DY8 ....119 L2
 WOLV WV1 ....3 L6
Corsican Cl BNTWD WS7 ....18 D5
 SHHTH WV12 ....38 C6
Corsican Dr HEDN WS12 ....12 E5
Corston Ms RLSS CV31 ....207 C7
Cort Dr BNTWD WS7 ....18 F5
Corunna Rd WWCK CV34 ....205 G6
Corvedale Rd SLYOAK B29 ....123 C7
Corve Gdns
 DUNHL/THL/PER WV6 ....35 J8
Corve Vw SEDG DY3 * 66 A4
Corville Gdns
 LGN/SDN/BHAMAIR B26 ...127 M1
Corville Rd RMSLY B62 ....104 D7
Corwen Cft NFLD/LBR B31 ....123 J7
Cory Cft TPTN/OCK DY4 ....67 L8
Coseley Rd BILS/COS WV14 ....51 C8
Cosford Cl REDE B98 ....203 K4
 RLSN CV32 ....206 F2
Cosford Crs CVALE B35 ....91 L2
Cosford Dr DUDS DY2 ....85 J8
Cosford La RRUGBY CV23 ....160 E3
Cossington Rd
 ERDW/GRVHL B23 ....72 B6
Costers La CBROM B36 ....203 K3
Costock Cl
 CHWD/FDBR/MGN B37 ....110 F5
Cotford Rd ALE/KHTH/YWD B14 146 E3
Cotheridge Cl SHLY B90 ....149 C7
Cot La STRBR DY8 ....101 H1
Cotleigh Gv KGSTG B44 ....71 H2
Cotman Dr BDWTH CV12 ....116 E1
 GTB/HAM B43 ....71 G2
Coton Gv SHLY B90 ....147 J3
Coton La CRTAM B79 ....31 H6
 ERDW/GRVHL B23 ....90 D1
Coton Rd RRUGBY CV23 ....161 G5
Coton Rd
 ETTPK/GDPK/PENN WV4 ......49 M8
 NUN CV11 ....99 C2
 RUGBYN/HIL CV21 ....187 L5
 WALM/CURD B76 ....75 J4
Cotsdale Rd
 ETTPK/GDPK/PENN WV4 ......65 J2
Cotsford SOLH B91 * 148 E2
Cotswold Av GTWY WS6 ....24 D2
 STRPT DY13 ....188 B4
Cotswold Cl ALDR WS9 ....41 G4
 KIDDW DY11 ....164 A3
 OLDBY B69 ....86 C8
 RBRY B45 ....143 L4
Cotswold Ct BKHL/PFLD WV2 ......49 L1
Cotswold Crs NUNW/HART CV10 ..97 M2
Cotswold Cft HALE B63 ....121 H1
Cotswold Dr COVS CV3 ....181 G2
Cotswold Gv SHHTH WV12 ....37 M4
Cotswold Rd BKHL/PFLD WV2 ......50 D6
 HEDN WS12 ....12 E5
 STRBR DY8 ....101 M7
Cotswold Wy BRGRVW B61 ....168 E8
Cottage Cl BNTWD WS7 ....18 F5
 HEDN WS12 ....17 H1
 RLSS CV31 ....207 G7
 WNSFLD WV11 ....37 G7
Cottage Dr BRGRVE B60 ....169 G4
Cottage Farm La BRGRVE B60 ...169 K4
Cottage Farm Rd COVN CV6 ....133 C4
 TAM/AM/WIL B77 ....46 B7
Cottage Gdns RBRY B45 ....143 K7
Cottage La BNTWD WS7 ....18 D8
 BRGRVE B60 ....169 G3
 CSHL/WTROR B46 ....76 B7
 WALM/CURD B76 ....74 D7
 WOLV WV10 ....36 B2
Cottage Leap
 RUGBYN/HIL CV21 ....187 H1
Cottage Ms ALDR WS9 ....55 J1
Cottage St BRLYHL DY5 ....102 B2
 KGSWFD DY6 ....83 H6
Cottage Vw CDSL WV8 ....34 F1
Cotterell Rd RUGBYN/HIL CV21 ..160 D7
Cotteridge Rd BVILLE B30 ....145 L1
Cotterills Av WASH/WDE B8 ......108 F1
Cotterills La WASH/WDE B8 ......109 G1
Cotterills Rd TPTN/OCK DY4 ....67 M6
Cottesbrook Cl COVS CV3 ....156 C4
Cottesbrook Rd ACGN B27 ....127 G1
Cottesfield Cl WASH/WDE B8 ....109 G1
Cottesmore Cl HHTH/SAND B71 ...69 K5
Cottle Cl WSLW WS2 ....52 D2
Cotton Arches Rbt NUN CV11 .....99 C3
Cotton Dr KNWTH CV8 ....180 A7
Cotton Gv HEDN WS12 ....12 E4
Cotton La MOS/BIL B13 ....125 L5
Cotton Mill Spinney RLSN CV32 .199 J7
Cotton Pool Rd BRGRVW B61 .....191 J3
Cottrell St HHTH/SAND B71 ....87 H1
Cottsmeadow Dr
 WASH/WDE B8 ....109 G1
Cotwall End Rd SEDG DY3 ....83 M1
Cotysmore Rd NUNW/HART CV10 .75 C8
Couchman Rd WASH/WDE B8 ....108 C1
Coughton Dr RLSS CV31 ....207 H8
Coulson Cl BNTWD WS7 ....18 C5
Coulter Gv
 DUNHL/THL/PER WV6 ....48 D1
Coulter La BNTWD WS7 ....19 J5
Coundon Gv COVN CV6 ....133 C5
Coundon St COV CV1 ....8 C3
Coundon Wedge Dr COVW CV5 ..133 G7
Counterfield Dr
 BLKHTH/ROWR B65 ....85 K8
Countess Dr RUSH/SHEL WS4 .....40 B6
Countess Rd NUN CV11 ....98 E1
The Countess's Cft COVS CV3 ....155 H6
Counting House Wy
 BRGRVE B60 ....191 J4
County Cl BVILLE B30 ....125 C3
 RIDG/WDGT B32 ....122 F8
County Dr POL/KGSB/FAZ B78 .....45 L1
County La KINVER DY7 ....119 H5
County Park Av RMSLY B62 ....122 A2
Courtaulds Wy COVN CV6 ....134 B7
Court Cl KIDDW DY11 ....137 M4
Court Crs KGSWFD DY6 ....83 C8
Court Dr LICHS WS14 ....21 M7
 STRPT DY13 ....188 D1
Courtenay Gdns GTB/HAM B43 ...70 C3
Courtenay Rd KGSTG B44 ....71 F3
Court Farm Rd
 ERDW/GRVHL B23 ....72 C7
Courthouse Cft KNWTH CV8 .....198 A1
Courtland Av COVN CV6 ....133 K8
Courtlands Cl DIG/EDG B5 ....107 C3
The Courtlands
 LGN La ERDW/GRVHL B23 ......72 C5
Court Leet Rd COVS CV3 ....157 H6
Court Leet Rd COVS CV3 ....155 L6
Courtney CL NUN CV11 ....81 K6
Court Oak Gv RIDG/WDGT B32 ..105 K7
Court Oak Rd RIDG/WDGT B32 ..105 K7
Court Pas DUDN DY1 * 85 G4
Court Rd BHTH/HG B12 ....107 J7
 DUNHL/THL/PER WV6 ....49 J1
 ETTPK/GDPK/PENN WV4 ......66 L1
 SPARK B11 ....126 A1
Court St CDYHTH B64 ....103 J4
 RLSS CV31 ....206 E6
Courtway Av
 ALE/KHTH/YWD B14 ....146 F4
The Courtyard
 CSHL/WTROR B46 * 93 K3
Cousins St BKHL/PFLD WV2 ....50 B6
Coveley Gv WSNGN B18 ....88 E8
Coven Cl BLOX/PEL WS3 ....25 L8
Coven Gv SLYOAK B29 ....123 M3
Coven Mill Cl COVEN WV9 ....22 A4
Coven St WOLV WV10 ....3 H1
Coventry Hay BDWTH CV12 ......202 E1
Coventry Point COV CV1 * 8 F5
Coventry Rd BDWTH CV12 ....116 H4
 BTACH/HAR CV33 ....199 J5
 COVE CV2 ....117 J7
 COVS CV3 ....157 J3
 CSHL/WTROR B46 ....111 L2
 HIA/OLT B92 ....129 M2
 KNWTH CV8 ....179 L7
 KNWTH CV8 ....181 G6
 KNWTH CV8 ....181 J2
 LGN/SDN/BHAMAIR B26 ......128 E1
 LGN/SDN/BHAMAIR B26 ......109 K5
 NUNW/HART CV10 ....99 G6
 POL/KGSB/FAZ B78 ....76 B1
 RCOVN/BALC/EX CV7 ....114 C3
 RCOVN/BALC/EX CV7 ....152 B3
 RRUGBY CV23 ....158 C3
 RRUGBY CV23 ....158 D8
 RRUGBY CV23 ....185 J1
 SMHTH B10 ....7 M8
 SMHTH B10 ....107 M4
 WWCK CV34 ....205 K5
Coventry Rd Exhall
 RCOVN/BALC/EX CV7 ....116 E6
Coventry St COVE CV2 ....155 L1
 DIG/EDG B5 ....7 J6
 KIDD DY10 ....138 C7
 NUN CV11 ....99 C1
 STRBR DY8 ....101 L8
 WOLV WV1 ....50 J3
Coventry Wy BDWTH CV12 ....116 B3
 KNWTH CV8 ....183 K2
 RCOVN/BALC/EX CV7 ....114 C5
 RCOVN/BALC/EX CV7 ....152 C1
Cover Cft WALM/CURD B76 ....73 L4
Coverdale Rd HIA/OLT B92 ....127 L1
Coverley Pl RUGBYS/DCH CV22 ..186 C2
The Covers STUD B80 ....203 J7
Covert La STRBR DY8 ....119 H4
The Covert CDSL WV8 ....35 J4
Covey Cl LICH WS14 ....21 H4
Cowan Cl RUGBYS/DCH CV22 ....185 M4
Cowdray Cl RLSS CV31 ....207 G6
Cow La POL/KGSB/FAZ B78 ....62 D2
Cowles Cft YDLY B25 ....109 J4
Cowley TAM/AM/WIL B77 ....47 G3
Cowley Cl CBROM B36 ....92 D4
 PENK ST19 ....10 D6
Cowley Dr ACGN B27 ....127 H1
 DUDN DY1 ....84 D3
Cowley Gn HEDN WS12 ....12 D5
Cowley Rd COVE CV2 ....156 B1
 SPARK B11 ....108 C8
Cowper Cl SHHTH WV12 ....38 C6
Cowslip Cl HWK/WKHTH B38 .....145 K5
 SLYOAK B29 ....123 L6
Coxcroft Av BRLYHL DY5 ....102 D5
Coxmoor Cl BLOX/PEL WS3 * 38 D2
Cox Rd BILS/COS WV14 ....67 J4
Cox's Cl NUNW/HART CV10 ....98 D7
Cox's La CDYHTH B64 ....103 K3
Cox St CBHAMNW B3 ....6 C1
 COV CV1 ....9 H3
Coxwell Av WOLV WV10 ....36 A8
Coxwell Gdns
 LDYWD/EDGR B16 ....88 A8
Coyne Cl TPTN/OCK DY4 ....67 H8
Coyne Rd WBROM B70 ....86 F3
Cozens Cl BDWTH CV12 ....116 E1
Crabbe St HAG/WOL DY9 ....102 D8
Crabbs Cross La REDW B97 ....202 B8
Crab La CNCK/NC WS11 ....16 E2
 SHHTH WV12 ....38 B4
Crabmill Cl DOR/KN B93 ....150 A6
Crab Mill La COVN CV6 ....134 D6
Crabmill La COVN CV6 ....134 C6
Crabourne Rd DUDS DY2 ....102 F3
Crabtree Cl HHTH/SAND B71 ....69 H6
 NFLD/LBR B31 ....145 G3
Crabtree Dr BRGRVW B61 ....191 K7
 CHWD/FDBR/MGN B37 ....110 D2
Crabtree Gv RLSS CV31 ....207 J7
Crabtree La BRGRVW B61 ....191 J2
Crabtree Rd WSL WS1 ....5 K3
 WSL WS1 ....88 E8
Crackley Cottages
 KNWTH CV8 * 179 M5
Crackley HI KNWTH CV8 * 179 M5
Crackley La KNWTH CV8 ....179 J1
Crackley Wy DUDS DY2 ....85 M2
Craddock Rd SMTHWKW B67 ....87 J7
Craddock St
 DUNHL/THL/PER WV6 ....49 L1
Cradley Cft REDE B98 ....203 M4
Cradley Cft HDSW B21 ....88 B2
Cradley Flds HALE B63 ....103 H8
Cradley Forge HALE B63 ....103 K6
Cradley Park Rd DUDS DY2 ....85 M2
Cradley Rd CDYHTH B64 ....103 G5
Cradock Rd WASH/WDE B8 ....90 D2
Craig Cft
 CHWD/FDBR/MGN B37 ....111 H3
Craigends Av COVS CV3 ....156 C7
Crail Gv GTB/HAM B43 ....70 F2
Crakston Cl COVE CV2 ....156 D3
Cramlington Rd PBAR/PBCH B42 ..70 F1
Cramore Cl TPTN/OCK DY4 ....67 L5
Cramper's Fld COVN CV6 ....133 C3

Cramp HI DARL/WED WS10 ....52 B7
Cranberry Dr STRPT DY13 ....188 C1
Cranbourne Cha COVE CV2 ....135 K8
Cranbourne Av
 ETTPK/GDPK/PENN WV4 ......66 C2
Cranbourne Cl RBRY B45 ....143 M3
Cranbourne Gv KGSTG B44 ....71 L5
Cranbourne Pl
 HHTH/SAND B71 * 87 H1
Cranbourne Rd KGSTG B44 ....71 K4
 STRBR DY8 ....119 L1
Cranbrook Gv
 DUNHL/THL/PER WV6 ....48 D2
Cranbrook Rd HDSW B21 ....88 A4
Cranby St WASH/WDE B8 ....90 A8
Cranberry Rd STETCH B33 ....110 C2
Cranbrook HI
 POL/KGSB/FAZ B78 ....59 G4
Cranbrook La LICHS WS14 ....27 K7
Crane Cl WWCK CV34 ....205 H4
Crane Dr BNTWD WS7 ....26 E1
Crane Fld LGN/SDN/BHAMAIR 20 E4
Crane Hollow WMBN WV5 * 64 C8
Cranehouse Rd KGSTG B44 ....71 L3
Cranemoor Cl VAUX/NECH B7 * ...90 A7
Crane Rd BILS/COS WV14 ....67 K2
Craner's Rd COV CV1 ....9 L1
Cranesbill Cl WOLV WV10 ....23 H3
Cranesbill Rd SLYOAK B29 ....123 L7
Cranes Park Rd
 LGN/SDN/BHAMAIR B26 ......110 A8
Crane St KIDDW DY11 ....138 A7
 DUNHL/THL/PER WV6 ....J8
Cranfield Cv
 LGN/SDN/BHAMAIR B26 ......109 K5
Cranfield Pl DSYBK/YTR WS5 ......69 K1
Cranfield Rd BNTWD WS7 ....18 E6
Cranford Gv SOLH B91 * 148 B7
Cranford Rd BDMR/CCFT WV3 .....49 G5
 COVW CV5 ....154 B1
Cranford St SMTHWK B66 ....88 A8
Cranford Wy SMTHWK B66 ....88 A8
Cranham Cl REDW B97 ....201 M5
Cranham Dr KGSWFD DY6 ....83 H8
Cranhill Cl HIA/OLT B92 ....127 M4
Crankhall La DARL/WED WS10 .....69 C2
Cranleigh Cl ALDR WS9 ....40 F8
 SHHTH WV12 ....38 A4
Cranleigh Gdns SOLH B91 * 148 C3
Cranleigh Pl KGSTG B44 ....71 J8
Cranley Dr CDSL WV8 ....34 D1
Cranmer Av SHHTH WV12 ....38 B8
Cranmer Cl GTWY WS6 ....24 A4
Cranmere Av
 DUNHL/THL/PER WV6 * 34 E7
Cranmere Cl
 DUNHL/THL/PER WV6 * 34 E7
Cranmoor Cl FOAKS/STRLY B74 ..42 D7
Cranmoor Crs HALE B63 ....103 L8
Cranmore Av HDSW B21 ....88 B6
 SHLY B90 ....148 C5
Cranmore Bvd SHLY B90 ....148 B5
Cranmore Dr SHLY B90 ....148 B5
Cranmore Rd BDMR/CCFT WV3 ...49 K2
 CBROM B36 ....92 C4
 SHLY B90 ....148 B5
Cransley Gv SOLH B91 ....148 E4
Cantock Cl SHHTH WV12 ....38 A4
Crantock Rd PBAR/PBCH B42 ......89 C1
Crantock Wy NUN CV11 ....99 K1
Cranwell Gn WMBN WV5 ....64 D8
Cranwell Gdr REDE/BCHGN B24 ...91 H2
Cranwell Wy CVALE B35 ....91 L2
Crateford La PENK ST19 ....14 A6
Crathie Cl COVE CV2 ....135 K7
Crathorne Av WOLV WV10 ....36 A4
Craufurd Ct STRBR DY8 ....119 L2
Craven La COVS CV3 ....157 H6
Craven Av COVS CV3 ....157 H6
Craven Rd RUGBYN/HIL CV21 ....186 F1
Craven St BKHL/PFLD WV2 * 50 D7
 COVW CV5 ....154 D3
Crawford Av DARL/WED WS10 .....52 A6
 ETTPK/GDPK/PENN WV4 ......66 D2
 SMTHWKW B67 ....87 H3
Crawford Cl RLSN CV32 ....206 F1
Crawford Rd BDMR/CCFT WV3 .....2 A5
 WALM/CURD B76 ....73 K5
Crawford St WASH/WDE B8 ....90 A8
Crawshaws Rd CBROM B36 ....92 A4
Crayford Rd KGSTG B44 ....71 L4
Craythorne Av
 BFLD/HDSWWD B20 ....70 C8
Crecy Cl WALM/CURD B76 ....73 J1
Crecy Rd COVS CV3 ....155 J6
Credenda Rd WBROM B70 ....86 E4
Crediton Cl NUN CV11 ....81 K9
Credon Gv EDG B15 ....106 D8
Cregoe St EDG B15 ....6 D8
Cremore Av WASH/WDE B8 ....90 C8
Cremorne Wk MGN/WHC B75 * 56 F5
Crendon Cl STUD B80 ....203 J8
Crendon Rd BLKHTH/ROWR B65 ...85 J1
Crescent Ar SOLH B91 * 149 G1
Crescent Rd BRLYHL DY5 ....102 A3
 COVS CV3 ....155 M3
The Crescent Grange Rd
 HAG/WOL DY9 * 120 A1
Crescent Rd DARL/WED WS10 .....52 B7
 DUDS DY2 ....84 F8
 KIDDW DY11 ....138 A7
 WLNHL WV13 ....51 K4
Crescent Studios WSNGN B18 * ...88 F7
The Crescent ATHST CV9 ....62 A2
 BILS/COS WV14 ....51 H7
 BLKHTH/ROWR B65 ....103 M3
 BNTWD WS7 ....18 D4
 BRGRVE B60 ....191 K6
 CDYHTH B64 ....103 L6
 CHWD/FDBR/MGN B37 ....111 J3
 DARL/WED WS10 ....68 E1
 DUDN DY1 ....85 J1
 DUNHL/THL/PER WV6 ....35 J3
 GTB/HAM B43 ....70 E4
 GTWY WS6 ....24 E3
 HAG/WOL DY9 ....120 A1
 HIA/OLT B92 ....129 M6
 KIDD DY10 ....138 F1
 RCOVN/BALC/EX CV7 ....115 K7
 RRUGBY CV23 ....185 G2
 SHLY B90 ....147 L1
 SOLH B91 ....148 F1
 WLNHL WV13 ....52 A4
 WSL WS1 ....5 J6
 WSL WS1 ....5 M6
 WSNGN B18 ....88 F7
Cressage Av NFLD/LBR B31 ....144 E4
Cressage Rd COVE CV2 ....135 L3
Cressett Av BRLYHL DY5 ....101 M4
Cressett La BRLYHL DY5 ....102 A3
Cressington Dr
 FOAKS/STRLY B74 ....56 E4
Cresswell Cl NUNW/HART CV10 ...81 C5
Cresswell Crs BLOX/PEL WS3 ....38 D3
Cresswell Gv ERDE/BCHGN B24 ...91 H1
The Crest NFLD/LBR B31 ....122 F7
 RLSN CV32 ....207 G1
Crest Vw ALE/KHTH/YWD B14 ...146 F1

FOAKS/STRLY B74 ....55 K4
Crestwood TAM/AM/WIL B77 ......32 E8
Crestwood Av KIDDW DY11 ....137 L8
Crestwood Dr KGSTG B44 ....71 K4
Crestwood Gln
 DUNHL/THL/PER WV6 ....35 J6
Creswell Rd HLGN/YWD B28 .....126 F6
Creswick Gv RBRY B45 ....144 A6
Crew La KNWTH CV8 ....180 C8
Crew Rd DARL/WED WS10 ....68 E1
Creynolds Cl SHLY B90 ....174 B1
Creynolds La SHLY B90 ....174 C1
Cricket Cl COWW CV5 ....154 C2
Cricketers Meadow
 CDYHTH B64 ....103 K6
Cricket La LICHS WS14 ....29 G1
Cricket Meadow SEDG DY3 ....66 C8
 WOLV WV10 ....36 B3
Crick La BFLD/HDSWWD B20 ......88 C5
Cricklewood Dr RMSLY B62 ....122 B2
Crigdon TAM/AM/WIL B77 ....32 E8
Crimmond Rd HALE B63 ....103 J8
Crimscote Cl SHLY B90 ....148 D3
Cringlebrook TAM/AM/WIL B77 ...46 B4
Cripps Rd WSLW WS2 ....52 C2
Crocketts Dr SHLY B90 * 88 B6
Crockett's La SMTHWK B66 ....87 L8
Crocketts Rd HDSW B21 ....88 B6
Crockett St DUDN DY1 ....84 E3
Crockford Dr MGN/WHC B75 ....56 E2
Crockford Rd HRBN B17 ....105 K7
Crocus Crs COVEN WV9 ....35 L2
Croft Av HEDN WS12 ....12 E4
Croft Cl REDE B98 ....203 H1
 RRUGBY CV23 ....183 K7
 WWCK CV34 ....206 B4
Croft Crs BRWNH WS8 ....26 B6
Croft Down Rd HIA/OLT B92 ....128 C4
Croftdown Rd HRBN B17 ....105 K7
Crofters Cl STRBR DY8 ....119 M1
Crofters Ct EDG B15 ....106 C7
Crofts Flds BDWTH CV12 ....116 F5
Croft Gdns BNTWD WS7 ....18 F5
Croft La WOLV WV10 ....14 B4
 WOLV WV10 ....36 B3
Croftleigh Gdns SOLH B91 * 148 C3
Croft Md NUNW/HART CV10 ....97 C3
Croft Pool BDWTH CV12 ....116 D3
The Crofts WALM/CURD B76 ....73 L6
Croft St CRTAM B79 ....31 M7
 WLNHL WV13 ....51 L3
 WSLW WS2 ....53 H4
The Croft BDWTH CV12 ....117 M3
 COVN CV6 ....134 C4
 DSYBK/YTR WS5 ....54 B5
 DUDS DY2 ....84 D7
 GTWY WS6 ....24 E3
 KIDD DY10 ....140 A3
 KIDDW DY11 ....163 L2
 NFLD/LBR B31 ....144 F2
 RCOVN/BALC/EX CV7 ....131 C4
 RUGBYN/HIL CV21 * 187 C5
 SEDG DY3 ....66 C4
 WLNHL WV13 ....51 L3
 WMBN WV5 ....64 B8
Croftway
 BFLD/HDSWWD B20 * 89 G2
Crompton Cl WSLW WS2 ....52 B2
Crompton Cl CDSL WV8 ....34 F1
Crompton Av
 BFLD/HDSWWD B20 ....70 C7
 RBRY B45 ....143 H4
 TPTN/OCK DY4 ....85 L1
 VAUX/NECH B7 ....90 A7
Crompton St WWCK CV34 ....205 H4
 WSLW WS2 ....52 C1
Cromwell Dr DUDS DY2 ....85 M2
Cromwell La RIDG/WDGT B32 ....121 J4
 TLHL/CAN CV4 ....153 G7
Cromwell Rd CRTAM B79 ....31 J4
 HEDN WS12 ....17 H4
 RUGBYS/DCH CV22 ....187 G4
 WOLV WV10 ....36 E3
Cromwells Meadow LICHS WS14 ..21 H4
Cromwell St COVN CV6 ....134 C7
 DUDS DY2 ....85 J1
 VAUX/NECH B7 ....89 M8
Crondal Pl EDG B15 ....106 C7
Crondal Rd
 RCOVN/BALC/EX CV7 ....114 C7
Cronehills Linkway WBROM B70 ...87 H2
Cronehills St WBROM B70 ....87 H1
Crookham Cl HRBN B17 ....105 H4
Crookhay La HHTH/SAND B71 .....68 E5
Crook House Yd
 RRUGBY CV23 * 158 D1
Crook La ALDR WS9 ....54 E7
Croome Cl COVN CV6 ....154 D1
 REDE B98 ....203 K3
 SPARK B11 ....125 M2
Cropredy Rd NFLD/LBR B31 ....144 L1
Cropthorne Cl REDE B98 ....202 E6
Cropthorne Dr HYWD B47 ....146 F6
Cropthorne Rd SHLY B90 ....148 C1
Crosbie Rd COVW CV5 ....154 C2
 HRBN B17 ....105 M7
Crosby Cl CBHAMW B1 ....6 D3
 DUNHL/THL/PER WV6 ....35 J6
Cross Cheaping COV CV1 ....8 E3
Cross Farm Rd HRBN B17 ....124 B1
Cross Farms La RBRY B45 ....143 K4
Crossfell LICH WS13 * 21 J1
Crossfield Rd LICH WS13 ....21 J1
 STETCH B33 ....109 L1
Cross Fields Rd WWCK CV34 .....205 K5
Crossgate Rd DUDS DY2 ....84 F8
 REDE B98 ....203 C6
The Crossings LICH WS13 ....21 H4
Cross In Hand La LICH WS13 ....19 L1
Crosskey Cl STETCH B33 ....110 C3
Cross Keys LICH WS13 ....20 F5
Crossland Crs
 DUNHL/THL/PER WV6 ....35 K7
Cross La GTB/HAM B43 ....70 C4
 LICHS WS14 ....21 H1

RLSN CV32 ....207 J1
SEDG DY3 ....66 B5
Crossley St DUDS DY3 * 103 H1
Cross Pl SEDG DY3 ....66 C4
Cross Rd COVN CV6 ....134 D5
 BLKHTH/ROWR B65 ....104 A4
 BLOX/PEL WS3 ....39 L4
 BNTWD WS7 ....18 C5
 CNCK/NC WS11 ....16 C8
 COV CV1 ....9 H2
 CRTAM B79 ....31 H8
 DARL/WED WS10 ....68 E2
 GTWY WS6 ....24 B3
 HALE B63 ....121 L2
 HDSW B21 ....88 A5
 HEDN WS12 ....17 J4
 KGSWFD DY6 ....83 H6
 LGLYGN/QTN B68 ....104 E1
 NUNW/HART CV10 ....98 F1
 RLSN CV32 ....206 E4
 RRUGBY CV23 ....159 L8
 RUGBYN/HIL CV21 ....187 G1
 STRBR DY8 ....101 M2
 STRBR DY8 ....101 J8
 TAM/AM/WIL B77 ....46 A2
 WLNHL WV13 ....51 L4
 WOLV WV1 ....3 M6
 WWCK CV34 ....205 K6
Cross St North WOLV WV1 ....3 H1
Cross St South BKHL/PFLD WV2 ...50 B1
Cross Wk POL/KGSB/FAZ B78 ......47 L7
Cross Walks Rd HAG/WOL DY9 ...102 C8
Crossway La KGSTG B44 ....71 K7
Crossway Rd COVS CV3 ....181 J4
Crosswells Rd LGLYGN/QTN B68 ..86 F8
Crowberry La
 POL/KGSB/FAZ B78 ....59 G4
Crowden Rd TAM/AM/WIL B77 .....46 E4
Crowesbridge Ms
 BILS/COS WV14 ....66 F5
Crowhill Rd NUN CV11 ....99 K3
Crowhurst Rd NFLD/LBR B31 .....144 C5
Crowland Av
 DUNHL/THL/PER WV6 ....48 C5
Crowle Dr HAG/WOL DY9 ....102 A8
Crowmere Rd COVE CV2 ....135 K6
Crown Br PENK ST19 ....10 C7
Crown Cl BLKHTH/ROWR B65 ....104 B1
 BRGRVW B61 ....191 K3
Crown Ct DARL/WED WS10 ....52 A5
Crown Gn COVN CV6 ....134 C3
Crown La FOAKS/STRLY B74 ....56 C3
 KIDD DY10 ....138 C2
 STRBR DY8 ....101 J2
 STRPT DY13 ....189 J5
Crown Meadow ALVE B48 ....170 E7
Crownmeadow Dr
 TPTN/OCK DY4 ....68 B6
Crown Rd BORD B9 ....108 B3
 BVILLE B30 ....145 L1
Crown St WOLV WV1 ....3 H6
 SEDG DY3 ....16 B8
Crown Ter RLSS CV31 ....206 D6
Crown Wk TPTN/OCK DY4 ....85 L3
Crown Wy RLSN CV32 ....206 F2
Crows Nest Cl WALM/CURD B76 ...73 J2
Crowther Gdns HALE B63 ....103 G6
Crowther Gv
 DUNHL/THL/PER WV6 ....49 K1
Crowther Rd
 DUNHL/THL/PER WV6 ....35 K8
 ERDW/GRVHL B23 ....72 B8
 WOLV WV10 ....50 C1
Crow Thorns RUGBYN/HIL CV21 ..161 G7
Croxall Dr CSHL/WTROR B46 ....94 E3
Croxall Wy SMTHWK B66 ....87 M8
Croxdene Av BLOX/PEL WS3 ....38 D4
Croxhall St BDWTH CV12 ....117 G3
Croxley Gdns WLNHL WV13 ....51 K3
Croxstalls Av BLOX/PEL WS3 ....38 E4
Croxstalls Cl BLOX/PEL WS3 ....38 E4
Croxstalls Pl BLOX/PEL WS3 ....38 E4
Croxstalls Rd BLOX/PEL WS3 ....38 E4
Croxton Gv STETCH B33 ....109 L1
Croyde Av PBAR/PBCH B42 ....70 D3
Croydon Cl COVS CV3 ....155 J7
Croydon Rd ERDE/BCHGN B24 .....90 E4
 SLYOAK B29 ....124 D2
Croy Dr CVALE B35 ....91 M1
The Crucible BILS/COS WV14 ....67 G3
Cruisehill La REDW B97 ....201 H8
Crummock Cl COVN CV6 ....134 B2
Crumpfields La REDW B97 ....201 J7
Crundals La BEWD DY12 ....136 F7
Crusader Cl OLDBY B69 ....86 B6
Crutch La DROIT WR9 ....190 A8
Crutchley Av POL/KGSB/FAZ B78 ..45 L4
Crychan Cl RBRY B45 ....143 M3
Cryersoak Cl SHLY B90 ....148 E6
Cryfield Grange Rd
 TLHL/CAN CV4 ....180 A3
Cryfield Hts TLHL/CAN CV4 ....180 A3
Crystal Av STRBR DY8 ....101 K4
Crystal Dr SMTHWK B66 ....87 G5
Cubbington Rd COVN CV6 ....134 C2
 RLSN CV32 ....206 E2
Cubley Rd HLGN/YWD B28 ....126 C4
Cuckoo Cl CNCK/NC WS11 ....161 C7
Cuckoo La COV CV1 ....9 G4
Cuckoo Rd VAUX/NECH B7 ....90 B5
Cuin Dr SMTHWK B66 ....88 A8
Cuin Rd SMTHWK B66 ....88 A8
Culey Gv STETCH B33 ....110 B3
Culford Dr RIDG/WDGT B32 ....123 G5
Culham Cl ACGN B27 ....127 H3
Culleywick St WOLV WV10 ....3 L6
Culmington Gv NFLD/LBR B31 ....144 C5
Culmington Rd NFLD/LBR B31 ....144 D5
Culmore Cl SHHTH WV12 ....38 A4
Culmore Rd RMSLY B62 ....104 C1
Culpepper Cl NUNW/HART CV10 ..98 C1
Culverhouse Dr STRBR DY8 ....101 L4
Culverley Crs DOR/KN B93 ....150 F4
Culwell St WOLV WV10 ....3 H3
Culworth Cl RLSS CV31 ....206 D8
 RUGBYN/HIL CV21 ....161 J6
Culworth Rw COVN CV6 ....133 J4
Cumberford Av STETCH B33 ......110 E2
Cumberland Av DIG/EDG B5 ....107 J2
Cumberland Cl KGSWFD DY6 ....83 J6
Cumberland Crs BNTWD WS7 ......18 E5
 RLSN CV32 ....207 G2
Cumberland Dr
 NUNW/HART CV10 ....98 C2
 POL/KGSB/FAZ B78 ....45 L4
Cumberland Rd BILS/COS WV14 ...51 H5
 CNCK/NC WS11 ....16 E5
 HHTH/SAND B71 ....68 D3
 LGLYGN/QTN B68 ....104 E1
 WLNHL WV13 ....52 B3
Cumberland St CBHAMW B1 ....6 B6
 LICHS WS14 ....21 H1
Cumbria Cl COV CV1 * 8 A4

Cumbrian Cft *HALE* B63 ....121 H3
Cumbria Wy *WASH/WDE* B8 ....90 B7
Cumming St *RLSS* CV31 ....206 E2
Cundall Cl *RLSS* CV31 ....206 F7
Cunningham Rd
 DUNHL/THL/PER WV6 ....48 C1
 WSLW WS2 ....52 C3
Cunningham Wy North
 RUGBYS/DCH CV22 ....186 A4
Cupfields Av *TPTN/OCK* DY4 ......68 A5
Cupfields Crs *TPTN/OCK* DY4 .....68 A6
Curborough Rd *PBAR/PBCH* B42 ...7 G7
Curborough Rd *LICH* WS13 ....20 F2
Curdale Rd *LICH* WS13 ....122 F5
Curdworth La *WALM/CURD* B76 ....74 D4
Curie *TAM/AM/WIL* B77 ....187 H7
Cur La *REDW* B97 ....200 F2
Curlew *TAM/AM/WIL* B77 ....46 E6
Curlew Cl *KIDD* DY10 ....164 F3
 LICHS WS14 ....21 J6
Curlew Hl *CNCK/NC* WS11 ....16 C1
Curlews Cl *ERDW/GRVHL* B23 ......72 C4
Curlieu Cl *RWWCK/WEL* CV35 .....204 D7
Curral Rd *BLKHTH/ROWR* B65 .....103 M2
Curriers Cl *TLHL/CAN* CV4 ....153 H6
Curslow Cottages *KIDD* DY10 *...165 K8
Curslow La *KIDD* DY10 ....165 K5
Curtin Dr *DARL/WED* WS10 ....67 M1
Curtis Cl *BRGRVE* B60 * 192 D5
Curtis Rd *COVE* CV2 ....135 H7
Curtiss Cl *BRGRVE* B60 * 192 D5
Curzon Av *COVN* CV6 ....134 C5
Curzon Circ *CBHAMNE* B4 ....7 L4
Curzon Gv *RLSS* CV31 ....207 G7
Curzon St *BKHL/PFLD* WV2 ....50 B6
 CBHAMNE B4 ....7 L4
Cuthbert Rd *WSNGN* B18 ....106 C1
Cutlers Rough Cl *NFLD/LBR* B31 ..123 K8
Cutler St *SMTHWK* B66 ....87 M8
Cutsdean Cl *NFLD/LBR* B31 ....123 K7
Cutshill Cl *CBROM* B36 ....92 A5
Cut Throat La *HOCK/TIA* B94 ....174 A1
The Cutting *RUSH/SHEL* WS4 ....53 K1
Cuttle Mill La *WALM/CURD* B76 ....75 H6
Cuttle Pool La *DOR/KN* B93 ....176 D1
Cutworth Cl *WALM/CURD* B76 ....73 L2
Cygnet Cl *ALVE* B48 ....13 G6
 HEDN WS12 ....13 J4
Cygnet Dr *BRWNH* WS8 ....26 C6
 CRTAM B79 ....31 K8
Cygnet Gv *ERDW/GRVHL* B23 ....71 L7
Cygnet La *BRLYHL* DY5 ....84 A6
Cygnet Rd *WBROM* B70 ....68 E8
Cygnus Wy *WBROM* B70 ....68 D8
Cymbeline Wy
 RUGBYS/DCH CV22 ....186 B7
Cypress Av *SEDG* DY3 ....66 D8
Cypress Cft *COVS* CV3 ....156 D5
Cypress Gdns *KGSWFD* DY6 ....101 G1
Cypress Gv *NFLD/LBR* B31 ....144 C4
Cypress Hl *HEDN* WS12 ....13 L1
Cypress Rd *DSYBK/YTR* WS5 ....70 A1
 DUDS DY2 ....85 K4
Cypress Sq *ACGN* B27 ....109 G8
Cypress Wy *NFLD/LBR* B31 ....144 D5
Cyprus Cl *SLYOAK* B29 ....123 L6
Cyprus St *BKHL/PFLD* WV2 ....49 M7
 OLDBY B69 ....86 E5
Cyril Gv *SMTHWK* B10 * 108 A5
Cyril Rd *SMTHWK* B10 * 108 A5

D

Dace *TAM/AM/WIL* B77 ....46 F6
Dacer Cl *BVILLE* B30 ....124 E6
Dace Rd *WOLV* WV1 ....5 H7
Dadford Vw *BRLYHL* DY5 ....101 M3
Dadleys Wd
 RCOVN/BALC/EX CV7 * 114 D8
Dad's La *MOS/BIL* B13 ....125 H1
Daffern Av *RCOVN/BALC/EX* CV7 ..96 E5
Daffern Rd
 RCOVN/BALC/EX CV7 ....116 E1
Daffodil Cl *SEDG* DY3 ....66 C6
Daffodil Pl *DSYBK/YTR* WS5 ....54 B5
Daffodil Rd *DSYBK/YTR* WS5 ....54 B5
Daffodil Wy *NFLD/LBR* B31 ....144 C5
Dagger La *HHTH/SAND* B71 ....69 J8
Dagnall Rd *ACGN* B27 ....127 H2
Dahlia Cl *WOLV* WV1 ....51 G4
Daimler Cl *CBROM* B36 ....92 C4
Daimler Rd *ALE/KHTH/YWD* B14 ...147 H2
 COVN CV6 ....134 A8
Dainton Gv *RIDG/WDGT* B32 ....123 C4
Daintree Cft *COVS* CV3 ....155 C6
Daintry Dr *POL/KGSB/FAZ* B78 .....26 F6
Dairy Cl *TPTN/OCK* DY4 ....67 M8
Dairy Ct *LGLYGN/QTN* B68 ....105 H6
Dairy La *REDW* B97 ....193 L8
Daisy Bank *HEDN* WS12 ....12 D5
Daisy Bank *BLOX/PEL* WS3 ....39 M3
Daisy Bank Crs *DSYBK/YTR* WS5 ..54 B5
Daisy Dr *ERDW/GRVHL* B23 ....71 L8
Daisy Farm Rd
 ALE/KHTH/YWD B14 ....146 F3
Daisy Meadow *TPTN/OCK* DY4 .....68 A7
Daisy Rd *LDYWD/EDGR* B16 ....106 D3
Daisy St *BILS/COS* WV14 ....67 J5
 DUNHL/THL/PER WV6 ....49 L1
Daisy Wk *COVEN* WV9 ....35 L2
Dalbeg Cl *CDSL* WV5 ....35 J2
Dalbury Rd *HLGN/YWD* B28 ....126 C8
Dalby Cl *COVS* CV3 ....156 C6
Dalby Rd *BLOX/PEL* WS3 ....39 K7
Dale Cl *BRGRVW* B61 ....168 B4
Dale Dr *BNTWD* WS7 ....18 F2
 DARL/WED WS10 ....52 B7
 NUNW/HART CV10 ....80 C8
Dale End *CBHAMNE* B4 ....7 H5
Dalecote Av *HIA/OLT* B92 ....128 C5
Dale Dr *BNTWD* WS7 ....18 F2
 DARL/WED WS10 ....52 B7
 NUNW/HART CV10 ....80 C8
Dale End *CBHAMNE* B4 ....7 H5
Dalehouse La *KNWTH* CV8 ....180 A7
Dale Meadow Cl
 RCOVN/BALC/EX CV7 ....151 M7
Dale Rd *REDE* B98 ....194 D8
 RMSLY B62 ....122 D5
 SLYOAK B29 ....124 C2
 STRBR DY8 ....119 K3
Dales Cl *DUNHL/THL/PER* WV6 .....35 M7
Dalesman Cl *KGSWFD* DY6 ....82 F6
Dale St *BDMR/CCFT* WV3 ....2 D7
 BILS/COS WV14 ....51 K8
 DARL/WED WS10 ....68 C7
 RLSN CV32 ....206 D5
 RUGBYS/DCH CV21 ....186 E1
 SMTHWK B66 ....105 J2
 WSL WS1 ....4 E7
Daleswood Pk *RMSLY* B62 * 142 D3

Dale Ter *OLDBY* B69 ....86 A5
Daleview Rd
 ALE/KHTH/YWD B14 ....147 G2
Daleway Rd *COVS* CV3 ....180 F2
Dalewood Cft
 LGN/SDN/BHAMAIR B26 ....109 K7
Dalewood Rd
 CHWD/FDBR/MGN B37 ....92 D8
Daley Cl *CBHAMW* B1 ....6 D5
Daley Rd *BILS/COS* WV14 ....67 K3
Dalkeith Av *RUGBYS/DCH* CV22 ..186 B6
Dalkeith Rd *SCFLD/BOLD* B73 ......72 C3
Dalkeith St *WSLW* WS2 ....4 A1
Dallas Rd *ERDW/GRVHL* B23 ....90 A1
Dallimore La *HIA/OLT* B92 ....127 K2
Dallington Rd *COVN* CV6 ....133 J7
Dalmeny Rd *TLHL/CAN* CV4 ....153 H6
Dalston Cl *DUDS* DY2 ....85 H7
Dalston Rd *ACGN* B27 ....127 G1
Dalton Cl *RUGBY* CV23 ....158 F7
Dalton Ct *WMBN* WV5 ....64 C6
Dalton Gdns *COVE* CV2 ....156 D1
Dalton Rd *BDWTH* CV12 ....116 D3
 COVW CV5 ....8 C9
 WSLW WS2 ....52 E2
Dalton St *BDMR/CCFT* WV3 ....2 E5
 CBHAMNE B4 ....7 H4
Dalton Wy *CBHAM* B2 ....7 G4
Dalvine Rd *DUDS* DY2 ....102 A3
Dalwood Cl *BILS/COS* WV14 ....66 F6
Damar Cft *ALE/KHTH/YWD* B14 ...146 B1
Dama Rd *POL/KGSB/FAZ* B78 ......45 K5
Dame Agnes Gv *COVN* CV6 ....134 F5
Damien Cl *SMTHWK* B67 ....87 K8
Damson Cl *REDW* B97 ....201 M7
 SHHTH WV12 ....37 L7
Damson Dr *SOLH* B91 ....37 H7
Damson Pkwy *HIA/OLT* B92 ....128 D2
Damson Rd *RWWCK/WEL* CV35 ..204 D7
Damson Wy *BEWD* DY12 ....162 F1
Dam St *LICH* WS13 ....20 F5
Danbury Cl *WALM/CURD* B76 ....73 L3
Danbury Rd *SHLY* B90 ....147 M2
Danby Dr *HEDN* WS12 ....18 J4
Danby Gv *ERDE/BCHGN* B24 ....90 F3
Dando Rd *DUDS* DY2 ....85 H5
Dandy Bank Rd *KGSWFD* DY6 ......83 L5
Dandy's Wk *WSL* WS1 ....5 G5
Dane Av *BILS/COS* WV14 ....67 J1
Danelagh Cl *CRTAM* B79 ....31 K6
Dane Rd *COVE* CV2 ....155 M1
Danesbury Crs *KGSTG* B44 ....71 L5
 RLSS CV31 ....207 H7
Danesdale Cl *WNSFLD* WV11 ....37 K1
Danescourt Rd
 DUNHL/THL/PER WV6 ....35 G7
Danescroft *STRPT* DY13 ....188 D1
Danewood Dr *ALDR* WS9 ....40 D2
Daneswood Rd *COVS* CV3 ....157 K6
Dane Ter *BLKHTH/ROWR* B65 ......86 A8
Daneways Cl *FOAKS/STRLY* B74 ...55 L5
Danford Cl *STRBR* DY8 ....119 L1
Danford Gdns *SMHTH* B10 ....108 A5
Danford La *SOLH* B91 ....148 C2
Danford Rd *HLYWD* B47 ....174 D7
Danford Wy *GTB/HAM* B43 ....70 D7
Dangerfield La *DARL/WED* WS10 ...52 A8
Daniel Av *NUNW/HART* CV10 ....98 A2
Daniel Rd *ATHST* CV9 ....63 K6
Daniels La *ALDR* WS9 ....55 C1
Daniels Rd *BORD* B9 ....108 E4
Danilo Rd *CNCK/NC* WS11 ....16 B4
Danks St *TPTN/OCK* DY4 ....85 L3
Danzey Cl *REDE* B98 ....202 F8
Danzey Green Rd *CBROM* B36 ......91 M4
Danzey Gv *BVILLE* B30 ....146 A2
Daphne Cl *COVE* CV2 ....135 G3
Darby Cl *BILS/COS* WV14 ....66 E3
Darby End Rd
 BLKHTH/ROWR B65 ....103 J1
Darby La *DARL/WED* WS10 ....68 F2
 LGLYGN/QTN B68 ....105 J8
Darbys Hill Rd *OLDBY* B69 ....85 M6
Darby St *BLKHTH/ROWR* B65 .....104 A2
Darell Cft *WALM/CURD* B76 ....73 J2
Daren Cl *CBROM* B36 ....92 D5
Dare Rd *ERDW/GRVHL* B23 ....90 C1
Darfield Ct *KNWTH* CV8 ....182 A8
Darfield Wk *BRTH/HG* B12 * 107 K5
Darges La *GTWY* WS6 ....24 D1
Dark La *BDWTH* CV12 ....116 B4
 BRGRVE B60 ....191 H7
 COV CV1 ....8 E1
 GTWY WS6 ....25 G4
 HAG/WOL DY9 ....141 J6
 HWK/WKHTH B38 ....146 B6
 KINVER DY7 ....118 A2
 POL/KGSB/FAZ B78 ....47 J5
 RMSLY B62 ....142 D1
 WNSFLD WV11 ....23 H6
 WOLV WV10 ....22 B5
Darlaston Cl *BILS/COS* WV14 ....51 L6
Darlaston La *BILS/COS* WV14 ....51 L6
Darlaston Rd *WSLW* WS2 ....52 E5
Darley Dr *DUNHL/THL/PER* WV6 ...35 M8
Darley Green Rd *DOR/KN* B93 ....175 M4
Darley Rd *FOAKS/STRLY* B74 ......55 K6
Darlington St *DARL/WED* WS10 ....52 B8
 WOLV WV1 ....2 E5
Darlington Yd *WOLV* WV1 * 2 E5
Darnel Cft *SMHTH* B10 ....107 M4
Darnel Hurst Rd *MGN/WHC* B75 ...57 G2
Darnford Cl *COVE* CV2 ....135 K6
 CSCFLD/WYGN B72 ....72 A1
 HLGN/YWD B28 ....126 E8
Darnford La *LICHS* WS14 ....21 J7
Darnford Moors *LICHS* WS14 ....21 J7
Darnford Vw *LICH* WS13 ....21 J4
Darnick Rd *SCFLD/BOLD* B73 ......73 D2
Darnley Rd *LDYWD/EDGR* B16 ....106 D3
Darrach Cl *COVE* CV2 ....135 L3
Darris Rd *SLYOAK* B29 ....124 E5
Dartmoor Rd *RBRY* B45 ....143 L3
Dart *TAM/AM/WIL* B77 ....46 E6
Dartington Wy *NUN* CV11 ....99 K5
Dartmoor Cl *RBRY* B45 ....143 L3
Dartmouth Av *BLOX/PEL* WS3 ......39 J6
 CNCK/NC WS11 ....16 A5
 STRBR DY8 ....100 D5
 WLNHL WV13 ....51 K3
Dartmouth Cir *AST/WIT* B6 ....89 K8
Dartmouth Cl *BLOX/PEL* WS3 ....39 J8
 CNCK/NC WS11 ....16 A5
Dartmouth Crs *BILS/COS* WV14 ....51 L6
Dartmouth Dr *ALDR* WS9 ....40 E3
 EDG B15 ....107 G6
Dartmouth Pl *BLOX/PEL* WS3 ....39 J8
Dartmouth Rd *CNCK/NC* WS11 .....16 B4
 COVE CV2 ....135 G8
 SLYOAK B29 ....124 D3
 SMTHWK B66 ....87 K5
Dartmouth St *BKHL/PFLD* WV2 ......3 H8
 WBROM B70 ....86 F2

Dart St *BORD* B9 ....107 M4
Darvel Rd *SHHTH* WV12 ....52 B1
Darwall St *WSL* WS1 ....4 F3
Darwin Cl *BNTWD* WS7 ....18 F4
 COVE CV2 ....135 L2
 HEDN WS12 ....17 J4
Darwin Dr *DUNHL/THL/PER* WV6 ...48 D1
Darwin Pl *WSLW* WS2 ....38 F7
Darwin St *BHTH/HG* B12 ....107 K5
Dassett Gv *BORD* B9 ....109 G3
Dassett Rd *DOR/KN* B93 ....175 K1
Datchet Cl *COVW* CV5 ....154 A1
Datteln Rd *CNCK/NC* WS11 ....16 E1
D'Aubeny Rd *TLHL/CAN* CV4 ......153 H7
Dauntsey Covert
 ALE/KHTH/YWD B14 ....146 B3
Davena Cl *DIG/EDG* B5 ....123 J3
Davena Gv *BILS/COS* WV14 ....67 H2
Davenham Rd *BRGRVE* B60 ....192 A4
Davenport Dr *BRGRVE* B60 ....191 H7
 CVALE B35 ....92 A2
Davenport Rd
 DUNHL/THL/PER WV6 ....34 F8
 WNSFLD WV11 ....37 J7
Daventry Gv *RIDG/WDGT* B32 ....105 G2
Daventry Rd *COVS* CV3 ....155 H6
Davey Rd *BFLD/HDSWWD* B20 .....89 J4
David Peacock Cl *TPTN/OCK* DY4 ..67 L1
David Rd *BFLD/HDSWWD* B20 .....88 D3
 COV CV1 ....9 K6
 RCOVN/BALC/EX CV7 ....116 D6
 RUGBYS/DCH CV22 ....186 B5
 TPTN/OCK DY4 ....67 L6
Davidson Av *RLSS* CV31 ....206 E6
Davidson Rd *LICHS* WS14 ....21 J6
The Davids *NFLD/LBR* B31 ....124 A7
Davies Av *BILS/COS* WV14 ....67 H2
Davies Rd *RCOVN/BALC/EX* CV7 ..116 D6
Davis Av *TPTN/OCK* DY4 ....85 J1
Davis Cl *RLSN* CV32 ....206 B3
Davis Gv
 LGN/SDN/BHAMAIR B26 ....109 J7
Davison Rd *SMTHWK* B67 ....105 K2
Davis Rd *SHHTH* WV12 ....38 B5
Davy Rd *WSLW* WS2 ....38 E8
Dawberry Cl
 ALE/KHTH/YWD B14 ....125 H8
Dawberry Fields Rd
 ALE/KHTH/YWD B14 ....125 G8
Dawberry Rd
 ALE/KHTH/YWD B14 ....125 G8
Daw End *RUSH/SHEL* WS4 ....40 A7
Daw End La *RUSH/SHEL* WS4 ....39 M6
Dawes Av *WBROM* B70 ....87 G4
Dawley Cl *COVE* CV2 ....155 L1
Dawley Brook Rd *KGSWFD* DY6 ...83 H5
Dawley Crs
 CHWD/FDBR/MGN B37 ....110 F4
Dawley Rd *KGSWFD* DY6 ....83 G5
Dawlish Cl *NUN* CV11 ....81 J8
Dawlish Dr *COVS* CV3 ....155 H8
Dawlish Rd *DUDN* DY1 ....66 F8
 SLYOAK B29 ....124 D3
 SMTHWK B66 ....87 M8
Dawn Dr *DARL/WED* WS10 ....68 A3
Dawney Dr *MGN/WHC* B75 ....56 E1
Dawn Rd *NFLD/LBR* B31 ....123 J7
Dawson Av *BILS/COS* WV14 ....66 D5
Dawson Rd *BRGRVW* B61 ....191 J5
 COVS CV3 ....155 L4
 HDSW B21 ....88 C5
Dawson Sq *BILS/COS* WV14 * 51 L8
Dawson St *BLOX/PEL* WS3 ....39 M5
 SMTHWK B66 ....105 L2
Day Av *WNSFLD* WV11 ....37 J5
Daybrook Cl *REDW* B98 ....193 M8
Dayhouse Bank *RMSLY* B62 ....142 F4
Daylesford Rd *HIA/OLT* B92 ....127 L2
Days Cl *COV* CV1 ....9 K3
Day's La *COV* CV1 ....9 K3
Day St *WSLW* WS2 ....4 E1
Daytona Dr *COVW* CV5 ....131 M5
Deacon Cl *RUGBYS/DCH* CV22 ..187 G4
Deacon St *NUN* CV11 ....99 C2
Deakin Av *BRWNH* WS8 ....26 D4
Deakin Rd *ERDE/BCHGN* B24 ......90 D2
 MGN/WHC B75 ....57 J6
Deakins Av *YDLY* B25 ....108 F6
Deakins Rd *YDLY* B25 ....108 E6
Deal Av *BNTWD* WS7 ....18 E5
Deal Dr *DUDS* DY2 ....85 G7
Deal Gv *NFLD/LBR* B31 ....144 E1
Deanbrook Cl *SHLY* B90 ....148 E7
Dean Cl *CSCFLD/WYGN* B72 ....72 E4
 KGSTG B44 ....71 M5
 STRBR DY8 ....101 M7
Dean Ct *CDSL* WV8 ....34 C8
Deane Pde *RUGBYS/DCH* CV21 ..187 L5
Deane Rd *RUGBYS/DCH* CV21 ....187 L5
Deanery Cl *WOLV* WV10 ....23 G3
Deanery Rw *WOLV* WV1 * 2 F3
Dean Rd *ERDW/GRVHL* B23 ....72 D8
 RUSH/SHEL WS4 ....40 A6
 WMBN WV5 ....64 D8
Deans Cl *REDE* B98 ....195 H8
Deans Cft *LICH* WS13 ....21 G6
Deansfield Rd *WOLV* WV1 ....50 D5
Deansford La *KIDD* DY10 ....139 K5
Deans Pl *BLOX/PEL* WS3 ....39 K7
Dean's Rd *WOLV* WV1 ....50 E2
Deans Slade Dr *LICHS* WS14 ....28 S1
Deanston Cft *COVE* CV2 ....135 K4
Dean St *COVE* CV2 ....135 L7
 DIG/EDG B5 ....7 H7
 SEDG DY3 ....66 B5
Deansway *BRGRVW* B61 ....191 H4
Deans Wy *RCOVN/BALC/EX* CV7 ..116 D7
Deansway *WWCK* CV34 ....205 H4
The Deansway *KIDD* DY10 ....138 C6
Dearman Rd *NFLD/LBR* B31 ....144 C6
Dearmont Rd *NFLD/LBR* B31 ....144 C6
Dearne Ct *SEDG* DY3 ....66 C6
Deasy Rd *COV* CV1 ....9 L8
Deavall Wy *CNCK/NC* WS11 ....16 F5
Debben Cl *DOR/KN* B93 ....175 L4
Debenham Crs *YDLY* B25 ....109 H4
Debenham Rd *YDLY* B25 ....109 H4
Deblen Dr *LDYWD/EDGR* B16 .....106 B4
Deborah Cl
 ETTPK/GDPK/PENN WV4 ....50 A7
De-Compton Cl
 RCOVN/BALC/EX CV7 ....115 C4
Deedmore Cl *COVE* CV2 ....135 K4
Deegan Cl *COVE* CV2 ....134 E7
Dee Gv *CNCK/NC* WS11 ....16 B5
Deelands Rd *RBRY* B45 ....143 J5
Deeley *TAM/AM/WIL* B77 ....46 E4
Deeley Cl *CDYHTH* B64 ....103 J4
 EDG B15 ....107 G6
Deeley Dr *TPTN/OCK* DY4 ....68 A4
Deeley Pl *BLOX/PEL* WS3 ....38 F7
Deeley St *BLOX/PEL* WS3 * 38 F5
 BRLYHL DY5 * 102 A4
Deepdale *BDWTH* CV12 ....116 E2
Deepdale Av
 LGN/SDN/BHAMAIR B26 ....127 M1

Deepdale La *DUDN* DY1 ....84 C2
Deepdales *WMBN* WV5 ....64 C7
Deepdale Wy *CSHL/WTROR* B46 ...76 D7
Deeplow Cl *CSCFLD/WYGN* B72 * ..73 G1
Deepmoor Rd *STECH* B33 ....109 K2
Deepmore Av *WSLW* WS2 ....52 E3
Deepmore Rd
 RUGBYS/DCH CV22 ....186 B5
Deepwood Cl *RUSH/SHEL* WS4 ....39 M5
Deer Barn Hl *REDE* B98 ....202 E4
Deer Cl *BLOX/PEL* WS3 ....39 G4
 LICHS WS14 ....17 L6
Deerdale Wy *COVS* CV3 ....156 D5
Deerfold Crs *BNTWD* WS7 ....18 F6
Deerhill *TAM/AM/WIL* B77 ....46 E4
Deerhurst *REDE* B98 ....195 G6
Deerhurst Rd
 BFLD/HDSWWD B20 ....70 D8
 COVN CV6 ....133 H3
The Deer Leap *KNWTH* CV8 ....179 M7
Deer Pk Rd *BLOX/PEL* WS3 ....39 J4
Deer Pk Wy *WWCK* CV34 ....205 H5
Deer Park Rd *POL/KGSB/FAZ* B78 ..45 J4
Deer Park Wy *SOLH* B91 ....149 G4
Defford Av *RUSH/SHEL* WS4 ....40 A4
Defford Cl *REDW* B97 ....201 J4
Defford Dr *LGLYGN/QTN* B68 ......104 F1
Dehavilland Cl *CVALE* B35 ....91 L3
De Havilland Dr *CVALE* B35 ....91 L3
Delage Cl *COVN* CV6 ....134 F1
Delamere Cl *CBROM* B36 ....92 B4
Delamere Dr *GTB/HAM* B43 ....70 A2
Delamere Rd *BDWTH* CV12 ....116 D3
 BEWD DY12 ....163 G1
 HLGN/YWD B28 ....126 D6
 SHHTH WV12 ....38 A6
Delamere Wy *RLSN* CV32 ....207 J7
Delancey Keep *MGN/WHC* B75 ....57 L8
Delaware Rd *COVS* CV3 ....155 G5
Delhi Av *COVN* CV6 ....134 D4
Delhurst Av
 ETTPK/GDPK/PENN WV4 ....66 C2
Delhurst Rd *KGSTG* B44 ....71 H4
Delius St *TLHL/CAN* CV4 ....153 J2
Della Dr *RIDG/WDGT* B32 ....123 H5
Dell Cl *COVS* CV3 ....155 M8
Dellow Gv *ALVE* B48 ....170 E8
Dellows Cl *HWK/WKHTH* B38 .....145 H6
Dell Rd *BRLYHL* DY5 ....83 M8
 BVILLE B30 ....124 E8
The Dell *CRTAM* B79 ....31 M7
 HIA/OLT B92 ....17 H1
 LDYWD/EDGR B16 * 106 D3
 LICH WS13 ....20 D6
 NFLD/LBR B31 ....123 H7
 STRBR DY8 ....101 J7
Delmore Wy *WALM/CURD* B76 .....73 J7
Delph Dr *BRLYHL* DY5 ....102 D5
Delphinium Cl *BORD* B9 ....108 D2
 KIDD DY11 ....138 A4
Delph Rd *BRLYHL* DY5 ....102 B5
Delrene Rd *HLGN/YWD* B28 ....147 K2
Delta Wy *CNCK/NC* WS11 ....16 F6
Deltic *TAM/AM/WIL* B77 ....46 E4
Delves Cr *ATHST* CV9 ....61 H4
Delves Crs *DSYBK/YTR* WS5 ....53 L7
Delves Green Rd
 DSYBK/YTR WS5 ....53 L7
Delves Rd *WSL* WS1 ....5 H9
Delville Rd *DARL/WED* WS10 ....68 D3
De Marnham Cl *WBROM* B70 ....87 J4
De Montfort Rd *KNWTH* CV8 ....179 J7
De Montfort Wy *TLHL/CAN* CV4 ...154 D8
De Moram Gv *HIA/OLT* B92 ....128 D6
Dempster Rd *BDWTH* CV12 ....116 C3
Demuth Wy *OLDBY* B69 ....69 J8
Denaby Gv *ALE/KHTH/YWD* B14 ..147 H1
Denbigh Cl *DUDN* DY1 ....84 D3
Denbigh Crs *HHTH/SAND* B71 ......68 F3
Denbigh Dr *DARL/WED* WS10 ....68 F1
 HHTH/SAND B71 ....68 F3
Denbigh Rd *COVN* CV6 ....133 J7
 TPTN/OCK DY4 ....86 A1
Denbigh St *BORD* B9 ....108 B3
Denbury Cl *HEDN* WS12 ....17 L4
Denby Cl *BORD* B9 ....109 G3
 RLSN CV32 ....207 G3
Denby Buildings *RLSN* CV32 * 206 D5
Denby Cl *SHLY* B90 ....148 F7
Dencer Cl *RBRY* B45 ....143 K5
Dencer Dr *KNWTH* CV8 ....198 A1
Dencil Cl *HALE* B63 ....103 H8
Dene Av *KGSWFD* DY6 ....101 G1
Dene Court Rd *HIA/OLT* B92 ....127 K4
Denefield Dr *STRPT* DY13 ....10 D5
Denegate Cl *WALM/CURD* B76 .....73 J7
Dene Hollow *MOS/BIL* B13 ....126 A7
Denehurst Wy
 NUNW/HART CV10 ....98 D2
Dene Rd
 ETTPK/GDPK/PENN WV4 ....64 D1
 STRBR DY8 ....119 K2
Denewood Av
 BFLD/HDSWWD B20 ....88 E3
Denewood Wy *KNWTH* CV8 ....180 A8
Denford Gv
 ALE/KHTH/YWD B14 ....125 H8
Dengate Dr
 RCOVN/BALC/EX CV7 ....151 M6
Denham Av *COVW* CV5 ....153 M1
Denham Ct *ATHST* CV9 ....61 J6
Denham Gdns *BDMR/CCFT* WV3 ...48 F5
Denham Rd *ACGN* B27 ....108 F8
Denholme Gv
 ALE/KHTH/YWD B14 ....146 E2
Denholm Rd *WALM/CURD* B76 .....73 J1
Denise Dr *BILS/COS* WV14 ....67 J4
 CHWD/FDBR/MGN B37 ....110 D1
 HRBN B17 ....124 A1
Denleigh Rd *KGSWFD* DY6 ....101 K1
Denmark Ri *HEDN* WS12 ....13 H5
Denmark Vls *LICH* WS13 * 20 F5
Denmead Dr *WNSFLD* WV11 ....37 K5
Denmore Gdns *WOLV* WV1 ....50 F3
Dennett Cl *WWCK* CV34 ....205 M3
Dennis *TAM/AM/WIL* B77 ....46 E4
Dennis Hall Rd *STRBR* DY8 ....101 L5
Dennis Rd *BHTH/HG* B12 ....125 M1
 COVE CV2 ....135 G2
Denshaw Cft *COVE* CV2 ....135 K4
Denshaw Rd
 ALE/KHTH/YWD B14 ....125 H7
Denton Cl *KNWTH* CV8 ....179 H7
Denton Cft *DOR/KN* B93 ....175 L2
Denton Gv *GTB/HAM* B43 ....70 D6
 STECH B33 ....109 J3
Denton Rd *HAG/WOL* DY9 ....120 E1
Dent St *CRTAM* B79 ....32 A7

Denver Rd *ALE/KHTH/YWD* B14 ...146 E3
Denville Cl *BILS/COS* WV14 ....51 J6
Denville Crs *BORD* B9 ....108 F2
Denville Rd *RLSN* CV32 ....206 E2
Depwo Gv *RIDG/WDGT* B32 ....105 G2
Derby Av *DUNHL/THL/PER* WV6 ...35 J6
Derby Dr
 CHWD/FDBR/MGN B37 ....110 F3
Derby Rd *LICHS* WS14 ....30 B2
Derby St *DIG/EDG* B5 ....7 M5
 WSLW WS2 ....53 H1
Dereham Cl *WASH/WDE* B8 ....108 A1
Dereham Ct *RLSN* CV32 ....206 E1
Dereham Wk *BILS/COS* WV14 ......51 H5
Dereton Cl *DUDN* DY1 ....84 C6
Dering Cl *COVE* CV2 ....135 H5
Deronda Cl *BDWTH* CV12 ....116 E2
Derrick Burchers Ml
 KIDD DY11 * 138 C7
Derron Av
 LGN/SDN/BHAMAIR B26 ....109 J3
Derry Cl *HRBN* B17 ....123 L2
 KNWTH CV8 ....180 D8
Derrydown Cl *ERDW/GRVHL* B23 ..90 C2
Derrydown Rd *PBAR/PBCH* B42 ...70 F8
Derry St *BKHL/PFLD* WV2 * 2 A3
 BRLYHL DY5 ....102 A3
Dersingham Dr *COVN* CV6 ....134 F3
Derwent *TAM/AM/WIL* B77 ....46 B4
Derwent Av *STRPT* DY13 ....163 K8
Derwent Cl *BRLYHL* DY5 ....83 M7
 COVW CV5 ....55 K3
 FOAKS/STRLY B74 ....55 L3
 RLSN CV32 ....206 B4
 WLNHL WV13 ....52 A3
Derwent Dr *BEWD* DY12 ....162 D1
Derwent Gv *BNTWD* WS7 ....19 H7
 BVILLE B30 ....125 G5
 CNCK/NC WS11 ....16 B5
 COVN CV6 ....133 L3
 DUNHL/THL/PER WV6 ....35 H5
Derwent Wy *BRGRVE* B60 ....191 K1
 NUN CV11 ....81 K7
Desford Av *PBAR/PBCH* B42 ....71 G6
Despard Rd *COVW* CV5 ....152 F2
Dettonford Rd *RIDG/WDGT* B32 ..122 F5
Devereux Cl *CBROM* B36 ....92 A4
 TLHL/CAN CV4 ....153 G4
Devereux Rd *MGN/WHC* B75 ....57 J4
 WBROM B70 ....87 J4
Devey Dr *TPTN/OCK* DY4 ....67 L8
Devine Cft *TPTN/OCK* DY4 ....67 L8
Devitts Cl *SHLY* B90 ....148 D6
Devon Cl *KIDDW* DY11 ....138 A4
 NUNW/HART CV10 ....80 D2
Devon Crs *ALDR* WS9 ....40 A4
 DUDS DY2 ....84 D6
 HHTH/SAND B71 ....68 F4
Devon Gv *COVE* CV2 ....134 F8
Devonport Cl *REDW* B97 ....193 M8
Devon Rd *CNCK/NC* WS11 ....16 D5
 DARL/WED WS10 ....69 G1
 RBRY B45 ....143 K4
 SMTHWK B67 ....87 H6
 STRBR DY8 ....101 H6
 WLNHL WV13 ....51 M3
 WOLV WV1 ....50 E5
Devonshire Av *WSNGN* B18 ....88 D7
Devonshire Dr *HHTH/SAND* B71 ...87 J2
 POL/KGSB/FAZ B78 ....45 L4
Devonshire Rd
 BFLD/HDSWWD B20 ....88 D3
 HRBN B17 ....87 J7
Devonshire St *WSNGN* B18 ....88 D7
Devon St *VAUX/NECH* B7 ....108 A1
Devoran Cl
 DUNHL/THL/PER WV6 ....49 M1
 RCOVN/BALC/EX CV7 ....116 E4
Dewar Gv *RUGBYS/DCH* CV21 ...187 J3
Dewberry Cl *STRBR* DY8 ....188 C1
Dewberry Dr *DSYBK/YTR* WS5 .....69 L2
Dewberry Rd *STRBR* DY8 ....101 K4
Dewhurst Cft *STECH* B33 ....109 M3
Dewsbury Av *COVS* CV3 ....154 F8
Dewsbury Cl *STRBR* DY8 ....101 J2
Dewsbury Dr *BNTWD* WS7 ....19 G7
 ETTPK/GDPK/PENN WV4 ....65 L2
Dewsbury Gv *PBAR/PBCH* B42 ....71 G8
Dexter La *ATHST* CV9 ....77 G2
Dexter Wy *POL/KGSB/FAZ* B78 ....47 K5
Deykin Av *AST/WIT* B6 ....89 L3
Deykin Rd *LICH* WS13 ....20 E7
D'Eyncourt Rd *WNSFLD* WV11 .....36 E6
Dial Cl *ALE/KHTH/YWD* B14 ......146 C3
Dial House La *COVW* CV5 ....153 K1
Dial La *STRBR* DY8 ....101 J5
 WBROM B70 ....68 C7
Diamond Gv *CNCK/NC* WS11 ....17 G3
Diamond Park Dr *STRBR* DY8 ......99 L5
Diana Cl *ALDR* WS9 ....40 F2
Diana Dr *COVE* CV2 ....135 L4
Dibble Cl *SHHTH* WV12 ....38 B8
Dibble Rd *SMTHWKW* B67 ....87 K7
Dibdale Rd *DUDN* DY1 ....84 D3
Dibdale St *DUDN* DY1 ....84 D4
Dice Pleck *NFLD/LBR* B31 ....145 G3
Dickens Cl *NUNW/HART* CV10 ......80 C1
 SEDG DY3 ....65 M8
Dickens Grn *ALE/KHTH/YWD* B14 ..146 E2
Dickens Heath Rd *SHLY* B90 ......147 L8
Dickens Rd *BILS/COS* WV14 ....51 K5
 COVN CV6 ....133 L5
 RUGBYS/DCH CV22 ....186 D7
 WOLV WV10 ....23 L8
 WWCK CV34 ....205 M5
Dickinson Av *WOLV* WV10 ....36 D6
Dickinson Ct
 RUGBYS/DCH CV22 ....186 E4
Dickinson Dr *WALM/CURD* B76 ....73 J1
 WSLW WS2 ....52 E1
Dickinson Rd *WMBN* WV5 ....82 E1
Dick Sheppard Av
 TPTN/OCK DY4 ....67 M5
Didcot Cl *REDW* B97 ....202 M8
Diddington Av *HLGN/YWD* B28 ...126 E8
Diddington La *HIA/OLT* B92 ....130 A5
Didgley Gv
 CHWD/FDBR/MGN B37 ....92 E8
Didgley La *RCOVN/BALC/EX* CV7 ..114 A1
Didsbury Rd
 RCOVN/BALC/EX CV7 ....116 E4
Digbeth *DIG/EDG* B5 ....7 H6
Digbeth *WSL* WS1 ....4 F5
Digby Cl *COVW* CV5 ....132 F7
Digby Crs *CSHL/WTROR* B46 ....93 H5
Digby Dr
 CHWD/FDBR/MGN B37 ....110 F7
Digby Rd *CSHL/WTROR* B46 ....93 H5
 KGSWFD DY6 ....83 H5
 SCFLD/BOLD B73 ....72 E2
Dilcock Wy *TLHL/CAN* CV4 ....153 K6
Dilke Rd *ALDR* WS9 ....39 G8
Dillam Cl *COVN* CV6 ....134 E1
Dillotford Av *COVS* CV3 ....155 G6

Dilloways La *WLNHL* WV13 ....51 J4
Dilwyn Cl *REDE* B98 ....203 K4
Dimbles Hl *LICH* WS13 ....20 F4
Dimbles La *LICH* WS13 ....20 E3
Dimmingsdale Bank
  RIDG/WDGT B32 ....123 G1
Dimmingsdale Rd
  ETTPK/GDPK/PENN WV4 ....48 B8
Dimminsdale La *WLNHL* WV13 ....51 L4
Dimmocks Av *BILS/COS* WV14 ....67 H5
Dimmock St
  ETTPK/GDPK/PENN WV4 ....50 B8
Dimsdale Gv *NFLD/LBR* B31 ....144 C2
Dimsdale Rd *NFLD/LBR* B31 ....144 C2
Dinedor Cl *REDE* B98 ....203 H2
Dingle Av *CDYHTH* B64 ....103 J5
Dingle Cl *BVILLE* B30 ....124 B6
  COVN CV6 ....133 L7
  DUDS DY2 ....85 J6
Dingle Hollow *OLDBY* B69 ....86 B5
Dingle La *CSHL/WTROR* B46 ....76 A4
  SOLH B91 ....148 D3
  WLNHL WV13 ....51 L1
Dingle Md *ALE/KHTH/YWD* B14 ....146 A1
Dingle Rd *BRWNH* WS8 ....9 G7
  DUDS DY2 ....85 J6
  HAG/WOL DY9 ....119 M3
  KCSWFD DY6 ....101 L1
  WMBN WV5 ....64 D8
Dingle St *OLDBY* B69 ....86 B5
The Dingle *BDMR/CCFT* WV3 ....49 H4
  NUNW/HART CV10 ....80 C7
  OLDBY B69 ....86 B5
  SHLY B90 ....148 B8
  SLYOAK B29 ....124 C3
Dingle Vw *SEDG* DY3 ....66 A6
Dingley Rd *BDWTH* CV12 ....117 M3
Dingleywell *WSL* WS10 ....52 E8
Dinham Gdns *DUDN* DY1 ....84 C2
Dinmore Av *NFLD/LBR* B31 ....144 F1
Dinmore Cl *REDE* B98 ....203 H2
Dippons Dr
  DUNHL/THL/PER WV6 ....48 E3
Dippons Mill Cl
  DUNHL/THL/PER WV6 ....48 E2
Dirtyfoot La
  ETTPK/GDPK/PENN WV4 ....48 B8
Discovery Cl *TPTN/OCK* DY4 ....68 A8
Discovery Dr *COVS* CV3 ....156 F5
The Ditch *WSL* WS1 ....5 G4
Ditton Cl *RUGBYS/DCH* CV22 ....186 A4
Ditton Gv *NFLD/LBR* B31 ....144 C2
Dixon Cl *CVALE* B35 ....91 L3
  TPTN/OCK DY4 ....68 A7
Dixon Rd *SMHTH* B10 ....107 M5
Dixon's Green Rd *DUDS* DY2 ....85 J5
Dixon St *BKHL/PFLD* WV2 ....50 C7
  KIDD DY10 ....138 C2
Dobbins Oak Rd *HAG/WOL* DY9 ....120 D4
Dobbs Mill Cl *SLYOAK* B29 ....124 F3
Dobbs St *BKHL/PFLD* WV2 ....2 A7
Dobes La *KIDD* DY10 ....166 A7
Dockar Rd *NFLD/LBR* B31 ....144 C2
Dockers Rd *RCOVN/BALC/EX* CV7 ....152 J4
Dock La *DUDN* DY1 ....84 F4
Dock Meadow Dr
  ETTPK/GDPK/PENN WV4 ....66 E1
Dock Rd *STRBR* DY8 ....101 K3
The Dock *BRGRVW* B61 ....168 E5
The Dock *BRGRVW* B61 ....102 D8
Doctors Hl *BRGRVW* B61 ....168 D4
  HAG/WOL DY9 ....120 A2
Doctors Piece *KCSWFD* DY6 ....82 D7
Doctor's Piece *WLNHL* WV13 ....51 M3
Dodd Av *WWCK* CV34 ....206 A6
Doddington Gv
  RIDG/WDGT B32 ....122 F5
Dodds La *LICH* WS13 ....19 L2
Dodford Cl *RBRY* B45 ....143 K6
Dodford Rd *BRGRVW* B61 ....168 B4
Dodgson Cl *COVN* CV6 ....134 C1
Doe Bank La *ALDR* WS9 ....55 H7
  COV CV1 ....8 A4
Doe Bank Rd *TPTN/OCK* DY4 ....68 A4
Dogberry Cl *COVS* CV3 ....156 A7
Dogge Lane Cft *ACGN* B27 ....126 D1
Dogkennel La *LGLYGN/QTN* B68 ....87 G8
Dog Kennel La *HALE* B63 ....121 M2
  SHLY B90 ....148 A6
  WSL WS1 ....5 H4
Dog La *BEWD* DY12 ....162 F5
  BRGRVW B61 ....190 A7
  CSHL/WTROR B46 ....76 A4
  LICHS WS14 ....43 L1
  TAM/AM/WIL B77 ....32 F7
Dogpool La *BVILLE* B30 ....124 F4
Doidge Rd *ERDW/GRVHL* B23 ....90 B2
Dolben La *REDE* B98 ....203 H4
Dollery Dr *DIG/EDG* B5 ....107 G8
Dollis Gv *KGSTG* B44 ....71 K2
Dollman St *VAUX/NECH* B7 ....107 M2
Dolman Rd *AST/WIT* B6 ....89 G1
Dolobran Rd *SPARK* B11 ....107 M6
Dolomite Av *COVW* CV5 ....154 C6
Dolphin Cl *BLOX/PEL* WS3 ....39 K4
Dolphin La *ACGN* B27 ....127 C4
Dolphin Rd *REDE* B98 ....194 E8
  SPARK B11 ....108 B8
Dolton Wy *TPTN/OCK* DY4 ....67 J7
Domar Rd *KIDDW* DY11 ....137 M6
Dominic Cl *BVILLE* B30 ....145 H1
Doncaster Cl *COVE* CV2 ....135 H6
Doncaster Wy *CBROM* B36 ....91 J5
Don Cl *EDG* B15 ....106 B5
Donegal Cl *TLHL/CAN* CV4 ....153 L6
Donegal Rd *FOAKS/STRLY* B74 ....55 J1
Dongan Rd *WWCK* CV34 ....205 L3
Don Gv *CNCK/NC* WS11 ....16 B6
Donibristle Cft *CVALE* B35 ....91 L1
Donnington Av *COVN* CV6 ....133 J8
Donnington Cl *REDE* B98 ....195 G8
Donnithorne Av
  NUNW/HART CV10 ....99 G4
Dooley Cl *WLNHL* WV13 ....51 J3
Doone Cl *COVE* CV2 ....135 J7
Dorado *TAM/AM/WIL* B77 ....46 D2
Doran Cl *HALE* B63 ....121 H4
Dora Rd *HDSW* B21 ....88 C6
  SMHTH B10 ....108 C6
  WBROM B70 ....87 G4
Dora St *WSLW* WS2 ....52 F6
Dorcas Cl *NUN* CV11 ....99 M5
Dorchester Av
  RWWCK/WEL CV35 ....204 C1
Dorchester Ct *SOLH* B91 ....148 E1
Dorchester Dr *HRBN* B17 ....123 H1
Dorchester Rd *CNCK/NC* WS11 ....15 M4
  HAG/WOL DY9 ....120 D4
  SHHTH WV12 ....38 C1
  SOLH B91 ....148 E1
Dorchester Wy *COVE* CV2 ....135 K6
  NUN CV11 ....81 L6
Dordale Cl *NFLD/LBR* B31 ....144 A4
Dordale Rd *HAG/WOL* DY9 ....167 K2
Dordon Cl *SHLY* B90 ....147 L4
Dordon Rd *POL/KGSB/FAZ* B78 ....47 K5

Doreen Gv *ERDE/BCHGN* B24 ....90 F3
Doris Rd *BORD* B9 ....108 B4
  CSHL/WTROR B46 ....93 K5
  SPARK B11 ....125 M1
Dorking St *LICH* WS13 6
Dorlcote Rd *WASH/WDE* B8 ....108 E1
Dorlecote Rd
  NUNW/HART CV10 ....99 G5
Dormer Harris Av
  TLHL/CAN CV4 ....153 K4
Dormer Av *TAM/AM/WIL* B77 ....32 C8
Dormie Cl *PRLSN* CV32 ....206 D3
Dormie Cl *HWK/WKHTH* B38 ....145 H4
Dormington Rd *KGSTG* B44 ....71 K2
Dormston Cl *REDE* B98 ....202 D4
  SOLH B91 ....149 G5
Dormston Dr *SEDG* DY3 ....66 B5
  SLYOAK B29 ....123 K3
Dormy Dr *NFLD/LBR* B31 ....144 E6
Dorncliffe Av *STETCH* B33 ....110 B6
Dorney Cl *COVW* CV5 ....154 C5
Dornton Rd *BVILLE* B30 ....125 G5
Dorothy Powell Wy *COVE* CV2 ....135 K4
Dorothy Rd *SMHTHKW* B67 ....106 F3
  SPARK B11 ....108 F8
Dorothy St *WSL* WS1 ....4 C9
Dorridge Cl *REDW* B97 ....201 M4
Dorridge Cft *DOR/KN* B93 ....175 K3
Dorridge Rd *DOR/KN* B93 ....175 L3
Dorrington Gn *PBAR/PBCH* B42 ....70 E8
Dorrington Rd *PBAR/PBCH* B42 ....70 E8
Dorset Cl *NUNW/HART* CV10 ....98 D2
  POL/KGSB/FAZ B78 ....45 L4
  RBRY B45 ....143 K3
Dorset Dr *ALDR* WS9 ....40 E4
Dorset Pl *BLOX/PEL* WS3 ....39 G6
Dorset Rd *COV* CV1 ....134 A8
  HEDN WS12 ....17 J4
  HRBN B17 ....105 M2
  STRBR DY8 ....101 H6
  WASH/WDE B8 ....90 A7
Dorset Tower *WSNGN* B18 * 6 A2
Dorsett Cl *DARL/WED* WS10 ....52 A7
  DARL/WED WS10 ....69 H3
Dorsett Rd *DARL/WED* WS10 ....52 A7
  STRPT DY13 ....163 K8
  STRPT DY13 ....188 E1
Dorsett Road Ter
  DARL/WED WS10 ....52 A7
Dorsheath Gdns
  ERDW/GRVHL B23 ....90 D1
Dorsington Cl
  RWWCK/WEL CV35 ....204 C2
Dorsington Rd *ACGN* B27 ....127 H4
Dorstone Covert
  ALE/KHTH/YWD B14 ....146 A3
Dorville Rd *HWK/WKHTH* B38 ....145 H5
Dosthill Rd (Two Gates)
  TAM/AM/WIL B77 ....46 B7
Dotterel Pl *KIDD* DY10 ....164 E4
Douay Rd *ERDE/BCHGN* B24 ....72 F7
Double Rw *DUDS* DY2 ....103 J1
Doughty St *TPTN/OCK* DY4 ....68 F6
Douglas Av *CBROM* B36 ....91 H7
  LGLYGN/QTN B68 ....87 H8
Douglas Davies Cl *SHHTH* WV12 ....52 A1
Douglas Pl *WOLVN* WV10 ....36 F2
Douglas Rd *ACGN* B27 ....126 F1
  BILS/COS WV14 ....67 H5
  CSCFLD/WYGN B72 ....73 C2
  HDSW B21 ....88 C5
  HLYWD B47 ....146 E6
  LGLYGN/QTN B68 ....105 H1
  RMSLY B62 ....104 C4
  RUGBYN/HIL CV21 ....161 G7
Douglass Rd *DUDS* DY2 ....85 H5
Doulton Cl *COVE* CV2 * 135 J4
  RIDG/WDGT B32 ....123 K2
Doulton Dr *SMTHWK* B66 ....87 L7
Doulton Rd *BLKHTH/ROWR* B65 ....85 M3
Dovebridge Cl *WALM/CURD* B76 ....73 K1
Dove Cl *BDWTH* CV12 ....116 C2
  BNTWD WS7 ....18 C4
  DARL/WED WS10 ....68 F1
  KIDD DY10 ....164 E3
  WSL WS1 ....5 J5
  YDLY B25 ....109 J5
Dovecote Av *BLOX/PEL* WS3 ....25 L7
  COVN CV6 ....134 D3
  SHHTH WV12 ....51 L1
  SHLY B90 ....147 M4
Dovedale Av *BLOX/PEL* WS3 ....25 L7
  COVN CV6 ....134 D3
  SHHTH WV12 ....51 L1
  SHLY B90 ....147 M4
Dovedale Dr *HLGN/YWD* B28 ....126 C3
Dovedale Rd *ERDW/GRVHL* B23 ....72 A7
  ETTPK/GDPK/PENN WV4 ....65 J5
Dove Dr *STRBR* DY8 ....101 L5
Dove Gdns *HWK/WKHTH* B38 ....145 K3
Dove Hollow *GTWY* WS6 ....24 D4
  HEDN WS12 ....17 H6
Dovehouse Flds *LICHS* WS14 ....20 F7
Dove House La *HIA/OLT* B92 ....127 K6
Dovehouse Pool Rd *AST/WIT* B6 ....89 J3
Dover Cl *RIDG/WDGT* B32 ....122 E6
Dovercourt Rd
  LGN/SDN/BHAMAIR B26 ....110 A8
Doverdale Av *HLGN/YWD* B28 ....138 F8
Doverdale Cl *HALE* B63 ....103 H8
  REDE B98 ....201 G8
Doveridge Pl *WSL* WS1 ....5 G7
Doveridge Rd *HLGN/YWD* B28 ....126 C3
Doversley Rd
  ALE/KHTH/YWD B14 ....125 G8
Dover St *BILS/COS* WV14 ....51 H7
  COV CV1 ....8 D4
  WSNGN B18 ....89 D7
Dovestone *POL/KGSB/FAZ* B78 ....47 H4
Dovey Dr *WALM/CURD* B76 ....73 L6
Dovey Rd *MOS/BIL* B13 ....125 M1
  OLDBY B69 ....86 B5
Dovey Tower *VAUX/NECH* B7 * 7 L2
Dowar Rd *RBRY* B45 ....144 A6
Dowells Gdns *STRBR* DY8 ....101 H2
The Doweries *RBRY* B45 ....143 K5
Dower Rd *MGN/WHC* B75 ....56 F8
Dowler's Hill Crs *REDE* B98 ....202 E5
Dowles Cl *SLYOAK* B29 ....123 M7
Dowles Rd *BEWD* DY12 ....162 D3
  KIDDW DY11 ....163 M3
Dowley Cft *COVS* CV3 ....156 F2
Downcroft Av
  HWK/WKHTH B38 ....145 J3
Downderry Wy *COVN* CV6 ....134 E7
Downend Cl *WOLVN* WV10 ....36 D1
Downes Ct *TPTN/OCK* DY4 ....67 J7
Downesway *CNCK/NC* WS11 ....16 A3

Downey Cl *SPARK* B11 ....107 M6
Downfield Cl *BLOX/PEL* WS3 * 38 E1
Downfield Dr *SEDG* DY3 ....66 C7
Downham Cl *DSYBK/YTR* WS5 ....54 C4
Downham Pl *BDMR/CCFT* WV3 ....49 K5
Downing Cl *BLKHTH/ROWR* B65 ....104 A4
  DOR/KN B93 ....175 L4
  WNSFLD WV11 ....37 H6
Downing Crs *BDWTH* CV12 ....117 G1
Downing Dr *CRTAM* B79 ....31 J8
Downing St *HALE* B63 ....103 H5
  SMTHWK B66 ....88 A6
Downland Cl *HWK/WKHTH* B38 ....145 K4
Downsell Rd *REDW* B97 ....201 L3
Downsfield Rd
  LGN/SDN/BHAMAIR B26 ....109 M6
Downside Rd *ERDE/BCHGN* B24 ....90 C4
Downs Rd *WLNHL* WV13 ....52 A5
The Downs *FOAKS/STRLY* B74 ....55 J3
  WOLVN WV10 ....36 A7
Downton Cl *COVE* CV2 ....135 L5
Downton Crs *STETCH* B33 ....110 C2
Downton Rd *BDWTH* CV12 ....116 B4
Dowty Wy *WOLVN* WV10 ....35 L2
Doyle Dr *COVN* CV6 ....134 D2
Dragoon Flds *BRGRVE* B60 ....191 M5
Drake Cl *PENK* ST19 ....10 D6
Drake Cl *BLOX/PEL* WS3 ....38 F4
Drake Crs *KIDDW* DY11 ....137 L5
Drake Cft *LICH* WS13 ....21 C5
Drake St *COVN* CV6 ....134 B6
  HHTH/SAND B71 ....69 G8
Drancy Av *SHHTH* WV12 ....38 B7
Draper Cl *KNWTH* CV8 ....198 A1
Draper's Flds *COV* CV1 ....8 F2
Drawbridge Rd *SHLY* B90 ....147 G5
Draycote Cl *HIA/OLT* B92 ....128 B6
Draycott Av *ERDW/GRVHL* B23 ....72 B8
Draycott Cl
  ETTPK/GDPK/PENN WV4 ....49 C8
  REDW B97 ....193 M8
Draycott Crs *TAM/AM/WIL* B77 ....46 A4
Draycott Dr *NFLD/LBR* B31 ....123 J2
Draycott Rd *COVE* CV2 ....134 F6
  SMTHWK B66 ....87 J6
Drayman Cl *WSL* WS1 ....5 C7
Drayton Cl *MGN/WHC* B75 ....56 F2
  NUNW/HART CV10 ....79 L5
  REDE B98 ....203 H5
Drayton Cl *BRGRVE* B60 ....191 M5
  NUNW/HART CV10 * 79 M3
  WWCK CV34 ....205 J3
Drayton Crs *COVW* CV5 ....132 B6
Drayton La *POL/KGSB/FAZ* B78 ....44 D8
Drayton Leys
  RUGBYS/DCH CV22 ....186 C6
Drayton Manor Dr
  POL/KGSB/FAZ B78 ....45 K4
Drayton Rd
  ALE/KHTH/YWD B14 ....125 J5
  BDWTH CV12 ....117 G3
  HAG/WOL DY9 ....141 H7
  KIDD DY10 ....138 C1
  SHLY B90 ....148 C5
  SMTHWK B66 ....105 L4
Drayton St *BKHL/PFLD* WV2 ....2 B7
  WSLW WS2 ....4 E3
Drayton Wy *NUNW/HART* CV10 ....80 A6
Dreadnought Rd *BRLYHL* DY5 ....83 M6
The Dreel *EDG* DY5 ....106 C6
Dreghorn Rd *CBROM* B36 ....91 J5
Drem Cft *CVALE* B35 ....91 L3
Dresden Cl
  ETTPK/GDPK/PENN WV4 ....66 C1
Drew Crs *HAG/WOL* DY9 ....120 B2
  KNWTH CV8 ....197 L1
Drew Rd *HAG/WOL* DY9 ....120 B2
Drews Holloway *HALE* B63 ....103 H8
Drews Holloway South
  HALE B63 ....103 H8
Drews La *WASH/WDE* B8 ....90 E7
Drews Meadow Cl
  ALE/KHTH/YWD B14 ....146 A3
Dreyer Cl *RUGBYS/DCH* CV22 ....186 A3
Driffield Cl *REDE* B98 ....203 H3
Driffold *SCFLD/BOLD* B73 ....72 F2
Driftwood Cl *HWK/WKHTH* B38 ....145 H6
Drive Flds
  ETTPK/GDPK/PENN WV4 ....48 F7
The Drive *ALVE* B48 ....170 F2
  BFLD/HDSWWD B20 ....88 B3
  BLOX/PEL WS3 ....39 J3
  BRLYHL DY5 ....84 B8
  CDSL WV8 ....34 D2
  COVE CV2 ....156 B2
  CSHL/WTROR B46 * 93 C2
  DUNHL/THL/PER WV6 * 50 C5
  ERDW/GRVHL B23 ....90 C3
  HALE B63 ....103 H8
  HALE B63 ....121 G2
  LICHS WS14 ....29 J5
  REDW B97 ....193 G2
  RUSH/SHEL WS4 ....40 A8
Droitwich Rd *KIDD* DY10 ....165 G8
Dronfield Rd *COVE* CV2 ....155 M2
Drovers Wy *BRGRVE* B60 ....191 J7
The Droveway *COVEN* WV9 ....35 K3
Droylsdon Park Rd *COVS* CV3 ....180 F2
Druid Park Rd *SHHTH* WV12 ....38 A3
Druid Rd *COVE* CV2 ....155 M2
Druids Av *ALDR* WS9 ....41 G5
  BLKHTH/ROWR B65 ....104 B1
Druids La *ALE/KHTH/YWD* B14 ....146 A4
Druids Wk *ALDR* WS9 ....40 E2
Druids Wy *PENK* ST19 ....10 D6
Drummond Cl *COVN* CV6 ....133 K6
  WNSFLD WV11 ....37 J3
Drummond Gv *GTB/HAM* B43 ....71 C2
Drummond Rd *BORD* B9 ....108 D3
  BRGRVE B60 ....191 J6
  HAG/WOL DY9 ....120 D1
Drummond St *WOLV* WV1 ....2 E3
Drummond Wy
  CHWD/FDBR/MGN B37 ....111 J3
Drury La *CDSL* WV8 ....34 D1
  RUGBYN/HIL CV21 * 186 E2
  SOLH B91 ....149 G2
  STRBR DY8 ....101 K6
Dryden Cl *TAM/AM/WIL* B77 ....47 C2
  WNSFLD WV11 ....37 L1
Dryden Gv *ACGN* B27 ....126 F3
Dryden Pl *BLOX/PEL* WS3 ....39 J6
Dryden Rd *BLOX/PEL* WS3 ....39 J6
  CRTAM B79 ....31 L6
  WOLVN WV10 ....36 D1
Dryden Wk *RUGBYS/DCH* CV22 ....186 C2

Drylea Gv *CBROM* B36 ....91 K5
Dry Mill La *BEWD* DY12 ....136 C5
Dual Wy *HEDN* WS12 ....12 A5
Dubarry Av *KGSWFD* DY6 ....83 G5
Duchess Pde *WBROM* B70 * 87 H2
Duchess Rd *LDYWD/EDGR* B16 ....106 E4
  WSL WS1 ....53 H8
Duckhouse Rd *WNSFLD* WV11 ....37 H6
Duck La *CDSL* WV8 ....34 D2
Duckpen Cottages *KIDD* DY10 * 139 J5
Duddeston Dr *WASH/WDE* B8 ....108 D1
Duddeston Manor Rd
  VAUX/NECH B7 ....7 M1
Duddeston Mill Rd
  VAUX/NECH B7 ....107 M1
Dudding Rd
  ETTPK/GDPK/PENN WV4 ....50 B8
Dudhill Rd *CDYHTH* B64 ....103 L2
Dudley Cl *BLKHTH/ROWR* B65 ....85 K7
Dudley Crs *WNSFLD* WV11 ....37 J7
Dudley Gn *RLSN* CV32 ....206 F3
Dudley Park Rd *ACGN* B27 ....127 C2
Dudley Port *TPTN/OCK* DY4 ....85 L2
  BLKHTH/ROWR B65 ....50 B6
  BRLYHL DY5 ....102 B1
  HALE B63 ....103 M7
  KCSWFD DY6 ....83 C5
  KNWTH CV8 ....197 K3
  OLDBY B69 ....86 D5
  SEDG DY3 ....66 B6
  SEDG DY3 ....83 C2
  TPTN/OCK DY4 ....67 H8
  WSNGN B18 ....106 B3
Dudley Rd East *OLDBY* B69 ....86 A3
Dudley Rd West *OLDBY* B69 ....85 M5
Dudley Rw *DUDS* DY2 ....85 H4
Dudley Southern By-Pass
  DUDS DY2 ....84 E6
Dudley St *ATHST* CV9 ....63 H6
  BILS/COS WV14 ....67 H1
  COVN CV6 ....134 C4
  DARL/WED WS10 ....68 C3
  DIG/EDG B5 ....7 G6
  KIDD DY10 ....138 C2
  SEDG DY3 ....83 C2
  WBROM B70 ....68 D8
  WOLV WV1 ....3 C5
  WSL WS1 ....4 F5
Dudley Wk
  ETTPK/GDPK/PENN WV4 ....50 A8
Dudley Wood Av *DUDS* DY2 ....103 G4
Dudley Wood Rd *DUDS* DY2 ....103 G4
Dudmaston Wy *DUDN* DY1 ....84 C2
Dudnill Gv *RIDG/WDGT* B32 ....122 E5
Duffield Cl *CDSL* WV8 ....35 K4
Duffy Pl *RUGBYN/HIL* CV21 ....187 C5
Dufton Rd *RIDG/WDGT* B32 ....105 H8
Dugdale Cl *HEDN* WS12 ....17 K2
Dugdale Crs *MGN/WHC* B75 ....57 C2
Dugdale St *NUN* CV11 ....99 G1
  WSNGN B18 ....106 B3
Duggins La
  RCOVN/BALC/EX CV7 ....152 F1
Duke Barn Fld *COVE* CV2 ....134 E8
Duke of Yk *NFLD/LBR* B31 * 125 H8
Dukes Rd *BVILLE* B30 ....145 K2
Duke St *BDMR/CCFT* WV3 ....49 L6
  BLKHTH/ROWR B65 ....85 M3
  COVN CV6 ....154 D3
  CSCFLD/WYGN B72 ....72 F1
  NUN CV11 ....98 E1
  RLSN CV32 ....206 F3
  RUGBYN/HIL CV21 ....186 E1
  SEDG DY3 ....66 B8
  STRBR DY8 ....101 L7
  WBROM B70 ....86 F1
  WNSFLD WV11 ....37 H8
  WOLV WV1 ....3 C5
Dukes Wy *POL/KGSB/FAZ* B78 ....47 L4
Dulverton Av *COVW* CV5 ....154 B1
Dulverton Rd *AST/WIT* B6 ....89 J1
  COVW CV5 ....154 B1
Dulwich Gv *KGSTG* B44 ....71 M5
Dulwich Rd *KGSTG* B44 ....71 L5
Dumbleberry Av *SEDG* DY3 ....66 A6
Dumbleberry La *ALDR* WS9 ....40 C5
Dumble Pit La *HLYWD* B47 ....172 C6
Dumolo's La *TAM/AM/WIL* B77 ....46 C2
Dumphouse La *ALVE* B48 ....195 C4
Dunard Rd *SHLY* B90 ....147 L2
Dunbar Cl *KIDD* DY10 ....149 K7
Dunbar Gv *GTB/HAM* B43 ....70 F1
Dunblane Dr *RLSN* CV32 ....199 C8
Duncalfe Dr *RUGBYS/DCH* CV22 ....186 B7
Duncan Dr *RUGBYS/DCH* CV22 ....186 B7
Duncan Edwards Cl *DUDN* DY1 ....84 D3
Duncan St *BKHL/PFLD* WV2 ....50 A6
Dunchurch Cl
  RCOVN/BALC/EX CV7 ....151 M6
  REDE B98 ....203 K4
Dunchurch Crs *SCFLD/BOLD* B73 ....72 A2
Dunchurch Dr *NFLD/LBR* B31 ....123 J2
Dunchurch Hwy *COVW* CV5 ....132 E7
Dunchurch Rd
  RUGBYS/DCH CV22 ....186 D6
Dunclent Crs *KIDD* DY10 ....138 F8
Dunclent La *KIDD* DY10 ....165 H2
Duncombe Gn *CSHL/WTROR* B46 ....93 K6
Duncombe Gv *HRBN* B17 ....105 K6
Duncombe St *STRBR* DY8 ....101 H7
Duncroft Av *COVN* CV6 ....133 K6
Duncroft Rd
  LGN/SDN/BHAMAIR B26 ....109 K5
Duncumb Rd *MGN/WHC* B75 ....57 J1
Dundalk La *GTWY* WS6 ....24 C5
Dundas Av *OLDBY* B69 ....85 K5
Dunedin *TAM/AM/WIL* B77 ....46 E4
Dunedin Dr *RBRY* B45 ....169 L4
Dunedin Rd *KGSTG* B44 ....71 J2
Dunhampton Dr *KIDD* DY10 ....138 F4
Dunhill Av *TLHL/CAN* CV4 ....153 J2
Dunkirk Av *WBROM* B70 ....86 C1
Dunkley St *WOLV* WV1 ....2 E1
Dunley Cft *SHLY* B90 ....148 B7
Dunlin Cl *ERDW/GRVHL* B23 ....90 B2
  KGSWFD DY6 ....83 J7
Dunlin Dr *KIDD* DY10 ....164 D3
Dunlop Rd *REDW* B97 ....202 A4
Dunlop Wy *ERDE/BCHGN* B24 ....91 J4
Dunmore Rd *BDWTH* CV12 ....137 G8
Dunnerdale *RUGBYN/HIL* CV21 ....161 H5
Dunnerdale Rd *BRWNH* WS8 ....26 B7
Dunnigan Rd *RIDG/WDGT* B32 ....123 K2
Dunnington Av *KIDD* DY10 ....138 F4
Dunn's Bank *BRLYHL* DY5 ....102 B5
Dunns La *POL/KGSB/FAZ* B78 ....47 K2
Dunrose Cl *COVE* CV2 ....156 C3
Dunsfold Cft *AST/WIT* B6 ....89 K1
Dunsford Cl *BRLYHL* DY5 ....101 M6
Dunsford Rd *SMTHWK* B66 ....105 L4
Dunsink Rd *AST/WIT* B6 ....89 J2
Dunslade Crs *BRLYHL* DY5 ....102 D5
Dunslade Rd *ERDW/GRVHL* B23 ....72 C6

Dunsley Dr *KINVER* DY7 ....118 A1
  STRBR DY8 ....101 J2
Dunsley Gv
  ETTPK/GDPK/PENN WV4 ....65 L1
Dunsley Rd *KINVER* DY7 ....100 B8
Dunsmore Av *COVS* CV3 ....156 A7
  RUGBYN/HIL CV21 ....187 C5
Dunsmore Dr *BRLYHL* DY5 ....102 B5
Dunsmore Gv *SOLH* B91 ....127 L3
Dunsmore Rd *HLGN/YWD* B28 ....126 C4
Dunstall Av
  DUNHL/THL/PER WV6 ....36 A8
Dunstall Cl *REDW* B97 ....201 M3
Dunstall Gv *SLYOAK* B29 ....123 K5
Dunstall Hl
  DUNHL/THL/PER WV6 ....36 A8
Dunstall La
  DUNHL/THL/PER WV6 ....35 M8
  POL/KGSB/FAZ B78 ....31 C8
Dunstall Rd
  DUNHL/THL/PER WV6 ....49 M1
  HALE B63 ....121 H2
Dunstan Cft *SHLY* B90 ....148 A5
Dunster *TAM/AM/WIL* B77 ....46 A6
Dunster Cl *BVILLE* B30 ....145 M1
Dunster Gv
  DUNHL/THL/PER WV6 ....48 D2
Dunster Pl *COVN* CV6 ....134 B2
Dunster Rd
  CHWD/FDBR/MGN B37 ....111 C2
Dunston Cl *GTWY* WS6 ....24 C5
  KCSWFD DY6 ....83 H6
Dunston Dr *BNTWD* WS7 ....18 E5
Dunsville Dr *COVE* CV2 ....135 K5
Dunton Cl *MGN/WHC* B75 ....56 F1
Dunton Coppice
  WALM/CURD B76 ....75 J5
Dunton Hall Rd *SHLY* B90 ....147 L5
Dunton La *WALM/CURD* B76 ....74 F4
Dunton Rd
  CHWD/FDBR/MGN B37 ....110 D1
Dunvegan Gv *COVS* CV3 ....156 A3
  KNWTH CV8 ....198 A1
Dunvegan Rd *ERDE/BCHGN* B24 ....90 E1
Durant Cl *RBRY* B45 ....143 H4
Durban Rd *SMTHWK* B66 ....106 A4
Durbar Av *COVN* CV6 ....134 B5
D'urberville Rd *BKHL/PFLD* WV2 ....50 D7
Durham Av *WLNHL* WV13 ....52 A2
Durham Cft *BRGRVW* B61 ....191 J1
  POL/KGSB/FAZ B78 ....45 L4
  RCOVN/BALC/EX CV7 ....133 K1
Durham Crs *COVW* CV5 ....132 B5
Durham Cft
  CHWD/FDBR/MGN B37 ....110 E3
Durham Dr *HHTH/SAND* B71 ....69 H6
Durham Pl *WSLW* WS2 ....52 B1
Durham Rd *BLKHTH/ROWR* B65 ....104 C1
  DARL/WED WS10 ....68 H1
  DUDS DY2 ....85 G8
  SPARK B11 ....125 M1
  STRBR DY8 ....101 K5
  WSLW WS2 ....52 F5
Durley Dean Rd *SLYOAK* B29 ....124 A3
Durley Dr *SCFLD/BOLD* B73 ....72 A2
Durley Rd *YDLY* B25 ....109 C8
Durliston Gv *HLGN/YWD* B28 ....126 F3
Durnford Cft
  ALE/KHTH/YWD B14 ....146 C4
Durrell Dr *RUGBYS/DCH* CV22 ....185 L5
Dursley Cl *HIA/OLT* B92 ....127 M5
  SHHTH WV12 ....52 B1
Dursley Dr *CNCK/NC* WS11 ....15 M3
Dursley La *REDE* B98 ....203 L2
Dursley Rd *BNTWD* WS7 ....18 E6
Dusthouse La *BRGRVE* B60 ....192 B6
Dutton Gv *COVE* CV2 ....135 H2
Dutton's La *MGN/WHC* B75 ....57 J1
Duxford Cl *REDW* B97 ....201 M5
Duxford Rd *PBAR/PBCH* B42 ....70 F5
Dwellings La *RIDG/WDGT* B32 ....104 F8
Dyas Av *PBAR/PBCH* B42 ....70 E6
Dyas Rd *HLYWD* B47 ....146 E6
  KGSTG B44 ....71 H5
Dyce Cl *CVALE* B35 ....91 L1
Dyers La *HOCK/TIA* B94 ....174 B5
  KNWTH CV8 ....183 L2
Dymoke St *BHTH/HG* B12 ....107 K5
Dymond Rd *COVN* CV6 ....134 A2
Dynes Wk *SMTHWKW* B67 ....87 L8
Dyott Cl *WSL* WS1 ....5 L4
Dyott Rd *MOS/BIL* B13 ....125 L4
Dysart Cl *COV* CV1 ....9 J2
Dyson Cl *RUGBYN/HIL* CV21 ....187 K4
  WSLW WS2 ....52 B1
Dysons Gdns *WASH/WDE* B8 ....90 C8
Dyson St *TLHL/CAN* CV4 ....153 J2

E

Eachelhurst Rd
  ERDE/BCHGN B24 ....91 J1
Eachus Rd *BILS/COS* WV14 ....67 H5
Eachway *RBRY* B45 ....143 K7
Eachway La *RBRY* B45 ....143 L7
Eacott Cl *COVN* CV6 ....133 L2
Eadie Ms *REDW* B97 ....202 A4
Eadie St *NUNW/HART* CV10 ....98 A1
Eagle Cl *BLKHTH/ROWR* B65 ....103 K1
  DUDN DY1 ....84 D4
  GTWY WS6 ....24 D4
  NUN CV11 ....99 M5
Eagle Cft *ALE/KHTH/YWD* B14 ....146 C3
Eagle Dr *TAM/AM/WIL* B77 ....46 F3
Eagle Gdns *ERDE/BCHGN* B24 ....90 E3
Eagle Gv *CBROM* B36 ....92 E5
  HEDN WS12 ....17 C4
Eagle La *TPTN/OCK* DY4 ....68 B7
Eagle Rd *REDE* B98 ....195 J8
Eagle St *BDMR/CCFT* WV3 ....49 L6
  BKHL/PFLD WV2 ....3 K8
  COV CV1 ....134 B8
  RLSS CV31 ....207 G7
  TPTN/OCK DY4 ....68 A7
Eagle St East *COV* CV1 ....134 B8
Ealing Gv *KGSTG* B44 ....71 L4
Ealingham *TAM/AM/WIL* B77 ....46 E4
Eardisley Gdns
  BFLD/HDSWWD B20 ....89 H4
Earls Cl *REDW* B97 ....201 K3
Earls Court Rd *HRBN* B17 ....105 J1
The Earl's Cft *COVS* CV3 ....155 G8
Earlsdon Av North *COVW* CV5 ....154 D4
Earlsdon Av South *COVW* CV5 ....8 A9
Earlsdon St *COVW* CV5 ....154 D5
Earls Ferry Gdns
  RIDG/WDGT B32 ....122 F6
Earlsmead Rd *HDSW* B21 ....88 A5
Earlsmere *HOCK/TIA* B94 ....173 M4
Earls Rd *NUN* CV11 ....80 C5

GTB/HAM B43 70 C6
STRPT DY13 163 K7
Ennersdale Bungalows
CSHL/WTROR B46 93 K4
Ennersdale Cl CSHL/WTROR B46 93 K4
Ennersdale Rd CSHL/WTROR B46 93 K4
Enright Cl RLSN CV32 206 C3
Ensall Dr STRBR DY8 101 J4
Ensbury Cl SHHTH WV12 52 B1
Ensdale Rw WLNHL WV13 51 L4
Ensdon Gv KGSTG B44 71 M4
Ensford Cl FOAKS/STRLY B74 56 C1
Ensign Cl TLHL/CAN CV4 153 G4
Ensor Cl NUN CV11 81 K7
Ensor Dr POL/KGSB/FAZ B78 47 K4
Enstone Rd DUDN DY1 84 D5
ERDW/GRVHL B23 72 E7
Enterprise Dr
FOAKS/STRLY B74 * 55 J6
HAG/WOL DY9 102 D7
WOLVN WV10 14 B8
Enterprise Gv BLOX/PEL WS3 25 M8
Enterprise Wy CBHAMNE B4 7 J1
Enville Cl BLOX/PEL WS3 38 E2
CHWD/FDBR/MGN B37 110 F4
Enville Gv SPARK B11 108 B8
Enville Pl STRBR DY8 * 101 K8
Enville Rd
ETTPK/GDPK/PENN WV4 49 G8
KGSWFD DY6 82 F5
SEDG DY3 84 B1
Enville St STRBR DY8 101 K8
Epping Cl BLOX/PEL WS3 39 K7
RBRY B45 143 M3
Epping Gv KGSTG B44 71 L6
Epping Wy RLSN CV32 207 G1
Epsom Cl BDWTH CV12 116 F1
DUNHL/THL/PER WV6 48 D1
LICHS WS14 21 H6
REDW B97 201 M5
TAM/AM/WIL B77 60 A2
Epsom Dr COVS CV3 156 A7
Epsom Gv KGSTG B44 71 M5
Epsom Rd BRGRVW B61 168 E4
RLSN CV32 207 G1
RUGBYS/DCH CV22 186 B4
Epwell Gv KGSTG B44 71 K7
Epwell Rd KGSTG B44 71 K7
Equipoint YDLY B25 * 109 H7
Erasmus Rd SPARK B11 107 L6
Ercall Cl ERDW/GRVHL B23 71 L7
Erdington Hall Rd
ERDE/BCHGN B24 90 D3
Erdington Rd ALDR WS9 54 F2
ATHST CV9 63 H6
Erica Av BDWTH CV12 116 C3
Erica Cl KIDDW DY11 138 B4
SLYOAK B29 123 L5
Erica Rd DSYBK/YTR WS5 69 M2
Eric Grey Cl COVE CV2 134 E8
Eringden TAM/AM/WIL B77 46 F4
Erithway Rd COVS CV3 180 F1
Ermington Crs CBROM B36 91 J6
Ermington Rd
ETTPK/GDPK/PENN WV4 50 B8
Erneley Cl STRPT DY13 188 D4
Ernest Clarke Cl SHHTH WV12 52 A1
Ernest Ct HWK/WKHTH B38 145 L4
Ernest Richards Rd
BDWTH CV12 116 F1
Ernest Rd BHTH/HG B12 125 M1
DUDS DY2 85 K4
SMTHWKW B67 87 J7
Ernest St CBHAMW B1 6 E8
Ernsford Av COVS CV3 155 L4
Ernsford Cl DOR/KN B93 175 K3
Erskine St VAUX/NECH B7 107 M2
Erwood Cl REDW B97 201 M3
Esher Dr COVS CV3 155 J6
Esher Rd HHTH/SAND B71 69 H7
KGSTG B44 71 K1
Eskdale RUGBYN/HIL CV21 161 G5
Eskdale Cl WOLV WV1 50 E3
Eskdale Wk BRLYHL DY5 101 M5
Eskrett St HEDN WS12 12 F8
Esme Rd SPARK B11 125 M1
Esmond Cl BVILLE B30 124 B8
Essendon Rd WASH/WDE B8 108 F1
Essex Av DARL/WED WS10 69 G1
KGSWFD DY6 82 F8
Essex Cl COVW CV5 153 M2
KNWTH CV8 197 J3
Essex Dr HEDN WS12 16 F1
Essex Gdns STRBR DY8 101 H6
Essex Rd DUDS DY2 84 D7
MGN/WHC B75 57 H4
Essex St DIG/EDG B5 6 F8
RUGBYN/HIL CV21 186 D1
WSLW WS2 39 H8
Essington Cl LICHS WS14 20 E8
LICHS WS14 28 E7
STRBR DY8 101 J5
Essington Rd SHHTH WV12 37 M4
Essington St LDYWD/EDGR B16 6 B7
Essington Wy WOLV WV1 50 F4
Este Rd LGN/SDN/BHAMAIR B26 109 L5
Esterton Cl COVN CV6 134 A3
Estone Wk AST/WIT B6 89 K6
Estria Rd EDG B15 106 F6
Estridge La GTWY WS6 24 E3
Etchell Rd POL/KGSB/FAZ B78 45 K2
Ethelfield Rd COVE CV2 155 M2
Ethelfleda Rd TAM/AM/WIL B77 46 D8
Ethelfleda Ter DARL/WED WS10 68 D2
Ethelred Cl FOAKS/STRLY B74 56 E2
Ethel Rd HRBN B17 106 B8
Ethel St CBHAM B2 6 F5
LGLYGN/QTN B68 104 E1
SMTHWKW B67 105 K3
Etheridge Rd BILS/COS WV14 66 E4
Eton Cl SEDG DY3 66 D6
Eton Dr STRBR DY8 119 L2
Eton Rd BHTH/HG B12 125 M1
Eton Wk HAG/WOL DY9 119 L7
Etruria Wy BILS/COS WV14 51 J6
Etta Gv KGSTG B44 71 J1
Ettingley Cl REDE B98 202 F8
Ettingshall Park Farm La
ETTPK/GDPK/PENN WV4 66 B1
Ettingshall Rd BILS/COS WV14 66 E4
BKHL/PFLD WV2 50 E6
Ettington Cl DOR/KN B93 175 H3
Ettington Rd AST/WIT B6 89 J5
COVW CV5 153 L2
Ettymore Cl SEDG DY3 66 B5
Ettymore Rd SEDG DY3 66 B5
Ettymore Rd West SEDG DY3 66 A5
Etwall Rd HLGN/YWD B28 126 C8
Euan Cl HRBN B17 106 A5
Eunal Ct REDW B97 202 C8
Europa Av WBROM B70 87 K3
Europa Wy LICHS WS14 21 K5
Euston Crs COVS CV3 156 A7
Euston Pl RLSN CV32 206 D5
Evans Cl BDWTH CV12 117 G2
KIDDW DY11 138 A2
TPTN/OCK DY4 67 G8
Evans Cft POL/KGSB/FAZ B78 45 L4
Evans Pl BILS/COS WV14 51 J6
Evans Rd RUGBYS/DCH CV22 186 A3
Evans St BILS/COS WV14 66 D4
DUNHL/THL/PER WV6 2 C1
WLNHL WV13 51 H4
Eva Rd LGLYGN/QTN B68 105 G3
WSNGN B18 88 C7
Eve La DUDN DY1 66 D8
Evelyn Av COVN CV6 134 C3
Evelyn Cft SCFLD/BOLD B73 72 E5
Evelyn Rd SPARK B11 126 A1
Evenlode Cl REDE B98 202 D4
Evenlode Crs COVN CV6 133 K8
Evenlode Gv WLNHL WV13 52 B4
Evenlode Rd HIA/OLT B92 127 L2
Everard Cl RRUGBY CV23 161 L8
Everdon Cl RUGBYS/DCH CV22 187 J5
Everdon Rd COVN CV6 133 M3
Everest Cl SMTHWK B66 87 J5
Everest Rd BFLD/HDSWWD B20 88 E2
RUGBYS/DCH CV22 186 C5
WSLW WS2 52 D2
Everglade Rd POL/KGSB/FAZ B78 60 F3
Evergreen Cl BILS/COS WV14 66 F5
Evergreen Hts HEDN WS12 12 E5
Everitt Dr DOR/KN B93 149 L7
Eversleigh Rd COVN CV6 133 J6
Eversley Dl ERDE/BCHGN B24 90 E3
Eversley Gv SEDG DY3 66 A3
WNSFLD WV11 37 G7
Eversley Rd BORD B9 108 B4
Evers St BRLYHL DY5 102 E5
Everton Rd WASH/WDE B8 109 G1
Eves Cft RIDG/WDGT B32 123 G4
Evesham Crs BLOX/PEL WS3 38 D2
Evesham Ri DUDS DY2 103 H2
Evesham Rd REDW B97 202 B5
Evesham St REDW B97 202 C2
Evesham Wk TLHL/CAN CV4 154 A8
Eveson Rd STRBR DY8 119 H3
Evington Pl YDLY B25 * 108 E6
Evreux Wy RUGBYN/HIL CV21 186 E2
Ewart Rd WSLW WS2 52 C2
Ewell Rd ERDE/BCHGN B24 90 F1
Ewhurst Av SLYOAK B29 124 D4
Ewhurst Cl WLNHL WV13 51 K5
Ewloe Cl KIDDW DY11 164 C4
Exbury Cl COVEN WV9 35 K3
Exbury Wy NUN CV11 99 J5
Excelsior Gv BLOX/PEL WS3 25 M8
Exchange St BRLYHL DY5 102 B1
KIDD DY10 138 C8
The Exchange BLOX/PEL WS3 * 38 F4
Exe Cft NFLD/LBR B31 144 F5
Exeter Cl COVS CV3 156 B5
KIDDW DY11 137 L7
Exeter Dr
CHWD/FDBR/MGN B37 110 D5
CRTAM B79 31 J8
Exeter Pas CBHAMW B1 6 F8
Exeter Pl WSLW WS2 52 F4
Exeter Rd CNCK/NC WS11 15 M5
DUDS DY2 103 H3
SLYOAK B29 124 D3
SMTHWK B66 87 M8
Exeter St CBHAMW B1 6 E8
Exford Cl BRLYHL DY5 101 M6
Exhall Basin COVN CV6 * 116 F7
Exhall Cl REDE B98 195 H8
SOLH B91 148 C3
Exhall Gn RCOVN/BALC/EX CV7 116 D6
Exhall Rd RCOVN/BALC/EX CV7 115 K7
Exham Cl WWCK CV34 205 J4
Exhibition Wy BHAMNEC B40 129 H1
Exley TAM/AM/WIL B77 46 B4
Exminster Rd COVS CV3 155 J8
Exmoor Dr BRGRVW B61 168 E8
RLSN CV32 207 G1
Exmoor Gn WNSFLD WV11 37 G6
Exmouth Cl COVE CV2 135 G6
The Expressway WBROM B70 87 G1
Exton Cl RCOVN/BALC/EX CV7 116 A6
WNSFLD WV11 37 K5
Exton Gdns SMTHWK B66 * 88 B7
Exton Wy WASH/WDE B8 90 B8
Eydon Cl RUGBYN/HIL CV21 161 J7
Eyffler Cl WWCK CV34 205 H6
Eyland Gv WSL WS1 5 G3
Eymore Cl SLYOAK B29 123 M7
Eyre St WSNGN B18 106 E2
Eyston Av TPTN/OCK DY4 68 B5
Eyton Cl REDE B98 203 H2
Eyton Cft BHTH/HG B12 107 K6
Ezekiel La SHHTH WV12 38 A7

F

Fabian Cl COVS CV3 156 B6
RBRY B45 143 K3
Fabian Crs SHLY B90 147 M4
Facet Rd HWK/WKHTH B38 145 L3
Factory La BRGRVW B61 191 J4
Factory Rd TPTN/OCK DY4 67 J7
WSNGN B18 88 D7
Factory St DARL/WED WS10 52 A7
Fairbanks Cl COVE CV2 135 L6
Fairbourne Av
BLKHTH/ROWR B65 104 C1
KGSTG B44 71 J3
Fairbourne Gdns REDW B97 202 A5
Fairbourne Wy COVN CV6 133 J5
Fairburn Crs BLOX/PEL WS3 25 M8
Faircroft KNWTH CV8 197 K2
Faircroft Av WALM/CURD B76 73 K7
Faircroft Rd CBROM B36 92 B4
Fairfax Rd MGN/WHC B75 73 K1
NFLD/LBR B31 144 E5
WOLVN WV10 36 B2
Fairfax St COV CV1 9 G4
Fairfield Cl HEDN WS12 17 H4
Fairfield Ct COVS CV3 155 L6
Fairfield Dr BLOX/PEL WS3 39 M1
CDSL WV8 34 C2
PENK ST19 10 C7
RMSLY B62 104 C4
Fairfield Gv RMSLY B62 104 C4
Fairfield La KIDDW DY11 137 M2
Fairfield Mt WSL WS1 5 G7
Fairfield Ri
RCOVN/BALC/EX CV7 131 G4
STRBR DY8 101 G8
Fairfield Rd
ALE/KHTH/YWD B14 125 J5
BRGRVW B61 168 B4
DUDS DY2 85 H6
HALE B63 121 L3
RMSLY B62 104 C4
STRBR DY8 101 G8
Fairfields Hl POL/KGSB/FAZ B78 47 K5
Fairford Cl REDE B98 195 J6
Fairford Gdns BNTWD WS7 19 G7
STRBR DY8 101 J2
Fairford Rd KGSTG B44 71 K7
Fairgreen Gdns BRLYHL DY5 84 A8
Fairgreen Wy FOAKS/STRLY B74 55 L4
SLYOAK B29 124 D4
Fairground Wy WSL WS1 4 D6
Fairhaven Cft RMSLY B62 104 C4
Fairhills SEDG DY3 66 B5
Fairhill Wy SPARK B11 107 M6
Fairholme Rd CBROM B36 90 F6
Fairhurst Dr RLSN CV32 206 C2
Fair Isle Dr NUNW/HART CV10 98 D2
Fair Lady Dr BNTWD WS7 18 B5
Fairlands Pk TLHL/CAN CV4 154 C8
Fairlawn EDG B15 * 106 E6
Fairlawn Cl SHHTH WV12 38 A4
Fairlawn Dr KGSWFD DY6 101 H1
Fairlawns
LGN/SDN/BHAMAIR B26 109 K4
WALM/CURD B76 73 L5
Fairlie Crs HWK/WKHTH B38 145 H4
Fairlight Dr RBRY B45 169 L4
Fairmead Ri HWK/WKHTH B38 145 J4
Fairmile Cl COVS CV3 156 A5
Fairmile Rd HALE B63 103 K7
Fairmont Rd BRGRVE B60 191 M5
Fairmount Dr CNCK/NC WS11 16 C5
Fairoak Dr BRGRVE B60 191 K7
DUNHL/THL/PER WV6 48 E2
Fair Oaks Dr GTWY WS6 24 E5
Fairview Av PBAR/PBCH B42 70 F7
Fairview Cl GTWY WS6 24 B3
TAM/AM/WIL B77 32 D8
WNSFLD WV11 36 F6
Fairview Crs KGSWFD DY6 83 K7
WNSFLD WV11 36 F6
Fairview Gv WNSFLD WV11 36 F6
Fairview Ms CSHL/WTROR B46 * 93 K6
Fairview Rd DUDN DY1 84 E3
ETTPK/GDPK/PENN WV4 65 G1
WNSFLD WV11 36 F6
Fairway CNCK/NC WS11 16 B7
NFLD/LBR B31 144 C3
NUN CV11 99 M5
RUSH/SHEL WS4 40 B4
TAM/AM/WIL B77 46 C8
Fairway Av OLDBY B69 85 L5
Fairway Dr RBRY B45 143 K7
Fairway Gn BILS/COS WV14 51 G6
Fairway Ri KNWTH CV8 180 A7
Fairway Rd LGLYGN/QTN B68 104 D4
Fairways Av STRBR DY8 119 J3
Fairways Cl COVW CV5 132 E7
STRBR DY8 119 J3
Fairways Dr BRGRVE B60 169 L8
The Fairways RLSN CV32 206 B3
The Fairway HWK/WKHTH B38 145 H3
Fairyfield Av GTB/HAM B43 70 B4
Fakenham Cft HRBN B17 105 K6
Falcon TAM/AM/WIL B77 46 E7
Falcon Av COVS CV3 156 D5
Falcon Cl CNCK/NC WS11 16 A3
GTWY WS6 24 A3
KIDD DY10 164 C2
NUN CV11 99 M5
Falcon Crs BILS/COS WV14 66 D3
Falcondale Rd SHHTH WV12 38 A4
Falconhurst Rd SLYOAK B29 124 A3
Falcon Lodge Crs MGN/WHC B75 57 L8
Falcon Pl OLDBY B69 86 A6
Falcon Ri STRBR DY8 101 G7
Falcon Rd LGLYGN/QTN B68 104 D3
The Falcons MGN/WHC B75 57 M8
Falcon Wy DUDN DY1 84 D4
Falfield Cl OLDBY B69 86 A7
Falfield Gv NFLD/LBR B31 144 C6
Falkland Cl TLHL/CAN CV4 153 H6
Falkland Cft BVILLE B30 124 F7
Falklands Cl SEDG DY3 82 C3
Falkland Wy CBROM B36 92 F8
Falkwood Gv DOR/KN B93 149 K7
Fallindale Rd
LGN/SDN/BHAMAIR B26 109 M7
Fallings Heath Cl
DARL/WED WS10 52 D6
Fallow Fld CNCK/NC WS11 16 C2
FOAKS/STRLY B74 55 M2
LICH WS13 20 F2
Fallowfield CDSL WV8 35 J3
DUNHL/THL/PER WV6 48 B1
Fallowfield Av HLGN/YWD B28 126 D8
Fallowfield Cl PENK ST19 10 C5
Fallow Field Rd
BLKHTH/ROWR B65 103 L2
Fallowfield Rd DSYBK/YTR WS5 54 C5
HALE B63 121 H2
HIA/OLT B92 128 A3
Fallowfields COVN CV6 134 A1
Fallowfields Cl BRGRVW B61 191 J2
Fallow Hl RLSS CV31 207 G7
Fallow Pk HEDN WS12 * 13 H5
Fallows Rd SPARK B11 108 A7
Fallow Wk RIDG/WDGT B32 122 E3
Falmouth Cl NUN CV11 81 L8
Falmouth Dr TAM/AM/WIL B77 32 D8
Falmouth Rd BKDE/SHDE B34 91 J8
DSYBK/YTR WS5 54 B6
Falna Crs CRTAM B79 31 K6
Falstaff Av HLYWD B47 146 E7
Falstaff Cl NUN CV11 99 L4
WALM/CURD B76 73 L6
Falstaff Dr RUGBYS/DCH CV22 186 B7
Falstaff Rd SHLY B90 148 A3
TLHL/CAN CV4 153 J3
Falstone Rd SCFLD/BOLD B73 72 B3
Fancott Dr KNWTH CV8 179 J7
Fancott Rd NFLD/LBR B31 123 L8
Fancourt Av
ETTPK/GDPK/PENN WV4 49 H8
Fane Rd WNSFLD WV11 37 L4
Fanshawe Rd ACGN B27 127 G4
Faraday Av RIDG/WDGT B32 105 H8
WALM/CURD B76 75 J8
Faraday Rd RUGBYS/DCH CV22 187 G4
WSLW WS2 38 F7
Faraday Whf VAUX/NECH B7 * 7 K1
Farber Rd COVE CV2 135 L7
Farbrook Wy SHHTH WV12 37 M7
Farcroft Av COVW CV5 153 H1
HDSW B21 88 B4
Farcroft Gv HDSW B21 88 B4
Farcroft Rd HDSW B21 88 B4
Fardon Wy ERDW/GRVHL B23 72 B5
Fareham Av RUGBYS/DCH CV22 187 J5
Fareham Crs
ETTPK/GDPK/PENN WV4 49 G7
Farewell La BNTWD WS7 19 J7
Farfield KIDD DY10 138 D8
Farfield Cl NFLD/LBR B31 144 F3
Far Gosford St COV CV1 9 K5
Far Highfield WALM/CURD B76 73 H1
Far Hill Cl HHTH/SAND B71 69 K5
Faringdon TAM/AM/WIL B77 46 D4
Farlands Dr STRBR DY8 119 L2
Farlands Gv GTB/HAM B43 70 D6
Farlands Rd STRBR DY8 119 L2
Farleigh Dr BDMR/CCFT WV3 48 E5
Farleigh Rd
DUNHL/THL/PER WV6 48 E2
Farley La HAG/WOL DY9 142 C5
Farley Rd ERDW/GRVHL B23 89 M1
Farley St RLSS CV31 206 E6
TPTN/OCK DY4 68 B8
Farlow Cl COVN CV6 * 134 E7
REDE B98 203 H1
Farlow Cft
CHWD/FDBR/MGN B37 110 D6
Farlow Rd NFLD/LBR B31 145 G2
Farmacre BORD B9 107 M3
Farman Rd COVW CV5 154 D3
Farm Av LGLYGN/QTN B68 104 E2
Farmbridge Cl WSLW WS2 52 B2
Farmbridge Rd WSLW WS2 52 B3
Farmbrook Av WOLVN WV10 36 B2
Farm Cl CDSL WV8 34 F3
COVN CV6 133 M2
CRTAM B79 32 A6
HEDN WS12 17 G2
HIA/OLT B92 128 A3
KIDDW DY11 163 M3
SEDG DY3 65 M6
STETCH B33 109 K2
Farmcote Rd COVE CV2 134 F1
STETCH B33 109 L1
Farm Cft LOZ/NWT B19 89 G7
Farmcroft Rd HAG/WOL DY9 120 C3
Farmdale Gv RBRY B45 143 L7
Farmer Rd SMTHWK B10 108 E6
Farmers Cl WALM/CURD B76 73 J1
Farmers Ct HALE B63 121 K1
Farmers Fold WOLV WV1 2 F5
Farmers Rd BRGRVE B60 191 J7
Farmers Wk HDSW B21 88 B6
Farmer Ward Rd KNWTH CV8 197 L2
Farmer Wy TPTN/OCK DY4 67 M4
Farm Gv RUGBYS/DCH CV22 187 G4
Farmhouse Rd SHHTH WV12 38 B8
Farm House Wy GTB/HAM B43 70 C1
Farmhouse Wy SHLY B90 148 F7
Farm La RRUGBY CV23 159 J1
Farmoor Gv BKDE/SHDE B34 92 C7
Far Moor La REDE B98 195 L8
Farmoor Wy WOLVN WV10 36 C1
Farm Pl COVS CV3 * 155 M5
Farm Rd BDMR/CCFT WV3 49 G5
BLKHTH/ROWR B65 103 L1
BRLYHL DY5 102 C4
KNWTH CV8 197 J3
LGLYGN/QTN B68 104 E2
REDE B98 202 E2
RLSN CV32 206 F2
SMTHWKW B67 105 J2
SPARK B11 107 M7
STRPT DY13 188 F1
TPTN/OCK DY4 67 M6
Farmside Cl HAG/WOL DY9 120 E2
Farmside Gn COVEN WV9 35 K3
Farmstead Cl WSL WS1 53 J8
Farmstead Rd HIA/OLT B92 128 A3
The Farmstead COVS CV3 155 M5
Farm St LOZ/NWT B19 89 G7
WBROM B70 87 G4
WSLW WS2 53 J1
Farnborough Cl REDE B98 203 K4
Farnborough Ct MGN/WHC B75 57 G3
Farnborough Dr SHLY B90 148 D7
Farnborough Rd CVALE B35 91 L3
Farnbury Cft HWK/WKHTH B38 145 M3
Farncote Dr FOAKS/STRLY B74 56 D2
Farndale Av COVN CV6 134 B2
DUNHL/THL/PER WV6 35 L8
Farndale Cl BRLYHL DY5 101 M7
Farndon Av
CHWD/FDBR/MGN B37 110 F6
Farndon Cl BDWTH CV12 117 M2
Farndon Rd WASH/WDE B8 90 D8
Farnham Cl GTB/HAM B43 70 D5
Farnham Rd HDSW B21 88 B3
Farnhurst Rd CBROM B36 90 F6
Farnol Rd
LGN/SDN/BHAMAIR B26 109 K5
Farnworth Gv CBROM B36 92 C4
Farquhar Rd EDG B15 106 D7
MOS/BIL B13 125 K2
Farquhar Rd East EDG B15 106 D7
Farr Dr TLHL/CAN CV4 153 M3
Farren Rd COVE CV2 135 J8
NFLD/LBR B31 144 B4
Farrier Cl BRGRVE B60 191 J6
WALM/CURD B76 73 K5
Farrier Rd GTB/HAM B43 71 H2
Farriers Ml BLOX/PEL WS3 39 J1
The Farriers
LGN/SDN/BHAMAIR B26 109 M8
Farriers Wy NUN CV11 99 K3
Farrier Wy KGSWFD DY6 82 E6
Farringdon St WSLW WS2 4 C2
Farrington Rd
ERDW/GRVHL B23 71 M8
ETTPK/GDPK/PENN WV4 66 C3
Farrow Rd KGSTG B44 71 J2
Farthing La CSCFLD/WYGN B72 72 F1
WALM/CURD B76 75 G7
Farthing Pools Cl
CSCFLD/WYGN B72 73 G1
Farthings La DUDS DY2 84 E6
The Farthings HRBN B17 106 B7
Farvale Rd WALM/CURD B76 74 A7
Far Vw ALDR WS9 40 F3
Farway Gdns CDSL WV8 34 D3
Far Wood Rd NFLD/LBR B31 123 J5
Faseman Av TLHL/CAN CV4 153 K3
Fashoda Rd SLYOAK B29 124 F4
Fasson Cl TAM/AM/WIL B77 46 A5
Fastlea Rd RIDG/WDGT B32 123 H4
Fastmoor Ov STETCH B33 110 C4
Fast Pits Rd YDLY B25 108 F5
Fatherless Barn Crs HALE B63 121 G1
Faulconbridge Av COVW CV5 153 J1
Faulkland Crs WOLV WV1 3 G3
Faulkner Cl STRBR DY8 119 K1
Faulkner Rd HIA/OLT B92 127 M4
Faulkners Farm Dr
ERDW/GRVHL B23 71 M7
Faulknor Dr BRLYHL DY5 83 M6
Faultlands Cl NUN CV11 99 K5
Faversham Cl CDSL WV8 35 J5
WSLW WS2 52 B2
Fawdry Cl SCFLD/BOLD B73 56 F8
Fawdry St DIG/EDG B5 7 M5
SMTHWK B66 88 A8
WOLV WV1 2 D2
Fawley Cl COVS CV3 156 A7
WLNHL WV13 51 K5
Fawley Gv ALE/KHTH/YWD B14 124 F8
Fawn Cl HEDN WS12 12 A7
Fawsley Leys
RUGBYS/DCH CV22 186 E6
Faygate Cl COVS CV3 156 D2
Fazeley Rd POL/KGSB/FAZ B78 45 M1
Fazeley St DIG/EDG B5 7 K5
Fearnings Cottages
REDW B97 * 202 B8
Fearon Pl SMTHWK B66 * 87 L7
Featherbed La LICH WS13 20 C2
REDW B97 201 M8
RUGBYN/HIL CV21 187 L4
Featherstone Cl
NUNW/HART CV10 99 G3
SHLY B90 148 B3
Featherstone Crs SHLY B90 148 B4
Featherstone La WOLVN WV10 22 F5
Featherstone Rd
ALE/KHTH/YWD B14 125 J7
Featherston Rd
FOAKS/STRLY B74 55 L3
Feckenham Rd REDW B97 202 A5
Fecknam Wy LICH WS13 21 G3
Feiashill Rd SEDG DY3 82 B2
Feilding Cl COVE CV2 135 L7
Feilding Wy NUNW/HART CV10 79 L8
Felbrigg Cl BRLYHL DY5 102 B5
The Feldings ERDE/BCHGN B24 91 G1
Feldon La RMSLY B62 104 C6
Felgate Cl SHLY B90 148 E7
Fellbrook Cl STETCH B33 109 K1
Fell Gv HDSW B21 88 A4
RLSN CV32 207 G2
Fellmeadow Rd STETCH B33 109 L3
Fellmeadow Wy SEDG DY3 66 C7
Fellmore Gv RLSS CV31 207 G6
Fellows Av KGSWFD DY6 83 G5
Fellows La HRBN B17 105 L7
Fellows Rd BILS/COS WV14 51 H6
Fellows St BKHL/PFLD WV2 2 E9
Fellows Wy RUGBYN/HIL CV21 187 K5
Felspar Rd TAM/AM/WIL B77 46 E2
Felstead Cl TAM/AM/WIL B77 60 A1
Felsted Wy VAUX/NECH B7 7 M2
Felstone Rd KGSTG B44 71 J4
Feltham Cl STETCH B33 110 C4
Felton Cl COVE CV2 135 J4
REDE B98 203 J4
Felton Cft STETCH B33 109 L2
Felton Gv SOLH B91 148 F4
Fenbourne Cl RUSH/SHEL WS4 40 A5
Fenchurch Cl WSLW WS2 53 H1
Fen Cl KIDDW DY11 138 C5
Fencote Av
CHWD/FDBR/MGN B37 110 E1
Fen End Rd
RCOVN/BALC/EX CV7 176 F1
Fenmere Cl
ETTPK/GDPK/PENN WV4 50 B8
Fennel Cl GTWY WS6 24 B2
Fennel Cft BKDE/SHDE B34 91 M6
Fennel Rd BRLYHL DY5 102 A6
Fennis Cl DOR/KN B93 175 K2
Fenn Ri SHHTH WV12 37 M7
STRBR DY8 101 G2
Fenn St TAM/AM/WIL B77 46 B4
Fens Crs BRLYHL DY5 84 A8
Fenside Av COVS CV3 181 H1
Fens Pool Av BRLYHL DY5 84 B8
The Fensway BKDE/SHDE B34 91 L8
Fenter Cl MOS/BIL B13 125 K1
Fentham Cl HIA/OLT B92 129 M7
Fentham Ct HIA/OLT B92 127 K4
Fentham Gn HIA/OLT B92 129 L6
Fentham Rd AST/WIT B6 89 H5
ERDW/GRVHL B23 90 B2
HIA/OLT B92 129 L6
Fenton Rd ACGN B27 108 F8
HLYWD B47 146 E6
Fenton St BRLYHL DY5 102 B2
SMTHWK B66 87 J6
Fenton Wy ACGN B27 126 F1
Fenwick Cl REDW B97 201 M4
Fenwick Dr RUGBYN/HIL CV21 187 L5
Fereday Rd ALDR WS9 40 F2
Fereday's Cft SEDG DY3 66 B6
Fereday St TPTN/OCK DY4 67 K5
Ferguson Dr KIDDW DY11 163 L4
TPTN/OCK DY4 67 M7
Ferguson Rd LGLYGN/QTN B68 87 H8
Ferguson St WNSFLD WV11 37 L4
Fern Av TPTN/OCK DY4 67 K6
Fernbank Cl HALE B63 121 H3
Fernbank Crs DSYBK/YTR WS5 70 A1
Fernbank Rd WASH/WDE B8 108 E1
Ferncliffe Rd HRBN B17 123 M1
Fern Cl BILS/COS WV14 66 F5
COVE CV2 135 G3
RRUGBY CV23 161 H5
RUSH/SHEL WS4 40 A4
Fern Cft LICH WS13 20 D4
Ferndale Av GTB/HAM B43 70 D6
Ferndale Cl BNTWD WS7 18 E7
BRGRVW B61 168 E4
HAG/WOL DY9 119 L8
NUN CV11 81 J8
STRPT DY13 189 G2
Ferndale Ct CSHL/WTROR B46 93 L8
Ferndale Crs BHTH/HG B12 107 L5
KIDDW DY11 137 L4
Ferndale Dr KNWTH CV8 197 L3
Ferndale Ms CSHL/WTROR B46 93 L8
Ferndale Pk HAG/WOL DY9 120 A5
Ferndale Rd COVS CV3 157 H6
CSHL/WTROR B46 93 L8
FOAKS/STRLY B74 55 K5
HLGN/YWD B28 126 D5
LGLYGN/QTN B68 104 E3
LICH WS13 20 D4
Fern Dale Rd
RCOVN/BALC/EX CV7 151 K7
Ferndale Rd WNSFLD WV11 37 M2
Fern Dell Cl CNCK/NC WS11 16 A3
Ferndene Rd SPARK B11 126 D2
Ferndown Av SEDG DY3 66 A6
Ferndown Cl BLOX/PEL WS3 38 F1
COVW CV5 153 K2
LGN/SDN/BHAMAIR B26 109 L4
Ferndown Ct
RUGBYS/DCH CV22 186 C4
Ferndown Gdns WNSFLD WV11 37 K8
Ferndown Rd
RUGBYS/DCH CV22 186 C4
SOLH B91 127 M7
Ferndown Ter
RUGBYS/DCH CV22 186 C4
Fern Dr GTWY WS6 24 E1
Ferney Hill Av REDW B97 202 A2
Fern Gv BDWTH CV12 116 C3
Fernhill Cl KNWTH CV8 179 J7
Fernhill Dr RLSN CV32 206 F4
Fernhill Gv KGSTG B44 71 K2
Fernhill La RCOVN/BALC/EX CV7 151 K7
Fernhill Rd HIA/OLT B92 127 J3
Fernhurst Dr BRLYHL DY5 83 M6
Fernhurst Rd WASH/WDE B8 108 E2
Fernleigh Av BNTWD WS7 18 E5
Fernleigh Gdns STRBR DY8 101 G2
Fernleigh Rd RUSH/SHEL WS4 5 M1
Fernley Rd SPARK B11 126 A1
Fern Leys BDMR/CCFT WV3 49 H4
Fern Rd BDMR/CCFT WV3 2 D8
DUDN DY1 85 G1
ERDE/BCHGN B24 90 E1
HEDN WS12 12 B8
Fernside Gdns SPARK B11 125 M2
Fern Vls DARL/WED WS10 * 52 C7
Fernwood Cl REDE B98 202 E8
SCFLD/BOLD B73 72 C4
Fernwood Cft
ALE/KHTH/YWD B14 125 J7
TPTN/OCK DY4 85 K1
Fernwood Rd SCFLD/BOLD B73 72 C5
Fernwoods RIDG/WDGT B32 122 F3
Ferrers Cl MGN/WHC B75 57 H3
TLHL/CAN CV4 153 K3

Ferrers Rd TAM/AM/WIL B77 46 B1
Ferrie Gv BRWNH WS8 26 C5
Ferris Gv ACGN B27 126 E4
Festival Av DARL/WED WS10 68 A1
Festival Ct CNCK/NC WS11 * 12 C8
Festival Ms HEDN WS12 12 D7
Festival Wy
DUNHL/THL/PER WV6 35 M8
Fetherston Crs KNWTH CV8 182 E4
Fetherston Gra HOCK/TIA B94 * 175 K8
Ffernfail Ct ERDW/GRVHL B23 72 C8
Fibbersley WLNHL WV13 51 K1
Fibbersley Bank WLNHL WV13 51 K1
Fiddlers Gn HIA/OLT B92 129 L6
Field Av NFLD/LBR B31 123 K8
Field Barn Rd
RWWCK/WEL CV35 204 D6
Field Cl BLOX/PEL WS3 39 G5
BLOX/PEL WS3 39 M3
KNWTH CV8 179 M8
LGN/SDN/BHAMAIR B26 109 L7
STRBR DY8 101 L3
WWCK CV34 205 M6
Field Cottage Dr STRBR DY8 119 M2
Field Cottages COVS CV3 * 156 A8
Field End STRPT DY13 188 C1
Fieldfare BNTWD WS7 19 H8
Fieldfare Cl BLKHTH/ROWR B65 103 K1
RRUGBY CV23 161 G5
Fieldfare Cl KIDD DY10 164 E4
Fieldfare Cft CBROM B36 92 E5
Fieldfare Rd HAG/WOL DY9 120 B1
Field Farm La REDE B98 203 H3
Field Farm Rd TAM/AM/WIL B77 46 B4
Fieldgate La KNWTH CV8 179 J6
Field Head La WWCK CV34 205 M7
Field Head Pl
DUNHL/THL/PER WV6 48 F1
Fieldhead Rd SPARK B11 126 E2
Fieldhouse La RMSLY B62 142 C1
Fieldhouse Rd BNTWD WS7 18 E6
ETTPK/GDPK/PENN WV4 66 C1
HEDN WS12 12 D6
YDLY B25 109 G5
Fielding Cl ATHST CV9 63 H3
Field La GTWY WS6 24 D2
HAG/WOL DY9 141 G1
RIDG/WDGT B32 122 E5
RUSH/SHEL WS4 39 M3
SOLH B91 128 E8
STRBR DY8 119 L2
Field Ms DUDS DY2 103 J3
Fieldon Br ATHST CV9 63 H2
Fieldon Cl SHLY B90 148 A2
Field Rd BLOX/PEL WS3 39 G4
DUDS DY2 85 J4
LICH WS13 20 F2
TPTN/OCK DY4 67 K5
Fields Ct WWCK CV34 205 K5
Fieldside La COVS CV3 156 D2
The Fields CDSL WV8 34 F1
Field St BILS/COS WV14 67 J2
CNCK/NC WS11 16 D2
WLNHL WV13 51 L3
WOLVN WV10 3 J2
Field Vw KNWTH CV8 182 E3
Fieldview Cl BILS/COS WV14 67 H3
Field View Cl
RCOVN/BALC/EX CV7 116 E5
Field View Dr
BLKHTH/ROWR B65 104 D3
Field Wk ALDR WS9 40 F6
Field Wy HOCK/TIA B94 175 G7
Fieldways Cl HLYWD B47 146 E6
Fiery Hill Dr RBRY B45 170 A5
Fiery Hill Rd RBRY B45 170 A5
Fife Rd COVW CV5 154 D3
Fife St NUN CV11 98 E1
Fifield Cl NUN CV11 99 H3
Fifield Gv STETCH B33 109 K2
Fifth Av BORD B9 108 D3
WOLVN WV10 36 B6
Filance Cl PENK ST19 10 D6
Filance La PENK ST19 10 D6
Filey TAM/AM/WIL B77 32 D8
Filey Cl CNCK/NC WS11 16 A5
Filey Rd WOLVN WV10 35 M3
Fillingham Cl
CHWD/FDBR/MGN B37 111 H4
Fillongley Rd CSHL/WTROR B46 94 F8
RCOVN/BALC/EX CV7 131 G4
Filton Av BNTWD WS7 18 E5
Filton Cft CVALE B35 91 L1
Fimbrell Cl STRBR DY8 101 L5
Finbury Cl HIA/OLT B92 127 K4
Finchall Cft HIA/OLT B92 128 C5
Fincham Cl COVEN WV9 35 L2
Finch Cl BLKHTH/ROWR B65 103 K1
Finch Cft RCOVN/BALC/EX CV7 151 M6
Finchdene Gv BDMR/CCFT WV3 49 L5
Finch Dr FOAKS/STRLY B74 55 L8
Finches End BKDE/SHDE B34 92 A8
Finchfield Cl STRBR DY8 119 G1
Finchfield Gdns
BDMR/CCFT WV3 49 J4
Finchfield Hl BDMR/CCFT WV3 49 H3
Finchfield La BDMR/CCFT WV3 49 G5
Finchfield Rd BDMR/CCFT WV3 49 J4
Finchfield Rd West
BDMR/CCFT WV3 49 G4
Finchley Av LOZ/NWT B19 * 89 G5
Finchley Cl SEDG DY3 84 B3
Finchley Rd KGSTG B44 71 M3
Finchmead Rd STETCH B33 110 C3
Finchpath Rd WBROM B70 68 E7
Finch Rd LOZ/NWT B19 89 G5
Findlay Rd ALE/KHTH/YWD B14 125 J4
Findley Cl ATHST CV9 63 K7
Findon Cl REDW B97 193 L8
Findon Rd WASH/WDE B8 90 F7
Findon St KIDD DY10 138 D7
Fineacre La RRUGBY CV23 183 G8
Finford Cft
RCOVN/BALC/EX CV7 151 M7
Fingal Cl COVS CV3 156 A7
Finger Post Dr BLOX/PEL WS3 25 L8
Fingest Cl COVW CV5 153 M1
Finham Crs KNWTH CV8 179 M7
Finham Green Rd COVS CV3 180 F2
Finham Gv COVS CV3 181 G2
Finham Rd KNWTH CV8 179 M7
Finings Ct RLSN CV32 * 206 D3
Finlarigg Dr EDG B15 106 D7
Finmere RUGBYN/HIL CV21 161 H7
Finmere Rd HLGN/YWD B28 126 D5
Finmere Wy SHLY B90 148 B3
Finnemore Cl COVS CV3 154 F8
Finnemore Rd BORD B9 108 E3
Finney Well Cl BILS/COS WV14 66 F2
Finsbury Dr BRLYHL DY5 102 A6
Finsbury Gv ERDW/GRVHL B23 72 B7
Finstall Cl CSCFLD/WYGN B72 73 G4
VAUX/NECH B7 7 M2
Finstall Rd BRGRVE B60 192 A5
Finwood Cl HIA/OLT B92 128 C5
Fir Av BHTH/HG B12 107 L8
Firbank Cl BVILLE B30 124 C6
Firbank Wy BLOX/PEL WS3 39 K3
Firbarn Cl WALM/CURD B76 73 H2
Firbeck Gv KGSTG B44 71 L4
Firbeck Rd KGSTG B44 71 L4
Fir Cl HEDN WS12 12 B5
Fir Cft BRLYHL DY5 102 A5
Fircroft BILS/COS WV14 67 L2
NFLD/LBR B31 123 K5
POL/KGSB/FAZ B78 60 A6
SOLH B91 127 K7
Fircroft Cl BRGRVE B60 191 H7
CNCK/NC WS11 16 E2
Firecrest Cl CNCK/NC WS11 17 G3
ERDW/GRVHL B23 71 M6
Firecrest Wy KIDD DY10 164 F4
Fir Gv ALE/KHTH/YWD B14 125 K8
BDMR/CCFT WV3 2 A7
STRBR DY8 101 G7
TLHL/CAN CV4 153 L3
Firhill Cft ALE/KHTH/YWD B14 146 B3
Firmstone St STRBR DY8 101 J6
Firsbrook Cl
DUNHL/THL/PER WV6 35 L8
Firs Cl BRGRVE B60 169 G4
SMTHWKW B67 87 L8
The Firs Cl KIDD DY10 138 E8
Firs Dr RUGBYS/DCH CV22 186 D3
SHLY B90 147 L4
Firs Farm Dr CBROM B36 91 K6
Firsholm Cl SCFLD/BOLD B73 72 E6
Firs Rd KGSWFD DY6 83 J7
Firs St DUDS DY2 85 H1
First Av BORD B9 108 C4
BRWNH WS8 26 E5
COVS CV3 156 A4
KGSWFD DY6 83 L5
SLYOAK B29 124 F2
WALM/CURD B76 73 L8
WOLVN WV10 36 C7
First Exhibition Av
BHAMNEC B40 129 H1
The Firs BDWTH CV12 116 C3
COVW CV5 154 F5
POL/KGSB/FAZ B78 60 B6
RCOVN/BALC/EX CV7 * 130 F4
SPARK B11 108 A7
First Meadow Piece
RIDG/WDGT B32 123 J1
Fir St SEDG DY3 65 K6
Firsvale Rd WNSFLD WV11 37 K8
Firsway DUNHL/THL/PER WV6 48 E4
Firswood Rd STETCH B33 110 A4
Firth Dr ALE/KHTH/YWD B14 125 M8
RMSLY B62 104 C5
Firth Park Crs RMSLY B62 104 C5
Fir Tree Av TLHL/CAN CV4 153 L3
Fir Tree Cl CRTAM B79 31 J6
KGSTG B44 71 J6
REDW B97 202 B1
Fir Tree Dr DSYBK/YTR WS5 69 M1
SEDG DY3 66 C6
Fir Tree Gv NUN CV11 99 H4
SCFLD/BOLD B73 72 D4
Firtree La RCOVN/BALC/EX CV7 96 E5
Fir Tree Rd BDMR/CCFT WV3 49 H6
Firtree Rd ERDE/BCHGN B24 90 F3
Fisher Av RUGBYS/DCH CV22 187 J5
Fisher Rd BLOX/PEL WS3 38 D3
COVN CV6 134 C5
OLDBY B69 87 G6
Fishers Dr SHLY B90 147 K8
Fisher St BDMR/CCFT WV3 2 C8
BRLYHL DY5 101 M2
DUDS DY2 85 H4
HEDN WS12 12 D5
TPTN/OCK DY4 68 A8
TPTN/OCK DY4 85 L2
WLNHL WV13 52 A3
Fishers Wk ATHST CV9 * 63 J6
Fish Hl REDW B97 202 C1
Fishing Line Rd REDE B98 194 C8
Fishley Cl BLOX/PEL WS3 39 G1
Fishley La BLOX/PEL WS3 39 G1
Fishponds Rd KNWTH CV8 197 J2
Fishpool Cl CBROM B36 91 G5
Fishpool La
RCOVN/BALC/EX CV7 111 M7
Fistral Gdns BDMR/CCFT WV3 49 K6
Fitters Mill Cl DIG/EDG B5 * 107 J7
Fitton Av KGSWFD DY6 83 L8
Fitton St NUN CV11 98 F2
Fitzalan Cl RRUGBY CV23 158 F7
Fitzgerald Pl BRLYHL DY5 101 M7
Fitzguy Cl WBROM B70 87 J4
Fitzmaurice Rd WNSFLD WV11 37 K6
Fitz Roy Av HRBN B17 105 K6
Fitzroy Cl COVE CV2 135 M7
Fitzroy Rd NFLD/LBR B31 144 A2
Five Broadway
LDYWD/EDGR B16 * 6 A8
Fivefield Rd
RCOVN/BALC/EX CV7 115 J8
Five Fields Rd SHHTH WV12 37 L8
Five Oaks Rd WLNHL WV13 51 J5
Fives Gv BNTWD WS7 18 A5
Five Ways EDG B15 6 A8
Flackwell Rd ERDW/GRVHL B23 72 C6
Fladbury Cl DUDS DY2 103 H2
REDE B98 202 F5
Fladbury Crs SLYOAK B29 124 B3
Fladbury Gdns
BFLD/HDSWWD B20 * 89 G5
Fladbury Pl LOZ/NWT B19 * 89 G6
Flamboro' Cl COVS CV3 156 D5
Flamborough Cl
BKDE/SHDE B34 91 L6
Flamborough Wy
BILS/COS WV14 66 F6
Flanders Cl REDE B98 195 G8
Flanders Dr KGSWFD DY6 83 H5
Flanders Hall Cottages
ATHST CV9 * 76 D3
Flash La WMBN WV5 64 C3
Flash Rd OLDBY B69 86 E6
Flatlea NFLD/LBR B31 144 D1
Flats La LICHS WS14 29 L7
The Flats BRGRVW B61 191 K2
The Flatts DARL/WED WS10 52 C6
Flaunden Cl COVW CV5 153 M2
Flavel Crs RLSS CV31 206 D6
Flavell Av BILS/COS WV14 67 H4
Flavell Cl RIDG/WDGT B32 122 F4
Flavells La SEDG DY3 83 M3
YDLY B25 109 G5
Flavell St DUDN DY1 66 F7
Flavel Rd BRGRVE B60 191 J6
Flax Cl HLYWD B47 146 E8
Flax Gdns HWK/WKHTH B38 145 K5
Flaxhall St WSLW WS2 52 F5
Flaxley Cl REDE B98 203 L2
Flaxley Rd STETCH B33 109 K2
The Flax Ovens PENK ST19 10 C3
Flaxton Gv STETCH B33 109 L1
Flecknoe Cl CBROM B36 92 A4
Flecknose St COVS CV3 156 A7
Fledburgh Dr WALM/CURD B76 73 H2
Fleet Crs RUGBYN/HIL CV21 187 J3
Fleet St CBHAMNW B3 6 D4
COV CV1 8 E5
Fleetwood Gv
LGN/SDN/BHAMAIR B26 109 L4
Fleming Pl WSLW WS2 38 E7
Fleming Rd RIDG/WDGT B32 105 H8
WSLW WS2 38 E7
Flemmynge Cl CDSL WV8 34 C1
Fletchamstead Hwy
TLHL/CAN CV4 154 A4
Fletcher Gv DOR/KN B93 175 M1
Fletcher Rd SHHTH WV12 38 B4
Fletcher's La WLNHL WV13 52 A3
Fletcher St HAG/WOL DY9 102 D8
Fletchworth Ga COVW CV5 154 B5
Fletton Gv ALE/KHTH/YWD B14 146 E2
Flinkford Cl DSYBK/YTR WS5 54 A7
Flinn Cl LICHS WS14 21 H6
Flint Cl ATHST CV9 63 J3
KIDDW DY11 164 C3
Flint Green Rd ACGN B27 126 F2
Flintham Cl ACGN B27 127 J2
The Flintway STETCH B33 109 J1
Floodgate St DIG/EDG B5 7 K7
Flood St DUDS DY2 85 H4
Flora Cl CRTAM B79 32 A6
Flora Rd YDLY B25 108 F6
Florence Av
ETTPK/GDPK/PENN WV4 66 D1
SPARK B11 107 M8
Florence Cl ATHST CV9 63 H4
RCOVN/BALC/EX CV7 116 D5
Florence Gv HHTH/SAND B71 69 J4
Florence Rd ACGN B27 127 H1
ALE/KHTH/YWD B14 125 K5
CDSL WV8 35 G2
ERDW/GRVHL B23 72 F6
HDSW B21 88 B5
OLDBY B69 86 B6
SMTHWK B66 105 M1
TPTN/OCK DY4 67 L6
WBROM B70 87 J4
Florence St CBHAMW B1 6 E8
HEDN WS12 12 E6
WSL WS1 5 J5
Florence Vls SPARK B11 * 108 A6
Florendine St TAM/AM/WIL B77 32 D8
Florian Gv DARL/WED WS10 52 C6
Florida Wy KGSWFD DY6 83 L8
Flowerdale Cl BILS/COS WV14 66 F5
Flowerdale Dr COVE CV2 134 F7
Floyd Gv RCOVN/BALC/EX CV7 152 A6
Floyds La RUSH/SHEL WS4 40 A7
Floyer Rd SMHTH B10 108 C4
Flude Rd RCOVN/BALC/EX CV7 116 A7
Flyford Cl REDE B98 202 D4
Flyford Cft SLYOAK B29 123 K3
Flynt Av COVW CV5 132 E7
Fockbury Mill La BRGRVW B61 168 C8
Fockbury Rd BRGRVW B61 167 L8
Foden Cl LICHS WS14 28 D7
Foden Rd PBAR/PBCH B42 70 E5
Foinavon Cl BLKHTH/ROWR B65 85 K7
Fold St WOLV WV1 2 E6
The Fold DARL/WED WS10 52 B7
ETTPK/GDPK/PENN WV4 65 K1
Foldyard Cl WALM/CURD B76 73 L5
Foleshill Rd COV CV1 8 F2
COVN CV6 134 B7
Foley Av DUNHL/THL/PER WV6 48 F2
KIDDW DY11 164 A5
Foley Church Cl
FOAKS/STRLY B74 55 L3
Foley Dr DUNHL/THL/PER WV6 49 G2
KIDDW DY11 163 M5
Foley Gv KIDDW DY11 163 M5
WMBN WV5 64 C8
Foley Rd HAG/WOL DY9 119 M3
WASH/WDE B8 90 F7
Foley Rd East FOAKS/STRLY B74 55 K4
Foley Rd West FOAKS/STRLY B74 55 H4
Foley St DARL/WED WS10 68 E2
Foley Wood Cl FOAKS/STRLY B74 55 J4
Foliot Flds YDLY B25 109 H5
Folkes Rd HAG/WOL DY9 102 E7
Folkestone Cft CBROM B36 91 J5
Folliott Rd STETCH B33 109 L2
Follyhouse Cl WSL WS1 * 5 G8
Follyhouse La WSL WS1 5 G8
Folly La ATHST CV9 62 C5
Fontenaye Rd CRTAM B79 31 J6
Fontley Cl
LGN/SDN/BHAMAIR B26 109 L4
Fontmell Cl COVS CV3 156 E1
Fontwell Rd WOLVN WV10 36 B1
Footherley La LICHS WS14 42 A1
Footherley Rd LICHS WS14 28 D8
Fordbridge Cl REDW B97 202 A4
Fordbridge Rd
CHWD/FDBR/MGN B37 110 D1
Ford Brook La BLOX/PEL WS3 39 M4
Forder Gv ALE/KHTH/YWD B14 146 E3
Forde Way Gdns
HWK/WKHTH B38 145 H6
Fordfield Rd STETCH B33 110 A1
Fordham Gv COVEN WV9 35 L2
Fordhouse La BVILLE B30 124 F7
Fordhouse Rd BRGRVE B60 191 L4
WOLVN WV10 36 B4
Ford La LICH WS13 19 L3
Fordraught La RMSLY B62 142 F4
The Fordrift
CHWD/FDBR/MGN B37 110 E8
Ford Rd BRGRVW B61 191 J4
Fordrough YDLY B25 108 D6
Fordrough Av BORD B9 108 C2
Fordrough La BORD B9 108 C2
The Fordrough
FOAKS/STRLY B74 56 E4
NFLD/LBR B31 144 F5
SHLY B90 147 G6
Fords Rd SHLY B90 147 J6
Ford St COV CV1 9 H3
NUNW/HART CV10 98 C1
SMTHWKW B67 87 K7
WSLW WS2 4 B9
WSNGN B18 88 F8
Fordwater Rd FOAKS/STRLY B74 55 K7
Fordwell Cl COVW CV5 154 D2
Foredraft Cl RIDG/WDGT B32 123 G3
Foredraft St HALE B63 103 H8
Foredrift Cl REDE B98 202 C4
Foredrove La HIA/OLT B92 128 C7
Forelands Gv BRGRVW B61 191 H5
Foreland Wy COVN CV6 133 L3
Forest Av BLOX/PEL WS3 39 H6
Forest Cl BEWD DY12 162 D2
BRGRVE B60 168 F7
FOAKS/STRLY B74 55 J6
SMTHWK B66 87 J6
Forest Ct DOR/KN B93 175 K2
Forest Dl RBRY B45 143 M7
Forest Dr CDYHTH B64 103 J3
HRBN B17 106 B7
Foresters Pl RUGBYN/HIL CV21 187 M6
Forester's Rd COVS CV3 155 J7
Forester Wy KIDD DY10 164 C2
Forest Ga SHHTH WV12 38 B5
Forest Gld GTWY WS6 * 24 D3
Forest Hill Rd
LGN/SDN/BHAMAIR B26 110 A8
Forest La BLOX/PEL WS3 39 J8
BRGRVE B60 200 C8
Forest Pk WALM/CURD B76 73 J1
Forest Pl BLOX/PEL WS3 39 J7
Fore St CBHAM B2 7 G5
Forest Rd DOR/KN B93 175 L2
DUDN DY1 85 G1
LGLYGN/QTN B68 105 G6
MOS/BIL B13 125 L2
YDLY B25 109 G7
Forest Vw REDW B97 202 B7
Forest Wy GTWY WS6 24 B3
HLYWD B47 146 F7
NUNW/HART CV10 98 C3
Forfield Pl RLSS CV31 206 E6
Forfield Rd COVN CV6 133 J8
Forge Cl BNTWD WS7 19 H8
CDSL WV8 35 J4
Forge Cft WALM/CURD B76 73 M7
Forge Dr BRGRVW B61 191 K2
Forge La ALDR WS9 41 K7
BNTWD WS7 19 K7
CDYHTH B64 102 F5
FOAKS/STRLY B74 42 A7
HAG/WOL DY9 141 H6
HHTH/SAND B71 69 L7
KGSWFD DY6 82 E5
KIDD DY10 139 M4
LICH WS13 20 E4
LICHS WS14 21 K6
RMSLY B62 104 A8
WALM/CURD B76 73 M7
Forge Leys WMBN WV5 64 C7
Forge Mill Rd REDE B98 194 D8
Forge Rd BLOX/PEL WS3 25 K8
CSHL/WTROR B46 94 D3
DARL/WED WS10 51 M7
KNWTH CV8 179 L7
SHHTH WV12 52 A1
STRBR DY8 101 K7
Forge St DARL/WED WS10 68 C1
HEDN WS12 17 G1
The Forge CRTAM B79 31 L8
HALE B63 102 E5
Forge Valley Wy WMBN WV5 64 C7
Forge Wy COVN CV6 134 A2
OLDBY B69 86 C7
Forknell Av COVE CV2 135 G8
Formans Rd SPARK B11 126 C2
Formby Av
DUNHL/THL/PER WV6 48 B1
Formby Wy BLOX/PEL WS3 38 E2
Fornside Cl RUGBYN/HIL CV21 161 H6
Forrell Gv NFLD/LBR B31 144 B4
Forrest Av CNCK/NC WS11 16 C6
WNSFLD WV11 37 L1
Forrester St WSLW WS2 4 B3
Forrester Street Prec WSLW WS2 4 B3
Forrest Rd KNWTH CV8 197 J1
Forshaw Heath La
HOCK/TIA B94 172 E7
Forshaw Heath Rd
HOCK/TIA B94 173 G5
Forster St SMTHWKW B67 87 J6
VAUX/NECH B7 7 L3
Forsythia Cl NFLD/LBR B31 123 K5
Forsythia Gv CDSL WV8 34 E2
Fort Crs ALDR WS9 40 F2
Forth Dr CHWD/FDBR/MGN B37 110 F1
Forth Gv HWK/WKHTH B38 145 J5
Forth Wy RMSLY B62 104 C5
Forties TAM/AM/WIL B77 46 C6
Fort-mahon Pl BEWD DY12 162 D2
Fortnum Cl STETCH B33 110 A3
Forton Cl DUNHL/THL/PER WV6 48 F3
Fort Pkwy ERDE/BCHGN B24 90 F5
ERDE/BCHGN B24 91 K3
Forum Dr RUGBYN/HIL CV21 160 E7
Forward Cottages ALVE B48 * 170 D7
Fosberry Cl WWCK CV34 205 M5
Fosbrooke Rd SMHTH B10 108 E5
Fossdale Rd TAM/AM/WIL B77 46 E5
Fosseway LICHS WS14 20 E8
Fosse Wy RRUGBY CV23 183 L7
Fosseway Dr ERDW/GRVHL B23 72 C5
Fosseway La LICH WS13 28 B1
Fosseway Rd COVS CV3 180 F1
Fossil Dr RBRY B45 143 L6
Foster Av BILS/COS WV14 66 F4
HEDN WS12 12 D7
Fosterd Rd RUGBYN/HIL CV21 160 D8
Foster Gdns WSNGN B18 * 88 D7
Foster Gn DUNHL/THL/PER WV6 48 C2
Foster Pl STRBR DY8 101 J7
Foster Rd COVN CV6 133 M6
WOLVN WV10 36 C7
Fosters Gn BRGRVE B60 200 B6
Foster St BLOX/PEL WS3 39 H5
DARL/WED WS10 52 B6
Foster St East STRBR DY8 101 L8
Foster Wy DIG/EDG B5 107 G8
Fotherley Brook Rd ALDR WS9 41 K8
Founder Cl TLHL/CAN CV4 153 K5
Foundry La BLOX/PEL WS3 39 G3
SMTHWK B66 87 M6
Foundry Rd KGSWFD DY6 82 F5
WSNGN B18 88 B8
Foundry St BILS/COS WV14 67 G4
KGSWFD DY6 82 F5
STRPT DY13 188 E1
TPTN/OCK DY4 67 J5
Fountain Arcade Chambers
DUDN DY1 * 85 G4
Fountain Cl NFLD/LBR B31 144 C7
Fountain Ct CBHAMNE B4 * 7 G3
Fountain La BILS/COS WV14 67 H5
OLDBY B69 86 D4
Fountain Rd HRBN B17 105 M4
Fountains Rd BLOX/PEL WS3 38 C3
Fountains Wy BLOX/PEL WS3 38 C3
Four Acres RIDG/WDGT B32 123 G1
Four Ashes Rd DOR/KN B93 175 H2
Four Crosses La WOLVN WV10 15 H7
Four Crosses Rd
RUSH/SHEL WS4 40 A4
Fourfields Wy
RCOVN/BALC/EX CV7 96 D6
Fourlands Av CSCFLD/WYGN B72 73 H6
Fourlands Rd NFLD/LBR B31 123 J7
Four Oaks Cl REDE B98 202 B5
Four Oaks Common Rd
FOAKS/STRLY B74 56 C2
Four Oaks Rd FOAKS/STRLY B74 56 D3
Four Pounds Av COVW CV5 154 D2
Four Stones Cl SOLH B91 148 E4
Four Stones Gv DIG/EDG B5 107 H7
Fourth Av BORD B9 108 D3
BRWNH WS8 26 E5
SLYOAK B29 125 G2
WOLVN WV10 36 B7
Fourways ATHST CV9 63 J5
Four Winds Rd DUDS DY2 85 J6
Fowey Cl WALM/CURD B76 73 L6
Fowey Rd BKDE/SHDE B34 91 K7
Fowgay Dr SOLH B91 148 D4
Fowler Cl CDSL WV8 34 C7
SMTHWK B66 87 L5
Fowler Pl STRPT DY13 163 L8
Fowler Rd COVN CV6 133 M8
MGN/WHC B75 57 L8
Fowler St BKHL/PFLD WV2 50 A7
VAUX/NECH B7 89 M8
Fowlmere Rd PBAR/PBCH B42 70 F5
Fownhope Cl REDE B98 203 J2
Fow Oak TLHL/CAN CV4 153 G3
Fox Av NUNW/HART CV10 81 C5
Foxbury Dr DOR/KN B93 175 L2
Fox Cl RUGBYN/HIL CV21 187 M4
TAM/AM/WIL B77 46 A5
Foxcote Av HDSW B21 88 C6
Foxcote Cl REDE B98 203 J1
SHLY B90 148 B5
Foxcote Dr SHLY B90 148 B5
Foxcote La HAG/WOL DY9 120 F2
Fox Covert STRBR DY8 101 J8
Fox Crs SPARK B11 * 126 B1
Foxcroft Cl BNTWD WS7 18 E8
Foxdale Dr BRLYHL DY5 101 M2
Foxdale Gv STETCH B33 110 A3
Foxdale Wk RLSS CV31 207 G7
Foxes Cl BRGRVE B60 169 M8
Foxes Meadow BVILLE B30 145 K1
WALM/CURD B76 73 L5
Foxes Rake CNCK/NC WS11 16 C2
Foxes Rdg CDYHTH B64 103 J5
Foxes Wy RCOVN/BALC/EX CV7 151 M7
Foxfield Dr STRBR DY8 119 L2
Foxfields Wy HEDN WS12 12 A6
Fox Foot Dr BRLYHL DY5 102 A1
Foxford Cl CBROM B36 92 B4
CSCFLD/WYGN B72 73 G6
Foxford Crs COVE CV2 134 F1
Foxglove TAM/AM/WIL B77 46 E1
Foxglove Cl BDWTH CV12 116 C4
BLOX/PEL WS3 25 L8
COVN CV6 134 A3
LICHS WS14 20 E8
RRUGBY CV23 161 J5
WNSFLD WV11 37 J8
WOLVN WV10 22 F6
Foxglove Crs
CHWD/FDBR/MGN B37 110 C2
Foxglove Rd DUDN DY1 84 D1
Foxglove Wy BRGRVE B60 169 G7
ERDW/GRVHL B23 71 M6
HDSW B21 88 B6
Fox Green Crs ACGN B27 126 E3
Fox Gv ACGN B27 126 E3
Fox Hl SLYOAK B29 124 A5
Foxhill Cl HEDN WS12 17 H3
Fox Hill Cl SLYOAK B29 124 A5
Foxhill La ALVE B48 170 B8
Fox Hill Rd MGN/WHC B75 57 K3
Foxhill's Cl BNTWD WS7 18 E8
Foxhills Pk DUDS DY2 103 G1
Foxhills Rd
ETTPK/GDPK/PENN WV4 65 G2
STRBR DY8 101 H4
Foxholes La REDW B97 201 L7
The Foxholes KIDD DY10 138 D5
Foxhollies Dr HALE B63 121 J1
Fox Hollies Rd ACGN B27 126 F2
WALM/CURD B76 73 K5
Fox Hollow
DUNHL/THL/PER WV6 49 G3
Foxhope Cl HWK/WKHTH B38 145 M4
Foxhunt Rd HALE B63 121 J3
Foxland Av GTWY WS6 24 E2
RBRY B45 144 A6
Foxland Cl
CHWD/FDBR/MGN B37 111 H3
SHLY B90 174 B1
Foxlands Av
ETTPK/GDPK/PENN WV4 65 H2
Foxlands Crs
ETTPK/GDPK/PENN WV4 65 G2
Foxlands Dr CSCFLD/WYGN B72 73 H6
ETTPK/GDPK/PENN WV4 65 G2
SEDG DY3 66 B8
Fox La BRGRVW B61 191 H5
KIDD DY10 166 B7
LICH WS13 20 E1
Foxlea Rd HALE B63 121 H4
Foxley Dr SOLH B91 128 F8
Foxlydiate Crs REDW B97 201 L1
Foxlydiate La REDW B97 201 K3
Foxlydiate Ms REDW B97 * 201 L1
Foxmeadow Cl SEDG DY3 66 C6
Foxoak St CDYHTH B64 103 G4
Foxons Barn Rd
RUGBYN/HIL CV21 161 G7
Fox's La WOLV WV1 36 B8
Fox St CBHAMNE B4 7 J4
DUDN DY1 67 G7
Foxtail Wy HEDN WS12 17 J1
Foxton Rd COVS CV3 156 C4
WASH/WDE B8 90 D8
Fox Wk ALDR WS9 40 F2
Foxwalks Av BRGRVW B61 191 H5
Foxwell Gv BORD B9 108 F3
Foxwell Rd BORD B9 108 F3
Foxwood Av GTB/HAM B43 70 F2
Foxwood Gv
CHWD/FDBR/MGN B37 92 D8
Foxwood Rd
CHWD/FDBR/MGN B37 92 D8
POL/KGSB/FAZ B78 47 K5
Foxyards Cl TPTN/OCK DY4 * 67 H8
Foxyards Rd TPTN/OCK DY4 67 H8
Foyle Rd HWK/WKHTH B38 145 K4
Fozdar Crs BILS/COS WV14 66 E4
Fradley Cl BVILLE B30 145 H1
Framefield Dr SOLH B91 128 C7
Framlingham Gv
DUNHL/THL/PER WV6 48 E2
KNWTH CV8 180 A7
Frampton Cl BVILLE B30 124 B6
CHWD/FDBR/MGN B37 111 H2
Frampton Wk COVE CV2 156 D1
Frampton Wy GTB/HAM B43 71 H1
Frances Av WWCK CV34 205 L6
Frances Crs BDWTH CV12 116 E2
Frances Dr BLOX/PEL WS3 38 F3
Frances Havergal Cl RLSS CV31 206 D7
Frances Rd BVILLE B30 124 E8
ERDW/GRVHL B23 90 B2
KNWTH CV8 181 J2
LOZ/NWT B19 89 G5
Franchecourt Dr KIDDW DY11 137 M4
Franche Rd KIDDW DY11 137 M4
Franchise Gdns DARL/WED WS10 52 D7
Franchise St DARL/WED WS10 52 C8
KIDDW DY11 138 A8
PBAR/PBCH B42 89 J3
Franciscan Rd COVS CV3 155 G5
Francis Cl FOAKS/STRLY B74 55 K5
KGSWFD DY6 83 H5
PENK ST19 10 D5
POL/KGSB/FAZ B78 47 L3
Francis Dr RUGBYS/DCH CV22 185 L4
Francis Green La PENK ST19 10 D4
Francis Rd BRGRVE B60 191 K6
LDYWD/EDGR B16 106 E4
LICH WS13 20 E3
SMTHWKW B67 87 H8
STETCH B33 109 H2
STRBR DY8 101 G8
STRPT DY13 163 J7
YDLY B25 108 E7
Francis St COVN CV6 134 C7

VAUX/NECH B7 7 M1
WBROM B70 87 H4
WOLV WV1 2 E1
Francis Wk NFLD/LBR B31 144 E6
Francis Ward Cl HHTH/SAND B71 68 E5
Frankburn Rd FOAKS/STRLY B74 55 J5
Frankfort St LOZ/NWT B19 89 H7
Frankholmes Dr SHLY B90 148 E7
Frankland Rd COVN CV6 134 E4
Frankley Av RMSLY B62 104 D8
Frankley Beeches Rd
NFLD/LBR B31 144 B2
Frankley Gn RMSLY B62 122 B8
Frankley Green La
RIDG/WDGT B32 122 D8
Frankley Hill La
RIDG/WDGT B32 143 K1
Frankley La NFLD/LBR B31 123 G7
Frankley Lodge Rd
NFLD/LBR B31 144 B1
Frankley Rd LGLYGN/QTN B68 104 E5
Frankley Ter HRBN B17 * 105 M8
Franklin Dr BNTWD WS7 18 F7
Franklin Gv TLHL/CAN CV4 153 J4
Franklin Rd BVILLE B30 124 D8
NUN CV11 99 H4
Franklins Gdns COVS CV3 156 F4
Franklin St WSNGN B18 88 C8
Franklin Wy BVILLE B30 124 D6
Franklyn Cl
DUNHL/THL/PER WV6 34 C8
Frankpledge Rd COVS CV3 155 J5
Frank Rd SMTHWKW B67 87 J7
Frank St BHTH/HG B12 107 K6
NUN CV11 98 F2
Franks Wy STETCH B33 109 J3
Frank Tommey Cl
BLKHTH/ROWR B65 * 104 A4
Frankton Av COVS CV3 155 H8
Frankton Cl HIA/OLT B92 127 M3
REDE B98 203 J5
Frankton Gv BORD B9 108 F3
Frankton La RRUGBY CV23 183 L8
Frankwell Dr COVE CV2 135 J4
Fraser Cl NUNW/HART CV10 79 M7
Fraser Rd COVN CV6 133 L4
SPARK B11 108 A8
Fraser St BILS/COS WV14 51 J7
Frayne Av KGSWFD DY6 83 G6
Freasley Cl SHLY B90 148 B2
Freasley Rd BKDE/SHDE B34 92 B8
Freda Ri OLDBY B69 86 B5
Freda Rd WBROM B70 87 H4
Fredas Gv HRBN B17 123 L1
Frederick Ct TAM/AM/WIL B77 46 C2
Frederick Neal Av COVW CV5 153 H1
Frederick Rd AST/WIT B6 89 J5
EDG B15 106 F5
ERDW/GRVHL B23 90 B3
KIDDW DY11 164 D4
LGLYGN/QTN B68 105 H6
PENK ST19 10 D3
RCOVN/BALC/EX CV7 96 D5
SCFLD/BOLD B73 72 E3
SLYOAK B29 124 B3
SPARK B11 126 A1
STETCH B33 109 G2
WNSFLD WV11 37 G8
Fredericks Cl STRBR DY8 119 J1
Frederick St BKHL/PFLD WV2 2 F8
CBHAMW B1 6 C2
RUGBYS/DCH CV22 186 D2
WBROM B70 87 G1
WSLW WS2 4 C4
Frederick William St
WLNHL WV13 51 M3
Fred Lee Gv COVS CV3 181 H1
Fred Smith Cl DARL/WED WS10 52 F8
Freeboard La KNWTH CV8 183 J6
Freeburn Cswy TLHL/CAN CV4 154 A6
Freeford Gdns LICHS WS14 21 J7
Freehold St COV CV1 155 K1
Freeland Gv KGSWFD DY6 101 K1
Freeman Cl NUNW/HART CV10 98 B1
Freeman Dr MGN/WHC B75 73 K1
Freeman Pl BILS/COS WV14 51 J5
Freeman Rd DARL/WED WS10 69 G2
VAUX/NECH B7 89 M8
Freemans Cl RLSN CV32 206 C4
Freeman St COVN CV6 134 D7
DIG/EDG B5 7 H5
WOLVN WV10 3 L4
Freemantle Rd
RUGBYS/DCH CV22 186 A3
Freer Dr BNTWD WS7 19 J6
Freer Rd AST/WIT B6 89 H5
Freer St NUN CV11 99 J3
WSL WS1 4 F3
Freesland Ri NUNW/HART CV10 79 M7
Freeth Rd BRWNH WS8 26 E4
Freeth St LDYWD/EDGR B16 106 E3
OLDBY B69 86 D5
Freezeland St BILS/COS WV14 50 F7
Fremantle Dr HEDN WS12 17 J3
Fremont Dr DUDN DY1 84 C2
French Av POL/KGSB/FAZ B78 45 G4
French Rd DUDS DY2 85 J4
Frensham Cl
CHWD/FDBR/MGN B37 111 G3
GTWY WS6 24 C1
Frensham Dr NUNW/HART CV10 79 M8
Frensham Wy HRBN B17 106 A7
Frenshaw Gv KGSTG B44 71 K5
Freshfield Cl COVW CV5 133 G4
Freshwater Dr BRLYHL DY5 101 M4
Freshwater Gv RLSS CV31 207 G7
Fretton Cl COVN CV6 134 D6
Freville Cl CRTAM B79 31 L7
Frevill Rd COVN CV6 134 F5
Friardale Cl DARL/WED WS10 69 H2
Friar Park Rd DARL/WED WS10 69 G2
Friars Cl COVS CV3 157 J6
STRBR DY8 101 G2
Friar's Ga ATHST CV9 63 H5
Friars Gorse KINVER DY7 101 G6
Friars' Rd COV CV1 8 F7
Friars St WWCK CV34 205 H7
Friar St DARL/WED WS10 68 F2
Friars Wk TAM/AM/WIL B77 46 A2
Friary Av LICH WS13 20 E6
SHLY B90 148 E7
Friary Cl RWWCK/WEL CV35 204 D7
Friary Crs RUSH/SHEL WS4 40 A7
Friary Dr FOAKS/STRLY B74 56 D2
Friary Gdns HDSW B21 88 B3
Friary Rd ATHST CV9 63 H4
HDSW B21 88 C3
Friary St NUN CV11 80 F8
The Friary LICH WS13 20 F6
Friary Vw LICH WS13 * 20 F6
Friday Acre LICH WS13 20 F3
Friday La HIA/OLT B92 150 B1
Friesland Dr WOLV WV1 50 F2
Friezeland Rd WSLW WS2 52 F3
Friezland La BRWNH WS8 26 E8
Friezland Wy BRWNH WS8 26 E8
Frilsham Wy COVW CV5 132 F8
Fringe Green Cl BRGRVE B60 191 L6
Fringe Meadow Rd REDE B98 195 K7
Frinton Gv HDSW B21 88 A6
Frisby Rd RIDG/WDGT B32 105 J8
TLHL/CAN CV4 153 J3
Friston Av LDYWD/EDGR B16 6 A7
Friswell Dr COVN CV6 134 D5
Frobisher Cl GTWY WS6 24 D4
Frobisher Rd COVS CV3 155 G8
RUGBYS/DCH CV22 186 A4
Frodesley Rd
LGN/SDN/BHAMAIR B26 109 M5
Froggatt Rd BILS/COS WV14 51 H6
Froggatts Ride WALM/CURD B76 73 K2
Frog La LICH WS13 20 F6
RCOVN/BALC/EX CV7 151 L8
Frogmere Cl COVW CV5 132 F7
COVW CV5 * 133 G7
Frogmill Rd NFLD/LBR B31 143 M3
Frogmore La KNWTH CV8 177 K2
Frome Cl DUDN DY1 84 B3
Frome Dr WNSFLD WV11 37 G8
Frome Wy ALE/KHTH/YWD B14 125 G7
Front Cottages ALVE B48 * 170 D7
Frost St BKHL/PFLD WV2 50 E7
Froxmere Cl SOLH B91 148 F5
Froyle Cl DUNHL/THL/PER WV6 35 G8
Froysell St WLNHL WV13 51 M3
Fryer Av RLSN CV32 206 C3
Fryer Rd NFLD/LBR B31 144 F6
Fryers Cl BLOX/PEL WS3 38 F6
Fryers Rd WSLW WS2 38 E7
Fryer St WOLV WV1 3 G4
Frythe Cl KNWTH CV8 180 A7
Fuchsia Dr COVEN WV9 35 K2
Fugelmere Cl HRBN B17 105 K6
Fulbrook Cl REDE B98 195 G8
Fulbrook Gv SLYOAK B29 123 K5
Fulbrook Rd COVE CV2 135 G4
DUDN DY1 84 E4
Fulford Dr WALM/CURD B76 73 M8
Fulford Gv
LGN/SDN/BHAMAIR B26 110 A7
Fulford Hall Rd HOCK/TIA B94 173 H2
Fulham Rd SPARK B11 107 M8
Fullbrook Cl SHLY B90 148 E8
Fullbrook Rd DSYBK/YTR WS5 53 J8
Fullelove Rd BRWNH WS8 26 E7
Fullers Cl COVN CV6 133 K6
Fullerton Cl CDSL WV8 35 J4
Fullmore Cl PENK ST19 10 D6
Fullwood Cl COVE CV2 135 J3
Fullwood Crs DUDS DY2 84 C7
Fullwoods End BILS/COS WV14 67 G5
Fulmar Crs KIDD DY10 164 F3
Fulmer Wk WSNGN B18 * 106 E2
Fulton Cl BRGRVE B60 191 M4
Fulwell Gv KGSTG B44 71 L5
Fulwell Ms
CHWD/FDBR/MGN B37 110 F5
Fulwood Av RMSLY B62 104 D5
Furber Pl KGSWFD DY6 83 K7
Furlong La HALE B63 103 G7
Furlong Meadow
NFLD/LBR B31 145 G3
Furlong Rd COV CV1 9 H8
Furlongs Rd SEDG DY3 66 B7
The Furlongs STRBR DY8 119 M2
WNSFLD WV11 36 F8
The Furlong DARL/WED WS10 52 C8
Furlong Wk SEDG DY3 84 B1
Furnace Cl BDWTH CV12 117 G2
WMBN WV5 64 C8
Furnace Hl HALE B63 103 M7
Furnace La HALE B63 103 M8
Furnace Pde TPTN/OCK DY4 67 J7
Furnace Rd BDWTH CV12 117 H2
DUDS DY2 85 G5
Furness TAM/AM/WIL B77 46 B3
Furness Cl BLOX/PEL WS3 38 D2
RUGBYN/HIL CV21 161 H6
Furnivall Crs LICH WS13 21 H4
Furrow Cl RUGBYN/HIL CV21 187 H1
The Furrows BRGRVE B60 191 H7
Furst St BRWNH WS8 26 E5
Furzebank Wy SHHTH WV12 52 C1
Furze La REDE B98 203 L1
Furze Wy DSYBK/YTR WS5 54 B5
Fynford Rd COVN CV6 133 M8

G

Gable Cft LICHS WS14 21 J7
Gables Cl RUGBYS/DCH CV22 186 B5
The Gables ERDE/BCHGN B24 91 H1
POL/KGSB/FAZ B78 47 L3
Gabor Cl RUGBYN/HIL CV21 161 G7
Gaddesby Rd
ALE/KHTH/YWD B14 125 K5
Gadds Dr BLKHTH/ROWR B65 104 B1
Gadsby Av WNSFLD WV11 37 L6
Gadsby St NUN CV11 99 J2
Gads Gn DUDS DY2 85 H8
Gads Green Crs DUDS DY2 85 J7
Gads La DUDN DY1 85 G4
WBROM B70 86 E2
Gadwall Cft ERDW/GRVHL B23 89 M2
Gaelic Rd CNCK/NC WS11 16 B1
Gagarin CRTAM B79 31 K8
Gaiafields Rd LICH WS13 20 F4
Gaialands Crs LICH WS13 20 F4
Gaia La LICH WS13 20 E5
Gail Cl ALDR WS9 40 F1
Gailey Cft KGSTG B44 71 J2
Gailey Lea La PENK ST19 14 F3
Gailey Pk WOLVN WV10 * 22 A7
Gail Pk BDMR/CCFT WV3 49 H6
Gainford Cl COVEN WV9 35 K4
Gainford Ri COVS CV3 156 D2
Gainford Rd KGSTG B44 72 A4
Gainsborough Crs DOR/KN B93 149 L7
GTB/HAM B43 71 H1
RUGBYN/HIL CV21 187 M4
Gainsborough Dr BDWTH CV12 116 E1
DUNHL/THL/PER WV6 48 D1
POL/KGSB/FAZ B78 44 F5
RLSS CV31 207 G6
Gainsborough Hl STRBR DY8 119 L2
Gainsborough Ms KIDDW DY11 137 M8
Gainsborough Pl DUDN DY1 84 C3
Gainsborough Rd
PBAR/PBCH B42 70 F7
Gainsbrook Crs CNCK/NC WS11 17 K8
Gainsford Dr RMSLY B62 103 M7
Gains La BLOX/PEL WS3 25 H3
Gairloch Rd SHHTH WV12 37 M4
Gaitskell Ter OLDBY B69 86 B3
Gaitswell Wy SMTHWK B66 87 K6
Galahad Wy DARL/WED WS10 68 E3
STRPT DY13 188 D2
Galbraith Cl BILS/COS WV14 67 H5
Galena Cl TAM/AM/WIL B77 46 F3
Galena Wy AST/WIT B6 89 J7
Gale Wk BLKHTH/ROWR B65 85 K8
Galey's Rd COVS CV3 155 H5
Gallagher Rd BDWTH CV12 116 E3
Gallery Sq WSL WS1 4 E3
The Galliards TLHL/CAN CV4 180 B1
Galliers Cl TAM/AM/WIL B77 46 D8
Galloway Av BKDE/SHDE B34 91 K7
Gallows Hl WWCK CV34 205 M8
Galmington Dr COVS CV3 154 F8
Galton Cl ERDE/BCHGN B24 91 K1
TPTN/OCK DY4 68 A7
Galton Dr DUDS DY2 84 F7
Galton Rd SMTHWKW B67 105 K4
Galtons La HAG/WOL DY9 141 L6
Galway Rd BNTWD WS7 18 E5
Gamesfield Gn BDMR/CCFT WV3 49 K4
Gammage St DUDS DY2 84 F5
Gamson Cl KIDD DY10 164 C1
Ganborough Cl REDE B98 203 J4
Gandy Rd SHHTH WV12 37 L7
Gannahs Farm Cl
WALM/CURD B76 73 K2
Gannow Green La RBRY B45 143 G4
Gannow Manor Crs RBRY B45 143 J4
Gannow Manor Gdns RBRY B45 143 K4
Gannow Rd RBRY B45 143 J6
Gannow Wk RBRY B45 143 J6
Ganton Rd BLOX/PEL WS3 38 E1
Garage Cl TAM/AM/WIL B77 32 B8
Garden Cl DOR/KN B93 149 K7
RBRY B45 143 L3
WASH/WDE B8 90 E8
Garden Ct WWCK CV34 205 J6
Garden Crs BLOX/PEL WS3 39 K2
Garden Cft ALDR WS9 40 F6
Gardeners Cl KIDDW DY11 138 A5
Gardeners Wy WMBN WV5 82 D1
Garden Gv BFLD/HDSWWD B20 70 C7
Gardenia Dr COVW CV5 132 E7
The Gardens ERDW/GRVHL B23 90 C2
KNWTH CV8 197 L2
RLSS CV31 207 J8
Garden St WSLW WS2 4 E1
Garden Wk BILS/COS WV14 51 K7
SEDG DY3 84 A3
Gardners Meadow BEWD DY12 162 F2
Gardner Wy KNWTH CV8 197 L3
Garfield Rd
LGN/SDN/BHAMAIR B26 109 M5
Garganey Ct KIDD DY10 164 D4
Garibaldi Ter BRGRVE B60 191 L4
Garland Crs RMSLY B62 104 C5
Garland Rd STRPT DY13 163 H7
Garlands Cft
RCOVN/BALC/EX CV7 115 L7
The Garlands WNSFLD WV11 37 G6
Garland St BORD B9 108 A2
Garland Wy NFLD/LBR B31 144 F1
Garlick Dr KNWTH CV8 180 A7
Garman Cl GTB/HAM B43 70 C3
Garner Cl BILS/COS WV14 67 H2
Garnet Av GTB/HAM B43 70 F2
Garnet Cl ALDR WS9 41 H1
Garnett Dr MGN/WHC B75 57 J7
Garnette Cl NUNW/HART CV10 79 M8
Garrard Gdns SCFLD/BOLD B73 56 F8
Garrat St BRLYHL DY5 84 C8
Garratt Cl LGLYGN/QTN B68 105 G1
RRUGBY CV23 159 M8
Garratt's La CDYHTH B64 103 K3
Garratt St HHTH/SAND B71 68 F8
Garratts Wk
ALE/KHTH/YWD B14 146 C4
Garret Cl KGSWFD DY6 83 H4
Garretts Green La
LGN/SDN/BHAMAIR B26 109 L6
Garrett St NUN CV11 99 J3
Garrick Cl COVW CV5 153 G1
DUDN DY1 84 D2
Garrick Ri BNTWD WS7 18 F6
Garrick Rd CNCK/NC WS11 16 B1
LICH WS13 20 D3
Garrick St WOLV WV1 3 G6
Garrigill TAM/AM/WIL B77 46 E4
Garrington St DARL/WED WS10 52 A6
Garrison La BORD B9 107 M3
Garrison St BORD B9 107 M3
Garth Crs COVS CV3 156 A5
The Garth ALE/KHTH/YWD B14 147 H1
LICH WS13 20 F3
Garway Cl REDE B98 203 J4
RLSN CV32 206 D1
Garway Gv YDLY B25 108 F7
Garwood Rd
LGN/SDN/BHAMAIR B26 109 K3
Garyth Williams Cl
RUGBYS/DCH CV22 186 C5
Gas Sq BRGRVW B61 191 J4
Gas St CBHAMW B1 6 C6
RLSS CV31 206 D6
RUGBYN/HIL CV21 186 F2
Gatacre St SEDG DY3 84 B2
Gatcombe Cl WOLVN WV10 36 D1
Gatcombe Rd DUDN DY1 84 C3
Gate Cl WMBN WV5 64 E8
Gatehouse Cl RUGBYN/HIL CV21 187 L5
Gatehouse Fold DUDS DY2 * 85 H4
Gatehouse La BDWTH CV12 116 E3
Gate La CSHL/WTROR B46 76 D7
HOCK/TIA B94 175 G2
SCFLD/BOLD B73 72 D3
Gateley Cl REDE B98 203 L1
Gateley Rd LGLYGN/QTN B68 105 H6
Gateside Rd COVN CV6 134 C3
Gate St SEDG DY3 66 C6
TPTN/OCK DY4 85 L3
WASH/WDE B8 90 B8
Gatis St DUNHL/THL/PER WV6 35 L8
Gatwick Rd CVALE B35 91 M1
Gauden Rd HAG/WOL DY9 120 B4
Gaulby Wk COVS CV3 156 E4
The Gaunts ALVE B48 170 F7
Gaveston Rd COVN CV6 133 J7
RLSN CV32 206 C4
Gavin Wy PBAR/PBCH B42 89 K1
Gawne La DUDS DY2 103 J1
Gawsworth CRTAM B79 31 H6
Gaydon Cl COVN CV6 134 E5
DUNHL/THL/PER WV6 34 C8
REDE B98 202 D4
Gaydon Gv SLYOAK B29 123 L3
Gaydon Pl SCFLD/BOLD B73 72 F1
Gaydon Rd ALDR WS9 54 E1
HIA/OLT B92 128 B2
Gayer St COVN CV6 134 D4
Gayfield Av BRLYHL DY5 102 B4
Gay Hill La HWK/WKHTH B38 145 M5
Gayhurst Cl COVS CV3 156 C5
Gayhurst Dr YDLY B25 109 J5
Gayle TAM/AM/WIL B77 46 E4
Gayle Gv ACGN B27 127 G5
Gayton Rd HHTH/SAND B71 69 H7
Gaywood Cft EDG B15 6 D9
Gaza Cl TLHL/CAN CV4 153 L4
Gazelle Cl COV CV1 9 J3
Geach St LOZ/NWT B19 89 H7
Gedney Cl ALE/KHTH/YWD B14 147 G2
Geeson Cl CVALE B35 91 M1
Gee St LOZ/NWT B19 89 H7
Gemini Dr CNCK/NC WS11 16 D7
Gem Vls SPARK B11 * 108 A6
Geneva Rd TPTN/OCK DY4 85 H1
Genge Av
ETTPK/GDPK/PENN WV4 66 C1
Genners La RIDG/WDGT B32 123 G5
Genthorn Cl
ETTPK/GDPK/PENN WV4 66 D1
Gentian Cl NFLD/LBR B31 123 K7
Gentian Wy RRUGBY CV23 161 J5
Geoffery Cl COVE CV2 134 F8
Geoffrey Cl WALM/CURD B76 73 M6
Geoffrey Pl SPARK B11 * 126 A2
Geoffrey Rd SHLY B90 147 K2
SPARK B11 126 A2
George Arthur Rd
WASH/WDE B8 108 B1
George Av BLKHTH/ROWR B65 104 B3
POL/KGSB/FAZ B78 45 G4
George Birch Cl RRUGBY CV23 158 C2
George Bird Cl SMTHWK B66 * 87 L7
George Cl DUDS DY2 85 J5
George Dance Cl KIDD DY10 * 138 F7
George Eliot Av BDWTH CV12 117 H3
George Eliot Rd COV CV1 134 B8
George Eliot St
NUNW/HART CV10 99 G3
George Frederick Rd
SCFLD/BOLD B73 71 L1
George Henry Rd TPTN/OCK DY4 68 C6
George Hodgkinson Cl
COVW CV5 153 K2
George La LICH WS13 20 F5
George Marston Rd COVS CV3 156 C4
George Park Cl COVE CV2 135 G4
George Rd ALVE B48 170 E7
BILS/COS WV14 67 H4
CSHL/WTROR B46 93 G2
ERDW/GRVHL B23 90 A2
GTB/HAM B43 70 D3
HALE B63 121 K1
LGLYGN/QTN B68 105 G3
SCFLD/BOLD B73 72 B4
SLYOAK B29 124 C3
SOLH B91 149 G2
WWCK CV34 205 L5
YDLY B25 108 E7
George Robertson Cl COVS CV3 156 C6
George Rose Gdns
DARL/WED WS10 51 M7
George St BHTH/HG B12 107 K8
BKHL/PFLD WV2 2 F7
BRGRVW B61 191 K3
CBHAMNW B3 6 C4
COV CV1 134 C8
CRTAM B79 45 M1
DUDN DY1 66 F7
HDSW B21 88 A5
HEDN WS12 17 G1
KIDD DY10 138 D7
LOZ/NWT B19 88 F6
NUN CV11 99 H3
RCOVN/BALC/EX CV7 96 E5
RLSS CV31 206 E6
RUGBYN/HIL CV21 186 D2
STRBR DY8 101 K4
WBROM B70 87 H3
WLNHL WV13 51 L1
WSL WS1 4 F5
George St Ringway
BDWTH CV12 116 F2
George St West WSNGN B18 106 E1
Georgina Av BILS/COS WV14 67 H2
Geraldine Rd YDLY B25 108 F6
Gerald Rd STRBR DY8 101 J6
Geranium Gv BORD B9 108 D2
Geranium Rd DUDS DY2 85 K5
Gerard CRTAM B79 31 J6
Gerard Av TLHL/CAN CV4 153 M5
Gerard Rd RUGBYS/DCH CV22 185 L5
Gerard Rw RUGBYS/DCH CV22 * 185 L5
Gerardsfield Rd STETCH B33 110 B2
Germander Dr DSYBK/YTR WS5 69 L2
Gerrard Cl LOZ/NWT B19 89 H6
Gerrard Rd WLNHL WV13 51 J4
Gerrard St LOZ/NWT B19 89 G7
WWCK CV34 205 J7
Gervase Dr DUDN DY1 85 G2
Geston Rd DUDN DY1 84 D5
Gheluvelt Av KIDD DY10 138 D5
Gheluvelt Ct STRPT DY13 188 D1
Gibbert Hill Rd TLHL/CAN CV4 153 M8
Gibbet Hill Rd TLHL/CAN CV4 180 A2
Gibbet La KINVER DY7 118 E1
Gibbins Rd SLYOAK B29 124 A4
Gibb La BRGRVW B61 168 E5
Gibbons Cl TLHL/CAN CV4 153 K3
Gibbons Crs STRPT DY13 188 D1
Gibbons Gv
DUNHL/THL/PER WV6 49 J1
Gibbons Hill Rd SEDG DY3 66 B3
Gibbons La BRLYHL DY5 83 L6
Gibbons Rd
DUNHL/THL/PER WV6 49 K1
MGN/WHC B75 56 F2
Gibbs Cl COVE CV2 135 M7
Gibbs Hill Rd NFLD/LBR B31 144 F6
Gibbs Rd HAG/WOL DY9 102 E8
REDE B98 194 E8
Gibbs St DUNHL/THL/PER WV6 49 L1
Gibb St BORD B9 7 K7
Gibson Crs BDWTH CV12 116 E3
Gibson Dr BFLD/HDSWWD B20 88 F4
RUGBYN/HIL CV21 187 K4
Gibson Rd BFLD/HDSWWD B20 88 F5
DUNHL/THL/PER WV6 48 C2
Gideon Cl
LGN/SDN/BHAMAIR B26 109 H7
Gideons Cl SEDG DY3 66 B8
Gielgud Wy
RCOVN/BALC/EX CV7 135 M5
Giffard Rd WOLV WV1 50 F6
WOLVN WV10 36 C2
Giffard Wy WWCK CV34 205 J4
Giffords Cft LICH WS13 20 E4
Giggetty La WMBN WV5 64 C7
Gigg La WALM/CURD B76 74 F2
Gigmill Wy STRBR DY8 119 J1
Gilbanks Rd STRBR DY8 101 H6
Gilberry Cl DOR/KN B93 149 L8
Gilbert Av OLDBY B69 85 M6
RUGBYS/DCH CV22 186 B3
Gilbert Cl COV CV1 9 K3
WNSFLD WV11 37 L6
Gilbert La WMBN WV5 64 F6
Gilbert Rd BRGRVE B60 191 J6
LICH WS13 21 G3
SMTHWK B66 105 M1
Gilbert Scott Wy KIDD DY10 138 C6
Gilbertstone Av
LGN/SDN/BHAMAIR B26 109 J8
Gilbertstone Cl REDE B98 202 C4
Gilbert St TPTN/OCK DY4 85 K3
Gilbeys Cl STRBR DY8 101 J4
Gilby Rd LDYWD/EDGR B16 106 E4
Gilchrist Dr EDG B15 106 C5
Gildas Av HWK/WKHTH B38 145 L4
Giles Cl COVN CV6 134 A3
HIA/OLT B92 128 D6
STETCH B33 109 J2
Giles Rd LGLYGN/QTN B68 86 F8
LICH WS13 20 E2
Gilfil Rd NUNW/HART CV10 98 F4
Gilgal STRPT DY13 188 E1
Gilldown Pl EDG B15 106 F6
Gillespie Cft AST/WIT B6 89 K6
Gillet Cl NUN CV11 98 F2
Gillhurst Rd HRBN B17 105 M6
Gillians Wk COVE CV2 135 L5
Gilling Gv BKDE/SHDE B34 91 L7
Gillingham Cl DARL/WED WS10 69 H1
Gillity Av DSYBK/YTR WS5 5 M7
Gillity Cl DSYBK/YTR WS5 5 M7
Gilliver Rd SHLY B90 147 M3
Gillman Cl
LGN/SDN/BHAMAIR B26 128 B1
Gillott Cl SOLH B91 149 J2
Gillott Rd LDYWD/EDGR B16 106 B3
Gillows Cft SHLY B90 148 E6
Gillquart Wy COV CV1 9 H8
Gillscroft Rd STETCH B33 109 L2
Gill St DUDS DY2 103 J2
WBROM B70 87 G4
Gillway CRTAM B79 31 M5
Gilmorton Cl HRBN B17 105 M6
SOLH B91 149 G4
Gilpin Cl CBROM B36 91 G7
Gilpin Crs BLOX/PEL WS3 39 L1
Gilpins Cft GTWY WS6 24 B4
Gilson Dr CSHL/WTROR B46 93 H5
Gilson Rd CSHL/WTROR B46 93 J5
Gilson St TPTN/OCK DY4 68 A5
Gilson Wy
CHWD/FDBR/MGN B37 92 E8
Gilwell Rd BKDE/SHDE B34 92 C7
Gimble Wk HRBN B17 105 K5
Ginkgo Wk RLSS CV31 206 D8
Gipsy Cl RCOVN/BALC/EX CV7 151 M8
Gipsy La ERDW/GRVHL B23 71 M8
NUNW/HART CV10 99 G7
RCOVN/BALC/EX CV7 152 A8
WLNHL WV13 51 M4
Girdlers Cl COVS CV3 154 F8
Girtin Cl BDWTH CV12 116 E1
Girton Rd CNCK/NC WS11 16 D5
Girvan Gv RLSN CV32 199 G8
Gisborn Cl SMHTH B10 * 107 M5
Gisburn Cl REDW B97 193 M8
WWCK CV34 205 K4
Gladeside Cl RUSH/SHEL WS4 40 A5
The Glades ALDR WS9 40 F6
The Glade CDSL WV8 35 J4
CNCK/NC WS11 16 A3
COVW CV5 153 K2
FOAKS/STRLY B74 55 J4
HAG/WOL DY9 102 C8
LGN/SDN/BHAMAIR B26 128 B1
Gladiator Wy RUGBYN/HIL CV21 160 D6
Gladstone Dr OLDBY B69 86 A2
Gladstone Gv KGSWFD DY6 83 H5
Gladstone Rd DOR/KN B93 175 L3
ERDW/GRVHL B23 90 B2
HEDN WS12 17 J4
LGN/SDN/BHAMAIR B26 109 H7
SPARK B11 107 M7
STRBR DY8 101 H7
Gladstone St AST/WIT B6 89 L5
DARL/WED WS10 52 C7
HHTH/SAND B71 69 G8
RUGBYN/HIL CV21 186 C1
WSLW WS2 53 H1
Gladys Rd SMTHWKW B67 105 K3
YDLY B25 108 F6
Gladys Ter SMTHWKW B67 * 105 L3
Glaisdale Av COVN CV6 134 C2
Glaisdale Gdns
DUNHL/THL/PER WV6 35 L8
Glaisdale Rd HLGN/YWD B28 126 E5
Glaisedale Gv WLNHL WV13 52 A3
Glaisher Dr WOLVN WV10 36 A7
Glamis Rd SHHTH WV12 37 M6
Glanville Dr MGN/WHC B75 56 E1
Glaramara Cl RUGBYN/HIL CV21 161 H7
Glasbury Cft HWK/WKHTH B38 145 J6
Glascote Cl SHLY B90 147 L2
Glascote Gv BKDE/SHDE B34 92 A7
Glascote La TAM/AM/WIL B77 46 D6
Glascote Rd TAM/AM/WIL B77 46 B2
Glasscroft Cottages BNTWD WS7 19 K6
Glasshouse Hl STRBR DY8 119 M2
Glasshouse La HOCK/TIA B94 175 J8
KNWTH CV8 180 A8
Glastonbury Cl KIDDW DY11 137 L7
Glastonbury Crs BLOX/PEL WS3 38 C3
Glastonbury Rd
ALE/KHTH/YWD B14 126 A8
HHTH/SAND B71 69 H5
Glastonbury Wy BLOX/PEL WS3 38 C4
Glaston Dr SOLH B91 148 E5
Gleads Cft RIDG/WDGT B32 122 E2
Gleave Rd SLYOAK B29 124 C4
Glebe Av BDWTH CV12 116 C4
Glebe Cl REDE B98 203 H3
TLHL/CAN CV4 153 L6
Glebe Crs KNWTH CV8 197 L2
RUGBYN/HIL CV21 186 C2
Glebe Dr SCFLD/BOLD B73 72 D5
Glebefarm Gv COVS CV3 156 D2
Glebe Farm Rd
RUGBYN/HIL CV21 160 D6
STETCH B33 91 L8
Glebe Flds WALM/CURD B76 74 F7
Glebefields Rd TPTN/OCK DY4 67 L5
Glebeland Cl LDYWD/EDGR B16 6 A7
Glebe La NUN CV11 81 K8
STRBR DY8 119 J1
Glebe Pl DARL/WED WS10 51 M7
RLSS CV31 206 F6
Glebe Rd ALVE B48 170 E6
NUN CV11 99 H1
SOLH B91 128 B8
WLNHL WV13 51 K5
Glebe St WSL WS1 4 E6
The Glebe HAG/WOL DY9 141 J7
RCOVN/BALC/EX CV7 115 G6
REDE B98 195 K6
Glebe Wy RCOVN/BALC/EX CV7 151 L6
Gledhill Pk LICHS WS14 21 G8
Gleeson Dr WWCK CV34 205 J3
Glenavon Rd
ALE/KHTH/YWD B14 146 E2
Glen Cl HEDN WS12 12 B8
RUSH/SHEL WS4 53 L2
Glencoe Dr CNCK/NC WS11 16 E1
Glencoe Rd COVS CV3 155 M4
SMTHWK B66 106 A1
Glen Ct BDMR/CCFT WV3 49 J3
Glencroft Rd HIA/OLT B92 128 B2
Glendale Av KNWTH CV8 179 L8
Glendale Cl BDMR/CCFT WV3 49 G5
HALE B63 121 M1
Glendale Ct TAM/AM/WIL B77 46 F7
Glendale Dr STETCH B33 109 K2
WMBN WV5 64 E7
Glendale Gdns CNCK/NC WS11 16 E1
Glendale Wy TLHL/CAN CV4 153 G3
Glendawn Cl CNCK/NC WS11 16 E2
Glendene Crs HWK/WKHTH B38 145 G6
Glendene Rd HEDN WS12 13 G7
Glen Devon Cl RBRY B45 143 L3
Glendon Rd ERDW/GRVHL B23 72 B7

Glendon Wy DOR/KN B93 ...... 175 J2
Glendower Av COVW CV5 ...... 154 B3
Glendower Rd ALDR WS9 ...... 40 F4
PBAR/PBCH B42 ...... 56 C8
Gleneagles Dr BRGRVE B60 ...... 169 L8
GTB/HAM B43 ...... 70 C1
MGN/WHC B75 ...... 57 G6
OLDBY B69 ...... 85 L6
Gleneagles Rd BLOX/PEL WS3 ...... 38 D2
COVE CV2 ...... 135 J7
DUNHL/THL/PER WV6 ...... 34 D8
LGN/SDN/BHAMAIR B26 ...... 109 J7
Glenelg Dr STRBR DY8 ...... 119 M3
Glenelg Ms DSYBK/YTR WS5 ...... 54 B8
Glenfern Gdns KNWTH CV8 ...... 182 C3
Glenfern Rd BILS/COS WV14 ...... 67 M2
Glenfield CDSL WV8 ...... 35 J3
Glenfield Av COVN/HART CV10 ...... 81 G6
SOLH B91 ...... 149 G5
WALM/CURD B76 ...... 73 J2
Glenfield Gv SLYOAK B29 ...... 130 E6
BDMR/CCFT WV3 ...... 49 K4
Glengarry Gdns
BDMR/CCFT WV3 ...... 49 K4
Glenhill Dr HWK/WKHTH B38 ...... 145 L5
Glenhurst Cl WSLW WS2 ...... 52 B2
Glenmead Rd KGSTG B44 ...... 71 H5
Glenmore Av BNTWD WS7 ...... 18 E1
Glenmore Cl BDMR/CCFT WV3 ...... 49 J6
Glenmore Dr COVN CV6 ...... 116 D8
HWK/WKHTH B38 ...... 145 H4
Glenmount Av COVN CV6 ...... 116 D8
Glenn St COVN CV6 ...... 134 D2
Glen Park Rd SEDG DY3 ...... 84 B3
Glenpark Rd WASH/WDE B8 ...... 90 C8
Glenridding Cl COVN CV6 ...... 116 D8
Glen Ri MOS/BIL B13 ...... 126 A7
Glen Rd SEDG DY3 ...... 66 C3
STRBR DY8 ...... 119 K2
Glenroy Cl COVE CV2 ...... 135 J7
Glenroyde HWK/WKHTH B38 ...... 145 J6
Glen Side RIDG/WDGT B32 ...... 123 H3
Glenside Av WOLVN WV10 ...... 127 M2
The Glen BRGRVE B60 * 169 M8
Glenthorne Dr GTWY WV6 ...... 24 C2
Glenthorne Rd ERDE/BCHGN B24 ... 90 E3
Glenthorne Wy
ERDE/BCHGN B24 ...... 90 E3
Glentworth Av COVN CV6 ...... 133 L3
Glentworth Rd WALM/CURD B76 ... 73 L3
Glentworth Gdns
DUNHL/THL/PER WV6 ...... 35 M8
Glenville Av ATHST CV9 ...... 61 C5
Glenville Dr ERDW/GRVHL B23 ...... 72 C8
Glenwood Cl BRLYHL DY5 ...... 102 B5
Glenwood Dr SHLY B90 ...... 174 B1
Glenwood Gdns BDWTH CV12 ...... 98 E3
Glenwood Ri ALDR WS9 ...... 41 H2
Glenwood Rd HWK/WKHTH B38 ... 145 H5
Globe St DARL/WED WS10 ...... 68 D4
Gloster Dr KNWTH CV8 ...... 179 K7
Gloucester Cl LICH WS13 ...... 20 C1
NUN CV11 ...... 81 L6
Gloucester Pl WLNHL WV13 ...... 52 B3
Gloucester Rd DARL/WED WS10 ... 69 G2
DSYBK/YTR WS5 ...... 55 M7
DUDS DY2 ...... 103 H3
Gloucester St COV CV1 ...... 8 C4
DIG/EDG B5 ...... 7 G7
DUNHL/THL/PER WV6 ...... 49 M1
RLSS CV31 ...... 206 D6
Gloucester Wy BEWD DY12 ...... 162 F1
CHWD/FDBR/MGN B37 ...... 110 E2
CNCK/NC WS11 ...... 16 F4
Glover Cl HLGN/YWD B28 ...... 126 D7
Glover Rd MGN/WHC B75 ...... 57 K8
Glover's Cl ATHST CV9 ...... 63 K6
HEDN WS12 ...... 13 L8
RCOVN/BALC/EX CV7 ...... 131 C4
Glovers Cft
CHWD/FDBR/MGN B37 ...... 110 D2
Glovers Field Dr VAUX/NECH B7 ... 90 A6
Glovers Rd SMHTH B10 ...... 108 A5
Glover St BORD B9 ...... 7 M6
COVS CV3 ...... 155 H5
HEDN WS12 ...... 17 K2
REDE B98 ...... 202 C2
WBROM B70 ...... 87 H4
Glyme Av DUNHL/THL/PER WV6 ... 35 J8
Glyn Av BILS/COS WV14 ...... 67 M2
Glyndebourne CRTAM B79 ...... 31 H6
Glyn Dr BILS/COS WV14 ...... 67 M2
Glyn Farm Rd RIDG/WDGT B32 .... 105 L3
Glynn Crs HALE B63 ...... 141 K6
Glynne Av KGSWFD DY6 ...... 101 H7
Glyn Rd RIDG/WDGT B32 ...... 105 H7
Glynside Av RIDG/WDGT B32 ...... 105 L3
Godfrey Cl RLSS CV31 ...... 207 J3
Godiva Pl COV CV1 ...... 9 J4
Godolphin CRTAM B79 ...... 31 H7
Godson Crs KIDDW DY11 ...... 163 M2
Godson Pl KIDDW DY11 ...... 164 A2
Goffs Cl RIDG/WDGT B32 ...... 123 K2
Gofton TAM/AM/WIL B77 ...... 46 C5
Gold Av RUGBYS/DCH CV22 ...... 185 M5
Goldborough Cl BILS/COS WV14 ... 67 H2
Gold Cl NUN CV11 ...... 99 J3
Goldcrest TAM/AM/WIL B77 ...... 46 C5
Goldcrest Cl DUDS DY2 ...... 103 H3
Goldcrest Cft CBROM B36 ...... 92 E5
Goldcrest Dr KIDD DY10 ...... 164 F3
Golden Acres La COVS CV3 ...... 156 D4
Goldencrest Dr OLDBY B69 ...... 86 C5
Golden Cross La BRGRVW B61 ...... 168 C5
Golden End Dr DOR/KN B93 ...... 150 F7
Golden Hillock Rd DUDS DY2 ...... 103 G2
SPARK B11 ...... 108 B8
Golden Hind Dr STRPT DY13 ...... 188 E3
Goldfinch Cl SLYOAK B29 ...... 124 B5
Goldfinch Rd HAG/WOL DY9 ...... 120 A2
Goldicroft Rd DARL/WED WS10 .... 68 E2
Goldieslie Cl SCFLD/BOLD B73 ...... 72 F1
Goldieslie Rd SCFLD/BOLD B73 .... 72 F1
Goldsborough TAM/AM/WIL B77 .. 46 A4
Golds Hill Gdns HDSW B21 ...... 88 D6
Golds Hill Rd HDSW B21 ...... 88 D5
Golds Hill Wy DARL/WED WS10 ... 68 B6
Goldsmith Av
RUGBYS/DCH CV22 ...... 186 D6
WWCK CV34 ...... 205 G8
Goldsmith Pl CRTAM B79 ...... 31 L6
Goldsmith Rd
ALE/KHTH/YWD B14 ...... 125 K5
BLOX/PEL WS3 ...... 39 J5
Goldstar Wy STECH B33 ...... 110 A3
Goldthorn Av
ETTPK/GDPK/PENN WV4 ...... 49 M8
Goldthorn Cl COVW CV5 ...... 153 H1
Goldthorn Crs
ETTPK/GDPK/PENN WV4 ...... 49 L7
Goldthorne Av CNCK/NC WS11 .... 16 B9
Goldthorn HI
ETTPK/GDPK/PENN WV4 ...... 49 M7
Goldthorn Pl KIDDW DY11 ...... 164 A3
Goldthorn Rd
ETTPK/GDPK/PENN WV4 ...... 49 M7
KIDDW DY11 ...... 163 M2
Golf Dr NUN CV11 ...... 99 M4
Golf La BILS/COS WV14 ...... 51 H6
Golson Cl MGN/WHC B75 ...... 57 J7
Gomeldon Av
ALE/KHTH/YWD B14 ...... 146 D4
Gomer St WLNHL WV13 ...... 51 L3
Gomer St West WLNHL WV13 ...... 51 L3
Gooch Cl DIG/EDG B5 ...... 107 L7
Gooch St North DIG/EDG B5 ...... 7 G8
Goodall Cl CRUGBY CV23 ...... 161 L8
Goodall Gv GTB/HAM B43 ...... 55 J8
Goodby Rd MOS/BIL B13 ...... 125 H2
Goode Av WSNGN B18 ...... 88 E8
Goode Cl LCLYGN/QTN B68 ...... 105 L3
WWCK CV34 ...... 205 G6
Goode Cft TLHL/CAN CV4 ...... 153 K3
Goodere Av POL/KCSB/FAZ B78 ... 47 L5
Goodere Dr POL/KCSB/FAZ B78 ... 47 L3
Goodeve Wk MGN/WHC B75 ...... 57 M8
Goodison Gdns
ERDE/BCHGN B24 ...... 72 F8
Goodman Cl HLGN/YWD B28 ...... 126 D7
Goodman St CBHAMW B1 ...... 6 A4
Goodman Wy TLHL/CAN CV4 ...... 153 C4
Goodrest Av LCLYGN/QTN B68 .... 104 E7
Goodrest Cft
ALE/KHTH/YWD B14 ...... 147 G1
Goodrest La HWK/WKHTH B38 .... 145 K7
Goodrich Av
DUNHL/THL/PER WV6 ...... 48 E2
Goodrich Cl REDE B98 ...... 203 K3
Goodrich Covert
ALE/KHTH/YWD B14 ...... 146 A3
Goodrich Wy VAUX/NECH B7 * 89 M7
Goods Station La PENK ST19 ...... 10 C3
Goodway Ct CBHAMNE B4 ...... 7 L3
Goodway Rd HIA/OLT B92 ...... 128 C2
KGSTG B44 ...... 71 J5
Goodwin Cl KIDDW DY11 ...... 138 A6
Goodwood Cl CBROM B36 ...... 91 H5
COVS CV3 ...... 156 A2
HEDN WS12 * 13 L8
Goodwood Dr FOAKS/STRLY B74 .. 55 K7
Goodwood Rd BRGRVW B61 ...... 168 B4
Goodwyn Av LCLYGN/QTN B68 ... 105 H6
Goodyear Av WOLVN WV10 ...... 36 C6
Goodyear Rd SMTHWKW B67 ...... 105 H3
Goodyers End La
RCOVN/BALC/EX CV7 ...... 116 B5
Goosehill Cft REDE B98 ...... 203 J4
Goosemoor La
ERDW/GRVHL B23 ...... 72 D6
Goostry Cl TAM/AM/WIL B77 ...... 46 B1
Goostry Rd TAM/AM/WIL B77 ...... 32 B8
Gopsal St CBHAMNE B4 ...... 7 L3
Gorcott La BDWTH CV12 ...... 147 L8
Gordon Av
ETTPK/GDPK/PENN WV4 ...... 66 D2
HHTH/SAND B71 ...... 69 G5
LOZ/NWT B19 ...... 89 H6
OLDBY B69 ...... 86 B3
Gordon Crs BRLYHL DY5 ...... 84 C8
Gordon Dr TPTN/OCK DY4 ...... 68 A8
Gordon Pl BILS/COS WV14 ...... 51 G8
Gordon Rd HRBN B17 ...... 106 B7
LOZ/NWT B19 ...... 89 G5
Gordon St BKHL/PFLD WV2 ...... 5 H7
BORD B9 * 107 M3
COV CV1 ...... 8 C7
DARL/WED WS10 ...... 52 B7
RLSS CV31 ...... 206 E6
Gorey Cl SHHTH WV12 ...... 37 M5
Gorge Rd SEDG DY3 ...... 66 C5
Goring Rd COVE CV2 ...... 155 L1
Gorleston Gv
ALE/KHTH/YWD B14 ...... 146 F3
Gorleston Rd
ALE/KHTH/YWD B14 ...... 146 F3
Gorsebrook Rd
DUNHL/THL/PER WV6 ...... 35 M8
Gorse Cl CHWD/FDBR/MGN B37 .. 110 D3
RUGBYS/DCH CV22 ...... 186 C4
SLYOAK B29 ...... 123 L5
Gorse Dr HEDN WS12 ...... 12 B8
Gorse Farm Rd GTB/HAM B43 ...... 70 C5
NUN CV11 ...... 99 K4
Gorsefield Rd BKDE/SHDE B34 .... 92 A8
Gorse La HAG/WOL DY9 ...... 141 M5
Gorse Lea LICH WS14 ...... 21 J7
Gorse Meadow Dr BRBR B45 ...... 169 M5
Gorsemoor Rd HEDN WS12 ...... 17 H4
Gorsemoor Wy WNSFLD WV11 ... 37 M2
Gorse Rd DUDN DY1 ...... 67 L5
WNSFLD WV11 ...... 37 L5
Gorseway BNTWD WS7 ...... 18 F8
COVW CV5 ...... 154 A2
Gorsey Cl BLOX/PEL WS3 ...... 25 K4
Gorsey La CNCK/NC WS11 ...... 15 M4
CNCK/NC WS11 ...... 25 C3
CSHL/WTROR B46 ...... 93 J3
GTWY WV6 ...... 24 D5
HLYWD B47 ...... 172 E1
Gorsey Piece RIDG/WDGT B32 .... 123 G1
Gorsey Wy ALDR WS9 ...... 40 E6
Gorstey Lea BNTWD WS7 ...... 19 G5
Gorstie Cft GTB/HAM B43 ...... 70 C5
Gorsty Av BRLYHL DY5 ...... 102 A1
Gorsty Bank LICHS WS14 ...... 21 J5
Gorsty Hayes CDSL WV8 ...... 35 G2
Gorsty Hill Rd RMSLY B62 ...... 103 M5
Gorsty Bank Rd
TAM/AM/WIL B77 ...... 46 E3
Gorsymead Gv NFLD/LBR B31 ..... 144 A3
Gorsy Rd RIDG/WDGT B32 ...... 123 H1
Gorsy Wy NUNW/HART CV10 ...... 80 B9
Gorton Cft
RCOVN/BALC/EX CV7 ...... 151 M6
Gorway Cl WSL WS1 ...... 5 H8
Gorway Gdns WSL WS1 ...... 5 J8
Gorway Rd WSL WS1 ...... 5 H8
Goscote Cl BLOX/PEL WS3 ...... 39 K6
REDW B97 ...... 193 L1
Goscote La BLOX/PEL WS3 ...... 39 J3
Goscote Lodge Crs
BLOX/PEL WS3 ...... 39 L6
Goscote Pl BLOX/PEL WS3 ...... 39 L6
Goscote Rd BLOX/PEL WS3 ...... 39 K4
Gosford St BHTH/HG B12 ...... 107 L5
COV CV1 ...... 9 J4
DOR/KN B93 ...... 176 C1
Gospel End Rd SEDG DY3 ...... 65 M5
Gospel End St SEDG DY3 ...... 66 B6
Gospel Farm Rd ACGN B27 ...... 126 D1
Gospel La ACGN B27 ...... 127 G6
Gospel Oak Rd COVN CV6 ...... 133 M1
TPTN/OCK DY4 ...... 67 M4
Gosport Cl WOLV WV1 ...... 51 G1
Gosport Rd COVN CV6 ...... 134 C5
Goss Cft SLYOAK B29 ...... 124 B4
Gossett La KNWTH CV8 ...... 157 K6
Gossey La STECH B33 ...... 110 A3
The Goss BRLYHL DY5 ...... 102 B4

Gotham Rd
LGN/SDN/BHAMAIR B26 ...... 109 J7
Gothersley La KINVER DY7 ...... 100 B3
Goths Cl BLKHTH/ROWR B65 ...... 104 A1
Golf Dr NUN CV11 ...... 99 M4
Gough Av WNSFLD WV11 ...... 36 F5
Gough Rd BILS/COS WV14 ...... 67 G4
EDG B15 ...... 107 G6
SPARK B11 ...... 108 B8
Gough St CBHAMW B1 ...... 6 E7
WLNHL WV13 ...... 52 A3
WOLV WV1 ...... 3 L8
Gould Av East KIDDW DY11 ...... 163 L5
Gould Av West KIDDW DY11 ...... 163 L5
Gould Firm La ALDR WS9 ...... 41 J7
Gould Rd RWWCK/WEL CV35 ...... 204 E6
Gower Av KGSWFD DY6 ...... 101 K1
Gower Rd RMSLY B62 ...... 104 E8
SEDG DY3 ...... 65 M4
Gower St BKHL/PFLD WV2 ...... 5 H8
LOZ/NWT B19 ...... 89 H6
WLNHL WV13 ...... 51 M3
WSLW WS2 ...... 52 F6
Gowland Dr CNCK/NC WS11 ...... 15 J4
Goya Cl CNCK/NC WS11 ...... 17 C3
Gozzard St BILS/COS WV14 ...... 51 J8
Gracemere Crs HLGN/YWD B28 ... 147 J1
Grace Rd COVS CV3 ...... 131 L5
OLDBY B69 ...... 86 A5
SPARK B11 ...... 108 A7
TPTN/OCK DY4 ...... 67 L3
Gracewell Rd MOS/BIL B13 ...... 126 B4
Grafton Cl REDE B98 ...... 202 F6
Grafton Ct TLHL/CAN CV4 * 153 M6
Grafton Crs BRGRVE B60 ...... 191 M6
Grafton Dr WLNHL WV13 ...... 51 H4
Grafton Gdns SEDG DY3 ...... 83 M2
Grafton Gv LOZ/NWT B19 * 89 G6
Grafton La BRGRVE B61 ...... 191 G6
Grafton Pl BILS/COS WV14 ...... 51 J6
Grafton Rd HDSW B21 ...... 88 B4
HHTH/SAND B71 ...... 87 H1
LGLYGN/QTN B68 ...... 104 D3
SHLY B90 ...... 147 G3
SPARK B11 ...... 107 M6
Grafton St COV CV1 ...... 9 K5
Graham Cl COVN CV6 ...... 134 F5
TPTN/OCK DY4 ...... 67 M4
Graham Crs RBRY B45 ...... 143 K6
Graham Rd HHTH/SAND B71 ...... 87 H1
RMSLY B62 ...... 104 A5
RUGBYN/HIL CV21 ...... 187 G1
STRBR DY8 ...... 119 K8
WASH/WDE B8 ...... 108 D2
YDLY B25 ...... 109 G7
Graham St CBHAMW B1 ...... 6 A3
LOZ/NWT B19 ...... 89 G5
NUN CV11 ...... 80 F8
Grainger Cl TPTN/OCK DY4 ...... 68 B7
Grainger Ct CNCK/NC WS11 * 16 B3
Grainge's La CDYHTH B64 ...... 103 C5
Grainger St DUDS DY2 ...... 85 H6
Graiseley Cl BDMR/CCFT WV3 ..... 2 D7
Graiseley Hl BDMR/CCFT WV3 ..... 2 D7
Graiseley La WNSFLD WV11 ...... 37 G8
Graiseley Rw BKHL/PFLD WV2 .... 2 D7
Graith Cl ALE/KHTH/YWD B14 .... 147 J2
Gramer Ct ATHST CV9 * 63 K7
Grammar School La HALE B63 ..... 121 L1
Grampian Rd STRBR DY8 ...... 101 L7
Granary Rd HEDN WS12 ...... 12 B8
Granary La WALM/CURD B76 ...... 73 K2
Granary Rd BRGRVE B60 ...... 191 J7
CDSL WV8 ...... 35 L3
The Granary ALDR WS9 ...... 40 F7
Granborough Cl COVS CV3 ...... 156 D5
Granbourne Rd SHHTH WV12 .... 52 B1
Granby Av STECH B33 ...... 110 A4
Granby Cl HIA/OLT B92 ...... 127 J4
REDE B98 ...... 203 K1
Granby Rd NUNW/HART CV10 .... 98 D1
Grandborough Dr SOLH B91 ...... 148 E4
Grand Cl SMTHWK B66 ...... 105 M4
Grand Junction Wy WSL WS1 ..... 53 H8
Grand Union Canal Wk
CBHAMW B4 ...... 6 F1
DOR/KN B93 ...... 150 B8
DOR/KN B93 ...... 176 C5
RLSS CV31 ...... 207 J7
SOLH B91 ...... 149 M2
SPARK B11 ...... 108 A4
WWCK CV34 ...... 205 M5
Grand Union Canal Wk
CBHAMNW B3 ...... 7 G1
Grandys Cft
CHWD/FDBR/MGN B37 ...... 110 D3
Grange Av ALDR WS9 ...... 40 E4
CNCK/NC WS11 ...... 15 C3
COVS CV3 ...... 156 D6
COVS CV3 ...... 181 G2
KNWTH CV8 ...... 179 J7
MGN/WHC B75 ...... 57 G2
PENK ST19 ...... 10 B3
WASH/WDE B8 * 90 F7
Grange Cl NUNW/HART CV10 ...... 80 A3
TAM/AM/WIL B77 ...... 46 A5
WWCK CV34 ...... 206 A3
Grange Ct BDMR/CCFT WV3 * 2 D7
HAG/WOL DY9 * 120 A2
KGSWFD DY6 ...... 101 K1
WSLW WS2 * 52 B3
Grange Crs HALE B63 ...... 121 H4
PENK ST19 ...... 10 B4
RBRY B45 ...... 143 J5
RUSH/SHEL WS4 ...... 39 M5
Grange Farm Dr
HWK/WKHTH B38 ...... 145 H4
Grangefield Cl CDSL WV8 ...... 35 K4
Grange Hl RMSLY B62 ...... 122 A3
Grange Hill Rd
HWK/WKHTH B38 ...... 145 J4
Grange La BRGRVE B60 ...... 193 L2
HAG/WOL DY9 ...... 120 B1
KGSWFD DY6 ...... 101 K1
LICH WS13 ...... 20 A7
LICH WS13 ...... 20 A7
MGN/WHC B75 ...... 57 G2
Grangemouth Rd COVN CV6 ...... 133 M4
Grange Ri HWK/WKHTH B38 ...... 145 K6
Grange Rd ALE/KHTH/YWD B14 .. 125 H5
AST/WIT B6 ...... 89 J5
BKHL/PFLD WV2 ...... 66 F6
BNTWD WS7 ...... 18 E8
BORD B9 ...... 108 B5
CDYHTH B64 ...... 103 L4
CNCK/NC WS11 ...... 17 M7
COVN CV6 ...... 134 F1
DOR/KN B93 ...... 176 C5
DUDN DY1 ...... 84 F4
DUNHL/THL/PER WV6 ...... 48 C8
ERDE/BCHGN B24 ...... 90 C3
HAG/WOL DY9 ...... 120 A2
HWK/WKHTH B38 ...... 145 A5
KGSWFD DY6 ...... 101 K1
LICH WS13 ...... 19 G2
LICHS WS14 ...... 21 J5
NUNW/HART CV10 ...... 78 C5
POL/KCSB/FAZ B78 ...... 47 H6
RCOVN/BALC/EX CV7 ...... 114 D7
RCOVN/BALC/EX CV7 ...... 151 M6

RLSN CV32 ...... 206 E2
RUGBYN/HIL CV21 ...... 160 C3
SLYOAK B29 ...... 124 D2
SMTHWK B66 ...... 105 L4
WSL WS1 ...... 5 H7
Grange Sq DUDN DY1 ...... 84 F4
The Grange WMBN WV5 ...... 64 E6
WWCK CV34 ...... 205 M6
Grange Wk COVN CV6 * 116 F5
Grangewood Ct HIA/OLT B92 * ... 127 J8
Granhill Cl REDE B98 ...... 202 E5
Granoe Cl COVS CV3 ...... 156 C5
Grant Cl HHTH/SAND B71 ...... 69 G8
KGSWFD DY6 ...... 83 K5
Grantham Cl BRLYHL DY5 ...... 101 M6
Grantham Rd SMTHWK B66 ...... 105 M2
SPARK B11 ...... 107 M7
Grantley Dr
CHWD/FDBR/MGN B37 ...... 110 E3
Granton Cl ALE/KHTH/YWD B14 .. 125 H8
Granton Rd
ALE/KHTH/YWD B14 ...... 125 H8
Grantown Gv GTWY WV6 ...... 38 E1
Grant Rd COVS CV3 ...... 155 M3
RCOVN/BALC/EX CV7 ...... 116 E5
Grant St BLOX/PEL WS3 ...... 38 F5
EDG B15 ...... 6 E7
Granville TAM/AM/WIL B77 ...... 46 F4
Granville Cl BKHL/PFLD WV2 ...... 3 H5
BRGRVE B60 ...... 191 M4
Granville Crest KIDD DY10 ...... 138 F7
Granville Dr KGSWFD DY6 ...... 83 K8
Granville Rd CDYHTH B64 ...... 103 M5
DOR/KN B93 ...... 175 L3
Granville Sq EDG B15 ...... 6 E7
Granville St BKHL/PFLD WV2 ...... 3 H5
CBHAMW B1 ...... 6 E7
RLSN CV32 ...... 206 E3
WLNHL WV13 ...... 51 L2
Grasdene Gv HRBN B17 ...... 124 A1
Grasmere Av COVS CV3 ...... 154 D1
DUNHL/THL/PER WV6 ...... 48 D1
FOAKS/STRLY B74 ...... 55 L2
Grasmere Cl NUN CV11 ...... 81 K6
Grasmere Gv STRPT DY13 ...... 163 K7
Grasmere Pl CNCK/NC WS11 ...... 12 C8
Grasmere Rd BDWTH CV12 ...... 116 E3
HDSW B21 ...... 88 D6
Grasscroft Dr COVS CV3 ...... 155 M6
Grassholme TAM/AM/WIL B77 .... 46 B5
Grassington Av WWCK CV34 ...... 205 K4
Grassington Dr
CHWD/FDBR/MGN B37 ...... 110 D4
NUN CV11 ...... 99 J3
Grassmere Ct STRBR DY8 * 119 K2
Grassmoor Rd
HWK/WKHTH B38 ...... 145 J3
Grassy La WOLVN WV10 ...... 36 F4
Graston Cl LDYWD/EDGR B16 .... 106 C3
Gratley Cft HEDN WS12 ...... 16 A1
Grattidge Rd HIA/OLT B92 ...... 127 H4
Gratton Ct COVS CV3 ...... 154 D7
Gravel Bank RIDG/WDGT B32 .... 123 H3
Gravel Hl TLHL/CAN CV4 ...... 153 K4
Gravel La HEDN WS12 ...... 11 M7
WMBN WV5 ...... 64 E5
Gravelly Hl North
ERDE/BCHGN B24 ...... 90 C2
Gravelly La ALDR WS9 ...... 41 J3
ERDW/GRVHL B23 ...... 72 C8
Gravel Pit La ALVE B48 ...... 194 C1
The Gravel WALM/CURD B76 ...... 74 F3
Gray Cl KIDD DY10 ...... 138 F7
Grayfield Av MOS/BIL B13 ...... 125 K2
Grayland Cl ACGN B27 ...... 126 F1
The Graylands COVS CV3 ...... 181 G1
Grayling TAM/AM/WIL B77 ...... 46 B3
Grayling Cl DARL/WED WS10 ...... 67 M4
Grayling Rd BRLYHL DY5 ...... 102 A3
Grayling Wk
CHWD/FDBR/MGN B37 ...... 111 G3
WOLV WV1 ...... 50 F1
Gray Rd HEDN WS12 ...... 12 D7
Grayshott Cl BRGRVW B61 ...... 191 H2
ERDW/GRVHL B23 ...... 72 C8
Grays Rd HRBN B17 ...... 106 B7
Grayston Av TAM/AM/WIL B77 ... 46 F4
Gray St BORD B9 ...... 107 M3
Grayswood Av COVW CV5 ...... 154 B1
Grayswood Park Rd
RIDG/WDGT B32 ...... 105 G2
Grazebrook Cft
RIDG/WDGT B32 ...... 123 H5
Grazebrook Rd DUDS DY2 ...... 85 G6
Grazewood Cl SHHTH WV12 ...... 37 M6
Grazier Av TAM/AM/WIL B77 ...... 46 A4
Grazing La REDW B97 ...... 201 J3
The Grazings KINVER DY7 ...... 118 A2
Greadier St SHHTH WV12 ...... 38 A1
Great Arthur St SMTHWK B66 ..... 87 K6
Great Balance RRUGBY CV23 ...... 158 E2
Great Barn La REDW B97 ...... 201 M4
Great Barr St BORD B9 ...... 7 M6
Great Borne RUGBYN/HIL CV21 .. 161 G6
Great Brickkiln St
BDMR/CCFT WV3 ...... 2 A7
Great Bridge TPTN/OCK DY4 ...... 68 B6
Great Bridge Rd BILS/COS WV14 .. 67 L5
Great Bridge St WBROM B70 ...... 68 C8
Great Brook St VAUX/NECH B7 .... 7 L1
Great Central Wy
RUGBYN/HIL CV21 ...... 187 G5
Great Charles St BRWNH WS8 .... 26 D5
Great Charles St Queensway
CBHAMNW B3 ...... 6 E4
Great Colmore St EDG B15 ...... 6 E7
Great Cornbow HALE B63 ...... 121 M2
Great Croft St DARL/WED WS10 .. 52 B7
Great Farley Dr NFLD/LBR B31 .... 144 A5
Great Francis St VAUX/NECH B7 .. 107 M1
Great Hampton Rw LOZ/NWT B19 ..6 D1
Great Hampton St WOLV WV1 ..... 3 G2
WSNGN B18 ...... 89 G8
Greatheed Rd RLSN CV32 ...... 206 D3
Great Hockings La REDW B97 ..... 201 J3
Great King St LOZ/NWT B19 ...... 89 G7
Great Lister St VAUX/NECH B7 ..... 7 L1
Greatmead TAM/AM/WIL B77 ..... 46 A4
Great Stone Rd NFLD/LBR B31 .... 144 E1
Great Tindal St
LDYWD/EDGR B16 ...... 106 C3
Great Western Ar CBHAMNW B3 ...7 G4

Great Western Cl WSNGN B18 ...... 88 C7
Great Western Dr CDYHTH B64 ... 103 L4
Great Western St
DARL/WED WS10 ...... 68 C3
WOLV WV1 ...... 3 K2
Great Western Wy STRPT DY13 .. 163 L8
Great Wood Rd BORD B9 ...... 108 A4
Greaves Av DSYBK/YTR WS5 ...... 54 A7
Greaves Cl DSYBK/YTR WS5 ...... 54 A7
WWCK CV34 ...... 206 A7
Greaves Crs SHHTH WV12 ...... 38 A3
Greaves Gdns KIDDW DY11 ...... 137 M4
Greaves Sq HWK/WKHTH B38 .... 145 M4
The Greaves WALM/CURD B76 ..... 73 F3
Grebe Cl ERDW/GRVHL B23 ...... 89 M2
Greenacre Dr CDSL WV8 ...... 34 F3
Greenacre Rd TPTN/OCK DY4 ..... 67 L4
Green Acres ACGN B27 ...... 126 F5
WMBN WV5 ...... 64 C7
Greenacres
DUNHL/THL/PER WV6 ...... 34 F8
SEDG DY3 ...... 65 L4
WALM/CURD B76 ...... 73 L1
Greenacres Av WOLVN WV10 ...... 37 G4
Greenacres Cl FOAKS/STRLY B74 .. 55 J3
Greenacres La BEWD DY12 ...... 162 C1
Greenacres Rd BRGRVW B61 ...... 191 J2
Green Acres Rd
HWK/WKHTH B38 ...... 145 H5
Greenaleigh Rd
ALE/KHTH/YWD B14 ...... 147 H2
Green Av HLGN/YWD B28 ...... 126 C4
Greenaway Cl GTB/HAM B43 ...... 71 G2
Greenbank RBRY B45 ...... 170 B5
Green Bank Av HLGN/YWD B28 .. 126 C4
Greenbank Gdns STRBR DY8 ...... 101 J3
Greenbank Rd BEWD DY12 ...... 162 A1
RCOVN/BALC/EX CV7 ...... 151 K7
Green Barns La LICHS WS14 ...... 43 J1
Green Bower Dr BRGRVW B61 ..... 168 B8
Greenbush Dr HALE B63 ...... 103 L8
Green Cl HLYWD B47 ...... 172 D2
RRUGBY CV23 ...... 185 K1
Green Cft HLGN/YWD B28 ...... 126 D5
Greencroft BILS/COS WV14 ...... 51 H7
KGSWFD DY6 ...... 101 H1
LICH WS13 ...... 20 C3
Greendale Cl ATHST CV9 ...... 63 J6
BRGRVW B61 ...... 168 F5
Greendale Rd ATHST CV9 ...... 63 J6
COVW CV5 ...... 153 L3
Green Dr RIDG/WDGT B32 ...... 123 G4
WOLVN WV10 ...... 36 A6
Greenend Rd MOS/BIL B13 ...... 125 J3
Greenfels Ri DUDS DY2 ...... 85 K5
Greenfield Av CDYHTH B64 ...... 102 F4
RCOVN/BALC/EX CV7 ...... 151 L6
STRBR DY8 ...... 101 K8
Greenfield Cft BILS/COS WV14 .... 67 H2
Greenfield La WOLVN WV10 ...... 22 B8
Greenfield Rd GTB/HAM B43 ...... 70 A6
HRBN B17 ...... 106 A8
SMTHWK B66 ...... 105 J1
Greenfields ALDR WS9 ...... 40 E6
CNCK/NC WS11 ...... 16 A6
REDE B98 ...... 202 C3
RUSH/SHEL WS4 ...... 40 B3
WMBN WV5 ...... 63 J6
The Green Fld COVS CV3 ...... 155 M5
Greenfield Vw SEDG DY3 ...... 65 M6
Greenfinch Cl KIDD DY10 ...... 138 E6
Greenfinch Rd CBROM B36 ...... 92 E6
HAG/WOL DY9 ...... 120 A2
Greenford Rd REDW B97 ...... 193 M8
Green Gables
ALE/KHTH/YWD B14 ...... 146 F2
HLYWD B47 ...... 172 F6
MGN/WHC B75 ...... 56 F6
Green Gables Dr HLYWD B47 * 146 E1
Greenheart TAM/AM/WIL B77 ..... 46 E1
Green Heath Rd HEDN WS12 ...... 12 F4
Greenhill BRGRVE B60 ...... 169 K7
WMBN WV5 ...... 64 F7
Greenhill Av KIDD DY10 ...... 138 D5
Green Hill Cl BRGRVE B60 ...... 169 G7
Greenhill Cl SHHTH WV12 ...... 37 M8
TAM/AM/WIL B77 ...... 46 A8
Greenhill Gdns GTB/HAM B43 ..... 70 B3
RMSLY B62 ...... 103 L8
WMBN WV5 ...... 64 F8
Greenhill Ms LICH WS13 ...... 21 G5
Greenhill Rd CSCFLD/WYGN B72 .. 72 E5
HDSW B21 ...... 88 A3
MOS/BIL B13 ...... 125 K4
RMSLY B62 ...... 104 B6
RUGBYS/DCH CV22 ...... 186 C8
SEDG DY3 ...... 66 C8
Greenhill Vls ALDR WS9 * 40 F4
Green Hill Wy SHLY B90 ...... 126 F8
Greenholm Rd KGSTG B44 ...... 71 J6
Greenhough Rd LICH WS13 ...... 20 D5
Greenhurst Dr BRBR B45 ...... 169 M4
Greening Dr EDG B15 ...... 106 F6
Greenland Av COVW CV5 ...... 132 D8
Greenland Cl KGSWFD DY6 ...... 83 J8
Greenland Ct COVW CV5 ...... 132 D8
Greenland Ri HIA/OLT B92 ...... 128 C6
Greenland Rd SLYOAK B29 ...... 124 E4
Greenlands WMBN WV5 ...... 64 C6
Greenlands Av REDE B98 ...... 202 E5
Greenlands Dr REDE B98 ...... 202 D4
Greenlands Rd
CHWD/FDBR/MGN B37 ...... 111 G3
Green La ALDR WS9 ...... 41 J3
ATHST CV9 ...... 62 D3
BLOX/PEL WS3 ...... 39 L1
BLOX/PEL WS3 ...... 39 L1
BNTWD WS7 ...... 19 H4
BNTWD WS7 ...... 19 H4
BORD B9 ...... 108 A4
BRGRVW B61 ...... 191 J4
CBROM B36 ...... 92 C5
CNCK/NC WS11 ...... 16 C5
COVS CV3 ...... 154 E7
CSHL/WTROR B46 ...... 93 J3
DUDN DY1 ...... 66 L6
DUNHL/THL/PER WV6 ...... 48 B7
GTB/HAM B43 ...... 70 B2
HAG/WOL DY9 ...... 102 B8
HDSW B21 ...... 87 L3
HWK/WKHTH B38 ...... 145 A5
KGSWFD DY6 ...... 101 G1
LICH WS13 ...... 19 G2
LICHS WS14 ...... 21 J5
NUNW/HART CV10 ...... 78 C5
POL/KCSB/FAZ B78 ...... 47 H6
POL/KCSB/FAZ B78 ...... 47 H6
RCOVN/BALC/EX CV7 ...... 114 D7
RCOVN/BALC/EX CV7 ...... 151 M6

REDW B97	201	K4
RIDG/WDGT B32	105	G7
RMSLY B62	104	B4
RRUGBY CV23	158	B2
RRUGBY CV23	158	F8
RUSH/SHEL WS4	40	E2
SHLY B90	147	J4
SLYOAK B29	123	K6
TAM/AM/WIL B77	47	G6
WSLW WS2		G2
WWCK CV34	205	J5
Green Lanes BILS/COS WV14	51	G4
SCFLD/BOLD B73	72	F6
Green Lea TAM/AM/WIL B77	46	C5
Greenleaf CI COWV CV6	153	L2
Greenleas Gdns HALE B63	122	A2
Green Leigh ERDW/GRVHL B23	72	D5
Greenleighs SEDG DY3	66	B2
Greenly Rd		
ETTPK/GDPK/PENN WV4	50	B8
Green Meadow HAG/WOL DY9	119	M5
Green Meadow WMBN WV5	64	C7
Green Meadow Rd SHHTH WV12	37	M6
SLYOAK B29	123	K6
Green Mdw HEDN WS12	17	G4
Greenmoor Rd		
NUNW/HART CV10	98	C2
SEDG DY3	66	E6
Green Oak Rd CDSL WV8	34	F3
Greenodd Dr COVN CV6	116	D8
Green Park Av BILS/COS WV14	50	F5
Green Park Dr BRGRVE B60	191	K4
DUDS DY2	85	K4
NFLD/LBR B31	144	C3
Greenridge Rd		
BFLD/HDSWWD B20	70	D3
Green Rd DUDS DY2	85	H6
MOS/BIL B13	126	D4
Green Rock La BLOX/PEL WS3	39	H4
Greenroyde HAG/WOL DY9	119	M4
Greensand Dr BILS/COS WV14	67	G3
Greensforge La KINVER DY7	100	B5
Greenside HRBN B17	106	A8
Greenside CI NUN CV11	99	M5
Greenside Rd ERDE/BCHGN B24	73	G8
Greenside Wy RUSH/SHEL WS5	55	L1
Greensill Av TPTN/OCK DY4	67	K5
Green Slade Crs BRGRVE B60	169	G4
Green Slade Cft NFLD/LBR B31	144	B3
Green Slade Rd DSYBK/YTR WS5	54	A6
SEDG DY3	66	M3
SHLY B90	147	G3
Greensleeves FOAKS/STRLY B74	56	D5
Greensleeves CI COVN CV6	133	M3
Greens Rd COVN CV6	133	L3
Greenstead Rd MOS/BIL B13	126	D4
The Greens		
DUNHL/THL/PER WV6 *	48	C1
Green St BHTH/HG B12	7	L8
BILS/COS WV14	51	K4
KIDD DY10	164	C1
OLDBY B69	86	E6
STRBR DY8	101	K8
WSLW WS2		G2
WBROM B70	87	G5
Greensward CI KNWTH CV8	179	M7
Green Sward La REDE B98	203	H4
The Greensward COVS CV3	156	F4
Greensway WNSFLD WV11	36	F5
Greens Yd BDWTH CV12 *	117	G2
The Green ALDR WS9	41	G7
BLOX/PEL WS3	38	F4
CBROM B36		L4
CNCK/NC WS11	16	B4
CRTAM B79	33	L2
CSCFLD/WYGN B72	73	H4
CSHL/WTROR B46	94	D3
DARL/WED WS10	52	B5
HWK/WKHTH B38	145	K3
KIDD DY10	166	C4
LGLYGN/QTN B68	104	F3
NUN CV11 *	99	J3
POL/KGSB/FAZ B78	47	L2
SEDG DY3	66	C4
WWCK CV34	205	J4
Greenvale Av		
LGN/SDN/BHAMAIR B26	110	B3
Greenway ALDR WS9	40	F3
BFLD/HDSWWD B20	70	D3
NUN CV11 *	99	M5
POL/KGSB/FAZ B78	47	L2
SEDG DY3	66	C4
WWCK CV34	205	J4
Greenway Av STRBR DY8	101	J8
Greenway Dr SCFLD/BOLD B73	72	A2
Greenway Gdns		
HWK/WKHTH B38	145	J3
SEDG DY3	66	C4
Greenway Rd BILS/COS WV14	108	G8
Greenways HALE B63	121	K5
NFLD/LBR B31	123	K5
PENK ST19	10	E5
STRBR DY8	101	J4
The Greenways RLSS CV31	206	F2
Greenway St BORD B9	108	A4
The Greenway		
CHWD/FDBR/MGN B37	110	E7
HAG/WOL DY9	119	K8
SCFLD/BOLD B73	71	M2
Greenwood YDLY B25	109	H5
Greenwood Av ACGN B27	126	E3
BLKHTH/ROWR B65	104	B3
LGLYGN/QTN B68	86	F8
Greenwood CI		
ALE/KHTH/YWD B14	125	J8
RRUGBY CV23	159	L4
HEDN WS12	12	F5
Greenwood Pk ALDR WS9	41	G4
Greenwood Pl ALDR WS9	41	F3
HHTH/SAND B71	68	F5
WOLVN WV10	36	A6
The Greenwoods STRBR DY8	101	J8
Greethurst Dr MOS/BIL B13	126	A3
Greets Green Rd WBROM B70	86	C3
Greetville Ct STECH B33	91	L8
Gregory Av COVS CV3	154	F1
SLYOAK B29	123	L5
Gregory CI DARL/WED WS10	68	A1
Gregory Dr DUDN DY1	84	E3
Gregory Hood Rd COVS CV3	155	H8
Gregory Rd BNTWD WS7	9	H8
STRBR DY8	101	G8
Greig Ct CNCK/NC WS11	17	C3
Grendon Cl REDE B98	203	H4
TLHL/CAN CV4	153	C4
Grendon Dr RUGBYS/DCH CV22	161	J6
SCFLD/BOLD B73	72	B2

Grendon Gdns BDMR/CCFT WV3	49	H7
Grendon Rd		
ALE/KHTH/YWD B14	146	E2
HIA/OLT B92	127	J4
POL/KGSB/FAZ B78	47	L4
Grenfell Cl RLSS CV31	207	G7
Grenfell Dr EDC B15	106	D5
Grenfell Rd BLOX/PEL WS3	39	J2
Grenville Av COVE CV2	155	M2
Grenville Cl RUGBYS/DCH CV22	186	A4
WSLW WS2		B2
Grenville Dr ERDW/GRVHL B23	89	M2
SMTHWK B66	87	H5
Grenville Pl WBROM B70	86	C2
Grenville Rd DUDN DY1	84	C4
SHLY B90	147	M3
Gresham Av RLSN CV32	206	F3
Gresham Pl RLSN CV32 *	206	F3
Gresham Rd CNCK/NC WS11	126	E7
HLGN/YWD B28	126	D7
LGLYGN/QTN B68	86	F8
NUNW/HART CV10	98	F5
Gresley TAM/AM/WIL B77	46	C4
Gresley CI MGN/WHC B75	56	L1
Gresley Rd COVE CV2	135	M3
Gresley Rw LICH WS13	21	G5
Gressel La STETCH B33	110	A4
Grestone Av BFLD/HDSWWD B20	88	C2
Greswold Cl TLHL/CAN CV4	153	L4
Greswolde Dr ERDE/BCHGN B24	90	F1
Greswolde Park Rd ACGN B27	126	F2
Greswolde Rd SOLH B91	127	J7
SPARK B11	126	A2
The Greswoldes RLSS CV31	207	K7
Greswold Gdns CBROM B36	91	L8
Greswold St HHTH/SAND B71	68	F8
Gretna Rd COVS CV3	180	D1
Gretton Crs ALDR WS9	40	D8
Gretton Rd ALDR WS9	40	D8
ERDW/GRVHL B23	72	B6
Greville Cl PENK ST19	10	D5
Greville Dr EDC B15	107	G7
Greville Rd KNWTH CV8	197	J1
WWCK CV34	205	M4
Grevis Cl MOS/BIL B13	125	K1
Grevis Rd STETCH B33	109	J4
Greycoat Rd COVN CV6	133	L3
Greyfort Crs HIA/OLT B92	127	K4
Greyfriars Cl DUDN DY1	84	C2
HIA/OLT B92	127	H6
Greyfriars Dr CRTAM B79	31	J8
Greyfriars La COV CV1	8	F5
Greyfriars Rd COV CV1	8	F5
Grey Green La BEWD DY12	136	F8
Greyhound La		
ETTPK/GDPK/PENN WV4	48	D3
STRBR DY8	119	H3
Greyhurst Cft SOLH B91	148	F5
Grey Mill Cl SHLY B90	148	D7
Greysbrook LICHS WS14 *	28	E8
Greystoke Av GTB/HAM B36	91	H6
Greystoke Dr KGSWFD DY6	83	H7
Greystone CI REDE B98	195	G2
Greystone Pas DUDN DY1	84	B4
Greystone St DUDS DY2	85	G4
Grey Tree Crs DOR/KN B93	175	J2
Grice St WBROM B70	87	G5
Griffin Cl BNTWD WS7	18	C5
Griffin Gdns HRBN B17	124	D1
Griffin Rd ERDW/GRVHL B23	72	A8
KIDD DY10	164	C1
RLSS CV31	206	A6
Griffins Brook Cl BVILLE B30	124	D7
Griffins Brook La BVILLE B30	124	D7
Griffin St DUDS DY2	103	G1
WBROM B70	87	H2
WOLV WV1	3	M6
Griffiths Dr WMBN WV5	64	C1
WNSFLD WV11	37	J4
Griffiths Rd DUDN DY1	66	E7
HHTH/SAND B71	69	G4
SHHTH WV12	38	B1
Griff La NUNW/HART CV10	98	B7
Grigg Gv NFLD/LBR B31	144	C4
Grimley Cl REDW B97	202	D4
Grimley La BRGRVE B60	192	C6
Grimley Rd NFLD/LBR B31	145	H3
Grimley Wy CNCK/NC WS11	16	D1
Grimpits La HWK/WKHTH B38	145	L6
Grimshaw Rd ACGN B27	126	A2
Grimstock Hl CSHL/WTROR B46 *	93	J4
Grimston Cl COVS CV3	156	E3
Grimstone St WOLVN WV10	3	J2
Grindleford Rd PBAR/PBCH B42	71	H6
Grindle Rd COVN CV6	134	D1
Grindsbrook TAM/AM/WIL B77	46	E5
Gristhorpe Rd SLYOAK B29	124	A3
Grizebeck Dr COVW CV5	132	E8
Grizedale RUGBYN/HIL CV21	161	G6
Grizedale Cl RBRY B45	143	M3
Grocott Cl PENK ST19	10	C3
Grocott Rd DARL/WED WS10	67	M1
Grosmont Rd BHTH/HG B12	107	L7
Grosvenor Av		
BFLD/HDSWWD B20	89	G3
FOAKS/STRLY B74	55	K4
KIDD DY10	138	D7
Grosvenor Cl LICHS WS14	21	H7
MGN/WHC B75	57	G4
PENK ST19	10	C4
WOLVN WV10	36	B3
Grosvenor Crs BRGRVE B61	168	F8
Grosvenor Gdns BRGRVE B61	168	F8
Grosvenor Pk		
ETTPK/GDPK/PENN WV4	49	K8
Grosvenor Rd AST/WIT B6	89	M5
BFLD/HDSWWD B20	89	G3
COV CV1		A7
ETTPK/GDPK/PENN WV4	66	C2
LGLYGN/QTN B68	104	E1
RLSS CV31	206	E8
RUGBYN/HIL CV21	187	G2
SEDG DY3	84	B3
SOLH B91	148	D4
WOLVN WV10	36	B3
Grosvenor Sq HLGN/YWD B28	126	D8
Grosvenor St CBHAMNE B4	7	J4
WOLV WV10	3	J3
Grosvenor St West		
LDYWD/EDGR B16	6	A7
Grosvenor Wd BRLYHL DY5	102	B6
Grotto La DUNHL/THL/PER WV6	35	J8
Groucutt Cl BILS/COS WV14	67	G5
Grounds Dr FOAKS/STRLY B74	56	D2
Grounds Rd FOAKS/STRLY B74	56	D2
Grout St WBROM B70	86	D2
Grove Av HALE B63	121	K2
HDSW B21	88	D5
MOS/BIL B13	125	L3
SLYOAK B29 *	124	A4
SOLH B91	148	C4
Grove CI CNCK/NC WS11	17	K8
Grove Cottage Rd BORD B9	108	D3
Grove Cft PBAR/PBCH B42 *	70	D7
Grove Crs BLOX/PEL WS3 *	84	A8
BRLYHL DY5		

Grove Cft RWWCK/WEL CV35	204	C8
Grove Farm Dr MGN/WHC B75	57	K8
Grovefield Crs		
RCOVN/BALC/EX CV7	152	A5
Grove Flds NUNW/HART CV10	81	G5
Grove Gdns BRGRVW B61	168	E7
HDSW B21		B4
Grove Hill Rd HDSW B21	88	D4
Grove House WSL WS1 *	5	G5
Groveland Rd TPTN/OCK DY4	85	G2
Grovelands Crs WOLVN WV10	36	B3
Grove La BFLD/HDSWWD B20	88	D3
BLOX/PEL WS3	25	J4
DUNHL/THL/PER WV6	48	J1
HOCK/TIA B94	175	L8
HRBN B17	123	A1
RCOVN/BALC/EX CV7	115	K6
SMTHWK B66	88	D4
WALM/CURD B76	74	E2
Groveley La NFLD/LBR B31	144	D7
RBRY B45	170	A1
Grove Ms NFLD/LBR B31	144	F5
Grove Pk KGSWFD DY6	83	G5
RWWCK/WEL CV35	204	B7
Grove Pl NUNW/HART CV10	98	B2
RLSS CV31		B8
Grove Rd ALE/KHTH/YWD B14	125	H6
ATHST CV9	63	H6
DOR/KN B93	175	M2
HAG/WOL DY9	120	D1
LGLYGN/QTN B68	105	H4
NUNW/HART CV10	98	B2
SOLH B91	128	A8
SPARK B11	126	A2
Groveside Wy BHTH/HG B12	25	L8
Grove St COV CV1	9	H4
DUDS DY2	85	J5
REDE B98	202	C2
RLSN CV32	206	C5
WOLVN WV10	3	M2
WSNGN B18	106	B1
Grove Ter WSL WS1	5	G5
The Grove BDWTH CV12	116	F2
BLKHTH/ROWR B65	104	A3
BNTWD WS7	18	B5
BRLYHL DY5	102	A4
CSHL/WTROR B46	111	K1
DSYBK/YTR WS5	55	M2
ETTPK/GDPK/PENN WV4	50	C8
FOAKS/STRLY B74	42	B6
GTB/HAM B43	70	C1
HIA/OLT B92	129	L5
LDYWD/EDGR B16 *	106	D3
NFLD/LBR B31	144	F5
RBRY B45	169	L3
STRPT DY13	189	G2
WASH/WDE B8	108	F1
WNSFLD WV11	36	F7
Grove Vale Av GTB/HAM B43	70	A4
Grove Wy FOAKS/STRLY B74	55	K6
Grovewood Dr		
HWK/WKHTH B38	145	J4
Guardhouse Rd COVN CV6	133	M5
Guardian Ct NFLD/LBR B31	144	B2
SOLH B91	149	H2
Guardians Wy NFLD/LBR B31	123	J5
Guernsey Dr CBROM B36	92	F7
Guest Av WNSFLD WV11	36	H6
Guest Gv LOZ/NWT B19	89	G7
Guild Av BLOX/PEL WS3	39	H6
Guild CI LOZ/NWT B19	89	H7
Guildford CI KIDDW DY11	137	L7
Guildford Cft		
CHWD/FDBR/MGN B37	110	D5
Guildford Dr LOZ/NWT B19	89	H7
Guildford St LOZ/NWT B19	89	G7
Guild Rd BRGRVE B60	191	K4
COVN CV6	134	B6
Guilsborough Rd COVS CV3	156	C4
Guinness Cl REDW B97	202	B5
Guiting Cl REDW B97	201	M4
Guiting Rd SLYOAK B29	123	L6
Gulistan Rd RLSN CV32	206	C4
Gullane CI HWK/WKHTH B38	145	H4
The Gullet POL/KGSB/FAZ B78	47	K4
Gullick Wy BNTWD WS7	18	B5
Gulliman's Wy RLSS CV31	207	H1
Gullswood Cl		
ALE/KHTH/YWD B14	146	B3
Gulson Rd COV CV1	9	K4
Gumbleberrys Cl		
WASH/WDE B8	109	G1
Gundry Cl RLSS CV31	206	E6
Gun Hi RCOVN/BALC/EX CV7	96	F5
Gun La COVE CV2	134	C2
Gunmakers Wk LOZ/NWT B19	89	H6
Gunner La RBRY B45	143	H6
Gunner Gv WLSN/HART CV10	57	L7
Gunns Wy HIA/OLT B92	127	H6
Guns La WBROM B70	86	F1
Gunstock Cft FOAKS/STRLY B74	55	J6
Gunter Rd ERDE/BCHGN B24	91	J2
Gunton Av COVS CV3	156	A6
Guphill Av COVW CV5	154	B3
Guphill La COVW CV5	154	B2
Gurnard TAM/AM/WIL B77	46	B7
Gurnard Cl SHHTH WV12	37	M4
Gurney Pl WSLW WS2	38	B1
Gurney Rd WSLW WS2	38	B1
Guthrie Cl LOZ/NWT B19	89	H7
Guthrum Cl		
DUNHL/THL/PER WV6	34	D8
ERDW/GRVHL B23	72	F2
Gutteridge Av COVN CV6	133	L3
The Gutter HAG/WOL DY9	142	C6
Guy Av WOLVN WV10	36	C7
Guy Pl East RLSN CV32	206	D4
Guy Pl West RLSN CV32	206	D4
Guy Rd KNWTH CV8	197	K5
Guy's Cliffe Av RLSN CV32	206	B4
WALM/CURD B76	73	K4
Guy's Cliffe Rd RLSN CV32	206	C5
Guy's Cliffe Ter WWCK CV34	205	K6
Guys Cl CRTAM B79	31	K6
WWCK CV34	205	K5
Guy's Cross Park Rd		
WWCK CV34	205	K5
Guy's La SEDG DY3	83	M3
Guy St RLSN CV32	206	C4
Guy's Wd BRLYHL DY5	102	E5
Gwalia Gv ERDW/GRVHL B23 *	90	D1
Gwendoline Wy ALDR WS9	40	F1
Gypsy La ATHST CV9	63	H5
CSHL/WTROR B46	94	D3
KNWTH CV8	197	K4
POL/KGSB/FAZ B78	61	L4
REDW B97	193	G8

H

Habberley La KIDDW DY11	137	K5

Habberley Rd BEWD DY12	137	J7
BLKHTH/ROWR B65	104	B3
Habberley St KIDDW DY11	138	A7
Habberly Cft SOLH B91	148	F6
Hackett Cl BILS/COS WV14	51	G4
Hackett Dr SMTHWK B66	87	H6
Hackett Rd BLKHTH/ROWR B65	104	C3
Hackett St TPTN/OCK DY4	68	A6
Hackford Rd		
ETTPK/GDPK/PENN WV4	66	D7
Hackmans Gate La		
HAG/WOL DY9	140	F6
Hack St BORD B9	7	L7
Hackwood Rd DARL/WED WS10	68	F3
Hadcroft Gra HAG/WOL DY9	120	B5
Haddock Rd BILS/COS WV14	51	G6
Haddon Crs SHHTH WV12	38	C6
Haddon Cft HALE B63	121	C4
Haddon End COVS CV3	155	H7
RLSN CV32	206	C5
Haddon St COVN CV6	134	E5
Haden Circ BHTH/HG B12	107	K6
Haden CI CDYHTH B64	103	K6
STRBR DY8	101	K3
Haden Cross Dr CDYHTH B64	103	J6
Hadendale CDYHTH B64	103	J6
Haden Hi BDMR/CCFT WV3	2	A1
Haden Hill Rd CDYHTH B64	103	K6
Haden Park Rd CDYHTH B64	103	J6
TPTN/OCK DY4	67	L4
Haden St BHTH/HG B12	107	K6
Haden Wy BHTH/HG B12	107	K7
Hadfield CI ERDE/BCHGN B24	91	H7
RRUGBY CV23	161	L8
Hadfield Wy		
CHWD/FDBR/MGN B37	110	L1
Hadland Rd STETCH B33	109	M4
Hadleigh Cft WALM/CURD B76	73	L7
Hadleigh Rd COVS CV3	181	G2
HLYWD B47	146	E8
Hadley Cl DUDS DY2	103	J1
HLYWD B47	146	E8
Hadley Cft SMTHWK B66	87	L6
Hadley Pl BILS/COS WV14	51	G6
Hadley Rd BILS/COS WV14	51	G6
WSLW WS2	38	D7
Hadley St LGLYGN/QTN B68	104	E1
Hadlow Cft STETCH B33	110	B6
Hadrian Cl RLSN CV32	206	F1
Hadrian Dr CSHL/WTROR B46	93	J4
Hadrians Cl TAM/AM/WIL B77	46	B5
Hadrians Wy RUGBYN/HIL CV21	160	D6
Hadyn		
LGN/SDN/BHAMAIR B26	109	M7
Hadzor Rd LGLYGN/QTN B68	105	H5
Hafren Cl RBRY B45	143	M3
Hafren Wy STRPT DY13	188	D1
Hafton Gv BORD B9	108	B4
Haggar St BKHL/PFLD WV2	50	D7
Hagley Cswy HAG/WOL DY9	120	C6
Hagley Pk HAG/WOL DY9	120	A7
Hagley Park Dr RBRY B45	143	L7
Hagley Rd HAG/WOL DY9	120	D5
HALE B63	121	C5
HALE B63	121	K2
HRBN B17	106	A4
STRBR DY8	119	M2
Hagley Rd West HRBN B17	105	L4
RIDG/WDGT B32	105	E7
Hagley St HALE B63	121	H4
Hailes Park Cl BKHL/PFLD WV2	50	D7
Hailsham Rd ERDW/GRVHL B23	72	D6
Hailstone Cl BLKHTH/ROWR B65	85	L7
Haines Cl TPTN/OCK DY4	68	A5
Haines St WBROM B70	87	H3
Hainfield Dr SOLH B91	128	C4
Hainge Rd OLDBY B69	86	A5
Hainult Cl STRBR DY8	101	H1
Halberton St WSNGN B18	106	C1
Haldon Gv NFLD/LBR B31	144	C6
Hale Ct WSL WS1 *	5	H4
Halecroft Av WNSFLD WV11	37	H4
Hale Gv ERDE/BCHGN B24	91	H1
Hales Crs SMTHWK B66	105	J1
Halescroft Sq NFLD/LBR B31	123	J7
Hales Gdns ERDW/GRVHL B23	72	A6
Hales La SMTHWK B66	105	J1
Halesmere Rd BRGRVW B61	169	G3
CDYHTH B64	103	K5
DUDS DY2	85	G8
RMSLY B62	104	C8
Hales Pk BEWD DY12	162	D2
Hales Rd DARL/WED WS10	68	E1
HALE B63	121	L1
Hales St COV CV1	9	H3
Haley Rd OLDBY B69	86	D5
Halesworth Rd WOLVN WV10	35	K3
Halewood Gv HLGN/YWD B28	126	E6
Haley St SHHTH WV12	38	A8
Halfcot Av HAG/WOL DY9	120	A6
Halford Crs BLOX/PEL WS3	39	K8
Halford La COVN CV6	133	L3
Halford Rd SOLH B91	127	J7
Halford's La SMTHWK B66	87	G1
Halford St CRTAM B79	31	J5
Halfshire La KIDD DY10	139	M4
Halfway La KGSTG B44	71	J7
Halifax Cl COVW CV5	132	C6
Halifax Gv WSNGN B18 *	106	C1
Halifax Rd SHLY B90	147	M5
Haling Cl PENK ST19	10	D5
Haling Rd PENK ST19	10	D5
Haliscombe Gv AST/WIT B6 *	89	J5
Halladale HWK/WKHTH B38	145	K4
Hallam Cl HHTH/SAND B71	87	J1
Hallam Crs WOLVN WV10	36	A1
Hallam Dr HHTH/SAND B71	69	H8
Hallam Rd COVN CV6	133	M2
Hallams Cl KNWTH CV8	157	K8
Hallbridge Cl BLOX/PEL WS3	39	K3
Hallbridge Wy OLDBY B69	85	M3
Hall Brook Rd		
RCOVN/BALC/EX CV7	133	C1
Halichurch Rd DUDS DY2	84	D6
Hall CI KNWTH CV8	180	F7
Hallcourt Cl CNCK/NC WS11	16	C1
Hallcourt Crs CNCK/NC WS11	16	C1
Hallcourt La CNCK/NC WS11	16	C1
Hall Crs HHTH/SAND B71	68	E4
Hallcroft Wy ALDR WS9	41	G8
DOR/KN B93	149	G7

Hall Dale Cl HLGN/YWD B28	126	D8
Hall Dr CHWD/FDBR/MGN B37	110	E6
STRBR DY8		
Hall End DARL/WED WS10	68	D2
NUNW/HART CV10	99	H3
Hallens Dr DARL/WED WS10	68	A2
Hallet Dr BDMR/CCFT WV3	2	B4
Hallewell Rd LDYWD/EDGR B16	106	B3
Hallfields RLSS CV31	207	J8
Hall Gdns ATHST CV9 *	63	L5
Hall Green Rd COV CV2	134	F3
HHTH/SAND B71	69	H4
Hallgreen St BILS/COS WV14	67	J2
Hall Gv BILS/COS WV14	67	C4
RRUGBY CV23	158	C1
Hall Hays Rd BKDE/SHDE B34	92	C6
Hall La ALDR WS9	40	C3
ATHST CV9	63	M5
BILS/COS WV14	66	C4
BLOX/PEL WS3	39	K2
BNTWD WS7	27	J1
COVE CV2	135	K7
GTWY WS6	24	C7
HAG/WOL DY9	120	B7
TPTN/OCK DY4	67	K5
Hall Meadow CNCK/NC WS11	15	M7
HAG/WOL DY9	120	B6
Hallmoor Rd STETCH B33	109	M2
Hallot Cl ERDW/GRVHL B23	72	B2
Halloughton Rd		
FOAKS/STRLY B74	56	C6
Hallowfields REDE B98	202	C4
Hall Park St BILS/COS WV14	50	F7
Hall Rd BFLD/HDSWWD B20	88	E6
CBROM B36	91	L5
RLSN CV32	206	D4
SMTHWK B67	105	J1
WASH/WDE B8	108	C2
Halls Farm La BEWD DY12	137	G5
Hallstead Rd MOS/BIL B13	125	M8
Hall St BILS/COS WV14	51	J3
CDYHTH B64	103	K3
DUDS DY2	85	J3
LGLYGN/QTN B68	86	F8
SEDG DY3	66	F8
STRBR DY8	119	L2
TPTN/OCK DY4	67	J8
WBROM B70	87	G3
WLNHL WV13	51	M4
WNSFLD WV11	37	L1
WSLW WS2	53	H2
WSNGN B18	6	D1
Hall St East DARL/WED WS10	52	A6
Hall St South WBROM B70	87	H5
Hall Wk CSHL/WTROR B46	111	K1
Halsbury Gv KGSTG B44	71	M5
Halstead Gv SOLH B91	148	E5
Halston Rd BNTWD WS7	18	F4
Halton Rd SCFLD/BOLD B73	72	D2
Halton St DUDS DY2	85	G2
Hamar Wy		
CHWD/FDBR/MGN B37	110	E4
Hamberley Ct WSNGN B18	106	B1
Hamble TAM/AM/WIL B77	46	B5
Hamble Cl BRLYHL DY5	83	L7
Hambledon Cl COVEN WV35	35	L3
Hamble Gv		
DUNHL/THL/PER WV6	48	C1
Hamble Rd		
ETTPK/GDPK/PENN WV4	49	G7
PBAR/PBCH B42	70	D4
Hambleton Rd HALE B63	121	H3
Hambletts Rd WBROM B70	86	E2
Hambrook Cl		
DUNHL/THL/PER WV6	35	L8
Hambury Dr		
ALE/KHTH/YWD B14	125	H6
Hamelin St CNCK/NC WS11	16	C2
Hamgreen La REDW B97	201	H8
Hamilton Av HRBN B17	105	L5
RMSLY B62	103	J7
STRBR DY8	101	H7
Hamilton Cl BDWTH CV12	116	A4
BRGRVE B60	191	C4
HEDN WS12	17	K1
SEDG DY3	66	A5
STRBR DY8	101	G3
Hamilton Dr OLDBY B69	86	A3
SLYOAK B29	124	A3
Hamilton Gdns WOLVN WV10	36	D2
Hamilton Lea CNCK/NC WS11	17	L2
Hamilton Rd COV CV2	155	L2
HDSW B21	88	B5
KIDDW DY11	163	M2
REDW B97	202	A5
RLSS CV31	207	J8
SMTHWKW B67	105	J3
TPTN/OCK DY4	68	A7
Hamilton St BLOX/PEL WS3	39	G4
Hamilton Ter RLSN CV32	206	D5
Ham La HAG/WOL DY9	120	B7
KGSWFD DY6	83	J4
Hamlet Cl NUN CV11	99	L4
RUGBYS/DCH CV22	186	B7
Hamlet Gdns HLGN/YWD B28	126	D5
Hamlet Rd HLGN/YWD B28	126	D6
The Hamlet CNCK/NC WS11	17	L8
RWWCK/WEL CV35	197	L6
Hammer Bank HALE B63	103	G6
Hammersley St BDWTH CV12	116	E2
Hammerwich La BNTWD WS7	27	K2
Hammerwich Rd BNTWD WS7	19	H7
Hammond Av WOLVN WV10	36	C5
Hammond Cl NUN CV11	99	J2
Hammond Dr ERDW/GRVHL B23	72	D8
Hammond Rd COVE CV2	9	M1
Hammond Wy STRBR DY8	101	L6
Hampden Retreat		
BHTH/HG B12	107	J7
Hampden Wy		
RUGBYS/DCH CV22	186	A6
Hamps Cl BNTWD WS7	19	H6
Hampshire Cl COVS CV3	156	D6
POL/KGSB/FAZ B78	45	K3
Hampshire Dr EDC B15	106	B7
Hampson Cl SPARK B11	107	M7
Hampstead Gld HALE B63	122	L4
Hampstead Gld HALE B63	122	L4
Hampton Av BRGRVE B60	191	L5
NUNW/HART CV10	98	B4
Hampton CI CRTAM B79	32	A6
REDE B98	203	J3
SCFLD/BOLD B73	72	A3
Hampton Court Rd HRBN B17	105	K4
Hampton Cft		
RWWCK/WEL CV35	204	C6
Hampton Dr FOAKS/STRLY B74	56	F5
Hampton Gdns HAG/WOL DY9	120	A2
Hampton Gn CNCK/NC WS11	16	B6
Hampton Gv BLOX/PEL WS3	39	J2
RLSN CV32	206	B4

Hampton La
RCOVN/BALC/EX CV7 ....130 D5
SOLH B91 ....128 F8
Hampton Rd AST/WIT B6 ....89 H5
COVN CV6 ....134 D7
DOR/KN B93 ....150 A6
ERDW/GRVHL B23 ....90 B1
RWWCK/WEL CV35 ....204 C7
WOLVN WV10 ....35 M4
Hampton Rd BILS/COS WV14 ....66 F5
CNCK/NC WS11 ....16 B6
DUDS DY2 ....84 F8
LOZ/NWT B19 ....6 E1
WWCK CV34 ....205 H7
Hams La WALM/CURD B76 ....75 K8
Hams Rd WASH/WDE B8 ....108 B1
Hamstead Hall Av
BFLD/HDSWWD B20 ....70 C8
Hamstead Hall Rd
BFLD/HDSWWD B20 ....88 C1
Hamstead HI
BFLD/HDSWWD B20 ....88 F4
GTB/HAM B43 ....70 D8
Hamstead Ter DARL/WED WS10 ....68 E3
Hanam Cl MGN/WHC B75 ....57 K7
Hanbury Cl BRGRVE B60 ....191 L5
HALE B63 * 121 K3
Hanbury Crs BDMR/CCFT WV3 .....49 J7
Hanbury Cft ACGN B27 ....127 J2
Hanbury HI STRBR DY8 ....119 L1
Hanbury Rd BDWTH CV12 ....117 C1
BRWNH WS8 ....26 C3
CNCK/NC WS11 ....17 K8
DOR/KN B93 ....175 K2
TAM/AM/WIL B77 ....46 D1
WBROM B70 ....86 E2
Hanch PI WSL WS1 ....5 H6
Hancock Gn TLHL/CAN CV4 ....153 K5
Hancock Rd WASH/WDE B8 ....108 D1
Hancox St LGLYGN/QTN B68 ....104 C3
Handcross Gv COVS CV3 ....154 E8
Handel Ct CNCK/NC WS11 ....17 G3
Handley Gv NFLD/LBR B31 ....144 A3
Handley's Cl KNWTH CV8 ....182 E4
Handley St DARL/WED WS10 ....68 E5
Handsworth Cl HDSW B21 ....88 B6
Handsworth Crs GTB/HAM B43 ......70 E2
Handsworth New Rd
WSNGN B18 ....88 C1
Handsworth Wood Rd
BFLD/HDSWWD B20 ....88 D2
Hanford Cl COVN CV6 ....134 D7
Hanging La NFLD/LBR B31 ....144 C4
Hangleton Dr SPARK B11 ....108 B7
Hangman's La CRTAM B79 ....33 L3
Hanley Cl HALE B63 ....121 J1
Hanley St LOZ/NWT B19 ....6 F1
Hanlith TAM/AM/WIL B77 ....46 E5
Hannaford Wy CNCK/NC WS11 ....16 D3
Hannafore Rd
LDYWD/EDGR B16 ....106 B2
Hannah Rd BILS/COS WV14 ....67 L2
Hanney Hay Rd BNTWD WS7 ....26 F2
Hannon Rd ALE/KHTH/YWD B14 ...125 J8
Hanover Cl AST/WIT B6 ....89 J6
Hanover Ct
DUNHL/THL/PER WV6 ....49 G1
REDE B98 * 202 B5
WSLW WS2 ....52 C4
Hanover Dr VAUX/NECH B7 ....90 D5
Hanover Gdns RLSN CV32 * 206 E4
RUGBYS/HIL 186 F1
Hanover PI CNCK/NC WS11 ....17 G4
Hanover Rd BLKHTH/ROWR B65 ...104 A1
Hanover St BRGRVE B61 ....191 K3
Hans Cl COV CV1 ....9 M1
Hansell Dr DOR/KN B93 ....175 J3
Hansom Rd RIDG/WDGT B32 ....105 G8
Hanson Cv HIA/OLT B92 ....109 K8
Hanson's Bridge Rd
ERDE/BCHGN B24 ....73 K8
Hanson Wy COVN CV6 ....116 E8
Hanstone Rd STRPT DY13 ....188 D4
Hanwell Cl WALM/CURD B76 ....75 M6
Hanwood Cl BHTH/HG B12 ....107 J5
COVW CV5 ....153 H1
Hanworth Cl RLSN CV32 ....206 F2
Hanworth Rd WWCK CV34 ....205 H5
Harald Cl DUNHL/THL/PER WV6 ......34 C1
Harbeck Av KGSTG B44 ....71 K5
Harborrow Cl HAG/WOL DY9 ....119 J3
Harbet Dr BHAMNEC B40 ....129 J1
Harbinger Rd HWK/WKHTH B38 ....145 M3
Harborne La SLYOAK B29 ....124 E5
Harborne Park Rd HRBN B17 ....106 A4
Harborne Rd EDG B15 ....106 C7
SMTHWKW B67 ....105 H4
Harborough Dr ALDR WS9 ....40 E8
CBROM B36 ....92 B4
Harborough Rd COVN CV6 ....133 M3
RUGBYN/HIL CV21 ....160 C6
Harborough Wk HAG/WOL DY9 .....119 M3
Harbours CI BRGRVE B60 ....191 H5
Harbours HI HAG/WOL DY9 ....142 C7
Harbury Cl REDE B98 ....203 H4
WALM/CURD B76 ....73 H7
Harbury La BHTH/HG B12 ....107 H8
Harby Cl CHWD/FDBR/MGN B37 ...110 F5
Harcourt COVS CV3 ....156 C8
Harcourt Dr DUDN DY1 ....84 B3
FOAKS/STRLY B74 ....56 C1
Harcourt Gdns NUN CV11 ....99 C2
Harcourt Rd CDYHTH B64 ....103 K5
DARL/WED WS10 ....68 C3
ERDW/GRVHL B23 ....72 C8
Harden Cl BLOX/PEL WS3 ....39 J6
Harden Gv BLOX/PEL WS3 ....39 H6
Harden Manor Ct HALE B63 * 122 A2
Harden Rd BLOX/PEL WS3 ....39 H6
Harden V HALE B63 * 103 J8
Hardie Gn CNCK/NC WS11 ....16 D2
Harding St BILS/COS WV14 ....67 H4
Hardingwood La
RCOVN/BALC/EX CV7 ....113 J2
Hardon Rd
ETTPK/GDPK/PENN WV4 ....65 H2
Hardware St WBROM B70 ....87 H1
Hardwick Cl COVW CV5 ....153 L1
Hardwick Ct CRTAM B79 ....32 L1
Hardwick Rd CDYHTH B64 ....103 L6
Hardwicke Wy HAG/WOL DY9 ....102 B9
Hardwick Rd FOAKS/STRLY B74 * ...55 K3
LGN/SDN/BHAMAIR B26 ....111 J3
Hardwike Wk
ALE/KHTH/YWD B14 ....146 A3
Hardwyn Cl COVS CV3 ....156 K4
Hardy Av KIDD DY10 ....138 E7
Hardy Cl NUNW/HART CV10 ....97 L1
RUGBYS/DCH CV22 ....186 A3
Hardy Sq BKHL/PFLD WV2 * 50 D7

Hare & Hounds La
NUNW/HART CV10 ....98 E3
Harebell TAM/AM/WIL B77 ....46 E1
Harebell Cl DSYBK/YTR WS5 ....69 L2
HEDN WV12 ....22 E1
WOLVN WV10 ....22 E1
Harebell Crs DUDN DY1 ....84 E1
Harebell Gdns
HWK/WKHTH B38 ....145 K5
Harebell Wy RRUGBY CV23 ....161 K5
Harefield La NUNW/HART CV10 ....98 D5
Harefield Rd COVE CV2 ....155 M2
NUN CV11 ....99 G1
Hare Gv NFLD/LBR B31 ....144 B2
Harefield Cl REDW B97 ....202 B3
Hare St BILS/COS WV14 ....51 K8
Harewell Dr MGN/WHC B75 ....57 J7
Harewood Av DARL/WED WS10 ....69 G2
GTB/HAM B43 ....70 A3
Harewood Cl HLGN/YWD B28 ....126 C8
Harewood Rd COVN CV5 ....154 A2
Harford St LOZ/NWT B19 ....6 D1
Hargate La HHTH/SAND B71 ....87 C1
Harger Ct KNWTH CV8 ....197 K1
Hargrave Cl COVS CV3 ....156 K4
CSHL/WTROR B46 ....92 F7
Hargrave Rd SHLY B90 ....147 H5
Hargreave Cl WALM/CURD B76 ....35 K6
Hargreaves St BKHL/PFLD WV2 ......50 D6
Harington Rd COVN CV6 ....133 L8
Harland Cl BRGRVW B61 ....191 K2
Harland Rd FOAKS/STRLY B74 ....56 C2
Harlech Cl KNWTH CV8 ....180 A8
OLDBY B69 ....85 L4
RIDG/WDGT B32 ....122 E7
Harlech Rd SHHTH WV12 ....38 A7
KIDDW DY11 ....164 C3
Harleston Rd KGSTG B44 ....71 K5
Harley Cl BRWNH WS8 ....26 B4
Harley Dr BILS/COS WV14 ....66 F1
Harley St COVE CV2 ....155 L2
Harlow Gv HLGN/YWD B28 ....126 E7
Harlstones Cl STRBR DY8 ....101 L6
Harlyn Cl BILS/COS WV14 ....67 L3
Harman Rd CSCFLD/WYGN B72 ......72 F4
Harmar Cl COVW CV5 ....205 H4
Harmer Cl COVE CV2 ....135 L6
Harmer St WSNGN B18 ....88 E8
Harmon Rd STRBR DY8 ....101 C8
Harmony Ct NUNW/HART CV10 ....98 F3
Harnall Cl SHLY B90 ....148 C6
Harnall La East COV CV1 ....9 H1
Harnall La West COV CV1 ....8 F1
Harnall Rw COV CV1 ....9 K4
Harness Cl DSYBK/YTR WS5 ....69 J1
Harold Davies Dr RUGBY CV21 ....188 D3
Harold Rd COVE CV2 ....156 B3
LDYWD/EDGR B16 ....106 D4
SMTHWKW B67 ....105 J2
Harold St NUN CV11 ....99 G2
Harold Ter LOZ/NWT B19 * 89 C5
Harpenden Dr COVW CV5 ....132 E8
Harper Av WNSFLD WV11 ....37 G6
Harper Rd BILS/COS WV14 ....51 H7
COV CV1 ....9 J4
Harpers La ATHST CV9 ....63 L7
Harper St WLNHL WV13 ....51 L3
Harpur Cl RUSH/SHEL WS4 ....53 L1
Harpur Rd RUSH/SHEL WS4 ....53 L1
Harrier Rd ACGN B27 ....127 K3
Harriers Gn KIDD DY10 ....138 F5
Harriet Cl BRLYHL DY5 ....83 M8
Harringay Dr STRBR DY8 ....119 J2
Harringay Rd LICH WS13 ....71 K3
Harrington Wk LICH WS13 ....20 F1
Harris Cl BLOX/PEL WS3 ....39 C4
GTWY WS6 ....24 B4
RUGBYN/HIL CV21 ....187 M5
Harrison Crs BDWTH CV12 ....116 E3
Harrison Rd CNCK/NC WS11 ....16 C6
ERDE/BCHGN B24 ....90 D1
FOAKS/STRLY B74 ....42 C4
REDW B97 ....202 A3
RUSH/SHEL WS4 ....40 A3
STRBR DY8 ....101 L4
Harrison's Fold DUDS DY2 ....85 G8
Harrison's Pleck BDWTH CV12 ....116 E3
Harrisons La PENK ST19 ....14 C4
Harrisons Pleck BILS/COS WV14 ...125 K2
Harrison's Rd EDG B15 ....106 C7
Harrison St BLOX/PEL WS3 ....39 C4
Harrison Wy RLSS CV31 ....206 D8
Harris Rd COVS CV3 ....155 M3
WWCK CV34 ....205 G5
Harrold Av BLKHTH/ROWR B65 ......104 C4
Harrold Rd BLKHTH/ROWR B65 ......104 C2
Harrold St TPTN/OCK DY4 ....68 A6
Harrold Ter LOZ/NWT B19 ....89 C5
Harrop Wy STRBR DY8 ....101 L5
Harrowby Dr TPTN/OCK DY4 ....85 L1
Harrowby PI WLNHL WV13 ....52 A4
Harrowby Rd BILS/COS WV14 ....67 L1
WOLVN WV10 ....35 L2
Harrow Cl BRGRVE B60 ....191 J7
COVN CV6 ....134 E3
HAG/WOL DY9 ....119 J2
Harrowfield Rd STECH B33 ....109 J1
Harrow Rd KGSWFD DY6 ....84 B3
SLYOAK B29 ....124 D2
Harrow St WOLV WV1 ....2 D1
Harry Perks St WLNHL WV13 ....51 L2
Harry Rose Rd COVE CV2 ....156 C2
Harry Truslove Cl COVN CV6 ....133 L6
Harry Weston Rd COVS CV3 ....156 K4
Hart Cl RUGBYN/HIL CV21 ....187 M5
Hart Dr SCFLD/BOLD B73 ....72 E4
Hartfield Crs ACGN B27 ....126 E4
Hartford Cl HRBN B17 ....105 J4
Hartford Rd BRGRVE B60 ....191 M4
Hartill Rd
ETTPK/GDPK/PENN WV4 ....65 H2
Hartill St WLNHL WV13 ....51 M5
Hattersley Gv SPARK B11 ....126 E2
Hatton Cl RWWCK/WEL CV35 ....204 B3
Hatton Crs WNSFLD WV11 ....36 D8
Hatton Gdns PBAR/PBCH B42 ....70 B6
Hatton Rd BDMR/CCFT WV3 * 15 K2
CNCK/NC WS11 ....15 L4
Hattons Gv CDSL WV8 ....34 F3
Hatton St BILS/COS WV14 ....67 L4
Haughton Rd
BFLD/HDSWWD B20 ....89 G8
Haunch La MOS/BIL B13 ....125 K7
WALM/CURD B76 ....75 L5
Haunchwood Dr
WALM/CURD B76 ....73 K6
Haunchwood Park Dr
NUNW/HART CV10 ....97 J1
Haunchwood Rd
NUNW/HART CV10 ....98 B3
Havacre La BILS/COS WV14 ....67 J1

Hartleyburn TAM/AM/WIL B77 ....46 E5
Hartley Dr ALDR WS9 ....54 F1
Hartley Gv KGSTG B44 ....71 M2
Hartley PI EDG B15 ....71 L2
Hartley Rd KGSTG B44 ....71 J2
Harton Wy ALE/KHTH/YWD B14 .....125 C8
Hartopp Rd FOAKS/STRLY B74 ....56 D4
WASH/WDE B8 ....108 A2
Hartridge Wk COVW CV5 ....153 M1
Harts Cl HRBN B17 ....106 B7
Harts Green Rd HRBN B17 ....105 L8
Hartshill Rd BKDE/SHDE B34 ....91 L7
HIA/OLT B92 ....127 H3
Hartshorn St BILS/COS WV14 ....51 H8
Hartside Cl HALE B63 ....121 G3
Hartslade LICHS WS14 ....21 J7
Harts Rd WASH/WDE B8 ....90 C8
Hart St WSL WS1 ....4 F6
Hartswell Dr MOS/BIL B13 ....125 K7
Hartwell Cl SOLH B91 ....148 F4
Hartwell La GTWY WS6 ....24 C2
Hartwell Rd ERDE/BCHGN B24 ....90 F3
Harvard Cl DUDN DY1 ....84 D1
Harvard Rd HIA/OLT B92 ....127 M1
Harvest Cl BRGRVE B60 ....124 F8
BVILLE B30 ....66 C3
SEDG DY3 ....66 C8
Harvesters Cl COVS CV3 ....156 E3
FOAKS/STRLY B74 ....55 J3
Harvesters Rd SHHTH WV12 ....38 B8
Harvester Wy KGSWFD DY6 ....82 E5
Harvest Fields Wy
MGN/WHC B75 ....57 J2
Harvest Gdns LGLYGN/QTN B68 ....104 E1
Harvest Hill Cl RLSS CV31 * 207 G3
Harvest Hill La COVW CV5 ....132 B3
Harvest Rd BLKHTH/ROWR B65 .....103 L1
SMTHWKW B67 ....105 H2
Harvey Cl COVW CV5 ....132 E6
Harvey Ct STECH B33 * 110 B2
Harvey Dr MGN/WHC B75 ....57 J7
Harvey Rd
LGN/SDN/BHAMAIR B26 ....109 H6
WSLW WS2 ....38 F1
Harvills Hawthorn WBROM B70 ....68 D6
Harvine Wk STRBR DY8 ....119 J2
Harvington Cl KIDDW DY11 ....193 H5
REDW B97 ....193 M8
Harvington Dr SHLY B90 ....148 F7
Harvington Hall La KIDD DY10 ....145 M3
Harvington Rd BILS/COS WV14 ....66 F4
BRGRVE B60 ....191 L5
HALE B63 ....121 J7
LGLYGN/QTN B68 ....104 E5
SLYOAK B29 ....123 L5
Harvington Wy WALM/CURD B76 ......73 K8
Harwell Cl CRTAM B79 ....32 A6
Harwin Cl DUNHL/THL/PER WV6 ....35 K6
Harwood Drive
TAM/AM/WIL B77 ....60 B1
Harwood Gv SHLY B90 ....148 A5
Harwood Rd WBROM B70 ....86 F2
Hasbury Cl HALE B63 ....121 J7
Hasbury Rd RIDG/WDGT B32 ....122 E5
Haselbech Rd COVS CV3 ....156 D4
Haselbury Cnr
NUNW/HART CV10 ....98 D1
Haseley Cl REDE B98 ....203 J5
RLSS CV31 ....206 F8
Haseley Rd COVE CV2 ....135 G4
HDSW B21 ....88 C6
SOLH B91 ....127 J7
Haselor Rd SCFLD/BOLD B73 ....72 C4
Haselour Rd
CHWD/FDBR/MGN B37 ....92 D3
Hasilwood Sq COVS CV3 ....155 M3
Haskell St WSL WS1 ....5 J5
Haslucks Cft SHLY B90 ....147 L2
Haslucks Green Rd SHLY B90 ....147 J5
Hassop Rd PBAR/PBCH B42 ....70 C4
Hastang Flds RLSS CV31 ....207 C8
Hastings Rd BRGRVE B60 ....191 J6
COVE CV2 ....155 L1
ERDW/GRVHL B23 ....71 M6
Haswell Rd HALE B63 ....121 H4
Hatcham Rd KGSTG B44 ....72 A3
Hatchett St LOZ/NWT B19 ....89 J8
Hatchford Av WNSFLD WV11 ....128 A2
Hatchford Brook Rd
HIA/OLT B92 ....128 A2
Hatch Heath Cl WMBN WV5 ....64 D5
Hateley Dr
ETTPK/GDPK/PENN WV4 ....66 C1
REDE B98 ....203 J4
Hatfield Cl ERDW/GRVHL B23 ....72 B6
REDE B98 ....203 J4
Hatfield Rd HAG/WOL DY9 ....120 A1
LOZ/NWT B19 ....89 H5
Hathaway Cl
RCOVN/BALC/EX CV7 ....151 M6
WLNHL WV13 ....51 K5
Hathaway Dr NUN CV11 ....99 J3
WWCK CV34 ....205 J3
Hathaway Ms STRBR DY8 * 101 J2
SHLY B90 ....147 M4
Hathaway Rd MGN/WHC B75 ....56 C2
GTWY WS6 ....24 A1
SHLY B90 ....147 M4
TLHL/CAN CV4 ....153 H4
Hatherden Dr WALM/CURD B76 ....73 L3
Hatherell Rd RLSS CV31 ....207 J8
Hathersage Rd PBAR/PBCH B42 ......70 B6
Hatherton Cft CNCK/NC WS11 ....16 A4
Hatherton Gdns WOLVN WV10 ....35 K4
Hatherton Gv SLYOAK B29 ....123 K4
Hatherton PI ALDR WS9 ....54 D4
Hatherton Rd BILS/COS WV14 ....51 K7
CNCK/NC WS11 ....15 M4
PENK ST19 ....10 M4
Hatherton St GTWY WS6 ....24 A1
WSL WS1 ....4 F4
Hatters Ct BDWTH CV12 ....117 C3

Havefield Av LICHS WS14 ....21 H6
Havelock Cl BDMR/CCFT WV3 ....49 J6
Havelock Rd BFLD/HDSWWD B20 ....89 C3
SPARK B11 ....126 C1
Haven Cft BFLD/HDSWWD B20 ....70 B5
Haven Cl RUGBYS/DCH CV22 * 186 C2
Haven Dr ACGN B27 ....126 F2
The Haven ALE/KHTH/YWD B14 ....147 H1
BKHL/PFLD WV2 ....2 F9
STRBR DY8 ....101 H3
WNSFLD WV11 ....51 H1
Haverford Dr RBRY B45 ....143 M7
Havergal Wk HALE B63 ....120 F1
Haverhill Cl BLOX/PEL WS3 ....38 E2
Hawbridge Cl SHLY B90 ....148 F7
Hawbush Rd BLOX/PEL WS3 ....39 J7
BRLYHL DY5 ....101 L3
Hawcroft Gv BKDE/SHDE B34 ....92 A7
Hawes Cl WSL WS1 ....5 K7
Hawes La BLKHTH/ROWR B65 ....103 M1
Hawes Rd WSL WS1 ....53 M1
Haweswater Dr KGSWFD DY6 ....83 H7
Hawfield Cl OLDBY B69 ....86 A6
Hawfield Gv CSCFLD/WYGN B72 .....73 C6
Hawfield Rd OLDBY B69 ....86 A6
Hawfinch TAM/AM/WIL B77 ....60 B4
Hawford Av KIDD DY10 ....164 E8
Hawford Av KIDD DY10 ....138 E8
Hawk Cl NUN CV11 ....99 M5
Hawker Dr CVALE B35 ....91 K3
Hawkesbury Cl REDE B98 ....195 H8
Hawkesbury La COVE CV2 ....117 L7
Hawkesbury Rd SHLY B90 ....147 K4
Hawkes Cl SLYOAK B29 ....124 E5
Hawkesford Cl CBROM B36 ....92 A6
FOAKS/STRLY B74 ....56 F4
Hawkesford Rd STECH B33 ....110 B2
Hawkeshead RUGBYN/HIL CV21 ....161 H6
Hawkes La HHTH/SAND B71 ....68 E6
Hawkesley Crs NFLD/LBR B31 ....144 D5
Hawkesley Dr NFLD/LBR B31 ....144 D5
Hawkesley End
HWK/WKHTH B38 ....145 H5
Hawkesley Mill La
NFLD/LBR B31 ....144 D3
Hawkesley Rd DUDN DY1 ....84 D5
Hawkesley Sq COVW CV5 ....132 E3
Hawkesmoor Dr DOR/KN B93 ....21 H5
Hawkes St BORD B10 ....68 D7
Hawkestone Crs WBROM B70 ....68 D7
Hawkestone Rd SLYOAK B29 ....123 L6
Hawkeswell Cl HIA/OLT B92 ....127 J5
Hawkeswell Dr KGSWFD DY6 ....83 D7
Hawkeswell La
CSHL/WTROR B46 ....111 M2
Hawkesworth Dr KNWTH CV8 ....179 L7
Hawkesyard Rd
ERDE/BCHGN B24 ....90 C4
Hawkhurst Rd
ALE/KHTH/YWD B14 ....146 D3
Hawkins Dr CVALE B35 ....91 L1
Hawkins Cl DIG/EDG B5 ....107 J3
LICH WS13 ....20 F3
RUGBYS/DCH CV22 ....186 C4
Hawkins Cft TPTN/OCK DY4 ....85 L2
Hawkins Rd CNCK/NC WS11 ....24 A1
COVW CV5 ....96 A6
Hawkins St WBROM B70 ....68 F3
Hawkley Cl WOLV WV1 ....50 F3
Hawkmoor Gdns
HWK/WKHTH B38 ....145 L5
Hawks Cl GTWY WS6 ....24 B8
Hawkshead Dr DOR/KN B93 ....149 K7
Hawkside TAM/AM/WIL B77 ....46 F5
Hawkswood Dr
DARL/WED WS10 ....67 M2
RCOVN/BALC/EX CV7 ....151 M6
Hawkswood Gv
ALE/KHTH/YWD B14 ....146 D3
Hawksworth Dr COV CV1 ....8 B3
Hawkyard Ct CNCK/NC WS11 ....16 E1
Hawlands RUGBYN/HIL CV21 ....161 H1
Hawley Cl RUSH/SHEL WS4 ....53 K1
Hawnby Gv WALM/CURD B76 ....73 L3
Hawne Cl HALE B63 ....103 J7
The Hawnelands HALE B63 * 103 K8
Hawne La HALE B63 ....103 J7
Hawksford Crs WOLVN WV10 ....36 B6
Hawthorn Av ATHST CV9 ....24 E4
GTWY WS6 ....24 E4
Hawthorn Brook Wy
ERDW/GRVHL B23 ....72 C5
Hawthorn Cl BORD B9 ....107 M4
ERDW/GRVHL B23 ....72 D4
LICH WS13 ....21 H5
Hawthorn Coppice
HAG/WOL DY9 ....119 L7
Hawthorn Crs BEWD DY12 ....162 C3
Hawthorn Cft LGLYGN/QTN B68 .....105 H6
Hawthorne Av CRTAM B79 ....31 L5
Hawthorne Cl
RCOVN/BALC/EX CV7 ....96 F5
Hawthorne Cl KNWTH CV8 ....183 L1
Hawthorne Crs BNTWD WS7 ....18 E4
Hawthorne Dr HLYWD B47 ....146 F4
Hawthorne Gv SEDG DY3 ....84 B3
Hawthorne La CDSL WV8 ....34 D4
Hawthorne Rd BKHL/PFLD WV2 ....50 B7
BVILLE B30 ....66 C5
CBROM B36 ....92 C6
DUDN DY1 ....85 G1
EDG B15 ....24 C1
GTWY WS6 ....24 C1
HALE B63 ....121 J6
HEDN WS12 ....12 B1
HEDN WS12 ....37 K2
SHHTH WV12 ....38 B2
WNSFLD WV11 ....51 H3
Hawthorne Ter
NUNW/HART CV10 ....80 D8
Hawthorn HI ATHST CV9 ....63 J3
Hawthorn Kinver KINVER DY7 ....118 A2
Hawthorn Gv KIDDW DY11 ....137 L3
LOZ/NWT B19 * 6 D8
Hawthorn La TLHL/CAN CV4 ....153 J3
Hawthorn Pk
BFLD/HDSWWD B20 ....88 D8
Hawthorn PI WSLW WS2 ....52 D8
Hawthorn Rd BRGRVW B61 ....168 E8
BRLYHL DY5 ....102 C5
CSCFLD/WYGN B72 ....73 G4
DARL/WED WS10 ....68 D8
DSYBK/YTR WS5 ....55 L6
FOAKS/STRLY B74 ....55 J6
KGSTG B44 ....71 L4
REDW B97 ....194 A8
TPTN/OCK DY4 ....68 A8
WOLVN WV10 ....50 F5

The Hawthorns KIDD DY10 * 138 E8
MOS/BIL B13 * 125 K2
POL/KGSB/FAZ B78 ....60 A6
Hawthorn Wy
RUGBYS/DCH CV22 ....185 M4
Haxby Av BKDE/SHDE B34 ....91 L7
The Haybarn WALM/CURD B76 ....73 L4
Haybridge Av STRBR DY8 ....119 K8
Haybridge Dr SPARK B11 ....126 D1
Haycock PI DARL/WED WS10 ....52 A6
Haycroft Av WASH/WDE B8 ....90 C4
Haycroft Dr MGN/WHC B75 ....56 E1
Haydn Sanders Sq WSL WS1 ....4 E7
Haydock Cl CBROM B36 ....91 K5
COVN CV6 ....133 G6
DUNHL/THL/PER WV6 ....35 M8
TAM/AM/WIL B77 ....60 B1
Haydock Rd BRGRVW B61 ....168 F4
Haydon Cl DOR/KN B93 ....175 K3
Haydon Cft STECH B33 ....109 L2
Haye House Gv CBROM B36 ....91 J6
Haye La STUD B80 ....203 L4
Hayes Cl RUGBYN/HIL CV21 ....161 H6
LGLYGN/QTN B68 ....87 H8
Hayes Crs HWK/WKHTH B38 ....145 J6
Hayes Green Rd
RCOVN/BALC/EX CV7 ....116 D4
Hayes Gv ERDE/BCHGN B24 ....73 H7
Hayes La HAG/WOL DY9 ....102 E2
RCOVN/BALC/EX CV7 ....116 D5
Hayes Meadow
WALM/CURD B76 ....73 H6
Hayes Rd KIDDW DY11 ....137 M2
LGLYGN/QTN B68 ....87 H8
NUNW/HART CV10 ....86 H1
Hayes St WBROM B70 ....86 F2
The Hayes HAG/WOL DY9 ....102 E8
NFLD/LBR B31 ....145 G6
SHHTH WV12 ....37 M7
Hayes View LICH WS13 ....20 D4
Hayes Wy CNCK/NC WS11 ....16 E4
HEDN WS12 ....17 C4
Hayfield Cl MOS/BIL B13 ....125 M3
Hayfield HI RUGE WS15 ....18 D1
Hayfield Rd MOS/BIL B13 ....125 M3
Hayford Cl REDE B98 ....194 E8
Hay Green Cl BVILLE B30 ....102 B3
Hay Green La BVILLE B30 ....124 A7
Hay Hall Rd SPARK B11 ....108 D8
Hayland Rd ERDW/GRVHL B23 ....72 C7
Hay La COV CV1 ....9 G5
SHLY B90 ....148 A7
Hayle TAM/AM/WIL B77 ....46 B3
Hayle Av WWCK CV34 ....205 K4
Hayle Cl HWK/WKHTH B38 ....145 M3
NUN CV11 ....81 J8
Hayley Green Rd
RIDG/WDGT B32 ....122 F5
Hayley Park Rd HALE B63 ....121 C5
Hayling Cl RBRY B45 ....143 K4
Hayling Gv BKHL/PFLD WV2 ....49 M7
Hayloft Cl BRGRVE B60 ....191 J7
The Haylofts HALE B63 ....121 G4
Haymoor LICHS WS14 ....21 J6
Haynes Cl BRGRVE B61 ....168 F5
Haynes La DSYBK/YTR WS5 ....69 M1
Haynestone Rd COVN CV6 ....133 J7
Haynes Wy RUGBYN/HIL CV21 ....160 D5
Hay Pk DIG/EDG B5 ....107 H1
Haypits Cl HHTH/SAND B71 ....87 J2
Hayrick Dr KGSWFD DY6 ....82 F6
Hay Rd YDLY B25 ....108 E6
Hayseech CDYHTH B64 ....103 L6
Hayseech Rd HALE B63 ....103 L5
The Hays Kent's Moat
LGN/SDN/BHAMAIR B26 ....109 L4
Hayton Gv TLHL/CAN CV4 ....153 K6
Haytor Av ALE/KHTH/YWD B14 ....125 H8
Haytor Ri COV CV1 ....35 K5
Hayton Cl COVEN WV9 ....35 K5
Hayward Cl RWWCK/WEL CV35 ....204 D7
Hayward Rd MGN/WHC B75 ....57 G6
Haywards Cl BLOX/PEL WS3 ....39 K2
ERDW/GRVHL B23 ....72 C8
Hayward St BILS/COS WV14 ....66 F5
Haywharf Rd BRLYHL DY5 ....83 M7
Haywood Dr
DUNHL/THL/PER WV6 ....49 C1
RMSLY B62 ....104 C1
Haywood Rd STECH B33 ....110 D3
Haywood's Farm
HHTH/SAND B71 ....69 K3
Hayworth Cl CRTAM B79 ....31 K5
Hayworth Rd LICH WS13 ....21 H5
Hazel Av DARL/WED WS10 ....68 E1
SCFLD/BOLD B73 ....72 A4
Hazelbank HWK/WKHTH B38 ....145 J3
Hazelbeach Rd WASH/WDE B8 ....90 D4
Hazelbeech Rd WBROM B70 ....86 F3
Hazel Cl NUNW/HART CV10 ....79 L6
RLSN CV32 ....206 E3
Hazel Cft
CHWD/FDBR/MGN B37 ....110 F4
NFLD/LBR B31 ....144 E2
Hazelcroft POL/KGSB/FAZ B78 ....60 A6
Hazeldene STRPT DY13 ....189 G2
Hazeldene Gv AST/WIT B6 * 89 J5
Hazeldene Rd HALE B63 ....121 J3
STECH B33 ....110 B6
Hazel Dr HEDN WS12 ....13 L7
HLYWD B47 ....146 F7
Hazeley Cl HRBN B17 ....105 K6
Hazel Gdns ACGN B27 * 127 C1
CDSL WV8 ....21 H3
Hazelgarth TAM/AM/WIL B77 ....46 E5
Hazel Gv BDWTH CV12 ....117 H2
BILS/COS WV14 ....51 G7
HOCK/TIA B94 ....175 J7
LICHS WS14 ....21 J6
STRBR DY8 ....119 G2
WBROM B70 ....87 G4
WMBN WV5 ....64 E6
Hazelhurst Rd
ALE/KHTH/YWD B14 ....125 J6
CBROM B36 ....92 C6
Hazel La GTWY WS6 ....24 F5
Hazell Wy NUNW/HART CV10 ....98 A4
Hazelmere Dr BDMR/CCFT WV3 ....48 E4
BNTWD WS7 ....26 D1
Hazelmere Rd HLGN/YWD B28 ....126 D5
Hazeloak Rd SHLY B90 ....147 L6
Hazel Rd BDMR/CCFT WV3 ....49 J6
COVN CV6 ....134 C4
DUDN DY1 ....85 G3
KGSWFD DY6 ....83 J8
NUNW/HART CV10 ....79 M6
RBRY B45 ....143 K7
REDW B97 ....194 A8
TPTN/OCK DY4 ....68 A6
Hazelton Cl BRGRVE B60 ....169 G5
SOLH B91 ....148 F4
Hazelton Rd BRGRVE B60 ....168 F4
Hazeltree Cft ACGN B27 ....126 F3
Hazeltree Gv DOR/KN B93 ....175 J2

Hazelville Gv HLGN/YWD B28 126 E7
Hazelville Rd HLGN/YWD B28 126 E7
Hazelwell Crs BVILLE B30 124 F7
Hazelwell Dr
ALE/KHTH/YWD B14 125 H7
Hazelwell Fordrough
BVILLE B30 124 F6
Hazelwell La BVILLE B30 124 E6
Hazelwell Rd BVILLE B30 124 E7
Hazelwood Cl GTWY WS6 24 B3
KIDDW DY11 163 L1
Hazelwood Dr WNSFLD WV11 36 E8
Hazelwood Gv SHHTH WV12 38 B8
Hazelwood Rd ACGN B27 126 F3
DUDN DY1 66 D8
FOAKS/STRLY B74 55 H4
Hazlemere Cl COVW CV5 153 M1
Hazlemere Dr FOAKS/STRLY B74 56 E4
Hazlemere Gv CNCK/NC WS11 15 M5
Hazlitt Gv BVILLE B30 145 H1
Headborough Rd COVE CV2 134 E8
Headingley Rd HDSW B21 88 C3
Headington Av COVN CV6 133 L3
Headland Dr WASH/WDE B8 90 B8
Headland Rd BDMR/CCFT WV3 48 D4
The Headlands COVW CV5 154 B1
FOAKS/STRLY B74 56 A2
Headless Cross Dr REDW B97 202 B4
Headley Cft HWK/WKHTH B38 145 H5
Headley Heath La
HWK/WKHTH B38 145 M6
Headley Ri SHLY B90 148 B3
Headway Rd WOLVN WV10 36 A2
Heale Cl HALE B63 102 E6
Healey TAM/AM/WIL B77 46 C3
Healey Cl RUGBYN/HIL CV21 161 G6
Health Centre Rd
TLHL/CAN CV4 180 A1
Heanley La ATHST CV9 61 H6
ATHST CV9 77 H1
Heanor Cft AST/WIT B6 89 M5
Heantun Ri WOLV WV1 * 2 E1
Heantun Rw WNSFLD WV11 * 37 M3
Hearsall Common COVW CV5 154 C3
Hearsall La COVW CV5 154 D3
Heartland Ms
BLKHTH/ROWR B65 103 M3
Heartlands Pkwy VAUX/NECH B7 90 A8
Heartlands Pl WASH/WDE B8 108 C1
Heart of England Wy
CSHL/WTROR B46 76 C8
CSHL/WTROR B46 95 J8
DOR/KN B93 176 F7
KNWTH CV8 177 H2
LICH WS13 19 M4
POL/KGSB/FAZ B78 45 K8
POL/KGSB/FAZ B78 76 C1
RCOVN/BALC/EX CV7 131 L2
WALM/CURD B76 59 L7
Heath Acres DARL/WED WS10 68 A1
Heath Av BDWTH CV12 116 C4
LICHS WS14 30 A2
Heathbank Dr HEDN WS12 12 A7
Heath Bridge Cl BLOX/PEL WS3 39 L5
Heathbrook Av KGSWFD DY6 82 F6
Heathcliff Rd DUDS DY2 85 K6
SPARK B11 126 D1
Heath Cl ALDR WS9 27 J8
BRGRVE B60 191 J7
BVILLE B30 124 B8
TPTN/OCK DY4 67 M8
Heathcote Av SOLH B91 148 C2
Heathcote La WWCK CV34 205 L8
Heathcote Rd BVILLE B30 124 E8
Heathcote St COVN CV6 133 L6
Heath Crs COVE CV2 134 D8
Heath Cft NFLD/LBR B31 144 E6
Heath Croft Rd MGN/WHC B75 57 G4
Heath Dr KIDD DY10 138 F4
Heath End Rd HAG/WOL DY9 142 A6
NUNW/HART CV10 98 C3
Heather Av DSYBK/YTR WS5 69 M1
Heather Cl CBROM B36 92 E5
LICH WS13 21 H4
NUNW/HART CV10 98 D2
RUGBYS/DCH CV22 186 C4
WNSFLD WV11 37 J8
Heather Court Gdns
FOAKS/STRLY B74 56 E5
Heather Cft KGSTG B44 71 K4
Heather Dl MOS/BIL B13 125 G3
Heather Dr BDWTH CV12 116 C3
HEDN WS12 12 B8
RBRY B45 143 K7
Heather Gv SHHTH WV12 52 C1
SOLH B91 128 C7
Heatherleigh Rd CBROM B36 92 D5
Heather Ms HEDN WS12 12 E5
Heather Rd BLOX/PEL WS3 38 D5
COVE CV2 134 F3
COVS CV3 157 G6
DUDN DY1 85 G1
GTB/HAM B43 70 A5
HEDN WS12 12 E4
SMHTH B10 108 D5
SMTHWKW B67 87 J8
Heather Va HEDN WS12 13 H7
Heath Farm Rd CDSL WV8 34 F3
STRBR DY8 119 J2
Heathfield Av
BFLD/HDSWWD B20 88 F5
Heathfield Cl CDYHTH B64 103 K3
DOR/KN B93 149 L8
Heathfield Crs KIDDW DY11 163 M1
Heathfield Dr BLOX/PEL WS3 38 F3
Heathfield Gdns STRBR DY8 119 K1
Heathfield La DARL/WED WS10 52 A7
Heathfield La West
DARL/WED WS10 51 M8
Heathfield Rd
ALE/KHTH/YWD B14 125 J5
BEWD DY12 163 G1
COVW CV5 154 A3
FOAKS/STRLY B74 56 D2
HALE B63 121 J2
LOZ/NWT B19 88 F6
REDW B97 201 L4
STRPT DY13 188 F4
Heathfield Wy CDYHTH B64 103 K4
Heath Gap Rd CNCK/NC WS11 16 D2
Heath Gdns SOLH B91 128 B7
Heath Gn DUDN DY1 66 D8
Heathgreen Cl
CHWD/FDBR/MGN B37 111 H2
Heath Green Gv WSNGN B18 * 106 C1
Heath Green Rd WSNGN B18 106 C1
Heath Green Wy TLHL/CAN CV4 153 K7
Heath Gv CDSL WV8 34 F2
Heath Hill Rd
DUNHL/THL/PER WV6 48 C4
Heath House Dr WMBN WV5 64 B8
Heath House La CDSL WV8 34 C5
Heathland Av BKDE/SHDE B34 91 L6
Heathland Cl HEDN WS12 17 H3
Heathlands WMBN WV5 64 B8
Heathlands Cl KGSWFD DY6 83 J5
Heathlands Rd SCFLD/BOLD B73 72 D3
The Heathlands
BLKHTH/ROWR B65 104 A4
RRUGBY CV23 * 161 L8
STRBR DY8 119 M1
STRPT DY13 188 F3
WMBN WV5 64 B8
Heath La HHTH/SAND B71 69 H6
KIDD DY10 165 G5
RRUGBY CV23 158 B3
STRBR DY8 119 L1
Heathleigh Rd
HWK/WKHTH B38 145 G5
Heathley La POL/KGSB/FAZ B78 45 H7
Heathmere Av YDLY B25 109 H5
Heathmere Dr
CHWD/FDBR/MGN B37 110 D3
Heath Mill Cl SEDG DY3 82 B1
Heath Mill La BORD B9 7 L7
Heath Mill Rd SEDG DY3 82 B1
Heath Pk WOLVN WV10 * 22 A7
Heath Ri ALE/KHTH/YWD B14 146 E4
Heath Rd BDWTH CV12 116 D4
BVILLE B30 145 G1
COVE CV2 155 K1
DARL/WED WS10 52 C5
DUDS DY2 102 F3
HLYWD B47 146 E6
SHHTH WV12 38 B5
SOLH B91 128 B7
Heath Rd South NFLD/LBR B31 144 F1
Heathside Dr BLOX/PEL WS3 39 L1
HWK/WKHTH B38 145 M4
Heath St BLKHTH/ROWR B65 104 A4
CRTAM B79 32 A8
HEDN WS12 12 F6
STRBR DY8 101 K8
WSNGN B18 88 B8
Heath St South WSNGN B18 * 106 D1
Heath Ter RLSN CV32 206 B4
Heath Vw BNTWD WS7 18 E4
HEDN WS12 * 17 K5
Heath Wy BKDE/SHDE B34 91 L7
CNCK/NC WS11 17 G4
RUGBYS/DCH CV22 187 H5
Heathy Farm Cl
RIDG/WDGT B32 122 F4
Heathy Ri RIDG/WDGT B32 122 E3
Heaton Cl WOLVN WV10 22 C8
Heaton Dr EDG B15 106 C5
Heaton Rd SOLH B91 127 K6
Heaton St WSNGN B18 88 F7
Hebden TAM/AM/WIL B77 46 F5
Hebden Av WWCK CV34 205 J4
Hebden Gv HLGN/YWD B28 147 H2
SHHTH WV12 37 M4
Hebden Wy NUN CV11 99 L3
Heckley Rd
RCOVN/BALC/EX CV7 116 E6
Heddle Gv COVN CV6 134 F5
Heddon Pl VAUX/NECH B7 7 M3
Hedera Cl DSYBK/YTR WS5 69 M2
Hedera Rd REDE B98 195 L7
Hedgefield Gv HALE B63 121 G1
Hedgefield Wy TLHL/CAN CV4 153 K5
Hedgerow Cl HEDN WS12 12 D6
Hedgerow Dr KGSWFD DY6 83 H4
The Hedgerows
NUNW/HART CV10 80 D7
RMSLY B62 142 D1
TAM/AM/WIL B77 46 D5
Hedgerow Wk COVN CV6 133 M1
The Hedges WMBN WV5 64 C7
Hedges Wy BRGRVE B60 191 M4
Hedgetree Cft
CHWD/FDBR/MGN B37 111 G3
Hedging La TAM/AM/WIL B77 46 C8
Hedgley Gv STETCH B33 109 L1
Hedingham Gv
CHWD/FDBR/MGN B37 111 H3
Hedley Cft CVALE B35 91 M1
Hednesford Rd BRWNH WS8 26 A3
CNCK/NC WS11 16 D3
CNCK/NC WS11 17 K6
HEDN WS12 17 H3
Hednesford St CNCK/NC WS11 16 C4
Heeley Rd SLYOAK B29 124 D3
Heemstede La RLSN CV32 206 E3
Heenan Gv LICH WS13 20 D3
Heera Cl COVN CV6 134 B5
Hefford Dr SMTHWK B66 87 L7
Heightington Pl STRPT DY13 188 C4
Heightington Rd BEWD DY12 162 D8
Helena Cl NUNW/HART CV10 98 D2
Helena St CBHAMW B1 6 C4
Helenny Cl WNSFLD WV11 36 E8
Helen St COVN CV6 134 D7
Hele Rd COVS CV3 155 H7
Helford Cl TPTN/OCK DY4 85 H1
Heligan Pl HEDN WS12 * 17 H3
Hellaby Cl CSCFLD/WYGN B72 72 F1
Hellidon Cl RLSN CV32 206 E3
Hellier Av TPTN/OCK DY4 85 M1
Hellier Dr WMBN WV5 64 C6
Hellier Rd WOLVN WV10 36 C3
Hellier St DUDS DY2 85 G5
Helmdon Cl RUGBYN/HIL CV21 161 H7
Helming Dr WOLV WV1 50 F2
Helmingham CRTAM B79 31 G6
Helmsdale Rd RLSN CV32 198 F8
Helmsdale Wy SEDG DY3 66 E6
Helmsley Cl BRLYHL DY5 102 A5
Helmsley Rd WNSFLD WV11 37 G5
Helmswood Dr
CHWD/FDBR/MGN B37 111 G5
Helston Cl CRTAM B79 32 A5
DSYBK/YTR WS5 54 B6
NUN CV11 81 K8
STRBR DY8 101 G3
Helstone Gv SPARK B11 126 E1
Helston Rd DSYBK/YTR WS5 54 A7
Helvellyn Wy RUGBYN/HIL CV21 161 H6
Hembs Crs GTB/HAM B43 70 A5
Hemdale NUN CV11 99 L1
Hemingford Rd COVE CV2 135 K5
Heming Rd REDE B98 203 J6
Hemlingford Cft
CHWD/FDBR/MGN B37 110 E6
Hemlingford Rd
CHWD/FDBR/MGN B37 92 C7
POL/KGSB/FAZ B78 76 B1
WALM/CURD B76 73 K6
Hemlock Wy CNCK/NC WS11 16 F3
Hemmings Cl RLSS CV31 207 J8
STRBR DY8 101 J8
WOLVN WV10 3 K2
Hemmings St DARL/WED WS10 52 A5
Hemming St KIDDW DY11 164 A1
Hemming Wy KIDD DY10 166 C5
Hemplands Rd STRBR DY8 101 K8
Hempole La TPTN/OCK DY4 68 B7
Hemsby Cl TLHL/CAN CV4 153 L6
Hemsworth Dr BDWTH CV12 117 M3
Hemyock Rd SLYOAK B29 123 M5
Henbury Rd ACGN B27 127 H2
Henderson Cl LICHS WS14 21 H6
Henderson Wk TPTN/OCK DY4 67 M5
Henderson Wy
BLKHTH/ROWR B65 104 A4
Hendon Cl SEDG DY3 84 B3
WOLVN WV10 36 C5
Hendon Rd SPARK B11 107 M8
Hendre Cl COVW CV5 154 B3
Heneage Pl VAUX/NECH B7 7 L2
Heneage St VAUX/NECH B7 7 L1
Heneage St West VAUX/NECH B7 7 K2
Henfield Cl WNSFLD WV11 37 H7
Hengham Rd
LGN/SDN/BHAMAIR B26 109 L4
Hen La COVN CV6 134 B2
Henley Cl BLOX/PEL WS3 39 J4
BNTWD WS7 18 F8
CRTAM B79 32 A7
NUN CV11 81 K5
SCFLD/BOLD B73 72 F5
TPTN/OCK DY4 68 B8
Henley Crs SOLH B91 127 M6
Henley Dr MGN/WHC B75 56 E2
Henley Mill La COVE CV2 135 G6
Henley Rd COVE CV2 135 G5
RLSS CV31 206 F8
WOLVN WV10 35 M4
Henley St SPARK B11 107 L6
Henley Vls BHTH/HG B12 * 107 M8
Henley Wk COVE CV2 * 135 G3
Henlow Cl TPTN/OCK DY4 67 H8
Henlow Rd ALE/KHTH/YWD B14 146 D3
The Hennalls CBROM B36 91 K6
Hennals Av REDW B97 201 K2
Henn Dr TPTN/OCK DY4 67 J4
Henne Dr BILS/COS WV14 67 G4
Henney Cl PENK ST19 * 10 D6
Henn St TPTN/OCK DY4 67 J5
Henrietta St CBHAMNW B3 6 E2
COVN CV6 134 C8
Henry Boteler Rd
TLHL/CAN CV4 153 M6
Henry Rd YDLY B25 109 G7
Henry St COV CV1 8 F3
KNWTH CV8 179 L8
NUN CV11 98 F3
RUGBYN/HIL CV21 * 186 E2
WSLW WS2 4 C4
Hensborough SHLY B90 147 L8
Hensel Dr BDMR/CCFT WV3 49 G5
Henshaw Gv YDLY B25 109 G6
Henshaw Rd SMHTH B10 108 B5
Henson Rd BDWTH CV12 116 C4
Henstead St DIG/EDG B5 6 F9
Hentland Cl REDE B98 203 H1
Henwood Cl
DUNHL/THL/PER WV6 49 H2
Henwood La SOLH B91 149 M1
Henwood Rd
DUNHL/THL/PER WV6 49 H2
Hepburn Cl ALDR WS9 54 E1
Hepburn Edge ERDE/BCHGN B24 90 F1
Hepworth Cl
DUNHL/THL/PER WV6 48 D1
Hepworth Rd COVS CV3 156 E4
Herald Av COVW CV5 154 B4
Herald Wy COVS CV3 156 E6
Herbert Austin Dr BRGRVE B60 169 J4
Herbert Rd ALDR WS9 40 E4
HDSW B21 88 D4
SMHTH B10 108 A4
SMTHWKW B67 105 L4
SOLH B91 148 F2
Herbert's La KNWTH CV8 179 L8
Herberts Park Rd
DARL/WED WS10 51 M7
Herbert St BILS/COS WV14 50 F7
NUNW/HART CV10 98 C2
REDW B97 202 C1
WBROM B70 87 H2
WOLV WV1 3 G3
Herbhill Cl
ETTPK/GDPK/PENN WV4 66 B1
Hereford Av BHTH/HG B12 107 L7
Hereford Cl ALDR WS9 40 E5
KIDDW DY11 137 L7
NUNW/HART CV10 98 C1
RBRY B45 143 L3
Hereford Pl HHTH/SAND B71 68 F6
Hereford Rd DUDS DY2 103 J2
HEDN WS12 16 F1
LGLYGN/QTN B68 104 F6
Hereford Sq WASH/WDE B8 90 A8
Hereford St WSLW WS2 53 J1
Hereford Wy POL/KGSB/FAZ B78 45 L3
Hereward Ri RMSLY B62 103 M8
Heritage Cl LGLYGN/QTN B68 105 G1
Heritage Ct LICHS WS14 21 H7
TLHL/CAN CV4 180 B2
Heritage Wy STETCH B33 110 B2
TPTN/OCK DY4 67 M8
Hermes Cl RLSS CV31 206 C8
Hermes Crs COVE CV2 135 J6
Hermes Rd
LGN/SDN/BHAMAIR B26 129 G1
LICH WS13 21 H3
Hermitage Dr WALM/CURD B76 73 L1
Hermitage La
POL/KGSB/FAZ B78 47 J4
Hermitage Rd COVE CV2 156 A1
EDG B15 106 A5
ERDW/GRVHL B23 90 B2
SOLH B91 128 A8
The Hermitage SOLH B91 128 A7
Hermitage Wy KNWTH CV8 197 L2
STRPT DY13 188 C4
Hermit's Cft COVS CV3 9 H9
Hermit St SEDG DY3 84 B1
Hernall Cft
LGN/SDN/BHAMAIR B26 109 L6
Herne Cl WSNGN B18 106 E1
Hernefield Rd BKDE/SHDE B34 91 L6
Hernehurst RIDG/WDGT B32 105 G7
Herne's Nest BEWD DY12 162 E3
Hern Rd BRLYHL DY5 102 A7
Heronbank TLHL/CAN CV4 153 G3
Heron Cl ALVE B48 170 E6
SHLY B90 174 B2
Herondale HEDN WS12 16 F1
Herondale Rd
LGN/SDN/BHAMAIR B26 109 K7
STRBR DY8 119 G1
Heron Dr PENK ST19 10 E7
Heronfield Cl REDE B98 195 G7
Heronfield Dr NFLD/LBR B31 144 D7
Heronfield Wy SOLH B91 128 C8
Heron Ml BLOX/PEL WS3 39 J2
Heron Rd LGLYGN/QTN B68 104 E3
The Heronry
DUNHL/THL/PER WV6 48 D3
Herons Wy SLYOAK B29 124 A2
Heronswood Dr BRLYHL DY5 102 B4
Heronswood Rd KIDD DY10 164 D3
RBRY B45 143 M7
Heronville Dr WBROM B70 68 E6
Heronville Rd WBROM B70 68 E7
Heron Wy RBRY B45 143 J6
Herrick Rd COVE CV2 156 B2
WASH/WDE B8 90 C8
Herrick St BDMR/CCFT WV3 2 D6
Herring Rd ATHST CV9 63 J6
Herringshaw Cft
WALM/CURD B76 73 J2
Hertford Pl COV CV1 8 C6
Hertford St BHTH/HG B12 107 L8
COV CV1 8 F5
Hertford Wy DOR/KN B93 175 M1
Hervey Gv ERDE/BCHGN B24 73 H7
Hesket Av LGLYGN/QTN B68 105 G4
Hesketh Crs ERDW/GRVHL B23 72 A8
Hesleden TAM/AM/WIL B77 46 F5
Heslop Cl COVS CV3 156 D5
Hessian Cl BILS/COS WV14 66 F3
Hestia Dr SLYOAK B29 124 C5
Heston Av PBAR/PBCH B42 70 E5
Hever Av KGSTG B44 71 L4
Hever Cl DUDN DY1 84 C3
Hewell Av BRGRVE B60 191 K6
Hewell Cl KGSWFD DY6 83 H4
NFLD/LBR B31 144 D6
REDW B97 193 G7
Hewell La BRGRVE B60 192 E3
RBRY B45 170 A5
REDW B97 193 J8
Hewell Pl RBRY B45 * 170 B5
Hewell Rd RBRY B45 170 B5
REDW B97 194 B8
Hewitson Gdns
SMTHWKW B67 * 105 K3
Hewitt Av COVN CV6 133 M8
Hewitt Cl LICH WS13 20 E3
Hewitt St DARL/WED WS10 52 A7
Hewston Cft HEDN WS12 17 H1
Hexby Cl COVE CV2 135 L7
Hexham Wy DUDN DY1 84 D3
Hexton Cl SHLY B90 147 H3
Hexworthy Av COVS CV3 154 F8
Heybarnes Rd SMHTH B10 108 E6
Heybrook Cl COVE CV2 135 G6
Heycott Gv HWK/WKHTH B38 146 A3
Heycroft TLHL/CAN CV4 180 B1
Heydon Rd BRGRVE B60 192 B4
BRLYHL DY5 83 M8
Heyford Cl COVE CV2 135 H2
Heyford Gv SOLH B91 149 G5
Heyford Leys
RUGBYS/DCH CV22 186 D7
Heyford Wy CVALE B35 91 L1
Heygate Wy ALDR WS9 40 F4
Heynesfield Rd STETCH B33 110 A2
Heythrop Gv MOS/BIL B13 126 B5
Heyville Cft KNWTH CV8 198 A2
Heywood Cl COVN CV6 * 134 E6
Hibbert Cl RUGBYS/DCH CV22 186 D4
Hickman Av WOLV WV1 50 E5
Hickman Gdns
LDYWD/EDGR B16 106 D4
Hickman Rd BILS/COS WV14 51 G8
BRLYHL DY5 102 A1
NUNW/HART CV10 97 K1
SPARK B11 107 M7
TPTN/OCK DY4 67 K5
Hickman's Av DUDS DY2 103 J3
Hickmans Cl RMSLY B62 104 E7
Hickman St HAG/WOL DY9 102 A7
Hickmerelands La SEDG DY3 66 B5
Hickory Ct CNCK/NC WS11 * 17 G3
Hickory Dr HRBN B17 105 M3
Hicks Cl WWCK CV34 205 J3
Hidcote Av WALM/CURD B76 73 L5
Hidcote Cl NUN CV11 99 K5
RLSS CV31 207 G8
Hidcote Gv
CHWD/FDBR/MGN B37 110 E6
STETCH B33 110 A5
Hidcote Rd KNWTH CV8 180 A7
Hidson Rd ERDW/GRVHL B23 90 A1
Higgins Av BILS/COS WV14 67 H3
Higgins La RIDG/WDGT B32 105 G8
Higgins Wk SMTHWK B66 87 M7
Higgs Field Crs
BLKHTH/ROWR B65 103 M4
Higgs Rd WNSFLD WV11 37 L4
Higham La NUN CV11 81 J7
Higham's Cl BLKHTH/ROWR B65 103 M2
Higham Wy WOLVN WV10 36 C7
High Arcal Dr SEDG DY3 66 D6
High Arcal Rd SEDG DY3 83 K1
High Ash Cl
RCOVN/BALC/EX CV7 116 D6
High Av CDYHTH B64 103 K5
High Bank CNCK/NC WS11 16 C5
High Beech COVW CV5 132 E7
High Beeches GTB/HAM B43 70 B4
Highbridge Rd DUDS DY2 102 F1
SCFLD/BOLD B73 72 E4
High Brink Rd CSHL/WTROR B46 93 K6
Highbrook Cl COVEN WV9 35 L3
High Broome Ct
POL/KGSB/FAZ B78 45 L2
High Brow HRBN B17 105 M6
High Bullen DARL/WED WS10 68 D2
Highbury Av
BLKHTH/ROWR B65 104 B2
HDSW B21 * 88 D5
Highbury Cl BLKHTH/ROWR B65 104 B2
Highbury Gn NUNW/HART CV10 80 A6
Highbury Rd
ALE/KHTH/YWD B14 125 H5
FOAKS/STRLY B74 56 A2
LGLYGN/QTN B68 86 F8
Highclere BEWD DY12 162 E3
High Clere CDYHTH B64 103 L6
Highclere Dr BEWD DY12 162 E3
Highcliffe Rd TAM/AM/WIL B77 46 B5
Highcrest Cl NFLD/LBR B31 144 E6
High Cft ALDR WS9 40 F3
GTB/HAM B43 70 A4
Highcroft BLOX/PEL WS3 * 25 M7
Highcroft Av STRBR DY8 100 F2
Highcroft Cl HIA/OLT B92 128 A3
Highcroft Crs RLSN CV32 206 A4
Highcroft Dr FOAKS/STRLY B74 56 C2
Highcroft Rd ERDW/GRVHL B23 90 C2
Highdown Cottages
KIDD DY10 * 118 E7
Highdown Crs SHLY B90 148 E7
Highdown Rd RLSS CV31 206 F7
High Elms La BRGRVE B60 200 C6
High Ercal Av BRLYHL DY5 102 A3
High Farm Rd HALE B63 121 K2
RMSLY B62 104 D5
Highfield RCOVN/BALC/EX CV7 131 G4
RWWCK/WEL CV35 204 C2
Highfield Av BILS/COS WV14 67 J1
BNTWD WS7 18 F6
REDW B97 202 B5
RUSH/SHEL WS4 40 A5
TAM/AM/WIL B77 32 E8
WOLVN WV10 36 E3
Highfield Cl BNTWD WS7 18 F6
HLGN/YWD B28 126 B8
KNWTH CV8 197 J1
Highfield Ct CNCK/NC WS11 12 F8
Highfield Crs
BLKHTH/ROWR B65 103 M5
HALE B63 103 H8
WNSFLD WV11 36 F7
Highfield Dr ERDW/GRVHL B23 72 D6
Highfield La HAG/WOL DY9 141 L2
HALE B63 121 L2
RCOVN/BALC/EX CV7 114 F4
RIDG/WDGT B32 122 F1
Highfield Rd
ALE/KHTH/YWD B14 126 B8
BLKHTH/ROWR B65 103 M4
BLOX/PEL WS3 39 L1
BNTWD WS7 18 F6
BRGRVW B61 191 J5
COVE CV2 9 M2
DUDS DY2 85 J4
EDG B15 106 E5
GTB/HAM B43 70 A6
HALE B63 103 H8
HEDN WS12 17 J4
KIDD DY10 138 E5
MOS/BIL B13 125 L2
NUN CV11 99 H3
REDW B97 202 B5
SEDG DY3 66 B4
SMTHWKW B67 87 K8
STRBR DY8 101 L3
TPTN/OCK DY4 67 L6
WASH/WDE B8 90 C8
Highfield Rd North
BLOX/PEL WS3 25 K8
Highfields BNTWD WS7 18 F6
BRGRVW B61 191 J4
CSHL/WTROR B46 * 76 E6
Highfields Ct
ETTPK/GDPK/PENN WV4 * 49 H7
Highfields Dr BILS/COS WV14 67 H2
WMBN WV5 64 E8
Highfields Gra GTWY WS6 24 B4
Highfields Pk GTWY WS6 24 B4
Highfields Rd BILS/COS WV14 67 H2
BNTWD WS7 26 D1
The Highfields
DUNHL/THL/PER WV6 48 E3
Highfield Ter RLSN CV32 206 B4
Highfield Wy ALDR WS9 40 F3
Highgate FOAKS/STRLY B74 55 M4
SEDG DY3 66 C8
Highgate Av
ETTPK/GDPK/PENN WV4 49 H7
WSL WS1 5 H7
Highgate Cl BHTH/HG B12 107 K6
KIDDW DY11 163 L1
WSL WS1 5 H8
Highgate Dr WSL WS1 5 H9
Highgate Middleway
BHTH/HG B12 107 K6
Highgate Pl BHTH/HG B12 107 L6
Highgate Rd BHTH/HG B12 107 L7
DUDS DY2 84 D7
WSL WS1 5 G9
Highgate Sq BHTH/HG B12 * 107 K6
Highgate St BHTH/HG B12 107 J6
CDYHTH B64 103 K3
High Gra LICH WS13 20 D4
High Gn CNCK/NC WS11 16 B4
High Green Ct CNCK/NC WS11 * 16 B4
Highgrove DUNHL/THL/PER WV6 49 G2
RUGBYS/DCH CV22 186 B6
TLHL/CAN CV4 153 K8
Highgrove Cl CRTAM B79 31 M6
SHHTH WV12 37 M7
Highgrove Ct KIDD DY10 138 E4
Highgrove Pl DUDN DY1 84 D3
High Haden Crs CDYHTH B64 103 L5
High Haden Rd CDYHTH B64 103 M5
High Heath Cl BVILLE B30 124 B8
High Hl WNSFLD WV11 37 L3
High Holborn SEDG DY3 66 B6
High House Dr RBRY B45 169 K2
High House La BRGRVE B60 192 E7
Highland Ms BILS/COS WV14 67 H4
Highland Rdg RMSLY B62 104 C8
High Land Rd ALDR WS9 40 F2
Highland Rd CDYHTH B64 103 J3
COVW CV5 154 D4
DUDN DY1 84 E2
ERDW/GRVHL B23 72 D8
GTB/HAM B43 70 C2
HEDN WS12 16 A1
KNWTH CV8 180 A6
RLSN CV32 206 F1
Highlands Cl KIDDW DY11 137 L8
WWCK CV34 205 K5
Highlands Rd BDMR/CCFT WV3 49 H5
SHLY B90 148 C5
The Highlands SHLY B90 * 148 C5
Highland Wy REDE B98 202 E6
High Leasowes HALE B63 121 L1
Highley Cl KIDDW DY11 163 M3
REDE B98 203 J1
Highlow Av KIDDW DY11 138 A4
High Meadow Rd
HWK/WKHTH B38 145 L3
High Mdw BRGRVE B60 191 H6
DUNHL/THL/PER WV6 49 G3
WMBN WV5 64 E7
Highmoor Cl BILS/COS WV14 67 H2
SHHTH WV12 37 M6
Highmoor Rd
BLKHTH/ROWR B65 103 M2
Highmore Dr RIDG/WDGT B32 123 G5
High Mount St HEDN WS12 12 F7
High Oak BRLYHL DY5 84 A7
Highover Dr MGN/WHC B75 56 E1
Highpark Av STRBR DY8 101 H8
High Park Cl COVW CV5 153 K2
SEDG DY3 66 B4
SMTHWK B66 87 M8
High Park Crs SEDG DY3 66 B4
High Park Rd HALE B63 102 F8
High Park St VAUX/NECH B7 89 M7
High Rdg ALDR WS9 40 D8
High Ridge Cl ALDR WS9 40 C8
DARL/WED WS10 67 L1
High Rd SHHTH WV12 38 A8
High St ALDR WS9 40 D2
ALDR WS9 40 F7
ALE/KHTH/YWD B14 125 J5
ATHST CV9 61 G8
BDWTH CV12 116 F3
BEWD DY12 162 F2
BILS/COS WV14 51 G8
BILS/COS WV14 67 L1
BLKHTH/ROWR B65 104 A4
BLOX/PEL WS3 38 F5
BLOX/PEL WS3 39 L2
BNTWD WS7 18 C4
BNTWD WS7 18 D8
BRGRVE B60 191 K3
BRLYHL DY5 84 A6
BRLYHL DY5 102 A1
BRLYHL DY5 102 D4
BRWNH WS8 26 C7
CBHAM B2 7 G5
CNCK/NC WS11 17 M8
COV CV1 8 F5
COVN CV6 133 K4
CSHL/WTROR B46 93 K6
DARL/WED WS10 52 A7
DARL/WED WS10 67 L1
DOR/KN B93 150 A7
DUDS DY2 85 G5
DUNHL/THL/PER WV6 49 H1
ERDE/BCHGN B24 90 D1
GTWY WS6 24 A3
HAG/WOL DY9 102 C8
HAG/WOL DY9 141 J6
HALE B63 121 M1

HIA/OLT B92 129 L7
HRBN B17 106 A8
KGSWFD DY6 82 F5
KGSWFD DY6 83 H7
KIDD DY10 138 C7
KNWTH CV8 179 J8
KNWTH CV8 182 F4
LOZ/NWT B19 89 J6
NUN CV11 98 F1
POL/KGSB/FAZ B78 47 M3
RIDG/WDGT B32 104 E7
RLSN CV32 199 J8
RLSS CV31 206 D6
RUGBYN/HIL CV21 187 L5
SCFLD/BOLD B73 57 G7
SEDG DY3 66 B4
SEDG DY3 82 C3
SHLY B90 147 G3
SMTHWK B66 87 L8
SOLH B91 149 G1
STRBR DY8 101 J3
STRBR DY8 101 K6
STRBR DY8 101 L8
STRPT DY13 188 E2
TAM/AM/WIL B77 60 A1
TPTN/OCK DY4 67 J8
TPTN/OCK DY4 67 K5
WASH/WDE B8 90 B8
WBROM B70 87 G1
WBROM B70 87 J3
WMBN WV5 64 F7
WNSFLD WV11 37 G8
WSL WS1 4 F4
WWCK CV34 205 J7
High St Bordesley BORD B9 7 L7
High St Deritend DIG/EDG B5 7 K7
Highters Cl ALE/KHTH/YWD B14 146 F3
Highter's Heath La
ALE/KHTH/YWD B14 146 E4
Highters Rd
ALE/KHTH/YWD B14 146 E2
High Timbers RBRY B45 143 K4
High Tower VAUX/NECH B7 * 89 M8
Hightree Cl RIDG/WDGT B32 122 F4
High Trees BFLD/HDSWWD B20 88 D2
High Trees Cl REDE B98 202 C6
High Trees Rd DOR/KN B93 149 L6
High Vw ATHST CV9 77 G1
BILS/COS WV14 66 D4
Highview Dr KGSWFD DY6 101 K1
High View Dr
RCOVN/BALC/EX CV7 116 A6
High View Rd RLSN CV32 199 G8
Highview St DUDS DY2 85 J4
Highwaymans Cft
TLHL/CAN CV4 154 B8
Highwood Av HIA/OLT B92 127 L4
High Wood Cl KGSWFD DY6 83 G7
Highwood Cft
HWK/WKHTH B38 145 H4
Hiker Gv CHWD/FDBR/MGN B37 111 H3
Hilary Bevins Cl
MKTBOS/BARL/STKG CV13 81 K1
Hilary Crs DUDN DY1 66 F7
Hilary Dr ALDR WS9 40 E8
BDMR/CCFT WV3 49 H6
WALM/CURD B76 73 L2
Hilary Gv NFLD/LBR B31 144 D1
Hilary Rd NUNW/HART CV10 80 C8
TLHL/CAN CV4 154 B7
Hilden Rd VAUX/NECH B7 7 M2
Hilderic Crs DUDN DY1 84 D6
Hilderstone Rd YDLY B25 109 G7
Hildicks Crs BLOX/PEL WS3 39 K6
Hildicks Pl BLOX/PEL WS3 39 K6
Hillaire Cl HWK/WKHTH B38 146 A4
Hillaries Rd ERDW/GRVHL B23 90 B3
Hillary Av DARL/WED WS10 69 G2
Hillary Crest SEDG DY3 * 66 C8
Hillary Rd RUGBYS/DCH CV22 186 C5
STRPT DY13 164 B6
Hillary St WSLW WS2 4 A9
Hill Av ETTPK/GDPK/PENN WV4 66 D2
Hill Bank HAG/WOL DY9 120 D1
Hillbank OLDBY B69 86 B5
Hill Bank Dr STETCH B33 109 H1
Hill Bank Rd HALE B63 103 H6
HWK/WKHTH B38 145 L3
Hillborough Rd HIA/OLT B92 127 H3
Hillbrook Gv STETCH B33 109 K2
Hillbury Dr SHHTH WV12 37 M5
Hill Cl NFLD/LBR B31 144 F4
RLSN CV32 206 E2
SEDG DY3 66 C4
Hill Crs RRUGBY CV23 183 K7
Hill Crest RLSN CV32 199 J8
SEDG DY3 83 M1
Hill Crest Av BRLYHL DY5 102 A4
Hillcrest Av GTB/HAM B43 70 C3
HALE B63 102 F6
WOLVN WV10 36 C5
Hillcrest Cl CRTAM B79 31 M7
DUDS DY2 85 G8
Hill Crest Dr LICH WS13 20 E4
Hillcrest Gdns SHHTH WV12 38 B8
Hill Crest Gv KGSTG B44 71 L6
Hillcrest Ri BNTWD WS7 26 F1
Hill Crest Rd DUDS DY2 85 J4
MOS/BIL B13 125 J3
Hillcrest Rd CSCFLD/WYGN B72 73 G5
GTB/HAM B43 70 C3
NUNW/HART CV10 80 B8
POL/KGSB/FAZ B78 47 K6
RMSLY B62 142 D1
Hill Croft Rd
ALE/KHTH/YWD B14 125 G7
Hillcroft Rd KGSWFD DY6 83 J6
Hillcross Wk CBROM B36 91 K6
Hilldene Rd KGSWFD DY6 101 G1
Hillditch La KIDDW DY11 189 J3
Hill Dr CNCK/NC WS11 16 E2
Hilldrop Gv HRBN B17 124 B2
Hilleys Cft
CHWD/FDBR/MGN B37 110 D2
Hill Farm Av NUN CV11 99 M4
Hillfield Ms SOLH B91 148 F5
Hillfield Rd RUGBYS/DCH CV22 186 A4
SOLH B91 148 F5
SPARK B11 126 B2
Hillfields SMTHWKW B67 105 H2
Hillfields Rd BRLYHL DY5 101 M6
Hill Fray Dr COVS CV3 155 L8
Hill Gv BFLD/HDSWWD B20 * 89 G3
Hill Grove Crs KIDD DY10 138 E8
Hillgrove Gdns KIDD DY10 164 E1
Hill Hook Rd FOAKS/STRLY B74 42 C7
Hill House La STETCH B33 109 K2
Hillhurst Gv CBROM B36 92 B4
Hilliard Cl BDWTH CV12 116 E1
Hilliards Cft PBAR/PBCH B42 70 E5
Hillingford Av GTB/HAM B43 71 H1
Hill La BNTWD WS7 18 C4
BRGRVE B60 191 K4
BRGRVE B60 200 C7
GTB/HAM B43 70 C3
HAG/WOL DY9 141 J1
HLYWD B47 172 C4
MGN/WHC B75 57 M3
Hillman TAM/AM/WIL B77 46 C3
Hillman Dr DUDS DY2 85 J6
Hillman Gv CBROM B36 92 C4
Hillmeads Dr DUDS DY2 85 J6
Hillmeads Rd HWK/WKHTH B38 145 L4
Hillmorton Cl REDE B98 195 J7
Hillmorton La RRUGBY CV23 187 L3
Hillmorton Rd COVE CV2 135 G3
DOR/KN B93 149 L8
FOAKS/STRLY B74 56 D1
RUGBYN/HIL CV21 187 H3
Hillmount Cl HLGN/YWD B28 126 C3
Hill Pk ALDR WS9 40 E1
Hill Pas CDYHTH B64 103 J3
Hill Pl WNSFLD WV11 37 L4
Hill Rise Vw BRGRVE B60 169 G7
Hill Rd HAG/WOL DY9 102 C8
OLDBY B69 85 L3
RCOVN/BALC/EX CV7 115 K7
WLNHL WV13 51 H4
Hill Side COVE CV2 134 E7
POL/KGSB/FAZ B78 76 B1
SEDG DY3 84 A1
Hillside BRWNH WS8 26 E7
LICHS WS14 21 H8
NUNW/HART CV10 79 L5
REDE B98 202 B3
WMBN WV5 64 C6
Hillside Av BLKHTH/ROWR B65 103 M5
BRLYHL DY5 102 E5
HALE B63 103 H7
Hillside Cl BNTWD WS7 18 C8
HEDN WS12 12 E6
KIDDW DY11 137 L6
RIDG/WDGT B32 122 E5
STRPT DY13 188 C5
Hillside Crs BLOX/PEL WS3 39 K3
Hillside Cft HIA/OLT B92 128 C1
Hillside Dr BRGRVE B60 168 F7
CHWD/FDBR/MGN B37 110 D1
FOAKS/STRLY B74 55 K6
KIDDW DY11 137 L6
NUNW/HART CV10 80 A6
PBAR/PBCH B42 70 E7
Hillside Gdns
CHWD/FDBR/MGN B37 * 110 D1
WOLV WV1 50 E2
Hillside Gv KIDD DY10 139 G2
Hillside Rd DUDN DY1 84 E1
ERDW/GRVHL B23 90 B3
FOAKS/STRLY B74 56 D1
GTB/HAM B43 70 B3
Hillstone Gdns WOLVN WV10 36 D5
Hillstone Rd BKDE/SHDE B34 92 B8
Hill St BDWTH CV12 98 F8
BILS/COS WV14 67 J2
BNTWD WS7 18 C8
BRLYHL DY5 102 B3
BRLYHL DY5 102 E5
CBHAM B2 6 E5
CNCK/NC WS11 17 K7
COV CV1 8 D4
DARL/WED WS10 52 C7
DUDS DY2 84 F8
GTWY WS6 24 A3
HAG/WOL DY9 102 D8
HALE B63 121 L2
HEDN WS12 17 G2
KIDDW DY11 138 B7
NUNW/HART CV10 98 B1
RLSN CV32 206 E4
RUGBYN/HIL CV21 186 E1
SEDG DY3 66 C8
SMTHWK B66 87 L7
STRBR DY8 101 K5
STRBR DY8 119 K1
TPTN/OCK DY4 85 K1
WNSFLD WV11 37 K2
WSL WS1 5 G5
WWCK CV34 205 M5
The Hill RIDG/WDGT B32 123 H3
Hill Top ATHST CV9 61 M3
COV CV1 9 G4
HHTH/SAND B71 68 E6
REDW B97 201 K4
Hilltop HAG/WOL DY9 120 C2
Hilltop Av BEWD DY12 163 H1
Hill Top Av CRTAM B79 31 M5
RMSLY B62 104 C6
Hill Top Cl KGSTG B44 71 J7
Hilltop Cl KNWTH CV8 177 J5
Hilltop Dr CBROM B36 91 H6
Hilltop Rd DUDS DY2 85 J5
Hill Top Rd LGLYGN/QTN B68 105 G3
NFLD/LBR B31 144 D2
Hill Top Wk ALDR WS9 41 G4
Hill Vw ALDR WS9 40 F3
Hillview Cl BRGRVE B60 169 G7
HALE B63 103 J7
Hillview Rd BRGRVE B60 169 G7
RBRY B45 143 J5
Hill Village Rd MGN/WHC B75 56 E1
Hillville Gdns STRBR DY8 119 M2
Hill Wd BLOX/PEL WS3 39 K3
Hillwood Av SHLY B90 148 E7
Hillwood Cl STRBR DY8 101 G1
Hillwood Common Rd
MGN/WHC B75 42 F8
Hill Wood Rd MGN/WHC B75 43 G8
Hillwood Rd NFLD/LBR B31 123 J6
RMSLY B62 104 A6
Hill Wootton Rd
RWWCK/WEL CV35 197 L7
Hillyfields Rd ERDW/GRVHL B23 90 A1
Hilly Rd BILS/COS WV14 67 J3
Hilmore Wy TAM/AM/WIL B77 46 C5
Hilsea Cl COVEN WV9 35 K4
Hilston Av
ETTPK/GDPK/PENN WV4 65 G1
HALE B63 121 K1
Hilton Av HLGN/YWD B28 147 J1
NUNW/HART CV10 79 M7
Hilton Cl BLOX/PEL WS3 38 D4
Hilton Ct COVW CV5 * 154 D3
Hilton Cross WOLVN WV10 22 F8
Hilton Dr CSCFLD/WYGN B72 73 G5
Hilton La GTWY WS6 24 E3
WOLVN WV10 23 H5
Hilton Pl BILS/COS WV14 51 J8
Hilton Rd BNTWD WS7 18 A5
ETTPK/GDPK/PENN WV4 66 D1
OLDBY B69 86 A5
SHHTH WV12 38 A5
WOLVN WV10 22 F6
Hilton St WBROM B70 86 E2
WOLVN WV10 3 J2
Himbleton Cl REDE B98 202 D4
Himbleton Cft SHLY B90 148 E7
Himley Av DUDN DY1 84 D3
Himley Cl GTB/HAM B43 70 A3
SHHTH WV12 37 L8
Himley Crs
ETTPK/GDPK/PENN WV4 50 A8
Himley Gdns SEDG DY3 83 K1
Himley Gv RBRY B45 143 M7
Himley La SEDG DY3 82 D3
Himley Rd BDWTH CV12 116 B3
DUDN DY1 84 C4
SEDG DY3 83 J2
Himley St DUDN DY1 84 E4
Hinbrook Rd DUDN DY1 84 C4
Hinchliffe Av BILS/COS WV14 66 F3
Hinckes Rd
DUNHL/THL/PER WV6 34 F8
Hinckley Ct LGLYGN/QTN B68 * 104 F6
Hinckley La
MKTBOS/BARL/STKG CV13 81 M2
Hinckley Rd NUN CV11 81 J8
RCOVN/BALC/EX CV7 135 M5
Hinckley St DIG/EDG B5 6 F7
Hincks St BKHL/PFLD WV2 50 E6
Hind Cl WWCK CV34 205 K3
Hinde Cl RUGBYN/HIL CV21 161 G6
Hindhead Rd
ALE/KHTH/YWD B14 147 G1
Hindlip Cl HALE B63 121 K3
REDE B98 203 L1
Hindlow Cl VAUX/NECH B7 107 M1
Hindon Gv ACGN B27 126 F6
Hindon Sq EDG B15 106 D5
Hingeston St WSNGN B18 6 A1
Hingley Cft FOAKS/STRLY B74 55 K2
Hingley Rd HALE B63 102 E7
Hingley St CDYHTH B64 103 H4
Hinksford Gdns SEDG DY3 82 C3
Hinksford La SEDG DY3 82 C4
Hinsford Cl KGSWFD DY6 83 J5
Hinstock Cl
ETTPK/GDPK/PENN WV4 65 L1
Hinstock Rd BFLD/HDSWWD B20 88 D4
Hintlesham Av EDG B15 106 B8
Hinton Av ALVE B48 170 E7
Hinton Flds BRGRVW B61 168 C6
Hinton Gv WNSFLD WV11 37 K8
Hintons Coppice DOR/KN B93 149 J7
Hints Ct POL/KGSB/FAZ B78 44 B3
Hints La POL/KGSB/FAZ B78 44 D2
Hints Rd POL/KGSB/FAZ B78 44 F3
Hipkins St TPTN/OCK DY4 67 J6
Hiplands Rd RMSLY B62 122 C1
Hipsley Cl CBROM B36 92 A4
Hipsley La ATHST CV9 61 J8
Hipsmoor Cl
CHWD/FDBR/MGN B37 110 D2
Hipswell Hwy COVE CV2 156 B1
Hirdemonsay SHLY B90 147 K8
Hiron Cft COVS CV3 155 G5
The Hiron COVS CV3 155 G5
Hirst Cl RRUGBY CV23 159 L8
Histons Dr CDSL WV8 34 D3
Histons Hl CDSL WV8 34 D3
Hitchcock Cl SMTHWKW B67 87 H8
Hitches La EDG B15 106 F6
Hitchman Ms RLSS CV31 206 E8
Hitchman Rd RLSS CV31 206 E7
Hither Green La REDE B98 194 D6
Hitherside SHLY B90 147 M7
Hoarestone Av NUN CV11 99 L6
Hoarstone STRBR DY8 119 K8
Hoarstone Cl BEWD DY12 137 G8
Hoarstone La BEWD DY12 137 G7
Hobacre Cl RBRY B45 143 L5
Hobart Cft VAUX/NECH B7 89 L8
Hobart Dr DSYBK/YTR WS5 54 A7
Hobart Rd HEDN WS12 17 J3
TPTN/OCK DY4 67 J4
Hobble End La GTWY WS6 24 E7
Hobgate Rd WOLVN WV10 3 L1
Hob Green Rd HAG/WOL DY9 120 C3
Hobhouse Cl GTB/HAM B43 70 D6
Hob La HIA/OLT B92 150 E5
RCOVN/BALC/EX CV7 152 C8
Hobley Cl RUGBYS/DCH CV22 186 B6
Hobley St WLNHL WV13 52 A3
Hobmoor Cft YDLY B25 109 H6
Hob Moor Rd
LGN/SDN/BHAMAIR B26 109 H6
SMHTH B10 108 E4
Hobnock Rd WNSFLD WV11 37 L1
Hobs Hole La ALDR WS9 41 H6
Hob's Meadow HIA/OLT B92 127 L3
Hob's Moat Rd HIA/OLT B92 127 M3
Hobson Cl WSNGN B18 88 E8
Hobson Rd SLYOAK B29 124 F4
Hobs Rd DARL/WED WS10 68 E1
LICH WS13 21 J4
Hobstone Hill La BNTWD WS7 19 J4
Hockett St COVS CV3 9 H9
Hocking Rd COVE CV2 156 C1
Hockley Brook Cl WSNGN B18 88 E8
Hockley Brook La
HAG/WOL DY9 167 J1
Hockley Cl LOZ/NWT B19 89 H7
Hockley Hl WSNGN B18 88 F7
Hockley La COVW CV5 132 A8
DUDS DY2 102 F2
Hockley Pool Cl WSNGN B18 88 F8
Hockley Rd BILS/COS WV14 66 E6
ERDW/GRVHL B23 90 B1
TAM/AM/WIL B77 46 D6
Hockley St LOZ/NWT B19 89 G8
WSNGN B18 6 C1
Hodge Hill Av HAG/WOL DY9 120 D2
Hodge Hill Rd BKDE/SHDE B34 91 J8
Hodge La TAM/AM/WIL B77 32 F7
Hodgetts Cl SMTHWKW B67 105 H2
Hodgetts Dr HALE B63 121 G5
Hodgett's La
RCOVN/BALC/EX CV7 152 D5
Hodgkins Cl BRWNH WS8 26 E7
Hodnell Cl CBROM B36 92 A4
Hodnet Cl BILS/COS WV14 50 F8
KNWTH CV8 179 M8
Hodnet Dr BRLYHL DY5 84 A7
Hodnet Gv DIG/EDG B5 7 G9
Hodnet Pl CNCK/NC WS11 16 F3
Hodson Av WLNHL WV13 52 A4
Hodson Cl WNSFLD WV11 37 K5
Hoff Beck Court Ct BORD B9 * 107 M3
Hogarth Cl BDWTH CV12 116 E1
GTB/HAM B43 55 H8
WLNHL WV13 51 J3
Hoggs La NFLD/LBR B31 144 C1
Hogrills End La
CSHL/WTROR B46 94 E1
Holbeache La KGSWFD DY6 83 H4
Holbeache Rd KGSWFD DY6 83 G5
KINVER DY7 100 E1
Holbeach Rd STETCH B33 109 M3
Holbeche Crs
RCOVN/BALC/EX CV7 114 C2
Holbeche Rd DOR/KN B93 149 L6
MGN/WHC B75 73 M1
Holbein Cl BDWTH CV12 116 E1
Holberg Gv WNSFLD WV11 37 K7
Holborn Av COVN CV6 134 A3
Holborn Hl VAUX/NECH B7 89 M5
Holbrook Av RUGBYN/HIL CV21 186 E1
Holbrook La COVN CV6 134 A3
Holbrook Rd RRUGBY CV23 159 M8
Holbrook Wy COVN CV6 134 B4
Holbury Cl COVEN WV9 35 L3
Holcombe Rd SPARK B11 126 E2
Holcot Leys RUGBYS/DCH CV22 186 E6
Holcroft Rd HAG/WOL DY9 120 A1
HALE B63 103 G8
KGSWFD DY6 83 G4
Holcroft St BKHL/PFLD WV2 50 E6
TPTN/OCK DY4 85 L3
Holden Cl ERDW/GRVHL B23 90 C3
Holden Crs BLOX/PEL WS3 39 J8
Holden Cft TPTN/OCK DY4 85 L2
Holden Pl BLOX/PEL WS3 53 J1
Holden Rd DARL/WED WS10 68 E3
ETTPK/GDPK/PENN WV4 65 H2
Holder Dr CNCK/NC WS11 15 M3
Holder Rd SPARK B11 108 A7
YDLY B25 109 G6
Holders Gdns MOS/BIL B13 125 G3
Holders La MOS/BIL B13 125 G3
Holdford Rd AST/WIT B6 89 K3
Holdgate Rd SLYOAK B29 123 M6
Hole Farm Rd NFLD/LBR B31 124 A8
Hole Farm Wy
HWK/WKHTH B38 145 K6
Hole La NFLD/LBR B31 124 A7
Holford Av WSLW WS2 53 G7
Holford Dr PBAR/PBCH B42 89 J1
Holford Wy AST/WIT B6 89 L2
Holifast Rd CSCFLD/WYGN B72 73 G6
Holioak Dr WWCK CV34 205 L7
Holland Av DOR/KN B93 149 M5
LGLYGN/QTN B68 105 G1
Holland Cl LICH WS13 21 L4
Holland Cft WALM/CURD B76 75 M3
Holland Rd BILS/COS WV14 51 J6
COVN CV6 133 L7
CSCFLD/WYGN B72 72 F2
GTB/HAM B43 70 B6
Holland Rd West AST/WIT B6 89 K7
Hollands Pl BLOX/PEL WS3 39 H4
Hollands Rd BLOX/PEL WS3 39 H4
Holland St CBHAMNW B3 6 C4
CSCFLD/WYGN B72 72 F1
DUDN DY1 84 F5
TPTN/OCK DY4 68 A6
Hollemeadow Av BLOX/PEL WS3 39 H6
Holliars Gv
CHWD/FDBR/MGN B37 92 D8
Hollick Crs RCOVN/BALC/EX CV7 96 E5
Hollicombe Ter COVE CV2 135 H5
Holliday Rd ERDE/BCHGN B24 90 E1
HDSW B21 88 D6
Holliday St CBHAMW B1 6 D6
Hollie Lucas Rd MOS/BIL B13 125 K6
Hollies Av CNCK/NC WS11 16 D4
Hollies Cft DIG/EDG B5 107 G8
Hollies Dr DARL/WED WS10 68 D2
RMSLY B62 * 104 C7
Hollies La KIDDW DY11 137 K2
Hollies Park Rd CNCK/NC WS11 16 D4
Hollies Ri CDYHTH B64 103 K5
Hollies Rd OLDBY B69 85 L5
POL/KGSB/FAZ B78 47 M5
Hollies St BRLYHL DY5 84 B6
The Hollies AST/WIT B6 89 M5
BKHL/PFLD WV2 2 E8
RBRY B45 169 L4
RRUGBY CV23 161 K4
SMTHWK B66 * 106 A1
STRPT DY13 163 J7
Hollin Brow Cl DOR/KN B93 175 M2
Hollingberry La
WALM/CURD B76 73 K2
Hollings Gv SOLH B91 148 F5
Hollington Rd WOLV WV1 50 F5
Hollington Wy SOLH B91 149 G6
Hollinwell Cl BLOX/PEL WS3 38 E2
Hollis La KNWTH CV8 179 J5
Hollis Rd COVS CV3 155 L3
Hollister Dr RIDG/WDGT B32 123 K2
Holloway CRTAM B79 45 M1
NFLD/LBR B31 123 J7
Holloway Bank DARL/WED WS10 68 D5
Holloway Circus Queensway
CBHAMW B1 6 F7
Holloway Dr REDE B98 202 D3
WMBN WV5 64 C8
Holloway Fld COVN CV6 133 L7
Holloway Head EDG B15 6 E8
Holloway La REDE B98 202 D2
Holloway Pk REDE B98 202 E2
Holloway St SEDG DY3 84 B1
WOLV WV1 50 E6
Holloway St West SEDG DY3 66 B8
The Holloway ALVE B48 194 A2
DUNHL/THL/PER WV6 48 F3
KIDD DY10 166 C3
SEDG DY3 82 B4
STRBR DY8 101 K6
WWCK CV34 205 H7
Hollow Crs COVN CV6 133 M8
Hollow Cft NFLD/LBR B31 144 F2
Hollow Croft Rd SHHTH WV12 37 M6
Hollowell Wy RUGBYN/HIL CV21 161 G6
The Hollow MOS/BIL B13 125 J1
Hollowtree La BRGRVE B60 192 E2
Holly Av BHTH/HG B12 107 L8
SLYOAK B29 124 F4
Holly Bank COVW CV5 * 8 A9
Hollybank Av WNSFLD WV11 37 L2
Hollybank Cl BLOX/PEL WS3 38 E4
Hollybank Gv HALE B63 121 H4
Hollybank Rd MOS/BIL B13 125 L7
Hollyberry Av SOLH B91 148 E5
Hollyberry Cl REDE B98 203 L1
Hollyberry Cft BKDE/SHDE B34 92 A7
Hollybrow SLYOAK B29 123 L6
Holly Bush Gv RIDG/WDGT B32 105 H6
Hollybush La CDSL WV8 34 B3
COVN CV6 134 E1
ETTPK/GDPK/PENN WV4 65 H1
STRBR DY8 101 K6
Holly Cl CRTAM B79 31 M6
SHHTH WV12 38 A7
WALM/CURD B76 73 K3
Hollycot Gdns BHTH/HG B12 107 K7
Hollycroft Rd HDSW B21 88 B4
Hollydale Rd
BLKHTH/ROWR B65 104 B2
ERDE/BCHGN B24 91 G2
Holly Dell HWK/WKHTH B38 145 M3
Holly Dr ACGN B27 126 F3
ATHST CV9 77 H1
HLYWD B47 146 F6
KNWTH CV8 182 F4
Hollyfaste Rd STETCH B33 109 M4
Hollyfast La
RCOVN/BALC/EX CV7 133 G1
Hollyfast Rd COVN CV6 133 J6
Hollyfield Av SOLH B91 148 C2
Hollyfield Ct MGN/WHC B75 57 J8
Hollyfield Crs MGN/WHC B75 73 J1
Hollyfield Dr MGN/WHC B75 57 J8
RBRY B45 169 L4
Hollyfield Rd MGN/WHC B75 57 J8
Holly Gv BDMR/CCFT WV3 49 K6
BRGRVW B61 191 K2
BVILLE B30 124 D5
LOZ/NWT B19 88 F5
RRUGBY CV23 158 F8
STRBR DY8 101 K8
TLHL/CAN CV4 154 A3
Holly Grove La BNTWD WS7 18 C4
Holly Hall Rd DUDS DY2 84 E7
Hollyhedge Cl NFLD/LBR B31 123 H7
WSLW WS2 4 B2
Hollyhedge La WSLW WS2 4 B1
Hollyhedge Rd HHTH/SAND B71 69 J6
Hollyhill La LICHS WS14 42 C1
Holly Hill Rd LICHS WS14 28 D8
RBRY B45 143 L3
Hollyhock Rd ACGN B27 126 D4
DUDS DY2 85 K4
Hollyhurst BDWTH CV12 116 D4
CSHL/WTROR B46 93 G3
Hollyhurst Dr STRBR DY8 101 J2
Hollyhurst Gv
LGN/SDN/BHAMAIR B26 109 J7
SHLY B90 147 M5
Hollyhurst Rd SCFLD/BOLD B73 71 M2
Hollyland CSHL/WTROR B46 94 D4
Holly La ALDR WS9 40 E1
ALDR WS9 41 K5
ALVE B48 172 D8
ATHST CV9 63 G4
CHWD/FDBR/MGN B37 110 D5
ERDE/BCHGN B24 72 E8
ERDE/BCHGN B24 91 G2
GTWY WS6 24 D5
HEDN WS12 12 A6
KNWTH CV8 177 M3
MGN/WHC B75 56 E2
SMTHWK B66 87 J6
WALM/CURD B76 74 B1
Hollymoor Wy NFLD/LBR B31 143 M4
Hollymount RMSLY B62 104 E6
Hollyoak Cft NFLD/LBR B31 144 F5
Hollyoake LGLYGN/QTN B68 104 E3
Hollyoake Cl LGLYGN/QTN B68 104 E2
Hollyoak Gv SOLH B91 148 E4
Hollyoak Rd FOAKS/STRLY B74 55 K7
Hollyoak St HHTH/SAND B71 87 H1
Hollyoak Wy CNCK/NC WS11 16 D4
Holly Park Dr ERDE/BCHGN B24 90 F2
Holly Pl AST/WIT B6 * 89 J5
SLYOAK B29 * 124 F3
Holly Rd BLKHTH/ROWR B65 103 M4
BRGRVW B61 191 K1
BVILLE B30 145 L1
DARL/WED WS10 52 D8
DUDN DY1 84 E2
HDSW B21 88 D5
HHTH/SAND B71 69 J5
LDYWD/EDGR B16 106 A4
LGLYGN/QTN B68 105 G5
STRPT DY13 188 F1
Holly Stitches Rd
NUNW/HART CV10 80 C7
Holly St CNCK/NC WS11 12 D7
DUDN DY1 84 C6
RLSN CV32 206 E4
SMTHWKW B67 87 K8
Holly Wk KNWTH CV8 181 J3
NUN CV11 99 K3
RLSN CV32 206 E5
Hollywell Rd DOR/KN B93 149 L8
LGN/SDN/BHAMAIR B26 109 M7
Hollywell St BILS/COS WV14 66 E4
Holly Wd GTB/HAM B43 70 E4
Hollywood By-Pass HLYWD B47 146 C8
Hollywood Cft PBAR/PBCH B42 70 D5
Hollywood Gdns HLYWD B47 146 E5
Hollywood La HLYWD B47 146 E5
Holman Cl WLNHL WV13 51 J3
Holman Rd WLNHL WV13 51 H3
Holman St KIDDW DY11 138 A8
Holman Wy NUN CV11 99 H2
Holmbridge Gv RUSH/SHEL WS4 40 B3
Holmcroft COVE CV2 135 K5
Holmcroft Gdns COVEN WV9 22 A3
Holmcroft Rd KIDD DY10 138 E7
Holme Cl RUGBYN/HIL CV21 161 G7
Holme Ml WOLVN WV10 36 B1
Holme Ri PENK ST19 10 E4
Holmes Dr COVW CV5 132 B8
RBRY B45 143 K7
Holmesfield Rd PBAR/PBCH B42 71 G6
Holmes Rd SHHTH WV12 38 B6
The Holmes WOLVN WV10 36 B2
Holme Wy RUSH/SHEL WS4 39 M6
Holmewood Cl KNWTH CV8 179 M8
Holmfield Rd COVE CV2 155 M3
Holmsdale Rd COVN CV6 134 C6
Holm View Cl LICHS WS14 28 D7
Holmwood Av KIDDW DY11 137 L7
Holmwood Dr REDW B97 202 A2
Holmwood Rd BORD B9 108 B4
Holston Cl HEDN WS12 17 K4
Holsworth Cl TAM/AM/WIL B77 46 B4
Holsworthy Cl NUN CV11 81 J8
Holt Ct North VAUX/NECH B7 * 7 K2
Holt Ct South VAUX/NECH B7 * 7 K2
Holt Crs CNCK/NC WS11 16 F3
Holte Dr MGN/WHC B75 57 H3
Holte Rd AST/WIT B6 89 L4
ATHST CV9 63 H4
SPARK B11 108 B8
Holtes Wk AST/WIT B6 * 89 M5
Holt Hl REDE B98 195 K5
Holt La RMSLY B62 142 B1
Holt Rd RMSLY B62 104 C4
Holtshill La WSL WS1 5 H3
Holt St VAUX/NECH B7 7 J1
The Holt RLSN CV32 206 F1
Holt Vls WALM/CURD B76 * 74 F6
Holwick TAM/AM/WIL B77 46 F5
Holy Cross Gn HAG/WOL DY9 141 J3
Holy Cross La HAG/WOL DY9 141 J5
Holyhead Chambers COV CV1 * 8 D4
Holyhead Rd CDSL WV8 34 B5
COVW CV5 8 B3
Holyhead Rd COVW CV5 133 H8
Holyhead Rd COVW CV5 133 J8
DARL/WED WS10 68 A1
DARL/WED WS10 68 C2
HDSW B21 88 A5
Holyhead Wy HDSW B21 88 B5
Holyoak Cl AST/WIT B6 89 K4
BDWTH CV12 116 D4
RUGBYS/DCH CV22 186 A5
Holyoakes La REDW B97 193 G7
Holy Oaks Cl REDE B98 203 J3
Holyrood Gv AST/WIT B6 * 89 J5
Holy Well Cl LDYWD/EDGR B16 106 E3
Holywell Cl TLHL/CAN CV4 153 H4
Holywell La RBRY B45 143 H7
Holywell Ri LICHS WS14 21 H7
Home Cl KNWTH CV8 182 A7
Homecroft Rd YDLY B25 109 J5
Homedene Rd NFLD/LBR B31 123 J6
Home Farm RWWCK/WEL CV35 197 K7
Home Farm Cl ATHST CV9 63 M5
Homefield Rd CDSL WV8 34 F2
Homelands PBAR/PBCH B42 70 F6
The Homelands WOLVN WV10 * 22 A7
Homelea Rd YDLY B25 109 H5
Homemead Gv RBRY B45 143 K6
Home Meadow La REDE B98 195 J7
Home Park Rd NUN CV11 99 G2
Homer Cl RLSS CV31 206 C8
Homer Hill Rd HALE B63 102 F6
Homer Rd MGN/WHC B75 57 G3
SOLH B91 148 F2
Homers Fold BILS/COS WV14 51 H8
Homer St BHTH/HG B12 107 K8
Homerton Rd KGSTG B44 71 M4

Homestead Cl *SEDG* DY3 ....66 C8
Homestead Dr *MGN/WHC* B75 ....57 G2
Homestead Rd *STETCH* B33 ....109 M4
Homeward Wy *COVS* CV3 ....156 C6
Homewood Cl *WALM/CURD* B76 ...73 J2
Homfray Rd *KIDD* DY10 ....138 D5
Honesty Cl *BRWNH* WS8 ....26 B6
Honeswode Cl
  BFLD/HDSWWD B20 ....88 E5
Honeyborne Rd *MGN/WHC* B75 ....57 H6
Honeybourne *TAM/AM/WIL* B77 ...46 B3
Honeybourne Cl *COVW* CV5 ....153 M2
  HALE B63 ....121 L2
Honeybourne Crs *WMBN* WV5 ......64 B8
Honeybourne Rd *HALE* B63 ....122 A2
  STETCH B33 ....109 M4
Honeybrook La *KIDDW* DY11 ....137 M4
Honeychurch Cl *REDE* B98 ....202 D2
Honeycomb Wy *NFLD/LBR* B31 ...144 C2
Honeyfield Rd *COV* CV1 ....156 A4
Honeysuckle Av *KGSWFD* DY6 ......83 J6
Honeysuckle Cl
  RIDG/WDGT B32 ....104 F8
Honeysuckle Dr *COVE* CV2 ....134 T3
  DSYBK/YTR WS5 ....69 L2
  WOLVN WV10 ....22 F6
Honeysuckle Gdns *ACGN* B27 ......109 G8
Honeysuckle Wy *GTWY* WS6 ....24 F1
Honeytree Cl *KGSWFD* DY6 ....101 K2
Honiley Dr *KNWTH* CV8 ....177 L4
Honiley Rd *KNWTH* CV8 ....177 L4
  STETCH B33 ....109 L3
Honiley Wy *COVE* CV2 ....135 H4
Honister Cl *BRLYHL* DY5 ....102 C1
Honiton Cl *NFLD/LBR* B31 ....144 C1
Honiton Crs *NFLD/LBR* B31 ....144 C1
Honiton Rd *COVE* CV2 ....134 F8
Honiton Wk *SMTHWK* B66 ....87 M8
Honiton Wy *ALDR* WS9 ....40 D8
Honnington Gdns SLYOAK B29 * ...123 K4
Honor Av
  ETTPK/GDPK/PENN WV4 ....50 A8
Hood Gv *BVILLE* B30 ....145 H1
Hood St *COV* CV1 ....9 J4
Hook Wy *RUGBYS/DCH* CV22 ......186 B4
Hook Dr *FOAKS/STRLY* B74 ....56 C1
Hook La *LICHS* WS14 ....42 A2
Hooper St *WSNGN* B18 ....106 D1
Hoo Rd *KIDD* DY10 ....164 C2
Hoosen Cl *RMSLY* B62 ....104 E7
Hope Cl *RCOVN/BALC/EX* CV7 ....152 C6
Hopedale Cl *COVE* CV2 ....156 C2
Hopedale Rd *RIDG/WDGT* B32 ....105 G8
Hope Pl *SLYOAK* B29 * 124 D3
Hope Rd *TPTN/OCK* DY4 ....68 A7
Hope St *COV* CV1 ....6 E6
  DIG/EDG B5 ....107 H5
  DUDS DY2 ....85 G5
  RMSLY B62 ....104 B5
  STRBR DY8 ....101 L2
  WBROM B70 ....87 J3
  WSL WS1 ....5 G5
Hopgardens Av *BRGRVE* B60 ....191 M3
Hopkins Dr *HHTH/SAND* B71 ....69 J6
Hopkins Rd *COVN* CV6 ....8 A1
Hopkins St *TPTN/OCK* DY4 ....85 L3
Hopley's Cl *TAM/AM/WIL* B77 ....46 C1
Hop Pole La *BEWD* DY12 ....162 C2
Hopstone Gdns
  ETTPK/GDPK/PENN WV4 ....49 K8
Hopstone Rd *SLYOAK* B29 ....123 L4
Hopton Cl *COVW* CV5 ....153 L1
  DUNHL/THL/PER WV6 ....48 D2
  TPTN/OCK DY4 ....68 A3
Hopton Crs *WOLVN* WV11 ....37 J7
Hopton Crofts *RLSN* CV32 ....206 A3
Hopton Dr *KIDDW* DY11 ....164 C4
Hopton Gdns *DUDN* DY1 ....84 E2
Hopton Gv *MOS/BIL* B13 ....125 L1
Hopton Meadow *HEDN* WS12 ....17 G4
Hopwas Gv
  CHWD/FDBR/MGN B37 ....110 E5
Hopwas Hl *POL/KGSB/FAZ* B78 ....30 E7
Hopwood Cl *HALE* B63 ....121 L3
Hopwood Gv *NFLD/LBR* B31 ....144 C1
Hopyard Cl *SEDG* DY3 ....66 B8
Hopyard Gdns *BILS/COS* WV14 .....66 F2
Hopyard La *REDE* B98 ....203 J1
  SEDG DY3 ....83 A3
Hopyard Rd *ALEW* WS2 ....52 C3
Horace Partridge Rd
  DARL/WED WS10 ....51 L8
Horace St *BILS/COS* WV14 ....66 L5
Horatio Dr *MOS/BIL* B13 ....125 K1
Hordern Cl *DUNHL/THL/PER* WV6...35 K8
Hordern Crs *BRLYHL* DY5 ....102 B5
Hordern Gv
  DUNHL/THL/PER WV6 ....35 K8
Hordern Pk *WOLVN* WV10 * 22 A7
Hordern Rd
  DUNHL/THL/PER WV6 ....35 K8
Hornbeam *TAM/AM/WIL* B77 ....46 E1
Hornbeam Cl *BRLYHL* DY12 ....162 C2
  SLYOAK B29 ....123 M6
Hornbeam Crs *HEDN* WS12 ....13 L7
Hornbeam Dr *TLHL/CAN* CV4 ....153 H4
Hornbeam Gv *RLSS* CV31 ....207 J3
Hornbeam Wk *RLSS* CV31 * 2 B6
Hornby Gv *ALE/KHTH/YWD* B14 ..147 G1
Hornby Rd
  ETTPK/GDPK/PENN WV4 ....66 A1
Hornchurch Cl *COV* CV1 ....8 F8
Horndean Cl *COVN* CV6 ....134 C5
Horne Cl *RUGBYN/HIL* CV21 ....187 L5
Horne Wy *BKDE/SHDE* B34 ....92 D3
Horning Dr *BILS/COS* WV14 ....67 G2
Horninglold Cl *COVS* CV3 ....156 C5
Hornsey Cl *COVE* CV2 ....135 M6
Hornsey Rd *KGSTG* B44 ....71 L3
Hornsey Rd *KGSTG* B44 ....71 L3
Hornton Cl *FOAKS/STRLY* B74 ....42 B8
Horobins Yd *BNTWD* WS7 * 18 F1
Horrell Rd
  LGN/SDN/BHAMAIR B26 ....109 M7
  SHLY B90 ....147 K3
Horse Bridge La *KINVER* DY7 ....118 A3
Horsecroft Dr *HHTH/SAND* B71 .....69 J7
Horse Fair *KIDD* DY10 ....138 C6
Horsehills Dr *BDMR/CCFT* WV3 .....49 J3
Horselea Cft *WASH/WDE* B8 ....108 G1
Horsley Flds *WOLV* WV1 ....5 K7
Horsley Heath *TPTN/OCK* DY4 ....85 M1
Horsley Rd *TPTN/OCK* DY4 ....85 M7
Horseshoe Cl *WSLW* WS2 ....52 F6
Horse Shoe Rd *COVN* CV6 ....134 C1
Horse Shoes La
  LGN/SDN/BHAMAIR B26 ....109 M8
The Horseshoe
  LGLYGN/QTN B68 ....105 J3
Horsfall Rd *MGN/WHC* B75 ....57 M8
Horsford Rd *COVS* CV3 ....155 J7
Horsham Av *STRBR* DY8 ....101 G2
Horsley La *LICHS* WS14 ....28 B5
Horsley Rd *FOAKS/STRLY* B74 ....71 H1
  GTB/HAM B43 ....71 H1
Horton Cl *DARL/WED* WS10 ....52 B6

Horton Crs *RUGBYS/DCH* CV22 ...186 E3
Horton Gv *SHLY* B90 ....160 E7
Horton Pl *DARL/WED* WS10 ....52 B6
Horton Sq *BHTH/HG* B12 ....107 J5
Horton St *DARL/WED* WS10 ....52 B6
  TPTN/OCK DY4 ....68 B8
  WBROM B70 ....87 G4
Hosiery St *BDWTH* CV12 ....117 G3
Hoskyn Cl *RUGBYN/HIL* CV21 .....187 K5
Hospital La *BDWTH* CV12 ....115 M4
  BILS/COS WV14 ....66 F6
  GTWY WS6 ....23 M3
Hospital Rd *BNTWD* WS7 ....26 F1
Hospital St *CRTAM* B79 ....31 M8
  LOZ/NWT B19 ....6 E1
  WOLV WV1 ....5 H1
  WSLW WS2 ....53 H1
Hossill La *HAG/WOL* DY9 ....141 H4
Hotchkiss Wy *COVS* CV3 ....156 C6
Hotel Buildings *LICHS* WS14 * 27 L3
Hothersall Dr *SCFLD/BOLD* B73 ....72 D5
Hothorpe Cl *COVS* CV3 ....156 D4
Hotspur Rd *KGSTG* B44 ....71 K4
Hough Pl *WSLW* WS2 ....52 E6
Hough Rd *ALE/KHTH/YWD* B14 ...125 H7
  WSLW WS2 ....52 E6
Houghton Ct *HLGN/YWD* B28 ....147 H1
Houghton St *OLDBY* B69 ....86 D7
  WBROM B70 ....87 H5
Houldey Rd *NFLD/LBR* B31 ....144 F4
Houldsworth Crs *COVN* CV6 ....134 A1
Houliston Cl *DARL/WED* WS10 ......52 E3
Houndsfield Cl *HLYWD* B47 ....147 G7
Houndsfield Gv *HLYWD* B47 ....146 E8
Houndsfield La *HLYWD* B47 ....146 E8
Housman Cl *BRGRVE* B60 ....191 J5
Houston Rd *RUGBYN/HIL* CV21 ...161 G7
Houting *TAM/AM/WIL* B77 ....46 B8
The Houx *STRBR* DY8 ....101 J5
Hove Av *COVW* CV5 ....153 J1
Hovelands Cl *COVE* CV2 ....135 G5
Hove Rd *ACGN* B27 ....126 F4
Hoveton Cl *REDE* B98 ....202 F4
Howard Av *BRGRVW* B61 ....191 J2
Howard Cl *RCOVN/BALC/EX* CV7...152 A5
Howard Rd *HEDN* WS12 ....13 G6
Howard Rd *ALE/KHTH/YWD* B14...125 H6
  BFLD/HDSWWD B20 ....88 E5
  BILS/COS WV14 ....67 K2
  GTB/HAM B43 ....70 A5
  HIA/OLT B92 ....127 J2
  NUNW/HART CV10 ....98 E2
  REDE B98 ....202 F5
  WNSFLD WV11 ....37 K5
  YDLY B25 ....109 G7
Howard Rd East
  ALE/KHTH/YWD B14 ....125 J6
Howard St *BKHL/PFLD* WV2 ....3 G8
  COV CV1 ....9 G1
  LOZ/NWT B19 ....6 E1
  TPTN/OCK DY4 ....67 M8
  WBROM B70 ....68 D6
Howard Wk *RLSS* CV31 ....206 B6
Howarth Wy *AST/WIT* B6 ....89 L6
Howat Rd *RCOVN/BALC/EX* CV7 ...115 K6
Howcotte Gn *TLHL/CAN* CV4 ....153 H4
Howden Pl *STETCH* B33 ....91 L8
Howdle's La *BRWNH* WS8 ....26 D3
Howe Crs *SHHTH* WV12 ....38 A7
Howe Green La
  NUNW/HART CV10 ....115 H2
Howell Dr *TPTN/OCK* DY4 ....67 L8
Howell Rd *BKHL/PFLD* WV2 ....50 C6
Howells Cl *BDWTH* CV12 ....116 B5
Howes Cft *CVALE* B35 ....91 L3
Howes La *COVS* CV3 ....181 G2
Howe St *CBHAMNE* B4 ....7 K3
Howford Gv *VAUX/NECH* B7 ....107 M1
Howkins Rd *RUGBYN/HIL* CV21 ...161 G7
Howland Cl *COVN* CV9 ....35 K3
Howlette Rd *TLHL/CAN* CV4 ....153 J3
Howley Av *KGSTG* B44 ....71 J4
Howley Grange Rd *RMSLY* B62 .....104 C5
Hoylake *TAM/AM/WIL* B77 ....46 F1
Hoylake Cl *BLOX/PEL* WS3 ....39 J4
  NUN CV11 ....99 M4
Hoylake Dr *OLDBY* B69 ....85 L6
Hoylake Rd
  DUNHL/THL/PER WV6 ....34 B8
Hoyland Wy *BVILLE* B30 ....124 C5
Huband Cl *REDE* B98 ....194 E8
Hubert Cft *SLYOAK* B29 ....124 C3
Hubert Rd *SLYOAK* B29 ....124 D3
Hubert St *AST/WIT* B6 ....89 K8
The Hub *SOLH* B91 * 149 G2
Hucker Cl *WSLW* WS2 ....52 A6
Hucker Rd *WSLW* WS2 ....52 A6
Huddesford Dr
  RCOVN/BALC/EX CV7 ....152 A5
Huddisdon Cl *WWCK* CV34 ....205 K4
Huddleston Cl *WOLVN* WV10 ....22 E7
Huddocks Vw *BLOX/PEL* WS3 ....25 K8
Hudson Av *CSHL/WTROR* B46 ....93 K7
Hudson Cl *CNCK/NC* WS11 ....19 G7
Hudson Dr *BNTWD* WS7 ....19 G7
Hudson Gv
  DUNHL/THL/PER WV6 ....34 C8
Hudson Rd *BFLD/HDSWWD* B20 ....88 B1
  RUGBYS/DCH CV22 ....186 C4
  TPTN/OCK DY4 ....86 A1
Hudson's Dr *BVILLE* B30 ....145 L1
Hudswell Dr *BRLYHL* DY5 ....102 B5
Huggins Cl
  RCOVN/BALC/EX CV7 ....152 A6
Hughes Av *BDMR/CCFT* WV3 ....49 K5
Hughes Cl *WWCK* CV34 ....205 H3
Hughes Pl *BILS/COS* WV14 ....51 H6
Hughes Rd *BILS/COS* WV14 ....51 H6
  DARL/WED WS10 ....51 L8
Hugh Rd *COVS* CV3 ....155 L3
  SMTH B10 ....108 C4
  SMTH B67 ....87 H8
Hugh Vls *SMTH* B10 * 108 C4
Huins Cl *REDE* B98 ....202 E1
Hulbert Dr *DUDS* DY2 ....84 F7
Hulland Pl *BRLYHL* DY5 ....102 A2
Hullbrook Rd *MOS/BIL* B13 ....126 A8
Hulme Cl *COVS* CV3 ....156 F4
Humber Av *COV* CV1 ....9 K7
  WALM/CURD B76 ....73 L4
Humber Gdns *HALE* B63 ....102 F8
Humber Gv *CBROM* B36 ....92 D4
Humber Rd *BDMR/CCFT* WV3 ....9 M6
  COVS CV3 ....9 J8
Humberstone Rd
  ERDE/BCHGN B24 ....91 J1
Hume St *KIDD* DY11 ....138 A8
  SMTHWK B66 ....106 D3
Humpage Rd *BORD* B9 ....108 C3
Humphrey Av *BRGRVE* B60 ....191 J6
Humphrey Burton's Rd
  COVS CV3 ....155 J6
Humphrey-Davy Rd
  BDWTH CV12 ....116 B5
Humphrey Middlemore Dr
  HRBN B17 ....124 B1
Humphrey St *SEDG* DY3 ....84 B2
Humphries Crs *BILS/COS* WV14 .....67 K3

Humphries Dr *KIDD* DY10 ....164 D1
Humphries Rd *WOLVN* WV10 ....36 B6
Humphris St *WWCK* CV34 ....205 M5
Hundred Acre Rd
  FOAKS/STRLY B74 ....55 K6
Hungary Cl *HAG/WOL* DY9 ....102 A8
Hungary Hl *HAG/WOL* DY9 ....102 A8
Hungerford Rd *CBROM* B36 ....92 A4
Hungerford Rd *STRBR* DY8 ....119 J3
Hungry La *LICHS* WS14 ....43 K1
Cunningham Gv *SOLH* B91 ....148 F5
Hunnington Cl *RIDG/WDGT* B32 ..122 E4
Hunnington Crs *HALE* B63 ....121 M3
Hunscote Cl *SHLY* B90 ....147 K4
Hunslet Cl *RIDG/WDGT* B32 ....123 J4
Hunslet Rd *BNTWD* WS7 ....18 F5
  RIDG/WDGT B32 ....123 K1
Hunstanton Av *HRBN* B17 ....105 K5
Hunstanton Cl *BRLYHL* DY5 ....102 A5
Hunt Cl *RWWCK/WEL* CV35 ....204 D7
Hunt End La *REDW* B97 ....202 A8
Hunter Av *BNTWD* WS7 ....18 F6
Hunter Cl *LICHS* WS14 ....21 H7
Hunter Crs *BLOX/PEL* WS3 ....39 K7
Hunter Rd *CNCK/NC* WS11 ....16 C5
Hunters Cl *BILS/COS* WV14 ....51 L6
  COVS CV3 ....156 E3
Hunters La *RUGBYN/HIL* CV21 ....160 E8
Hunters Pk *ATHST* CV9 ....62 A5
Hunter's Ride *KINVER* DY7 ....100 F3
Hunters Rd *LOZ/NWT* B19 ....88 F7
  RUGBYN/HIL CV21 ....187 G1
Hunters V *LOZ/NWT* B19 ....88 F7
Hunters Wk *ATHST* CV9 ....63 M6
Hunter Ter *COVS* CV5 ....154 A5
Huntingdon Cl
  POL/KGSB/FAZ B78 ....45 K3
  REDE B98 ....203 J3
Huntingdon Gdns *HALE* B63 ....103 G6
Huntingdon Rd *COVW* CV5 ....8 C3
  HHTH/SAND B71 ....68 F6
Huntington Wy
  NUNW/HART CV10 ....98 C2
Huntington Rd *SHHTH* WV12 ....38 B6
Huntington Terrace Rd
  CNCK/NC WS11 ....16 D1
Huntingtree Rd *HALE* B63 ....121 J1
Huntlands Rd *HALE* B63 ....121 J3
Hunt La *ATHST* CV9 ....63 M6
Huntley Dr *SOLH* B91 ....148 F3
Hunton HI *ERDW/GRVHL* B23 ....90 B2
Hunton Rd *ERDW/GRVHL* B23 ....90 C2
Hunt Paddocks *KNWTH* CV8 ....197 J4
Hunt's La *SHHTH* WV12 ....38 B7
Huntsmans Cl *COVS* CV14 * 67 H5
Huntsmans Ga *BNTWD* WS7 ....18 E3
Huntsmans Ri *HEDN* WS12 ....12 A5
Hunts Mill Dr *BRLYHL* DY5 ....84 A4
Hunts Ri *BEWD* DY12 ....163 G2
Hunts Rd *BVILLE* B30 ....124 E6
Hunt Ter *TLHL/CAN* CV4 ....153 M6
Hurcott La *BDWTH* CV12 ....139 G4
Hurcott Rd *KIDD* DY10 ....138 E5
Hurdis Rd *SHLY* B90 ....147 L3
Hurdlow Av *WSNGN* B18 ....88 F8
Hurley Cl *CSCFLD/WYGN* B72 ....73 G5
  DSYBK/YTR WS5 ....69 M2
  RLSN CV32 ....206 E2
Hurley Common *ATHST* CV9 ....61 G7
Hurley Gv *CHWD/FDBR/MGN* B37...92 D8
Hurley La *CSHL/WTROR* B46 ....77 J8
Hurleys Fold *DUDS* DY2 ....84 F8
Hurlingham Rd *KGSTG* B44 ....71 L4
Hurn Wy *COVN* CV6 ....134 F1
Huron Cl *CNCK/NC* WS11 ....16 F3
Hursey Dr *TPTN/OCK* DY4 ....67 L8
Hurstbourne Crs *WOLV* WV1 ....51 G1
Hurst Cl *CBROM* B36 ....92 C6
Hurstcroft Rd *STETCH* B33 ....109 M2
Hurst Green Rd *DOR/KN* B93 ....175 K1
  RMSLY B62 ....104 C5
  WALM/CURD B76 ....74 D7
Hurst La *BKDE/SHDE* B34 ....92 B7
  BRLYHL DY5 ....102 D2
  TPTN/OCK DY4 ....67 H8
Hurst La North *BKDE/SHDE* B34 ....92 C2
Hurst Rd *BDWTH* CV12 ....116 F2
  BILS/COS WV14 ....66 F4
  COVN CV6 ....134 C1
  SMTHWK B67 ....105 H3
Hurst St *DIG/EDG* B5 ....6 F7
The Hurst *HLYWD* B47 ....146 E7
  MOS/BIL B13 ....126 A4
The Hurstway
  ERDW/GRVHL B23 ....72 A3
Hurstwood Rd *ERDW/GRVHL* B23 ..72 A3
Hussey Rd *CNCK/NC* WS11 ....10 C3
Hussey Rd *BRWNH* WS8 ....26 C5
  CNCK/NC WS11 ....19 G7
Husum Wy *KIDD* DY10 ....139 G6
Hut Hill La *GTWY* WS6 ....24 E1
Hutton Av *WASH/WDE* B8 ....90 B4
Hutton Rd *BFLD/HDSWWD* B20 ......90 B4
  WASH/WDE B8 ....90 B4
Huxbey Dr *HIA/OLT* B92 ....128 D5
Huxley Cl *COVEN* WV9 ....35 L3
Hyatt Sq *BRLYHL* DY5 ....102 A6
Hyde Pl *BRGRVE* B60 ....191 M6
Hyde Pl *RLSN* CV32 ....206 C5
Hyde Rd *COVE* CV2 ....156 C1
  WNSFLD WV11 ....89 J3
Hydes Rd *DARL/WED* WS10 ....68 C2
  HHTH/SAND B71 ....69 G4
The Hyde *HAG/WOL* DY9 ....120 B3
Hyett Wy *TPTN/OCK* DY4 ....67 M3
Hylda Rd *BFLD/HDSWWD* B20 ....88 B1
Hylstone Crs *WNSFLD* WV11 ....37 H7
Hylton St *WSNGN* B18 ....89 G8
Hypericum Gdns *COVE* CV2 * 135 G8
Hyperion Dr
  ETTPK/GDPK/PENN WV4 ....65 L2
Hyperion Rd *CBROM* B36 ....91 J4
  KINVER DY7 ....101 G3
Hyron Hall Rd *ACGN* B27 ....127 G3
Hyssop Cl *CNCK/NC* WS11 ....16 F3
  VAUX/NECH B7 ....32 A7
Hytall Rd *SHLY* B90 ....147 G3
Hythe Gv *YDLY* B25 ....109 H5

Ibberton Rd
  ALE/KHTH/YWD B14 ....146 C1
Ibis Cl *KIDD* DY10 ....164 D1
Ibis Gdns *KGSWFD* DY6 ....83 L7
Ibstock Cl *REDE* B98 ....203 J1
Ibstock Dr *STRBR* DY8 ....119 L1
Ibstock Rd *COVN* CV6 ....116 D8
Icknield Cl *FOAKS/STRLY* B74 ....55 L4

Icknield Port Rd
  LDYWD/EDGR B16 ....106 C2
Icknield Sq *LDYWD/EDGR* B16 .....106 C2
Icknield St *ALVE* B48 ....171 M3
  HWK/WKHTH B38 ....145 M5
  REDE B98 ....195 G6
  WSNGN B18 ....106 D1
Icknield Street Dr *REDE* B98 ....203 H1
Ida Rd *WBROM* B70 ....87 H4
Idbury Rd *KGSTG* B44 ....71 L6
Iden Rd *COV* CV1 ....134 C8
Idmiston Cft
  ALE/KHTH/YWD B14 ....146 D3
Idonia Rd *DUNHL/THL/PER* WV6 ....34 C8
Ilam Pk *KNWTH* CV8 ....180 A8
Ilex Ct *WWCK* CV34 ....205 L6
Ilford Cl *BDWTH* CV12 ....116 C2
Ilford Dr *COVS* CV3 ....154 F8
Ilford Rd *ERDW/GRVHL* B23 ....72 B7
Ilfracombe Gv *COVS* CV3 ....154 E8
Iliffe Wy *HRBN* B17 ....124 D1
Ilkley Gv *CHWD/FDBR/MGN* B37 ...110 D3
Illey Cl *NFLD/LBR* B31 ....143 M4
Illey La *RMSLY* B62 ....122 A4
Illshaw *COVEN* WV9 ....35 L2
Illshaw Cl *REDE* B98 ....203 L1
Illshaw Heath Rd *HOCK/TIA* B94 ..174 B2
Ilmer Cl *RUGBYN/HIL* CV21 ....161 J2
Ilmington Cl *SCFLD/BOLD* B73 ....72 A2
Ilmington Rd *SLYOAK* B29 ....123 K4
Ilsham Gv *NFLD/LBR* B31 ....144 C7
Ilsley Rd *ERDW/GRVHL* B23 ....90 C1
Imber Rd *KIDD* DY10 ....164 E4
Imperial Av *KIDD* DY10 ....138 D5
Imperial Gv *KIDD* DY10 ....138 D5
Imperial Ri *CSHL/WTROR* B46 ....93 J3
Imperial Rd *BORD* B9 ....108 C4
Impney Cl *REDE* B98 ....195 H7
Impsley Cl *CBROM* B36 ....91 M5
Inca Cl *COVS* CV3 ....156 D5
Ince Rd *DARL/WED* WS10 ....52 A6
Incestre Dr *GTB/HAM* B43 ....70 A4
Inchbrook Rd *KNWTH* CV8 ....180 A6
Inchcape Av *BFLD/HDSWWD* B20 ...88 E2
Inchford Cl *NUN* CV11 ....99 K4
Inchford Rd *HIA/OLT* B92 ....128 C6
Inchlaggan Rd *WOLVN* WV10 ....36 D7
Infantry Pl *MGN/WHC* B75 ....57 L7
Ingatestone Dr *STRBR* DY8 ....101 G2
Ingestre Dr *GTB/HAM* B43 ....70 A4
Ingestre Gv *HLGN/YWD* B28 ....126 D6
  WOLVN WV10 ....36 A4
Ingham Wy *HRBN* B17 ....105 K6
Ingleby Gdns
  DUNHL/THL/PER WV6 ....35 L8
Ingledew Cl *WSLW* WS2 ....52 B2
Inglefield Rd *STETCH* B33 ....109 K2
Inglemere Gv *SLYOAK* B29 ....123 K8
Inglenook Dr
  BFLD/HDSWWD B20 ....88 F3
Ingleside Vls *SPARK* B11 * 108 A3
Ingleton Cl *NUN* CV11 ....115 J4
Ingleton Rd *WASH/WDE* B8 ....90 B6
Inglewood Av *BDMR/CCFT* WV3 .....49 K5
Inglewood Cl *KGSWFD* DY6 * 83 L7
  RLSN CV32 ....206 E2
Inglewood Gv *FOAKS/STRLY* B74 ...55 K4
Inglewood Rd *SPARK* B11 ....108 A3
Ingoldsby Rd *NFLD/LBR* B31 ....145 G2
Ingot Cl *WSLW* WS2 ....38 F7
Ingram Crs *BEWD* DY12 ....162 D1
Ingram Gv *ACGN* B27 ....126 E3
Ingram Pit La *TAM/AM/WIL* B77 .....32 E8
Ingram Pl *BLOX/PEL* WS3 ....39 H4
Ingram Rd *BLOX/PEL* WS3 ....39 H4
  COVW CV5 ....154 A3
Inhedge St *SEDG* DY3 ....66 C8
The Inhedge *DUDN* DY1 ....85 G4
Inkberrow Rd *HALE* B63 ....121 K3
Inkerman Gv *WOLVN* WV10 ....3 J1
Inkerman St *VAUX/NECH* B7 ....107 M1
  WOLVN WV10 ....19 J3
Inland Rd *ERDE/BCHGN* B24 ....91 H3
Innage Cl *RLSS* CV31 ....206 E5
Innage Rd *NFLD/LBR* B31 ....144 F1
Innage St *ATHST* CV9 * 63 H5
Innis Rd *COVW* CV5 ....154 C6
Inn La *KIDD* DY10 ....189 L3
Innsworth Dr *CVALE* B35 ....91 L1
Insetton Cl *REDE* B98 ....203 H1
Inshaw Cl *STETCH* B33 ....109 J2
Instate Cl
  ALE/KHTH/YWD B14 ....125 K5
Instone Rd *COVN* CV6 ....134 C7
  HALE B63 ....121 K2
Instow Cl *SHHTH* WV12 ....37 M5
Insull Av *ALE/KHTH/YWD* B14 ......146 E4
Intended St *HALE* B63 ....103 G6
International Dr
  LGN/SDN/BHAMAIR B26 ....129 C1
International Sq
  CHWD/FDBR/MGN B37 * 111 G7
Intown WSL WS1 ....5 G3
Intown Rw *WSL* WS1 ....5 G3
Inverary Cl *KNWTH* CV8 ....198 A1
Inverclyde Rd
  BFLD/HDSWWD B20 ....88 C2
Inverness Cl *COVW* CV5 ....153 L1
Inverness Rd *NFLD/LBR* B31 ....144 D2
Invicta Rd *COVS* CV3 ....156 D5
Inworth *COVEN* WV9 ....35 M2
Ipsley Church La *REDE* B98 ....203 H3
Ipsley Gv *ERDW/GRVHL* B23 ....71 L8
Ipsley La *REDE* B98 ....203 H3
Ipstones Av *STETCH* B33 ....109 K1
Ipswich Crs *PBAR/PBCH* B42 ....71 G5
Ireland Green Rd *WBROM* B70 ....86 E2
Ireton Cl *TLHL/CAN* CV4 ....153 H4
Ireton Rd *BFLD/HDSWWD* B20 ....88 B1
  WOLVN WV10 ....36 B2
Iris Cl *CRTAM* B79 ....32 A7
  DUDS DY2 ....85 K4
  SLYOAK B29 ....123 M5
Iris Dr *ALE/KHTH/YWD* B14 ....146 B1
Irnham Rd *FOAKS/STRLY* B74 ....56 A4
Iron Bridge Wk *HAG/WOL* DY9 ....119 M5
Iron La *STETCH* B33 ....109 H1
Ironmonger Rw *COV* CV1 ....6 F4
Ironstone Cl *BEWD* DY12 ....162 C1
Ironstone Rd *HEDN* WS12 ....18 A2
Irvan Av *WBROM* B70 ....86 E2
Irvine Cl *BLOX/PEL* WS3 ....38 F5
Irvine Rd *BLOX/PEL* WS3 ....38 F5
Irving Cl *LICH* WS13 ....20 C3
  SEDG DY3 ....83 J7
Irving Rd *COV* CV1 ....135 K7
  HIA/OLT B92 ....128 C1
  TPTN/OCK DY4 ....67 L4
Irving St *EDG* B15 ....6 D6

Irwell *TAM/AM/WIL* B77 ....46 C3
Irwin Av *RBRY* B45 ....144 A7
Isaac Walton Pl *WBROM* B70 ....86 E3
Isambard Dr *COVN* CV6 ....116 D8
Isbourne Wy *BORD* B9 ....107 M2
Isis Gv *CBROM* B36 ....92 D5
  WLNHL WV13 ....52 A3
Island Dr *KIDD* DY10 ....164 C1
Island Rd *HDSW* B21 ....88 A4
Islington Cl *HALE* B63 ....63 L1
Islington Crs *ATHST* CV9 ....61 G4
Islington Rw *EDG* B15 ....6 A6
Ismere Rd *ERDE/BCHGN* B24 ....90 F3
Ismere Wy *KIDD* DY10 ....138 D8
Itchen Gv *DUNHL/THL/PER* WV6 .....48 C2
Ithon Gv *HWK/WKHTH* B38 ....145 J5
Ivanhoe Av *NUN* CV11 ....99 J4
Ivanhoe Rd *BKHL/PFLD* WV2 ....50 D7
  GTB/HAM B43 ....71 G3
  LICHS WS14 ....27 J3
Ivanhoe St *DUDS* DY2 ....84 E6
Ivatt *TAM/AM/WIL* B77 ....46 D5
Ivatt Cl *RUSH/SHEL* WS4 ....39 M6
Iverley Dr *KIDD* DY10 ....119 G8
Iverley Rd *HALE* B63 ....122 A2
Iverley Wk *HAG/WOL* DY9 ....119 M3
Ivor Rd *ATHST* CV9 ....62 D6
  COVN CV6 ....134 D3
  REDW B97 ....202 B3
  SPARK B11 ....125 M1
Ivy Av *BHTH/HG* B12 ....107 L8
Ivy Bank *ATHST* CV9 * 62 B7
Ivybridge Gv *PBAR/PBCH* B42 ....89 G2
Ivybridge Rd *COVS* CV3 ....155 H8
Ivy Cl *CNCK/NC* WS11 ....16 A5
Ivy Cft *COVEN* WV9 ....35 K2
Ivydale Av
  LGN/SDN/BHAMAIR B26 ....110 A8
Ivy Farm La *TLHL/CAN* CV4 ....154 B7
Ivyfield Rd *ERDW/GRVHL* B23 ....71 M8
Ivy Gv *BRWNH* WS8 ....40 E1
  NUNW/HART CV10 ....80 D7
  WSNGN B18 ....88 F8
Ivyhouse La *BILS/COS* WV14 ....66 F5
Ivyhouse Rd *HWK/WKHTH* B38 ....145 G5
Ivy House Rd *OLDBY* B69 ....86 B7
Ivy La *CBHAMNE* B4 ....7 K4
  RMSLY B62 ....121 H8
Ivy Lodge Cl
  CHWD/FDBR/MGN B37 ....110 E5
Ivy Rd *BVILLE* B30 ....124 E7
  DUDN DY1 ....84 E1
  HDSW B21 ....88 E6
  SCFLD/BOLD B73 ....73 G5
  SHLY B90 ....67 K6
Ivy Wy *SHLY* B90 ....147 L7
Izod St *REDW* B97 ....202 B1
Izons La *WBROM* B70 ....86 B4
Izons Rd *WBROM* B70 ....86 E4

Jacey Rd *LDYWD/EDGR* B16 ....106 B3
  SHLY B90 ....147 M1
Jackdaw Cl *SEDG* DY3 ....66 A5
Jackdaw Dr *CBROM* B36 ....92 D5
Jacker's Rd *COVN* CV6 ....134 F1
Jack Hayward Wy *WOLV* WV1 ....4 D3
Jack Holden Av *BILS/COS* WV14 .....66 E3
Jacklin Dr *COVS* CV3 ....181 G1
Jackson Cl *CNCK/NC* WS11 ....25 J1
  LGLYGN/QTN B68 ....86 F8
  RCOVN/BALC/EX CV7 ....115 L6
  RWWCK/WEL CV35 ....204 D7
  SPARK B11 * 107 M6
  TPTN/OCK DY4 ....67 M4
  WOLVN WV10 ....19 L1
Jackson Crs *STRPT* SY13 ....188 C4
Jackson Dr *SMTHWKW* B67 ....87 H8
Jackson Rd *COVN* CV6 ....134 B4
  LICH WS13 ....20 F2
  RUGBYN/HIL CV21 ....187 L4
  WASH/WDE B8 ....90 B6
Jackson St *DUNHL/THL/PER* WV6 ..49 M1
  HAG/WOL DY9 ....102 C8
  LGLYGN/QTN B68 ....86 F8
Jackson Wk *CVALE* B35 ....91 L3
Jacmar Crs *SMTHWKW* B67 ....87 J7
Jacob Dr *TLHL/CAN* CV4 ....153 H4
Jacobean La *DOR/KN* B93 ....149 M4
Jacob's Hall La *GTWY* WS6 ....24 C4
Jacoby Pl *EDG* B15 ....107 G8
Jacox Crs *KNWTH* CV8 ....198 A1
Jade Cl *COV* CV1 ....17 H1
Jade Gv *CNCK/NC* WS11 ....17 G3
Jaffray Crs *ERDE/BCHGN* B24 ....90 D2
Jaffray Rd *ERDE/BCHGN* B24 ....90 D2
Jaguar *TAM/AM/WIL* B77 ....46 C3
Jakeman Cl *REDE* B98 ....203 J1
James Bridge Cl *WSLW* WS2 * 52 F6
James Cl *DARL/WED* WS10 ....52 D6
  SMTHWK B67 ....87 J8
Jamescroft *COVS* CV3 ....156 C1
James Dawson Dr *COVW* CV5 ....131 M5
James Eaton Cl *BRLYHL* DY5 ....102 D4
James Eaton Cl *HHTH/SAND* B71 ..69 G8
James Galloway Cl *COVS* CV3 ......156 C6
James Green Rd *TLHL/CAN* CV4 ...153 K3
Jameson Rd *AST/WIT* B6 ....90 A5
Jameson St
  DUNHL/THL/PER WV6 ....49 M1
James Rd *CSHL/WTROR* B46 ....93 K5
  GTB/HAM B43 ....70 C6
  KIDD DY10 ....108 D7
  SPARK B11 ....108 A2
James Samuel Pl *BHTH/HG* B12 ...107 K6
James Scott Rd *HALE* B63 ....102 E7
James St *BILS/COS* WV14 ....51 J7
  CBHAMW B1 ....6 D3
  CNCK/NC WS11 ....12 D8
  NUN CV11 ....80 E8
  RCOVN/BALC/EX CV7 ....96 C5
  RUGBYN/HIL CV21 ....186 F2
  WLNHL WV13 ....51 L3
James Turner St *WSNGN* B18 ....88 F7
James Watt Dr *BFLD/HDSWWD* B20...88 F0
James Watt Queensway
  ....7 H3
James Watt St *HHTH/SAND* B71 .....68 F5
Jane Lane Cl *WSLW* WS2 ....52 D1
Janice Gv *ALE/KHTH/YWD* B14 .....146 F1
Janine Av *WNSFLD* WV11 ....37 H3
Jaques Cl *CSHL/WTROR* B46 ....93 J5
Jardine Crs *TLHL/CAN* CV4 ....153 K3
Jardine Rd *AST/WIT* B6 ....89 K4
Jared Wy *AST/WIT* B6 ....89 L6
Jarvis Crs *OLDBY* B69 ....104 C1
Jarvis Rd *ERDW/GRVHL* B23 ....90 D4
Jasmin Cft *ALE/KHTH/YWD* B14 ...146 C2
Jasmine Cl *COVEN* WV9 ....35 K2
Jasmine Gv *BRGRVW* B61 ....191 K1
  CDSL WV8 ....20 F6

COVS CV3 ...156 A5
RLSN CV32 ...206 E3
Jasmine Pl COVS CV3 * ...156 A5
Jasmine Rd DUDS DY2 ...85 K4
TAM/AM/WIL B77 ...46 E1
Jason Cl TAM/AM/WIL B77 ...32 B8
Jason Rd HAG/WOL DY9 ...120 D1
Jayne Cl HHTH/SAND B71 ...69 J4
WNSFLD WV11 ...37 H6
Jay Park Crs KIDD DY10 ...164 E3
Jay Rd KGSWFD DY6 ...83 H5
Jays Av TPTN/OCK DY4 ...85 M1
Jays Cl REDE B98 ...203 L2
Jayshaw Av GTB/HAM B43 ...70 C5
Jean Dr TPTN/OCK DY4 ...68 B7
Jean St ATHST CV9 ...62 A4
Jeavons Pl BILS/COS WV14 ...51 G8
Jedburgh Av
  DUNHL/THL/PER WV6 ...48 C3
Jedburgh Gv COVS CV3 ...180 C1
Jeddo St BKHL/PFLD WV2 ...2 E8
Jeffcock Rd BDMR/CCFT WV3 ...49 L5
Jefferson Cl HHTH/SAND B71 ...68 C1
Jeffrey Av
  ETTPK/GDPK/PENN WV4 ...50 D7
Jeffrey Cl BDWTH CV12 ...116 B5
Jeffrey Rd BLKHTH/ROWR B65 ...104 C2
Jeffs Av BKHL/PFLD WV2 ...3 H9
Jeliff St TLHL/CAN CV4 ...153 K4
Jelleyman Cl KIDDW DY11 ...137 M7
Jenkins Cl BILS/COS WV14 ...51 G8
Jenkinson Rd DARL/WED WS10 ...68 B4
Jenkins Rd RUGBYN/HIL CV21 ...187 L4
Jenkins Rd SMHTH B10 ...108 A5
Jenks Av WOLVN WV10 ...36 C5
Jenks Rd WMBN WV5 ...64 D8
Jennens Rd CBHAMNE B4 ...7 K3
Jenner Cl WSLW WS2 ...38 D7
Jenner Rd WSLW WS2 ...38 D7
Jenner St BKHL/PFLD WV2 ...3 J7
COV CV1 ...9 H1
Jennings St COYHTH B64 ...103 H3
Jenny Cl BILS/COS WV14 ...67 J4
Jenny Walkers La
  DUNHL/THL/PER WV6 ...48 B5
Jensen TAM/AM/WIL B77 ...46 C3
Jenton Rd RLSS CV31 ...206 F3
Jephcott Rd WASH/WDE B8 ...108 E2
Jephson Dr
  LGN/SDN/BHAMAIR B26 ...109 K6
Jephson Pl RLSS CV31 * ...206 F6
Jeremy Gv HIA/OLT B92 ...127 M1
Jeremy Rd
  ETTPK/GDPK/PENN WV4 ...50 A8
Jerome Dr CNCK/NC WS11 ...17 K8
Jerome Rd CNCK/NC WS11 ...17 K8
  CSCFLD/WYGN B72 ...73 H1
  WSLW WS2 ...52 F4
Jerome Wy BNTWD WS7 ...18 F6
Jerrard Dr MGN/WHC B75 ...57 G8
Jerrard Ms MGN/WHC B75 * ...57 G8
Jerry's La ERDW/GRVHL B23 ...72 B6
  LICHS WS14 ...30 A5
Jersey Cl REDE B98 ...195 H6
Jersey Cft CBROM B36 ...92 F7
Jersey Rd WASH/WDE B8 ...108 B1
Jerusalem Wk KIDD DY10 ...138 C6
Jervis Cl BRLYHL DY5 ...84 A6
Jervis Crs FOAKS/STRLY B74 ...56 A2
Jervis Pk FOAKS/STRLY B74 ...56 A1
Jervis Rd TAM/AM/WIL B77 ...46 D8
Jervis Ter HDSW B21 * ...88 B5
Jervoise Dr NFLD/LBR B31 ...123 H4
Jervoise La HHTH/SAND B71 ...69 L4
Jervoise Rd SLYOAK B29 ...123 K4
Jervoise St WBROM B70 ...86 E1
Jesmond Gv HEDN WS12 ...13 L8
Jesmond Gv ERDE/BCHGN B24 ...91 H1
Jesmond Rd COV CV1 ...9 K2
Jessel Rd WSLW WS2 ...4 E3
Jessie Rd ALDR WS9 ...40 E4
Jesson Cl WSL WS1 ...5 K8
Jesson Rd MGN/WHC B75 ...57 G7
  SEDG DY3 ...66 E2
  WSL WS1 ...5 J5
Jesson St WBROM B70 ...87 J3
Jessop Dr TAM/AM/WIL B77 ...32 B8
Jevon St BILS/COS WV14 * ...66 F5
Jevons Rd SCFLD/BOLD B73 ...72 A2
Jew's La DUDN DY3 ...84 C1
Jiggins La RIDG/WDGT B32 ...123 G5
Jill Av GTB/HAM B43 ...70 A4
Jillcot Rd HIA/OLT B92 ...127 M2
Jim Forrest Cl COVS CV3 ...156 A5
Jinnah Cl BHTH/HG B12 ...107 L6
Jinnah Rd REDE B98 ...202 C3
Joanna Dr COVS CV5 ...181 G1
Joan St BKHL/PFLD WV2 ...50 C7
Joan Ward St COVS CV3 ...9 G9
Job's La TLHL/CAN CV4 ...153 L3
Jockey Fld SEDG DY3 ...66 C2
Jockey Hl LICHS WS14 * ...21 K8
Jockey La DARL/WED WS10 * ...68 A4
Jockey Rd SCFLD/BOLD B73 ...72 B3
Jodrell St NUN CV11 ...80 D7
Joe Obrien Cl COVS CV3 ...156 A7
Joeys La CDSL WV8 ...33 J3
John Bosco Cl HHTH/SAND B71 ...68 F6
John Bright Cl DSYBK/YTR DY4 ...67 K5
John Bright St CBHAM B2 ...6 E6
Johndory TAM/AM/WIL B77 ...46 D7
John Fletcher Cl
  DARL/WED WS10 ...68 F1
John Grace St COVS CV3 ...9 G7
John Harper St WLNHL WV13 ...51 M3
John Kempe Wy BHTH/HG B12 ...107 L6
John Knight Rd BDWTH CV12 ...98 F8
John McGuire Crs COVS CV3 ...156 C6
John Nash Sq KNWTH CV8 ...197 K2
John O'gaunt Rd KNWTH CV8 ...197 J2
John Riley Dr SHHTH WV12 ...38 A8
John Rd RMSLY B62 ...122 D1
John Rous Av TLHL/CAN CV4 ...153 M6
John Shelton Dr COVN CV6 ...134 A1
John Simpson Cl KNWTH CV8 ...183 L2
Johns La GTWY WS6 ...24 D2
  OLDBY B69 ...86 A3
  TPTN/OCK DY4 ...85 M1
  WNSFLD WV11 ...37 K6
Johnson Cl CBROM B36 ...91 K5
  DARL/WED WS10 ...52 B8
  LICH WS13 ...21 G4
  REDE B98 ...194 D3
  SPARK B11 ...108 A8
Johnson Dr CVALE B35 ...91 K2
Johnson Pl BILS/COS WV14 ...51 K6
Johnson Rd BDWTH CV12 ...117 G2
  BNTWD WS7 ...18 D5
  CNCK/NC WS11 ...16 B1
  COVN CV6 ...134 C5
  DARL/WED WS10 ...52 B8
  DARL/WED WS10 ...69 C3

ERDW/GRVHL B23 ...72 D8
  SHHTH WV12 ...38 B6
Johnsons Bridge Rd
  HHTH/SAND B71 ...69 G7
Johnsons Gv LGLYGN/QTN B68 ...105 G5
Johnson St ATHST CV9 ...61 G4
  BILS/COS WV14 ...66 D4
  BKHL/PFLD WV2 ...3 G1
  VAUX/NECH B7 ...90 A7
Johnstone St LOZ/NWT B19 ...89 H5
Johnston St WBROM B70 ...87 H4
John St BDWTH CV12 ...116 E3
  BKHL/PFLD WV2 ...50 F2
  BLKHTH/ROWR B65 ...104 A4
  BRLYHL DY5 ...102 B1
  CNCK/NC WS11 ...12 D8
  HEDN WS12 ...17 K2
  LOZ/NWT B19 ...88 F6
  NUN CV11 ...99 C3
  NUNW/HART CV10 ...98 C2
  OLDBY B69 ...86 E6
  RLSN CV32 ...206 D5
  STRBR DY8 ...101 K4
  TAM/AM/WIL B77 ...46 C2
  WBROM B70 ...68 D8
  WLNHL WV13 ...51 L4
  WSL WS1 ...4 E1
John St North HHTH/SAND B71 ...68 F8
John Thwaites Cl
  RUGBYS/DCH CV22 ...186 E3
Joiners Cft SOLH B91 ...128 C5
Joinings Bank LGLYGN/QTN B68 ...104 F1
Jolyffe Park Rd COVE CV2 ...135 K5
Jones Field Crs WOLV WV1 ...5 K1
Jones' La BNTWD WS7 ...19 K6
  GTWY WS6 ...24 F4
Jones Rd RCOVN/BALC/EX CV7 ...116 E4
  SHHTH WV12 ...38 B4
  WOLVN WV10 ...36 A7
Jones Wood Cl WALM/CURD B76 ...73 K6
Jonkel Av TAM/AM/WIL B77 ...46 D8
Jonquil Cl ERDW/GRVHL B23 ...72 A6
Jordan Cl KNWTH CV8 ...197 M3
  MGN/WHC B75 ...56 F1
  SMHTH B66 ...87 M8
Jordan Leys TPTN/OCK DY4 ...67 M8
Jordan Pl BILS/COS WV14 ...67 J2
Jordan Rd MGN/WHC B75 ...56 F1
Jordans Cl REDW B97 ...202 B7
The Jordans COVW CV5 ...154 A1
Jordan Wy ALDR WS9 ...40 F4
Jordan Well COV CV1 ...9 G5
Jorden's Wk BEWD DY12 ...163 G1
Joseph Creighton Cl COVS CV3 ...156 C6
Joseph Dewsbury Cl ...18 C5
Joseph Luckman Rd
  BDWTH CV12 ...116 E1
Joseph St OLDBY B69 ...86 D7
Josiah Houses BILS/COS WV14 * ...67 G5
Josiah Rd NFLD/LBR B31 ...144 B5
Jowett TAM/AM/WIL B77 ...46 B3
Jowett's La HHTH/SAND B71 ...68 F5
Joyberry Dr STRBR DY8 ...119 K2
Joyce Pool WWCK CV34 ...205 J6
Joyce Wy RUGBYS/DCH CV22 ...185 L5
Joynson St DARL/WED WS10 ...52 C8
Jubilee Av HHTH/SAND B71 ...68 F2
  REDW B97 ...202 B6
Jubilee Cl BLOX/PEL WS3 ...39 J7
  GTWY WS6 ...24 F2
Jubilee Crs COVN CV6 ...133 M6
Jubilee Dr North KIDD DY11 ...163 M3
Jubilee Dr South KIDD DY11 ...163 M3
Jubilee Gdns ERDW/GRVHL B23 ...71 M6
Jubilee Rd BILS/COS WV14 ...67 L1
  RBRY B45 ...143 J3
  TPTN/OCK DY4 ...67 L6
Jubilee St HHTH/SAND B71 ...68 F8
  RUGBYN/HIL CV21 ...185 C2
Jubilee Ter BDWTH CV12 * ...116 F1
Judd Cl BDWTH CV12 ...116 D2
Judds La COVN CV6 ...134 C1
Judge Cl OLDBY B69 ...86 E6
Judge Rd BRLYHL DY5 ...102 D6
Judith Wy RUGBYS/DCH CV22 ...185 L5
Juggins La HOCK/TIA B94 ...172 F6
Julia Av ERDE/BCHGN B24 ...91 K1
Julia Gdns HHTH/SAND B71 ...68 F2
Julian Cl BRGRVW B61 ...168 E5
  COVE CV2 ...135 K5
  GTWY WS6 ...24 E2
  WOLV WV1 ...50 F3
Julian Rd WOLV WV1 ...50 F3
Julie Cft BILS/COS WV14 ...67 J4
Juliet Cl NUN CV11 ...99 L4
Juliet Dr RUGBYS/DCH CV22 ...186 B7
Juliet Rd RMSLY B62 ...122 C1
Julius Dr CSHL/WTROR B46 ...93 K4
Junction One
  RUGBYN/HIL CV21 * ...160 E7
Junction Rd BKHL/PFLD WV2 ...50 F6
  BRGRVW B61 ...191 J2
  HDSW B21 ...88 A5
  STRBR DY8 ...101 J5
  STRBR DY8 ...119 M1
Junction St DUDS DY2 ...84 F5
  OLDBY B69 ...86 B4
  WSL WS1 ...4 D8
Junction St South OLDBY B69 ...86 B8
The Junction STRBR DY8 ...101 J5
June Crs TAM/AM/WIL B77 ...32 C8
June Cft
  LGN/SDN/BHAMAIR B26 ...110 B8
Junewood Cl RUGBYN/HIL CV21 ...161 H6
Juniper TAM/AM/WIL B77 ...46 B3
Juniper Cl ACGN B27 ...108 F8
  BDWTH CV12 ...116 B3
  HEDN WS12 ...13 L7
Juniper Dr COVW CV5 ...132 D8
  DSYBK/YTR DY6 ...69 M1
  WALM/CURD B76 ...73 L6
Juniper Ri HALE B63 ...103 L8
Jury Rd BRLYHL DY5 ...102 D6
Jury St WWCK CV34 ...205 J7
Jutland Rd MOS/BIL B13 ...125 M6

K

Kalfs Dr RUGBYS/DCH CV22 ...185 M5
Kanzan Rd COVE CV2 ...135 G1
Kareen Gv COVS CV3 ...157 G6
Karen Cl NUNW/HART CV10 ...80 C6
Karen Wy BRLYHL DY5 ...102 B5
Karlingford Cl COVW CV5 ...154 B5
Katherine Rd SMTHWK B67 ...105 K3
Kathleen Av BDWTH CV12 ...116 C4
Kathleen Rd CSCFLD/WYGN B72 ...73 G1
  YDLY B25 ...109 G6
Katie Rd SLYOAK B29 ...124 C4
Katmandu Rd BRGRVE B60 ...192 C4
Katrine Cl NUNW/HART CV10 ...80 A8
Katrine Rd STRPT DY13 ...163 J7

Kay Cl RUGBYN/HIL CV21 ...161 G6
Kayne Cl KGSWFD DY6 ...83 G6
Kaysbrook Dr RRUGBY CV23 ...183 L2
Kean Cl LICH WS13 ...20 C3
Keanscott Dr LGLYGN/QTN B68 ...105 K1
Keasdon Gv WLNHL WV13 ...52 A3
Keating Gdns MGN/WHC B75 ...56 F1
Keats Av CNCK/NC WS11 ...12 C1
  SMHTH B10 ...108 B6
Keats Cl CRTAM B79 ...31 K5
  FOAKS/STRLY B74 ...42 D7
  NUNW/HART CV10 ...79 J8
  SEDG DY3 ...66 D3
  STRBR DY8 ...101 L5
Keats Dr BILS/COS WV14 ...67 H3
Keats Gv ACGN B27 ...126 F4
  WOLVN WV10 ...36 A5
Keats Pl KIDD DY10 ...138 F7
Keats Rd BLOX/PEL WS3 ...39 J1
  COVE CV2 ...156 B3
  SHHTH WV12 ...38 C5
Keble Gv
  LGN/SDN/BHAMAIR B26 ...109 M7
  WSL WS1 ...5 K9
Keble Wk CRTAM B79 ...31 L1
Kebull Gn TLHL/CAN CV4 ...153 J5
Kedleston Cl BLOX/PEL WS3 * ...38 C2
Kedleston Rd HLGN/YWD B28 ...126 D7
Keel Dr MOS/BIL B13 ...126 B4
Keele Cl REDE B98 ...195 H1
Keeley St BORD B9 ...107 M3
Keeling Dr CNCK/NC WS11 ...15 M4
Keeling St KNWTH CV8 ...179 M8
Keenan Dr BDWTH CV12 ...116 B4
Keen St SMTHWK B66 ...106 A1
Keepers Cl CDSL WV8 ...34 E5
Keepers Gate Cl MGN/WHC B75 * ...57 G6
Keepers Rd FOAKS/STRLY B74 ...42 A8
Keepers Wk BDWTH CV12 * ...116 B3
Keer Ct BORD B9 * ...107 M2
Kegworth Cl COVN CV6 ...134 C7
Kegworth Rd ERDW/GRVHL B23 ...90 A4
Keir Cl RLSN CV32 ...206 A5
Keir Pl STRBR DY8 ...101 J3
Keir Rd DARL/WED WS10 ...69 G3
Keith Rd RLSN CV32 ...206 F1
Kelby Cl NFLD/LBR B31 ...144 C2
Kelby Rd NFLD/LBR B31 ...144 C1
Keldy Cl DUNHL/THL/PER WV6 ...35 H8
Kele Rd TLHL/CAN CV4 ...153 K6
Kelfield Av HRBN B17 ...123 M1
Kelia Dr SMTHWK B67 ...87 K7
Kelling Cl BRLYHL DY5 ...102 A5
Kellington Cl WASH/WDE B8 ...108 D1
Kelmarsh Dr SOLH B91 ...148 F4
Kelmscote Rd COVN CV6 ...133 K5
Kelmscott Rd HRBN B17 ...105 H6
Kelsall Cl WOLV WV1 ...50 F3
Kelsall Cft CBHAMW B1 ...6 A4
Kelsey Cl NUN CV11 ...99 J2
  VAUX/NECH B7 * ...107 M1
Kelsey La RCOVN/BALC/EX CV7 ...152 B8
Kelsey's Cl KNWTH CV8 ...183 K2
Kelso Gdns
  DUNHL/THL/PER WV6 ...48 B3
Kelsull Cft
  CHWD/FDBR/MGN B37 ...110 E4
Kelton Ct EDG B15 ...106 C7
Kelverdale Gv
  ALE/KHTH/YWD B14 ...146 A1
Kelverley Gv HHTH/SAND B71 ...69 L4
Kelvin Av COVE CV2 ...135 H8
Kelvin Cl KIDD DY11 ...137 L5
Kelvin Dr CNCK/NC WS11 ...16 E1
Kelvin Pl BLOX/PEL WS3 ...38 F7
Kelvin Rd NFLD/LBR B31 ...144 A4
  RLSN CV32 ...198 F8
  WSLW WS2 ...38 C7
Kelvin Wy WBROM B70 ...87 G4
Kelway COVS CV3 ...157 H4
Kelway Av GTB/HAM B43 ...70 F2
Kelwood Dr HALE B63 ...103 K8
Kelynmead Rd STETCH B33 ...109 J3
Kemberton Cl BDMR/CCFT WV3 ...49 G4
Kemberton Rd BDMR/CCFT WV3 ...49 G4
  SLYOAK B29 ...123 L3
Kemble Cl SHHTH WV12 ...52 B1
Kemble Cft CVALE B35 ...91 G2
Kemelstowe Crs HALE B63 ...121 G5
Kemerton Wy SHLY B90 ...148 D8
Kempe Rd STETCH B33 ...109 J1
Kempley Av COVE CV2 ...156 A3
Kempsey Cl HALE B63 ...121 J1
  HIA/OLT B92 ...127 K2
  OLDBY B69 ...104 D1
  REDE B98 ...202 F6
Kempsey Covert
  HWK/WKHTH B38 ...145 J6
Kempsford Cl REDE B98 ...202 D7
Kemps Green Rd
  RCOVN/BALC/EX CV7 ...151 M7
Kempson Av CSCFLD/WYGN B72 ...73 G4
  HHTH/SAND B71 ...68 F8
Kempson Rd CBROM B36 ...91 K5
Kempsons Gv BILS/COS WV14 ...66 F2
Kempthorne Av WOLVN WV10 ...36 C5
Kempthorne Gdns
  BLOX/PEL WS3 ...38 E3
Kempthorne Rd BILS/COS WV14 ...51 K7
Kempton Cl HEDN WS12 ...13 L1
Kempton Ct BRGRVW B61 ...168 E4
Kempton Crs RLSN CV32 ...207 G1
Kempton Dr GTWY WS6 ...25 G2
Kempton Park Rd CBROM B36 ...91 H5
Kempton Wy STRBR DY8 ...119 J2
Kemsey Dr BILS/COS WV14 ...67 J1
Kemshead Av NFLD/LBR B31 ...144 C5
Kemsley Rd
  ALE/KHTH/YWD B14 ...146 D3
Ken St NUN CV11 ...99 G5
Kenchester Cl REDE B98 ...203 K3
Kendai Av CSHL/WTROR B46 ...93 K5
  RBRY B45 ...143 J3
  RLSN CV32 ...206 A5
Kendal Cl BRGRVE B60 ...191 M4
  DUNHL/THL/PER WV6 ...35 K7
  NUN CV11 ...81 L7
  REDE B98 ...203 L2
Kendal Ct ALDR WS9 * ...40 D7
  YDLY B25 ...109 G7
Kendal Dr RBRY B45 ...170 A4
Kendal End Rd RBRY B45 ...170 A3
Kendal Gv HIA/OLT B92 ...128 C3
Kendal Ri COVN CV6 ...133 K8

Kendal Ri COVW CV5 ...154 A1
  DUNHL/THL/PER WV6 ...35 K7
  LGLYGN/QTN B68 ...104 F2
Kendal Rise Rd RBRY B45 ...143 M6
Kendal Rd SPARK B11 ...107 M8
Kendlewood Rd KIDD DY10 ...138 F4
Kendon Av COVN CV6 ...133 J7
Kendrick Av
  HIA/OLT B92 ...128 D7
Kendrick Cl CRTAM B79 ...31 K5
  COVN CV6 ...134 C1
Kendrick Pl BILS/COS WV14 ...67 L1
Kendrick Rd BILS/COS WV14 ...67 K8
  ERDE/BCHGN B24 ...73 K8
  WOLVN WV10 ...36 D1
Kendricks Rd DARL/WED WS10 ...52 D6
Kenelm Rd BILS/COS WV14 ...67 L2
  LGLYGN/QTN B68 ...104 E2
  SCFLD/BOLD B73 ...72 F1
  SMHTH B10 ...108 C5
Kenelm's Ct RMSLY B62 ...121 L8
Kenilworth Cl FOAKS/STRLY B74 ...56 E5
  PENK ST19 ...14 B8
  REDW B97 ...202 B7
  STRBR DY8 ...101 H3
  TPTN/OCK DY4 ...85 H1
Kenilworth Crs
  ETTPK/GDPK/PENN WV4 ...66 C1
  WSLW WS2 ...38 C7
Kenilworth Dr CNCK/NC WS11 ...16 E1
  KIDD DY11 ...164 C3
  NUN CV11 ...98 E2
Kenilworth Rd
  BFLD/HDSWWD B20 ...89 J3
  COVS CV5 ...154 E6
  DOR/KN B93 ...150 B7
  DUNHL/THL/PER WV6 ...48 D1
  KNWTH CV8 ...178 C3
  LGLYGN/QTN B68 ...105 H5
  LICHS WS14 ...20 F7
  RCOVN/BALC/EX CV7 ...130 A3
  RLSN CV32 ...198 C6
  RLSN CV32 ...199 G5
  TAM/AM/WIL B77 ...46 D8
  TLHL/CAN CV4 ...180 A4
Kenilworth St RLSN CV32 ...206 D5
Kenley Gv RUGBYS/DCH CV22 ...186 A3
Kenley Gv SHLY B90 ...148 B3
Kenmare Wy WNSFLD WV11 ...51 G1
Kenmore Av HEDN WS12 ...12 D6
Kenmore Dr MGN/WHC B75 ...57 G6
Kennan Av RLSS CV31 ...206 D7
Kennedy Cl KIDD DY10 ...164 C2
  SEDG DY3 ...84 B1
Kennedy Cft
  LGN/SDN/BHAMAIR B26 ...109 L6
Kennedy Crs DARL/WED WS10 ...52 A6
Kennedy Gv BVILLE B30 ...124 F7
Kennedy Rd WOLVN WV10 ...3 H3
Kennedy Sq RLSN CV32 * ...206 E4
Kennel La ATHST CV9 ...63 H6
Kennerley Rd
  LGN/SDN/BHAMAIR B26 ...109 L6
Kennet Cl COVS CV3 ...156 A4
Kennet Cl BRWNH WS8 ...26 A3
  WSLW WS2 ...52 F2
Kenneth Gv ERDW/GRVHL B23 ...71 L8
Kennford Cl OLDBY B69 ...86 A7
Kennington Rd WOLVN WV10 ...37 H7
Kenpas Hwy COVS CV3 ...154 D8
Kenrick Cft CVALE B35 ...91 K3
Kenrick Wy SMTHWK B66 ...87 K5
  WBROM B70 ...87 H6
Kensington Av
  BHTH/HG B12 ...107 J8
Kensington Ct
  NUNW/HART CV10 ...80 A7
Kensington Dr CRTAM B79 ...31 L5
  FOAKS/STRLY B74 ...42 D8
Kensington Gdns STRBR DY8 ...101 G4
Kensington Rd COVW CV5 ...8 C1
  NUNW/HART CV10 ...80 A7
  SHHTH WV12 ...37 M5
  SLYOAK B29 ...124 E4
Kensington St LOZ/NWT B19 ...89 H2
Kenswick Dr HALE B63 ...121 L3
Kent Av POL/KGSB/FAZ B78 ...45 L4
  WSLW WS2 ...52 F2
Kent Cl ALDR WS9 ...40 H4
  BLOX/PEL WS3 ...39 J8
  COVS CV3 ...155 J7
  HHTH/SAND B71 ...68 F6
  KIDD DY10 ...164 C2
Kenthurst Cl COVW CV5 ...153 G1
Kentish Rd HDSW B21 ...88 A5
Kentmere Cl COVE CV2 ...135 J3
Kentmere Rd BRGRVE B60 ...191 M4
Kenton Av DUNHL/THL/PER WV6 ...48 E7
Kent Pl DUDS DY2 ...85 G4
  HEDN WS12 ...17 K4
Kenton Wk SLYOAK B29 ...124 A4
Kent Rd BKHL/PFLD WV2 ...50 C6
  DARL/WED WS10 ...69 H1
  RBRY B45 ...143 K4
  RMSLY B62 ...104 B7
  STRBR DY8 ...101 H5
Kent's Cl HIA/OLT B92 ...127 K1
Kent St DIG/EDG B5 ...7 G7
  SEDG DY3 ...66 C3
  WSL WS1 ...39 J8
Kent St North WSNGN B18 ...88 D8
The Kent CRTAM B79 ...31 J6
Kentwell CRTAM B79 ...31 J6
Kenward Cft HRBN B17 ...105 J6
Kenway HLYWD B47 ...146 E5
Kenwick Rd HRBN B17 ...123 H1
Kenwood Rd BORD B9 ...108 F3
Kenyon Cl BRGRVE B60 ...191 M4
  STRBR DY8 ...101 J7
Kenyon St CBHAMNW B3 ...6 C3
Kepler CRTAM B79 ...31 J6
Keppel Cl RUGBYS/DCH CV22 ...186 A4
Keppel St COV CV1 ...134 C8
Kerby Rd ERDW/GRVHL B23 ...90 E5
Keresley Brook Rd COVN CV6 ...133 J5
Keresley Cl COVN CV6 ...133 K6
  SOLH B91 ...128 C4
Keresley Green Rd COVN CV6 ...133 J6
Keresley Gv SLYOAK B29 ...123 K5
Keresley Rd COVN CV6 ...133 J5
Kernthorpe Rd
  ALE/KHTH/YWD B14 ...146 A3
Kerr Dr TPTN/OCK DY4 ...67 J5
Kerria Rd TAM/AM/WIL B77 ...46 F3
Kerridge Cl COVEN WV9 ...22 E8
Kerris Wy COVS CV3 ...156 C3
Kerry Cl BRLYHL DY5 ...84 A6
  NFLD/LBR B31 ...123 J7
Kerry Croft Cl REDW B97 ...202 B3
Kerry Gdns WNSFLD WV11 ...51 H1
Kerswell Cl REDW B97 ...193 M8
Kerswell Dr SHLY B90 ...176 B3
Kesterton Rd FOAKS/STRLY B74 ...42 A8
Kesteven Cl EDG B15 ...106 C7

Kesteven Rd HHTH/SAND B71 ...69 G6
Keston Rd KGSTG B44 ...71 K1
Kestrel TAM/AM/WIL B77 ...46 F1
Kestrel Av YDLY B25 ...108 F5
Kestrel Cl ERDW/GRVHL B23 ...72 B7
  KIDD DY10 ...164 C3
Kestrel Cft COVS CV3 ...155 H7
Kestrel Dr FOAKS/STRLY B74 ...42 D8
Kestrel Gv HEDN WS12 ...17 J2
  SHHTH WV12 ...38 A5
  SLYOAK B29 ...123 M7
Kestrel Ri DUNHL/THL/PER WV6 ...35 H8
Kestrel Rd DUDN DY1 ...84 E5
  HALE B63 ...120 F4
  LGLYGN/QTN B68 ...104 D3
Kestrel Wy GTWY WS6 ...24 F2
Keswick Cl NUN CV11 ...81 L7
Keswick Dr KGSWFD DY6 ...83 H7
  RUGBYS/DCH CV21 ...161 G5
Keswick Gn RLSN CV32 ...206 B4
Keswick Gv FOAKS/STRLY B74 ...55 K3
  HIA/OLT B92 ...127 K1
Keswick Wk COVE CV2 ...156 D1
Ketley Cft BHTH/HG B12 ...107 K6
Ketley Fids KGSWFD DY6 ...83 L8
Ketley Hill Rd DUDN DY1 ...84 D5
Ketley Rd KGSWFD DY6 ...83 L8
Kettlebrook Rd SHLY B90 ...148 F7
  TAM/AM/WIL B77 ...46 A1
Kettlehouse Rd KGSTG B44 ...71 K1
Kettlesbank Rd SEDG DY3 * ...84 C5
Kettlewell Cl WWCK CV34 ...205 J4
Kettlewell Wy
  CHWD/FDBR/MGN B37 ...110 D3
Ketton Gv STETCH B33 ...110 B6
Kevilik St COVS CV3 ...155 H7
Kew Cl CHWD/FDBR/MGN B37 ...110 D3
  KNWTH CV8 ...180 A8
Kew Dr DUDN DY1 ...84 E3
Kew Gdns STETCH B33 ...109 H4
Kew Rd RUGBYN/HIL CV21 ...186 E1
Kewstoke Cl SHHTH WV12 ...37 J4
Kewstoke Rd SHHTH WV12 ...37 J4
Keyes Dr KGSWFD DY6 ...83 H4
Keyham Ct RUGBYS/DCH CV22 ...186 A5
  RLSN CV32 ...206 A3
Key Hill WSNGN B18 ...88 F8
Key Hill Circ WSNGN B18 ...6 A1
Key Hill Dr WSNGN B18 ...88 F8
Keynell Covert BVILLE B30 ...146 A3
Keynes Dr BILS/COS WV14 ...51 L8
Keys Crs HHTH/SAND B71 ...69 G7
Keys Hl ATHST CV9 ...62 A4
Keys Park Rd HEDN WS12 ...17 J2
Keyte TPTN/OCK DY4 ...67 L8
The Keyway WLNHL WV13 ...51 L5
Keyworth Cl TPTN/OCK DY4 ...67 M8
Khyber Cl DARL/WED WS10 ...52 A5
Kidd Cft DARL/WED WS10 ...52 A8
Kidderminster Rd BEWD DY12 ...163 G1
  BRGRVW B61 ...191 J2
  HAG/WOL DY9 ...119 M8
  KGSWFD DY6 ...82 F6
  KIDD DY10 ...119 G6
Kidderminster Rd South
  HEDN WS12 ...140 C2
Kielder Cl DSYBK/YTR WS5 ...70 A2
  HEDN WS12 ...17 J3
Kielder Dr NUNW/HART CV10 ...98 D3
Kielder Gdns HAG/WOL DY9 ...119 M4
Kier's Bridge Cl TPTN/OCK DY4 ...85 L2
Kilburn Dr COVW CV5 ...154 D2
  KGSWFD DY6 ...83 K4
Kilburn Gv KGSTG B44 ...71 K2
Kilburn Pl DUDS DY2 ...85 H7
Kilburn Rd KGSTG B44 ...71 K2
Kilby Av LDYWD/EDGR B16 ...6 A6
Kilby Gv RLSS CV31 ...207 G8
Kilby Gv BFLD/HDSWWD B20 ...88 D3
Kilcote Rd SHLY B90 ...147 G3
Kildale Cl COV CV1 ...9 J3
Kilderkin Ct COV CV1 ...9 H8
Kildwick Wy WWCK CV34 ...205 J4
Kilmet Wk SMTHWK B67 * ...87 K8
Kilmore Cft CBROM B36 ...91 J4
Kilmorie Rd ACGN B27 ...109 G6
  CNCK/NC WS11 ...16 A3
Kiln Cl NUNW/HART CV10 ...98 C3
Kiln La SHLY B90 ...173 K1
  YDLY B25 ...108 F7
Kilnsey Gv WWCK CV34 ...205 J4
Kiln Wy POL/KGSB/FAZ B78 ...47 K4
Kilpeck Cl REDE B98 ...203 K3
Kilsby Gv SOLH B91 ...149 G5
Kilvert Rd DARL/WED WS10 ...68 A3
Kimberlee Av KIDD DY10 ...138 F1
Kimberley Av WASH/WDE B8 ...90 C8
Kimberley Cl COVW CV5 ...153 K1
  FOAKS/STRLY B74 ...194 F6
Kimberley Pl BILS/COS WV14 ...66 F6
Kimberley Rd BDWTH CV12 ...116 F6
  HIA/OLT B92 ...127 L3
  KNWTH CV8 ...180 D1
  RUGBYS/DCH CV21 ...186 F1
  SMTHWK B66 ...87 G5
Kimberley St BDMR/CCFT WV3 ...2 B7
Kimble Cl COVW CV5 ...153 M1
Kimble Gv ERDE/BCHGN B24 ...91 H2
Kimbley Rd HHTH/SAND B71 ...68 F6
Kimpton Cl ALE/KHTH/YWD B14 ...146 C3
Kimsan Cft FOAKS/STRLY B74 ...55 L6
Kinchford Cl SOLH B91 ...148 F5
Kineton Cl REDE B98 ...203 H4
Kineton Cft RIDG/WDGT B32 ...123 G5
Kineton Green Rd HIA/OLT B92 ...127 H5
Kineton La HOCK/TIA B94 ...174 A3
Kineton Ri SEDG DY3 ...66 A3
Kineton Rd COVE CV2 ...135 M1
  RBRY B45 ...143 J3
  SCFLD/BOLD B73 ...72 C4
Kinfare Dr DUNHL/THL/PER WV6 ...48 F1
Kinfare Ri DUDN DY3 ...84 C1
King Charles Av WSLW WS2 ...52 C3
King Charles Cl KIDD DY11 ...138 A1
King Charles Ct KGSTG B44 ...71 M3
King Charles Rd RMSLY B62 ...122 E1
King Charles Sq KIDD DY10 * ...138 C2
King Edmund St DUDN DY1 ...84 D2
King Edward Av BRGRVW B61 ...191 H1
King Edward Rd BRGRVW B61 ...168 D8
  COV CV1 ...9 L4
  MOS/BIL B13 ...125 K2
  NUN CV11 ...99 H1
  RUGBYN/HIL CV21 ...186 F1
King Edwards Cl
  BFLD/HDSWWD B20 * ...88 F5
King Edwards Gdns
  BFLD/HDSWWD B20 * ...98 F6
King Edward's Rw
  BKHL/PFLD WV2 * ...2 F9

King Edward's Sq
SCFLD/BOLD B73 57 G8
King Edward St
DARL/WED WS10 52 B8
Kingfield Rd COVN CV6 134 B7
SHLY B90 147 G3
Kingfisher TAM/AM/WIL B77 46 E7
Kingfisher Av NUNW/HART CV10 80 A8
Kingfisher Cl
LGN/SDN/BHAMAIR B26 109 L7
SEDG DY3 66 A3
Kingfisher Ct ALVE B48 170 E6
Kingfisher Dr CBROM B36 92 E5
HEDN WS12 17 G1
STRBR DY8 119 G1
Kingfisher Gv KIDD DY10 164 F2
SHHTH WV12 37 M5
Kingfisher Rd ERDW/GRVHL B23 72 A6
Kingfisher Veiw STETCH B33 91 L8
Kingfisher Wk PENK ST19 10 D5
Kingfisher Wy SLYOAK B29 124 B5
King George Av BRGRVW B61 191 K1
King George Cl BRGRVW B61 191 J1
King George Crs
RUSH/SHEL WS4 39 M7
King George Pl RUSH/SHEL WS4 39 M7
King George's Av BDWTH CV12 98 F8
COVN CV6 134 C3
King George VI Av
DSYBK/YTR WS5 54 A5
Kingham Cl REDE B98 203 L1
SEDG DY3 84 A3
Kingham Covert
ALE/KHTH/YWD B14 146 B3
Kingland Dr RLSN CV32 206 A4
King Richard St COVE CV2 9 L3
Kings Arms La STRPT DY13 188 B6
Kings Av ATHST CV9 63 J5
HEDN WS12 17 G1
OLDBY B69 85 M3
Kingsbridge Rd
NUNW/HART CV10 81 H7
RIDG/WDGT B32 123 H4
Kingsbridge Wk SMTHWK B66 87 M8
Kingsbrook Dr SOLH B91 148 F5
Kingsbury Av ERDE/BCHGN B24 91 H2
Kingsbury Cl RUSH/SHEL WS4 53 M1
WALM/CURD B76 74 B8
Kingsbury Link
POL/KGSB/FAZ B78 * 60 E3
Kingsbury Rd COVN CV6 133 H7
ERDE/BCHGN B24 90 C3
TPTN/OCK DY4 67 L5
WALM/CURD B76 74 A8
WALM/CURD B76 75 L3
Kingsclere Wk
ETTPK/GDPK/PENN WV4 49 G6
Kingscliff Rd SMHTH B10 108 E5
Kings Cl ALE/KHTH/YWD B14 125 G7
STUD B80 * 203 L4
Kingscote Cl REDE B98 195 H6
Kingscote Gv COVS CV3 180 E1
Kingscote Rd DOR/KN B93 175 J3
EDG B15 106 B6
King's Ct CHWD/FDBR/MGN B37 111 J4
NUN CV11 * 98 F1
STRBR DY8 101 J8
Kings Cft CBROM B36 92 D6
HEDN WS12 17 J1
LGN/SDN/BHAMAIR B26 109 L8
Kingscroft Cl FOAKS/STRLY B74 55 L5
Kingscroft Rd
FOAKS/STRLY B74 55 L6
Kingsdene Av STRBR DY8 101 G1
Kingsdown Av PBAR/PBCH B42 70 D7
Kingsdown Rd BNTWD WS7 18 C4
NFLD/LBR B31 123 J4
Kingsfield Rd
ALE/KHTH/YWD B14 125 J5
Kingsford Cl CBROM B36 92 B4
Kingsford Nouveau
KGSWFD DY6 83 L8
Kings Gdn BVILLE B30 145 J1
Kings Gdns BDWTH CV12 117 G3
Kings Green Av
HWK/WKHTH B38 145 K3
Kings Gv COVE CV2 155 M2
Kingshayes Rd ALDR WS9 40 F3
Kingshill Dr HWK/WKHTH B38 145 K3
King's Hill Fld DARL/WED WS10 52 C8
King's Hill La COVS CV3 180 D4
King's Hill Rd LICHS WS14 21 G7
Kingsholm Cl COVS CV3 156 F4
Kingshurst RLSS CV31 207 J7
Kingshurst Rd NFLD/LBR B31 144 E2
SHLY B90 147 K4
Kingshurst Wy
CHWD/FDBR/MGN B37 92 D8
Kingsland Av COVW CV5 154 D3
Kingsland Dr DOR/KN B93 175 J2
Kingsland Rd KGSTG B44 71 J1
WOLV WV1 2 C2
Kingslea Rd SOLH B91 148 C3
Kingsleigh Cft MGN/WHC B75 56 F3
Kingsleigh Dr CBROM B36 91 L5
Kingsleigh Rd
BFLD/HDSWWD B20 88 F3
Kingsley Av
DUNHL/THL/PER WV6 48 F1
HEDN WS12 13 G6
REDE B98 202 E2
RUGBYN/HIL CV21 187 J4
Kingsley Cl CRTAM B79 31 L7
Kingsley Ct YDLY B25 * 109 J5
Kingsley Crs BDWTH CV12 117 M2
Kingsley Gdns CDSL WV8 34 C2
Kingsley Gv SEDG DY3 65 L8
Kingsley Rd BHTH/HG B12 107 L8
BVILLE B30 145 H1
KGSWFD DY6 83 G8
Kingsley St DUDS DY2 85 G8
WSLW WS2 52 F6
Kingsley Ter COVE CV2 135 J5
Kingsley Wk COVE CV2 135 K5
Kingslow Av
ETTPK/GDPK/PENN WV4 49 H7
Kingsmead Ms COVS CV3 156 A7
King's Meadow HAG/WOL DY9 141 J3
Kingsmere Cl ERDE/BCHGN B24 90 C3
Kings Mill Cl DARL/WED WS10 52 C8
Kings Newnham La
RRUGBY CV23 158 E6
Kings Newnham Rd
RRUGBY CV23 158 F7
Kings Park Dr COVS CV3 156 F4
Kings Rd ALE/KHTH/YWD B14 125 G7
ERDW/GRVHL B23 90 A1
KGSTG B44 71 J2
KGSTG B44 72 A3
KIDDW DY11 138 A7
RUSH/SHEL WS4 40 A6
SEDG DY3 66 C5
SPARK B11 108 E8
WOLVN WV10 14 F7
Kings Sq BILS/COS WV14 * 66 E5
Kings Street Prec
DARL/WED WS10 52 B7
Kingstanding Rd KGSTG B44 71 K3
Kings Ter ALE/KHTH/YWD B14 125 G7
Kingsthorpe Rd
ALE/KHTH/YWD B14 146 E2
Kingston Cl CRTAM B79 32 A6
Kingston Ms RLSS CV31 207 G7
Kingston Rd BORD B9 107 M4
COVW CV5 154 D3
Kingston Rw CBHAMW B1 6 C5
Kingston Wy KGSWFD DY6 83 G6
King St ALDR WS9 40 D3
BDWTH CV12 117 G3
BILS/COS WV14 66 E5
BILS/COS WV14 67 J2
BNTWD WS7 18 D8
BRLYHL DY5 102 D5
CDYHTH B64 103 K4
CRTAM B79 45 M1
DARL/WED WS10 68 C3
DUDS DY2 85 G4
HAG/WOL DY9 120 D1
HALE B63 121 L1
RLSN CV32 206 E4
RUGBYN/HIL CV21 186 E1
SMTHWK B66 87 M6
SPARK B11 107 L7
STRBR DY8 101 J7
WLNHL WV13 51 M3
WOLV WV1 2 F5
WSL WS1 4 D9
King Street Pas BRLYHL DY5 102 E5
DUDS DY2 85 H4
Kingsway CNCK/NC WS11 16 E1
COVE CV2 155 L2
LGLYGN/QTN B68 104 F6
NUN CV11 98 F1
POL/KGSB/FAZ B78 60 A7
RLSS CV31 206 D7
RUGBYS/DCH CV22 186 E4
STRBR DY8 101 H5
STRPT DY13 163 J6
WNSFLD WV11 37 L1
WOLVN WV10 36 E7
Kingsway Av TPTN/OCK DY4 67 L5
Kingsway Dr HWK/WKHTH B38 145 K3
Kingsway North ALDR WS9 * 40 C7
Kingsway Rd WOLVN WV10 36 E7
Kingsway South ALDR WS9 * 40 C7
Kingsway Ter WNSFLD WV11 * 37 L1
Kingswear Av
DUNHL/THL/PER WV6 48 D2
Kingswinford Rd BRLYHL DY5 84 C6
Kingswood Av CNCK/NC WS11 16 A6
RCOVN/BALC/EX CV7 114 F5
Kingswood Cl COVN CV6 134 B4
HOCK/TIA B94 176 C8
SHLY B90 148 B4
Kingswood Cft VAUX/NECH B7 90 A6
Kingswood Dr BVILLE B30 146 A2
CNCK/NC WS11 17 K8
FOAKS/STRLY B74 71 K1
GTWY WS6 24 E1
Kingswood Gdns
BDMR/CCFT WV3 49 K7
Kingswood Rd MOS/BIL B13 125 L1
NFLD/LBR B31 144 D7
NUNW/HART CV10 97 M2
STRBR DY8 101 G1
Kingswood Ter YDLY B25 * 108 F6
Kington Cl SHHTH WV12 37 M5
Kington Gdns
CHWD/FDBR/MGN B37 110 D3
Kington Wy STETCH B33 109 J4
King William St COV CV1 9 J2
STRBR DY8 101 K5
Kiniths Crs HHTH/SAND B71 87 J1
Kiniths Wy HHTH/SAND B71 87 J1
RMSLY B62 104 C4
Kinlet Cl BDMR/CCFT WV3 48 E5
REDE B98 203 J2
Kinlet Gv NFLD/LBR B31 145 G3
Kinloch Dr DUDN DY1 84 D2
Kinman Wy RUGBYN/HIL CV21 161 G7
Kinnerley St WSL WS1 5 J5
Kinnersley Cl REDE B98 203 J2
Kinnersley Crs OLDBY B69 86 B8
Kinnerton Crs SLYOAK B29 123 K3
Kinross Av HEDN WS12 12 D6
Kinross Cl NUNW/HART CV10 98 D3
Kinross Crs GTB/HAM B43 70 F1
Kinross Rd RLSN CV32 206 F1
Kinsall Gn TAM/AM/WIL B77 47 G7
Kinsey Gv ALE/KHTH/YWD B14 146 D1
Kinsham Dr SOLH B91 148 F5
Kintore Cft RIDG/WDGT B32 122 F6
Kintyre Cl RBRY B45 143 J4
The Kintyre COVE CV2 135 M6
Kinver Av KIDDW DY11 163 L5
SHHTH WV12 37 M8
Kinver Cl COVE CV2 135 J4
Kinver Crs ALDR WS9 41 G4
Kinver Cft BHTH/HG B12 107 J7
WALM/CURD B76 73 K5
Kinver Dr
ETTPK/GDPK/PENN WV4 49 G8
HAG/WOL DY9 120 A6
Kinver Rd NFLD/LBR B31 145 H3
Kinver St STRBR DY8 101 H4
Kinwalsey La
RCOVN/BALC/EX CV7 113 J7
Kinwarton Cl
LGN/SDN/BHAMAIR B26 109 H7
Kipling Av BILS/COS WV14 66 F4
Kipling Cl NUNW/HART CV10 79 L8
TPTN/OCK DY4 67 L5
Kipling Ri CRTAM B79 31 K5
Kipling Rd COVN CV6 133 K5
NFLD/LBR B31 145 G1
SEDG DY3 65 L8
SHHTH WV12 38 C6
WOLVN WV10 36 B3
Kirby Av WWCK CV34 205 K4
Kirby Cl BILS/COS WV14 67 J2
COV CV1 134 B7
KNWTH CV8 157 K8
Kirby Corner Rd TLHL/CAN CV4 153 M8
Kirby Dr DUDN DY1 84 C2
Kirby Rd COVW CV5 154 D3
WSNGN B18 88 C7
Kirkby Cl RUGBYN/HIL CV21 161 J7
Kirkby Gn SCFLD/BOLD B73 72 E2
Kirkby Rd RUGBYN/HIL CV21 187 K5
Kirkdale Av COVN CV6 134 B2
Kirkham Gdns BRLYHL DY5 84 A7
Kirkham Gv STETCH B33 109 K1
Kirkham Wy TPTN/OCK DY4 67 L8
Kirkland Wy POL/KGSB/FAZ B78 44 F5
Kirkside Gv BRWNH WS8 26 D6
Kirkstall BLOX/PEL WS3 38 D3
Kirkstall Crs BLOX/PEL WS3 38 D3
Kirkstone RUGBYN/HIL CV21 161 H6
Kirkstone Ct BRLYHL DY5 101 M5
Kirkstone Crs GTB/HAM B43 70 D7
WMBN WV5 64 D7
Kirkstone Rd BDWTH CV12 116 E3
Kirkstone Wy BRLYHL DY5 101 M5
Kirkwall Rd RIDG/WDGT B32 123 H4
Kirkwood Av ERDW/GRVHL B23 72 D6
Kirstead Gdns
DUNHL/THL/PER WV6 48 F2
Kirtley TAM/AM/WIL B77 46 C3
Kirton Cl COVN CV6 133 K4
Kirton Gv DUNHL/THL/PER WV6 49 G1
SOLH B91 148 E4
STETCH B33 109 L1
Kitchener Rd COVN CV6 134 C4
DUDS DY2 85 K4
SLYOAK B29 124 F4
Kitchener St SMTHWK B66 88 B7
Kitchen La WNSFLD WV11 37 J5
WNSFLD WV11 37 L3
Kitebrook Cl REDE B98 203 J1
SHLY B90 148 E6
Kite La REDW B97 193 L8
Kites Cl WWCK CV34 205 J3
Kites Nest La RWWCK/WEL CV35 196 A4
Kitsland Rd BKDE/SHDE B34 92 C7
Kitswell Gdns RIDG/WDGT B32 122 E5
Kittermaster Rd
RCOVN/BALC/EX CV7 130 F3
Kittiwake Dr BRLYHL DY5 102 A6
KIDD DY10 164 F2
Kittoe Rd FOAKS/STRLY B74 56 D2
Kitt's Green Rd STETCH B33 109 M2
Kitwell La RIDG/WDGT B32 122 E5
Kitwood Av POL/KGSB/FAZ B78 47 K7
Kitwood Dr HIA/OLT B92 128 B6
Kixley La DOR/KN B93 150 A7
Klevedon Cl NUN CV11 99 L4
Knaresdale Cl BRLYHL DY5 102 A5
Knaves Castle Av BRWNH WS8 26 D3
Knebley Crs NUNW/HART CV10 99 G4
Knebworth Cl KGSTG B44 71 J5
The Knibbs WWCK CV34 * 205 J6
Knight Av COV CV1 9 K7
Knightcote Dr SOLH B91 148 F5
Knightley Cl RLSN CV32 199 J8
Knightley Rd SOLH B91 148 D3
Knightlow Av COVS CV3 156 A8
Knightlow Cl KNWTH CV8 198 A2
Knightlow Rd HRBN B17 105 M5
Knighton Cl FOAKS/STRLY B74 56 D2
Knighton Dr FOAKS/STRLY B74 56 D3
Knighton Rd DUDS DY2 103 H1
FOAKS/STRLY B74 42 B8
HEDN WS12 17 J2
NFLD/LBR B31 145 G1
Knight Rd BNTWD WS7 18 C4
KIDDW DY11 138 A2
Knights Av
DUNHL/THL/PER WV6 35 J7
Knightsbridge Av BDWTH CV12 98 F8
Knightsbridge Cl
FOAKS/STRLY B74 56 D1
Knightsbridge La SHHTH WV12 37 M7
Knightsbridge Rd HIA/OLT B92 127 K4
Knights Cl ERDW/GRVHL B23 90 C3
PENK ST19 10 D6
Knights Ct
CHWD/FDBR/MGN B37 111 J5
CNCK/NC WS11 25 L1
Knights Crs
DUNHL/THL/PER WV6 35 J6
Knightsfield Cl SCFLD/BOLD B73 72 A2
Knightsford Cl REDW B97 201 K3
Knights Hl ALDR WS9 54 F2
Knights Rd SPARK B11 126 E1
Knights Templar Wy
TLHL/CAN CV4 153 L4
Knightstone Av WSNGN B18 106 E1
Knights Wood Cl MGN/WHC B75 57 H6
Knightwick Crs
ERDW/GRVHL B23 72 A8
Knipersley Rd ERDW/GRVHL B23 72 E7
Knob Hl RRUGBY CV23 183 K7
Knoll Cl BNTWD WS7 18 E8
Knoll Cft ALDR WS9 41 G4
COVS CV3 155 G7
LDYWD/EDGR B16 * 106 E3
SHLY B90 174 B1
Knoll Dr COVS CV3 155 G7
WWCK CV34 205 J3
The Knoll KGSWFD DY6 83 J8
RIDG/WDGT B32 123 G4
Knottsall La LGLYGN/QTN B68 104 F2
Knotts Farm Rd KGSWFD DY6 101 L1
Knowesley Cl BRGRVE B60 191 M3
Knowlands Rd SOLH B91 148 E6
Knowle Cl RBRY B45 144 B6
REDE B98 195 G7
Knowle Hl ATHST CV9 77 G1
KNWTH CV8 180 A7
Knowle Hill Rd DUDS DY2 102 F1
Knowle La LICHS WS14 28 F3
Knowle Rd BLKHTH/ROWR B65 103 K1
HIA/OLT B92 150 C3
SPARK B11 126 B2
Knowles Av NUNW/HART CV10 98 A1
Knowles Dr FOAKS/STRLY B74 56 E6
Knowles Rd WOLV WV1 3 L6
Knowles St DARL/WED WS10 68 E2
Knowle Wood Rd DOR/KN B93 175 M3
Knox Crs NUN CV11 81 K6
Knox Rd BKHL/PFLD WV2 50 A7
Knox's Grave La LICHS WS14 29 M6
Knutswood Cl MOS/BIL B13 * 126 B6
Kohima Dr STRBR DY8 101 J8
Kossuth Rd BILS/COS WV14 66 E4
Kurtus TAM/AM/WIL B77 46 B7
Kyle Cl WOLVN WV10 35 M4
Kylemilne Wy STRPT DY13 189 G2
Kyles Wy RIDG/WDGT B32 122 F6
Kynaston Crs CDSL WV8 34 F3
Kyngsford Rd STETCH B33 110 B2
Kynner Wy COVS CV3 156 F5
Kyotts Lake Rd SPARK B11 107 L6
Kyrwicks La BHTH/HG B12 107 L6
Kyter La CBROM B36 91 M5

L

Laburnham Rd KGSWFD DY6 83 J7
Laburnum Av
CHWD/FDBR/MGN B37 92 D7
CNCK/NC WS11 16 B6
COVN CV6 133 K8
CRTAM B79 31 M5
KNWTH CV8 197 L1
SMTHWKW B67 105 J1
Laburnum Cl BDWTH CV12 116 C3
BLOX/PEL WS3 39 K3
CHWD/FDBR/MGN B37 92 D7
CNCK/NC WS11 16 C6
HLYWD B47 146 E8
POL/KGSB/FAZ B78 60 B7
REDE B98 202 C3
Laburnum Cft OLDBY B69 85 M3
Laburnum Dr WALM/CURD B76 73 L2
Laburnum Gv BNTWD WS7 18 D7
BRGRVW B61 191 K1
KIDDW DY11 137 L5
MOS/BIL B13 * 125 K2
NUNW/HART CV10 80 B7
RUGBYS/DCH CV22 186 C5
WSLW WS2 52 D2
WWCK CV34 205 M4
Laburnum Rd ALDR WS9 40 E2
BVILLE B30 124 D6
DARL/WED WS10 68 F2
DSYBK/YTR WS5 54 A8
DUDN DY1 84 F1
ETTPK/GDPK/PENN WV4 66 C2
TPTN/OCK DY4 67 K6
WOLV WV1 50 F5
Laburnum St BDMR/CCFT WV3 2 B7
STRBR DY8 101 J6
Laburnum Vls SPARK B11 * 108 A8
Laburnum Wy NFLD/LBR B31 144 E4
Lacell Cl WWCK CV34 205 H4
Laches Cl WOLVN WV10 14 B8
Laches La WOLVN WV10 22 C3
Ladbroke Dr WALM/CURD B76 73 K3
Ladbroke Gv ACGN B27 127 G5
Ladbroke Pk WWCK CV34 * 205 J5
Ladbrook Cl REDE B98 202 C6
Ladbrook Gv SEDG DY3 83 L2
Ladbrook Rd COVW CV5 153 L1
SOLH B91 149 G2
Ladbury Gv DSYBK/YTR WS5 69 L1
Ladbury Rd DSYBK/YTR WS5 69 L1
Ladeler Gv STETCH B33 110 B3
Ladies Wk SEDG DY3 66 B5
Lady Bank CRTAM B79 * 45 M1
RIDG/WDGT B32 122 F6
Lady Br POL/KGSB/FAZ B78 45 L1
Lady Bracknell Ms
NFLD/LBR B31 145 G1
Lady Byron La DOR/KN B93 149 K6
Ladycroft LDYWD/EDGR B16 6 A6
RLSN CV32 199 J8
Ladyfields Wy
RCOVN/BALC/EX CV7 133 M1
Lady Grey's Wk STRBR DY8 101 H8
Ladygrove Cl REDE B98 202 E5
Lady Harriet's La REDE B98 202 D1
Lady La COVN CV6 134 D1
HOCK/TIA B94 173 L3
Ladymead Dr COVN CV6 133 M3
Lady Meadow Cl
POL/KGSB/FAZ B78 45 L2
Ladymoor Rd BILS/COS WV14 67 G3
Ladypool Av SPARK B11 * 107 M7
Ladypool Cl RMSLY B62 122 A1
Ladypool Pl RUSH/SHEL WS4 39 L8
Ladypool Rd BHTH/HG B12 107 L8
Ladysmith Rd HALE B63 103 G7
Ladysmock RRUGBY CV23 161 H5
Lady Warwick Av BDWTH CV12 117 G3
Ladywell Cl WMBN WV5 64 E5
Ladywell Wk DIG/EDG B5 7 G7
Ladywood Circ
LDYWD/EDGR B16 106 E3
Ladywood Cl BRLYHL DY5 102 D3
Ladywood Middleway
LDYWD/EDGR B16 106 E3
Ladywood Rd FOAKS/STRLY B74 56 E5
LDYWD/EDGR B16 106 D4
Laggan Cl NUNW/HART CV10 80 A8
Lagonda TAM/AM/WIL B77 46 B2
Lagrange CRTAM B79 31 J7
The Lair POL/KGSB/FAZ B78 47 K5
Lake Av DSYBK/YTR WS5 5 M9
Lake Cl DSYBK/YTR WS5 54 A6
Lakedown Cl
ALE/KHTH/YWD B14 146 C4
Lakefield Cl HLGN/YWD B28 126 F6
Lakefield Rd WNSFLD WV11 37 J8
Lakehouse Gv
HWK/WKHTH B38 145 H2
Lakehouse Rd ERDW/GRVHL B23 72 C5
Lakeland Dr TAM/AM/WIL B77 46 E6
Lakenheath CRTAM B79 32 A6
Lakes Cl KIDDW DY11 138 A6
Lakes Ct BEWD DY12 162 D2
Lakeside BDWTH CV12 116 E3
CHWD/FDBR/MGN B37 111 J5
FOAKS/STRLY B74 41 M8
REDW B97 193 H6
Lakeside Cl WLNHL WV13 51 J2
Lakeside Ct BRLYHL DY5 101 M5
Lakeside Dr CNCK/NC WS11 17 L7
SHLY B90 148 D6
Lakeside Rd WBROM B70 68 E7
Lakes Rd ERDW/GRVHL B23 71 L7
The Lakes Rd BEWD DY12 162 D2
Lake St SEDG DY3 84 B2
Lake View Rd COVW CV5 154 D1
Lakewood Dr RBRY B45 143 M4
Lakey La HLGN/YWD B28 126 E5
Lakin Ct WWCK CV34 205 K5
Lakin Rd WWCK CV34 205 K5
Lambah Cl BILS/COS WV14 51 J6
Lamb Cl BKDE/SHDE B34 92 C8
Lamb Crs WMBN WV5 64 D8
Lambert Cl ERDW/GRVHL B23 72 B8
Lambert Ct KGSWFD DY6 83 H5
Lambert Dr BNTWD WS7 18 E6
Lambert End WBROM B70 86 F2
Lambert Fold DUDS DY2 85 J5
Lambert Rd WOLVN WV10 36 D7
Lambert St WBROM B70 86 F2
Lambeth Cl
CHWD/FDBR/MGN B37 110 F1
COVE CV2 135 J6
Lambeth Rd BILS/COS WV14 50 F6
KGSTG B44 71 J2
Lambourn Crs RLSS CV31 207 G7
Lambourne Cl COVW CV5 153 L1
GTWY WS6 24 D2
LICHS WS14 21 J5
Lambourne Gv STETCH B33 110 C3
Lambourne Wy BRLYHL DY5 101 M5
CNCK/NC WS11 17 L8
Lambourn Rd ERDW/GRVHL B23 90 B1
WLNHL WV13 52 B4
Lambscote Cl SHLY B90 147 G3
Lamb St COV CV1 8 E3
Lamerton Cl COVE CV2 135 G7
Lamintone Dr RLSN CV32 206 A3
Lammas Cl HIA/OLT B92 128 A4
Lammas Ct KNWTH CV8 183 L2
Lammas House COVN CV6 * 8 A2
Lammas Rd COVN CV6 154 D1
STRBR DY8 101 G2
Lammermoor Av GTB/HAM B43 70 D3
Lamont Av RIDG/WDGT B32 123 K2
Lamorna Cl BDMR/CCFT WV3 48 F5
NUN CV11 99 K1
Lamp La RCOVN/BALC/EX CV7 96 D7
Lamprey TAM/AM/WIL B77 46 B7
Lanark Cft CVALE B35 91 K2
Lancaster Av ALDR WS9 40 F5
DARL/WED WS10 69 G2
RBRY B45 143 L5
Lancaster Circus Queensway
CBHAMNE B4 7 H2
Lancaster Cl ATHST CV9 63 J4
BVILLE B30 124 E7
Lancaster Dr CVALE B35 91 M3
Lancaster Gdns
ETTPK/GDPK/PENN WV4 49 J8
Lancaster Pl BLOX/PEL WS3 39 G3
KNWTH CV8 197 J3
Lancaster Rd BEWD DY12 162 D2
BRLYHL DY5 102 A3
RUGBYN/HIL CV21 186 E1
Lancaster St CBHAMNE B4 7 H1
Lance Dr BNTWD WS7 18 C4
Lancelot Cl WASH/WDE B8 108 C2
Lanchester Cl CRTAM B79 31 J6
Lanchester Rd COVN CV6 133 M7
HWK/WKHTH B38 145 L4
Lanchester Wy CBROM B36 92 D4
Lancia Cl COVN CV6 134 F1
Lander Cl RBRY B45 143 L7
Landgate Rd HDSW B21 88 A3
Land La CHWD/FDBR/MGN B37 110 E6
Land Oak Dr KIDD DY10 138 F6
Landor Rd DOR/KN B93 149 L7
REDE B98 202 E4
WWCK CV34 205 H5
Landor St WASH/WDE B8 107 M2
Landport Rd WOLV WV1 3 L8
Landrake Rd KGSWFD DY6 83 K8
Landsdown Pl WSNGN B18 88 E8
Landseer Cl RUGBYN/HIL CV21 187 M5
Landseer Gv GTB/HAM B43 71 H1
Landsgate STRBR DY8 119 L4
Landswood Cl KGSTG B44 71 L4
Landswood Rd
LGLYGN/QTN B68 105 G1
Landywood Gn GTWY WS6 24 C3
Landywood La GTWY WS6 24 B3
Lane Av WSLW WS2 52 F2
Lane Cl WSLW WS2 52 F2
Lane Cft WALM/CURD B76 73 L5
Lane Green Av CDSL WV8 35 G4
Lane Green Rd CDSL WV8 35 G3
Lane Rd ETTPK/GDPK/PENN WV4 66 E2
Lanes Cl WMBN WV5 64 B8
Lanesfield Dr
ETTPK/GDPK/PENN WV4 66 E1
Laneside COVS CV3 156 C7
Laneside Av FOAKS/STRLY B74 55 K6
Laneside Gdns WSLW WS2 52 E3
Lane St BILS/COS WV14 67 H2
Langbank Av COVS CV3 156 B6
Langcliffe Av WWCK CV34 205 K4
Langcomb Rd SHLY B90 147 L5
Langdale Av COVN CV6 134 B2
Langdale Cl BRWNH WS8 26 C7
RLSN CV32 207 H2
RUGBYN/HIL CV21 161 G6
Langdale Ct TAM/AM/WIL B77 32 E7
Langdale Cft HDSW B21 88 C6
Langdale Dr BILS/COS WV14 51 H6
CNCK/NC WS11 15 M6
NUN CV11 81 L7
Langdale Rd GTB/HAM B43 70 D6
STRPT DY13 188 B4
Langdale Wy HAG/WOL DY9 120 B1
Langdon St BORD B9 107 M3
Langfield Rd DOR/KN B93 149 L6
Langford Av GTB/HAM B43 70 C5
Langford Cl WSL WS1 5 H5
Langford Cft SOLH B91 149 G3
Langford Gv HRBN B17 124 A2
Langham Cl
LGN/SDN/BHAMAIR B26 109 L6
Langham Gn FOAKS/STRLY B74 55 K4
Langholm Dr HEDN WS12 17 J3
SCFLD/BOLD B73 72 B4
Langland Dr SEDG DY3 66 A5
Langley Av BILS/COS WV14 67 G5
Langley Cl REDE B98 203 H4
Langley Crs LGLYGN/QTN B68 104 F1
Langley Cft TLHL/CAN CV4 153 K2
Langley Dr CVALE B35 91 L4
Langley Gdns BDMR/CCFT WV3 49 H6
Langley Green Rd OLDBY B69 104 E1
Langley Gv SMHTH B10 * 108 B5
Langley Hall Dr MGN/WHC B75 57 M7
Langley Hall Rd HIA/OLT B92 127 G6
MGN/WHC B75 57 M8
Langley Heath Dr
WALM/CURD B76 73 K2
Langley High St OLDBY B69 86 E8
Langley Ri HIA/OLT B92 128 B2
Langley Rd
ETTPK/GDPK/PENN WV4 48 C7
LGLYGN/QTN B68 104 E1
SMHTH B10 108 B5
Langleys Rd SLYOAK B29 124 C4
Langlodge Rd COVN CV6 133 M3
Langmead Cl WSLW WS2 52 B2
Langnor Rd COVE CV2 135 G6
Langsett Rd WOLVN WV10 3 J1
Langstone Rd
ALE/KHTH/YWD B14 146 F3
DUDN DY1 84 C4
Langton Cl CBROM B36 92 F7
COVS CV3 156 C5
Langton Pl BILS/COS WV14 51 L7
Langton Rd RUGBYN/HIL CV21 187 J4
WASH/WDE B8 108 C1
Langtree Av SOLH B91 148 F4
Langtree Cl HEDN WS12 17 H4
Langwood Cl TLHL/CAN CV4 153 M6
Langwood Ct CBROM B36 91 M5
Langworth Av ACGN B27 109 G8
Lannacombe Rd NFLD/LBR B31 144 C7
Lansbury Av DARL/WED WS10 68 A1
Lansbury Dr CNCK/NC WS11 16 C1
Lansbury Gn CDYHTH B64 103 M5
Lansbury Rd CDYHTH B64 103 M5
Lansdale Av HIA/OLT B92 128 D5
Lansdowne Av CDSL WV8 34 C3
Lansdowne Circ RLSN CV32 206 E4
Lansdowne Cl BDWTH CV12 116 E2
BILS/COS WV14 66 E6
DUDS DY2 85 K7
Lansdowne Crs RLSN CV32 * 206 E4
TAM/AM/WIL B77 46 B4
Lansdowne Pl
RUGBYN/HIL CV21 187 H3
Lansdowne Rd BILS/COS WV14 51 J6
ERDE/BCHGN B24 90 D2
HALE B63 121 H3
HDSW B21 88 E6
RLSN CV32 206 E4
RMSLY B62 104 D5
WOLV WV1 2 D3
Lansdowne St COVE CV2 9 L4
RLSN CV32 206 E4
WSNGN B18 106 D1
Lansdown Gn KIDDW DY11 137 M8
Lansdown Pl WSNGN B18 * 88 E8
Lant Cl RCOVN/BALC/EX CV7 152 F6
Lantern Rd DUDS DY2 103 G3
Lapal La RIDG/WDGT B32 122 E3
Lapal La North RMSLY B62 122 C2
Lapal La South RMSLY B62 122 C2
Lapley Cl WOLV WV1 50 F3
Lapper Av
ETTPK/GDPK/PENN WV4 66 D3
Lapwing TAM/AM/WIL B77 46 E7
Lapwing Cl GTWY WS6 24 A4
KIDD DY10 164 F4
Lapwing Cft ERDW/GRVHL B23 72 A6
Lapwing Dr HIA/OLT B92 129 M6
Lapwood Av KGSWFD DY6 83 L8
Lapworth Cl REDE B98 202 D6
Lapworth Dr SCFLD/BOLD B73 72 A2

Lapworth Gv BHTH/HG B12 107 K7
Lapworth Rd COVE CV2 135 G4
Lara Cl HRBN B17 105 M5
Lara Gv TPTN/OCK DY4 85 L3
Larch Av HDSW B21 88 B3
Larch Cl KINVER DY7 118 A2
LICHS WS14 21 J6
RUGBYS/DCH CV22 185 M3
Larch Cft
CHWD/FDBR/MGN B37 110 F3
OLDBY B69 85 M3
Larches Cottage Gdns
KIDDW DY11 * 164 B2
Larches La BDMR/CCFT WV3 2 A5
Larches Rd KIDDW DY11 164 B2
Larches St SPARK B11 107 L7
The Larches POL/KGSB/FAZ B78 60 B6
RCOVN/BALC/EX CV7 116 E5
Larchfield Cl BFLD/HDSWWD B20 88 F2
Larchfields KNWTH CV8 183 L1
Larch Gv SEDG DY3 66 C6
WWCK CV34 205 L3
Larchmere Dr BRGRVW B61 191 H2
HLGN/YWD B28 126 D5
WNSFLD WV11 37 L2
Larch Rd KGSWFD DY6 83 J6
Larch Tree Av COVW CV5 153 L2
Larchwood Crs
FOAKS/STRLY B74 55 J5
Larchwood Dr CNCK/NC WS11 16 E1
Larchwood Gn DSYBK/YTR WS5 69 L1
Larchwood Rd DSYBK/YTR WS5 69 L1
RCOVN/BALC/EX CV7 116 F5
Larcombe Dr
ETTPK/GDPK/PENN WV4 50 B8
Larford Wk STRPT DY13 188 D4
Large Av DARL/WED WS10 68 A1
Lark Cl ALE/KHTH/YWD B14 146 E3
Larkfield Av CBROM B36 91 M5
Larkfield Rd REDE B98 202 E4
Larkfield Wy COVW CV5 132 E7
Larkhill KIDD DY10 138 C6
Larkhill Rd STRBR DY8 119 G1
Larkhill Wk ALE/KHTH/YWD B14 146 B4
Larkin Cl BDWTH CV12 117 M2
WOLVN WV10 36 E4
Larkin Gv COVE CV2 135 K7
Lark Meadow Dr
CHWD/FDBR/MGN B37 110 C2
Larkspur RRUGBY CV23 161 H5
TAM/AM/WIL B77 60 B1
Larkspur Av BNTWD WS7 18 E8
Larkspur Cft CBROM B36 91 H5
Larkspur Dr WOLVN WV10 22 F6
Larkspur Rd DUDS DY2 85 K5
Larkspur Wy BRWNH WS8 26 B7
Larkswood Dr
ETTPK/GDPK/PENN WV4 65 G2
SEDG DY3 66 B6
Larne Rd
LGN/SDN/BHAMAIR B26 109 L6
Lassington Cl REDE B98 203 J2
Latches Cl DARL/WED WS10 52 C7
Latchford Cl REDE B98 195 J7
Latelow Rd STETCH B33 109 L3
Latham Av GTB/HAM B43 70 C6
Latham Crs TPTN/OCK DY4 85 L2
Latham Rd COVW CV5 8 A5
Latherford Cl WOLVN WV10 14 C8
Latherford La WOLVN WV10 14 F8
Lath La SMTHWK B66 87 H5
Lathom Gv STETCH B33 91 K8
Latimer Cl KNWTH CV8 197 K3
Latimer Gdns EDG B15 107 H6
Latimer Pl WSNGN B18 88 C7
Latimer Rd ALVE B48 170 E8
Latimer St WLNHL WV13 51 L2
Latymer Cl WALM/CURD B76 73 L6
Lauder Cl SEDG DY3 66 A4
WLNHL WV13 51 H4
Lauderdale Av COVN CV6 134 B2
Lauderdale Cl BRWNH WS8 26 C7
RUGBYN/HIL CV21 185 M1
Lauderdale Gdns WOLVN WV10 36 C2
Laughton Cl NFLD/LBR B31 144 F6
Launceston Cl DSYBK/YTR WS5 54 B6
TAM/AM/WIL B77 46 B3
Launceston Dr NUN CV11 99 K1
Launceston Rd DSYBK/YTR WS5 54 B6
The Launde
ALE/KHTH/YWD B14 147 H2
Laundry Rd SMTHWK B66 106 A2
Laural Dr SMTHWK B66 87 M5
Laureates Wk FOAKS/STRLY B74 56 E4
Laurel Av BHTH/HG B12 107 L8
POL/KGSB/FAZ B78 47 L6
Laurel Bank CRTAM B79 31 M7
Laurel Cl COVE CV2 135 J3
LICH WS13 21 H5
REDE B98 202 C3
Laurel Dr BNTWD WS7 19 G6
FOAKS/STRLY B74 55 J5
HEDN WS12 17 J1
NUNW/HART CV10 79 L6
RUGBYS/DCH CV22 185 M4
SMTHWK B66 87 L5
Laurel Gdns HDSW B21 88 C4
RUGBYS/DCH CV22 186 D5
Laurel Gv BDMR/CCFT WV3 49 J7
BILS/COS WV14 67 L1
BRGRVW B61 191 K1
BVILLE B30 124 C7
Laurel La HALE B63 121 M2
Laurel Rd BVILLE B30 145 L1
DSYBK/YTR WS5 53 M8
DUDN DY1 84 E1
HDSW B21 88 C3
TPTN/OCK DY4 67 K6
Laurels Crs
RCOVN/BALC/EX CV7 152 A7
The Laurels BDWTH CV12 116 C3
LGN/SDN/BHAMAIR B26 110 A8
POL/KGSB/FAZ B78 60 B6
SMTHWK B66 * 106 A1
Laurence Gv
DUNHL/THL/PER WV6 35 J6
Lauriston Cl DUDN DY1 84 D2
Lavender Av COVN CV6 133 K8
Lavender Cl BDWTH CV12 116 C4
COVEN WV9 35 K2
RRUGBY CV23 161 J5
Lavender Gdns
ERDW/GRVHL B23 71 M6
Lavender Gv BILS/COS WV14 51 K7
BLOX/PEL WS3 39 J8
Lavender Hall La
RCOVN/BALC/EX CV7 151 M4
Lavender La STRBR DY8 119 H2
Lavender Rd DUDN DY1 84 F2
TAM/AM/WIL B77 46 C1
Lavendon Rd PBAR/PBCH B42 70 E8
Lavinia Rd RMSLY B62 122 C2
Law Cliff Rd PBAR/PBCH B42 70 F7
Law Cl OLDBY B69 86 B3
Lawden Rd SMHTH B10 107 M5
Lawford Av LICHS WS14 21 J6
Lawford Cl COVS CV3 156 C4
VAUX/NECH B7 7 M3
Lawford Gv DIG/EDG B5 107 J5
SHLY B90 147 H3
Lawford Heath La
RRUGBY CV23 184 F8
Lawford La RUGBYS/DCH CV22 185 M4
Lawford Rd RLSS CV31 206 F8
RUGBYN/HIL CV21 186 D2
Lawfred Av WNSFLD WV11 37 H8
Lawley Cl RUSH/SHEL WS4 39 M4
TLHL/CAN CV4 153 L3
Lawley Middleway
VAUX/NECH B7 7 L2
Lawley Rd BILS/COS WV14 50 F7
Lawley St DUDN DY1 84 E4
WBROM B70 86 D2
The Lawley HALE B63 121 G4
Lawn Av STRBR DY8 119 J1
Lawnoaks Cl BRWNH WS8 26 B3
Lawn Rd BKHL/PFLD WV2 50 C7
Lawnsdale Cl CSHL/WTROR B46 93 K7
Lawnsdown Rd BRLYHL DY5 102 D6
Lawnsfield Gv ERDW/GRVHL B23 72 B6
Lawnside Gn BILS/COS WV14 51 H5
The Lawns BDWTH CV12 116 B3
Lawn St STRBR DY8 119 J1
Lawnswood KINVER DY7 100 E1
WALM/CURD B76 73 L5
Lawnswood Av BNTWD WS7 26 D1
DUNHL/THL/PER WV6 35 J5
ETTPK/GDPK/PENN WV4 66 C1
SHLY B90 148 B2
STRBR DY8 101 G1
Lawnswood Cl HEDN WS12 17 H4
Lawnswood Dr ALDR WS9 40 E2
KINVER DY7 100 E3
Lawnswood Gv HDSW B21 88 A4
Lawnswood Ri
DUNHL/THL/PER WV6 35 K5
Lawnswood Rd SEDG DY3 66 B8
STRBR DY8 101 G2
Lawnwood Rd DUDS DY2 103 G3
Lawrence Av WNSFLD WV11 37 K7
WOLVN WV10 50 E1
Lawrence Ct CRTAM B79 31 L7
Lawrence Dr WALM/CURD B76 74 B7
Lawrence Gdns KNWTH CV8 179 K7
Lawrence La CDYHTH B64 103 J4
Lawrence Rd RUGBYN/HIL CV21 187 H2
Lawrence Saunders Rd
COVN CV6 133 M8
Lawrence Sheriff St
RUGBYS/DCH CV22 186 E3
Lawrence St HAG/WOL DY9 102 A7
WLNHL WV13 51 L2
Lawrence Wk GTB/HAM B43 71 H1
Lawson Cl ALDR WS9 54 F1
Lawson St CBHAMNE B4 7 H2
Law St HHTH/SAND B71 69 G8
Lawton Cl OLDBY B69 86 A7
Laxey Rd LDYWD/EDGR B16 106 A2
Laxford Cl BHTH/HG B12 107 J7
Laxton Cl KGSWFD DY6 83 L8
Laxton Dr BEWD DY12 162 D2
Laxton Gv YDLY B25 109 H4
Layamon Wk STRPT DY13 188 D3
Lay Gdns RLSS CV31 207 J8
Lazy Hl ALDR WS9 41 G3
HWK/WKHTH B38 145 M3
Lazy Hill Rd ALDR WS9 41 G4
Lea Av DARL/WED WS10 68 B4
Lea Bank Av KIDDW DY11 137 L8
Lea Bank Rd DUDS DY2 102 F2
Leabon Gv HRBN B17 124 A1
Leabrook
LGN/SDN/BHAMAIR B26 109 K5
Leabrook Rd DARL/WED WS10 68 B4
Leabrook Rd North
DARL/WED WS10 68 B4
Lea Castle Cl KIDD DY10 138 E4
Lea Castle Dr KIDD DY10 139 G3
The Lea Cswy KIDDW DY11 163 L1
Leach Green La RBRY B45 143 M7
Leach Heath La RBRY B45 143 K6
Leacliffe Wy FOAKS/STRLY B74 55 K2
Leacote Dr
DUNHL/THL/PER WV6 49 G1
Lea Crs RUGBYN/HIL CV21 160 B8
Leacrest Rd COVN CV6 133 L3
Leacroft SHHTH WV12 38 A6
Leacroft Av WOLVN WV10 36 C5
Leacroft Cl ALDR WS9 40 F4
Leacroft Gv HHTH/SAND B71 68 F5
Leacroft La CNCK/NC WS11 16 D8
Leacroft Rd KGSWFD DY6 83 J5
PENK ST19 10 D3
Lea Croft Rd REDW B97 202 B8
Leadbetter Dr BRGRVW B61 191 K3
Lea Dr LGN/SDN/BHAMAIR B26 109 L7
Lea End La ALVE B48 171 G1
Leafdown Cl HEDN WS12 17 H1
Leafenden Av BNTWD WS7 18 E8
Leafield Cl COVE CV2 135 K5
Leafield Crs STETCH B33 91 L8
Leafield Gdns RMSLY B62 104 B5
Leafield Rd HIA/OLT B92 127 M4
Leaf La COVS CV3 155 K7
Lea Ford Rd STETCH B33 110 A1
Leaford Wy KGSWFD DY6 83 K8
Leafy Gld FOAKS/STRLY B74 55 L2
Leafy Ri SEDG DY3 84 A1
Lea Gdns BDMR/CCFT WV3 2 D9
Leagh Cl KNWTH CV8 179 M6
Lea Green Av TPTN/OCK DY4 67 G8
Lea Green La HLYWD B47 147 G7
Lea Hall Dr BNTWD WS7 18 D4
Lea Hall Rd STETCH B33 109 L3
Leahill Cft
CHWD/FDBR/MGN B37 110 D3
Lea Hill Rd BFLD/HDSWWD B20 89 G3
Leaholme Gdns HAG/WOL DY9 119 M3
Leahouse Gdns
LGLYGN/QTN B68 104 E2
Lea House Rd BVILLE B30 124 E6
Leahouse Rd LGLYGN/QTN B68 104 E2
Leahurst Crs HRBN B17 124 A1
Lea La GTWY WS6 24 E3
KIDD DY10 138 C2
Lea Manor Dr
ETTPK/GDPK/PENN WV4 65 J2
Leam Cl NUN CV11 99 K4
Leam Crs HIA/OLT B92 128 A4
Leam Dr BNTWD WS7 19 H6
Leam Gn TLHL/CAN CV4 154 B8
Leamington Cl CNCK/NC WS11 16 A5
Leamington Rd BHTH/HG B12 107 M8
COVS CV3 155 G6
KNWTH CV8 182 C7
KNWTH CV8 197 L3
KNWTH CV8 199 L3
Leamore Cl WSLW WS2 38 E6
Leamore La WSLW WS2 38 E6
Leamount Dr KGSTG B44 72 A3
Leam Rd RLSS CV31 206 A6
Leam St RLSS CV31 206 F6
Leam Ter RLSS CV31 206 F5
Leander Cl BNTWD WS7 18 F4
GTWY WS6 24 D4
Leander Gdns
ALE/KHTH/YWD B14 125 K8
Leander Rd HAG/WOL DY9 120 D1
Lea Park Ri BRGRVW B61 168 D8
Leapgate La STRPT DY13 164 C8
Lea Rd BDMR/CCFT WV3 49 L6
SPARK B11 126 B1
Lear Rd WMBN WV5 64 F6
Leas Cl BDWTH CV12 116 E2
Leason La WOLVN WV10 36 E5
Leasow Dr EDG B15 124 B2
Leasowe Rd RBRY B45 143 K5
TPTN/OCK DY4 85 J1
Leasowe's Av COVS CV3 180 D1
Leasowes Ct HALE B63 121 K3
Leasowes Dr BDMR/CCFT WV3 49 H7
DUNHL/THL/PER WV6 48 B1
Leasowes La RMSLY B62 104 A8
Leasowes Rd
ALE/KHTH/YWD B14 125 K4
The Leasowe LICH WS13 20 E4
The Leasow ALDR WS9 40 C8
The Leas WOLVN WV10 23 G6
Lea St KIDD DY10 138 D8
The Lea KIDDW DY11 137 L8
STETCH B33 109 L2
Leatherhead Cl AST/WIT B6 89 K7
Leathermill La
NUNW/HART CV10 80 B2
Lea Vale Rd STRBR DY8 119 K3
Leavesden Gv
LGN/SDN/BHAMAIR B26 109 L8
Lea Vw ALDR WS9 40 C8
SHHTH WV12 37 L8
Lea Village STETCH B33 109 M3
Lea Wk KNWTH CV8 182 F4
RBRY B45 143 K5
Leaward Cl NUNW/HART CV10 98 C3
Lea Wood Gv KIDDW DY11 137 L8
Lea Yield Cl SLYOAK B29 124 E6
Lebanon Gv BNTWD WS7 18 D5
Lechlade Cl REDE B98 195 G6
Lechlade Rd GTB/HAM B43 70 C5
Leckie Rd WSLW WS2 53 J1
Ledbrook Rd RLSN CV32 199 H8
Ledbury Cl ALDR WS9 41 G4
LDYWD/EDGR B16 106 E3
REDE B98 203 K3
Ledbury Dr WOLV WV1 50 F4
Ledbury Rd RLSS CV31 207 G7
Ledbury Wy WALM/CURD B76 73 L5
Ledsam Gv RIDG/WDGT B32 105 K7
Ledsam St LDYWD/EDGR B16 106 E3
Ledwell SHLY B90 147 L8
Lee Bank Middleway EDG B15 6 D9
Leebank Rd HALE B63 121 J3
Leech St TPTN/OCK DY4 68 A8
Lee Cl WWCK CV34 205 J3
Lee Crs EDG B15 107 G5
Leeder Cl COVN CV6 134 A3
Leedham Av TAM/AM/WIL B77 32 C8
Lee Gdns SMTHWKW B67 87 J8
Leeming Cl TLHL/CAN CV4 154 A7
Lee Mt EDG B15 * 107 G5
Lee Rd CDYHTH B64 103 K5
HLYWD B47 146 E6
RLSS CV31 206 C6
Leeson Wk HRBN B17 106 B8
Lees Rd BILS/COS WV14 67 K2
Lees St WSNGN B18 88 D8
Lees Ter BILS/COS WV14 67 K2
Lee St WBROM B70 68 E5
The Lee COVW CV5 154 A1
Legge La BILS/COS WV14 67 H3
CBHAMW B1 6 B3
Legge St AST/WIT B6 7 J1
BKHL/PFLD WV2 50 C7
WBROM B70 87 H2
Legion Cl CNCK/NC WS11 17 L7
Legion Rd RBRY B45 143 J6
Legs La WOLVN WV10 36 D2
Le Hanche Cl
RCOVN/BALC/EX CV7 115 L6
Leicester Cswy COV CV1 134 B8
Leicester Cl SMTHWKW B67 105 J4
Leicester Crs ATHST CV9 63 J4
Leicester La RLSN CV32 199 G6
Leicester Pl HHTH/SAND B71 69 G6
Leicester Rd BDWTH CV12 116 F1
NUN CV11 99 G1
RUGBYN/HIL CV21 160 F6
Leicester Rw COV CV1 8 F2
Leicester St BDWTH CV12 116 F2
DUNHL/THL/PER WV6 2 C1
RLSN CV32 206 E4
WSL WS1 4 F3
Leigham Dr HRBN B17 105 K6
Leigh Av BNTWD WS7 18 F6
COVS CV3 181 G2
Leigh Cl RUSH/SHEL WS4 53 L1
Leigh Rd MGN/WHC B75 57 M7
RUGBYN/HIL CV21 160 D5
RUSH/SHEL WS4 53 L1
WASH/WDE B8 90 C7
Leighs Cl RUSH/SHEL WS4 40 A4
Leighs Rd RUSH/SHEL WS4 39 M4
Leigh St COV CV1 9 K2
Leighswood Av ALDR WS9 40 F6
Leighswood Cl CNCK/NC WS11 17 K8
Leighswood Gv ALDR WS9 40 E6
Leighswood Rd ALDR WS9 40 F7
Leighton Cl DUDN DY1 84 C3
GTB/HAM B43 71 G2
RLSN CV32 207 G1
TLHL/CAN CV4 180 B3
Leighton Rd BDMR/CCFT WV3 49 K7
BILS/COS WV14 67 L1
MOS/BIL B13 125 K3
Leith Gv HWK/WKHTH B38 145 J5
Lelant Gv HRBN B17 105 L8
Lellow St HHTH/SAND B71 69 G5
Le More FOAKS/STRLY B74 56 E3
Lemox Rd WBROM B70 68 E5
Lench Cl REDW B97 193 L8
RMSLY B62 104 A4
Lench's Cl MOS/BIL B13 125 K3
Lenchs Gn DIG/EDG B5 107 J6
Lench St CBHAMNE B4 7 G2
Lenchs Trust Houses
BHTH/HG B12 * 107 K6
Len Davies Rd SHHTH WV12 37 L6
Lennard Gdns SMTHWK B66 * 88 B7
Lennox Cl COVS CV3 156 B7
Lennox Gdns BDMR/CCFT WV3 2 A8
Lennox Gv SCFLD/BOLD B73 72 E6
Lennox St LOZ/NWT B19 89 H7
Lenton Cft
LGN/SDN/BHAMAIR B26 127 J1
Lenton's La COVE CV2 135 H1
Lenwade Rd LGLYGN/QTN B68 105 H5
Leofric St COVN CV6 133 L8
Leomansley Cl LICH WS13 20 D6
Leomansley Rd LICH WS13 20 D6
Leomansley Vw LICH WS13 20 C6
Leominster Rd SPARK B11 126 C2
Leonard Av KIDD DY10 138 E4
LOZ/NWT B19 89 G5
Leonard Gv LOZ/NWT B19 89 H8
Leonard Rd LOZ/NWT B19 89 G5
STRBR DY8 101 M7
Leopold Av BFLD/HDSWWD B20 70 C8
Leopold Rd COV CV1 9 L1
Leopold St BHTH/HG B12 107 K5
Lepid Gv SLYOAK B29 124 B3
Lerryn Cl KGSWFD DY6 83 K8
Lerwick Cl KGSWFD DY6 83 K8
Lesingham Dr TLHL/CAN CV4 153 J4
Lesley Dr KGSWFD DY6 101 J1
Leslie Dr TPTN/OCK DY4 67 L4
Leslie Ri OLDBY B69 86 A5
Leslie Rd BFLD/HDSWWD B20 89 H3
FOAKS/STRLY B74 55 M3
LDYWD/EDGR B16 106 D3
WOLVN WV10 50 D1
Lesscroft Cl COVEN WV9 35 L2
Lester Gv ALDR WS9 55 J3
Lester St BILS/COS WV14 51 K8
Lestock Cl RUGBYS/DCH CV22 186 A3
Leswell Gv KIDD DY10 138 D7
Leswell La KIDD DY10 138 D7
Leswell St KIDD DY10 138 D7
Letchlade Cl COVE CV2 135 G5
Levante Gdns STETCH B33 109 H3
Levedale Rd RSTAF ST18 10 A2
Leve La WLNHL WV13 51 M4
Level St BRLYHL DY5 102 C2
Leven Cft WALM/CURD B76 73 L6
Leven Dr WNSFLD WV11 37 M4
Leven Wy COVE CV2 135 L5
Levenwick Wy KGSWFD DY6 83 L8
The Leverretts HDSW B21 88 A2
Lever Rd RUGBYN/HIL CV21 187 L4
Lever St BKHL/PFLD WV2 3 G8
Leverton Ri WOLVN WV10 36 A7
Leveson Av GTWY WS6 24 C3
Leveson Cl DUDS DY2 85 J5
Leveson Crs
RCOVN/BALC/EX CV7 151 M7
Leveson Dr TPTN/OCK DY4 67 J7
Leveson Rd WNSFLD WV11 37 K5
Leveson St WLNHL WV13 51 L3
Levett Rd LICHS WS14 30 A4
TAM/AM/WIL B77 32 F8
Levetts Flds LICH WS13 21 G6
Levetts Hollow HEDN WS12 17 H2
Levetts Sq LICH WS13 * 20 F6
Levington Cl
DUNHL/THL/PER WV6 34 D8
Levy Cl RUGBYN/HIL CV21 186 D2
Lewis Av WOLV WV1 50 F2
Lewis Cl LICHS WS14 21 J6
SHHTH WV12 38 B8
Lewis Ct ATHST CV9 63 K7
Lewis Gv WNSFLD WV11 37 H7
Lewisham Rd SMTHWK B66 87 L6
WOLVN WV10 35 M3
Lewisham St HHTH/SAND B71 87 H1
Lewis Rd BVILLE B30 125 G6
COV CV1 134 B8
HAG/WOL DY9 102 B8
LGLYGN/QTN B68 104 F6
RLSS CV31 207 J8
Lewis St BILS/COS WV14 51 J7
TPTN/OCK DY4 68 B8
WSLW WS2 53 H2
Lewthorn Ri
ETTPK/GDPK/PENN WV4 66 B1
Lexington Gn BRLYHL DY5 102 A6
Leybourne Crs COVEN WV9 35 K3
Leybourne Gv YDLY B25 108 F7
Leybrook Rd RBRY B45 143 M5
Leyburn Cl COVN CV6 134 B2
NUN CV11 99 L3
SHHTH WV12 52 B1
WWCK CV34 205 J4
Leyburn Rd LDYWD/EDGR B16 106 E4
Leycester Cl NFLD/LBR B31 144 E6
Leycester Rd KNWTH CV8 197 K3
Leycroft Av STETCH B33 110 B2
Leyes La KNWTH CV8 180 A8
The Leyes RRUGBY CV23 161 L4
Leyfields LICH WS13 20 F3
Ley Hill Farm Rd NFLD/LBR B31 123 J8
Ley Hill Rd MGN/WHC B75 57 G4
Leylan Cft MOS/BIL B13 126 B6
Leyland Av BDMR/CCFT WV3 49 K4
Leyland Cft BLOX/PEL WS3 39 K1
Leyland Rd BDWTH CV12 117 M3
COVW CV5 154 B1
NUN CV11 99 J4
TAM/AM/WIL B77 46 C3
Leyman Cl ALE/KHTH/YWD B14 147 G1
Leymere Cl
RCOVN/BALC/EX CV7 131 G4
Ley Ri SEDG DY3 66 A4
Leys Cl HAG/WOL DY9 120 A3
Leys Crs BRLYHL DY5 101 M2
Leysdown Gv ACGN B27 127 G5
Leysdown Rd ACGN B27 127 G5
Leyside COVS CV3 156 C8
Leys La RCOVN/BALC/EX CV7 131 G4
Leys Rd BRLYHL DY5 101 M2
Leysters Cl REDE B98 203 J2
The Leys DARL/WED WS10 52 A7
NFLD/LBR B31 123 M8
Leys Wood Cft
LGN/SDN/BHAMAIR B26 109 L7
Leyton Cl BRLYHL DY5 102 B5
Leyton Gv KGSTG B44 71 L4
Leyton Rd HDSW B21 88 D5
Libbards Ga SOLH B91 149 G5
Libbards Wy SOLH B91 148 F5
Liberty Rd TAM/AM/WIL B77 46 D8
Liberty Wy NUN CV11 99 K2
Libra Cl CRTAM B79 31 K6
Library Rd TLHL/CAN CV4 153 M8
Library Wy RBRY B45 143 K6
Lich Av WNSFLD WV11 37 J6
Lichen Cl HEDN WS12 12 A8
Lichen Gn TLHL/CAN CV4 154 B8
Lichfield Av KIDDW DY11 137 K7
Lichfield Cl NUN CV11 81 L6
RCOVN/BALC/EX CV7 96 E5
Lichfield Crs POL/KGSB/FAZ B78 30 F6
Lichfield Rd ALDR WS9 40 E1
AST/WIT B6 89 L7
BLOX/PEL WS3 25 M8
BLOX/PEL WS3 39 G3
BNTWD WS7 19 H7
BRWNH WS8 26 D5
CNCK/NC WS11 16 D5
COVS CV3 155 H5
CSHL/WTROR B46 93 J5
FOAKS/STRLY B74 42 D8
LICHS WS14 27 G4
POL/KGSB/FAZ B78 30 F6
POL/KGSB/FAZ B78 58 E8
RUSH/SHEL WS4 53 L1
SHHTH WV12 38 B5
WALM/CURD B76 75 H8
WNSFLD WV11 37 J7
Lichfield St BILS/COS WV14 51 J7
CRTAM B79 31 L8
POL/KGSB/FAZ B78 45 K4
STRPT DY13 188 E2
TPTN/OCK DY4 67 K5
WOLV WV1 2 F5
WSL WS1 5 G3
Lichwood Rd WNSFLD WV11 37 K6
Lickey Coppice RBRY B45 170 A1
Lickey Grange Dr BRGRVE B60 169 J4
Lickey Gv KIDDW DY11 163 M3
Lickey Rd RBRY B45 143 M8
STRBR DY8 101 M7
Lickey Rock BRGRVE B60 169 H4
Lickey Sq RBRY B45 169 K3
Lickhill Rd STRPT DY13 188 D1
Lickhill Rd North STRPT DY13 163 H7
Liddon Gv ACGN B27 127 G5
Liddon Rd ACGN B27 127 G5
Lifford Cl ALE/KHTH/YWD B14 145 M1
Lifford La BVILLE B30 124 E8
Lifford Wy COVS CV3 156 E6
Lifton Cft KGSWFD DY6 83 K8
Light Ash WOLVN WV10 22 A2
Lighthorne Av
LDYWD/EDGR B16 106 E2
Lighthorne Rd SOLH B91 127 M7
Light La COV CV1 8 E2
Lightning Wy NFLD/LBR B31 144 F6
Lightoak Cl REDW B97 202 A7
Lightwood Cl DOR/KN B93 149 M5
Lightwood Rd DUDN DY1 84 E2
Lightwoods Hl SMTHWKW B67 105 J5
Lightwoods Rd HAG/WOL DY9 120 A4
SMTHWKW B67 105 K4
Lilac Av BHTH/HG B12 107 L8
CNCK/NC WS11 16 B6
COVN CV6 133 K8
DSYBK/YTR WS5 69 L1
FOAKS/STRLY B74 55 J6
KGSTG B44 71 J6
TPTN/OCK DY4 67 J6
Lilac Cl REDE B98 202 C3
Lilac Dr RUGBYS/DCH CV22 185 M3
WMBN WV5 64 D7
Lilac Gv BNTWD WS7 18 D6
DARL/WED WS10 68 E3
STRPT DY13 188 C1
WSLW WS2 52 C2
WWCK CV34 205 L4
Lilac La GTWY WS6 24 D5
Lilac Rd BDWTH CV12 99 H8
CRTAM B79 31 L5
DUDN DY1 84 F1
SHHTH WV12 38 C6
WOLV WV1 50 F5
Lilac Wy RMSLY B62 104 D5
Lilbourne Rd RRUGBY CV23 161 L8
Lilian Gv BILS/COS WV14 67 J4
Lilleshall Cl REDE B98 203 J2
Lilleshall Crs BKHL/PFLD WV2 50 B6
Lilleshall Rd
LGN/SDN/BHAMAIR B26 109 M6
Lilley Cl COVN CV6 134 A3
Lilley Green Rd ALVE B48 195 G2
Lilley La NFLD/LBR B31 144 F5
Lillington Av RLSN CV32 206 D3
Lillington Cl LICH WS13 20 E5
RLSN CV32 206 E2
Lillington Gv BKDE/SHDE B34 92 B8
Lillington Rd COVE CV2 135 H4
RLSN CV32 206 E1
SHLY B90 147 M5
Lilycroft La HWK/WKHTH B38 145 L6
Lily Green La REDW B97 193 L8
Lily Rd LGN/SDN/BHAMAIR B26 109 H7
Lily St HHTH/SAND B71 69 G8
Limberlost Cl
BFLD/HDSWWD B20 88 E2
Limbrick Av TLHL/CAN CV4 153 L4
Limbrick Cl SHLY B90 147 K3
Limbury Gv HIA/OLT B92 * 128 D5
Lime Av RLSN CV32 206 E1
SLYOAK B29 * 124 D3
WSLW WS2 52 C2
Lime Cl HLYWD B47 146 E8
TPTN/OCK DY4 67 J8
WBROM B70 86 E1
WSLW WS2 52 C2
Lime Ct SPARK B11 126 A1
Lime Gv ATHST CV9 76 F1
BHTH/HG B12 107 K8
BILS/COS WV14 51 G5
BNTWD WS7 19 G7
BRGRVW B61 191 K1
CHWD/FDBR/MGN B37 110 F4
KINVER DY7 118 A2
KNWTH CV8 197 L1
LGN/SDN/BHAMAIR B26 109 H7
LICH WS13 21 H5
LOZ/NWT B19 89 G5
NUNW/HART CV10 80 C8
RUSH/SHEL WS4 40 A7
SCFLD/BOLD B73 72 F6
SMTHWK B66 105 M1
TLHL/CAN CV4 153 M3
Limehurst Av BDMR/CCFT WV3 49 G4
Limehurst Rd RUSH/SHEL WS4 40 A8
Lime Kiln Cl HWK/WKHTH B38 145 H6
Limekiln La ALE/KHTH/YWD B14 146 E1
HOCK/TIA B94 174 A4
Lime Kilns POL/KGSB/FAZ B78 47 L5
Lime La BLOX/PEL WS3 25 L4
Limepit La DUDN DY1 84 E2
HEDN WS12 12 C7
Lime Rd DARL/WED WS10 68 D1
HEDN WS12 12 B5
SEDG DY3 66 D4
Limes Av BLKHTH/ROWR B65 104 A3
BRLYHL DY5 84 A8
Limes Coppice
NUNW/HART CV10 79 J6
Limescroft Cl RUSH/SHEL WS4 39 M6
Limes Rd DUDN DY1 84 F2
DUNHL/THL/PER WV6 49 G1
The Limes BDWTH CV12 116 C3
ERDE/BCHGN B24 90 D2
LDYWD/EDGR B16 * 106 D2
RCOVN/BALC/EX CV7 * 133 K1
SPARK B11 108 A7
WSL WS1 5 K3
Limestone Hall La
RRUGBY CV23 184 E1
Lime St BDMR/CCFT WV3 2 B8
BILS/COS WV14 66 E5
WSL WS1 5 H4
Limes Vw SEDG DY3 66 B6
Lime Tree Av
DUNHL/THL/PER WV6 48 E2
RUGBYS/DCH CV22 185 M6
TLHL/CAN CV4 153 L3
Lime Tree Crs REDW B97 201 M1
Lime Tree Gdns CDSL WV8 34 F2
Lime Tree Gv NFLD/LBR B31 145 G3
Lime Tree Rd ACGN B27 109 G8
CDSL WV8 34 F2
DSYBK/YTR WS5 69 L1
WASH/WDE B8 90 D7
Limetree Rd FOAKS/STRLY B74 55 H4
Lime Tree Wk STRPT DY13 163 J8
Linaker Rd COVS CV3 156 A8
Linchmere Rd HDSW B21 88 A3
Lincoln Av NUNW/HART CV10 79 M6
WLNHL WV13 52 B3
Lincoln Cl ACGN B27 127 J2
LICH WS13 21 G2
WWCK CV34 205 J4
Lincoln Crs KIDDW DY11 137 K7
Lincoln Cft LICHS WS14 28 D7

Lincoln Dr *CNCK/NC* WS11 ....16 D5
Lincoln Gn *WOLVN* WV10 ....36 B3
Lincoln Gv
  CHWD/FDBR/MGN B37 ....110 E5
Lincoln Rd *BRGRVW* B61 ....191 J1
  DUDS 103 H2
  HHTH/SAND B71 ....69 H4
  HIA/OLT B92 ....127 H3
  SMTHWK B66 ....105 J3
  WSL WS1 ....5 J3
Lincoln Rd North *HIA/OLT* B92 ....127 J2
Lincoln St *BHTH/HG* B12 ....107 J7
  COV CV1 ....3 G5
  WOLVN WV10 ....3 K3
Lincomb Bank *STRPT* DY13 ....189 H7
Lincomb La *STRPT* DY13 ....189 G8
Lincroft Crs *COVW* CV5 ....154 D1
Lindale *RUGBYN/HIL* CV21 ....161 G5
Lindale Av *CBROM* B36 ....91 G7
Lindale Crs *BRLYHL* DY5 ....101 M7
Lindale Dr *WMBN* WV5 ....64 D7
Linden Av *BNTWD* WS7 ....18 D5
  GTB/HAM B43 ....70 B5
  KIDD DY10 ....138 E6
  OLDBY B69 ....86 B5
  RMSLY B62 ....104 C6
  STRPT DY13 ....188 D5
Linden CI *TAM/AM/WIL* B77 ....46 D1
  WSLW WS2 ....52 B3
  WWCK CV34 ....205 J3
Linden Dr *STRBR* DY8 ....119 L2
Linden Gdns *KIDD* DY10 ....138 E6
Linden La *SHHTH* WV12 ....38 B1
Linden Lea *BDMR/CCFT* WV3 ....49 H4
  BDWTH CV12 ....116 F2
Linden Rd *DUDN* DY1 ....84 F2
  SLYOAK B29 ....124 C5
  SMTHWK B66 ....105 L3
Lindens Dr *FOAKS/STRLY* B74 ....55 K8
The Lindens
  DUNHL/THL/PER WV6 ....49 J2
  RIDG/WDGT B32 ....105 J4
Linden Vw *HEDN* WS12 ....16 F1
Lindenwood *SCFLD/BOLD* B73 ....56 F7
Lindale *TAM/AM/WIL* B77 ....47 J2
The Lindfield *COVS* CV3 ....156 A5
Lindford Wy *HWK/WKHTH* B38 ....145 M3
Lindhurst Dr *HOCK/TIA* B94 ....174 F8
Lindisarne *TAM/AM/WIL* B77 ....46 B3
Lindisfarne Dr *KNWTH* CV8 ....198 A1
Lindley Av *TPTN/OCK* DY4 ....85 K2
Lindley Rd *BDWTH* CV12 ....116 B3
  COVS CV3 ....155 M3
Lindon CI *BRWNH* WS8 ....26 E7
Lindon Dr *BRWNH* WS8 ....26 D7
Lindon Rd *BRWNH* WS8 ....26 E8
Lindon Vw *BRWNH* WS8 ....26 E8
Lindrick CI *BLOX/PEL* WS3 ....38 D2
Lindridge CI *REDE* B98 ....203 L2
Lindridge Dr *WALM/CURD* B76 ....72 A8
Lindridge Rd *ERDW/GRVHL* B23 ....72 A8
  MGN/WHC B75 ....57 K6
  SHLY B90 ....147 K4
Lindrosa Rd *FOAKS/STRLY* B74 ....55 K2
Lindsay Rd *PBAR/PBCH* B42 ....70 F4
Lindsey Av *NFLD/LBR* B31 ....145 G1
Lindsey Crs *KNWTH* CV8 ....197 L4
Lindsey PI *BRLYHL* DY5 ....102 A2
Lindsey Rd *HHTH/SAND* B71 ....69 G6
Lindsworth Ap *BVILLE* B30 ....146 A2
Lindsworth Rd *BVILLE* B30 ....145 M2
Lineholt CI *REDE* B98 ....202 E7
Linehouse La *BRGRVE* B60 ....169 H6
Linen St *WWCK* CV34 ....205 H7
Linfield Gdns *SEDG* DY3 ....66 A4
Linford Av *YDLY* DY5 ....109 H4
Linford Wk *COVE* CV2 ....135 K4
Linforth Dr *FOAKS/STRLY* B74 ....55 L6
Lingard CI *VAUX/NECH* B7 ....89 M8
Lingard Rd *MGN/WHC* B75 ....57 K8
Lingen CI *REDE* B98 ....203 J2
Lingfield Av *KGSTG* B44 ....71 J4
  WOLVN WV10 ....22 B8
Lingfield CI *GTWY* WS6 ....24 D3
Lingfield Dr *GTWY* WS6 ....24 D3
Lingfield Gdns *BKDE/SHDE* B34 ....91 M7
Lingfield Gv
  DUNHL/THL/PER WV6 ....48 D1
Lingfield Rd *BEWD* DY12 ....137 H8
  CNCK/NC WS11 ....17 G8
Lingfield Wy *KGSWFD* DY6 ....83 L8
Lingham CI *HIA/OLT* B92 ....128 B6
Ling Rd *WOLVN* WV10 ....22 C7
Lingwood Dr *NUNW/HART* CV10 ....98 D2
Linhope Dr *KGSWFD* DY6 ....83 L8
Link Rd *COVW* CV6 ....133 M5
  ETTPK/GDPK/PENN WV4 ....65 L2
  HLYWD B47 ....146 E4
  LGLYGN/QTN B68 ....104 F5
Links Dr *RBRY* B45 ....143 L7
  SOLH B91 ....127 M7
  STRBR DY8 ....119 J3
Links Rd *COVN* CV6 ....133 M5
  ETTPK/GDPK/PENN WV4 ....65 L2
  HLYWD B47 ....146 E4
  LGLYGN/QTN B68 ....104 F5
Links Side Wy *ALDR* WS9 ....41 G5
Links Vw *FOAKS/STRLY* B74 ....55 L4
  RMSLY B62 ....122 A3
Linkswood CI *BMSL* B13 ....125 M4
The Link *ACGN* WS11 ....126 D4
Linkway *RLSS* CV31 ....206 C7
Linley CI *ALDR* WS9 ....40 A2
Linley Dr *WOLVN* WV10 ....36 C4
Linley Gv *ALE/KHTH/YWD* B14 ....125 G7
  SEDG DY3 ....83 M3
Linley Rd *RUSH/SHEL* WS4 ....40 F6
Linley Wood Rd *ALDR* WS9 ....40 E4
Linnell Rd *RUGBYN/HIL* CV21 ....187 J3
Linnet CI *COVS* CV3 ....156 A5
  HEDN WS12 ....12 B6
  RMSLY B62 ....103 M1
  SLYOAK B29 ....124 C5
Linnet Gv *SHHTH* WV12 ....38 A5
Linnet Rd *KIDD* DY10 ....164 D1
Linpole Wk *ALE/KHTH/YWD* B14 ....146 A2
Linsey Rd *HIA/OLT* B92 ....128 A3
Linslade CI
  ETTPK/GDPK/PENN WV4 ....66 B1
Linstock Wy *COVN* CV6 ....134 F1
Linthouse La *WNSFLD* WV11 ....37 J5
Linthurst Newtown
  BRGRVE B60 ....169 L8
Linthurst Rd *BRGRVE* B60 ....169 L7
Linton Av *SOLH* B91 ....148 E4
Linton CI *HALE* B63 ....103 G8
  REDE B98 ....203 K3
Linton Ct *RBRS/COS* WS14 ....67 G1
Linton Ms *REDE* B98 ....203 K3
Linton Rd *CDYHTH* B64 ....103 K2
  ETTPK/GDPK/PENN WV4 ....49 J8
  GTB/HAM B43 ....71 G1
  SPARK B11 ....126 E1
Linwood Dr *COVE* CV2 ....135 K4
  HEDN WS12 ....12 D6
Linwood Rd *DUDN* DY1 ....66 F3

HDSW B21 ....88 C5
SOLH B91 ....127 H8
Lionel St *CBHAMNW* B3 ....6 E2
Lion Fields Av *COWW* CV5 ....132 F7
Lion HI *STRPT* DY13 ....188 E2
Lion Pas *STRBR* DY8 ....101 K8
Lion's Den *LICHS* WS14 ....27 J3
Lion Sq *KIDD* DY10 ....138 C7
Lion St *KIDD* DY10 ....138 C7
  STRBR DY8 ....101 K8
Liskeard CI *NUN* CV11 ....81 L8
Liskeard Rd *DSYBK/YTR* WS5 ....54 B6
Lisko CI *STRBR* DY8 ....101 L5
Lisle Av *KIDD* DY10 ....138 A4
Lisle St *DIG/EDG* B5 ....7 K6
Lismore Cft
  RCOVN/BALC/EX CV7 ....135 M6
Lismore Dr *HRBN* B17 ....123 L2
Lisson Gv *KGSTG* B44 ....71 K1
Listelow CI *CBROM* B36 ....91 M5
Lister CI *TPTN/OCK* DY4 ....85 L1
  WSLW WS2 ....38 F8
Lister Rd *ATHST* CV9 ....63 H4
  DUDS DY2 ....85 G6
  KIDDW DY11 ....163 M2
  WSLW WS2 ....38 F8
Lister St *NUN* CV11 ....99 H2
  VAUX/NECH B7 ....7 J1
  WLNHL WV13 ....51 M4
Listowel Rd
  ALE/KHTH/YWD B14 ....125 H7
Lisures Dr *WALM/CURD* B76 ....73 H1
Little Acre *REDW* B97 ....202 B8
Little Albert St *WSL* WS1 * 4 F7
Little Ann St *DIG/EDG* B5 ....7 K6
Little Aston Hall Dr
  FOAKS/STRLY B74 ....41 L8
Little Aston La *FOAKS/STRLY* B74 ....42 B7
Little Aston Park Rd
  FOAKS/STRLY B74 ....55 L2
Little Aston Rd *ALDR* WS9 ....41 G6
Little Barrow Wk *LICH* WS13 ....20 E4
Little Barr St *BORD* B9 ....7 M5
Little Bell Hall Cottages
  HAG/WOL DY9 * 141 H7
Little Birches *BDMR/CCFT* WV3 ....49 K5
Little Bricklin St *BKHL/PFLD* WV2 ....2 E7
Little Bromwich Rd *BORD* B9 ....108 F4
Little Brum *ATHST* CV9 ....62 A3
Little Caldmore *WSL* WS1 ....4 F6
Little Checkhill La *KINVER* DY7 ....100 B1
Little Church St *COV* CV1 * 9 G1
  RUGBYN/HIL CV21 ....186 E2
Little Clothier St *WLNHL* WV13 ....51 L2
Little Clover CI *VAUX/NECH* B7 ....90 A7
Little Cornbow *HALE* B63 ....121 M2
Littlecote *CRTAM* B79 ....31 H7
Littlecote Cft
  ALE/KHTH/YWD B14 ....146 E2
Littlecote Dr *ERDW/GRVHL* B23 ....72 D6
Little Cottage St *BRLYHL* DY5 ....102 B2
Little Cft *GTB/HAM* B43 ....70 B4
Little Cross St *DARL/WED* WS10 ....52 A6
Little Cryfield *TLHL/CAN* CV4 ....180 A3
Little Duke St *NUN* CV11 ....98 F1
Little Edward St *BORD* B9 ....7 M6
Little Elborow St
  RUGBYN/HIL CV21 ....186 E2
Little Fld *COVE* CV2 ....134 E8
Little Fields Wy *OLDBY* B69 ....86 D6
Little Forge Rd *REDE* B98 ....203 G6
Little Francis Gv *VAUX/NECH* B7 ....89 M8
Little Gra *LICH* WS13 ....20 D4
Little Grebe Rd *KIDD* DY10 * 164 D1
Little Green La *BORD* B9 ....108 A4
Little Green Lanes
  SCFLD/BOLD B73 ....72 F6
Little Gv *RUGBYS/DCH* CV22 ....187 D1
Little Hardwick Rd *ALDR* WS9 ....55 H3
Little Hay La *LICHS* WS14 ....42 F5
Little Heath Cft *BKDE/SHDE* B34 ....91 M7
Little Heath La *BRGRVE* B60 ....169 J7
Littleheath La *BRGRVE* B60 ....169 J7
Little HI *DARL/WED* WS10 ....68 D2
Little Hill Gv *KGSWFD* DY6 ....82 F7
Little Hill Wy *RIDG/WDGT* B32 ....122 F1
Little Johnson's La *ALDR* WS9 ....54 F4
Little John St *BRLYHL* DY5 ....102 B1
Little La *HHTH/SAND* B71 ....69 H8
  SHHTH WV12 ....38 D1
Little Lawford La *RUGBY* CV23 ....159 J6
Little Lawns CI *BRWNH* WS8 ....26 D8
Little London *WSL* WS1 ....4 F8
Little London La *RUGBY* CV23 ....161 L4
Little Marsh Gv *PENK* ST19 ....10 D1
Littlemead Av *NFLD/LBR* B31 ....145 G4
Little Meadow Cft
  NFLD/LBR B31 ....123 K8
Littlemead Rd *SHLY* B90 ....147 J5
Little Moor HI *SMTHWK* B67 ....87 K3
Little Newport St *WSL* WS1 * 4 F5
Little Oaks Rd *AST/WIT* B6 ....89 J1
Littleover Av *ALE/KHTH/YWD* B28 ....126 D7
Little Pk *RIDG/WDGT* B32 ....122 F1
Little Park St *COV* CV1 ....9 G3
  WOLV WV1 ....3 H5
Little Pennington St
  RUGBYN/HIL CV21 ....186 D2
Little Pipe La *LICH* WS13 ....19 L1
Little Pitts Cft *ERDE/BCHGN* B24 ....73 H8
Little Potter St *BRLYHL* DY5 ....102 B2
Little Pountney St
  BKHL/PFLD WV2 * 2 F8
Little Shadwell St *CBHAMNE* B4 * 7 G2
Littleshaw Cft *HLYWD* B47 ....173 G1
Littleshaw La *HLYWD* B47 ....173 G1
Little's La *WOLV* WV1 ....3 G3
Little South St *COV* CV1 * 9 K4
Little Station St *WSL* WS1 * 4 E5
Little St *DUDS* DY2 ....85 H5
Little Sutton La *MGN/WHC* B75 ....57 H5
Little Sutton Rd *MGN/WHC* B75 ....57 H3
Littlethorpe *COVS* CV3 ....156 B8
Little Park St *COV* CV1 * 3 H5
Littleton CI *KNWTH* CV8 ....179 L6
  WALM/CURD B76 ....58 A7
Littleton Crs *PENK* ST19 ....10 D4
Littleton Crt *SOLH* B91 ....149 G5
Littleton Dr *HEDN* WS12 ....12 A6
Littleton Rd *SHHTH* WV12 ....38 A6
Littleton St East *WSL* WS1 ....4 F5
Littleton St West *WSLW* WS2 ....4 E5
Littlewood La *WSL* WS1 ....40 B4
Littlewood CI *SOLH* B91 ....148 F5
Littlewood La *GTWY* WS6 ....24 C1
Littlewood Rd *GTWY* WS6 ....24 C1
Little Woods *REDW* B97 ....202 D6
Little Wood St *WLNHL* WV13 ....51 L3
Littleworth Av *DUDN* DY1 ....66 A5
Littleworth Gv *WALM/CURD* B76 ....73 K1
Littleworth HI *HEDN* WS12 ....17 H1
Littleworth Rd *HEDN* WS12 ....17 H1
Litton *TAM/AM/WIL* B77 ....47 H1
Liveridge CI *DOR/KN* B93 ....149 K7
Liverpool Cft
  CHWD/FDBR/MGN B37 ....110 D4
Liverpool St *BORD* B9 ....7 L4

Livery St *CBHAMNW* B3 ....6 E2
  RLSN CV32 ....206 D5
Livingstone Av
  DUNHL/THL/PER WV6 ....34 C8
  RUGBY CV23 ....185 K1
Livingstone Rd
  ALE/KHTH/YWD B14 ....125 J7
  BFLD/HDSWWD B20 ....89 G4
  BILS/COS WV14 ....50 F8
  BLOX/PEL WS3 ....39 J3
  COVN CV6 ....134 B6
  DOR/KN B93 ....162 B8
Liza Ct *RUGBYN/HIL* CV21 ....161 F5
Llangorse CI *STRPT* DY13 ....163 J6
Llewellyn Rd *RLSS* CV31 ....206 E7
Lloyd CI *NUN* CV11 ....99 H3
Llangorse CI *STRPT* DY13 ....163 J6
Lloyd Cres *COVE* CV2 ....156 C2
Lloyd Dr
  ETTPK/GDPK/PENN WV4 ....65 G3
Lloyd George Gv *CNCK/NC* WS11 ....17 G3
Lloyd HI
  ETTPK/GDPK/PENN WV4 * 65 G3
  DUNHL/THL/PER WV6 ....35 H8
  RUGBYN/HIL CV21 ....161 G2
Lloyd Rd *BFLD/HDSWWD* B20 ....88 E1
  DUNHL/THL/PER WV6 ....35 H8
  HHTH/SAND B71 ....87 J1
  SMTH B10 ....108 B5
Lloyd Sq *EDG* B15 * 106 C5
Lloyds Rd *RMSLY* B62 ....104 A6
Lloyd St *CNCK/NC* WS10 ....16 B4
  DARL/WED WS10 ....68 C2
  DUDS DY2 ....85 H5
  DUNHL/THL/PER WV6 ....35 K1
  HHTH/SAND B71 ....87 J1
Loach Dr *COVE* CV2 ....134 F1
Load St *BEWD* DY12 ....162 F2
Lobelia CI *KIDDW* DY11 ....138 A4
Locarno Rd *TPTN/OCK* DY4 ....67 M4
Lochalsh Gv *WNSFLD* WV11 ....37 M4
Lochranza Cft *REDE* B98 ....203 G6
Lochsong CI *TAM/AM/WIL* B77 ....60 B1
Lockd Dr *STETCH* B33 ....109 H2
Locke CI *COVN* CV6 ....133 L4
Locke PI *VAUX/NECH* B7 ....7 M3
Locket CI *WSLW* WS2 ....51 D1
Lockfield CI *STRBR* DY8 ....101 K3
Lockhart CI *KNWTH* CV8 ....197 L5
Lockhart Dr *MGN/WHC* B75 ....57 L4
Lockheed CI *RLSS* CV31 ....206 D8
Lockhurst La *COVN* CV6 ....134 B6
Locking Cft *CVALE* B35 ....91 M2
Lockington Cft *RMSLY* B62 ....104 D2
Lock Keepers CI *CNCK/NC* WS11 ....17 K8
Lock Keepers Reach *ALVE* B48 * 170 D7
Lock La *WWCK* CV34 ....205 H4
Lockley Cl *WOLVN* WV10 ....50 D1
Lock Rd *PENK* ST19 ....10 D6
Lockside *ALDR* WS9 ....40 D6
  WMBN WV5 ....64 C6
Locksmith CI *WLNHL* WV13 ....51 M3
The Locks *RUGBY* CV23 ....187 M4
Lock St *WOLV* WV1 ....3 H3
Locks Vw *STRBR* DY8 ....101 H4
Lockton Rd *NFLD/LBR* B31 ....144 D1
Lockwood Rd *NFLD/LBR* B31 ....144 D2
Lode La *HIA/OLT* B92 ....128 A6
  SOLH B91 ....128 A6
Lodge CI *ATHST* CV9 ....63 L7
  BEWD DY12 ....163 H1
  DSYBK/YTR WS5 ....54 B7
  RMSLY B62 ....122 B2
Lodge Crs *DUDS* DY2 ....102 E1
  HAG/WOL DY9 ....119 M8
Lodge Cft *DOR/KN* B93 ....149 M7
  NFLD/LBR B31 ....123 J8
Lodge Dr
  LGN/SDN/BHAMAIR B26 ....109 J5
Lodge Farm CI *WALM/CURD* B76 ....73 K2
Lodgefield Rd *RMSLY* B62 ....103 M6
Lodge Green La
  RCOVN/BALC/EX CV7 ....131 J2
Lodge Green La North
  RCOVN/BALC/EX CV7 ....131 J2
Lodge Gv *ALDR* WS9 ....40 E8
Lodge Hill Rd *SLYOAK* B29 ....124 B8
Lodge La *KGSWFD* DY6 ....82 F7
  LICH WS13 ....19 H2
Lodgepool CI *KGSTG* B44 ....71 J7
Lodge Pool Dr *REDE* B98 ....202 D4
Lodge Rd *AST/WIT* B6 ....89 J5
  BILS/COS WV14 ....67 K1
  BNTWD WS7 ....18 C3
  COVS CV3 ....155 M4
  DARL/WED WS10 ....52 B8
  DOR/KN B93 ....149 M7
  DSYBK/YTR WS5 ....54 B8
  REDE B98 ....202 C2
  RUGBYN/HIL CV21 ....186 F1
  RUSH/SHEL WS4 ....39 M4
  SMTHWK B67 ....87 J6
  STRPT DY13 ....188 E2
  WBROM B70 ....86 F2
  WOLVN WV10 ....35 M5
  WSNGN B18 ....88 C8
Lodge St *OLDBY* B69 ....86 E6
  SHHTH WV12 ....38 A8
Lodge Vw *GTWY* WS6 ....24 A2
Loeless Rd *STETCH* B33 ....109 L2
Lofthouse Crs *NFLD/LBR* B31 ....144 D2
Lofthouse Gv *NFLD/LBR* B31 ....144 D2
Lofthouse Rd
  BFLD/HDSWWD B20 ....88 C3
Loftus CI *NFLD/LBR* B31 ....123 K5
Loftus Ct *BNTWD* WS7 ....18 D1
Logan CI *WOLVN* WV10 ....36 A7
Logan Rd *COVE* CV2 ....135 M4
Lole CI *COVN* CV6 ....133 M1
Lollard Cft *COVS* CV3 ....155 H5
Lomaine Dr *BVILLE* B30 ....145 J1
Loman Rd *NFLD/LBR* B31 ....122 E7
Lomas La *LICH* WS13 ....20 E4
Lomax CI *LICH* WS13 ....20 E4
Lomax Rd *HEDN* WS12 ....12 F6
Lombard Av *DUDS* DY2 ....103 H2
Lombard Gdns *LICH* WS13 * 20 E4
Lombard St *BHTH/HG* B12 ....7 J9
  LICH WS13 ....20 E5
  STRPT DY13 ....188 E2
  WBROM B70 ....87 G2
Lombard St West *WBROM* B70 * 87 G2
Lombardy Cft *RMSLY* B62 ....104 E7
Lombardy Gdns *SHHTH* WV12 ....38 C6
Lombardy Gv *BNTWD* WS7 ....18 C2
Lomita Crs *TAM/AM/WIL* B77 ....46 B5
Lomond CI *BKDE/SHDE* B34 ....92 C2
  CRTAM B79 ....31 K5
Lomond Rd *SEDG* DY3 ....66 A4
Lomond Wy *NUNW/HART* CV10 ....80 A3
Lomsey CI *TLHL/CAN* CV4 ....153 L4
Londonderry Gv *SMTHWKW* B67 * 87 K3
Londonderry La *SMTHWKW* B67 ....87 K3
London Hts *DUDN* DY1 ....84 E3
London Rd *BFLD/HDSWWD* B20 * 9 G9
  COV CV1 ....9 G6
  COVS CV3 ....155 K6
  KNWTH CV8 ....183 H4

LICHS WS14 ....21 G8
MGN/WHC B75 ....57 L1
RRUGBY CV23 ....184 A6
London St *SMTHWK* B66 ....88 A8
Lones St *HHTH/SAND* B71 ....69 M5
Long Acre *CDSL* WV8 ....34 C5
  KIDD DY10 ....138 D7
  VAUX/NECH B7 ....89 M7
Longacre *WLNHL* WV13 ....51 L5
Longacres *HEDN* WS12 ....13 K8
  WLNHL WV13 ....51 L5
Long Acre St *WSLW* WS2 ....4 D1
Long Bank *BEWD* DY12 ....162 B3
Longbank Rd *OLDBY* B69 ....86 A5
Longboat La *STRBR* DY8 ....101 K8
Longboat Quay *DUDS* DY2 ....103 H1
Longborough CI *REDW* B97 ....201 M7
Longbow Rd *NFLD/LBR* B31 ....144 A7
Longbridge La *NFLD/LBR* B31 ....144 D6
Long Bridge Rd *LICHS* WS14 ....21 G8
Long Brook La *KNWTH* CV8 ....177 J1
Long CI Av *COVW* CV5 ....132 F7
Long Close Av *COVW* CV5 ....132 F7
Long Close Wk *CVALE* B35 ....91 L2
Long Compton Dr
  HAG/WOL DY9 ....119 L7
Long Cft *HEDN* WS12 ....16 A1
Longcroft CI *CVALE* B35 ....91 L2
The Longcroft *HALE* B63 ....121 J1
  RUSH/SHEL WS4 ....40 A6
Longdales Rd *HWK/WKHTH* B38 ....145 H6
London Av
  ETTPK/GDPK/PENN WV4 ....50 B3
Longdon CI *REDE* B98 ....202 F6
Longdon CI *FOAKS/STRLY* B74 ....56 C1
Longdon Rd *DOR/KN* B93 ....149 L7
Longfellow CI *REDW* B97 ....202 A6
Longfellow PI *CNCK/NC* WS11 ....16 C1
Longfellow Rd *BNTWD* WS7 ....18 D4
  BVILLE B30 ....145 H2
  COVE CV2 ....156 A2
  SEDG DY3 ....65 L8
Longfield CI *HLGN/YWD* B28 ....126 D7
  TAM/AM/WIL B77 ....46 C1
Longfield Rd *HAG/WOL* DY9 ....102 B8
  NFLD/LBR B31 ....123 J6
  RLSS CV31 ....206 F7
Longford CI *DOR/KN* B93 ....175 M2
  RIDG/WDGT B32 ....122 E6
  WMBN WV5 ....64 B8
Longford Gn *KGSTG* B44 ....71 L2
Longford Gv *KGSTG* B44 ....71 L2
Longford Rd *CNCK/NC* WS11 ....16 C1
  COVN CV6 ....134 E2
  KGSTG B44 ....71 L2
  RCOVN/BALC/EX CV7 ....116 E7
  WOLVN WV10 ....50 D1
Longford St *COVN* CV6 ....134 D1
Long Furlong
  RUGBYS/DCH CV22 ....186 E6
Longham Cft *RIDG/WDGT* B32 ....123 K1
Longhope CI *REDE* B98 ....203 K5
Longhurst Cft *NFLD/LBR* B31 ....144 E6
Long Hyde Rd *SMTHWK* B67 ....105 H4
Long Innage *HALE* B63 ....103 F7
Long Knowle La *WNSFLD* WV11 ....36 E1
Longlake Av
  DUNHL/THL/PER WV6 ....48 E1
Longlands Dr *TAM/AM/WIL* B77 ....47 G4
Longlands Rd *RMSLY* B62 ....122 C4
The Longlands *RBRY* B45 ....170 B6
  WMBN WV5 ....64 E7
Long La *BLKHTH/ROWR* B65 ....104 D1
  RCOVN/BALC/EX CV7 ....133 H5
  WNSFLD WV11 ....24 D1
Long Leasow *SLYOAK* B29 ....123 M6
Longleat *CRTAM* B79 ....31 H6
  GTB/HAM B43 ....70 A4
Longleat Dr *DUDN* DY1 ....84 C3
  SHLY B90 ....148 C8
Longleat Gv *RLSS* CV31 ....207 J3
Longleat Rd *ALDR* WS9 ....40 E3
Long Ley *WOLVN* WV10 ....3 L1
Longley Av *WALM/CURD* B76 ....74 B0
Longley Crs
  LGN/SDN/BHAMAIR B26 ....127 J1
Long Leys CI *CSHL/WTROR* B46 * 92 F3
Long Leys Cft *CSHL/WTROR* B46 ....92 F3
Longmeadow CI *MGN/WHC* B75 ....57 L8
Longmeadow Crs
  BKDE/SHDE B34 ....92 C2
Longmeadow Gv
  NFLD/LBR B31 ....144 E7
Long Meadow Rd *BRGRVE* B60 ....169 G7
Longmeadow Rd
  DSYBK/YTR WS5 ....54 C5
Long Mill Av *WNSFLD* WV11 ....36 F6
Long Mill North *WNSFLD* WV11 ....36 F6
Long Mill South *WNSFLD* WV11 ....36 F6
Longmoor CI *REDW* B97 ....193 M7
  WNSFLD WV11 ....37 K8
Longmoor Rd *HALE* B63 ....121 H4
  SCFLD/BOLD B73 ....71 M2
Longmore Av *WSLW* WS2 ....52 C4
Longmore CI *SCFLD/BOLD* B73 ....55 L8
Longmore HI *STRPT* DY13 ....188 D3
Longmore Rd *SHLY* B90 ....147 L3
Longmore St *BHTH/HG* B12 ....106 F5
  DARL/WED WS10 ....68 C2
Long Mynd *HALE* B63 ....121 H4
Long Mynd CI *SHHTH* WV12 * 37 M1
Long Mynd Rd *NFLD/LBR* B31 ....123 J7
Longmynd Wy *STRPT* DY13 ....188 D3
Long Nuke Rd *NFLD/LBR* B31 ....123 J6
Longrood Rd
  RUGBYS/DCH CV22 ....186 B2
Long Saw Dr *NFLD/LBR* B31 ....144 B4
Longshaw Gv *BKDE/SHDE* B34 ....92 B7
The Long Shoot *NUN* CV11 ....81 M1
Longstaff Av *HEDN* WS12 ....18 A1
Longstaff Cft *LICH* WS13 ....19 J4
Longstone CI *SHLY* B90 ....148 F7
Longstone Rd *PBAR/PBCH* B42 ....71 H4
Long St *ATHST* CV9 ....63 G4
  POL/KGSB/FAZ B78 ....47 L5
  SPARK B11 ....107 J2
  WOLV WV1 ....3 G4
  WSLW WS2 ....4 F5
Long Wd *BVILLE* B30 ....124 C8
Longwood CI *TLHL/CAN* CV4 ....153 K7
Longwood La *RUSH/SHEL* WS4 ....54 C3
Longwood Ri *SHHTH* WV12 ....38 C6
Longwood Rd *ALDR* WS9 ....54 F3
  RBRY B45 ....143 L6
Lonicera CI *DSYBK/YTR* WS5 ....69 G2
Lonscale Dr *COVS* CV3 ....154 F8
Lonsdale CI *SHHTH* WV12 ....37 M1
  TAM/AM/WIL B77 ....46 C1
Lonsdale Rd *BDMR/CCFT* WV3 ....51 K7
  BILS/COS WV14 ....51 K7
  DSYBK/YTR WS5 ....54 B7
  RBRY B45 ....143 L6
  RLSN CV32 ....206 F1
  SMTHWK B66 ....88 A6
Lord Austin Dr *BRGRVE* B60 ....169 J4
Lord Cromwell Ct
  CNCK/NC WS11 * 12 E8

Lord Lytton Av *COVE* CV2 ....156 B3
Lord's Dr *WSLW* WS2 ....4 F1
Lords La *KINVER* DY7 ....100 C4
Lordsmore CI *BILS/COS* WV14 ....67 H4
Lord St *BDMR/CCFT* WV3 ....2 A7
  BILS/COS WV14 ....67 J2
  COVW CV5 ....154 D3
  VAUX/NECH B7 ....7 K1
  WSL WS1 ....4 F9
Lord St West *BILS/COS* WV14 ....67 J2
Lordswood CI *REDW* B97 ....201 L5
Lordswood Rd *HRBN* B17 ....105 L5
Lordswood Sq *HRBN* B17 * 105 M6
Lorenzo CI *COVS* CV3 ....156 B7
Lorimer Wy *GTB/HAM* B43 ....55 H8
Lorne Gv *KIDD* DY10 ....138 E7
Lorne St *BNTWD* WS7 ....18 E8
  KIDD DY10 ....138 E8
  STRPT DY13 ....163 L8
  TPTN/OCK DY4 ....67 K5
Lorrainer Av *STRBR* DY8 ....101 L5
Lorton *CRTAM* B79 ....31 H6
Lothersdale *TAM/AM/WIL* B77 ....46 B5
Lothians Rd *BLOX/PEL* WS3 ....25 L1
  DUNHL/THL/PER WV6 ....35 H7
Lottie Rd *SLYOAK* B29 ....124 C4
Lotus *TAM/AM/WIL* B77 ....46 D1
Lotus Cft *SMTHWK* B67 ....105 K1
Lotus Dr *CNCK/NC* WS11 ....12 C8
Lotus Wy *BLKHTH/ROWR* B65 ....103 K1
Loudon Av *COVN* CV6 ....133 L8
Loughshaw *TAM/AM/WIL* B77 ....47 G4
Loughton Gv *HALE* B63 ....121 K1
Louisa St *CBHAMNW* B1 ....6 C4
Louise Cft *ALE/KHTH/YWD* B14 ....146 C3
Louise Lorne Rd *MOS/BIL* B13 ....125 K1
Louise Rd *HDSW* B21 ....88 C6
Louise St *SEDG* DY3 ....83 M2
Lount Wk *LOZ/NWT* B19 ....89 J8
Lovage Rd *REDE* B98 ....195 K7
Loveday St *CBHAMNE* B4 ....7 G2
  CBHAMNW B4 ....7 G2
Lovelace Av *SOLH* B91 ....149 H5
Love La *DUNHL/THL/PER* WV6 ....35 H7
  GTWY WS6 ....24 F1
  HAG/WOL DY9 ....102 C6
  HLYWD B47 ....172 C8
  STRBR DY8 ....119 L2
  WSL WS1 ....4 F9
Lovell *CRTAM* B79 ....31 K7
Lovell CI *RCOVN/BALC/EX* CV7 ....116 E5
  SLYOAK B29 ....123 L7
Lovell Rd *BDWTH* CV12 ....116 E2
Love Lyne *REDW* B97 ....201 L8
Lovett Av *OLDBY* B69 ....85 M4
Loveridge CI *CDSL* WV8 ....21 K6
Loverock Crs *RUGBYN/HIL* CV21 ....187 J3
Lovett Av *OLDBY* B69 ....85 M4
Lowans Hill Vw *REDW* B97 ....202 A1
Low Av *GTB/HAM* B43 ....70 D5
Lowbridge CI *SHHTH* WV12 ....38 A3
Lowbrook La *SHLY* B90 ....173 H1
Lowden Cft
  LGN/SDN/BHAMAIR B26 ....127 J1
Lowdham *TAM/AM/WIL* B77 ....47 G4
Lowe Av *DARL/WED* WS10 ....51 M6
Lowe Dr *KGSWFD* DY6 ....101 J1
  SCFLD/BOLD B73 ....72 B2
Lowe La *KIDDW* DY11 ....137 M2
Lower Av *RLSS* CV31 ....206 D6
Lower Beeches Rd
  NFLD/LBR B31 ....144 A3
Lower Bentley La *BRGRVE* B60 ....200 C4
Lower Cape *WWCK* CV34 ....205 H3
Lower Chapel St *OLDBY* B69 ....86 D6
Lower Church St *TPTN/OCK* DY4 ....67 L7
Lower City Rd *OLDBY* B69 ....86 D6
Lower Common La *REDW* B97 ....201 M3
Lowercroft Wy
  FOAKS/STRLY B74 ....42 C7
Lower Dartmouth St *BORD* B9 ....107 L4
Lower Darwin St *BHTH/HG* B12 ....7 J9
Lower Derry St *BRLYHL* DY5 ....102 B3
Lower Eastern Green La
  COVW CV5 ....153 K1
Lower End *KNWTH* CV8 ....182 A7
Lower Essex St *DIG/EDG* B5 ....7 G8
Lower Ford St *COV* CV1 ....9 J1
Lower Forster St *WSL* WS1 ....5 G2
Lower Gambolds La
  BRGRVE B60 ....191 K7
Lower Gn *TPTN/OCK* DY4 * 67 J8
Lower Grinsty La *REDW* B97 ....202 A5
Lower Ground CI *AST/WIT* B6 * 89 K4
Lower Gungate *CRTAM* B79 ....31 M8
Lower Hall La *WSL* WS1 ....4 F4
Lower Hall St *WLNHL* WV13 ....51 L3
Lower High St *CDYHTH* B64 ....103 G5
  DARL/WED WS10 ....68 D3
  STRBR DY8 ....101 K7
Lower Higley CI
  RIDG/WDGT B32 ....123 J1
Lower Hillmorton Rd
  RUGBYN/HIL CV21 ....187 G3
Lower Holyhead Rd *COV* CV1 ....8 D4
Lower Horseley Flds *WOLV* WV1 ....3 L3
Lower House La *ATHST* CV9 ....61 K3
Lower Ladies Hills *KNWTH* CV8 ....179 L7
Lower La *LICH* WS13 ....19 G3
Lower Leam St *RLSS* CV31 ....206 E6
Lower Lichfield St *WLNHL* WV13 ....51 M3
Lower Lickhill Rd *STRPT* DY13 ....188 D1
Lower Loveday St *LOZ/NWT* B19 ....6 F1
Lower Mill RLSN CV32 * 206 D5
Lower Mill St *KIDD* DY10 ....138 B7
Lower Moor *SLYOAK* B29 ....124 C5
Lower North St *RUSH/SHEL* WS4 ....53 J2
Lower Prec *COV* CV1 ....8 F5
The Lower Pde
  CSCFLD/WYGN B72 ....57 G8
Lower Pk *REDE* B98 ....162 F2
Lowerpark *TAM/AM/WIL* B77 ....46 A4
Lower Parklands *KIDDW* DY11 ....138 B8
Lower Prec *COV* CV1 ....8 E5
Lower Prestwood Rd
  WNSFLD WV11 ....37 G6
Lower Queen St
  CSCFLD/WYGN B72 ....73 G1
Lower Reddicroft
  SCFLD/BOLD B73 ....57 H8
Lower Rd *HEDN* WS12 ....17 G2
  RCOVN/BALC/EX CV7 ....117 M7
Lower Rushall St *WSL* WS1 ....5 G3
Lower Sandford St *LICH* WS13 ....20 C6
Lower Severn St *CBHAMW* B1 ....6 E6
Lower Shepley La *BRGRVE* B60 ....169 H5
Lowerstack Cft
  CHWD/FDBR/MGN B37 ....110 D2
Lower St *DUNHL/THL/PER* WV6 ....35 H8
  RUGBYN/HIL CV21 ....187 M5
Lower Temple St *CBHAMW* B1 ....6 E5
Lower Tower St *LOZ/NWT* B19 ....89 H8

Lower Trinity St BORD B9 7 L7
Lower Valley Rd BRLYHL DY5 101 L3
Lower Vauxhall WOLV WV1 2 A4
Lower Villiers St
BKHL/PFLD WV2 50 A6
RLSN CV32 206 E4
Lower Walsall St WOLV WV1 3 L6
Lower White Rd
RIDG/WDGT B32 105 H8
Lowes Av WWCK CV34 205 J4
Lowesmoor Rd
LGN/SDN/BHAMAIR B26 109 M6
Lowe St BHTH/HG B12 7 M9
DUNHL/THL/PER WV6 2 B1
Loweswater Cl NUN CV11 81 L7
Loweswater Dr SEDG DY3 84 B2
Loweswater Rd COVS CV3 156 C4
STRPT DY13 163 J6
Lowfield Cl RIDG/WDGT B32 122 E2
Lowfield La REDW B97 193 M8
Lowforce TAM/AM/WIL B77 47 G4
Low Hill Crs WOLVN WV10 36 C5
Lowhill La RBRY B45 144 A7
Lowland Cl CDYHTH B64 103 K4
Lowland Rd HEDN WS12 12 A8
Lowlands Av
DUNHL/THL/PER WV6 35 J7
FOAKS/STRLY B74 55 J5
Lowlands La REDE B98 203 H2
Lowndes Rd STRBR DY8 101 J7
Lowry Cl BDWTH CV12 116 E1
DUNHL/THL/PER WV6 48 D1
SMTHWKW B67 87 K7
WLNHL WV13 51 H3
Low St GTWY WS6 24 A2
Low Thatch HWK/WKHTH B38 145 J6
Lowther St COVE CV2 9 M2
Low Town OLDBY B69 86 E6
Low Wood Rd ERDW/GRVHL B23 72 C8
Loxdale Sidings BILS/COS WV14 67 K1
Loxdale St BILS/COS WV14 67 K1
DARL/WED WS10 68 D3
Loxley Av ALE/KHTH/YWD B14 147 G3
SHLY B90 147 K4
Loxley Cl COVE CV2 135 H3
NFLD/LBR B31 123 J5
REDE B98 195 H7
Loxley Rd MGN/WHC B75 57 H2
SMTHWKW B67 105 K4
Loxley Wy RLSN CV32 206 E2
Loxton Cl FOAKS/STRLY B74 42 B8
Loynells Rd RBRY B45 143 L6
Loyns Cl CHWD/FDBR/MGN B37 110 C2
Lozells Rd LOZ/NWT B19 88 F6
Lozells St LOZ/NWT B19 89 G6
Lozells Wood Cl LOZ/NWT B19 88 F6
Lucas Circ LOZ/NWT B19 89 G7
Lucas Ct RLSN CV32 206 B5
RUGBYN/HIL CV21 186 F1
Luce Cl CVALE B35 91 M1
Lucerne Cl COVE CV2 135 G2
Luce Rd WOLVN WV10 36 C7
Lucian Cl COVE CV2 135 L6
Lucknow Rd SHHTH WV12 37 M8
Luddington Rd HIA/OLT B92 128 C6
Ludford Cl MGN/WHC B75 57 J6
NUNW/HART CV10 96 F1
Ludford Rd NUNW/HART CV10 80 A7
RIDG/WDGT B32 122 E4
Ludgate CRTAM B79 31 L8
Ludgate Av KIDDW DY11 163 L1
Ludgate Cl CSHL/WTROR B46 92 E2
OLDBY B69 85 M5
Ludgate Hl CBHAMNW B3 6 E3
Ludgate St DUDN DY1 * 84 F4
Lud La CRTAM B79 31 L8
Ludlow Cl
CHWD/FDBR/MGN B37 111 G3
CNCK/NC WS11 17 G3
SHHTH WV12 37 M7
Ludlow La WSLW WS2 52 E1
Ludlow Rd COVW CV5 8 A6
KIDD DY10 164 C3
REDW B97 202 B2
WASH/WDE B8 108 D2
Ludlow Wy DUDN DY1 84 C3
Ludmer Wy BFLD/HDSWWD B20 89 G3
Ludstone Av
ETTPK/GDPK/PENN WV4 49 H8
Ludstone Rd SLYOAK B29 123 K4
Ludworth Av
CHWD/FDBR/MGN B37 110 F4
Luff Cl COVS CV3 155 M5
Lugtrout La SOLH B91 128 D7
Lulworth Cl HALE B63 103 G7
Lulworth Pk KNWTH CV8 180 A7
Lulworth Rd BNTWD WS7 18 E6
HLGN/YWD B28 126 E5
Lumley Gv
CHWD/FDBR/MGN B37 111 H3
Lumley Rd WSL WS1 5 K5
Lumsden Cl COVE CV2 135 K5
Lunar Cl TLHL/CAN CV4 154 B8
Lundy Vw CBROM B36 92 F7
Lunn Av KNWTH CV8 197 J2
Lunns Cft LICH WS13 21 G5
Lunt Gv RIDG/WDGT B32 105 H8
Lunt Pl BILS/COS WV14 51 L7
Lunt Rd BILS/COS WV14 51 L6
Lupin Gv BORD B9 108 D2
DSYBK/YTR WS5 69 M1
Lupin Rd DUDS DY2 85 K4
Lupton Av COVS CV3 155 G7
Lusbridge Cl HALE B63 120 F1
Luscombe Rd COVE CV2 135 J5
Luther Wy COVW CV5 153 K1
Lutley Av HALE B63 121 J1
Lutley Cl BDMR/CCFT WV3 49 J6
Lutley Dr HAG/WOL DY9 120 A2
Lutley Gv RIDG/WDGT B32 122 F4
Lutley La HALE B63 121 G3
Lutley Mill Rd HALE B63 121 J1
Luton Rd SLYOAK B29 124 D2
Lutterworth Rd COVE CV2 135 G8
NUN CV11 99 K4
Luttrell Rd FOAKS/STRLY B74 56 D5
Luxor La COVW CV5 131 M5
Lyall Gdns RBRY B45 143 J4
Lyall Gv ACGN B27 126 E3
Lychgate Av HAG/WOL DY9 120 A4
Lydate Rd RMSLY B62 122 D1
Lydbrook Covert
HWK/WKHTH B38 145 J5
Lydbury Gv STETCH B33 109 L1
Lyd Cl WNSFLD WV11 36 F8
Lydd Cft CVALE B35 91 M1
Lyddington Dr RMSLY B62 103 M6
Lyde Gn HALE B63 103 G6
Lydford Cl COVE CV2 135 G6
Lydford Gv ERDE/BCHGN B24 90 E3
Lydford Rd BLOX/PEL WS3 38 F3
Lydgate Rd COVN CV6 133 M8
KGSWFD DY6 83 K8
Lydget Gv ERDW/GRVHL B23 72 B6
Lydham Cl BILS/COS WV14 66 F1
ERDW/GRVHL B23 71 L7
REDE B98 194 C8
Lydia Cft FOAKS/STRLY B74 42 C7
Lydian Cl DUNHL/THL/PER WV6 2 D1
Lydiate Ash Rd BRGRVW B61 169 G2
Lydiate Av NFLD/LBR B31 144 B4
Lydiates Cl SEDG DY3 65 M6
Lydney Cl REDE B98 195 H7
SHHTH WV12 52 B1
Lydney Gv NFLD/LBR B31 144 D2
Lydstep Gv RLSS CV31 207 G6
Lye Av RIDG/WDGT B32 122 E3
Lye By-pass HAG/WOL DY9 102 C7
Lye Close La RIDG/WDGT B32 122 D3
Lyecroft Av
CHWD/FDBR/MGN B37 111 H3
Lye Cross Rd OLDBY B69 85 M6
Lygon Cl REDE B98 194 E8
Lygon Gv RIDG/WDGT B32 123 J1
Lymedene Rd PBAR/PBCH B42 70 F8
Lyme Green Rd STETCH B33 109 K1
Lymer Rd WOLVN WV10 36 A4
Lymesy St COVS CV3 155 H7
Lymington Cl COVN CV6 134 B5
Lymington Dr COVN CV6 116 F7
Lymington Rd BNTWD WS7 18 D4
WLNHL WV13 52 B3
Lymore Cft COVE CV2 135 L5
Lymsey Cft STRBR DY8 101 G2
Lyn Av LICH WS13 20 D4
Lynbrook Cl DUDS DY2 85 H7
HLYWD B47 146 E5
Lynbrook Rd COVW CV5 154 B5
Lynchgate Ct TLHL/CAN CV4 * 154 A7
Lynchgate Rd TLHL/CAN CV4 154 A7
The Lynch NUN CV11 99 H3
POL/KGSB/FAZ B78 47 K4
Lyncourt Gv RIDG/WDGT B32 104 F7
Lyncroft Rd SPARK B11 126 D3
Lyndale TAM/AM/WIL B77 46 D7
Lyndale Cl COVW CV5 154 A2
Lyndale Dr WNSFLD WV11 37 K8
Lyndale Rd COVW CV5 154 A2
DUDS DY2 85 J7
SEDG DY3 65 M3
Lynden Cl BRGRVW B61 191 J2
Lyndenwood REDW B97 201 L3
Lyndholm Rd KIDD DY10 138 E7
Lyndhurst Cl COVN CV6 116 F8
Lyndhurst Cft COVW CV5 153 G1
Lyndhurst Dr KIDD DY10 138 C5
STRBR DY8 101 K4
Lyndhurst Rd BDMR/CCFT WV3 49 L6
ERDE/BCHGN B24 90 D3
HEDN WS12 17 H4
HHTH/SAND B71 69 J6
RUGBYN/HIL CV21 187 K4
Lyndon HHTH/SAND B71 69 H8
Lyndon Cl BFLD/HDSWWD B20 88 F3
CBROM B36 92 A5
HALE B63 103 J8
SEDG DY3 66 C4
Lyndon Ct RLSN CV32 * 206 C5
Lyndon Cft
CHWD/FDBR/MGN B37 110 F6
Lyndon Gv HHTH/SAND B71 87 H1
KGSWFD DY6 82 F5
Lyndon Rd HIA/OLT B92 127 K3
RBRY B45 143 J6
SCFLD/BOLD B73 56 F8
STETCH B33 109 J2
Lyndworth Rd BVILLE B30 125 G6
Lyneham Cl CRTAM B79 31 M5
Lyneham Gdns WALM/CURD B76 73 L7
Lyneham Wy CVALE B35 91 K2
Lynehill La PENK ST19 10 B7
Lynfield Cl HWK/WKHTH B38 145 K6
Lynfield Rd LICH WS13 20 D4
Lyng Cl COVW CV5 153 L2
Lyng La WBROM B70 87 G3
Lynmouth Cl ALDR WS9 40 D8
NUN CV11 81 J8
Lynmouth Rd COVE CV2 135 J5
Lynn Gv SLYOAK B29 124 A2
Lynn La ALDR WS9 27 J7
Lynton Av DUNHL/THL/PER WV6 35 J6
HHTH/SAND B71 69 G6
SMTHWK B66 87 L7
Lynton Cl WWCK CV34 205 J4
Lynton Rd AST/WIT B6 89 L6
COVN CV6 134 D4
Lynval Rd BRLYHL DY5 102 D6
Lynwood Av KGSWFD DY6 82 F5
Lynwood Cl SHHTH WV12 38 C5
Lynwood Dr KIDD DY10 139 M3
Lynwood Wk HRBN B17 124 A1
RLSS CV31 207 G7
Lyons Gv SPARK B11 126 A2
Lysander Rd RBRY B45 143 L3
Lysander St COVS CV3 156 B7
Lysander Wy CNCK/NC WS11 16 C2
Lyster Cl WWCK CV34 204 F5
Lysways St WSL WS1 5 G6
Lythall Cl RLSS CV31 207 K8
Lythalls La COVN CV6 134 C3
Lytham TAM/AM/WIL B77 33 G8
Lytham Cl STRBR DY8 119 L3
WALM/CURD B76 73 M7
Lytham Cft EDG B15 6 E8
Lytham Gv BLOX/PEL WS3 38 E1
Lytham Rd DUNHL/THL/PER WV6 48 B1
RUGBYS/DCH CV22 186 B4
Lythwood Dr BRLYHL DY5 102 A5
Lyttelton Rd BEWD DY12 162 E1
LDYWD/EDGR B16 106 B4
STETCH B33 109 H3
STRBR DY8 101 H8
WWCK CV34 205 J5
Lyttleton Av BRGRVE B60 191 J6
RMSLY B62 104 C6
Lyttleton Cl COVS CV3 156 E4
DUDS DY2 103 G1
Lyttleton St WBROM B70 87 G3
Lytton Av
ETTPK/GDPK/PENN WV4 65 H1
Lytton Gv ACGN B27 126 F4
Lytton La RIDG/WDGT B32 123 K2

M

Maas Rd NFLD/LBR B31 144 E1
Mabey Av REDE B98 194 D8
Macadam Cl BNTWD WS7 18 F5
Macarthur Rd CDYHTH B64 103 G5
Macaulay Rd COVE CV2 156 B1
RUGBYS/DCH CV22 186 C6
Macbeth Cl RUGBYS/DCH CV22 186 C7
Macdonald Cl OLDBY B69 86 B3
Macdonald Rd COVE CV2 156 B2
Macdonald St DIG/EDG B5 7 H9
Macefield Cl COVE CV2 135 H3
Mace St CDYHTH B64 103 J4
Mac Gregor Crs
TAM/AM/WIL B77 46 D1
Macgregor Tithe CRTAM B79 31 M8
Machin Rd ERDW/GRVHL B23 90 D1
Mackadown La STETCH B33 110 B3
Mackay Rd BLOX/PEL WS3 39 H3
Mackenzie Cl COVW CV5 132 E6
Mackenzie Rd SPARK B11 126 A3
Mackmillan Rd
BLKHTH/ROWR B65 104 A3
Macmillan Cl OLDBY B69 86 A3
Macrome Rd
DUNHL/THL/PER WV6 35 J5
Madam's Hill Rd SHLY B90 148 B6
Madden Pl RUGBYS/DCH CV22 186 A3
Maddocks Hl CSCFLD/WYGN B72 73 G3
Madehurst Rd ERDW/GRVHL B23 72 C7
Madeira Av CDSL WV8 34 E3
Madeira Cft COVW CV5 154 C3
Madeley Rd HAG/WOL DY9 142 C6
KGSWFD DY6 101 L1
REDE B98 195 K8
SPARK B11 108 A8
Madin Rd TPTN/OCK DY4 85 J1
Madison Av CBROM B36 91 H7
WSLW WS2 52 F3
Madley Cl RBRY B45 143 J5
Madox Cl CRTAM B79 31 J5
Madresfield Dr HALE B63 121 M3
Madrona TAM/AM/WIL B77 46 F1
Maer Cl BLKHTH/ROWR B65 104 A2
Mafeking Rd SMTHWK B66 87 L6
Mafeking Vls RMSLY B62 * 103 M6
Magdala St WSNGN B18 88 C8
Magdalen Cl DUDN DY1 84 E3
Magdalene Rd WSL WS1 5 K9
Magna Cl GTWY WS6 24 C2
Magness Crs SHHTH WV12 38 A8
Magnet La RUGBYS/DCH CV22 186 A5
Magnolia TAM/AM/WIL B77 46 E1
Magnolia Cl COVS CV3 154 F8
SLYOAK B29 123 L6
Magnolia Dr DSYBK/YTR WS5 69 K1
Magnolia Gv CDSL WV8 34 E2
Magnolia Wy STRBR DY8 101 K5
Magnum Cl FOAKS/STRLY B74 * 55 K6
Magnus TAM/AM/WIL B77 46 C7
Magpie Cl DUDS DY2 103 J2
Magpie La RCOVN/BALC/EX CV7 151 J7
Magpie Wy KIDD DY10 164 F3
Magyar Crs NUN CV11 99 K5
Maidavale Crs COVS CV3 155 G8
Maidendale Rd KGSWFD DY6 82 F6
Maidenhair Dr RRUGBY CV23 161 H5
Maidensbridge Gdns
KGSWFD DY6 82 F4
Maidensbridge Rd KGSWFD DY6 82 F4
Maidstone Dr BNTWD WS7 19 H7
STRBR DY8 101 J2
Maidstone Rd
BFLD/HDSWWD B20 89 J4
Maidwell Dr SHLY B90 148 C5
Main Rd ATHST CV9 61 L6
ATHST CV9 62 C7
ATHST CV9 63 L2
CRTAM B79 33 M3
LGN/SDN/BHAMAIR B26 128 D2
RCOVN/BALC/EX CV7 131 G4
Mainstone Cl REDE B98 203 J2
Mainstream Wy VAUX/NECH B7 108 A1
Main St ALDR WS9 41 J1
CRTAM B79 31 M4
KNWTH CV8 183 L1
LICHS WS14 28 D7
MKTBOS/BARL/STKG CV13 81 K2
RRUGBY CV23 159 J1
RRUGBY CV23 159 M2
RRUGBY CV23 161 K8
RRUGBY CV23 161 L4
RRUGBY CV23 185 L1
RUGBYN/HIL CV21 160 B6
RUGBYS/DCH CV22 186 A5
SPARK B11 107 L6
Main Ter BHTH/HG B12 * 107 L6
Mainwaring Dr MGN/WHC B75 57 J3
Maisemore Cl REDE B98 195 H7
Maisonettes CDSL WV8 * 34 F2
The Maisonettes
ERDE/BCHGN B24 * 90 C3
Maitland TAM/AM/WIL B77 46 D3
Maitland Rd DUDN DY1 84 B4
WASH/WDE B8 108 D1
Majestic Wy
BLKHTH/ROWR B65 104 A1
Major St BKHL/PFLD WV2 50 C6
Majuba Rd LDYWD/EDGR B16 106 A1
Makepeace Av WWCK CV34 205 K4
Malam Cl TLHL/CAN CV4 153 L4
Malcolm Av BRGRVW B61 191 J2
ERDE/BCHGN B24 73 G8
Malcolm Gv RBRY B45 143 L6
Malcolm Rd SHLY B90 147 M3
Malcolmson Cl EDG B15 106 D6
Maldale TAM/AM/WIL B77 47 G4
Malfield Av REDW B97 201 K3
Malfield Dr ACGN B27 127 J2
Malham Cl NUN CV11 99 L3
Malham Rd STRPT DY13 163 J6
TAM/AM/WIL B77 47 G4
WWCK CV34 205 K4
Malins Rd
ETTPK/GDPK/PENN WV4 50 B8
HRBN B17 106 B8
The Malins WWCK CV34 205 M7
Malkit Cl WSLW WS2 52 C1
Mallaby Cl SHLY B90 147 L5
Mallard Av KIDD DY10 164 F2
NUNW/HART CV10 80 A8
Mallard Cl ACGN B27 127 G2
BLOX/PEL WS3 25 L7
BRLYHL DY5 102 A6
REDE B98 194 D8
Mallard Cft LICH WS13 21 G5
Mallard Dr ERDW/GRVHL B23 89 M2
OLDBY B69 104 D2
Mallender Dr DOR/KN B93 149 K6
Mallen Dr OLDBY B69 85 M4
Mallerin Cft NUNW/HART CV10 79 M8
Mallets Cnr LICHS WS14 * 21 J8
Mallicot Cl LICH WS13 21 H4
Mallin St SMTHWK B66 87 H6
Mallory Crs BLOX/PEL WS3 39 H3
Mallory Dr KIDDW DY11 138 B4
WWCK CV34 205 H6
Mallory Ri MOS/BIL B13 126 A4
Mallory Rd DUNHL/THL/PER WV6 48 C2
Mallory Wy
RCOVN/BALC/EX CV7 116 C8
Mallow Cl DSYBK/YTR WS5 69 K2
Mallow Ct
DUNHL/THL/PER WV6 * 35 M8
Mallow Ri ERDW/GRVHL B23 71 M6
Mallows Cl DARL/WED WS10 * 52 B7
Mallow Wy RRUGBY CV23 161 G5
Malmesbury Rd COVN CV6 133 L3
SMHTH B10 108 C7
Malpas Dr RIDG/WDGT B32 123 G5
Malpass Gdns CDSL WV8 34 C1
Malpass Rd BRLYHL DY5 102 D6
Malpas Wk WOLVN WV10 50 E1
Malt Cl EDG B15 106 B7
Malthouse Cl NUNW/HART CV10 96 F1
Malthouse Cft AST/WIT B6 89 J5
Malthouse Dr DUDN DY1 84 E3
Malthouse Gdns LOZ/NWT B19 89 H6
Malthouse Gv YDLY B25 109 J4
Malthouse La
DUNHL/THL/PER WV6 35 H7
HOCK/TIA B94 173 J7
KNWTH CV8 179 J7
PBAR/PBCH B42 71 H5
WASH/WDE B8 90 C7
Malt House La WOLVN WV10 14 F8
Malthouse Rd TPTN/OCK DY4 67 J8
Malthouse Rw
CHWD/FDBR/MGN B37 110 E5
The Maltings ALDR WS9 * 41 G7
NUN CV11 * 81 J8
RLSN CV32 206 D3
WMBN WV5 * 64 E7
WOLV WV1 3 G2
Malt Mill La RMSLY B62 104 A5
Malton Gv MOS/BIL B13 125 M6
Malvern Av HAG/WOL DY9 102 A8
NUNW/HART CV10 97 M2
RUGBYS/DCH CV22 187 H4
Malvern Cl HHTH/SAND B71 69 H8
SHHTH WV12 51 M1
STRPT DY13 188 B5
Malvern Ct ACGN B27 * 127 G1
WOLVN WV10 36 B5
Malvern Crs DUDS DY2 84 D7
Malvern Dr ALDR WS9 41 G5
KIDD DY10 164 C2
WALM/CURD B76 73 L5
WOLV WV1 50 F4
Malvern Hill Rd VAUX/NECH B7 90 A6
Malvern Park Av SOLH B91 149 H2
Malvern Rd ACGN B27 127 G1
BRGRVE B60 191 H6
COVW CV5 154 C1
LGLYGN/QTN B68 104 F5
RBRY B45 169 L3
RCOVN/BALC/EX CV7 152 A7
REDW B97 202 B5
Malvern St BHTH/HG B12 107 L8
Malvern Vw KIDD DY10 166 C4
KIDDW DY11 163 M4
Malvern View Rd SEDG DY3 84 B1
Mamble Rd STRBR DY8 101 J8
Mammoth Dr WOLVN WV10 36 B7
Manby Cl DUNHL/THL/PER WV6 2 C1
Manby Rd CVALE B35 91 L1
Manby St TPTN/OCK DY4 67 K5
Mancetter Rd ATHST CV9 63 L7
NUNW/HART CV10 80 B5
SHLY B90 148 A2
Manchester St AST/WIT B6 89 J8
OLDBY B69 86 F6
Mancroft Cl KGSWFD DY6 82 F6
Mancroft Gdns
DUNHL/THL/PER WV6 35 G8
Mancroft Rd
DUNHL/THL/PER WV6 35 G8
Mandale Rd WOLVN WV10 36 D7
Mandarin Av KIDD DY10 164 F2
Manderley Cl COVW CV5 132 A8
SEDG DY3 66 A3
Manders Est WOLV WV1 * 3 M3
Mander St BDMR/CCFT WV3 2 D8
Manderville Gdns KGSWFD DY6 83 G7
Mandeville Gdns WSL WS1 5 H6
Mandeville Wy BRGRVW B61 168 D8
Maney Cnr CSCFLD/WYGN B72 72 F1
Maney Hill Rd
CSCFLD/WYGN B72 73 G2
Manfield Av COVE CV2 135 L6
Manfield Rd WLNHL WV13 51 G2
Manifold Cl BNTWD WS7 19 H7
Manilla Rd SLYOAK B29 124 F4
Manitoba Cft HWK/WKHTH B38 145 K5
Manley Cl WBROM B70 * 86 E2
Manley Rd LICH WS13 21 H4
Manlove St BDMR/CCFT WV3 2 B8
Manningford Rd
ALE/KHTH/YWD B14 146 D3
Mann's Cl KNWTH CV8 182 F5
Manor Abbey Dr RMSLY B62 122 C2
Manor Abbey Rd RMSLY B62 122 C1
Manor Av CNCK/NC WS11 16 B4
GTWY WS6 24 E1
KIDDW DY11 137 L6
Manor Av South KIDDW DY11 137 L7
Manor Cl ATHST CV9 61 M3
CDSL WV8 34 F2
ETTPK/GDPK/PENN WV4 65 K1
KIDDW DY11 137 L7
STRPT DY13 163 M8
WLNHL WV13 51 K2
Manor Ct DOR/KN B93 * 175 K3
KNWTH CV8 * 179 L7
WSLW WS2 * 4 A4
Manor Court Av NUN CV11 80 F8
Manor Court Rd BRGRVE B60 191 J5
NUN CV11 98 E1
Manor Dr SCFLD/BOLD B73 72 F1
SEDG DY3 82 C3
SEDG DY3 83 M2
SLYOAK B29 * 123 M6
WOLVN WV10 23 H3
Manor Est KNWTH CV8 183 K2
Manor Farm Dr SHHTH WV12 38 B8
Manor Farm Rd SPARK B11 126 C1
Manorfield Cl PENK ST19 10 C5
Manor Fold CDSL WV8 34 B3
Manorford Av HHTH/SAND B71 69 L4
Manor Gdns STETCH B33 109 H4
WMBN WV5 * 64 F6
Manor Gv NFLD/LBR B31 144 A4
Manor Hall Ms COVS CV3 156 A7
Manor Hl SCFLD/BOLD B73 72 F1
Manor House Cl
RUGBYN/HIL CV21 160 B6
SLYOAK B29 123 K4
Manor House Dr COV CV1 8 E6
Manor House La
CSHL/WTROR B46 92 F2
LGN/SDN/BHAMAIR B26 109 J7
Manor House Pk CDSL WV8 34 F1
Manor House Rd
DARL/WED WS10 68 D1
Manor Houses RMSLY B62 * 104 D8
Manor La BRGRVW B61 143 G8
CRTAM B79 31 J2
KIDDW DY11 189 M5
RMSLY B62 122 C1
STRBR DY8 119 H2
Manor Pk KGSWFD DY6 83 H7
NFLD/LBR B31 144 A3
Manor Park Rd CBROM B36 92 B6
NUN CV11 80 E8
Manor Ri BNTWD WS7 18 E8
LICHS WS14 21 G7
Manor Rd AST/WIT B6 89 K4
ATHST CV9 63 J7
COV CV1 8 F7
DARL/WED WS10 69 H3
DOR/KN B93 175 K2
ETTPK/GDPK/PENN WV4 50 E8
ETTPK/GDPK/PENN WV4 65 K1
FOAKS/STRLY B74 55 L5
HLYWD B47 172 E2
KNWTH CV8 179 K7
LDYWD/EDGR B16 106 B4
POL/KGSB/FAZ B78 45 H4
REDW B97 200 E4
RLSN CV32 206 F2
RUGBYN/HIL CV21 186 F1
SCFLD/BOLD B73 56 F8
SMTHWKW B67 87 H8
SOLH B91 127 M8
STETCH B33 109 J2
STRBR DY8 101 H3
STRPT DY13 163 M8
TAM/AM/WIL B77 46 A1
TPTN/OCK DY4 67 K8
WOLVN WV10 36 A6
WSLW WS2 4 A3
Manor Rd North
LDYWD/EDGR B16 106 B4
Manor Road Prec WSLW WS2 4 A3
Manor Stables DOR/KN B93 * 176 F4
Manor St DUNHL/THL/PER WV6 35 G8
Manor Terrace Flats
KNWTH CV8 * 179 L7
Manor Vw KNWTH CV8 * 183 K2
Manor Wy HALE B63 121 K4
RMSLY B62 122 A3
Mansard Cl BDMR/CCFT WV3 49 K5
WNSFLD WV11 36 F5
Manse Cl RCOVN/BALC/EX CV7 116 E4
Mansell Cl HALE B63 102 F6
Mansell Rd REDW B97 202 B6
TPTN/OCK DY4 67 L5
Mansel Rd SMHTH B10 108 C5
Mansel St COVN CV6 134 C5
Mansfield Cl CRTAM B79 31 J7
Mansfield Rd AST/WIT B6 89 H5
YDLY B25 109 G8
Mansion Cl DUDN DY1 84 E2
Mansion Crs SMTHWKW B67 105 J1
Mansion Dr BNTWD WS7 27 H1
TPTN/OCK DY4 68 A8
Manston Dr
DUNHL/THL/PER WV6 34 C8
Manston Hl PENK ST19 10 C6
Manston Rd
LGN/SDN/BHAMAIR B26 109 M6
Manston Vw CRTAM B79 32 A5
Manta Rd TAM/AM/WIL B77 46 B7
Mantilla Dr COVS CV3 154 F8
Manton Cft DOR/KN B93 175 J2
Manway Cl BFLD/HDSWWD B20 70 D8
Manwoods Cl
BFLD/HDSWWD B20 88 F3
Maple Av DARL/WED WS10 69 G1
RCOVN/BALC/EX CV7 116 F4
Maple Bank EDG B15 * 106 E6
Maplebeck Cl COVW CV5 8 A4
Maplebeck Ct SOLH B91 * 128 A8
Maple Cl BILS/COS WV14 66 E6
BNTWD WS7 18 D6
HDSW B21 88 C4
KIDDW DY11 137 M5
STRBR DY8 119 H3
STRPT DY13 188 C1
Maple Crs CNCK/NC WS11 16 A5
Maple Cft ALE/KHTH/YWD B14 125 K7
Mapledene Rd
LGN/SDN/BHAMAIR B26 110 B7
Maple Dr DSYBK/YTR WS5 69 M1
HEDN WS12 12 B5
KGSTG B44 71 M5
POL/KGSB/FAZ B78 60 B6
RUSH/SHEL WS4 39 M5
SEDG DY3 83 M3
Maple Gn DUDN DY1 66 E8
Maple Gv BDMR/CCFT WV3 49 G3
BILS/COS WV14 67 K1
CHWD/FDBR/MGN B37 92 D7
KGSWFD DY6 83 J7
LICHS WS14 21 J6
LOZ/NWT B19 89 G5
RUGBYN/HIL CV21 186 E1
WWCK CV34 205 L4
Maple Leaf Dr
CHWD/FDBR/MGN B37 110 F5
Maple Leaf Rd DARL/WED WS10 68 A4
Maple Ri LGLYGN/QTN B68 105 G3
TAM/AM/WIL B77 46 E1
Maple Rd BDMR/CCFT WV3 49 J5
BLOX/PEL WS3 39 K3
BVILLE B30 124 C5
CSCFLD/WYGN B72 73 G2
DUDN DY1 85 G2
NUNW/HART CV10 80 C8
RBRY B45 143 K7
RLSS CV31 206 D7
RMSLY B62 104 B5
The Maples BDWTH CV12 116 C3
Maple St BLOX/PEL WS3 39 H3
Mapleton Gv HLGN/YWD B28 126 F6
Mapleton Rd COVN CV6 133 K5
HLGN/YWD B28 126 F7
Maple Tree La HALE B63 103 G7
Maple Wy NFLD/LBR B31 144 D5
Maplewood WALM/CURD B76 73 L5
Mapperley Cl COVE CV2 135 L5
Mapperley Gdns MOS/BIL B13 125 G2
Mappleborough Rd SHLY B90 147 J4
Marans Cft HWK/WKHTH B38 145 H6
Marbury Cl HWK/WKHTH B38 145 H3
Marbury Ms BRLYHL DY5 102 B4
Marchant Rd BDMR/CCFT WV3 49 K3
BILS/COS WV14 51 G6
March Cl GTWY WS6 24 B4
March End Rd WNSFLD WV11 37 H8
Marchfont Cl NUN CV11 99 K3
March Gv BEWD DY12 162 F1
Marchmont Rd BORD B9 108 E3
Marchmount Rd
CSCFLD/WYGN B72 73 G5
March Wy ALDR WS9 41 G4
COVS CV3 156 B6
Marchwood Cl REDW B97 193 L8
Marcliff Crs SHLY B90 147 G3
Marconi Pl HEDN WS12 13 G6
Marcos Dr CBROM B36 92 D4
Marcot Rd HIA/OLT B92 109 K8
Marcroft Pl RLSS CV31 207 H7
Marden Cl WLNHL WV13 51 K4
Marden Gv NFLD/LBR B31 144 E6
Mardol Cl COVE CV2 135 H6
Mardon Rd
LGN/SDN/BHAMAIR B26 109 M8
Maree Gv WNSFLD WV11 37 M4
Marfield Cl WALM/CURD B76 73 L7
Margam Crs BLOX/PEL WS3 38 D3
Margam Ter BLOX/PEL WS3 38 D3
Margam Wy BLOX/PEL WS3 38 D3
Margaret Av BDWTH CV12 116 E2
HALE B63 121 K1
Margaret Cl BRLYHL DY5 102 C5
Margaret Dr CNCK/NC WS11 12 C7
STRBR DY8 119 M1
Margaret Gdns SMTHWKW B67 87 J8
Margaret Gv HRBN B17 106 A6
Margaret Rd ATHST CV9 63 J6
DARL/WED WS10 68 A1
HRBN B17 106 A8
SCFLD/BOLD B73 72 B4
WSLW WS2 52 C2
Margaret St CBHAMNW B3 6 E4

WBROM B70 ....86 F3
Margaret V TPTN/OCK DY4 ....68 A4
Margeson Cl COVE CV2 ....156 C3
Margesson Dr RBRY B45 ....170 B4
Margetts Cl KNWTH CV8 ....197 K1
Marholm Cl COVEN WV9 ....35 K3
Marian Cft
LGN/SDN/BHAMAIR B26 ......110 B8
Maria St WBROM B70 ....87 H5
Marie Brock Cl TLHL/CAN CV4 ..153 L3
Marie Cl ATHST CV9 ....63 L6
Marie Dr ACCN S27 ....126 F5
Marigold Cl CNCK/NC WS11 * 17 G2
Marigold Crs DUDN DY1 ....84 E1
Marina Cl TLHL/CAN CV4 ....153 J6
Marina Crs HEDN WS12 ....12 E8
Marine Dr KGSTG B44 ....71 J7
Marine Gdns STRBR DY8 ....101 L4
Mariner CRTAM B79 ....31 J6
Mariner Av LDYWD/EDGR B16 ...106 C4
Marion Cl BRLYHL DY5 ....102 C3
Marion Rd COVN CV6 ....134 B6
SMTHWK B67 ....87 H7
Marion Wy HLGN/YWD B28 ....126 C6
Marita Cl DUDS DY2 ....103 J2
Marjoram Cl HWK/WKHTH B38 ..145 K5
Marjorie Av BVILLE B30 ....145 M2
Mark Av DARL/WED WS10 ....68 C2
Markby Rd WSNGN B18 ....88 B3
Mark Cl REDE B98 ....202 C3
Market Cnr RLSS CV31 ....206 F7
Market End Cl BDWTH CV12 .....116 A3
Market Hall Bils/COS WV14 * 51 H8
Market La
ETTPK/GDPK/PENN WV4 ......48 D7
LICHS WS14 ....28 C3
Market Pl BLKHTH/ROWR B65 * ..104 A4
BLOX/PEL WS3 ....38 F4
CNCK/NC WS11 ....16 C1
DARL/WED WS10 ....68 C3
PENK ST19 * 10 C1
REDW B97 ....202 C1
TPTN/OCK DY4 ....67 G8
WLNHL WV13 ....51 L3
Market Sq CDYHTH B64 * 103 G5
Market St ATHST CV9 ....63 H5
BRGRVW B61 ....191 L3
CRTAM B79 ....45 M1
HEDN WS12 ....13 G8
KGSWFD DY6 ....83 L7
KIDD DY10 ....138 C8
LICH WS13 ....20 F6
OLDBY B69 ....86 E5
PENK ST19 ....10 D3
SOLH B91 ....149 J2
WOLWN WV10 ....35 M3
WSLW WS2 ....4 C3
Market Wy COV CV1 ....8 C5
HAG/WOL DY9 ....120 A7
Markfield Rd
LGN/SDN/BHAMAIR B26 ......109 M5
Markford Wk LOZ/NWT B19 ....89 H7
Markham Crs HIA/OLT B92 ....128 D4
Markham Cft COVEN WV9 ....35 L5
Markham Dr KGSWFD DY6 ....101 J9
Marklew Cl BRWNH WS8 ....26 E4
Marklin Av WOLWN WV10 ....36 M6
Mark Rd DARL/WED WS10 ....68 C2
Marksbury Cl
DUNHL/THL/PER WV6 ....35 L8
Marks Ms WWCK CV34 * 205 J7
Marlbank Rd STRBR DY8 ....101 L4
Marlborough Av
FOAKS/STRLY B74 ....42 C7
Marlborough Ct LICH WS13 ....20 F6
Marlborough Dr RLSS CV31 ....207 G2
STRBR DY8 ....119 L2
STRPT DY13 ....188 C5
Marlborough Gdns
DUNHL/THL/PER WV6 ....49 J1
STRBR DY8 ....101 L4
Marlborough Gv YDLY B25 ....109 H4
Marlborough Rd BORD B9 ....108 C4
CBROM B36 ....92 E2
COVE CV2 ....155 L3
NUN CV11 ....98 F1
RUGBYS/DCH CV22 ....186 C5
SEDG DY3 ....66 D7
SMTHWK B66 ....105 L2
Marlborough St BLOX/PEL WS3 ..38 F4
KIDD DY10 ....138 C8
Marlborough Wy
TAM/AM/WIL B77 ....46 C3
Marlbrook Cl HIA/OLT B92 ....128 A1
Marlbrook Dr
ETTPK/GDPK/PENN WV4 ......49 M7
Marlbrook Gdns BRGRVW B61 ..168 F4
Marlbrook La BRGRVE B60 ....169 H4
Marlburn Wy WMBN WV5 ....64 C7
Marlcliff Gv MOS/BIL B13 ....125 L7
Marldon Rd
ALE/KHTH/YWD B14 ....125 J8
Marlene Cft
CHWD/FDBR/MGN B37 ....111 G4
Marler Rd TLHL/CAN CV4 ....153 K6
Marley Rd KGSWFD DY6 ....101 L1
Marlfield La REDE B98 ....194 F8
Marlin TAM/AM/WIL B77 ....46 B4
Marling Cft HIA/OLT B92 ....128 C6
Marlissa Dr COVN CV6 ....134 C3
Marloes Wk RLSS CV31 ....207 G7
Marlow Cl COVW CV6 ....153 M1
DUDS DY2 ....103 J2
Marlowe Cl KIDD DY10 ....138 C7
NUNW/HART CV10 ....79 K8
Marlowe Dr SHHTH WV12 ....37 L6
Marlow Rd ATHST CV9 ....61 G8
ERDW/GRVHL B23 ....91 J7
TAM/AM/WIL B77 ....32 C8
Marlow St BLKHTH/ROWR B65 ..103 M4
WSLW WS2 ....4 B6
Marlpit La MGN/WHC B75 ....57 H2
REDW B97 ....201 M4
Marlpool Cl KIDD DY11 ....137 M4
Marlpool Dr BLOX/PEL WS3 ....39 K4
REDW B97 ....202 A2
Marlpool La KIDD DY11 ....138 A4
Marlpool Pl KIDD DY11 ....138 A4
REDW B97 ....202 A2
Marlwood Cl COVN CV6 ....134 D1
Marl Top HWK/WKHTH B38 ....145 K3
Marmion Dr GTB/HAM B43 ....70 D3
Marmion Gv DUDN DY1 ....84 E5
Marmion Wy WBROM B70 ....68 D7
Marne Cl WWCK CV34 ....205 J1
Marnel Dr BDMR/CCFT WV3 ......49 H5
Marner Rd BDWTH CV12 ....116 C2
NUNW/HART CV10 ....98 F4
Marnhull Cl COVE CV2 ....156 D1

Marpool Ct KIDD DY11 ....138 A5
Marquis Dr CDYHTH B64 ....103 L6
Marquis's Dr HLYWD B47 ....13 J2
Marrick TAM/AM/WIL B77 ....47 G5
Marriners La COVW CV5 ....132 F8
Marriott Rd BDWTH CV12 ....116 B3
COVN CV6 ....8 A1
SEDG DY3 ....103 C1
SMTHWK B67 ....87 H4
Marrowfat La HDSW B21 ....88 D6
Mars Cl RLSS CV31 ....206 F7
Marsdale Dr NUNW/HART CV10 ..98 C2
Marsden Cl HIA/OLT B92 ....127 J4
Marsden Dr REDE B98 ....202 D2
Marsett TAM/AM/WIL B77 ....47 G5
Marshall Cl ALDR WS9 ....54 F1
Marshall Gv KGSTG B44 ....71 K6
Marshall Lake Rd SHLY B90 ......148 B5
Marshall Rd LGLYGN/QTN B68 ..105 C4
RCOVN/BALC/EX CV7 ....116 E5
WLNHL WV13 ....51 H4
Marshall St CBHAMW B1 ....6 E7
SMTHWK B67 ....87 H6
TAM/AM/WIL B77 ....32 C8
Marsham Cl WWCK CV34 ....205 M5
Marsham Court Rd SOLH B91 ....127 K6
Marsham Rd
ALE/KHTH/YWD B14 ....146 D2
Marshbrook Cl COVE CV2 ....135 J3
Marshbrook Rd
ERDW/GRVHL B23 ....91 J1
Marsh Crs STRBR DY8 ....101 H2
Marsh End HWK/WKHTH B38 ....145 L5
Marshfield SHLY B90 ....147 L8
Marshfield Dr TLHL/CAN CV4 ....180 B3
Marshfield Gdns
ERDW/GRVHL B23 ....90 C3
Marsh Gv KIDD DY11 ....138 C5
Marsh Hl ERDW/GRVHL B23 ......90 A1
Marshland Wy WSLW WS2 ....52 C4
Marsh La CSHL/WTROR B46 ......92 F2
ERDW/GRVHL B23 ....69 H5
HHTH/SAND B71 ....69 M7
HIA/OLT B92 ....130 B8
LICHS WS14 ....20 F8
LICHS WS14 ....21 L8
PENK ST19 ....10 D3
SOLH B91 ....149 J2
WOLWN WV10 ....35 M3
WSLW WS2 ....4 D1
Marsh Lane Pde WOLWN WV10 ..4 D1
Marshmont Wy
ERDW/GRVHL B23 ....72 B5
Marsh St WSLW WS2 ....4 C3
The Marsh DARL/WED WS10 ......68 C2
Marshwood Cft CNCK/NC WS11 ..16 E3
Marshwood Cft
RIDG/WDGT B32 ....122 E2
Marsland Rd HRBN B17 ....106 A5
Marston Av DARL/WED WS10 .....52 A7
Marston Cl RLSN CV32 ....206 F3
STRBR DY8 ....119 C1
Marston Cft
CHWD/FDBR/MGN B37 ....110 D5
Marston Dr
CHWD/FDBR/MGN B37 ....92 E8
Marston Gv GTB/HAM B43 ....70 A5
Marston La BDWTH CV12 ....116 F1
WALM/CURD B76 ....75 J4
Marston Rd BKHL/PFLD WV2 .....50 A6
DUDN DY1 ....84 B5
HEDN WS12 ....12 D7
SCFLD/BOLD B73 ....72 E6
SLYOAK B29 ....123 L5
Marten Cl RWWCK/WEL CV35 ...204 E6
Martham Dr
DUNHL/THL/PER WV6 ....48 F3
Martin Cl BILS/COS WV14 ....67 K2
BRGRVW B61 ....191 J4
COVW CV6 ....153 J1
LGN/SDN/BHAMAIR B26 ......109 H7
Martin Cft LICH WS13 ....20 E4
Martindale CNCK/NC WS11 ....16 E3
Martindale Rd
RCOVN/BALC/EX CV7 ....117 C5
Martindale Wk BRLYHL DY5 .....101 M7
Martin Dr SHHTH WV12 ....38 A7
Martineau Pl CBHAM B2 * 7 J1
Martineau Sq CBHAM B2 * 7 J1
Martingale Cl BRGRVE B60 ....191 J7
DSYBK/YTR WS5 ....69 K1
Martin Hill St DUDS DY2 ....85 G5
Martin La RUGBYS/DCH CV22 ..186 B6
Martin Ri
CHWD/FDBR/MGN B37 ....110 D5
Martin Rd BILS/COS WV14 ....67 K2
DSYBK/YTR WS5 ....54 A5
TPTN/OCK DY4 ....67 L8
Martins Dr ATHST CV9 ....63 H3
Martins Rd BDWTH CV12 ....116 C4
Martin St
ETTPK/GDPK/PENN WV4 ......50 D7
Martins Wy STRPT DY13 ....188 C3
Mart La STRPT DY13 ....188 E3
Martlesham Sq CVALE B35 ....91 L1
Martley Cl REDE B98 ....202 F6
Martley Cft RIDG/WDGT B32 ....123 J1
SOLH B91 ....148 F5
Martley Dr HAG/WOL DY9 ....120 A1
Martley Rd OLDBY B69 ....86 B7
RUSH/SHEL WS4 ....40 A4
STRPT DY13 ....188 B5
Marton Av BNTWD WS7 ....18 E5
Marton Cl VAUX/NECH B7 ....89 M7
The Martyrs' Cl COVS CV3 ....9 G9
Marwood Cl NUN CV11 ....99 M3
Marwood Cft FOAKS/STRLY B74 ..55 L1
Mary Ann St CBHAMNW B3 ....3 J6
WOLV WV1 * 3 J6
Mary Herbert St COVS CV3 ....8 B7
Mary Rd HDSW B21 ....88 C6
OLDBY B69 ....86 A3
STETCH B33 ....109 H2
WBROM B70 ....87 H4
Mary Slessor St COVS CV3 ....156 B6
Marystow Cl COVW CV5 ....132 C3
Mary St BHTH/HG B12 ....107 J8
CBHAMNW B3 ....6 D2
HEDN WS12 ....13 H1
WSLW WS2 ....53 H2
Mary Vale Rd BVILLE B30 ....124 C7
Marywell Cl RIDG/WDGT B32 ......67 C6
Masefield Av DUDN DY1 ....67 C6
Masefield Cl BILS/COS WV14 ......67 L4

BNTWD WS7 ....18 E4
LICHS WS14 ....20 F7
Masefield Dr CRTAM B79 ....31 L7
Masefield Gv CNCK/NC WS11 ....16 C1
Masefield Ri BLOX/PEL WS3 ......39 J5
SEDG DY3 ....66 E4
WOLWN WV10 ....36 E4
Masefield Sq NFLD/LBR B31 .....145 C1
Mashaw Cl STETCH B33 ....109 J3
Mashie Gdns HWK/WKHTH B38 ..145 H4
Maslen Pl HALE B63 ....103 M3
Maslin Dr BILS/COS WV14 ....66 F4
Mason Av RLSN CV32 ....207 G2
Mason Cl REDW B97 ....202 B6
Mason Crs
ETTPK/GDPK/PENN WV4 ......49 J8
Mason La HOCK/TIA B94 ....173 K4
Masonleys Rd NFLD/LBR B31 ....144 B2
Mason Rd COVN CV6 ....134 D4
ERDE/BCHGN B24 ....90 E7
KIDD DY11 ....138 A7
REDW B97 ....202 B5
WSLW WS2 ....38 D8
Masons Cl HALE B63 ....103 C3
Masons Cottages
ERDE/BCHGN B24 * 72 F8
Mason St BILS/COS WV14 ....66 F6
BKHL/PFLD WV2 ....50 A6
WBROM B70 ....86 F1
Masons Wy HIA/OLT B92 ....127 J3
Massbrook Gv WOLWN WV10 .....36 D7
Massbrook Rd WOLWN WV10 .....36 D7
Masser Rd COVN CV6 ....134 A1
Masshouse La
HWK/WKHTH B38 ....145 K4
Masters Rd RMSLY B62 ....104 C4
Matchborough Wy REDE B98 ....203 J4
Matchlock Cl FOAKS/STRLY B74 ..55 J6
Matfen Av SCFLD/BOLD B73 ......72 D3
Mathe Cft RLSS CV31 ....207 G8
Math Meadow RIDG/WDGT B32 ..155 K8
Matlock Cl BLOX/PEL WS3 ....39 G2
DUDS DY2 ....103 H2
RUGBYN/HIL CV21 ....161 G6
Matlock Dr CNCK/NC WS11 ....16 E1
COV CV1 ....134 B7
SPARK B11 ....107 C8
Matlock Vls BHTH/HG B12 * 107 M8
Matterson Rd COVN CV6 ....133 L8
Matthew La KIDD DY11 ....164 D4
Matthews Cl
BLKHTH/ROWR B65 ....103 M4
Mattox Rd WOLWN WV10 ....37 H7
Matty Rd LGLYGN/QTN B68 ......105 C1
Maud Rd CSHL/WTROR B46 ......93 H2
WBROM B70 ....87 G4
Maudslay Rd COVW CV5 ....154 C3
Maughan St BRLYHL DY5 ....102 E5
DUDN DY1 ....84 E4
Maund Cl BRGRVE B60 ....191 J6
Maureen Cl TLHL/CAN CV4 ....153 C4
Maurice Gv WOLWN WV10 ....36 A3
Maurice Rd ALE/KHTH/YWD B14 125 J7
SMTHWK B67 ....105 H3
Mavis Gdns LGLYGN/QTN B68 ..104 F5
Mavis Rd HEDN WS12 ....12 F6
NFLD/LBR B31 ....144 C4
Mavor Av BNTWD WS7 ....18 E4
Mawby Rd BDWTH CV12 ....116 B4
Mawnan Cl
RCOVN/BALC/EX CV7 ....116 F5
Maw St WSL WS1 ....53 K7
Maxholm Rd FOAKS/STRLY B74 ..55 K7
Max Rd COVN CV6 ....133 K8
RIDG/WDGT B32 ....105 H8
Maxstoke Cl BLOX/PEL WS3 ......38 F2
RCOVN/BALC/EX CV7 ....130 F4
REDE B98 ....203 H4
TAM/AM/WIL B77 ....60 A1
Maxstoke Cft SHLY B90 ....148 A5
Maxstoke La RLSS CV31 ....206 D6
Maxstoke La CSHL/WTROR B46 ..93 L7
RCOVN/BALC/EX CV7 ....130 F3
Maxstoke Rd SCFLD/BOLD B73 ..72 C3
Maxstoke St BORD B9 ....107 M3
Maxted Rd ERDW/GRVHL B23 ....72 A5
Maxtock Av LICH WS13 ....20 E2
Maxwell Av BFLD/HDSWWD B20 ..88 F4
Maxwell Cl LICH WS13 ....21 C6
Maxwell Rd BKHL/PFLD WV2 ....3 H4
Mayall Dr MGN/WHC B75 ....57 C1
Mayama Rd POL/KGSB/FAZ B78 ..45 K5
May Av BHTH/HG B12 ....107 L8
Maybank BORD B9 ....108 D2
Maybank Cl LICHS WS14 ....21 J5
Maybank Pl PBAR/PBCH B42 ......71 J7
Maybank Rd DUDS DY2 ....103 G2
Mayberry Cl
ALE/KHTH/YWD B14 ....146 F3
STRPT DY13 ....188 C1
Maybridge Dr SOLH B91 ....148 F5
Maybrook Rd BRWNH WS8 ....26 D8
WALM/CURD B76 ....73 L2
Maybury Cl CDSL WV8 ....34 C1
Maybush Gdns WOLWN WV10 .....36 A4
May Cl BNTWD WS7 ....18 D4
Maycock Rd COVN CV6 ....134 B6
Maycroft Cl HEDN WS12 ....12 D6
Maydene Cft BHTH/HG B12 * 107 J8
Mayfair HAG/WOL DY9 ....120 B3
Mayfair Cl DUDN DY1 ....84 E3
KGSTG B44 ....71 M6
Mayfair Dr KGSWFD DY6 ....83 C6
NUNW/HART CV10 ....97 K1
Mayfair Gdns BDMR/CCFT WV3 ..49 H3
TPTN/OCK DY4 ....85 L1
Mayfield Av BDWTH CV12 ....116 F2
BRGRVW B61 ....168 D4
Mayfield Cl BDWTH CV12 ....116 F2
BRGRVW B61 ....191 L4
RLSS CV31 ....207 G7
SOLH B91 ....149 G4
Mayfield Crs
BLKHTH/ROWR B65 ....103 L2
Mayfield Dr KNWTH CV8 ....198 A1
Mayfield Rd BVILLE B30 ....124 E7
COVW CV5 ....8 A1
DUDN DY1 ....84 F1
FOAKS/STRLY B74 ....55 H3
HALE B63 ....121 H3
NUNW/HART CV10 ....79 L5
RIDG/WDGT B32 ....104 F2
RMSLY B62 ....104 A3
RUGBYN/HIL CV21 ....160 B7
SMTHWKW B67 ....105 K1
WWCK CV34 ....205 J7
Mayflower Dr BRLYHL DY5 ....83 L6
COVE CV2 ....156 B3
STRPT DY13 ....188 C1
Mayford Gv MOS/BIL B13 ....125 M7

Maygrove Rd KGSWFD DY6 ....83 G6
TPTN/OCK DY4 ....67 L5
Mayhurst Cl HLYWD B47 ....147 G7
Mayhurst Rd HLYWD B47 ....146 F6
Mayland Dr BFLD/HDSWWD B20 ..88 E4
Mayland Rd LDYWD/EDGR B16 ..106 A3
May La ALE/KHTH/YWD B14 ......125 K8
HLYWD B47 ....146 F6
RUGBYS/DCH CV22 ....186 B4
Maynard Av BDWTH CV12 ....116 B5
STRBR DY8 ....119 H2
WWCK CV34 ....205 L6
Mayne Cl RWWCK/WEL CV35 ...204 E3
Mayor's Cft TLHL/CAN CV4 ....153 M6
Maypole Cl BEWD DY12 ....163 G2
CDYHTH B64 ....102 F5
Maypole Dr STRBR DY8 ....101 J8
Maypole Flds HALE B63 ....102 E5
Maypole Gv
ALE/KHTH/YWD B14 ....146 F3
Maypole Hl HALE B63 ....102 E5
Maypole La
ALE/KHTH/YWD B14 ....146 F3
ATHST CV9 ....62 A4
Maypole Rd OLDBY B69 ....86 A4
Maypole St WMBN WV5 ....64 F6
May St BLOX/PEL WS3 ....39 J4
COVN CV6 ....134 C5
Mayswood Dr
DUNHL/THL/PER WV6 ....48 D4
Mayswood Gv RIDG/WDGT B32 ..123 H1
Mayswood Rd HIA/OLT B92 ......128 D3
Maythorn Av WALM/CURD B76 ...73 L7
Maythorn Gdns CDSL WV8 ....34 E1
DUNHL/THL/PER WV6 ....49 G1
Maythorn Gv SOLH B91 ....148 F5
Maytree Cl
CHWD/FDBR/MGN B37 ....110 D3
May Tree Gv BFLD/HDSWWD B20 88 D2
Maywell Dr HIA/OLT B92 ....128 D5
Maywood Cl KGSWFD DY6 ....82 F7
McBean Rd
DUNHL/THL/PER WV6 ....49 K1
McConnell Cl BRGRVE B60 ....191 M6
McConnell Dr
RCOVN/BALC/EX CV7 ....116 D7
McDougall Rd DARL/WED WS10 ..69 G2
McGhie St HEDN WS12 ....12 F7
McGregor Cl AST/WIT B6 ....89 K6
McKean Rd OLDBY B69 ....86 A3
McKen Ct WBROM B70 * 87 G3
McKinnell Crs
RUGBYN/HIL CV21 ....187 J3
McLean Rd WOLWN WV10 ....36 A3
McMahon Rd BDWTH CV12 ......116 C5
Meaburn Cl SLYOAK B29 ....123 L6
Mead Cl ALDR WS9 ....40 F7
Mead Crs BORD B9 ....108 F2
Meadfoot Av
ALE/KHTH/YWD B14 ....146 D2
Meadfoot Dr KGSWFD DY6 ....82 F6
Meadfoot Rd COVS CV3 ....156 B7
The Meadlands WMBN WV5 ....64 C7
Meadow Av HHTH/SAND B71 .....69 K4
Meadowbrook Gdns CDSL WV8 ..34 F1
Meadowbrook Rd HALE B63 .....121 H2
LICH WS13 ....20 F7
Meadow Brook Rd
NFLD/LBR B31 ....123 K8
Meadow Cl FOAKS/STRLY B74 ...55 K4
HOCK/TIA B94 ....175 C4
HRBN B17 ....105 M4
PENK ST19 ....10 D1
POL/KGSB/FAZ B78 ....60 B8
RLSN CV32 ....207 G1
RUGBY CV23 ....183 C1
RUSH/SHEL WS4 * 40 A1
Meadow Ct NUN CV11 ....98 F1
Meadow Cft
DUNHL/THL/PER WV6 ....48 B2
HAG/WOL DY9 ....140 D1
HEDN WS12 ....16 A4
HLYWD B47 ....172 E2
LICH WS13 ....21 K4
RCOVN/BALC/EX CV7 ....96 C4
Meadow Dr
DUNHL/THL/PER WV6 ....48 B2
HAG/WOL DY9 ....140 D1
HIA/OLT B92 ....127 H3
Meadow Grange Dr
SHHTH WV12 ....37 M6
Meadow Gv GTWY WS6 ....24 C3
HIA/OLT B92 ....127 H3
Meadow Hill Cl KIDD DY11 ....137 L8
Meadow Hill Crs REDE B98 ......194 D8
Meadow Hill Dr CNCK/NC WS11 ..16 E3
Meadowhill Dr STRBR DY8 ....101 J3
Meadow Hill Rd
HWK/WKHTH B38 ....145 J3
Meadowhill Rd REDE B98 ....194 D8
Meadowlands Dr
RUSH/SHEL WS4 ....40 A5
Meadow La ALVE B48 ....170 F7
BILS/COS WV14 ....66 F4
SHHTH WV12 ....38 A7
WMBN WV5 ....64 C5
WOLWN WV10 ....22 A7
Meadow Lark Cl HEDN WS12 .....16 F1
Meadowpark Rd STRBR DY8 ....101 H5
Meadow Pleck La SHLY B90 .....147 K2
Meadow Ri BEWD DY12 ....137 H8
BVILLE B30 ....124 D6
RCOVN/BALC/EX CV7 * 152 A6
Meadow Rd ALDR WS9 ....54 C1
ATHST CV9 ....61 G8
BDMR/CCFT WV3 ....49 G5
BRGRVW B61 ....168 D5
COVW CV6 ....133 M1
DUDN DY1 ....84 F1
HLYWD B47 ....172 E2
HRBN B17 ....105 M4
KNWTH CV8 ....183 L1
LGLYGN/QTN B68 ....104 F3
NUNW/HART CV10 ....79 L5
RIDG/WDGT B32 ....104 D2
RMSLY B62 ....104 A4
RUGBYN/HIL CV21 ....160 D3
SMTHWKW B67 ....105 K1
WWCK CV34 ....205 L6
Meadows Gv CDSL WV8 ....34 E1
Meadowside NUN CV11 ....99 M5
Meadowside Cl GTB/HAM B43 ....70 D2
Meadowside Rd
FOAKS/STRLY B74 ....56 D7
The Meadows ALDR WS9 ....40 C8
HAG/WOL DY9 ....119 M6
RWWCK/WEL CV35 ....197 L6
Meadow St ATHST CV9 ....63 H5
CDYHTH B64 ....103 K5
COV CV1 ....8 A5
NUN CV11 ....98 F1
TAM/AM/WIL B77 ....46 A2
WSL WS1 ....4 D5
WSLW WS2 ....4 C3
Meadowsweet RRUGBY CV23 ...161 G2

Meadowsweet Av
HWK/WKHTH B38 ....145 K5
Meadowsweet Wy KGSWFD DY6 ..83 L7
Meadow V CDSL WV8 ....34 F4
Meadowvale Rd BRGRVE B60 ....169 G2
Meadow Vw BNTWD WS7 ....19 H7
MOS/BIL B13 ....126 A5
SEDG DY3 ....66 E4
STRPT DY13 ....188 C5
Meadow View Whf
DUNHL/THL/PER WV6 * 49 J1
Meadow Wk
ALE/KHTH/YWD B14 ....146 C4
CDYHTH B64 ....103 H5
Meadow Wy CDSL WV8 ....34 F4
HEDN WS12 ....17 G4
RRUGBY CV23 ....159 M2
RWWCK/WEL CV35 ....196 A3
STRBR DY8 ....101 G3
Mead Ri EDG B15 ....106 D7
The Mead SEDG DY3 ....66 H5
Meadthorpe Rd KGSTG B44 ....71 H5
Meadvale Rd RBRY B45 ....143 M7
Meadway COVE CV2 ....134 F7
STETCH B33 ....109 K3
Meadway Cl HEDN WS12 ....17 G4
Meadway St BNTWD WS7 ....18 E8
The Meadway
DUNHL/THL/PER WV6 ....34 E8
REDW B97 ....202 A4
Mears Cl ERDW/GRVHL B23 ......72 B5
Mears Coppice BRLYHL DY5 .....102 C3
Mears Dr STETCH B33 ....109 H1
Mearse Cl WSNGN B18 ....88 E1
Mearse La HAG/WOL DY9 ....141 K7
RBRY B45 ....169 K4
Mease Av BNTWD WS7 ....19 H7
Mease Cft BORD B9 ....107 M3
Measham Gv
LGN/SDN/BHAMAIR B26 ......109 J8
Measham Wy WNSFLD WV11 .....37 J5
Medcroft Av BFLD/HDSWWD B20 ..88 C1
Medici Rd BRGRVE B60 ....192 A3
Medina Rd COVN CV6 ....134 C4
Medina Rd COVN CV6 ....134 C4
SPARK B11 ....126 C1
Medina Wy KGSWFD DY6 ....83 C7
Medland Av COVS CV3 ....154 D8
Medley Rd SPARK B11 ....108 B8
Medlicott Rd SPARK B11 ....108 A8
Medway TAM/AM/WIL B77 ....46 B4
Medway Cft CBROM B36 ....92 C3
Medway Gv HWK/WKHTH B38 ..145 J5
Medway Rd BRWNH WS8 ....26 A3
Medwin Gv ERDW/GRVHL B23 ....72 B6
Meerash La BNTWD WS7 ....27 G2
Meer End HWK/WKHTH B38 .....145 J6
Meer End Rd KNWTH CV8 ....178 A3
Meerhill Av SHLY B90 ....148 D7
Meeting House La
NFLD/LBR B31 ....144 E1
RCOVN/BALC/EX CV7 ....152 A7
Meeting La BRLYHL DY5 ....101 M4
Meeting St DARL/WED WS10 ......68 C2
DUDS DY2 ....103 C1
TPTN/OCK DY4 ....68 A7
Meg La BNTWD WS7 ....18 F4
Melbourne Av BRGRVW B61 .....191 J1
LOZ/NWT B19 ....89 G7
SMTHWK B66 ....87 M6
Melbourne Cl BRGRVW B61 .....191 J1
KGSWFD DY6 ....101 J1
NUN CV11 ....99 J5
WBROM B70 ....68 E5
Melbourne Crs HEDN WS12 ....17 J3
Melbourne Gdns
DSYBK/YTR WS5 ....53 M7
Melbourne Rd BRGRVW B61 .....191 J1
COVW CV5 ....8 A5
HALE B63 ....103 M8
SMTHWK B66 ....87 L6
Melbury Cl BDMR/CCFT WV3 * 2 B7
Melbury Gv
ALE/KHTH/YWD B14 ....125 J8
Melbury Wy CNCK/NC WS11 ......16 D3
Melchett Rd BVILLE B30 ....145 K2
Melcote Gv KGSTG B44 ....71 J5
Meldon Dr BILS/COS WV14 ....67 L3
Melen St REDW B97 ....202 B1
Melford CRTAM B79 ....31 H7
Melford Cl SEDG DY3 ....66 A3
Melford Hall Rd SOLH B91 ....127 K6
Melford Ri BNTWD WS7 ....18 C4
Melfort Cl COVS CV3 ....156 D3
Melksham Sq CVALE B35 ....91 L2
Mellis Gv ERDW/GRVHL B23 ......71 L8
Mellish Ct RUGBYS/DCH CV22 ..186 C4
Mellish Dr RUSH/SHEL WS4 ....53 M2
Mellish Rd RUGBYS/DCH CV22 ..186 C4
RUSH/SHEL WS4 ....53 M2
Mellor Dr FOAKS/STRLY B74 ......56 C2
Mellor Rd RUGBYN/HIL CV21 ....187 M5
Mellors Cl HRBN B17 ....123 H2
Mellowdew Rd COVE CV2 ....156 A1
STRBR DY8 ....101 G3
Mellowship Rd COVW CV5 ....132 A8
Mell Sq SOLH B91 ....149 G1
Mellwaters TAM/AM/WIL B77 ....47 G5
Melplash Av SOLH B91 ....148 E1
Melrose Av BDWTH CV12 ....116 B5
BHTH/HG B12 ....107 L7
HHTH/SAND B71 ....69 H4
SCFLD/BOLD B73 ....72 C3
SPARK B11 ....108 A7
STRBR DY8 ....119 L3
SMTHWK B66 ....145 K4
Melrose Dr
DUNHL/THL/PER WV6 ....48 B1
HEDN WS12 ....12 C5
KNWTH CV8 ....183 L1
Melrose Gv LOZ/NWT B19 ....88 F6
Melrose Rd BFLD/HDSWWD B20 ..88 F4
Melstock Cl TPTN/OCK DY4 ....67 H8
Melstock Rd
ALE/KHTH/YWD B14 ....125 H6
Melton Av HIA/OLT B92 ....127 L1
Melton Dr EDG B15 ....106 D7
Melton Rd ALE/KHTH/YWD B14 ..125 K5
RLSN CV32 ....206 F1
Melverley Gv KGSTG B44 ....71 K6
Melverton Av RCOVN/BALC/EX CV7 ..116 E3
RUGBYS/DCH CV22 ....186 C4
Melville Hall
LDYWD/EDGR B16 * 106 B4
Melville Rd COV CV1 ....8 B4
COVW CV5 ....133 H7
Melverton Av VAUX/NECH B7 ....107 M1
Membury Rd BORD B9 ....108 B4
Memory La DARL/WED WS10 ......52 B5
WNSFLD WV11 ....36 F8
Menai Cl SHHTH WV12 ....37 M5

Mendip Av WASH/WDE B8 ....90 C8
Mendip CI BKHL/PFLD WV2 ....50 D7
  BRGRVW B61 ....168 E8
  SEDG DY3 ....84 B2
Mendip Rd HALE B63 ....121 H4
  HEDN WS12 ....12 E4
  STRBR DY8 ....101 M7
  WASH/WDE B8 ....108 C1
Menin Wy TAM/AM/WIL B77 ....47 G4
Menin Crs MOS/BIL B13 ....125 M6
Menin Rd MOS/BIL B13 ....125 M6
  TPTN/OCK DY4 ....67 H8
Menteith CI STRPT DY13 ....163 J2
Meon Gv DUNHL/THL/PER WV6 ....48 C1
  STETCH B33 ....109 M5
Meon Ri HAG/WOL WD9 ....120 A2
Meon Wy WNSFLD WV11 ....37 K6
Meranti CI SHHTH WV12 ....38 A5
Mercer Av COVE CV2 ....134 E8
  CSHL/WTROR B46 ....92 E2
Mercer Ct RUGBYN/HIL CV21 ....187 G5
Mercer Gv WNSFLD WV11 ....37 H6
Mercers Meadow
  RCOVN/BALC/EX CV7 ....115 L7
Mercia Av KNWTH CV8 ....197 J1
Mercia CI BRGRVE B60 ....191 J6
  CRTAM B79 ....31 J6
Mercia Dr ALE/KHTH/YWD B14 ....125 H7
  DUNHL/THL/PER WV6 ....47 F8
Mercian Wy TAM/AM/WIL B77 ....32 F8
Mercia Wy WWCK CV34 ....205 L6
Mercot CI REDE B98 ....202 E7
Mercury Rd CNCK/NC WS11 ....12 E8
Mere Av CVALE B35 ....91 L2
Mere CI SHHTH WV12 ....37 L5
Merecote Rd HIA/OLT B92 ....127 H6
Meredith CI KIDDW DY11 ....163 L4
Meredith Pool CI WSNGN B18 * 88 D7
Meredith Rd COVE CV2 ....156 B3
  SEDG DY3 ....65 L8
  WNSFLD WV11 ....37 G5
Meredith St CDYHTH B64 ....103 H4
Mere Dr MGN/WHC B75 ....56 F3
Mere Green CI MGN/WHC B75 ....57 G3
Mere Green Rd MGN/WHC B75 ....57 G3
Mere La PENK ST19 ....14 A1
Mere Oak Rd
  DUNHL/THL/PER WV6 ....34 C8
Mere Pool Rd MGN/WHC B75 ....57 H3
Mere Rd ERDW/GRVHL B23 ....90 B2
  STRBR DY8 ....119 J1
Mereside Wy HIA/OLT B92 ....127 J5
Meres Rd HALE B63 ....105 G3
Merevale Av NUN CV11 ....98 E1
Merevale CI REDE B98 ....203 H5
Merevale Rd ATHST CV9 ....63 G4
  HIA/OLT B92 ....127 M3
Merevale Vw ATHST CV9 ....63 G6
Mere Vw RUSH/SHEL WS4 ....40 A5
Merganser TAM/AM/WIL B77 ....46 F7
Merganser CI KIDD DY10 ....164 F2
Meriden Av STRBR DY8 ....101 H7
Meriden CI CNCK/NC WS11 ....15 M5
  REDE B98 ....203 L2
  STRBR DY8 ....101 H6
Meriden Dr
  CHWD/FDBR/MGN B37 ....92 E8
Meriden Ri HIA/OLT B92 ....128 E3
Meriden Rd HIA/OLT B92 ....130 A6
  RCOVN/BALC/EX CV7 ....113 M6
  RCOVN/BALC/EX CV7 ....131 G8
  WOLVN WV10 ....35 L5
Meriden St COV CV1 ....8 C3
  DIG/EDG B5 ....7 J8
Meridian PI BRGRVE B60 * 191 L4
Merino Av NFLD/LBR B31 ....144 D6
Merlin Av NUNW/HART CV10 ....79 M7
Merlin CI CNCK/NC WS11 ....16 A3
  CVALE B35 ....91 L2
  DUDN DY1 ....84 D5
  RRUGBY CV23 ....161 G5
  TAM/AM/WIL B77 ....46 F7
Merlin Dr KIDD DY10 ....164 F2
Merlin Gv
  LGN/SDN/BHAMAIR B26 ....109 M8
Merrick CI HALE B63 ....121 H3
Merrick Rd WNSFLD WV11 ....37 L7
Merricks CI BEWD DY12 ....162 D2
Merricks La BEWD DY12 ....162 D2
Merridale Av BDMR/CCFT WV3 ....49 K3
Merridale Crs BDMR/CCFT WV3 ....2 A6
Merridale Gdns BDMR/CCFT WV3 ....2 A6
Merridale La BDMR/CCFT WV3 ....49 J4
Merridale Rd BDMR/CCFT WV3 ....49 K4
Merridale St BDMR/CCFT WV3 ....2 D7
Merridale St West
  BDMR/CCFT WV3 2
Merriemont Dr RBRY B45 ....169 L4
Merrill CI GTWY WS6 ....24 C3
Merrill Gdns BRGRVE B60 ....169 H3
Merrills Hall WLNHL WV13 ....51 M1
Merrill's Hall La WNSFLD WV11 ....51 J1
Merrington CI SOLH B91 ....149 G5
Merrion's CI GTB/HAM B43 ....70 C1
Merrishaw Rd NFLD/LBR B31 ....144 B1
Merritts Brook La SLYOAK B29 ....123 L8
Merritt's Brook La
  NFLD/LBR B31 ....123 J8
Merritt's HI NFLD/LBR B31 ....123 J1
Merrivale Rd COVW CV5 ....154 C2
  RMSLY B62 ....104 D5
Merryfield CI HIA/OLT B92 ....128 B6
Merryfield Gv HRBN B17 ....124 A1
Merryfield Rd DUDN DY1 ....84 B4
Merryfields Wy COVE CV2 ....135 L4
Merry HI BRLYHL DY5 ....102 A3
Merryhill Dr WSNGN B18 ....88 D7
Merse Rd REDE B98 ....203 J5
Mersey Gv HWK/WKHTH B38 ....145 J5
Mersey Rd BILS/COS WV14 ....67 L3
  BLOX/PEL WS3 ....39 J4
Merstal Dr HIA/OLT B92 ....128 D6
Merstone CI BILS/COS WV14 ....51 L4
Merstowe CI ACGN B27 ....126 F2
Merton CI BEWD DY12 ....162 C1
  KIDD DY10 ....138 F6
  LGLYGN/QTN B68 ....104 D3
Merton Rd MOS/BIL B13 ....125 M2
Mertens Dr RUGBYS/DCH CV22 ....186 D6
Mervyn PI BILS/COS WV14 ....67 K2
Mervyn Rd BILS/COS WV14 ....67 K2
  HDSW B21 ....88 B4
Meryhurst Rd DARL/WED WS10 ....68 F1
Merynton Av TLHL/CAN CV4 ....154 F7
Meschines St COVS CV3 ....155 H7
Mesnes Gn LICHS WS14 ....21 G7
Messenger Rd SMTHWK B66 ....87 H2

Metchley La EDG B15 ....124 B5
  HRBN B17 ....106 B8
Metchley Park Rd EDG B15 ....124 B1
Metfield Cft HRBN B17 ....124 B1
  KGSWFD DY6 ....83 K7
Metlin Gv STETCH B33 ....110 C2
Metric Wk SMTHWK B66 ....88 A6
Metro Triangle VAUX/NECH B7 * 90 B6
Metro Wy SMTHWK B66 ....88 A6
Mews Rd RLSN CV32 ....206 B5
The Mews BDWTH CV12 ....116 F3
  BLKHTH/ROWR B65 ....103 M3
  KNWTH CV8 ....197 J2
  RLSN CV32 * 206 C5
Meyrick Rd WBROM B70 ....68 C7
Meyrick Wk LDYWD/EDGR B16 ....106 D4
Miall Park Rd SOLH B91 ....127 J8
Miall Rd HLGN/YWD B28 ....126 E5
Mica CI TAM/AM/WIL B77 ....46 F3
Michael Blanning Pl
  RCOVN/BALC/EX CV7 * 151 M6
Michael Ct EDG B15 ....107 G6
Michaelmas Rd COVS CV3 ....8 A8
Michael Rd DARL/WED WS10 ....51 M6
  SMTHWK B67 ....87 J7
Michaelwood CI REDW B97 ....201 K3
Michell CI COVS CV3 ....155 M5
Michelle CI MOS/BIL B13 ....125 L3
Michigan CI CNCK/NC WS11 ....16 F3
Micklehill Dr SHLY B90 ....147 M5
Mickle Meadow
  CSHL/WTROR B46 ....92 F2
Mickleover Rd WASH/WDE B8 ....91 G8
Mickleton TAM/AM/WIL B77 ....47 G5
Mickleton Av STETCH B33 ....110 A5
Mickleton CI REDE B98 ....202 C6
Mickleton Dr
  RWWCK/WEL CV35 ....204 B3
  HIA/OLT B92 ....127 H5
Micklewood CI PENK ST19 ....10 C4
Micklewood La PENK ST19 ....14 F1
Mickley Av WOLVN WV10 ....36 C8
Midacre WLNHL WV13 ....51 L4
Midd CI NUN CV11 ....99 L5
Middle Acre Rd
  RIDG/WDGT B32 ....123 J3
Middle Av WLNHL WV13 ....51 J5
Middle Bickenhill La
  HIA/OLT B92 ....129 L1
Middlecotes TLHL/CAN CV4 ....153 M4
Middle Crs BLOX/PEL WS3 ....39 K6
Middle Cross WOLV WV1 ....3 H6
Middle Dr RBRY B45 ....170 B1
Middle Entry CRTAM B79 ....31 M8
Middlefield CDSL WV8 ....35 J2
Middlefield Av DOR/KN B93 ....175 M1
  RMSLY B62 ....104 D5
Middlefield CI RMSLY B62 ....104 D4
Middlefield Gdns RMSLY B62 ....104 D5
Middlefield La HAG/WOL DY9 ....119 M7
Middlefield Rd BRGRVE B60 ....191 M6
Middlefield Dr COVS CV3 ....156 E4
Middle Gdns WLNHL WV13 ....51 M3
Middlehill RIDG/WDGT B32 ....122 F4
Middle House Dr BRGRVE B60 ....169 H4
Middlehouse La REDE B98 ....194 C7
Middle La CDSL WV8 ....34 A3
  CSHL/WTROR B46 ....76 C7
  HLYWD B47 ....172 D2
  HWK/WKHTH B38 ....146 A6
Middle Leaford STETCH B33 ....91 L8
Middle Leasowe
  RIDG/WDGT B32 ....123 G1
Middle Lock La
  RWWCK/WEL CV35 ....203 G5
Middlemarch Rd COVN CV6 ....133 M7
  NUNW/HART CV10 ....98 F4
Middle Meadow Av
  RIDG/WDGT B32 ....105 G8
Middlemist Gv GTB/HAM B43 ....70 D7
Middlemore La ALDR WS9 ....40 D7
Middlemore La West ALDR WS9 ....40 C7
Middlemore Rd NFLD/LBR B31 ....144 F3
  SMTHWK B66 ....87 H6
Middle Park CI SLYOAK B29 ....123 M5
Middlepark Rd DUDN DY1 ....84 C5
Middle Park Rd SLYOAK B29 ....123 M5
Middle Piece Dr REDW B97 ....201 L5
Middle Ride COVS CV3 ....156 C7
Middle Rd BRGRVE B60 ....200 B3
  BRGRVW B61 ....168 D1
Middlesmoor TAM/AM/WIL B77 ....47 G5
Middleton CI DSYBK/YTR WS5 ....53 K8
  REDE B98 ....203 K3
Middleton Gdns BVILLE B30 ....145 H1
Middleton Gra NFLD/LBR B31 ....145 G1
Middleton Hall Rd BVILLE B30 ....145 J1
Middleton La POL/KGSB/FAZ B78 ....58 D7
Middleton Rd
  ALE/KHTH/YWD B14 ....125 J6
  BRGRVW B61 ....191 K1
  BRWNH WS8 ....26 E4
  FOAKS/STRLY B74 ....55 L4
  KIDDW DY11 ....138 A4
  SHLY B90 ....147 L3
Middletree Rd HALE B63 ....103 G6
Middleway HEDN WS12 ....13 J6
Middleway Av STRBR DY8 ....101 G2
Middleway Rd BILS/COS WV14 ....51 G5
Middleway Vw WSNGN B18 ....106 C1
Midford Gv EDG B15 ....6 D9
Midgley Dr FOAKS/STRLY B74 ....56 E3
Midhill Dr OLDBY B69 ....86 B2
Midhurst Dr HEDN WS12 ....13 G6
Midhurst Gv
  DUNHL/THL/PER WV6 ....35 G8
Midhurst Rd BVILLE B30 ....145 M2
Midland CI HDSW B21 ....88 D6
Midland Dr SUT B72 ....57 G8
Midland Rd BVILLE B30 ....124 D8
  COVN CV6 ....134 C8
  DARL/WED WS10 ....52 A5
  FOAKS/STRLY B74 ....56 E6
  HEDN WS12 ....12 A8
  NUN CV11 ....80 B7
  WSL WS1 ....4 E7
Midland St WASH/WDE B8 ....108 A2
Midpoint Pk WALM/CURD B76 * 74 A8
Midvale Dr ALE/KHTH/YWD B14 ....146 B3
Milburn TAM/AM/WIL B77 ....46 F5
Milburn Hill Rd TLHL/CAN CV4 ....153 M8
Milburn Rd KGSTG B44 ....71 L2
Milby Dr NUN CV11 ....81 K5
Milcote CI SCFLD/BOLD B73 ....72 A2
Milcote Dr HEDN WS12 ....13 G6
  SHLY B90 ....147 H4
Milcote Rd SLYOAK B29 ....123 G5
  SMTHWK B67 ....105 K3
  SOLH B91 ....148 B5
Milcote Wy KGSWFD DY6 ....82 F5
Mildenhall CRTAM B79 ....31 K5
Mildenhall Rd PBAR/PBCH B42 ....70 E4

Mildred Rd CDYHTH B64 ....103 J3
Mildred Wy OLDBY B69 ....86 A3
Milebrook Gv RIDG/WDGT B32 ....122 F5
Milebush Av CBROM B36 ....92 B4
Mile Flat KGSWFD DY6 ....82 B9
Mile La COVS CV3 ....8 H9
Miles Gv MOS/BIL B13 ....85 K6
Miles Meadow COVN CV6 ....134 E4
Miles Meadow CI SHHTH WV12 ....38 A5
Milestone Dr HAG/WOL DY9 ....140 E1
  RUGBYS/DCH CV22 ....186 D5
Milestone La BHTH/HG B12 ....88 B5
Milestone Wy SHHTH WV12 ....37 M5
Mile Tree La COVE CV2 ....117 J7
Milford Av BHTH/HG B12 ....107 L7
  WNSFLD WV12 ....37 L8
  STRPT DY13 ....163 J7
Milford CI COVW CV5 ....132 F7
  REDW B97 ....201 M6
  STRBR DY8 ....101 J2
Milford Copse HRBN B17 ....105 M4
Milford Ct LOZ/NWT B19 ....89 H8
Milford Cft BLKHTH/ROWR B65 ....85 K7
  REDW B97 ....201 M6
Milford Gv SHLY B90 ....148 C3
Milford PI ALE/KHTH/YWD B14 * 125 J5
  HRBN B17 ....105 M8
Milford St NUNW/HART CV10 ....98 F3
Milhill Rd REDE B98 ....203 J4
Milholme Gn HIA/OLT B92 ....128 B6
Milking Bank DUDN DY1 ....84 C3
Milk St DIG/EDG B5 ....7 L7
Millais CI BDWTH CV12 ....116 E1
Millard Rd BILS/COS WV14 ....66 F7
Millbank CSHL/WTROR B46 ....95 H2
  SEDG DY3 ....65 L6
Millbank Gv ERDW/GRVHL B23 ....71 M7
Mill Bank Ms KNWTH CV8 ....179 M7
Millbank St WNSFLD WV11 ....37 K4
Millbeck RUGBYN/HIL CV21 ....161 L6
Millbrook CI CNCK/NC WS11 ....16 D3
Millbrook Dr NUN CV11 ....99 L5
Millbrook Rd
  ALE/KHTH/YWD B14 ....125 G7
Millbrook Wy BRLYHL DY5 ....101 M5
Mill Burn Wy BORD B9 ....107 M3
Mill CI BRGRVE B60 ....191 K7
  COVE CV2 ....134 F2
  HLYWD B47 ....146 E6
  KIDD DY10 ....139 M3
  KNWTH CV8 ....183 K2
  NUN CV11 ....99 K4
  SEDG DY3 ....66 B7
  STRPT DY13 ....188 F2
Mill Crs CNCK/NC WS11 ....16 F3
  POL/KGSB/FAZ B78 ....76 B1
Mill Cft BILS/COS WV14 ....51 G8
Millcroft CI RIDG/WDGT B32 ....123 J3
Millcroft Rd FOAKS/STRLY B74 ....55 L5
Milldale CI KIDD DY10 ....138 C5
Milldale Crs WOLVN WV10 ....36 B1
Milldale Rd WOLVN WV10 ....36 B1
Mill Dr SMTHWK B66 ....87 M8
Mill End KNWTH CV8 ....179 L7
Millenium CI BLOX/PEL WS3 ....39 L1
Millennium Gdns CDYHTH B64 ....103 J3
Millennium Pk WBROM B70 * 68 D8
Millennium CI BLOX/PEL WS3 ....39 L1
Millennium Wy CDSL WV8 ....34 F1
  KNWTH CV8 ....183 K2
Miller CI BRGRVE B60 ....191 J7
Miller Crs BILS/COS WV14 ....66 F7
Millers CI WSL WS2 ....52 D4
Millers Dale CI
  RUGBYN/HIL CV21 ....161 G6
Millersdale Dr HHTH/SAND B71 ....69 K3
Millers Green Dr KGSWFD DY6 ....82 E5
Millers Rd WWCK CV34 ....205 H5
Miller St AST/WIT B6 ....89 J8
Millers V HEDN WS12 ....17 H4
  WMBN WV5 ....64 B8
Millers Wk BLOX/PEL WS3 ....39 J2
Mill Farm Rd HRBN B17 ....124 A1
Millfield NFLD/LBR B31 ....144 E1
Millfield Av BLOX/PEL WS3 ....39 H3
  RUSH/SHEL WS4 ....39 M4
Millfield Gdns KIDDW DY11 ....138 D2
Millfield Rd BFLD/HDSWWD B20 ....70 D8
  BRGRVW B61 ....191 H4
  BRWNH WS8 ....26 E6
Millfields STETCH B33 ....110 C2
Millfields Av RUGBYN/HIL CV21 ....187 K5
Millfields Rd HHTH/SAND B71 ....68 F4
  WNSFLD WV11 ....37 H4
Millfield Vw HALE B63 ....121 J1
Millford CI HLGN/YWD B28 ....126 E8
Mill Gdns SMTHWK B67 ....105 K3
Mill Gn WOLVN WV10 ....36 B1
Mill Gv CDSL WV8 ....35 G2
Mill HI COVS CV3 ....181 H2
Millhaven Av BVILLE B30 ....124 F7
Millhouse Ct COVN CV6 ....134 D6
Millhouse Dr RLSN CV32 ....206 A3
Millhouse Gdns PENK ST19 ....10 C4
Millhouse Rd YDLY B25 ....108 A5
Millicent CI HEDN WS12 ....13 G5
Millichip Rd WLNHL WV13 ....51 J1
Milliners Ct ATHST CV9 ....63 H5
Millington Rd CBROM B36 ....91 J3
  TPTN/OCK DY4 ....67 K4
  WOLVN WV10 ....36 C7
Million St WSLW WS2 ....53 G2
Mill La ALDR WS9 ....41 K1
  ALDR WS9 ....41 L2
  ATHST CV9 ....63 L5
  BDWTH CV12 ....117 G2
  BNTWD WS7 ....27 H2
  BRGRVW B61 ....168 A2
  BRGRVW B61 ....191 K5
  COVS CV3 ....156 D5
  CRTAM B79 ....32 A8
  DIG/EDG B5 ....7 J7
  DOR/KN B93 ....175 J1
  DUNHL/THL/PER WV6 ....35 J6
  HOCK/TIA B94 ....172 F4
  KIDD DY10 ....139 M3
  KIDDW DY11 ....164 D3
  KIDDW DY11 ....138 D3
  LICHS WS14 ....32 F5
  NFLD/LBR B31 ....144 D4
  POL/KGSB/FAZ B78 ....45 L5
  RCOVN/BALC/EX CV7 ....96 A3
  RIDG/WDGT B32 ....123 J3
  RLSN CV32 ....199 J3
  RMSLY B62 ....122 A3
  RRUGBY CV23 ....161 J4
  SHHTH WV12 ....38 A4
  SOLH B91 ....149 G1
  STRPT DY13 ....188 F1
  WMBN WV5 ....62 B5
  WNSFLD WV11 ....36 F2
Mill Lane Ar SOLH B91 * 149 G2

Millmead Rd SLYOAK B29 ....123 J3
Mill Pk CNCK/NC WS11 ....16 E3
Mill Pl BLOX/PEL WS3 ....53 J1
Mill Pool CI HAG/WOL DY9 ....140 E1
Mill Pool La DOR/KN B93 ....175 D1
Millpool Gdns
  ALE/KHTH/YWD B14 ....146 D2
Millpool Hill Alcester Rd South
  ALE/KHTH/YWD B14 ....146 D1
Mill Pool La DOR/KN B93 ....175 D1
Millpool Wy SMTHWKW B67 ....105 L1
Mill Race La COVN CV6 ....134 E2
  STRBR DY8 ....101 L1
Millrace Rd REDE B98 ....194 C8
Mill Race Vw ATHST CV9 ....63 H3
Millridge Wy KIDDW DY11 ....189 L4
Mill Rd BRWNH WS8 ....26 C6
  CDYHTH B64 ....103 J6
  RLSS CV31 ....206 E5
  RUGBYS/DCH CV22 ....187 G1
  RUSH/SHEL WS4 ....39 M4
  STRPT DY13 ....188 F1
Mills Av WALM/CURD B76 ....73 J1
Millsborough Rd REDE B98 ....202 C2
Mills CI WNSFLD WV11 ....36 F5
Mills Crs BKHL/PFLD WV2 ....3 J7
Millside HLGN/YWD B28 ....147 J2
Mills Rd BKHL/PFLD WV2 ....3 J9
Millstone CI WALM/CURD B76 ....73 K4
Mill St AST/WIT B6 ....89 G4
  BDWTH CV12 ....116 F2
  BILS/COS WV14 ....51 G8
  BRLYHL DY5 ....102 B3
  CDYHTH B64 ....103 G6
  CNCK/NC WS11 ....16 C3
  COV CV1 ....8 D2
  CSCFLD/WYGN B72 ....57 G8
  DARL/WED WS10 ....52 A7
  KIDD DY10 ....138 A7
  NUN CV11 ....99 G1
  PENK ST19 ....10 C4
  REDW B97 ....202 B3
  RLSS CV31 ....206 E6
  STRPT DY13 ....188 F2
  TPTN/OCK DY4 ....68 B8
  WBROM B70 ....87 G1
  WLNHL WV13 ....51 J2
  WSL WS2 ....53 J2
  WWCK CV34 ....205 K7
Mill Ter BDWTH CV12 ....98 F8
Millthorpe CI WASH/WDE B8 ....90 D8
Mill Vw STETCH B33 ....110 A3
Mill Wk WOLV WV1 ....99 L1
Millwalk Dr COVEN WV9 ....35 L2
The Mill Wk NFLD/LBR B31 ....144 D4
Millward Rd BORD B9 ....108 A4
Millwright CI TPTN/OCK DY4 ....67 M8
Milner CI COVE CV2 ....135 L4
Milner Crs COVE CV2 ....135 M4
Milner Dr CRTAM B79 ....31 J8
Milner Rd SLYOAK B29 ....124 E4
Milner Wy MOS/BIL B13 ....125 L3
Milo Crs POL/KGSB/FAZ B78 ....45 L3
Milrose Wy TLHL/CAN CV4 ....153 K5
Milsom Gv BKDE/SHDE B34 ....92 D2
Milstead Rd
  LGN/SDN/BHAMAIR B26 ....109 L4
Milton Av BHTH/HG B12 ....107 L7
  CRTAM B79 ....31 L6
  WWCK CV34 ....205 G8
Milton CI BDWTH CV12 ....117 H4
  DOR/KN B93 ....175 L1
  REDW B97 ....202 B3
  SHHTH WV12 ....38 C6
  STRBR DY8 ....101 L6
  WSL WS1 ....53 H7
Milton Ct DUNHL/THL/PER WV6 ....48 E1
Milton Gv HDSW B21 * 88 C5
Milton PI WSL WS1 ....53 H7
Milton Rd BILS/COS WV14 ....67 L4
  BRGRVW B61 ....168 E5
  CNCK/NC WS11 ....16 C1
  DOR/KN B93 ....175 L1
  SMTHWK B67 ....87 H6
  WOLVN WV10 ....36 E8
Milton St BRLYHL DY5 ....84 D9
  COVE CV2 ....155 L1
  HHTH/SAND B71 ....68 F8
  LOZ/NWT B19 ....6 B1
  WSNGN B18 ....88 C8
Milverton CI HALE B63 ....103 J1
  WALM/CURD B76 ....73 K6
Milverton Crs RLSN CV32 ....206 D1
Milverton Crs West RLSN CV32 ....206 D1
Milverton HI RLSN CV32 ....206 D5
Milverton Lawn RLSN CV32 ....206 B5
Milverton Rd COVE CV2 ....135 G3
  ERDW/GRVHL B23 ....71 J8
  SOLH B91 ....150 A8
Milverton Ter RLSN CV32 ....206 D5
Mimosa CI SLYOAK B29 ....123 M5
Mimosa Wk KGSWFD DY6 ....83 J5
Mincing La BLKHTH/ROWR B65 ....104 A2
Mindelsohn Wy EDG B15 ....124 B3
Minden Gv SLYOAK B29 ....123 J4
Minehead Rd DUDN DY1 ....84 B5
  WOLVN WV10 ....36 C7
Miner St WSLW WS2 ....53 G2
Miners Wk POL/KGSB/FAZ B78 ....45 K4
Minerva CI SHHTH WV12 ....52 F1
  TAM/AM/WIL B77 ....32 B8
Minewood CI BLOX/PEL WS3 ....38 D2
Minions CI ATHST CV9 ....63 H5
Minith Rd BILS/COS WV14 ....67 H5
Miniva Dr WALM/CURD B76 ....73 L1
Minivet Dr BHTH/HG B12 ....107 J5
Minley Av HRBN B17 ....105 H6
The Minories CBHAMNW B3 ....7 G4
Minors HI LICHS WS14 ....21 H7
Minstead Rd ERDE/BCHGN B24 ....90 B4
Minster CI BLKHTH/ROWR B65 ....104 A2
  DOR/KN B93 ....175 L4
Minster Ct MOS/BIL B13 * 125 L3
Minster Dr SMHTH B10 ....108 B6
Minsterley CI BDMR/CCFT WV3 ....49 J5
Minster Rd COV CV1 ....154 A4
  STRPT DY13 ....188 C1
The Minster WLNHL WV13 ....51 J2
Mintern Rd YDLY B25 ....108 B5
Minton CI WOLV WV1 ....51 M3
Minton Rd COV CV3 ....135 M4
  RIDG/WDGT B32 ....123 J3
Minworth Rd CSHL/WTROR B46 ....92 D4
Mira Dr
  MKTBOS/BARL/STKG CV13 ....81 G2
Miranda CI COVS CV3 ....156 B6
  RBRY B45 ....143 L5
Mirfield CI COVEN WV9 ....35 L2

Mirfield Rd SOLH B91 ....127 L7
  STETCH B33 ....109 M3
Mission CI CDYHTH B64 ....103 L4
Mission Dr TPTN/OCK DY4 ....85 L1
Mistletoe Dr DSYBK/YTR WS5 ....69 L2
Mitcham CI HEDN WS12 ....12 D6
Mitcham Gv KGSTG B44 ....71 M4
Mitcheldean CI REDE B98 ....202 C6
Mitcheldean Covert
  ALE/KHTH/YWD B14 ....146 D2
Mitchell Av BILS/COS WV14 ....66 F4
  TLHL/CAN CV4 ....153 L7
Mitchell Rd BDWTH CV12 ....116 F3
Mitchells Ct CRTAM B79 * 31 M8
Mitchel Rd KGSWFD DY6 ....101 K1
Mitford Dr HIA/OLT B92 ....128 B6
Mitre CI SHHTH WV12 ....38 B6
  WNSFLD WV11 ....37 L2
Mitre Fold WOLV WV1 ....2 E4
Mitre Rd GTWY WS6 ....24 B3
  HAG/WOL DY9 ....102 C8
Mitten Av RBRY B45 ....143 K4
Mitton CI STRPT DY13 ....188 E1
Mitton Gdns STRPT DY13 ....188 C2
Mitton Rd BFLD/HDSWWD B20 ....88 C3
Mitton St STRPT DY13 ....188 E2
Moat Av COVS CV3 ....180 D1
Moat Brook Av CDSL WV8 ....34 C1
Moatbrook La CDSL WV8 ....34 B1
Moat CI KNWTH CV8 ....182 K7
Moat Coppice RIDG/WDGT B32 ....122 E4
Moat Cft
  CHWD/FDBR/MGN B37 ....92 D4
  WALM/CURD B76 ....73 M6
Moat Dr POL/KGSB/FAZ B78 ....45 J3
  RMSLY B62 ....104 D4
Moat Farm Dr BDWTH CV12 ....116 A4
  RIDG/WDGT B32 ....122 E4
  RUGBYN/HIL CV21 ....187 L6
Moat Farm Wy BLOX/PEL WS3 ....25 L8
Moatfield Ter DARL/WED WS10 ....68 E2
Moat Green Av WNSFLD WV11 ....37 J4
Moat House La CSHL/WTROR B46 ....94 F4
  TLHL/CAN CV4 ....154 A6
Moat House La East
  WNSFLD WV11 ....37 H6
Moathouse La West
  WNSFLD WV11 ....37 H6
Moat La DIG/EDG B5 ....7 H6
  GTWY WS6 ....24 E3
  LGN/SDN/BHAMAIR B26 ....109 J2
  SOLH B91 ....128 A7
Moat Mdw RIDG/WDGT B32 ....123 J3
Moat Rd LGLYGN/QTN B68 ....104 F2
  TPTN/OCK DY4 ....67 L6
  WSLW WS2 ....4 A3
Moatside CI BLOX/PEL WS3 ....25 L8
Moat St WLNHL WV13 ....51 J2
Mockley Wood Rd DOR/KN B93 ....149 M6
Mob La RUSH/SHEL WS4 ....40 A3
Modbury Av RIDG/WDGT B32 ....123 H4
Modbury CI COVS CV3 ....155 H8
Moden CI SEDG DY3 ....66 B8
Moden HI SEDG DY3 ....66 A7
Moffit Wy STRPT DY13 ....188 C1
Mogul La HALE B63 ....103 G3
Moillett CI WSNGN B18 ....106 B1
Moilliett Ct SMTHWK B66 ....88 A7
Moira Crs
  ALE/KHTH/YWD B14 ....147 G1
Moises Hall Rd WMBN WV5 ....64 F7
Molands
  RCOVN/BALC/EX CV7 ....130 B4
Moland St AST/WIT B6 ....7 H1
Mole St SPARK B11 ....107 M7
Molesworth Av COVS CV3 ....155 L4
Molineux St WOLV WV1 ....3 J5
Mollington Crs SHLY B90 ....148 A2
Mollington Gv
  RWWCK/WEL CV35 ....204 B2
Molyneux Rd DUDS DY2 ....103 J3
Momus Bvd COVE CV2 ....156 A3
Monarch Dr TPTN/OCK DY4 ....68 A7
Monarch's Wy
  BLKHTH/ROWR B65 ....103 K1
  BRGRVE B61 ....192 A5
  BRGRVW B61 ....191 H3
  HAG/WOL DY9 ....120 A2
  KGSWFD DY6 ....82 C7
  KIDD DY10 ....86 A3
  OLDBY B69 ....86 A3
  REDW B97 ....201 H5
  WNSFLD WV11 ....37 H2
  WSL WS1 ....52 E2
Monarch Wy DUDS DY2 ....102 F1
Mona Rd ERDW/GRVHL B23 ....72 D8
Monastery Dr SOLH B91 ....127 H8
Monckton Rd LGLYGN/QTN B68 ....104 E6
Moncreiffe CI DUDS DY2 ....85 J5
Moncrieffe St WSL WS1 ....5 J5
Mondrian Rd BRGRVE B60 ....192 A4
Money La BRGRVW B61 ....142 E7
Monica Rd SMHTH B10 ....108 B6
Monins Av TPTN/OCK DY4 ....85 L2
Monk CI TPTN/OCK DY4 ....85 M2
Monk Rd WASH/WDE B8 ....91 F8
Monks CI RUGBYS/DCH CV22 ....185 L5
  WMBN WV5 ....64 C7
The Monk's Cft COVS CV3 ....155 G6
Monkseaton Rd
  CSCFLD/WYGN B72 ....72 F3
Monksfield Av GTB/HAM B43 ....70 F4
Monks Field CI TLHL/CAN CV4 ....153 L4
Monkshood Ms
  ERDW/GRVHL B23 ....71 M5
Monkshood Retreat
  HWK/WKHTH B38 ....145 K5
Monks Kirby Rd
  WALM/CURD B76 ....73 K2
Monks Pth REDW B97 ....201 K1
Monkspath SHLY B90 ....148 E3
  WALM/CURD B76 ....73 K5
Monkspath CI SHLY B90 ....148 D7
Monkspath Hall Rd SHLY B90 ....148 D7
Monks Rd COV CV1 ....157 G6
  COVS CV3 ....157 G6
Monksway HWK/WKHTH B38 ....145 M5
Monks Wy TAM/AM/WIL B77 ....32 D8
  WWCK CV34 ....205 H7
Monkswell CI BRLYHL DY5 ....102 B4
  SMHTH B10 ....108 B6
Monkswood Crs COVE CV2 ....135 J3
Monkswood Rd NFLD/LBR B31 ....145 G3
Monkton CI SLYOAK B29 ....123 H6
Monmer CI WLNHL WV13 ....51 M1
Monmer La WLNHL WV13 ....51 M2
Monmore Rd WOLV WV1 ....50 E5
Monmouth CI COVW CV5 ....154 A3
  KNWTH CV8 ....179 K7
Monmouth Dr HHTH/SAND B71 ....68 F4
  SCFLD/BOLD B73 ....72 A1
Monmouth Gdns
  NUNW/HART CV10 ....79 M6
Monmouth Rd RIDG/WDGT B32 ....123 H5
  SMTHWKW B67 ....105 H3
  WSLW WS2 ....52 C2
Monsal Av WOLVN WV10 ....3 J1

Monsaldale Cl BRWNH WS8 ....26 B7
Monsal Rd PBAR/PBCH B42 ....71 G6
Monsieurs Hall La BRGRVW B61 ..190 D7
Mons Rd DUDS DY1 ....85 J4
Montague Rd ERDE/BCHGN B24 ...90 E4
  HDSW B21 ....88 D5
  LDYWD/EDGR B16 ....106 C4
  RUGBYS/DCH CV22 ....186 C8
  SMTHWK B66 ....105 M2
  WWCK CV34 ....205 L4
Montague St AST/WIT B6 ....89 M5
  DIG/EDG B5 ....7 M5
Montalt Rd COVS CV3 ....155 J6
Montana Av NUNW/HART CV10 ...98 C2
Montcrieff Dr RLSS CV31 ....207 C8
Monteagle Dr KGSWFD DY6 ....83 H4
Montford Gv SHHTH WV12 ....38 C6
Montford Rd CSHL/WTROR B46 ...93 K8
  WSLW WS2 ....52 F7
Montgomery Av RWWCK/WEL CV35 ...204 C7
Montgomery Cl BRGRVW B61 ...168 E4
  COVS CV3 ....182 A1
Montgomery Cft WWCK CV34 * ...205 K6
Montgomery Crs BRLYHL DY5 ...102 D6
Montgomery Cft SPARK B11 ...108 A6
Montgomery Dr RUGBYS/DCH CV22 ...186 A4
Montgomery Rd WSLW WS2 ....52 C3
Montgomery St SPARK B11 ...107 M6
Montpelier Rd ERDE/BCHGN B24 ...90 E4
Montpellier Cl COVS CV3 ....155 G1
Montpellier Gdns DUDN DY1 ...84 C3
Montpellier St BHTH/HG B12 ...107 L7
Montrose Av RLSN CV32 ....206 E1
Montrose Cl CNCK/NC WS11 ...12 D8
Montrose Dr CVALE B35 ....91 J3
  DUDN DY1 ....84 E5
  NUNW/HART CV10 ....98 D2
Montrose Rd RUGBYS/DCH CV22 ...186 E4
Montsford Cl DOR/KN B93 ...149 K7
Monument Av HAG/WOL DY9 ...120 C1
Monument Dr WOLVN WV10 ...23 C5
Monument La HAG/WOL DY9 ...120 B6
  RBRY B45 ....169 K1
  SEDG DY3 ....66 C4
Monument Rd LDYWD/EDGR B16 ...106 B4
Monway Ter DARL/WED WS10 ...68 C2
Monwode Lea La CSHL/WTROR B46 ...95 M1
Monwood Gv SLYOAK B91 ...148 D3
Moorhull Hall Rd BKDE/SHDE B34 ...145 M2
Moodyscroft Rd STETCH B33 ...110 A2
Moon's La GTWY WS6 ....13 G6
Moons Moat Dr REDE B98 ...195 J8
Moorbrooke NUNW/HART CV10 ...79 M4
Moorcroft Cl NUN CV11 ...99 M4
Moorcroft Dr DARL/WED WS10 ...68 C3
Moorcroft Gdns REDW B97 ...201 M7
Moorcroft Rd MOS/BIL B13 ...125 H2
Moordown Av HIA/OLT B92 ...127 L3
Moore Cl COVN CV6 ....134 E1
  DUNHL/THL/PER WV6 ....48 D1
  FOAKS/STRLY B74 ....42 D7
  WWCK CV34 ....205 J3
Moore Crs LGLYGN/QTN B68 ...105 C2
Moorend Av CHWD/FDBR/MGN B37 ...110 E4
Moor End La ERDE/BCHGN B24 ...90 E1
Moore's Rw DIG/EDG B5 ....7 K7
Moore St WOLV WV1 ....13 G6
  WOLV WV1 ....3 J5
Moore Wk WWCK CV34 ....206 H4
Moor Farm Cl RUGBY CV23 ...183 K7
Moorfield Dr BRGRVW B61 ...191 K1
  HALE B63 ....103 L8
  SCFLD/BOLD B73 ....72 C5
Moorfield Rd BKDE/SHDE B34 ...91 L7
  BKHL/PFLD WV2 ....49 M6
The Moorfield COVS CV3 ....155 L5
Moorfoot Av HALE B63 ....121 G4
Moorgate CRTAM B79 ....31 L8
Moorgate Cl REDE B98 ....195 J7
Moor Green La MOS/BIL B13 ...125 C4
Moor Hall Dr HAG/WOL DY9 ...141 L4
  MGN/WHC B75 ....57 J4
Moor Hall La PENK ST19 ...10 E6
Moorhills Cft SHLY B90 ...147 M5
The Moorings BRLYHL DY5 ...102 D1
  COVEN WV9 ....10 A1
  OLDBY B69 ....86 C5
  RLSS CV31 ....206 B6
Moorland Av WOLVN WV10 ...36 A7
Moorland Rd BLOX/PEL WS3 ...38 C8
  CNCK/NC WS11 ....12 C8
  LDYWD/EDGR B16 ....106 B4
Moorlands Ct KNWTH CV8 ...197 K2
Moorlands Dr SHLY B90 ...148 A3
Moorlands Rd HHTH/SAND B71 ...69 G4
The Moorlands FOAKS/STRLY B74 ...56 D5
Moor La AST/WIT B6 ....71 K7
  BLKHL/ROWR B65 ....103 L2
  CRTAM B79 ....32 E7
  LICHS WS14 ....42 C4
  TAM/AM/WIL B77 ....32 B8
Moor Leasow NFLD/LBR B31 ...145 C3
Moor Meadow Rd MGN/WHC B75 ...57 H6
Moor Pk BLOX/PEL WS3 ...38 C8
  DUNHL/THL/PER WV6 ...34 B8
Moorpark Rd NFLD/LBR B31 ...144 E4
Moor Pool Av HRBN B17 ...106 A4
Moor Rd NUNW/HART CV10 ...189 M3
Moors Av KIDDW DY11 ...189 M3
Moors Cft RIDG/WDGT B32 ...122 F4
Moorside Av ALE/KHTH/YWD B14 ...147 G1
Moors La NFLD/LBR B31 ...123 J5
Moors Mill La TPTN/OCK DY4 ...68 A4
Moorsom St AST/WIT B6 ....89 J8
Moorsom Wy BRGRVE B60 ...191 M6
The Moors CBROM B36 ...91 K5
Moor St BRLYHL DY5 ....7 H5
  CBHAMNE B4 ....7 H5
  COVW CV5 ....154 D4
  CRTAM B79 ....31 L8
  DARL/WED WS10 ....87 G3
  WBROM B70 ....87 G3
Moor St South BKHL/PFLD WV2 ...50 A5
The Moor WALM/CURD B76 ...73 L5
Moorville Wk SPARK B11 ...107 L6
Moorwood Crs NUNW/HART CV10 ...79 L5

Moorwood La NUNW/HART CV10 ...79 L5
Morar Cl CBHAMW B1 ....91 M1
Moray Cl RMSLY B62 ....104 C5
Morcom Rd SPARK B11 ....108 C8
Morcroft BILS/COS WV14 ....67 L2
Mordaunt Dr MGN/WHC B75 ...57 H3
Morden Rd STETCH B33 ....109 H3
Moreall Mdw TLHL/CAN CV4 ...153 J7
The Morelands NFLD/LBR B31 ...144 F4
Morella Cl BEWD DY12 ....162 D2
Moreton Av ETTPK/GDPK/PENN WV4 ...66 C1
  GTB/HAM B43 ....71 C3
Moreton Cl RIDG/WDGT B32 ...105 K8
  TPTN/OCK DY4 ....67 M3
Moreton Rd SHLY B90 ....148 A3
  WOLVN WV10 ....36 B4
Moreton St CNCK/NC WS11 ...6 A2
  LGN/SDN/BHAMAIR B26 ...110 A8
Morford Rd ALDR WS9 ....40 E6
Morgan Cl OLDBY B69 ....86 B5
  RCOVN/BALC/EX CV7 ....96 D5
  WLNHL WV13 ....51 M1
Morgan Gv CBROM B36 ....92 A4
Morgan Rd POL/KGSB/FAZ B78 ...45 L3
Morgans Rd COVW CV5 ....153 G1
Morgrove Av DOR/KN B93 ...149 K7
Morillon Ct KIDD DY10 ...164 E4
Morjon Dr GTB/HAM B43 ...70 D3
Morland Rd COVN CV6 ...134 A2
  GTB/HAM B43 ....70 D3
Morley Gv DUNHL/THL/PER WV6 ...50 A1
Morley Rd BNTWD WS7 ...18 F6
  WASH/WDE B8 ....90 F1
Morlich Ri BRLYHL DY5 ...101 M5
Morlings Dr BNTWD WS7 ...18 F5
Morning Pines STRBR DY8 ...119 J1
Morningside COVW CV5 ...56 F7
  SCFLD/BOLD B73 ....56 F7
Mornington Rd SMTHWK B66 ...87 M6
Morpeth TAM/AM/WIL B77 ...46 A6
Morrell St RLSN CV32 ...206 D4
Morris Av COVE CV2 ...116 B1
  WSLW WS2 ....52 C3
Morris Cl ACCN B27 ....127 H1
  RUGBYN/HIL CV21 ....160 D7
Morris Cft CBROM B36 ...92 C4
Morris Dr NUN CV11 ...99 H4
Morris Field Cft HLGN/YWD B28 ...147 J1
Morris Hl POL/KGSB/FAZ B78 ...47 K6
Morris Rd WASH/WDE B8 ...90 F1
Morris St WBROM B70 ...87 G4
Morsefield La BDMR/CCFT WV3 ...203 H4
Morson Crs RUGBYN/HIL CV21 ...187 J3
Morston TAM/AM/WIL B77 ...46 B1
Mortimers Cl ALE/KHTH/YWD B14 ...146 F4
Morton Cl COVN CV6 ...133 L4
Morton Gdns RUGBYN/HIL CV21 ...186 F3
Morton La REDW B97 ...201 M7
Morton Rd BRLYHL DY5 ...102 B6
  KIDD DY10 ....165 M3
Morton St RLSN CV32 ...206 D4
Morvale Gdns HAG/WOL DY9 ...102 C8
Morvale St HAG/WOL DY9 ...102 C8
Morven Rd SCFLD/BOLD B73 ...72 D2
Morville Cft ETTPK/GDPK/PENN WV4 ...66 F1
Morville Rd DUDS DY2 ...103 H1
Morville St LDYWD/EDGR B16 ...6 A7
Mosborough Crs LOZ/NWT B19 ...89 G4
Mosedale RUGBYN/HIL CV21 ...161 H6
Mosedale Dr WNSFLD WV11 ...37 K8
Moseley Av WNSFLD WV11 ...37 K2
Moseley Ct CHWD/FDBR/MGN B37 ...110 D5
Moseley Old Hall La WOLVN WV10 ...22 E8
Moseley Rd BHTH/HG B12 ...7 L9
  KNWTH CV8 ....197 M2
  WLNHL WV13 ....51 H4
  WOLVN WV10 ....22 E8
Mossbank Av BNTWD WS7 ...18 E7
Moss Cl ALDR WS9 ...40 E8
  HEDN WS12 ....12 E5
  RUGBYS/DCH CV22 ....186 C4
  RUSH/SHEL WS4 ....53 L2
Mossdale TAM/AM/WIL B77 ...47 G5
Mossdale Crs NUNW/HART CV10 ...98 D3
Mossdale Wy SEDG DY3 ...66 C6
Moss Dr SCFLD/BOLD B73 ...73 G2
Mossfield Rd ALE/KHTH/YWD B14 ...125 J6
Moss Gdns BILS/COS WV14 ...66 F2
Moss Gv ALE/KHTH/YWD B14 ...125 H7
  KGSWFD DY6 ....83 H6
  KNWTH CV8 ....179 M6
Moss House Cl EDG B15 ...6 B8
Mossley Cl BLOX/PEL WS3 ...38 C4
Mossley La BLOX/PEL WS3 ...38 D3
Moss Rd CNCK/NC WS11 ...16 E2
Moss St CNCK/NC WS11 ...16 E1
  RLSS CV31 ....206 E6
Mossvale Cl CDYHTH B64 ...103 J4
Mossvale Gv WASH/WDE B8 ...90 D8
Mosswood Rd CNCK/NC WS11 ...16 B6
Mostyn Crs HHTH/SAND B71 ...68 C4
Mostyn Rd HDSW B21 ...88 D3
  LDYWD/EDGR B16 ....106 D4
Mostyn St WOLV WV1 ...7 J2
Mottram Cl WBROM B70 ...86 D3
Mottrams Ct SCFLD/WYGN B72 ...73 C3
Mott's Cft LOZ/NWT B19 ...6 E1
Mott's Wy CSHL/WTROR B46 ...93 L7
Moule Cl KIDDW DY11 ...137 M7
Moundsley Gv ALE/KHTH/YWD B14 ...146 E2
Mountain Ash Dr HAG/WOL DY9 ...120 A3
Mountain Ash Rd BRWNH WS8 ...26 C8
Mountain Pine Cl HEDN WS12 * ...12 E5
Mount Av BRLYHL DY5 ...102 A1
  HEDN WS12 ....12 D5
Mountbatten Av KNWTH CV8 ...198 A2
Mountbatten Cl BNTWD WS7 ...18 E7
  WBROM B70 ....87 K3
Mountbatten Rd WSLW WS2 ...52 B3
Mount Cl GTWY WS6 ...24 B3
  MOS/BIL B13 ....125 K1

  SEDG DY3 ....84 A3
  WMBN WV5 ....64 E6
Mount Cottages ETTPK/GDPK/PENN WV4 * ...65 K2
Mount Ct DUNHL/THL/PER WV6 * ...48 D2
Mount Dr BDWTH CV12 ...116 E2
  WMBN WV5 ....64 E6
Mountfield Cl ALE/KHTH/YWD B14 ...146 E3
Mountford Cl BLKHTH/ROWR B65 ...104 A2
Mountford Crs ALDR WS9 ...40 F5
Mountford Dr MGN/WHC B75 ...57 G5
Mountford La BILS/COS WV14 ...51 H6
Mountford Rd SHLY B90 ...147 H4
Mount Gdns COVW CV5 ...154 C4
Mountjoy Crs HIA/OLT B92 ...128 A2
Mount La HAG/WOL DY9 ...141 J1
  SEDG DY3 ....84 A3
Mount Nod Wy COVW CV5 ...153 F1
Mount Pleasant ALE/KHTH/YWD B14 ...125 J4
  BILS/COS WV14 ....51 J7
  BKHL/PFLD WV2 * 50 D6
  BRLYHL DY5 ....102 C4
  ETTPK/GDPK/PENN WV4 * ...65 K2
  ETTPK/GDPK/PENN WV4 * ...66 D3
  HDSW B21 ....88 D2
  OLDBY B69 ....86 A5
  STRBR DY8 ....101 L8
  STRBR DY8 ....101 M8
  WLNHL WV13 ....51 J5
  WMBN WV5 ....64 D6
Mount Pleasant Rd BDWTH CV12 ...116 E2
Mount Pleasant St BILS/COS WV14 ...66 F5
  WBROM B70 ....87 G3
Mount Pleasant Ter NUNW/HART CV10 ...80 D7
Mountrath St WSL WS1 ...4 E5
Mount Rd BLKHTH/ROWR B65 ...104 C2
  BLOX/PEL WS3 ....18 F7
  BNTWD WS7 ....18 F7
  BRGRVW B61 ....168 B4
  DUNHL/THL/PER WV6 ...48 D3
  ETTPK/GDPK/PENN WV4 ...65 J1
  ETTPK/GDPK/PENN WV4 ...66 D3
  HDSW B21 ....88 D3
  OLDBY B69 ....86 A5
  STRBR DY8 ....101 L8
  STRBR DY8 ....101 M8
  TPTN/OCK DY4 ....68 A7
  VAUX/NECH B7 ....90 A4
  WSL WS1 ....4 E6
Mounts Wy VAUX/NECH B7 ...90 A4
The Mount CDYHTH B64 ...103 J4
  COVS CV3 ....155 H5
  ERDW/GRVHL B23 ....90 B4
  WALM/CURD B76 ....75 G8
Mount Vernon Dr BRGRVW B61 ...168 B4
Mount Wy MGN/WHC B75 ...73 J1
Mountwood Covert DUNHL/THL/PER WV6 ...48 F2
Mousehall Farm Rd BRLYHL DY5 ...102 B6
Mouse Hl BLOX/PEL WS3 ...39 K2
Mouse La KIDDW DY11 ...137 M5
Mousesweet Cl DUDS DY2 ...103 J1
Mousesweet La DUDS DY2 ...103 J2
Mousesweet Wk CDYHTH B64 ...102 F5
Mowbray Cl BRLYHL DY5 ...84 C4
Mowbray St BNTWD WS7 ...18 C4
  COVS CV3 ....9 M3
  DIG/EDG B5 ....107 J5
Mowe Cft CHWD/FDBR/MGN B37 ...110 E6
Moxhull Cl SHHTH WV12 ...38 A4
Moxhull Dr WALM/CURD B76 ...73 J5
Moxhull Gdns SHHTH WV12 ...38 A4
Moxhull Rd CHWD/FDBR/MGN B37 ...92 C8
Moxley Rd DARL/WED WS10 ...67 M1
Moyeady Av RUGBYN/HIL CV21 ...187 J5
Moyle Crs COVW CV5 ...153 H1
Moyle Dr HALE B63 ...102 F6
Moyses Cft SMTHWK B66 ...87 L5
Mozart Ct CNCK/NC WS11 ...17 G3
Muchall Rd ETTPK/GDPK/PENN WV4 ...49 L8
Much Park St COV CV1 ...9 H5
Mucklow Hl RMSLY B62 ...104 B8
Muirfield TAM/AM/WIL B77 ...32 F5
Muirfield Cl BLOX/PEL WS3 ...38 E2
Muirfield Crs OLDBY B69 ...85 L6
Muirfield Gdns HWK/WKHTH B38 ...145 H4
Muirville Cl STRBR DY8 ...101 H2
Mulberry Cl RLSN CV32 ...206 E3
Mulberry Dr MOS/BIL B13 ...125 L4
  WWCK CV34 ....205 K4
Mulberry Gn DUDN DY1 ...66 D8
Mulberry Pl BLOX/PEL WS3 ...38 D4
Mulberry Rd BLOX/PEL WS3 ...38 D4
  CNCK/NC WS11 ....16 C2
  COVN CV6 ....134 E7
  NFLD/LBR B31 ....124 A4
  RUGBYS/DCH CV22 ....185 M3
Mulberry Wy NUNW/HART CV10 ...79 K5
Muldoon Cl CNCK/NC WS11 ...16 A4
Mull Cl RBRY B45 ...143 J4
Mull Cft CBROM B36 ...92 E6
Mullensgrove Rd CHWD/FDBR/MGN B37 ...92 C8
Mullett Rd WNSFLD WV11 ...36 F6
Mullett St BRLYHL DY5 ...83 M8
Mulliners Cl CHWD/FDBR/MGN B37 * ...111 H3
Mulliner St COVN CV6 ...134 D4
Mullion Cft HWK/WKHTH B38 ...145 J4
Mulroy Rd FOAKS/STRLY B74 ...56 F7
Mulwych Rd STETCH B33 ...110 C2
Munches La HAG/WOL DY9 ...142 A5
Muncie Cl KIDD DY10 ...139 G8
Munsley Cl REDE B98 ...203 K3
Munslow Gv NFLD/LBR B31 ...144 B4
Muntz Crs HOCK/TIA B94 ...175 G7
Muntz St SMTHH B10 ...108 B5
Murcott Rd HAG/WOL DY9 ...120 M4
Murcroft Rd HAG/WOL DY9 ...120 B4
Murdock Gv HDSW B21 ...88 C6
Murdock Pl SMTHWK B66 ...88 D3
Murdock Rd WSLW WS2 ...38 D1
Murray Ct SCFLD/BOLD B73 ...72 C2
Murrayfield Wy COVS CV3 ...156 F4

Murrayian Cl RUGBYN/HIL CV21 ...186 F2
Murray Rd COVN CV6 ...133 L6
  RUGBYN/HIL CV21 ....187 G1
Murrell Cl DIG/EDG B5 ...107 H6
Murton TAM/AM/WIL B77 ...47 G5
Musborough Cl CBROM B36 ...92 A4
Muscott Gv HRBN B17 ...105 K3
Muscovy Rd ERDW/GRVHL B23 ...90 A2
Musgrave Cl WALM/CURD B76 ...73 J2
Musgrave Rd WSNGN B18 ...88 D8
Mushroom Hall Rd LGLYGN/QTN B68 ...86 F8
Musk La SEDG DY3 ...83 M2
Musk La West SEDG DY3 ...83 M2
Muskoka BEWD DY12 ...162 D4
Muswell Cl SOLH B91 ...128 B8
Muxloe Cl BLOX/PEL WS3 ...38 C8
Myatt Av ALDR WS9 ...40 D8
  BKHL/PFLD WV2 ....50 C2
  BNTWD WS7 ....18 E6
Myatt Cl BKHL/PFLD WV2 ...50 C2
Myddleton St WSNGN B18 ...106 E1
Myles Ct BRLYHL DY5 ...102 C1
Mylgrove COVS CV3 ...181 H1
Mynors Crs HLYWD B47 ...146 E8
Myring Dr MGN/WHC B75 ...57 H6
Myrtle Av ALE/KHTH/YWD B14 ...146 D3
  BHTH/HG B12 ....107 L8
  REDE B98 ....202 C3
Myrtle Cl SHHTH WV12 ...38 C6
Myrtle Gv BDMR/CCFT WV3 ...49 J7
  COVW CV5 ....154 D4
Myrtle Pl SLYOAK B29 ...124 F3
Myrtle Rd DUDN DY1 ...84 E2
Myrtle St BKHL/PFLD WV2 ...50 D7
Myrtle Ter TPTN/OCK DY4 ...67 M3
Mythe La ATHST CV9 ...63 L5
Mythe Vw ATHST CV9 ...63 L5
Myton Crs WWCK CV34 ...206 A4
Myton Crofts RLSS CV31 ...206 B6
Myton Dr SHLY B90 ...147 H3
Myton Gdns WWCK CV34 ...205 L4
Myton La WWCK CV34 ...206 A4
Myton Rd WWCK CV34 ...205 L4
Mytton Cl DUDS DY2 ...85 J4
Mytton Gv TPTN/OCK DY4 ...67 J8
Mytton Rd BVILLE B30 ...124 D4
  CSHL/WTROR B46 ....92 D2

N

Naden Rd LOZ/NWT B19 ...88 F7
Nadin Rd SCFLD/BOLD B73 ...72 C6
Naesby Rd DUNHL/THL/PER WV6 ...48 D2
Nafford Gv ALE/KHTH/YWD B14 ...146 D3
Nagersfield Rd BRLYHL DY5 ...101 J3
Nagington Dr PENK ST19 ...10 D6
Nailcote Av TLHL/CAN CV4 ...153 G4
Nailcote La RCOVN/BALC/EX CV7 ...152 E6
Nailers Cl BRGRVE B60 ...191 J7
  RIDG/WDGT B32 ....122 D3
  WMBN WV5 * 64 C3
Nailers Dr BNTWD WS7 ...19 L3
Nailers Fold BILS/COS WV14 ...67 G3
Nailers Rw WMBN WV5 * ...64 D3
Nailstone Crs ACGN B27 ...127 C5
Nailsworth Rd DOR/KN B93 ...175 H3
  REDE B98 ....202 B3
Nairn Cl HLGN/YWD B28 ...126 D3
  NUNW/HART CV10 ....98 E3
  REDE B98 ....203 J2
Nairn Rd BLOX/PEL WS3 ...38 E1
Nally Dr BILS/COS WV14 ...66 E3
Nanaimo Wy KGSWFD DY6 ...101 L3
Nansen Rd SPARK B11 ...126 A2
  WASH/WDE B8 ....90 A6
Nantmel Gv RIDG/WDGT B32 ...123 C5
Naomi Wy ALDR WS9 ...40 F3
Napier TAM/AM/WIL B77 ...46 C2
Napier Dr TPTN/OCK DY4 ...68 A4
Napier Gn BKHL/PFLD WV2 ...50 B6
Napier Rd RLSN CV32 ...206 C4
  WSLW WS2 ....52 F6
Napier St COV CV1 ...9 K4
Napton Cl REDE B98 ...203 H4
Napton Dr RLSN CV32 ...206 E1
Napton Gn COVW CV5 ...153 C2
Napton Gv SLYOAK B29 ...123 J3
Narberth Wy COVE CV2 ...135 K6
Nares Cl RUGBYS/DCH CV22 ...186 C4
Narraway Gv TPTN/OCK DY4 ...68 B5
Narrowboat Wy DUDS DY2 ...84 B8
Narrow La BRWNH WS8 ...26 E6
  RMSLY B62 ....104 C3
  WSLW WS2 ....52 F6
Naseby Cl COVS CV3 ...156 D5
  REDE B98 ....195 H7
Naseby Dr HALE B63 ...121 H3
Naseby Rd RUGBYS/DCH CV22 ...187 G4
  SOLH B91 ....127 M7
  WASH/WDE B8 ....90 D4
Nash Av DUNHL/THL/PER WV6 ...48 D3
Nash Cl BLKHTH/ROWR B65 ...104 A4
Nash Cft CHWD/FDBR/MGN B37 ...111 F5
Nashe Cl KIDD DY10 ...139 G8
Nash La HAG/WOL DY9 ...141 H6
Nash Rd BRLYHL DY5 ...202 F4
Nash Sq PBAR/PBCH B42 ...89 H1
Nash Wk SMTHWK B66 ...88 A4
Nately Gv SLYOAK B29 ...123 M2
Nathan Cl MGN/WHC B75 ...57 G5
Naunton Cl SLYOAK B29 ...123 M6
Naunton Rd WSLW WS2 ...52 B5
Navenby Cl BRLYHL DY5 ...102 E1
Navigation La DARL/WED WS10 ...69 K3
Navigation St CBHAMW B1 ...6 E5
  WOLV WV1 ....3 J3
  WSLW WS2 ....52 F3
Navigation Wy CNCK/NC WS11 ...16 E3
  COVN CV6 ....134 E5
  WBROM B70 ....86 D3
  WSNGN B18 ....88 D8
Nayland Cft HLGN/YWD B28 ...126 E4
Nayler Cl RUGBYN/HIL CV21 ...161 G7
Naylor Cl KIDDW DY11 ...163 M2
Naylors Gv SEDG DY3 ...84 C3
Neachell Ct WNSFLD WV11 * ...51 J4
Neachells La WLNHL WV13 ...37 H9
  WNSFLD WV11 ....37 H9
Neachless Av WMBN WV5 ...64 D6
Neachley Gv STETCH B33 ...109 K1
Neal Ct COVE CV2 * ...116 C8
Neale Av COVW CV5 ...132 C4
Neale St CRTAM B79 ...31 K7
Neander CRTAM B79 ...31 K7
Nearhill Rd HWK/WKHTH B38 ...144 F5
Near Lands Cl RIDG/WDGT B32 ...122 F3
Nearmoor Rd BKDE/SHDE B34 ...91 M5
Neasden Gv KGSTG B44 ...72 B8
Neath Rd BLOX/PEL WS3 ...38 D5
Neath Wy BLOX/PEL WS3 ...38 D5
  SEDG DY3 ....66 B2

Nebsworth Cl SHLY B90 ...127 H8
Nechells Park Rd VAUX/NECH B7 ...90 A6
Nechells Pkwy VAUX/NECH B7 * ...7 J4
Nechells Pl VAUX/NECH B7 ...89 M7
Needham St VAUX/NECH B7 ...90 A6
Needhill Cl DOR/KN B93 ...149 K7
Needle Mill La REDE B98 ...194 C7
Needlers End La RCOVN/BALC/EX CV7 ...151 K7
Needless House STUD B80 * ...203 J8
Neilston St RLSS CV31 ...206 E6
Nelson Av BILS/COS WV14 ...51 G6
  WWCK CV34 ....205 L4
Nelson Dr HEDN WS12 ...12 D3
Nelson La WWCK CV34 ...205 L5
Nelson Rd AST/WIT B6 ...89 L4
  DUDN DY1 ....84 F4
  STRPT DY13 ....188 F4
Nelson St CBHAMW B1 ...6 B4
  COV CV1 ....9 K2
  HHTH/SAND B71 ....69 J3
  OLDBY B69 ....86 F7
  WLNHL WV13 ....51 M2
Nelson Wy RUGBYS/DCH CV22 ...186 A4
Nemesia TAM/AM/WIL B77 ...46 C2
Nene Cl COVS CV3 ...156 B6
  STRBR DY8 ....119 L1
Nene Wy CBROM B36 ...92 D5
Neptune St TPTN/OCK DY4 ...67 M3
Nesbit Gv BORD B9 ...108 F2
Nesfield Cl HWK/WKHTH B38 ...145 G4
Nesfield Gv HIA/OLT B92 ...129 M6
Nesscliffe Gv ERDW/GRVHL B23 ...72 B6
Neston Gv STETCH B33 ...109 H3
Netheravon Cl ALE/KHTH/YWD B14 ...146 B4
Nether Beacon LICH WS13 ...20 D4
Netherbridge Av LICHS WS14 ...21 J5
Netherby Rd SEDG DY3 ...66 C5
Nethercote Gdns SHLY B90 ...147 J2
Netherdale Cl CSCFLD/WYGN B72 ...73 G6
Netherdale Rd ALE/KHTH/YWD B14 ...146 B4
Netherend Cl HALE B63 ...102 E6
Netherend La HALE B63 ...102 E6
Netherend Sq HALE B63 ...102 E6
Netherfield REDE B98 ...202 E5
Netherfield Gdns ACCN B27 ...126 F2
Nethergate SEDG DY3 ...66 D8
Nether La BNTWD WS7 ...19 H5
Nethermill Rd COVN CV6 ...133 L8
Nethersole St POL/KGSB/FAZ B78 ...47 L3
Netherstone Gv FOAKS/STRLY B74 ...42 D8
Netherstowe LICH WS13 ...21 G3
Netherstowe La LICH WS13 ...21 G3
Netherton Gv STETCH B33 ...110 A2
Netherton La BEWD DY12 ...163 G3
Netherwood Cl SOLH B91 ...127 J7
Netherwood La DOR/KN B93 ...176 E6
Nethy Dr DUNHL/THL/PER WV6 ...34 F8
Netley Gv SPARK B11 ...126 A2
Netley Rd BLOX/PEL WS3 ...38 C5
Netley Wy BLOX/PEL WS3 ...38 C5
Nevada Wy CHWD/FDBR/MGN B37 ...111 G4
Neve Av WOLVN WV10 ...36 D4
Nevill Cl RLSS CV31 ...206 E1
Neville Av ETTPK/GDPK/PENN WV4 ...50 B7
  KIDDW DY11 ....164 B2
Neville Ct REDE B98 ...194 C7
Neville Cl WWCK CV34 * ...205 J3
Neville Gv WWCK CV34 ...205 K4
Neville Rd CBROM B36 ...92 A2
  ERDW/GRVHL B23 ....90 A2
  SHLY B90 ....147 K4
Neville St TAM/AM/WIL B77 ...46 C2
Nevill St CRTAM B79 ...31 L8
Nevin Gv PBAR/PBCH B42 ...71 G8
Nevis Ct BDMR/CCFT WV3 ...49 J5
Nevis Gv SHHTH WV12 ...37 M4
Nevison Gv GTB/HAM B43 ...70 F1
Newall Cl RUGBY CV23 ...161 J8
Newark Cft LGN/SDN/BHAMAIR B26 ...109 M7
Newark Rd DUDS DY2 ...103 H3
  SHHTH WV12 ....38 A6
New Ash Dr COVW CV5 ...132 C6
Newbank Gv BORD B9 ...108 F2
New Barns La LICHS WS14 ...41 M1
New Bartholomew St DIG/EDG B5 ...7 H5
New Birmingham Rd OLDBY B69 ...85 L4
Newbold Cl COVS CV3 ...156 D4
  DOR/KN B93 ....149 K8
Newbold Pl VAUX/NECH B7 ...89 M8
Newbold Rd RUGBYN/HIL CV21 ...160 C2
Newbolds Rd WOLVN WV10 ...36 E7
Newbold Ter RLSN CV32 ...206 E5
Newbold Ter East RLSN CV32 ...206 F4
Newbolt Rd BILS/COS WV14 ...51 J7
Newbolt St WSYBK/YTR WS5 ...53 J8
New Bond St BORD B9 ...107 M4
  DUDS DY2 ....85 H5
Newborough Gv HLGN/YWD B28 ...147 K1
Newborough Rd HLGN/YWD B28 ...147 K1
  SHLY B90 ....147 K1
Newbourne Hl ALVE B48 ...194 C1
Newbridge Av DUNHL/THL/PER WV6 ...49 J2
Newbridge Crs DUNHL/THL/PER WV6 ...49 J1
Newbridge Gdns DUNHL/THL/PER WV6 ...49 J1
Newbridge Ms DUNHL/THL/PER WV6 * ...49 K1
Newbridge Rd BORD B9 ...108 F2
  KGSWFD DY6 ....83 C5
Newbridge St DUNHL/THL/PER WV6 ...49 K1
New Brook St RLSN CV32 ...206 C5
New Buildings COV CV1 ...8 F4
  WOLVN WV10 * 22 A4
Newburn Cft RIDG/WDGT B32 ...104 F5
Newbury Cl BRGRVW B61 ...168 F4
  GTWY WS6 ....24 D2
  RLSS CV31 ....207 G7
  RMSLY B62 ....122 B2
Newbury La OLDBY B69 ...85 M7
Newbury Rd CNCK/NC WS11 ...17 L8
  STRBR DY8 ....100 E5
  WOLVN WV10 ....36 A3
Newby Cl COVS CV3 ...155 J7
Newby Gv CHWD/FDBR/MGN B37 ...110 F1

New Canal St *DIG/EDG* B5 ....7 J6
Newcastle Cft *CVALE* B35 ....92 A2
New Church Rd
  SCFLD/BOLD B73 ....72 E5
New Cl *RWWCK/WEL* CV35 ......204 E7
New College Cl *WSL* WS1 ....5 K9
Newcombe Rd *COVW* CV6 ....8 B3
  HDSW B21 ....88 B3
  BNTWD WS7 ....19 G5
Newcomen Dr *TPTN/OCK* DY4 ....85 K2
Newcomen Rd *BDWTH* CV12 ......116 B6
New Cottages
  ETTPK/GDPK/PENN WV4 * 48 B7
  NUNW/HART CV10 * 98 D2
Newcott Cl *COVEN* WV9 ....35 K3
New Coventry Rd
  LGN/SDN/BHAMAIR B26 ....109 K8
New Cft *LOZ/NWT* B19 ....89 J6
Newcroft Gv
  LGN/SDN/BHAMAIR B26 ....109 J6
New Cross Av *WNSFLD* WV11 ....50 F1
New Cross St *DARL/WED* WS10 ..52 D8
  TPTN/OCK DY4 ....67 J8
Newdegate Rd *BDWTH* CV12 .....116 E1
Newdegate St *NUN* CV11 ....99 G1
Newdigate *RLSS* CV31 ....207 G3
Newdigate Rd *COVN* CV6 ....134 D8
  MGN/WHC B75 ....73 L1
New Dudley Rd *KGSWFD* DY6 ....83 G5
Newells Dr *TPTN/OCK* DY4 ....68 B6
Newells Rd
  LGN/SDN/BHAMAIR B26 ....109 L6
New England *RMSLY* B62 ....104 C6
New England Cl *OLDBY* B69 ....86 C4
Newent Cl *REDE* B98 ....203 L2
  SHHTH WV12 ....37 L7
Newey Av *BDWTH* CV12 ....116 B6
Newey Cl *RBRY* B45 ....143 L7
Newey Dr *KNWTH* CV8 ....197 L3
Newey Rd *COVE* CV2 ....156 B1
  HLGN/YWD B28 ....37 L5
  WNSFLD WV11 ....37 L5
New Farm Rd *HAG/WOL* DY9 .....102 A8
Newfield Cl *KNWTH* CV8 ....197 M2
  SOLH B91 ....128 B7
  WSLW WS2 ....39 C8
Newfield Crs *HALE* B63 ....103 L8
Newfield Dr *KGSWFD* DY6 ....101 J1
Newfield Gdns *HAG/WOL* DY9 ...140 E1
  HALE B63 ....103 L8
Newfield Pl *HAG/WOL* DY9 ....140 E1
Newfield Rd *COV* CV1 ....134 A8
  HAG/WOL DY9 ....140 E1
  OLDBY B69 ....86 B4
New Forest Rd *BLOX/PEL* WS3 ....39 J7
Newgale Wk *BILS/COS* WV14 ......207 D6
New Gas St *WBROM* B70 ....68 E7
Newgate St *BNTWD* WS7 ....19 K6
New Green Pk *COVE* CV2 * 135 H6
Newhall Cl *CBHAMNW* B3 * 6 C3
Newhall Crs *CNCK/NC* WS11 ....16 C3
New Hall Dr *WALM/CURD* B76 .....73 H1
Newhall Farm Cl
  WALM/CURD B76 ....73 H1
Newhall Gdns *CNCK/NC* WS11 * ..16 D3
Newhall Hl *CBHAMNW* B1 ....6 C3
Newhall Pl *DARL/WED* WS10 * 68 E2
  COVE CV2 ....135 H6
New Hall St *WLNHL* WV13 ....51 L3
Newham Gn *NUNW/HART* CV10 ...80 A6
New Hampton Rd East
  WOLV WV1 ....2 C2
Newhaven Cl *COVN* CV6 ....133 J7
  VAUX/NECH B7 ....7 L1
Newhay Cft *LOZ/NWT* B19 ....89 G6
New Hayes Rd *HEDN* WS12 ....18 A1
New Heath Cl *WNSFLD* WV11 ......36 F8
New Henry St *LGLYGN/QTN* B68 104 E1
Newhope Cl *EDG* B15 ....107 H5
New Hope Rd *SMTHWK* B66 ....106 E4
New Horse Rd *GTWY* WS6 ....24 C2
Newhouse Cft
  RCOVN/BALC/EX CV7 ....151 M7
Newhouse Farm Cl
  WALM/CURD B76 ....73 K2
Newhouse La *BRGRVW* B61 ....190 B6
Newick Av *FOAKS/STRLY* B74 ......55 H4
Newick Gv
  ALE/KHTH/YWD B14 * 125 G8
Newick St *DUDS* DY2 ....103 G1
Newington Cl *COVN* CV6 ....133 H7
Newington Rd
  CHWD/FDBR/MGN B37 ....110 F5
New Inn La *LOZ/NWT* B19 ....89 H4
New Inns Cl *HDSW* B21 ....88 B5
New Inns La *RBRY* B45 ....143 J4
New John St *AST/WIT* B6 ....89 J8
  RMSLY B62 ....104 C6
New John St West *LOZ/NWT* B19 88 F7
New King St *DUDS* DY2 * 85 G4
Newland Cl *REDE* B98 ....202 F6
  RUSH/SHEL WS4 ....40 A3
Newland Gdns *CDYHTH* B64 ......103 J5
Newland Gv *DUDS* DY2 ....84 D6
Newland La
  RCOVN/BALC/EX CV7 ....115 M6
  COV CV1 ....134 B8
  RLSN CV32 ....207 H3
  SMHTH B10 ....108 D4
Newlands Cl *KIDDW* DY11 ....138 A4
  PENK ST19 ....10 D6
  WLNHL WV13 ....51 L4
Newlands Ct *HEDN* WS12 ....17 J5
Newlands Dr *RMSLY* B62 ....104 C6
Newlands La
  CHWD/FDBR/MGN B37 ....110 E7
  CNCK/NC WS11 ....17 G6
  BVILLE B30 ....124 F6
  DOR/KN B93 ....162 A1
Newland St *RUGBYS/DCH* CV22 186 C2
Newlands Wk
  LGLYGN/QTN B68 * 104 F1
New Landywood La
  WNSFLD WV11 ....24 C7
Newlyn Cl *LICHS* WS14 ....21 H6
  NUN CV11 ....99 K1
Newlyn Rd *CDYHTH* B64 ....103 H4
  NFLD/LBR B31 ....144 D2
Newman Av
  ETTPK/GDPK/PENN WV4 ....66 D1
Newman Cl *BDWTH* CV12 ....116 D1
Newman College Cl
  RIDG/WDGT B32 ....123 G5
Newman Pl *BILS/COS* WV14 ....68 B5
Newman Rd *ERDE/BCHGN* B24 ....90 D1
  TPTN/OCK DY4 ....68 A4
  WOLV WV10 ....36 E4
Newmans Cl *SMTHWK* B66 * 106 A1
Newman Wy *RBRY* B45 ....143 L6

Newmarket Cl *COVN* CV6 ....134 F1
  DUNHL/THL/PER WV6 ....49 M1
Newmarket Rd *CNCK/NC* WS11 ...17 L8
New Market St *CBHAMNW* B3 * 6 E4
Newmarsh Rd *WALM/CURD* B76 ..73 L7
New Meadow Cl *NFLD/LBR* B31 .144 F1
New Meadow Rd *REDE* B98 ....202 F2
New Meeting St *OLDBY* B69 ....86 B6
New Mill La *WALM/CURD* B76 ....54 A7
New Mill St *DUDS* DY2 ....85 H4
Newmore Gdns *DSYBK/YTR* WS5 54 A7
New Moseley Rd *BHTH/HG* B12 .107 H5
Newnham Rd *COV* CV1 ....134 D8
Newnham Ri *SHLY* B90 ....148 D3
  LDYWD/EDGR B16 ....106 D1
  RLSN CV32 ....206 F2
New Penkridge Rd
  CNCK/NC WS11 ....15 M3
New Pool Rd *CDYHTH* B64 ....102 F5
Newport Rd *BHTH/HG* B12 ....125 L1
  CBROM B36 ....91 K5
  COVN CV6 ....134 B4
Newport St *WOLV* WV10 ....50 C1
  WSL WS1 ....4 C6
Newquay Cl *DSYBK/YTR* WS5 ......54 C6
  NUN CV11 ....81 K8
Newquay Rd *DSYBK/YTR* WS5 .....54 B6
New Rd *ALDR* WS9 ....40 E8
  BDWTH CV12 ....115 K3
  BEWD DY12 ....17 H8
  BNTWD WS7 ....18 F7
  BRGRVE B60 ....191 L4
  BRGRVW B61 ....168 C3
  BRWNH WS8 ....26 D6
  COVN CV6 ....133 K4
  CRTAM B79 ....33 J4
  CSHL/WTROR B46 ....92 F2
  DUDS DY2 ....85 G6
  DUNHL/THL/PER WV6 ....49 J1
  HALE B63 ....121 M1
  HLYWD B47 ....146 D5
  KIDD DY10 ....138 C8
  KIDD DY10 ....139 G2
  KIDD DY10 ....164 C1
  LICHS WS14 ....28 D1
  PENK ST19 ....10 C4
  RBRY B45 ....143 J4
  RCOVN/BALC/EX CV7 ....115 M7
  SOLH B91 ....149 G2
  STRBR DY8 ....101 L8
  TAM/AM/WIL B77 ....46 D6
  TPTN/OCK DY4 ....68 B7
  WLNHL WV13 ....51 H5
  WNSFLD WV11 ....22 B4
  WOLVN WV10 ....23 C5
New Rw *POL/KGSB/FAZ* B78 * 45 J8
New Rowley Rd *DUDS* DY2 ....85 J6
Newsholme Cl *WWCK* CV34 ....205 J4
New Spring St North
  WSNGN B18 ....88 E8
Newstead *CRTAM* B79 ....31 H1
Newstead Cl *NUN* CV11 ....99 K3
Newstead Gv *KGSTG* B44 ....79 J3
Newstead Wy *COVS* CV3 ....156 F4
New St *ATHST* CV9 ....62 A4
  BDMR/CCFT WV3 ....49 H7
  BDWTH CV12 ....117 G3
  BKHL/PFLD WV2 ....50 E7
  BLOX/PEL WS3 ....38 F4
  BNTWD WS7 ....18 C6
  BRLYHL DY5 ....102 A1
  CBROM B36 ....91 M5
  CNCK/NC WS11 ....16 B7
  CNCK/NC WS11 ....16 C4
  DARL/WED WS10 ....52 B7
  DUDN DY1 ....85 G4
  ERDW/GRVHL B23 ....72 D8
  ETTPK/GDPK/PENN WV4 ....50 C3
  GTWY WS6 ....24 E4
  HEDN WS12 ....17 G1
  KGSWFD DY6 ....83 G5
  KGSWFD DY6 ....101 H1
  KNWTH CV8 ....179 K7
  POL/KGSB/FAZ B78 ....45 M5
  POL/KGSB/FAZ B78 ....47 H5
  POL/KGSB/FAZ B78 ....47 L8
  RBRY B45 ....143 J5
  RLSN CV32 ....199 J8
  RLSS CV31 ....206 E6
  RUGBYS/DCH CV22 ....186 C2
  RUSH/SHEL WS4 ....39 M6
  RUSH/SHEL WS4 ....40 B4
  SEDG DY3 ....84 A2
  SMTHWK B66 ....87 M7
  STRBR DY8 ....101 H5
  STRBR DY8 ....101 L8
  STRPT DY13 ....188 D2
  TAM/AM/WIL B77 ....46 A5
  TAM/AM/WIL B77 ....46 C2
  TPTN/OCK DY4 ....67 J8
  WBROM B70 ....68 E6
  WBROM B70 ....87 H2
  WLNHL WV13 ....51 J4
  WNSFLD WV11 ....37 L2
  WSL WS1 ....5 H6
  WWCK CV34 ....205 J7
New St North *HHTH/SAND* B71 ....87 H2
New Summer St *LOZ/NWT* B19 * 6 F1
New Swan La *WBROM* B70 ....68 B8
Newton Cl *BEWD* DY12 ....162 D1
  COVE CV2 ....135 K6
  GTB/HAM B43 ....70 A5
  NUNW/HART CV10 ....79 M3
  REDE B98 ....202 D7
Newton Gdns *GTB/HAM* B43 ....69 M5
Newton Gv *SLYOAK* B29 * 124 D3
Newton La *CRTAM* B79 ....33 L2
  RRUGBY CV23 ....161 C2
Newton Manor Cl *GTB/HAM* B43 70 B5
Newton Manor La
  RRUGBY CV23 ....161 G5
Newton Pl *WSLW* WS2 ....38 F7
  WSNGN B18 ....88 D6
Newton Rd *BRGRVE* B60 ....191 L6
  DOR/KN B93 ....149 M6
  GTB/HAM B43 ....70 A5
  LICH WS13 ....20 D3
  RRUGBY CV23 ....161 L5
  SPARK B11 ....107 M8
  WSLW WS2 ....38 F7
Newton Sq *GTB/HAM* B43 ....70 C4
Newton St *CBHAMNE* B4 ....7 H3
  HHTH/SAND B71 ....69 J4
New Town *BRLYHL* DY5 ....101 K4
  DUDS DY2 ....103 H4
Newtown Dr *LOZ/NWT* B19 ....6 A1
Newtown La *CDYHTH* B64 ....103 H4

HAG/WOL DY9 ....142 B5
  RBRY B45 ....143 G4
Newtown Middleway
  AST/WIT B6 ....89 J8
Newtown Rd *BDWTH* CV12 ....116 E3
  NUN CV11 ....81 G8
New Town Rw *LOZ/NWT* B19 ....89 J7
Newtown St *CDYHTH* B64 ....103 H3
New Union St *COV* CV1 ....8 F6
New Village *DUDS* DY2 ....103 G4
New Vls *WNSFLD* WV11 * 36 F8
New Wood Cl *KINVER* DY7 ....101 G5
New Wood Gv *ALDR* WS9 ....40 G5
New Wood La *KIDD* DY10 ....139 L5
Niall Cl *EDG* B15 ....106 D5
Nibletts Hl *BRGRVW* B61 ....167 M6
Nicholas Everton Cl
  KNWTH CV8 ....157 L8
Nicholas Rd *FOAKS/STRLY* B74 ...55 J5
Nicholas Wk *WALM/CURD* B76 .....74 F7
Nicholds Cl *BILS/COS* WV14 ....66 F4
Nicholls Fold *WNSFLD* WV11 ....37 H5
Nicholls Rd *TPTN/OCK* DY4 ....67 J4
Nicholls St *COV* CV1 ....9 L2
  WBROM B70 ....87 H3
Nichols Wy *HEDN* WS12 ....17 J4
Nichols Cl *HIA/OLT* B92 ....128 D6
Nickson Rd *TLHL/CAN* CV4 ....153 K4
Nigel Av *NFLD/LBR* B31 ....123 L8
Nigel Rd *DUDN* DY1 ....84 D3
  WASH/WDE B8 ....90 C7
Nightingale *TAM/AM/WIL* B77 .....46 C3
Nightingale Av *CBROM* B36 ....92 E5
Nightingale Cl *ATHST* CV9 ....63 J4
  ERDW/GRVHL B23 ....72 A6
  HEDN WS12 ....17 H5
Nightingale Crs *BRLYHL* DY5 .....102 B6
  TPTN/OCK DY4 ....68 A8
Nightingale La *COVW* CV5 ....154 B5
Nightingale Pl *BILS/COS* WV14 ...51 H5
Nightingale Wk *BNTWD* WS7 ....19 K6
Nightjar Gv *ERDW/GRVHL* B23 ....72 A7
Nighwood Dr *FOAKS/STRLY* B74 ..55 K6
Nijon Cl *HDSW* B21 ....88 B5
Nimbus *TAM/AM/WIL* B77 ....60 B1
Nimmings Cl *NFLD/LBR* B31 ......144 D7
Nimmings Rd *RMSLY* B62 ....104 B4
Nina Cl *STRPT* DY13 ....188 F2
Nineacres Dr
  CHWD/FDBR/MGN B37 ....110 E3
Nine Days Cl *REDE* B98 ....202 F7
Nine Elms La *WOLV* WV10 ....50 C1
Ninefoot La *TAM/AM/WIL* B77 .....46 D6
Nine Leasowes *SMTHWK* B66 .....87 J1
Nine Locks Rdg *BRLYHL* DY5 .....102 B3
Nineveh Av *HDSW* B21 ....88 C6
Nineveh Rd *HDSW* B21 ....88 C6
Ninfield Rd *ACGN* B27 ....126 E1
Ninian Wy *TAM/AM/WIL* B77 ....46 C7
Nirvana Cl *CNCK/NC* WS11 ....16 A3
Nith Pl *DUDN* DY1 ....84 F3
Niton Rd *NUNW/HART* CV10 ....81 H7
Niven Cl *COVW* CV5 ....132 E7
Noble Cl *WWCK* CV34 ....205 H5
Noble Dr *RUGBYS/DCH* CV22 ....185 L5
Nocke Rd *WNSFLD* WV11 ....37 K4
Nock St *TPTN/OCK* DY4 * 68 A6
Noddy Cl *HDSW* B21 ....88 A5
Noddy Park Rd *ALDR* WS9 ....40 F6
Nod Ri *COVW* CV5 ....153 M2
Noel Av *BHTH/HG* B12 ....107 H5
Noele Gordon Gdns *WSL* WS1 * ...4 E7
Noel Rd *LDYWD/EDGR* B16 ....106 B3
Nolan Cl *COVN* CV6 ....116 B8
Nolton Cl *GTB/HAM* B43 ....70 C4
No Name Rd *BNTWD* WS7 ....18 C6
Nooklands Cft *STECH* B33 ....109 L3
The Nook *BRLYHL* DY5 ....83 M8
  GTWY WS6 ....24 D1
  NUN CV11 ....99 J3
Noonan Cl *REDW* B97 ....201 M3
Noose Crs *WLNHL* WV13 ....51 J3
Noose La *WLNHL* WV13 ....51 K2
Nora Rd *SPARK* B11 ....126 A2
Norbiton Rd *KGSTG* B44 ....71 L5
Norbreck Cl *GTB/HAM* B43 ....70 D5
Norbury Av *BLOX/PEL* WS3 ....39 K2
Norbury Cl *REDE* B98 ....194 F6
Norbury Crs
  ETTPK/GDPK/PENN WV4 ....66 D1
Norbury Dr *BRLYHL* DY5 ....102 B4
Norbury Gv *HIA/OLT* B92 ....127 L2
Norbury Rd *BILS/COS* WV14 ....51 K7
  KGSTG B44 ....71 K2
  WBROM B70 ....68 D4
  WOLVN WV10 ....36 D7
Norcombe Gv *SHLY* B90 ....148 E8
Nordic Drift *COVE* CV2 ....135 L7
Nordley Rd *WNSFLD* WV11 ....37 G3
Norfolk Av *HHTH/SAND* B71 ....69 H6
Norfolk Cl *BVILLE* B30 ....124 F6
Norfolk Crs *ALDR* WS9 ....40 F5
  NUNW/HART CV10 ....98 C2
Norfolk Dr *DARL/WED* WS10 ....69 H1
  TAM/AM/WIL B77 ....46 C2
Norfolk Gdns *MGN/WHC* B75 ......56 D5
Norfolk New Rd *WSLW* WS2 ....52 C1
Norfolk Pl *WSLW* WS2 ....39 M8
Norfolk Rd *BDMR/CCFT* WV3 * 2 B5
  DUDS DY2 ....84 E6
  EDG B15 ....106 B5
  ERDW/GRVHL B23 ....72 D8
  LGLYGN/QTN B68 ....104 F6
  MGN/WHC B75 ....57 G6
  RBRY B45 ....143 K4
  STRBR DY8 ....101 K4
Norfolk Ter *TLHL/CAN* CV4 ....154 A6
  RLSN CV32 ....206 D1
Norfolk Tower *WSNGN* B18 ....88 E8
Norgrave Rd *HIA/OLT* B92 ....128 A3
Norgrove La *REDW* B97 ....201 G6
Norland Rd *ACGN* B27 ....127 G4
Norley Gv *MOS/BIL* B13 ....126 A6
Norman Ashman Coppice
  COVS CV3 ....157 G6
Norman Av *COVE* CV2 ....135 K4
  NUN CV11 ....98 D1
  RIDG/WDGT B32 ....105 J6
Norman Cl *CRTAM* B79 ....31 H2
Norman Pl *WWCK* CV34 ....205 K1
Norman Rd
  RWWCK/WEL CV35 ....204 E6
Normandy Rd
  BFLD/HDSWWD B20 ....89 H4
Norman Place Rd *COVN* CV6 .....133 H4
Norman St *DSYBK/YTR* WS5 ....54 A6
  NFLD/LBR B31 ....144 E2
  PENK ST19 ....10 D5
  RUGBYN/HIL CV21 ....160 D7
Norman Ter *BLKHTH/ROWR* B65 104 A1

Normanton Av
  LGN/SDN/BHAMAIR B26 ....110 B8
Norrington Gv *NFLD/LBR* B31 ...144 A1
Norrington Rd *NFLD/LBR* B31 ....144 A1
Norris Dr *STECH* B33 ....109 J1
Norris Rd *AST/WIT* B6 ....89 K4
Norris Wy *MGN/WHC* B75 ....57 H3
Northampton St *WSNGN* B18 ....6 C1
Northam Wk
  DUNHL/THL/PER WV6 ....49 M1
Northanger Rd *ACGN* B27 ....126 F3
North Av *BDWTH* CV12 ....117 H3
  BHAMNEC B40 ....111 K8
  COVE CV2 ....155 L2
  WNSFLD WV11 ....37 G7
Northbourne Dr *NUN* CV11 ....99 L6
North Brook Rd *COVS* CV5 ....133 H5
Northbrook Rd *SHLY* B90 ....127 G8
Northbrook St
  LDYWD/EDGR B16 ....106 D1
North Cl *RLSN* CV32 ....199 J8
Northcote Rd
  RUGBYS/DCH CV22 ....186 D3
  STECH B33 ....109 H1
Northcote St *RLSS* CV31 ....206 F6
Northcote Wk *ATHST* CV9 ....63 H5
Northcroft Rd *BILS/COS* WV14 .....63 H8
  DUDS DY2 ....103 H1
North Crs *WOLVN* WV10 ....22 F6
Northdown Rd *SOLH* B91 ....148 A6
North Dr *BFLD/HDSWWD* B20 ......88 F5
  BHAMNEC B40 ....111 K8
  MGN/WHC B75 ....57 G7
Northey Rd *COVN* CV6 ....134 B5
Northfield Cl *REDE* B98 ....194 F8
Northfield Gv *BDMR/CCFT* WV3 ..49 G6
Northfield Rd *BVILLE* B30 ....145 H1
  COV CV1 ....9 K6
  DUDS DY2 ....85 H8
  HRBN B17 ....123 L2
Northfields Wy *BRWNH* WS8 ....26 B6
Northgate *ALDR* WS9 ....40 E5
  CDYHTH B64 ....103 H5
North Ga *HRBN* B17 ....106 A6
Northgate St *KIDDW* DY11 ....163 L1
Northgate St *WWCK* CV34 ....205 J6
Northgate Wy *ALDR* WS9 ....40 E5
North Gn
  ETTPK/GDPK/PENN WV4 ....49 H7
North Holme *BORD* B9 ....108 A3
Northland Rd *SHLY* B90 ....148 C5
Northlands Rd *MOS/BIL* B13 ......125 L4
Northleach Av
  ALE/KHTH/YWD B14 ....146 B3
Northleach Cl *REDE* B98 ....194 F8
Northleigh Rd *WASH/WDE* B8 .....90 E7
Northolt Dr *CVALE* B35 ....92 C1
Northolt Gv *PBAR/PCH* B42 ....70 D1
North Oval *WOLV* WV10 ....36 C8
Northover Cl *COVEN* WV9 ....35 J4
North Park Rd *ERDW/GRVHL* B23 89 M2
North Pathway *HRBN* B17 ....105 M6
North Rd *BFLD/HDSWWD* B20 ......89 J3
  BNTWD WS7 ....18 D4
  BRLYHL DY5 ....102 A3
  CNCK/NC WS11 ....16 C7
  COVE CV2 ....134 E8
  DARL/WED WS10 ....68 D2
  HRBN B17 ....106 B7
  RRUGBY CV23 ....186 E2
  SMTHWK B67 ....87 K8
  WOLV WV1 ....4 F4
  WSL WS1 ....53 J7
North Roundhay *STECH* B33 .....109 L1
Northside Cl *REDE* B98 ....202 D6
Northside Dr *FOAKS/STRLY* B74 ..55 K5
North Springfield *SEDG* DY3 ....66 C4
North St *ATHST* CV9 ....63 H5
  BNTWD WS7 ....18 D4
  BRLYHL DY5 ....102 A3
  CNCK/NC WS11 ....16 C7
  COVE CV2 ....134 E8
  DARL/WED WS10 ....68 D2
  DUDS DY2 ....103 H1
  NUNW/HART CV10 ....98 D2
  RUGBYN/HIL CV21 ....186 E2
  SMTHWK B67 ....87 K8
  WOLV WV1 ....4 F4
  WSL WS1 ....53 J7
Northumberland Av
  KIDD DY10 ....164 A2
  NUNW/HART CV10 ....98 C2
Northumberland Cl
  POL/KGSB/FAZ B78 ....45 L4
  RLSN CV32 ....206 B3
Northumberland St
  VAUX/NECH B7 ....7 M3
Northvale Cl *KNWTH* CV8 ....179 M4
North Vw *RCOVN/BALC/EX* CV7 135 L4
North View Dr *BRLYHL* DY5 ....102 A3
North Villiers St *RLSN* CV32 ....206 D1
North Warwick St *BORD* B9 * 108 B4
Northway *BHAMNEC* B40 ....111 K8
  RLSS CV31 ....206 F3
  SEDG DY3 ....66 B5
North Western Ar *CBHAM* B2 ....7 G4
North Western Rd *SMTHWK* B66 ..87 K7
North Western Ter *WSNGN* B18 ...88 D6
Northwick Crs *SOLH* B91 ....148 F4
Northwood La *BEWD* DY12 ....136 D4
  BEWD DY12 ....162 F1
Northwood Park Cl
  WOLVN WV10 ....36 C3
Northwood Park Rd
  WOLVN WV10 ....36 C3
North Wood St *CBHAMNW* B1 ....6 D2
North Worcestershire Pth
  HAG/WOL DY9 ....119 M7
  HAG/WOL DY9 ....142 A1
  RBRY B45 ....169 L1
Northycote La *WOLVN* WV10 ....36 D1
Norton Cl *CRTAM* B79 ....32 A6
  ETTPK/GDPK/PENN WV4 ....65 G2
  REDE B98 ....203 H1
  SMTHWK B66 ....88 A8
Norton Crs *BILS/COS* WV14 ....67 H4
  BORD B9 ....108 F2
  DUDS DY2 ....103 H3
Norton East Rd *CNCK/NC* WS11 ..17 M8
Norton Ga *HWK/WKHTH* B38 .....145 J4
Norton Gra *CNCK/NC* WS11 ....17 K1
Norton Green La *CNCK/NC* WS11 17 M3
  DOR/KN B93 ....175 M3
Norton Hall La *CNCK/NC* WS11 ...16 E1
Norton Hill Dr *COVE* CV2 ....135 J7
Norton Leys *RUGBYS/DCH* CV22 186 D7
Norton Rd *BLOX/PEL* WS3 ....39 J5
  CSHL/WTROR B46 ....93 K5
  KIDD DY10 ....138 F7
  STRBR DY8 ....101 J4
Norton Springs *CNCK/NC* WS11 ..17 K8

Norton St *WSNGN* B18 ....88 D8
  CNCK/NC WS11 ....16 D8
Norton Ter *BVILLE* B30 ....124 E7
Nortune Cl *HWK/WKHTH* B38 ....145 H3
Norwich Av *KIDDW* DY11 ....137 K2
Norwich Cl *LICH* WS13 ....21 G2
  NUN CV11 ....81 L5
Norwich Cft
  CHWD/FDBR/MGN B37 ....110 D4
Norwich Dr *COVS* CV3 ....154 F8
  HRBN B17 ....105 K5
Norwich Rd *DUDS* DY2 ....103 H3
  WSLW WS2 ....52 F4
Norwood Av *CDYHTH* B64 ....103 K6
Norwood Gv *COVN* CV6 ....133 L4
  LOZ/NWT B19 ....88 F6
Norwood Rd *BORD* B9 ....108 C3
  BRLYHL DY5 ....102 A2
Nottingham Dr *SHHTH* WV12 ......38 A6
Nottingham Rd *LICHS* WS14 ....30 A2
Nottingham Wy *BRLYHL* DY5 .....102 D3
Nova Cft *PBAR/PBCH* B42 ....70 F4
Nova Cft *COVW* CV5 ....153 G1
Nova Scotia St *CBHAMNE* B4 ....7 J4
Nowell St *DARL/WED* WS10 ....52 C8
Nuffield Rd *COVE* CV6 ....134 E6
Nugent Cl *AST/WIT* B6 ....89 J8
Nugent Gv *SHLY* B90 ....174 B2
Nuneaton La
  MKTBGS/BARL/STKG CV13 .....81 K3
Nuneaton Rd *ATHST* CV9 ....63 L8
  BDWTH CV12 ....99 M8
  BDWTH CV12 ....116 F1
  CSHL/WTROR B46 ....95 J2
  NUNW/HART CV10 ....79 M3
  RCOVN/BALC/EX CV7 ....114 C2
Nunts La *COVN* CV6 ....133 M2
Nunts Park Av *COVN* CV6 ....133 M1
Nursery Av *ALDR* WS9 ....40 F8
  BHTH/HG B12 ....107 K8
Nursery Cl *BVILLE* B30 ....124 D8
  HAG/WOL DY9 ....119 L8
  KIDD DY11 ....137 M5
Nursery Cft *LICH* WS13 ....20 D4
Nursery Dr *PENK* ST19 ....10 C3
  WMBN WV5 ....82 D1
Nursery Gdns *CDSL* WV8 ....34 D1
  SHLY B90 ....147 J5
  STRBR DY8 ....101 K4
Nursery La *FOAKS/STRLY* B74 .....55 J3
  POL/KGSB/FAZ B78 ....50 F7
  RLSS CV31 ....206 E8
Nursery Rd *ATHST* CV9 ....63 K6
  BEWD DY12 ....162 F1
  BLOX/PEL WS3 ....38 F5
  BVILLE B30 ....124 C8
  EDG B15 ....106 B6
  LOZ/NWT B19 ....88 F7
  NUNW/HART CV10 ....79 J5
Nursery Vw Cl *ALDR* WS9 ....55 J3
Nursery Wk
  DUNHL/THL/PER WV6 ....35 H8
Nutbrook Av *TLHL/CAN* CV4 ......153 J3
Nutbush Dr *NFLD/LBR* B31 ....123 H7
Nutfield Wk *RIDG/WDGT* B32 ....105 K8
Nutgrove Cl
  ALE/KHTH/YWD B14 ....125 K6
Nuthatch Dr *BRLYHL* DY5 ....83 L1
Nuthurst *MGN/WHC* B75 ....73 L1
Nuthurst Crs *NUNW/HART* CV10 ..97 G2
Nuthurst Gv
  ALE/KHTH/YWD B14 ....146 B3
  DOR/KN B93 ....175 L1
Nuthurst La *NUNW/HART* CV10 ...97 G3
  NUNW/HART CV10 ....97 J6
Nuthurst Rd *NFLD/LBR* B31 ....144 D2
Nutley Dr *TPTN/OCK* DY4 ....68 B5
Nutmeg Gv *WSL* WS1 ....5 K3
Nuttall Gv *HDSW* B21 ....88 A6
Nymet *TAM/AM/WIL* B77 ....46 C3

O

Oakalls Av *BRGRVE* B60 ....191 M3
Oak Apple Cl *STRPT* DY13 ....188 C6
Oak Apple Rd *BRGRVW* B61 ......168 C5
Oak Av *BHTH/HG* B12 ....107 L8
  GTWY WS6 ....24 E4
  HEDN WS12 ....17 J5
  RCOVN/BALC/EX CV7 ....96 C5
  WBROM B70 ....86 F2
  WSL WS2 ....52 C2
Oak Bank *WSNGN* B18 ....88 E7
Oak Barn Rd *RMSLY* B62 ....104 B5
Oak Cl *BDWTH* CV12 ....117 G1
  HRBN B17 ....123 M3
  KINVER DY7 ....118 A2
  STRBR DY8 ....101 K5
  TPTN/OCK DY4 ....67 L4
Oak Ct *HALE* B63 ....121 K3
Oak Crs *BLOX/PEL* WS3 ....39 H7
  OLDBY B69 ....85 M4
Oak Cft *CHWD/FDBR/MGN* B37 .110 C2
Oakcroft Rd *MOS/BIL* B13 ....125 M6
Oakdale Cl *BRLYHL* DY5 ....83 L8
  LGLYGN/QTN B68 ....104 E3
Oakdale Rd *CBROM* B36 ....91 J3
  COVS CV3 ....157 G3
  LGLYGN/QTN B68 ....104 D3
Oakdene Cl *STRPT* DY13 ....188 D3
Oakdene Crs *NUNW/HART* CV10 ..81 H6
Oakdene Dr *RBRY* B45 ....170 A5
Oakdene Rd *BNTWD* WS7 ....18 E7
Oak Dr *ERDW/GRVHL* B23 ....72 A6
Oaken Covert *CDSL* WV8 ....34 C3
Oaken Dr *CDSL* WV8 ....34 A3
  SHHTH WV12 ....38 C6
  SOLH B91 ....127 M8
Oakenfield *LICH* WS13 ....20 D3
Oaken Gdns *BNTWD* WS7 ....18 E6
Oaken Gv *CDSL* WV8 ....34 C3
Oakenhayes Crs *BRWNH* WS8 .....26 A8
Oaken La *CDSL* WV8 ....34 A2
Oaken Lanes *CDSL* WV8 ....34 A2
Oaken Pk *CDSL* WV8 ....34 C4
Oakenshaw Rd *REDE* B98 ....202 D5
  SHLY B90 ....148 A3
Oakeswell St *DARL/WED* WS10 ....68 A2
Oakeywell St *DUDS* DY2 ....85 H4
Oak Farm Cl *COVS* CV3 ....85 L1
Oak Farm Rd *WALM/CURD* B76 ...73 L8
Oakfield Av *BHTH/HG* B12 ....107 L8
  DUDN DY1 ....68 F7
  KGSWFD DY6 ....83 J3
  SPARK B11 ....107 M8
Oakfield Cl *SMTHWK* B66 ....88 A7
  STRBR DY8 ....101 K4
Oakfield Dr *BLOX/PEL* WS3 ....25 L8

RBRY B45 ....170 B1
Oakfield Gdns *ATHST* CV9 ....63 J6
Oakfield Rd *BHTH/HG* B12 .....125 J1
　CDSL WV8 ....34 F3
　COVN CV6 ....133 K8
　ERDE/BCHGN B24 ....90 D2
　KIDD DY11 ....120 D3
　RUGBYS/DCH CV22 ......186 D3
　SLYOAK B29 ....124 E2
　SMTHWK B66 ....88 B4
　STRBR DY8 ....101 L4
Oakfields *SOLH* B91 ....128 F6
Oakford Dr *COVW* CV5 ......132 D7
Oak Gn *DUDN* DY1 ....66 E8
　DUNHL/THL/PER WV6 .....48 F2
Oak Gv *KIDD* DY10 ....138 E8
　NFLD/LBR B31 ....144 C4
　WNSFLD WV11 ....36 F6
Oakhall Dr *DOK/KN* B93 ....175 K1
Oakham Av *DUDS* DY2 ....85 J6
Oakham Cl *REDE* B98 ......202 E8
Oakham Crs *DUDS* DY2 ......85 J6
Oakham Dr *DUDS* DY2 ....85 K5
Oakhampton Rd *STRPT* DY13 188 D3
Oakham Rd *DUDS* DY2 ....85 K5
　HRBN B17 ....105 H6
Oak HI *BDMR/CCFT* WV3 .....49 G7
Oakhill Av *KIDD* DY10 ....164 C1
Oakhill Dr *HRBN* B17 .....105 M5
Oakhill Dr *BRLYHL* DY5 ...101 M6
Oak Hill Dr *EDG* B15 .....106 C6
Oakhill Rd *CNCK/NC* WS11 ..16 D3
Oakhurst *LICHS* WS14 ......21 G6
Oakhurst Dr *BRGRVE* B60 ..191 L2
Oakhurst Rd *ACGN* B27 ....126 F4
　CSCFLD/WYGN B72 ....72 F5
Oakland Cl *SOLH* B91 .....149 L1
Oakland Dr *SEDG* DY3 ......83 M3
Oakland Gv *BRGRVW* B61 ...191 L1
Oakland Rd *BLOX/PEL* WS3 ..39 J6
　HDSW B21 ....88 C2
　MOS/BIL B13 ....125 L2
Oaklands *NFLD/LBR* B31 ...144 D1
　RMSLY B62 ....122 E1
　WALM/CURD B76 ....74 F8
Oaklands Av *HRBN* B17 ....105 J6
Oaklands Cl *HEDN* WS12 ....12 A7
Oaklands Cft *WALM/CURD* B76 .73 M6
Oaklands Dr *BFLD/HDSWWD* B20 .88 D3
Oaklands Gn *BILS/COS* WV14 .51 L5
Oaklands Rd *BDMR/CCFT* WV3 ..2 C9
　FOAKS/STRLY B74 ....56 F5
The Oaklands *BDMR/CCFT* WV3 *..2 F7
　CHWD/FDBR/MGN B37 ....110 C6
　KIDD DY10 ....138 E6
　TLHL/CAN CV4 ....153 L3
Oaklands Wy *BLOX/PEL* WS3 ..39 M2
　NFLD/LBR B31 ....144 A4
Oak La *BNTWD* WS7 ....18 D4
　COVW CV5 ....132 A5
　HIA/OLT B92 ....150 F3
　KGSWFD DY6 ....83 J4
　PENK ST19 ....15 G5
　WBROM B70 ....86 F2
Oaklea Dr *CDYHTH* B64 ....103 K3
Oak Leaf Dr *MOS/BIL* B13 .125 L2
Oak Leasow *RIDG/WDGT* B32 .122 F1
Oakleigh *NFLD/LBR* B31 ...145 G3
Oakleigh Dr *CDSL* WV8 .....34 C2
　SEDG DY3 ....66 A6
Oak Leigh Rd *STRBR* DY8 ..119 L3
Oakleighs *STRBR* DY8 .....101 C4
Oakleigh Wk *KNWTH* CV8 ...177 K4
Oakley Av *ALDR* WS9 ....60 E8
　TPTN/OCK DY4 ....67 K4
Oakley Cl *PENK* ST19 ......10 E4
Oakley Gv
　ETTPK/GDPK/PENN WV4 ...49 H8
Oakley Rd *BVILLE* B30 ....124 F8
　ETTPK/GDPK/PENN WV4 ...49 H8
　SMHTH B10 ....108 A4
Oak Leys *BDMR/CCFT* WV3 ...49 G4
Oakley Wood Dr *SOLH* B91 .149 J1
Oakly Rd *REDW* B97 ....202 B2
Oakmeadow Cl
　LGN/SDN/BHAMAIR B26 ...109 H8
　STETCH B33 ....110 B3
Oakmeadow Wy
　ERDE/BCHGN B24 ....91 H2
Oakmoor Rd *COVN* CV6 .....134 C2
Oakmount Cl *BLOX/PEL* WS3 .39 K4
Oakmount Rd *FOAKS/STRLY* B74 .55 L4
Oak Park Rd *STRBR* DY8 ...101 K4
Oak Pl *RLSS* CV31 ....206 F6
Oakridge Cl *REDE* B98 ....195 G6
　SHHTH WV12 ....52 A1
Oakridge Dr *GTWY* WS6 .....24 C3
Oakridge Rd *RLSN* CV32 ...207 C1
Oak Ri *CSHL/WTROR* B46 ....93 K8
Oak Rd *ALDR* WS9 ....40 E2
　BLOX/PEL WS3 ....25 K8
　BRGRVW B61 ....168 F5
　DUDN DY1 ....85 G2
　LGLYGN/QTN B68 ....105 C6
　RUSH/SHEL WS4 ....40 A5
　TPTN/OCK DY4 ....67 J7
　WBROM B70 ....86 F3
　WLNHL WV13 ....51 J3
Oakroyd Crs *NUNW/HART* CV10 .80 B6
Oaks Cnr *RLSN* CV32 *.....206 D3
Oaks Crs *BDMR/CCFT* WV3 .....2 A5
Oaks Dr *BDMR/CCFT* WV3 2
　CNCK/NC WS11 ....16 A4
　WMBN WV5 ....64 E8
　WOLVN WV10 ....22 D5
Oakslade Dr *HIA/OLT* B92 .128 C5
Oaks Pl *COVN* CV6 ....134 E2
Oaks Rd *KNWTH* CV8 ....197 J5
The Oaks *BDMR/CCFT* WV3 *....2
　BDWTH CV12 ....116 D4
　BKDE/SHDE B34 ....91 M6
　BLOX/PEL WS3 ....38 E4
　HWK/WKHTH B38 ....145 K7
　RLSN CV32 *............206 B5
　SMTHWK B67 *............87 K8
Oak St *BDMR/CCFT* WV3 *......3
　BILS/COS WV14 ....66 F6
　BRLYHL DY5 ....102 D4
　CDYHTH B64 ....103 J1
　DUDS DY2 ....103 J1
　KGSWFD DY6 ....83 G8
　RUGBYS/DCH CV22 ....186 E3
Oakthorpe Dr
　CHWD/FDBR/MGN B37 .....92 D8
Oakthorpe Gdns *OLDBY* B69 .85 L3
Oak Tree Av *COVS* CV3 ....154 E4
　REDW B97 ....201 M4
Oak Tree Cl *DOR/KN* B93 ..175 J1
　RLSN CV32 ....206 A2
Oaktree Cl *ALVE* B48 ......70 E6
　POL/KGSB/FAZ B78 ....60 D1
Oak Tree Crs *RMSLY* B62 ..104 D7
Oak Tree Gdns *STRBR* DY8 .101 L4
Oak Tree La *HLYWD* B47 ...146 F7
　SLYOAK B29 ....124 C4

Oak Tree Rd *COVS* CV3 ....156 E6
　WASH/WDE B8 ....90 B7
Oaktree Rd *DARL/WED* WS10 .68 B7
The Oak Wk *NFLD/LBR* B31 .144 E4
Oak Wy *TLHL/CAN* CV4 .....153 H3
　WALM/CURD B76 ....73 K3
Oakwood Cl *ALDR* WS9 ......40 C1
　ATHST CV9 ....28 E7
　LICHS WS14 ....28 C7
　WNSFLD WV11 ....37 M2
Oakwood Crs *DUDS* DY2 .....84 D7
Oakwood Cft *SOLH* B91 ....149 L6
Oakwood Dr
　ALE/KHTH/YWD B14 ......146 B1
　FOAKS/STRLY B74 ....55 J5
Oakwood Gv *WWCK* CV34 ....205 L4
Oakwood Rd *BEWD* DY12 ....162 D2
　BLOX/PEL WS3 ....39 J6
　HLYWD B47 ....146 E7
　SCFLD/BOLD B73 ....72 C4
　SMTHWK B67 ....105 K1
　SPARK B11 ....126 A2
Oakwoods *CNCK/NC* WS11 ....16 A5
Oakwood St *WBROM* B70 .....68 F8
Oakworth Cl *COVE* CV2 ....135 K5
Oasthouse Cl
　KGSWFD DY6 ....82 C6
Oaston Rd *CBROM* B36 ......92 B5
　NUN CV11 ....99 H1
Oatfield Cl *BNTWD* WS7 ....26 C1
Oatlands Cl *CNCK/NC* WS11 .133 M1
Oatlands Wk
　ALE/KHTH/YWD B14 ......146 A3
Oatmill Cl *DARL/WED* WS10 *.52 C8
Oban Dr *NUNW/HART* CV10 ...98 A1
Oban Rd *COVN* CV6 ....116 D8
　HIA/OLT B92 ....127 K4
Oberon Cl *NUN* CV11 ....99 L4
　RBRY B45 ....143 L3
　RUGBYS/DCH CV22 ....188 B7
Oberon Dr *SHLY* B90 ......147 L4
Occupation Rd *BRWNH* WS8 ..40 F1
　COVE CV2 ....156 A2
Occupation St *DUDN* DY1 ...84 E3
Ocean Dr *DARL/WED* WS10 ...84 A8
Ockam Cft *NFLD/LBR* B31 ..145 G3
Ocker Hill Rd *TPTN/OCK* DY4 .67 M4
O'Connor Dr *TPTN/OCK* DY4 .68 A4
Oddicombe Cft *COVS* CV3 ..155 L6
Oddingley Rd *NFLD/LBR* B31 .145 G3
Odell Crs *BLOX/PEL* WS3 ...39 G6
Odell Pl *DIG/EDG* B5 .....107 G8
Odell Rd *BLOX/PEL* WS3 ....38 F6
Odensil Gn *HIA/OLT* B92 ..127 M3
Odiham Cl *CRTAM* B79 ......32 A5
Odin Cl *HEDN* WS12 ....12 E8
Odnall La *HAG/WOL* DY9 ...141 J1
Offa Dr *CRTAM* B79 ....31 M8
　KNWTH CV8 ....179 L8
Offa Rd *RLSS* CV31 ....207 G5
Offa's Dr *DUNHL/THL/PER* WV6 .34 C8
Offa St *CRTAM* B79 ....31 M8
Offchurch La *RLSS* CV31 ..207 K7
Offchurch Rd *RLSN* CV32 ..207 J1
Offenham Cl *REDE* B98 ....194 F7
Offenham Covert
　HWK/WKHTH B38 ....145 J5
Offini Cl *WBROM* B70 ......87 K3
Offmoor Rd *RIDG/WDGT* B32 .122 F5
Offmore Farm Cl *KIDD* DY10 .139 C7
Offmore La *KIDD* DY10 ....138 E7
Offwell Rd *REDE* B98 .....203 H4
Ogbury Cl *ALE/KHTH/YWD* B14 .146 A4
Ogley Crs *BRWNH* WS8 ......26 A8
Ogley Dr *MGN/WHE* B75 .....57 L8
Ogley Hay Rd *BNTWD* WS7 ...18 E3
　BNTWD WS7 ....26 E3
Ogley Rd *BRWNH* WS8 ....26 A8
Ogley V *BNTWD* WS7 ....18 F5
O'Keeffe Cl *SPARK* B11 ...107 M7
Okehampton Dr
　HHTH/SAND B71 ....69 G7
Okehampton Rd *COVS* CV3 ..155 J8
Okement Dr *WNSFLD* WV11 ...36 F8
Okement Gv *RRUGBY* CV23 ..159 M8
Oken Ct *WWCK* CV34 ....205 H6
Oken Rd *WWCK* CV34 ....205 H5
Olaf Pl *COVE* CV2 ....135 L6
Old Abbey Gdns *HRBN* B17 .124 B1
Old Acre Cl *WALM/CURD* B76 .73 H7
Old Acre Dr *HDSW* B21 .....88 B3
Oldacre Rd *LGLYGN/QTN* B68 .104 E6
Oldany Wy *NUNW/HART* CV10 .98 D3
Old Bank Rd *NFLD/LBR* B31 .144 F3
Old Barn Rd *BVILLE* B30 ..124 A6
　DUDN DY1 ....85 L1
Old Beeches *ERDW/GRVHL* B23 .72 A5
Old Bell Rd *ERDW/GRVHL* B23 .72 F7
Oldberrow Cl *SHLY* B90 ...148 E7
Old Birchills *WSLW* WS2 ....52 C2
Old Birmingham Rd *ALVE* B48 .170 E5
　BRGRVE B60 ....169 G6
Old Bridge St *LOZ/NWT* B19 .88 F7
Old Bridge Wk
　BLKHTH/ROWR B65 ....85 K8
Old Bromford La *CBROM* B36 .90 F7
Old Brookside *STETCH* B33 .109 J3
Old Budbrooke Rd
　RIWWCK/WEL CV35 ......204 D7
Old Burcot La *BRGRVE* B60 .192 A1
Oldbury Cl *REDE* B98 .....194 F7
Oldbury Rd *CRTAM* B79 .....31 M8
Oldbury Ring Wy *OLDBY* B69 .86 D6
Oldbury Rd *BLKHTH/ROWR* B65 .104 B5
　NUNW/HART CV10 ....79 G4
　SMTHWK B66 ....87 G6
　WBROM B70 ....86 D2
Oldbury St *DARL/WED* WS10 .68 F2
Oldbury Vw *NUNW/HART* CV10 .79 M4
Old Bush St *BRLYHL* DY5 ..102 C2
Old Camp HI *SPARK* B11 ....7 M9
Old Cannock Rd *WOLVN* WV10 .23 H4
Old Castle Gv *BRWNH* WS8 ..26 D3
Old Chapel Rd *SMTHWKW* B67 .105 K2
Old Chester Rd South
　KIDD DY11 ....164 C3
Old Church Gn *STETCH* B33 .109 J3
Old Church Rd *COVN* CV6 ..134 D4
　CSHL/WTROR B46 ....92 F2
Old Crest Av *REDE* B98 ...202 C2
Old Croft La *CBROM* B36 ...91 M6
Old Cross St *TPTN/OCK* DY4 .67 M5
Old Crown Cl *RIDG/WDGT* B32 .122 F4
Old Crown Ms *COVE* CV2 ...117 H8
Old Damson La *HIA/OLT* B92 .128 D3
Old Dickens Heath Rd
　SHLY B90 ....147 L8
Olde Hall Ct *WOLVN* WV10 *.23 G6
Olde Hall La *WOLVN* WV10 ..23 G6
Old Fallings Crs *WOLVN* WV10 .36 D7
Old Fallings La *WOLVN* WV10 .36 D5
Old Fallow Av *CNCK/NC* WS11 .16 C2
Old Fallow Rd *CNCK/NC* WS11 .16 C2
Old Falls Cl *GTWY* WS6 ....24 B2
Old Farm Dr *CDSL* WV8 .....34 C4

Old Farm Gv
　ALE/KHTH/YWD B14 ......126 A8
Old Farm La *CSHL/WTROR* B46 .94 E1
Old Farm Meadow
　BDMR/CCFT WV3 ....49 G5
Old Farm Rd *ATHST* CV9 ....63 M5
　STETCH B33 ....109 J1
Oldfield Dr *STRBR* DY8 ...119 L2
Oldfield Rd *BHTH/HG* B12 .107 J7
　BILS/COS WV14 ....66 E5
　COVW CV5 ....154 B2
Oldfields *CDYHTH* B64 ....103 H5
　HAG/WOL DY9 ....119 M7
Old Fordrove *WALM/CURD* B76 .73 H2
Old Forest Wy *BKDE/SHDE* B34 .91 M7
Old Forge Dr *REDE* B98 ...202 F4
Old Forge Gdns *KIDD* DY11 .189 L3
Old Grange Rd *SPARK* B11 .126 A1
Old Green La *DOR/KN* B93 .176 F3
Old Grove Gdns *HAG/WOL* DY9 .120 B2
Old Hall Cl *STRBR* DY8 ...101 L6
Old Hall La *ALDR* WS9 .....54 F8
　CNCK/NC WS11 ....16 F6
　GTWY WS6 ....24 D7
Old Hall St *WOLV* WV1 ......3 G6
Old Ham La *HAG/WOL* DY9 ..120 A3
Old Hampton La *WNSFLD* WV11 .37 J3
Old Hawne La *HALE* B63 ...103 L8
Old Heath Crs *WOLV* WV1 ...50 A4
Old Heath Rd *WOLV* WV1 ....50 A3
Old Hedging La
　TAM/AM/WIL B77 ....46 B8
Old Hednesford Rd
　CNCK/NC WS11 ....16 E7
Old HI *DUNHL/THL/PER* WV6 .35 H8
Old Hinckley Rd
　NUNW/HART CV10 ....81 H8
Old Hobicus La *LGLYGN/QTN* B68 .86 F5
Old Holly La *ATHST* CV9 ...63 G3
Old Horns Crs *PBAR/PBCH* B42 .71 G3
Oldhouse Farm Cl
　HLGN/YWD B28 ....126 D7
Old House La
　RCOVN/BALC/EX CV7 ....114 E6
　RMSLY B62 ....142 F4
Oldington Gv *SOLH* B91 ...148 E6
Oldington La *STRPT* DY13 .163 M5
Old Kingsbury Rd
　WALM/CURD B76 ....74 A8
Oldknow Rd *SMHTH* B10 ....108 C7
Old Landywood La
　WOLVN WV11 ....24 A7
Old La *ALVE* B48 ....195 H1
　BLOX/PEL WS3 ....39 G6
　DUNHL/THL/PER WV6 .....48 D3
　WOLVN WV10 ....23 G6
Old Leicester Rd
　RUGBYN/HIL CV21 ....160 E6
Old Level Wy *DUDS* DY2 ...103 H1
Old Lime Gdns
　HWK/WKHTH B38 ....145 J5
Old Lindens Cl *FOAKS/STRLY* B74 .55 J4
Old Lode La *HIA/OLT* B92 .127 M3
Old London Rd *LICHS* WS14 .29 H4
Old Manor Cl *POL/KGSB/FAZ* B78 .45 J8
The Old Mnr
　DUNHL/THL/PER WV6 *....35 H8
Old Masters Cl *WSL* WS1 ....5 L1
Old Meadow Rd *NFLD/LBR* B31 *.144 F6
Old Meeting Rd *BILS/COS* WV14 .67 G5
Old Meeting St *HHTH/SAND* B71 .68 F8
Old Meeting Yd *BDWTH* CV12 *.116 F2
Old Mill Av *TLHL/CAN* CV4 .154 D8
Old Mill Br *WWCK* CV34 ...205 K7
Old Mill Cl *SHLY* B90 ....147 H3
Old Mill Gdns *RUSH/SHEL* WS4 .40 D7
Old Mill Gv *BFLD/HDSWWD* B20 *.89 C3
Old Mill Rd *CSHL/WTROR* B46 .93 K6
Old Milverton La *RLSN* CV32 .206 C1
Old Milverton Rd *RLSN* CV32 .206 A2
Old Moat Dr *NFLD/LBR* B31 .144 F2
Old Moat Wy *WASH/WDE* B8 .90 F7
Oldnall Cl *HAG/WOL* DY9 .120 D1
Oldnall Rd *HAG/WOL* DY9 .120 D1
　KIDD DY10 ....164 D1
Old Oak Cl *ALDR* WS9 ......40 F5
Old Oak Rd *HWK/WKHTH* B38 .145 L5
Old Oscott HI *KGSTG* B44 ..71 J4
Old Oscott La *KGSTG* B44 ..71 J5
Old Pk *SLYOAK* B29 ....123 L8
Old Park La *OLDBY* B69 ....86 B8
Old Park Rd *DARL/WED* WS10 .52 C7
　DUDN DY1 ....84 D1
　HEDN WS12 ....13 L8
Old Park Wk *LOZ/NWT* B19 ..89 J6
Old Penkridge Rd
　CNCK/NC WS11 ....16 A3
Old Pleck Rd *WSLW* WS2 .....4 A7
Old Port Cl *TPTN/OCK* DY4 *.85 M3
Old Portway *HWK/WKHTH* B38 *.145 L4
Old Postway *LOZ/NWT* B19 ..89 H6
Old Quarry Cl *RBRY* B45 ..143 K5
Old Quarry Dr *SEDG* DY3 ...66 B8
Old Rectory Gdns *ALDR* WS9 .41 G7
Old Rectory La *ALVE* B48 .170 F6
Old Rd *RCOVN/BALC/EX* CV7 .131 J4
Old Ruiton *WLNHL* WV13 ....51 L3
Old School Dr
　BLKHTH/ROWR B65 ....103 M2
Old School Ms *RLSN* CV32 .206 F2
Old Scott Cl *STETCH* B33 .110 A3
Old Smithy Pl *WSNGN* B18 ..88 B8
Old Snow HI *CBHAMNW* B3 ....6 F7
Old Sq *CBHAMNE* B4 ....7 G4
Old Stables Wk *VAUX/NECH* B7 .90 A6
Old Stafford Rd *WOLVN* WV10 .22 A1
Old Station Rd *BRGRVE* B60 .191 L5
　HIA/OLT B92 ....129 K3
　STETCH B33 ....109 H1
Old Stone Cl *RBRY* B45 ...143 K4
Old Stowheath La
　WLNHL WV13 *............51 G4
Old Stratford Rd *BRGRVE* B60 *.192 A3
Old Tokengate *HRBN* B17 ..106 B7
Old Town Cl *HWK/WKHTH* B38 .145 K3
Old Town La *BLOX/PEL* WS3 ..39 K2
Old Vicarage Cl *BLOX/PEL* WS3 .39 L3
Old Walsall Rd *GTB/HAM* B43 .70 D5
Old Warstone La *WOLVN* WV11 *.23 M5
Old Warwick Ct *HIA/OLT* B92 .127 J4
Old Warwick Rd *HIA/OLT* B92 .127 J4
　HOCK/TIA B94 ....175 H8
　RLSS CV31 ....207 J4
Old Waste La
　RCOVN/BALC/EX CV7 ....152 C7
Oldway Dr *SOLH* B91 ......149 J3
Old Well Rd *RUSH/SHEL* WS4 .39 M6
Old Wharf Rd *STRBR* DY8 ..101 K7
Oldwich La East *KNWTH* CV8 .177 J4
Oldwich La West *DOR/KN* B93 .177 G5
Old Winnings Rd
　RCOVN/BALC/EX CV7 ....115 K6
Olga Dr *TPTN/OCK* DY4 .....67 M4
Olinthus Av *WNSFLD* WV11 ..37 J6
Olive Av *COVE* CV2 ....135 H6
Olive Dr *RMSLY* B62 ......104 A5

Olive Hill Rd *RMSLY* B62 .104 B5
Olive La *RMSLY* B62 ......104 A5
Olive Pl *ALE/KHTH/YWD* B14 *.125 J1
Oliver Cl *DUDS* DY2 ....85 J5
Oliver Ct *BLKHTH/ROWR* B65 .103 M3
Oliver Crs *BILS/COS* WV14 .67 J3
Oliver Rd *ERDW/GRVHL* B23 .72 D7
　SMTHWK B66 ....87 K4
Oliver St *COVN* CV6 ......134 D7
　RUGBYN/HIL CV21 ....186 D2
　VAUX/NECH B7 ....89 L8
Olivier Wy *RCOVN/BALC/EX* CV7 *.135 M5
Ollerton Rd
　LGN/SDN/BHAMAIR B26 ...109 K6
Ollison Dr *FOAKS/STRLY* B74 .55 K5
Olliver Cl *RIDG/WDGT* B32 .122 D3
Olorenshaw Rd
　LGN/SDN/BHAMAIR B26 ...110 B8
Olton Av *COVW* CV5 ....153 J1
Olton Bvd East *ACGN* B27 .127 C3
Olton Bvd West *SPARK* B11 .126 C2
Olton Cft *ACGN* B27 ......127 F4
　CNCK/NC WS6 ....16 F6
Olton Mere *HIA/OLT* B92 * .127 H3
Olton Pl *NUNW/HART* CV10 ..98 A1
Olton Rd *SHLY* B90 ....126 F8
Olton Whf *HIA/OLT* B92 ...127 G3
Olympus Av *RLSS* CV31 ....206 F7
Olympus Cl *COVW* CV5 .....131 H5
Olympus Dr *TPTN/OCK* DY4 ..68 B7
Olympus Gdns *STRPT* DY13 .189 G2
Omar Rd *COVE* CV2 ....135 G4
Ombersley Cl *OLDBY* B69 ...86 B8
　REDE B98 ....202 F6
Ombersley Rd *BHTH/HG* B12 .107 J7
　HALE B63 ....121 K3
Onibury Rd *HDSW* B21 ......88 B4
Onley La *RUGBYS/DCH* CV22 .187 H8
Onley Ter *TLHL/CAN* CV4 ..154 A6
Onslow Crs *HIA/OLT* B92 ..127 L4
Onslow Cft *RLSN* CV32 ....206 D3
Onslow Rd *SPARK* B11 .....126 A4
Ontario Cl *HWK/WKHTH* B38 .145 L5
Oozells Sq *CBHAMW* B1 ......6 B6
Oozells St *CBHAMW* B1 ......6 B6
Open Field Cl *NFLD/LBR* B31 .144 F5
Openfield Cft *CSHL/WTROR* B46 *.93 L3
The Orangery *HAG/WOL* DY9 .120 B6
Oratory Cl *COVS* CV3 .....156 A7
Orbital Wy *CNCK/NC* WS11 ..16 C7
Orchard Av *WALM/CURD* B76 .73 K7
　SOLH B91 ....128 B8
Orchard Ct *ATHST* CV9 .....63 H6
　BDMR/CCFT WV3 ....48 E5
　COVS CV3 ....156 D4
　KGSWFD DY6 ....83 H7
Orchard Crs *COVS* CV3 ......8 C9
　PENK ST19 ....10 D4
Orchard Cft *RBRY* B45 ....170 B5
Orchard Dr *COVW* CV5 .....153 G1
　NFLD/LBR B31 ....144 B5
Orchard Gv *ALDR* WS9 ......54 F1
　ETTPK/GDPK/PENN WV4 ...65 G7
　FOAKS/STRLY B74 ....56 D2
　SEDG DY3 ....83 M2
Orchard La *CDSL* WV8 ......34 F2
　HAG/WOL DY9 ....102 C7
　WOLVN WV10 ....23 G2
Orchard Meadow Wk
　CVALE B35 ....91 M2
Orchard Ri *STUD* B80 .....203 K5
Orchard Rd *ATHST* CV9 .....62 A3
　BEWD DY12 ....162 E2
　LGN/SDN/BHAMAIR B26 ...109 K6
　BRGRVW B61 ....191 K1
　DSYBK/YTR WS5 ....69 M2
　DUDS DY2 ....103 G3
　ERDE/BCHGN B24 ....72 E8
　HOCK/TIA B94 ....175 G7
　KIDD DY10 ....139 G1
　WLNHL WV13 ....51 M4
　WNSFLD WV11 ....37 G6
The Orchards *FOAKS/STRLY* B74 .56 B6
　HLYWD B47 ....146 E6
　KIDDW DY11 ....137 M4
　RRUGBY CV23 ....161 K4
　SHLY B90 ....174 B1
Orchard St *BDWTH* CV12 .....98 F8
　BRLYHL DY5 ....102 B3
　CRTAM B79 ....31 M8
　KIDD DY10 ....138 C2
　NUN CV11 ....99 H1
　OLDBY B69 ....85 K3
　REDE B98 ....202 C2
　SEDG DY3 ....84 C5
　SMTHWKW B67 ....105 G3
Orchards Wy *BHTH/HG* B12 .107 J7
The Orchard *ATHST* CV9 ....62 A6
　BEWD DY12 ....162 C2
　BILS/COS WV14 ....51 J8
　BLOX/PEL WS3 ....39 H3
　BNTWD WS7 *.............18 E5
　BNTWD WS7 *.............18 F5
　BRGRVW B61 ....191 J1
　CHWD/FDBR/MGN B37 ....110 D5
　DUNHL/THL/PER WV6 .....35 J7
Orchard Vis *HLYWD* B47 ...172 D4
Orchard Wy *ACGN* B27 .....126 F1
　GTB/HAM B43 ....126 F1
　HLYWD B47 ....146 E6
　KNWTH CV8 ....182 A7
　NUNW/HART CV10 ....80 A7
　RRUGBY CV23 ....183 K7
　RUGBYS/DCH CV22 ....186 D5
Orcheston Wk
　ALE/KHTH/YWD B14 ......146 A1
Orchid Cl *SMTHWK* B66 .....87 H6
Orchid Dr *LOZ/NWT* B19 ....89 J4
Orchid Wy *RRUGBY* CV23 ...161 K5
Ordnance Rd *COVN* CV6 ....134 C8
Oregon Cl *KGSWFD* DY6 .....83 K7
Oregon Dr *SHHTH* WV12 .....38 C6
Oregon Gdns *BNTWD* WS7 ....18 D1
Orford Gv *HDSW* B21 ....88 A6
Orford Ri *NUNW/HART* CV10 .97 J1
Oriel Cl *CNCK/NC* WS11 ....16 C4
Oriel Dr *WOLVN* WV10 ......23 G2
Oriel Vis *SPARK* B11 * ...108 A8
Oriole Cv *KIDD* DY10 .....164 E5
Orion Cl *GTWY* WS6 ....24 B3
　WASH/WDE B8 ....108 C1
Orion Crs *COVE* CV2 ......135 J3
Orion Wy *CNCK/NC* WS11 ....12 G5

Orkney Av *BKDE/SHDE* B34 ..91 K7
Orkney Cl *NUNW/HART* CV10 .98 E3
Orkney Cft *CBROM* B36 .....92 F6
Orkney Dr *TAM/AM/WIL* B77 .46 D6
Orlando Cl *RUGBYS/DCH* CV22 *.186 F6
　WSL WS1 ....4 F6
Orlescote Rd *TLHL/CAN* CV4 .154 B7
Ormande Cl *HALE* B63 .....121 G6
Orme Cl *STRBR* DY8 ....101 L5
Ormes La *ATHST* CV9 ....63 H1
　DUNHL/THL/PER WV6 .....49 C2
Ormond Pl *BILS/COS* WV14 ..51 J7
Ormond Rd *RBRY* B45 ......143 J4
Ormonds Cl *LICH* WS13 .....20 C7
Ormsby Gv *ACGN* B27 ......126 F6
Ormscliffe Rd *RBRY* B45 ..143 K6
Orphanage Rd
　CSCFLD/WYGN B72 ....73 G6
　ERDE/BCHGN B24 ....73 G7
Orpington Dr *COVN* CV6 ...134 B1
Orpington Rd *KGSTG* B44 ...71 J2
Orpwood Rd *STETCH* B33 ..109 L3
Orson Leys *RUGBYS/DCH* CV22 .186 C6
Orton Av *WALM/CURD* B76 ...73 K7
Orton Cl *CSHL/WTROR* B46 ..92 E2
Orton Gv
　ETTPK/GDPK/PENN WV4 ...65 H1
Orton La
　ETTPK/GDPK/PENN WV4 ...64 D2
Orton Rd *COVN* CV6 ....134 A2
Orton Wy *CVALE* B35 ....91 L3
Orwell Cl *NUNW/HART* CV10 .79 L8
　RRUGBY CV23 ....161 L3
　STRBR DY8 ....119 H1
　WNSFLD WV11 ....37 K8
Orwell Pas *DIG/EDG* B5 .....7 H7
Orwell Rd *COV* CV1 ....5 L7
　WSL WS1 ....5 L5
Osbaston Cl *COVW* CV5 ....153 J1
Osberton Dr *DUDN* DY1 .....84 D3
Osborne *CRTAM* B79 * 31 H6
Osborne Cl *AST/WIT* B6 ....89 L5
　BRLYHL DY5 ....102 D5
　KIDD DY10 ....138 F7
Osborne Dr *DARL/WED* WS10 .52 C8
Osborne Gv *LOZ/NWT* B19 *..89 G6
Osborne Rd *COVW* CV5 ....8 A9
　ERDW/GRVHL B23 ....72 A7
　ETTPK/GDPK/PENN WV4 ...49 K8
　HDSW B21 ....88 D5
　HHTH/SAND B71 ....68 A5
　SHLY B90 ....148 B8
Osborn Rd *SPARK* B11 .....107 A7
Osbourne Cft *SHLY* B90 ...148 B8
Oscott Rd *PBAR/PBCH* B42 ..89 J2
Oscott School La *KGSTG* B44 .71 J3
Osier Gv *ERDW/GRVHL* B23 ..71 M7
Osier Pl *WOLV* WV1 ....3 M4
Osier St *WOLV* WV1 ....3 M4
Osler St *LDYWD/EDGR* B16 .106 D3
Oslo Gdns *COVE* CV2 ......135 L6
Osmaston Rd *HRBN* B17 ....123 L2
　STRBR DY8 ....119 J3
Osmington Gv *HALE* B63 ...103 H7
Osprey *TAM/AM/WIL* B77 ....46 E7
Osprey Cl *COVE* CV2 ......135 K6
　NUN CV11 ....99 M5
Osprey Dr *DUDN* DY1 ....84 D4
Osprey Gv *HEDN* WS12 ......17 G4
Osprey Park Dr *KIDD* DY10 .146 F4
Osprey Rd *ERDW/GRVHL* B23 .72 A7
　HIA/OLT B92 ....127 H3
Ostler Cl *KGSWFD* DY6 .....82 F6
Oswald Rd *RLSN* CV32 .....206 B4
Oswald St *REDW* B97 ......202 C2
Oswald Wy *RUGBYS/DCH* CV22 .186 D2
Oswestry Cl *REDW* B97 ....202 A5
Oswin Gv *COVE* CV2 ....156 A1
Oswin Pl *BLOX/PEL* WS3 ....39 K8
Oswin Rd *BLOX/PEL* WS3 ....39 K8
Othello Cl *RUGBYS/DCH* CV22 .186 E8
Otley Gv *BORD B9 ....
Otter Cft *BKDE/SHDE* B34 ..92 B8
Otters Rest *RLSS* CV31 ...207 G8
Otterstone Cl *SEDG* DY3 ...66 A3
Otter St *TAM/AM/WIL* B77 ..46 E7
Oughton Rd *BHTH/HG* B12 .107 L6
Oulton Cl *KIDDW* DY11 ....138 B5
Oundle Rd *KGSTG* B44 ......71 K6
Ounsdale Crs *WMBN* WV5 ....64 E6
Ounsdale Rd *WMBN* WV5 .....64 D7
Ounty John La *STRBR* DY8 .119 L5
Ousterne La
　RCOVN/BALC/EX CV7 ....114 B2
Outermarch Rd *COVN* CV6 ..134 A7
Outmore Rd *STETCH* B33 ..109 M4
Outwood Cl *REDE* B98 .....202 C1
Out Wood Dr *NFLD/LBR* B31 .144 B4
Outwoods Cl *ATHST* CV9 ....63 G6
Oval Rd *ERDE/BCHGN* B24 ...90 C4
　RUGBYS/DCH CV22 ....187 H5
　TPTN/OCK DY4 ....68 D7
The Oval *DARL/WED* WS10 ...84 C5
　DUDN DY1 ....84 D3
　SMTHWKW B67 ....105 H2
Overberry Cl *COVE* CV2 ...135 K3
Overbrook Cl *SEDG* DY3 ....84 A3
The Overbury *ATHST* CV9 ...62 A3
Overbury Rd *NFLD/LBR* B31 .145 G2
Overbury Rd *NFLD/LBR* B31 .145 G2
　RMSLY B62 ....121 M3
Overdale Av *WALM/CURD* B76 .73 K3
Overdale Cl *SHHTH* WV12 ...52 A2
Overdale Dr *WSLW* WS2 .....52 A2
Overdale Rd *COVW* CV5 ....154 A2
　RIDG/WDGT B32 ....
Overend Gv *RLSN* CV32 ....206 A3
Overend Rd *HALE* B63 .....103 H7
Overend St *WBROM* B70 .....87 H2
Overfield Dr *BILS/COS* WV14 .51 G7
Overfield Rd *DUDN* DY1 ....84 C5
　RIDG/WDGT B32 ....
Over Green Dr
　CHWD/FDBR/MGN B37 .....92 D8
Overhill Rd *BNTWD* WS7 ....18 E8
Overlea Av *ACGN* B27 .....126 F2
Over Mill Dr *SLYOAK* B29 .124 F3
Overmoor Cl *LOZ/NWT* B19 ..89 G6
Over Pool Rd *WASH/WDE* B8 .90 E7
Overseal Rd *WNSFLD* WV11 ..37 J3
Overslade Crs *COVN* CV6 ..133 J6
Overslade La
　RUGBYS/DCH CV22 ....186 B6
Overslade Manor Dr
　RUGBYS/DCH CV22 ....186 D5
Overslade Rd *SOLH* B91 ...148 D3
Oversley Rd *WALM/CURD* B76 .73 K3
Overstrand *COVN* CV6 ......133 K1
Over St *COVN* CV6 ....134 C5
Overton Cl *HLGN/YWD* B28 .126 D1
Overton Dr *CSHL/WTROR* B46 .93 G2
Overton Gv *ACGN* B27 .....127 C6
Overton La *BNTWD* WS7 ......9 M5

Overton Pl HHTH/SAND B71 ....69 H7
 VAUX/NECH 7 L2
Overton Rd ACGN B27 ....126 F5
Overtons Cl RLSS CV31 ....207 K8
Overwood Cft WASH/WDE B8..108 C2
Owenford Rd COVN CV6 ....134 A6
Owen Pl BILS/COS WV14 ....51 H7
Owen Rd BDMR/CCFT WV3 ....2 B1
 BILS/COS WV14 ....51 H6
 WLNHL WV13 ....51 M4
Owens Cft ATHST CV9 ....145 L4
Owen St ATHST CV9 ....63 H5
 DARL/WED WS10 ....52 B6
 DUDS DY2 ....7 J7
 TPTN/OCK DY4 ....67 H8
Owens Wy CDYHTH B64 ....103 L4
Ownall Rd BKDE/SHDE B34 ....92 A7
Oxbarn Av BDMR/CCFT WV3 ....49 L6
Oxbow Wy KIDDW DY11 ....138 C5
Oxbridge Wy CRTAM B79 ....31 H7
Ox Cl COVE CV2 ....134 E7
Oxendon Wy COVS CV3 ....156 C5
Oxenton Cft HALE B63 ....121 H3
Oxford Canal Pth
 RUGBYN/HIL CV21 ....160 F6
Oxford Canal Wk RRUGBY CV23..158 E1
Oxford Cl GTWY WS6 ....24 D2
 NUN CV11 ....81 K5
 WASH/WDE B8 ....90 F8
Oxford Dr ACGN B27 ....127 H1
 STRBR DY8 ....119 K1
Oxford Gn CNCK/NC WS11 ....16 D5
Oxford Pl RLSN CV32 ....206 E4
Oxford Rd ACGN B27 ....127 G2
 CNCK/NC WS11 ....16 D5
 ERDW/GRVHL B23 ....90 D1
 KNWTH CV8 ....192 D4
 MOS/BIL B13 ....125 L3
 RRUGBY CV23 ....183 G8
 SMTHWK B67 ....87 L5
 WBROM B70 ....86 F2
Oxford St BILS/COS WV14 ....51 H8
 BVILLE B30 ....124 E6
 COV CV1 ....9 K4
 DARL/WED WS10 ....68 F3
 DIG/EDG B5 ....7 H7
 DUDN DY10 ....138 C8
 KIDD DY10 ....138 C8
 RLSN CV32 ....206 D4
 RUGBYN/HIL CV21 ....187 G2
 WOLV WV1 ....3 H6
 WSLW WS2 ....4 A8
Oxhayes Cl
 RCOVN/BALC/EX CV7 ....152 A7
Oxhill Cl REDE B98 ....203 J4
Oxhill Rd HDSW B21 ....88 B3
 SHLY B90 ....147 G3
Ox Leasow RIDG/WDGT B32 ....123 G3
Oxleasow Rd REDE B98 ....195 J8
Oxley Av WOLVN WV10 ....35 M5
Oxley Cl DUDS DY2 ....102 F3
 GTWY WS6 ....24 C1
Oxley Dr COVS CV3 ....181 G2
Oxley Gv SLYOAK B29 ....123 L5
Oxley La WOLV WV1 ....2 F1
Oxley Links Rd WOLVN WV10 ....35 M5
Oxley Moor Rd COVEN WV9 ....35 L5
Ox Leys Rd MGN/WHC B75 ....73 M1
Oxley St WOLV WV1 ....2 F1
Oxlip Cl DSYBK/YTR WS5 ....69 H7
Oxpiece Dr CBROM B36 ....91 H5
Oxstall Cl WALM/CURD B76 ....74 B8
Ox St SEDG DY3 ....66 B8
Oxted Cl WNSFLD WV11 ....37 M7
Oxted Cft ERDW/GRVHL B23 ....90 C2
Oxwood La RMSLY B62 ....143 H1
Oxygen St VAUX/NECH 7 J1

P

Pace Crs BILS/COS WV14 ....67 K3
Pacific Av DARL/WED WS10 ....68 B4
Packenham Dr WALM/CURD B76..73 K5
Packhorse La HWK/WKHTH B38..146 B7
Packington Av BKDE/SHDE B34 ..92 A8
 COVW CV5 ....132 F7
Packington La
 CSHL/WTROR B46 ....111 L1
 POL/KGSB/FAZ B78 ....30 D8
 RCOVN/BALC/EX CV7 ....112 F4
Packington Pl RLSN CV32 ....206 E6
Packmores SHLY B90 ....147 L8
Packmore St WWCK CV34 ....205 H5
Packwood Av
 RUGBYN/HIL CV21 ....187 M5
Packwood Cl
 BFLD/HDSWWD B20 ....88 D3
 DOR/KN B93 ....175 J1
 NUN CV11 ....99 K5
 REDW B97 ....201 K4
 RLSS CV31 ....207 L8
 WLNHL WV13 ....51 K5
Packwood Cottages
 DOR/KN B93 * 175 K4
Packwood Ct SLYOAK B29 ....123 K4
Packwood Dr GTB/HAM B43 ....70 B4
Packwood Gn COVW CV5 ....153 L2
Packwood La HOCK/TIA B94 ....175 L7
Packwood Ms WWCK CV34 * 205 M5
Packwood Rd
 LGN/SDN/BHAMAIR B26 ....109 M5
 OLDBY B69 ....85 L4
Padarn Cl SEDG DY3 ....66 A4
Padbury COVEN WV9 ....35 M2
Padbury La BNTWD WS7 ....18 D2
Paddiford Pl NUNW/HART CV10..98 A4
Paddington Rd HDSW B21 ....88 A4
Paddock Dr DOR/KN B93 ....175 J1
Paddock La ALDR WS9 ....40 E8
 GTWY WS6 ....24 C1
 REDE B98 ....202 C6
 WSL WS1 ....5 H4
The Paddock BILS/COS WV14 ....67 K6
 POL/KGSB/FAZ B78 ....47 L2
Paddocks Gn WSNGN B18 ....88 E8
The Paddocks BDWTH CV12 ....117 M2
 RRUGBY CV23 ....183 K8
 WSL WS4 ....205 K6
The Paddock BILS/COS WV14 ....67 K6
 BRGRVE B60 ....191 H4
 CDSL WS8 ....34 E3
 DUNHL/THL/PER WV6 ....35 L8
 HAG/WOL DY9 ....119 M5
 LICHS WS14 ....21 G8
 SEDG DY3 ....66 C4
Paddock Vw
 DUNHL/THL/PER WV6 ....35 L8
Paddox Cl RUGBYN/HIL CV21 ..187 K5

Paddys Rw WALM/CURD B76 * 75 L6
Padgate Cl CVALE B35 ....91 M2
Padgets Ct RLSS CV31 ....203 H1
Padmore Ct RLSS CV31 ....206 F7
Padstow TAM/AM/WIL B77 ....32 D8
Padstow Cl NUN CV11 ....81 K8
Padstow Rd ERDE/BCHGN B24 ..91 H1
 TLHL/CAN CV4 ....153 J6
Padua Rd BRGRVE B60 ....192 A4
Paganal Dr WBROM B70 ....87 J4
Paganel Dr DUDN DY1 ....85 G2
Paganel Rd SLYOAK B29 ....123 L3
Page Rd TLHL/CAN CV4 ....153 J6
Pages Cl MGN/WHC B75 ....57 G8
Pages La GTB/HAM B43 ....70 C4
Paget Cl BILS/COS WV14 * 66 F5
 BRGRVW B61 ....191 J3
 LICH WS13 ....20 F5
 PENK ST19 ....20 F5
Paget Ct COVE CV2 ....134 E2
Paget Dr BNTWD WS7 ....2 A4
Paget Rd DUNHL/THL/PER WV6 ..49 H2
 ERDE/BCHGN B24 ....91 H2
Pagets Cha HEDN WS12 ....18 A1
Paget's La KNWTH CV8 ....182 B8
Paget St WOLV WV1 ....2 D1
Pagham Cl COVEN WV9 ....35 K3
Pagnell Gv MOS/BIL B13 ....126 A7
Paignton Rd LDYWD/EDGR B16..106 B2
Pailton Cl COVE CV2 ....135 G3
Pailton Gv SLYOAK B29 ....123 L4
Pailton Rd RRUGBY CV23 ....159 M1
 SHLY B90 ....126 F8
Painswick Cl DSYBK/YTR WS5 ....69 M2
 REDE B98 ....202 C1
Painswick Rd HLGN/YWD B28 ..126 C6
Painters Cft BILS/COS WV14 ....67 J4
Pakefield Rd BVILLE B30 ....145 M2
Pakenham Cl WALM/CURD B76 ..73 K5
Pakenham Rd EDG B15 ....7 G6
Pake's Cft COVN CV6 ....133 L8
Pakfield Wk AST/WIT B6 * 89 K4
Palace Cl BLKHTH/ROWR B65 ....104 B3
Palace Dr SMTHWK B66 ....87 G5
Palace Rd BORD B9 ....108 C4
Palefield Rd SHLY B90 ....148 D7
Pale La HRBN B17 ....105 K5
Palermo Av COVS CV3 ....155 J7
Pale St SEDG DY3 ....66 C8
Palethorpe Rd TPTN/OCK DY4 ..67 L5
Palfrey Rd STRBR DY8 ....119 L3
Pallett Dr NUN CV11 ....81 L6
Palmcourt Av HLGN/YWD B28 ..126 C6
Palm Cft BRLYHL DY5 ....102 A5
Palmer Cl WNSFLD WV11 ....37 K4
Palmer La COV CV1 ....8 F3
Palmers Cl CDSL WV8 ....35 G3
 RUGBYN/HIL CV21 ....187 M5
 SHLY B90 ....126 F8
Palmers Gv CBROM B36 ....91 J5
Palmers Rd REDE B98 ....195 K8
Palmerston Dr OLDBY B69 ....86 A6
Palmerston Rd COVW CV5 ....154 D5
 SPARK B11 ....107 M7
Palmer St BORD B9 ....7 M6
Palmers Wy CDSL WV8 ....35 G4
Palm Tree Av COVE CV2 ....135 G3
Palmvale Cft
 LGN/SDN/BHAMAIR B26 ....109 L7
Palmyra Rd BRGRVE B60 ....192 A3
Palomino Pl LDYWD/EDGR B16..106 D3
Pamela Rd NFLD/LBR B31 ....144 E3
Pancras Cl COVE CV2 ....135 J4
Pan Cft CBROM B36 ....91 G6
Pandora Rd COVE CV2 ....135 J6
Pangbourne Cl COVE CV2 ....135 G5
Pangfield Pk COVW CV5 ....154 A1
Panjab Gdns SMTHWKW B67 * ..87 K1
Pannel Cft LOZ/NWT B19 ....89 H7
Panther Cft BKDE/SHDE B34 ....92 B8
Pantolf Pl RUGBYN/HIL CV21 ..160 C6
Papenham Gn TLHL/CAN CV4 ..153 J6
Paper Mill End PBAR/PBCH B42..71 H7
Papworth Dr BRGRVW B61 ....168 D8
Papyrus Wy CBROM B36 ....91 K4
Parade RLSN CV32 ....206 D5
The Parade BRWNH WS8 ....26 C4
 CDYHTH B64 ....103 J3
 DUDN DY1 ....84 F3
 KGSWFD DY6 ....82 F6
 KIDD DY10 * 138 D5
 NUN CV11 ....99 G2
 WALM/CURD ....2 A3 (* WV11 *)
Paradise DUDS DY2 ....85 H5
Paradise Circus Queensway
 CBHAMNW B3 ....6 D5
Paradise Gv BLOX/PEL WS3 ....39 K2
Paradise La BLOX/PEL WS3 ....39 K2
 HLGN/YWD B28 ....126 C1
 WOLVN WV10 ....22 C4
Paradise Pl CBHAMNW B3 * 6 E5
Paradise Rw BRGRVE B60 ....191 K4
Paradise St CBHAM B3 ....6 E5
 COV CV1 ....9 H7
 RUGBYN/HIL CV21 ....187 G2
 WBROM B70 ....87 H2
 WWCK CV34 ....205 K5
Paradise Wy
 RCOVN/BALC/EX CV7 ....135 L4
Paragon Wy
 RCOVN/BALC/EX CV7 ....116 F5
Parbrook Cl TLHL/CAN CV4 ....153 J5
Parbury TAM/AM/WIL B77 ....46 D8
The Parchments LICH WS13 ....20 F4
Pardington Cl HIA/OLT B92 ....128 C5
Pargeter Rd SMTHWKW B67 ....105 K3
Pargeter St STRBR DY8 ....119 K1
 WSLW WS2 ....4 A2
Par Gn NFLD/LBR B31 ....145 G4
Parish Gdns HAG/WOL DY9 ....119 M4
Parish Hl BRGRVW B61 ....168 B4
Park Aly BEWD DY12 ....162 F2
Park Av BLKHTH/ROWR B65 ....104 A2
 BNTWD WS7 ....18 F8
 BVILLE B30 ....124 F7
 CNCK/NC WS11 ....17 L8
 COVS CV3 ....134 A2
 CSHL/WTROR B46 ....93 K7
 ETTPK/GDPK/PENN WV4 ....50 A6
 LGLYGN/QTN B68 ....104 F2
 NUN CV11 ....99 J2
 POL/KGSB/FAZ B78 ....45 J4
 SMTHWKW B67 ....105 K1
 SOLH B91 ....149 H2
 STRPT DY13 ....188 D1
 TPTN/OCK DY4 ....67 J8
 WMBN WV5 ....51 M4
 WOLV WV1 ....2 D1
 WSNGN B18 ....88 E6
Park Cl BEWD DY12 ....162 F2
 BILS/COS WV14 ....66 F6
 BRWNH WS8 ....26 B5
 BNTWD WS7 ....18 C5
 BNTWD WS7 ....18 F8
 BLOX/PEL WS3 ....38 F4
 GTWY WS6 ....24 C2
 HIA/OLT B92 ....128 B3

KNWTH CV8 ....179 M5
 OLDBY B69 ....86 A6
Park Ct REDE B98 ....202 E2
 RUGBYN/HIL CV21 * 186 E1
Park Crs HHTH/SAND B71 ....87 H1
 STRPT DY13 ....188 D1
Park Cft BNTWD WS7 ....2 A4
 HLYWD B47 ....146 E8
Park Dale DARL/WED WS10 ....68 E1
Parkdale Av ERDE/BCHGN B24 ..90 D3
Parkdale Dr NFLD/LBR B31 ....144 E6
Park Dale Ct WOLV WV1 ....2 A3
Park Dl East WOLV WV1 ....2 A3
Parkdale Rd
 LGN/SDN/BHAMAIR B26 ....110 A7
Park Dl West WOLV WV1 ....2 A3
Park Dr ETTPK/GDPK/PENN WV4 ..50 A8
 FOAKS/STRLY B74 ....56 A1
 FOAKS/STRLY B74 ....56 D3
 RLSS CV31 ....206 D3
Park Edge HRBN B17 ....106 A6
Parkend LICHS WS14 ....21 J6
Parkend Rd RUGBYN/HIL CV21 ..160 F6
Park End Dr RIDG/WDGT B32 ....123 H4
Parker Pl STRPT DY13 ....164 A6
Parker Rd WNSFLD WV11 ....37 K4
Parkers Ct COVEN WV9 ....22 A4
Parker St BLOX/PEL WS3 ....38 E4
 LDYWD/EDGR B16 ....106 D4
Parkes Av CDSL WS8 ....34 F5
Parkes Cl DSYBK/YTR WS5 ....69 M2
Parkes Hall Rd DUDN DY1 ....51 L1
Parkes La SEDG DY3 ....66 E6
 TPTN/OCK DY4 ....67 K5
Parkes Pas STRPT DY13 ....188 E2
Parkes Quay STRPT DY13 ....188 E2
Parkes St BRLYHL DY5 ....102 B3
 SMTHWKW B67 ....105 K1
 WALM/CURD B76 ....51 M4
 WWCK CV34 ....205 H6
Parkeston Crs KGSTG B44 ....71 M4
Park Farm Cl
 RUGBYS/DCH CV22 ....186 B3
Park Farm Rd GTB/HAM B43 ....70 B3
 TAM/AM/WIL B77 ....46 A4
Parkfield RIDG/WDGT B32 ....122 D3
Parkfield Chalet Land
 BKHL/PFLD WV2 * 50 B7
Parkfield Cl EDG B15 ....107 L8
 KIDDW DY11 ....189 L3
 REDE B98 ....194 F7
 RMSLY B62 ....104 B8
 WALM/CURD B76 ....46 A5
Parkfield Colliery
 ETTPK/GDPK/PENN WV4 ....50 D8
Parkfield Crs BKHL/PFLD WV2 ..50 C7
 TAM/AM/WIL B77 ....46 A5
Parkfield Dr CBROM B36 ....92 A4
 KNWTH CV8 ....179 M8
Parkfield Gv BKHL/PFLD WV2 ..50 C7
Parkfield Rd CSHL/WTROR B46..93 K6
 DUDS DY2 ....85 H7
 ETTPK/GDPK/PENN WV4 ....50 C7
 LGLYGN/QTN B68 ....104 E2
 RCOVN/BALC/EX CV7 ....115 J7
 RUGBYN/HIL CV21 ....160 B7
 STRBR DY8 ....101 M8
 WASH/WDE B8 ....108 C2
Parkgate Rd COVN CV6 ....133 H7
Park Gate Rd KIDDW DY11 ....138 F3
Park Gv CSHL/WTROR B46 ....93 G2
 SMTHH B10 * 108 B5
Park Hall Cl DSYBK/YTR WS5 ....54 F5
Park Hall Crs CBROM B36 ....91 M5
Parkhall Cft BKDE/SHDE B34 ....92 B8
Park Head Crs DUDS DY2 * 84 F7
Parkhead Locks DUDS DY2 * 84 E7
Park Head Rd DUDS DY2 ....84 F7
Park Hl BLKHTH/ROWR B65 ....103 M4
 DARL/WED WS10 ....69 G1
 MOS/BIL B13 ....125 J1
Park Hill Dr BFLD/HDSWWD B20..70 B8
Parkhill Dr COVW CV5 ....132 D6
Park Hill Rd HRBN B17 ....106 A7
 SMTHWKW B67 ....87 H5
Parkhill St BNTWD WS7 ....18 C5
 WALM/CURD B76 ....73 K7
Park Hill St DUDS DY2 ....85 J5
Parkhouse Av WNSFLD WV11 ..36 F7
Parkhouse Dr ERDW/GRVHL B23..71 L8
Parkhouse Gdns SEDG DY3 ....84 A1
Parkinson Dr ATHST CV9 ....63 J3
Parkland Av KIDDW DY11 ....137 M8
Parklands Av RLSN CV32 ....207 G1
Parklands Cft REDW B97 ....193 H4
Parklands Dr FOAKS/STRLY B74..56 G6
Parklands Gdns WSL WS1 ....5 L3
Parklands Rd BILS/COS WV14 ..67 H2
 DARL/WED WS10 ....52 C8
 WOLV WV1 ....50 A1
The Parklands BDMR/CCFT WV3..49 H5
 ERDW/GRVHL B23 ....72 B7
 HAG/WOL DY9 ....120 B2
Park La AST/WIT B6 ....89 H7
 BEWD DY12 ....162 D3
 CVALE B35 ....73 H4
 DARL/WED WS10 ....52 D5
 GTWY WS6 ....24 D2
 HALE B63 ....102 E7
 HHTH/SAND B71 ....87 M1
 KGSWFD DY6 ....83 J6
 KIDD DY10 ....165 L3
 LICHS WS14 ....28 E8
 NUN CV11 ....99 J2
 NUNW/HART CV10 ....97 K1
 OLDBY B69 ....86 E7
 POL/KGSB/FAZ B78 ....45 J4
 RCOVN/BALC/EX CV7 ....96 E8
 RCOVN/BALC/EX CV7 ....151 M3
 WOLVN WV10 ....36 C3
Park La East TPTN/OCK DY4 ....85 M1
Park La West TPTN/OCK DY4 ....85 J1
Park Lime Dr RUSH/SHEL WS4 ..53 M1
Park Meadow Av BILS/COS WV14..51 J8
Park Ms SLYOAK B29 ....123 M4
The Park Paling COVS CV3 ....155 J1
Park Pl VAUX/NECH B7 ....90 A6
Park Retreat SMTHWK B66 ....105 H1
Park Rdg FOAKS/STRLY B74 ....56 E6
Park Ri HALE B63 ....102 F7
Park Ridge Dr HALE B63 ....102 F7
Park Rd AST/WIT B6 ....89 L4
 ATHST CV9 ....116 F3
 BILS/COS WV14 ....66 F6
 BLOX/PEL WS3 ....38 F4
 BNTWD WS7 ....18 C5
 BNTWD WS7 ....18 F8
 BRLYHL DY5 ....102 D5

CNCK/NC WS11 ....16 B4
 CNCK/NC WS11 ....17 J7
 COV CV1 ....8 F7
 CSHL/WTROR B46 ....93 K7
 DARL/WED WS10 ....52 C6
 DSYBK/YTR WS5 ....54 D8
 DUDN DY1 ....85 G7
 DUDS DY2 ....85 G7
 ERDW/GRVHL B23 ....90 A3
 HAG/WOL DY9 ....119 M8
 HALE B63 ....102 F7
 KNWTH CV8 ....179 L7
 MOS/BIL B13 ....125 K1
 OLDBY B69 ....86 A6
 POL/KGSB/FAZ B78 ....47 M5
 RLSN CV32 ....206 D1
 RUGBYN/HIL CV21 ....186 E1
 RUSH/SHEL WS4 ....53 M1
 SCFLD/BOLD B73 ....56 F8
 SEDG DY3 ....83 M1
 SMTHWKW B67 ....105 K4
 SPARK B11 ....108 A4
 STRBR DY8 ....101 H8
 TAM/AM/WIL B77 ....46 A8
 WLNHL WV13 ....51 H5
 WOLVN WV10 ....23 H5
 WSNGN B18 ....88 D8
Park Rd East WOLV WV1 ....2 C2
Park Rd South WSNGN B18 ....88 D8
Park Rd West STRBR DY8 ....101 G8
 WOLV WV1 ....2 C1
Parkside COV CV1 ....9 H6
 RIDG/WDGT B32 ....123 G4
 TAM/AM/WIL B77 ....46 D7
 WWCK CV34 ....205 K6
Parkside Av WLNHL WV13 ....51 J3
Parkside Cl DARL/WED WS10 ....52 F2
Parkside La RUSH/SHEL WS4 ....15 L2
Parkside Rd BFLD/HDSWWD B20..70 C8
 HALE B63 ....104 B8
Parkside Wy FOAKS/STRLY B74..55 L4
 NFLD/LBR B31 ....144 A4
Park Sq CHWD/FDBR/MGN B37..111 H5
Parkstone Av HLYWD B47 ....146 B7
Parkstone Cl RUSH/SHEL WS4 ..40 A4
Parkstone Rd COVN CV6 ....134 D5
Park St AST/WIT B6 ....89 L6
 BLKHTH/ROWR B65 ....104 B4
 CDYHTH B64 ....103 H3
 CNCK/NC WS11 ....16 C4
 COVN CV6 ....134 C6
 CRTAM B79 ....31 L8
 DARL/WED WS10 ....68 D2
 GTWY WS6 ....24 C2
 HAG/WOL DY9 ....102 B7
 KGSWFD DY6 ....83 H7
 KIDD DY10 ....138 D5
 NUN CV11 ....99 J2
 OLDBY B69 ....86 H2
 RLSN CV32 ....206 D5
 STRBR DY8 ....101 K5
 STRBR DY8 ....119 L1
 TPTN/OCK DY4 ....67 L1
Park St South BKHL/PFLD WV2 ....4 E3
Park Ter DARL/WED WS10 ....51 M7
 HDSW B21 ....88 C5
The Park REDW B97 ....193 G6
Park Vw DARL/WED WS10 ....52 A7
 HOCK/TIA B94 ....175 J8 (HOCK/SHEL)
 SCFLD/BOLD B73 ....56 E7
Park View Cl
 RCOVN/BALC/EX CV7 ....116 E6
Parkview Ct KGSWFD DY6 ....82 F5
Park View Crs WSLW WS2 ....52 F5
Parkview Dr WASH/WDE B8 ....90 E8
Parkview Rd BILS/COS WV14 ....51 G5
Park View Rd FOAKS/STRLY B74..56 E2
 HAG/WOL DY9 ....119 M7
 NFLD/LBR B31 ....144 D2
Park Vls BORD B9 * 107 M3
Parkville Av HRBN B17 ....123 H3
Parkville Cl COVN CV6 ....134 A2
Parkville Hwy COVN CV6 ....133 M3
Park Wk BRLYHL DY5 ....102 B5
 RUGBYN/HIL CV21 ....186 E1
Park Wy RBRY B45 ....143 M5
 REDE B98 ....194 F7
 WNSFLD WV11 ....37 L4
Parkway RCOVN/BALC/EX CV7..135 M5
 WASH/WDE B8 ....90 E8
Parkway Rd DUDN DY1 ....84 E3
The Parkway CDSL WV8 ....34 B7
 DUNHL/THL/PER WV6 ....35 L8
 RUSH/SHEL WS4 ....40 A5
Parkwood Cft PBAR/PBCH B42 ..70 D4
Parkwood Dr SCFLD/BOLD B73 ..72 A3
Park Wood La TLHL/CAN CV4 ..153 H6
Parkwood Rd BRGRVW B61 ....191 D2
Parkyn St BKHL/PFLD WV2 ....3 J9
Parliament St AST/WIT B6 ....89 K7
 SMHTH B10 ....108 A5
 WBROM B70 ....87 H4
Parlows End HWK/WKHTH B38..145 L4
Parmington Cl REDW B97 ....201 H4
Parnell Cl RUGBYN/HIL CV21 ..186 D2
Parr Cl RLSS CV31 ....206 E1
Parrotts Gv COVE CV2 ....117 H8
Parry Rd COVE CV2 ....134 F5
 KIDDW DY11 ....163 M2
 WNSFLD WV11 ....37 L5
Parsonage Dr HALE B63 ....102 F6
 RBRY B45 ....170 B1
Parsonage St HHTH/SAND B71..87 H7
 OLDBY B69 ....86 F7
Parson's Hl BVILLE B30 ....145 H4
 LGLYGN/QTN B68 ....104 F4
Parsons Hollow
 TAM/AM/WIL B77 ....46 C5
Parson's Nook COVE CV2 ....134 E6
Parsons Rd REDE B98 ....202 C3
Parsons St DUDN DY1 ....84 E4
Parson St TAM/AM/WIL B77 ....46 D8
Partons Rd KHTH/KHTH/YWD B14..125 H7
Partridge Av DARL/WED WS10 ..51 M7
Partridge Cl
 CHWD/FDBR/MGN B37 ....111 G2
 HEDN WS12 ....12 B6
 LICH WS14 ....21 G5
Partridge Gv KIDD DY10 ....164 E3
Partridge Rd REDW B97 ....201 H4
 STETCH B33 ....108 E1
Partridge Mll BLOX/PEL WS3 ....39 J2
Partridge Rd
 LGN/SDN/BHAMAIR B26 ....109 J4
 STRBR DY8 ....119 L1
Passey Rd MOS/BIL B13 ....126 B3
Passfield Av HEDN WS12 ....11 H3
Passfield Rd STETCH B33 ....109 K2
The Pastures
 TAM/AM/WIL B77 ....46 B1
Pasture Ga CNCK/NC WS11 ....15 J4
Pasture Vw BLOX/PEL WS3 ....39 K4
Patch La REDE B98 ....202 D7

Pat Davis Ct KIDD DY10 ....138 C6
Patent Dr DARL/WED WS10 ....68 A3
Paternoster Rw DIG/EDG B5 * 7 H5
 KIDDW DY11 ....138 D7
 WOLV WV1 ....3 G3
Paterson Pl BRWNH WS8 ....26 A3
Pathlow Crs SHLY B90 ....147 L4
The Patios KIDDW DY11 ....138 C6
Paton Gv BHTH/HG B13 ....125 K3
Patricia Cl TLHL/CAN CV4 ....153 G4
Patricia Av KHTH/KHTH/YWD B14..147 G1
 ETTPK/GDPK/PENN WV4 ....50 A8
Patricia Crs DUDN DY1 ....66 F7
Patricia Dr TPTN/OCK DY4 ....85 L3
Patrick Br HIA/OLT B92 ....130 B6
Patrick Gregory Rd
 WNSFLD WV11 ....37 K6
Patrick Ms LICH WS13 ....20 D4
Patrick Rd
 LGN/SDN/BHAMAIR B26 ....109 J6
Patriot Cl WSL WS1 ....53 H8
Patshull Av WOLVN WV10 ....35 M7
Patshull Cl GTB/HAM B43 ....70 B4
Patshull Gv WOLVN WV10 ....35 M7
Patshull Pl LOZ/NWT B19 * 89 M8
Pattens Rd WWCK CV34 ....205 M4
Patterdale RUGBYN/HIL CV21 ..161 H6
Patterdale Dr CNCK/NC WS11 ..16 E1
 ERDW/GRVHL B23 ....90 B1
Patterdale Wy BRLYHL DY5 ....101 M5
Patterton Dr WALM/CURD B76 ..73 K5
Pattingham Rd
 DUNHL/THL/PER WV6 ....48 A3
Pattison Gdns ERDW/GRVHL B23..90 B1
Pattison St DSYBK/YTR WS5 ....53 J8
Paul Byrne Ct
 BFLD/HDSWWD B20 ....88 F4
Pauline Av COVN CV6 ....134 F3
Pauls Coppice BRWNH WS8 ....26 B5
Paul St BILS/COS WV14 ....66 E4
 BKHL/PFLD WV2 ....2 ...
 DARL/WED WS10 ....68 E3
Paul V TPTN/OCK DY4 ....67 M8
Pavenham Dr DIG/EDG B5 ....125 G1
Pavilion Av SMTHWKW B67 ....105 J2
Pavilion Dr PBAR/PBCH B42 ....89 G2
Pavilion End KINVER DY7 ....100 C4
Pavilion Gdns BRGRVW B61 ....168 D8
 DUDS DY2 ....103 G3
The Pavilions CBHAMNE B4 * 7 H1
 CHWD/FDBR/MGN B37 ....111 H5
Pavilion Wy COVN CV6 ....154 D2
Pavillion Cl ALDR WS9 ....40 F5
Pavior's Rd BNTWD WS7 ....26 C1
Paxford Cl REDE B98 ....194 F7
Paxford Wy NFLD/LBR B31 ....123 L3
Paxmead Cl COVN CV6 ....133 L3
Paxton Av COVN CV6 ....8 ...
 HAG/WOL DY9 ....120 E1
 WSNGN B18 ....88 E8
Payne Cl RLSN CV32 ....206 C3
Paynell Cl COVN CV6 ....133 M3
Payne's La COV CV1 ....9 L4
 RUGBYN/HIL CV21 ....186 B2
Payne St BLKHTH/ROWR B65 ....104 A4
Payton Cl OLDBY B69 ....86 B5
Payton Rd HDSW B21 ....88 B5
Peace Cl GTWY WS6 ....24 C2
Peach Av DARL/WED WS10 ....52 A7
Peachley Cl HALE B63 ....121 M3
Peach Ley Rd SLYOAK B29 ....123 K6
Peach Rd SHHTH WV12 ....37 L7
Peacock Av COVE CV2 ....135 K4
 WNSFLD WV11 ....37 L7
Peacock Cl TPTN/OCK DY4 ....85 M1
Peacock Ms KIDDW DY11 ....138 C5
Peacock Rd DARL/WED WS10 ....52 A7
 MOS/BIL B13 ....125 K7
Peacocks Est BHTH/HG B64 * ..103 G4
Peak Cft CBROM B36 ....91 H5
Peak Dr SEDG DY3 ....83 M2
Peake Av NUN CV11 ....81 J5
Peake Crs BRWNH WS8 ....26 D8
Peake Dr TPTN/OCK DY4 ....85 M1
Peake Rd BRWNH WS8 ....26 D8
Peak House Rd GTB/HAM B43 ..70 C2
Peakman Cl RBRY B45 ....143 L7
Peakman St REDW B97 ....202 C1
Peak Rd STRBR DY8 ....101 M7
Peal St WSL WS1 ....5 G4
Pearce Cl DUDN DY1 ....84 C5
Pearl Gv ACGN B27 ....126 F2
Pearl La STRPT DY13 ....188 B5
Pearman Rd RBRY B45 ....143 H4
 SMTHWK B66 ....105 L2
Pearmans Cft HLYWD B47 ....146 E1
Pearsall Dr OLDBY B69 ....86 C5
Pears Cl KNWTH CV8 ....179 K8
Pearson Av COVN CV6 ....134 F4
Pearson St BRLYHL DY5 ....102 B2
 CDYHTH B64 ....103 J4
 HAG/WOL DY9 ....120 B2
 WBROM B70 ....86 F1
Pear Tree Av NUNW/HART CV10..80 F7
 POL/KGSB/FAZ B78 ....60 B8
 TPTN/OCK DY4 ....51 M4
Peartree Av WLNHL WV13 ....51 M4
Pear Tree Cl CRTAM B79 ....69 M4
 HEDN WS12 ....12 B6
 KIDD DY10 ....138 F6
 SHLY B90 ....147 H3
 STETCH B33 ....109 H3
Pear Tree Ct
 BLKHTH/ROWR B65 ....104 B2
Pear Tree Crs SHLY B90 ....147 G2
Pear Tree Dr
 BLKHTH/ROWR B65 ....104 B2
 GTB/HAM B43 ....70 A4
Peartree Dr STRBR DY8 ....119 L3
Pear Tree Gv SHLY B90 ....147 G2
Pear Tree La BILS/COS WV14 ....67 H5
 BRWNH WS8 ....26 A3 (BLKHTH)
Peartree La CDYHTH B64 ....103 J4
 DUDS DY2 ....85 H7
 GTB/HAM B43 ....70 A4
 SMTHWK B67 ....105 J1
Pear Tree Wy
 RUGBYS/DCH CV22 ....185 M4
Peascroft La BILS/COS WV14 ....51 J7
Peasefield Cl HDSW B21 ....88 C4
Peat Cl RUGBYS/DCH CV22 ....186 C4
Pebblebrook Wy BDWTH CV12..117 J3
Pebble Cl STRBR DY8 ....101 M8
Pebble Island Wy RLSS CV31 ..207 G8
Pebble Mill Cl CNCK/NC WS11 ..16 D3
Pebble Mill Dr CNCK/NC WS11..16 D3
Pebble Mill Rd DIG/EDG B5 ....124 F1
Pebworth Av SHLY B90 ....148 F7
Pebworth Cl COVW CV5 ....153 ?

REDE B98 .....195 G6
SLYOAK B29 .....124 F2

Pebworth Dr
RWWCK/WEL CV35 .....204 C2
Pebworth Gv DUDN DY1 .....84 E2
STETCH B33 .....110 A5
Peckham Rd KGSTG B44 .....71 L5
Peckover Cl BLKHTH/ROWR B65...103 M4
Peckstone Cl COV CV1 .....6 D8
Peddimore La WALM/CURD B76 .....74 B7
Pedmore Cl REDE B98 .....202 F6
Pedmore Court Rd STRBR B79 .....119 M4
Pedmore Gv KGSTG B44 .....71 K3
Pedmore Hall La HAG/WOL DY9 ...120 A4
Pedmore La HAG/WOL DY9 .....120 A4
HAG/WOL DY9 .....120 A4
Pedmore Rd BRLYHL DY5 .....102 D1
HAG/WOL DY9 .....102 D1
Peel Cl COVN CV6 .....134 C7
Peel Dr HEDN WS12 .....12 F1
DARL/WED WS10 .....52 B5
HIA/OLT B92 .....129 M7
POL/KGSB/FAZ B78 .....45 J8
WLNHL WV13 .....51 L4
Peel La COVN CV6 .....134 C7
Peel St BDMR/CCFT WV3 .....2 E6
COVN CV6 .....134 D7
DUDS DY2 .....85 J1
HHTH/SAND B71 .....69 G8
KIDDW DY11 .....138 B8
TPTN/OCK DY4 .....85 L1
WLNHL WV13 .....51 L4
WSNGN B18 .....88 C8
Peel Wk HRBN B17 .....105 K6
Pegasus Wk SLYOAK B29 .....124 B4
Peglee Wk ALE/KHTH/YWD B14 ...146 A3
Pegmill Cl COVS CV3 .....155 K5
Pelham Dr DUDN DY1 .....84 E2
Pelham Ldg KIDD DY10 .....138 D8
Pelham Rd WASH/WDE B8 .....108 F1
Pelsall La BLOX/PEL WS3 .....39 L7
RUSH/SHEL WS4 .....39 M6
Pelsall Rd BRWNH WS8 .....26 B6
Pemberly Gv ACGN B27 .....126 E4
Pemberton Cl SMTHWK B66 .....105 M2
Pemberton Crs DARL/WED WS10...69 G1
KIDD DY10 .....139 G2
Pemberton Rd BILS/COS WV14 .....67 H4
WBROM B70 .....68 C6
Pemberton St WSNGN B18 .....6 A2
Pembridge Cl BRLYHL DY5 .....102 D4
REDE B98 .....203 H3
RIDG/WDGT B32 .....122 D4
Pembridge Rd DOR/KN B93 .....175 J2
Pembroke Av BKHL/PFLD WV2 .....50 C6
Pembroke Cl BDWTH CV12 .....116 A4
CRTAM B79 .....31 H4
SHHTH WV12 .....37 M7
WWCK CV34 .....204 E3
Pembroke Cft HLGN/YWD B28 ...126 E8
Pembroke Gdns STRBR DY8 .....101 G3
Pembroke Rd BHTH/HG B12 .....125 L1
HHTH/SAND B71 .....68 F6
Pembroke Wy HHTH/SAND B71 .....68 F6
HLGN/YWD B28 .....126 E8
NUN CV11 .....99 K5
STRPT DY13 .....163 J7
Pembrook Rd COVN CV6 .....134 A3
Pembury Av COVN CV6 .....134 C6
Pembury Cl FOAKS/STRLY B74 .....55 K7
Pembury Cft KGSTG B44 .....71 L4
Penarth Gv COVS CV3 .....156 D6
Pencombe Dr
ETTPK/GDPK/PENN WV4 .....50 A8
Pencraig Cl KNWTH CV8 .....179 M8
Pencroft Rd BKDE/SHDE B34 .....91 M6
Penda Gv DUNHL/THL/PER WV6..34 D8
Pendeen Rd
ALE/KHTH/YWD B14 .....147 G1
Pendeford Cl
DUNHL/THL/PER WV6 .....35 J5
Pendeford La COVEN WV9 .....35 L1
Pendeford Mill La CDSL WV8 .....35 G2
Pendennis Cl COVN CV6 .....134 C5
Pendennis Dr OLDBY B69 .....85 L5
Penderel Cl BVILLE B30 .....124 B8
Penderel St BLOX/PEL WS3 .....39 G4
Pendigo Wy BHAMNEC B40 .....129 K2
Pendinas Dr CDSL WV8 .....21 G1
Pendle Hl HEDN WS12 .....17 G1
Pendleton Gv ACGN B27 .....126 F5
Pendragon Rd PBAR/PBCH B42 ...89 G1
Pendred Rd RUGBYS/DCH CV22..186 A4
Pendrel Cl GTWY WS6 .....24 C5
Pendrell Cl
CHWD/FDBR/MGN B37 .....110 E2
Pendrell Ct CDSL WV8 .....34 E2
Pendrill Rd WOLVN WV10 .....36 D2
Penfields Rd STRBR DY8 .....101 L1
Penge Gv KGSTG B44 .....71 J2
Penhallow Dr
ETTPK/GDPK/PENN WV4 .....51 J1
Penhurst Av BFLD/HDSWWD B20..89 H4
Penk Dr BNTWD WS7 .....19 H7
Penkridge Bank HEDN WS12 .....12 C1
Penkridge Cl WSLW WS2 .....53 H1
Penkridge Gv STETCH B33 .....109 K1
Penkridge La PENK ST19 .....11 H6
Penkridge St WSLW WS2 .....53 H1
Penkridge Whf PENK ST19 .....10 D5
Penk Ri DUNHL/THL/PER WV6 .....48 E1
Penleigh Gdns WMBN WV5 .....64 D6
Penley Gv WASH/WDE B8 .....90 F7
Penmanor BRGRVE B60 .....192 B5
Penmire Rd ATHST CV9 .....
Pennant Rd BLKHTH/ROWR B65..103 H4
CDYHTH B64 .....103 H4
Pennard Gv RIDG/WDGT B32 ...123 K1
Penn Cl BLOX/PEL WS3 .....39 G4
Penn Common Rd
ETTPK/GDPK/PENN WV4 .....65 J4
Penncricket La
BLKHTH/ROWR B65 .....104 C2
Penn Croft La
ETTPK/GDPK/PENN WV4 .....65 L4
Pennhouse Av
ETTPK/GDPK/PENN WV4 .....49 K8
Pennine Dr CNCK/NC WS11 .....16 C3
Pennine Rd BRGRVW B61 .....168 E8
Pennine Wy NUNW/HART CV10 ...72 B1
SHHTH WV12 .....52 B1
STRBR DY8 .....101 L2
TAM/AM/WIL B77 .....46 F5
WASH/WDE B8 .....90 A4
Pennington Cl WBROM B70 .....86 E3
Pennington Ms
RUGBYN/HIL CV21 .....186 C2
Pennington Wy COVN CV6 .....134 C2
Penn Rd BKHL/PFLD WV2 .....2 E8

BLKHTH/ROWR B65 .....104 C2
ETTPK/GDPK/PENN WV4 .....65 J1
SEDG DY3 .....
Penn Rd Island BDMR/CCFT WV3 ...2 E7
Penns Cl RUSH/SHEL WS4 .....40 A5
Penns Lake Rd WALM/CURD B76..73 J8
Penns La CSCFLD/WYGN B72 .....73 H6
CSHL/WTROR B46 .....93 K6
Penns Wood Cl SEDG DY3 .....66 A3
Penns Wood Dr
WALM/CURD B76 .....73 K6
Pennwood La
ETTPK/GDPK/PENN WV4 .....65 K2
Pennyacre Rd
ALE/KHTH/YWD B14 .....146 B3
Pennycress Gdns WOLVN WV10..22 F6
Pennycress Gn CNCK/NC WS11 ...25 L1
Pennyfield Cft STETCH B33 .....109 J2
Pennyford Cl REDW B97 .....193 L8
Pennyhill La HHTH/SAND B71 .....69 J6
Pennymoor Rd
TAM/AM/WIL B77 .....46 F6
Penny Park La COVN CV6 .....133 K2
Pennyroyal Cl DSYBK/YTR WS5...69 L2
Penny Royal Cl SEDG DY3 .....84 B3
Pennystone Cl RLSS CV31 .....207 H7
Penrice Dr DUDS DY2 .....85 K4
Penrith Cl BRLYHL DY5 .....101 M5
RLSN CV32 .....206 A3
Penrith Cft RIDG/WDGT B32 .....122 E5
Penrith Gv
CHWD/FDBR/MGN B37 .....111 G3
Penrose Cl TLHL/CAN CV4 .....153 L6
Penryhn Cl KNWTH CV8 .....180 A8
Penryn Cl DSYBK/YTR WS5 .....54 B6
NUN CV11 .....81 L8
Penryn Rd DSYBK/YTR WS5 .....54 B6
Pensan Vls DARL/WED WS10 * ...52 B7
Pensby Cl MOS/BIL B13 .....126 A5
Pensford Rd NFLD/LBR B31 .....145 G2
Pensham Cft SHLY B90 .....148 E7
Penshaw Cl COVEN WV9 .....35 L3
Penshaw Gv MOS/BIL B13 .....126 A4
Penshurst Av NUN CV11 .....99 K5
Penshurst Rd BRLYHL DY5 .....101 M5
Pensilva Wy COV CV1 .....7 L1
Penstock Dr OLDBY B69 .....104 D1
Penstone La
ETTPK/GDPK/PENN WV4 .....64 C5
Pentire Cl NUN CV11 .....81 J8
Pentire Rd LICHS WS14 .....21 H7
Pentland Cft BHTH/HG B12 .....107 H5
Pentlands Gdns
BDMR/CCFT WV3 .....49 J3
Pentos Dr SPARK B11 .....126 B3
Pentridge Cl WALM/CURD B76 ...73 K8
Penzance Wy NUN CV11 .....81 K8
Penzer Dr RBRY B45 .....170 B5
Penzer St KGSWFD DY6 .....83 L1
Peolsford Rd BLOX/PEL WS3 .....39 L1
Peplins Wy BVILLE B30 .....145 M2
Peplow Rd STETCH B33 .....109 L1
Pepperbox Dr TPTN/OCK DY4 ...67 G7
Pepper Hl STRBR DY8 .....119 L1
Pepper La COV CV1 .....6 E7
Pepperwood Cl BRGRVW B61 ...168 B2
Pepper Wood Dr NFLD/LBR B31..144 A4
Pepys Cnr TLHL/CAN CV4 .....153 J2
Perch Av
CHWD/FDBR/MGN B37 .....110 E2
Perch Cl WOLV WV1 .....50 F1
Perchfoot Cl COV CV1 .....8 H8
Perch Rd WSLW WS2 .....52 L1
Percival Rd LDYWD/EDGR B16...106 A4
RUGBYS/DCH CV22 .....187 H5
Percy Crs KNWTH CV8 .....197 J3
SPARK B11 .....126 B2
WWCK CV34 .....205 J5
Percy St COV CV1 .....8 C4
Peregrine Dr DUDN DY1 .....84 D4
Peregrine Gv COVW CV5 .....132 E8
Peregrine Gv DUDY DY10 .....164 E3
Pereira Rd HRBN B17 .....106 A6
Perimeter Rd BHAMNEC B40 .....129 L1
Perivale Gv BILS/COS WV14 .....67 H4
Perivale Wy STRBR DY8 .....101 L5
Periwinkle Cl BRWNH WS8 .....26 B7
Perkins Cl DUDN DY1 .....67 G7
Perkins Gv RUGBYN/HIL CV21..187 K4
Perks Rd WNSFLD WV11 .....37 K7
Permian Ct RUGBYN/HIL CV21..161 G7
Perott Dr MGN/WHC B75 .....57 H3
Perrett Wk KIDD DY11 .....138 A7
Perrins Av HAG/WOL DY9 .....120 D1
Perrins Ri HAG/WOL DY9 .....120 D1
Perrott Gdns STRBR DY8 .....101 M4
Perrott St WSNGN B18 .....88 B7
Perry Av PBAR/PBCH B42 .....89 G1
Perry Barr Locks
PBAR/PBCH B42 * 70 F7
Perry Cl DUDS DY2 .....85 H5
Perry Common Rd
ERDW/GRVHL B23 .....71 M7
Perry Ct LGLYGN/QTN B68 .....104 F6
Perrycrofts Crs CRTAM B79 .....32 A6
Perryfields Cl REDE B98 .....202 D7
Perryfields Rd BRGRVW B61 ...168 D8
Perryfields Rd BRGRVW B61 ...168 H2
Perryford Dr SOLH B91 .....148 F5
Perry Hall Dr SHHTH WV12 .....37 M8
Perry Hall Rd WNSFLD WV11 .....37 K7
Perry Hill Crs LGLYGN/QTN B68..104 F6
Perry Hill La LGLYGN/QTN B68 * ..104 F6
Perry Hill Rd LGLYGN/QTN B68..105 G6
Perry La BRGRVW B61 .....191 K3
KIDD DY10 .....164 F9
Perryman Dr POL/KGSB/FAZ B78..60 D5
Perry Park Crs PBAR/PBCH B42..70 F7
Perry Park Rd CDYHTH B64 .....103 M4
Perry St BILS/COS WV14 .....67 J2
DARL/WED WS10 .....52 D8
SMTHWK B66 .....87 L6
TPTN/OCK DY4 .....85 L1
Perry Villa Dr PBAR/PBCH B42..71 H4
Perry Wk ERDW/GRVHL B23 .....71 M7
Perrywell Rd PBAR/PBCH B42 ...89 J1
Perry Wood Rd PBAR/PBCH B42..70 E6
Persehouse St WSL WS1 .....5 H1
Pershore Cl WS8 .....38 D3
Pershore Pl TLHL/CAN CV4 .....154 C7
Pershore Rd BLOX/PEL WS3 .....38 E2
BVILLE B30 .....145 K1
DIG/EDG B5 .....107 H7
HALE B63 .....121 L3
KIDDW DY11 .....137 L2
Pershore Rd South BVILLE B30..145 K2
Pershore St DIG/EDG B5 .....6 E7
Pershore Wy BLOX/PEL WS3 .....38 D3
Perth Ri COVW CV5 .....153 L1
Perth Rd SHHTH WV12 .....37 M7

Perton Brook V
DUNHL/THL/PER WV6 .....48 D3
Perton Gv DUNHL/THL/PER WV6..48 D3
SLYOAK B29 .....123 L4
Perton Rd DUNHL/THL/PER WV6..48 D3
Pestilence La ALVE B48 .....171 H5
Petard Ct TAM/AM/WIL B77 * 46 A5
Petchells Cl BRLYHL DY5 .....83 M8
Peter Av RLSN CV32 .....199 J8
Peterborough Dr CNCK/NC WS11..17 G4
Peterbrook Ri SHLY B90 .....147 H4
Peterbrook Rd SHLY B90 .....147 H4
Peterdale Dr
ETTPK/GDPK/PENN WV4 .....65 K2
Peterhead TAM/AM/WIL B77 .....32 D8
Peters Av NFLD/LBR B31 .....144 D3
Petersfield CNCK/NC WS11 .....16 D1
Petersfield Ct HLGN/YWD B28 * ..126 D5
Petersfield Dr
BLKHTH/ROWR B65 .....104 C2
Petersfield Rd HLGN/YWD B28 ...126 D5
Petersham Pl EDG B15 .....106 C7
Petersham Rd KGSTG B44 .....72 A4
Peter's Finger BRGRVW B61 .....191 K4
Peter's Hill Rd BRLYHL DY5 .....102 A6
Petershouse Dr
FOAKS/STRLY B74 .....42 D8
Peter's La BEWD WS7 .....19 L8
Peters St WBROM B70 .....68 E6
Peters Wk CDYHTH B64 .....134 E1
Petford St CDYHTH B64 .....103 J4
Petitor Crs COVE CV2 .....135 G4
Pettit Cl ALE/KHTH/YWD B14..146 C4
Pettiver Crs RUGBYN/HIL CV21..187 K4
Petton Cl REDE B98 .....203 J2
Pettyfield Cl
LGN/SDN/BHAMAIR B26 .....109 L7
Pettyfields Cl DOR/KN B93 .....149 L8
Petworth Cl WLNHL WV13 .....51 K5
Petworth Gv
LGN/SDN/BHAMAIR B26 .....109 J7
Pevensey Cl DUDS DY2 .....85 K5
Pevensey Rd BRGRVE B60 .....192 A4
Peverel Dr HLGN/YWD B28 .....126 D6
Peveril Dr COVS CV3 .....154 F8
Peveril Gv WALM/CURD B76 .....73 J1
Peveril Rd DUNHL/THL/PER WV6..48 D1
Pevril Wy GTB/HAM B43 .....70 D3
Peyto Cl COVN CV6 .....134 A3
Pheasant Cl BDWTH CV12 .....116 B4
KIDD DY10 .....164 E3
Pheasant Cft CBROM B36 .....92 E5
Pheasant La REDE B98 .....202 D6
Pheasant Oak TLHL/CAN CV4 ...153 G3
Pheasant St BRLYHL DY5 .....102 A2
Pheasant St SMTHWKW B67 .....105 H3
Philip Gv CNCK/NC WS11 .....16 D1
Philip Rd HALE B63 .....121 K2
TPTN/OCK DY4 .....68 B8
Philip Sidney Rd SPARK B11 .....125 M2
Philip St BILS/COS WV14 .....67 H4
Philip Victor Rd
BFLD/HDSWWD B20 .....88 D4
Phillimore Rd WASH/WDE B8 .....90 B8
Phillippes Rd WWCK CV34 .....205 K4
Phillip Rd WSLW WS2 .....52 D3
Phillips Av WNSFLD WV11 .....37 K4
Phillips St AST/WIT B6 .....89 J7
Phillips Ter REDE B98 .....202 D1
Phipps Av RUGBYN/HIL CV21..187 K4
Phipson Rd SPARK B11 .....125 M2
Phoenix Gn EDG B15 .....106 C4
Phoenix Pk BLKHTH/ROWR B65..104 B4
Phoenix Ri DARL/WED WS10 .....68 A1
ERDW/GRVHL B23 .....71 M6
TPTN/OCK DY4 .....67 K7
WLNHL WV13 .....51 H2
Phoenix St BKHL/PFLD WV2 .....50 D4
WBROM B70 .....68 D8
Phoenix Wy COVN CV6 .....134 C3
Picasso Cl CNCK/NC WS11 .....17 H3
Piccadilly Ar DRBM B2 .....6 F5
Piccadilly Cl
CHWD/FDBR/MGN B37 .....111 G4
Piccadilly Crs POL/KGSB/FAZ B78..60 D5
Pickard Cl RUGBYN/HIL CV21 ...161 J6
Pickard St WWCK CV34 .....205 L6
Pickenham Rd
ALE/KHTH/YWD B14 .....146 E4
Pickering Cft RIDG/WDGT B32..123 G4
Pickering Rd WNSFLD WV11 .....37 H8
Pickersleigh Cl HALE B63 .....121 L2
Pickford Cl NUN CV11 .....99 L4
Pickford Grange La COVW CV5..132 A6
Pickford Green La COVW CV5 ...132 A7
Pickford St DIG/EDG B5 .....7 K6
Pickford Wy COVW CV5 .....132 F7
Pickrell Rd BILS/COS WV14 .....66 F4
Pickwick Gv MOS/BIL B13 .....126 A3
Pickwick Pl BILS/COS WV14 .....67 J1
Picton Cft
CHWD/FDBR/MGN B37 .....111 H4
Picton Gv MOS/BIL B13 .....125 M8
Picturedrome Wy
DARL/WED WS10 .....52 B7
Piddock Rd SMTHWK B66 .....87 L8
Pierce Av HIA/OLT B92 .....127 J2
Piercy St WBROM B70 .....86 E2
Piers Cl WWCK CV34 .....205 K5
Piers Rd WSNGN B18 .....88 E6
Piggots Cft
CHWD/FDBR/MGN B37 .....110 D2
Pike Cl BFLD/HDSWWD B20 .....89 G3
Pike Dr CHWD/FDBR/MGN B37..111 G2
Pikehelve St TPTN/OCK DY4 .....68 C6
Pike Hl BRGRVE B60 .....169 L7
Pikehorne Cft CBROM B36 .....92 B5
Pike Rd WSLW WS2 .....52 E1
Pikers La COVW CV5 .....132 E2
Pikes Pool La BRGRVE B60 .....192 B4
The Pikes RBRY B45 .....143 K5
Pilgrims La RUGBY CV23 .....161 K4
Pilkington Av CSCFLD/WYGN B72..72 E4
Pilkington Rd COVW CV5 .....146 C
Pillaton Cl PENK ST19 .....10 C5
Pillaton Dr HEDN WS12 .....12 C1
Pilling Cl COVE CV2 .....135 K4
Pilson Cl CBROM B36 .....92 E4
Pimbury Rd SHHTH WV12 .....38 B6
Pimlico Ct SEDG DY3 .....84 C4
Pimpernel Dr DSYBK/YTR WS5...69 L2
Pinbury Cft
CHWD/FDBR/MGN B37 .....110 D3
Pinchers Cl HAG/WOL DY9 .....141 J6
Pinders La RUGBYN/HIL CV21 * ..186 F7
Pineapple Cl
ALE/KHTH/YWD B14 .....125 G7
Pineapple Gv BVILLE B30 .....125 G6
Pineapple Rd BVILLE B30 .....125 G7
Pine Av DARL/WED WS10 .....52 B8
SMTHWK B66 .....87 G6
Pine Cl BDMR/CCFT WV3 .....2 A1
Pine Gn DY1 .....66 F8

KINVER DY7 .....118 A2
SOLH B91 .....148 D3
Pinedene STRPT DY13 .....188 F2
Pine Gn DY1 .....66 F8
Pine Gv ALE/KHTH/YWD B14 ...125 L6
BNTWD WS7 .....18 D4
RBRY B45 .....169 K3
RUGBYN/HIL CV32 .....187 L4
Pinehurst RLSN CV32 .....199 J8
Pinehurst Dr HWK/WKHTH B38...145 K2
Pine Leigh FOAKS/STRLY B74 .....56 F4
Pineneedle Cft SHHTH WV12 .....52 C1
Pineridge Dr KIDDW DY11 .....137 M8
Pine Rd DUDN DY1 .....67 G8
The Pines BDMR/CCFT WV3 .....49 H4
BDWTH CV12 .....116 C3
LICHS WS14 .....21 K6
RBRY B45 .....143 L4
SHLY B90 .....147 J6
TLHL/CAN CV4 * 153 H6
Pine Sq WS6 .....95 G6
Pine St BLOX/PEL WS3 .....39 G4
Pinetree Av FOAKS/STRLY B74...55 H4
Pine Tree Av TLHL/CAN CV4 ...153 K4
Pine Tree Cl HEDN WS12 .....12 E4
Pinetree Rd BEWD DY12 .....162 D3
Pine Tree Rd BEWD DY12 .....162 D3
Pineview NFLD/LBR B31 .....144 D3
Pine Wk CDSL WV8 .....34 D3
HAG/WOL DY9 .....120 B2
NFLD/LBR B31 .....144 D2
STRPT DY13 .....188 C1
Pinewall Av HWK/WKHTH B38...145 K4
Pineways FOAKS/STRLY B74 .....56 A2
STRBR DY8 .....101 G3
Pineways Dr
DUNHL/THL/PER WV6 .....49 J2
The Pineways OLDBY B69 .....86 A8
Pinewood Av BILS/COS WV14 .....67 J6
CNCK/NC WS11 .....16 B1
Pinewood Cl BDMR/CCFT WV3 ...48 E5
BRWNH WS8 .....26 C5
KGSWFD DY6 .....83 L3
KGSTG B44 .....71 L3
RBRY B45 .....143 H5
SHHTH WV12 .....38 B6
WMBN WV5 .....64 C7
Pinewood Dr COVS CV3 .....157 G6
SOLH B91 .....148 D3
Pine Woods RIDG/WDGT B32 ...122 E3
SLYOAK B29 .....123 K5
Pinewoods Av HAG/WOL DY9 ...140 D1
Pinewoods Cl HAG/WOL DY9 ...140 D1
Pinfield Dr BRGRVE B60 .....169 M4
Pinfold CNCK/NC WS11 .....16 C3
Pinfold Ct DARL/WED WS10 .....52 D8
Pinfold Crs
ETTPK/GDPK/PENN WV4 .....49 K8
Pinfold Gdns WNSFLD WV11 .....37 H8
Pinfold Gv BDMR/CCFT WV3 .....49 H7
Pinfold La ALDR WS9 .....54 F6
CNCK/NC WS11 .....25 J1
ETTPK/GDPK/PENN WV4 .....49 J8
GTWY WS6 .....24 E2
PENK ST19 .....10 D5
Pinfold Rd LICH WS13 .....20 D4
SOLH B91 .....128 C4
Pinfold St BILS/COS WV14 .....51 H8
CBHAM B2 .....6 C5
DARL/WED WS10 .....52 A8
OLDBY B69 .....86 A4
RUGBYN/HIL CV21 .....186 D6
Pingle Cl HHTH/SAND B71 .....69 H4
Pingle Ct NUN CV11 .....99 H6
Pingle La BNTWD WS7 .....27 H1
Pink Green La REDE B98 .....195 M3
Pinkney Pl LGLYGN/QTN B68 ...105 G2
Pinley Flds COVS CV3 .....155 M5
Pinley Gv GTB/HAM B43 .....70 F2
Pinley Wy SOLH B91 .....148 E5
Pinner Gv RIDG/WDGT B32 .....123 J1
Pinner's Cft COVE CV2 .....134 E8
Pinnock Pl TLHL/CAN CV4 .....153 K4
Pinson Rd WLNHL WV13 .....51 K4
Pinta Dr STRPT DY13 .....188 F2
Pintail Dr ERDW/GRVHL B23 .....90 A3
Pintail Gv KIDD DY10 .....164 F2
Pinto Cl LDYWD/EDGR B16 .....106 D3
Pinwall La ATHST CV9 .....63 K1
Pinza Cft CBROM B36 .....92 A6
Pioli Pl WSLW WS2 .....39 H8
Pioneer Cl REDW B97 .....202 B1
Pioneer Ct REDW B97 .....
Piper Cl DUNHL/THL/PER WV6 ...48 D1
Piper Pl STRBR DY8 .....101 K5
Piper Rd BDMR/CCFT WV3 .....48 E5
Pipers Cl BRGRVE B60 .....191 H6
Pipers Cft LICH WS13 .....21 J2
Piper's La KNWTH CV8 .....197 L5
NUNW/HART CV10 .....79 G5
Pipers Rw WOLV WV1 3
Pipes Meadow BILS/COS WV14..51 J8
Pipewell Cl RUGBYS/DCH CV22..186 A4
Pipit Ct KIDD DY10 .....164 E3
Pipkin Ct COV CV1 .....
Pippin Av HALE B63 .....102 F6
Pirbright Cl BILS/COS WV14 .....52 A8
Pirrey Cl BILS/COS WV14 .....67 H4
Pitcairn Cl BVILLE B30 .....125 J8
Pitcairn Dr RMSLY B62 .....103 M7
Pitcairn Rd SMTHWKW B67 .....105 J4
Pitcheroak Cottages
REDW B97 * 201 L2
Pitclose Rd NFLD/LBR B31 .....144 F4
Pitfield Rd STETCH B33 .....110 B4
Pitfield Rw DUDN DY1 .....84 D5
Pitfields Cl LGLYGN/QTN B68 ...104 E5
Pitfields Rd LGLYGN/QTN B68 ...104 E5
Pitfield St DUDN DY1 * 84 D5
Pithall Rd BKDE/SHDE B34 .....92 B2
Pit Hl KNWTH CV8 .....182 A8
Pit Leasow Cl BVILLE B30 .....124 F7
Pitman Rd RIDG/WDGT B32 .....105 G8
Pitmaston Rd HLGN/YWD B28 ...126 C6
Pitsford St WSNGN B18 .....6 H1
Pitt La HIA/OLT B92 .....127 J1
Pitts Farm Rd CBROM B36 .....92 C3
Pitt St CBHAMNE B4 * 7 L3
KIDD DY10 .....138 D
Pixall Dr EDG B15 .....106 C8
Pixhall Wk CVALE B35 .....91 M2
Plainview Cl FOAKS/STRLY B74..55 H3
Plaistow Av CBROM B36 .....91 G6
Plane Gv
CHWD/FDBR/MGN B37 .....110 D4
Planetary Rd WLNHL WV13 .....50 F1
Planetree Cl BRGRVE B60 .....190 M3
Plane Tree Cl KIDD DY10 .....138 D6
Planetree Rd DSYBK/YTR WS5..69 M1
Plane Tree Rd FOAKS/STRLY B74 ...55 H5

Planet Rd BRLYHL DY5 .....102 B1
Plank La CSHL/WTROR B46 .....92 E3
Planks La WMBN WV5 .....64 D7
Plantagenet Dr
RUGBYS/DCH CV22 .....186 C7
Plantation Dr MGN/WHC B75 .....57 H3
Plantation La POL/KGSB/FAZ B78..30 F6
SEDG DY3 .....
Plantation Rd DSYBK/YTR WS5..69 K1
The Plantation BRLYHL DY5 .....83 M6
Planter Cl RUGBYS/DCH CV22..185 L5
Plant La BNTWD WS7 .....18 B6
Plants Brook Rd
WALM/CURD B76 .....73 K7
Plants Cl GTWY WS6 .....24 E5
SCFLD/BOLD B73 .....72 E4
Plants Gv ERDE/BCHGN B24 .....73 H7
Plants Hill Crs TLHL/CAN CV4..153 J4
Plants Hollow BRLYHL DY5 .....102 D4
Plant St STRBR DY8 .....101 H3
STRBR DY8 .....101 J3
Plant Wy BLOX/PEL WS3 .....39 K1
Plascom Rd WOLV WV1 .....50 E4
Plato Cl WWCK CV34 .....206 D8
Platts Crs STRBR DY8 .....101 J3
Platts Dr STRBR DY8 .....101 J3
Platts Rd STRBR DY8 .....101 J3
Platt St CNCK/NC WS11 .....12 E8
DARL/WED WS10 .....52 B8
Playdon Gv
ALE/KHTH/YWD B14 .....146 E2
Pleasant Cl KGSWFD DY6 .....101 L3
Pleasant Gv ERDE/BCHGN B24..73 H7
Pleasant Harbour BEWD DY12..162 D3
Pleasant Md ALDR WS9 .....40 C8
Pleasant St HKD DY10 .....138 C6
WBROM B70 .....68 B5
WBROM B70 .....87 G4
Pleasant Vw SEDG DY3 .....84 B3
Pleasant Wy RLSN CV32 .....206 E3
Pleck Rd WSLW WS2 .....52 E6
Plestowes Cl SHLY B90 .....126 F8
Plexfield Rd RUGBYS/DCH CV22..186 A4
Pleydell Cl COVS CV3 .....156 A8
Plimsoll Gv RIDG/WDGT B32 ...105 G8
Plimsoll St KIDD DY11 .....138 B8
Plomer Cl RUGBYS/DCH CV22..186 A5
Plott La RUGBY CV23 .....183 J7
Plough & Harrow Rd
LDYWD/EDGR B16 .....106 D4
Plough Av RIDG/WDGT B32 .....123 G3
Plough Hill Rd
NUNW/HART CV10 .....79 K7
Ploughmans Pl MGN/WHC B75..57 H1
Ploughmans Wk BRGRVE B60 ...191 H1
KGSWFD DY6 .....21 G2
LICH WS13 .....21 G2
Plover Cl WOLVN WV10 .....36 C5
Ploverdale Crs KGSWFD DY6 ...83 L7
Plover Gv KIDD DY10 .....164 F4
Plowden Rd STETCH B33 .....109 K1
Plowman St RUGBYN/HIL CV21..186 D2
Plume St AST/WIT B6 .....89 M6
Plumstead Rd KGSTG B44 .....71 L5
Plym Cl WNSFLD WV11 .....37 L7
Plymouth Cl REDW B97 .....202 A3
COVS CV3 .....157 G8
Plymouth Cl COVS CV3 .....135 G6
NFLD/LBR B31 .....144 E6
REDW B97 .....202 A3
Plymouth Ct RBRY B45 .....169 L5
Plymouth Pl RLSN CV32 .....206 E3
Plymouth Rd BVILLE B30 .....124 F6
RBRY B45 .....169 L4
REDW B97 .....202 B3
Pochard Cl KIDD DY10 .....164 E3
Pocklington Pl NFLD/LBR B31 * ..124 A7
Pointon Cl BILS/COS WV14 .....66 C3
Poitiers Rd COVS CV3 .....155 H7
Polden Cl HALE B63 .....121 G4
Polesworth Cl REDE B98 .....203 H4
Polesworth Rd BKDE/SHDE B34..91 M7
Police Cottages
CSHL/WTROR B46 * 94 B3
Pollard Rd ACGN B27 .....126 F3
The Pollards ERDW/GRVHL B23..72 C5
Polo Flds HAG/WOL DY9 .....119 M4
Pomeroy Cl TLHL/CAN CV4 .....153 H6
Pomeroy Rd GTB/HAM B43 .....71 H1
RIDG/WDGT B32 .....123 G4
Pommel Cl DSYBK/YTR WS5 .....69 K1
Pond Crs BKHL/PFLD WV2 .....50 C6
Pond Gv BKHL/PFLD WV2 .....50 C6
Pond La BKHL/PFLD WV2 .....3 H9
Pondthorpe COVS CV3 .....156 C5
Ponesfield Rd LICH WS13 .....20 C7
Ponesgreen LICH WS13 .....20 C7
Pontypool Av COVS CV3 .....156 D7
Pool Av CNCK/NC WS11 .....17 M8
Pool Bank BDWTH CV12 .....116 C4
Pool Bank St NUN CV11 .....98 F1
Pool Cl RUGBYS/DCH CV22 .....186 B5
WOLVN WV10 .....23 H4
Pool Cottages KNWTH CV8 * 181 J3
Pool End Cl DOR/KN B93 .....149 K7
Poole Rd COVN CV6 .....133 L2
Pooles Cl KIDD DY10 .....138 C6
Pooles La SHHTH WV12 .....38 C6
Poole St STRBR DY8 .....119 J1
Pooley La RUGBYN/HIL CV21 .....47 L3
Pooley Vw POL/KGSB/FAZ B78..47 L3
Pool Farm Rd ACGN B27 .....127 G4
Poolfield Av SOLH B91 .....148 D2
Poolfield Rd LICH WS13 .....20 C7
Pool Furlong HAG/WOL DY9 .....141 M4
Pool Gn ALDR WS9 .....40 C8
Pool Hall Crs BDMR/CCFT WV3..48 B5
Pool Hall Rd BDMR/CCFT WV3..48 B5
Pool Hayes La SHHTH WV12 .....37 L8
Poolhead La HOCK/TIA B94 .....172 F6
Pool House Rd WMBN WV5 .....64 B7
Pool La OLDBY B69 .....104 D1
Pool Meadow GTWY WS6 .....24 B4
WALM/CURD B76 .....73 L5
Pool Meadow Cl MOS/BIL B13..126 A4
SOLH B91 .....149 K4
Pool Rd BRWNH WS8 .....26 B3
HALE B63 .....121 M2
NUNW/HART CV10 .....80 D8
SMTHWK B66 .....87 M8
WNSFLD WV11 .....37 L7
Poolside Gdns COVS CV3 .....154 E8
Pool St AST/WIT B6 .....89 K5
BKHL/PFLD WV2 .....
DUDN DY1 .....66 E7
WSL WS1 .....
Pool Vw GTWY WS6 .....24 E1
Pope Gv WHE WS12 .....
Pope Rd WOLVN WV10 .....36 E5
Popes La HWK/WKHTH B38 .....145 H2
OLDBY B69 .....86 F2
Pope St CBHAMW B1 .....
RUGBYS/DCH CV22 .....186 C2

SMTHWK B66 ....87 M6
Poplar Ar *SOLH B91* * 149 G1
Poplar Av *ALE/KHTH/YWD B14* ..125 J5
BDWTH B46 ....117 H3
BHTH/HG B12 ....125 L1
BNTWD WS7 ....18 D7
BRWNH WS8 ....26 E5
CHWD/FDBR/MGN B37 ...111 C5
CNCK/NC WS11 ....16 D1
DSYBK/YTR WS5 ....69 L1
ERDW/GRVHL B23 * 90 D1
HRBN B17 ....105 H3
LOZ/NWT B19 * 89 G5
MGN/WHC B75 ....57 K6
OLDBY B69 ....85 M5
OLDBY B69 ....86 E8
TPTN/OCK DY4 ....67 H4
WBROM B70 ....87 J3
WNSFLD WV11 ....58 F6
WSLW WS2 ....52 B1
Poplar Cl *BRGRVW B61* 168 D6
OLDBY B69 ....86 A4
WMBN WV5 ....64 F7
WSLW WS2 ....52 C1
Poplar Crs *DUDN DY1* 84 F2
STRBR DY8 ....119 J2
Poplar Dr *AST/WIT B6* 71 H4
RBRY B45 ....170 B5
WASH/WDE B8 ....90 B7
Poplar Gn *DUDN DY1* * 84 E7
Poplar Gv *KNWTH CV8* 182 F4
LOZ/NWT B19 * 89 G5
RUGBYN/HIL CV21 ....186 E1
SMTHWK B66 ....105 M2
Poplar La *CNCK/NC WS11* 15 K5
RMSLY B62 ....142 E2
Poplar Rd *ALE/KHTH/YWD B14* ..125 J5
BDMR/CCFT WV3 ....49 L7
BILS/COS WV14 ....51 K6
BRWNH WS8 ....26 E5
COVW CV5 ....154 D4
DARL/WED WS10 ....52 E7
DOR/KN B93 ....175 K2
GTWY WS6 ....24 D4
KGSWFD DY6 ....83 J8
KIDD DY11 ....164 A1
OLDBY B69 ....86 E5
REDW B97 ....201 L2
SMTHWK B66 ....105 L4
SOLH B91 ....149 G1
SPARK B11 ....107 M8
STRBR DY8 ....119 J2
Poplars Dr *CBROM B36* 91 M5
CDSL WV8 ....34 D3
The Poplars *CNCK/NC WS11* ..16 C1
LDYWD/EDGR B16 * 106 D2
NUNW/HART CV10 ....98 B2
SPARK B11 ....108 A7
STRBR DY8 ....101 K3
Poplar St *BKHL/PFLD WV2* ...50 B7
CNCK/NC WS11 ....17 J1
SMTHWK B66 ....87 F3
Poplarwoods *RIDG/WDGT B32* ..122 F5
Poppy Cl *COVS CV3* * 156 D7
Poppy Dr *DSYBK/YTR WS5* 69 K2
RRUGBY 161 D3
Poppyfield Ct *TLHL/CAN CV4* ..180 B2
Poppy Gv *WASH/WDE B8* 108 A1
Poppy La *ERDE/BCHGN B24* 73 G8
Poppymead *ERDW/GRVHL B23* ..71 M5
Porchester Cl *ALDR WS9* 40 E3
Porchester Dr *LOZ/NWT B19* ...89 H7
Porchester St *LOZ/NWT B19* ..89 H7
Porlock Cl *COVS CV3* * 155 E3
Porlock Crs *NFLD/LBR B31* ...144 B2
Porlock Rd *STRBR DY8* 101 K3
Portal Rd *WSLW WS2* 52 D3
Portchester Dr *WNSFLD WV11* ..37 H3
Porter Av *CSCFLD/WYGN B72* ..72 F6
TLHL/CAN CV4 ....153 J5
Porters Cft *HRBN B17* 105 L5
Porters Fld *DUDS DY2* 85 H4
Portersfield Rd *CDYHTH B64* ..103 G5
Portershill Dr *SHLY B90* 148 A5
Porter St *DUDS DY2* 85 H4
Porter St South *DUDS DY2* ...85 H4
Porters Wy *BORD B9* 108 C3
Portfield Dr *TPTN/OCK DY4* ...85 L2
Portfield Gv *ERDW/GRVHL B23* ..72 E7
Porthkerry Gv *COVS DY3* 65 M6
Port Hope Rd *SPARK B11* 107 L6
Porthouse Gv *BILS/COS WV14* * ..66 F2
Portia Av *SHLY B90* 147 M3
Portia Cl *NUN CV11* 99 L5
Portland Av *ALDR WS9* 31 K5
CRTAM B79 ....31 K3
Portland Crs *HAG/WOL DY9* ...119 M4
Portland Dr *HAG/WOL DY9* 119 M4
NUNW/HART CV10 ....98 A1
Portland House *RLSS CV32* 206 D5
Portland Ms *RLSS CV32* 206 D5
Portland Pl *BILS/COS WV14* ...66 F6
CNCK/NC WS11 ....16 A6
RUGBYN/HIL CV21 ....187 H3
Portland Pl East *RLSN CV32* ..206 D5
Portland Pl West *RLSN CV32* ..206 D5
Portland Rd *ALDR WS9* 40 F7
LDYWD/EDGR B16 ....106 A3
RUGBYN/HIL CV21 ....187 H3
Portland Rd *AST/WIT B6* 89 L6
RLSN CV32 ....206 D5
WSLW WS2 ....4 C1
Portland Ter *WSNGN B18* 88 D8
Portleys La *POL/KGSB/FAZ B78* ..59 H1
Portman Rd *ALE/KHTH/YWD B14* ..125 K6
Portobello Cl *WLNHL WV13* ...51 H4
Portobello Rd *WBROM B70* 68 D5
Portree Av *COVS CV3* 156 D5
Portrush Av *NFLD/LBR B31* ...145 G4
Portrush Rd *DUNHL/THL/PER WV6* ..48 B1
Portsdown Cl *WOLVN WV10* ...36 D6
Portsdown Rd *HALE B63* 121 H4
Portsea Cl *COVS CV3* 155 H7
Portswood Cl *COVEN WV9* 36 A1
Portway Cl *KGSWFD DY6* 83 J8
RLSS CV31 ....207 H7
SOLH B91 ....148 C4
TLHL/CAN CV4 ....153 J5
Portway Hl *OLDBY B69* 85 M7
Portway Rd *BILS/COS WV14* ..51 K6
BLKHTH/ROWR B65 ....103 H1
DARL/WED WS10 ....68 C1
OLDBY B69 ....86 B8
The Portway *KGSWFD DY6* 83 J8
Portwrinkle Av *COVN CV6* 134 E7
Posey Cl *HDSW B21* 88 A2
Postbridge Rd *COVS CV3* 155 H6
Post Office La *ATHST CV9* 63 H6
Post Office Rd *ATHST CV9* 62 A4
Post Office Yd *RRUGBY CV23* * ..158 D1
Pottal Pool Rd *HEDN WS12* ...11 M4
Potter Cft *ERDW/GRVHL B23* ..72 B5

Potters Cl *RRUGBY CV23* 158 C2
Potters Green Rd *COVE CV2* ..135 J4
Potters La *AST/WIT B6* 89 J6
POL/KGSB/FAZ B78 ....47 L5
Pottery Rd *LGLYGN/QTN B68* ..105 G4
SMTHWK B66 ....87 L6
Potton Cl *COVS CV3* 156 C7
Potts Cl *KNWTH CV8* 198 A1
Pouk Hill Cl *WSLW WS2* 52 E2
Pouk La *LICHS WS14* 27 J5
Poultney Rd *COVN CV6* 133 L7
Poultney St *WBROM B70* 68 D6
Poulton Cl *MOS/BIL B13* 125 L3
Pound Cl *LGLYGN/QTN B68* ...104 D2
Pound La *CSHL/WTROR B46* ...111 H1
CSHL/WTROR B46 ....111 L1
RIDG/WDGT B32 ....143 K2
RLSN CV32 ....206 E2
Poundley Cl *CBROM B36* 93 G2
Pound Rd *ALE/KHTH/YWD B14* ..146 C4
DARL/WED WS10 ....68 C2
LGLYGN/QTN B68 ....104 D2
Pountney St *BKHL/PFLD WV2* ...2 F8
Powell Av *RIDG/WDGT B32* 104 E7
Powell Cl *BILS/COS WV14* 67 J2
TPTN/OCK DY4 ....68 A8
Powell Pl *BILS/COS WV14* 67 J2
Powell Rd *COVE CV2* 155 L1
Powell St *CBHAMW B1* 121 M2
HALE B63 ....121 M2
WOLVN WV10 ....50 D1
Powell Wy *NUN CV11* 98 F1
Power Crs *LDYWD/EDGR B16* * ..106 E4
Powers Ct *RLSN CV32* 206 D4
Power Station Rd *STRPT DY13* ..188 F1
Powick Pl *LOZ/NWT B19* * 89 G6
Powick Rd *ERDW/GRVHL B23* ...90 B4
Powis Av *TPTN/OCK DY4* 67 M6
Powis Gv *KNWTH CV8* 180 A8
Powke La *BLKHTH/ROWR B65* ..103 L3
Powlers Cl *HAG/WOL DY9* 120 C3
Powlett St *BKHL/PFLD WV2* ...3 G1
Poxon Rd *ALDR WS9* 40 E2
The Poynings
DUNHL/THL/PER WV6 ....35 G8
Poyser Rd *NUNW/HART CV10* ..99 G5
Pratts La *STUD B80* 203 L5
Premier Cl *BVILLE B30* 106 A8
Premier St *VAUX/NECH B7* 90 B5
Premier Wy *SCFLD/BOLD B73* ..72 B2
Prentice Cl *RUGBYN/HIL CV21* ..159 M8
Prescelly Cl *NUNW/HART CV10* ..97 M2
Prescot Rd *HAG/WOL DY9* 119 J2
Prescott Rd *DE PENK ST19* 10 E4
Prestbury Cl *REDE B98* 203 L2
Prestbury Rd *AST/WIT B6* 89 J5
Presthope Rd *SLYOAK B29* 123 M6
Preston Av *WALM/CURD B76* ...73 J2
Preston Cl *REDE B98* 194 F7
TLHL/CAN CV4 ....153 K6
Preston Rd
LGN/SDN/BHAMAIR B26 .....109 H7
WSNGN B18 ....88 C7
Prestons Rw *BILS/COS WV14* ..66 E2
Prestwick Rd *MGN/WHC B75* ..57 G6
Prestwick Rd *CVALE B35* 91 M1
KGSWFD 83 G7
Prestwood Av *WNSFLD WV11* ..37 H5
Prestwood Dr *KINVER DY7* 100 D5
Prestwood Rd *KINVER DY7* 100 C7
WOLVN WV10 ....50 C1
Prestwood Rd West
WNSFLD WV11 ....36 F7
Pretorian Wy
RUGBYN/HIL CV21 ....160 E6
Pretoria Rd *BORD B9* 108 C2
Priam Gv *BLOX/PEL WS3* 25 M8
Price Av *DARL/WED WS10* 45 H4
Price Crs *BILS/COS WV14* 51 H6
Price Rd *DARL/WED WS10* 69 G2
HAG/WOL DY9 ....102 E2
Prices Rd *SEDG DY3* 84 A2
Price St *BILS/COS WV14* 51 K8
CBHAMNE B4 ....7 G2
CNCK/NC WS11 ....16 C4
DUDS DY2 ....85 J5
SMTHWK B66 ....87 M8
WBROM B70 ....87 G2
Pridmore Rd *COVN CV6* 134 B6
Priestfield Cl *KGSTG B44* 71 H3
Priestfield Rd *REDW B97* 202 B8
Priestfield St *BILS/COS WV14* ..50 F7
Priestland Rd *BKDE/SHDE B34* ..91 M6
Priestley Cl *BFLD/HDSWWD B20* ..88 E4
HALE B63 ....102 F2
Priestley Rd *SPARK B11* 107 L6
WSLW WS2 ....38 E8
Priest St *CDYHTH B64* 103 K4
Primley Av *CBROM B36* 91 H6
TAM/AM/WIL B77 ....46 D3
WSLW WS2 ....52 F5
Primley Cl *WSLW WS2* 52 F3
Primrose Av *SPARK B11* 108 A4
TPTN/OCK DY4 ....68 A5
WOLVN WV10 ....36 B2
Primrose Bank
LGLYGN/QTN B68 ....104 F1
Primrose Cl *BLOX/PEL WS3* ...25 L8
BRGRVE B60 ....169 G7
CDYHTH B64 ....102 F5
RRUGBY CV23 ....161 D3
Primrose Crs *DUDN DY1* 85 G1
Primrose Cft *HLGN/YWD B28* ..126 D8
Primrose Dr *BDWTH CV12* 116 C4
Primrose Gdns *CDSL WV8* 34 E2
HWK/WKHTH B38 ....145 K5
WOLVN WV10 ....36 B2
Primrose Hl *HWK/WKHTH B38* ..145 K4
STRBR DY8 ....101 J3
WWCK CV34 ....205 H3
Primrose Hill St *COV CV1* 9 H2
Primrose La *HLGN/YWD B28* ...126 D8
WOLVN WV10 ....36 D5
Primrose Meadow
CNCK/NC WS11 ....17 G3
Primrose Pk *BRLYHL DY5* 84 A4
Primrose Rd *DUDS DY2* 103 G1
The Primroses *DSYBK/YTR WS5* ..69 M1
Primrose Woods
RIDG/WDGT B32 ....122 F3
Primsland Cl *SOLH B91* 149 G6
Prince Albert St *BORD B9* 108 C2
Prince Andrew Crs *RBRY B45* ..143 J3
Princefield Av *PENK ST19* 10 D5
Prince George Rd
DARL/WED WS10 ....52 E8
Prince of Wales La *SHLY B90* ..147 M3
Prince of Wales Rd *COVW CV5* ..154 C2
Princep Cl *GTB/HAM B43* 71 H1

Prince Philip Cl *RBRY B45* 143 J3
Prince Rd *BVILLE B30* 145 K2
Prince Rupert Ms *LICH WS13* * ..20 C1
Prince Rupert Rd *STRPT DY13* ..188 D2
Prince Ruperts Wy *LICH WS13* ..20 C5
Prince's Av *NUN CV11* 98 F2
WSL WS1 ....5 J3
Princes Cl *COVS CV3* 155 M5
Princes Dr *CDSL WV8* 34 B2
KNWTH CV8 ....179 L5
RLSN CV32 ....206 B5
Princes Ga *SOLH B91* 148 F1
Princes Rd *ATHST CV9* 61 G8
OLDBY B69 ....85 L5
POL/KGSB/FAZ B78 ....47 M3
STRBR DY8 ....119 H3
Princess Alice Dr
SCFLD/BOLD B73 ....72 B3
Princess Anne Rd
BILS/COS WV14 ....67 K2
WSLW WS2 ....52 D2
Princess Crs *HALE B63* 103 J1
Princess Dr *COVN CV6* * 134 F4
Princess Gv *HHTH/SAND B71* ..69 H6
Princess Pde *WBROM B70* * ...87 H2
Princess Pde *ATHST CV9* 63 J5
DIG/EDG B5 ....107 J7
LGLYGN/QTN B68 ....105 H3
Princess Rd *ATHST CV9* 63 J5
Princess Sq *BILS/COS WV14* ...67 K2
Princess St *BNTWD WS7* 18 C5
CNCK/NC WS11 ....12 C1
COVN CV6 ....134 D6
WOLV WV1 ....3 G5
Prince's St *CBHAMNE B4* 7 K3
NUN CV11 ....98 F2
RLSN CV32 ....206 F4
RUGBYN/HIL CV21 ....186 D1
STRPT DY13 ....188 C5
Princess Wy *DARL/WED WS10* ..52 A5
Princethorpe Cl *BKDE/SHDE B34* ..92 B6
SHLY B90 ....126 D8
Princethorpe Rd *SLYOAK B29* ..123 M4
Princethorpe Wy *COVS CV3* ...156 B6
Princeton Gdns *COVEN WV9* ...35 K3
Prince William Ct *COV CV1* * ..8 B3
Princip St *CBHAMNE B4* 7 G2
Printing House St *CBHAMNE B4* * ..7 G3
Prior Cl *KIDD DY10* 139 G8
Prior Deram Wk *TLHL/CAN CV4* ..153 G5
Priors Cl *RCOVN/BALC/EX CV7* ..151 M7
Priorsfield Rd North *COVN CV6* ..8 B1
Priorsfield Rd South *COVN CV6* ..8 B1
Priors Harnall *COV CV1* 9 J1
Priors Mi *SEDG DY3* 66 C7
The Priors *BDWTH CV12* 117 G3
Priors Wy *ERDW/GRVHL B23* ..72 A5
Priory Av *SLYOAK B29* 124 F3
Priory Chambers *DUDN DY1* * ..85 G4
Priory Cl *CSHL/WTROR B46* * ..93 L8
DUDN DY1 ....84 F3
HOCK/TIA B94 ....176 B8
SMTHWK B66 ....106 A1
WBROM B70 ....87 K3
Priory Ct *COVW CV5* * 8 A8
Priory Cft *KNWTH CV8* 197 K1
Priory Dr *LGLYGN/QTN B68* ...87 G3
Priory Field Cl *BILS/COS WV14* ..66 D8
Priorygate Wy *BORD B9* 108 C2
Priory La *SEDG DY3* 66 B6
Priory Ms *WWCK CV34* 205 J6
Priory Pl *COV CV1* 9 G4

Prospect Rd South *REDE B98* ..202 E1
Prospect Rw *DUDS DY2* 85 H3
STRBR DY8 ....119 L2
Prospect St *BILS/COS WV14* ..51 J7
CRTAM B79 ....31 L8
TPTN/OCK DY4 ....68 A3
Prospect Wy *RUGBYN/HIL CV21* ..161 G8
Prosper Meadow *KGSWFD DY6* ..83 J6
Prospero Cl *RBRY B45* 143 J3
Prosser St *BILS/COS WV14* 51 H6
WOLVN WV10 ....36 C8
Prossers Wk *CSHL/WTROR B46* ..93 K6
Proud Cross Ringway
KIDD DY10 ....138 A6
Proud's La *BILS/COS WV14* 51 H5
Provence Cl *WOLVN WV10* 50 D1
Providence Cl *BLOX/PEL WS3* ..39 G5
Providence La *BLOX/PEL WS3* ..39 G5
Providence Pl
NUNW/HART CV10 * 78 B3
Providence Rd *BRGRVW B61* ..191 K6
Providence Rw *BILS/COS WV14* ..66 F5
Providence St *CDYHTH B64* ...103 H4
COVW CV5 ....154 D5
HAG/WOL DY9 ....102 C7
TPTN/OCK DY4 ....68 A8
Providence Ter
DARL/WED WS10 ....52 E7
Pruden Av
ETTPK/GDPK/PENN WV4 .....66 D2
Pryor Rd *LGLYGN/QTN B68* ...105 G2
Ptarmigan Pl *NUN CV11* 99 K2
Puckering's La *WWCK CV34* ...205 H7
Pudsey Dr *MGN/WHC B75* 57 G2
Pugh Crs *WSLW WS2* 52 C3
Pugh Rd *AST/WIT B6* 89 L6
BILS/COS WV14 ....67 J2
ETTPK/GDPK/PENN WV4 .....66 D3
Pugin Cl *DUNHL/THL/PER WV6* ..48 B2
Pugin Gdns *ERDW/GRVHL B23* ..72 B3
Pullman Cl *STRPT DY13* 188 E1
TAM/AM/WIL B77 ....46 E3
Puma Wy *COV CV1* 9 H7
Pumphouse La *BRGRVE B60* ...169 K5
REDW B97 ....200 F1
Pump La *RCOVN/BALC/EX CV7* ..114 A2
Pump St *BKHL/PFLD WV2* 50 E6
KIDD DY10 ....164 C1
Puppy Gn *TPTN/OCK DY4* 67 M8
Purbeck Cl *HALE B63* 121 H4
Purbeck Cft *RIDG/WDGT B32* ..105 K8
Purbrook *TAM/AM/WIL B77* ...46 C5
Purbrook Rd *WOLV WV1* 3 H5
Purcell Av *LICH WS13* 20 F5
NUN CV11 ....99 K2
Purcell Cl *RLSN CV32* 206 E5
Purcell Rd *COVN CV6* 134 F5
WOLVN WV10 ....36 B5
Purdy Rd *BILS/COS WV14* 67 J4
Purefoy Rd *COVS CV3* 155 H5
Purley Chase La *ATHST CV9* ..79 H1
Purley Gv *ERDW/GRVHL B23* ..71 L8
Purley Vw *ATHST CV9* 63 K7
Purlieu La *KNWTH CV8* 179 G8
Purnells Wy *DOR/KN B93* 149 L8
Purshall Cl *REDW B97* 202 A4
Purslet Rd *WOLV WV1* 50 E3
Purslow Gv *NFLD/LBR B31* ...144 A2
Purton Ms *RLSS CV31* 207 G7
Putney Av *BFLD/HDSWWD B20* ..89 G4
Putney La *RMSLY B62* 142 F3
Putney Rd *BFLD/HDSWWD B20* ..89 G4
Puxton Dr *KIDD DY11* 138 B4
Puxton La *KIDD DY11* 138 B4
Pye Green Rd *CNCK/NC WS11* ..16 C2
Pype Hayes Rd *ERDE/BCHGN B24* ..91 H1
Pype Hayes Rd
ERDE/BCHGN B24 ....91 H1
Pytchley Rd *RUGBYS/DCH CV22* ..187 D4
Pytman Dr *WALM/CURD B76* ..73 L6
Pyt Pk *COVW CV5* 154 A1

Q

The Quadrangle *BVILLE B30* * ..124 D7
The Quadrant *COV CV1* * 8 E5
SEDG DY3 ....66 B4
Quadrille Lawns *COVEN WV9* ..35 K3
Quail Gn *DUNHL/THL/PER WV6* ..48 D3
Quail Park Dr *KIDD DY10* 164 E3
Qualcast Rd *WOLV WV10* 3 L4
Quantock Cl *BRWNH WS8* 26 C8
RBRY B45 ....143 M3
Quantock Dr *KIDD DY10* 138 E7
NUNW/HART CV10 ....97 M2
Quantock Rd *STRBR DY8* 101 M7
Quantry La *HAG/WOL DY9* 142 C6
Quarrington Gv
ALE/KHTH/YWD B14 ....146 E2
Quarry Bank *KIDD DY11* 189 L3
Quarry Brow *SEDG DY3* 66 C8
Quarry Cl *GTWY WS6* 13 G5
RUGBYN/HIL CV21 ....160 D7
RWWCK/WEL CV35 ....197 K6
Quarry Cottages
RWWCK/WEL CV35 * 197 K6
Quarryfield La *COV CV1* 9 J3
Quarry Flds *RWWCK/WEL CV35* ..197 K6
Quarry Hl *HALE B63* 121 K3
Quarry Hills La *LICHS WS14* ..21 H8
Quarry House Cl *RBRY B45* ...143 K4
Quarry La *ATHST CV9* 79 J1
BRGRVW B61 ....191 H5
NFLD/LBR B31 ....144 D2
NUN CV11 ....99 H5
RMSLY B62 ....121 K3
Quarry Park Rd *STRBR DY8* ..119 L5
Quarry Ri *OLDBY B69* 85 M5
Quarry Rd *DUDS DY2* 102 F3
KNWTH CV8 ....179 J2
SLYOAK B29 ....123 K4
Quarry St *RLSN CV32* 206 A4
The Quarry *KIDD DY10* 138 D5
Quarry Wk *RBRY B45* 143 K4
Quarrywood Gv *COVE CV2* 155 L1
Quasar Centre *WSL WS1* * 98 A2
Quasar Centre *WSL WS1* * 5 H4
Quayle Gv *STRBR DY8* 101 H2
Quayside Cl *OLDBY B69* 86 C5
Quayside Dr *WSLW WS2* 4 B6
Queen Eleanors Dr
DOR/KN B93 ....149 M5
Queen Elizabeth Rd *WSLW WS2* ..52 D3
Queen Elizabeth Rd *KIDD DY10* ..138 F7
NUNW/HART CV10 ....80 A7
RBRY B45 ....143 J3
Queen Isabel's Av *COVS CV3* ..155 M6
Queen Margaret's Rd
TLHL/CAN CV4 ....153 M5
Queen Mary's Rd *BDWTH CV12* ..99 C8
COVN CV6 ....134 B5

Queen Mary St *WSL WS1* 53 H7
Queen Philippa St *COVS CV3* ..155 H7
Queens Ar *NUN CV11* * 99 G5
WOLV WV1 ....2 F5
Queens Av
ALE/KHTH/YWD B14 * 125 J5
OLDBY B69 ....85 M4
SHLY B90 ....147 M3
WSNGN B18 ....18 *
Queensbridge Rd *MOS/BIL B13* ..125 H6
KNWTH CV8 ....197 G2
SMTHWKW B67 ....87 L8
Queens Cl *ERDE/BCHGN B24* * ..106 D8
SOLH B91 ....149 J1
Queens Crs *BILS/COS WV14* ..66 E4
STRBR DY8 ....101 L6
Queen's Cross *DUDS DY2* 84 F5
Queens Dr *BLKHTH/ROWR B65* ..104 B1
BNTWD WS7 ....18 D8
BVILLE B30 ....145 L1
DIG/EDG B5 ....107 *
Queensferry Cl
RUGBYS/DCH CV22 ....186 A5
Queens Gdns *BILS/COS WV14* ..51 H6
CDSL WV8 ....34 D2
DUDS DY2 ....102 F1
Queens Head Rd *HDSW B21* ..88 C8
Queens Hl *HAG/WOL DY9* 141 H6
Queens Hospital Cl *EDG B15* ...6 C8
Queensland Av *COVW CV5* 154 D3
Queen's Lea *SHHTH WV12* 38 A3
Queen's Park Rd *HRBN B17* ...105 H7
Queen Sq *WOLV WV1* 2 F5
Queen's Ride *MOS/BIL B13* ...125 G1
Queens Rd *AST/WIT B6* 89 L5
ATHST CV9 ....63 J5
COV CV1 ....8 C5
DSYBK/YTR WS5 ....53 M7
ERDW/GRVHL B23 ....90 A2
LGLYGN/QTN B68 ....87 H8
LGN/SDN/BHAMAIR B26 .....109 K4
NUN CV11 ....98 F1
RRUGBY CV23 ....158 C6
RUSH/SHEL WS4 ....53 H6
SEDG DY3 ....66 C5
STRBR DY8 ....101 K7
STRPT DY13 ....188 C4
WOLVN WV10 ....14 F7
Queen's Sq *WWCK CV34* 205 H6
Queens Tower *VAUX/NECH B7* * ..89 M8
Queen St *ALDR WS9* 40 D3
BDWTH CV12 ....117 G3
BHTH/HG B12 ....107 H6
BILS/COS WV14 ....51 J8
BNTWD WS7 ....18 D8
BRLYHL DY5 ....84 B7
BRLYHL DY5 ....102 E5
CDYHTH B64 ....103 H4
CNCK/NC WS11 ....16 B4
COV CV1 ....9 H1
CSCFLD/WYGN B72 ....72 F1
DARL/WED WS10 ....52 B5
DARL/WED WS10 ....67 M1
GTWY WS6 ....24 B3
HALE B63 ....121 H4
KGSWFD DY6 ....83 H6
KIDD DY10 ....138 C4
LICH WS13 ....20 C5
OLDBY B69 ....86 E5
REDE B98 ....202 C1
RLSN CV32 ....199 H8
RLSN CV32 ....206 E4
RUGBYN/HIL CV21 ....186 E2
STRBR DY8 ....101 H2
STRBR DY8 ....119 H3
TPTN/OCK DY4 ....67 K5
WBROM B70 ....87 H2
WOLV WV1 ....3 G5
Queensway *ATHST CV9* 77 G1
BEWD DY12 ....137 G8
POL/KGSB/FAZ B78 ....47 K7
Queensway *CBHAMNE B4* * 7 J4
CRTAM B79 ....31 L5
FOAKS/STRLY B74 ....55 L5
HAG/WOL DY9 ....120 C3
HALE B63 ....121 H4
LGLYGN/QTN B68 ....104 F4
NUNW/HART CV10 ....81 H7
RLSS CV31 ....206 D8
Queensway Cl *LGLYGN/QTN B68* ..104 F4
Queenswood Rd *MGN/WHC B75* ..56 F4
MOS/BIL B13 ....125 L1
Queen Victoria Rd *COV CV1* * ..8 B4
Queen Victoria St
RUGBYN/HIL CV21 ....187 G2
Quenby Dr *DUDN DY1* 84 D5
Quendale *WMBN WV5* 64 C7
Quentin Dr *DUDN DY1* 84 D5
Queslade Cl *GTB/HAM B43* 70 D4
Queslett Rd *GTB/HAM B43* 70 F3
KGSTG B44 ....71 J2
Queslett Rd East
FOAKS/STRLY B74 ....55 K8
Quibery Cl *REDE B98* 203 K2
Quicksand La *ALDR WS9* 54 D1
Quigley Av *BORD B9* 107 M3
Quildes Rd *STRBR DY8* 101 H2
Quilletts Cl *COVN CV6* 134 C4
Quilter Cl *BILS/COS WV14* 66 E6
WSLW WS2 ....52 C2
Quilter Rd *ERDE/BCHGN B24* ..90 F3
Quince *TAM/AM/WIL B77* 46 F2
Quincey Dr *ERDE/BCHGN B24* ..91 C2
Quincy Ri *BRLYHL DY5* 102 A6
Quinn Cl *COVS CV3* 155 M6
Quinneys La *REDE B98* 202 F2
Quinton Av *GTWY WS6* 24 D2
Quinton Cl *HIA/OLT B92* 128 E1
Quinton Ct *HRBN B17* 105 G3
REDE B98 ....202 B2
RWWCK/WEL CV35 ....204 B2
Quinton Expy *RIDG/WDGT B32* ..104 F3
Quinton La *RIDG/WDGT B32* ..105 H7
Quinton Pk *COVS CV3* 155 H6
Quinton Rd *COV CV1* 9 G8
HRBN B17 ....123 H7
Quinton Rd West
RIDG/WDGT B32 ....104 F3
Quorn Crs *STRBR DY8* 101 G2
Quorn Gv *ERDE/BCHGN B24* ...90 F3
Quorn Wy *COVS CV3* 156 C6

R

Rabbit La *WOLVN WV10* 22 E6
Rabone La *SMTHWK B66* 87 M7
Raby Cl *OLDBY B69* 85 K5
Raby St *BKHL/PFLD WV2* 3 H8
Racecourse La *STRBR DY8* 119 J4

Racecourse Rd
DUNHL/THL/PER WV6 35 L8
Racemeadow Rd ATHST CV9 63 K4
Rachael Gdns DARL/WED WS10 69 G1
Rachel Cl TPTN/OCK DY4 68 A4
Rachel Gdns SLYOAK B29 124 B3
Radbourn Dr FOAKS/STRLY B74 57 G7
Radbourne Dr HALE B63 102 E6
Radbourne Rd SHLY B90 148 B2
Radbrook Wy RLSS CV31 207 H7
Radcliffe Dr RMSLY B62 104 C7
Radcliffe Gdns RLSS CV31 * 206 E7
Radcliffe Rd COVW CV5 154 D5
Raddens Rd RMSLY B62 122 D2
Raddington Dr HIA/OLT B92 127 H5
Raddlebarn Farm Dr
SLYOAK B29 124 D4
Raddlebarn Rd SLYOAK B29 124 D4
Radford Av KIDD DY10 138 C6
Radford Cl ATHST CV9 63 J3
DSYBK/YTR WS5 69 L2
Radford Cottages RLSS CV31 * 206 F6
Radford Dr RUSH/SHEL WS4 40 A3
Radford La
ETTPK/GDPK/PENN WV4 48 D6
Radford Ri SOLH B91 128 C8
Radford Rd ALVE B48 171 G7
COVN CV6 133 L7
RLSS CV31 206 F6
SLYOAK B29 123 L6
Radley Dr NUNW/HART CV10 98 E4
Radley Gv SLYOAK B29 123 L3
Radley Rd HAG/WOL DY9 120 D1
RUSH/SHEL WS4 40 A7
The Radleys STETCH B33 110 B6
Radlow Crs
CHWD/FDBR/MGN B37 110 F5
Radmore Cl BNTWD WS7 18 B5
Radnor Cl RBRY B45 143 M3
Radnor Cft DSYBK/YTR WS5 70 A2
Radnor Dr NUNW/HART CV10 98 C3
Radnor Gn HHTH/SAND B71 69 G6
Radnor Ri HEDN WS12 16 F1
Radnor Rd BFLD/HDSWWD B20 88 F5
LGLYGN/QTN B68 104 F6
SEDG DY3 66 A5
Radnor St WSNGN B18 88 E7
Radnor Wk COVE CV2 135 K5
Radstock Av CBROM B36 91 G6
Radstock Rd SHHTH WV12 38 A4
Radway Cl REDE B98 194 F7
Radway Rd SHLY B90 148 C6
Raeburn Rd GTB/HAM B43 71 G1
Raford Rd ERDW/GRVHL B23 72 B7
Ragees Rd STRBR DY8 101 K2
Raglan Av DUNHL/THL/PER WV6 48 D2
SMTHWK B66 106 A1
Raglan Cl FOAKS/STRLY B74 55 K2
NUN CV11 99 H1
SEDG DY3 65 M6
Raglan Gv KNWTH CV8 179 M8
Raglan Rd DIG/EDG B5 107 H7
HDSW B21 88 A5
SMTHWK B66 106 A1
Raglan St BDMR/CCFT WV3 2 D5
BRLYHL DY5 102 A1
COV CV1 9 J4
Raglan Wy
CHWD/FDBR/MGN B37 111 H3
Ragley Cl BLOX/PEL WS3 38 E4
DOR/KN B93 149 M6
Ragley Crs BRGRVE B60 191 L5
Ragley Dr GTB/HAM B43 70 B3
LGN/SDN/BHAMAIR B26 110 A7
WLNHL WV13 51 K5
Ragley Wy NUN CV11 99 K3
Raglis Cl REDW B97 201 L3
Ragnall Av STETCH B33 110 B6
Raikes La LICHS WS14 27 M7
Railswood Dr BLOX/PEL WS3 39 L2
Railway Dr BILS/COS WV14 51 J8
WOLV WV1 3 H4
Railway La BNTWD WS7 18 C4
WLNHL WV13 51 L4
Railway Rd BFLD/HDSWWD B20 89 K3
SCFLD/BOLD B73 56 F8
Railwayside Cl SMTHWK B66 87 J6
Railway St BILS/COS WV14 51 J8
CNCK/NC WS11 16 C5
CNCK/NC WS11 17 L8
RRUGBY CV23 185 L1
TPTN/OCK DY4 68 A8
WBROM B70 86 F1
WOLV WV1 3 H4
Railway Ter ATHST CV9 * 63 H5
BDWTH CV12 * 117 G3
DARL/WED WS10 68 D3
PBAR/PBCH B42 * 70 D7
RUGBYN/HIL CV21 186 F1
VAUX/NECH B7 89 M6
Railwharf Sidings DUDS DY2 103 H1
Rainbow St BILS/COS WV14 67 H2
BKHL/PFLD WV2 3 G9
Rainham Cl TPTN/OCK DY4 67 H8
Rainsbrook Av
RUGBYS/DCH CV22 187 J5
Rainsbrook Dr NUN CV11 99 L4
SHLY B90 148 D7
Rainscar TAM/AM/WIL B77 46 F6
Raison Av NUN CV11 81 K5
Rake Hl BNTWD WS7 18 F5
Rake Wy EDG B15 6 B7
Raleigh Cl HDSW B21 87 M4
Raleigh Cft GTB/HAM B43 70 C2
Raleigh Rd BILS/COS WV14 67 K2
BORD B9 108 B3
COVE CV2 155 M2
Raleigh St HHTH/SAND B71 87 G1
WSLW WS2 4 A2
Ralph Crs POL/KGSB/FAZ B78 60 A7
Ralph Rd COVN CV6 133 K8
SHLY B90 148 B1
WASH/WDE B8 108 B1
Ralphs Meadow
RIDG/WDGT B32 123 H3
Ralston Cl BLOX/PEL WS3 38 E1
Ramillies Crs GTWY WS6 24 D4
Ramp Rd
CHWD/FDBR/MGN B37 111 G8
Ramsay Cl HHTH/SAND B71 69 K5
Ramsay Crs COVW CV5 132 F6
Ramsay Rd LGLYGN/QTN B68 105 G4
TPTN/OCK DY4 67 J6
WSLW WS2 38 E8
Ramsden Av NUNW/HART CV10 80 A6
Ramsden Cl SLYOAK B29 123 M6
Ramsden Ct NUNW/HART CV10 * 80 A6
Ramsden Rd ATHST CV9 63 L6
Ramsey Cl RBRY B45 143 J4
Ramsey Rd RLSS CV31 206 F7
VAUX/NECH B7 90 A6
Ranby Rd COVE CV2 9 L2
Randall Av ALVE B48 170 E7
Randall Cl KGSWFD DY6 101 K1
Randall Rd KNWTH CV8 197 K2
Randle Dr MGN/WHC B75 57 G2
Randle Rd HAG/WOL DY9 120 A1
NUNW/HART CV10 98 B1
Randle St COVN CV6 133 M8
Randolph Cl RLSS CV31 207 G7
Randwick Gv KGSTG B44 71 H4
Ranelagh Rd BKHL/PFLD WV2 50 A7
Ranelagh St RLSS CV31 206 E7
Ranelagh Ter RLSS CV31 206 D7
Range Meadow Cl RLSN CV32 206 A2
Range Wy POL/KGSB/FAZ B78 60 B8
Rangeways Rd KGSWFD DY6 101 K2
KIDDW DY11 137 L5
Rangeworthy Cl REDW B97 202 A6
Rangifer Rd POL/KGSB/FAZ B78 45 K5
Rangoon Rd HIA/OLT B92 128 C1
Rankine Cl RUGBYN/HIL CV21 160 B6
Ranleigh Av KGSWFD DY6 101 K1
Rann Cl LDYWD/EDGR B16 106 E4
Rannoch Cl BRLYHL DY5 101 M5
STRPT DY13 163 J6
Rannoch Dr NUNW/HART CV10 80 A8
Rannock Cl COVS CV3 156 D3
Ranscombe Dr SEDG DY3 84 A3
Ransome Rd
RCOVN/BALC/EX CV7 96 E5
Ransom Rd COVN CV6 134 C5
ERDW/GRVHL B23 90 A1
Ranulf Cft COVS CV3 155 G6
Ranworth Ri
ETTPK/GDPK/PENN WV4 66 B1
Raphael Cl COVW CV5 154 A2
Rashwood Cl HOCK/TIA B94 174 F7
Ratcliffe Br ATHST CV9 63 K3
Ratcliffe Cl SEDG DY3 66 D6
Ratcliffe La ATHST CV9 63 K1
Ratcliffe Rd ATHST CV9 63 K4
SOLH B91 128 A6
WNSFLD WV11 37 L7
Ratcliffe St ATHST CV9 63 H5
Ratcliff Wk OLDBY B69 * 86 D6
Ratcliff Wy TPTN/OCK DY4 68 A7
Rathbone Cl BILS/COS WV14 51 H8
DIG/EDG B5 107 J6
RCOVN/BALC/EX CV7 115 L7
RUGBYN/HIL CV21 187 L5
Rathbone Rd SMTHWKW B67 105 K3
Rathlin Cl COVEN WV9 35 L2
Rathlin Cft CBROM B36 92 F8
Rathmore Cl STRBR DY8 119 J3
Rathwell Cl COVEN WV9 35 L3
Ratliffe Rd RUGBYS/DCH CV22 186 D6
Rattle Cft STETCH B33 109 J2
Raveloe Dr NUN CV11 99 H4
Ravenall Cl BKDE/SHDE B34 91 M6
Raven Cl GTWY WS6 24 B3
HEDN WS12 12 A6
HEDN WS12 17 J1
Raven Cragg Rd COVW CV5 154 C5
Raven Crs WNSFLD WV11 37 K5
Ravenfield Cl WASH/WDE B8 90 D8
Ravenglass RUGBYN/HIL CV21 161 H6
Ravenhayes La RIDG/WDGT B32 122 E7
Raven Hays Rd NFLD/LBR B31 144 A3
Ravenhill Dr CDSL WV8 34 E2
Ravenhurst Dr GTB/HAM B43 70 C2
Ravenhurst Ms
ERDW/GRVHL B23 90 C2
Ravenhurst Rd HRBN B17 106 A6
Ravenhurst St BHTH/HG B12 7 L9
Raven Rd DSYBK/YTR WS5 53 M7
Ravens Bank Dr REDE B98 195 H6
Ravensbourne Gv WLNHL WV13 52 A3
Ravenscroft STRBR DY8 101 G7
Ravenscroft Rd HIA/OLT B92 127 L5
SHHTH WV12 37 M8
Ravensdale Av RLSN CV32 206 A3
Ravensdale Cl DSYBK/YTR WS5 5 L9
Ravensdale Gdns
DSYBK/YTR WS5 53 M7
Ravensdale Rd COVE CV2 156 A2
SMHTH B10 108 D6
Ravenshaw La SOLH B91 149 L1
Ravenshaw Rd
LDYWD/EDGR B16 106 A3
Ravenshaw Wy SOLH B91 149 L3
Ravenshill Rd
ALE/KHTH/YWD B14 147 G1
Ravensholme
DUNHL/THL/PER WV6 48 D3
Ravensholst TLHL/CAN CV4 * 154 B7
Ravensitch Wk BRLYHL DY5 102 C4
Ravensmere Rd REDE B98 202 F4
Ravensthorpe Cl COVS CV3 156 C5
Ravenstone TAM/AM/WIL B77 46 F5
Raven St STRPT DY13 188 D2
Ravenswood EDG B15 106 C5
Ravenswood Cl
FOAKS/STRLY B74 56 F5
Ravenswood Dr SOLH B91 148 C4
Ravenswood Hl
CSHL/WTROR B46 93 K6
Raven Wy NUN CV11 99 K3
Rawdon Gv KGSTG B44 71 M5
Rawlings Rd SMTHWKW B67 105 L3
Rawlins Cft CVALE B35 91 M2
Rawlinson Rd RLSN CV32 206 F3
Rawlins St LDYWD/EDGR B16 106 E4
Rawnsley Dr KNWTH CV8 180 A7
Rawnsley Rd HEDN WS12 13 J6
Rawn Vw ATHST CV9 63 K7
Raybolds Bridge Rd WSLW WS2 53 G1
Raybolds Bridge St WSLW WS2 53 G1
Raybon Cft RBRY B45 * 143 L7
Raybould's Fold DUDS DY2 85 G8
Rayford Dr HHTH/SAND B71 69 K3
Raygill TAM/AM/WIL B77 46 F5
Ray Hall La GTB/HAM B43 69 M5
Rayleigh Rd BDMR/CCFT WV3 2 A9
Raymond Av PBAR/PBCH B42 70 F7
Raymond Cl COVN CV6 116 D8
WSLW WS2 39 H8
Raymond Gdns WNSFLD WV11 37 J8
Raymond Rd WASH/WDE B8 108 C1
Raymont Gv GTB/HAM B43 70 F1
Rayners Cft
LGN/SDN/BHAMAIR B26 109 K3
Raynor Crs BDWTH CV12 116 B4
Raynor Rd WOLVN WV10 36 D7
Raynsford Wk WWCK CV34 205 H4
The Raywoods
NUNW/HART CV10 98 D2
Rea Av RBRY B45 143 J5
Reabrook Rd NFLD/LBR B31 144 D5
Rea Cl NFLD/LBR B31 144 E6
Readers Wk GTB/HAM B43 70 D4
Reading Av NUN CV11 81 K5
Reading Cl COVE CV2 134 F2
Read St COV CV1 9 K4
Rea Fordway RBRY B45 143 K4
Reansway Sq
DUNHL/THL/PER WV6 49 L1
Reapers Cl SHHTH WV12 38 B8
Reardon Ct WWCK CV34 205 J4
Reaside Crs
ALE/KHTH/YWD B14 124 F8
Reaside Cft BHTH/HG B12 * 107 J7
Reaside Dr RBRY B45 143 M5
Rea St DIG/EDG B5 7 J8
Rea St South DIG/EDG B5 7 H9
Rea Ter DIG/EDG B5 7 K6
Rea Valley Dr NFLD/LBR B31 144 F3
Reaview Dr SLYOAK B29 124 F3
Reaymer Cl WSLW WS2 38 F6
Reay Nadin Dr SCFLD/BOLD B73 71 M1
Rebecca Dr SLYOAK B29 124 C3
Rebecca Gdns
ETTPK/GDPK/PENN WV4 65 K1
Recreation Rd BRGRVW B61 191 K2
COVN CV6 134 E2
Recreation St DUDS DY2 85 H8
Rectory Av DARL/WED WS10 52 B7
Rectory Cl COVW CV5 133 G7
POL/KGSB/FAZ B78 45 J8
RCOVN/BALC/EX CV7 116 E4
STRBR DY8 119 M2
Rectory Cottages
RCOVN/BALC/EX CV7 * 96 C4
Rectory Dr
RCOVN/BALC/EX CV7 116 E4
Rectory Gdns KIDDW DY11 189 L2
SOLH B91 149 H2
STRBR DY8 119 M2
Rectory Gv WSNGN B18 88 C7
Rectory La CBROM B36 91 L5
COVW CV5 133 G7
KIDDW DY11 189 L2
STRPT DY13 188 B3
Rectory Park Av MGN/WHC B75 73 J1
Rectory Park Cl MGN/WHC B75 73 J1
Rectory Park Rd
LGN/SDN/BHAMAIR B26 110 A8
Rectory Rd MGN/WHC B75 57 G8
NFLD/LBR B31 144 F2
RCOVN/BALC/EX CV7 96 C4
REDW B97 202 A4
SOLH B91 149 G2
STRBR DY8 119 M2
Rectory St STRBR DY8 101 H2
Redacre Rd SCFLD/BOLD B73 72 D3
Redacres DUNHL/THL/PER WV6 35 J7
Redbank Av ERDW/GRVHL B23 90 A2
Redbourn Rd BLOX/PEL WS3 38 E1
Red Brick Cl CDYHTH B64 * 103 H6
Redbrook Cl HEDN WS12 17 H4
Redbrook Covert
HWK/WKHTH B38 145 J6
Red Brook Rd WSLW WS2 38 E8
Redbrooks Cl SOLH B91 148 E4
Redburn Dr
ALE/KHTH/YWD B14 146 B3
Redcap Cft COVN CV6 * 134 B1
Redcar Cl BRGRVW B61 168 E4
RLSN CV32 206 F1
Redcar Cft CBROM B36 91 G5
Redcar Rd COV CV1 155 J1
WOLVN WV10 36 B1
Redcliff TAM/AM/WIL B77 32 D8
Redcliffe Dr WMBN WV5 64 F7
Redcotts Cl WOLVN WV10 36 E6
Redcroft Dr ERDE/BCHGN B24 73 G8
Redcroft Rd DUDS DY2 85 J7
Reddal Hill Rd CDYHTH B64 103 J4
Red Deeps NUN CV11 99 H5
Reddicap Heath Rd
MGN/WHC B75 73 K1
Reddicap Hl WALM/CURD B76 73 H1
Reddicroft SCFLD/BOLD B73 57 G8
Reddings La CSHL/WTROR B46 76 E8
HLGN/YWD B28 126 C3
Reddings Rd MOS/BIL B13 125 H3
The Reddings HLYWD B47 146 E8
Redditch Ringway REDW B97 202 B2
Redditch Rd ALVE B48 170 F2
ALVE B48 170 F5
BRGRVE B60 191 H8
HWK/WKHTH B38 145 J4
STUD B80 203 H8
Redesdale Av COVN CV6 133 K8
Redfern Av KNWTH CV8 179 L7
Redfern Cl HIA/OLT B92 127 M4
Redfern Dr BNTWD WS7 18 F8
Redfern Park Wy SPARK B11 108 E8
Redfern Rd SPARK B11 108 E8
Redfly La BRLYHL DY5 84 A7
Redford Cl MOS/BIL B13 125 M3
Redgate Cl HWK/WKHTH B38 145 H3
Redgrave Cl
RCOVN/BALC/EX CV7 135 M5
Redhall Rd LGLYGN/QTN B68 105 J6
SEDG DY3 84 A3
Red Hl BEWD DY12 162 F3
REDE B98 202 D3
STRBR DY8 119 M1
Redhill Av WMBN WV5 64 E7
Redhill Cl CRTAM B79 31 L6
STRBR DY8 119 M1
Red Hill Cl STUD B80 203 J7
Red Hill Gv HWK/WKHTH B38 145 K6
Redhill La BRGRVW B61 143 G8
Red Hill Pl RMSLY B62 121 L6
Redhill Rd CNCK/NC WS11 16 D1
HWK/WKHTH B38 145 H6
NFLD/LBR B31 144 F5
YDLY B25 108 E7
Red Hill St WOLV WV1 2 F2
Red House Av DARL/WED WS10 68 F2
Redhouse Cl DOR/KN B93 149 J8
Red House La ALDR WS9 40 C8
Red House Park Rd
GTB/HAM B43 70 C3
Redhouse Rd
DUNHL/THL/PER WV6 34 F8
Red House Rd STETCH B33 109 J2
STRPT DY13 188 B5
Redhouse St WSL WS1 4 F9
Redhurst Dr WOLVN WV10 35 M2
Redlake TAM/AM/WIL B77 46 C5
Redlake Dr HAG/WOL DY9 119 M5
Redlake Rd STRBR DY8 119 M4
Redland Cl BRGRVE B60 169 G4
COVE CV2 135 H3
Redland La KNWTH CV8 182 E2
Redland Rd RLSS CV31 206 F8
Redlands Cl SOLH B91 128 B8
Redlands Rd SOLH B91 128 A8
Redlands Wy FOAKS/STRLY B74 55 L4
Red La COVN CV6 134 C8
KNWTH CV8 178 F1
KNWTH CV8 179 H5
NUNW/HART CV10 97 J6
SEDG DY3 65 M5
WNSFLD WV11 38 A3
Red Leasowes Rd HALE B63 121 K2
Redliff Av CBROM B36 92 B4
Red Lion Av CNCK/NC WS11 25 L1
Red Lion Cl OLDBY B69 85 L4
Red Lion Crs CNCK/NC WS11 25 L1
Red Lion La CNCK/NC WS11 25 L1
Red Lion St ALVE B48 170 F7
REDE B98 202 C1
WOLV WV1 2 E4
Redlock Fld LICHS WS14 20 E8
Red Lodge Dr
RUGBYS/DCH CV22 186 C5
Redmead Cl NFLD/LBR B31 145 G1
Redmoor Gdns
ETTPK/GDPK/PENN WV4 49 L8
Redmoor Rd RUGE WS15 18 D2
Redmoor Wy WALM/CURD B76 74 B7
Rednal Hill La RBRY B45 143 L7
Rednall Dr MGN/WHC B75 57 G2
Rednal Mill Dr RBRY B45 144 A6
Rednal Rd HWK/WKHTH B38 145 G5
Redpine Crest SHHTH WV12 52 B1
Red River Rd WSLW WS2 38 E8
Red Rock Dr CDSL WV8 34 D3
Redruth Cl COVN CV6 134 E5
DSYBK/YTR WS5 54 B6
KGSWFD DY6 83 H5
NUN CV11 99 K1
Redruth Rd DSYBK/YTR WS5 54 B6
Red Sands Rd KIDDW DY11 138 C5
Redstart Av KIDD DY10 164 F3
Redstone Cl REDE B98 195 G7
Redstone Dr WNSFLD WV11 37 K8
Redstone Farm Rd
HLGN/YWD B28 126 F7
Redstone La STRPT DY13 188 C5
Redthorn Gv STETCH B33 109 H2
Redvers Rd BORD B9 108 C4
Redwell Cl TAM/AM/WIL B77 32 B8
Redwing TAM/AM/WIL B77 46 E7
Redwing Cl BNTWD WS7 19 H8
Redwing Ct KIDD DY10 164 E4
Redwing Dr HEDN WS12 12 A6
Redwing Gv ERDW/GRVHL B23 71 M6
Redwood Av DUDN DY1 66 D8
Redwood Cl BVILLE B30 145 J1
FOAKS/STRLY B74 55 K3
Redwood Cft
ALE/KHTH/YWD B14 125 J6
NUNW/HART CV10 98 E3
Redwood Dr BNTWD WS7 18 D5
CNCK/NC WS11 16 D2
OLDBY B69 85 M3
POL/KGSB/FAZ B78 60 B6
Redwood Gdns ACGN B27 * 108 F8
Redwood Rd BILS/COS WV14 67 H3
BVILLE B30 145 J1
DSYBK/YTR WS5 69 M1
KINVER DY7 118 A2
Redwood Wy SHHTH WV12 37 M5
Reedham Gdns
ETTPK/GDPK/PENN WV4 49 H7
Reedly Rd SHHTH WV12 38 A4
Reedmace TAM/AM/WIL B77 46 A3
Reedmace Cl HWK/WKHTH B38 145 K5
Reedswood Cl WSLW WS2 53 G2
Reedswood Gdns WSLW WS2 53 G2
Reedswood La WSLW WS2 53 G2
Reedswood Wy WSLW WS2 52 E1
Rees Dr COVS CV3 181 G1
WMBN WV5 64 F6
Reeve Ct KIDD DY10 164 E4
Reeve Dr KNWTH CV8 197 L1
Reeve La LICH WS13 20 F5
Reeves Gdns CDSL WV8 34 E1
Reeves Rd ALE/KHTH/YWD B14 125 G7
Reeves St BLOX/PEL WS3 38 F5
Reform St HHTH/SAND B71 87 H2
Regal Cl TAM/AM/WIL B77 46 A5
Regal Cft CBROM B36 90 F5
Regal Dr WSLW WS2 4 B7
Regan Av SHLY B90 147 L4
Regan Crs ERDW/GRVHL B23 72 C7
Regan Dr OLDBY B69 86 B5
Regency Cl BORD B9 108 B4
NUNW/HART CV10 81 H7
Regency Ct COVW CV5 154 D5
Regency Dr COVS CV3 154 D8
HWK/WKHTH B38 145 J3
KNWTH CV8 197 K2
Regency Gdns
ALE/KHTH/YWD B14 147 G2
Regency Ms RLSN CV32 * 206 E5
Regency Wk FOAKS/STRLY B74 42 B8
Regent Av OLDBY B69 85 L4
Regent Cl DIG/EDG B5 107 H7
HALE B63 121 L1
KGSWFD DY6 83 G7
OLDBY B69 85 L5
Regent Ct SMTHWK B66 87 L8
Regent Dr OLDBY B69 85 L4
Regent Gv RLSN CV32 206 D5
Regent Ms BRGRVW B61 * 191 J5
Regent Pde CBHAMW B1 6 C2
Regent Park Rd SMHTH B10 108 A5
Regent Pl CBHAMW B1 6 C2
OLDBY B69 85 M3
RLSS CV31 206 E6
RUGBYN/HIL CV21 186 E1
Regent Rd
ETTPK/GDPK/PENN WV4 49 J8
HDSW B21 88 B5
HRBN B17 106 A7
OLDBY B69 85 L4
Regents Ct BKHL/PFLD WV2 * 2 F7
Regents Park Rd BRGRVE B60 192 A3
Regent St BDWTH CV12 117 G1
BILS/COS WV14 51 H7
BVILLE B30 124 E6
CBHAMW B1 6 C2
CDYHTH B64 103 K3
COV CV1 8 C7
DUDN DY1 67 G7
NUN CV11 99 H1
RLSN CV32 206 D5
RUGBYN/HIL CV21 186 E2
SMTHWK B66 87 L7
TPTN/OCK DY4 67 J5
WLNHL WV13 51 L2
Regiment Ct COVN CV6 133 L4
Regina Av KGSTG B44 71 H5
Regina Cl RBRY B45 143 J4
Regina Crs COVE CV2 135 L6
DUNHL/THL/PER WV6 48 F1
Regina Dr PBAR/PBCH B42 89 H2
RUSH/SHEL WS4 53 L1
Reginald Rd SMTHWKW B67 105 K3
WASH/WDE B8 108 B1
Regis Beeches
DUNHL/THL/PER WV6 * 35 G8
Regis Gdns BLKHTH/ROWR B65 104 A4
Regis Heath Rd
BLKHTH/ROWR B65 104 B3
Regis Rd BLKHTH/ROWR B65 104 A3
DUNHL/THL/PER WV6 34 F8
Regis Wk COVE CV2 135 K6
Reid Av SHHTH WV12 38 B7
Reid Rd LGLYGN/QTN B68 105 G4
Reigate Av WASH/WDE B8 109 G1
Reindeer Rd POL/KGSB/FAZ B78 45 J4
Relay Dr TAM/AM/WIL B77 47 G6
Relko Dr CBROM B36 91 G6
Rembrandt Cl COVW CV5 154 A2
HEDN WS12 17 H3
Remburn Gdns WWCK CV34 205 K5
Remembrance Rd COVS CV3 156 B7
DARL/WED WS10 69 G2
Remington Dr CNCK/NC WS11 16 D5
Remington Pl WSLW WS2 39 G8
Remington Rd WSLW WS2 38 F7
Rendermore Cl PENK ST19 10 C6
Rene Rd TAM/AM/WIL B77 32 C8
Renfrew Cl STRBR DY8 101 G2
Renfrew Gdns KIDDW DY11 138 A8
Renfrew Sq CVALE B35 91 M1
Renison Rd BDWTH CV12 116 C4
Rennie Gv RIDG/WDGT B32 105 H8
Rennison Dr WMBN WV5 64 E7
Renolds Cl COVW CV5 154 A3
Renown Av COVW CV5 154 A4
Renown Cl BRLYHL DY5 83 M6
Renton Gv WOLVN WV10 35 L4
Renton Rd WOLVN WV10 35 L4
Repington Av ATHST CV9 63 H3
Repington Rd North
TAM/AM/WIL B77 32 E8
Repington Rd South
TAM/AM/WIL B77 32 E8
Repington Wy MGN/WHC B75 57 M8
Repton Av DUNHL/THL/PER WV6 48 B2
Repton Cl CNCK/NC WS11 15 M5
Repton Dr COVN CV6 134 F3
Repton Gv BORD B9 108 F2
Repton Rd BORD B9 108 F2
Reservoir Cl WSLW WS2 52 F5
Reservoir Dr CSHL/WTROR B46 94 D3
Reservoir Pas DARL/WED WS10 68 D2
Reservoir Pl WSLW WS2 52 F5
Reservoir Retreat
LDYWD/EDGR B16 106 D4
Reservoir Rd
BLKHTH/ROWR B65 104 B2
ERDW/GRVHL B23 90 B1
HEDN WS12 17 H1
HIA/OLT B92 127 K5
KIDDW DY11 164 A2
LDYWD/EDGR B16 106 D3
LGLYGN/QTN B68 105 G1
RBRY B45 170 A2
RUGBYN/HIL CV21 161 G7
SLYOAK B29 124 A2
Reservoir St WSLW WS2 52 F5
Resolution Wy STRPT DY13 188 F3
Retallack Cl SMTHWK B66 87 M5
Retford Dr WALM/CURD B76 73 J1
Retford Gv YDLY B25 109 G7
Retreat Gdns SEDG DY3 66 C6
The Retreat CDYHTH B64 103 J6
Revesby Wk VAUX/NECH B7 7 M2
Revival St BLOX/PEL WS3 38 F4
Rex Cl TLHL/CAN CV4 153 H5
Reyde Cl REDW B97 201 K3
Reynard Cl REDW B97 201 K2
Reynards Cl REDW B97 201 K2
SEDG DY3 66 E6
Reynolds Cl LICH WS13 20 F3
RUGBYN/HIL CV21 187 M5
SEDG DY3 82 C3
Reynolds Gv
DUNHL/THL/PER WV6 34 D8
Reynolds Rd BDWTH CV12 116 E1
HDSW B21 88 C6
Reynoldstown Rd CBROM B36 91 G5
Reynolds Wk WNSFLD WV11 37 L5
Rhayader Rd NFLD/LBR B31 123 J8
Rhodes Cl SEDG DY3 83 L1
Rhone Cl SPARK B11 126 A2
Rhoose Cft CVALE B35 91 M3
Rhuddlan Wy KIDDW DY11 164 C4
Rhys Thomas Cl SHHTH WV12 52 B1
Ribbesford Av WOLVN WV10 35 M5
Ribbesford Cl HALE B63 103 H8
Ribbesford Crs BILS/COS WV14 67 H4
Ribbesford Dr STRPT DY13 188 C1
Ribbesford Rd STRPT DY13 188 B3
Ribble Cl BDWTH CV12 117 M3
Ribble Rd COVS CV3 9 M6
Ribblesdale TAM/AM/WIL B77 46 F6
Ribblesdale Rd BVILLE B30 124 E6
Ribbonfields NUN CV11 99 H2
Richard Cooper Rd LICHS WS14 28 D8
Richard Joy Cl COVN CV6 134 A3
Richard Pl DSYBK/YTR WS5 54 A5
Richard Rd DSYBK/YTR WS5 54 A5
Richards Cl KNWTH CV8 179 K8
NFLD/LBR B31 144 D7
OLDBY B69 104 C1
Richards Gv RLSS CV31 206 E8
Richardson Cl WWCK CV34 205 K4
Richardson Dr STRBR DY8 101 J5
Richards Rd TPTN/OCK DY4 67 K4
Richards St DARL/WED WS10 52 B6
Richard St VAUX/NECH B7 89 K8
WBROM B70 86 F2
Richard St South WBROM B70 87 G3
Richard St West WBROM B70 86 F3
Richard Williams Rd
DARL/WED WS10 68 F3
Richborough Dr DUDN DY1 84 C2
Rich Cl WWCK CV34 205 L6
Riches St DUNHL/THL/PER WV6 49 K2
Richford Gv STETCH B33 110 B3
Richmond Aston Dr
TPTN/OCK DY4 67 L8
Richmond Av BDMR/CCFT WV3 49 K4
BHTH/HG B12 * 107 K8
Richmond Cl
BFLD/HDSWWD B20 88 E3
CNCK/NC WS11 12 E8
CRTAM B79 31 L8
Richmond Cft PBAR/PBCH B42 70 D7
Richmond Dr BDMR/CCFT WV3 49 J4
DUNHL/THL/PER WV6 48 D2
LICHS WS14 21 H6
Richmond Gdns WMBN WV5 64 E8
Richmond Gv STRBR DY8 101 J5
Richmond Hl LGLYGN/QTN B68 87 G8
Richmond Hill Gdns EDG B15 106 C7
Richmond Hill Rd EDG B15 106 C7
Richmond Pk KGSWFD DY6 83 G5
Richmond Pl
ALE/KHTH/YWD B14 125 K5
Richmond Rd ATHST CV9 63 H6
BDMR/CCFT WV3 49 J4
BEWD DY12 162 D2
DUDS DY2 84 F5
HIA/OLT B92 127 J3
HLYWD B47 147 G6
NUN CV11 98 E2
RBRY B45 143 J6
RUGBYN/HIL CV21 187 G3
SCFLD/BOLD B73 56 F7
SEDG DY3 66 C6
SMTHWK B66 105 L3
WSNGN B18 88 F7
YDLY B25 109 H3
Richmond St COVE CV2 155 L2
HALE B63 121 L1
WBROM B70 68 D7
WSL WS1 5 H5
Richmond St South WBROM B70 68 C8
Richmond Wy
CHWD/FDBR/MGN B37 111 G2
Rickard Cl DOR/KN B93 149 J8
Rickets Cl STRPT DY13 163 M6
Ricketts Pl BEWD DY12 162 F2
Rickman Dr EDG B15 107 H5
Rickyard Cl POL/KGSB/FAZ B78 47 L3
SLYOAK B29 123 L7
YDLY B25 109 H4
Rickyard La REDE B98 195 H8
Rickyard Piece RIDG/WDGT B32 123 J1
Riddfield Rd CBROM B36 91 J5
Ridding Gdns POL/KGSB/FAZ B78 47 L5
Ridding La DARL/WED WS10 68 D3
Riddings Cl BEWD DY12 137 G8
Riddings Crs BLOX/PEL WS3 39 K1

Riddings Hl
RCOVN/BALC/EX CV7 ....152 H5
Riddings La ATHST CV9 ....62 U3
The Riddings ATHST CV9 ....62 K3
COVW CV5 ....154 B6
HAG/WOL DY9 ....120 B3
STETCH B33 ....109 J1
TAM/AM/WIL B77 ....32 C8
WALM/CURD B76 ....73 H5
WOLVN WV10 ....36 E6
Ridgacre La RIDG/WDGT B32 .....105 C8
Ridgacre Rd HHTH/SAND B71 .....68 F7
RIDG/WDGT B32 ....104 E7
Ridgacre Rd West
RIDG/WDGT B32 ....104 E7
WSLW WS2 ....52 B2
Ridge Cl MOS/BIL B13 ....126 A7
Ridge Cl COVW CV5 ....132 E2
Ridge Dr RUGBYN/HIL CV21 ......187 H1
Ridgefield Rd RMSLY B62 ....104 A5
Ridge Gv HAG/WOL DY9 ....102 A8
Ridge La NUNW/HART CV10 ....78 E3
WNSFLD WV11 ....37 H6
Ridgeley Cl WWCK CV34 ....52 D4
Ridgemount Dr
HWK/WKHTH B38 ....145 H6
Ridge Rd KGSWFD DY6 ....83 C8
Ridge St STRBR DY8 ....101 C7
Ridgethorpe COVS CV3 ....156 C8
Ridgewater Cl RBRY B45 ....143 M7
Ridge Wy ALDR WS9 ....54 F1
Ridgeway HRBN B17 ....105 M3
SEDG DY3 ....66 B6
Ridgeway Av COVS CV3 ....155 C5
RMSLY B62 ....104 E7
Ridgeway Ct WSLW WS2 ....52 D4
Ridgeway Dr
ETTPK/GDPK/PENN WV4 ....65 K2
Ridgeway Rd STRBR DY8 ....101 K3
TPTN/OCK DY4 ....67 L5
The Ridgeway BNTWD WS7 ....18 B8
ERDW/GRVHL B23 ....71 L7
STRPT DY13 ....163 M8
WWCK CV34 ....205 L4
Ridgewood BKDE/SHDE B34 ....107 M7
Ridgewood Av STRBR DY8 ....101 C7
Ridgewood Cl RLSN CV32 ....206 A4
WSL WS1 ....5 G6
Ridgewood Dr MGN/WHC B75 ....56 F4
Ridgewood Gdns KGSTG B44 ....71 K6
Ridgewood Ri TAM/AM/WIL B77 ....32 E8
Ridgley Rd TLHL/CAN CV4 ....153 J5
Ridgmont Cft RIDG/WDGT B32 ....105 J8
Riding Cl HHTH/SAND B71 ....69 K6
Ridings Brook Dr CNCK/NC WS11 ..16 E3
Ridings La REDE B98 ....194 F6
Ridings Pk CNCK/NC WS11 * 16 E2
Riding Wy SHHTH WV12 ....38 B7
Ridleys Cross STRPT DY13 ......188 C2
Ridley St CBHAMW B1 ....8 D8
Ridpool Rd STETCH B33 ....109 M2
Rifle Range Rd KIDDW DY11 .....163 M2
Rifle St BILS/COS WV14 ....5 G6
Rigby Dr CNCK/NC WS11 ....16 C1
Rigby La BRGRVE B60 ....191 M5
Rigby St DARL/WED WS10 ....68 D4
Rigdale Cl COVE CV2 ....156 C3
Riland Rd MGN/WHC B75 ....57 H8
Riley Cl KNWTH CV8 ....198 A1
Riley Crs BDMR/CCFT WV3 ....49 L7
Riley Dr CBROM B36 ....92 E4
Riley Rd ALE/KHTH/YWD B14 .....147 H2
Riley St WLNHL WV13 ....51 M3
Rilstone Rd RIDG/WDGT B32 .....105 K8
Rindleford Av
Ringhills Rd CDSL WV8 ....34 F3
Ringinglow Rd KGSTG B44 ....71 G3
Ringmere Av CBROM B36 ....91 M5
Ringwood Rd BNTWD WS7 ....18 B6
Ring Road St Andrews WOLV WV1 ...2 D5
Ring Road St Davids WOLV WV1 ....3 H4
Ring Road St Georges
BKHL/PFLD WV2 ....3 G7
Ring Road St Johns
BKHL/PFLD WV2 ....2 E7
Ring Road St Marks
BDMR/CCFT WV3 ....2 D6
Ring Road St Patricks WOLV WV1 ..3 G3
Ring Road St Peters WOLV WV1 ....2 E6
Ringswood Rd HIA/OLT B92 ......127 J1
The Ring YDLY B25 ....109 G5
Ringway CNCK/NC WS11 ....16 C4
Ringway Hill Cross COV CV1 ......8 D5
Ringway Queens COV CV1 ....8 D5
Ringway Rudge COV CV1 ....8 D5
Ringway St Johns COV CV1 ....9 G5
Ringway St Nicholas COV CV1 .....8 F3
Ringway St Patricks COV CV1 .....8 F7
Ringway Swanswell COV CV1 ....9 G2
The Ringway YDLY B25 ....138 C2
Ringway Whitefriars COV CV1 .....9 H3
Ringwood Av ALDR WS9 ....40 F8
Ringwood Dr RBRY B45 ....143 L4
Ringwood Hwy COVE CV2 ....135 J3
Ringwood Rd WOLVN WV10 ....36 C3
Ripley Cl DUDS DY2 ....85 K5
Ripley Gv ERDW/GRVHL B23 ....71 M8
Ripon Dr HHTH/SAND B71 ....69 H4
Ripon Rd ALE/KHTH/YWD B14 .....147 G1
WOLVN WV10 ....36 A6
WSLW WS2 ....52 F2
River Ct COV CV1 ....5 J3
Riverbank Rd WNSFLD WV11 ....37 L2
Riverdrive TAM/AM/WIL B77 ......63 H3
Riverfield Gv TAM/AM/WIL B77 ...32 D8
Riverford Cft TLHL/CAN CV4 ....180 B2
River Lee Rd SPARK B11 * 108 C8
Rivermead NUN CV11 ....98 E1
Rivermead Pk BKDE/SHDE B34 .....91 H7
Riversdale Rd
ALE/KHTH/YWD B14 ....147 H2
ATHST CV9 ....63 K5
Riverside ATHST CV9 ....63 L6

RLSS CV31 * 206 C5
Riverside Cl BRGRVE B60 ....169 G7
COVS CV3 ....155 K7
Riverside Ct HWK/WKHTH B38 ....145 H2
Riverside Crs HLGN/YWD B28 ....147 H1
Riverside Dr SOLH B91 ....149 J3
STETCH B33 ....93 K5
Riverside North BEWD DY12 .....162 F1
Riversleigh Dr STRBR DY8 ......101 J5
Riversley Rd NUN CV11 ....99 G2
River St DIG/EDG B5 ....7 L6
Riverway DARL/WED WS10 ....68 F3
Riverway Dr BEWD DY12 ....162 F1
Rivington Cl STRBR DY8 ....119 J1
Rivington Crs KGSTG B44 ....72 A4
Roach TAM/AM/WIL B77 ....46 B7
Roach Cl BRLYHL DY5 ....84 B8
CHWD/FDBR/MGN B37 ....111 G2
Roach Crs WNSFLD WV11 * 37 K5
Roach Pool Cft
LDYWD/EDGR B16 ....106 A3
Road Eastwood DUDS DY2 ....85 J7
Road No 1 KIDDW DY11 ....164 C3
Road No 2 KIDDW DY11 ....164 C3
Road No 3 KIDDW DY11 ....164 C3
Roanne Ringway NUN CV11 ....98 F1
Robbins Ct RUGBYN/HIL CV21 ....187 H5
Robert Av ERDW/GRVHL B23 ....72 C7
Robert Cl COVS CV3 ....182 A1
CRTAM B79 ....31 K6
Robert Cramb Av
TLHL/CAN CV4 ....153 K5
Robert Hill Cl RUGBYN/HIL CV21 187 L4
Robert Rd BFLD/HDSWWD B20 ......88 F4
RCOVN/BALC/EX CV7 ....116 D1
TPTN/OCK DY4 ....67 K7
Roberts Cl ALDR WS9 ....40 D3
RRUGBY CV23 ....183 K7
Roberts Green Rd SEDG DY3 ......84 C1
Roberts La HAG/WOL DY9 ....119 M5
Robertson Cl RRUGBY CV23 ......160 D6
Robertson Knoll CBROM B36 ......91 K5
Robertsons Gdns VAUX/NECH B7 ..90 A6
Roberts Rd ACGN B27 ....127 G2
BLOX/PEL WS3 ....39 K8
DARL/WED WS10 ....69 J2
Robert St SEDG DY3 ....84 C1
Robert Wynd BILS/COS WV14 ......66 D4
Robeson Cl TPTN/OCK DY4 ....67 H7
Robey's La FAZ/KGSB/FAZ B78 ....33 H8
Robin Cl CBROM B36 ....92 E5
HEDN WS12 ....13 J7
KGSWFD DY6 ....83 L7
Robin Ct KIDD DY10 ....164 E3
Robin Gv WNSFLD WV11 ....37 L5
Robin Hood Cft HLGN/YWD B28 ...126 F6
Robin Hood La HLGN/YWD B28 ....126 C6
Robin Hood Rd BRLYHL DY5 ......102 D3
Robinia TAM/AM/WIL B77 ....46 C1
Robinia Cl RLSN CV32 ....206 F3
Robin Rd ERDW/GRVHL B23 ....90 C1
Robins Cl GTWY WS6 ....19 L2
STRBR DY8 ....119 L2
Robinsfield Dr NFLD/LBR B31 ...144 B6
Robins Hill Dr ALVE B48 ....170 B8
Robinson Cl CRTAM B79 ....31 K4
Robinson Rd BDWTH CV12 ....116 B5
BNTWD WS7 ....18 D7
Robinson's Wy WALM/CURD B76 ....74 B8
Robins Rd BNTWD WS7 ....18 B7
Robins Wy NUNW/HART CV10 ....97 L2
Robotham Cl RUGBYN/HIL CV21 ...160 D8
Robottom Cl WSLW WS2 ....38 F7
Rocester Av WNSFLD WV11 ....37 J6
Rochdale Wk SMHTH B10 ....108 A6
Rocheberie Wy
RUGBYS/DCH CV22 ....186 D5
Roche Dr BLOX/PEL WS3 ....38 C4
Rochester Av BNTWD WS7 ....18 E5
Rochester Ct NUNW/HART CV10 ...98 F2
REDW B97 ....202 A5
Rochester Cft WSLW WS2 ....52 E1
Rochester Rd COVW CV5 ....154 C5
NFLD/LBR B31 ....144 E1
Rochester Wy HEDN WS12 ....17 G4
The Roche BNTWD WS7 ....19 L5
Roche Wy BLOX/PEL WS3 ....38 C3
Rochford Cl HALE B63 ....121 K3
RBRY B45 ....143 J6
WALM/CURD B76 ....73 L5
WSLW WS2 ....4 A8
Rochford Ct SHLY B90 ....148 E2
Rochford Gv
ETTPK/GDPK/PENN WV4 ....49 J8
Rock Av RBRY B45 ....144 A6
Rock Cl COVN CV6 ....134 F4
NUNW/HART CV10 ....97 K1
Rocken End COVN CV6 ....134 B5
Rockford Cl REDE B98 ....202 D8
Rockford Rd PBAR/PBCH B42 .....70 E6
Rock Gv HIA/OLT B92 ....127 J2
Rock Hl BRGRVE B61 ....191 H6
Rockingham Cl BLOX/PEL WS3 * ..38 F4
DOR/KN B93 ....175 H3
SEDG DY3 ....83 M2
Rockingham Dr
DUNHL/THL/PER WV6 ....48 C2
NUN CV11 ....99 K6
Rockingham Gdns
FOAKS/STRLY B74 ....56 F7
Rockingham Hall Gdns
HAG/WOL DY9 ....120 B6
Rockingham Rd YDLY B25 ....109 H5
Rockland Dr STETCH B33 ....109 H1
Rockland Gdns WLNHL WV13 ......51 M3
Rocklands Crs LICH WS13 ....21 H5
Rocklands Dr MGN/WHC B75 ......56 F5
Rock La RCOVN/BALC/EX CV7 ....115 C6
Rockley Rd BLKHTH/ROWR B65 ....87 J3
Rockmead Av KGSTG B44 ....71 K3
Rock Mill La WSLW WS2 ....206 A4
Rockmoor Cl STETCH B33 ....110 C2
Rock Rd BILS/COS WV14 ....66 C5
HIA/OLT B92 ....127 J2
Rockrose Gdns WOLVN WV10 ......22 G6
Rock St SEDG DY3 ....84 C1
The Rock DUNHL/THL/PER WV6 ....35 H8
Rockville Rd WASH/WDE B8 .....108 C1
Rockwell La ALVE B48 ....194 C1
Rocky La ACGN B27 ....127 K3
BRGRVW B61 ....191 L7
KNWTH CV8 ....198 B3
PBAR/PBCH B42 ....71 G4
Rodbaston Dr PENK ST19 ....10 C8
Rodborough Rd DOR/KN B93 .....175 J2
CHWD/FDBR/MGN B37 ....109 M7
Rodbourne Rd HRBN B17 ....124 A2
Roddis Cl ERDW/GRVHL B23 ......72 D5
Roden Av KIDD DY10 ....138 D6
Roderick Dr WNSFLD WV11 ....37 H6
Roderick Rd SPARK B11 ....108 A3
Rodhouse Cl TLHL/CAN CV4 .....153 H4

Rodlington Av KGSTG B44 ....71 K4
Rodman Cl BLOX/PEL WS3 ....106 B5
Rodney Cl HIA/OLT B92 * 127 M4
LDYWD/EDGR B16 ....106 C3
RUGBYS/DCH CV22 ....186 A4
Rodney Rd HIA/OLT B92 ....127 M4
Rodway Cl BRLYHL DY5 ....102 B6
ETTPK/GDPK/PENN WV4 ....89 H6
LOZ/NWT B19 ....89 H6
Rodway Dr COVW CV5 ....153 H1
Roe Cl BR BRWNH WS8 ....26 C8
Roebuck Cl BKDE/SHDE B34 .....110 C1
Roebuck Gld SHHTH WV12 ....52 C1
Roebuck La WBROM B70 ....87 J4
Roebuck Pl BLOX/PEL WS3 ....39 J7
Roebuck Rd BLOX/PEL WS3 ....39 J7
Roebuck St WBROM B70 ....87 K4
Roe Cl WWCK CV34 ....205 K5
Roedean Ct KGSTG B44 ....205 K5
Roford Ct SEDG DY3 ....66 C8
Rogerfield Rd ERDW/GRVHL B23 ...72 E7
Rogers Rd WASH/WDE B8 ....90 F8
Rokeby Cl WALM/CURD B76 ....73 J1
Rokeby Rd GTB/HAM B43 ....70 D3
Rokeby St RUGBYN/HIL CV21 ....187 G2
Rokewood Cl KGSWFD DY6 ....83 H4
Rokholt Crs CNCK/NC WS11 ....16 A4
Roland Av COVN CV6 ....133 M2
Roland Gdns LOZ/NWT B19 ....89 J2
Roland Gv LOZ/NWT B19 ....89 J2
Roland Mt COVN CV6 ....134 A2
Rolan Dr SHLY B90 ....147 J5
Roland Rd LOZ/NWT B19 ....89 J2
Roland Ter LOZ/NWT B19 ....89 J2
Rolfe St SMTHWK B66 ....87 L7
Rollason Cl COVN CV6 ....134 A2
Rollason Rd COVN CV6 ....133 M5
DUDS DY2 ....85 H5
ERDE/BCHGN B24 ....90 C2
Rollasons Yd COVN CV6 * 134 E2
Rollesby Dr WLNHL WV13 ....51 K5
Rolling Mill Cl DIG/EDG B5 * ..107 J6
Rollingmill St WSLW WS2 ....4 A5
Rollswood Dr SOLH B91 ....148 D1
Roman Cl BRWNH WS8 ....26 C3
Roman La FOAKS/STRLY B74 ......55 M2
Roman Pk FOAKS/STRLY B74 ......55 M1
Roman Rd COVE CV2 ....155 M2
FOAKS/STRLY B74 ....42 A8
Roman Rd (Sandy La)
STRBR DY8 ....119 G1
Roman Vw CNCK/NC WS11 ....16 D8
Roman Wy BLKHTH/ROWR B65 .....104 A2
BRGRVE B60 ....191 M1
COVS CV3 ....181 B2
CRTAM B79 ....31 J6
CSHL/WTROR B46 ....93 J3
EDG B15 ....124 B2
LICHS WS14 ....21 H6
POL/KGSB/FAZ B78 ....47 L7
RUGBYN/HIL CV21 ....160 E6
Romany Rd RBRY B45 ....143 H4
Romany Wy STRBR DY8 ....119 G2
Roma Rd SPARK B11 ....108 C8
Romford Cl
LGN/SDN/BHAMAIR B26 ....109 M7
Romford Rd COVN CV6 ....133 M3
Romilly Av BFLD/HDSWWD B20 .....88 F3
Romilly Cl STRBR DY8 ....101 J7
WALM/CURD B76 ....73 L1
Romney TAM/AM/WIL B77 ....46 D5
Romney Cl HLGN/YWD B28 ....126 D6
Romney Wy GTB/HAM B43 ....71 H1
Romsey Av NUNW/HART CV10 ....81 H5
Romsey Gv WOLVN WV10 ....36 A2
Romsey Rd WOLVN WV10 ....36 A2
Romsey Wy BLOX/PEL WS3 ....38 D2
Romsley Cl RBRY B45 ....143 J5
REDE B98 ....203 K2
RMSLY B62 ....121 M3
RUSH/SHEL WS4 ....40 A3
Romsley Dr
HAG/WOL DY9 ....102 A8
LGLYGN/QTN B68 ....85 L8
RIDG/WDGT B32 ....122 F5
Romulus Cl BFLD/HDSWWD B20 .....88 F2
Ronald Gv CBROM B36 ....92 E5
Ronald Pl BORD B9 ....108 C3
Ronald Rd BORD B9 ....108 B3
Ron Davis Cl SMTHWK B66 * 87 M4
Ro-oak Rd COVN CV6 ....133 K8
Rood End Rd LGLYGN/QTN B68 .....87 G7
Rooker Av BKHL/PFLD WV2 ....50 C7
Rooker Crs BKHL/PFLD WV2 ....50 C7
Rookery Cl REDW B97 ....202 B4
Rookery La BKHL/PFLD WV2 ....50 C7
COVN CV6 ....133 M2
POL/KGSB/FAZ B78 ....44 A3
Rookery Pk BRLYHL DY5 ....83 M8
Rookery Rd
ETTPK/GDPK/PENN WV4 ....66 C2
HDSW B21 ....88 C4
SLYOAK B29 ....124 D3
WMBN WV5 ....64 F7
Rookery St WNSFLD WV11 ....37 G8
The Rookery NUNW/HART CV10 ....78 D5
NUNW/HART CV10 ....78 D5
RIDG/WDGT B32 ....122 E3
Rooks Meadow HAG/WOL DY9 .....119 M7
Rooks Nest RRUGBY CV23 ....158 C2
Rookwood Dr
DUNHL/THL/PER WV6 ....48 D4
NUN CV11 ....99 K6
Roosevelt Dr TLHL/CAN CV4 ....153 H4
Rooth St DARL/WED WS10 ....68 F1
Roper Cl RUGBYN/HIL CV21 .....187 L5
Roper Wy SEDG DY3 ....83 H6
Rosafield Av HALE B63 ....104 D7
Rosalind Av DUDN DY1 ....67 L2
Rosalind Gv WNSFLD WV11 ....37 L8
Rosamond St WSL WS1 ....4 C7
Rosary Rd ERDW/GRVHL B23 ....90 B3
Rosary Vls SPARK B11 * 108 C4
Rosaville Crs COVW CV5 ....132 E7
Rose Av ALVE B48 ....170 E8
COVN CV6 ....133 K8
KGSWFD DY6 ....83 K8
LGLYGN/QTN B68 ....85 L8
Rose Bank Dr BLOX/PEL WS3 * ...53 J1
Rosebay Av HWK/WKHTH B38 .....145 K5
Rose Bay Meadow
CNCK/NC WS11 ....17 G3
Roseberry Av COVE CV2 ....134 F4
Roseberry Gdns KIDD DY10 .....139 G2
Roseberry Rd SMTHWK B66 ......106 A1
TAM/AM/WIL B77 ....60 A1
Rosebery Rd BDMR/CCFT WV3 ......2 C7
Rosebery St LDYWD/EDGR B16 ....106 C1
WSNGN B18 ....6 A2
Rose Cft KNWTH CV8 ....179 J7
Rose Cottages
RUGBYN/HIL CV21 ....186 C2
SLYOAK B29 * 124 D3
Rose Ct SMTHWK B66 ....88 A8

Rosecroft Rd
LGN/SDN/BHAMAIR B26 ....110 A7
Rosedale Av ERDW/GRVHL B23 .....90 C2
SMTHWK B66 ....88 A8
Rosedale Gv YDLY B25 ....109 G5
Rosedale Pl WLNHL WV13 ....51 L5
Rose Dene STRPT DY13 ....188 C1
Rosedene Dr
BFLD/HDSWWD B20 ....88 D3
Rose Dr BRWNH WS8 ....26 C8
Rosefield Cft AST/WIT B6 ....89 K7
Rosefield Pl RLSN CV32 ....206 C8
Rosefield Rd SMTHWK B67 ....105 L5
Rosefield St RLSN CV32 ....206 E5
Rosegreen Cl COVS CV3 ....155 J7
Rosehall Cl REDE B98 ....202 C7
SOLH B91 ....148 D4
Rose Hl ATHST CV9 ....63 J6
BRLYHL DY5 ....85 M5
RBRY B45 ....169 L1
WLNHL WV13 ....51 L4
Rose Hill Cl CBROM B36 ....12 D5
Rose Hill Gdns WLNHL WV13 .....51 L4
Rose Hill Rd HDSW B21 ....88 E6
Rosehip Cl DSYBK/YTR WS5 ......107 J6
Rosehip Dr COVE CV2 ....134 F7
Roseland Av DUDS DY2 ....85 K4
Roseland Rd KNWTH CV8 ....197 K5
Roselands Av COVE CV2 ....135 H5
Roseland Wy EDG B15 ....6 B8
Rose La BNTWD WS7 ....19 G6
NUN CV11 ....99 G2
Roseleigh Rd RBRY B45 ....143 M7
Rosemary Av BILS/COS WV14 ......51 K7
GTWY WS6 ....24 B2
Rosemary Cl BRWNH WS8 ....26 B7
COVW CV5 ....153 J2
Rosemary Crs DUDN DY1 ....66 D7
ETTPK/GDPK/PENN WV4 ....50 A8
Rosemary Crs West
ETTPK/GDPK/PENN WV4 ....49 M8
Rosemary Dr FOAKS/STRLY B74 ...56 A2
HEDN WS12 ....12 D8
Rosemary Hl KNWTH CV8 ....179 K8
Rosemary Hill Rd
FOAKS/STRLY B74 ....42 B8
Rosemary La STRBR DY8 ....119 H2
Rosemary Nook
FOAKS/STRLY B74 ....42 A8
Rosemary Rd GTWY WS6 ....24 B2
HALE B63 ....121 H3
KIDD DY10 ....138 F6
STETCH B33 ....109 K3
TAM/AM/WIL B77 ....46 C1
TPTN/OCK DY4 ....67 L8
Rosemoor Dr BRLYHL DY5 ....101 M6
Rosemount Cl COVE CV2 ....135 J6
Rosemullion Cl
RCOVN/BALC/EX CV7 ....116 C5
Rosenhurst Dr BEWD DY12 ......162 E5
Rose Rd CSHL/WTROR B46 ....93 K5
HRBN B17 ....106 B7
Rose St BILS/COS WV14 ....52 B6
Rose Vis YDLY B25 * 108 E6
Rosetti Cl KIDD DY10 ....139 G7
Roseville Gdns CDSL WV8 ....34 D1
Roseville Prec CDSL WV8 * 34 D1
Rosewood NUN CV11 ....99 K4
Rosewood Av RUGBYS/DCH CV22 ..186 D5
Rosewood Cl TAM/AM/WIL B77 ....46 B1
Rosewood Crs RLSN CV32 ....206 F3
Rosewood Dr ERDW/GRVHL B23 .....37 M5
SHHTH WV12 ....37 M5
Rosewood Gdns WNSFLD WV11 .....37 M2
Rosewood Pk GTWY WS6 ....24 B3
Rosewood Rd DUDN DY1 ....66 F8
Roshven Rd BHTH/HG B12 ....125 L1
Roslin Cl BRGRVE B60 ....109 J6
Roslin Gv LOZ/NWT B19 ....89 J3
Roslyn Cl SMTHWK B66 ....87 L7
Ross BLKHTH/ROWR B65 ....103 M3
Ross Cl BDMR/CCFT WV3 ....49 J5
COVW CV5 ....132 E8
Ross Dr KGSWFD DY6 ....83 G6
Rosse Ct HIA/OLT B92 ....128 D5
Rossendale Cl HALE B63 ....103 H7
Rossendale Wy
NUNW/HART CV10 ....98 B3
Ross Hts BLKHTH/ROWR B65 .....103 M3
Rosslyn Av COVN CV6 ....133 J7
Rosslyn Rd WALM/CURD B76 ....73 K7
Ross Rd BLOX/PEL WS3 ....39 K7
Ross Wy NUN CV11 ....99 K6
Rostrevor Rd SMHTH B10 ....108 D4
Rosy Cross CRTAM B79 ....31 K4
Rothay TAM/AM/WIL B77 ....46 D5
Rothbury Gn HEDN WS12 ....17 J3
Rotherby Gv
CHWD/FDBR/MGN B37 ....110 F6
Rotherfield Cl RLSS CV31 .....206 F6
Rotherfield Rd
LGN/SDN/BHAMAIR B26 ....109 M5
Rotherhams HI ATHST CV9 ....62 B1
Rotherhams Oak La
HOCK/TIA B94 ....174 D7
Rothesay Cl NUNW/HART CV10 ....98 E3
Rothesay Cft RIDG/WDGT B32 ...122 F6
Rothesay Dr STRBR DY8 ....101 G2
Rothesay Wy SHHTH WV12 ....37 M7
Rothley Dr RUGBYN/HIL CV21 ...161 J6
Rothwell Dr SHLY B90 ....127 H8
Rothwell Rd WWCK CV34 ....205 G4
Rotten Rw LICH WS13 ....21 G5
Rotton Park Rd
LDYWD/EDGR B16 ....106 A3
Rotton Park St
LDYWD/EDGR B16 ....106 D2
Rough Hay Pl DARL/WED WS10 ....52 A6
Rough Hay Rd DARL/WED WS10 ....52 A6
Rough Hill Dr
BLKHTH/ROWR B65 ....85 K7
REDE B98 ....202 D4
Rough Hills Rd BKHL/PFLD WV2 ..50 D7
Roughknowles Rd
TLHL/CAN CV4 ....153 H7
Roughlea Av CBROM B36 ....91 K6
Roughley Dr MGN/WHC B75 ....57 G3
Roughley Farm Rd
MGN/WHC B75 ....71 G2
Rough Rd KGSTG B44 ....71 L2
The Rough REDW B97 ....202 B5
Rouncil Cl HIA/OLT B92 ....128 D2
Rouncil La KNWTH CV8 ....197 G5
The Roundabout
NFLD/LBR B31 ....144 B4
Round Av RRUGBY CV23 ....159 L8
Round Cl SHLY B90 ....147 K7
Round Ct WLNHL WV13 ....51 K3
Round Hl SEDG DY3 ....66 B3
Round Hill Av WAG/WOL DY9 ....120 A4
Roundhill Cl WALM/CURD B76 ....73 J1
Roundhills Rd RMSLY B62 ......104 D5
Roundhill Ter RMSLY B62 ......104 C4

Roundhill Wy BRWNH WS8 ....26 E3
Round House Rd COVS CV3 ....155 H7
SEDG DY3 ....84 C1
Roundlea Cl SHHTH WV12 ....37 L1
Roundlea Rd NFLD/LBR B31 .....123 M8
Round Rd ERDE/BCHGN B24 ....90 F3
Round Saw Cft RBRY B45 ....143 K5
Rounds Gdns
RUGBYN/HIL CV21 ....186 D5
Rounds Green Rd OLDBY B69 ......86 C6
Rounds Hl KNWTH CV8 ....197 J3
Rounds Hill Rd BILS/COS WV14 ..67 H5
Rounds Rd BILS/COS WV14 ....67 H5
Round St DUDS DY2 ....85 G7
RUGBYN/HIL CV21 ....186 D2
Roundway Down
DUNHL/THL/PER WV6 ....48 C2
Rounton Cl FOAKS/STRLY B74 ....56 B1
Rousay Cl RBRY B45 ....143 K4
Rousdon Gv GTB/HAM B43 ....70 B5
Rover Dr ACGN B27 ....127 H1
CBROM B36 ....92 B4
Rover Rd COV CV1 * 8 C5
Rowallan Rd MGN/WHC B75 ....57 H3
Rowanberry Cl STRPT DY13 .....188 C1
Rowan Cl BRGRVE B61 ....191 J3
COVS CV3 ....157 H6
HLYWD B47 ....146 F8
LICH WS13 ....21 H5
POL/KGSB/FAZ B78 ....60 B7
WALM/CURD B76 ....73 K3
Rowan Ct BVILLE B30 ....145 L3
Rowan Crs BDMR/CCFT WV3 ....49 J6
BILS/COS WV14 ....66 F4
Rowan Dr HLGN/YWD B28 ....126 E8
RUGBYS/DCH CV22 ....185 M3
WNSFLD WV11 ....37 M2
WWCK CV34 ....205 K5
Rowan Gdns POL/KGSB/FAZ B78 ...47 M5
Rowan Gv BNTWD WS7 ....18 D7
COVE CV2 ....135 J3
Rowan Ri KGSWFD DY6 ....83 J7
Rowan Rd CNCK/NC WS11 ....16 A3
CSCFLD/WYGN B72 ....73 C3
DSYBK/YTR WS5 ....69 K1
NUNW/HART CV10 ....80 A7
REDW B97 ....201 L1
SEDG DY3 ....201 L1
The Rowans BDWTH CV12 ....116 C3
Rowantrees RBRY B45 ....143 M8
Rowan Wy
CHWD/FDBR/MGN B37 ....111 J4
NFLD/LBR B31 ....144 D4
Roway La OLDBY B69 ....86 C4
Rowborough*
RWWCK/WEL CV35 ....204 C3
Rowbrook Cl SHLY B90 ....147 J5
Rowchester Ct CBHAMNE B4 * 7 J3
Rowcroft Covert
ALE/KHTH/YWD B14 ....146 A2
Rowcroft Rd COVE CV2 ....135 L7
Rowdale Rd PBAR/PBCH B42 ......71 G6
Rowden Dr ERDW/GRVHL B23 ......72 E7
SOLH B91 ....148 C3
Rowena Gdns SEDG DY3 ....66 A3
Rowheath Rd BVILLE B30 ....145 K1
Rowington Av
BLKHTH/ROWR B65 ....104 A3
Rowington Cl COVW CV5 ....133 H7
Rowington Rd BKDE/SHDE B34 ....92 C7
Rowington Ter RBRY B25 * 108 F6
Rowland Av POL/KGSB/FAZ B78 ...47 L2
Rowland Ct RCOVN/BALC/EX CV7 ..96 C4
Rowland Gdns WSLW WS2 ....4 A1
Rowland Hill Av TPTN/OCK DY4 .137 M8
Rowland Hill Dr TPTN/OCK DY4 ...86 A1
Rowlands Av WOLV WV1 ....52 C2
WSLW WS2 ....52 C2
Rowlands Cl WSLW WS2 ....52 C2
Rowlands Rd SOLH B91 ....127 M5
Rowland St
BLKHTH/ROWR B65 ....104 A2
Rowland Wy KIDDW DY11 ....164 C4
Rowley Cl HEDN WS12 ....17 J3
Rowley Dr COVS CV3 ....181 M1
Rowley Gv STETCH B33 ....110 B2
Rowley Hall Av
BLKHTH/ROWR B65 ....104 A2
Rowley Hill Vw CDYHTH B64 ....103 K5
Rowley La COVS CV3 ....182 B2
Rowley PI RUSH/SHEL WS4 ....39 M6
Rowley Rd KNWTH CV8 ....181 K2
Rowley's Green La COVN CV6 ...134 C1
Rowley Vw WSL WS1 ....5 H3
Rowley Vw BILS/COS WV14 ....67 H2
WBROM B70 ....86 F2
Rowley Village
BLKHTH/ROWR B65 ....104 A2
Rowney Cft HLGN/YWD B28 ......147 J4
Rowney Green La ALVE B48 .....194 B2
Rowood Dr HIA/OLT B92 ....128 A6
Rowse Cl RUGBYN/HIL CV21 .....186 B3
The Row KNWTH CV8 * 181 K3
Rowthorn Cl FOAKS/STRLY B74 ...55 L6
Rowthorn Dr SHLY B90 ....148 E7*
Rowton Av
DUNHL/THL/PER WV6 ....48 C2
Rowton Dr FOAKS/STRLY B74 .....55 K8
Roxall Cl KIDD DY10 ....140 K4
Roxburgh Cft RLSN CV32 ....198 F8
Roxburgh Gv GTB/HAM B43 ....71 G1
Roxburgh Rd NUN CV11 ....99 J4
CSCFLD/WYGN B72 ....72 E2
Roxby Gdns
DUNHL/THL/PER WV6 ....35 L8
Royal Cl BLKHTH/ROWR B65 ......86 A8
BRLYHL DY5 ....102 A5
Royal Ct RUGBYN/HIL CV21 .....186 D2
Royal Mail St CBHAMW B1 ....6 E6
Royal Meadow Dr ATHST CV9 .....63 J6
Royal Oak La
RCOVN/BALC/EX CV7 ....116 A6
Royal Oak Rd
BLKHTH/ROWR B65 ....85 K8
RMSLY B62 ....104 C4
Royal Oak Yd BDWTH CV12 * 116 F1
Royal Priors RLSN CV32 * 206 D4
Royal Rd MGN/WHC B75 ....57 G5
Royal Scot Gv WSL WS1 ....53 H8
Royal Star Cl STETCH B33 .....110 A3
Royal Wy TPTN/OCK DY4 ....85 L3
Royal Worcester Crs
BRGRVE B60 ....192 A4
Royal Gn ACGN B27 ....127 G5
Roylesden Crs SCFLD/BOLD B73 ..72 A3
Royston Cha SCFLD/BOLD B73 ....56 C8
Royston Cl COVS CV3 ....156 C2
Royston Cl BHTH/HG B12 ....87 K7
Royston Wy SEDG DY3 ....66 A5
Rozel Av KIDD DY10 ....138 D2
Rubens Cl COVW CV5 ....154 A2
Rubery Cl BVILLE B30 ....145 K1
Rubery Farm Gv RBRY B45 .....143 K5
Rubery Field Cl RBRY B45 .....143 K4
Rubery La RBRY B45 ....143 K4

Rubery La South RBRY B45 143 K5
Rubery St DARL/WED WS10 52 B5
Ruckley Av LOZ/NWT B19 * 89 G6
Ruckley Rd SLYOAK B29 123 L5
Rudd Gdns WOLV WV1 50 F1
Ruddington Wy LOZ/NWT B19 89 J8
Rudgard Rd COVN CV6 134 E1
Rudge Av WOLV WV1 50 F2
Rudge Cl SHHTH WV12 52 A1
Rudge Cft STETCH B33 109 L1
Rudge Wk WSNGN B18 * 106 E2
Rudgewick Cft AST/WIT B6 89 K7
Rudyard Cl WOLVN WV10 36 C1
Rudyard Gv STETCH B33 109 M2
Rudyngfield Dr STETCH B33 109 K2
Rufford CRTAM B79 31 J7
Rufford Cl ERDW/GRVHL B23 72 B5
Rufford Rd HAG/WOL DY9 120 A1
Rufford St HAG/WOL DY9 102 B7
Rufford Wy ALDR WS9 40 C6
Rugby La RRUGBY CV23 183 L7
Rugby Rd BTACH/HAR CV33 199 K7
COVS CV3 157 G5
RLSN CV32 206 B5
RRUGBY CV23 158 D2
RRUGBY CV23 158 F8
RRUGBY CV23 159 K2
RRUGBY CV23 159 M3
RRUGBY CV23 185 G1
RRUGBY CV23 185 M1
STRBR DY8 101 H6
Rugby St WOLV WV1 2 C2
Rugeley Av SHHTH WV12 38 B5
Rugeley Cl TPTN/OCK DY4 67 J8
Rugeley Rd BNTWD WS7 18 D5
BNTWD WS7 19 G3
HEDN WS12 13 G7
Ruislip Cl CVALE B35 91 L1
Ruiton St SEDG DY3 84 B1
Rumbow HALE B63 121 M1
Rumbow La RMSLY B62 142 B1
Rumbush La HOCK/TIA B94 173 H4
Rumer Hill Rd CNCK/NC WS11 16 C6
Runcorn Cl
CHWD/FDBR/MGN B37 111 G1
REDE B98 202 D5
Runcorn Rd BHTH/HG B12 107 K8
Runneymede Gdns
NUNW/HART CV10 98 D2
Runnymede Dr
RCOVN/BALC/EX CV7 152 A8
Runnymede Rd SPARK B11 126 C2
Rupert Brooke Rd
RUGBYS/DCH CV22 186 C6
Rupert Rd COVN CV6 133 M5
Rupert St BDMR/CCFT WV3 2 A4
VAUX/NECH B7 89 L8
Rushall Cl RUSH/SHEL WS4 53 M1
STRBR DY8 101 J5
Rushall Manor Cl
RUSH/SHEL WS4 53 M1
Rushall Manor Rd
RUSH/SHEL WS4 53 M1
Rushall Rd WOLVN WV10 36 C3
Rushbrook Cl BRWNH WS8 26 C7
HIA/OLT B92 127 J3
Rushbrooke Cl MOS/BIL B13 125 K1
Rushbrooke Dr SCFLD/BOLD B73 72 A1
Rushbrook Gv
ALE/KHTH/YWD B14 146 A2
Rushbury Cl BILS/COS WV14 50 F8
SHLY B90 148 B1
Rushden Cft KGSTG B44 71 K4
Rushes Ml BLOX/PEL WS3 39 J2
Rushey La SPARK B11 108 E8
Rushford Av WMBN WV5 64 E7
Rushford Cl SHLY B90 148 E6
Rush Gn RIDG/WDGT B32 123 J3
Rush La REDE B98 194 F7
TAM/AM/WIL B77 60 B2
Rushleigh Rd SHLY B90 147 J5
Rushmead Gv RBRY B45 143 L6
Rushmere Rd TPTN/OCK DY4 67 L5
Rushmoor Cl FOAKS/STRLY B74 56 F7
Rushmoor Dr COVW CV5 8 A4
Rushmore St RLSS CV31 206 F6
Rushmore Ter RLSS CV31 206 F7
Rushock Cl REDE B98 203 G7
Rushton Cl
RCOVN/BALC/EX CV7 152 A6
Rushwater Cl WMBN WV5 64 C7
Rushwick Gv SHLY B90 148 E7
Rushwood Cl RUSH/SHEL WS4 53 L2
Rushy Piece RIDG/WDGT B32 123 H2
Rusina Ct RLSS CV31 * 206 D7
Ruskin Av BLKHTH/ROWR B65 104 B3
ETTPK/GDPK/PENN WV4 66 D3
KIDD DY10 139 G7
SEDG DY3 65 L8
Ruskin Cl AST/WIT B6 89 K6
COVN CV6 133 H7
NUNW/HART CV10 79 L8
RUGBYS/DCH CV22 186 D7
Ruskin Gv ACGN B27 126 F3
Ruskin Hall Gv AST/WIT B6 89 K6
Ruskin Rd WOLVN WV10 36 D5
Ruskin St HHTH/SAND B71 69 G8
Russel Cft BRGRVE B60 191 L6
Russell Bank Rd
FOAKS/STRLY B74 56 C1
Russell Cl OLDBY B69 86 B3
TPTN/OCK DY4 68 A4
WNSFLD WV11 37 K4
Russell Rd BILS/COS WV14 51 K6
HLGN/YWD B28 126 C3
KIDD DY10 164 D1
MOS/BIL B13 125 H2
Russell's Hall Rd DUDN DY1 84 C4
The Russells MOS/BIL B13 125 H2
Russell St BDMR/CCFT WV3 2 D7
COV CV1 9 G2
DARL/WED WS10 68 D3
DUDN DY1 84 F4
RLSN CV32 206 D4
WLNHL WV13 51 M3
Russell St North COV CV1 * 9 G1
Russell Ter RLSS CV31 206 E6
Russelsheim Wy
RUGBYS/DCH CV22 186 E3
Russet Gv TLHL/CAN CV4 * 180 B2
Russett Cl BNTWD WS7 18 E7
DSYBK/YTR WS5 54 B5
Russett Wy BEWD DY12 162 D1
BRLYHL DY5 83 L6
Russet Wy NFLD/LBR B31 123 J7
Ruston St LDYWD/EDGR B16 106 E4
Ruthall Cl SLYOAK B29 124 A6
Ruth Cl DARL/WED WS10 68 A3
Rutherford Gln NUN CV11 99 K4
Rutherford Rd BRGRVE B60 191 M7
ERDW/GRVHL B23 72 C6
WSLW WS2 38 E7
Rutherglen Av COVS CV3 155 L7
Rutland Av
ETTPK/GDPK/PENN WV4 65 H1
NUNW/HART CV10 98 D1
Rutland Crs ALDR WS9 40 F4
BILS/COS WV14 51 H6
Rutland Cft COVS CV3 156 D5
Rutland Dr BRGRVE B60 191 L5
LGN/SDN/BHAMAIR B26 109 J6
POL/KGSB/FAZ B78 45 L4
Rutland Pl STRBR DY8 101 H5
Rutland Rd DARL/WED WS10 69 G1
HEDN WS12 17 J4
HHTH/SAND B71 69 G6
SMTHWK B66 105 L4
Rutland St BLOX/PEL WS3 39 J8
Rutland Ter WSNGN B18 * 88 E8
Rutley Gv RIDG/WDGT B32 123 K1
Rutters Meadow
RIDG/WDGT B32 122 F1
Rutter St WSL WS1 4 E8
Ryan Av WNSFLD WV11 37 L6
Ryan Pl DUDS DY2 85 G7
Rycroft Gv STETCH B33 110 A3
Rydal TAM/AM/WIL B77 46 E6
Rydal Av NUN CV11 81 L7
Rydal Cl COVW CV5 132 F5
FOAKS/STRLY B74 55 K3
HEDN WS12 12 E5
RUGBYN/HIL CV21 161 H7
STRPT DY13 163 K7
WNSFLD WV11 37 G6
Rydal Dr DUNHL/THL/PER WV6 48 D1
Rydding La HHTH/SAND B71 69 G5
Rydding Sq HHTH/SAND B71 68 F5
Ryde Av NUNW/HART CV10 81 H7
Ryde Gv ACGN B27 126 E4
Ryde Park Rd RBRY B45 144 A7
Ryder Cl RWWCK/WEL CV35 204 D7
Ryder Rw RCOVN/BALC/EX CV7 96 E5
Ryders Green Rd WBROM B70 86 D1
Ryders Hayes La BLOX/PEL WS3 39 L1
Ryders Hill Crs
NUNW/HART CV10 80 A6
Ryder St CBHAMNE B4 * 7 H3
STRBR DY8 101 H3
WBROM B70 68 D8
Ryebank Cl BVILLE B30 124 A8
Ryeclose Cft
CHWD/FDBR/MGN B37 111 H2
Rye Cft ACGN B27 109 G8
HAG/WOL DY9 120 C3
HLYWD B47 146 E8
Ryecroft Av
ETTPK/GDPK/PENN WV4 49 M8
Ryecroft Cl SEDG DY3 66 A5
Ryecroft Dr BNTWD WS7 18 E5
Ryecroft Pk WSLW WS2 53 J2
Ryecroft Pl BLOX/PEL WS3 39 K7
Ryecroft St WSLW WS2 53 J2
Ryefield CDSL WV8 35 J4
Ryefield Cl HAG/WOL DY9 140 E1
SOLH B91 127 J8
Ryefield La WALM/CURD B76 74 F4
Ryegrass La REDW B97 202 A7
Rye Grass Wk CVALE B35 91 M2
Rye Gv SPARK B11 126 D1
Rye Hl COVW CV5 132 E7
The Ryelands RRUGBY CV23 185 G6
Rye Meadow KNWTH CV8 179 J3
Rye Piece Ringway
BDWTH CV12 116 F2
Ryhope Cl BDWTH CV12 116 A4
Ryknild Cl FOAKS/STRLY B74 42 C7
Ryknild St LICHS WS14 21 J7
Ryland Cl HALE B63 121 J3
RLSS CV31 206 F7
TPTN/OCK DY4 67 M8
Ryland Rd EDG B15 107 G6
ERDE/BCHGN B24 90 D4
SPARK B11 126 B1
Rylands Dr
ETTPK/GDPK/PENN WV4 65 L1
Ryland St LDYWD/EDGR B16 6 A7
Ryle St BLOX/PEL WS3 39 H3
Rylston Av COVN CV6 133 L4
Rylstone Wy WWCK CV34 * 205 J4
Rymond Rd BKDE/SHDE B34 91 J7
Ryton TAM/AM/WIL B77 46 D5
Ryton Br KNWTH CV8 182 B2
Ryton Cl REDE B98 203 H4
SCFLD/BOLD B73 56 F8
TLHL/CAN CV4 153 M5
WNSFLD WV11 36 E8
Ryton Gv BKDE/SHDE B34 92 B6
Ryvere Cl STRPT DY13 188 D3

S

Sabell Rd SMTHWKW B67 87 K7
Sabrina Dr BEWD DY12 162 E1
Sabrina Rd
DUNHL/THL/PER WV6 48 C4
Saddington Rd COVS CV3 156 C5
Saddlers Cl HALE B63 102 F8
LICHS WS14 21 J5
Saddlers Ms SOLH B91 149 G4
The Saddlestones
DUNHL/THL/PER WV6 48 B1
Saddleworth Rd GTWY WS6 38 E1
Sadler Gdns BDWTH CV12 117 G3
Sadler Rd BRWNH WS8 26 E5
COVN CV6 133 L4
MGN/WHC B75 57 K6
Sadlers Ct WSLW WS2 52 F6
Sadlers Ml BRWNH WS8 * 26 E6
Sadlers Wk LDYWD/EDGR B16 106 E4
Sadlerswell La HOCK/TIA B94 174 F7
Saffron TAM/AM/WIL B77 46 F1
Saffron Cl RRUGBY CV23 161 J5
Saffron Gdns
ETTPK/GDPK/PENN WV4 65 L1
Sage Cft NFLD/LBR B31 123 K8
St Agatha's Rd COVE CV2 155 L2
WASH/WDE B8 90 F8
St Agnes Cl MOS/BIL B13 125 M3
St Agnes La COV CV1 * 8 F3
St Agnes Rd MOS/BIL B13 125 M3
St Agnes Wy NUN CV11 99 K1
St Aidan's Rd CNCK/NC WS11 16 C1
St Aidans Wk SMHTH B10 * 108 A5
St Alban's Av KIDDW DY11 137 L6
St Albans Cl RLSN CV32 206 A3
SMTHWKW B67 * 87 J7
WNSFLD WV11 37 L5
St Albans Rd MOS/BIL B13 125 L1
SMTHWKW B67 87 J7
St Alphege Cl SOLH B91 * 149 G2
St Ambrose Cl RMSLY B62 104 A5
St Andrew Cl HEDN WS12 13 L8
St Andrews TAM/AM/WIL B77 46 F1
St Andrews Av BLOX/PEL WS3 25 L8
St Andrews Cl HRBN B17 123 L2
SEDG DY3 83 L2
STRBR DY8 119 K3
St Andrews Crs
RUGBYS/DCH CV22 186 E5
St Andrews Dr
DUNHL/THL/PER WV6 34 B8
NUN CV11 99 M4
OLDBY B69 85 M6
St Andrew's Rd BORD B9 107 M3
COVW CV5 154 D5
MGN/WHC B75 57 G6
RLSN CV32 198 F8
St Andrew's St BORD B9 107 M3
DUDS DY2 85 G8
St Andrews Wy
BRGRVW B61 191 H5
St Annes Cl BFLD/HDSWWD B20 88 D1
BNTWD WS7 26 C1
St Anne's Ct MOS/BIL B13 125 J1
St Annes Gv DOR/KN B93 149 L7
St Anne's Rd CDYHTH B64 103 G4
LICH WS13 20 F2
RUGBYS/DCH CV22 186 C4
WLNHL WV13 51 M2
WOLVN WV10 35 M4
St Annes Wy KGSTG B44 71 L6
St Ann's Rd COVE CV2 155 L2
St Anthonys Dr BLOX/PEL WS3 25 M8
St Athan Cft CVALE B35 91 M2
St Augustine's Rd
LDYWD/EDGR B16 106 B4
St Augustine's Wk COVN CV6 133 L6
St Augustus Cl HHTH/SAND B71 87 K2
St Austell Cl CRTAM B79 31 L7
NUN CV11 81 L8
St Austell Rd COVE CV2 156 C2
DSYBK/YTR WS5 54 B6
St Bartholemews Cl COVS CV3 156 E3
St Bartholomew's Rd
STRPT DY13 188 C3
St Bartholomew Ter
DARL/WED WS10 68 D2
St Benedicts Cl ATHST CV9 63 H5
WBROM B70 87 K3
St Benedict's Rd BNTWD WS7 18 F7
SMHTH B10 108 D5
WMBN WV5 64 E6
St Bernards Cl HEDN WS12 18 A1
St Bernards Rd
CSCFLD/WYGN B72 73 G3
SOLH B91 127 H8
St Bernards Wk COVS CV3 156 B7
St Blaise Av CSHL/WTROR B46 92 F3
St Blaise Rd MGN/WHC B75 57 H2
St Brades Cl OLDBY B69 86 A6
St Brides Cl SEDG DY3 66 A5
WMBN WV5 64 D7
Saintbury Dr SOLH B91 149 G6
St Caroline Cl WBROM B70 87 K2
St Catharines Cl WSL WS1 5 J9
St Catherine's Cl COVS CV3 155 M5
DUDS DY2 * 85 L4
MGN/WHC B75 57 K6
St Catherine's Crs
ETTPK/GDPK/PENN WV4 65 K1
St Catherine's Rd BRGRVE B60 169 K7
LICH WS13 20 F2
St Cecilia Cl KIDD DY10 164 C3
St Chad's Circus Queensway
CBHAMNW B3 6 F3
St Chad's Cl CNCK/NC WS11 16 E1
SEDG DY3 83 M2
St Chads Queensway
CBHAMNE B4 7 G2
St Chad's Rd BILS/COS WV14 51 K6
LICH WS13 20 F4
MGN/WHC B75 57 J8
RBRY B45 143 K6
WOLVN WV10 36 D5
St Christian's Cft COVS CV3 9 H9
St Christian's Rd COVS CV3 155 J5
St Christopher Cl HEDN WS12 13 L8
WBROM B70 87 J3
St Christophers
BFLD/HDSWWD B20 88 D1
St Christopher's Cl WWCK CV34 205 H5
St Christopher's Dr
TAM/AM/WIL B77 46 A4
St Clement's Av BLOX/PEL WS3 39 G6
St Clement's La HHTH/SAND B71 87 H1
St Clements Rd VAUX/NECH B7 90 A7
St Columba's Cl COV CV1 8 E2
St Columbas Dr RBRY B45 144 B6
St Cuthbert's Cl WBROM B70 87 K3
St David Cl HEDN WS12 13 L7
St Davids Cl BLOX/PEL WS3 25 M8
STRPT DY13 163 J7
WBROM B70 87 K3
St Davids Dr RIDG/WDGT B32 104 F8
St Davids Gv BFLD/HDSWWD B20 88 D1
St Davids Orch COVS CV3 156 D6
St Davids Pl BLOX/PEL WS3 39 H3
St Davids Wy NUNW/HART CV10 98 E7
St Denis Rd SLYOAK B29 123 L7
St Dominic's Rd
ERDE/BCHGN B24 90 C4
St Edburghs Rd STETCH B33 109 J4
St Editha's Cl CRTAM B79 31 M8
St Edithas Rd POL/KGSB/FAZ B78 47 L5
St Ediths Gn WWCK CV34 * 205 M5
St Edmonds Rd ATHST CV9 61 G8
St Edmund's Cl
DUNHL/THL/PER WV6 * 49 K2
WBROM B70 87 K3
St Edward's Rd SLYOAK B29 124 D3
Sainte Foy Av LICH WS13 20 E8
St Eleanor Cl WBROM B70 87 K2
St Elizabeth's Rd COVN CV6 134 C6
St Francis Av SOLH B91 127 J7
St Francis Cl BLOX/PEL WS3 25 M8
HEDN WS12 13 L8
St Fremund Wy RLSS CV31 207 G8
St George Dr HEDN WS12 13 L8
SMTHWK B66 * 87 L6
St Georges Av ERDW/GRVHL B23 72 E8
RUGBYS/DCH CV22 186 D5
St Georges Cl EDG B15 106 E6
MGN/WHC B75 57 K7
St Georges Ct FOAKS/STRLY B74 42 C8
St Georges Ml KIDD DY10 * 138 C7
St Georges Pde BKHL/PFLD WV2 3 G6
St Georges Pl WBROM B70 87 G1
St George's Rd ATHST CV9 63 H3
COV CV1 9 M7
DUDS DY2 85 H7
REDE B98 202 D1
RLSS CV31 206 D7
SHLY B90 148 B5
STRBR DY8 119 H3
St George's St DARL/WED WS10 52 B6
LOZ/NWT B19 6 E1
St George's Ter KIDD DY10 138 D7
St Georges Wy
NUNW/HART CV10 98 F5
TAM/AM/WIL B77 46 C1
St Gerards Rd SOLH B91 148 C3
St Giles Av BLKHTH/ROWR B65 103 M1
St Giles Cl BLKHTH/ROWR B65 103 M1
St Giles Crs WOLV WV1 50 E3
St Giles Rd BNTWD WS7 18 F7
RCOVN/BALC/EX CV7 116 B7
STETCH B33 110 B3
WLNHL WV13 51 M4
WOLV WV1 50 E3
St Giles Rw STRBR DY8 * 101 L7
St Giles St DUDS DY2 85 G8
St Godwald's Crs BRGRVE B60 191 M5
St Godwald's Rd BRGRVE B60 191 M6
St Helens Av TPTN/OCK DY4 68 A8
St Helens Rd LICH WS13 20 F2
RLSS CV31 206 D8
SOLH B91 127 L7
St Helen's Wy COVW CV5 132 F5
St Heliers Rd NFLD/LBR B31 144 C1
St Ives Cl CRTAM B79 31 M7
St Ives Rd COVE CV2 156 B2
DSYBK/YTR WS5 54 B6
St Ives Wy NUN CV11 99 K1
St James Av BLKHTH/ROWR B65 103 L1
St James Cl BLOX/PEL WS3 * 25 M8
WBROM B70 87 K3
St James' La COVS CV3 156 B7
St James Meadow Rd
RLSN CV32 206 A4
St James Pk WOLVN WV10 * 22 D4
St James Pl SHLY B90 147 M3
VAUX/NECH B7 7 M3
St James Rd CNCK/NC WS11 16 A5
CNCK/NC WS11 17 M8
EDG B15 6 A9
HDSW B21 88 B5
MGN/WHC B75 57 G3
OLDBY B69 86 B5
St James's Rd DUDN DY1 84 F3
St James's Ter DUDN DY1 84 E3
St James St DARL/WED WS10 68 C3
SEDG DY3 84 B2
WOLV WV1 3 J6
St James Wk BRWNH WS8 26 D6
St John Cl MGN/WHC B75 57 H1
St Johns WWCK CV34 205 K6
St Johns Av BLKHTH/ROWR B65 103 M1
KIDDW DY11 137 L7
KNWTH CV8 197 L2
RUGBYS/DCH CV22 187 J5
St John's Cl ALDR WS9 40 D2
CNCK/NC WS11 16 B5
DOR/KN B93 149 M7
LICH WS13 * 20 F7
NUNW/HART CV10 79 J5
SEDG DY3 82 B3
WBROM B70 87 K3
St John's Ct HEDN WS12 17 J4
LICHS WS14 * 20 F6
NFLD/LBR B31 144 F4
St John's Dr LICHS WS14 28 D8
St Johns Gv
CHWD/FDBR/MGN B37 110 D2
St John's Hl LICHS WS14 28 D8
St John's La RRUGBY CV23 159 L8
St Johns Rd BLOX/PEL WS3 25 M8
BRWNH WS8 26 E8
CNCK/NC WS11 16 B5
DARL/WED WS10 52 A8
DUDS DY2 85 H5
HALE B63 121 J1
HRBN B17 106 B7
LGLYGN/QTN B68 87 G8
RLSS CV31 206 E7
SPARK B11 108 A8
STRBR DY8 101 L7
STRPT DY13 163 L8
TPTN/OCK DY4 67 K6
WNSFLD WV11 37 L2
WSLW WS2 52 F5
St John's Sq BKHL/PFLD WV2 2 F7
St Johns St COV CV1 9 G6
DUDS DY2 85 G8
KIDDW DY11 138 A7
KNWTH CV8 197 K2
St Johns Ter RLSS CV31 * 206 E7
St John St BRGRVW B61 191 K3
CRTAM B79 31 M8
RUGBYN/HIL CV21 186 E1
St Johns Wk PBAR/PBCH B42 89 H1
St Johns Wd RBRY B45 143 M8
St Josephs Av NFLD/LBR B31 123 M8
St Josephs Cl BLOX/PEL WS3 39 L1
St Josephs Rd WASH/WDE B8 90 F8
St Joseph St DUDS DY2 85 H4
St Judes Cl ALE/KHTH/YWD B14 146 D3
MGN/WHC B75 57 K7
St Jude's Crs COVS CV3 156 B6
St Jude's Pas DIG/EDG B5 * 6 F7
St Jude's Rd
DUNHL/THL/PER WV6 49 K2
St Jude's Rd West
DUNHL/THL/PER WV6 49 K2
St Katherine's Rd
LGLYGN/QTN B68 105 G3
St Kenelms Av HALE B63 121 H4
St Kenelm's Cl WBROM B70 87 K3
St Kenelm's Rd RMSLY B62 121 H8
St Kilda's Rd WASH/WDE B8 * 90 C8
St Laurence Av WWCK CV34 205 H8
St Laurence Cl ALVE B48 170 F7
St Laurence Rd NFLD/LBR B31 123 L8
St Lawrence Cl DOR/KN B93 149 M8
St Lawrence Dr CNCK/NC WS11 16 F3
St Lawrence Rd
NUNW/HART CV10 96 F1
NUNW/HART CV10 97 G1
St Lawrence's Rd COVN CV6 134 D4
St Lawrence Wy
DARL/WED WS10 52 B7
St Leonards Cl
CHWD/FDBR/MGN B37 110 E6
St Leonards Vw
POL/KGSB/FAZ B78 47 L5
St Leonard's Wk KNWTH CV8 182 E4
St Loye's Cl RMSLY B62 104 B6
St Lukes Cl BLKHTH/ROWR B65 103 M1
CNCK/NC WS11 16 A5
St Luke's Rd BNTWD WS7 19 G7
COVN CV6 134 B3
Saint Luke's Rd DARL/WED WS10 68 F2
St Luke's Rd DIG/EDG B5 107 J6
St Lukes St CDYHTH B64 103 H4
St Lukes Wy NUNW/HART CV10 98 A2
St Margaret Rd COV CV1 9 L6
St Margaret's FOAKS/STRLY B74 56 A2
St Margarets Av WASH/WDE B8 90 F7
St Margarets Dr HALE B63 121 K3
St Margarets Rd BLOX/PEL WS3 39 L1
CRTAM B79 31 M6
GTB/HAM B43 70 D3
HIA/OLT B92 127 J4
LICH WS13 20 F2
RLSS CV31 206 E8
WASH/WDE B8 90 E7
St Mark's Av RUGBYS/DCH CV22 186 A6
St Marks Cl NUNW/HART CV10 98 A1
St Marks Crs CBHAMW B1 106 E2
St Mark's Ms RLSN CV32 206 C4
St Mark's Rd BDMR/CCFT WV3 2 C6
BLOX/PEL WS3 39 L1
BNTWD WS7 19 G7
BRWNH WS8 26 E8
DUDS DY2 85 K4
HAG/WOL DY9 102 B8
RLSN CV32 206 B4
SMTHWKW B67 105 H2
TPTN/OCK DY4 67 L5
St Mark's St BDMR/CCFT WV3 2 D6
CBHAMW B1 6 A3
St Martin's Cl BKHL/PFLD WV2 50 C7
WBROM B70 87 K3
St Martin's Dr TPTN/OCK DY4 67 L8
St Martin's Rd COVS CV3 180 F2
MGN/WHC B75 57 K8
St Martin's St EDG B15 6 B8
St Martin's Ter BILS/COS WV14 67 J2
St Marys Cl ACGN B27 126 F2
BILS/COS WV14 66 D5
ERDE/BCHGN B24 91 H1
WOLVN WV10 23 G3
WWCK CV34 205 H5
St Marys Ct WLNHL WV13 * 51 L3
St Mary's Crs RLSS CV31 206 F6
St Mary's La STRBR DY8 119 M2
St Marys Ringway KIDDW DY11 138 B7
St Mary's Rd ATHST CV9 63 J5
DARL/WED WS10 68 D2
HRBN B17 106 A8
LICH WS13 20 F2
NUN CV11 80 F8
RCOVN/BALC/EX CV7 114 C1
RLSS CV31 206 F7
St Mary's Rw CBHAMNE B4 7 G3
MOS/BIL B13 125 K2
St Mary's Ter RLSS CV31 206 F6
St Mary St COV CV1 9 G5
St Mary's Wy ALDR WS9 40 E8
TAM/AM/WIL B77 46 C1
St Matthew Cl HEDN WS12 13 L8
St Matthew's Av BNTWD WS7 19 K6
St Matthews Cl BLOX/PEL WS3 * 25 M8
WSL WS1 5 G5
St Matthew's Rd BNTWD WS7 19 K6
LGLYGN/QTN B68 104 E3
SMTHWK B66 88 A8
St Matthew St WOLV WV1 3 M6
St Mawes Rd
DUNHL/THL/PER WV6 48 D2
St Mawgen Cl CVALE B35 92 A1
St Michael Rd LICH WS13 21 G5
St Michael's Cl ATHST CV9 61 G4
ATHST CV9 63 K4
BLOX/PEL WS3 39 K3
PENK ST19 10 C5
RCOVN/BALC/EX CV7 96 D5
STRPT DY13 188 E1
St Michael's Ct
DUNHL/THL/PER WV6 35 J8
St Michael's Crs OLDBY B69 104 D1
St Michaels Dr HEDN WS12 13 L8
St Michael's Gv DUDS DY2 85 K4
St Michael's Rd COVE CV2 155 L2
PENK ST19 10 C5
SCFLD/BOLD B73 72 D5
SEDG DY3 65 K8
WSNGN B18 88 E6
WWCK CV34 205 H5
St Michael's Sq PENK ST19 10 C4
St Michael St WBROM B70 87 G2
WSL WS1 4 F7
St Michael's Wy
NUNW/HART CV10 98 A1
TPTN/OCK DY4 85 L2
St Modwena Wy PENK ST19 10 D6
St Nicholas Av KNWTH CV8 197 K2
St Nicholas Church St
WWCK CV34 205 K6
St Nicholas Cl BLOX/PEL WS3 39 L1
St Nicholas Ct WWCK CV34 * 205 K7
St Nicholas St COV CV1 8 E1
St Nicolas Gdns
HWK/WKHTH B38 145 K3
St Nicolas Park Dr NUN CV11 81 J6
St Nicolas Rd NUN CV11 81 H8
St Osburg's Rd COVE CV2 155 L2
St Oswalds Cl KIDD DY10 138 D5
St Oswalds Rd SMHTH B10 108 C5
St Patrick Cl HEDN WS12 13 L8
St Patricks Cl
ALE/KHTH/YWD B14 125 J7
St Paul's Av BHTH/HG B12 107 L8
KIDDW DY11 137 L7
St Paul's Cl CNCK/NC WS11 16 F4
COVEN WV9 22 A3
WWCK CV34 * 205 H7
St Paul's Ct TAM/AM/WIL B77 * 60 A1
St Pauls Crs BLOX/PEL WS3 25 M8
CSHL/WTROR B46 93 L6
WBROM B70 68 C6
St Pauls Dr RMSLY B62 104 B4
TPTN/OCK DY4 85 M1
St Paul's Rd BHTH/HG B12 107 K7
BNTWD WS7 19 G7
COVN CV6 134 C7
DARL/WED WS10 52 F8
DUDS DY2 85 H8
HEDN WS12 17 J2
NUNW/HART CV10 98 A2
SMTHWK B66 87 H6
St Paul's Sq CBHAMNW B3 6 E2
St Paul's St WSL WS1 4 F3
St Pauls Ter WWCK CV34 * 205 H7
St Peter's Av ATHST CV9 63 M6
St Peter's Cl ALDR WS9 41 J1
ATHST CV9 63 M6
CSCFLD/WYGN B72 72 F2
CSHL/WTROR B46 92 F3
HLGN/YWD B28 126 B7
REDW B97 202 B8
TAM/AM/WIL B77 46 A4
TPTN/OCK DY4 86 B1
St Peters Ct BLOX/PEL WS3 38 F4
COV CV1 * 9 J2
St Peters Cft SCFLD/BOLD B73 * 72 F2
St Peters Dr BLOX/PEL WS3 39 L1
NUNW/HART CV10 97 K1
St Peters La HIA/OLT B92 129 H5
St Peters Rd ATHST CV9 63 L6
BFLD/HDSWWD B20 89 G4
BNTWD WS7 19 G7
DUDS DY2 85 H7
HAG/WOL DY9 120 A4
HEDN WS12 17 H1
HRBN B17 105 M8
RUGBYN/HIL CV21 187 G3
St Peters Sq WOLV WV1 2 F4
St Peters Ter WSLW WS2 53 J1
St Philips Av BDMR/CCFT WV3 49 L6
St Philips Pl CBHAMNW B3 7 G4
St Phillips Av BDMR/CCFT WV3 49 K6
St Phillip's Gv BDMR/CCFT WV3 49 K6
St Quentin St WSLW WS2 4 A8
St Saviour's Cl BKHL/PFLD WV2 50 D7
St Saviour's Rd WASH/WDE B8 108 B1
St Silas' Sq LOZ/NWT B19 88 F6
St Simons Cl MGN/WHC B75 57 K7
St Stephen's Av WLNHL WV13 51 K3
St Stephens Ct HEDN WS12 * 17 G1
St Stephens Gdns REDE B98 194 D8
WLNHL WV13 * 51 L4
St Stephen's Rd BNTWD WS7 18 F7
HHTH/SAND B71 87 M5
SLYOAK B29 124 F5
St Stephens St AST/WIT B6 89 J7
Saints Wy NUNW/HART CV10 81 H8
St Thomas' Cl ALDR WS9 40 F4
BLOX/PEL WS3 39 J7
MGN/WHC B75 57 K8
St Thomas Ct COV CV1 * 8 C6

St Thomas Dr HEDN WS12 .....13 L8
St Thomas' Rd CNUW CV6 ....134 D2
  ERDW/GRVHL B23 ....90 B3
St Thomas Ct NUNW/HART CV10 ..98 A2
St Thomas's Ct 8 C5
St Thomas's Dr DUDS DY2 .....85 G8
St Valentines Cl WBROM B70 ...87 K5
St Vincent Crs WBROM B70 .....68 D7
St Vincent St LDYWD/EDGR B16 ...6 C5
St Vincent St West
  LDYWD/EDGR B16 ....106 E3
St Wilfreds Cottages
  RCOVN/BALC/EX CV7 * 96 C3
Saladin Av OLDBY B69 ....86 C8
Salcombe Gv
  LGN/SDN/BHAMAIR B26 ......110 A8
Salcombe Cl CNCK/NC WS11 .....15 M5
  COVS CV3 ....156 B2
  NUN CV11 ....81 K8
Salcombe Dr BRLYHL DY5 ....102 A4
Salcombe Gv BILS/COS WV14 .....67 H4
Salcombe Rd SMTHWK B66 ....87 M8
Salem St TPTN/OCK DY4 ....68 D8
Salford Cl COVE CV2 ....134 E8
Salford St AST/WIT B6 ....89 G8
  REDE B98 ....202 F7
Salisbury Av COVS CV3 ....155 G7
Salisbury Chambers
  MOS/BIL B13 * 125 K1
Salisbury Cl DUDN DY1 ....84 D2
  LICH WS13 ....21 G2
  MOS/BIL B13 ....125 J2
Salisbury Dr CNCK/NC WS11 .....16 F5
  CSHL/WTROR B46 ....93 G3
  KIDDW DY11 ....137 K7
  NUNW/HART CV10 ....79 M6
Salisbury Gv CSCFLD/WYGN B72 ..73 G6
Salisbury Rd LOZ/NWT B19 ......89 H5
  MOS/BIL B13 ....125 J2
  SMTHWK B66 ....105 M1
  WASH/WDE B8 ....90 C8
  WBROM B70 ....87 J4
Salisbury St BDMR/CCFT WV3 .....2 C7
  DARL/WED WS10 ....52 C6
Sallow Gv BRWNH WS8 ....26 D4
Sally Ward Dr ALDR WS9 ....40 E1
Salop Cl HHTH/SAND B71 ....68 D5
Salop Dr CNCK/NC WS11 ....16 D5
  LGLYGN/QTN B68 ....105 G2
Salop Rd LGLYGN/QTN B68 ......105 G2
  WBROM B70 ....202 B3
Salop St BHTH/HG B12 ....107 K5
  BILS/COS WV14 ....67 J1
  BKHL/PFLD WV2 ....2 E6
  DUDN DY1 ....84 E5
  OLDBY B69 ....86 C8
Salstar Cl AST/WIT B6 ....89 J7
Saltash Gv YDLY B25 ....109 G4
Saltbrook Rd HAG/WOL DY9 .....102 E6
Salter Rd TPTN/OCK DY4 ....67 K6
Salter's La CRTAM B79 ....31 M7
  HHTH/SAND B71 ....87 J1
  REDW B97 ....201 L1
Salter's St ALDR WS9 ....40 E2
Salter St HOCK/TIA B94 ....174 A4
Salters V WBROM B70 ....87 J4
Saltisford WWCK CV34 ....205 H5
Salt La COV CV1 ....8 F5
Saltley Cottages
  ERDE/BCHGN B24 * 90 D4
Saltley Rd VAUX/NECH B7 ....89 M8
Saltley Viad VAUX/NECH B7 .....90 A8
Salts La POL/KCSB/FAZ B78 .....59 K1
Saltwells Rd DUDS DY2 ....102 E3
Saltwells Rd DUDS DY2 ....102 F5
Salwarpe Gv SLYOAK B29 ....123 K3
Salwarpe Rd BRGRVE B60 ....191 M3
Sam Barber Ct HEDN WS12 * 17 J5
Sambar Cl BKDE/SHDE B34 ....92 B6
Sambourn Cl SOLH B91 ....25 K4
Sambourne Dr BKDE/SHDE B34 ....92 B6
Sambrook Rd WOLVN WV10 ....36 E7
Sam Gault Cl COVS CV3 ....156 C6
Sammons Wy TLHL/CAN CV4 .....153 H4
Sampson Cl COVE CV2 ....135 G2
  HDSW B21 ....88 A4
  OLDBY B69 ....86 C8
Sampson Rd SPARK B11 ....107 M6
Sampson Rd North SPARK B11 ...107 M5
Sampson St DARL/WED WS10 .....68 F2
Sams La WBROM B70 ....87 J4
Sam Spencer Ct KIDD DY10 ....165 L4
Samuel Cl LICH WS13 ....21 G3
Samuel St BLOX/PEL WS3 ....38 F4
Samuels Rd RIDG/WDGT B32 ....104 E8
Sanby Cl BDWTH CV12 ....116 E1
Sanda Cft CBROM B36 ....92 F7
Sandals Cl NFLD/LBR B31 ......144 A8
Sandal Ri SOLH B91 ....149 J2
Sandals Ri RMSLY B62 ....122 B2
Sandalwood Cl SHHTH WV12 ......37 M5
Sand Bank BLOX/PEL WS3 ....38 F4
Sandbarn Cl SHLY B90 ....148 D7
Sandbeds Rd SHHTH WV12 ....52 A1
Sandbourne Rd WASH/WDE B8 ...108 L1
Sanderling Cl WOLVN WV10 ......22 F6
Sanderling Cl KIDD DY10 ......164 L4
Sanderling Ri BNTWD WS7 ....18 F5
  BRLYHL DY5 ....63 J7
Sanders Cl ATHST CV9 ....85 J6
  DUDS DY2 ....85 J6
  REDW B97 ....201 L1
Sanders Cl BRGRVW B61 ....191 J4
  COVN CV6 ....116 F7
Sandfield Cl SHLY B90 ....147 M5
Sandfield Gv SEDG DY3 ....83 M3
Sandfield Rd HHTH/SAND B71 ....69 J4
  STRBR DY8 ....101 K3
Sandfields Rd LGLYGN/QTN B68 ..105 G3
Sandford Av
  BLKHTH/ROWR B65 ....104 A2
Sandford Cl COVE CV2 ....135 H2
Sandford Ri
  DUNHL/THL/PER WV6 ....35 J7
  MOS/BIL B13 ....125 L2
Sandford St LICH WS13 ....20 D5
Sandgate Crs COVE CV2 ....156 B3
Sandgate Rd HLGN/YWD B28 ....147 K1
  TPTN/OCK DY4 ....68 B5
Sandhills Crs SOLH B91 ....148 F5
Sandhills Gn RBRY B45 ....170 G6
Sandhills La RBRY B45 ....170 G6
Sandhills Rd RBRY B45 ....170 G5
Sandhill St BLOX/PEL WS3 ......38 E4
Sandhurst Av CBROM B36 ....91 M7
  HAG/WOL DY9 ....120 B3
Sandhurst Rd REDE B98 ....195 G7
Sandhurst Dr
  ETTPK/GDPK/PENN WV4 ....65 L1
  STRBR DY8 ....101 J2
Sandhurst Gv FOAKS/STRLY B74 ..42 C8
  KGSWFD DY6 ....101 L1

MOS/BIL B13 ....125 J3
Sandicliffe Cl KIDDW DY11 ....138 A5
Sandilands Cl COVE CV2 ....156 C5
Sandland Cl BILS/COS WV14 .....51 K7
Sandland Rd SHHTH WV12 ....38 A5
Sandmartin Cl DUDS DY2 ....103 G3
Sandmartin Wy KIDD DY10 .....164 G3
Sandmere Gv
  ALE/KHTH/YWD B14 ....147 L5
Sandmere Rd
  ALE/KHTH/YWD B14 ....147 L5
Sandon Cl REDE B98 ....202 E2
Sandon Gv ERDE/BCHGN B24 ......90 E1
Sandon Rd HAG/WOL DY9 ....120 D1
  HRBN B17 ....105 L4
  NUN CV11 ....80 F8
  WOLVN WV10 ....35 M3
Sandown TAM/AM/WIL B77 ....32 D8
Sandown Av COVN CV6 ....134 C4
  GTWY WS6 ....24 B2
Sandown Cl BNTWD WS7 ....18 D4
  HEDN WS12 ....13 J1
  RLSN CV32 ....207 G1
Sandown Dr BRGRVW B61 * 58 F4
  DUNHL/THL/PER WV6 ....48 D1
Sandown Rd CBROM B36 ....91 H5
  RUGBYN/HIL CV21 ....187 G1
Sandpiper TAM/AM/WIL B77 ......46 F8
Sandpiper Cl COVE CV2 ....134 F2
Sandpiper Wy BRDR/GRVHL B23 ...72 A7
Sandpit SLYOAK B29 * 124 C5
Sandpits La
  RCOVN/BALC/EX CV7 ....133 J3
Sandra Cl ALDR WS9 ....40 F8
Sandringham Av SHHTH WV12 .....37 M7
Sandringham Cl BNTWD WS7 ......18 C4
  TLHL/CAN CV4 ....153 H4
Sandringham Dr ALDR WS9 ....27 G7
  BLKHTH/ROWR B65 ....104 A1
Sandringham Pl STRBR DY8 ....101 K3
Sandringham Rd
  ETTPK/GDPK/PENN WV4 ....65 L1
  PBAR/PBCH B42 ....70 F7
  RMSLY B62 ....103 M6
  STRBR DY8 ....101 G4
  WMBN WV5 ....64 D7
Sandstone Av BRGRVW B61 ....58 D4
Sandstone Cl SEDG DY3 ....67 L3
Sandstone Rd BEWD DY12 ......163 G2
Sand St WBROM B70 ....86 C5
Sandway Gdns WASH/WDE B8 ......90 B7
Sandway Gv MOS/BIL B13 ....126 A6
Sandwell Av DARL/WED WS10 .....51 M8
Sandwell Pl SHHTH WV12 ....38 B7
  WBROM B70 ....87 G1
Sandwell Rd HDSW B21 ....88 B4
Sandwell Rd North
  HHTH/SAND B71 ....87 H1
Sandwell St WSL WS1 ....5 G6
Sandwell Wk WSL WS1 ....5 G7
Sandwick Cl COVS CV3 ....156 D5
Sandwood Dr KGSTG B44 ....71 K7
Sandyacre Wy STRBR DY8 ......101 M8
Sandy Bank BEWD DY12 ....162 G4
Sandy Crs BNSFLD WV11 ....37 L5
Sandy Cft CSCFLD/WYGN B72 .....73 G2
  MOS/BIL B13 ....126 A6
Sandyfields Rd SEDG DY3 ....65 K8
Sandy Gv REDW B97 ....201 K3
Sandy Gv BRWNH WS8 ....26 D4
Sandy Hill Ri SHLY B90 ....147 M2
Sandy Hill Rd SHLY B90 ....147 L1
Sandy Hollow
  DUNHL/THL/PER WV6 ....49 G3
Sandy La AST/WIT B6 ....89 L8
  BRGRVW B61 ....142 D8
  CDSL WV8 ....34 D7
  CNCK/NC WS11 ....15 L4
  COVN CV6 ....134 A8
  CSHL/WTROR B46 ....95 J1
  DARL/WED WS10 ....51 J7
  DUNHL/THL/PER WV6 ....48 F7
  KIDD DY10 ....139 M5
  KIDDW DY11 ....137 L6
  LICHS WS14 ....30 A1
  PBAR/PBCH B42 ....71 H3
  RCOVN/BALC/EX CV7 ....114 D2
  RLSN CV32 ....206 A2
  RUGBYN/HIL CV21 ....186 C2
  STRPT DY13 ....188 F4
Sandy Mt WMBN WV5 ....64 F6
Sandy Mount Rd WSL WS1 ....55 H7
Sandy Rd STRBR DY8 ....119 H4
Sandys Gv TPTN/OCK DY4 ....67 J3
Sandy Wy EDG B15 ....6 B7
  TAM/AM/WIL B77 ....46 F3
Sangwin Rd TPTN/OCK DY4 ....67 G6
Sankey Rd CNCK/NC WS11 ....16 D2
Sansome Ri SHLY B90 ....147 K3
Sansome Rd SHLY B90 ....147 K3
Sanstone Cl BLOX/PEL WS3 ......39 G2
Sanstone Rd BLOX/PEL WS3 ......38 F2
Santa Maria Wy STRPT DY13 ...188 F2
Santolina Dr DSYBK/YTR WS5 ....69 L2
Santos Cl COVS CV3 ....156 D5
Santridge La BRGRVW B61 .....191 L1
Sapcote Gv COVN CV6 ....134 F1
The Saplings PENK ST19 ....10 D4
Sapphire Ct
  RCOVN/BALC/EX CV7 * 155 M4
Sapphire Dr CNCK/NC WS11 ......17 G2
  RLSN CV31 ....206 D8
Sapphire Ga COVE CV2 ....156 A3
Saracen Dr MGN/WHC B75 ....57 K7
  RCOVN/BALC/EX CV7 ....151 J7
Sara Cl FOAKS/STRLY B74 ....56 E7
Sarah Cl BILS/COS WV14 ....67 J4
Sarah Gdns DSYBK/YTR WS5 ......69 L1
Sarah Seager Cl STRPT DY13 * ..163 J7
Saredon St BORD B9 ....107 H3
Saredon Cl BLOX/PEL WS3 ....39 L4
Saredon Rd CNCK/NC WS11 ....23 M1
  WOLVN WV10 ....23 H3
Sarehole Rd HLGN/YWD B28 ....126 D6
Sargeaunt St RLSS CV31 ....206 D6
Sark Dr CBROM B36 ....92 F7
Satchwell Pl RLSS CV31 ....206 E6
Satchwell Ct RLSN CV32 ......206 D5
Saturn Rd CNCK/NC WS11 ....12 D4
Saumur Wy RLSS CV31 ....206 F7
Saunders Av BDWTH CV12 ......116 F3
Saunders Cl HEDN WS12 ....13 K7
Saunton Cl COVW CV5 ....132 F4

Saunton Rd RUGBYS/DCH CV22 ..186 D4
Saunton Wy SLYOAK B29 ....124 A4
Saveker Dr WALM/CURD B76 ......73 J1
Savernake Cl RBRY B45 ....143 L3
Saville Cl RBRY B45 ....143 M6
Saville Gv KNWTH CV8 ....180 A7
Saw Mill Cl RUSH/SHEL WS4 ......4 C1
Saxelby Cl ALE/KHTH/YWD B14 ..146 E3
Saxilby Pl STRPT DY13 ....188 F1
Saxon Cl COVS CV3 ....157 H6
  CTWY WS6 ....24 C3
  POL/KCSB/FAZ B78 ....47 K4
  RUGBYS/DCH CV22 ....185 L5
  STUD B80 ....203 J8
  TAM/AM/WIL B77 ....46 D7
Saxoncourt
  DUNHL/THL/PER WV6 ....35 G8
Saxondale Av
  LGN/SDN/BHAMAIR B26 ......109 K7
Saxon Dr BLKHTH/ROWR B65 ....104 A1
  CRTAM B79 ....46 A1
Saxonfields
  DUNHL/THL/PER WV6 ....35 G8
Saxon Mill La CRTAM B79 ....46 A1
Saxon Rd COVE CV2 ....155 M1
  PENK ST19 ....10 D5
Saxons Wy ALE/KHTH/YWD B14 ..146 E3
Saxon Wk WLS WS13 ....20 C7
Saxon Wy
  CHWD/FDBR/MGN B37 ....110 D2
Saxon Wood Cl NFLD/LBR B31 ..144 E1
Saxon Wood Rd SHLY B90 ......148 B6
Saxton Dr FOAKS/STRLY B74 .....42 D7
Scafell Cl COVW CV5 ....155 L1
Scafell Dr BILS/COS WV14 ......51 K6
  ERDW/GRVHL B23 ....72 A8
Scafell Rd STRBR DY8 ....101 M7
Scaife Rd BRGRVE B60 ....191 M6
Scammerton TAM/AM/WIL B77 ....46 F6
Scampton Cl
  DUNHL/THL/PER WV6 ....34 C8
Scampton Wy CRTAM B79 ....32 A5
Scar Bank WWCK CV34 ....205 J4
Scarborough Cl WSLW WS2 ......52 F5
Scarborough Rd WSLW WS2 ......52 F5
Scarecrow La MGN/WHC B75 ......57 J5
Scarfield Hl ALVE B48 ....170 F2
Scarman Rd KNWTH CV8 ....179 L1
Scarsdale Rd PBAR/PBCH B42 ....71 H5
Schofield Av HHTH/SAND B71 ....68 C5
Schofield Rd
  CHWD/FDBR/MGN B37 ....92 D8
Scholars Ga BNTWD WS7 ....19 H7
Scholars Cl
  STECH B33 ....109 M3
Schofield Rd
  RCOVN/BALC/EX CV7 ....115 L7
Schoolacre Ri FOAKS/STRLY B74 ..55 J4
Schoolacre Rd BKDE/SHDE B34 ...91 M7
School Brwnh WS8 ....26 A1
School Bell Ms KNWTH CV8 * ..180 F7
School Cl BDMR/CCFT WV3 ....48 F5
  BNTWD WS7 ....18 A5
  CDSL WV8 ....34 C1
  CHWD/FDBR/MGN B37 ....92 E7
  CNCK/NC WS11 ....17 L7
  COVS CV3 ....9 M6
  OLDBY B69 ....86 A6
  WMBN WV5 ....64 D8
School Cottages WOLVN WV10 * ..35 M5
School Crs CNCK/NC WS11 ....17 L4
School Dr BILS/COS WV14 ....67 L3
  BRGRVE B60 ....191 M2
  HLYWD B47 ....172 E2
  STRBR DY8 ....101 K5
The School Dr DUDS DY2 ....85 H6
Schoolfield Gv
  RUGBYN/HIL CV21 ....186 D2
Schoolfields Rd LICHS WS14 ....28 E8
School Gdns RUGBYN/HIL CV21 ..187 L4
Schoolgate Cl RUSH/SHEL WS4 ...40 B4
  WASH/WDE B8 ....90 E7
School Gn BILS/COS WV14 ....51 G5
School Hl BTACH/HAR CV33 ....207 M5
  NUNW/HART CV10 ....79 L6
Schoolhouse Cl
  HWK/WKHTH B38 ....145 M3
School House La COVE CV2 ....135 L7
School La ALVE B48 ....170 F4
  BKDE/SHDE B34 ....91 M6
  BLOX/PEL WS3 ....39 K1
  BNTWD WS7 ....18 B5
  BRGRVE B60 ....168 F7
  BRLYHL DY5 ....101 M1
  CRTAM B79 ....33 K6
  HAG/WOL DY9 ....120 D7
  HALE B63 ....121 K3
  KNWTH CV8 ....177 J8
  KNWTH CV8 ....179 K8
  NUNW/HART CV10 ....79 J8
  POL/KCSB/FAZ B78 ....30 F6
  POL/KCSB/FAZ B78 ....47 K4
  RCOVN/BALC/EX CV7 ....116 C6
  RLSS CV31 ....207 J1
  RRUGBY CV23 ....183 K7
  SOLH B91 ....149 L1
  STECH B33 ....109 K4
  TAM/AM/WIL B77 ....46 B8
  WALM/CURD B76 ....75 L6
  WOLVN WV10 ....23 H3
  WOLV WV1 ....36 E3
Selcombe Wy HWK/WKHTH B38 ...145 M8
School St BRLYHL DY5 ....84 B6
  CDYHTH B64 ....103 H4
  DARL/WED WS10 ....52 A7
  DARL/WED WS10 ....52 D7
  DUDN DY1 ....84 F4
  KNWTH CV8 ....183 L1
  RRUGBY CV23 ....158 F8
  RUGBYN/HIL CV21 ....185 L1
  RUSH/SHEL WS4 ....40 B4
  SEDG DY3 ....66 C5
  STRBR DY8 ....101 J8
  TAM/AM/WIL B77 ....46 B8
  WLNHL WV13 ....51 K3
  WOLV WV1 ....3 J3
School St West BILS/COS WV14 ..67 G5
Scholars Ter SLYOAK B29 * ...124 D3
School Wk BILS/COS WV14 ....51 G5
  BNTWD WS7 ....18 B5
  NUN CV11 ....99 J3

Scimitar Cl CRTAM B79 ....31 J6
Scorers Cl HIA/OLT B92 ....126 F7
Scotchill Cl COVN CV6 ....133 K4
The Scotchings CBROM B36 ......91 J5
Scotch Orch LICH WS13 ....21 H4
Scotia Rd CNCK/NC WS11 ....16 E2
Scotland La RIDG/WDGT B32 ...122 F5
Scotland St CBHAMW B1 ....6 D3
Scots La COVN CV6 ....133 K7
  STRPT DY13 ....188 D8
Scott Av DARL/WED WS10 ....68 F3
  ETTPK/GDPK/PENN WV4 ....65 J1
Scott Cl LICHS WS14 ....20 F7
Scott Gv HIA/OLT B92 ....127 J2
Scott Rd DSYBK/YTR WS5 ....54 E7
  GTB/HAM B43 ....70 D3
  HIA/OLT B92 ....127 J3
  KNWTH CV8 ....197 J2
  REDW B97 ....202 A5
  RLSS CV31 ....206 F7
  TAM/AM/WIL B77 ....46 C1
Scott's Green Cl DUDN DY1 .....84 D5
Scott's Rd STRBR DY8 ....101 K7
Scott St HEDN WS12 ....17 K7
  TPTN/OCK DY4 ....68 A8
Scotwell Cl
  BLKHTH/ROWR B65 ....103 M2
Scout Cl STETCH B33 ....110 A3
Scribbans Cl SMTHWK B66 .....105 M1
Scribers La HLGN/YWD B28 ....147 G1
Sculthorpe Cl KIDD DY10 .....139 M3
Seabroke Av
  RUGBYS/DCH CV22 ....186 D2
Seacroft Av STETCH B33 ....109 J4
Seafield TAM/AM/WIL B77 ....32 D8
Seafield Cl KGSWFD DY6 ....101 J1
Seafield La ALVE B48 ....172 C7
Seaford Cl COVN CV6 ....134 F1
Seaforth Gv SHHTH WV12 ....37 M4
Seagar St HHTH/SAND B71 ....87 H1
Seagers La BRLYHL DY5 ....102 B3
Seagrave Rd COV CV1 ....9 J6
Seagull Bay Dr BILS/COS WV14 ..67 H4
Sealand Dr BDWTH CV12 ....116 D2
Seal Cl WALM/CURD B76 ....73 J2
Seals Gn HWK/WKHTH B38 ......145 H6
Sear Hills Cl
  RCOVN/BALC/EX CV7 ....151 M7
Seathwaite RUGBYN/HIL CV21 ..161 G6
Seaton Cl NUN CV11 ....81 K8
  WNSFLD WV11 ....37 K8
Seaton Gv MOS/BIL B13 ....125 H4
Seaton Pl STRBR DY8 ....101 G3
Sebastian Cl COVS CV3 ....155 M8
Sebright Gn KIDDW DY11 ....138 A2
Sebright Rd KIDDW DY11 ....138 A2
Second Av BORD B9 ....108 C4
  BRWNH WS8 ....26 A6
  COVS CV3 ....156 A4
  KGSWFD DY6 ....101 J1
  SLYOAK B29 ....124 F2
  WOLVN WV10 ....36 D7
Second Exhibition Av
  BHAMNEC B40 ....129 H1
Sedge Av HWK/WKHTH B38 ......145 K2
Sedgeberrow Covert
  HWK/WKHTH B38 ....145 J5
Sedgeberrow Rd HALE B63 .....121 L7
Sedgebourne Cl NFLD/LBR B31 ..144 A4
Sedge Dr BRGRVW B61 ....168 E7
Sedgefield Cl DUDN DY1 ....84 C2
Sedgefield Gv
  DUNHL/THL/PER WV6 ....48 A1
Sedgefield Wk BRGRVW B61 * ...168 F4
Sedgefield Wy CNCK/NC WS11 ....15 L1
Sedgeford Cl BRLYHL DY5 .....102 B5
Sedgehill Av HRBN B17 ....123 H1
Sedgemere Gv
  RCOVN/BALC/EX CV7 ....152 A8
  RUSH/SHEL WS4 ....40 A5
Sedgemere Rd
  LGN/SDN/BHAMAIR B26 ......109 K4
Sedgemoor Rd COVS CV3 ....155 M8
Sedgley Gv BFLD/HDSWWD B20 ...88 C1
Sedgley Hall Av SEDG DY3 ......66 B5
Sedgley Rd
  ETTPK/GDPK/PENN WV4 ....65 K1
  HAG/WOL DY9 ....120 C6
Sedgley Rd East TPTN/OCK DY4 ..67 L1
Sedgley Rd West TPTN/OCK DY4 ..67 G7
Sedgley St BKHL/PFLD WV2 ......50 A6
Sedlescombe Pk
  RUGBYS/DCH CV22 ....186 D5
Seed Field Cft COVS CV3 .....155 H6
Seedgreen Cl STRPT DY13 .....188 C5
Seedhouse Ct CDYHTH B64 .....103 L3
Seeds La BRWNH WS8 ....26 A1
Seeleys Rd SPARK B11 ....107 M4
Seeney La WALM/CURD B76 ....75 M2
Seeswood Cl NUNW/HART CV10 ...98 A3
Sefton Dr BLKHTH/ROWR B65 ....85 K7
Sefton Gv DARL/WED WS10 ....68 A3
Sefton Rd LDYWD/EDGR B16 ....106 D4
  TAM/AM/WIL B77 ....60 D1
  TLHL/CAN CV4 ....154 C7
Segbourne Rd RBRY B45 ....143 J5
Segundo Cl DSYBK/YTR WS5 .....69 J1
Segundo Rd DSYBK/YTR WS5 .....69 J1
Seiba Dr KIDDW DY11 ....137 K7
Selborne Cl WSL WS1 * 5 J4
Selborne Gv MOS/BIL B13 .....126 A4
Selborne Rd BFLD/HDSWWD B20 ..88 E3
  DUDS DY2 ....85 H6
  RUGBYS/DCH CV22 ....186 B5
Selborne St WSL WS1 ....5 J4
Selbourne Crs WOLV WV1 ....50 F1
Selby Cl STECH B33 ....109 K4
Selby Gv MOS/BIL B13 ....126 B5
Selby Wy BLOX/PEL WS3 ....38 D5
  NUNW/HART CV10 ....78 A8
Selcombe Wy HWK/WKHTH B38 ...145 M8
Selcroft Av RIDG/WDGT B32 ...122 D3
Selecta Av KGSTG B44 ....71 J3
Selkirk Cl HHTH/SAND B71 ......68 D6
Sell La ALE/KHTH/YWD B14 ....126 B8
Selly Av SLYOAK B29 ....124 E5
Selly Cl SLYOAK B29 ....124 E5
Selly Hall Cft BVILLE B30 ...124 C6
Selly Hill Rd SLYOAK B29 ....124 D5
Selly Oak Rd BVILLE B30 .....124 B6
Selly Park Rd SLYOAK B29 ....124 E5
Selly Whf SLYOAK B29 ....124 D5
Sellywick Rd SLYOAK B29 .....124 E5
Sellywood Rd SLYOAK B29 .....124 C6
Selma Gv ALE/KHTH/YWD B14 ...147 M3
Selmans Hl BLOX/PEL WS3 ......39 G2
Selmans Pde BLOX/PEL WS3 * ...39 G2
Selsdon Cl HLYWD B47 ....147 G8
  RBRY B45 ....143 M8
Selsdon Rd BLOX/PEL WS3 ......38 D4
Selsey Av HRBN B17 ....123 J1
Selsey Cl COVS CV3 ....182 A1
Selsey Rd HRBN B17 ....123 J1
Selside RUGBYN/HIL CV21 .....161 H6

Selston Rd AST/WIT B6 ....89 J6
Selvey Av GTB/HAM B43 ....70 F2
Selworthy Rd CBROM B36 ....92 D6
  COVN CV6 ....134 B2
Selwyn Cl BKHL/PFLD WV2 ....50 A6
Selwyn Rd BILS/COS WV14 ....51 K7
  BNTWD WS7 ....19 J5
  LDYWD/EDGR B16 ....106 B2
Selwyn Wk FOAKS/STRLY B74 .....56 A1
Semele Cl RLSS CV31 ....207 J8
Seneschal Cl COVS CV3 ....155 J6
Senneleys Park Rd
  NFLD/LBR B31 ....123 J5
Sennen Cl NUN CV11 ....81 L8
  WLNHL WV13 ....51 K4
Sensall Rd HAG/WOL DY9 ......120 D2
Sentry Wy MGN/WHC B75 ....57 H1
Septnon Dr COVN CV6 ....117 G7
Serin Cl KIDD DY10 ....164 D4
The Serpentine KIDDW DY11 ...164 A5
Settle Av BKDE/SHDE B34 ....91 K7
Settle Cft
  CHWD/FDBR/MGN B37 ....110 D4
Setton Dr SEDG DY3 ....66 C6
Seven Acres ALDR WS9 ....40 F8
Seven Acres La REDE B98 .....195 G8
Seven Acres Rd NFLD/LBR B31 ..145 G4
  RMSLY B62 ....104 E8
Sevendwellings Vw
  BRLYHL DY5 ....102 A4
Sevenhills Dr STRPT DY13 ....188 B5
Sevens Rd HEDN WS12 ....18 A4
Seven Star Rd SOLH B91 ......127 L8
Seven Stars Rd OLDBY B69 ......86 E7
Severn Cl BRGRVW B61 ....168 E5
  CBROM B36 ....92 D6
  RLSN CV32 ....206 F1
  SHHTH WV12 ....37 L6
  TPTN/OCK DY4 ....67 G8
Severn Dr BNTWD WS7 ....19 H7
  BLOX/PEL WS3 ....39 H5
  BRWNH WS8 ....26 A3
  COV CV1 ....9 L7
  HALE B63 ....102 F8
  STRBR DY8 ....119 K2
Severn Gv ACGN B27 ....127 G4
Severne Rd ACGN B27 ....127 G5
Severn Gv KIDDW DY11 ....163 M2
  LOZ/NWT B19 ....89 G6
  SPARK B11 * 108 A7
Severn Rd BDWTH CV12 ....117 L2
  BLOX/PEL WS3 ....39 H5
  BRWNH WS8 ....26 A3
  COV CV1 ....9 L7
  HALE B63 ....102 F8
  STRBR DY8 ....119 K2
Severn Side STRPT DY13 ......188 E3
Severn Side North BEWD DY12 ..162 F1
Severn Side South BEWD DY12 ..162 F2
Severn St CBHAMW B1 ....6 E7
Severn Wy BEWD DY12 ....162 D2
  HLYWD B47 ....172 D2
Sevington Cl SOLH B91 ....149 G5
Sewage Cottages
  NUNW/HART CV10 * 80 A2
Sewall Hwy COVN CV6 ....134 C5
Seward Cl LICHS WS14 ....21 H7
Seymour Cl COVS CV3 ....156 A8
  GTWY WS6 ....24 B4
  RWWCK/WEL CV35 ....204 D7
  SLYOAK B29 ....124 F5
Seymour Dr REDE B98 ....194 E8
Seymour Gdns FOAKS/STRLY B74 ..56 E2
Seymour Gv RLSS CV31 ....206 B7
Seymour Rd HAG/WOL DY9 ......102 D8
  KIDDW DY11 ....137 M5
  NUN CV11 ....99 J2
  OLDBY B69 ....87 G6
  RUGBYN/HIL CV21 ....161 G2
  TPTN/OCK DY4 ....68 A4
Shackleton Dr
  DUNHL/THL/PER WV6 ....34 B7
Shackleton Rd BLOX/PEL WS3 ...39 H3
Shadowbrook La HIA/OLT B92 ..129 G8
Shadowbrook Rd COVN CV6 .....133 L8
Shadwell Dr SEDG DY3 ....84 B3
Shadwell St CBHAMNE B4 ....7 G2
Shady La KGSTG B44 ....71 H3
Shadymoor Dr BRLYHL DY5 .....102 A5
Shaftesbury Av HAG/WOL DY9 ..120 A2
  RCOVN/BALC/EX CV7 ....131 J7
Shaftesbury Cl BRGRVE B60 ...191 M3
Shaftesbury Dr HEDN WS12 .....13 G6
Shaftesbury Rd COVW CV5 .....154 D5
  DARL/WED WS10 ....68 F3
Shaftesbury Sq HHTH/SAND B71 ..87 J1
Shaftmoor La HLGN/YWD B28 ...126 C3
Shaftsbury Cl BILS/COS WV14 ...51 M3
Shaftsbury Dr BNTWD WS7 ....19 K6
Shaftsbury Rd
  LGN/SDN/BHAMAIR B26 ......110 A8
Shahjalal Rd ASH BDWTH CV12 ..117 H3
Shakespeare Av BDWTH CV12 ...117 H3
  LICHS WS14 ....21 H7
  REDE B98 ....202 E3
  WWCK CV34 ....205 G8
Shakespeare Crs BILS/COS WV14 ..67 H3
  CRTAM B79 ....31 J7
Shakespeare Dr KIDD DY10 ....138 F7
  NUN CV11 ....99 L4
  SHLY B90 ....147 M4
Shakespeare Gdns
  RUGBYS/DCH CV22 ....186 C6
Shakespeare Pl SLYOAK B29 ...124 E6
Shakespeare Rd AST/WIT B6 .....89 M2
  BNTWD WS7 ....18 D5
  SEDG DY3 ....83 L1
  SHLY B90 ....148 A8
  SMTHWK B67 ....105 K5
  TPTN/OCK DY4 ....67 L5
Shakespeare St COVE CV2 .....155 M2
  SPARK B11 ....108 A3
  WOLV WV1 ....3 J6
Shakespear Gv CNCK/NC WS11 ...16 D3
Shaldon Wk SMTHWK B66 ....87 M8
The Shales WMBN WV5 ....64 C8
Shale St BILS/COS WV14 ....51 G8
Shalford Rd HIA/OLT B92 .....127 J1
Shallcross La SEDG DY3 ....84 B2
Shalnecote Gv
  ALE/KHTH/YWD B14 ....125 G8
Shandon Cl RIDG/WDGT B32 .....85 J6
Shanklin Cl GTWY WS6 ....24 D2
Shanklin Dr NUNW/HART CV10 ...81 M1
Shanklin Rd COVS CV3 ....181 M1
Shannon TAM/AM/WIL B77 ....46 E6
Shannon Dr BRWNH WS8 ....26 A3
Shannon Rd HWK/WKHTH B38 ....145 K5
Shapfell RUGBYN/HIL CV21 ....161 H6
Shapinsay Dr RBRY B45 ....143 K4
Shard End Crs BKDE/SHDE B34 ..92 A8
Shardlow Rd WNSFLD WV11 ......37 J5

The Shardway *BKDE/SHDE* B34 .....92 A8
Sharesacre St *WLNHL* WV1 .....51 M2
Sharington Cl *DUDS* DY2 .....85 J5
Sharman Cl *WOLVN* WV10 .....36 C7
Sharmans Cross Rd *SOLH* B91 .....148 C1
Sharon Cl
  ETTPK/GDPK/PENN WV4 .....50 C8
Sharon Wy *HEDN* WS12 .....17 H2
Sharp Cl *COVN* CV6 .....134 A3
Sharpe Cl *WWCK* CV34 .....205 J5
Sharpe St *TAM/AM/WIL* B77 .....E8
Sharpley Ct *COVE* CV5 .....135 L5
Sharps Cl *RBRY* B45 .....143 L6
Sharrat Fld *MGN/WHC* B75 .....57 H3
Sharratt Rd *BDWTH* CV12 .....116 D3
Sharrocks St *WOLV* WV1 .....3 J7
Shaw Av *KIDD* DY10 .....138 F7
Shawbank Rd *REDE* B98 .....202 F1
Shawberry Av *CVALE* B35 .....91 L2
Shawberry Rd
  CHWD/FDBR/MGN B37 * 92 D8
Shawbrook Gv
  ALE/KHTH/YWD B14 .....146 E2
Shawbury Cl *REDE* B98 .....203 J2
Shawbury Gv *BKTH/HG* B12 .....107 K5
  DUNHL/THL/PER WV6 .....34 C8
Shawbury La *WOLVN* WV10 .....36 D8
Shawbury Village
  CSHL/WTROR B46 .....95 J6
Shaw Dr *BNTWD* WS7 .....18 E4
  STETCH B33 .....109 J3
Shawfield *HLYWD* B47 .....146 E8
Shaw Hall La *COVEN* WV9 .....22 A6
Shaw Hedge Rd *BEWD* DY12 .....163 G1
Shaw Hellier Cft *BRLYHL* DY5 .....102 C3
Shaw Hill Rd *WASH/WDE* B8 .....108 E1
Shawhurst Cft *HLYWD* B47 .....146 E6
Shaw La *DUNHL/THL/PER* WV6 .....48 F2
  LICH WS13 .....20 C5
  RUGE WS15 .....18 E1
Shawley Cft *ACGN* B27 .....127 J1
Shaw Rd *BILS/COS* WV14 .....66 F4
  BKHL/PFLD WV2 .....50 A7
  DUDS DY2 .....84 F6
  TPTN/OCK DY4 .....86 A1
  WOLVN WV10 .....36 B7
Shaws Cl *REDW* B97 .....201 L3
Shawsdale Rd *CBROM* B36 .....94 F3
Shaw's La *GTWY* WS6 .....24 E8
Shaw's Pas *DIG/EDG* B5 .....7 J3
Shaw St *WBROM* B70 .....68 C5
  WSLW WS2 .....4 E2
Shayler Gv *BKHL/PFLD* WV2 .....50 B4
Sheaf La
  LGN/SDN/BHAMAIR B26 .....127 M1
  RBRY B45 .....143 K7
Shearwater Cl *KIDD* DY10 .....164 F3
Shearwater Wk
  ERDW/GRVHL B23 .....71 M7
Sheaves Cl
  ETTPK/GDPK/PENN WV4 .....66 E2
Shedden St *DUDS* DY2 .....85 H5
Sheddington Rd
  ERDW/GRVHL B23 .....72 B6
Sheen Rd *KGSTG* B44 .....71 J1
Sheepclose Dr
  CHWD/FDBR/MGN B37 .....110 E2
Sheepcote Cl *RLSN* CV32 .....206 E4
Sheepcote Gra *BRGRVW* B61 .....168 D8
Sheepcote La *TAM/AM/WIL* B77 .....46 D2
Sheepcote St *LDYWD/EDGR* B16 .....6 A5
Sheepcroft Cft *REDW* B97 .....201 K3
Sheepfold Cl
  BLKHTH/ROWR B65 .....103 L1
Sheepmoor Cl *HRBN* B17 .....105 K5
Sheepwash La *TPTN/OCK* DY4 .....68 B3
Sheepy Rd *ATHST* CV9 .....63 H2
Sheerwater Dr *BRLYHL* DY5 .....102 A4
Sheffield Rd *SCFLD/BOLD* B73 .....72 E6
Sheffield St *BRLYHL* DY5 .....102 E4
Shefford Rd *AST/WIT* B6 .....89 K8
Sheila Av *WNSFLD* WV11 .....37 K8
Shelah Rd *HALE* B63 .....103 L7
Shelbourne Cl *OLDBY* B69 .....86 B3
Sheldon Av *DARL/WED* WS10 .....68 A4
Sheldon Cl *BILS/COS* WV14 .....67 H2
Sheldon Dr *NFLD/LBR* B31 .....144 B4
Sheldonfield Rd
  LGN/SDN/BHAMAIR B26 .....128 B1
Sheldon Gv
  LGN/SDN/BHAMAIR B26 .....109 M8
  WWCK CV34 .....205 K3
Sheldon Hall Av *STETCH* B33 .....110 D2
Sheldon Heath Rd *STETCH* B33 .....110 B1
Sheldon Rd *HHTH/SAND* B71 .....69 J5
  REDE B98 .....202 F4
  WOLVN WV10 .....35 L4
Sheldrake Cl *COVS* CV3 .....156 F4
Shelduck Cl *KIDD* DY10 * 164 F2
Shelfield Cl *COVW* CV5 .....153 M2
  HOCK/TIA B94 .....175 G7
Shelfield Rd
  ALE/KHTH/YWD B14 .....146 A2
Shelley Av *KIDD* DY10 .....138 C6
  TPTN/OCK DY4 .....67 L5
Shelley Cl *BDWTH* CV12 .....117 H4
  BRGRVW B61 .....168 A3
  REDW B97 .....202 A4
  SEDG DY3 .....65 L8
  STRBR DY8 .....101 L5
Shelley Dr *AST/WIT* B6 .....89 M7
  FOAKS/STRLY B74 .....42 D7
Shelley Rd *BNTWD* WS7 .....18 E4
  CNCK/NC WS11 .....12 C6
  COVE CV2 .....156 A2
  CRTAM B79 .....31 K6
  SHHTH WV12 .....37 K3
  WOLVN WV10 .....36 B5
Shelly Cl *COVS* CV3 .....156 F4
Shelly Cl *CHWD/FDBR/MGN* B37 .....110 D3
Shelly Crs *SHLY* B90 .....148 F7
Shelly Cft *STETCH* B33 .....109 L2
Shelly La *SHLY* B90 .....148 F7
Shelsley Av *OLDBY* B69 .....86 B6
Shelsley Cl *PENK* ST19 .....10 E4
Shelsley Dr *MOS/BIL* B13 .....125 M4
Shelsley Wy *SOLH* B91 .....148 F4
Shelton Cl *DARL/WED* WS10 .....53 G8
Shelton La *HALE* B63 .....103 J8
Shelton Sq *COV* CV1 .....6 D6
Shelton St *TAM/AM/WIL* B77 .....46 C6
Sheltwood Cl *REDW* B97 .....201 L3
Sheltwood La *BRGRVW* B60 .....200 D5
Shelwick Gv *DOR/KN* B93 .....175 K1
Shenley Cl *DUDN* DY1 .....66 F7
Shenley Fields Dr
  NFLD/LBR B31 .....123 J5
Shenley Fields Rd *SLYOAK* B29 .....123 L6
Shenley Gdns *SLYOAK* B29 .....123 J8
Shenley Gn *NFLD/LBR* B31 .....123 J7
Shenley La *SLYOAK* B29 .....123 J5
Shenstone Av *RMSLY* B62 .....122 C1
  RUGBYN/HIL CV21 .....187 J4
  STRBR DY8 .....119 H3
Shenstone Cl *BRGRVE* B60 .....191 L2
  FOAKS/STRLY B74 .....42 C7

Shenstone Ct *BDMR/CCFT* WV3 .....49 L7
Shenstone Dr *ALDR* WS9 .....40 E5
  RCOVN/BALC/EX CV7 .....151 L7
Shenstone Rd
  ALE/KHTH/YWD B14 .....146 E4
  GTB/HAM B43 .....70 C5
  LDYWD/EDGR B16 .....106 A2
Shenstone Valley Rd
  RMSLY B62 .....104 D7
Shenton Wk
  CHWD/FDBR/MGN B37 .....92 D8
Shepheard Rd
  LGN/SDN/BHAMAIR B26 .....110 B8
Shepherd Cl *LICH* WS13 .....21 G3
  TLHL/CAN CV4 .....153 K2
Shepherd Dr *SHHTH* WV12 .....37 M8
Shepherds Brook Rd
  HAG/WOL DY9 .....102 B8
Shepherds Fold
  BLKHTH/ROWR B65 .....103 M3
Shepherds Gdns *EDG* B15 .....6 B7
Shepherds Green Rd
  ERDE/BCHGN B24 .....90 D3
Shepherds La
  RCOVN/BALC/EX CV7 .....130 C2
Shepherds Pool Rd
  MGN/WHC B75 .....57 J3
Shepherds Standing
  BKDE/SHDE B34 * 91 M7
Shepherds Wy
  ERDW/GRVHL B23 .....72 A5
Shepley Rd *BRGRVE* B60 .....169 L6
  RBRY B45 .....143 M7
Shepperton St *NUN* CV11 .....99 G3
Sheppey Dr *CBROM* B36 .....92 F8
Shepwell Gdns *WOLVN* WV10 .....23 G5
Shepwell Gn *WLNHL* WV13 .....52 A4
Sherard Cft *CBROM* B36 .....92 F7
Sheraton Cl *ALDR* WS9 .....40 F7
  HEDN WS12 .....12 D6
Sheraton Dr *KIDD* DY10 .....138 E7
Sheraton Gra *STRBR* DY8 .....119 K3
Sheraton Rd *BRGRVE* B60 .....192 A4
  CSHL/WTROR B46 .....111 L1
Sherborne Gdns *CDSL* WV8 .....34 C4
Sherborne Gv *CBHAMW* B1 .....106 C2
Sherborne Rd *WOLVN* WV10 .....36 B4
Sherborne St *LDYWD/EDGR* B16 .....6 A6
Sherbourne Av *HEDN* WS12 .....17 J1
Sherbourne Cr *NUNW/HART* CV10 .....79 M8
Sherbourne Crs *COVW* CV5 .....154 C1
Sherbourne Dr *ACGN* B27 .....127 G1
Sherbourne Pl *RLSN* CV32 * 206 E4
Sherbourne Rd *ACGN* B27 .....126 F1
  BHTH/HG B12 .....107 J6
  CDYHTH B64 .....103 L5
  STRBR DY8 .....119 M1
Sherbourne St *SCV* CV1 * 8 B5
Sherbourne Ter *RLSN* CV32 * 206 E4
Sherbrooke Av *TAM/AM/WIL* B77 .....46 C7
Sherdmore Cft *SHLY* B90 .....148 D7
Sheridan Cl *RUGBYS/DCH* CV22 .....186 D6
  WSLW WS2 .....52 F6
Sheridan Dr *NUNW/HART* CV10 .....79 K8
Sheridan Gdns *SEDG* DY3 .....65 K8
Sheridan St *HHTH/SAND* B71 .....87 H4
  WSLW WS2 .....52 F6
Sheridan Wk *CVALE* B35 * 91 L2
Sheriff Av *TLHL/CAN* CV4 .....153 M6
Sheriff Dr *BRLYHL* DY5 .....102 D3
Sheriff Rd *RUGBYN/HIL* CV21 .....187 H3
Sheriffs Cl *LICHS* WS14 .....21 J7
Sheriffs Orch *COV* CV1 .....8 E6
Sheriffoot La *MGN/WHC* B75 .....56 F2
Sheringham *EDG* B15 .....106 C6
Sheringham Rd *BVILLE* B30 .....145 M2
Sherington Av *COVW* CV5 .....154 A2
Sherington Dr
  ETTPK/GDPK/PENN WV4 .....50 B8
Sherlock Cl *SHHTH* WV12 .....38 B4
Sherlock Rd *COVW* CV5 .....154 B2
Sherlock St *DIG/EDG* B5 .....107 J5
Sherrans Dell
  ETTPK/GDPK/PENN WV4 .....66 B2
Sherratt Cl *WALM/CURD* B76 .....73 K5
Sherringham Dr *SHHTH* WV12 .....38 A4
Sherron Gdns *BHTH/HG* B12 .....107 K8
Sherston Covert *BVILLE* B30 .....146 A3
Shervale Cl
  ETTPK/GDPK/PENN WV4 .....49 L7
Sherwin Av *BILS/COS* WV14 .....66 E3
Sherwood Av *TPTN/OCK* DY4 .....85 K1
Sherwood Cl *ATHST* CV9 .....60 F4
  HIA/OLT B92 .....127 K5
  HLGN/YWD B28 .....126 D8
  CNCK/NC WS11 .....16 E2
Sherwood Dr *BRLYHL* DY5 .....102 D4
Sherwood Jones Cl *COVN* CV6 .....133 M7
Sherwood Ms *HLGN/YWD* B28 .....126 C7
Sherwood Rd *BRGRVE* B60 .....191 L6
  HLGN/YWD B28 .....126 C7
  SMTHWKW B67 .....105 L4
  STRBR DY8 .....101 J6
Sherwood St *WOLV* WV1 .....36 E7
Sherwood Wk *RLSN* CV32 .....207 L1
  RUSH/SHEL WS4 .....40 B6
Shetland Cl *TAM/AM/WIL* B77 .....46 D6
Shetland Dr *COVN* CV6 .....133 L1
  DUNHL/THL/PER WV6 .....35 M7
  LDYWD/EDGR B16 .....106 D3
Shetland Dr *NUNW/HART* CV10 .....98 D3
  SMTHWK B66 .....87 H6
Shevlock Wy *COVN* CV6 .....134 C7
Shidas La *OLDBY* B69 .....86 C6
Shifnal Wk *MGN/WHC* B75 .....57 K6
Shillcock Gv *LOZ/NWT* B19 .....89 J8
Shillingstone Cl *COVE* CV2 .....156 E1
Shillingstone Dr
  NUNW/HART CV10 .....98 A4
Shilton Cl *SHLY* B90 .....148 D1
Shilton Gv *SLYOAK* B29 .....123 K5
Shilton La *COVE* CV2 .....135 J3
Shinwell Crs *OLDBY* B69 .....86 A5
Shipbourne Cl *RIDG/WDGT* B32 .....105 K6
Shipley Flds *ERDE/BCHGN* B24 .....90 E2
Shipley Gv *SLYOAK* B29 .....123 L5
Shipston Rd *COVE* CV2 .....135 G2
  NFLD/LBR B31 .....144 F4
Shipton Cl *DUDN* DY1 .....84 C2
Shipton Rd *SCFLD/WYGN* B72 .....73 G2
Shipway Rd *YDLY* B25 .....108 B6
Shire Brook Cl *AST/WIT* B6 .....89 K3
Shirebrook Cl *COVN* CV6 .....134 F3
Shireland Cl
  WSNGN B18 * 106 B2
Shireland La *REDW* B97 .....201 J2
Shireland Rd *SMTHWK* B66 .....105 M1
Shirelea Cl *BNTWD* WS7 .....18 F2

Shire Rdg *ALDR* WS9 .....40 E1
The Shires *RUGBY* CV23 * 158 F7
Shirestone Rd *STETCH* B33 .....110 C3
Shireview Gdns *BLOX/PEL* WS3 * 39 M1
Shirewood Cl *DOR/KN* B93 .....175 M3
Shirland Rd
  CHWD/FDBR/MGN B37 .....110 E4
Shirlett Cl *COVN* CV6 .....134 F1
Shirley Dr *CSCFLD/WYGN* B72 .....73 H2
Shirley La *RCOVN/BALC/EX* CV7 .....131 L8
Shirley Park Rd *SHLY* B90 .....147 M3
Shirley Rd *BVILLE* B30 .....124 E8
  COVE CV2 .....135 K6
  DUDS DY2 .....85 G7
  HLGN/YWD B28 .....126 C5
  LGLYGN/QTN B68 .....87 G7
Shirral Gv *CHWD/FDBR/MGN* B37 .....92 D8
Shirrall Dr *POL/KGSB/FAZ* B78 .....58 B1
Shoal Hill Cl *CNCK/NC* WS11 .....15 M4
Sholing Cl *CDSL* WV8 .....35 K4
Shooters Cl *DIG/EDG* B5 .....107 H6
Shooters Hl *CSCFLD/WYGN* B72 .....73 K5
Shop La *CDSL* WV8 .....34 B4
Shopton Rd *BKDE/SHDE* B34 .....91 L6
Shoreham Cl *WLNHL* WV13 .....51 H4
Shorncliffe Rd *COVN* CV6 .....133 J7
Short Acre St *WSLW* WS2 .....4 E1
Shortbutts La *LICHS* WS14 .....20 F8
Shorters Av
  ALE/KHTH/YWD B14 .....146 F1
Shortfield Cl
  RCOVN/BALC/EX CV7 .....151 M6
Short Heath Rd
  ERDW/GRVHL B23 .....72 C7
  SHHTH WV12 .....37 K4
Shortland Cl *DOR/KN* B93 .....149 L7
Shortlands
  RCOVN/BALC/EX CV7 .....116 B7
Shortlands Cl *BVILLE* B30 .....145 L3
Shortlands La *BLOX/PEL* WS3 .....39 K1
Short La *GTWY* WS6 .....24 C2
Shortley Rd *COVS* CV3 .....155 J5
Short Rd *SMTHWKW* B67 .....105 H2
  WOLVN WV10 .....36 C4
Short St *BILS/COS* WV14 .....51 H7
  BLKHTH/ROWR B65 .....104 A4
  BRWNH WS8 .....26 D6
  CNCK/NC WS11 .....16 D2
  COV CV1 .....9 H6
  DARL/WED WS10 .....52 D6
  DUDN DY1 .....84 E3
  HALE B63 .....121 K1
  NUNW/HART CV10 .....98 A1
  SHHTH WV12 .....38 A8
  STRBR DY8 .....101 K8
  WOLV WV1 .....3 G4
  WSLW WS2 .....4 C4
The Shortwoods
  POL/KGSB/FAZ B78 .....47 L8
The Shortyard *KIDD* DY11 .....138 E1
Shorwell Pl *BRLYHL* DY5 .....102 A4
Shottery Cl *COVS* CV3 .....155 M2
Shottery Gv *WALM/CURD* B76 .....73 K4
Shottery Rd *SHLY* B90 .....147 M4
Shotteswell Rd *SHLY* B90 .....147 M6
Showell Circ *WOLVN* WV10 .....36 B6
Showell Green La *SPARK* B11 .....125 M2
Showell La
  ETTPK/GDPK/PENN WV4 .....64 C2
  RCOVN/BALC/EX CV7 .....131 K4
Showell Rd *WOLVN* WV10 .....36 B6
Showells Gdns *VAUX/NECH* B7 .....90 A6
Shrawley Av *KIDD* DY10 .....163 M2
Shrawley Cl *HALE* B63 .....121 L3
  RBRY B45 .....143 K6
Shrawley Crs *STETCH* B33 .....110 C5
Shrewley Crs *STETCH* B33 .....110 C5
Shrewsbury Cl *BLOX/PEL* WS3 .....38 D4
Shrewsbury Rd *RUGBYN/HIL* CV21 .....137 L8
Shrewton Av
  ALE/KHTH/YWD B14 .....146 B3
The Shrubberies *TLHL/CAN* CV4 .....180 C1
Shrubbery Av *TPTN/OCK* DY4 .....67 H8
Shrubbery Cl *WALM/CURD* B76 .....73 H7
Shrubbery Rd *BRGRVE* B61 .....191 J4
Shrubbery St *KIDD* DY10 .....138 D6
The Shrubbery *DUDN* DY1 * 84 F3
  LDYWD/EDGR B16 * 106 D2
Shrublands Av
  LGLYGN/QTN B68 .....104 F6
Shrub La *ERDE/BCHGN* B24 .....90 E1
Shuckburgh Crs
  RUGBYS/DCH CV22 .....187 H5
Shuckburgh Gv *RLSN* CV32 .....206 E3
Shugborough Dr *DUDN* DY1 .....84 C3
Shugborough Wy
  CNCK/NC WS11 .....16 F4
Shulman's Wk *COVE* CV2 .....135 H6
Shultern La *TLHL/CAN* CV4 .....180 C1
Shuna Cft *COVE* CV2 .....154 A7
Shustoke La *DSYBK/YTR* WS5 .....69 M1
Shustoke Rd *BKDE/SHDE* B34 .....92 A7
  SOLH B91 .....128 B8
Shutlock La *MOS/BIL* B13 .....125 H4
Shut Mill La *RMSLY* B62 .....142 B4
Shuttington Br *CRTAM* B79 .....33 H6
Shuttington Rd *CRTAM* B79 .....32 F7
Shutt La *HOCK/TIA* B94 .....173 M4
Shuttle St *COVN* CV6 .....134 C1
Shuttleworth Rd *RRUGBY* CV23 * 161 K8
Shyltons Cft *LDYWD/EDGR* B16 .....106 E3
Sibdon Gv *NFLD/LBR* B31 .....144 E5
Sibree Rd *COVS* CV3 .....181 M1
Sibton Cl *COVE* CV2 .....135 G4
Sidaway Cl *OLDBY* B69 .....86 A3
Sidaway St *CDYHTH* B64 .....103 J1
Sidbury Gv *DOR/KN* B93 .....175 J2
Sidcup Cl *BILS/COS* WV14 .....66 A7
Sidcup Rd *KGSTG* B44 .....71 L4
Siddeley Av *COVS* CV3 .....155 L2
  KNWTH CV8 .....197 J2
Siddons Cl *LICH* WS13 .....20 D3
Siddons Rd *BILS/COS* WV14 .....67 H3
Siddons Wy *HHTH/SAND* B71 .....68 E6
Sidenhill Cl *SHLY* B90 .....147 M3
The Sidings *RUGBYN/HIL* CV21 .....186 F3
Sidlaw Cl *HALE* B63 .....121 H3
  WOLVN WV10 .....35 M7
Sidmouth Cl *COVE* CV2 .....135 G4
  NUN CV11 .....99 H3
Sidney Rd *RUGBYS/DCH* CV22 .....187 G5
Sidney St *BKHL/PFLD* WV2 .....4 C8
Sidon Hill Wy *CNCK/NC* WS11 .....17 G2
Sidwick Crs *BKHL/PFLD* WV2 .....50 F2
Sigmund Cl *WOLV* WV1 .....37 G7
Signal Hayes Rd
  WALM/CURD B76 .....73 L4
Signal Wk *TAM/AM/WIL* B77 .....46 E3
Silesbourne Cl *CBROM* B36 * 92 A4
Silhill Hall Rd *SOLH* B91 .....127 L8
Silica Rd *TAM/AM/WIL* B77 .....46 F1
Silksby St *COVS* CV3 .....9 L9
Sillins Av *REDE* B98 .....202 E2
Sillins La *REDW* B97 .....201 J1
Silva Av *KGSWFD* DY6 .....83 K6

Silver Birch Av *BDWTH* CV12 .....116 C3
Silverbirch Cl *NUNW/HART* CV10 .....79 L6
Silver Birch Coppice
  FOAKS/STRLY B74 .....42 B8
Silver Birch Rd *HLYWD* B47 .....146 F7
  KIDD DY10 .....139 G8
Silver Birch Rd *BKHL/PFLD* WV2 .....50 B6
  CHWD/FDBR/MGN B37 .....92 D7
  CNCK/NC WS11 .....15 J7
  ERDE/BCHGN B24 .....72 F7
  FOAKS/STRLY B74 .....55 K6
  HEDN WS12 .....12 B5
Silvercroft Av *HDSW* B21 .....88 A1
Silverdale *BRGRVW* B61 .....191 K1
Silverdale Cl *COVE* CV2 .....134 F1
Silverdale Dr *WOLVN* WV10 .....36 C1
Silverdale Gdns *STRBR* DY8 .....101 G2
Silverdale Rd *ERDE/BCHGN* B24 .....71 M1
Silverfield Cl
  ALE/KHTH/YWD B14 .....125 J5
Silver Fir Cl *HEDN* WS12 .....12 C5
Silver Innage *HALE* B63 .....103 G6
Silverlands Av *LGLYGN/QTN* B68 .....104 E4
Silverlands Cl *HLGN/YWD* B28 .....126 D4
Silver Link Rd *TAM/AM/WIL* B77 .....46 D4
Silvermead Ct *HLYWD* B47 .....146 C8
Silvermead Rd *SCFLD/BOLD* B73 .....72 C4
Silvermere Rd
  LGN/SDN/BHAMAIR B26 .....110 B7
Silver's Cl *BLOX/PEL* WS3 .....25 L8
Silverstone Av *KIDD* DY11 .....138 B5
Silverstone Cl *WSLW* WS2 .....52 B2
Silverstone Dr *FOAKS/STRLY* B74 * 55 K7
  RCOVN/BALC/EX CV7 .....116 D1
Silver St *ALE/KHTH/YWD* B14 .....125 J5
  BRLYHL DY5 .....101 M3
  BRWNH WS8 .....26 B6
  COV CV1 .....6 F3
  CNCK/NC WS11 .....16 D2
  COV CV1 .....9 H6
  DARL/WED WS10 .....52 D6
  DUDN DY1 .....84 E3
  HALE B63 .....121 K1
  NUNW/HART CV10 .....98 A1
  SHHTH WV12 .....38 A8
  STRBR DY8 .....101 K8
Silver St (Above) *REDW* B97 .....202 C2
Silverthorne Av *TPTN/OCK* DY4 .....67 H8
Silverthorne La *CDYHTH* B64 .....102 F4
Silverton Crs *MOS/BIL* B13 .....126 B4
Silverton Hts *SMTHWKW* B67 * 87 K7
Silverton Rd *COVN* CV6 .....134 C1
  SMTHWKW B67 .....87 J7
Silverton Wy *WNSFLD* WV11 .....37 K8
Silvertrees Rd *TPTN/OCK* DY4 .....67 K8
Silvester Rd *BILS/COS* WV14 .....51 J7
Silvester Wy *STRBR* DY8 .....100 D5
Silvington Cl *SLYOAK* B29 .....124 A6
Simcox Gdns *RIDG/WDGT* B32 .....123 H5
Simcox Rd *DARL/WED* WS10 .....52 D8
Simcox St *HEDN* WS12 .....17 H1
Simeon Bissell Cl *TPTN/OCK* DY4 .....67 L8
Simeon's Wk *BRLYHL* DY5 .....102 D5
Simmonds Cl *BLOX/PEL* WS3 .....39 H2
Simmonds Pl *DARL/WED* WS10 .....52 D6
Simmonds Rd *BLOX/PEL* WS3 .....39 H1
Simmonds Wy *ATHST* CV9 .....63 K3
  BRWNH WS8 .....26 E8
Simmons Dr *POL/KGSB/FAZ* B78 .....58 F4
Simmons Leasow *RIDG/WDGT* B32 .....123 H3
Simmons Rd *WNSFLD* WV11 .....37 M4
Simms La *DUDS* DY2 .....85 G8
  HLYWD B47 .....146 E8
Simon Cl *HHTH/SAND* B71 .....69 J4
Simon Rd *HLYWD* B47 .....146 E6
Simon Stone St *COVN* CV6 .....134 D5
Simpkins Cl *ALDR* WS9 .....40 E2
Simpson Gv *COVS* CV3 .....156 A7
  WOLVN WV10 .....36 C7
Simpson Rd *CSCFLD/WYGN* B72 .....73 G4
  LICH WS13 .....20 C7
  WOLVN WV10 .....36 C7
  WSLW WS2 .....38 F1
Simpson St *OLDBY* B69 .....86 B6
Singer Cl *COVN* CV6 .....134 E5
Singer Cft *CBROM* B36 .....92 D4
Sion Av *KIDD* DY10 .....138 E4
Sion Gdns *STRPT* DY13 .....188 D2
Sion Hl *KIDD* DY10 .....138 E4
Sir Alfreds Wy *WALM/CURD* B76 .....73 J2
Sir Harrys Rd *EDG* B15 .....107 G7
Sir Henry Parkes Rd *COVW* CV5 .....154 B6
Sir Hilton's Rd *NFLD/LBR* B31 .....144 F6
Sir John's Rd *SLYOAK* B29 .....125 G2
Sir Richards Dr *HRBN* B17 .....105 K6
Sir Thomas White's Rd
  COVW CV5 .....154 D3
Sir William Lyons Rd
  TLHL/CAN CV4 .....153 M7
Sir Winston Churchill Pl
  COVS CV3 .....157 G2
Sisefield Rd *HWK/WKHTH* B38 .....145 L4
Siskin Cl *BNTWD* WS7 .....19 H8
  RRUGBY CV23 .....161 G5
Siskin Dr *BHTH/HG* B12 .....107 J3
  KNWTH CV8 .....182 A3
Siskin Pkwy East *KNWTH* CV8 .....181 M4
Siskin Pkwy West *KNWTH* CV8 .....181 M4
Siskin Rd *HAG/WOL* DY9 .....120 A2
Siskin Wy *KIDD* DY10 .....164 F4
Sister Dora Av *BNTWD* WS7 .....19 K6
Sister Dora Buildings *WSL* WS1 * 4 F4
Sister Dora Gdns *WSL* WS1 .....4 F4
Siviter's Cl *BLKHTH/ROWR* B65 .....103 M3
Siviter's La *BLKHTH/ROWR* B65 .....103 M3
Siviter St *HALE* B63 .....121 M1
Six Acres *RIDG/WDGT* B32 .....123 C1
Skelcher Rd *SHLY* B90 .....147 L1
Skelwith Ri *NUN* CV11 .....81 L7
Skemp Ct *BILS/COS* WV14 .....67 H1
Sketchley Cl *SMTHWK* B66 .....87 L3
Sketchley La *ATHST* CV9 .....63 K1
Skidmore Av *BDMR/CCFT* WV3 .....49 K5
  TAM/AM/WIL B77 .....46 D2
Skidmore Dr *WBROM* B70 .....86 F2
Skidmore Rd *BILS/COS* WV14 .....67 J2
Skilts Av *REDE* B98 .....202 B6
Skinner La *DIG/EDG* B5 .....7 H7
Skinner St *WOLV* WV1 .....2 E4
Skip La *DSYBK/YTR* WS5 .....54 C1
Skipness *TAM/AM/WIL* B77 .....32 C7
Skipton Gdns *COVE* CV2 .....134 F7
Skipton Pl *CNCK/NC* WS11 .....15 M2
  DUNHL/THL/PER WV6 .....35 J4
Skipton Rd *LDYWD/EDGR* B16 .....106 D4
Skipwith Cl *RRUGBY* CV23 .....158 B2
Skipworth Rd *COVS* CV3 .....156 E3
Skomer Cl *RBRY* B45 .....143 J4
Sky Blue Wy *COV* CV1 .....9 J5
Skye Cl *CBROM* B36 .....92 D5
  NUNW/HART CV10 .....79 L6
  TAM/AM/WIL B77 .....46 C6
Skye Wk *CDYHTH* B64 .....103 J4
Skylark Cl *BRLYHL* DY5 .....84 B5
  ERDW/GRVHL B23 * 72 A4

  HEDN WS12 .....12 A6
Skylark Wk *KIDD* DY10 .....164 E3
Slack La *HDSW* B21 .....88 C3
Slack's Av *ATHST* CV9 .....63 H6
Slacky La *BLOX/PEL* WS3 .....39 K4
Sladd La *KIDDW* DY11 .....137 M1
Slade Av *BNTWD* WS7 .....18 E5
Sladefield Rd *WASH/WDE* B8 .....90 E8
Slade Gdns *CDSL* WV8 .....34 E1
Slade Gv *DOR/KN* B93 .....160 D7
Slade Hl *DUNHL/THL/PER* WV6 * 49 K2
  RWWCK/WEL CV35 .....204 D6
Slade La *ALE/KHTH/YWD* B28 .....147 J2
  MGN/WHC B75 .....57 J1
  RUGBY CV23 .....158 E4
Slade Lanker *BKDE/SHDE* B34 .....91 L8
Slade Meadow *RLSS* CV31 .....207 J3
Sladepool Farm Rd
  ALE/KHTH/YWD B14 .....146 D2
Slade Rd *ERDW/GRVHL* B23 .....90 B3
  HALE B63 .....103 G7
  MGN/WHC B75 .....57 J2
  RUGBYN/HIL CV21 .....187 G3
  WOLVN WV10 .....36 A2
Slade View Ri *HEDN* WS12 .....13 L7
The Slad *STRPT* DY13 .....164 B7
Slaithwaite Rd *HHTH/SAND* B71 .....87 H1
Slaney Ct *WSLW* WS2 .....4 A9
Slaney Rd *WSLW* WS2 .....52 F7
Slatch House Rd
  SMTHWK B67 .....105 J3
Slateley Crs *SHLY* B90 .....148 D7
Slater Rd *DOR/KN* B93 .....175 J1
Slater St *BILS/COS* WV14 .....52 F6
  DARL/WED WS10 .....52 A9
  TPTN/OCK DY4 .....85 L1
  WLNHL WV13 .....52 A2
Sleaford Gv *HLGN/YWD* B28 .....126 E6
Sleaford Rd *HLGN/YWD* B28 .....126 E6
Sleath's Yd *BDWTH* CV12 .....116 E2
Sledmere Cl *COVE* CV2 .....134 F2
Sledmore Rd *DUDS* DY2 .....85 H6
Sleets Yd *BDWTH* CV12 .....116 D3
Slideslow Av *BRGRVE* B60 .....191 M3
Slideslow Dr *BRGRVE* B60 .....191 M4
The Slieve *BFLD/HDSWWD* B20 .....88 E2
Slim Av *BILS/COS* WV14 .....67 J4
Slimbridge Cl *REDW* B97 .....202 C8
  SHLY B90 .....148 E7
Slim Rd *WSLW* WS2 .....52 C3
Slims Ga *HALE* B63 .....121 L1
Slingfield Rd *NFLD/LBR* B31 .....145 G4
Slingsby *TAM/AM/WIL* B77 .....46 A6
Slingsby Cl *NUN* CV11 .....99 J3
The Sling *DUDS* DY2 .....85 G3
  KIDD DY10 .....138 C2
Sloane St *CBHAMW* B1 .....6 C3
Slowley Hl *RCOVN/BALC/EX* CV7 .....95 L4
Smallbrook La *BRWNH* WS8 .....26 B5
  WMBN WV5 .....64 F6
Smallbrook Queensway
  DIG/EDG B5 .....6 F7
Small Cl *SMTHWKW* B67 .....87 H4
Smalldale Rd *PBAR/PBCH* B42 .....71 H6
Smalley Cl *CNCK/NC* WS11 .....12 E8
Small Heath Br *SPARK* B11 .....107 J4
Small Heath Hwy *SMTH* B10 .....107 M5
  YDLY B25 .....108 D7
Small La *HOCK/TIA* B94 .....173 J7
Smallridge *LICH* WS13 .....20 D1
Smallshire Cl *WNSFLD* WV11 .....37 K8
Smallshire Wy *STRBR* DY8 .....101 H5
Small St *HHTH/SAND* B71 .....68 F8
  WSL WS1 .....4 E6
Smallwood Cl *ERDE/BCHGN* B24 * 91 H2
  WALM/CURD B76 .....73 J2
Smallwood Rd *CDSL* WV8 .....35 J3
Smallwood St *REDE* B98 .....202 C2
Smarts Av *LICHS* WS14 .....44 C4
Smarts Rd *BDWTH* CV12 .....116 D4
Smeaton Gdns *WSNGN* B18 .....106 C1
Smedley Crooke Pl *ALVE* B48 .....171 G3
Smeed Gv *ERDE/BCHGN* B24 .....90 F2
Smercote Cl *BDWTH* CV12 .....116 B4
Smestow La *SEDG* DY3 .....82 A9
Smestow St *WOLVN* WV10 .....36 E5
Smillie Pl *CNCK/NC* WS11 .....16 D2
Smirrells Rd *HLGN/YWD* B28 .....126 C8
Smith Av *DARL/WED* WS10 .....68 B1
Smith Cl *BILS/COS* WV14 .....66 F6
  SMTHWK B67 .....105 H2
Smithfield Ri *LICH* WS13 .....21 G4
Smithfield Rd *BLOX/PEL* WS3 .....39 H4
Smithford Wy *COV* CV1 .....8 F4
Smithmoor Crs *HHTH/SAND* B71 .....69 M4
Smith Rd *DARL/WED* WS10 .....68 C4
  WSLW WS2 .....53 G7
Smiths Cl *SMTHWK* B67 .....18 B6
  RIDG/WDGT B32 .....122 F1
Smiths La *DOR/KN* B93 .....160 A6
Smiths Orch *RUGBYN/HIL* CV21 .....187 G2
Smith St *ATHST* CV9 .....61 G4
  BDWTH CV12 .....116 C4
  BILS/COS WV14 .....51 H8
  COVN CV6 .....134 D8
  DUDS DY2 .....85 H4
  LOZ/NWT B19 .....89 G8
  RLSS CV31 .....206 D1
  WWCK CV34 .....205 J7
Smiths Wy *CSHL/WTROR* B46 .....92 E1
Smiths Yd *BDWTH* CV12 * 116 F1
Smithy Dr *BLOX/PEL* WS3 .....39 J1
Smithy La *ATHST* CV9 .....62 A7
  BRLYHL DY5 .....84 A3
  LICH WS13 .....20 E4
  RRUGBY CV23 .....158 F8
  TAM/AM/WIL B77 .....46 D6
The Smithy
  LGN/SDN/BHAMAIR B26 .....109 M7
Smorrall La *BDWTH* CV12 .....115 J4
  BDWTH CV12 .....116 B4
Smout Crs *BILS/COS* WV14 .....67 H4
Smythe Gv *WWCK* CV34 .....205 J4
Snakes Lake La *BRGRVW* B61 .....168 C1
Snapdragon Dr *DSYBK/YTR* WS5 .....69 K2
Snape Rd *COVE* CV2 .....135 J8
  WNSFLD WV11 .....37 L4
Sneyd Hall Cl *BLOX/PEL* WS3 * 38 E4
Sneyd Hall Rd *BLOX/PEL* WS3 .....38 E4
Sneyd La *BLOX/PEL* WS3 .....38 D4
  WNSFLD WV11 .....38 A4
Snipe Cl *WOLVN* WV10 .....22 F6
Snowberry Dr *BRLYHL* DY5 .....84 A4
Snowberry Gdns *ACGN* B27 * 126 F1
Snowdon Cl *KIDDW* DY11 .....138 A4
  NUNW/HART CV10 .....97 L2
Snowdon Gv *HALE* B63 .....121 H4
Snowdon Ri *SEDG* DY3 .....84 B2
Snowdon Rd *CNCK/NC* WS11 .....12 C7
  STRBR DY8 .....101 M7
Snowdon Wy *SHHTH* WV12 .....37 M4
  WOLVN WV10 .....35 M2
Snowdrop Cl *BRWNH* WS8 .....26 F1
Snowford Cl *SHLY* B90 .....147 K4
Snow Hl *BKHL/PFLD* WV2 .....3 G6

Snow Hill Jct BKHL/PFLD WV2 ....3 G7
Snow Hill Queensway
CBHAMNE B4 ....6 F3
Snows Drive Hl SHLY B90 ....148 B8
Snowshill Cl NUN CV11 ....99 K5
REDE B98 ....194 F7
Snowshill Gdns DUDN DY1 ....84 D1
Snuff Mill Wk BEWD DY12 ....162 E3
Soberton Cl WNSFLD WV11 ....37 K6
Soden Cl COVS CV3 ....156 B7
Soden's Av KNWTH CV8 ....182 E4
Soho Av WSNGN B18 ....88 E6
Soho Cl SMTHWK B66 ....88 A7
Soho Hl WSNGN B18 ....88 E6
Soho Pool Wy WSNGN B18 ....88 E7
Soho Rd HDSW B21 ....88 C5
Soho Wy SMTHWK B66 ....87 M7
Solari Cl TPTN/OCK DY4 ....68 A5
Solent Cl COVEN WV9 ....35 K3
Solent Dr COVE CV2 ....135 L4
Solihull By-Pass SOLH B91 ....128 B8
Solihull La HLGN/YWD B28 ....126 E7
Solihull Pkwy
CHWD/FDBR/MGN B37 ....111 J6
Solihull Rd HIA/OLT B92 ....129 H7
SHLY B90 ....148 A2
SPARK B11 ....126 B2
Solihull Wy CBROM B36 ....91 M4
HIA/OLT B92 ....128 A4
HOCK/TIA B94 ....174 A3
Solly Gv TPTN/OCK DY4 ....68 B6
Solva Cl WOLV WV1 ....50 F4
Solway Cl CRTAM B79 ....31 L6
DARL/WED WS10 ....69 G1
RLSS CV31 ....207 G7
Somerby Dr SOLH B91 ....148 E5
Somercotes Rd PBAR/PBCH B42 ..71 H5
Somerdale Rd NFLD/LBR B31 ....145 G1
Somerfield Cl RUSH/SHEL WS4 ....40 A4
Somerfield Dr GTWY WS6 ....24 C4
Somerfield Rd BLOX/PEL WS3 ....38 F5
Somerford Gdns WOLVN WV10 ....36 C3
Somerford Pl WLNHL WV13 ....51 K4
Somerford Rd SLYOAK B29 ....123 K5
Somerford Wy BILS/COS WV14 ....66 F5
Somerland Rd
LGN/SDN/BHAMAIR B26 ....109 L4
Somerleyton Av KIDD DY10 ....138 E8
Somerly Cl COVS CV3 ....156 D5
Somerset Cl POL/KGSB/FAZ B78 ....45 L4
Somerset Crs DARL/WED WS10 ....69 H1
Somerset Dr KIDDW DY11 ....138 A4
NFLD/LBR B31 ....144 D6
NUNW/HART CV10 ....98 C1
STRBR DY8 ....101 H6
Somerset Pl CNCK/NC WS11 ....16 C1
Somerset Rd
BFLD/HDSWWD B20 ....88 D3
COV CV1 ....134 A8
EDG B15 ....106 C7
ERDW/GRVHL B23 ....72 C7
HHTH/SAND B71 ....69 H7
RUSH/SHEL WS4 ....53 L1
WLNHL WV13 ....52 B3
Somers Pl RLSN CV32 ....206 C5
Somers Rd
RCOVN/BALC/EX CV7 ....115 K7
RCOVN/BALC/EX CV7 ....130 D4
RMSLY B62 ....104 A8
RUGBYS/DCH CV22 ....186 B3
WSLW WS2 ....52 E6
Somerton Dr
CHWD/FDBR/MGN B37 ....110 F6
ERDW/GRVHL B23 ....72 E7
Somerville Ct CRTAM B79 ....31 H7
Somerville Rd SCFLD/BOLD B73 ....72 E1
SMHTH B10 ....108 C5
Somery Rd DUDN DY1 ....85 G2
SLYOAK B29 ....123 L3
Sommerfield Rd
RIDG/WDGT B32 ....123 H2
Sommerville Dr SCFLD/BOLD B73 ..72 E1
Sommerville Rd COVE CV2 ....156 A1
Sonata Rd BRGRVE B60 ....192 A4
Sonning Dr COVEN WV9 ....35 K3
Sopwith Cft CVALE B35 ....91 L3
Sorbus TAM/AM/WIL B77 ....46 F1
Soredale Cft COVS CV3 ....156 E4
Sorrel TAM/AM/WIL B77 ....32 F8
Sorrel Cl OLDBY B69 ....85 M3
TLHL/CAN CV4 ....153 J4
WOLVN WV10 ....22 F6
Sorrel Dr ACGN B27 ....126 F3
DSYBK/YTR WS5 ....69 L2
POL/KGSB/FAZ B78 ....60 B6
RRUGBY CV23 ....161 H5
Sorrel Gv ERDE/BCHGN B24 ....91 H2
Sorrell Dr ACGN B27 * 126 F3
Sorrell Pl NUNW/HART CV10 ....99 H5
Sorrell Rd NUNW/HART CV10 ....99 G5
Soudan REDW B97 ....202 B3
Southacre Av DIG/EDG B5 ....107 J5
Southall Crs BILS/COS WV14 ....67 G4
Southall Dr KIDDW DY11 ....189 L4
Southall Rd WNSFLD WV11 ....37 L5
Southall's La DUDN DY1 ....84 F4
Southam Cl HLGN/YWD B28 ....126 C5
TLHL/CAN CV4 ....153 J6
Southam Dr SCFLD/BOLD B73 ....72 F4
Southampton St WOLV WV1 ....3 G3
Southam Rd HLGN/YWD B28 ....126 C5
RLSS CV31 ....207 L8
South Av COVE CV2 ....155 L3
STRBR DY8 ....119 K1
WNSFLD WV11 ....37 G8
South Bank Rd CDYHTH B64 ....103 K5
Southbank Rd COVN CV6 ....133 J8
KNWTH CV8 ....197 K1
Southbank Vw KGSWFD DY6 ....101 J1
Southborough Ter RLSS CV31 * ..206 E7
Southbourne Av
BKDE/SHDE B34 ....91 H7
WSLW WS2 ....52 F4
Southbourne Cl SLYOAK B29 ....124 E3
Southbourne Pl CNCK/NC WS11 ....16 B3
Southbourne Rd WOLVN WV10 ....36 A2
Southbrook Rd
RUGBYS/DCH CV22 ....186 E4
South Car Park Rd
BHAMNEC B40 ....129 K2
South Cl CNCK/NC WS11 ....16 A5
Southcote Gv HWK/WKHTH B38 ..145 H4
Southcott Av BRLYHL DY5 ....102 B5
Southcott Wy COVE CV2 ....135 K4
South Crs WOLVN WV10 ....23 G7
Southcrest Gdns REDE B98 ....202 B4
Southcrest Rd REDE B98 ....202 D3
South Dene SMTHWKW B67 * 87 K8
Southdown Av WSNGN B18 ....88 E7
South Dr CSHL/WTROR B46 ....93 J7
DIG/EDG B5 ....125 G1
MGN/WHC B75 ....57 G7
Southern Cl KGSWFD DY6 ....101 K2
Southerndown Rd SEDG DY3 ....65 M5
Southern Rd WASH/WDE B8 ....91 G8
Southern Wy DARL/WED WS10 ....68 A2
Southey Cl SHHTH WV12 ....38 C5
SOLH B91 ....148 F5
Southey Rd RUGBYS/DCH CV22 ..186 C6
Southfield Av CBROM B36 ....91 M5
LDYWD/EDGR B16 ....106 B2
Southfield Cl ALDR WS9 ....40 E8
NUNW/HART CV10 ....81 H7
Southfield Dr HLGN/YWD B28 ....126 E8
KNWTH CV8 ....179 L7
Southfield Gv BDMR/CCFT WV3 ....49 G6
Southfield Rd
LDYWD/EDGR B16 ....106 A2
RUGBYS/DCH CV22 ....187 G4
WNSFLD WV11 ....37 K8
Southfields Cl CSHL/WTROR B46 ..93 L8
Southfields Rd SOLH B91 ....148 D4
Southfield Wy GTWY WS6 ....24 D3
South Gdns HAG/WOL DY9 ....140 E1
Southgate CDYHTH B64 ....103 H5
CNCK/NC WS11 ....15 M6
WOLV WV1 ....2 D4
Southgate Cl KIDDW DY11 ....163 L1
Southgate End CNCK/NC WS11 ....15 M6
Southgate Rd KGSTG B44 ....71 J3
South Gn
ETTPK/GDPK/PENN WV4 ....49 H8
South Gv ERDW/GRVHL B23 ....72 D8
LOZ/NWT B19 ....88 F5
South Holme BORD B9 ....108 A4
Southlands ATHST CV9 ....63 J6
RLSS CV31 ....206 F6
Southlands Rd MOS/BIL B13 ....125 L4
Southlea Av RLSS CV31 ....206 C7
Southlea Cl RLSS CV31 ....206 C7
Southleigh Av COVW CV5 ....154 D7
Southmead Crs REDE B98 ....202 D2
Southmead Dr BRGRVE B60 ....168 F7
Southminster Dr
ALE/KHTH/YWD B14 ....125 J7
Southorn Ct RLSN CV32 * 207 H2
South Ov SEDG DY3 ....66 C8
South Pde CSCFLD/WYGN B72 ....57 G8
South Park Ms BRLYHL DY5 ....102 A3
Southport Cl COVS CV3 ....155 M8
South Range SPARK B11 ....107 M7
South Rdg COVW CV5 ....153 M1
South Rd ALE/KHTH/YWD B14 ....125 J5
BRGRVE B60 ....191 M6
ERDW/GRVHL B23 ....90 D1
HAG/WOL DY9 ....140 E1
NFLD/LBR B31 ....144 D3
RRUGBY CV23 ....161 K8
SMTHWKW B67 ....87 K8
SPARK B11 ....107 M6
STRBR DY8 ....119 K1
TPTN/OCK DY4 ....67 M5
WSNGN B18 ....88 E7
South Road Av WSNGN B18 ....88 E7
South Roundhay STETCH B33 ....109 L2
South St ATHST CV9 ....63 H5
BRLYHL DY5 ....102 A3
COV CV1 ....9 K4
HRBN B17 ....106 B7
KIDD DY10 ....138 D7
REDE B98 ....202 C2
RUGBYN/HIL CV21 ....187 H1
WLNHL WV13 ....51 J4
WOLVN WV10 ....36 A7
WSL WS1 ....4 D7
South Street Gdns WSL WS1 ....4 D7
South Tower VAUX/NECH B7 * 107 M1
South Vw GTB/HAM B43 ....70 C6
POL/KGSB/FAZ B78 ....76 B1
RRUGBY CV23 * 158 D1
RWWCK/WEL CV35 * 204 E7
South View Cl CDSL WV8 ....34 F3
WOLVN WV10 ....22 F7
South View Rd RLSN CV32 ....199 G8
RRUGBY CV23 ....185 K1
SEDG DY3 ....65 M5
Southville Bungalows
ALE/KHTH/YWD B14 * 146 F1
Southwark Cl LICH WS13 ....21 G2
South Wy BHAMNEC B40 ....129 K2
Southway RLSS CV31 ....206 E8
Southway Ct KGSWFD DY6 ....101 K1
Southwick Pl BILS/COS WV14 ....51 H6
Southwick Rd RMSLY B62 ....104 B5
Southwold Av BVILLE B30 ....146 A2
Southwood Av BKDE/SHDE B34 ....91 L6
Southwood Cl KGSWFD DY6 ....83 J8
Southwood Covert
ALE/KHTH/YWD B14 ....146 A3
Sovereign Cl KNWTH CV8 ....197 K4
Sovereign Dr DUDN DY1 ....84 B3
Sovereign Hts NFLD/LBR B31 ....144 A4
Sovereign Rd BVILLE B30 ....145 K1
COVW CV5 ....154 D3
Sovereign Rw COV CV1 ....8 B5
Sovereign Wk WSL WS1 ....5 H3
Sovereign Wy MOS/BIL B13 ....125 H3
Sowerby March
ERDE/BCHGN B24 ....91 H1
Sowers Cl SHHTH WV12 ....38 B8
Sowers Ct MGN/WHC B75 ....57 H1
Sowers Gdns SHHTH WV12 ....38 B8
Spade Gn LICH WS13 * 19 L5
Spadesbourne Rd BRGRVE B60 ..169 G7
Spa Gv BVILLE B30 ....125 G5
Sparkbrook St COV CV1 ....9 K3
Spark St SPARK B11 ....107 L7
Sparrey Dr SLYOAK B29 ....124 E5
Sparrow Cl DARL/WED WS10 ....52 F8
Sparrow Cock La DOR/KN B93 ....177 G4
Sparta Cl RUGBYN/HIL CV21 ....160 E7
Speakers Cl OLDBY B69 ....85 M6
Spearhill LICHS WS14 ....21 J6
Speed Rd TPTN/OCK DY4 ....67 J7
Speedway La KNWTH CV8 ....157 K6
Speedwell Cl ALDR WS9 ....40 D8
RRUGBY CV23 ....161 J6
WNSFLD WV11 ....37 J8
Speedwell Dr
RCOVN/BALC/EX CV7 ....151 L7
Speedwell Gdns BRLYHL DY5 ....101 M7
WOLVN WV10 ....22 F5
Speedwell La ATHST CV9 ....61 M5
Speedwell Rd DIG/EDG B5 ....107 H7
YDLY B25 ....108 E7
Speedy Cl CNCK/NC WS11 ....12 C8
Spencer Av BEWD DY12 ....163 G1
BILS/COS WV14 ....67 G5
COVW CV5 ....8 B8
Spencer Cl HHTH/SAND B71 ....69 K5
OLDBY B69 ....85 M5
SEDG DY3 ....83 L1
Spencer Dr BNTWD WS7 ....18 C5
Spencer Rd COVW CV5 ....8 D8
LICHS WS14 ....20 F7
Spencer's La
RCOVN/BALC/EX CV7 ....152 B3
Spencer St KIDDW DY11 ....164 A1
RLSS CV31 ....206 D6
WSNGN B18 ....6 C1
Spencer Yd RLSS CV31 ....206 D6
Spennells Valley Rd KIDD DY10 ....164 E2
Spenser Av
DUNHL/THL/PER WV6 ....48 C1
Spenser Cl CRTAM B79 ....31 L7
Spernall Gv SLYOAK B29 ....123 L4
Spetchley Cl REDW B97 ....202 A7
Spey Cl DIG/EDG B5 ....107 H7
Sphinx Dr COVS CV3 ....155 M4
Spiceland Rd NFLD/LBR B31 ....123 K7
Spicer Pl RUGBYS/DCH CV22 ....186 B4
Spiers Cl DOR/KN B93 ....149 L7
Spies Cl RMSLY B62 ....104 D7
Spies La RMSLY B62 ....104 D8
Spills Meadow SEDG DY3 ....66 C8
Spilsbury Cl RLSN CV32 ....206 C3
Spilsbury Cft SOLH B91 ....148 E5
Spindle Cl KIDDW DY11 ....138 B4
Spindle La SHLY B90 ....147 L7
Spindle St COV CV1 ....134 B7
Spindlewood Cl HEDN WS12 ....17 H4
Spinners End Dr CDYHTH B64 ....103 H4
Spinney Cl BLOX/PEL WS3 ....39 L3
BNTWD WS7 ....18 E4
CNCK/NC WS11 ....17 K8
COVS CV3 ....157 J6
KIDDW DY11 ....137 L7
NFLD/LBR B31 ....144 E2
POL/KGSB/FAZ B78 ....47 K5
RCOVN/BALC/EX CV7 ....96 C5
STRBR DY8 ....100 F2
Spinney Dr SHLY B90 ....174 B1
Spinney Farm Rd CNCK/NC WS11 ..15 M6
Spinney Hl WWCK CV34 ....205 L4
Spinney La BNTWD WS7 ....18 D4
NUNW/HART CV10 ....98 A1
The Spinney ATHST CV9 ....63 L6
BDMR/CCFT WV3 ....49 H4
BFLD/HDSWWD B20 ....88 C1
FOAKS/STRLY B74 ....41 M7
HLYWD B47 ....172 F1
RLSN CV32 ....206 B4
RRUGBY CV23 ....159 L8
SEDG DY3 ....84 A3
SOLH B91 ....149 G5
TLHL/CAN CV4 ....180 C2
Spinning School La CRTAM B79 ....31 M8
Spiral Cl RMSLY B62 ....104 C5
Spiral Gn ERDE/BCHGN B24 ....91 G1
Spirehouse La BRGRVE B60 ....169 H8
Spires Cft WOLVN WV10 ....23 H4
The Spires LICHS WS14 ....21 J7
NUNW/HART CV10 ....98 A1
Spire Vw BRGRVW B61 ....191 K2
Spitfire Rd ERDE/BCHGN B24 ....91 G3
Spitfire Wy CVALE B35 ....91 L3
Splash La HEDN WS12 ....17 G2
Spode Pl CNCK/NC WS11 ....16 F3
Spondon Gv BKDE/SHDE B34 ....92 A8
Spondon Rd WNSFLD WV11 ....37 J5
Spon End COV CV1 ....8 A4
Spon La ATHST CV9 ....62 B1
WBROM B70 ....87 H4
Spon La South SMTHWK B66 ....87 H5
Spon St COV CV1 ....8 D4
Spoon Dr HWK/WKHTH B38 ....145 H3
Spooner Cft DIG/EDG B5 ....107 J5
Spooners Cl HIA/OLT B92 ....128 D6
Spottiswood Cl
RUGBYS/DCH CV22 ....185 L5
Spouthouse La GTB/HAM B43 ....70 C6
Spout La WSL WS1 ....4 F7
Spreadbury Cl HRBN B17 ....105 K5
Sprengers Cl PENK ST19 ....10 E4
Sprig Cft CBROM B36 ....91 G5
Spring Av BLKHTH/ROWR B65 ....104 A3
Springavon Cft HRBN B17 ....105 M7
Springbank BORD B9 ....108 D2
Springbank Rd EDG B15 ....107 G6
Springbrook Cl CBROM B36 ....92 B4
Springbrook La HOCK/TIA B94 ....173 K6
Spring Cl COV CV1 ....9 K3
HAG/WOL DY9 ....140 D1
RUSH/SHEL WS4 ....40 A3
SOLH B91 ....148 D2
Spring Coppice Dr DOR/KN B93 ..175 L2
Spring Ct WSL WS1 ....5 K7
Spring Crs CDYHTH B64 ....103 K6
Springcroft Rd SPARK B11 ....126 D3
Springdale Ct NUN CV11 * 99 H2
Springfield ERDW/GRVHL B23 ....90 B2
Springfield Av BHTH/HG B12 ....107 L7
BRGRVE B60 ....191 L6
HAG/WOL DY9 ....120 C1
SEDG DY3 ....66 C4
Springfield Cl
BLKHTH/ROWR B65 ....85 L8
Springfield Ct HLGN/YWD B28 * ..126 D5
Springfield Crs BDWTH CV12 ....116 F3
DUDS DY2 ....85 K5
HIA/OLT B92 ....128 A2
WALM/CURD B76 ....73 L1
WBROM B70 ....87 J4
Springfield Dr
ALE/KHTH/YWD B14 * 125 J4
Springfield Gv SEDG DY3 ....66 B4
Springfield La
BLKHTH/ROWR B65 ....85 K8
KIDD DY10 ....138 D5
WOLVN WV10 ....36 B1
Springfield Pl COV CV1 * 9 G1
Springfield Ri HEDN WS12 ....13 G7
Springfield Rd
ALE/KHTH/YWD B14 ....125 K5
BILS/COS WV14 ....51 J6
CBROM B36 ....92 B5
COV CV1 ....9 G1
MOS/BIL B13 ....126 B4
NUN CV11 ....99 J3
RMSLY B62 ....104 B6
TAM/AM/WIL B77 ....46 B5
WALM/CURD B76 ....73 L2
WOLVN WV10 ....3 J1
Springfields CSHL/WTROR B46 ....93 K8
RUSH/SHEL WS4 ....39 M6
Springfields Rd BRLYHL DY5 ....101 M3
LGLYGN/QTN B68 ....105 G1
Springfield St WSNGN B18 ....106 E2
Springfield Ter
BLKHTH/ROWR B65 ....85 K8
Spring Gdns DUDS DY2 ....85 H5
HDSW B21 * 88 D6
Spring Gv BEWD DY12 * 163 H2
LOZ/NWT B19 * 88 F7
Spring Grove Crs KIDDW DY11 ....163 M2
Spring Grove Gdns WSNGN B18 ....88 D7
Spring Grove Rd KIDDW DY11 ....163 M2
Spring Head DARL/WED WS10 ....68 D3
Spring Hl ERDE/BCHGN B24 ....90 D2
KNWTH CV8 ....182 A8
RCOVN/BALC/EX CV7 ....96 D6
WSNGN B18 ....106 E1
Springhill NUNW/HART CV10 ....79 L5
Springhill Av
ETTPK/GDPK/PENN WV4 ....65 L1
Spring Hill Circ CBHAMW B1 ....6 A3
WSNGN B18 ....106 E2
Springhill Cl RUSH/SHEL WS4 ....40 B4
SHHTH WV12 ....38 B6
Springhill Gdns REDW B97 ....201 K3
Springhill Gv
ETTPK/GDPK/PENN WV4 ....65 G1
Spring Hill La
ETTPK/GDPK/PENN WV4 ....64 E1
Springhill Pk
ETTPK/GDPK/PENN WV4 ....64 F2
Spring Hill Pas WSNGN B18 ....106 E2
Springhill Ri BEWD DY12 ....163 G1
Spring Hill Rd NUNW/HART CV10 ..80 A7
Springhill Rd BNTWD WS7 ....18 E7
BRWNH WS8 ....26 E6
WNSFLD WV11 ....37 H5
WSL WS1 ....5 H5
Spring La ERDE/BCHGN B24 ....90 E2
HOCK/TIA B94 ....174 E8
KNWTH CV8 ....179 L8
RLSS CV31 ....207 J8
RMSLY B62 ....142 B1
RUSH/SHEL WS4 ....40 A3
SHHTH WV12 ....51 M1
Springle Styche La BNTWD WS7 ..19 G4
Spring Meadow CDYHTH B64 ....103 K4
GTWY WS6 ....24 B4
HALE B63 ....121 K3
TPTN/OCK DY4 ....68 A7
Springmeadow Gv LOZ/NWT B19 ..89 H7
Spring Meadow Rd DUDS DY2 ....103 G3
Spring Meadows Cl CDSL WV8 ....34 F1
Spring Parklands DUDN DY1 ....84 E5
Spring Pool WWCK CV34 ....205 J6
Spring Rd COVN CV6 ....134 D5
DUDS DY2 ....85 H7
EDG B15 ....107 H6
ETTPK/GDPK/PENN WV4 ....50 E8
LICH WS13 ....21 H3
RCOVN/BALC/EX CV7 ....117 L7
RUSH/SHEL WS4 ....40 B4
SMTHWK B66 ....87 H5
SPARK B11 ....126 D2
Springs Av BRGRVW B61 ....168 D4
Springslade RIDG/WDGT B32 ....105 K8
Springslade Dr
ERDE/BCHGN B24 ....91 H2
The Springs CDYHTH B64 ....103 L4
Spring St CNCK/NC WS11 ....16 C5
EDG B15 ....107 H5
HAG/WOL DY9 ....120 C1
HALE B63 ....103 G7
RUGBYN/HIL CV21 ....186 F2
TPTN/OCK DY4 ....67 L8
TPTN/OCK DY4 ....68 A5
Springthorpe Gn
ERDE/BCHGN B24 ....91 G1
Springthorpe Rd
ERDE/BCHGN B24 ....91 H2
Springvale Av BILS/COS WV14 ....66 F1
DSYBK/YTR WS5 ....54 A6
Spring Vale Cl BILS/COS WV14 ....66 E4
Spring Vale Rd
BLKHTH/ROWR B65 * 85 L8
Springvale Rd REDW B97 ....201 K3
Springvale St WLNHL WV13 ....51 M2
Springvale Wy BILS/COS WV14 ....67 G1
Spring Wk HALE B63 ....121 H4
OLDBY B69 ....86 E8
WSLW WS2 ....52 F2
Springwell Rd RLSS CV31 ....207 H7
Sproat Av DARL/WED WS10 ....52 A8
Spruce TAM/AM/WIL B77 ....46 F1
Spruce Gv ERDE/BCHGN B24 ....90 F3
RLSS CV31 ....206 D8
Spruce Rd DSYBK/YTR WS5 ....69 M2
HEDN WS12 ....12 D4
Spruce Wy BDMR/CCFT WV3 ....49 H4
Spur Tree Av BDMR/CCFT WV3 ....48 E4
Squadron Cl CVALE B35 ....92 A1
Square Cl RIDG/WDGT B32 ....123 G2
Square La RCOVN/BALC/EX CV7 ..114 F4
The Square ALVE B48 ....170 F7
BKHL/PFLD WV2 ....3 H9
COVE CV2 * 135 L6
HRBN B17 ....105 M7
KNWTH CV8 ....197 K1
NUN CV11 ....99 J3
SHHTH WV12 * 38 B5
SOLH B91 ....149 G2
TPTN/OCK DY4 ....68 B6
Squires Ct BRLYHL DY5 ....102 A4
Squires Cft COVE CV2 ....135 K4
WALM/CURD B76 ....73 L4
Squires Ga BNTWD WS7 ....19 G5
Squires Rd RRUGBY CV23 ....183 K7
Squires Wy TLHL/CAN CV4 ....154 B8
Squirhill Pl RLSS CV31 * 206 F6
Squirrel Cl HEDN WS12 ....12 A7
HEDN WS12 ....17 H3
Squirrel Hollow
WALM/CURD B76 ....73 L3
Squirrels Hollow BNTWD WS7 ....18 E4
LGLYGN/QTN B68 ....105 H6
Squirrel Wk
ETTPK/GDPK/PENN WV4 ....65 L1
FOAKS/STRLY B74 ....42 A8
Stable Ct SEDG DY3 ....66 C7
Stable Cft HHTH/SAND B71 ....69 K6
Stableford Cl REDW B97 ....202 B6
RIDG/WDGT B32 ....123 K2
Stable La WOLVN WV10 ....14 E6
The Stables SLYOAK B29 ....124 E3
Stable Wk NUN CV11 ....99 K3
Stable Wy BRGRVE B60 ....191 J7
Stable Yd KNWTH CV8 * 181 J3
Stacey Cl CDYHTH B64 ....103 J4
Stacey Grange Gdns
RBRY B45 * 143 L7
Stackhouse Cl ALDR WS9 ....40 E1
Stackhouse Dr BLOX/PEL WS3 ....39 L1
Stadium Cl COVN CV6 ....134 B3
KIDD DY10 ....164 D1
WLNHL WV13 ....51 M2
Stafford Cl BLOX/PEL WS3 ....39 G3
Stafford Crs LICHS WS14 ....30 B2
Stafford Dr HHTH/SAND B71 ....68 F6
Stafford La CDSL WV8 ....34 B4
HEDN WS12 ....12 F8
Stafford Rd CNCK/NC WS11 ....16 B1
COVEN WV9 ....22 A5
DARL/WED WS10 ....51 M7
GTWY WS6 ....24 B8
HDSW B21 ....88 D5
HEDN WS12 ....12 B4
LICH WS13 ....20 C4
PENK ST19 ....10 C4
WOLVN WV10 ....36 A5
Staffordshire Pool Cl
AST/WIT B6 * 89 K4
Staffordshire Wy PENK ST19 ....10 E4
Stafford St ATHST CV9 ....63 H6
CBHAMNE B4 ....7 H3
DARL/WED WS10 ....68 C3
DUDN DY1 ....84 F4
HEDN WS12 ....17 J4
WOLV WV1 ....2 F1
WSLW WS2 ....4 E2
Stafford Street Jct WOLV WV1 ....2 F3
Stafford Wy GTB/HAM B43 ....70 C6
Stagborough Wy HEDN WS12 ....16 F1
STRPT DY13 ....188 C1
Stag Crs BLOX/PEL WS3 ....39 J7
CNCK/NC WS11 ....17 L7
Stag Dr HEDN WS12 ....12 A7
Stag Hill Rd BLOX/PEL WS3 ....39 J6
Stag Wk WALM/CURD B76 ....73 H6
Staines Cl NUN CV11 ....81 K6
Stainforth Cl NUN CV11 ....99 K3
Stainsby Av LOZ/NWT B19 ....89 G8
Stainsby Cft SHLY B90 ....148 F8
Staircase La COVW CV5 ....133 G6
Stakenbridge La KIDD DY10 ....140 A1
Staley Cft HEDN WS12 ....16 A1
Stalling's La KGSWFD DY6 ....83 H5
Stambermill Cl HAG/WOL DY9 ....102 B8
Stamford Av COVS CV3 ....155 G7
Stamford Ct NUN CV11 * 80 F8
Stamford Crs BNTWD WS7 ....18 E5
Stamford Cft SOLH B91 ....148 F3
Stamford Gdns RLSN CV32 ....206 C4
Stamford Gv
BFLD/HDSWWD B20 ....89 G3
Stamford Rd
BFLD/HDSWWD B20 ....89 G4
BRLYHL DY5 ....102 A7
STRBR DY8 ....101 M8
Stamford St STRBR DY8 ....101 K6
Stanbrook Rd SHLY B90 ....148 E8
Stanbury Av DARL/WED WS10 ....51 M7
Stanbury Rd
ALE/KHTH/YWD B14 ....146 F1
Stancroft Gv
GN/SDN/BHAMAIR B26 ....109 L5
Standard Av TLHL/CAN CV4 ....153 L4
Standard Wy VAUX/NECH B7 ....90 D5
Standbridge Wy TPTN/OCK DY4 ....67 L8
Standedge TAM/AM/WIL B77 ....46 E6
Standhills Rd KGSWFD DY6 ....83 K8
Standish Cl COVE CV2 ....156 C3
Standlake Av CBROM B36 ....91 H6
Standlake Ms RLSS CV31 ....207 G8
Stand St WWCK CV34 ....205 H7
Stanfield Rd GTB/HAM B43 ....55 H8
RIDG/WDGT B32 ....105 J6
Stanford Av PBAR/PBCH B42 ....70 E6
Stanford Cl PENK ST19 ....10 C4
REDW B97 ....201 M7
Stanford Ct NUN CV11 * 99 H3
Stanford Gv HALE B63 ....121 G4
Stanford Rd BKHL/PFLD WV2 ....50 A6
BLKHTH/ROWR B65 ....103 M2
Stanhoe Cl BRLYHL DY5 ....102 B5
Stanhope Rd SMTHWKW B67 ....105 K2
Stanhope St BDMR/CCFT WV3 ....2 D6
BHTH/HG B12 ....107 K6
DUDS DY2 ....103 J1
Stanhope Wy GTB/HAM B43 ....71 H1
Stanhurst Wy HHTH/SAND B71 ....69 L3
Stanier Av COV CV1 ....8 B3
Stanier Cl RUSH/SHEL WS4 ....39 M6
Stanier Gv BFLD/HDSWWD B20 ....88 F3
Staniforth St AST/WIT B6 ....7 H1
Stanklyn La KIDD DY10 ....164 E5
Stanley Av MGN/WHC B75 ....73 K1
RIDG/WDGT B32 ....105 J6
SHLY B90 ....147 M1
Stanley Cl HLGN/YWD B28 ....126 E6
REDE B98 ....194 E8
WNSFLD WV11 ....37 K5
Stanley Ct DUNHL/THL/PER WV6 ..48 C1
Stanley Dr SEDG DY3 ....82 C3
Stanley Pl BILS/COS WV14 ....50 F8
MOS/BIL B13 * 125 K2
RUSH/SHEL WS4 ....39 M7
Stanley Rd ALE/KHTH/YWD B14 ..125 H6
ATHST CV9 ....63 H6
COVW CV5 ....154 D5
DARL/WED WS10 ....52 B8
HEDN WS12 ....12 F7
HHTH/SAND B71 ....69 J6
LGLYGN/QTN B68 ....105 G6
NUN CV11 ....80 E8
RUGBYN/HIL CV21 ....187 J4
RUSH/SHEL WS4 ....39 M7
STRBR DY8 ....119 K2
VAUX/NECH B7 ....90 A6
WOLVN WV10 ....36 B4
Stanley St BLOX/PEL WS3 ....39 G5
Stanmore Gv RIDG/WDGT B32 ....122 E2
Stanmore Rd LDYWD/EDGR B16 ..106 A4
Stansfield Gv KNWTH CV8 ....198 B1
Stanton Av DUDN DY1 ....66 D7
Stanton Gv
LGN/SDN/BHAMAIR B26 ....109 K5
SHLY B90 ....147 L1
TPTN/OCK DY4 ....67 L8
Stanton Rd GTB/HAM B43 ....70 B5
RLSS CV31 ....207 G7
SHLY B90 ....147 L1
WOLV WV1 ....3 M5
Stanton Wk WWCK CV34 ....205 H4
Stanville Rd
LGN/SDN/BHAMAIR B26 ....110 A7
Stanway Gdns HHTH/SAND B71 ....69 H7
Stanway Gv KGSTG B44 ....71 K2
Stanway Rd COVW CV5 ....8 B9
HHTH/SAND B71 ....69 H7
SHLY B90 ....148 B1
Stanwell Gv ERDW/GRVHL B23 ....72 C7
Stanwick Av STETCH B33 ....110 C2
Stapenhall Rd SHLY B90 ....148 E8
Staple Flat BRGRVE B60 ....169 G5
Stapleford Cft
ALE/KHTH/YWD B14 ....146 A3
Stapleford Gdns BNTWD WS7 ....19 H7
Stapleford Gv STRBR DY8 ....101 J3
Staple Hall Rd NFLD/LBR B31 ....144 F3
Staplehurst Rd HLGN/YWD B28 ..126 D5
Staple Lodge Rd NFLD/LBR B31 ..144 F4
Stapleton Cl REDE B98 ....203 H2
WALM/CURD B76 ....73 M7
Stapleton Dr
CHWD/FDBR/MGN B37 ....110 E2
Stapleton Rd ALDR WS9 ....40 D8
Stapylton Av HRBN B17 ....105 M8
Starbank Rd SMHTH B10 ....108 E5
Starbold Crs DOR/KN B93 ....149 M8
Star Cl TPTN/OCK DY4 ....68 A8
WSLW WS2 ....52 D1
Starcross Cl COVE CV2 ....135 G6
Starcross Rd ACGN B27 ....127 G3
Stare Gn TLHL/CAN CV4 ....154 B8
Stareton Cl TLHL/CAN CV4 ....154 C7
Star Hl EDG B15 ....106 F5
Starkey Cft
CHWD/FDBR/MGN B37 ....111 G3
Starkie Dr LGLYGN/QTN B68 ....105 G1
Starley Rd COV CV1 ....8 D5
Starley Wy
CHWD/FDBR/MGN B37 ....111 G7
Star St BDMR/CCFT WV3 ....49 J5
HAG/WOL DY9 ....102 D8
Startin Rd RCOVN/BALC/EX CV7 ..116 D6
Statham Dr LDYWD/EDGR B16 ....106 A3
Station Ap DOR/KN B93 ....175 K2
FOAKS/STRLY B74 ....42 D7
KIDD DY10 ....138 D8
LICH WS13 * 21 K5
RBRY B45 ....170 B5
RLSS CV31 ....206 D6
SCFLD/BOLD B73 ....56 F7
SOLH B91 ....148 E1
Station Av LDYWD/EDGR B16 ....106 A4
TLHL/CAN CV4 ....153 H5
WWCK CV34 ....205 K6
Station Buildings
DUNHL/THL/PER WV6 * 49 J1
Station Cl BLOX/PEL WS3 ....38 F5

CDSL WV8 ....34 C2
Station Dr BRLYHL DY5.......101 M4
FOAKS/STRLY B74 ....56 F5
HAG/WOL DY9 ....119 L8
HOCK/TIA B94 ....173 H4
KIDD DY11 ....139 M3
TPTN/OCK DY4 ....85 M1
WOLVN WV10 ....14 A8
Stationfields CRTAM B79 ....32 A8
Station HI KIDDW DY11.........189 M3
Station Link Rd
CHWD/FDBR/MGN B37 ....129 H4
Station PI BLOX/PEL WS3.......38 D5
Station Rd ACGN B27..........127 G2
ALDR WS9 ....40 F8
ALE/KHTH/YWD B14 ....125 H5
ALVE B48 ....70 E8
AST/WIT B6 ....89 K4
BEWD DY12 ....163 G2
BILS/COS WV14 ....51 J8
BLKHTH/ROWR B65 ....104 B3
BLOX/PEL WS3 ....39 L2
BNTWD B60 ....169 L8
BRGRVE B60 ....169 L8
BRLYHL DY5 ....102 A1
BVILLE B30 ....124 C8
CDSL WV8 ....34 C2
CDYHTH B64 ....103 K5
CHWD/FDBR/MGN B37 ....110 E8
CSHL/WTROR B46 ....93 K4
CSHL/WTROR B46 ....94 B2
DOR/KN B93 ....175 L2
ERDW/GRVHL B23 ....72 D8
GTWY WS6 ....24 D1
HAG/WOL DY9 ....102 C7
HAG/WOL DY9 ....119 L7
HDSW B21 ....88 A5
HEDN WS12 ....13 G7
HIA/OLT B92 ....129 L6
HLYWD B47 ....172 E2
HRBN B17 ....106 A7
HWK/WKHTH B38 ....145 K1
KIDDW DY11 ....189 M3
KNWTH CV8 ....197 K1
LICH WS13 ....21 C6
LICHS WS14 ....14 D8
MKTBOS/BARL/STKG CV13 ....81 K1
NFLD/LBR B31 ....144 E3
OLDBY B69 ....10 C4
PENK ST19 ....10 C4
POL/KGSB/FAZ B78 ....47 M2
RCOVN/BALC/EX CV7 ....96 B5
RCOVN/BALC/EX CV7 ....151 L7
RCOVN/BALC/EX CV7 ....152 A6
RRUGBY CV22 ....161 K8
RUSH/SHEL WS4 ....39 L7
SCFLD/BOLD B73 ....72 E4
SOLH B91 ....148 F1
STECH B33 ....109 H2
WMBN WV5 ....64 E5
WOLVN WV10 ....10 E1
WOLVN WV10 ....14 B8
WWCK CV34 ....205 K6
Station Sq COV CV1 4
Station St ATHST CV9 ....63 H5
BLOX/PEL WS3 ....38 F5
BRGRVE B60 ....191 K3
CDYHTH B64 ....103 C5
DARL/WED WS10 ....52 C7
DIG/EDG B5 ....4 D8
GTWY WS6 ....24 C2
SCFLD/BOLD B73 ....56 F8
TPTN/OCK DY4 ....67 M8
WSL WS1 ....4 E3
Station St East COVN CV6 .....134 C6
Station St West COVN CV6 ....134 C6
Station Tower COV CV1 * 8 E7
Staunton Rd BLOX/PEL WS3 ..38 E2
RLSS CV31 ....206 E8
Staveley Rd
ALE/KHTH/YWD B14 ....125 H7
DUNHL/THL/PER WV6 ....2 F7
Staveley Wy RUGBYN/HIL CV21.161 H7
Staverton CI COVS CV5 ....153 K2
Staverton Leys
RUGBYS/DCH CV22 ....186 E6
Stead CI TPTN/OCK DY4 *........67 M4
WSLW WS2 ....39 C8
Steadman St WSNGN B18 ......106 E2
Steatite Wy STRPT DY13 ....163 J8
Stechford La WASH/WDE B8 ....91 H1
Stechford Rd BKDE/SHDE B34 ..91 H1
Steel Bright Rd SMTHWK B66 ..88 A7
Steel Dr WOLVN WV10 ....10 B5
Steel St RUGBYS/DCH CV22 ..186 B2
Steel Gv YDLY B25 ....92 A8
Steelhouse La BKHL/PFLD WV2 ..3 J8
CBHAMNE B4 ....7 H1
Steelpark Rd RMSLY B62 ....103 M6
Steel Rd NFLD/LBR B31 ....144 D3
Steene Gv NFLD/LBR B31 ......144 A2
Steeping Wy RRUGBY CV23 ....159 M8
Steeplefield Rd COVN CV6 * 133 L8
The Steeples STRPT DY13 ....119 M2
Steepwood Cft BVILLE B30 .....145 H1
Steere Av CRTAM B79 ....32 A6
Stella Cft
CHWD/FDBR/MGN B37 ....111 G3
Stella Gv GTB/HAM B43 ....70 A5
Stella Rd TPTN/OCK DY4 ....67 K7
Stenbury CI WOLVN WV10 ....36 D1
Stencills Dr RUSH/SHEL WS4 ...53 M2
Stencills Rd RUSH/SHEL WS4 ..53 M1
Stennels Av RMSLY B62 ....122 C1
Stennels CI COVW CV5 ....133 K5
Stennels Crs RMSLY B62 ....122 C1
Stephens CI WNSFLD WV11 ....37 K5
Stephens CI TAM/AM/WIL B77 ...46 E3
Stephenson Dr
CHWD/FDBR/MGN B37 ....110 F3
DUNHL/THL/PER WV6 ....34 C8
Stephenson Rd
RCOVN/BALC/EX CV7 ....116 F6
Stephenson Sq WLSW WS2 ....38 F8
Stephenson St BDMR/CCFT WV3 ..2 D6
CBHAMNW B2 6
Stephens Rd WNSFLD WV12 .....37 L1
Stephens Rd MGN/WHC B75 ......73 L1
Stephens St RUGBYN/HIL CV21.186 D3
Stepney Rd COVE CV2 ....155 L1
Stepping Stones CI WSLW WS2 ..52 C1
Stepping Stones STRBR DY8 ...101 M8
Stepping Stones Rd COVW CV5 ..154 D2
Steppingstone St DUDN DY1 ....84 F4
Sterling Pk RLSS CV31 * 102 D1
Sterndale Rd PBAR/PBCH B42 ..71 G7
Steven Dr BILS/COS WV14 ....67 J4
Stevens Av RIDG/WDGT B32 ....123 H3
Stevens Dr HEDN WS12 ....13 H1
Stevens Ga BKHL/PFLD WV2 ....2 F9
Stevens Av REDE B98 ....202 D2
Stevenson Av REDE B98 ....202 D2
Stevenson CI COVN CV6 ....133 L5
CRTAM B79 ....32 B6
Stevenson Wk LICHS WS14 ....20 C1

Stevens Rd HAG/WOL DY9 ......120 B3
Steward St WSNGN B18 ....106 E2
Stewart CI COVW CV5 ....154 A3
Stewart CI KIDD DY10 ....138 D1
RCOVN/BALC/EX CV7 * 96 C5
Stewart Rd ALDR WS9 ....40 C2
KGSWFD DY6 ....101 H1
Stewarts Rd RMSLY B62 ....104 B6
Stewart St BKHL/PFLD WV2 ....2 F8
WOLVN WV10 ....98 F2
Stewkins STRBR DY8 ....101 J5
Steyning Rd
LGN/SDN/BHAMAIR B26 ....109 J8
Stickley La SEDG DY3 ....84 A1
Stidfall Gv RLSS CV31 ....207 H7
Stilehouse Crs
BLKHTH/ROWR B65 ....104 A3
Stilthouse Gv RBRY B45 ....143 L6
Stiper's HI CRTAM B79 ....47 M8
Stirling Rd HAG/WOL DY9 ....119 H1
Stirling CI COVS CV5 ....156 D5
Stirling PI CNCK/NC WS11 ....15 M5
Stirling Rd BILS/COS WV14 ....67 K2
DUDS DY2 ....85 J7
LDYWD/EDGR B16 ....106 D1
SCFLD/BOLD B73 ....72 E8
SHLY B90 ....148 C5
Stirrup CI DSYBK/YTR WS5 ....69 K1
Stivichall Cft COVS CV3 ....154 F7
Stockbridge CI
DUNHL/THL/PER WV6 ....48 D3
Stockdale PI EDG B15 ....106 B5
Stock Exchange Buildings
CBHAMNW B3 * 6 E4
Stockfield Rd ACGN B27 ....126 F1
Stockhay La BNTWD WS7 ....19 H6
Stockhill Dr RBRY B45 ....143 K7
Stocking St HAG/WOL DY9 .....102 D8
Stockland Rd ERDW/GRVHL B23 ..90 A1
Stockley Crs SHLY B90 ....148 A2
Stockmans CI HWK/WKHTH B38 .145 J5
Stocks CI RUGBYS/DCH CV22 ...186 E5
Stockton CI DOR/KN B93 ....175 M1
WALM/CURD B76 ....74 A8
WSLW WS2 ....53 H1
Stockton Rd COV CV1 ....9 J1
WALM/NE BRLYHL DY5 ....102 B5
Stockwell End
DUNHL/THL/PER WV6 ....35 H7
WMBN B21 ....88 C3
Stockwell Ri HIA/OLT B92 ....128 B6
Stockwell Rd
DUNHL/THL/PER WV6 ....35 H8
WMBN B21 ....88 C3
Stoke Gn COVS CV3 ....155 L3
Stoke La
MKTBOS/BARL/STKG CV13 .....81 M1
REDE B98 ....194 F6
Stoke Park Ms COVE CV2 * 155 L3
Stoke Rd BRGRVE B60 ....191 K6
Stoke Row COVE CV2 ....155 L1
Stokes Av TPTN/OCK DY4 ....67 L5
Stokesay Av
DUNHL/THL/PER WV6 ....48 D2
Stokesay CI KIDDW DY11 ....164 C3
NUNW/HART CV10 ....98 E2
OLDBY B69 ....85 L5
Stokesay Ri DUDN DY1 ....84 C2
Stoke's La CNCK/NC WS11 ....7 J5
Stokesay Gdns NFLD/LBR B31 ..144 D5
Stom Rd BILS/COS WV14 ....50 F8
Stoneacre CI BDMR/CCFT WV3 ...48 E4
Stone Av MGN/WHC B75 ....57 L4
Stonebow Av SOLH B91 ....148 F5
Stonebridge Crs
CHWD/FDBR/MGN B37 ....110 D1
Stonebridge Hwy COVS CV3 .....181 G1
Stonebridge Rd
CSHL/WTROR B46 ....93 K6
Stonebrook Wy COVN CV6 ....134 D2
Stonechat Cl KIDD DY10 ....164 A3
Stonechat Dr ERDW/GRVHL B23 ..90 A3
Stonecrop CI BRWNH B38 ....26 B7
HWK/WKHTH B38 ....145 K5
Stone Cross PENK ST19 ....10 C4
Stonedown CI
ETTPK/GDPK/PENN WV4 ....66 D2
Stonefield CI COVE CV2 ....135 L5
Stonefield Dr BRLYHL DY5 ......102 B5
Stonefield Rd BILS/COS WV14 * ..51 H8
Stoneford Rd SHLY B90 ....147 L1
Stonehall Rd
RUGBYS/DCH CV22 ....185 L5
Stonehaven TAM/AM/WIL B77 ...32 D8
Stonehaven Dr COVS CV3 ....181 G2
Stonehaven Gv HLGN/YWD B28 ..126 F1
Stonehenge Cft
ALE/KHTH/YWD B14 ....146 B4
Stonehill CI SHLY B90 ....148 D7
Stonehills CI SHLY B90 ....148 D7
Stonehills RUGBYN/HIL CV21 ..161 G6
Stonehouse Av WLNHL WV13 .....51 K2
Stonehouse CI REDW B97 ....202 A4
RLSS CV32 ....199 H8
Stonehouse Crs
DARL/WED WS10 ....68 F3
Stonehouse Dr
FOAKS/STRLY B74 ....55 M1
Stonehouse HI SLYOAK B29 .....123 L3
Stonehouse La ALVE B48 ....71 A1
COVS CV3 ....182 A1
RCOVN/BALC/EX CV7 ....96 B6
RIDG/WDGT B32 ....123 H3
SCFLD/BOLD B73 ....72 D2
Stonehouse Rd BRGRVE B60 ....191 L1
Stonehurst Rd GTB/HAM B43 .....71 F2
Stonelea ALDR WS9 ....40 F8
Stonelea CI HHTH/SAND B71 ......69 J5
Stoneleigh Av KNWTH CV8 ....179 L5
Stoneleigh CI FOAKS/STRLY B74 ..56 C6
KNWTH CV8 ....180 F7
REDE B98 ....202 D8
Stoneleigh Gdns CDSL WV8 ....34 D1
Stoneleigh Rd
BFLD/HDSWWD B20 ....89 J4
KNWTH CV8 ....180 F7
RLSN CV32 ....198 D7
SOLH B91 ....147 L1
TLHL/CAN CV4 ....180 B3
Stoneleigh Wy SEDG DY3 ....66 B7
Stone Pine HEDN WS12 ....12 D5
Stonerwood Av HLGN/YWD B28 .126 D1
Stone St DUDN DY1 ....84 F6
OLDBY B69 ....86 E6
Stoneton Crs
RCOVN/BALC/EX CV7 ....151 L7
Stoneton Gv SLYOAK B29 ....123 L5

Stone Upper CI
WALM/CURD B76 * 73 H1
Stonewell Crs NUN CV11 * 207 G7
Stonewell Crs NUN CV11 ....99 M5
Stone Yd DIG/EDG B5 ....7 K7
Stoney Brook Leys WMBN WV5 ..64 C8
Stoney CI HIA/OLT B92 ....128 C6
Stoney CI COVS CV3 ....156 E6
Stoney Cft CNCK/NC WS11 ....16 D4
Stoneyfields CI CNCK/NC WS11 ..16 D3
Stoneyford Gv
ALE/KHTH/YWD B14 ....146 F1
Stoneyhurst Rd
ERDE/BCHGN B24 ....90 D4
Stoney La BHTH/HG B12 ....107 M8
BLOX/PEL WS3 ....39 H2
BRGRVE B60 ....193 G5
DUDS DY2 ....103 G2
HAG/WOL DY9 ....140 C2
HHTH/SAND B71 ....87 H1
KIDD DY11 ....138 C5
RIDG/WDGT B32 ....104 F7
STECH B33 ....109 J4
STRPT DY13 ....189 J1
Stoney Lea Rd CNCK/NC WS11 ..16 D3
Stoneymoor Dr CBROM B36 ......92 D4
Stoney Rd COV CV1 ....8 F8
NUNW/HART CV10 ....80 F7
Stoney Stanton Rd COVN CV6 ..134 D6
Stoneythorpe CI SOLH B91 ......148 F4
Stoneywood Rd COVE CV2 ....135 K4
Stonleigh Av COVW CV5 ....154 D6
Stonnal Gv ERDW/GRVHL B23 ...72 E7
Stonnall Gv ALDR WS9 ....40 F5
Stonnall Rd ALDR WS9 ....41 G5
Stonor Park Rd SOLH B91 ....127 K7
Stonor Rd HLGN/YWD B28 ....147 L1
Stonydelph La TAM/AM/WIL B77 ..47 J8
Stony La SMTHWK B67 ....87 J8
Stony St SMTHWK B67 ....87 K7
Stornaway Rd CVALE B35 ....91 M1
Storrage La ALVE B48 ....194 C2
Storrs CI BORD B9 ....108 A4
Storrs PI BORD B9 ....108 B4
The Storrs RIDG/WDGT B32 .....122 F6
Stot Fold Rd
ALE/KHTH/YWD B14 ....146 D3
Stour TAM/AM/WIL B77 ....46 E8
Stour CI BRGRVW B61 ....168 C3
BRLYHL DY5 ....84 C8
HAG/WOL DY9 ....120 A6
HALE B63 ....103 K8
KIDD DY11 ....118 D8
KIDD DY11 ....138 C5
SEDG DY3 ....83 C1
WMBN WV5 ....65 G4
Stour Ct BNTWD WS7 ....19 H7
HALE B63 ....103 J7
Stourdale Rd CDYHTH B64 ....103 G6
Stourdell Rd HALE B63 ....103 H7
Stour HI BRLYHL DY5 ....102 E6
Stour La STRPT DY13 ....188 E2
Stourmore CI SHHTH WV12 ....38 B7
Stourport Rd BEWD DY12 ....163 G2
KIDDW DY11 ....163 M5
STRPT DY13 ....188 E1
Stour Rd WBROM B70 ....86 C2
Stourton CI DOR/KN B93 ....149 M6
WALM/CURD B76 ....73 K1
Stourton Crs KINVER DY7 ....100 D7
Stourton Dr BRLYHL DY5 ....101 M7
Stour Vale Rd HAG/WOL DY9 ....102 D7
Stour Valley CI BRLYHL DY5 ....102 B6
Stow Dr BRLYHL DY5 ....101 M7
Stowecroft CI COVN CV6 ....134 F6
Stowe Hill Gdns LICH WS13 ......21 G4
Stowell Rd SEDG B44 ....71 K6
Stowe PI TLHL/CAN CV4 ....153 G4
Stowe Rd BLOX/PEL WS3 ....20 F5
Stowe St BLOX/PEL WS3 ....39 G6
LICH WS13 ....21 G4
Stow Gv CBROM B36 ....91 J6
Stow Heath La WOLV WV1 ....50 F6
Stow Heath PI WOLV WV1 ....50 F6
Stowmans CI BILS/COS WV14 ....66 F2
Strachey Av RLSN CV32 ....206 C3
Straight Mile WOLVN WV10 ....14 D1
Straight Rd SHHTH WV12 ....38 A7
Straits Gn SEDG DY3 ....83 M1
Straits Rd SEDG DY3 ....83 M2
The Straits BRGRVE B60 ....191 L2
The Strand BRGRVE B60 ....191 L2
Stratford Av ATHST CV9 ....63 G6
Stratford CI DUDN DY1 ....84 C3
Stratford PI ALDR WS9 ....41 G5
Stratford PI BHTH/HG B12 ....107 L7
Stratford Rd BRGRVE B60 ....191 J3
HLGN/YWD B28 ....126 C3
HOCK/TIA B94 ....174 F2
SHLY B90 ....147 M2
SPARK B11 ....107 M7
Stratford St COVE CV2 ....155 L1
Stratford St North SPARK B11 ..107 L5
Stratford Wy CNCK/NC WS11 .....12 C1
Stratdhene Rd SLYOAK B29 ......124 A3
Strathearn Rd RLSN CV32 ....206 C4
Strathern Dr BILS/COS WV14 .....66 E4
Strathmore Av COV CV1 ....9 J6
Strathmore Crs WMBN WV5 ....64 E4
Strathmore Rd CNCK/NC WS11 ..16 C3
Strathmore Rd TPTN/OCK DY4 ...67 L5
Stratton St WOLVN WV10 ....50 D1
Strawberry CI OLDBY B69 ....86 A6
Strawberry Flds
RCOVN/BALC/EX CV7 ....130 F4
Strawberry La GTWY WS6 ....24 C5
WLNHL WV13 ....51 G2
Strawberry Wk COVE CV2 ....135 H3
Stream Meadow
RUSH/SHEL WS4 ....40 A4
Stream Pk KGSWFD DY6 ....101 H1
Stream Rd KGSWFD DY6 ....83 H8
Streamside CI COVW CV5 ....132 C5
Streamside Wy HIA/OLT B92 .....128 D1
Streatham Gv RLSN CV32 ....206 C3
Streather Rd MGN/WHC B75 ......57 G4
Streetly Crs FOAKS/STRLY B74 ...56 C5
Streetly Dr FOAKS/STRLY B74 ....56 C5
Streetly La FOAKS/STRLY B74 ....56 F5
Streetly Rd ERDW/GRVHL B23 ...72 C5
Streetly Wd FOAKS/STRLY B74 ...56 C5
Streetsbrook Rd SHLY B90 ......126 F6
SOLH B91 ....127 J8
Streets Corner Gdns ALDR WS9 ..40 E5
Streetsway RIDG/WDGT B32 ....104 A8
Strensham HI MOS/BIL B13 ......125 J1
Strensham Rd MOS/BIL B13 .....125 J1
Stretton Av COVS CV3 ....156 A5
Stretton Dr RBRY B45 ....169 J3
Stretton Gdns CDSL WV8 ....34 D1
Stretton Gv LOZ/NWT B19 * 89 G6
SPARK B11 ....108 A7

WASH/WDE B8 ....90 F7
Stretton PI BILS/COS WV14 ....66 F6
DUDS DY2 ....85 H1
Stretton Rd KIDDW DY11 ....163 M1
KNWTH CV8 ....183 L2
NUNW/HART CV10 ....98 E2
SHHTH WV12 ....38 A5
SHLY B90 ....147 M5
Stringer HI HEDN WS12 ....13 H6
Stringer CI MGN/WHC B75 ....56 E1
Stringers HI HEDN WS12 ....13 H6
Stringes CI WLNHL WV13 ....51 M2
Stringes La WLNHL WV13 ....51 M3
Stroma Wy NUNW/HART CV10 ...80 A7
Stronsay CI RBRY B45 ....143 K4
Stroud Av SHHTH WV12 ....38 A8
Stroud CI SHHTH WV12 ....52 A1
Stroud Rd SHLY B90 ....147 K3
Strutt CI EDG B15 ....106 A5
Stuart CI WWCK CV34 ....205 H4
RLSN CV32 ....206 C4
Stuart Crs DUDS DY2 ....85 J4
Stuart Rd BLKHTH/ROWR B65 ..104 B3
HALE B63 ....104 A8
RMSLY B62 ....104 B4
Stuart's Dr STECH B33 ....109 H4
Stuarts Gn HAG/WOL DY9 ....119 M5
Stuarts Rd STECH B33 ....109 H3
Stuart St BLOX/PEL WS3 ....38 F5
VAUX/NECH B7 ....90 A6
Stuarts Wy RIDG/WDGT B32 .....122 F6
Stubbers Green Rd ALDR WS9 ...40 E6
Stubbington CI WLNHL WV13 .....51 H4
Stubbs CI BDWTH CV12 ....116 E1
Stubbs Gv COVE CV2 ....134 F8
Stubbs Rd BDMR/CCFT WV3 ......48 D5
Stubby La WNSFLD WV11 ....37 L7
Stubley Dr WOLVN WV10 ....36 C8
Studfall Av RUGBYN/HIL CV21 ..187 K4
Studland Gn COVE CV2 ....156 E1
Studland Rd HLGN/YWD B28 ....126 D1
Studley Cft HIA/OLT B92 ....128 A2
Studley Dr BRLYHL DY5 ....102 A5
Studley Ga STRBR DY8 ....101 H8
Studley Rd BDMR/CCFT WV3 .....49 G5
REDE B98 ....202 E3
Studley St BHTH/HG B12 ....107 L7
Sturgeon's HI LICHS WS14 ....21 G7
Sturley Cft KNWTH CV8 ....179 M7
Sturman Dr BLKHTH/ROWR B65 ..135 H4
Sturminster CI COVS CV3 ....156 D1
Stychbrook Gdns LICH WS13 ......20 F3
Styles CI RLSS CV31 ....206 D1
RWWCK/WEL CV35 ....204 D6
Styvechale Av COVW CV5 ....154 D5
Suckling Green La CDSL WV8 .....34 D3
Sudbury CI RLSN CV32 ....207 G3
WNSFLD WV11 ....37 J5
Sudbury Gv KGSTG B44 ....71 M3
Sudeley CI CBROM B36 ....91 M4
Sudeley Gdns SEDG DY3 ....84 B3
Sudeley Rd NUNW/HART CV10 ...99 G5
Suffield Gv ERDW/GRVHL B23 ...71 J2
Suffolk CI BDWTH CV12 ....116 D2
COVW CV5 ....153 M2
Suffolk Dr BRLYHL DY5 ....102 A6
Suffolk Gv ALDR WS9 ....40 F5
Suffolk PI CBHAMW B1 * 6 C4
DUDS DY2 ....85 H7
WSLW WS2 ....39 H8
Suffolk Rd DARL/WED WS10 ....69 G2
DUDS DY2 ....84 E6
Suffolk St RLSN CV32 ....206 E4
Suffolk St Queensway
CBHAMW B1 ....6 D5
Suffrage St SMTHWK B66 ....87 M8
Sugarbrook La BRGRVE B60 .....191 M8
Sugarbrook Rd BRGRVE B60 .....191 M8
Sugar Loaf La KINVER DY7 ....118 F5
Sugden Gv DIG/EDG B5 ....7 G9
Sulgrave CI DUDN DY1 ....84 C2
Sullivan Rd COVN CV6 ....134 F6
Sumburgh Cft CVALE B35 ....91 M1
Summercourt Dr KGSWFD DY6 ...83 J8
Summercourt Sq KGSWFD DY6 ..83 H8
Summer Cft LOZ/NWT B19 ....89 H7
Summercroft STRPT DY13 ....188 C5
Summer Dr SEDG DY3 ....84 A2
Summerfield Av KGSWFD DY6 ....83 J4
WBROM B70 ....87 G1
Summerfield CI
TAM/AM/WIL B77 ....45 L4
Summerfield Crs
LDYWD/EDGR B16 ....106 C2
Summerfield Dr SLYOAK B29 ....123 H8
Summerfield Gv WSNGN B18 * ..106 C1
Summerfield La KIDDW DY11 ....164 D6
Summerfield Rd BNTWD WS7 .....18 B8
DUDS DY2 ....85 H5
HAG/WOL DY9 ....141 J3
HIA/OLT B92 ....127 L4
LDYWD/EDGR B16 ....106 C2
STRPT DY13 ....188 F1
TAM/AM/WIL B77 ....46 B1
Summerfields Av RMSLY B62 ....104 D5
Summergate SEDG DY3 ....84 B2
Summer Gv LICH WS13 ....21 H3
Summer HI HALE B63 ....121 M1
KGSWFD DY6 ....83 G7
Summerhill Av HEDN WS12 ....18 A1
Summerhill Rd KIDDW DY11 .....137 L7
Summerhill Rd BILS/COS WV14 ..67 H4
CBHAMW B1 ....6 A3
Summer Hill St CBHAMW B1 ....6 B4
Summer Hill Ter CBHAMW B1 * 6 B4
Summerhouse La LICH WS13 ....19 H2
Summerhouse Rd
BILS/COS WV14 ....66 E4
Summer La LOZ/NWT B19 ....6 F1
RUSH/SHEL WS4 ....39 M3
WALM/CURD B76 ....74 B7
Summerlea Rd YDLY B25 ....92 C5
Summeree Rd
ERDE/BCHGN B24 ....90 F3
Summer Rd ACGN B27 ....126 E3
BLKHTH/ROWR B65 ....84 E1
EDG B15 ....7 G6
ERDW/GRVHL B23 ....72 C5
HHTH/SAND B71 * 68 A4
Summer Rw BKHL/PFLD WV2 ....2 F8
CBHAMW B3 ....6 C4
Summersend Av HEDN WS12 ......18 A1
Summerside Av HEDN WS12 ....12 D5
HHTH/SAND B71 ....69 M6
KGSWFD DY6 ....83 H1
REDE B98 ....201 K8
STRBR DY8 ....101 K8
WSL WS1 ....5 J3
Summerton Rd OLDBY B69 ....86 B5
Summervale CI HAG/WOL DY9 ...119 L8
Summervale Rd HAG/WOL DY9 ..119 L8

Summerville Ter HRBN B17 * 106 A8
Summerway La KIDDW DY11 .....164 D3
Summit Crs SMTHWK B66 ....87 J5
Summit Gdns HALE B63 ....121 K2
Summit PI SEDG DY3 ....83 M3
The Summit HAG/WOL DY9 ....120 B1
Suncliffe Dr KNWTH CV8 ....197 L3
Suncroft RIDG/WDGT B32 ....105 G8
Sundbury Ri NFLD/LBR B31 ......123 M8
Sunderland Dr STRBR DY8 ....101 L5
Sunderton Rd
ALE/KHTH/YWD B14 ....146 C1
Sundew CI CBROM B36 ....91 H5
Sundew St COVE CV2 ....135 H3
Sundial La GTB/HAM B43 ....70 D4
Sundorne CI COVW CV5 ....153 L1
Sundour Crs WNSFLD WV11 ....36 F4
Sundridge Rd KGSTG B44 ....71 J1
Sunfield Rd CNCK/NC WS11 ....15 L4
Sunfields CI POL/KGSB/FAZ B78 ..47 L5
Sunleigh Gv ACGN B27 ....127 J1
Sunny Dr HEDN WS12 ....13 H6
Sunningdale RMSLY B62 ....122 C1
Sunningdale Av COVN CV6 ....134 D3
DUNHL/THL/PER WV6 ....2 D8
KNWTH CV8 ....197 M3
Sunningdale CI
BFLD/HDSWWD B20 ....88 C1
NUN CV11 ....99 L4
SCFLD/BOLD B73 ....72 E3
STRBR DY8 ....119 K3
Sunningdale Dr OLDBY B69 ....85 M6
Sunningdale Rd BRGRVW B61 ...191 L4
SEDG DY3 ....65 M4
SPARK B11 ....126 E2
Sunningdale Wy BLOX/PEL WS3 ..38 E2
Sunny Av BHTH/HG B12 ....107 L8
Sunnybank Av COVS CV3 ....155 M8
KGSTG B44 ....71 M1
Sunnybank CI ALDR WS9 ....55 J3
Sunny Bank Rd
LCGLYGN/QTN B68 ....105 G6
Sunnybank Rd SCFLD/BOLD B73 ..72 D2
SEDG DY3 ....66 C8
Sunnydene WASH/WDE B8 ....90 B8
Sunny Hill CI WMBN WV5 ....64 F7
Sunnymead BRGRVE B60 ....191 L4
Sunnymead Rd
LGN/SDN/BHAMAIR B26 ....109 K7
Sunnymead Wy
FOAKS/STRLY B74 ....55 K6
Sunnymede Rd KGSWFD DY6 ....101 L1
OLDBY B69 ....85 M6
Sunnyside ALDR WS9 ....40 D3
OLDBY B69 ....85 M6
Sunnyside Av ERDW/GRVHL B23 .90 C2
Sunnyside CI COVS CV3 ....154 D2
RCOVN/BALC/EX CV7 ....152 A6
Sunnyside Ct
NUNW/HART CV10 * 99 J4
Sunnyside Gdns KIDDW DY11 ...137 M4
Sunnyside La
RCOVN/BALC/EX CV7 ....152 A7
Sunridge Av LOZ/NWT B19 ....89 H7
WMBN WV5 ....64 E6
Sunrise HI HEDN WS12 ....12 F7
Sunset CI CRTAM B79 ....45 L1
GTWY WS6 ....24 D2
POL/KGSB/FAZ B78 ....47 L5
Sunset PI
ETTPK/GDPK/PENN WV4 ....66 D2
Sunshine CI KNWTH CV8 ....197 L3
Sun St BRLYHL DY5 ....102 D4
RUGBYN/HIL CV21 ....187 G2
WOLVN WV10 ....14 D7
WSL WS1 ....4 D8
Sunway Gv COVS CV3 ....154 A7
Surfeit HI CDYHTH B64 ....103 J5
Surfeit Hill Rd CDYHTH B64 .....103 H5
Surrey CI CNCK/NC WS11 ....16 D5
NUNW/HART CV10 ....98 C2
Surrey Crs HHTH/SAND B71 ....68 E5
Surrey Dr BDMR/CCFT WV3 ....49 J4
POL/KGSB/FAZ B78 ....47 L4
STRBR DY8 ....101 J1
Surrey Rd DUDS DY2 ....85 J4
KGSTG B44 ....71 J1
Surrey Wk ALDR WS9 ....40 E5
Sussex Av ALDR WS9 ....40 E5
DARL/WED WS10 ....68 G7
HHTH/SAND B71 ....69 G7
Sussex Dr BDMR/CCFT WV3 ....49 J4
HEDN WS12 ....12 F8
Sussex Rd COVW CV5 ....153 L1
SHLY B90 ....147 M1
Sutherland CI GTB/HAM B43 ....71 H1
WWCK CV34 ....205 K6
Sutherland Dr BDWTH CV12 ....116 E1
MOS/BIL B13 ....125 L1
WMBN WV5 ....64 E5
Sutherland Gv
DUNHL/THL/PER WV6 ....48 D2
Sutherland PI BKHL/PFLD WV2 ....3 H7
ETTPK/GDPK/PENN WV4 ....49 M8
GTWY WS6 ....24 C2
Sutherland St AST/WIT B6 ....89 M5
Sutton Ap WASH/WDE B8 ....108 E1
Sutton Av COVW CV5 ....153 H1
POL/KGSB/FAZ B78 ....47 L4
Sutton CI REDE B98 ....203 H3
Sutton Crt
ETTPK/GDPK/PENN WV4 ....66 C3
MGN/WHC B75 ....86 E2
Sutton Crs WBROM B70 ....86 E2
Sutton New Rd
ERDW/GRVHL B23 ....90 D1
Sutton Oak Rd SCFLD/BOLD B73 ..55 L8
SCFLD/BOLD B73 ....72 B1
Sutton Park Gv KIDDW DY11 ....164 A2
Sutton Park Ri KIDDW DY11 .....163 L2
Sutton Park Rd KIDDW DY11 ....163 L1
Sutton Rd DARL/WED WS10 ....52 D4
DSYBK/YTR WS5 ....54 D2
ERDE/BCHGN B24 ....90 F4
KIDDW DY11 ....138 A8
POL/KGSB/FAZ B78 ....44 D7
WSL WS1 ....5 L2
Sutton's Dr GTB/HAM B43 ....70 D1
Sutton Stop COVN CV6 ....116 F8
Sutton St AST/WIT B6 ....89 K7
DIG/EDG B5 ....6 E8
STRBR DY8 ....101 J4
Swadling St RLSS CV31 ....206 D7
Swain Crofts RLSS CV31 ....206 M1

Swains Gv KGSTG B44 ... 71 K1
Swaledale Cl BRGRVE B60 ... 191 J7
Swale Gv HWK/WKHTH B38 ... 145 K5
  WLNHL WV13 ... 52 B3
Swale Rd WALM/CURD B76 ... 73 L4
Swallow Av CBROM B36 ... 92 E5
Swallow Cl BHTH/HG B12 ... 107 M8
  DARL/WED WS10 ...
  DUDS DY2 ... 103 H5
Swallow Ct WOLVN WV10 ... 36 B6
Swallow Cft LICH WS13 ... 20 E4
Swallowdale ALDR WS9 ... 40 E1
  DUNHL/THL/PER WV6 ... 48 D3
Swallowdean Rd COVN CV6 ... 133 J5
Swallow Dr DY10 ... 164 E3
Swallowfall Av STRBR DY8 ... 119 G5
Swallowfield CRTAM B79 ... 31 J7
Swallowfields Dr HEDN WS12 ... 16 F2
Swallow Rd SEDG DY3 ... 66 A2
Swallow Rd COVN CV6 ... 133 M4
Swallows Cl BLOX/PEL WS3 ... 25 L8
Swallows' Meadow SHLY B90 ... 148 B5
Swallow St CBHAM B2 ... 6 E6
  WBROM B70 ... 86 E1
Swanage Gn COVE CV2 ... 156 F5
Swanage Rd SMHTH B10 ... 108 B5
Swan Av SMTHWK B66 ... 87 J6
Swan Bank
  ETTPK/GDPK/PENN WV4 ... 65 K1
Swan Cl GTWY WS6 ... 24 A3
  KIDD DY10 ... 139 M4
Swan Copse YDLY B25 ... 109 G8
Swancote Dr
  ETTPK/GDPK/PENN WV4 ... 49 G8
Swancote Rd DUDN DY1 ... 84 E5
  STETCH B33 ... 91 K8
Swan Ctyd
  LGN/SDN/BHAMAIR B26 * ... 109 H7
Swan Crs OLDBY B69 ... 104 D1
Swancroft Rd COVE CV2 ... 134 E8
  TPTN/OCK DY4 ... 67 K5
Swan Dr BRWNH WS8 ... 26 C6
Swanfield Rd STRBR DY8 ... 101 L4
Swanfields BNTWD WS7 ... 19 G7
Swan Gdns ERDW/GRVHL B23 ... 90 D3
Swan La BRGRVW B61 ... 168 B2
  BRGRVW B61 ... 190 C8
  COVE CV2 ... 9 M2
  STRBR DY8 ... 101 L3
  WBROM B70 ... 68 B9
  WOLVN WV10 ... 23 G4
Swanley Cl RIDG/WDGT B32 ... 122 E2
Swanmore Cl BDMR/CCFT WV3 ... 49 J6
Swann Rd BILS/COS WV14 ... 66 E3
Swanmote CRTAM B79 ... 31 K8
Swann Pool Dr RUSH/SHEL WS4 ... 40 F4
Swan Rd LICH WS13 ... 20 E6
Swansbrook Gdns
  HWK/WKHTH B38 ... 146 A3
Swanshurst La MOS/BIL B13 ... 126 A5
Swans Length ALVE B48 ... 170 E6
Swan St ALVE B48 ... 170 F7
  BRLYHL DY5 ...
  DUDS DY2 ... 85 G7
  RLSN CV32 ... 206 E4
  STRBR DY8 ... 101 J8
  WOLV WV1 ... 3 L5
  WWCK CV34 ... 205 M4
Swanswell Rd ACGN B27 ... 127 H5
Swanswell St COVE CV1 ... 9 H2
Swanswood Gv
  CHWD/FDBR/MGN B37 * ... 111 G2
Swarthmore Rd SLYOAK B29 ... 123 M6
Sweetbriar La SHHTH WV12 ... 38 B8
Sweetbriar Rd BKHL/PFLD WV2 ... 50 E6
Sweetbriar Wy HEDN WS12 ... 17 H5
Sweetman Pl
  DUNHL/THL/PER WV6 ... 2 E1
Sweetman St
  DUNHL/THL/PER WV6 ... 49 L1
Sweetmoor Cl CBROM B36 ... 92 A5
Sweetpool La HAG/WOL DY9 ... 119 K8
Swift Cl BRGRVW B61 ... 191 J5
  CBROM B36 ... 92 E5
  KNWTH CV8 ... 197 L3
Swift Pk RUGBYN/HIL CV21 ... 160 E6
Swift Park Gv KIDD DY10 ... 164 F3
Swift's Cnr COVS CV3 ... 155 J5
Swillington Rd COVN CV6 ... 133 M8
Swinbrook Gv KGSTG B44 ... 71 J4
Swinbrook Wy SHLY B90 ... 148 B5
Swincombe Rd COVE CV2 ... 156 B3
Swinburne Cl
  NUNW/HART CV10 ... 79 L8
Swinburne Rd REDW B97 ... 202 A6
Swincross Rd STRBR DY8 ... 119 M2
Swindale HAG/WOL DY9 ... 119 K8
Swindell Rd HAG/WOL DY9 ... 120 A4
Swindon Rd HRBN B17 ... 105 M2
  KGSWFD DY6 ... 82 D5
Swinfen Broun Rd LICH WS13 ... 20 E5
Swinford Gv DOR/KN B93 ... 175 J2
Swinford Leys WMBN WV5 ... 64 B8
Swinford Rd SLYOAK B29 ... 123 L2
  STRBR DY8 ... 119 L3
  WOLVN WV10 ... 36 C8
Swin Forge Wy SEDG DY3 ... 82 C3
Swiss Dr STRBR DY8 ... 101 K3
Swiss Hts STRPT DY13 ... 188 C1
Swiss Lodge Dr
  POL/KGSB/FAZ B78 ...
Swynnerton Dr WNSFLD WV11 ... 37 K1
Sycamore TAM/AM/WIL B77 ... 46 C3
Sycamore Av BHTH/HG B12 ... 107 L8
  POL/KGSB/FAZ B78 ... 47 L5
  REDE B98 ... 202 C3
Sycamore Cl ERDE/BCHGN B24 ... 90 D2
  KIDD DY10 ... 138 C6
  RUSH/SHEL WS4 ... 39 M5
  STRBR DY8 ... 119 H3
  WALM/CURD B76 ... 73 G3
Sycamore Crs
  CHWD/FDBR/MGN B37 ... 110 E5
  ERDE/BCHGN B24 ... 90 D2
  RCOVN/BALC/EX CV7 ... 96 F5
Sycamore Dr BDMR/CCFT WV3 ... 49 H4
  HLYWD B47 ... 146 F8
Sycamore Dr CNCK/NC WS11 ... 12 C7
  DUDN DY1 ... 66 D8
Sycamore Gv
  RUGBYN/HIL CV21 ... 186 E1
  WWCK CV34 ... 205 L4
Sycamore Paddock
  STRBR DY8 ... 101 L4
Sycamore Pl BILS/COS WV14 ... 67 L2
  SMTHWK B66 ... 87 H5
Sycamore Rd AST/WIT B6 ... 89 G5
  BNTWD WS7 ... 18 D6
  BVILLE B30 ... 124 D6
  COVE CV2 ... 9 L7
  DARL/WED WS10 ... 53 K8
  DSYBK/YTR WS5 ... 53 K8
  ERDW/GRVHL B23 ... 90 D2
  GTB/HAM B43 ... 70 C2
  HDSW B21 ... 88 B5
  HEDN WS12 ... 17 K1
  KGSWFD DY6 ... 83 J7
  NUNW/HART CV10 ... 80 B7
  OLDBY B69 ... 104 D1
  POL/KGSB/FAZ B78 ... 60 B6
  RUSH/SHEL WS4 ... 39 M5
  SMTHWK B66 ... 105 M2
  WSL WS1 ... 67 K6
The Sycamores BDWTH CV12 ... 116 C3
  WOLVN WV10 ... 36 D5
Sycamore Ter
  ALE/KHTH/YWD B14 * ... 125 G6
Sycamore Wy ACGN B27 ... 127 G1
  HEDN WS12 ... 12 B5
Sydenham Dr RLSS CV31 ... 206 F7
Sydenham Rd SMTHWK B66 ... 87 L6
  SPARK B11 ... 108 A7
  WOLV WV1 ... 50 F3
Sydnall Cl REDW B97 ... 201 K3
Sydnall Flds COVN CV6 ... 134 D1
Sydnall Rd COVN CV6 ... 116 D8
Sydney Cl WBROM B70 ... 68 E6
Sydney Rd BORD B9 ... 108 A3
  BRGRVW B61 ... 191 J2
  CDYHTH B64 ... 102 F4
  SMTHWK B66 ... 105 J3
Syerscote La CRTAM B79 ... 32 B3
Sykesmoor TAM/AM/WIL B77 ... 46 F4
Sylvan Av NFLD/LBR B31 ... 144 D2
Sylvan Dr COVS CV3 ... 154 D7
Sylvan Gn RMSLY B62 ... 104 B8
Sylvia Av NFLD/LBR B31 ... 144 F5
Symphony Ct CBHAMW B1 ... 6 A5
Synkere Cl
  RCOVN/BALC/EX CV7 ... 115 L1
Sytch La WMBN WV5 ... 64 E8
Sywell Leys RUGBYS/DCH CV22 ... 186 D7

T

Tabbs Gdns KIDD DY10 ... 138 C5
Tabeners La ATHST CV9 ... 63 H6
Table Oak La KNWTH CV8 ... 177 L3
Tachbrook Cl COVE CV2 ... 135 G3
Tachbrook Park Dr RLSS CV31 ... 206 C7
Tachbrook Rd RLSS CV31 ... 206 D7
Tachbrook St RLSS CV31 ... 206 E7
Tack Farm Rd STRBR DY8 ... 101 H4
Tackford Cl CBROM B36 ... 92 A4
Tackford Rd COVN CV6 ... 134 E6
Tackley Cl SHLY B90 ... 147 M5
Tadmore Cl BILS/COS WV14 ... 51 G8
Tadworth Cl WOLV WV1 ... 50 E3
Tainters Hl KNWTH CV8 ... 179 K7
Tait Cft HIA/OLT B92 ... 128 D5
Talaton Cl COVEN WV9 ... 35 L3
Talbot TAM/AM/WIL B77 ... 46 C2
Talbot Av KNWTH CV8 ... 179 J2
Talbot Cl ERDW/GRVHL B23 ... 72 B5
  KIDDW DY11 ... 189 L4
  WSL WS1 ... 39 G7
Talbot Pl BILS/COS WV14 ... 51 G7
Talbot Rd BKHL/PFLD WV2 ... 50 D7
  BRGRVE B61 ... 190 B5
  DUDS DY2 ... 102 F1
  SMTHWK B66 ... 105 L4
Talbotshill La KIDD DY10 ... 139 G1
Talbots La BRLYHL DY5 ... 102 C4
Talbot St BRLYHL DY5 ... 102 B2
  HAG/WOL DY9 ... 102 D8
  HALE B63 ... 103 G7
  KIDDW DY11 ... 164 A1
  STRBR DY8 ... 101 L8
  WSNGN B18 ... 88 D7
Talbot Wy SMTHWK B10 ... 108 D6
Talford St AST/WIT B6 ... 89 J7
Talfourd St BORD B9 ... 108 B4
Talgarth Covert
  HWK/WKHTH B38 ... 145 J6
Talisman Cl KNWTH CV8 ... 197 K2
Talke Rd DSYBK/YTR WS5 ... 53 K8
Talladale RIDG/WDGT B32 ... 122 F6
Talland Av COVN CV6 ... 134 E6
  TAM/AM/WIL B77 ... 32 C8
Tallants Cl COVN CV6 ... 134 E5
Tallants Rd COVN CV6 ... 134 D5
Tallington Rd
  LGN/SDN/BHAMAIR B26 ... 110 A6
Tall Trees Cl BRGRVW B61 * ... 168 D5
  FOAKS/STRLY B74 ... 56 B1
  SHHTH WV12 ... 38 B7
Tall Trees Dr HAG/WOL DY9 ... 120 B3
Talton Cl SHLY B90 ... 148 E8
Tamar Cl BRWNH WS8 ... 26 A3
  RRUGBY CV23 ... 159 M8
Tamar Dr CBROM B36 ... 92 D5
  SEDG DY3 ... 66 A7
  WALM/CURD B76 ... 73 H6
Tamar Gv DUNHL/THL/PER WV6 ... 48 C1
  WLNHL WV13 ... 52 A3
Tamarisk Cl SLYOAK B29 ... 123 M5
Tamar Ri STRBR DY8 ... 101 L5
Tamar Rd BDWTH CV12 ... 117 L3
  TAM/AM/WIL B77 ... 46 A3
Tame Av BNTWD WS7 ... 19 G7
  DARL/WED WS10 ... 69 G1
Tame Bank POL/KGSB/FAZ B78 ... 60 A7
Tame Br DSYBK/YTR WS5 ... 69 K1
Tame Cl WSL WS1 ... 69 L6
Tame Crs HHTH/SAND B71 ... 69 G7
Tame Dr BLOX/PEL WS3 ... 39 L4
Tamedrive POL/KGSB/FAZ B78 ... 45 L1
Tame Gv CNCK/NC WS11 ... 16 B5
Tame Ri LGLYGN/QTN B68 ... 104 F5
Tame Rd AST/WIT B6 ... 89 L3
  LGLYGN/QTN B68 ... 104 E5
  TPTN/OCK DY4 ... 68 A3
Tamerton Rd RIDG/WDGT B32 ... 123 H4
Tameside Dr CVALE B35 ... 89 K1
Tame St BILS/COS WV14 ... 51 K8
  TAM/AM/WIL B77 ... 46 A2
  WBROM B70 ... 68 D5
  WSL WS1 ... 53 J7
Tame St East WSL WS1 ... 53 K7
Tamhorn House Br LICHS WS14 ... 30 F2
Tamworth Cl BRWNH WS8 ... 26 D3
Tamworth Rd ATHST CV9 ... 61 G4
  MGN/WHC B75 ... 21 G8
  POL/KGSB/FAZ B78 ... 57 H6
  POL/KGSB/FAZ B78 ... 47 J1
  RCOVN/BALC/EX CV7 ... 95 K4
  RCOVN/BALC/EX CV7 ... 114 E5
  TAM/AM/WIL B77 ... 46 A5
Tamworth Rd (Amington)
  TAM/AM/WIL B77 ... 32 C8
Tamworth Rd (Dosthill)
  TAM/AM/WIL B77 ...
Tamworth St LICH WS13 ... 20 A7
Tancred St DSYBK/YTR WS5 ... 69 L2
Tancred Cl RLSS CV31 ... 206 D8
Tandy Dr ALE/KHTH/YWD B14 ... 146 D2
Tandy's La KIDD DY10 ... 166 C5

Tanfield Cl DUNHL/THL/PER WV6 ... 48 F2
Tanfield Rd DUDS DY2 ... 84 F6
  STETCH B33 ... 109 H2
Tanford Rd HIA/OLT B92 ... 128 A2
Tanglewood Cl BKDE/SHDE B34 ... 92 A3
  BRGRVW B60 ... 169 L7
  RIDG/WDGT B32 ... 122 D7
Tanglewood Gv SEDG DY3 ... 66 A3
Tangmere Cl
  DUNHL/THL/PER WV6 ... 34 C3
Tangmere Dr CVALE B35 ... 91 L2
Tanhill TAM/AM/WIL B77 ... 46 E4
Tanhouse Av GTB/HAM B43 ... 70 A6
Tanhouse Farm Rd
  HIA/OLT B92 ... 128 A3
Tanhouse La HALE B63 ... 103 G8
Tan La STRPT DY13 ... 188 E1
Tanners Cl MGN/WHC B75 ... 57 J6
Tanners Green La HLYWD B47 ... 172 A5
Tanner's Hl BEWD DY12 ... 162 B2
Tanners' La
  RCOVN/BALC/EX CV7 ... 152 F4
Tannery Cl ATHST CV9 ... 63 J5
  WSLW WS2 ... 4 D1
Tansey Green Rd BRLYHL DY5 ... 83 M5
Tansley Cl DOR/KN B93 ... 175 K1
Tansley Gv KGSTG B44 ... 71 K4
Tansley Hill Av DUDS DY2 ... 85 K5
Tansley Hill Rd DUDS DY2 ... 85 K4
Tansley Rd KGSTG B44 ... 71 K5
Tansy TAM/AM/WIL B77 ... 46 A2
Tantany La HHTH/SAND B71 ... 68 B5
Tantarra St WSL WS1 ... 5 H6
Tanwood Cl REDW B97 ... 201 L7
  SOLH B91 ... 148 F5
Tanworth Gv BHTH/HG B12 ... 107 K7
Tanworth La SHLY B90 ... 147 M7
Tanyard LICH WS13 ... 21 G5
  TLHL/CAN CV4 ... 153 G4
Tanyard Cl ALVE B48 ... 170 F7
Tanyard Gdns ALVE B48 ... 170 E7
Tapcon Wy COVE CV2 ... 135 K8
Tapestries Av WBROM B70 ... 86 E1
Taplow Pl CNCK/NC WS11 ... 16 D1
Tappinger Gv KNWTH CV8 ... 180 A8
Tapton Cl BLOX/PEL WS3 ... 39 G2
Tardebigge Cl REDW B97 * ... 193 G5
Tarlington Rd COVN CV6 ... 133 H7
Tarmac Rd
  ETTPK/GDPK/PENN WV4 ... 50 F8
Tarn Cl BDWTH CV12 ... 116 E3
Tarquin Cl COVS CV3 ... 156 B7
Tarragon Cl COVE CV2 ... 135 H4
Tarragon Gdns NFLD/LBR B31 ... 144 A5
Tarrant Gv RIDG/WDGT B32 ... 105 K8
Tarrant Wk COVE CV2 ... 135 L8
Tarrington Covert
  HWK/WKHTH B38 ... 145 J5
Tarry Hollow Rd BRLYHL DY5 ... 83 M1
Tarry Rd WASH/WDE B8 ... 108 C1
Tarvin Ms BRLYHL DY5 ... 102 B4
Taryn Dr DARL/WED WS10 ... 52 B6
Tasker St WBROM B70 ... 86 C1
  WSL WS1 ... 4 D6
Tasman Dr
  DUNHL/THL/PER WV6 ... 34 C8
Tat Bank Rd OLDBY B69 ... 86 F7
Tatnall Gv WWCK CV34 ... 205 J5
Taunton Av WOLVN WV10 ... 36 B1
Taunton Cl NFLD/LBR B31 ... 144 A2
Taunton Rd BHTH/HG B12 ... 125 L1
Taunton Wy COVN CV6 ... 133 L3
Taverners Cl SHHTH WV12 ... 38 A4
Taverner's Gn
  BFLD/HDSWWD B20 ... 88 D2
Tavistock Cl CRTAM B79 ... 32 A6
Tavistock Rd ACGN B27 ... 127 G6
Tavistock St RLSN CV32 ... 206 D4
Tavistock Wk COVE CV2 ... 135 G6
Tavistock Wy NUN CV11 ... 81 J8
Taw Cl CBROM B36 ... 92 D6
Tay Cft CHWD/FDBR/MGN B37 ... 111 G3
Tay Gv HWK/WKHTH B38 ... 145 K5
  RMSLY B62 ... 104 C5
Taylor Av BLOX/PEL WS3 ... 39 H5
  RLSN CV32 ... 206 F3
Taylor Cl KNWTH CV8 ... 179 M7
Taylor Gv WWCK CV34 * ... 205 J3
Taylor Rd ALE/KHTH/YWD B14 ... 125 K8
  DUDS DY2 ... 85 J8
  ETTPK/GDPK/PENN WV4 ... 50 D8
Taylor's La HHTH/SAND B71 ... 87 H1
  OLDBY B69 ... 86 C5
  SMTHWK B67 ... 86 D4
Taylors Orch ERDW/GRVHL B23 ... 89 H4
Taylor St WNSFLD WV11 ... 37 G8
Taylor Wy OLDBY B69 ... 85 M5
Taysfield Rd NFLD/LBR B31 ... 123 J7
Taywood Dr SMHTH B10 ... 108 A6
Teachers Cl COVN CV6 ... 133 L8
The Tea Gdn
  RCOVN/BALC/EX CV7 ... 116 C5
Tealby Gv SLYOAK B29 ... 124 E4
Teal Cl RRUGBY CV23 ... 161 H5
Teal Dr ERDW/GRVHL B23 ... 89 M2
Teal Gv DARL/WED WS10 ... 67 M2
Teall Rd WASH/WDE B8 ... 90 C8
Tean Cl BNTWD WS7 ... 19 H7
  SPARK B11 ... 126 E2
Teasdale Wy HAG/WOL DY9 ... 120 B1
Teasel Cl RRUGBY CV23 ... 161 H5
Teasel Gv WOLVN WV10 ... 23 G8
Teasel Rd WNSFLD WV11 ... 37 L8
Teazel Av BVILLE B30 ... 124 B7
Tebworth Cl COVEN WV9 ... 35 K3
Tedbury Crs ERDW/GRVHL B23 ... 72 C7
Tedder Rd WSLW WS2 ... 52 D3
Teddesley Cl CNCK/NC WS11 ... 16 B2
Teddesley Gv STETCH B33 ... 110 A1
Teddesley Rd PENK ST19 ... 10 D4
Teddesley St RUSH/SHEL WS4 ... 5 G1
Teddesley Wy HEDN WS12 ... 12 A7
Teddington Gv PBAR/PBCH B42 ... 89 G2
Ted Pitts La COVW CV5 ... 132 F3
Tedstone Rd RIDG/WDGT B32 ... 105 J8
Teesdale Av CBROM B36 ... 91 J8
Teesdale Cl WOLV WV1 ... 50 E3
Tees Gv HWK/WKHTH B38 ... 145 K5
Teeswater Cl BRGRVE B60 ... 191 J7
Teign TAM/AM/WIL B77 ... 46 E4
Teignmouth Rd SLYOAK B29 ... 124 D3
Telephone Rd COVS CV3 ... 156 A4
Telfer Rd COVN CV6 ... 133 M6
Telford Av GTWY WS6 ...
  RLSN CV32 ... 198 F8
Telford Cl BEWD DY12 ... 162 E2
Telford Gdns BDMR/CCFT WV3 ... 49 H6
Telford Gv HEDN WS12 ... 12 C3
Telford Rd CRTAM B79 ... 31 K7
  HHTH/SAND B71 ... 68 D1
  SMTHWK B67 ... 105 H4
  WSL WS2 ... 38 F8
Telford Wy KIDDW DY11 ... 163 M2
Teme Av WLNHL WV13 ... 52 A3
Teme Rd HALE B63 ... 102 F8
  STRBR DY8 ... 119 K2

RCOVN/BALC/EX CV7 ... 117 G5
  WSLW WS2 ... 38 E8
Teme Av KIDDW DY11 ... 87 K6
Tempest St BKHL/PFLD WV2 ... 3 G5
  CRTAM B79 ... 31 J3
Templar Av TLHL/CAN CV4 ... 153 L4
Templars' Flds TLHL/CAN CV4 ... 153 M6
The Templars OLDBY B69 ... 86 C9
  WWCK CV34 ... 205 K8
Templars Wk WLNHL WV13 ... 51 L3
Templars Wy PENK ST19 ... 10 D5
Temple Av BILS/COS WV14 ... 126 E7
  RCOVN/BALC/EX CV7 ... 151 K7
Temple Bar WLNHL WV13 ... 51 L2
Temple Cl REDE B98 ... 202 D1
Templefield Gdns BORD B9 ... 108 A4
Templefield Sq EDG B15 ... 106 F6
Templefield St BORD B9 ... 108 A4
Temple Gv WWCK CV34 ... 205 H8
Temple La DOR/KN B93 ... 176 B7
Temple Meadows Rd
  HHTH/SAND B71 ... 69 J8
Templemore Dr GTB/HAM B43 ... 70 C2
Temple Pas CBHAM B2 ... 6 E5
Temple Rw DOR/KN B93 ... 175 L2
  WLNHL WV13 ... 51 L2
Temple Rw West CBHAMNW B3 ... 6 E4
Temple Sq WLNHL WV13 ... 51 L2
Temple St BILS/COS WV14 ... 51 J8
  BKHL/PFLD WV2 ... 2 E5
  DOR/KN B93 ... 187 G2
  RUGBYN/HIL CV21 ... 187 G2
  SEDG DY3 ... 66 F6
  WBROM B70 ... 87 G1
Templeton Cl DOR/KN B93 ... 175 J2
Templeton Rd KGSTG B44 ... 71 J3
Temple Wy CSHL/WTROR B46 ... 93 K4
  OLDBY B69 ... 86 A3
Tenacre La SEDG DY3 ... 66 C8
Ten Acres End BVILLE B30 ... 124 F5
Tenacres La REDE B98 ... 203 K2
Ten Ashes La RBRY B45 ... 170 A1
Tenbury Cl ALDR WS9 ... 41 G5
  REDE B98 ... 195 G1
  WSLW WS2 ... 52 B2
Tenbury Ct
  ETTPK/GDPK/PENN WV4 ... 49 H8
Tenbury Gdns
  ETTPK/GDPK/PENN WV4 ... 65 H1
Tenbury Rd
  ALE/KHTH/YWD B14 ... 125 H7
Tenby Cl BDWTH CV12 ... 116 A4
Tenby Rd MOS/BIL B13 ... 126 B3
Tenby St CBHAMW B1 ... 6 B2
Tenby St North CBHAMW B1 ... 6 B2
Tenby Wy STRPT DY13 ... 163 J7
Teneriffe Rd COVN CV6 ... 134 D4
Tenlands Rd HALE B63 ... 121 K2
Tenlons Rd NUNW/HART CV10 ... 98 D3
Tennal Gv RIDG/WDGT B32 ... 105 K7
Tennal La RIDG/WDGT B32 ... 105 J8
Tennal Rd RIDG/WDGT B32 ... 105 J7
Tennant St EDG B15 ... 6 B8
  NUN CV11 ... 99 J3
Tennis Ct BVILLE B30 ... 145 H1
Tennis Ct EDG B15 * ... 106 E8
Tennscore Av GTWY WS6 ... 24 C2
Tennyson Av CRTAM B79 ... 31 L7
  RUGBYS/DCH CV22 ... 186 C6
Tennyson Cl KNWTH CV8 ... 180 A8
Tennyson Rd BRLYHL DY5 ... 84 B7
  COVE CV2 ... 156 A2
  REDW B97 ... 202 A5
  SEDG DY3 ... 65 G8
  SMHTH WV12 ... 38 C5
  SMHTH B10 ... 108 C6
  WOLVN WV10 ... 36 E4
Tennyson St BRLYHL DY5 ... 84 B7
Tennyson Wy KIDD DY10 ... 138 F7
Tenter Ct HALE B63 ... 121 M1
Tenter Dr HALE B63 ... 122 A2
Tenterfields HALE B63 ... 121 M1
Tern Cl ETTPK/GDPK/PENN WV4 ... 65 H5
Tern Gv HWK/WKHTH B38 ... 145 J5
Terrace Rd ATHST CV9 ... 63 J5
  BRLYHL DY5 ... 84 C2
  DARL/WED WS10 ... 68 E6
The Terrace BDMR/CCFT WV3 ... 49 G4
  CDYHTH B64 ... 103 J5
Terracotta Dr COVE CV2 ... 155 L1
Terrence Vls DARL/WED WS10 * ... 52 C6
Terry Av RLSN CV32 ... 206 A4
Terry Cl LICH WS13 ... 20 C3
Terry Dr WALM/CURD B76 ... 73 K4
Terry Rd COV CV1 ... 9 K7
Terrys Cl REDE B98 ... 194 D8
Terrys La ERDE/BCHGN B24 ... 91 G2
Terryspring Ct REDE B98 * ... 202 D2
Terry St DUDS DY2 ... 85 H4
Tessall La NFLD/LBR B31 ... 144 A4
Tetbury Gv NFLD/LBR B31 ... 144 B2
Tetley Av RUSH/SHEL WS4 ... 53 L1
Tetley Rd SPARK B11 ... 126 C2
Tetnall St DUDS DY2 ... 85 H5
Tettenhall Rd
  DUNHL/THL/PER WV6 ... 49 K2
Teveray Dr PENK ST19 ... 10 D6
Teviot Gdns BRLYHL DY5 ... 83 M6
Teviot Gv HWK/WKHTH B38 ... 145 K5
Tewkesbury Dr BDWTH CV12 ... 117 G2
  DUDS DY2 ... 103 J3
Tewkesbury Rd
  BFLD/HDSWWD B20 ... 89 J4
  BLOX/PEL WS3 ... 38 C5
Tew Park Rd HDSW B21 ... 88 B6
Thackeray Cl NUNW/HART CV10 ... 97 L1
  RUGBYS/DCH CV22 ... 186 D6
Thackeray Dr CRTAM B79 ... 31 L6
Thackeray Rd BVILLE B30 ... 124 D8
Thackhall St COVE CV2 ... 9 L2
Thame Ct HLYWD B47 ... 172 C6
Thames Cl BDWTH CV12 ... 117 G3
Thames Ct RUGBYN/HIL CV21 ...
  BRLYHL DY5 ... 83 M6
Thames Rd BLOX/PEL WS3 ... 39 H5
Thamley Rd COVN CV6 ... 133 H6
Thanet Cl KGSWFD DY6 ... 83 G7
Thanet Gv PBAR/PBCH B42 ... 89 G1
The Thatchers RMSLY B62 ... 104 C1
Thatchway Gdns
  HWK/WKHTH B38 ... 145 J6
Thaxted Cl STETCH B33 ... 110 C2
Theatre Ap WWCK CV34 * ... 205 H7
Theatre St WWCK CV34 ... 205 H7
Thebes Cl COVW CV5 ... 131 M5
Theddingworth Cl COVS CV3 ... 156 C5
Thelbridge Rd NFLD/LBR B31 ... 144 C7

Thelma Rd TPTN/OCK DY4 ... 67 J7
Thelma St WSL WS1 ... 4 D8
Thelsford Wy SOLH B91 ... 128 D5
Thena Gdns COVN CV6 ... 134 E4
Theodore Cl HRBN B17 ... 123 H1
  OLDBY B69 ...
The Pavilions CSHL/WTROR B46 ... 111 H5
Theresa Rd SPARK B11 ... 107 H6
Thetford Cl TPTN/OCK DY4 ... 67 H8
Thetford Gdns WNSFLD WV11 ... 37 H7
Thetford Rd PBAR/PBCH B42 ... 70 F3
Thetford Wy DSYBK/YTR WS5 ... 70 A2
Thickett Cl WSLW WS2 ... 52 F5
Thicknall Dr HAG/WOL DY9 ... 119 M3
Thicknall La HAG/WOL DY9 ... 140 F3
Thicknall Ri HAG/WOL DY9 ... 140 E1
Thickthorn Cl KNWTH CV8 ... 197 M2
Thimble End Rd
  WALM/CURD B76 ... 73 L3
Thimble Mill La AST/WIT B6 ... 89 M6
Thimblemill Rd SMTHWK B67 ... 105 H1
Thimbler Rd TLHL/CAN CV4 ... 154 A3
Third Av BORD B9 ... 108 D3
  BRWNH WS8 ... 26 E4
  KGSWFD DY6 ... 83 K5
  SLYOAK B29 ... 125 G2
  WOLVN WV10 ... 36 D6
Third Exhibition Av
  BHAMNEC B40 ... 111 H8
Third Rd BRGRVW B61 ... 168 D1
Thirlestane Cl KNWTH CV8 ... 180 A7
Thirlmere RUGBYN/HIL CV21 ... 161 G6
Thirlmere Av NUN CV11 ... 81 K7
Thirlmere Cl CNCK/NC WS11 ... 16 C4
  COVW CV5 ... 153 J2
  DUNHL/THL/PER WV6 ... 35 H5
  WNSFLD WV11 ... 37 L3
Thirlmere Gv
  DUNHL/THL/PER WV6 ... 48 D3
Thirlmere Rd BDWTH CV12 ... 116 E3
  STRPT DY13 ... 163 K1
Thirlmere Wk BRLYHL DY5 ... 101 M8
Thirsk Cft CBROM B36 ... 91 J5
Thirsk Rd COVS CV3 ... 155 G8
Thirsk Wy BRGRVW B61 ... 168 F4
Thirston Cl WNSFLD WV11 ... 37 L8
Thistle Cl SEDG DY3 ... 66 D7
Thistle Cl WNSFLD WV11 ... 37 H8
Thistledown Av BNTWD WS7 ... 18 E7
Thistle Down Cl
  FOAKS/STRLY B74 ... 55 L3
Thistledown Dr HEDN WS12 ... 17 G4
  WOLVN WV10 ... 23 G8
Thistledown Rd BKDE/SHDE B34 ... 92 A4
Thistle Gn HWK/WKHTH B38 ... 145 J6
Thistlegreen Cl
  BLKHTH/ROWR B65 ... 85 K8
Thistlegreen Rd DUDS DY2 ... 103 J1
Thistle La BRGRVW B61 ... 168 F4
Thistle Wy RIDG/WDGT B32 ... 122 F5
Thistlewood Gv DOR/KN B93 * ... 176 F7
Thistley Fld East COVN CV6 ... 133 K2
Thistley Fld North COVN CV6 ... 133 K2
Thistley Fld South COVN CV6 ... 133 K2
Thistley Fld West COVN CV6 ... 133 K2
Thistley Nook LICH WS13 * ... 20 E4
Thomas Crs SMTHWK B66 ... 88 A4
Thomas Guy Rd WBROM B70 ... 68 C5
Thomas Landsdail St COVS CV3 ... 9 G8
Thomas Lane St COVN CV6 ... 134 C1
Thomas Mason Cl WNSFLD WV11 ... 37 H6
Thomas Naul Cft TLHL/CAN CV4 ... 153 K2
Thomas Sharp St
  TLHL/CAN CV4 ... 153 L1
Thomas St AST/WIT B6 ... 89 K7
  BDWTH CV12 ... 116 E3
  BKHL/PFLD WV2 ... 2 F5
  COV CV1 * ... 8 C5
  RLSN CV32 ... 206 E4
  SMTHWK B66 ... 87 M4
  TAM/AM/WIL B77 ... 46 B1
  WBROM B70 ... 87 H3
Thomas St West
  STRBR DY8 ... 4 C2
Thomas Wy RRUGBY CV23 ... 159 L8
Thompson Av BKHL/PFLD WV2 ... 50 B6
Thompson Cl DUDS DY2 ... 102 F5
  WLNHL WV13 ... 51 L2
Thompson Dr VAUX/NECH B7 ... 90 D5
Thompson Gdns
  SMTHWK B67 ... 105 K1
Thompson Rd LGLYGN/QTN B68 ... 104 F1
  SMTHWK B67 ... 105 K1
Thompson's Rd
  RCOVN/BALC/EX CV7 ... 115 J7
Thomson Av NFLD/LBR B31 ... 123 L1
  WLNHL WV13 ... 51 L2
Thomson Cl RUGBYN/HIL CV21 ... 160 F7
Thor Cl CNCK/NC WS11 ... 12 B8
Thoresby CRTAM B79 ... 31 J7
Thoresby Cft DUDN DY1 ... 84 D2
Thornberry Dr DUDN DY1 ... 84 B5
Thornberry Wk VAUX/NECH B7 ... 90 D5
Thornbridge Av PBAR/PBCH B42 ... 71 G6
Thornbury Ct
  DUNHL/THL/PER WV6 ... 48 D3
Thornbury La REDE B98 ... 195 G6
Thornbury Rd
  BFLD/HDSWWD B20 ... 89 H3
  BLOX/PEL WS3 ... 38 C5
  TAM/AM/WIL B77 ... 46 C5
Thornby Av SOLH B91 ... 127 M8
  TAM/AM/WIL B77 ... 46 C5
Thornby Rd ERDW/GRVHL B23 ... 72 A5
Thorncliffe Rd REDW B97 ... 201 L7
Thorncliffe Rd KGSTG B44 ... 71 J3
Thorn Cft
  NUNW/HART CV10 ... 79 J5
Thorn Cl DARL/WED WS10 ... 68 C1
  RUGBYN/HIL CV21 ... 161 G7
Thorncroft Wy DSYBK/YTR WS5 ... 69 M1
Thorne Av WOLVN WV10 ... 36 C6
Thorne Rd WLNHL WV13 ... 51 L1
Thornes Cft ALDR WS9 ... 41 J4
Thorne St BKHL/PFLD WV2 ... 50 E6
Thorneycroft La WOLVN WV10 ... 36 E6
Thorneycroft Rd BILS/COS WV14 ... 67 L2
Thorney Rd COVE CV2 ... 134 D7
  FOAKS/STRLY B74 ... 55 J4
Thornfield Crs BNTWD WS7 ... 18 E5
Thornfield Rd ACGN B27 ... 127 G3
Thorngrove Av SOLH B91 ... 149 G5
Thornham Wy
  ALE/KHTH/YWD B14 ... 146 B4
Thornhill Ct COV CV1 * ... 134 C1
Thornhill Dr NUN CV11 ... 99 M5
Thornhill Gv HDSW B21 ... 88 B5
Thornhill Pk FOAKS/STRLY B74 ... 55 L5
Thornhill Rd BRLYHL DY5 ... 102 C4
  COV CV1 ... 134 C1
  DUDN DY1 ... 84 D1
  FOAKS/STRLY B74 ... 55 L5
  HALE B63 ... 121 J2
  HDSW B21 ... 88 B5
  HEDN WS12 ... 12 D6
  REDE B98 ... 195 J6
  SOLH B91 ... 128 A6

SPARK B11 ....126 B2
Thornhurst Av RIDG/WDGT B32 ....105 J6
Thornleigh SEDG DY3 ....66 B8
Thornley Cl MOS/BIL B13 ....125 L4
RLSS CV31 * 207 K8
WNSFLD WV11 ....37 K4
Thornley Cft GTWY WS6 ....24 B4
Thornley Gv WALM/CURD B76 ....74 A7
Thornley St WOLV WV1 ....3 C3
Thorn Rd BVILLE B30 ....124 C6
Thorns Av BRLYHL DY5 ....102 C4
Thornsett Gv HIA/OLT B92 ....126 F7
Thorns Rd BRLYHL DY5 ....102 C5
Thorn Stile Cl RLSN CV32 ....199 J7
Thornthwaite Cl RBRY B45 ....153 G1
Thornton Cl COVW CV5 ....143 M3
OLDBY B69 ....86 A3
WWCK CV34 ....205 K4
Thornton Dr BRLYHL DY5 * 102 C4
Thornton Rd B90 ....148 D7
WASH/WDE B8 ....90 F8
WOLV WV1 ....50 F4
Thorntons Wy
NUNW/HART CV10 ....97 L2
Thornwood Cl LGLYGN/QTN B68....87 G8
Thornyfield Cl SHLY B90 ....148 A2
Thornyhill Rd SHLY B90 ....148 A2
Thornyhurst La LICHS WS14 ....27 L8
Thorpe Av BNTWD WS7 ....18 B5
MGN/WHC B75 ....57 G6
Thorpe Ct SOLH B91 ....127 K6
Thorpe Rd WSL WS1 ....4 F7
Thorpe St BNTWD WS7 ....18 B5
Thorp St DIG/EDG B5 ....6 E7
Threadneedle St COV CV1 ....134 A7
Three Acres La SHLY B90 ....147 K7
Three Broadway
LDYWD/EDGR B16 * 6 A8
Three Corner Cl SHLY B90 ....147 J5
Three Cornered Cl RLSN CV32 ......199 J3
Three Oaks Rd HLYWD B47 ....172 F1
Three Shires Oak Rd
SMTHWKW B67 ....105 K3
Three Spires Av COVN CV6 ....133 L8
Three Tuns La WOLN WV10 ....36 A3
Threlfall Dr BEWD DY12 ....163 H1
Threshers Dr SHHTH WV12 ....13 M8
Throckmorton Rd REDE B98 ....202 E6
Throne Cl BLKHTH/ROWR B65 ....86 A8
Throne Crs BLKHTH/ROWR B65 ....86 B8
Throne Rd BLKHTH/ROWR B65 ....86 A8
Throstles Cl GTB/HAM B43 ....70 D2
Thrush Rd LGLYGN/QTN B68 ....104 D3
Thruxton Cl
ALE/KHTH/YWD B14 ....146 D2
REDE B98 ....203 J2
Thurcroft Cl WASH/WDE B8 ....108 D1
Thuree Rd SMTHWKW B67 ....105 H5
Thurleigh Cl HAG/WOL DY9 ....119 M3
Thurlestone Rd COVN CV6 ....133 K5
NFLD/LBR B31 ....144 C6
Thurloe Crs RBRY B45 ....143 J4
Thurlow Cl ATHST CV9 ....63 H3
Thurlston Av HIA/OLT B92 ....127 K1
Thurlstone Dr
ETTPK/GDPK/PENN WV4 ....65 K1
Thurlstone Rd BLOX/PEL WS3 ....38 C7
Thurnmill Rd RUGBYN/HIL CV21 ....159 M8
Thursfield Rd HHTH/SAND B71 ....69 J6
RLSN CV32 ....206 F2
TPTN/OCK DY4 ....67 L7
Thurso TAM/AM/WIL B77 ....32 C8
Thurston Av OLDBY B69 ....87 J3
Thynne St WBROM B70 ....87 J3
Tibbats Cl RIDG/WDGT B32 ....123 G2
Tibberton Cl BDMR/CCFT WV3 ....49 H6
HALE B63 ....122 A2
SOLH B91 ....148 E5
Tibberton Ct BRGRVE B60 ....191 H4
Tibbets La HRBN B17 ....123 L1
Tibbington Rd TPTN/OCK DY4 ....67 J4
Tibbington Ter TPTN/OCK DY4 ....67 J4
Tiberius Cl CSHL/WTROR B46 ....93 K4
Tiber Wy RUGBYN/HIL CV21 ....160 D6
Tibland Rd ACGN B27 ....127 H4
Ticknall Cl REDW B97 ....201 L1
Tidbury Cl REDW B97 ....202 A7
Tiddington Cl CBROM B36 ....91 M4
Tideswell Cl COVS CV3 ....156 E4
Tideswell Rd PBAR/PBCH B42 ....71 G7
Tidmarsh Cl
RCOVN/BALC/EX CV7 ....151 L7
Tidmarsh Rd
RWWCK/WEL CV35 ....197 L6
Tidmington Cl
RWWCK/WEL CV35 ....204 C3
Tidworth Cft
ALE/KHTH/YWD B14 ....146 E2
Tierney Dr TPTN/OCK DY4 ....68 A7
Tiffany La COVEN WV9 ....35 K3
Tiffield Rd YDLY B25 ....125 G8
Tigley Av RIDG/WDGT B32 ....123 H4
Tilbury Cl BDMR/CCFT WV3 ....48 E8
Tilbury Gv MOS/BIL B13 ....125 H4
Tildasley St WBROM B70 ....68 D8
Tildesley Cl PENK ST19 ....10 C5
Tildesley Dr SHHTH WV12 ....37 M8
Tile Cross Rd STETCH B33 ....110 C4
Tiled House La BRLYHL DY5 ....83 M7
Tile Gv CHWD/FDBR/MGN B37 ....92 E8
Tile Hill La TLHL/CAN CV4 ....153 J4
Tilehouse REDW B97 ....202 B3
Tilehouse Green La
DOR/KN B93 ....149 K6
Tilehouse La SHLY B90 ....147 L8
The Hurst Dr TLHL/CAN CV4 ....153 H5
Tilehurst Dr TLHL/CAN CV4 ....153 H5
Tilesford Cl SHLY B90 ....148 B8
Tilewood Av COVW CV5 ....153 J1
Tilia Rd TAM/AM/WIL B77 ....32 E8
Tiller Gv MGN/WHC B75 ....57 H1
Tilley St DARL/WED WS10 ....52 C7
Tillington Cl REDE B98 ....203 J3
Tillyard Cft SLYOAK B29 ....124 A4
Tilshead Cl ALE/KHTH/YWD B14 ....146 C2
Tilsley Gv ERDW/GRVHL B23 ....71 M8
Tilston Dr BRLYHL DY5 ....84 C1
Tilton Rd BORD B9 ....108 A4
Timberdine Cl HALE B63 ....103 H1
Timberhonger La BRGRVW B61 ......190 D4
Timberlake Cl SHLY B90 ....148 F7
Timber La STRPT DY13 ....163 M8
Timberley La BKDE/SHDE B34 ....92 A3
Timbers Wy ERDW/GRVHL B24 ....91 K1
SPARK B11 ....107 J2
Timbertree Crs CDYHTH B64 ....103 J6
Timbertree Rd CDYHTH B64 ....103 J6
Times Square WSL WS1 4
Timmins Cl SOLH B91 ....128 C8
Timmis Rd BILS/COS WV14 ....66 D2
Timmins Rd HAG/WOL DY9 ....102 A4
Timothy Gv TLHL/CAN CV4 ....153 M2
Timothy Rd OLDBY B69 ....86 A6
Tinacre HI DUNHL/THL/PER WV6 .....48 D1
Tinchbourne St DUDN DY1 * 85 G4
Tindal St BHTH/HG B12 ....107 H3

Tink-a-Tank WWCK CV34 * 205 J6
Tinkers Farm Gv NFLD/LBR B31 .....144 C2
Tinkers Farm Rd NFLD/LBR B31 .....144 C2
Tinkers Green Rd
TAM/AM/WIL B77 ....46 D7
Tinkers La HOCK/TIA B94 ....174 C5
Tinmeadow Crs RBRY B45 ....144 A6
Tinsley St TPTN/OCK DY4 ....68 C8
Tintagel Cl DUNHL/THL/PER WV6 ....48 D2
Tintagel Dr DUDN DY1 ....84 C3
Tintagel Gv KNWTH CV8 ....197 M1
Tintagel Wy ALDR WS9 ....40 B6
NUN CV11 ....81 L8
Tintern Cl BRGRVW B61 ....191 J3
FOAKS/STRLY B74 ....42 C5
KIDDW DY11 ....137 K7
Tintern Crs BLOX/PEL WS3 ....38 D3
Tintern Rd BFLD/HDSWWD B20 ....38 D3
Tintern Vls BHTH/HG B12 * 107 M8
Tintern Wy BDWTH CV12 ....117 G3
BLOX/PEL WS3 ....38 D3
Tipperary Cl CBROM B36 ....91 J5
Tipper's Hill La
RCOVN/BALC/EX CV7 ....96 B7
Tippett Cl NUN CV11 ....81 L8
Tipping's HI REDW B97 ....202 A8
Tipps Stone Cl TPTN/OCK DY4 ....85 J1
Tipton Rd OLDBY B69 ....86 A3
SEDG DY3 ....66 C6
TPTN/OCK DY4 ....85 J1
Tirley Rd STETCH B33 ....109 L1
Tisdale Ri KNWTH CV8 ....179 M7
Titania Cl RBRY B45 ....143 L2
Titan Wy LICHS WS14 ....21 K5
Titchfield Cl WOLVN WV10 * 36 C1
Titford La OLDBY B69 ....104 C1
Titford Rd OLDBY B69 ....104 D1
Tithe Barn Cl
RWWCK/WEL CV35 ....204 D6
Tithe Barn La HOCK/TIA B94 ....173 M6
Tithe Cft WOLVN WV10 ....3 M2
Tithe Rd WNSFLD WV11 ....37 H7
Titterstone Rd NFLD/LBR B31 ....144 E5
Tiverton Cl KGSWFD DY6 ....101 L2
Tiverton Dr HHTH/SAND B71 ....69 C7
NUN CV11 ....81 J8
Tiverton Gv COVE CV2 ....135 H8
SMTHWKW B67 * 87 K7
Tiverton Rd COVE CV2 ....135 H8
SLYOAK B29 ....124 D3
SMTHWK B66 ....87 M8
Tiveycourt Rd COVN CV6 ....134 E2
Tividale Cft OLDBY B69 ....85 L3
Tividale St TPTN/OCK DY4 ....85 L2
Tixall Rd HLGN/YWD B28 ....126 C8
Toberland BLOX/PEL WS3 * 38 F6
Tocil Cft TLHL/CAN CV4 ....180 B1
Todenham Wy
RWWCK/WEL CV35 ....204 C3
Toler Rd NUN CV11 ....80 F8
Tollard Cl COVE CV2 ....135 K8
Toll End Rd TPTN/OCK DY4 ....68 A5
Tolley Rd KIDDW DY11 ....163 M4
Tollgate Cl NFLD/LBR B31 ....144 D5
Tollgate Dr BFLD/HDSWWD B20 ....88 D6
Tollgate La CRTAM B79 ....31 J2
Tollhouse Rd BRGRVE B60 ....191 J7
Toll House Rd RBRY B45 ....144 A6
Tollhouse Wy SMTHWK B66 ....86 F8
WMBN WV5 ....64 C6
Tolman Dr TAM/AM/WIL B77 ....46 A2
Tolson Av PDL/KGSB/FAZ B78 ....45 M5
Tolson Cft TAM/AM/WIL B77 ....46 A3
Tolworth Gdns BKHL/PFLD WV2 ....50 C6
Tolworth Hall Rd
ERDE/BCHGN B24 ....90 F2
Tom Brown St
RUGBYN/HIL CV21 ....186 F1
Tomey Rd SPARK B11 ....108 B3
Tom Henderson Cl COVS CV3 ....156 D6
Tomkinson Dr KIDDW DY11 ....163 M1
Tomkinson Rd
NUNW/HART CV10 ....98 C1
Tomlan Rd NFLD/LBR B31 ....145 G6
Tomlinson Rd CBROM B36 ....92 B4
Tompstone Rd HHTH/SAND B71 ....69 K5
Tomson Av COVN CV6 ....8 C1
Tom Ward Cl COVS CV3 ....156 B6
Tom Williams Wy
TAM/AM/WIL B77 ....46 A5
Tonadine Cl WNSFLD WV11 ....37 L4
Tonbridge Rd COVS CV3 ....155 L7
ERDE/BCHGN B24 ....90 E4
Tong St WSL WS1 ....5 K4
Top Croft Rd ERDW/GRVHL B23 ....72 C2
Topfield Wk
ALE/KHTH/YWD B14 ....146 D3
Topland Gv NFLD/LBR B31 ....144 A5
Topp's Dr BDWTH CV12 ....116 C4
Topp's Heath BDWTH CV12 ....116 C4
Top Rd BRGRVW B61 ....168 B3
RCOVN/BALC/EX CV7 ....117 L6
Topsham Cft
ALE/KHTH/YWD B14 ....125 H8
Topsham Rd SMTHWKW B67 ....87 J7
Torbay Av TAM/AM/WIL B77 ....32 C8
Torbay Rd COVW CV5 ....154 A1
Torcastle Cl COVN CV6 ....134 D6
Torc Av TAM/AM/WIL B77 ....46 C1
Torcross Av COVE CV2 ....135 G4
Torfield CDSL WV8 ....35 J3
Toronto Gdns RIDG/WDGT B32 ....105 J3
Torpoint Cl COVE CV2 ....135 G6
Torquoise Cl CNCK/NC WS11 ....17 G2
Torrance Rd RUGBYN/HIL CV21 .....186 B2
Torre Av NFLD/LBR B31 ....144 C3
Torrey Gv WASH/WDE B8 ....109 G1
Torridge TAM/AM/WIL B77 ....46 A8
Torridge Dr WNSFLD WV11 ....37 H8
Torridon Cl STRPT DY13 ....163 J6
Torridon Cft MOS/BIL B13 ....125 J4
Torridon Rd SHHTH WV12 ....37 M4
Torrington Av TLHL/CAN CV4 ....153 K5
Torrs Cl REDE B98 ....202 B3
Torside TAM/AM/WIL B77 ....46 F6
Torton La DUDN DY1 ....113 L4
Torvale Rd DUNHL/THL/PER WV6 .....47 L7
Tor Wy BLOX/PEL WS3 ....39 K2
Torwood Cl TLHL/CAN CV4 ....153 K7
Totnes Cl COVE CV2 ....135 G2
Totnes Gv SLYOAK B29 * 124 D3
Totnes Rd SMTHWKW B67 ....87 K7
Tottenham Crs KGSTG B44 ....71 M3
Touchwood Hall Cl SOLH B91 ....149 G1
Tove Ct RRUGBY CV23 ....159 M8
Towbury Cl REDE B98 ....202 D3
Towcester Cft CBROM B36 ....91 H5
Tower Cft
CHWD/FDBR/MGN B37 ....110 D1
Tower Dr BRGRVW B61 ....168 B2
Tower HI PBAR/PBCH B42 ....70 E7
Tower Rd AST/WIT B6 ....89 K6
BDWTH CV12 ....116 E5
HEDN WS12 ....12 C1
MGN/WHC B75 ....57 K6
OLDBY B69 ....86 B6

RUGBYS/DCH CV22 ....187 G4
Towers Buildings KIDD DY10 * 138 C7
Towers Cl KIDD DY10 ....138 F6
KNWTH CV8 ....197 K4
Tower St COV CV1 ....8 F3
DUDN DY1 ....85 G4
LOZ/NWT B19 ....89 H7
RLSS CV31 * 206 E6
SEDG DY3 ....66 B4
WOLV WV1 ....3 G5
WSL WS1 ....4 F3
Tower View Crs
NUNW/HART CV10 ....97 M2
Tower View Rd GTWY WS6 ....24 C5
Townend Sq WSL WS1 * 4 E4
Townend St WSLW WS2 ....4 E3
Townesend Cl WWCK CV34 ....205 K4
Town Feilds Cl COVW CV5 ....132 A6
Townfields LICH WS13 ....20 E6
Townfold BLOX/PEL WS3 ....39 L1
Townley Gdns AST/WIT B6 ....89 J4
Townsend Av BRGRVE B60 ....191 M1
SEDG DY3 ....66 B5
Townsend Cft COVS CV3 ....155 G6
Townsend Dr NUN CV11 ....99 K2
WALM/CURD B76 ....73 K6
Townsend La RRUGBY CV23 ....185 M1
Townsend Rd
RUGBYN/HIL CV21 ....187 H2
Townsend Wy DCHAMW B1 ....6 B4
Townsend Gv
CHWD/FDBR/MGN B37 ....110 D1
Townson Rd WNSFLD WV11 ....37 K5
Townwell Fold WOLV WV1 * 3 F4
Towpath Cft NFLD/LBR B31 ....126 A5
Town Rd MOS/BIL B13 ....103 G8
Toys La HALE B63 ....103 G8
Tozer St TPTN/OCK DY4 ....67 K6
Traceys Meadow RBRY B45 ....143 L6
Trafalgar Cl HEDN WS12 ....17 J1
Trafalgar Gv YDLY B25 * 108 A3
Trafalgar Rd ERDE/BCHGN B24 ....90 D2
HDSW B21 ....88 C5
MOS/BIL B13 ....125 K2
OLDBY B69 ....85 M4
SMTHWK B66 ....105 M1
Trafford Cl ATHST CV9 ....63 H3
Trafford Dr NUNW/HART CV10 ....80 A7
Trajan HI CSHL/WTROR B46 ....93 J4
Tram Cl KIDD DY10 ....138 C3
Tram Wy SMTHWK B66 ....87 G6
Tramway Cl BILS/COS WV14 ....51 K6
DARL/WED WS10 ....52 C6
Tranter Crs CNCK/NC WS11 ....16 F1
Tranter Rd WASH/WDE B8 ....90 E8
Tranwell Cl COVEN WV9 ....9 J2
Traquain Dr DUDN DY1 ....84 C2
Travellers Wy
CHWD/FDBR/MGN B37 ....92 F7
Treaford La WASH/WDE B8 ....108 F1
Treasure Cl TAM/AM/WIL B77 ....46 C1
Tredington Cl RBRY B45 ....143 J6
Tredington Pk
RWWCK/WEL CV35 ....204 C2
Tredington Rd COVW CV5 ....153 K1
Tree Acre Gv HALE B63 ....121 G1
Treedale Cl TLHL/CAN CV4 ....153 H5
Treeford Cl SOLH B91 ....148 D4
Trees Rd WSL WS1 ....5 K7
Treeton Cft STETCH B33 ....109 L1
Treetops Dr SHHTH WV12 ....38 C8
Trefoil TAM/AM/WIL B77 ....32 F6
Trefoil Cl SLYOAK B29 ....123 L6
Treforest Rd COVS CV3 ....156 A5
Tregarron Rd HALE B63 ....103 G8
Tregea Ri GTB/HAM B43 ....70 A6
Tregony Ri LICHS WS14 ....21 H7
Tregorrick Rd
RCOVN/BALC/EX CV7 ....116 E5
Tregullan Rd
RCOVN/BALC/EX CV7 ....116 F5
Trehern Cl DOR/KN B93 ....149 L3
Treherne Rd COVN CV6 ....133 M5
Trehernes Dr HAG/WOL DY9 ....119 M4
Trehurst Av PBAR/PBCH B42 ....71 G4
Trejon Rd CDYHTH B64 ....103 J5
Trelawney Rd
RCOVN/BALC/EX CV7 ....116 E6
Tremaine Gdns WOLVN WV10 ....3 H1
Tremelling Wy
RCOVN/BALC/EX CV7 ....96 D5
Tremont St WOLVN WV10 ....3 K3
Trenance Cl LICHS WS14 ....21 H6
Trenance Rd
RCOVN/BALC/EX CV7 ....116 E6
Trenchard Cl MGN/WHC B75 ....57 K8
Treneere Rd
RCOVN/BALC/EX CV7 ....116 E5
Trensale Av COVN CV6 ....154 D1
Trent Cl BNTWD WS7 ....19 H7
DUNHL/THL/PER WV6 ....48 C1
STRBR DY8 ....119 L1
Trent Crs HLYWD B47 ....172 C3
Trent Dr CBROM B36 ....92 D5
Trentham Av SHHTH WV12 ....37 L8
Trentham Cl CNCK/NC WS11 ....15 F4
NUN CV11 ....99 K3
Trentham Gdns KNWTH CV8 ....180 A8
Trentham Gv
LGLYGN/QTN B68 ....109 J8
Trentham Ri BKHL/PFLD WV2 ....50 D6
Trentham Rd COV CV1 ....155 K1
NUNW/HART CV10 ....80 E1
Trent PI BLOX/PEL WS3 ....39 H5
Trent Rd BDWTH CV12 ....117 L3
BLOX/PEL WS3 ....39 L4
CNCK/NC WS11 ....81 C8
NUN CV11 ....81 J8
Trent St DIG/EDG B5 ....7 K6
Trent Valley Rd LICH WS13 ....21 G5
Trenville Av BHTH/HG B12 ....107 M8
Tresco Cl RBRY B45 ....143 J4
Trescott Rd NFLD/LBR B31 ....144 B2
REDE B98 ....202 D2
Tresham Rd KGSTG B44 ....71 J4
COVE CV2 ....87 H5
Tresillian Rd
RCOVN/BALC/EX CV7 ....116 F5
Trevanie Av RIDG/WDGT B32 ....105 J3
Treville Cl REDE B98 ....203 J3
Treviscoe Cl
RCOVN/BALC/EX CV7 ....116 E6
Trevithick Cl BNTWD WS7 ....19 H5
Trevorne Cl BHTH/HG B12 ....107 K8
Trevor Rd BLOX/PEL WS3 ....39 K1
Trevor St WASH/WDE B8 ....90 A7
Trevor St West VAUX/NECH B7 ....90 A7
Trevor White Dr
RUGBYS/DCH CV22 ....186 A1
Trevose Av
RCOVN/BALC/EX CV7 ....116 F6
Trevose Cl BLOX/PEL WS3 * 38 F1
Trevose Retreat BHTH/HG B12 ....107 K8
Trewman Cl WALM/CURD B76 ....73 K5
Treyamon Rd DYSBK/YTR WS5 ....54 B6

Treynham Cl WLNHL WV13 ....51 G4
The Triangle COVW CV5 ....153 M1
WSNGN B18 * 88 D7
Trianon Rd BRGRVE B60 ....192 A4
Trickley Dr MGN/WHC B75 * 57 K7
Trident Cl ERDW/GRVHL B23 ....72 E6
WALM/CURD B76 ....73 K6
Trident Ct
LGN/SDN/BHAMAIR B26 ....129 G3
Trident Dr DARL/WED WS10 ....68 D2
OLDBY B69 ....86 E7
Trident Rd
LGN/SDN/BHAMAIR B26 ....129 G1
Trigo Cft CBROM B36 ....91 J5
Trimpley Cl DOR/KN B93 ....175 J2
Trimpley Dr KIDDW DY11 ....137 L6
Trimpley Gdns
ETTPK/GDPK/PENN WV4 ....65 J2
Trimpley La BEWD DY12 ....137 G2
BEWD DY12 ....137 G2
Trindle Cl DUDN DY1 ....85 H3
Trindle Rd DUDN DY1 ....85 H3
Tring Ct DUNHL/THL/PER WV6 ....49 K1
Trinity Cl CNCK/NC WS11 ....16 C3
STRBR DY8 ....101 H3
Trinity Ct CROSS B79 ....31 H7
Trinity Fids KIDD DY10 ....138 D7
Trinity Gv DARL/WED WS10 ....68 D2
Trinity Hl CSCFLD/WYGN B72 ....57 G8
Trinity La COV CV1 ....8 F4
NUN CV11 ....99 J4
Trinity Pk BHAMNEC B40 ....129 G2
Trinity PI CSCFLD/WYGN B72 * 57 G8
Trinity Rd AST/WIT B6 ....89 J4
BILS/COS WV14 ....51 K8
DUDN DY1 ....85 G4
MGN/WHC B75 ....55 H4
POL/KGSB/FAZ B78 ....60 B7
SHHTH WV12 ....38 B7
STRBR DY8 ....101 L5
Trinity Rd North WBROM B70 ....87 H4
Trinity Rd South WBROM B70 ....87 H4
Trinity St BRLYHL DY5 ....102 B2
COV CV1 ....9 G4
CRADH B64 ....103 J6
OLDBY B69 ....86 E5
RLSN CV32 ....206 D4
SMTHWK B67 ....87 H4
Trinity Ter SPARK B11 ....7 M9
Trinity Wk NUN CV11 ....99 J3
Trinity Wy WBROM B70 ....87 H4
Trippleton Av RIDG/WDGT B32 ....144 F4
Tristram Av NFLD/LBR B31 ....144 F4
Triton Cl GTWY WS6 ....25 H2
Trittiford Rd MOS/BIL B13 ....126 A3
Triumph TAM/AM/WIL B77 ....46 C2
Triumph Cl COVE CV2 ....156 C2
Trojan TAM/AM/WIL B77 ....46 C2
Tromans Cl CDYHTH B64 ....103 J6
Troon TAM/AM/WIL B77 ....47 G1
Troon Cl BLOX/PEL WS3 ....38 E2
MGN/WHC B75 ....57 H1
Troon Ct DUNHL/THL/PER WV6 ....34 B8
Troon PI STRBR DY8 ....101 G2
Trossachs Rd COVW CV5 ....153 K2
Trotter's La HHTH/SAND B71 ....68 E6
Troughton Crs COVN CV6 ....133 L8
Trouse La DARL/WED WS10 ....52 B4
Troutbeck Av RLSN CV32 ....206 A3
Troutbeck Dr BRLYHL DY5 ....101 M5
Troutbeck Rd COVW CV5 ....153 K1
Troyes Cl COVS CV3 ....155 H6
Troy Gv ALE/KHTH/YWD B14 ....146 B1
Truda St WSL WS1 ....4 D8
Trueman Cl WWCK CV34 * 205 J6
Truemans Heath La HLYWD B47 .....146 F6
Truggist La
RCOVN/BALC/EX CV7 ....152 B5
Truro Cl BLKHTH/ROWR B65 ....104 C1
LICH WS13 ....20 E7
NUN CV11 ....81 K8
Truro Dr KIDDW DY11 ....137 L8
Truro Rd DYSBK/YTR WS5 ....54 B6
Trussell Wy RUGBYS/DCH CV22 .....185 K5
Trustin Crs HIA/OLT B92 ....128 C3
Tryan Rd NUNW/HART CV10 ....80 B1
Tryon PI BILS/COS WV14 ....51 J7
Trysull Av
LGN/SDN/BHAMAIR B26 ....128 A1
Trysull Gdns BDMR/CCFT WV3 ....49 H6
Trysull Holloway WMBN WV5 ....64 A2
Trysull Rd BDMR/CCFT WV3 ....49 G6
WMBN WV5 ....64 C2
Trysull Wy DUDS DY2 ....103 J3
Tudbury Rd NFLD/LBR B31 ....144 B1
Tudman Cl WALM/CURD B76 ....73 L6
Tudor Av COVW CV5 ....132 F8
Tudor Cl BNTWD WS7 ....19 F7
DUNHL/THL/PER WV6 ....48 C1
STRBR DY8 ....101 L1
Tudor Ct TPTN/OCK DY4 ....85 L1
WNSFLD WV11 ....37 K2
WWCK CV34 ....205 K4
Tudor Crs BHAMAIR WV2 ....49 M7
BKHL/PFLD WV2 ....49 M7
TAM/AM/WIL B77 ....32 F6
Tudor Cft
CHWD/FDBR/MGN B37 ....110 D4
Tudor Gdns ERDW/GRVHL B23 ....90 C2
STRBR DY8 ....101 L1
Tudor Gv FOAKS/STRLY B74 ....55 L5
Tudor HI SCFLD/BOLD B73 ....56 E7
Tudor PI SEDG DY3 ....66 A4
Tudor Rd BEWD DY12 ....162 D2
BLKHTH/ROWR B65 ....86 A8
BNTWD WS7 ....19 J7
DARL/WED WS10 ....52 C6
HEDN WS12 ....12 D5
LGLYGN/QTN B68 ....105 G1
MOS/BIL B13 ....125 K2
NUNW/HART CV10 ....80 A7
SCFLD/BOLD B73 ....56 E7
SEDG DY3 ....66 A4
WOLVN WV10 ....50 A1
Tudor Rw LICH WS13 * 20 E7
Tudors Cl SMHTH B10 * 108 A5
Tudor St DARL/WED WS10 ....85 L1
WSNGN B18 ....88 B7
Tudor Ter DUDS DY2 ....85 L5
HRBN B17 * 106 B7
Tudor Wy GTWY WS6 ....24 D5
CNCK/NC WS11 ....16 A4
Tufnell Gv WASH/WDE B8 ....90 D2
Tugford Rd NFLD/LBR B31 ....124 A4
Tugwood La STRPT DY13 ....189 M7
Tuke PI LICH WS13 ....20 D1
Tulip Tree Av KNWTH CV8 ....179 M8
Tulliver Cl BDWTH CV12 ....116 F1
Tulliver Rd NUNW/HART CV10 ....99 M8
Tulliver St COVN CV6 ....133 M8
Tulyar Cl CBROM B36 ....91 H5
Tunnel Dr REDE B98 ....202 C3

Tunnel La ALE/KHTH/YWD B14 ....145 M1
Tunnel Rd NUNW/HART CV10 ....97 G2
WBROM B70 ....68 E5
Tunstall Rd KGSWFD DY6 ....83 L8
Tunstall Wy DARL/WED WS10 ....73 L5
Turchil Rd RUGBYS/DCH CV22 ....185 G5
Turf Cl CNCK/NC WS11 ....25 L1
Turfpits La ERDW/GRVHL B23 ....72 B7
Turf Pitts La HOCK/TIA B94 ....57 K2
Turlands Cl COVE CV2 ....135 L2
Turley St DUDN DY1 ....66 E7
Turls Hill Rd SEDG DY3 ....66 C5
Turls St SEDG DY3 ....66 C6
Turnberry Av WALM/CURD B77 ....32 F8
Turnberry Gv CDSL WV8 ....34 B8
Turnberry Rd BLOX/PEL WS3 ....38 F1
PBAR/PBCH B42 ....70 F5
Turner Av
ETTPK/GDPK/PENN WV4 ....66 D3
Turner Cl BDWTH CV12 ....116 K1
CNCK/NC WS11 ....16 C3
RUGBYN/HIL CV21 ....187 M5
Turner Dr BRLYHL DY5 ....102 B6
Turner Gv DUNHL/THL/PER WV6 ....48 D1
Turner Rd COVW CV5 ....153 K8
Turners Cft HHTH/SAND B71 ....69 L5
Turner's Gv SEDG DY3 ....84 A1
Turner's HI BLKHTH/ROWR B65 ....86 M7
Turner's Hill Rd SEDG DY3 ....84 A1
Turner's La BRLYHL DY5 ....102 A5
Turner St DUDN DY1 * 84 B2
SEDG DY3 ....84 B2
SPARK B11 ....107 L2
TPTN/OCK DY4 ....86 E1
WBROM B70 ....86 E1
Turney Rd STRBR DY8 ....101 K7
Turnham Gn
DUNHL/THL/PER WV6 ....48 C2
Turnhouse Rd CVALE B35 ....91 M1
Turnley Rd BKDE/SHDE B34 ....92 B1
Turnpike Cl
RCOVN/BALC/EX CV7 ....151 M6
SPARK B11 ....107 L2
Turnpike Dr CSHL/WTROR B46 ....93 C2
Turnpike La REDW B97 ....201 L1
Turnpike Wy COVEN WV9 ....22 F6
Turnstone Dr WOLVN WV10 ....22 F6
Turnstone Rd KIDD DY10 ....164 B6
Turpin Ct RLSS CV31 * 206 D7
Turton Cl BLOX/PEL WS3 ....38 E1
Turton Rd TPTN/OCK DY4 ....67 K4
WBROM B70 ....86 F5
Turtons Cft BILS/COS WV14 ....51 J5
Turton St KIDD DY10 ....138 E5
Turton Wy KNWTH CV8 ....198 A1
Turves Gn NFLD/LBR B31 ....144 D5
Turville Rd BFLD/HDSWWD B20 ....89 C4
Tustin Gv ACGN B27 ....127 G5
Tutbury TAM/AM/WIL B77 ....46 A6
Tutbury Av
DUNHL/THL/PER WV6 ....48 D2
TLHL/CAN CV4 ....154 D8
Tutbury Cl CNCK/NC WS11 ....17 G2
Tutehill CNCK/NC WS11 * 17 G2
Tutnall Cl BRGRVE B60 ....192 D4
Tutnall Dr HOCK/TIA B94 ....174 F7
Tutnall La BRGRVE B60 ....192 D4
Tuttle HI NUNW/HART CV10 ....80 C7
Tuxford Cl WOLVN WV10 ....3 L1
Twatling Rd RBRY B45 ....169 L4
Tweeds Well RIDG/WDGT B32 ....122 F6
Twenty One Oaks ATHST CV9 ....62 C7
Twickenham Ct STRBR DY8 * 101 G6
Twickenham Wk COVS CV3 ....202 D4
Twiners Rd REDE B98 ....202 D4
Two Gates HALE B63 ....102 F8
Two Gates La HALE B63 ....103 G8
Two Locks BRLYHL DY5 ....102 B6
Two Oaks Av BNTWD WS7 ....18 B5
Two Woods La BRLYHL DY5 ....102 C6
Twycross Gv CBROM B36 ....91 H6
Twycross Wk WWCK CV34 ....205 H3
Twydale Av OLDBY B69 ....85 M4
Twyford Cl ALDR WS9 ....40 F6
Twyford Gv WNSFLD WV11 ....37 K6
Twyford Rd WASH/WDE B8 ....90 E8
Twyning Rd BVILLE B30 ....124 F6
LDYWD/EDGR B16 ....106 D1
Tybalt Cl COVS CV3 ....156 A3
Tyber Dr BFLD/HDSWWD B20 ....88 F2
Tyberry Cl SHLY B90 ....147 L6
Tyburn Gv ERDE/BCHGN B24 ....91 H2
Tyburn Rd ERDE/BCHGN B24 ....90 D4
WOLV WV1 ....51 G4
Tyburn Sq ERDE/BCHGN B24 ....91 H2
Tyebeams BKDE/SHDE B34 ....92 A8
Tye Gdns HAG/WOL DY9 ....119 M4
Tyler Ct ERDE/BCHGN B24 ....90 E1
Tyler Gdns WLNHL WV13 ....51 M4
Tyler Gv PBAR/PBCH B42 ....70 E1
Tyler Rd WLNHL WV13 ....51 L4
Tylers Gn HWK/WKHTH B38 ....145 M4
Tylers Gv SHLY B90 ....148 D7
Tylney Cl COVS CV3 ....156 F5
DIG/EDG B5 ....107 H6
Tyndale Crs GTB/HAM B43 ....71 G2
Tyndall Wk RIDG/WDGT B32 ....122 F3
Tyne Cl BRWNH WS8 ....26 A3
CHWD/FDBR/MGN B37 ....110 F1
Tynedale Crs
ETTPK/GDPK/PENN WV4 ....66 D3
Tynedale Rd SPARK B11 ....126 D2
Tyne Gv YDLY B25 ....109 H8
Tynemouth Cl COVE CV2 ....117 H8
Tyne PI BRLYHL DY5 ....102 D3
The Tynes BRGRVE B60 ....191 H6
Tyning Cl COVEN WV9 ....35 L5
Tyninghame Av
DUNHL/THL/PER WV6 ....35 H7
Tynings La ALDR WS9 ....40 E8
Tynings La ALDR WS9 * 40 K3
Tynsall Av REDW B97 ....201 K3
Tynward Cl COVS CV3 ....154 F8
Tyrley Cl DUNHL/THL/PER WV6 ....48 D1
Tyrol Cl STRBR DY8 ....101 H7
Tyseley Hill Rd SPARK B11 ....126 E3
Tyseley La SPARK B11 ....126 E3
Tysoe Cl HOCK/TIA B94 ....175 G7
REDE B98 ....203 H4
Tysoe Cft COVS CV3 ....156 D5
Tysoe Dr MGN/WHC B75 ....71 K6
Tysoe Rd KGSTG B44 ....71 K6
Tythe Barn Cl BRGRVE B60 ....191 H6
Tythebarn Dr KGSWFD DY6 ....82 E6
Tythebarn La SHLY B90 ....147 L7
Tyzack Cl BRLYHL DY5 ....102 A3

U

Udall Rd BILS/COS WV14 ....67 H2
Uffculme Rd BVILLE B30 ....125 H3
Uffmoor Est HALE B63 ....121 J3

Uffmoor La RMSLY B62 ....121 H7
Ufton Cl SHLY B90 ....148 C2
Ufton Crs SHLY B90 ....148 B2
Ufton Cft COVW CV5 ....153 L2
Ullapool Cl REDW B97 * 202 B8
Ullenhall Rd DOR/KN B93 ....149 L7
WALM/CURD B76 ....73 K5
Ullenwood HDSW B21 ....88 B6
Ulleries Rd HIA/OLT B92 ....127 L3
Ullrik Gn ERDE/BCHGN B24 ....90 D3
Ullswater TAM/AM/WIL B77 ....46 F6
Ullswater Av NUN CV11 ....81 K7
RLSN CV32 ....206 A3
STRPT DY13 ....163 K7
Ullswater Cl RIDG/WDGT B32 ....123 K3
Ullswater Gdns KGSWFD DY6 ....83 H7
Ullswater Pl CNCK/NC WS11 ....16 C4
Ullswater Ri BRLYHL DY5 ....84 B8
Ullswater Rd BDWTH CV12 ....116 E3
COVS CV3 ....156 C4
SHHTH WV12 ....37 M4
Ulster Cl CNCK/NC WS11 ....16 E2
Ulster Dr KGSWFD DY6 ....101 J1
Ulverley Crs HIA/OLT B92 ....127 K5
Ulverley Green Rd HIA/OLT B92 ....127 K5
Ulverscroft Rd COVS CV3 ....155 G6
Ulverston RUGBYN/HIL CV21 ....161 H6
Ulwine Dr NFLD/LBR B31 ....144 E1
Umberslade Rd HOCK/TIA B94 ....173 M5
SLYOAK B29 ....124 E5
Underhill Cl REDE B98 ....202 D7
Underhill La WOLVN WV10 ....36 E2
Underhill Rd TPTN/OCK DY4 ....68 A7
WASH/WDE B8 ....108 D2
Underhill St OLDBY B69 ....86 E8
Underley Cl KGSWFD DY6 ....82 F6
The Underpass BHAMNEC B40 ....129 J1
Underwood Cl EDG B15 ....124 B2
ERDW/GRVHL B23 ....90 A1
REDW B97 ....201 L6
Underwood Rd
BFLD/HDSWWD B20 ....70 C8
Unett St LOZ/NWT B19 ....89 G8
SMTHWK B66 ....106 A1
Unett Wk LOZ/NWT B19 ....89 G8
Unicorn Av COVW CV5 ....153 J1
Unicorn Hl REDW B97 ....202 B1
Unicorn La COVW CV5 ....153 K1
Union Cl TAM/AM/WIL B77 ....46 A2
Union La WMBN WV5 ....64 B4
Union Mill St WOLV WV1 ....3 J5
Union Pl COVN CV6 ....134 D1
Union Rd AST/WIT B6 ....89 M5
OLDBY B69 ....86 C3
RLSN CV32 ....206 C4
SHLY B90 ....148 A3
SOLH B91 ....149 G1
Union Rw HDSW B21 ....88 D5
Union St BILS/COS WV14 ....51 G8
BLKHTH/ROWR B65 ....104 A4
BNTWD WS7 ....18 C8
CBHAM B2 ....7 G5
CNCK/NC WS11 ....16 C7
DARL/WED WS10 ....68 C6
DUDS DY2 ....85 G4
HAG/WOL DY9 ....102 C8
KIDD DY10 ....138 C6
REDE B98 ....202 D2
RUGBYS/DCH CV22 ....186 E3
STRBR DY8 ....119 L1
TPTN/OCK DY4 ....67 K4
TPTN/OCK DY4 ....67 K8
WBROM B70 ....87 H5
WLNHL WV13 ....51 L3
WOLV WV1 ....3 H5
WSL WS1 ....5 H3
Unity Cl DARL/WED WS10 ....68 A1
Unity Pl OLDBY B69 * 86 E5
SLYOAK B29 * 124 D3
University Rd TLHL/CAN CV4 ....153 M8
Unketts Rd SMTHWKW B67 ....105 J2
Unwin Crs STRBR DY8 ....101 J8
Upavon Cl CVALE B35 ....91 L1
Upland Gv BRGRVW B61 ....191 L1
Upland Rd BRGRVW B61 ....191 L1
SLYOAK B29 ....124 E3
Uplands COVE CV2 ....134 E8
HALE B63 ....121 H3
Uplands Av BDMR/CCFT WV3 ....49 H5
BLKHTH/ROWR B65 ....104 B2
WLNHL WV13 ....51 H4
Uplands Cl DUDS DY2 ....85 J6
PENK ST19 ....10 C3
Uplands Dr BDMR/CCFT WV3 ....49 J5
SEDG DY3 ....66 B5
Uplands Gv WLNHL WV13 ....51 G4
Uplands Rd DUDS DY2 ....85 K6
HDSW B21 ....88 B3
WLNHL WV13 ....51 G4
The Uplands SMTHWKW B67 ....105 K1
Upleadon Cl REDW B97 ....201 L7
Upper Abbey St NUN CV11 ....80 F8
Upper Ashley St RMSLY B62 ....104 A4
Upper Balsall Heath Rd
BHTH/HG B12 ....107 K7
Upper Brook St WSLW WS2 ....4 C4
Upper Cape WWCK CV34 ....205 H5
Upper Chapel St OLDBY B69 ....85 M3
Upper Church La TPTN/OCK DY4 ....67 K6
Upper Clifton Rd
SCFLD/BOLD B73 ....56 F8
Upper Cl RIDG/WDGT B32 ....123 H2
Upper Coneybere St
BHTH/HG B12 ....107 K6
Upper Crossgate Rd REDE B98 ....203 G5
Upper Dean St DIG/EDG B5 ....7 G7
Upper Eastern Green La
COVW CV5 ....132 A8
Upper Ettingshall Rd
BILS/COS WV14 ....66 E5
Upper Field Cl REDE B98 ....195 G7
Upperfield Wy COVS CV3 ....156 E4
Upper Forster St RUSH/SHEL WS4 ....5 G1
Upper Gambolds La
BRGRVE B60 ....192 A8
Upper Gough St CBHAMW B1 ....6 E8
Upper Gn DUNHL/THL/PER WV6 ....35 H8
Upper Green La WSLW WS2 ....53 G1
Upper Grosvenor Rd
BFLD/HDSWWD B20 ....88 F3
Upper Grove St RLSN CV32 ....206 C4
Upper Gungate CRTAM B79 ....31 M7
Upper Hall Cl REDE B98 ....203 H4
Upper Hall La WSL WS1 ....4 F5
Upper Highgate St
BHTH/HG B12 ....107 K6
Upper High St CDYHTH B64 ....103 H4
DARL/WED WS10 ....68 D2
Upper Hill St COV CV1 ....8 D3
RLSN CV32 * 206 E3
Upper Holland Rd
CSCFLD/WYGN B72 ....73 G1
Upper Holly Wk RLSN CV32 ....206 F4
Upper Landywood La GTWY WS6 ....24 C5
Upper Lea Cottages
KIDD DY10 * 138 D1
Upper Lichfield St WLNHL WV13 ....51 L3
Upper Ml RLSN CV32 * 206 D5
Upper Marshall St CBHAMW B1 ....6 E7
Upper Meadow Rd
RIDG/WDGT B32 ....105 G8
Upper Navigation St WSLW WS2 ....4 D3
Upper Pk COVS CV3 ....156 B8
Upper Prec COV CV1 ....8 F4
Upper Ride COVS CV3 ....156 B8
Upper Rosemary Hl
KNWTH CV8 ....179 K8
Upper Rushall St WSL WS1 ....5 G4
Upper Russell St
DARL/WED WS10 ....68 D3
Upper St John St LICHS WS14 ....20 F7
Upper St Mary's Rd
SMTHWKW B67 ....105 K4
Upper Short St WSLW WS2 ....4 C4
Upper Sneyd Rd WNSFLD WV11 ....37 M3
Upper Spon St COV CV1 ....8 B5
Upper Spring La KNWTH CV8 ....179 K6
Upper St DUNHL/THL/PER WV6 ....35 H8
Upper Sutton St AST/WIT B6 ....89 K6
Upper Thomas St AST/WIT B6 ....89 K7
Upper Trinity St BORD B9 ....7 L7
Upper Vauxhall WOLV WV1 ....2 B4
Upper Villiers St
ETTPK/GDPK/PENN WV4 ....49 M7
Upper Well St COV CV1 ....8 E3
Upper William St CBHAMW B1 ....6 C7
Upper York St COV CV1 ....8 C6
Upper Zoar St BDMR/CCFT WV3 ....2 C8
Upton Cl REDE B98 ....203 K2
Upton Dr NUN CV11 ....99 K6
Upton Gdns BILS/COS WV14 ....51 G8
Upton Gv YDLY B25 ....109 G4
Upton Rd KIDD DY10 ....138 D4
RUGBYS/DCH CV22 ....186 B2
STETCH B33 ....109 G3
Upton St DUDS DY2 ....85 G8
Upwey Av SOLH B91 ....148 E1
Usk Wy CBROM B36 ....92 D5
Usmere Rd KIDD DY10 ....138 D5
Utrillo Cl COVW CV5 ....154 A2
Uttoxeter Cl
DUNHL/THL/PER WV6 ....35 M8
Uxbridge Av COVS CV3 ....156 A3
Uxbridge Cl SEDG DY3 ....84 B3
Uxbridge Ct BNTWD WS7 * 18 D8
Uxbridge St HEDN WS12 ....17 G1
LOZ/NWT B19 ....89 H8

V

Valbourne Rd
ALE/KHTH/YWD B14 ....146 A1
Vale Av ALDR WS9 ....55 H3
Vale Cl LICH WS13 ....20 F4
RIDG/WDGT B32 ....123 K2
RUGBYN/HIL CV21 ....187 L5
Vale Ct CDYHTH B64 * 103 H6
Vale Gdns PENK ST19 ....10 C6
Valencia Cft CVALE B35 ....91 M1
Valencia Rd BRGRVE B60 ....192 B4
Valentine Cl FOAKS/STRLY B74 ....55 K6
Valentine Rd
ALE/KHTH/YWD B14 ....125 J4
LGLYGN/QTN B68 ....105 G3
Valepits Rd STETCH B33 ....110 A4
Valerie Gv GTB/HAM B43 ....70 A5
Vale Ri PENK ST19 ....10 C5
Vale Rd DUDS DY2 ....103 J1
STRPT DY13 ....188 E2
Vale Rw SEDG DY3 ....66 B8
Vales Cl WALM/CURD B76 ....73 J6
Vale St BKHL/PFLD WV2 ....50 E7
HHTH/SAND B71 ....69 J7
SEDG DY3 ....66 B8
STRBR DY8 ....101 K5
The Vale COVS CV3 ....155 M5
SPARK B11 ....125 M3
Vale Vw ALDR WS9 ....54 F2
NUNW/HART CV10 ....98 C1
Valley Cl KIDDW DY11 ....137 J5
REDW B97 ....201 L7
Valley Dr RUGBYN/HIL CV21 ....160 E4
Valley Farm Rd RBRY B45 ....143 K7
Valley Gn GTWY WS6 ....24 C3
Valley La HOCK/TIA B94 ....176 B6
LICH WS13 ....21 H5
TAM/AM/WIL B77 ....46 C6
Valley Rd BLOX/PEL WS3 ....39 H5
BRGRVW B61 ....168 C6
CDYHTH B64 ....103 J6
COVE CV2 ....134 E7
FOAKS/STRLY B74 ....55 K6
GTB/HAM B43 ....70 A6
HAG/WOL DY9 ....102 D8
HEDN WS12 ....13 H7
HIA/OLT B92 ....128 A1
HOCK/TIA B94 ....173 L4
NUNW/HART CV10 ....97 K1
RLSN CV32 ....206 F3
RMSLY B62 ....104 D5
SEDG DY3 ....66 C7
SMTHWKW B67 ....105 K2
WOLVN WV10 ....36 D8
Valley Side BLOX/PEL WS3 ....39 K3
The Valley BNTWD WS7 ....18 B5
Valley Vw BEWD DY12 ....162 C3
BRWNH WS8 ....26 E6
Vallian Cft CBROM B36 ....91 K6
Vanborough Wk DUDN DY1 ....84 E3
Vanbrugh Ct
DUNHL/THL/PER WV6 ....48 C2
Van Diemans Rd WMBN WV5 ....64 C8
Van Dyke Cl COVW CV5 ....154 A2
Van Gogh Cl CNCK/NC WS11 ....17 H3
Vanguard TAM/AM/WIL B77 ....46 B7
Vanguard Av COVW CV5 ....154 A4
Vanguard Cl CBROM B36 ....91 J5
Vanguard Rd
LGN/SDN/BHAMAIR B26 ....129 G1
Vann Cl SMTHH B10 ....108 A5
Vantage Point WBROM B70 * 87 G3
Varden Cft DIG/EDG B5 ....107 H6
Vardon Dr COVS CV3 ....181 H1
Vardon Wy HWK/WKHTH B38 ....145 H4
Varley Rd ERDE/BCHGN B24 ....91 H1
Varley V ERDE/BCHGN B24 ....91 H1
Varlins Wy HWK/WKHTH B38 ....145 H7
Varney Av WBROM B70 ....87 H3
Vaughan Cl FOAKS/STRLY B74 ....42 D7
Vaughan Gdns CSHL WV8 ....34 D1
Vaughan Rd WLNHL WV13 ....51 H4
Vaughton Dr MGN/WHC B75 ....57 J7
Vaughton St BHTH/HG B12 ....107 K5
Vaughton St South DIG/EDG B5 ....107 J6
Vauxhall Av COVW CV5 ....154 A4
WOLV WV1 ....2 B4
Vauxhall Cl COV CV1 ....9 K3
Vauxhall Crs CBROM B36 ....92 D4
Vauxhall Gdns DUDS DY2 ....85 J6
Vauxhall Gv VAUX/NECH B7 ....107 M2
Vauxhall Pl VAUX/NECH B7 ....7 M3
Vauxhall Rd STRBR DY8 ....101 L8
VAUX/NECH B7 ....7 M3
Vauxhall St COV CV1 ....9 K3
DUDN DY1 ....84 F5
Vawdrey Cl STRPT DY13 ....188 C4
Vaynor Dr REDW B97 ....202 B5
Veasey Cl NUN CV11 ....99 J2
Vecqueray St COV CV1 ....9 K5
Velsheda Rd SHLY B90 ....147 L3
Venetia Rd BORD B9 ....108 A3
Venning Gv GTB/HAM B43 ....70 B6
Ventnor Av CBROM B36 ....91 H6
LOZ/NWT B19 ....89 G6
Ventnor Cl COVE CV2 ....156 C2
LGLYGN/QTN B68 ....105 G6
Ventnor Rd HIA/OLT B92 ....128 A2
Ventnor St NUNW/HART CV10 ....81 G7
Ventura Park Rd
POL/KGSB/FAZ B78 ....45 L2
Venture Centre CNCK/NC WS11 * 16 C7
Venture Wy VAUX/NECH B7 ....7 K1
Venus Bank BEWD DY12 ....162 E2
Vera Rd
LGN/SDN/BHAMAIR B26 ....109 J6
Vera Roberts Wy KIDDW DY11 ....163 M2
Verbena Gdns VAUX/NECH B7 ....89 L8
Verbena Rd NFLD/LBR B31 ....123 K8
Vercourt FOAKS/STRLY B74 ....55 M2
Verdi Ct LICH WS13 ....21 G3
Verdon Cl PENK ST19 ....10 E6
Vere Rd RUGBYN/HIL CV21 ....187 K4
Vere St DIG/EDG B5 ....107 H5
Verity Wk STRBR DY8 ....101 J4
Vermont Gn CNCK/NC WS11 ....16 E2
Vermont Gv RLSS CV31 ....207 H7
Verney Av STETCH B33 ....110 B6
Vernier Av KGSWFD DY6 ....83 L8
Vernolds Cft DIG/EDG B5 ....7 G9
Vernon Av BFLD/HDSWWD B20 ....88 D1
BRWNH WS8 ....26 E6
RUGBYS/DCH CV22 ....187 J5
TPTN/OCK DY4 ....85 J1
Vernon Cl COV CV1 ....9 K3
FOAKS/STRLY B74 ....42 C8
REDE B98 ....194 D8
RLSN CV32 ....206 C2
RMSLY B62 ....104 A5
WLNHL WV13 ....51 J4
WNSFLD WV11 ....37 K1
Vernon Ct LDYWD/EDGR B16 ....106 C4
LGLYGN/QTN B68 * 104 F6
Vernon Rd BILS/COS WV14 ....51 K7
LDYWD/EDGR B16 ....106 B4
LGLYGN/QTN B68 ....87 G7
RMSLY B62 ....104 A5
STRPT DY13 ....188 E1
Vernons La NUNW/HART CV10 ....98 D1
Vernons Pl WOLVN WV10 ....23 H4
Vernon St WBROM B70 ....86 C2
Vernon Wy BLOX/PEL WS3 ....38 C4
Verona Cl NUN CV11 ....99 L4
Verona Rd BRGRVE B60 ....192 A4
Veronica Av
ETTPK/GDPK/PENN WV4 ....50 C8
Veronica Cl SLYOAK B29 ....123 K7
Veronica Rd KGSWFD DY6 ....83 L7
Verstone Cft NFLD/LBR B31 ....144 E3
Verstone Rd SHLY B90 ....148 A1
Verwood Cl WLNHL WV13 ....51 H4
Vesey Cl CSHL/WTROR B46 ....92 F3
FOAKS/STRLY B74 ....56 D3
Vesey Rd SCFLD/BOLD B73 ....72 F4
Vesey St CBHAMNE B4 ....7 G2
Vestry Cl CDYHTH B64 ....103 K4
Vestry Ct STRBR DY8 ....101 J7
Viaduct Dr DUNHL/THL/PER WV6 ....35 M7
Viaduct St VAUX/NECH B7 ....7 M4
Vibart Rd
LGN/SDN/BHAMAIR B26 ....109 K5
Vicarage Cl ATHST CV9 ....63 J6
BRGRVE B60 ....191 M5
BRLYHL DY5 ....102 A6
BRWNH WS8 ....26 E5
BVILLE B30 ....124 F6
PBAR/PBCH B42 ....71 H6
POL/KGSB/FAZ B78 ....47 K8
TPTN/OCK DY4 ....67 J8
Vicarage Crs KIDD DY10 ....138 D8
REDW B97 ....202 A2
Vicarage Fld WWCK CV34 ....205 M5
Vicarage Gdns KNWTH CV8 * 197 L3
RMSLY B62 ....104 B4
WALM/CURD B76 ....73 K6
Vicarage Hl POL/KGSB/FAZ B78 ....58 F4
RUGBYN/HIL CV21 ....187 J1
Vicarage La BRLYHL DY5 ....84 B5
CSHL/WTROR B46 ....92 F3
RCOVN/BALC/EX CV7 ....116 B6
Vicarage Pl WSL WS1 ....4 E5
Vicarage Prospect DUDN DY1 ....84 F4
Vicarage Rd
ALE/KHTH/YWD B14 ....125 G6
AST/WIT B6 ....89 L6
BILS/COS WV14 ....67 G6
BKHL/PFLD WV2 ....3 H8
BLOX/PEL WS3 ....39 L3
BRWNH WS8 ....26 D6
DARL/WED WS10 ....68 D2
EDG B15 ....106 D5
ETTPK/GDPK/PENN WV4 ....65 J2
HAG/WOL DY9 ....102 D8
HHTH/SAND B71 ....69 H7
HOCK/TIA B94 ....174 A2
HOCK/TIA B94 ....175 J6
HRBN B17 ....105 M8
KIDD DY10 ....165 J3
KNWTH CV8 ....180 F1
LGLYGN/QTN B68 ....104 F1
RLSN CV32 ....206 E2
RMSLY B62 ....104 A5
RUGBYS/DCH CV22 ....186 D3
SEDG DY3 ....66 C8
SMTHWKW B67 ....87 K8
STETCH B33 ....109 J4
STRBR DY8 ....101 H6
WNSFLD WV11 ....36 F7
WOLVN WV10 ....14 C7
WSNGN B18 ....88 E6
Vicarage Rd West DUDN DY1 ....67 G7
Vicarage St LGLYGN/QTN B68 ....86 F8
NUN CV11 ....99 G1
Vicarage Ter WSLW WS2 ....4 A6
Vicarage Vw REDW B97 ....202 B2
Vicarage Wk WSL WS1 ....4 E5
Vicar St DARL/WED WS10 ....68 E2
DUDS DY2 ....85 G5
KIDD DY10 ....138 C7
SEDG DY3 ....66 C8
Vicars Wk HAG/WOL DY9 ....120 C3
Viceroy Cl EDG B15 ....107 G7
KGSWFD DY6 ....83 L8
Victor Cl BKHL/PFLD WV2 ....50 F7
Victoria Ar WOLV WV1 ....2 F5
Victoria Av BLOX/PEL WS3 ....39 G4
RMSLY B62 ....104 D7
RUGBYN/HIL CV21 ....186 D2
SMTHH B10 * 108 B6
SMTHWK B66 ....87 L8
Victoria Br BEWD DY12 ....136 B2
RLSS CV31 ....206 D5
Victoria Ct COVW CV5 * 154 B1
Victoria Dr POL/KGSB/FAZ B78 ....45 L5
Victoria Gdns CDYHTH B64 * 103 K3
LICH WS13 ....20 D7
Victoria Gv WMBN WV5 ....64 E5
Victoria Ms OLDBY B69 ....104 D2
RUSH/SHEL WS4 ....53 L2
Victoria Park Rd SMTHWK B66 ....87 M8
Victoria Pas WOLV WV1 ....2 F5
Victoria Pl DARL/WED WS10 * 52 B5
KIDDW DY11 ....163 M2
Victoria Rd ACGN B27 ....127 G3
AST/WIT B6 ....89 J6
ATHST CV9 ....63 K7
BDMR/CCFT WV3 ....49 J6
BLOX/PEL WS3 ....39 L2
BRGRVW B61 ....167 K6
BRGRVW B61 ....191 L2
BRLYHL DY5 ....102 E4
BVILLE B30 ....124 E6
CDYHTH B64 ....103 K3
CRTAM B79 ....32 A8
CSCFLD/WYGN B72 ....57 G8
DARL/WED WS10 ....52 B7
DUNHL/THL/PER WV6 ....35 J8
ERDW/GRVHL B23 ....90 B2
HDSW B21 ....88 C6
HRBN B17 ....105 M8
LGLYGN/QTN B68 ....87 G7
NUNW/HART CV10 ....79 M5
RLSS CV31 ....206 C5
RMSLY B62 ....104 B5
SEDG DY3 ....66 C5
STETCH B33 ....109 H2
TPTN/OCK DY4 ....67 K8
WOLVN WV10 ....36 D8
Victoria Sq CBHAMNW B3 ....6 E5
Victoria St BORD B9 ....108 B3
BRLYHL DY5 ....84 A6
BRLYHL DY5 ....102 B2
CNCK/NC WS11 ....16 B5
CNCK/NC WS11 ....16 C1
COV CV1 ....9 H2
DARL/WED WS10 ....68 C3
HALE B63 ....121 L1
HEDN WS12 ....13 G8
KGSWFD DY6 ....82 F4
NUN CV11 ....98 F1
REDE B98 ....202 C1
RLSS CV31 ....206 C6
RUGBYN/HIL CV21 ....186 C2
STRBR DY8 ....101 L8
WBROM B70 ....68 D8
WBROM B70 ....87 G2
WLNHL WV13 ....51 L2
WOLV WV1 ....2 F6
WWCK CV34 ....205 H6
Victoria Ter RLSS CV31 ....206 D6
RUSH/SHEL WS4 ....53 K2
Victor Rd HIA/OLT B92 ....128 C2
WSNGN B18 ....88 C7
Victor St BLOX/PEL WS3 ....39 L4
WSL WS1 ....4 E8
Victory Av BNTWD WS7 ....18 D6
DARL/WED WS10 ....68 A1
Victory Cl HEDN WS12 ....17 J1
STRPT DY13 ....188 F3
Victory La WSLW WS2 ....52 E1
Victory Ri HHTH/SAND B71 ....69 H8
Victory Rd COVN CV6 ....134 C5
View Dr DUDS DY2 ....85 J5
Viewfield Av HEDN WS12 ....12 D6
Viewfield Crs SEDG DY3 ....66 B6
Viewlands Dr
DUNHL/THL/PER WV6 ....48 E3
View Point OLDBY B69 ....85 M5
View St HEDN WS12 ....12 D7
Vigo Cl ALDR WS9 ....40 D3
Vigo Pl ALDR WS9 ....40 E6
Vigo Rd ALDR WS9 ....40 D3
Vigo Ter ALDR WS9 ....40 D2
Viking Ri BLKHTH/ROWR B65 ....104 A1
Villa Cl BDWTH CV12 ....117 M4
Villa Crs BDWTH CV12 ....117 M4
Village Rd AST/WIT B6 ....89 L4
The Village KGSWFD DY6 ....83 J6
Village Wy BILS/COS WV14 ....50 F8
Villa Rd COVN CV6 ....133 M7
LOZ/NWT B19 ....88 F6
Villa St LOZ/NWT B19 ....88 F6
STRBR DY8 ....101 L5
Villa Wk LOZ/NWT B19 ....89 G7
Villette Gv ALE/KHTH/YWD B14 ....147 G1
Villiers Av BILS/COS WV14 ....51 H7
Villiers Rd BRGRVE B60 ....191 H6
KNWTH CV8 ....179 M8
Villiers St COVE CV2 ....9 M3
KIDD DY10 ....138 E8
NUN CV11 ....81 H8
RLSN CV32 ....206 E4
WLNHL WV13 ....51 L3
WSL WS1 ....4 E8
WSNGN B18 ....88 C8
Vimy Rd DARL/WED WS10 ....68 E1
MOS/BIL B13 ....125 M5
Vincent Cl BHTH/HG B12 ....107 K7
Vincent Dr EDG B15 ....124 B2
Vincent Pde BHTH/HG B12 ....107 K7
Vincent Rd MGN/WHC B75 ....57 J6
Vincent St BHTH/HG B12 ....107 K8
COV CV1 ....8 C5
RLSN CV32 ....206 E4
WSL WS1 ....5 G8
Vince St SMTHWK B66 ....105 L2
Vinculum Wy WLNHL WV13 ....51 M5
Vine Av BHTH/HG B12 ....107 L8
Vinecote Rd COVN CV6 ....134 D1
Vine Ct WWCK CV34 * 205 K5
Vine Crs HHTH/SAND B71 ....69 H7
Vine Gdns CDYHTH B64 ....103 K3
Vine La CNCK/NC WS11 ....16 B8
HAG/WOL DY9 ....141 K2
HALE B63 ....121 M2
STRBR DY8 * 101 J4
WWCK CV34 ....205 J5
The Vineries ACGN B27 ....127 J1
Vine St AST/WIT B6 ....89 M6
BRLYHL DY5 ....84 C8
COV CV1 ....9 H3
KIDD DY10 ....138 E5
REDW B97 ....202 B1
STRBR DY8 ....101 J4
Vineyard Rd NFLD/LBR B31 ....123 K8
Vinnall Gv RIDG/WDGT B32 ....122 F5
Vintage Cl BKDE/SHDE B34 ....91 L8
Vinyard Cl WSNGN B18 ....88 D6
Violet Cl COVE CV2 ....135 G3
RRUGBY CV23 ....161 J5
Violet Cft TPTN/OCK DY4 ....67 M4
Violet La HAG/WOL DY9 ....141 J1
Virginia Dr
ETTPK/GDPK/PENN WV4 ....65 K1
Virginia Pl NUNW/HART CV10 ....98 C2
Virginia Rd COV CV1 ....9 J3
Viscount Cl CVALE B35 ....91 L3
RLSS CV31 ....206 D7
Viscount Rd BNTWD WS7 ....18 C4
Vista Gn HWK/WKHTH B38 ....145 M4
The Vista SEDG DY3 ....66 B4
Vittoria St CBHAMW B1 ....6 C2
SMTHWK B66 ....88 B7
Vivian Cl HRBN B17 ....106 A8
Vivian Rd HRBN B17 ....106 A8
Vixen Cl WALM/CURD B76 ....73 H6
Vogue Cl COV CV1 ....9 J3
Voyager Dr CNCK/NC WS11 ....16 D7
Vulcan Rd BILS/COS WV14 ....51 K8
LICH WS13 ....21 J4
SOLH B91 ....128 A7
Vyrnwy Gv HWK/WKHTH B38 ....145 J5
Vyse St AST/WIT B6 ....89 M5
WSNGN B18 ....6 C1

W

Wackrill Dr RLSN CV32 ....207 G2
Waddell Cl BILS/COS WV14 ....66 D4
Waddens Brook La
WNSFLD WV11 ....37 J8
Waddington Av GTB/HAM B43 ....70 C4
Wade Av COVS CV3 ....154 F8
Wadebridge Dr NUN CV11 ....99 K1
Wade Gv WWCK CV34 ....205 J3
Wadesmill Lawns WOLVN WV10 ....36 C1
Wade St LICH WS13 ....20 F6
Wadham Cl OLDBY B69 ....86 A7
Wadhurst Rd HRBN B17 ....105 M3
Wadleys Rd SOLH B91 ....127 K7
Waen Cl TPTN/OCK DY4 ....67 M5
Waggoners Cl BRGRVE B60 ....191 J7
KNWTH CV8 ....182 A8
Waggoner's La
POL/KGSB/FAZ B78 ....44 C5
Waggon La KIDD DY10 ....139 J2
Waggon St CDYHTH B64 ....103 K3
Waggon Wk HWK/WKHTH B38 ....145 G5
Wagoners Cl WASH/WDE B8 ....90 D7
Wagon La HIA/OLT B92 ....127 K1
LGN/SDN/BHAMAIR B26 ....109 L8
Wagstaff Cl BILS/COS WV14 ....67 H5
Wainbody Av North COVS CV3 ....154 E8
Wainbody Av South COVS CV3 ....180 D1
Wainrigg TAM/AM/WIL B77 ....46 F6
Wainwright Cl KGSWFD DY6 ....82 E6
Wainwright St AST/WIT B6 ....89 L6
Waite Rd WLNHL WV13 ....51 J5
Wakefield Cl ATHST CV9 ....76 F1
COVS CV3 ....156 D6
SCFLD/BOLD B73 ....72 E3
Wakefield Ct MOS/BIL B13 * 125 M3
Wakefield Gv CSHL/WTROR B46 ....92 F2
Wakeford Cl NUNW/HART CV10 ....78 E2
Wakeford Rd NFLD/LBR B31 ....145 G4
Wake Green Pk MOS/BIL B13 ....125 M3
Wake Green Rd MOS/BIL B13 ....125 L3
TPTN/OCK DY4 ....67 L4
Wake Gv WWCK CV34 ....204 F8
Wakehurst Cl NUN CV11 ....99 K5
Wakelam Gdns GTB/HAM B43 ....70 B4
Wakeley Hl
ETTPK/GDPK/PENN WV4 ....65 L2
Wakelin Rd SHLY B90 ....147 M6
Wakeman Ct WNSFLD WV11 ....37 K2
Wakeman Dr OLDBY B69 ....85 M5
Wakeman Gv STETCH B33 ....110 B6
Wakes Cl WLNHL WV13 ....51 M4
Wakes Rd DARL/WED WS10 ....68 E3
Walcot Cl MGN/WHC B75 ....56 F2
Walcot Dr GTB/HAM B43 ....70 C7
Walcot Gdns BILS/COS WV14 ....50 F8
Walcot Gn DOR/KN B93 ....175 L3
Waldale Cl SHHTH WV12 ....38 A4
Walden Gdns
ETTPK/GDPK/PENN WV4 ....49 J7
Walden Rd SPARK B11 ....126 E2
Waldeve Gv HIA/OLT B92 ....128 D5
Waldley Gv ERDE/BCHGN B24 ....91 G2
Waldron Av BRLYHL DY5 ....101 M3
Waldron Cl DARL/WED WS10 ....52 D7
Waldrons Moor
ALE/KHTH/YWD B14 ....125 G8
Walford Av BDMR/CCFT WV3 ....49 K5
Walford Dr HIA/OLT B92 ....128 B2
Walford Gv WWCK CV34 ....205 K4
Walford Pl RUGBYN/HIL CV21 ....187 K5
Walford Rd SPARK B11 ....108 A7
Walford St OLDBY B69 ....85 K3
Walhouse Cl WSL WS1 ....5 H3
Walhouse Dr PENK ST19 ....10 D6
Walhouse Rd WSL WS1 ....5 H3
Walhouse St CNCK/NC WS11 ....16 C5
Walker Av BRLYHL DY5 ....102 B6
HAG/WOL DY9 ....120 B2
OLDBY B69 ....86 A6
WOLVN WV10 ....36 C5
Walker Dr KIDD DY10 ....138 E4
VAUX/NECH B7 ....90 C5
Walker Pl BLOX/PEL WS3 ....39 J5
Walker Rd BLOX/PEL WS3 ....39 H5
Walkers Cft LICH WS13 ....21 G3
Walkers Fold SHHTH WV12 ....38 B7
Walkers Heath Rd
HWK/WKHTH B38 ....145 M4
Walkers Orch KNWTH CV8 ....180 F7
Walkers Ri HEDN WS12 ....13 H5
Walkers Rd REDE B98 ....195 J7
Walker St DUDS DY2 ....103 G1
TPTN/OCK DY4 ....68 A6
Walkers Wy CSHL/WTROR B46 ....93 L7
RCOVN/BALC/EX CV7 ....116 D4
Walk La WMBN WV5 ....64 E7
Walkmill La CNCK/NC WS11 ....16 B8
The Walk SEDG DY3 ....66 B4
Walkwood Crs REDW B97 ....202 A7
Walkwood Rd REDW B97 ....202 A7
Wallace Cl CNCK/NC WS11 ....17 K8
OLDBY B69 ....86 B7
Wallace Ct GTWY WS6 ....24 B4
Wallace Ri CDYHTH B64 ....103 J6
Wallace Rd BILS/COS WV14 ....67 L2
BRWNH WS8 ....26 C5
COVN CV6 ....133 L5
OLDBY B69 ....86 B7
SLYOAK B29 ....124 F3
Wall Av CSHL/WTROR B46 ....93 K8
Wallbank Rd WASH/WDE B8 ....90 E7
Wallbrook St BILS/COS WV14 ....67 H5
Wall Cft ALDR WS9 ....40 F6
Wall Dr FOAKS/STRLY B74 ....56 D1
Wall End Cl WSLW WS2 ....38 E6
Waller Cl RWWCK/WEL CV35 ....197 K6
Waller St RLSN CV32 ....206 E3
Wallface HHTH/SAND B71 ....68 E6
Wallheath Crs ALDR WS9 ....27 J8
Wall Heath La ALDR WS9 ....41 K1
Wall Hill Ct
RCOVN/BALC/EX CV7 * 96 C3
Wall Hill Rd
RCOVN/BALC/EX CV7 ....114 A6
Wallhouse La BRGRVE B60 ....200 D8
REDW B97 ....201 G8
Walling Cft BILS/COS WV14 ....66 F2
Wallingford Av NUN CV11 ....81 K6
Wallington Cl BLOX/PEL WS3 ....38 F3

Wallington Heath
  BLOX/PEL WS3 ....38 F3
Wall Island LICHS WS14 * ...28 C1
Wall La LICHS WS14 ....28 C2
Wallows La WS1 ....53 G7
Wallows Pl BRLYHL DY5 ....84 A8
Wallows Rd BRLYHL DY5 ....102 A1
Wallows Wd SEDG DY3 ....83 L1
Wallsgrove Cl RLSN CV32 ....206 F2
Wall St WOLV WV1 ....50 E3
Wall Well HALE B63 ....121 K2
Wall Well La HALE B63 ....121 K2
Walmead Cft HRBN B17 ....105 K6
Walmer Wy ERDW/GRVHL B23 ...71 M8
The Walmers ALDR WS9 ....40 F6
Walmer Meadow ALDR WS9 ...40 F6
Walmer Wy
  CHWD/FDBR/MGN B37 ....111 G2
Walmesley Wy NFLD/LBR B31 ...144 G2
Walmley Ash Rd
  WALM/CURD B76 ....73 K6
Walmley Cl HALE B63 ....102 F6
  WALM/CURD B76 ....73 K5
Walmley Rd MGN/WHC B75 ...73 J1
Walnut Av CDSL WV8 ....34 C7
Walnut Cl
  CHWD/FDBR/MGN B37 ....110 F4
  CNCK/NC WS11 ....16 D2
  HAG/WOL DY9 ....119 M4
  NUNW/HART CV10 ....79 L5
  NUNW/HART CV10 ....80 C7
Walnut Cft ATHST CV9 ....62 A5
Walnut Dr BDMR/CCFT WV3 ...49 H4
  CNCK/NC WS11 ....16 D3
  RLSN CV32 ....206 F2
  SMTHWK B66 ....87 M8
Walnut Gv LICHS WS14 ....21 K6
  STRPT DY13 ....189 G1
Walnut La BRGRVE B60 ....192 B5
  DARL/WED WS10 ....68 E3
Walnut Rd DSYBK/YTR WS5 ...69 G2
Walnut St COVE CV2 ....134 F3
Walnut Tree Cl KNWTH CV8 ...197 L2
Walnut Wy NFLD/LBR B31 ....144 D5
  RUGBYS/DCH CV22 ....185 M4
Walpole St DUNHL/THL/PER WV6 ...2 B2
Walpole Wk WBROM B70 ....87 H4
Walsal End La HALE/OLT B92 ...31 M4
Walsall End La HALE/OLT B92 ...31 M4
Walsall Rd ALDR WS9 ....40 C3
Walsall St ALDR WS9 ....54 D1
  ALDR WS9 ....40 D1
  BLOX/PEL WS3 ....39 L3
  CNCK/NC WS11 ....15 G1
  DARL/WED WS10 ....52 C7
  DSYBK/YTR WS5 ....69 K1
  FOAKS/STRLY B74 ....42 A4
  GTWY WS6 ....24 E1
  HHTH/SAND B71 ....69 J8
  LICHS WS13 ....21 J5
  LICHS WS14 ....27 J5
  PBAR/PBCH B42 ....70 E5
  WLNHL WV13 ....51 M3
Walsall St BILS/COS WV14 ....51 H8
  DARL/WED WS10 ....52 B7
  DARL/WED WS10 ....68 D2
  TLHL/CAN WS13 ....153 L6
  WBROM B70 ....87 H2
  WLNHL WV13 ....51 M3
  WOLV WV1 ....3 J6
Walsall Wood Rd ALDR WS9 ...40 E8
Walsgrave Cl HALE/OLT B92 ...128 B6
Walsgrave Gdns COVE CV2 ...135 L6
Walsgrave Rd COVE CV2 ....9 L2
Walsham Cft BKDE/SHDE B34 ...92 A8
Walsh Dr WALM/CURD B76 ....73 K1
Walsh Gv ERDW/GRVHL B23 ...72 B5
Walsh La RCOVN/BALC/EX CV7 ...131 J3
Walsingham Dr
  NUNW/HART CV10 ....98 E2
Walsingham St WSL WS1 ....5 J5
Walstead Rd DSYBK/YTR WS5 ...53 K8
Walstead Rd West
  DSYBK/YTR WS5 ....53 J8
Waltdene Cl GTB/HAM B43 ....70 C3
Walter Cobb Dr SCFLD/BOLD B73...72 E4
Walter Nash Rd East
  KIDDW DY11 ....163 L4
Walter Nash Rd West
  KIDDW DY11 ....163 L4
Walter Rd BILS/COS WV14 ....51 K8
  SMTHWK B67 ....87 J7
Walters Cl NFLD/LBR B31 ....144 D7
Walter Scott Rd BDWTH CV12 ...117 G4
Walters Rd LGLYGN/QTN B68 ...104 E6
Walters Rw DUDN DY1 ....84 E4
Walter St BLOX/PEL WS3 ....39 L4
  VAUX/NECH B7 ....89 M7
  WBROM B70 ....87 H3
Waltham Gv ERDRVW B61 ....191 J4
Waltham Crs NUNW/HART CV10...79 M8
Waltham Gv KGSTG B44 ....71 J3
Walthamstow Ct BRLYHL DY5...102 B4
Walton Av BLKHTH/ROWR B65 ...103 H5
Walton Cl BLKHTH/ROWR B65 ...103 L1
  COVS CV3 ....156 C6
  HALE B63 ....121 J5
  KIDDW DY11 ....163 M3
  NUN CV11 ....99 L6
  REDE B98 ....203 J2
  STRPT DY13 ....188 B4
Walton Crs
  ETTPK/GDPK/PENN WV4 ....50 C8
Walton Cft SOLH B91 ....148 F4
Walton Dr HAG/WOL DY9 ....102 A8
Walton Gdns CDSL WV8 ....34 C7
Walton Heath BLOX/PEL WS3 ...38 D2
Walton Heath Rd WS3 ...145 M3
Walton Pool La HAG/WOL DY9 ...141 L8
Walton Ri HAG/WOL DY9 ....141 L2
Walton Rd ALDR WS9 ....40 E4
  BRGRVW B61 ....191 L1
  DARL/WED WS10 ....69 G3
  ETTPK/GDPK/PENN WV4 ....50 D8
  LGLYGN/QTN B68 ....105 G4
  STRBR DY8 ....101 L7
Walton St TPTN/OCK DY4 ....67 K8
Wanderers Av BKHL/PFLD WV2 ...3 M7
Wanderer Wk ERDE/BCHGN B24 ...91 J4
Wandle Gv SPARK B11 ....126 E2
Wandsworth Rd KGSTG B44 ....71 J1
Wanley Rd COVS CV3 ....155 H7
Wannerton Rd KIDD DY10 ....139 H4
Wansbeck Gv HWK/WKHTH B38 ...145 J5
Wansbeck Wk SEDG DY3 ....66 D7
Wansfell Cl TLHL/CAN WS13 ...153 L6
Wanstead Rd WS9 ...93 J4
Wantage Rd CSHL/WTROR B46 ...93 J4
Wappenbury Cl COVS CV3 ....135 G5
Wappenbury Rd COVE CV2 ....135 G5
Wapping La REDE B98 ....195 M6
Warbage La BDMR/HAM DY9...165 K5
Warbank Cl ALVE B48 ....170 E7
Ward Cl WASH/WDE B8 ....90 E8
Warden Av SCFLD/BOLD B73...72 D5
Warden Rd COVN CV6 ....133 M7
Ward End Cl WASH/WDE B8 ...90 E7
Ward End Hall Gv WASH/WDE B8...90 E7
Ward End Park Rd
  WASH/WDE B8 ....90 D8

Wardend Rd WASH/WDE B8 ....90 E8
Warden Rd COVN CV6 ....133 M7
  SCFLD/BOLD B73 ....72 D5
The Wardens Av COVW CV5 ....132 F7
The Wardens KNWTH CV8 ....180 A8
Ward Gv
  ETTPK/GDPK/PENN WV4 ....49 M7
  WWCK CV34 ....205 M6
Wardle Rd MGN/WHC B75 ....56 E1
Wardle Pl HEDN WS12 ....12 B8
Wardles La GTWY WS6 ....24 D3
Wardle St CRTAM B79 ....31 L8
Wardlow Cl
  ETTPK/GDPK/PENN WV4 ....49 M7
Wardlow Rd VAUX/NECH B7 ...89 L8
Wardour Cl
  CHWD/FDBR/MGN B37 ....111 G3
Wardour Dr
  CHWD/FDBR/MGN B37 ....111 G3
Wardour Gv KGSTG B44 ....72 A5
Ward Rd CDSL WV8 ....34 C7
  ETTPK/GDPK/PENN WV4 ....50 B8
  STRPT DY13 ....188 F4
Ward St BILS/COS WV14 ....66 F5
  BKHL/PFLD WV2 ....50 F7
  HEDN WS12 ....12 D7
  LOZ/NWT B19 ....7 G1
  WLNHL WV13 ....51 M2
  WOLV WV1 ....3 J3
Wareham Gn COVE CV2 ....135 L8
Wareham Rd RBRY B45 ....143 M3
Wareing Dr ERDW/GRVHL B23 ...72 B5
Waresley Court Rd
  KIDDW DY11 ....189 L1
Waresley Pk KIDDW DY11 ....189 M5
Waresley Rd KIDDW DY11 ....189 L1
Warewell Cl WSL WS1 ....5 J5
Warewell St WSL WS1 ....5 G4
Waring Cl TPTN/OCK DY4 ....67 J5
Waring Rd TPTN/OCK DY4 ....67 L5
Warings Green Rd
  HOCK/TIA B94 ....174 B5
The Warings WMBN WV5 ....82 D1
War La HRBN B17 ....105 M8
Warley Cft LGLYGN/QTN B68 ...105 H5
Warley Hall Rd
  LGLYGN/QTN B68 ....105 H4
Warley Rd LGLYGN/QTN B68 ...87 G3
Warmington Cl COVS CV3 ....156 C5
Warmington Dr
  SCFLD/BOLD B73 ....72 F1
Warmington Gv
  RWWCK/WEL CV35 ....204 F5
Warmington Rd HLYWD B47 ...146 E2
  LGN/SDN/BHAMAIR B26 ....110 A8
Warmley Cl
  DUNHL/THL/PER WV6 ....35 M8
  SOLH B91 ....128 B8
Warmwell Cl COVE CV2 ....156 D1
Warneford Ms RLSS CV31 * 206 E6
Warner Cl WWCK CV34 ....205 H4
Warner Dr BRLYHL DY5 ....102 B4
Warner Pl BLOX/PEL WS3 * 39 K7
  CDSL WV8 ....34 D2
  DARL/WED WS10 ....52 D8
Warner Rw COVN CV6 ....134 D6
Warner St BHTH/HG B12 ....7 L9
Warners Wk SMTHWK B10 ....108 A5
Warple Rd RIDG/WDGT B32 ...105 G8
Warren Av ERDW/GRVHL B23 ...72 B8
  WOLVN WV10 ....36 D8
Warren Cl HEDN WS12 ....13 J8
  LICHS WS14 ....21 J7
  RLSN CV32 ....206 D2
  TPTN/OCK DY4 ....67 K6
Warren Dr BLKHTH/ROWR B65 ...85 K8
  DOR/KN B93 ....175 L2
  SEDG DY3 ....66 A3
Warren Farm Rd KGSTG B44 ...71 K5
Warren Fld KNWTH CV8 ....182 E4
Warren Gdns KGSWFD DY6 ....83 G7
Warren Gn TLHL/CAN CV4 ....153 K5
Warren Gv WASH/WDE B8 * 90 C7
Warren Hill Rd KGSTG B44 ....71 L6
Warren House Wk
  WALM/CURD B76 ....73 K4
Warren La RBRY B45 ....169 M2
Warren Pl BRWNH WS8 ....26 E6
Warren Rd BNTWD WS7 ....18 E3
  BVILLE B30 ....124 E6
  KGSTG B44 ....71 L7
  RUGBYS/DCH CV22 ....187 H4
  WASH/WDE B8 ....90 C7
Warrens Cft DSYBK/YTR WS5 ...54 B8
Warrens End WHK/WKHTH B38 ...145 K5
Warrens Hall Rd DUDS DY2 ...85 J4
Warrington Cl WALM/CURD B76...73 L4
Warrington Dr
  ERDW/GRVHL B23 ....72 B6
Warsash Cl WOLV WV1 ....50 F1
Warstock La
  ALE/KHTH/YWD B14 ....146 E1
Warstock Rd
  ALE/KHTH/YWD B14 ....146 E1
Warston Av RIDG/WDGT B32 ...123 H4
Warstone Cl BEWD DY12 ....163 H1
Warstone Dr HHTH/SAND B71 ...87 J1
Warstone La CBHAMW B1 ....6 C2
Warstone Ms WSNGN B18 * ...6 C2
Warstone Pde East WSNGN B18...6 C2
Warstone Rd WOLVN WV10 ...23 M4
Warstones Crs
  ETTPK/GDPK/PENN WV4 ....49 H8
Warstones Dr
  ETTPK/GDPK/PENN WV4 ....49 G8
Warstones Gdns
  ETTPK/GDPK/PENN WV4 ....49 G7
Warstones Rd
  ETTPK/GDPK/PENN WV4 ....65 H1
Warstone Ter HDSW B21 ....88 C5
Wartell Bank KGSWFD DY6 ....83 H6
Warton Cl KNWTH CV8 ....198 A1
Warwards La SLYOAK B29 ....124 E4
Warwell La
  LGN/SDN/BHAMAIR B26 ....109 H7
Warwick Av BRGRVE B60 ....191 L5
  DARL/WED WS10 ....69 G2
  DUNHL/THL/PER WV6 ....48 D7
  WLNHL WV13 ....52 B3
Warwick Cl CNCK/NC WS11 ...16 D5
  LGLYGN/QTN B68 ....104 F3
  WBROM B70 ....68 C5
Warwick Ct RLSN CV32 * 206 D4
  DARL/WED WS10 ....69 G2
Warwick Crest EDG B15 * 106 F1
Warwick Dr ATHST CV9 ....63 H1
  CDSL WV8 ....34 C2
Warwick Gdns
  NUNW/HART CV10 ....98 C1
  OLDBY B69 ....86 A3
Warwick Gra KIDD DY10 ....127 K6
Warwick Hall Gdns BRGRVE B60...191 L5
Warwick Hwy REDE B98 ....202 F4
Warwick La COV CV1 ....8 E5
Warwick New Rd RLSN CV32 ...206 B5
Warwick Pas CBHAM B2 ....7 G5
Warwick Pl RLSN CV32 ....206 B5
  WOLVN WV10 ....3 H1

Warwick Rd COVS CV3 ....8 D9
  DOR/KN B93 ....149 M6
  DUDS DY2 ....103 J2
  KNWTH CV8 ....183 L1
  KNWTH CV8 ....197 K2
  LGLYGN/QTN B68 ....105 H6
  SCFLD/BOLD B73 ....72 A3
  SOLH B91 ....127 K6
  SOLH B91 ....149 H2
  SPARK B11 ....108 A8
  STRBR DY8 ....101 H4
  TAM/AM/WIL B77 ....46 C1
Warwick Rw COV CV1 ....8 C6
Warwick St BHTH/HG B12 ....7 L8
  BILS/COS WV14 ....51 J8
  COVW CV5 ....154 D5
  RLSN CV32 ....206 E3
  RUGBYS/DCH CV22 ....186 E3
  RUSH/SHEL WS4 ....5 G1
  STRPT DY13 ....163 L8
  WOLV WV1 ....3 J6
Warwick Ter RLSN CV32 ....206 C4
Warwick Wy ALDR WS9 ....40 E4
Wasdale Cl RLSN CV32 ....206 A5
Wasdale Dr KGSWFD DY6 ....83 G6
Wasdale Rd BRWNH WS8 * 26 D3
  NFLD/LBR B31 ....144 D1
Waseley Rd RBRY B45 ....143 J5
Washbrook La CNCK/NC WS11 ...21 M1
  COVW CV5 ....132 C4
Washbrook Rd WASH/WDE B8 ...90 E7
Washford Av YDLY B25 ....108 F5
Washford Gv YDLY B25 ....108 F5
Washford La REDE B98 ....203 M5
Washington Dr
  BFLD/HDSWWD B20 ....88 F2
Washington St CBHAMW B1 ....6 D7
  DUDS DY2 ....103 H2
  KIDDW DY11 ....138 D2
Washington Whf CBHAMW B1 ...6 D7
Wash La YDLY B25 ....109 G5
Washwood Heath Rd
  WASH/WDE B8 ....90 B4
Wasperton Cl CBROM B36 ....91 M5
  COVS CV3 ....156 C5
Wassell Cl HALE B63 ....121 J3
Wassell Dr BEWD DY12 ....163 G1
Wassell Grove Rd
  HAG/WOL DY9 ....120 D4
Wassell Rd BILS/COS WV14 ....51 H6
  HAG/WOL DY9 ....120 C3
  HALE B63 ....121 J3
Waste La ATHST CV9 ....62 D4
  COVN CV6 ....133 J4
  RCOVN/BALC/EX CV7 ....152 C8
Wast Hill Gv HWK/WKHTH B38 ...145 K4
Wasthill La HWK/WKHTH B38 ...145 H8
Wastwater Ct
  DUNHL/THL/PER WV6 ....48 D1
Watchbury Cl CBROM B36 ....92 A4
Watch Cl COV CV1 ....8 C4
Watchman Av BRLYHL DY5 ...102 D6
Watchtower Rd STRPT DY13...164 E1
Watcombe Rd COVE CV2 ....135 J5
Waterbrook Cl PENK ST19 ....10 C6
Watercall Av COVS CV3 ....155 G8
Water Dl BDMR/CCFT WV3 ....49 J3
Waterdale SHLY B90 ....148 B8
  WMBN WV5 ....64 C8
Waterfall Cl
  RCOVN/BALC/EX CV7 ....131 G4
  SMTHWK B66 ....87 J4
Waterfall La CDYHTH B64 ....103 L4
Waterfall Rd BRLYHL DY5 ....102 A6
Waterfield Cl TPTN/OCK DY4 ...67 G8
Waterfield Pl STETCH B33 ....110 A3
Waterford Rd KGSWFD DY6 ....83 H6
Waterfront East BRLYHL DY5 ...102 C1
The Waterfront BRLYHL DY5 * ...102 C1
Waterfront Wy BRLYHL DY5 ...102 C1
Waterglade La WLNHL WV13 ...51 L4
Waterhaynes Cl RBRY B45 ....143 L7
Waterhead Cl WOLVN WV10 ...36 F3
Waterhead Dr WOLVN WV10 ...36 F3
Waterlade Cl KIDDW DY11 ....189 L3
Waterlade Rd KIDDW DY11 ....189 L3
Water La HHTH/SAND B71 ....69 M6
Waterlinks Bvd AST/WIT B6 ...89 L6
Waterloo Av
  CHWD/FDBR/MGN B37 ....110 F1
Waterloo Bvd HEDN WS12...17 J1
Waterloo Ct WWCK CV34 ....205 H4
Waterloo Pl RLSN CV32 * 206 D4
Waterloo Rd
  ALE/KHTH/YWD B14 ....125 J3
  BEWD DY12 ....162 D2
  SMTHWK B66 ....105 J2
  WOLV WV1 ....2 F1
  YDLY B25 ....108 F7
Waterloo St East
  TPTN/OCK DY4 * 67 K8
Waterloo St CBHAM B2 ....6 F5
  COV CV1 ....84 E5
  DUDN DY1 ....84 E5
  KIDD DY10 ....138 C7
  RLSS CV31 ....206 F6
  TPTN/OCK DY4 ....67 K8
Waterman Rd COVN CV6 ....134 D7
Watermead Gra BRWNH WS8 ...26 A3
Watermeadow Dr
  RUSH/SHEL WS4 ....40 A4
Watermere RUSH/SHEL WS4...40 B5
Water Mill Cl SLYOAK B29 ....124 B2
Water Mill Crs WALM/CURD B76...73 K4
Watermill Cl WOLVN WV10 ...36 B2
Watermint Cl HEDN WS12 ....17 J2
Water Orton La
  WALM/CURD B76 ....74 B8
Water Orton Rd CBROM B36...92 A5
Water Rd SEDG DY3 ....84 A3
Watersbridge Gdns
  NUNW/HART CV10 ....99 G4
Waters Dr FOAKS/STRLY B74 ...56 B2
The Waters Edge CBHAMW B1...6 B6
Waterside COVN CV6 ....117 G2
Waterside Cl BORD B9 ....107 M5
  ERDE/BCHGN B24 ....92 A3
  WOLVN WV10 ....22 D3
  TAM/AM/WIL B77 ....46 D1
Waterside Ct RUGBYS/HIL CV21...161 G2
  WSNGN B18 ....88 D8
Waterside Gra KIDD DY10 ....138 C5
Waterside Orch ALVE B48 * ...170 F3
Waterside Pk TPTN/OCK DY4 ...68 B6
Waterside Rd WLNHL WV13 ...51 M4
Water Side Wy COVN CV6 ....117 J5
Water Side Wy CSCFLD/WYGN B72...88 A2
Watersmeet Gv COVE CV2 ....134 F2
Watersmeet Rd COVE CV2 ....134 F2
Waterson Cft
  CHWD/FDBR/MGN B37 ....111 H2
Water St BNTWD WS7 ....18 D4
  CBHAMNW B3 ....6 E3
  KGSWFD DY6 ....83 H1
  WBROM B70 ....87 J3
  WOLVN WV10 ....3 H1

Waters Vw BLOX/PEL WS3 ....25 M8
Water Tower La KNWTH CV8 ...179 K7
Waterward Cl HRBN B17 ....106 A8
Waterways Dr OLDBY B69 ....86 C4
Waterways Gdns STRBR DY8 ...100 F8
Waterworks Dr NFLD/LBR B31...123 H8
Waterworks Rd
  LDYWD/EDGR B16 ....106 D4
  SMTHWK B66 * 89 M5
Watery La ALVE B48 ....171 J3
  ATHST CV9 ....172 A5
  CSHL/WTROR B46 ....94 B3
  DOR/KN B93 ....176 C2
  HAG/WOL DY9 ....140 D6
  LICH WS13 ....18 F2
  LICH WS13 ....21 G2
  RCOVN/BALC/EX CV7 ....114 B8
  RCOVN/BALC/EX CV7 ....133 L1
  REDE B98 ....202 F3
  RIDG/WDGT B32 ....122 E2
  SHLY B90 ....174 A1
  STRBR DY8 ....101 J3
  TPTN/OCK DY4 ....67 K8
  WLNHL WV13 ....51 J2
  WSL WS1 ....53 H7
Watery La Middleway
  BORD B9...107 M3
Watford Gap Rd MGN/WHC B75...42 E6
Watford Rd BVILLE B30 ....124 D8
Wathan Av BILS/COS WV14 ...66 C5
Wathen Rd RLSN CV32 ....206 E3
  WWCK CV34 ....205 J3
Watkins Gdns NFLD/LBR B31...144 F2
Watkins Rd SHHTH WV12 ....52 A8
Watland Gn BKDE/SHDE B34 ...91 L8
Watling Dr KNWTH CV8 ....179 M7
Watling St ATHST CV9 ....62 B2
  BRWNH WS8 ....26 F4
  CNCK/NC WS11 ....16 A7
  NUN CV11 ....81 M5
  POL/KCSB/FAZ B78 ....47 J8
  TAM/AM/WIL B77 ....46 A5
Watney Gv KGSTG B44 ....72 A5
Watson Cl CSCFLD/WYGN B72...88 A1
Watson Rd BILS/COS WV14 ...66 C5
  COVW CV5 ....154 B3
  DARL/WED WS10 ....51 L8
  VAUX/NECH B7 ....90 C5
  WOLVN WV10 ....35 M3
Watsons Cl DUDS DY2 ....85 J5
Watson's Green Flds DUDS DY2...85 J5
Watson's Green Rd DUDS DY2...85 J5
Watson Wy
  RCOVN/BALC/EX CV7 * 152 A6
Watt Ct STRPT DY13 ....163 L8
Wattisham Sq CVALE B35 ....91 L1
Wattis Rd SMTHWK B67 ....105 L3
Wattle Rd WBROM B70 ....68 D5
Watton Cl BILS/COS WV14 ....66 E4
Watton Gn CVALE B35 ....91 L1
Watton La CSHL/WTROR B46 ...93 G3
Watton St WBROM B70 ....87 G3
Watts Cl TPTN/OCK DY4 ....67 G8
Watts La RUGBYN/HIL CV21...187 M5
Watt's Rd SMTH B10 ....108 B5
Watt St SMTHWK B66 ....87 M7
Wattville Av HDSW B21 * 88 A5
Wattville Rd HDSW B21 ....88 A5
Watwood Rd SHLY B90 ....147 K2
Waugh Cl
  CHWD/FDBR/MGN B37 ....110 F3
Waugh Dr HALE B63 ....121 H6
Wavebeck Ct RUGBY CV23 ...159 M8
Waveley Rd COV CV1 ....8 A4
Wavell Rd BRLYHL DY5 ....102 D6
  WASH/WDE B8 ....90 C8
  WSLW WS2 ....52 C3
Wavendon Cl COVE CV2 ....135 K4
Waveney Av
  DUNHL/THL/PER WV6 ....48 C1
Waveney Cft CBROM B36 ....92 C5
Waveney CNCK/NC WS11 ....16 A7
Waverhill Rd HDSW B21 ....88 D6
Waverley Av GTB/HAM B43 ...70 F1
  NUN CV11 ....99 K5
Waverley Cl KIDD DY10 ....138 D5
Waverley Crs
  ETTPK/GDPK/PENN WV4 ....49 M7
  ETTPK/GDPK/PENN WV4 * 49 M7
  RMSLY B62 ....142 D1
Waverley Gdns WMBN WV5 ...64 C2
Waverley Rd BLOX/PEL WS3 ...38 D3
  DARL/WED WS10 ....52 B7
  KNWTH CV8 ....180 C3
  RLSS CV31 ....206 F7
  RUGBYN/HIL CV21 ....187 L4
  SMTH B10 ....108 B6
Waverley Sq NUN CV11 ....99 K5
Waverley St DUDS DY2 ....84 E5
Waverley Wk LICHS WS14 * ...21 G7
Waverton Ms RLSS CV31 ....207 G8
Waxtree Cl WWCK CV34 ....205 H6
Waxland Rd HALE B63 ....121 M3
Way Cft KIDDW DY11 ....163 L5
Wayfield Cl SHLY B90 ....148 A2
Wayfield Rd SHLY B90 ....148 A2
Wayford Dr CSCFLD/WYGN B72...88 A2
Wayford Gld WLNHL WV13 ...51 K5
Wayside CHWD/FDBR/MGN B37...110 E5
Wayside Acres CDSL WV8 ....34 D3
Wayside Dr FOAKS/STRLY B74 ...56 A2
Wayside Gdns SHHTH WV12 ...52 C8
Waystone La HAG/WOL DY9...167 G3
Wealden Hatch WOLVN WV10 ...23 J6
Wealdstone Dr SEDG DY3 ....84 B3
Weale Gv WWCK CV34 ....205 K3
Weaman St CBHAMNE B4 ....7 G3
Weather La STRPT DY13 ....188 C8
Weatheroak Cl REDW B97 ....201 L4
Weatheroak Rd SPARK B11 * ...108 C8
Weatheroak Rd ALVE B48 ....171 M4
Weather Oaks HRBN B17 ....105 M8
Weatheroaks ALDR WS9 ....41 G6
  RMSLY B62 * 104 E6
Weaver Av
  LGN/SDN/BHAMAIR B26 ....109 M7
  WALM/CURD B76 ....73 L4
Weaver Cl BRLYHL DY5 ....83 M7
Weaver Dr RUGBYN/HIL CV21...186 A1
Weaver Gv WLNHL WV13 ....52 B3
Weavers Hill RBRY B45 ....169 G5
Weavers Ri DUDS DY2 ....103 H2
Weavers Wk COVN CV6 ....135 G3
Weaving Gdns CNCK/NC WS11 * ...16 C4
Webb Croft Rd STECH B33 ....109 J1
Webb Ellis Rd
  RUGBYS/DCH CV22 ....186 C3
Webb La HLGN/YWD B28 ....126 C5
Webb Rd TPTN/OCK DY4 ....67 M8
Webb St BILS/COS WV14 ....67 G6
  NUNW/HART CV10 ....98 A2

WLNHL WV13 ....51 K3
Webley Ri WOLVN WV10 ....36 D1
Webster Av KNWTH CV8 ....179 M7
Webster Cl CSCFLD/WYGN B72...72 F6
  SPARK B11 ....107 M7
Webster Rd WLNHL WV13 ....51 L3
  WSLW WS2 ....39 H8
Webster St COVN CV6 ....134 C4
Webster Wy WALM/CURD B76...73 M6
Weddington Wynd BILS/COS WV14...67 J4
Weddington La
  NUNW/HART CV10 ....80 E2
Weddington Rd
  NUNW/HART CV10 ....81 H8
Weddington Ter
  NUNW/HART CV10 ....81 H8
Wedgbury Wy BRLYHL DY5...101 M4
Wedge St WSL WS1 ....5 J4
Wedgewood Av WBROM B70 ...68 D6
Wedgewood Cl BNTWD WS7 ...19 G6
  COVE CV2 ....135 L3
Wedgewood Dr
  BFLD/HDSWWD B20 ....88 F3
Wedgewood Pl WBROM B70 ...68 D6
Wedgewood Rd
  RIDG/WDGT B32 ....105 G8
Wedgnock Gn WWCK CV34 ...205 H5
Wedgnock La WWCK CV34 ....205 G4
Wedgwood Cl WOLV WV1 ....50 E4
Wednesbury Oak Rd
  TPTN/OCK DY4 ....67 L4
Wednesbury One
  DARL/WED WS10 * 68 D2
Wednesbury Rd WSLW WS2 ....4 E3
Wednesfield Rd WLNHL WV13 ...51 L2
  WOLVN WV10 ....3 K3
Wednesfield Wy WNSFLD WV11...51 J7
  WOLVN WV10 ....50 E1
Wedon Cl TLHL/CAN CV4 ....153 J6
Weeford Dell MGN/WHC B75 ...57 J2
Weeford Dr BFLD/HDSWWD B20...88 D1
Weeford Rd MGN/WHC B75 ...57 J4
Weights La REDE B98 * 194 A6
Weights La SLYOAK B29 ....123 M6
Welbeck Av WOLVN WV10 ....36 B6
Welbeck Cl RMSLY B62 ....104 C8
Welbeck Dr KIDDW DY11 ....137 M6
  RUSH/SHEL WS4 ....40 B5
Welbeck Gv ERDW/GRVHL B23 ...71 M3
Welbury Gdns
  DUNHL/THL/PER WV6 ....35 K8
Welby Ga RCOVN/BALC/EX CV7...151 L3
Welby Rd HLGN/YWD B28 ....126 C4
Welches Cl NFLD/LBR B31 ....123 L8
Welcombe Dr WALM/CURD B76...73 J5
Welcome Dr SOLH B91 ....148 D2
Welcome Gv BRGRVW B61 ....168 E4
Welcome St ATHST CV9 ....63 H5
Welford Av
  LGN/SDN/BHAMAIR B26 ....109 K5
Welford Cl REDE B98 ....202 D8
Welford Gv FOAKS/STRLY B74 ...56 D2
  RWWCK/WEL CV35 ....204 B2
Welford Pl COVN CV6 ....134 B6
Welford Rd BFLD/HDSWWD B20...88 E5
  RUGBYN/HIL CV21 ....172 C4
  SCFLD/BOLD B73 ....72 C4
  SHLY B90 ....148 A1
  TAM/AM/WIL B77 ....46 A8
Welgarth Av COVN CV6 ....133 J7
Welham Cft SHLY B90 ....148 E7
Welland Cl CSHL/WTROR B46 ...92 E2
  RUGBYN/HIL CV21 ....159 M8
Welland Dr STRBR DY8 ....101 L3
Welland Gv ERDE/BCHGN B24...91 G2
  WLNHL WV13 ....52 A3
Welland Rd COV CV1 ....9 L7
  HALE B63 ....121 L3
Welland Wy WALM/CURD B76...73 L6
Well Cl CBROM B36 * 91 J5
  REDW B97 ....202 C8
Wellcroft Rd BKDE/SHDE B34 ...91 L6
Wellcroft St DARL/WED WS10 ...68 C2
Wellesbourne CRTAM B79 ....32 A5
Wellesbourne Cl
  BDMR/CCFT WV3 ....48 F5
  REDE B98 ....202 C1
Wellesbourne Dr BILS/COS WV14...66 F4
Wellesbourne Rd
  BFLD/HDSWWD B20 ....88 F4
  COVW CV5 * 153 K8
Wellesley Dr TPTN/OCK DY4 ...67 K8
Wellesley Gdns MOS/BIL B13 ...126 B4
Wellesley Rd LGLYGN/QTN B68 ...86 F7
  RCOVN/BALC/EX CV7 * 152 B8
Wellfield Cl CNCK/NC WS11 ...15 M6
  RCOVN/BALC/EX CV7 * 152 B8
Wellfield Gdns DUDS DY2 ....85 J7
Wellfield Rd ALDR WS9 ....40 F6
  HLGN/YWD B28 ....126 F2
Wellhead La PBAR/PBCH B42 ...89 G1
Wellington Av BDMR/CCFT WV3...49 K6
Wellington Cl KGSWFD DY6 ...101 J1
Wellington Crs LICH WS13 ....21 M1
Wellington Dr CNCK/NC WS11 ...15 M5
Wellington Gdns COV CV1 ....8 A7
Wellington Gv SOLH B91 ....127 K7
Wellington Pl WLNHL WV13 ...51 K2
Wellington Rd
  BFLD/HDSWWD B20 ....88 F6
  BILS/COS WV14 ....50 F8
  BRGRVE B60 ....192 A4
  DSYBK/YTR WS5 ....54 A7
  DUDN DY1 ....84 F7
  EDG B15 ....107 G2
  RLSN CV32 ....206 F2
  SMTHWK B67 ....105 J1
  TPTN/OCK DY4 ....67 G6
Wellington St CDYHTH B64 ....103 K2
  COV CV1 ....9 J2
  HHTH/SAND B71 ....87 H1
  OLDBY B69 ....86 F6
  REDE B98 ....202 C2
  WSLW WS2 ....52 F2
  WSNGN B18 ....6 A2
Wellington St South
  WBROM B70 * 87 G1
Wellington Ter LOZ/NWT B19 * ...88 F8
  WLNHL WV13 ....51 L1
Wellington Wy CVALE B35 ....91 M3
Well La BLOX/PEL WS3 ....39 H1
  DIG/EDG B5 ....7 H7
  GTWY WS6 ....24 D3
  WNSFLD WV11 ....37 H5
Wellman Cft SLYOAK B29 ....124 B6
Wellmans Rd SHHTH WV12 ...52 A4
Well Meadow RBRY B45 ....143 L8
Well Pl BLOX/PEL WS3 * 39 J1
Wells Av DARL/WED WS10 ....52 A6
Wells Cl CNCK/NC WS11 ....12 C4
  HHTH/SAND B71 ....69 H2
  KIDDW DY11 ....137 L6
  NUNW/HART CV10 ....79 M3
Wellsford Av HALE/OLT B92 ...127 L1
Wells Green Rd HALE/OLT B92 ...127 L1
Well Spring Cl ATHST CV9 ....63 H5
Wells Rd BILS/COS WV14 ....67 J5

BLKHTH/ROWR B65 104 C2
BRLYHL DY5 101 M2
ETTPK/GDPK/PENN WV4 49 K8
LGN/SDN/BHAMAIR B26 128 E1
Wells St RUGBYN/HIL CV21 186 F2
Well St COV CV1 8 F3
DARL/WED WS10 52 C7
LOZ/NWT B19 89 G8
Welney Gdns COVEN WV9 35 L2
Welsby Av GTB/HAM B43 70 C6
Welsh Cl WWCK CV34 205 J3
Welsh House Farm Rd
RIDG/WDGT B32 123 K1
Welshmans Hl SCFLD/BOLD B73 71 M3
Welsh Rd COVE CV2 155 M1
RLSN CV32 207 K2
Welton Cl WALM/CURD B76 73 L3
Welton Pl RUGBYS/DCH CV22 187 H5
Welton Rd WWCK CV34 205 H4
Welwyndale Rd
CSCFLD/WYGN B72 73 G7
Wembley Gv YDLY B25 109 G5
Wembley La BNTWD WS7 18 A5
Wembrook Cl NUN CV11 99 H3
Wembury TAM/AM/WIL B77 32 C8
Wem Gdns WNSFLD WV11 37 H7
Wendell Crest WOLVN WV10 36 D2
Wendiburgh St TLHL/CAN CV4 153 L6
Wendover Ri COVW CV5 154 A1
Wendover Rd
BLKHTH/ROWR B65 85 L7
ERDW/GRVHL B23 72 A6
ETTPK/GDPK/PENN WV4 66 C3
Wendron Cl BRGRVE B60 191 M3
Wendron Gv
ALE/KHTH/YWD B14 146 B1
Wenlock TAM/AM/WIL B77 46 B2
Wenlock Av BDMR/CCFT WV3 49 J5
Wenlock Cl HALE B63 121 H3
SEDG DY3 66 A6
Wenlock Dr BRGRVW B61 168 E8
Wenlock Gdns BLOX/PEL WS3 39 J8
Wenlock Rd BFLD/HDSWWD B20 89 J4
STRBR DY8 101 M7
Wenlock Wy NUNW/HART CV10 97 M1
STRPT DY13 188 C4
Wenman St BHTH/HG B12 107 K7
Wensley Cft HIA/OLT B92 126 F7
Wensleydale Rd PBAR/PBCH B42 70 F7
Wensley Rd
LGN/SDN/BHAMAIR B26 109 K7
Wentbridge Rd WLNHL WV13 51 G4
Wentworth Av CBROM B36 91 M5
Wentworth Cl BNTWD WS7 19 G6
Wentworth Dr BRGRVE B60 169 L8
COVN CV6 133 M1
LICHS WS14 21 H8
NUN CV11 99 L4
OLDBY B69 85 L6
Wentworth Ga HRBN B17 105 M7
Wentworth Gv
DUNHL/THL/PER WV6 34 B8
Wentworth Park Av HRBN B17 105 M7
Wentworth Ri RMSLY B62 122 B2
Wentworth Rd BLOX/PEL WS3 38 D1
FOAKS/STRLY B74 56 E5
HIA/OLT B92 127 K2
HRBN B17 105 M7
RLSS CV31 207 H7
RUGBYS/DCH CV22 186 D4
STRBR DY8 101 H6
WOLVN WV10 36 D3
Wentworth Wy
RIDG/WDGT B32 123 K2
Wenyon Cl TPTN/OCK DY4 85 M1
Weoley Av SLYOAK B29 124 A3
Weoley Castle Rd SLYOAK B29 123 L4
Weoley Hl SLYOAK B29 124 A5
Weoley Park Rd SLYOAK B29 123 M4
Wergs Dr DUNHL/THL/PER WV6 34 E6
Wergs Gdns CDSL WV8 * 34 D4
Wergs Hall Rd CDSL WV8 34 D4
Wergs Rd DUNHL/THL/PER WV6 34 F7
Werneth Gv BLOX/PEL WS3 38 E1
Wesley Av CDSL WV8 34 F3
GTWY WS6 24 B2
HALE B63 102 F6
STRPT DY13 188 C4
Wesley Cl BNTWD WS7 18 D4
CDYHTH B64 103 K4
Wesley Gv DARL/WED WS10 68 C2
Wesley Pl HEDN WS12 13 G6
TPTN/OCK DY4 68 A6
Wesley Rd BRLYHL DY5 83 M8
CDSL WV8 34 F3
ERDW/GRVHL B23 72 D8
RUGBYN/HIL CV21 187 L5
Wesley's Fold DARL/WED WS10 52 B7
Wesley St BILS/COS WV14 67 J3
BKHL/PFLD WV2 50 E7
OLDBY B69 86 E5
WBROM B70 86 F2
Wesley Wy TAM/AM/WIL B77 46 C1
Wessenden TAM/AM/WIL B77 46 F6
Wessex Cl BDWTH CV12 116 E1
BRWNH WS8 26 D6
Wessex Dr CNCK/NC WS11 16 D3
Wessex Rd BKHL/PFLD WV2 50 D7
Wesson Gdns HALE B63 121 L2
Wesson Rd DARL/WED WS10 52 A6
West Acre WLNHL WV13 51 K4
Westacre Crs BDMR/CCFT WV3 48 F5
Westacre Dr BRLYHL DY5 102 D5
Westacre Gdns STETCH B33 109 K3
West Av BDWTH CV12 117 H3
BFLD/HDSWWD B20 88 D1
CBROM B36 92 B5
COVE CV2 155 L3
OLDBY B69 85 M5
RCOVN/BALC/EX CV7 115 L8
REDE B98 202 C2
WNSFLD WV11 37 G7
Westbook Wy WMBN WV5 64 D8
West Bvd RIDG/WDGT B32 105 J8
Westbourne Av BKDE/SHDE B34 91 J7
CNCK/NC WS11 16 B3
GTWY WS6 24 C1
Westbourne Cl BRGRVW B61 191 J4
Westbourne Crs BNTWD WS7 18 F6
EDG B15 106 E5
Westbourne Gdns EDG B15 106 E6
Westbourne Gv HDSW B21 * 88 D6
RUGBYS/DCH CV22 186 D4
Westbourne Rd
DARL/WED WS10 52 D6
EDG B15 106 D5
ETTPK/GDPK/PENN WV4 49 L8
HDSW B21 88 B4
HIA/OLT B92 127 K6
RMSLY B62 104 C7
RUSH/SHEL WS4 53 K1
WBROM B70 86 F4
Westbourne St BEWD DY12 162 F2
RUSH/SHEL WS4 53 K2
Westbourne Ter BRGRVW B61 * 191 J4
West Bromwich Ringway
WBROM B70 87 G2
West Bromwich Rd
DSYBK/YTR WS5 69 K1
WSL WS1 53 J7
West Bromwich St OLDBY B69 86 D4
WSL WS1 4 F7
Westbrook Av ALDR WS9 40 D8
Westbury Av DARL/WED WS10 52 D7
Westbury Ms COVE CV2 * 155 L2
Westbury Rd COVW CV5 133 H8
DARL/WED WS10 52 D7
HRBN B17 105 M2
NUNW/HART CV10 98 B1
Westbury St WOLV WV1 3 G4
West Cannock Wy HEDN WS12 13 H4
Westcliff Dr WWCK CV34 205 J3
Westcliffe Dr COVS CV3 154 F8
Westcliff Pl NFLD/LBR B31 144 D1
Westcombe Gv
RIDG/WDGT B32 122 E4
West Coppice Rd BRWNH WS8 26 A5
Westcote Av NFLD/LBR B31 144 A3
Westcote Cl HIA/OLT B92 127 L3
Westcotes TLHL/CAN CV4 153 M4
Westcott Cl STRBR DY8 101 K2
Westcott Rd
LGN/SDN/BHAMAIR B26 109 L5
Westcroft Av WOLVN WV10 36 E4
Westcroft Gv NFLD/LBR B31 145 G2
Westcroft Rd CDSL WV8 34 D7
SEDG DY3 65 M3
Westcroft Wy
ALE/KHTH/YWD B14 146 F4
Westdean Cl RMSLY B62 122 A1
West Dr BFLD/HDSWWD B20 88 F5
DIG/EDG B5 125 G1
POL/KGSB/FAZ B78 45 J3
West End Av SMTHWK B66 87 H6
West End Ct WWCK CV34 * 205 H7
Westerdale Cl SEDG DY3 66 E6
Westerham Cl DOR/KN B93 149 K7
Westeria Cl CBROM B36 92 A5
Westering Pkwy WOLVN WV10 36 C1
Westerings BFLD/HDSWWD B20 89 G3
Western Av BRLYHL DY5 101 M3
RMSLY B62 122 C1
SEDG DY3 65 M5
WSLW WS2 52 B2
Western By-Pass LICH WS13 20 D5
Western Cl WSLW WS2 52 B2
Western Rd CDYHTH B64 103 H5
ERDE/BCHGN B24 90 E2
HAG/WOL DY9 140 F1
HEDN WS12 12 F7
OLDBY B69 86 F8
SCFLD/BOLD B73 72 E4
STRBR DY8 119 K1
WSNGN B18 106 D1
Western Wy DARL/WED WS10 68 A2
KIDDW DY11 137 L8
Westfield Av
ALE/KHTH/YWD B14 146 F3
Westfield Cl DOR/KN B93 175 J3
NUNW/HART CV10 81 H7
Westfield Dr ALDR WS9 40 E7
WMBN WV5 64 D6
Westfield Gra
ALE/KHTH/YWD B14 125 J4
Westfield Gv BDMR/CCFT WV3 49 G5
Westfield Mnr MGN/WHC B75 56 E1
Westfield Rd ACGN B27 126 F2
ALE/KHTH/YWD B14 125 H5
BILS/COS WV14 50 F6
BRLYHL DY5 102 D5
DUDS DY2 85 H6
EDG B15 106 B5
RMSLY B62 104 C4
RUGBYS/DCH CV22 186 D3
SEDG DY3 66 B4
SMTHWKW B67 87 K8
WLNHL WV13 51 J5
Westfields BRGRVW B61 168 C5
Westford Gv HLGN/YWD B28 147 J2
Westgate ALDR WS9 40 C6
HEDN WS12 13 K7
West Ga LDYWD/EDGR B16 106 C2
Westgate Cl SEDG DY3 66 C6
WWCK CV34 205 H7
Westgate Rd RUGBYN/HIL CV21 187 J4
West Gn
ETTPK/GDPK/PENN WV4 49 G8
West Green Cl EDG B15 106 F5
Westgrove Av SHLY B90 148 D7
Westgrove Ter RLSN CV32 206 B5
Westhaven Dr NFLD/LBR B31 123 J6
Westhaven Rd FOAKS/STRLY B74 57 G7
Westhay Rd HLGN/YWD B28 126 F6
Westhead Rd KIDD DY10 138 E1
Westhead Rd North KIDD DY10 138 E1
West Heath Rd NFLD/LBR B31 144 F4
WSNGN B18 106 B1
Westhill BDMR/CCFT WV3 49 G3
West Hill Av HEDN WS12 12 F8
Westhill Cl HIA/OLT B92 127 J5
Westhill Rd COVN CV6 133 K7
HWK/WKHTH B38 145 K2
RLSN CV32 198 E7
West Holme BORD B9 108 A3
Westholme Cft BVILLE B30 124 C6
Westhouse Gv
ALE/KHTH/YWD B14 146 B1
Westland Av BDMR/CCFT WV3 49 K3
Westland Cl ERDW/GRVHL B23 72 D8
Westland Gdns BDMR/CCFT WV3 49 K3
STRBR DY8 101 K6
Westland Rd BDMR/CCFT WV3 49 K3
Westlands Rd MOS/BIL B13 125 L4
WALM/CURD B76 73 K7
Westlea Rd RLSS CV31 206 C7
Westleigh Av COVW CV5 154 D6
Westleigh Rd WMBN WV5 64 D8
Westley Cl HLGN/YWD B28 126 F7
West Leyes RUGBYN/HIL CV21 186 D2
Westley Rd ACGN B27 126 F2
Westley St BORD B9 7 M6
DUDN DY1 84 F5
Westmead Crs ERDE/BCHGN B24 91 G1
West Mead Dr
ALE/KHTH/YWD B14 125 J7
Westmead Dr LGLYGN/QTN B68 104 F1
West Ms KGSTG B44 71 H3
West Midlands Freeport
LGN/SDN/BHAMAIR B26 * 128 D2
West Mill Cft HWK/WKHTH B38 145 J6
Westminster Rd KIDDW DY11 137 L7
Westminster Av
ETTPK/GDPK/PENN WV4 49 M8
Westminster Cl BRGRVW B61 191 H4
DUDN DY1 84 E3
Westminster Dr
ALE/KHTH/YWD B14 125 H7
NUNW/HART CV10 79 M7
Westminster Rd
BFLD/HDSWWD B20 89 G3
CNCK/NC WS11 12 C7
COV CV1 8 D7
HHTH/SAND B71 69 H4
KIDDW DY11 137 K7
RUSH/SHEL WS4 39 M6
SLYOAK B29 124 E4
STRBR DY8 101 G3
Westmore Wy DARL/WED WS10 53 H8
Westmorland Av
NUNW/HART CV10 98 C1
Westmorland Cl
POL/KGSB/FAZ B78 45 L4
Westmorland Rd COVE CV2 156 D1
HHTH/SAND B71 69 G7
Weston Av LOZ/NWT B19 * 89 G6
OLDBY B69 85 M4
SPARK B11 108 A7
Westonbirt Cl KNWTH CV8 180 A7
Weston Cl CNCK/NC WS11 17 G4
DOR/KN B93 175 L3
RLSS CV31 207 G7
WSL WS1 53 J7
WWCK CV34 205 K6
Weston Crs ALDR WS9 54 F1
Weston Dr BILS/COS WV14 67 G1
DARL/WED WS10 68 A3
GTWY WS6 24 C5
Weston La BDWTH CV12 117 M2
SPARK B11 126 C1
Weston Rd LICH WS13 20 E3
LOZ/NWT B19 88 F6
SMTHWKW B67 105 K3
Weston St COV CV1 9 H2
WSL WS1 53 J7
Weston Ter LOZ/NWT B19 * 89 H5
Westover Rd
BFLD/HDSWWD B20 88 C1
West Park Av NFLD/LBR B31 144 C3
West Park Rd SMTHWKW B67 87 H6
West Pathway HRBN B17 106 A7
Westport Crs WNSFLD WV11 37 K8
Westray Cl RBRY B45 143 J4
West Rdg COVW CV5 132 E8
Westridge SEDG DY3 66 A5
Westridge Rd MOS/BIL B13 126 A7
West Ri MGN/WHC B75 57 G7
West Rd BRGRVE B60 191 L3
GTB/HAM B43 70 C6
HALE B63 102 F7
TPTN/OCK DY4 67 M5
West Rd South HALE B63 102 F7
Westside Dr RIDG/WDGT B32 123 H4
West St BLKHTH/ROWR B65 104 A4
BLOX/PEL WS3 39 G6
BRLYHL DY5 102 D5
CNCK/NC WS11 16 C7
COV CV1 9 K4
CRTAM B79 32 A8
DUDN DY1 84 F3
DUNHL/THL/PER WV6 36 A8
REDW B97 202 C2
RRUGBY CV23 185 L1
STRBR DY8 101 K8
TAM/AM/WIL B77 46 A2
VAUX/NECH B7 * 7 K2
WWCK CV34 205 H8
Westthorpe Gv LOZ/NWT B19 89 G8
West Vw NUNW/HART CV10 79 J5
WASH/WDE B8 109 G1
WOLVN WV10 22 F6
West View Dr KGSWFD DY6 83 J8
West View Rd MGN/WHC B75 57 J7
RLSN CV32 199 G8
RUGBYS/DCH CV22 186 B3
Westville Av KIDDW DY11 137 L8
Westville Rd WSLW WS2 52 E2
Westward Cl KGSTG B44 71 K5
West Wy RUSH/SHEL WS4 39 M3
Westwick Cl ALDR WS9 41 J1
West Winds WOLVN WV10 23 G6
Westwood Av SPARK B11 126 C1
STRBR DY8 119 H2
Westwood Crs ATHST CV9 63 H6
Westwood Dr RBRY B45 143 M4
Westwood Gv SOLH B91 148 D2
Westwood Heath Rd
TLHL/CAN CV4 153 G7
Westwood Rd AST/WIT B6 89 L3
ATHST CV9 63 H6
RUGBYS/DCH CV22 187 K6
SCFLD/BOLD B73 71 L1
Westwoods Hollow BNTWD WS7 18 F5
Westwood St BRLYHL DY5 101 L4
Westwood Vw
ERDE/BCHGN B24 91 G2
Westwood Wy TLHL/CAN CV4 153 J7
Wetherby Cl WOLVN WV10 36 B1
Wetherby Rd ACGN B27 127 G3
BLOX/PEL WS3 38 E1
Wetherell Wy
RUGBYN/HIL CV21 161 G6
Wetherfield Rd SPARK B11 126 E2
Wexford Cl DUDN DY1 84 D3
Wexford Rd COVE CV2 135 H4
Weybourne Rd KGSTG B44 71 J3
Weycroft Rd ERDW/GRVHL B23 71 M6
Weyhill Cl COVEN WV9 35 J3
Weymoor Rd HRBN B17 123 L2
Weymouth Dr
FOAKS/STRLY B74 56 D1
Whaley's Cft COVN CV6 133 L5
Wharf Ap ALDR WS9 40 D6
Wharf Cl LICHS WS14 * 21 G6
Wharf Cottages ATHST CV9 * 62 F4
Wharfdale Rd SPARK B11 108 E8
Wharfedale Cl KGSWFD DY6 82 F6
Wharfedale St DARL/WED WS10 68 D3
Wharf La BRGRVE B60 192 F4
SOLH B91 128 B7
WSNGN B18 88 E8
Wharf Rd BVILLE B30 145 L3
COV CV1 134 D8
YDLY B25 108 F8
Wharfside OLDBY B69 86 D6
Wharfside St CBHAMW B1 6 D7
Wharf St AST/WIT B6 89 L6
WOLV WV1 3 J6
WSLW WS2 4 B5
WSNGN B18 88 E7
WWCK CV34 205 L5
Whar Hall Rd HIA/OLT B92 128 C5
Wharrington Cl REDE B98 202 E5
Wharrington Hl REDE B98 202 E5
Wharton Av HIA/OLT B92 128 C6
Wharton St VAUX/NECH B7 90 B5
Wharwell La GTWY WS6 24 E4
Whatcote Gn HIA/OLT B92 128 B5
Whateley Av BLOX/PEL WS3 39 K7
Whateley Crs CBROM B36 92 B5
Whateley Gn FOAKS/STRLY B74 56 B5
Whateley Hall Cl DOR/KN B93 * 150 A6
Whateley Hall Rd DOR/KN B93 149 M6
Whateley La TAM/AM/WIL B77 60 D1
Whateley Pl BLOX/PEL WS3 * 39 K7
Whateley Rd BLOX/PEL WS3 39 K7
HDSW B21 88 C5
Whateley's Dr KNWTH CV8 197 L1
Wheatcroft Av BEWD DY12 163 G1
Wheatcroft Cl BNTWD WS7 18 E8
MGN/WHC B75 57 J2
PENK ST19 10 C5
RMSLY B62 104 D5
Wheatcroft Dr
CHWD/FDBR/MGN B37 111 G4
Wheatcroft Gv DUDS DY2 85 K4
Wheatcroft Rd STETCH B33 109 K3
Wheate Cft TLHL/CAN CV4 153 K3
Wheaten Cl
CHWD/FDBR/MGN B37 111 H2
Wheatfield Av
RUGBYS/DCH CV22 186 A4
Wheatfield Cl CBROM B36 92 E6
Wheatfield Vw NFLD/LBR B31 123 H8
Wheat Hl DSYBK/YTR WS5 54 C5
Wheathill Cl
ETTPK/GDPK/PENN WV4 65 J2
RLSN CV32 206 C3
Wheatlands Cl HEDN WS12 17 G4
Wheatlands Cft STETCH B33 110 C2
The Wheatlands
DUNHL/THL/PER WV6 48 B2
Wheatley Cl HIA/OLT B92 128 C5
LGLYGN/QTN B68 105 G5
MGN/WHC B75 57 G2
Wheatley Rd LGLYGN/QTN B68 105 G5
Wheatley St BKHL/PFLD WV2 50 C7
WBROM B70 86 E1
Wheatmill Cl KIDD DY10 139 M3
Wheatmoor Ri MGN/WHC B75 57 J7
Wheatmoor Rd MGN/WHC B75 57 K6
Wheaton Cl WOLVN WV10 36 A6
Wheaton V BFLD/HDSWWD B20 88 C2
Wheatridge Cl KGSWFD DY6 82 F2
Wheatridge Rd BRGRVE B60 191 H7
Wheats Av HRBN B17 123 M2
Wheatsheaf Rd CDSL WV8 35 J4
LDYWD/EDGR B16 106 B3
OLDBY B69 85 L5
Wheatstone Cl SEDG DY3 66 C7
Wheatstone Gv STETCH B33 91 K8
Wheat St NUN CV11 99 G1
Wheel Av CDSL WV8 34 D2
Wheeler Cl CDSL WV8 34 C1
DOR/KN B93 176 F6
Wheeler Rd WNSFLD WV11 37 G5
Wheeler's Fold WOLV WV1 3 G5
Wheelers La MOS/BIL B13 125 K6
Wheeler St LOZ/NWT B19 89 H7
STRBR DY8 101 K8
Wheeley Moor Rd
CHWD/FDBR/MGN B37 92 E8
Wheeley Rd ALVE B48 170 B8
HIA/OLT B92 128 B6
Wheeley's La EDG B15 6 C9
Wheeley's Rd EDG B15 106 F6
Wheel La LICH WS13 20 D4
Wheelock Cl FOAKS/STRLY B74 55 K6
Wheelwright Cl BRGRVE B60 191 J6
Wheelwright La COVN CV6 134 A1
Wheelwright Rd
ERDE/BCHGN B24 90 C3
Wheldrake Av BKDE/SHDE B34 92 A8
Wheler Rd COVS CV3 155 L5
Whernside RUGBYN/HIL CV21 161 G6
Whernside Dr
DUNHL/THL/PER WV6 35 L8
Wherretts Well La SOLH B91 128 C8
Whetstone Cl EDG B15 * 106 D8
Whetstone Dr
RUGBYN/HIL CV21 161 J6
Whetstone Gn WOLVN WV10 * 36 B4
Whetstone Gv WOLVN WV10 36 B5
Whetstone La ALDR WS9 40 F8
Whetstone Rd WOLVN WV10 36 B5
Whettybridge Rd RBRY B45 143 J7
Whetty La RBRY B45 143 J6
Whichcote Av
RCOVN/BALC/EX CV7 131 G4
Whichford Cl WALM/CURD B76 73 H7
Whichford Gv BORD B9 108 F3
While Rd CSCFLD/WYGN B72 72 F1
Whiley Cl RRUGBY CV23 161 K8
Whilmot Cl WOLVN WV10 22 F7
Whimbrel Gv KIDD DY10 164 E4
Whinberry Ri BRLYHL DY5 84 A4
Whinchat Gv KIDD DY10 164 E3
Whinfield Rd BRGRVW B61 167 M7
Whinyates Ri CNCK/NC WS11 16 D5
Whisley Brook La
HLGN/YWD B28 126 D3
Whiston Av WNSFLD WV11 37 L6
Whiston Gv SLYOAK B29 123 M5
Whitacre La LICHS WS14 27 J6
Whitacre Rd BORD B9 108 C2
DOR/KN B93 149 M6
NUN CV11 81 J8
RLSN CV32 206 E3
Whitaker Rd COVW CV5 154 A1
Whitbourne Cl BTHH/HG B12 107 M8
Whitburn Av PBAR/PBCH B42 70 E8
Whitburn Cl COVEN WV9 35 L3
KIDDW DY11 137 M7
Whitburn Rd BDWTH CV12 116 A4
Whitby Cl BLOX/PEL WS3 38 D2
Whitby Rd BTHH/HG B12 125 L1
Whitby Wy CNCK/NC WS11 16 A5
Whitchurch Cl REDE B98 202 D7
Whitchurch Wy TLHL/CAN CV4 153 K6
Whitcot Gv NFLD/LBR B31 * 144 D5
White Bark Cl HEDN WS12 12 E5
Whitebeam Cl BRWNH WS8 26 C7
SEDG DY3 84 A1
TLHL/CAN CV4 153 H4
Whitebeam Cft
HWK/WKHTH B38 145 J5
White Beam Rd
CHWD/FDBR/MGN B37 111 G5
White City Rd BRLYHL DY5 102 E4
White Cl HAG/WOL DY9 120 A3
Whitecrest GTB/HAM B43 70 D3
Whitecroft Rd
LGN/SDN/BHAMAIR B26 110 B8
White Falcon Ct SOLH B91 148 D3
White Farm Rd
FOAKS/STRLY B74 56 C1
White Field Av HRBN B17 105 L7
Whitefield Cl CDSL WV8 34 F3
TLHL/CAN CV4 153 H7
Whitefields Crs SOLH B91 148 F3
Whitefields Ga SOLH B91 148 E4
Whitefields Rd SOLH B91 148 E4
Whitefriars Dr HALE B63 121 L1
White Friars La COV CV1 9 H6
White Friars St COV CV1 9 H5
Whitegate Dr KIDDW DY11 163 L2
Whitegates Rd BILS/COS WV14 67 H3
Whitehall Cl NUNW/HART CV10 79 L3
Whitehall Dr DUDN DY1 84 E3
HALE B63 121 M1
Whitehall Rd BORD B9 108 B4
CDYHTH B64 103 G4
ETTPK/GDPK/PENN WV4 65 M1
HALE B63 121 M1
HDSW B21 88 E6
KGSWFD DY6 83 G7
RUGBYN/HIL CV21 186 F2
STRBR DY8 119 M3
TPTN/OCK DY4 68 B8
WBROM B70 86 C1
WSL WS1 4 F8
Whitehead Dr KNWTH CV8 180 A7
WALM/CURD B76 74 B7
Whitehead Gv
RCOVN/BALC/EX CV7 151 M6
Whitehead Rd AST/WIT B6 89 J6
Whiteheads Ct RLSN CV32 * 206 D4
White Heart Cl BEWD DY12 162 D2
Whitehill La SLYOAK B29 123 L8
Whitehill Rd KIDDW DY11 163 L2
White Hollies BLOX/PEL WS3 39 J1
Whitehorn Dr RLSN CV32 206 F3
Whitehorse Cl COVN CV6 116 F7
White Horse Rd BRWNH WS8 26 C3
Whitehouse Av BDMR/CCFT WV3 49 G5
DARL/WED WS10 51 M6
DARL/WED WS10 68 D2
White House Av WNSFLD WV11 37 K6
White House Cl RBRY B45 169 L4
SOLH B91 148 D2
Whitehouse Common Rd
MGN/WHC B75 57 J6
Whitehouse Crs BNTWD WS7 * 18 F6
MGN/WHC B75 57 J5
NUNW/HART CV10 98 B2
WNSFLD WV11 37 K4
Whitehouse Dr SMTHWK B66 87 L6
White House Gn SOLH B91 148 D2
Whitehouse La REDE B98 203 J2
Whitehouse Pl RBRY B45 143 K7
Whitehouse Rd KIDDW DY11 164 B1
POL/KGSB/FAZ B78 47 K6
White Houses La WOLVN WV10 22 E7
Whitehouse St AST/WIT B6 89 K7
BILS/COS WV14 67 G5
TPTN/OCK DY4 85 L3
WSLW WS2 53 H2
Whitehouse Wy ALDR WS9 54 D1
White House Wy SOLH B91 148 E2
Whitelaw Crs COVW CV5 132 F7
Whitemoor Dr SOLH B91 148 E6
Whitemoor Rd KNWTH CV8 197 L1
White Oak Dr BDMR/CCFT WV3 49 G4
KGSWFD DY6 83 G7
Whitepits La ALVE B48 195 K1
White Rd RIDG/WDGT B32 105 H7
SMTHWKW B67 87 K7
SPARK B11 108 A6
White Rw WMBN WV5 64 A4
Whitesands Cl TAM/AM/WIL B77 32 C8
White's Dr SEDG DY3 66 C5
Whiteside Cl COVS CV3 156 D5
Whiteslade Cl DOR/KN B93 149 L6
Whitesmith Cl SEDG DY3 66 B5
White's Rd HHTH/SAND B71 69 G7
Whites Rw KNWTH CV8 197 L3
Whitestitch La
RCOVN/BALC/EX CV7 130 F3
Whitestone Rd HALE B63 103 L7
NUN CV11 99 L6
White St BTHH/HG B12 107 L8
COV CV1 9 G3
WSL WS1 5 L5
Whites Wd WMBN WV5 64 E8
Whitethorn Cl HEDN WS12 12 E5
Whitethorn Crs
FOAKS/STRLY B74 55 H4
Whitethorn Rd STRBR DY8 101 L4
Whitewood Gld SHHTH WV12 52 C1
Whitfield Gv EDG B15 107 H5
Whitfield Rd HEDN WS12 13 G6
Whitford Cl BRGRVW B61 191 H5
Whitford Dr SHLY B90 148 F6
Whitford Gdns BRGRVW B61 191 H3
Whitford Rd BRGRVW B61 191 H3
Whitgreave Av WOLVN WV10 22 F6
WOLVN WV10 36 C5
Whitgreave Ct WOLVN WV10 * 22 F7
Whitgreave St WBROM B70 86 C2
Whiting TAM/AM/WIL B77 46 B6
Whitland Cl RBRY B45 143 M7
Whitland Dr
ALE/KHTH/YWD B14 146 D2
Whitley Av TAM/AM/WIL B77 32 C8
Whitley Cl DUNHL/THL/PER WV6 48 F3
Whitley Court Rd
RIDG/WDGT B32 105 G7
Whitley Dr FOAKS/STRLY B74 55 L5
Whitley St DARL/WED WS10 68 C2
Whitley Village COVS CV3 155 K6
Whitlock Gv
ALE/KHTH/YWD B14 146 E2
Whitminster Av
ERDE/BCHGN B24 90 F2
Whitminster Cl SHHTH WV12 52 A1
Whitmore Hl WOLV WV1 2 E4
Whitmore Park Rd COVN CV6 134 A2
Whitmore Rd SMTHDH B10 108 A5
STRBR DY8 101 H8
Whitmore St WOLV WV1 3 G4
WSL WS1 4 C9
WSNGN B18 88 F8
Whitnash Cl
RCOVN/BALC/EX CV7 151 L7
Whitnash Gv COVE CV2 135 H8
Whitney Av STRBR DY8 101 H7
Whittaker St BKHL/PFLD WV2 50 C6
Whittall Dr East KIDDW DY11 163 M4
Whittall Dr West KIDDW DY11 163 L4
Whittall St CBHAMNE B4 7 G3
Whittimere St WSL WS1 5 G3
Whittingham Gv WNSFLD WV11 37 K7
Whittingham Rd HALE B63 103 L8
Whittington Cl
ALE/KHTH/YWD B14 125 J8
HHTH/SAND B71 69 K5
WWCK CV34 205 M5
Whittington Common Rd
LICHS WS14 29 L1
Whittington Gv STETCH B33 109 K3
Whittington Hall Cottages
KINVER DY7 * 118 C3
Whittington Hall La
KINVER DY7 118 C3
Whittington La ATHST CV9 62 E3
Whittington Ov STETCH B33 109 L3
Whittington Rd STRBR DY8 119 H2
Whittle Cl COVS CV3 156 D5
RUGBYS/DCH CV22 186 B6
Whittle Cft CVALE B35 91 K2
Whittleford Gv CBROM B36 92 A4
Whittleford Rd
NUNW/HART CV10 98 A1
Whitton St DARL/WED WS10 52 C7
Whitville Cl KIDDW DY11 138 A6
Whitwell Cl SHLY B90 148 E7
Whitworth Av COVS CV3 155 M4
Whitworth Cl DARL/WED WS10 52 C6
Whitworth Dr HHTH/SAND B71 69 J4
Whoberley Av COVW CV5 154 B2
Whoberley Ct COVW CV5 * 154 A2
Whyley St OLDBY B69 86 E8
WBROM B70 86 E1
Whyley Wk OLDBY B69 86 E8
Whynot St HALE B63 102 F8
Wibert Cl SLYOAK B29 124 E4
Wichnor Rd HIA/OLT B92 109 K8
Wicket La KINVER DY7 100 C4
Wickham Cl COVN CV6 133 K3
Wickham Ct RLSN CV32 * 206 F2
Wickham Gdns WNSFLD WV11 36 E7
Wicklow Cl HALE B63 121 H4
Wickmans Dr TLHL/CAN CV4 153 G3
Wiclif Wy NUNW/HART CV10 97 M2
Widdecombe Cl COVE CV2 135 H5
Widdrington Rd COV CV1 134 A8

Wideacre Dr KGSTG B44 71 J6
Wide Acres RBRY B45 143 K4
Widney Av ALDR WS9 40 F4
SLYOAK B29 124 A3
Widney Cl DOR/KN B93 149 K8
Widney La SOLH B91 148 C4
Widney Manor Rd SOLH B91 149 G3
Widney Rd DOR/KN B93 149 J8
Wigeon Gv WOLVN WV10 22 F6
Wigford Rd TAM/AM/WIL B77 46 A8
Wiggins Cft WALM/CURD B76 73 K2
Wiggins Hill Rd WALM/CURD B76 74 D5
Wigginsmill Rd DARL/WED WS10 68 B4
Wiggin St LDYWD/EDGR B16 106 D2
Wigginton Ldg CRTAM B79 * 31 K6
Wigginton Rd CRTAM B79 31 H7
Wight Cft CBROM B36 92 F7
Wightman Cl LICHS WS14 21 J7
Wightwick Bank
DUNHL/THL/PER WV6 48 D3
Wightwick Cl BLOX/PEL WS3 38 F4
Wightwick Gv
DUNHL/THL/PER WV6 48 E3
Wightwick Hall Rd
DUNHL/THL/PER WV6 48 C4
Wigmore Gv KGSTG B44 71 M5
Wigmore La HHTH/SAND B71 69 L5
Wigorn La HAG/WOL DY9 119 M5
Wigorn Rd SMTHWKW B67 105 K4
Wigston Hl ATHST CV9 62 A8
Wigston Rd COVE CV2 135 K4
RUGBYN/HIL CV21 187 L4
Wilberforce Wy HIA/OLT B92 128 C6
Wilbraham Rd WSLW WS2 4 A4
Wilcote Gv ACGN B27 127 G5
Wilcox Av HEDN WS12 12 F6
Wildacres STRBR DY8 101 G7
Wilday Cl TPTN/OCK DY4 67 L8
Wildcroft Rd COVW CV5 154 A3
Wilde Cl ALE/KHTH/YWD B14 146 B1
Wilden Cl NFLD/LBR B31 144 A2
Wilden La STRPT DY13 189 G1
Wilden Top Rd STRPT DY13 189 H1
Wilderness La GTB/HAM B43 70 B2
Wildey Rd BDWTH CV12 116 B3
Wildfell Rd ACGN B27 127 H3
Wild Goose La REDE B98 203 H5
Wildmoor Cl COVE CV2 134 F1
Wildmoor La BRGRVW B61 168 E4
Wildmoor Rd SHLY B90 126 F8
Wildtree Av WOLVN WV10 36 E3
Wiley Av DARL/WED WS10 52 A7
Wiley Av South DARL/WED WS10 52 A8
Wilford Gv SOLH B91 148 F3
WALM/CURD B76 73 M7
Wilford Rd HHTH/SAND B71 69 H7
Wilkes Av WSLW WS2 52 D3
Wilkes Cl BLOX/PEL WS3 39 J2
Wilkes Cft SEDG DY3 66 B6
Wilkes Rd CDSL WV8 34 D2
Wilkes St HHTH/SAND B71 69 J6
WLNHL WV13 51 L4
Wilkin Rd BRWNH WS8 26 A3
Wilkinson Av BILS/COS WV14 67 J2
Wilkinson Cl BNTWD WS7 18 F5
SCFLD/BOLD B73 72 F3
Wilkinson Cft CBROM B36 91 G7
Wilkinson Rd DARL/WED WS10 51 L8
Wilkinson Wy CSHL/WTROR B46 94 E3
Wilkins Rd BILS/COS WV14 51 H6
Willard Rd YDLY B25 109 G7
Willaston Rd STETCH B33 110 B6
Willclare Rd
LGN/SDN/BHAMAIR B26 109 L7
Willcock Rd BKHL/PFLD WV2 50 C6
Willday Dr ATHST CV9 63 H3
Willenhall La COVS CV3 156 D6
WSLW WS2 38 D6
Willenhall Rd BILS/COS WV14 51 K7
DARL/WED WS10 52 B5
WOLV WV1 50 F4
Willenhall St DARL/WED WS10 52 A7
Willerby Fold WOLVN WV10 36 D1
Willersey Rd MOS/BIL B13 126 B5
Willes Rd RLSN CV32 206 E5
WSNGN B18 88 C7
Willes Ter RLSS CV31 206 F5
Willett Av BNTWD WS7 18 C8
Willett Rd HHTH/SAND B71 69 J5
Willetts Dr HALE B63 120 F1
Willetts Rd NFLD/LBR B31 144 E4
Willetts Wy CDYHTH B64 103 K3
Willey Gv ERDE/BCHGN B24 90 F3
William Arnold Cl COVE CV2 155 L1
William Booth La CBHAMNE B4 6 F4
William Bree Rd COVW CV5 132 A8
William Bristow Rd COVS CV3 155 J6
William Bullock Cl STRPT DY13 188 D2
William Coley Pl STRPT DY13 188 D4
William Cook Rd WASH/WDE B8 90 F8
William Cree Cl KNWTH CV8 183 K2
William Edward St
BHTH/HG B12 * 107 K5
William Green Rd
DARL/WED WS10 69 G2
William Groubb Cl COVS CV3 156 C6
William Harper Rd WLNHL WV13 51 M4
William Henry St VAUX/NECH B7 89 L7
William Ker Rd TPTN/OCK DY4 68 A8
William McKee Cl COVS CV3 156 C6
William Morris Gv
CNCK/NC WS11 16 B1
William Rd SMTHWKW B67 105 H2
Williams Cl SHHTH WV12 38 A8
Williamson Av HEDN WS12 18 A1
Williamson St BDMR/CCFT WV3 2 D8
William St BDWTH CV12 117 H3
BRLYHL DY5 102 A2
EDG B15 6 C8
NUN CV11 99 J2
REDW B97 202 C1
RLSN CV32 206 E5
RUGBYN/HIL CV21 186 F2
RUSH/SHEL WS4 53 K2
WBROM B70 68 C8
William St North LOZ/NWT B19 6 F1
William St West SMTHWK B66 87 M6
William Tarver Cl WWCK CV34 205 L6
William Wiggin Av
BLOX/PEL WS3 38 F3
Willingsworth Rd
DARL/WED WS10 68 A4
Willington Rd CRTAM B79 31 M6
Willington St NUN CV11 * 80 E8
Willingworth Cl
ETTPK/GDPK/PENN WV4 66 E2
Willis Gv BDWTH CV12 117 G2
Willis Pearson Av
BILS/COS WV14 67 K3
Willis St KIDDW DY11 138 A8
Willmore Gv HWK/WKHTH B38 145 K5
Willmore Rd BFLD/HDSWWD B20 89 H3
Willmott Cl MGN/WHC B75 57 H2
Willmott Rd MGN/WHC B75 57 H2
Willoughby Av KNWTH CV8 197 J2
Willoughby Cl COVS CV3 156 C5
PENK ST19 10 D6
Willoughby Dr SOLH B91 148 F4
Willoughby Gv SLYOAK B29 123 L4
Willoughby Pl
RUGBYS/DCH CV22 187 H5
Willoughby Rd CRTAM B79 31 J6
Willow Av BNTWD WS7 19 G7
DARL/WED WS10 68 D1
HRBN B17 105 L3
WNSFLD WV11 36 F5
Willow Bank BDMR/CCFT WV3 49 G4
Willowbank POL/KGSB/FAZ B78 45 M4
Willow Bank Rd DOR/KN B93 149 K7
Willow Brook Rd ALVE B48 170 E6
KNWTH CV8 183 L1
Willow Cl BDWTH CV12 98 E8
BRGRVW B61 191 J3
CDYHTH B64 103 J4
HAG/WOL DY9 119 K8
NUNW/HART CV10 79 L6
POL/KGSB/FAZ B78 60 B7
Willow Coppice
RIDG/WDGT B32 123 G4
Willow Ct SMTHWK B66 87 H5
Willow Ctyd COVE CV2 135 H6
Willowdale Gra
DUNHL/THL/PER WV6 35 J8
Willowdene STRPT DY13 188 F2
Willow Dr CDSL WV8 34 F2
HDSW B21 88 A4
OLDBY B69 86 A6
SHLY B90 174 B1
Willow End HAG/WOL DY9 120 B2
Willowfield Dr KIDDW DY11 138 A5
Willowfields Rd NUN CV11 99 L4
Willow Gdns BRGRVW B61 191 J2
LDYWD/EDGR B16 106 D1
Willow Gv TLHL/CAN CV4 154 A3
WNSFLD WV11 37 M2
Willow Hts CDYHTH B64 103 L5
Willowherb Cl CNCK/NC WS11 17 G3
COVS CV3 156 D5
DSYBK/YTR WS5 69 L2
Willowherb Wy SHLY B90 147 L8
Willow Meer KNWTH CV8 179 M8
Willow Ms SLYOAK B29 123 M4
Willow Park Dr STRBR DY8 119 L3
Willow Ri BRLYHL DY5 102 A4
Willow Rd BDMR/CCFT WV3 49 H5
BRGRVW B61 191 J3
BVILLE B30 124 D5
DUDN DY1 84 E1
GTB/HAM B43 70 D4
NUNW/HART CV10 80 C8
SOLH B91 148 C3
Willowsbrook Rd RMSLY B62 104 D5
Willows Crs BHTH/HG B12 107 H8
Willow Sheets Meadow
RLSN CV32 199 J7
Willowside RUSH/SHEL WS4 40 A5
Willowsmere Dr LICHS WS14 21 K6
Willows Rd BHTH/HG B12 107 J8
RUSH/SHEL WS4 40 A5
WSL WS1 5 K4
The Willows ACGN B27 126 F3
ATHST CV9 63 J3
BDWTH CV12 116 C3
CNCK/NC WS11 16 A4
HLYWD B47 146 E7
STRPT DY13 188 F2
WALM/CURD B76 73 K3
WMBN WV5 64 D8
Willowtree Cl LICH WS13 20 F3
Willow Tree Dr RBRY B45 170 B5
Willow Wk RUGBYS/DCH CV22 187 G3
Willow Wy
CHWD/FDBR/MGN B37 110 F3
REDW B97 201 M1
Wills Av HHTH/SAND B71 68 F6
Willsbridge Covert
ALE/KHTH/YWD B14 146 A2
Willson Cft ALE/KHTH/YWD B14 147 H2
Wills St LOZ/NWT B19 88 F6
Wills Wy SMTHWK B66 106 A1
Wilmcote Cl BHTH/HG B12 107 J7
Wilmcote Ct BRGRVW B61 191 H5
Wilmcote Dr MGN/WHC B75 56 F2
Wilmcote Gn COVW CV5 153 L2
Wilmcote Rd SOLH B91 127 K7
Wilmhurst Rd WWCK CV34 205 G5
Wilmington Rd RIDG/WDGT B32 104 F7
Wilmore La HLYWD B47 172 C1
Wilmot Av CSHL/WTROR B46 93 K7
Wilmot Cl RCOVN/BALC/EX CV7 151 M5
Wilmot Dr ERDW/GRVHL B23 72 E7
TPTN/OCK DY4 67 J7
Wilmot Gdns DUDN DY1 84 E3
Wilmott Cl LICH WS13 20 E6
Wilnecote Gv PBAR/PBCH B42 89 G1
RLSS CV31 206 F8
Wilnecote La TAM/AM/WIL B77 46 B3
Wilner's Vw BLOX/PEL WS3 25 K8
Wilsford Cl ALE/KHTH/YWD B14 146 B4
RUSH/SHEL WS4 40 A5
Wilson Cl RUGBYS/DCH CV22 186 A3
Wilson Dr MGN/WHC B75 57 L8
Wilson Gn COVS CV3 156 D4
Wilson Gv CNCK/NC WS11 17 G3
KNWTH CV8 198 A1
Wilson Rd BILS/COS WV14 67 G6
BRLYHL DY5 102 A1
KIDDW DY11 189 L4
LGLYGN/QTN B68 105 H5
LOZ/NWT B19 89 H4
SMTHWK B66 105 M2
Wilson's La COVN CV6 116 D8
Wilsons Rd DOR/KN B93 150 A7
Wilson St TPTN/OCK DY4 67 L8
Wiltell Rd LICHS WS14 20 F7
Wilton Av KIDDW DY11 137 L6
Wilton Cl SEDG DY3 66 C6
Wilton Rd BFLD/HDSWWD B20 88 F4
ERDW/GRVHL B23 72 D8
RCOVN/BALC/EX CV7 151 M7
SPARK B11 107 M8
Wilton St LOZ/NWT B19 89 H5
Wiltshire Cl BDWTH CV12 116 E2
COVW CV5 153 M2
WSLW WS2 38 F4
Wiltshire Dr HALE B63 102 F6
Wiltshire Wy HHTH/SAND B71 69 G6
Wimblebury Rd HEDN WS12 17 K2
Wimbledon Dr STRBR DY8 119 M3
Wimborne Dr COVE CV2 156 D1
Wimborne Rd WOLVN WV10 36 E7
Wimbourne Cl
NUNW/HART CV10 79 L8
Wimbourne Rd
LDYWD/EDGR B16 106 B2
WALM/CURD B76 73 L1
Wimperis Wy GTB/HAM B43 71 G1
Wimpole Gv KGSTG B44 71 M6
Wimshurst Meadow
WOLVN WV10 36 D1
Winbrook BEWD DY12 162 E2
Wincanton Cft CBROM B36 91 G5
Winceby Pl TLHL/CAN CV4 153 H4
Winceby Rd
DUNHL/THL/PER WV6 48 D2
Winchat Cl COVS CV3 156 D4
Winchcombe Cl DUDN DY1 84 C2
HIA/OLT B92 127 M3
Winchcombe Rd HIA/OLT B92 127 M3
Winchester Av KIDDW DY11 137 L7
NUNW/HART CV10 81 G5
Winchester Cl
BLKHTH/ROWR B65 104 C1
HAG/WOL DY9 119 L6
LICH WS13 21 G2
Winchester Dr
CHWD/FDBR/MGN B37 110 E3
STRBR DY8 119 L2
Winchester Gdns
NFLD/LBR B31 144 E2
Winchester Gv HDSW B21 * 88 A4
Winchester Ms ALDR WS9 54 F1
Winchester Ri DUDN DY1 84 E3
Winchester Rd
BFLD/HDSWWD B20 89 H4
CNCK/NC WS11 16 E2
HHTH/SAND B71 68 F5
POL/KGSB/FAZ B78 45 K2
WOLVN WV10 36 A3
Winchester St COV CV1 9 J3
Winchfield Dr HRBN B17 105 K6
Wincote Dr
DUNHL/THL/PER WV6 49 G1
Wincrest Wy BKDE/SHDE B34 92 A8
Windermere TAM/AM/WIL B77 46 E6
Windermere Av COVS CV3 156 C4
COVW CV5 153 J1
NUN CV11 81 K7
Windermere Cl
RUGBYN/HIL CV21 161 G6
Windermere Dr
FOAKS/STRLY B74 55 K2
KGSWFD DY6 83 H7
RLSN CV32 206 B3
Windermere Pl CNCK/NC WS11 16 C4
Windermere Rd
DUNHL/THL/PER WV6 35 H5
HDSW B21 88 C3
MOS/BIL B13 125 M4
Windermere Wy STRPT DY13 163 J7
Winderton Av
RWWCK/WEL CV35 204 B3
Winding House La COVN CV6 134 B1
Winding Ml North
BRLYHL DY5 * 102 C6
Winding Ml South
BRLYHL DY5 * 102 C6
The Windings LICH WS13 20 F4
Windlass Cft NFLD/LBR B31 123 K8
Windleaves Rd CBROM B36 92 C6
Windmill Av CSHL/WTROR B46 93 K6
RBRY B45 143 J5
Windmill Bank WMBN WV5 64 E6
Windmill Cl CRTAM B79 31 L5
KNWTH CV8 179 L7
LICH WS13 20 E3
NFLD/LBR B31 124 A8
STRPT DY13 188 D4
Windmill Cottages
PBAR/PBCH B42 * 70 E8
Windmill Crs BDMR/CCFT WV3 48 E4
SMTHWK B66 88 A8
Windmill Dr REDW B97 201 M5
Windmill End DUDS DY2 85 J8
Windmill Gdns REDW B97 201 L7
Windmill Gv KGSWFD DY6 82 E5
Windmill Hl HALE B63 103 H8
NFLD/LBR B31 123 M8
RLSN CV32 199 H8
The Windmill Hl COVW CV5 132 E6
Windmill La ATHST CV9 62 B7
BDMR/CCFT WV3 48 E4
DOR/KN B93 175 K4
LICH WS13 20 E3
NUNW/HART CV10 97 J7
RCOVN/BALC/EX CV7 114 B7
RUGE WS15 18 E1
SMTHWK B66 105 M1
Windmill Pk
RCOVN/BALC/EX CV7 * 178 B1
Windmill Prec SMTHWK B66 87 M8
Windmill Rd ATHST CV9 63 H4
COVN CV6 134 E2
NUNW/HART CV10 80 B6
RCOVN/BALC/EX CV7 116 E6
RLSS CV31 206 D8
SHLY B90 147 J3
Windmill St CBHAMW B1 6 F8
DARL/WED WS10 68 D2
DUDN DY1 84 E3
SEDG DY3 66 B8
WSL WS1 4 F6
Windmill Vw BILS/COS WV14 66 F6
Windridge Cl COVS CV3 156 A7
Windridge Crs HIA/OLT B92 128 D5
The Windrow
DUNHL/THL/PER WV6 48 B1
Windrush Cl REDW B97 202 B7
Windrush Gv SLYOAK B29 124 E5
Windrush Rd CNCK/NC WS11 12 C7
HLYWD B47 146 F6
Windrush Wy RRUGBY CV23 159 M8
Windsor Av
ETTPK/GDPK/PENN WV4 49 J7
LGLYGN/QTN B68 104 E2
Windsor Cl BLKHTH/ROWR B65 104 A1
BNTWD WS7 18 C4
CRTAM B79 32 A6
HALE B63 121 K2
NFLD/LBR B31 144 E7
RBRY B45 143 L3
Windsor Ct SEDG DY3 83 M4
Windsor Crs DUDS DY2 85 H7
Windsor Dr ERDE/BCHGN B24 73 G8
HIA/OLT B92 127 M3
KIDD DY10 138 C6
STRPT DY13 188 D5
Windsor Gdns BDMR/CCFT WV3 48 E6
BRGRVE B60 191 L3
CDSL WV8 34 D2
Windsor Ga SHHTH WV12 52 A1
Windsor Gv RUSH/SHEL WS4 40 A3
STRBR DY8 101 J4
Windsor Holloway KINVER DY7 118 A4
Windsor Pl ERDW/GRVHL B23 90 C2
RLSN CV32 206 D4
VAUX/NECH B7 7 M3
Windsor Rd BLKHTH/ROWR B65 86 A8
BVILLE B30 124 F8
CBROM B36 92 D6
ETTPK/GDPK/PENN WV4 50 D8
GTWY WS6 24 C1
HALE B63 121 K1
HHTH/SAND B71 68 F5
LGLYGN/QTN B68 104 E2
POL/KGSB/FAZ B78 47 L2
REDW B97 194 B8
SCFLD/BOLD B73 72 B4
STRBR DY8 119 H2
TPTN/OCK DY4 67 L5
WMBN WV5 64 D7
Windsor St BILS/COS WV14 51 G7
BRGRVE B60 191 K3
COV CV1 8 C5
NUN CV11 98 F1
REDW B97 202 B1
RLSN CV32 206 D4
RUGBYN/HIL CV21 187 G2
VAUX/NECH B7 89 K8
WSL WS1 4 F8
Windsor St South VAUX/NECH B7 7 L2
Windsor Ter
LDYWD/EDGR B16 * 106 D4
Windsor Vw RIDG/WDGT B32 122 F6
Windsor Wk DARL/WED WS10 52 B5
Windsor Wy RUSH/SHEL WS4 40 B6
Winds Point HAG/WOL DY9 119 L7
Windward Wy CBROM B36 92 D6
Windy Arbour KNWTH CV8 197 M2
Windy Arbour La WOLVN WV10 23 J1
Windyridge Rd WALM/CURD B76 73 K7
Winfield Rd NUN CV11 80 F8
Winfield St RUGBYN/HIL CV21 187 H2
Winford Av KGSWFD DY6 101 J1
Winforton Cl REDE B98 203 J2
Wingate Cl BVILLE B30 145 K1
Wingate Rd WSLW WS2 52 C3
Wing Cl WSLW WS2 52 D1
Wingfield Cl
CHWD/FDBR/MGN B37 110 D2
Wingfield Rd CSHL/WTROR B46 93 K8
PBAR/PBCH B42 71 G6
Wingfield Wy COVN CV6 133 L3
Wingfoot Av WOLVN WV10 36 B5
Wingrave Cl COVW CV5 132 E7
Winifred Av COVW CV5 8 B7
Winkle St WBROM B70 86 F1
Winleigh Rd BFLD/HDSWWD B20 88 D3
Winnall Cl BILS/COS WV14 67 H3
Winnallthorpe COVS CV3 156 C7
Winnie Rd SLYOAK B29 124 C4
Winnington Rd WASH/WDE B8 90 E6
Winnipeg Rd HWK/WKHTH B38 145 L5
Winrush Cl SEDG DY3 84 B2
Winsford Av COVW CV5 153 M1
Winsford Cl HALE B63 103 L7
RCOVN/BALC/EX CV7 151 L7
WALM/CURD B76 73 J2
Winsham Gv HDSW B21 88 B5
Winsham Wk COVS CV3 181 G2
Winslow Cl REDE B98 203 K3
RLSN CV32 206 A4
Winslow Dr
DUNHL/THL/PER WV6 49 J1
Winson Green Rd WSNGN B18 88 C8
Winson St WSNGN B18 106 B1
Winsor Av HEDN WS12 12 F7
Winstanley Rd STETCH B33 109 H3
Winster Av DOR/KN B93 175 J1
Winster Cl RCOVN/BALC/EX CV7 115 L6
Winster Gv KGSTG B44 71 H3
Winster Rd GTB/HAM B43 70 B5
WOLV WV1 50 F4
Winston Av COVE CV2 135 H4
Winston Cl COVE CV2 * 135 H5
Winston Crs RLSN CV32 * 207 G2
Winston Dr BFLD/HDSWWD B20 88 F3
RMSLY B62 142 E1
Winstone Cl REDE B98 202 E1
Winston Rd SEDG DY3 82 C3
Winterborne Gdns
NUNW/HART CV10 98 D4
Winterbourne Cft
ALE/KHTH/YWD B14 146 A3
Winterbourne Rd SOLH B91 148 D1
Winter Cl BRGRVW B61 168 D7
LICH WS13 21 H3
Winterfold Cl KIDD DY10 138 F7
Winterley Gdns SEDG DY3 66 C7
Winterley La RUSH/SHEL WS4 40 A6
Winterton Rd KGSTG B44 71 L2
Winthorpe Dr SOLH B91 149 G5
Wintney Cl HRBN B17 105 L6
Winton Gv WALM/CURD B76 73 L7
Winward Rd REDE B98 203 K4
Winwick Pl RUGBYS/DCH CV22 186 A5
Winwood Heath Rd RMSLY B62 142 C3
Winwood Rd
BLKHTH/ROWR B65 104 C2
Winwoods Gv RIDG/WDGT B32 122 E5
Winyate Hl REDE B98 202 E3
Winyates Wy REDE B98 203 J2
Wirehill Dr REDE B98 202 E4
Wiremill Cl KGSTG B44 71 J7
Wirral Rd NFLD/LBR B31 123 K7
Wiscombe Av PENK ST19 10 D4
Wiseacre Cft SHLY B90 147 J3
Wise Gv RUGBYN/HIL CV21 187 K3
WWCK CV34 205 J3
Wiseman Gv ERDW/GRVHL B23 72 B4
Wisemore WSL WS1 4 E2
Wise St RLSS CV31 206 D6
Wise Ter RLSS CV31 206 D6
Wishaw Cl REDE B98 202 E5
SHLY B90 147 J3
Wishaw Gv
CHWD/FDBR/MGN B37 92 D8
Wishaw La POL/KGSB/FAZ B78 58 F5
WALM/CURD B76 74 C6
Wisley Gv KNWTH CV8 180 A8
Wisley Wy RIDG/WDGT B32 105 K8
Wissage Ct LICH WS13 21 H5
Wissage Cft LICH WS13 21 G4
Wissage La LICH WS13 21 H4
Wissage Rd LICH WS13 21 H5
Wistaria Cl NFLD/LBR B31 123 L7
Wisteria Dr DSYBK/YTR WS5 69 K1
Wisteria Gv KGSTG B44 71 J3
Wistmans Cl DUDN DY1 84 B4
Wistwood Hayes WOLVN WV10 36 D1
Witham Cft SOLH B91 149 G4
Withdean Cl SPARK B11 108 B8
Witherford Cl SLYOAK B29 124 A5
Witherford Cft SHLY B90 148 B3
Witherford Wy SLYOAK B29 124 A4
Witherley Rd ATHST CV9 63 L6
Withern Wy SEDG DY3 84 A2
Withers Rd CDSL WV8 34 F2
Withers Wy HHTH/SAND B71 87 H1
Withington Covert
ALE/KHTH/YWD B14 146 B3
Withington Gv DOR/KN B93 175 J1
Withybed Cl ALVE B48 170 E7
Withybed La ALVE B48 170 D7
Withybrook Cl COVE CV2 135 H3
Withybrook Rd SHLY B90 147 M5
Withy Gv CHWD/FDBR/MGN B37 92 C8
Withy Hill Rd MGN/WHC B75 57 M5
Withymere La WMBN WV5 65 G5
Withymoor Rd DUDS DY2 103 J1
STRBR DY8 101 L6
Withy Rd BILS/COS WV14 67 G2
Withywood Cl SHHTH WV12 37 M4
Witley Av HALE B63 121 J1
SOLH B91 149 G3
Witley Cl KIDDW DY11 163 M3
Witley Crs OLDBY B69 86 C8
Witley Farm Cl SOLH B91 149 G3
Witley Rd NFLD/LBR B31 145 H3
Witley Wy STRPT DY13 188 B5
Witnell Rd COVN CV6 134 A7
Witney Cl CRTAM B79 31 K6
Witney Dr
CHWD/FDBR/MGN B37 110 D3
Witney Gv WOLVN WV10 35 M2
Witton Bank RMSLY B62 * 104 D7
Witton La AST/WIT B6 89 K4
HHTH/SAND B71 68 E5
Witton Lodge Rd
ERDW/GRVHL B23 71 M6
Witton Rd AST/WIT B6 89 J5
ETTPK/GDPK/PENN WV4 49 L7
Witton St BORD B9 107 M3
STRBR DY8 119 J1
Wivelden Av STRPT DY13 164 B7
Wixford Gv SHLY B90 148 B3
Wobaston Rd CDSL WV8 35 H2
Woburn TAM/AM/WIL B77 46 B2
Woburn Av SHHTH WV12 37 M7
Woburn Cl BRGRVW B61 191 H4
RLSS CV31 207 G7
Woburn Crs GTB/HAM B43 70 B4
Woburn Dr BRLYHL DY5 101 M5
CDYHTH B64 103 L6
NUNW/HART CV10 98 E3
Woburn Gv ACGN B27 127 G4
Wodehouse Cl WMBN WV5 64 C8
Wodehouse La SEDG DY3 65 J5
Woden Av WNSFLD WV11 37 G7
Woden Cl WMBN WV5 64 D6
Woden Crs WNSFLD WV11 37 G7
Woden Rd WOLVN WV10 3 L1
Woden Rd East DARL/WED WS10 52 F8
Woden Rd North
DARL/WED WS10 52 C8
Woden Rd South
DARL/WED WS10 68 D4
Woden Rd West
DARL/WED WS10 68 B1
Wold Wk MOS/BIL B13 125 M7
Wolfe Rd TLHL/CAN CV4 153 K6
Wolfsbane Dr DSYBK/YTR WS5 69 L2
Wolfson Dr EDG B15 124 B1
Wolgarston Wy PENK ST19 10 D6
Wollaston Ct STRBR DY8 101 G7
Wollaston Crs WNSFLD WV11 37 H7
Wollaston Rd KINVER DY7 101 G6
Wollerton Gv MGN/WHC B75 57 K7
Wollescote Rd HAG/WOL DY9 120 B2
Wollscote Dr SOLH B91 148 F3
Wolmer Rd WNSFLD WV11 37 K3
Wolseley TAM/AM/WIL B77 46 D3
Wolseley Av ACGN B27 127 H1
Wolseley Bank WOLVN WV10 36 D6
Wolseley Cl CBROM B36 92 E4
WOLVN WV10 36 D6
Wolseley Dr WASH/WDE B8 90 E6
Wolseley Ga WOLVN WV10 36 D6
Wolseley Rd BILS/COS WV14 50 F6
WBROM B70 68 D7
Wolseley St BORD B9 107 M3
Wolsey Rd LICH WS13 20 D3
RUGBYS/DCH CV22 186 B8
Wolston Cl SHLY B90 126 F8
Wolston La KNWTH CV8 183 G4
Wolverhampton Rd
BLOX/PEL WS3 38 F4
BLOX/PEL WS3 39 J2
CDSL WV8 34 D2
CNCK/NC WS11 15 M8
KIDD DY10 138 E4
KINVER DY7 100 D6
LGLYGN/QTN B68 104 E2
PENK ST19 10 C6
SEDG DY3 66 B2
SEDG DY3 83 G3
WNSFLD WV11 37 K2
WOLVN WV10 23 M4
WSLW WS2 4 A3
Wolverhampton Rd East
ETTPK/GDPK/PENN WV4 50 B8
Wolverhampton Rd South
LGLYGN/QTN B68 105 J6
Wolverhampton Rd West
WSLW WS2 52 D3
Wolverhampton St
BILS/COS WV14 51 G7
DARL/WED WS10 51 M7
DUDN DY1 84 F4
WLNHL WV13 51 K4
WSLW WS2 4 D3
Wolverley Av
ETTPK/GDPK/PENN WV4 49 H8
STRBR DY8 101 G7
Wolverley Crs OLDBY B69 86 B8
Wolverley Rd HALE B63 * 121 K3
HIA/OLT B92 128 B3
KIDD DY10 138 C2
KIDDW DY11 137 M4
RIDG/WDGT B32 122 F5
Wolverly Rd KIDD DY10 138 F3
Wolverson Cl SHHTH WV12 52 A1
Wolverson Rd ALDR WS9 40 E1
Wolverton Cl REDE B98 203 H3
Wolverton Rd
CHWD/FDBR/MGN B37 110 F6
COVW CV5 153 L2
DUDS DY2 85 J4
RBRY B45 144 A7
Wombourne Cl SEDG DY3 66 A5
Wombourne Pk WMBN WV5 82 D1
Wombourne Rd SEDG DY3 82 D2
Wombrook Dl WMBN WV5 64 B7
Woodacre Rd ERDE/BCHGN B24 91 G1
Woodall Rd AST/WIT B6 89 K4
Woodall St BLOX/PEL WS3 39 G5
CDYHTH B64 103 G4
Woodard Rd TPTN/OCK DY4 68 A6
Wood Av SEDG DY3 84 A1
WNSFLD WV11 37 G7
Woodbank Dr BRGRVW B61 168 D5
Wood Bank La PENK ST19 10 F3
Wood Bank Rd BDMR/CCFT WV3 48 E5
Woodbank Rd SEDG DY3 66 A6
Woodberrow La REDW B97 202 B7
Woodberry Dr WALM/CURD B76 73 L3
Woodberry Wk ACGN B27 127 H2
Woodbine Av SMHTH B10 * 108 B5
Woodbine Cottages RLSN CV32 206 C5
Woodbine Cft
LGN/SDN/BHAMAIR B26 109 L7
Woodbine St RLSN CV32 206 C5
Woodbourne EDG B15 106 B5
Woodbourne Rd HRBN B17 105 M5
SMTHWKW B67 105 J3
Woodbridge Cl BLOX/PEL WS3 38 E2
RUSH/SHEL WS4 40 B4
Woodbridge Rd MOS/BIL B13 125 K2
Woodbrooke Rd BVILLE B30 124 B6
Woodburn Cl COVW CV5 153 M1
Woodburn Rd SMTHWK B66 88 B6
Woodbury Cl BRLYHL DY5 102 C4
KIDDW DY11 189 K4
REDW B97 201 L7
RMSLY B62 104 D5
Woodbury Gv SOLH B91 148 F5
Woodbury Rd KIDDW DY11 163 M3
RMSLY B62 104 E5
STRPT DY13 163 K8
Woodbury Rd North
STRPT DY13 163 J8
Woodbury Rd West
STRPT DY13 163 K8
Woodchester HAG/WOL DY9 140 F1
Woodchester Rd DOR/KN B93 175 J3

Woodchurch Gra
SCFLD/BOLD B74 .....72 D5
Wood Cl CSHL/WTROR B46 .....93 K6
Woodclose Av COVN CV6 .....133 K2
Woodclose Rd
CHWD/FDBR/MGN B37 .....110 D2
Woodcock Cl NFLD/LBR B31 .....144 A4
Woodcock Gdns WOLVN WV10 .....22 F6
Woodcock La North ACGN B27 .....127 L2
NFLD/LBR B31 .....123 J5
Woodcock St VAUX/NECH B7 .....7 K2
Woodcombe Cl BRLYHL DY5 .....101 M6
Wood Common Gra
BLOX/PEL WS3 .....39 J1
Woodcote Av KNWTH CV8 .....179 H7
NUN CV11 .....81 K5
Woodcote Dr DOR/KN B93 .....175 M3
RWWCK/WEL CV35 .....197 K6
WASH/WDE B8 .....90 D8
Woodcote La KIDD DY10 .....167 H1
KNWTH CV8 .....197 J6
Woodcote PI LOZ/NWT B19 * 89 G6
Woodcote Rd
DUNHL/THL/PER WV6 .....49 C1
ERDE/BCHGN B24 .....73 H8
RLSN CV32 .....206 D2
WWCK CV34 .....205 K5
Woodcote Wy FOAKS/STRLY B74 .....55 K7
WSNGN B18 .....106 E1
Wood Cl BFLD/HDSWWD B20 .....88 E3
Woodcraft Cl TLHL/CAN CV4 .....153 L3
Wood Cft HLYWD B47 .....146 F7
Woodcroft Av
BFLD/HDSWWD B20 .....88 C2
CRTAM B79 .....31 M7
TPTN/OCK DY4 .....67 G8
Woodcroft Cl BRGRVE B60 .....169 K8
CDYHTH B64 .....103 K5
Woodcross La BILS/COS WV14 .....66 E3
Woodcross St BILS/COS WV14 .....66 D3
Woodend BFLD/HDSWWD B20 .....70 C7
Woodend Cft TLHL/CAN CV4 .....153 J4
Wood End Dr RBRY B45 .....169 L5
Wood End La ERDE/BCHGN B24 .....90 D2
HOCK/TIA B94 .....173 J8
RCOVN/BALC/EX CV7 .....114 E1
Woodend Pl
DUNHL/THL/PER WV6 .....48 F1
Wood End Rd DSYBK/YTR WS5 .....54 B5
ERDE/BCHGN B24 .....90 D2
WNSFLD WV11 .....37 H6
Woodfall Av BVILLE B30 .....124 D8
Woodfield Rd HAG/WOL DY9 .....141 H6
Woodfield Av BRLYHL DY5 .....83 K6
CDYHTH B64 .....103 H5
ETTPK/GDPK/PENN WV4 .....49 K7
HAG/WOL DY9 .....120 D3
OLDBY B69 .....104 E1
Woodfield Cl CNCK/NC WS11 .....17 K6
DSYBK/YTR WS5 .....54 C8
MGN/WHC B75 .....56 F5
REDE B98 .....194 E8
Woodfield Crs BHTH/HG B12 .....107 L7
KIDDW DY11 .....138 A8
Woodfield Dr CNCK/NC WS11 .....17 K6
Woodfield Hts
DUNHL/THL/PER WV6 .....49 H1
Woodfield La RMSLY B62 .....142 B5
Woodfield Rd
ALE/KHTH/YWD B14 .....125 K5
BHTH/HG B12 .....107 L7
COVW CV5 .....154 C5
SEDG DY3 .....84 A1
SOLH B91 .....127 K4
Woodfields Dr LICHS WS14 .....21 J7
Woodfields St KIDDW DY11 .....138 E4
Woodfold Cft ALDR WS9 .....40 F6
Woodford Av CBROM B36 .....91 G3
Woodford Br ATHST CV9 .....80 A1
Woodford Cl COVEN WV9 .....35 K3
NUNW/HART CV10 .....98 A1
RCOVN/BALC/EX CV7 .....116 D4
Woodford Crs BNTWD WS7 .....18 F6
Woodford La CNCK/NC WS11 .....16 D1
Woodford Green Rd
HLGN/YWD B28 .....126 C5
Woodford La NUNW/HART CV10 .....79 M2
WMBN WV5 .....64 B5
Woodford Wy HEDN WS12 .....17 C4
Woodfort Rd TPTN/OCK DY4 .....70 C6
Woodgate Dr RIDG/WDGT B32 .....122 E4
Woodgate Gdns
RIDG/WDGT B32 .....122 E3
Woodgate La RIDG/WDGT B32 .....122 E3
Woodgate Rd BRGRVE B60 .....200 A4
Woodgate Wy HAG/WOL DY9 .....141 J6
Woodglade Cft
HWK/WKHTH B38 .....145 J3
Woodgreen GTWY WS6 .....16 C8
Woodgreen Cl REDW B97 .....201 M7
Woodgreen Cft
LGLYGN/QTN B68 .....105 G6
Wood Green Rd
DARL/WED WS10 .....68 D2
WSNGN B18 .....106 B1
Woodgreen Rd
LGLYGN/QTN B68 .....105 G6
Woodhall Cl NUN CV11 .....99 K3
TPTN/OCK DY4 .....67 L7
Woodhall Cft HIA/OLT B92 .....127 K2
Woodhall Rd
ETTPK/GDPK/PENN WV4 .....65 J1
Woodham Cl RBRY B45 .....143 J4
Woodhampton Cl STRPT DY13 .....188 D5
Woodhams Rd KNWTH CV8 .....182 K2
Woodhaven CNCK/NC WS11 .....15 M7
RUSH/SHEL WS4 .....40 B4
Wood Hayes Rd WOLVN WV10 .....36 F5
Woodhill Cl WMBN WV5 .....64 D7
Wood Hill Ri COVN CV6 .....134 A3
Woodhouse Cl COVS CV3 .....156 C5
Woodhouse Fold WNSFLD WV11 .....37 H8
Woodhouse La TAM/AM/WIL B77 .....32 E8
Woodhouse Orch
HAG/WOL DY9 .....141 J6
Woodhouse Rd
DUNHL/THL/PER WV6 .....48 D2
RIDG/WDGT B32 .....105 J7
Woodhouse Rd North
DUNHL/THL/PER WV6 .....48 D2
Woodhouses La BNTWD WS7 .....19 J7
Woodhouses Rd BNTWD WS7 .....19 L6
Woodhurst Rd MOS/BIL B13 .....125 L1
Wooding Crs TPTN/OCK DY4 .....67 M4
Woodington Rd MGN/WHC B75 .....57 L8
Woodland Av BRLYHL DY5 .....102 A4
COVS CV3 .....154 D6
DUDN DY1 .....85 G3
KIDDW DY11 .....137 M6
Woodland Cl HAG/WOL DY9 .....120 B4
HEDN WS12 .....12 F5

SHHTH WV12 .....38 B7
Woodland Cottages
ETTPK/GDPK/PENN WV4 * 65 K1
Woodland Ct HEDN WS12 .....16 A1
LICHS WS14 .....21 H8
Woodland Crs BDMR/CCFT WV3 .....49 H6
Woodland Dr RBRY B45 .....169 L3
SMTHWK B66 .....87 J6
Woodland Gv GTB/HAM B43 .....55 J3
KIDD DY10 .....139 G2
SEDG DY3 .....83 M2
Woodland Ri CDYHTH B64 .....103 K5
SCFLD/BOLD B73 .....72 F1
Woodland Rd BDMR/CCFT WV3 .....49 H6
BRGRVW B61 .....167 K6
HDSW B21 .....88 A5
KNWTH CV8 .....179 M6
NFLD/LBR B31 .....144 F2
REDW B97 .....201 M2
RMSLY B62 .....104 B5
TAM/AM/WIL B77 .....46 E1
Woodlands Cottages
DSYBK/YTR WS5 .....54 C8
Woodlands Crs BLOX/PEL WS3 .....25 K8
Woodlands Paddock
ETTPK/GDPK/PENN WV4 .....65 J1
Woodlands Park Rd BVILLE B30 .....124 A8
Woodlands Rd BDWTH CV12 .....116 C1
COVS CV3 .....157 H6
KIDD DY10 .....138 F1
RBRY B45 .....143 H6
SPARK B11 .....126 A2
WASH/WDE B8 .....108 D1
WMBN WV5 .....64 E8
Woodlands St SMTHWK B66 .....88 A8
The Woodlands ATHST CV9 .....61 G4
CDYHTH B64 .....103 L6
LICH WS13 .....21 H5
MKBR/MHC B75 .....57 L7
NUNW/HART CV10 * 79 L5
STRBR DY8 .....119 L3
Woodlands Wy
CHWD/FDBR/MGN B37 .....111 H2
Wood La ALDR WS9 .....41 L5
BFLD/HDSWWD B20 .....88 D3
BLOX/PEL WS3 .....25 K8
BRGRVW B61 .....168 A2
CHWD/FDBR/MGN B37 .....110 E5
FOAKS/STRLY B74 .....90 F4
HEDN WS12 .....17 C1
HIA/OLT B92 .....150 D4
HOCK/TIA B94 .....173 J4
HRBN B17 .....105 L7
MKTBOS/BARL/STKG CV13 .....81 H2
NUNW/HART CV10 * 79 L5
RCOVN/BALC/EX CV7 .....96 B3
RIDG/WDGT B32 .....122 E4
SHHTH WV12 .....38 C6
WBROM B70 .....86 E2
WOLVN WV10 .....36 E3
WOLVN WV10 .....36 B3
Wood Lane Cl SHHTH WV12 * 38 C6
Woodlawn Gv KGSWFD DY6 .....83 H8
Woodlea Dr ERDE/BCHGN B24 .....90 D3
SOLH B91 .....127 J8
Wood Leasow RIDG/WDGT B32 .....123 K3
Woodleigh Av HRBN B17 .....124 D1
Woodleigh Cl HALE B63 .....103 L7
Woodleigh Rd
CSCFLD/WYGN B72 .....72 F4
TLHL/CAN CV4 .....153 L8
The Woodleys
ALE/KHTH/YWD B14 .....146 F1
Woodloes Av North
WWCK CV34 .....205 J3
Woodloes Av South
WWCK CV34 .....205 J4
Woodloes La
RWWCK/WEL CV35 .....205 J2
Woodloes Rd SHLY B90 .....147 M6
Woodman Cl DARL/WED WS10 .....68 F1
HALE B63 .....104 B2
Woodman La CGTWY WS6 .....24 C1
HAG/WOL DY9 .....141 H1
Woodman Rd
ALE/KHTH/YWD B14 .....146 E4
HALE B63 .....104 B2
Woodmeadow Rd BVILLE B30 .....145 L2
Woodmill Meadow KNWTH CV8 .....180 B1
Woodnorton Dr MOS/BIL B13 .....125 J3
Woodnorton Rd
BLKHTH/ROWR B65 .....104 D3
Woodpecker Gv CBROM B36 .....92 E6
Woodpecker Wy CNCK/NC WS11 .....17 C2
Woodperry Av SOLH B91 .....149 G4
Wood Piece La REDE B98 .....195 H6
Woodridge AST/WIT B6 .....89 J4
Woodridge Dr MOS/BIL B13 .....125 K3
Woodridge Rd HALE B63 .....103 L8
Wood Ridings LICH WS13 .....20 E4
Wood Rd CDSL WV8 .....34 B1
DUNHL/THL/PER WV6 .....48 A2
SEDG DY3 .....84 A2
WMBN WV5 .....64 F6
Woodroffe Wk COVN CV6 .....134 E1
Woodrough Dr MOS/BIL B13 .....125 K3
Woodrow Crs DOR/KN B93 .....149 M8
Woodrow Dr REDE B98 .....202 E7
Woodrow La BRGRVW B61 .....168 D4
KIDD DY10 .....166 A1
Woodrow North REDE B98 .....202 E6
Woodrow North Ter
REDE B98 * 202 E6
Woodrow South REDE B98 .....202 F6
Woodrow Wk REDE B98 .....202 E7
Woodruff Wy DSYBK/YTR WS5 .....69 K1
Woodrush Dr HLYWD B47 .....146 D5
Woods Bank Ter
DARL/WED WS10 .....52 A8
Woods Crs BRLYHL DY5 .....102 E4
Woods Cft LICH WS13 .....20 E4
Woodsetton Cl DUDN DY1 .....66 F7
Woodshires Rd COVN CV6 .....134 E7
Woodsia Cl RRUGBY CV23 .....161 H5
Woodside ATHST CV9 .....62 A5
FOAKS/STRLY B74 .....56 C3
RCOVN/BALC/EX CV7 .....96 B4
Wood Side WNSFLD WV11 .....37 H5
Woodside Av North COVS CV3 .....154 D9

Woodside Av South COVS CV3 .....154 D8
Woodside Cl ATHST CV9 .....61 G4
DSYBK/YTR WS5 .....54 B8
Woodside Dr DOR/KN B93 .....175 J3
RBRY B45 .....169 M5
Woodside Gv CDSL WV8 .....34 F2
Woodside Pk HOCK/TIA B94 .....172 F6
KNWTH CV8 * 182 F7
Woodside Pl HEDN WS12 .....12 B8
Woodside Rd DSYBK/YTR WS5 .....54 C7
DUDS DY2 .....84 F6
SLYOAK B29 .....124 E4
Woodside Wy ALDR WS9 .....40 F8
RIDG/WDGT B32 .....122 E5
SHHTH WV12 .....38 C6
SOLH B91 .....127 J8
Woods La BRLYHL DY5 .....102 B6
CDYHTH B64 .....103 G5
Woodsome Gv
ERDW/GRVHL B23 .....72 A6
Woodsorrel Rd DUDN DY1 .....84 D1
Woods Piece RCOVN/BALC/EX CV7 .....115 K7
The Woods MOS/BIL B13 .....125 K2
Woodstile SKDE/SHDE B34 .....91 M7
Woodstile Cl MGN/WHC B75 .....56 C7
Woodstock Cl DSYBK/YTR WS5 .....69 L2
DUDN DY1 .....84 E5
STRBR DY8 .....101 G4
Woodstock Crs DOR/KN B93 .....175 K2
Woodstock Dr FOAKS/STRLY B74 .....56 B1
HEDN WS12 .....12 A6
STRBR DY8 .....101 G3
Woodstock Rd COVS CV3 .....155 H6
HDSW B21 .....88 B3
MOS/BIL B13 .....125 L1
NUN CV11 .....99 J4
WOLV WV1 .....50 F4
Woodston Gv SOLH B91 .....149 G5
Wood St ATHST CV9 .....61 G5
BDWTH CV12 .....116 E1
BILS/COS WV14 .....51 H8
DARL/WED WS10 .....52 F1
DUDS DY2 .....84 D7
ETTPK/GDPK/PENN WV4 .....66 E2
HAG/WOL DY9 .....102 D8
KIDDW DY11 .....138 B7
RLSN CV32 .....206 B5
RUGBYN/HIL CV21 .....160 E8
STRBR DY8 .....101 H6
TPTN/OCK DY4 .....67 J7
WLNHL WV13 .....51 L3
WOLVN WV10 .....36 C8
Woodthorne Cl PENK ST19 .....10 D6
Woodthorne Rd South
DUNHL/THL/PER WV6 .....34 E7
Woodthorne Rd
DUNHL/THL/PER WV6 .....34 E8
Woodthorpe Dr BEWD DY12 .....162 E1
HAG/WOL DY9 .....120 B2
Woodthorpe Gdns
ALE/KHTH/YWD B14 .....125 J8
Woodthorpe Rd
ALE/KHTH/YWD B14 .....125 H8
Woodvale Rd HLGN/YWD B28 .....147 L1
Woodvale Rd HLGN/YWD B28 .....147 J1
RIDG/WDGT B32 .....122 E4
Woodview Rd EDG B15 .....107 G6
Woodview Rd ATHST CV9 .....63 J6
Woodville Gdns SEDG DY3 .....84 C4
Woodville Rd
ALE/KHTH/YWD B14 .....125 K4
HRBN B17 .....105 L7
WWCK CV34 .....205 J5
Woodward Pl HAG/WOL DY9 .....120 A1
Woodward Rd KIDDW DY11 .....164 A2
Woodwards Cl WSLW WS2 .....52 F5
Woodwards Pl WSLW WS2 .....52 F5
Woodwards Rd WSLW WS2 .....52 F5
Woodward St HHTH/SAND B71 .....87 H1
Woodway ERDE/BCHGN B24 .....72 F8
RWWCK/WEL CV35 .....206 C6
Woodway Av RWWCK/WEL CV35 .....205 D7
Woodway Cl COVE CV2 .....135 K2
Woodway La COVE CV2 .....135 K2
Woodway Wk COVE CV2 .....135 K3
Woodwells Rd WASH/WDE B8 .....90 E8
Woody Bank GTWY WS6 .....24 C3
Woolacombe Lodge Rd
SLYOAK B29 .....124 A3
Woolaston Rd REDE B98 .....203 G5
Woolgrove St COVN CV6 .....134 E2
Woolhope Cl REDE B98 .....203 G2
Woolmore Rd
ERDW/GRVHL B23 .....90 A1
Woolpack Cl
BLKHTH/ROWR B65 .....103 L1
The Woolpack WWCK CV34 * 205 H7
Woolpack Wy ATHST CV9 .....63 H5
Wooton Cl REDW B97 .....201 L1
Wooton Ct CNCK/NC WS11 .....16 F2
Wootton Ct RLSN CV32 .....206 B2
Wootton Green La
RCOVN/BALC/EX CV7 .....151 L4
Wootton La
RCOVN/BALC/EX CV7 .....151 K3
Wootton Rd BDMR/CCFT WV3 .....49 G6
NFLD/LBR B31 .....144 A6
Woottons Ct CNCK/NC WS11 .....16 D4
Wootton St BDWTH CV12 .....117 G2
Worcester Bar CBHAMW B1 * 6 B6
Worcester Cl CNCK/NC WS11 .....16 D5
COVW CV5 .....132 F6
HAG/WOL DY9 .....119 J8
LICH WS13 .....20 F2
MGN/WHC B75 .....57 H2
Worcester Ct BDMR/CCFT WV3 .....49 J7
Worcester Gn HHTH/SAND B71 .....69 G6
Worcester Gv
DUNHL/THL/PER WV6 .....48 B1
Worcester La MGN/WHC B75 .....57 H2
STRBR DY8 .....119 M3
Worcester Ri SLYOAK B29 .....124 F4
Worcester Rd BRGRVW B61 .....191 K4
DUDS DY2 .....103 J2
HAG/WOL DY9 .....119 L8
KIDD DY10 .....138 F5
KIDD DY10 .....165 H6
KIDDW DY11 .....137 G8
KNWTH CV8 .....197 N5
LGLYGN/QTN B68 .....105 K4
LICHS WS14 .....30 A2
STRPT DY13 .....188 B5
WLNHL WV13 .....52 B2
Worcester St BKHL/PFLD WV2 .....2 E7
KIDD DY10 .....138 C7
RUGBYN/HIL CV21 .....186 E1
STRBR DY8 .....119 L4
STRPT DY13 .....188 B4
Worcester Wk CBHAM B2 * 7 G6

Word HI HRBN B17 .....105 K6
Wordsley Rd REDE B98 .....194 F6
Wordsworth Av CRTAM B79 .....31 L7
ETTPK/GDPK/PENN WV4 .....66 C1
REDW B97 .....202 A5
WWCK CV34 .....205 K3
Wordsworth Cl CNCK/NC WS11 .....16 A1
LICHS WS14 .....20 F3
TPTN/OCK DY4 .....67 K5
Wordsworth Ct
DUNHL/THL/PER WV6 .....48 C1
Wordsworth Crs KIDD DY10 .....138 F1
Wordsworth Dr KNWTH CV8 .....198 A1
Wordsworth Rd CDYHTH B64 .....117 H8
BLOX/PEL WS3 .....39 J5
BNTWD WS7 .....18 E3
COVE CV2 .....156 A1
RUGBYS/DCH CV22 .....186 C7
SEDG DY3 .....65 M8
SHHTH WV12 .....38 C6
SMHTH B10 .....108 B6
WOLVN WV10 .....36 C8
Wordsworth St HHTH/SAND B71 .....69 G8
Worfield Cl RUSH/SHEL WS4 .....40 D3
Worfield Gdns BDMR/CCFT WV3 .....49 K8
World's End Av
RIDG/WDGT B32 .....105 H7
World's End La RIDG/WDGT B32 .....105 H8
Worlds End Rd
BFLD/HDSWWD B20 .....88 E2
Worleys Wharf Av
DARL/WED WS10 .....69 J3
Worsdell Cl COV CV1 .....8 C2
Worsey Dr TPTN/OCK DY4 .....68 B7
Worsfold Cl COVW CV5 .....132 E6
Worth Crs STRPT DY13 .....163 H7
Worthen Gv NFLD/LBR B31 .....144 E5
Worthy Down WNSFLD WV11 .....37 K8
Wortley Av WOLVN WV10 * 36 C7
Worton Rd HAG/WOL DY9 .....120 C5
Wragby Cl COVEN WV9 .....35 M2
Wrekin Cl HALE B63 .....121 G4
KIDD DY10 .....163 M3
Wrekin Dr BDMR/CCFT WV3 .....49 J8
BRGRVW B61 .....168 E3
DUNHL/THL/PER WV6 .....34 E8
HAG/WOL DY9 .....120 B1
Wrekin Gv SHHTH WV12 .....37 M8
Wrekin La DUNHL/THL/PER WV6 .....34 E8
Wrekin Rd KCSTG B44 .....71 K7
SCFLD/BOLD B73 .....72 E4
Wrekin Vw BRWNH WS8 .....26 C6
HEDN WS12 .....12 D4
Wrekin View Rd SEDG DY3 .....66 A5
Wrekin Wk STRPT DY13 .....188 B4
Wren Av DUNHL/THL/PER WV6 .....48 D2
Wrenbury Dr COVN CV6 .....134 E1
Wrens Av KGSWFD DY6 .....101 L1
TPTN/OCK DY4 .....67 G2
Wrens Hill Rd DUDN DY1 .....66 F8
Wren's Nest Cl SHLY B90 .....147 L8
Wrens Nest Rd DUDN DY1 .....66 F8
Wrens Park Av WALM/CURD B76 .....73 J6
Wren St COVE CV2 .....135 M3
DUDN DY1 .....66 F7
DUDS DY2 .....84 F8
Wrentham St CBHAM B5 .....6 F9
Wretham Rd LOZ/NWT B19 .....88 F7
Wrexham Av WSLW WS2 .....52 D4
Wright Av WNSFLD WV11 .....37 M6
Wright Cl POL/KGSB/FAZ B78 .....60 B8
Wrighton Cl SHHTH WV12 .....38 A5
Wright Rd WASH/WDE B8 .....90 A4
Wright's Av CNCK/NC WS11 .....16 D1
Wright's La CDYHTH B64 .....103 K3
Wright St BILS/COS WV14 .....67 J1
COV CV1 .....134 C8
HALE B63 .....121 M1
SMHTH B10 .....108 B5
WOLVN WV10 * 50 B1
Wrigsham St COVS CV3 .....9 G8
Wrottesley Park Rd CDSL WV8 .....34 A1
Wrottesley Rd
DUNHL/THL/PER WV6 .....34 F7
GTB/HAM B43 .....70 D4
Wrottesley Rd West
DUNHL/THL/PER WV6 .....34 F7
Wrottesley St DIG/EDG B5 .....7 G7
Wroxall Cl BRLYHL DY5 .....101 M5
Wroxall Dr COVS CV3 .....156 B8
Wroxall Gv MOS/BIL B13 .....125 L4
Wroxall Rd SOLH B91 .....127 J7
Wroxham Gln WLNHL WV13 .....51 K5
Wroxton Cl WOLV WV1 .....3 K8
Wulfric Cl PENK ST19 .....10 E5
Wulfruna Gdns BDMR/CCFT WV3 .....49 K4
Wulfruna St WOLV WV1 .....2 F3
Wulfrun Sq WOLV WV1 .....3 G5
Wulfrun Wy WOLV WV1 .....2 F4
Wyatt Cl DIG/EDG B5 .....107 G8
Wyatt Cl BDWTH CV12 * 116 F2
Wyatt Rd MGN/WHC B75 .....57 M7
Wychall Dr WOLVN WV10 .....36 C1
Wychall La HWK/WKHTH B38 .....145 H3
Wychall Park Gv
HWK/WKHTH B38 .....145 H3
Wychall Rd NFLD/LBR B31 .....144 F2
Wychbold Cl REDW B97 .....201 L2
SHHTH WV12 .....38 B1
Wychbold Crs STETCH B33 .....110 A3
Wychbury Ct HALE B63 .....121 L2
Wychbury Dr HAG/WOL DY9 .....119 L5
Wychbury Rd BDMR/CCFT WV3 .....49 G6
BRLYHL DY5 .....102 C5
HAG/WOL DY9 .....120 C4
RIDG/WDGT B32 .....122 E5
Wyche Av ALE/KHTH/YWD B14 .....146 B1
Wych-Elm Cl
RUGBYS/DCH CV22 .....185 M4
Wych Elm Rd RLSS CV31 .....206 D3
Wychelm Farm Rd
ALE/KHTH/YWD B14 .....146 E4
Wych Elm Rd BRWNH WS8 .....26 B8
Wychnor Gv HHTH/SAND B71 .....69 G6
Wychwood Av COVS CV3 .....181 G1
DOR/KN B93 .....149 M5
Wychwood Crs
LGN/SDN/BHAMAIR B26 .....109 L7
Wychwood Dr REDW B97 .....202 B7
Wyckham Cl HRBN B17 .....123 L1
Wyckham Rd CBROM B36 .....92 D4
Wycliffe Gv COVE CV2 .....155 M1
Wycliffe Rd West COVE CV2 .....134 F7
Wycome Rd HLGN/YWD B28 .....126 F7
Wye Cl BDWTH CV12 .....117 M3
DUNHL/THL/PER WV6 .....48 D1
RLSN CV32 .....207 L2
WALM/CURD B76 .....73 J6
Wye Rd BLOX/PEL WS3 .....39 J4
Wyegate Cl COVN CV6 .....133 M2
Wykeham Gv
DUNHL/THL/PER WV6 .....48 B1
Wykeley Rd COVE CV2 .....156 A1
Wyken Av COVE CV2 .....135 H8

Wyken Cl DOR/KN B93 .....175 J3
Wyken Cft COVE CV2 .....135 H8
Wyken Grange Rd COVE CV2 .....135 G8
Wyken Rd COVE CV2 .....134 E8
Wyke Rd COVE CV2 .....156 A1
Wylde Cl HTH/SAND B71 .....68 E5
Wyld Ct COVE CV2 .....132 E6
Wylde Crs BLKHTH/ROWR B65 .....104 A1
Wylde Green Rd
CSCFLD/WYGN B72 .....73 G4
Wyley Rd COVN CV6 .....133 M8
Wymering Av WNSFLD WV11 .....37 K6
Wynall La HAG/WOL DY9 .....120 D1
Wynall La South
HAG/WOL DY9 .....120 E1
Wynbrook Gv SHLY B90 .....148 E7
Wynchcombe Av
ETTPK/GDPK/PENN WV4 .....65 K1
Wyncote Cl KNWTH CV8 .....197 L1
Wyndcliff Rd BORD B9 .....108 A4
Wyndham Rd
LDYWD/EDGR B16 .....106 D4
Wyndhurst Rd STETCH B33 .....109 J1
Wyndley Cl SCFLD/BOLD B73 .....72 F1
Wyndley La SCFLD/BOLD B73 .....72 E1
Wyndmill Crs HHTH/SAND B71 .....69 K4
Wynd ham Rd
ALE/KHTH/YWD B14 .....125 J8
Wyndshiels CSHL/WTROR B46 .....93 L7
Wynds Point NFLD/LBR B31 .....123 M8
The Wynd SEDG DY3 .....66 B4
Wynfield Gdns
ALE/KHTH/YWD B14 .....125 J8
Wynford Rd ACGN B27 .....127 L1
Wyn-Griffith Dr TPTN/OCK DY4 .....85 L2
Wynn Cl BORD B9 .....137 H8
Wynne Crs
ETTPK/GDPK/PENN WV4 .....65 G2
Wynn Rd
ETTPK/GDPK/PENN WV4 .....49 K7
Wynn St EDG B15 .....6 E9
Wynstead Covert
ALE/KHTH/YWD B14 .....146 A3
Wynter Rd RUGBYS/DCH CV22 .....186 B2
Wyntor La HHTH/SAND B71 .....68 F5
Wynyates CRTAM B79 .....31 J7
Wyre Cl ALDR WS9 .....40 D1
Wyre Ct BEWD DY12 * 162 D3
Wyre Hl BEWD DY12 .....162 C3
Wyre Rd STRBR DY8 .....101 J6
Wyrley Brook Pk
CNCK/NC WS11 * 16 B7
Wyrley Cl BRWNH WS8 .....26 A3
LICHS WS14 .....20 E8
SHHTH WV12 .....38 A6
Wyrley La BLOX/PEL WS3 .....25 L8
Wyrley Rd AST/WIT B6 .....89 L2
MGN/WHC B75 .....57 H4
WNSFLD WV11 .....37 L7
Wyrley St WOLVN WV10 .....3 L4
Wyrley Wy ERDW/GRVHL B23 .....71 L7
Wythall Green Wy HLYWD B47 .....172 C2
Wythall Rd HALE B63 .....121 L3
Wythburn Wy
RUGBYN/HIL CV21 .....161 H6
Wythwood Gv HAG/WOL DY9 .....120 D1
Wythwood Rd HLYWD B47 .....146 F7
TPTN/OCK DY4 .....67 L5
Wyton Av LGLYGN/QTN B68 .....105 G3
Wyver Crs COVE CV2 .....156 A2
Wyvern Cl FOAKS/STRLY B74 .....56 A1
LGLYGN/QTN B68 .....104 F1
SHHTH WV12 .....37 L6
Wyvern Gv HEDN WS12 .....12 E8
SLYOAK B29 .....124 A3
Wyvern Rd FOAKS/STRLY B74 .....56 A1
Wyvis Cl BDMR/CCFT WV3 .....49 J3

Y

Yale Dr WNSFLD WV11 .....37 J8
Yardley Cl LGLYGN/QTN B68 .....104 F4
REDE B98 .....203 J3
WWCK CV34 .....205 K3
Yardley Fields Rd STETCH B33 .....109 H3
Yardley Green Rd BORD B9 .....108 D4
Yardley Rd ACGN B27 .....127 C4
Yardley St BRLYHL DY5 .....102 K7
COV CV1 .....9 J2
DARL/WED WS10 .....52 F1
Yardley Wood Rd
ALE/KHTH/YWD B14 .....146 F1
MOS/BIL B13 .....125 M3
Yare Gv WLNHL WV13 .....52 A4
Yarmouth Gn TLHL/CAN CV4 .....153 C5
Yarnborough H STRBR DY8 .....119 L3
Yarnbury Cl
ALE/KHTH/YWD B14 .....146 E4
Yarn Cl HLYWD B47 .....146 E8
Yarner Cl DUDN DY1 .....84 C4
Yarnfield Rd SPARK B11 .....126 E2
Yarningale Cl REDE B98 .....202 D7
Yarningale Rd
ALE/KHTH/YWD B14 .....125 G8
COVS CV3 .....156 A8
Yarnold La BRGRVW B61 .....168 A6
Yarranton Cl STRPT DY13 .....188 C5
Yarrow Cl BLOX/PEL WS3 .....25 L8
RRUGBY CV23 * 161 H5
WNSFLD WV11 .....37 K8
Yarrow Dr HWK/WKHTH B38 .....145 H5
Yarwell Cl WOLVN WV10 .....3 H1
Yateley Av PBAR/PBCH B42 .....70 E6
Yateley Crs PBAR/PBCH B42 .....70 E6
Yateley Rd EDG B15 .....106 C6
Yates Av RUGBYN/HIL CV21 .....160 E5
Yatesbury Av CVALE B35 .....91 K2
Yates Cft FOAKS/STRLY B74 .....42 D7
Yates La RMSLY B62 .....104 F3
Yeadon Cl REDW B97 .....201 L4
Yeadon Gdns BDMR/CCFT WV3 .....49 G8
Yeames Cl GTB/HAM B43 .....55 G8
Yellowhammer Cft KIDD DY10 .....164 A4
Yelverton Cl BLOX/PEL WS3 .....38 F1
Yelverton Dr EDG B15 .....106 C6
Yelverton Rd COVN CV6 .....134 A5
Yeman Rd LGLYGN/QTN B68 .....105 J2
Yemscroft GTWY WS6 .....25 H2
Yemscroft Flats
RUSH/SHEL WS4 * 39 L7
Yenton Cl POL/KGSB/FAZ B78 .....45 L2
Yenton Gv CSCFLD/WYGN B72 .....72 C2
Yeoman Cl KIDD DY10 .....164 C2
Yeomanry Cl MGN/WHC B75 .....57 H2
WWCK CV34 .....205 K3
Yeomans Wy MGN/WHC B75 .....57 K7
Yeovilton Cl CRTAM B79 .....31 J5
Yerbury Gv ERDW/GRVHL B23 .....71 J8
Yew Cl COVS CV3 .....156 A1
Yew Croft Av HRBN B17 .....105 L7
Yewdale HRBN B17 .....124 A1

Yewdale Crs *COVE* CV2 ....135 J4
Yewhurst Rd *SOLH* B91 ....148 B1
The Yews *BDWTH* CV12 ....116 C3
Yew St *BDMR/CCFT* WV3 ....2 A2
Yew Tree Av *HAG/WOL* DY9 ....141 H5
  LICHS WS14 ....21 J6
Yew Tree Cl *BEWD* DY12 ....162 D2
  CNCK/NC WS11 ....17 L8
  REDW B97 ....201 L1
Yew Tree Ct *RLSS* CV31 * 206 D8
Yewtree Dr *BRGRVE* B60 ....191 M3
Yew Tree Gdns *CDSL* WV8 ....34 E1
Yew Tree Hill *RUGBY* CV23 ....158 C2
Yew Tree Hills *DUDS* DY2 ....103 G2
Yewtree La *BLKHTH/ROWR* B65 ....103 M3
Yew Tree La *BEWD* DY12 ....162 D2
  BILS/COS WV14 ....67 H4
  BRGRVW B61 ....168 B3
  DARL/WED WS10 ....68 E3
  DUNHL/THL/PER WV6 ....34 D7
  LGN/SDN/BHAMAIR B26 ....109 J6
  RMSLY B62 ....143 J2
  SOLH B91 ....128 C8

Yew Tree Pl *RMSLY* B62 ....121 K8
Yew Tree Ri *WALM/CURD* B76 ....73 K2
Yewtree Rd *FOAKS/STRLY* B74 ....55 H5
  SCFLD/BOLD B73 ....72 E6
Yew Tree Rd *AST/WIT* B6 ....89 L4
  CBROM B36 ....92 C5
  DSYBK/YTR WS5 ....53 L8
  DUDS DY2 ....103 G1
  EDG B15 ....6 C9
  HALE B63 ....121 J2
  KIDD DY10 ....138 D8
  MOS/BIL B13 ....125 H3
  RUSH/SHEL WS4 ....39 M4
  SMTHWKW B67 ....105 J1
Yew Tree Vis *SCFLD/BOLD* B73 * 72 E6
Yew Tree Wk *STRPT* DY13 ....188 C1
Yockleton Rd *STECH* B33 ....110 A2
York Av *ATHST* CV9 ....63 J4
  BDMR/CCFT WV3 ....49 J4
  BDWTH CV12 ....117 H3
  BRGRVW B61 ....191 J1
  WLNHL WV13 ....52 B3
  WSLW WS2 ....52 F3

Yorkbrooke Dr
  LGN/SDN/BHAMAIR B26 ....109 M8
York Cl *BVILLE* B30 ....124 E7
  COVS CV5 ....156 A8
  LICH WS13 ....21 G2
  TPTN/OCK DY4 ....85 H1
Yorkdale Cl *SEDG* DY3 ....84 B2
York Dr *ERDE/BCHGN* B24 ....90 F5
Yorke Av *BRLYHL* DY5 ....101 L4
York Gdns *BDMR/CCFT* WV3 ....49 J4
Yorklea Cl
  CHWD/FDBR/MGN B37 ....110 D3
Yorklea Cft
  CHWD/FDBR/MGN B37 ....110 D3
Yorkminster Dr
  CHWD/FDBR/MGN B37 ....111 G2
York Pl *KIDD* DY10 * 138 C6
York Rd *ALE/KHTH/YWD* B14 ....125 J5
  BDMR/CCFT WV3 ....48 F5

  BEWD DY12 ....162 D1
  BLKHTH/ROWR B65 ....104 C2
  BRGRVW B61 ....191 K1
  CNCK/NC WS11 ....16 D6
  DUDS DY2 ....103 J2
  ERDW/GRVHL B23 ....90 D7
  HDSW B21 ....88 D5
  HLGN/YWD B28 ....126 D4
  LDYWD/EDGR B16 ....106 B4
  RLSS CV31 ....206 D1
  RUSH/SHEL WS4 ....40 B6
Yorksand Rd *POL/KGSB/FAZ* B78 ....45 K5
York St *COV* CV1 ....8 C6
  HRBN B17 ....106 B7
  KIDD DY10 ....138 C6
  NUN CV11 ....98 E1
  RUGBYN/HIL CV21 ....186 D2
  STRPT DY13 ....188 D2
  WOLV WV1 ....3 J6
Yorks Wood Dr
  CHWD/FDBR/MGN B37 ....92 C8
York Ter *WSNGN* B18 ....89 G8
Young Cl *WWCK* CV34 ....204 F8

Young St *WBROM* B70 ....86 E2
Yoxall Gv *STECH* B33 ....109 L2
Yoxall Rd *SHLY* B90 ....148 B3
Yule Rd *COVE* CV2 ....135 H8

Yvonne Rd *REDW* B97 ....202 A7

Z

Zion Cl *GTWY* WS6 ....24 B2
Zions Cl *CDYHTH* B64 ....103 K4
Zoar St *BDMR/CCFT* WV3 ....2 A2
  SEDG DY3 ....84 A2
Zorrina Cl *NUNW/HART* CV10 ....79 M8
Zortech Av *STRPT* DY13 ....163 L5
Zouche Cl *STRBR* DY8 ....101 J5

Index - featured places

The 3b Business Village
  HDSW B21 ....88 B6
A1 Trading Estate
  SMTHWK B66 ....87 L6
A1 Trading Estate
  SMTHWKW B67 ....105 K3
Abberley Industrial Centre
  SMTHWK B66 ....88 B8
Abberley Industrial Centre
  NUN CV11 ....80 F8
Abbey Clinic
  COVW CV6 ....8 A4
Abbey CP School
  BLOX/PEL WS3 ....38 C2
Abbey Fields Swimming Pool
  KNWTH CV8 ....179 J8
Abbeygate Shopping Centre
  NUN CV11 ....99 G1
The Abbey Hotel
  Golf & Country Club
  REDE B98 ....194 D6
Abbey Industrial Estate
  COVE CV2 ....135 J8
Abbey Infant School
  SMTHWKW B67 ....105 J3
Abbey Junior School
  SMTHWKW B67 ....105 J4
Abbey Stadium
  REDE B98 ....194 C6
Abbey Trading Centre
  REDE B98 ....194 C8
Abbey Tutorial College
  CBHAMNE B3 ....6 E3
Abbots Farm Infant School
  RUGBYN/HIL CV21 ....187 J3
Abbots Farm Junior School
  RUGBYN/HIL CV21 ....187 K3
Abbotsford School
  KNWTH CV8 ....179 K7
Ace Business Park
  STECH B33 ....110 A3
Acocks Green J & I School
  ACGN B27 ....126 F2
Acton Business Park
  NUNW/HART CV10 ....80 D8
Acupoint Magneto Clinic
  SMHTH B10 ....108 C6
Adams Hotel
  RLSS CV31 ....206 D5
Adderley Primary School
  WASH/WDE B8 ....108 B2
Adderley Trading Estate
  WASH/WDE B8 ....108 A1
Advance Business Park
  CNCK/NC WS11 ....16 C7
The Alan Morton Track
  STRPT DY13 ....163 L7
Albert Bradbeer Infant School
  NFLD/LBR B31 ....144 D6
Albert Bradbeer Junior School
  NFLD/LBR B31 ....144 D6
Albert Pritchard Infant School
  DARL/WED WS10 ....52 E8
Albion Business Park
  SMTHWK B66 ....87 J5
Albion Industrial Estate
  COVN CV6 ....134 C4
Albion Industrial Estate
  WBROM B70 ....86 E3
Albion Junior School
  HHTH/SAND B71 ....87 L5
Albion Road Junior School
  WLNHL WV13 ....51 M3
Alcott Hall Primary School
  CHWD/FDBR/MGN B37 ....110 F4
Alderbrook School
  SOLH B91 ....148 D3
Alder Coppice Primary School
  SEDG DY3 ....66 A4
Aldergate Medical Centre
  CRTAM B79 ....31 H4
Alderman Callow School
  TLHL/CAN CV4 ....153 L7
Alderman Green
  Primary School
  COVE CV2 ....135 G2
Alderman Harris
  Primary School
  TLHL/CAN CV4 ....153 K6
Aldermans Green Industrial Est
  COVE CV2 ....135 J3
Alderman Smith School
  NUNW/HART CV10 ....98 B3
Aldermoor Farm
  Primary School
  COVS CV3 ....155 M5
Aldermoor Lane Welfare Clinic
  COVS CV3 ....155 L4
Aldersley High School
  CDSL WV8 ....35 J4
Aldersley Leisure Village
  DUNHL/THL/PER WV6 ....35 K7
Aldersley Stadium
  DUNHL/THL/PER WV6 ....35 K7
Aldridge & Brownhills
  Magistrates Court
  ALDR WS9 ....40 C4
Aldridge School
  ALDR WS9 ....40 E8
Alexander Industrial Park
  BILS/COS WV14 ....67 G1
The Alexander Patterson
  Special School
  KIDD DY10 ....139 G2
Alexandra High School &
  Sixth Form Centre
  TPTN/OCK DY4 ....67 M7

The Alexandra Hospital
  REDE B98 ....203 G7
Alexandra Industrial Estate
  TPTN/OCK DY4 ....67 K7
Alexandra Medical Centre
  HALE B63 ....103 K8
Alexandra Theatre
  DIG/EDG B5 ....6 F6
Al-Furqan Community College
  SPARK B11 ....126 D1
Al-Furqan Primary School
  SPARK B11 ....126 D1
Al Hijrah School
  BORD B9 ....108 C3
Al Huda Girls School
  WASH/WDE B8 ....90 B8
Alice Stevens Special School
  COVS CV3 ....155 L8
Allens Croft Primary School
  ALE/KHTH/YWB B14 ....124 F8
Allens Rough JMI School
  SHHTH WV12 ....38 A4
Allesley Hall Primary School
  COVW CV5 ....153 M1
Allesley Hotel
  COVW CV5 ....132 F7
Allesley Park Medical Centre
  COVW CV5 ....154 A1
Allesley Primary School
  COVW CV5 ....132 E6
Alliance Business Park
  NUN CV11 ....99 K2
All Saints CE Infant School
  BDWTH CV12 ....117 G3
All Saints CE J & I School
  HHTH/SAND B71 ....87 L5
All Saints CE Junior School
  WWCK CV34 ....205 L4
All Saints CE Primary School
  COV CV1 ....9 K7
All Saints CE Primary School
  NUNW/HART CV10 ....99 G4
All Saints Industrial Estate
  WSNGN B18 ....88 E8
All Saints Primary School
  RWWCK/WEL CV35 ....197 L8
All Souls RC Primary School
  COVW CV5 ....154 C3
Alma Industrial Estate
  DARL/WED WS10 ....52 A7
Alpha Business Park
  COVE CV2 ....135 H4
Alston Primary School
  BORD B9 ....108 E2
Althorpe Industrial Estate
  RLSS CV31 ....206 E6
Alumrock Medical Centre
  WASH/WDE B8 ....108 C1
Alumwell Community School
  WSLW WS2 ....52 F3
Alumwell Infant School
  WSLW WS2 ....52 F3
Alumwell Junior School
  WSLW WS2 ....52 F3
Alvechurch CE Middle School
  ALVE B48 ....170 F7
Alvis Retail Park
  COVW CV5 ....8 A3
Amblecote Primary School
  STRBR DY8 ....101 K5
AMC Cinema
  LDYWD/EDGR B16 ....106 E4
Amington Industrial Estate
  TAM/AM/WIL B77 ....46 E2
Amington Industrial Estate
  TAM/AM/WIL B77 ....47 G3
Ammond Business Centre
  NUN CV11 ....99 J2
Amptronik Trading Estate
  SEDG DY3 ....82 B1
Anchor Brook Industrial Park
  ALDR WS9 ....40 F7
Anderton Park
  Primary School
  BHTH/HG B12 ....125 L1
Angel Croft Hotel
  LICH WS13 ....20 E5
Angel Hotel
  RLSN CV32 ....206 E5
Anglesey Business Park
  HEDN WS12 ....17 J1
Anglesey Primary School
  LOZ/NWT B19 ....89 G6
Anglo African Industrial Park
  OLDBY B69 ....86 C3
Anita Myatt Health Centre
  ETTPK/GDPK/PENN WV4 ....65 H1
Ankermoor Primary School
  TAM/AM/WIL B77 ....32 C8
Ankerside Shopping Centre
  CRTAM B79 ....45 M1
Annie Lennard Infant School
  SMTHWKW B67 ....105 J2
Annie Osborn Primary School
  COVE CV2 ....135 H6
Apex Business Park
  CNCK/NC WS11 ....17 L8
Apollo Cinema
  RLSN CV32 ....206 C5
Arboretum
  RUSH/SHEL WS4 ....5 K2
Arbury Hall
  NUNW/HART CV10 ....98 A6
Arbury Medical Centre
  NUNW/HART CV10 ....98 C2
Arcadian Shopping Centre
  DIG/EDG B5 ....7 G7

Archbishop Grimshaw
  RC School
  CHWD/FDBR/MGN B37 ....110 D2
Archbishop Ilsey Catholic
  Technology College &
  6th Form Centre
  ACGN B27 ....127 G2
Arches Business Centre
  RUGBYN/HIL CV21 ....161 G8
Arches Industrial Estate
  COVW CV5 ....8 A4
Arches Industrial Estate
  RUGBYN/HIL CV21 ....161 G8
Arden Forest Infant School
  BDWTH CV12 ....117 L2
Arden Hill Infant School
  ATHST CV9 ....63 J6
Arden Hotel & Leisure Club
  HIA/OLT B92 ....129 G3
Arden Industrial Estate
  WASH/WDE B8 ....90 F6
Arden Primary School
  SPARK B11 ....108 A8
Arden School
  DOR/KN B93 ....149 M8
Areley Common First School
  STRPT DY13 ....188 C4
Areley Kings the Windmill
  First School
  STRPT DY13 ....188 C4
The Arena
  COV CV1 ....8 D5
Argyle Street Clinic
  TAM/AM/WIL B77 ....46 C1
Arley Industrial Estate
  RCOVN/BALC/EX CV7 ....96 D5
Arley Sports Centre
  RCOVN/BALC/EX CV7 ....96 C3
Armoury Trading Estate
  SPARK B11 ....108 B7
Arnold Lawn School
  RLSN CV32 ....206 D3
Arran Medical Centre
  CBROM B36 ....92 E6
Arriva Business Park
  KIDDW DY11 ....164 A4
Arrow Business Park
  REDE B98 ....202 F2
Arrow Industrial Estate
  SHHTH WV12 ....37 M6
Arrow Vale Community
  High School
  REDE B98 ....203 J3
Arthur Terry School
  FOAKS/STRLY B74 ....56 E3
Arts Centre
  CRTAM B79 ....31 M8
  LICH WS13 ....20 C5
  NUN CV11 ....98 F1
Arts Centre Cinema
  TLHL/CAN CV4 ....179 M1
Ashbourne Centre
  ERDW/GRVHL B23 ....90 C2
Ashcroft County
  Infants School
  CRTAM B79 ....32 A6
Ash End House Childrens Farm
  POL/KGSB/FAZ B78 ....58 F6
Ashford Industrial Estate
  BKHL/PFLD WV2 ....50 D6
Ashfurlong Health Centre
  MGN/WHC B75 ....57 J5
Ash Green School
  RCOVN/BALC/EX CV7 ....116 B7
Ashlawn School
  RUGBYS/DCH CV22 ....187 J6
Ashmore Industrial Estate
  WSLW WS2 ....4 E1
Ashmore Park Clinic
  WNSFLD WV11 ....37 L5
Ashmores Industrial Estate
  DUDN DY1 ....85 H2
Ashtree Medical Centre
  BVILLE B30 ....124 E7
Ashworth Park Primary School
  STRBR DY8 ....101 H4
Astley Castle
  NUNW/HART CV10 ....97 J5
Astley CE Primary School
  STRPT DY13 ....188 A8
Astley CE School
  NUNW/HART CV10 ....97 J6
Aston Cross Business Park
  AST/WIT B6 ....89 L7
Aston Expressway
  Industrial Estate
  AST/WIT B6 ....89 J8
Aston Fields Industrial Estate
  BRGRVE B60 ....191 L7
Aston Fields Middle School
  BRGRVE B60 ....192 A5
Aston Fields Trading Estate
  BRGRVE B60 ....191 K7
Aston Hall
  AST/WIT B6 ....89 K5
Aston Health Centre
  AST/WIT B6 ....89 K7
Aston Manor Cricket &
  Lucas Sports Club
  PBAR/PBCH B42 ....71 H4
Aston Manor School
  AST/WIT B6 ....89 K7
Aston Newtown Pool
  & Fitness Centre
  LOZ/NWT B19 ....89 H8

Aston Park Industrial Estate
  NUN CV11 ....80 F7
Aston Science Park
  VAUX/NECH B7 ....7 K1
Aston Tower Primary School
  AST/WIT B6 ....89 K6
Aston University
  CBHAMNE B4 ....7 J2
Aston University
  (Institute of Art & Design)
  CBHAMNE B4 ....7 J1
Aston Villa FC (Villa Park)
  AST/WIT B6 ....89 K4
Aston Wood Golf Club
  LICHS WS14 ....42 G5
Astoria Hotel
  LDYWD/EDGR B16 ....106 B4
A7 Sports Centre
  COVN CV6 ....134 E6
Atherstone College
  ATHST CV9 ....63 H5
Atherstone Golf Club
  ATHST CV9 ....63 H7
Atherstone Town Cricket Club
  ATHST CV9 ....63 K4
Atherstone United FC
  ATHST CV9 ....63 H5
Atlas Trading Estate
  BILS/COS WV14 ....67 K3
Atlas Trading Estate
  SPARK B11 ....108 B8
Attleborough Fields
  Industrial Estate
  NUN CV11 ....99 K2
Attleborough Sports Club
  NUN CV11 ....99 J3
Attock Community
  Sports & Cricket Club
  MOS/BIL B13 ....126 A4
Attwood Business Centre
  HAG/WOL DY9 ....102 D8
Audley J & I School
  STECH B33 ....109 L1
Autobase Industrial Estate
  TPTN/OCK DY4 ....85 M2
Avenue Clinic
  NUN CV11 ....80 E8
Avery Dell Industrial Estate
  BVILLE B30 ....124 D7
Avon Business Park
  CNCK/NC WS11 ....16 A6
Avoncroft Museum of
  Historic Buildings
  BRGRVE B60 ....191 J8
Avon Industrial Estate
  RUGBYN/HIL CV21 ....161 G8
Avon Valley School
  RUGBYN/HIL CV21 ....160 C7
Axcess 10 Business Park
  WSLW WS2 ....52 C4
Bablake Junior School
  COV CV1 ....8 D2
Bablake School
  COV CV1 ....8 C2
Baddesley Ensor CE
  Infant School
  ATHST CV9 ....62 B4
Baddesley Ensor Junior School
  ATHST CV9 ....62 B4
Baggeridge Country Park
  SEDG DY3 ....65 J7
Baginton Fields Special School
  COVS CV3 ....181 M1
Bagley Industrial Park
  DUDS DY2 ....103 H1
Balliol Business Park
  COVEN WV9 ....35 J2
Balsall Common Health Clinic
  RCOVN/BALC/EX CV7 ....151 M6
Balsall Common Primary School
  RCOVN/BALC/EX CV7 ....151 M6
Banners Gate Infant School
  SCFLD/BOLD B73 ....71 M1
Banners Gate Junior School
  SCFLD/BOLD B73 ....71 L1
Bantock House Museum
  BDMR/CCFT WV3 ....49 J3
Barber Institute of Fine Arts
  EDG B15 ....124 D1
Barford Primary School
  LDYWD/EDGR B16 ....106 C2
Barkers Butts RFC
  COVW CV5 ....132 K5
Barnfield Trading Estate
  TPTN/OCK DY4 ....67 G7
Barnt Green Cricket Club
  RBRY B45 ....170 A4
Barnt Green St Andrews
  CE First School
  RBRY B45 ....170 A5
Baron Business Centre
  HAG/WOL DY9 ....102 C8
Barons Court Industrial Estate
  ALDR WS9 ....40 C3
Barons Court Trading Estate
  ALDR WS9 ....40 C3
The Barr Beacon School
  ALDR WS9 ....54 F8
Barrs Hill School &
  Community College
  COV CV1 ....8 D1
Bartley Green FC
  RIDG/WDGT B32 ....123 G4
Bartley Green Health Centre
  RIDG/WDGT B32 ....122 F4
Bartley Green Technology College
  RIDG/WDGT B32 ....123 G4

Barton Industrial Estate
  BILS/COS WV14 ....51 J6
Baskerville Special School
  HRBN B17 ....105 L7
Batchley First School
  REDW B97 ....201 M1
Bath Walk Industrial Estate
  BHTH/HG B12 ....107 J8
Baverstock Gm School
  ALE/KHTH/YWD B14 ....146 C3
Baxter College
  KIDDW DY11 ....137 M7
Bayer Hall Clinic
  BILS/COS WV14 ....67 G5
Bayton Road Industrial Estate
  RCOVN/BALC/EX CV7 ....116 F6
Beacon CP School
  SHHTH WV12 ....38 B5
Beacon Hill Cemetery
  ETTPK/GDPK/PENN WV4 ....66 C3
Beaconside Primary School
  RBRY B45 ....143 J7
Beacon Trading Estate
  ALDR WS9 ....40 D7
Bean Road Industrial Estate
  TPTN/OCK DY4 ....67 G7
Bearwood Medical Centre
  SMTHWKW B67 ....105 K3
Bearwood Primary School
  SMTHWK B66 ....105 L3
Bearwood Shopping Centre
  SMTHWK B66 ....105 L4
Beauchamp Industrial Park
  TAM/AM/WIL B77 ....46 B5
Beau Desert Golf Club
  HEDN WS12 ....13 M5
Beaufort Special School
  CBROM B36 ....91 H8
Beauty Bank Primary School
  STRBR DY8 ....101 K7
Bede Shopping Arcade
  BDWTH CV12 ....116 F2
Bedworth Health Centre
  BDWTH CV12 ....116 F3
Bedworth Leisure Centre
  BDWTH CV12 ....117 G3
Bedworth RFC
  BDWTH CV12 ....116 D4
Beechdale CP School
  BVILLE B30 ....39 G8
Beeches Hospital
  BRGRVE B60 ....2 A3
The Beeches Infant School
  RBRY B45 ....143 M3
Beeches Pool & Fitness Centre
  PBAR/PBCH B42 ....70 F6
Beechwood Business Park
  HEDN WS12 ....16 F2
Beecroft Hill Special School
  CNCK/NC WS11 ....16 B3
Belbroughton CE First School
  HAG/WOL DY9 ....141 J7
Belfont Trading Estate
  RMSLY B62 ....122 A1
The Belfry Golf Club
  WALM/CURD B76 ....75 G2
Belgrade Theatre
  COV CV1 ....8 E4
Belgrave High School
  TAM/AM/WIL B77 ....46 D4
Belgrave Recreation Centre
  TAM/AM/WIL B77 ....46 C4
Bell Barn Shopping Centre
  EDG B15 ....6 D9
Belle Vue Medical Centre
  EDG B15 ....107 H6
Belle Vue Primary School
  STRBR DY8 ....101 G2
Bellfield J & I School
  NFLD/LBR B31 ....144 D1
Bell Green Health Centre
  COVE CV2 ....135 G4
Bells Farm Primary School
  ALE/KHTH/YWD B14 ....146 A3
The Bell Shopping Centre
  NFLD/LBR B31 ....144 E1
Bennetts Well
  Primary School
  CHWD/FDBR/MGN B37 ....110 D2
Bennick Trading Estate
  CNCK/NC WS11 ....16 C7
Benson Community School
  WSNGN B18 ....88 D7
Benson Industrial Estate
  WSNGN B18 ....88 D7
Bentley Bridge Business Park
  WNSFLD WV11 ....37 G8
Bentley Drive
  Primary School
  WSLW WS2 ....52 F2
Bentley Heath CE
  Primary School
  DOR/KN B93 ....149 K8
Bentley Lane Industrial Park
  WSLW WS2 ....52 F2
Bentley Mill Industrial Estate
  WSLW WS2 ....52 D3
Bentley West Primary School
  WSLW WS2 ....52 C2
Beoley First School
  REDE B98 ....195 J5
Berkswell CE Primary School
  RCOVN/BALC/EX CV7 ....152 A2
Berkswell Windmill
  RCOVN/BALC/EX CV7 ....178 D1
Bermuda Business Park
  NUNW/HART CV10 ....98 E6

Bermuda Park Industrial Estate
NUNW/HART CV10 ....98 D4

Bescot Hotel
WSLW WS2 ....52 F7

Bescot Industrial Estate
DARL/WED WS10 ....68 B2

Bevan Industrial Estate
BRLYHL DY5 ....101 L2

Beverley Hotel
RUSH/SHEL WS4 ....53 L1

Bewdley CC
BEWD DY12 ....162 F3

Bewdley High School
BEWD DY12 ....163 G3

Bewdley Medical Centre
BEWD DY12 ....162 F2

Bewdley Museum
BEWD DY12 ....162 F2

Bewdley Rowing Club
BEWD DY12 ....162 F1

Bewdley Tennis Club
BEWD DY12 ....163 G2

BGW Business Park
BRGRVE B60 ....191 K7

Bhylls Acre Primary School
BDMR/CCFT WV3 ....48 B5

Bickenhill Trading Estate
CHWD/FDBR/MGN B37 ....111 H8

Bickford Road Industrial Estate
AST/WIT B6 ....89 L4

Bilbrook CE Middle School
CDSL WV8 ....34 F1

Bilbrook Medical Centre
CDSL WV8 ....34 F2

Billesley Primary School
MOS/BIL B13 ....126 A7

Bilston Central Industrial Estate
BILS/COS WV14 ....51 J8

Bilston CE Primary School
BILS/COS WV14 ....50 F1

Bilston Health Centre
BILS/COS WV14 ....51 H1

Bilston Industrial Estate
BILS/COS WV14 ....67 L1

Bilston Key Industrial Estate
BILS/COS WV14 ....51 L8

Bilston Leisure Centre
BILS/COS WV14 ....51 H7

Bilston Public Library & Art Gallery
BILS/COS WV14 ....51 J7

Bilston Town FC
BILS/COS WV14 ....51 K7

Bilton CE Junior School
RUGBYS/DCH CV22 ....186 B4

Bilton High School
RUGBYS/DCH CV22 ....185 M4

Bilton Industrial Estate
COVS CV3 ....9 M7

Bilton Industrial Estate
HWK/WKHTH B38 ....145 L4

Bilton Infant School
RUGBYS/DCH CV22 ....186 A5

Bingley Primary School
BDMR/CCFT WV3 ....2 B9

Binley Business Park
COVS CV3 ....156 E4

Binley Industrial Estate
COVS CV3 ....156 E6

Binley Woods Primary School
KNWTH CV8 ....157 J6

Birchbrook Industrial Park
LICHS WS14 ....28 C7

Birch Business Park
CNCK/NC WS11 ....16 D7

Birch Coppice Industrial Estate
POL/KGSB/FAZ B78 ....47 J8

Birchen Coppice F & M School
KIDDW DY11 ....163 L3

Birchensale Middle School
REDW B97 ....202 A1

Birches First School
CDSL WV8 ....34 F4

Birches Green J & I School
ERDE/BCHGN B24 ....90 F2

Birchfield Independent Girls School
AST/WIT B6 ....89 J5

Birchfield Primary School
AST/WIT B6 ....89 H4

Birchills CE School
WSLW WS2 ....4 C2

Birchills Health Centre
WSLW WS2 ....4 B1

Birchley Industrial Estate
OLDBY B69 ....86 C8

Birch Road East Industrial Estate
AST/WIT B6 ....89 M3

Birchwood Primary School
POL/KGSB/FAZ B78 ....47 K6

Birds Bush County Primary School
TAM/AM/WIL B77 ....46 C5

Birmingham Alexander Stadium
PBAR/PBCH B42 ....71 K3

The Birmingham and Midland Hospital for Woman
SPARK B11 ....126 A2

Birmingham Area Civil Service Sports Club
HIA/OLT B92 ....128 C4

Birmingham Botanical Gardens & Glasshouses
EDG B15 ....106 D6

Birmingham Business Centre
WBROM B70 ....87 K3

Birmingham Business Park
CSHL/WTROR B46 ....111 J3

Birmingham City FC (St Andrews Stadium)
BORD B9 ....107 M4

Birmingham Community College
CBHAMNW B3 ....6 F4
CSCFLD/WYGN B72 ....57 G8

Birmingham Conservatoire (UCE)
CBHAMNW B3 ....6 D5

The Birmingham Crematorium
PBAR/PBCH B42 ....71 G8

Birmingham Crown Court
CBHAMNE B4 ....7 G3

Birmingham Heartlands Hospital
BORD B9 ....108 F3

Birmingham International Airport
LGN/SDN/BHAMAIR B26 ....110 D4

Birmingham Marriott Hotel
LDYWD/EDGR B16 ....6 A8

The Birmingham Mint
WSNGN B18 ....6 B1

The Birmingham Nuffield Hospital
EDG B15 ....106 D8

Birmingham One Industrial Estate
CBHAMNW B1 ....6 B4

Birmingham Repertory Theatre
CBHAMNW B1 ....6 D5

Birmingham Wheels Adventure Park
BORD B9 ....108 A3

Birmingham Womens Hospital
EDG B15 ....106 B8

Birmingham (Yardley) Crematorium
LGN/SDN/BHAMAIR B26 ....109 H8

Bishop Ashbury's Cottage
GTB/HAM B43 ....69 M4

The Bishop Challoner RC School
ALE/KHTH/YWD B14 ....125 K3

Bishopgate Business Park
COV CV1 ....134 B8

Bishop Milner RC Secondary School
DUDN DY1 ....84 E2

Bishop Ullathorne RC Comprehensive School
COVS CV3 ....180 C1

Bishop Veseys Grammar School
FOAKS/STRLY B74 ....57 G7

Bishop Walsh Catholic School
WALM/CURD B76 ....73 H3

Bishop Wilson CE Primary School
CHWD/FDBR/MGN B37 ....111 G3

Bishop Wulstan RC High School
RUGBYS/DCH CV22 ....186 E3

Bi-tec Industrial Park
WOLV WV1 ....3 M6

Black Boy Hotel
BEWD DY12 ....162 F2

Blackbrook Valley Industrial Estate
DUDS DY2 ....84 E7

Blackbrook Valley Industrial Park
DUDS DY2 ....84 E8

Black Country Living Museum
DUDN DY1 ....85 H1

Blackheath Primary School
BLKHTH/ROWR B65 ....103 M4

Blackheath Trading Estate
BLKHTH/ROWR B65 ....104 C3

Black Lake Industrial Estate
WBROM B70 ....68 E7

The Blackwell Golf Club
BRGRVE B60 ....169 M8

Blackwood School
ALDR WS9 ....55 H3

Blakebrook Special School
KIDDW DY11 ....138 A7

Blakedown CE First School
KIDD DY10 ....140 A4

Blake High School
HEDN WS12 ....12 E7

Blakeley Heath Primary School
WMBN WV5 ....64 E8

Blakenall FC
BLOX/PEL WS3 ....39 G6

Blakenall Heath Junior School
BLOX/PEL WS3 ....39 G5

Blakenhale Infant School
STECH B33 ....109 M4

Blakenhale Junior School
STECH B33 ....109 M4

Blakenhall Industrial Estate
BKHL/PFLD WV2 ....49 M6

Blakesley Hall & Museum
YDLY B25 ....109 H4

Blakesley Hall Primary School
YDLY B25 ....109 H4

Blanford Mere Primary School
KGSWFD DY6 ....83 J6

Bleakhouse Clinic
LGLYGN/QTN B68 ....105 G4

Bleakhouse Junior School
LGLYGN/QTN B68 ....105 G4

Blossomfield Infant School
SHLY B90 ....148 B2

Blowers Green Primary School
DUDS DY2 ....84 F5

Bloxwich Business Park
WSLW WS2 ....38 F6

Bloxwich CE Primary School
BLOX/PEL WS3 ....38 F4

Bloxwich Golf Club
BLOX/PEL WS3 ....38 F1

Bloxwich Hospital
BLOX/PEL WS3 ....38 F5

Bloxwich Lane Industrial Estate
WSLW WS2 ....52 C2

Bloxwich Leisure Centre
BLOX/PEL WS3 ....39 G5

Blue Coat CE Comprehensive School
WSL WS1 ....5 G5

Blue Coat CE Infant School
WSL WS1 ....5 G6

Blue Coat CE Junior School
WSL WS1 ....5 H5

Blue Coat CE School
COV CV1 ....9 L8

The Blue Coat School
EDG B15 ....106 C7

Blythe Business Park
HOCK/TIA B94 ....174 D2

Blythe Special School
CSHL/WTROR B46 ....111 L1

BMI Priory Hospital
EDG B15 ....106 F8

Boat Club
WWCK CV34 ....205 K7

Boating Lakes
WOLV WV1 ....2 C3

Boddis Industrial Park
CDYHTH B64 ....103 L3

Bodmin Road Industrial Estate
COVE CV2 ....135 J8

Boldmere Clinic
SCFLD/BOLD B73 ....72 D4

Boldmere Golf Club
SCFLD/BOLD B73 ....72 D4

Boldmere J & I School
SCFLD/BOLD B73 ....72 D4

Boldmere St Michaels FC
SCFLD/BOLD B73 ....72 D5

Bond's Hospital & Bablake Old School
COV CV1 ....8 D4

Bonehill Industrial Estate
POL/KGSB/FAZ B78 ....45 K4

Boney Hay Primary School
HEDN WS7 ....18 E4

Bordesley Abbey (remains of)
REDE B98 ....194 D7

Bordesley Abbey Visitors Centre
REDE B98 ....194 D7

Bordesley Green Girls School
WASH/WDE B8 ....108 C2

Bordesley Green Primary School
BORD B9 ....108 E3

Bordesley Green Trading Estate
WASH/WDE B8 ....108 B2

Borough Cemetery
DUDS DY2 ....84 F5

Boscomoor Industrial Estate
PENK ST19 ....10 C6

Boscomoor Shopping Centre
PENK ST19 ....10 B6

Boswells Monument
LICH WS13 ....20 F5

Bosworth Wood Primary School
CBROM B36 ....92 D4

Boughton Leigh County Junior School
RUGBYN/HIL CV21 ....161 G6

Boughton Leigh Infant School
RUGBYN/HIL CV21 ....161 H6

Boughton Road Industrial Estate
RUGBYN/HIL CV21 ....160 F7

Boulton Industrial Centre
WSNGN B18 ....88 F8

The Boundary Hotel
WSL WS1 ....5 L9

Boundary Industrial Estate
WOLVN WV10 ....22 A8

Bourneville Infant School
BVILLE B30 ....124 C6

Bourneville Junior School
BVILLE B30 ....124 C6

Bournville College of FE
NFLD/LBR B31 ....124 A6

Bournville School of Art & Craft
BVILLE B30 ....124 C6

Bournville School & Sixth Form Centre
NFLD/LBR B31 ....124 A7

Bowling Alley
BRLYHL DY5 ....102 B3

Bowling Alley
COVS CV3 ....181 H1

Bowling Alley
LDYWD/EDGR B16 ....106 E4

Bowling Alley
POL/KGSB/FAZ B78 ....45 M1

Bowling Alley
RCOVN/BALC/EX CV7 ....135 M5

Bowling Alley
RLSS CV31 ....206 B7

Bowling Alley
RUGBYN/HIL CV21 ....160 F7

Brackendale Shopping Centre
SHHTH WV12 ....52 B1

Bradford Street Clinic
WSL WS1 ....4 E5

Braidwood School for Deaf Children
ERDW/GRVHL B23 ....71 M7

Bramford Primary School
DUDN DY1 ....66 E7

Brandhall Clinic
LGLYGN/QTN B68 ....104 F5

Brandhall Golf Club
LGLYGN/QTN B68 ....104 E3

Brandhall Primary School
LGLYGN/QTN B68 ....104 F4

Brandon Court Leofric Business Park
COVS CV3 ....156 E6

The Brandon Hall Hotel
KNWTH CV8 ....157 J8

Brandon Way Industrial Estate
WBROM B70 ....86 D2

Brandwood End Cemetery
ALE/KHTH/YWD B14 ....125 J8

Brandwood End Cemetery
COVW CV5 ....8 B4

Brasshouse Infant School
SMTHWK B66 ....87 K6

Brays Special School
LGN/SDN/BHAMAIR B26 ....109 M1

Breener Industrial Estate
STRBR DY8 ....101 M4

Briars Country Club
KIDDW DY11 ....137 L6

Brickhouse J & I School
BLKHTH/ROWR B65 ....103 L2

Bridge Industrial Estate
HIA/OLT B92 ....128 A5

The Bridge Medical Centre
STRPT DY13 ....188 D3

Bridgeside Industrial Estate
TAM/AM/WIL B77 ....46 A2

Bridgeside Trading Estate
TAM/AM/WIL B77 ....46 A2

Bridge Special School
ERDW/GRVHL B23 ....90 C1

Bridge Street Industrial Estate
DARL/WED WS10 ....68 D4

The Bridge Trading Estate
SMTHWK B66 ....87 M6

Bridge Works Industrial Estate
KNWTH CV8 ....197 L1

Bridgtown Business Centre
CNCK/NC WS11 ....16 F2

Bridgtown County Primary School
CNCK/NC WS11 ....16 E1

The Brierley Hill Health Centre
BRLYHL DY5 ....102 B2

Brierley Hill Primary School
BRLYHL DY5 ....102 C3

The Brierley Trading Estate
BRLYHL DY5 ....102 A2

Brierly Hill Leisure Centre
BRLYHL DY5 ....102 C3

The Brier Special School
BRLYHL DY5 ....102 C2

Brindley Business Park
CNCK/NC WS11 ....16 F2

Brindley Place
CBHAMNW B1 ....6 C6

Brineton Industrial Estate
WSLW WS2 ....4 B6

Brinklow CE First School
RRUGBY CV23 ....158 D1

Bristnall Hall High School
LGLYGN/QTN B68 ....105 H2

Britannia High School
BLKHTH/ROWR B65 ....104 B3

Broad Heath Community Primary School
COVN CV6 ....134 C2

Broad Heath School
COVN CV6 ....134 C6

Broad Lane Trading Estate
COVW CV5 ....153 G1

Broadmeadow J & I School
BVILLE B30 ....145 M3

Broad Street Gallery
WOLV WV1 ....3 G4

Broad Street Health Centre
COVN CV6 ....134 D6

Broad Street Old Boys RFC
COVS CV3 ....156 F5

Broad Street RFC
COVE CV2 ....135 G5

Broadwalk Retail Park
DUDS DY2 ....84 F5

Broadway Medical Centre
DSYBK/YTR WS5 ....53 K7

Broadway Plaza
LDYWD/EDGR B16 ....106 E4

Broadway School
BFLD/HDSWWD B20 ....89 J3

Broadwell Industrial Park
OLDBY B69 ....86 D5

Broadwyn Trading Estate
CDYHTH B64 ....103 L4

Brockencote Hall Country House Hotel
KIDD DY10 ....166 B6

Brockmoor Industrial Estate
KGSWFD DY6 ....101 L2

Brockmoor Primary School
BRLYHL DY5 ....102 A2

Bromford J & I School
CBROM B36 ....91 H6

Bromford Road Industrial Estate
OLDBY B69 ....86 A4

Bromley Hills Primary School
KGSWFD DY6 ....101 K1

Bromley Primary School
BRLYHL DY5 ....83 H8

Bromsgrove Business Centre
BRGRVW B61 ....191 K3

Bromsgrove Clinic
BRGRVW B61 ....191 K2

Bromsgrove Golf Club
BRGRVE B60 ....192 A3

Bromsgrove Lower School
BRGRVE B60 ....191 K4

Bromsgrove Museum & Tourist Information Centre
BRGRVW B61 ....191 L2

Bromsgrove Private Hospital
BRGRVE B60 ....192 F4

Bromsgrove RFCI
BRGRVE B60 ....192 A5

Bromsgrove Rovers FC
BRGRVW B61 ....191 L2

Bromsgrove Upper School
BRGRVE B60 ....191 K4

Brooke Special School
RUGBYS/DCH CV22 ....186 D4

Brooke Special School (Sec Site)
RUGBYS/DCH CV22 ....186 D4

Brook Farm Industrial Estate
HOCK/TIA B94 ....173 M3

Brookfields Primary School
WSNGN B18 ....6 A1

Brookhurst Primary School
RLSN CV32 ....206 B4

Brooklands Grange Hotel
COVW CV6 ....133 H8

Brooklands Hospital
CHWD/FDBR/MGN B37 ....110 F3

The Brook Primary School
STRBR DY8 ....101 K4

Brookside Industrial Estate
DARL/WED WS10 ....68 F2

Brook Street Business Centre
TPTN/OCK DY4 ....67 J7

Brookvale Primary School
ERDW/GRVHL B23 ....89 M1

Brookvale Trading Estate
AST/WIT B6 ....89 L2

Broomfield Park Surgery
COVW CV5 ....8 B4

Brownhills Business Park
BRWNH WS8 ....26 A5

Brownhills Clinic
BRWNH WS8 ....26 D6

Brownhills Comprehensive School
BRWNH WS8 ....26 D4

Brownhills West JMI School
BRWNH WS8 ....26 A3

Browning Street Industrial Estate
LDYWD/EDGR B16 ....6 A6

Brownmead Primary School
BKDE/SHDE B34 ....91 M7

Brownsover Community School
RRUGBY CV23 ....161 H5

Brownsover Hall Hotel
RUGBYN/HIL CV21 ....160 F5

Brunswick Park Trading Estate
DARL/WED WS10 ....68 F1

Brymill Industrial Estate
TPTN/OCK DY4 ....67 J6

BSA Business Park
SPARK B11 ....108 B7

BT Tower
CBHAMNW B3 ....6 D1

Budbrooke Industrial Estate
WWCK CV34 ....205 G5

Budbrooke Medical Centre
RWWCK/WEL CV35 ....204 D5

Budbrooke Primary School
RWWCK/WEL CV35 ....204 D5

Bullring Shopping Centre
DIG/EDG B5 ....7 H6

Bull Ring Trading Estate
BORD B9 ....7 K7

Bull Street Trading Estate
BRLYHL DY5 ....101 M4

Buntsford Hill Business Park
BRGRVE B60 ....191 K7

The Burlington Hotel
CBHAM B2 ....6 F5

Burlish Middle School
STRPT DY13 ....163 K7

The Burlish Park First School
STRPT DY13 ....163 K8

Burman Infant School
SHLY B90 ....147 J3

Burnsall Road Industrial Estate
COVW CV5 ....154 A5

Burnt Tree Industrial Estate
TPTN/OCK DY4 ....85 M3

Burnt Tree J & I School
OLDBY B69 ....85 L2

Burntwood Baths
BNTWD WS7 ....18 D7

Burntwood Health Centre
BNTWD WS7 ....19 G2

Burntwood Town Shopping Centre
BNTWD WS7 ....18 C6

Burton Green CE Primary
KNWTH CV8 ....178 F2

Burton Industrial Estate
CDYHTH B64 ....103 J5

Bushbury Baths
WOLVN WV10 ....36 C4

Bushbury Health Centre
WOLVN WV10 ....36 C3

Bushbury Hill J & I School
WOLVN WV10 ....36 D4

Busill Jones JMI School
BLOX/PEL WS3 ....38 D5

Butlers Leap Industrial Estate
RUGBYN/HIL CV21 ....187 H1

Butts JMI School
RUSH/SHEL WS4 ....5 G1

Cadbury College
HWK/WKHTH B38 ....145 K4

Cadbury World
BVILLE B30 ....124 D6

Calderfields Golf Club & Academy
RUSH/SHEL WS4 ....54 A3

Caldmore JMI School
WSL WS1 ....4 F7

Caldmore Medical Centre
WSL WS1 ....4 F7

Calthorpe Special School
BHTH/HG B12 ....107 L5

Caludon Castle School
COVE CV2 ....156 C1

Cambrian Wharf
CBHAMNW B1 ....6 C5

Cambridge Tutorial College
SMTHWK B10 ....108 B5

Campanile Hotel
AST/WIT D6 ....89 K8
COVE CV2 ....135 L5
REDE B98 ....195 L8

Camp Hill Clinic
NUNW/HART CV10 ....80 B7

Camp Hill Old Edwardians RFC
SHLY B90 ....147 M2

Camp Hill Primary School
NUNW/HART CV10 ....80 C7

Camping & Caravanning Club Site
KIDD DY10 ....138 D2
RMSLY B62 ....142 C1

Campion School
RLSS CV31 ....207 G8

Canal Side Industrial Estate
BRLYHL DY5 ....101 M4

Canal View Industrial Estate
BRLYHL DY5 ....101 L4

Canley Gardens Crematorium
TLHL/CAN CV4 ....154 B7

Canning Wharf
CBHAMNW B3 ....6 D4

Cannock Centre
CNCK/NC WS11 ....16 C4

Cannock Chase Country Park
HEDN WS12 ....13 H3

Cannock Chase FC
CNCK/NC WS11 ....12 F5

Cannock Chase High School
CNCK/NC WS11 ....16 C3

Cannock Chase Hospital
CNCK/NC WS11 ....16 C3

Cannock Chase Technical College
CNCK/NC WS11 ....16 B4

Cannock Chase Technical College
CNCK/NC WS11 ....16 C6

Cannock Industrial Centre
CNCK/NC WS11 ....16 C6

Cannock Motor Racing Stadium
HEDN WS12 ....13 K8

Cannock Park Golf Club
CNCK/NC WS11 ....16 B3

Cannock & Rugeley Cricket Club
HEDN WS12 ....13 L8

Cannock Sports Stadium
CNCK/NC WS11 ....12 D8

Cannon Business Park
BILS/COS WV14 ....67 G4

Cannon Park Primary School
TLHL/CAN CV4 ....154 B8

Canon Evans CE Infant School
BDWTH CV12 ....116 E3

Canon Maggs CE Junior School
BDWTH CV12 ....116 E3

Canterbury Cross Primary NC School
BFLD/HDSWWD B20 ....89 J2

Cape Hill Medical Centre
SMTHWK B66 ....106 A1

Cape Industrial Estate
WWCK CV34 ....205 J5

Cape Primary School
SMTHWK B66 ....106 A1

Cardinal Griffin RC School
CNCK/NC WS11 ....16 B2

Cardinal Newman RC School & Community College
COVN CV6 ....133 K3

Cardinal Wiseman Catholic School
KGSTG B44 ....71 K3

Cardinal Wiseman RC School
COVE CV2 ....135 J4

Carlton Business Centre
VAUX/NECH B7 ....90 A8

Carlyle Business Park
WBROM B70 ....68 D8

Carlyon Road Industrial Estate
ATHST CV9 ....63 K4

Carters Green Medical Centre
WBROM B70 ....87 G1

Cash's Business Centre
COV CV1 ....134 B8

Caslon Primary School
HALE B63 ....120 F1

Castle Bromwich Business Park
CVALE B35 ....91 K4

Castle Bromwich CC
CBROM B36 ....92 A5

Castle Bromwich Hall Gardens
CBROM B36 ....91 L5

Castle Bromwich Infant School
CBROM B36 ....92 C5

Castle Bromwich Junior School
CBROM B36 ....92 B6

Castlecroft J & I School
BDMR/CCFT WV3 ....48 F4

Castle High School
DUDN DY1 ....84 E2

Castle Hills
RCOVN/BALC/EX CV7 ....114 D4

Castle Museum
CRTAM B79 ....45 L1

Castle Place Industrial Estate
COV CV1 ....9 J2

Castle Pleasure Grounds
TAM/AM/WIL B77 ....45 M1

The Castle Pool & Adventure Play Centre
CVALE B35 ....91 K3

Castle Sixth Form Centre (Kenilworth School)
KNWTH CV8 ....197 K3

Castle Special School
BLOX/PEL WS3 ....38 F6
Castle Vale Health Centre
CVALE B35 ....91 K2
Castle Vale Industrial Estate
WALM/CURD B76 ....73 L8
Castle Vale School
CVALE B35 ....91 M2
Castle Vale Shopping Centre
CVALE B35 ....91 K2
Castle View Industrial Estate
TPTN/OCK DY4 ....85 K2
Cathedral Lanes
Shopping Centre
COV CV1 ....8 F4
Catshill Clinic
BRGRVW B61 ....168 E5
Catshill First School
BRGRVW B61 ....168 E5
Catshill Middle School
BRGRVW B61 ....168 D5
Causeway Green
Primary School
LGLYGN/QTN B68 ....104 D2
Cedars Business Centre
CNCK/NC WS11 ....16 A6
Cedars Hotel
KIDD DY11 ....138 A6
Centech Business Park
REDE B98 ....195 K7
Centenary Business Centre
NUN CV11 ....99 J2
Central Business Park
STETCH B33 ....110 B4
Central City Industrial Estate
COVN CV6 ....134 D8
Central Clinic
DUDS DY2 ....85 H4
Central Hall
CBHAMNE B4 ....7 H3
Central Industrial Estate
BKHL/PFLD WV2 ....50 C6
Central Park Industrial Estate
BRLYHL DY5 ....102 D2
DUDS DY2 ....103 G1
DUDS DY2 ....103 J2
Central Six Retail Park
COV CV1 ....8 D7
Central Trading Estate
KGSWFD DY6 ....83 K4
Centre Link Industrial Estate
VAUX/NECH B7 ....89 M7
Centrovell Industrial Estate
NUN CV11 ....99 G3
Century Industrial Estate
KGSTG B44 ....71 J2
The Chace Hotel
COVS CV3 ....155 M8
Chace Primary School
COVS CV3 ....156 A7
Chaddesley Corbett
Endowed First School
KIDD DY10 ....166 C5
Chadsgrove Special School
BRGRVW B61 ....168 D5
Chadsmead Primary School
LICH WS13 ....20 E4
Chadsmoor CE Junior School
CNCK/NC WS11 ....16 E1
Chadsmoor Infants School
CNCK/NC WS11 ....16 E1
Chad Vale Primary School
EDG B15 ....106 B6
Chadwick Bank
Industrial Estate
STRPT DY13 ....189 H5
Chadwick Business Park
STRPT DY13 ....189 H5
Chadwick Industrial Estate
STRPT DY13 ....189 H5
Challenge Business Park
COV CV1 ....134 B8
Chamber of Commerce
WSL WS1 ....5 H2
Chamber of Commerce
& Industry
BDMR/CCFT WV3 ....2 A4
Chancel Industrial Estate
DARL/WED WS10 ....52 B8
KGSWFD DY6 ....83 H4
WLNHL WV13 ....51 M3
WOLV WV1 ....50 D4
Chancel Way Industrial Estate
PBAR/PBCH B42 ....71 K8
Chandos Primary School
DIG/EDG B5 ....107 J6
Chantry Industrial Estate
WALM/CURD B76 ....74 F6
Chapel Fields Junior School
HIA/OLT B92 ....127 K2
Chapel Street
Industrial Estate
DUDS DY2 ....103 H1
Charford First School
BRGRVE B60 ....191 K6
Charlemont Primary School
HHTH/SAND B71 ....69 J5
Charles Street Industrial Estate
TPTN/OCK DY4 ....68 C8
Charnwood Business Park
BILS/COS WV14 ....51 G8
Charnwood County
Primary School
LICH WS13 ....21 G2
Charterfield Shopping Centre
KGSWFD DY6 ....83 H5
Chase Leisure Centre
CNCK/NC WS11 ....16 B3
Chase Park Industrial Estate
BNTWD WS7 ....18 B6
Chaseside Industrial Estate
HEDN WS12 ....16 F2
Chase Terrace High School
BNTWD WS7 ....18 C5
Chase Terrace High School
BNTWD WS7 ....18 E6
Chase Terrace High School
BNTWD WS7 ....18 D5
Chase Terrace
Technology College
BNTWD WS7 ....18 D5
Chase Town CP School
BNTWD WS7 ....18 C8
Chase Town High School
BNTWD WS7 ....26 C1
Chasetown Industrial Estate
BNTWD WS7 ....18 C6
Chasewater Country Park
BNTWD WS7 ....18 A8
Chasewater Heaths
Business Park
BNTWD WS7 ....18 A6
BNTWD WS7 ....18 D4
Chasewater Industrial Estate
BNTWD WS7 ....18 C7
Chasewater Light Railway
CNCK/NC WS11 ....26 A2
Chase Watersports Centre
BRWNH WS8 ....26 A2

Chasewood Park
Business Centre
HEDN WS12 ....17 J4
Cheapside Industrial Estate
BHTH/HG B12 ....7 K8
Chelmsley Wood
Industrial Estate
CHWD/FDBR/MGN B37 ....92 B8
Chelmsley Wood
Shopping Centre
CHWD/FDBR/MGN B37 ....110 F3
Chelsea Trading Estate
AST/WIT B6 ....89 L7
Cherry Oak Special School
SLYOAK B29 ....124 B3
Cherry Orchard
Primary School
BFLD/HDSWWD B20 ....88 C2
Cherry Tree Sports Club
COVN CV6 ....134 C3
Cherry Trees Special School
WMBN WV5 ....64 D7
Cherrywood Industrial Estate
WASH/WDE B8 ....108 B2
Chesford Grange Hotel
KNWTH CV8 ....198 A5
Cheslyn Hay High School
GTWY WS6 ....23 M2
Cheslyn Hay Primary School
GTWY WS6 ....23 M2
Cheston Industrial Estate
AST/WIT B6 ....89 M6
Cheswick Green
Primary School
SHLY B90 ....148 C8
Chetwynd Junior School
NUN CV11 ....99 K6
Cheylesmore Welfare Clinic
COVS CV3 ....155 J7
Chilcote Primary School
HLGN/YWD B28 ....147 K1
Chillington Works
Industrial Estate
WOLV WV1 ....3 M7
Chilvers Coton Community
Infant School
NUNW/HART CV10 ....98 F2
Chinese Quarter
DIG/EDG B5 ....7 G7
The Chiropody Surgery
YDLY B25 ....109 H4
Chivenor Primary School
CVALE B35 ....91 L3
Christ Church CE Infant School
DUNHL/THL/PER WV6 ....2 D1
Christ Church CE Junior School
DUNHL/THL/PER WV6 ....49 G1
Christ Church CE
Primary School
BLOX/PEL WS3 ....39 H6
LICH WS13 ....20 D6
OLDBY B69 ....86 C5
SPARK B11 ....107 M6
Christ Church Infant School
DUNHL/THL/PER WV6 ....48 F1
Christ Church Primary School
BILS/COS WV14 ....67 H4
Christ Church School
PENK ST19 ....14 A3
Christ the King Catholic
Infant School
COVN CV6 ....133 K7
Christ the King RC
Junior School
COVN CV6 ....133 K6
Christ the King RC
Primary School
KGSTG B44 ....71 J4
Chuckery Primary School
WSL WS1 ....5 J4
Churchbridge Industrial Estate
OLDBY B69 ....86 D7
Churchfield Industrial Estate
DUDS DY2 ....85 G5
Church Hill Middle School
REDE B98 ....195 H7
Churchill & Blakedown
Golf Club
KIDD DY10 ....139 L3
Churchill Precinct
DUDS DY2 ....85 H4
Church Lane Health Centre
STETCH B33 ....109 K2
Church Lane Industrial Estate
HHTH/SAND B71 ....69 G7
Church Lawford
Business Centre
RRUGBY CV23 ....158 E8
Church of Ascension CE
Primary School
KGSWFD DY6 ....82 F5
Cineworld Cinema
RUGBYN/HIL CV21 ....160 F7
Cineworld Cinema
SOLH B91 ....149 G2
City Arcade
COV CV1 ....8 E5
City College Coventry
TLHL/CAN CV4 ....153 K4
City College East Birmingham
STETCH B33 ....109 M5
City Estate
CDYHTH B64 ....103 H5
City Farm
COV CV1 ....9 J2
City Hospital NHS Trust
WSNGN B18 ....106 D1
City of Coventry-
Brandon Wood Golf Club
KNWTH CV8 ....157 G8
City Plaza Shopping Centre
CBHAM B2 ....6 F5
City Road Primary School
LDYWD/EDGR B16 ....106 B2
The City Technology College
CHWD/FDBR/MGN B37 ....110 E1
City Trading Estate
LDYWD/EDGR B16 ....106 D2
City Walls & Gate
COV CV1 ....9 G3
Clapham Terrace County
Primary School
RLSS CV31 ....206 E6
Claregate Primary School
DUNHL/THL/PER WV6 ....35 K6
Clarendon House Hotel
KNWTH CV8 ....179 K7
Clarkes Industrial Estate
SCFLD/BOLD B73 ....72 E4
Clay Brook First School
REDE B98 ....203 K4
Clearwater Industrial Estate
BKHL/PFLD WV2 ....50 D6
Clent Hills
HAG/WOL DY9 ....120 L8
Clent Parochial First School
HAG/WOL DY9 ....141 K3
Cleton Street Business Centre
TPTN/OCK DY4 ....85 M2

Clifford Bridge Primary School
COVS CV3 ....156 E2
Clifton Infant School
BHTH/HG B12 ....107 L8
Clifton Junior School
BHTH/HG B12 ....107 L8
Clifton Road Industrial Estate
BHTH/HG B12 ....107 K8
Clifton upon Dunsmore CE
Primary School
RRUGBY CV23 ....161 K8
Clinton Combined School
KNWTH CV8 ....197 J2
The Clock Towers
Shopping Centre
RUGBYN/HIL CV21 ....186 E2
Closers Business Centre
NUN CV11 ....99 H3
Clothier Street Primary School
WLNHL WV13 ....51 L2
Cmt Industrial Estate
OLDBY B69 ....86 C5
Coach House Evening
Prep School
SCFLD/BOLD B73 ....72 D3
Coach House Special School
BRGRVE B60 ....190 F8
Coalpool Clinic
BLOX/PEL WS3 ....39 K7
Cobham Business Centre
WASH/WDE B8 ....108 B2
Cockshut Hill Technology
College
LGN/SDN/BHAMAIR B26 ....109 L5
Cocks Moors Woods
Leisure Centre
ALE/KHTH/YWD B14 ....146 D1
Codsall Clinic
CDSL WV8 ....34 E2
Codsall High School
CDSL WV8 ....34 E2
Codsall Middle School
CDSL WV8 ....34 D2
Cofton Medical Centre
NFLD/LBR B31 ....144 E6
Cofton Primary School
NFLD/LBR B31 ....144 E7
Coldand Colts FC
SOLH B91 ....128 D7
Colebourne Primary School
BKDE/SHDE B34 ....91 J8
Coleshill CE Primary School
CSHL/WTROR B46 ....93 K7
Coleshill Clinic
CSHL/WTROR B46 ....93 L7
Coleshill Heath Primary School
CHWD/FDBR/MGN B37 ....111 G4
Coleshill Industrial Estate
CSHL/WTROR B46 ....93 K3
Coleshill Leisure Centre
CSHL/WTROR B46 ....93 K5
Coleshill School
CSHL/WTROR B46 ....111 L2
Coleshill Town FC
CSHL/WTROR B46 ....111 L2
The College High School
ERDW/GRVHL B23 ....71 L7
College of Adult Education
WOLV WV1 ....3 G6
College of Continuing
Education
BLOX/PEL WS3 ....39 H7
Colley Lane Health Clinic
HALE B63 ....103 G7
Colley Lane Primary School
HALE B63 ....102 F7
Collingwood Primary School
WOLVN WV10 ....36 C3
Colmers Farm J & I School
RBRY B45 ....143 M5
Colmers Farm
Secondary School
RBRY B45 ....143 M5
Colmore J & I School
ALE/KHTH/YWD B14 ....125 H6
Colonial Industrial Park
CDYHTH B64 ....103 H6
Colton Hills School
ETTPK/GDPK/PENN WV4 ....65 M1
Combe Abbey Country Park
COVS CV3 ....156 F2
Comberton F & M School
KIDD DY10 ....164 F1
Combined Courts
WOLV WV1 ....3 H5
Comfort Inn
LDYWD/EDGR B16 ....106 B4
Common Lane
Industrial Estate
KNWTH CV8 ....180 A6
Community Leisure Centre
TPTN/OCK DY4 ....67 H7
Conduit Road Industrial Estate
CNCK/NC WS11 ....25 L1
Coneygre Industrial Estate
TPTN/OCK DY4 ....85 K2
Connect Business Park
WASH/WDE B8 ....108 A3
Conway Primary School
SPARK B11 ....107 M7
Cookley Wharf
Industrial Estate
BRLYHL DY5 ....101 L2
Cooper & Jordan CE
J & I School
ALDR WS9 ....41 G7
Copperfield House Hotel
SLYOAK B29 ....124 B2
Coppice High
Community School
WNSFLD WV11 ....37 L6
Coppice Junior School
HIA/OLT B92 ....128 C6
Coppice Primary School
HLYWD B47 ....146 E7
Coppice Primary School
MGN/WHC B75 ....57 G4
Coppice Side Industrial Estate
BRWNH WS8 ....26 B6
Coppice Trading Estate
KIDDW DY11 ....163 M5
Copt Heath Golf Club
DOR/KN B93 ....149 L5
Copthorne Hotel
BRLYHL DY5 ....102 C1
Copthorne Hotel
CBHAMNW B3 ....6 D5
Corbett Hospital
STRBR DY8 ....101 L6
Corbett Industrial Estate
DUDS DY2 ....85 G7
Corbett Infant School
SMTHWK B66 ....87 M8
Corley Cricket Club
RCOVN/BALC/EX CV7 ....115 G7
Corley School
RCOVN/BALC/EX CV7 ....114 F7
Corngreaves Hall Golf Club
CDYHTH B64 ....103 K5

Corngreaves J & I School
CDYHTH B64 ....103 H4
Corngreaves Trading Estate
CDYHTH B64 ....103 H6
Cornwall Industrial Estate
SMTHWK B66 ....88 A6
Cornwall Industrial Estate
WASH/WDE B8 ....108 A1
Cornwall Road Industrial Estate
SMTHWK B66 ....88 A6
Corpus Christi RC
Primary School
COVS CV3 ....156 B6
STETCH B33 ....109 H3
WNSFLD WV11 ....37 L5
Coseley Medical Centre
BILS/COS WV14 ....67 G5
The Coseley School
BILS/COS WV14 ....66 F4
Coseley Swimming Pool &
Supachute
BILS/COS WV14 ....67 G5
Coten End Primary School
WARW CV34 ....205 K6
Coton Green Primary School
CRTAM B79 ....31 K6
Cotteridge Primary School
BVILLE B30 ....124 E8
Cottesbrooke Infant School
ACGN B27 ....127 G1
Cottesbrooke Junior School
ACGN B27 ....127 G1
Cotwall End Primary School
SEDG DY3 ....66 A6
Coundon Court School &
Community College
COVN CV6 ....133 G3
COVN CV6 ....134 C6
Coundon Primary School
COVN CV6 ....133 J8
County Bridge
Primary School
WSLW WS2 ....52 C4
Courtfield Primary School
ERDW/GRVHL B23 ....72 C7
Courthouse Green
Primary School
COVN CV6 ....134 E5
Courtyard by Marriott
KNWTH CV8 ....182 B2
WWCK CV34 ....206 B8
Coventry Airport
COVS CV3 ....181 L4
Coventry Athletics Track
TLHL/CAN CV4 ....153 M7
Coventry Business Park
COVW CV5 ....154 D4
Coventry Cathedral &
Visitor Centre
COV CV1 ....9 G4
Coventry City FC
(Highfield Road Stadium)
COVE CV2 ....9 L3
Coventry Golf Club
KNWTH CV8 ....181 H3
Coventry Grammar School
COVW CV5 ....154 D4
Coventry Hearsall Golf Club
COVW CV5 ....154 D5
Coventry Muslim School
COVN CV6 ....134 C4
Coventry Preparatory School
COVW CV5 ....154 F5
Coventry RFC
COVW CV5 ....8 B2
Coventry Sports Centre
COV CV1 ....9 H4
Coventry Technical College
COV CV1 ....8 B6
The Coventry Toy Museum
COV CV1 ....9 H5
Coventry Trading Estate
KNWTH CV8 ....182 A3
Coventry University
COV CV1 ....9 H5
Coventry University
Technocentre
COV CV1 ....9 G7
Coventry & Warwickshire
Hospital
COV CV1 ....9 G1
Coventry Welsh RFC
COVN CV6 ....134 B1
c/PLEX (Under Development)
WBROM B70 ....87 H2
Crabbs Cross Medical Centre
REDW B97 ....202 C7
Crabtree Clinic
CHWD/FDBR/MGN B37 ....110 D3
Cradley CE Primary School
HALE B63 ....103 G6
Cradley Heath Community
Recreation Centre
DUDS DY2 ....103 J3
Cradley High School
HALE B63 ....102 F7
Cradley Town FC
HALE B63 ....121 G1
Craig Croft Child Health Clinic
CHWD/FDBR/MGN B37 ....111 G3
Craig Croft Medical Centre
CHWD/FDBR/MGN B37 ....111 G3
Cranmore Industrial Estate
SHLY B90 ....148 C5
Cranmore Infant School
SOLH B91 ....148 C4
Crescent Industrial Park
DUDS DY2 ....84 F6
The Crescent School
RUGBYS/DCH CV22 ....186 B5
Crescent Theatre
LDYWD/EDGR B16 ....6 B6
Crescent Works Industrial Park
DARL/WED WS10 ....52 B4
Crestwood Park
Primary School
KGSWFD DY6 ....83 L8
The Crestwood
Secondary School
KGSWFD DY6 ....83 K8
Criterion Theatre
COVW CV5 ....8 A9
Crocketts Lane Primary School
SMTHWK B66 ....87 L8
Croft Foundry Industrial Estate
WLNHL WV13 ....51 L3
Croft Industrial Estate
CHWD/FDBR/MGN B37 ....110 F3
Croft Industrial Estate
CHWD/FDBR/MGN B37 ....111 G3
Croft Junior School
NUNW/HART CV10 ....98 C2
Croft Medical Centre
RLSS CV31 ....207 G8
Croft Street JMI School
WSLW WS2 ....53 H1
Cromwell Primary School
VAUX/NECH B7 ....89 L7

Cronehill Primary School
WBROM B70 ....87 G1
Cronehills Health Centre
WBROM B70 ....87 G2
Crossfield Industrial Estate
LICH WS13 ....21 J5
Crossings Industrial Estate
BLOX/PEL WS3 ....38 F5
Crossley Retail Park
KIDDW DY11 ....138 C6
Cross Quays Business Park
OLDBY B69 ....86 A3
Cross Road Industrial Estate
COVN CV6 ....134 D6
Cross Street Health Centre
DUDN DY1 ....85 G4
Crossways Shopping Centre
WOLVN WV10 ....50 E2
Crowne Plaza Hotel
CBHAMW B1 ....6 D6
Crown Meadow First School
ALVE B48 ....170 E7
Crown Wharf Shopping Centre
WSLW WS2 ....4 C7
Crown Wharf Shopping Park
WSLW WS2 ....53 G1
Crystal Leisure Centre
STRBR DY8 ....101 K8
Cubbington CE Primary School
RLSN CV32 ....199 J3
Culwell Industrial Park
WOLVN WV10 ....3 J5
Culwell Trading Estate
WOLVN WV10 ....3 L1
Curdworth Primary School
WALM/CURD B76 ....75 G7
Dadsford Bridge
Industrial Estate
STRBR DY8 ....101 J3
Dalehouse Lane
Industrial Estate
KNWTH CV8 ....180 A6
Dame Elizabeth Cadbury
School
BVILLE B30 ....124 C6
Dame Ellen Pinsent School
HRBN B17 ....105 M3
Damson Wood Infant School
HIA/OLT B92 ....128 B6
Danesmore Park
Primary School
WNSFLD WV11 ....37 K4
Darlaston Central
Trading Estate
DARL/WED WS10 ....52 C6
Darlaston Clinic
DARL/WED WS10 ....52 B7
Darlaston Community School
DARL/WED WS10 ....51 M7
Darlaston FC
DARL/WED WS10 ....52 B7
Darlaston Road
Industrial Estate
DARL/WED WS10 ....52 B7
Dartmouth Golf Club
HHTH/SAND B71 ....69 J7
Dartmouth High School
GTB/HAM B43 ....70 B2
Dartmouth Special School
COV CV2 ....135 H7
Davenport Lodge School
COVW CV5 ....8 C7
David Lloyd Birmingham
KGSTG B44 ....71 J2
Daw End School
RUSH/SHEL WS4 ....39 K7
Dawley Brook Primary School
KGSWFD DY6 ....83 G6
Dawley Trading Estate
KGSWFD DY6 ....83 H5
Daylesford Infant School
HIA/OLT B92 ....127 L2
Days Inn
CBHAMW B1 ....6 D7
Deanery CE Primary School
WALM/CURD B76 ....73 K5
Deansfield High School
WOLV WV1 ....51 G3
Deedmore Special School
COVE CV2 ....135 G5
Deeleys Industrial Estate
WSLW WS2 ....38 F7
Deepdale Industrial Estate
DUDN DY1 ....84 C2
The Dell Stadium
BRLYHL DY5 ....83 M8
Delph Road Industrial Estate
BRLYHL DY5 ....102 B4
Delta Business Centre
CNCK/NC WS11 ....16 B7
Delta Trading Estate
BKHL/PFLD WV2 ....3 L8
Delves J & I School
DSYBK/YTR WS5 ....53 L8
De Montfort Hotel
KNWTH CV8 ....197 K1
Dental Health Centre
KGSTG B44 ....71 K3
Dental Hospital
CBHAMNE B4 ....7 G2
Department of Art (UCE)
CBHAMNW B3 ....6 E4
The De Vere Belfry Hotel
WALM/CURD B76 ....74 F2
Devonshire J & I School
SMTHWK B67 ....87 J8
Deykin Avenue J & I School
AST/WIT B6 ....89 L3
D'Eyncourt Primary School
WNSFLD WV11 ....36 F7
Diana Princess of Wales
Hospital (for Children)
CBHAMNE B4 ....7 G3
Dickens Heath
Primary School
SHLY B90 ....147 K7
Digbeth Coach Station
DIG/EDG B5 ....7 J7
Dingle Primary School
KGSWFD DY6 ....101 L1
Dingleside Middle School
REDE B98 ....202 F5
Dock Lane Industrial Estate
DUDN DY1 ....84 F4
Dock Meadow Drive
Industrial Estate
ETTPK/GDPK/PENN WV4 ....66 C1
Dodford First School
BRGRVW B61 ....167 L8
Dolphin Sports Centre
BRGRVE B60 ....191 L3
Doranda Way Industrial Park
HHTH/SAND B71 ....87 K4
Dordon Primary School
POL/KGSB/FAZ B78 ....47 L7
Dormston Secondary School
SEDG DY3 ....66 C6
Dormston Trading Estate
DUDN DY1 ....84 D1

Dorothy Pattison Hospital
WSLW WS2 ....52 F4
Dorothy Purcell Junior School
BILS/COS WV14 ....67 M2
Dorridge Cricket Club
DOR/KN B93 ....175 J4
Dorridge J & I School
DOR/KN B93 ....175 L2
Dorrington Primary School
PBAR/PBCH B42 ....70 E7
Dosthill Primary School
TAM/AM/WIL B77 ....46 A8
Doulton Trading Estate
BLKHTH/ROWR B65 ....103 K1
Dovecote J & I School
CDSL WV8 ....35 J4
The Dovecote Surgery
LGLYGN/QTN B68 ....105 H6
Downing Close Health Clinic
DOR/KN B93 ....175 L1
Drayton Court Hotel
POL/KGSB/FAZ B78 ....45 L5
Drayton Manor Theme Park & Zoo
POL/KGSB/FAZ B78 ....45 K5
Drayton Park Golf Club
POL/KGSB/FAZ B78 ....45 K6
Dreamwell Industrial Estate
YDLY B25 ....108 D7
Driffold Gallery
SCFLD/BOLD B73 ....72 F2
Dr J's Monument
LICH WS13 ....20 F5
Droicon Industrial Estate
BLKHTH/ROWR B65 ....85 M8
The Dr Phillips Shopping Centre
COVE CV2 ....135 H4
Druids Heath Golf Club
ALDR WS9 ....41 G5
Duddeston Mill Trading Estate
WASH/WDE B8 ....108 A1
Dudley Central Trading Estate
DUDS DY2 ....84 F5
Dudley College
DUDN DY1 ....84 F3
Dudley College (Mons Hill Campus)
DUDN DY1 ....84 F1
Dudley County Court
BRLYHL DY5 ....102 C1
Dudley Golf Club
BLKHTH/ROWR B65 ....85 L7
Dudley Kingswinford RFC
KGSWFD DY6 ....82 E6
Dudley Leisure Centre
DUDN DY1 ....84 F4
Dudley Museum & Art Gallery
DUDN DY1 ....85 G4
Dudley Town Hall
DUDN DY1 ....85 G4
Dudley Water Sports Centre
DUDS DY2 ....102 F2
Dudley Wood Primary School
DUDS DY2 ....103 G3
Dudley Zoo & Castle
DUDN DY1 ....85 H3
Dunstall Hill Industrial Estate
DUNHL/THL/PER WV6 ....36 A8
Dunstall Hill Primary School
DUNHL/THL/PER WV6 ....50 A1
Dunton Trading Estate
VAUX/NECH B7 ....90 B6
Durbar Avenue Industrial Estate
COVN CV6 ....134 B5
Durberville Road Industrial Estate
BKHL/PFLD WV2 ....50 D6
Eagle Industrial Estate
WBROM B70 ....68 C5
Eagle Trading Estate
HALE B63 ....121 L1
Earl Place Business Park
TLHL/CAN CV4 ....153 M4
Earlsdon Business Centre
COVW CV5 ....154 D5
Earlsdon Primary School
COVW CV5 ....8 A8
Earls High School
HALE B63 ....121 M1
Earlswood School
ERDW/GRVHL B23 ....90 C3
Earlswood Trading Estate
HOCK/TIA B94 ....173 G7
Eastbourne House School
ACGN B27 ....127 G1
East Cannock Industrial Estate
HEDN WS12 ....16 F2
Eastern Green Junior School
COVW CV5 ....132 B8
Eastfield Primary School
WOLV WV1 ....3 M5
Eastlands County Primary School
RUGBYN/HIL CV21 ....187 H3
Eastlands Court Business Centre
RUGBYN/HIL CV21 ....187 G2
East Park J & I School
WOLV WV1 ....50 F5
East Park Trading Estate
WOLV WV1 ....3 M8
Eastwood Business Village
COVS CV3 ....156 D4
Eaton Wood Medical Centre
ERDE/BCHGN B24 ....91 H2
Ebrook Adult Training Centre
CSCFLD/WYGN B72 ....73 H2
Eclipse Industrial Estate
TPTN/OCK DY4 ....67 J8
Eclipse Trading Estate
TPTN/OCK DY4 ....67 J8
Edgar Stammers J & I School
BLOX/PEL WS3 ....39 K6
Edgbaston Golf Club
EDG B15 ....106 F7
Edgbaston Health Clinic
EDG B15 ....106 C8
Edgbaston Health Clinic
SOLH B91 ....127 K7
Edgbaston High School for Girls & Prep Department
EDG B15 ....106 D6
Edgbaston Shopping Centre
LDYWD/EDGR B16 ....106 E5
Edgewick Community Primary School
COVN CV6 ....134 C5
Edgewood Road Clinic
RBRY B45 ....143 M7
Edgwick Park Industrial Estate
COVN CV6 ....134 D5
Edmondscote Track
RLSN CV32 ....206 B6
Edward Street Hospital
WBROM B70 ....87 G2
Electra Park Industrial Estate
AST/WIT B6 ....89 M4
Electric Cinema
DIG/EDG B5 ....6 F6
Elgar House Surgery
REDW B97 ....202 C1
Elliott's Field Retail Park
RUGBYN/HIL CV21 ....160 F6
The Ellowes Hall School
SEDG DY3 ....66 A8
Elmdon Trading Estate
CHWD/FDBR/MGN B37 ....111 G7
Elmore Green JMI School
BLOX/PEL WS3 ....38 E4
Elms Farm Primary School
LGN/SDN/BHAMAIR B26 ....110 A6
Elms Health Centre
HALE B63 ....102 F7
Elm Street Infant School
WLNHL WV13 ....52 A2
Elm Terrace Clinic
OLDBY B69 ....85 M4
Elston Hall Primary School
WOLVN WV10 ....36 B3
Ely House Hotel
BDMR/CCFT WV3 ....2 B5
Embassy Industrial Estate
HAG/WOL DY9 ....102 D8
Empire Industrial Park
ALDR WS9 ....40 D4
Emscote County Infant School
WWCK CV34 ....205 M5
Emscote House School
RLSN CV32 ....206 B5
Enfield Industrial Estate
REDW B97 ....194 B8
English Martyrs RC Primary School
RUGBYN/HIL CV21 ....187 K6
SPARK B11 ....126 A1
Ensign Business Centre
TLHL/CAN CV4 ....153 K7
Enterprise Industrial Park
LICHS WS14 ....21 K5
Erasmus Darwin Centre
LICH WS13 ....20 E5
Erdington Hall Primary School
ERDE/BCHGN B24 ....90 D3
Erdington Industrial Park
ERDE/BCHGN B24 ....91 K1
Erdington Medical Centre
ERDE/BCHGN B24 ....90 C3
Erdington Pool & Turkish Suite
ERDW/GRVHL B23 ....90 E1
Ernesford Grange Primary School
COVS CV3 ....156 C4
Ernesford Grange School & Community School
COVS CV3 ....156 B5
Essington Light Industrial Estate
WNSFLD WV11 ....37 K1
Etone Community School
NUN CV11 ....81 H8
Etone Sports Centre
NUN CV11 ....81 H8
Ettingshall Primary School
BILS/COS WV14 ....50 F6
Euro Business Park
OLDBY B69 ....86 C4
European Business Park
OLDBY B69 ....86 C6
Eversfield Preparatory School
SOLH B91 ....149 G1
Exchange Industrial Estate
CNCK/NC WS11 ....16 C7
Exhall Business Park
RCOVN/BALC/EX CV7 ....116 F5
Exhall Cedars Infant School
RCOVN/BALC/EX CV7 ....116 F5
Exhall Grange Special School
RCOVN/BALC/EX CV7 ....116 B8
Express by Holiday Inn
COVS CV3 ....180 F1
CSHL/WTROR B46 ....111 K6
CVALE B35 ....91 L4
GTB/HAM B43 ....70 C1
HLGN/YWD B28 ....126 E7
LICHS WS14 ....28 E7
RUGBYN/HIL CV21 ....160 F6
Express by Holiday Inn (Birchley Park)
OLDBY B69 ....86 C7
Expressway Industrial Estate
AST/WIT B6 ....89 J7
Eye Infirmary
BDMR/CCFT WV3 ....2 B5
Fairey Industrial Estate
TAM/AM/WIL B77 ....46 B5
Fairfax School
MGN/WHC B75 ....57 K8
Fairfield First School
BRGRVW B61 ....168 B2
Fairfield Villa FC
BRGRVW B61 ....168 B2
Fairhaven Primary School
STRBR DY8 ....101 H2
The Fairlawns at Aldridge Hotel
ALDR WS9 ....41 J7
Fair View Industrial Estate
WALM/CURD B76 ....74 F6
Fairway Primary School
HWK/WKHTH B38 ....145 H3
Falcon Lodge Clinic
MGN/WHC B75 ....57 L8
Fallings Park Industrial Estate
WOLVN WV10 ....36 D8
Fallings Park Primary School
WOLVN WV10 ....36 E6
Falstaff Hotel
RLSN CV32 ....206 B5
Fazeley Health Centre
POL/KGSB/FAZ B78 ....45 L5
Fazeley Industrial Estate
DIG/EDG B5 ....7 K5
Featherstone Health Centre
WOLVN WV10 ....22 F6
Featherstone Primary School
ERDW/GRVHL B23 ....90 C1
Feldon Lane Clinic
RMSLY B62 ....104 C6
Fernbank Medical Centre
WASH/WDE B8 ....108 E1
Ferndale Primary School
GTB/HAM B43 ....70 C5
Field Road Industrial Estate
BLOX/PEL WS3 ....39 G5
Fillongley CE School
RCOVN/BALC/EX CV7 ....114 B2
Finham Park School
COVS CV3 ....180 E1
Finham Primary School
COVS CV3 ....180 F2
Finstall First School
BRGRVE B60 ....191 M4
Firs Industrial Estate
STRPT DY13 ....164 A6
Firs Primary School
CBROM B36 ....91 J5
Fir Tree Primary School
DSYBK/YTR WS5 ....69 L1
Five Ways Primary School
HEDN WS12 ....17 H3
Five Ways Shopping Centre
EDG B15 ....6 A8
Flax Hill Junior School
CRTAM B79 ....31 M6
Flemings Hotel
HIA/OLT B92 ....127 J4
Fletchamstead Highway Industrial Estate
COVW CV5 ....154 B6
Fletchworth Gate Industrial Estate
COVW CV5 ....154 A5
Florendine Primary School
TAM/AM/WIL B77 ....32 D8
Foleshill Cemetery
COVN CV6 ....134 E3
Foleshill CE Primary School
COVN CV6 ....134 E3
Foleshill Leisure Centre
COVN CV6 ....134 B6
Foley Business Park
KIDDW DY11 ....163 M5
Foley Industrial Estate
KIDDW DY11 ....164 A3
Foley Industrial Park
KIDDW DY11 ....164 A4
Foley Park First School
KIDDW DY11 ....164 A2
The Foot Clinic
CBHAMNW B3 ....6 E4
Fordbridge Infant School
CHWD/FDBR/MGN B37 ....92 F8
Fordhouse Road Industrial Estate
WOLVN WV10 ....36 A5
Fordhouses Cricket Club
WOLVN WV10 ....36 B1
Fords Hospital
COV CV1 ....8 E5
Forest Glades Leisure Centre
KIDD DY10 ....138 C7
Forest Hotel
DOR/KN B93 ....175 K3
Forest Oak School
CBROM B36 ....92 C4
Forge Mill Needle Museum
REDE B98 ....194 D7
Forge Trading Estate
RMSLY B62 ....104 A8
Formans Trading Estate
SPARK B11 ....126 B2
Fort Industrial Park
ERDE/BCHGN B24 ....91 K4
The Fort Shopping Park
ERDE/BCHGR B24 ....91 G4
Forum Health Centre
COVE CV2 ....156 B1
Fosse Wayside Industrial Estate
RUGBYN/HIL CV21 ....187 H1
Foundry Primary School
WSNGN B18 ....88 B7
Fountain Court Hotel
LDYWD/EDGR B16 ....106 A4
Four Dwellings High School
RIDG/WDGT B32 ....104 F8
Four Dwellings Infant School
RIDG/WDGT B32 ....104 F8
Four Dwellings Junior School
RIDG/WDGT B32 ....104 F8
Four Oaks J & I School
FOAKS/STRLY B74 ....56 C1
Four Oaks Medical Centre
MGN/WHC B75 ....56 F3
Four Oaks Saints Cricket Club
FOAKS/STRLY B74 ....42 C8
Four Seasons Art Gallery
ERDE/BCHGN B24 ....72 E8
Foxford School & Community Arts College
COVN CV6 ....116 E8
Fox & Goose Shopping Centre
WASH/WDE B8 ....91 G8
The Fox Hollies Leisure Centre
ACGN B27 ....126 E4
Fox Hollies Special School
ACGN B27 ....126 E4
Fox Hotel International
BKHL/PFLD WV2 ....2 E7
Foxmill Estate
SPARK B11 ....126 B3
Foxyards Primary School
TPTN/OCK DY4 ....67 G8
Franche Clinic
KIDDW DY11 ....137 M5
Franche First School
KIDDW DY11 ....137 M5
Franche Middle School
KIDDW DY11 ....137 M5
Frank F Harrison Comprehensive School
WSLW WS2 ....38 D6
Frank Halfpenny Hall
LICH WS13 ....21 G5
Frankley Community High School
RBRY B45 ....143 K3
Frankley Health Centre
RBRY B45 ....143 L4
Frankley Industrial Park
RBRY B45 ....143 M4
Frank Whittle Primary School
COVE CV2 ....135 K5
Frederick Bird Primary School
COV CV1 ....134 D8
Friar Park Clinic
DARL/WED WS10 ....69 H2
Friary Grange Sports Centre
LICH WS13 ....20 D3
The Friary School
LICH WS13 ....20 C3
Frogmill Junior School
RBRY B45 ....143 M3
Fulfen Primary School
BNTWD WS7 ....19 H6
Fulford Heath Golf Club
HLYWD B47 ....172 F3
Gainsborough House Hotel
KIDDW DY11 ....137 M8
Gainsborough Trading Estate
STRBR DY8 ....119 M1
Gallagher Business Park
RCOVN/BALC/EX CV7 ....134 C1
Gallagher Retail Park
COVN CV6 ....134 D5
Galley Common Infant School
NUNW/HART CV10 ....79 K8
Galley Common Medical Centre
NUNW/HART CV10 ....97 K1
Gannow Middle School
RBRY B45 ....143 H6
Garretts Green Trading Estate
STETCH B33 ....110 A4
Gas Street Basin
CBHAMW B1 ....6 C6
Gatehouse Trading Estate
BRWNH WS8 ....26 E4
Gate Medical Centre
WASH/WDE B8 ....90 B7
Gay Hill Golf Club
HLYWD B47 ....146 E5
George Auden School
NFLD/LBR B31 ....123 K8
George Betts Primary School
SMTHWK B66 ....87 G6
George Dixon Lower School
HRBN B17 ....106 A4
George Dixon School & 6th Form
HRBN B17 ....106 A3
The George Eliot Hospital NHS Trust
NUNW/HART CV10 ....98 F3
George Eliot School
NUN CV11 ....99 H4
George Fentham J & I School
HIA/OLT B92 ....129 L7
The George Hotel
BEWD DY12 ....162 E2
The George Hotel
LICH WS13 ....20 F5
George Salter High School
WBROM B70 ....86 E1
Gibbons Industrial Park
KGSWFD DY6 ....83 L6
The Giffard RC Primary School
DUNHL/THL/PER WV6 ....35 K8
Gig Mill Primary School
STRBR DY8 ....119 J2
Gilbertstone Primary School
LGN/SDN/BHAMAIR B26 ....109 H8
G K Davies Industrial Estate
HAG/WOL DY9 ....102 E7
Glascote Comprehensive School
TAM/AM/WIL B77 ....46 D4
Glascote Health Centre
TAM/AM/WIL B77 ....46 D3
Glascote Heath Primary School
TAM/AM/WIL B77 ....46 D3
Glebe Farm Industrial Estate
RUGBYN/HIL CV21 ....160 D6
Glebefields Health Centre
TPTN/OCK DY4 ....67 L5
Glebe Fields Primary School
TPTN/OCK DY4 ....67 L4
Glendale Infant School
NUNW/HART CV10 ....98 D3
Glenmead J & I School
PBAR/PBCH B42 ....71 H5
Glenthorne CP School
GTWY WS6 ....24 C2
Glynne Primary School
KGSWFD DY6 ....101 G1
Godiva Trading Estate
COVN CV6 ....134 D5
Golden Hillock School
SPARK B11 ....108 B7
The Golden Lion Inn
RRUGBY CV23 ....159 J1
Goldtel Industrial Estate
ETTPK/GDPK/PENN WV4 ....50 E8
Goldthorne Medical Centre
ETTPK/GDPK/PENN WV4 ....50 A7
Goldthorn Park Primary School
ETTPK/GDPK/PENN WV4 ....50 B8
Good Hope Hospital
MGN/WHC B75 ....57 H7
Good Shepherd RC Primary School
COVN CV6 ....134 D4
Goodyers End Primary School
RCOVN/BALC/EX CV7 ....116 C5
Gornal Wood Crematorium
SEDG DY3 ....83 M4
Gorsemoor Primary School
HEDN WS12 ....17 H4
Goscote Hospital
BLOX/PEL WS3 ....39 K5
Goscote Industrial Estate
BLOX/PEL WS3 ....39 J4
Gosford Industrial Estate
COV CV1 ....9 K5
Gosford Park Primary School
COVS CV3 ....9 M6
Gossey Lane J & I School
STETCH B33 ....110 A3
The GPT Golf Club
COVS CV3 ....156 B4
Gracechurch Shopping Centre
SCFLD/BOLD B73 ....56 F8
Grace Mary Primary School
OLDBY B69 ....86 A6
Grafton Manor House
BRGRVW B61 ....190 F6
Graiseley Primary School
BKHL/PFLD WV2 ....2 E9
The Granary Hotel
KIDD DY10 ....165 H5
Granby Business Park
STETCH B33 ....110 B4
Grand Theatre
WOLV WV1 ....3 G4
The Grange Arts & Media Centre
WSL WS1 ....4 F2
Grange Farm Primary School
COVS CV3 ....154 F8
Grangehurst Primary School
COVN CV6 ....134 F1
The Grange Playhouse
DSYBK/YTR WS5 ....5 M4
The Grange School
HAG/WOL DY9 ....120 B1
Gravel Hill Surgery
WMBN WV5 ....64 F7
Gravelly Industrial Park
VAUX/NECH B7 ....90 C5
Grazebrook Industrial Estate
DUDS DY2 ....84 E7
Grazebrook Industrial Park
DUDS DY2 ....84 F7
Great Barr Business Park
PBAR/PBCH B42 ....70 E8
Great Barr Golf Club
GTB/HAM B43 ....70 D1
Great Barr Hotel & Conference Centre
GTB/HAM B43 ....69 M4
Great Barr School
KGSTG B44 ....71 H4
Great Bridge Industrial Estate
TPTN/OCK DY4 ....68 A6
Great Bridge Primary School
TPTN/OCK DY4 ....68 A7
Great Central Way Industrial Estate
RUGBYN/HIL CV21 ....187 H1
Great Western Industrial Estate
WSNGN B18 ....88 C7
Great Wyrley High School
GTWY WS6 ....24 D1
Green Acres Primary School
BILS/COS WV14 ....51 K7
Greenacres Primary School
TAM/AM/WIL B77 ....32 F8
Greenfield Primary School
RUSH/SHEL WS4 ....40 A5
Greenfield Primary School
STRBR DY8 ....101 K8
Greenfield Surgery
STRBR DY8 ....101 K8
Greenhill Health Centre
LICH WS13 ....21 G5
Greenhill Industrial Estate
KIDD DY10 ....138 E6
Greenholm J & I School
KGSTG B44 ....71 J6
Green Industrial Estate
HEDN WS12 ....13 G6
Greenlands Business Centre
REDE B98 ....202 F4
Green Lane Industrial Estate
BORD B9 ....108 C3
Green Meadow Primary School
SLYOAK B29 ....123 K6
Green Rock J & I School
BLOX/PEL WS3 ....39 J4
Green Street Trading Estate
KIDD DY10 ....138 C8
Greet Primary School
SPARK B11 ....126 B1
Greets Green Road Industrial Estate
WBROM B70 ....86 D1
Gregston Industrial Estate
OLDBY B69 ....86 F5
Grendon Primary School
ALE/KHTH/YWD B14 ....146 E2
Grestone Primary School
BFLD/HDSWWD B20 ....88 C1
Greswold Primary School
SOLH B91 ....127 M7
Greysbrooke CP School
LICHS WS14 ....28 E7
Griff Clara Industrial Estate
NUNW/HART CV10 ....98 D6
Griffin Business Park
CHWD/FDBR/MGN B37 ....111 G2
Griffin Industrial Estate
OLDBY B69 ....104 D2
Griffins Brook Medical Centre
SLYOAK B29 ....124 A6
The Griff School
BDWTH CV12 ....116 F2
Grimstock Country House Hotel
CSHL/WTROR B46 ....93 J4
The Grinnall Business Centre
STRPT DY13 ....188 F4
Grosvenor Hotel
RUGBYN/HIL CV21 ....186 F2
Grosvenor Shopping Centre
NFLD/LBR B31 ....144 E1
Grovelands Industrial Estate
RCOVN/BALC/EX CV7 ....116 E7
Grove Medical Centre
BKHL/PFLD WV2 ....3 J9
Grove Park Industrial Estate
CNCK/NC WS11 ....16 C7
Grove Primary School
BKHL/PFLD WV2 ....3 J9
Grove School
HDSW B21 ....88 D5
Grove Vale Primary School
GTB/HAM B43 ....70 B4
Guardian Angels RC Primary School
BKDE/SHDE B34 ....92 B7
Guest Hospital
DUDN DY1 ....85 J2
Gulson Hospital
COV CV1 ....9 J6
Gulson Road Clinic
COV CV1 ....9 J5
Gun Barrel Industrial Centre
CDYHTH B64 ....103 K6
Gun Hill Infant School
RCOVN/BALC/EX CV7 ....96 E5
Guns Village Primary School
WBROM B70 ....86 E2
Gunter Primary School
ERDE/BCHGN B24 ....91 J1
Gupta Trading Estate
OLDBY B69 ....86 D4
Guy Motors Industrial Park
WOLVN WV10 ....36 C8
GWS Industrial Estate
DARL/WED WS10 ....68 B4
GWS Trading Estate
TPTN/OCK DY4 ....68 B4
Habberley Golf Club
KIDDW DY11 ....137 J4
Haden Hill Leisure Centre
CDYHTH B64 ....103 K5
Hadley Stadium
SMTHWK B66 ....105 L2
Hagley F & M School
HAG/WOL DY9 ....119 M8
Hagley Golf & Country Club
HAG/WOL DY9 ....120 E5
Hagley Hall
HAG/WOL DY9 ....120 C7
Hagley RC High School
STRBR DY8 ....119 K7
Haigs Hotel
RCOVN/BALC/EX CV7 ....151 M6
Halas Industrial Estate
HALE B63 ....103 M8
Halcyon Gallery
CBHAM B2 ....6 F6
Halesbury Special School
RMSLY B62 ....104 C5
Hales Industrial Park
COVN CV6 ....134 C1
Halesowen CC
HALE B63 ....121 M3
Halesowen CE Primary School
HALE B63 ....121 L1
Halesowen College
HALE B63 ....103 M8
Halesowen FC (The Grove Recreation Ground)
HALE B63 ....103 L8
Halesowen Golf Club
RMSLY B62 ....104 B8
Halesowen Harriers FC
HALE B63 ....102 F8
Halesowen Health Centre
HALE B63 ....121 M2
Halesowen Industrial Park
RMSLY B62 ....103 M7
Halesowen Leisure Centre
HALE B63 ....121 M2
Halesowen Magistrates Court
HALE B63 ....121 M2
Hale Trading Estate
TPTN/OCK DY4 ....67 M8

Hallfield School
EDG B15 ....106 E6
Hall Green J & I School
HHTH/SAND B71 ....69 G8
Hall Green Little Theatre
HLGN/YWD B28 ....126 C6
Hall Green Little Theatre
ACGN B27 ....126 E3
Hall Green Secondary School
HLGN/YWD B28 ....126 C5
Hall Green Stadium
HLGN/YWD B28 ....126 D4
Hallmoor Special School
STECH B33 ....109 M2
Hall of Memory
CBHAMW B1 ....6 D5
Hamd House School
SMHTH B10 ....108 C5
Ham Dingle Primary School
HAG/WOL DY9 ....120 A3
Hamilton Special School
HDSW B21 ....88 B5
Hammerwich Hospital
BNTWD WS7 ....18 F8
Hammond Business Centre
NUN CV11 ....99 J2
Hams Hall International
Freight Terminal
CSHL/WTROR B46 ......93 L2
Hams Hall National
Distribution Park
WALM/CURD B76 ....93 M1
Hamstead Hall School
BFLD/HDSWWD B20 ....70 C7
Hamstead J & I School
GTB/HAM B43 ....70 B6
Hanburys Farm Community
Primary School
TAM/AM/WIL B77 ....46 B4
Handsworth Boys
Grammar School
HDSW B21 ....88 C5
Handsworth Cemetery
HDSW B21 ....87 M3
Handsworth Golf Club
BFLD/HDSWWD B20 ....88 B1
Handsworth Leisure Centre
BFLD/HDSWWD B20 ....88 D5
Handsworth Rugby Club
DSYBK/YTR WS5 ....70 E1
Handsworth Technical College
HDSW B21 ....88 C5
Handsworth Wood Girls School
& Sixth Form Centre
BFLD/HDSWWD B20 ....88 D3
Hanford Close
Industrial Estate
COVN CV6 ....134 C7
Hanover International Hotel
& Club
BRGRVW B61 ....191 H3
Harborne Church Farm
Golf Club
HRBN B17 ....123 M1
Harborne Golf Club
RIDG/WDGT B32 ....105 L8
Harborne Hill School
EDG B15 ....106 C7
Harborne Pool &
Fitness Centre
HRBN B17 ....105 M8
Harborne Primary School
HRBN B17 ....106 A7
Harden Primary School
BLOX/PEL WS3 ....39 J1
Hargate Primary School
HHTH/SAND B71 ....87 H2
Harriers Industrial Estate
KIDD DY10 ....138 D8
Harnall Lane Industrial Estate
COV CV1 ....9 H1
Harnall Lane Medical Centre
COV CV1 ....9 H1
The Harper Bell School
BHTH/HG B12 ....107 L5
Harris CE High School
RUGBYS/DCH CV22 .....186 D4
Harrisons Institute & Sports Club
GTWY WS6 ....24 E4
Harry Mitchell Leisure Centre
SMTHWKW B67 ....87 K8
The Harry Taylor First School
REDW B97 ....202 C7
Hartlebury Castle
KIDDW DY11 ....189 K2
Hartlebury CE School
KIDDW DY11 ....189 K2
Hartshill Hayes Country Park
NUNW/HART CV10 ....79 L4
Hartshill School
NUNW/HART CV10 ....79 M5
Harvey Road Health Centre
LGN/SDN/BHAMAIR B26 ...109 J4
Harvey Works
Industrial Estate
HALE B63 ....103 K7
Harvills Hawthorn
Primary School
WBROM B70 ....68 D6
Harvington Hall
KIDD DY10 ....165 M4
Hasbury CE Primary School
HALE B63 ....121 K3
Haslucks Green Junior School
SHLY B90 ....147 L2
Hastingwood Industrial Park
ERDE/BCHGN B24 ....90 F4
Hatchford Brook Golf Club
LGN/SDN/BHAMAIR B26 ...128 C1
Hatchford Brook
Primary School
HIA/OLT B92 ....128 A2
Hatchford Gm Primary School
CHWD/FDBR/MGN B37 ...110 D3
Hateley Heath Primary School
HHTH/SAND B71 ....68 F6
Hatherton Lane Primary School
WSLW WS2 ....38 D7
Haunchwood Park
Industrial Estate
NUNW/HART CV10 ....97 J1
Havergal CE Primary School
WOLVN WV10 ....23 G3
Hawbush Primary School
BRLYHL DY5 ....101 M3
Hawkesbury Field School
COVE CV2 ....135 G2
Hawkesbury Lock
Industrial Centre
RCOVN/BALC/EX CV7 ...116 F7
Hawkes Green Medical Centre
CNCK/NC WS11 ....17 G3

Hawkins Sports Club
GTWY WS6 ....24 B1
Hawksmill Industrial Estate
BORD B9 ....108 A4
Hawthorne Primary School
KGSTG B44 ....71 L6
Hawthorns Business Centre
SMTHWK B66 ....87 L5
Hawthorns Industrial Estate
HDSW B21 ....87 M5
Haybridge High School
STRBR DY8 ....119 K7
Hayes Trading Estate
HAG/WOL DY9 ....102 E3
The Hayes Trading Estate
HAG/WOL DY9 ....102 E3
Hayley Green Hospital
HALE B63 ....121 H5
Hayward Industrial Park
ALDR WS9 ....40 E6
Hazelhead Industrial Estate
COV CV1 ....9 J4
Hazell Way Industrial Estate
NUNW/HART CV10 ....98 D4
Hazel Oak School
SHLY B90 ....147 L3
Hazel Slade Primary School
HEDN WS12 ....13 L7
Hearsall Primary School
COVW CV5 ....8 A4
The Heartlands High School
VAUX/NECH B7 ....7 M1
Heart of England Crematorium
NUN CV11 ....99 K2
Heart of England School
RCOVN/BALC/EX CV7 ...151 M1
Heath Business Park
KNWTH CV8 ....184 B4
Heath Clinic
SOLH B91 ....128 B8
Heathcote Industrial Estate
WWCK CV34 ....206 B8
Heathfield Foundation
Technology College
CDYHTH B64 ....103 K3
Heathfield Primary School
BFLD/HDSWWD B20 ......89 G5
Heathfield School
KIDD DY10 ....138 D3
Heathfields Infant School
TAM/AM/WIL B77 ....46 D7
Heath Hayes Primary School
HEDN WS12 ....17 K3
Heathlands (NC) School
BKDE/SHDE B34 ....91 K6
Heath Lane Cemetery
HHTH/SAND B71 ....69 H6
Heath Lane Hospital
HHTH/SAND B71 ....69 H6
Heath Lodge Hotel
CHWD/FDBR/MGN B37 ...111 H3
Heath Mount Primary School
BHTH/HG B12 ....107 J7
Heath Park High School
WOLVN WV10 ....36 E8
Heath Street Industrial Estate
SMTHWK B66 ....88 B8
Heath Town Leisure Centre
WOLVN WV10 ....50 E1
Hebrew Congregation
CBHAMW B1 ....6 E7
Hedging Lane Industrial Estate
TAM/AM/WIL B77 ....46 B8
Hednesford Town FC
(Keys Park)
HEDN WS12 ....17 H2
Hemdale Business Park
NUN CV11 ....99 K2
Henley College
COVN CV6 ....135 G5
Henley Industrial Park
COVE CV2 ....135 J6
Henry Bellairs CE
Junior School
BDWTH CV12 ....117 H2
Henry Hinde Infant School
RUGBYS/DCH CV22 ....186 A4
Henry Hinde Junior School
RUGBYS/DCH CV22 ....185 M3
Henry Parkes Primary School
TLHL/CAN CV4 ....154 A5
Herald Business Park
COVS CV3 ....156 D6
Herbert Art Gallery &
Museum
COV CV1 ....9 G5
Herbert Fowler Junior School
RCOVN/BALC/EX CV7 .....96 D3
Hereford & Worcester County
Museum
KIDDW DY11 ....189 G2
Hereward College of FE
TLHL/CAN CV4 ....153 K4
Hewell Road Swimming Pool
REDW B97 ....194 A8
H Hayes Clinic
HEDN WS12 ....17 J4
Higham Lane School
NUNW/HART CV10 ....81 J7
Higham on the Hill
Primary School
MKTBOS/BARL/STKG CV13 ...81 L1
The High Arcal
Secondary School
SEDG DY3 ....66 D7
Highclare St Paul's School
FOAKS/STRLY B74 ....56 D1
Highclare the Abbey School
ERDW/GRVHL B23 ....72 E8
Highclare Woodfield School
CSCFLD/WYGN B72 ....73 G4
Highcroft Hospital
ERDW/GRVHL B23 ....90 B2
Highfield Primary School
WASH/WDE B8 ....90 C8
Highfields Primary School
BILS/COS WV14 ....67 G3
Highfields Primary School
BLKHTH/ROWR B65 ....104 A5
Highfields Primary School
BNTWD WS7 ....19 G6
Highfields School
ETTPK/GDPK/PENN WV4 ...48 F8
Highgate Business Centre
BHTH/HG B12 ....107 M7
Highgate Medical Centre
BHTH/HG B12 ....107 K6
Highgate Primary School
DUDS DY2 ....84 D7
Highgate Retail Park
BHTH/HG B12 ....107 K6
Highgate Trading Estate
BHTH/HG B12 ....107 L6
Highgate United FC
SHLY B90 ....147 J7
High Meadow Infant School
CSHL/WTROR B46 ....93 K5
Highters Heath J & I School
ALE/KHTH/YWD B14 ......146 F2

Hillary Primary School
WSLW WS2 ....4 A9
Hill Avenue Primary School
ETTPK/GDPK/PENN WV4 ...66 D2
Hillcrest Business Park
DUDS DY2 ....85 G6
Hillcrest Industrial Estate
CDYHTH B64 ....103 H5
Hillcrest School &
Community College
DUDS DY2 ....84 F8
Hillcrest School &
6th Form Centre
RIDG/WDGT B32 ....123 J2
Hill Farm Primary School
COVN CV6 ....133 M6
Hillfields Health Centre
COV CV1 ....9 H2
Hillmeads Health Centre
HWK/WKHTH B38 ....145 L4
Hillmorton Manor Hotel
& Restaurant
RUGBYN/HIL CV21 ....187 L6
Hillmorton Primary School
RUGBYN/HIL CV21 ....187 M5
Hillstone Primary School
BKDE/SHDE B34 ....92 B8
Hill Top Industrial Estate
WBROM B70 ....68 D5
Hilltop Medical Centre
LGLYGN/QTN B68 ....105 G3
Hilltop Public Golf Course
BFLD/HDSWWD B20 ....88 A1
Himley Country Hotel
SEDG DY3 ....82 F2
Himley Hall
SEDG DY3 ....83 H2
Himley Hall Golf Centre
SEDG DY3 ....83 J1
Himley Hall & Park
SEDG DY3 ....83 H1
Himley House Hotel
SEDG DY3 ....83 G2
Hingley Industrial Estate
DUDS DY2 ....103 G4
Hippodrome Theatre
DIG/EDG B5 ....6 F8
Hive Industrial Centre
WSNGN B18 ....88 E6
HM Prison
REDW B97 ....193 H5
HM Prison
WOLVN WV10 ....22 D6
HM Prison
WSNGN B18 ....88 C8
Hob Green Primary School
HAG/WOL DY9 ....120 C3
Hobmoor Primary School
YDLY B25 ....109 H5
Hobs Moat Medical Centre
HIA/OLT B92 ....127 L3
Hockley Brook Trading Estate
HSNGN B18 ....88 E8
Hockley Heath Pavilion
(Sports Centre)
HOCK/TIA B94 ....175 G7
Hockley Heath Primary School
HOCK/TIA B94 ....174 F7
Hockley Hill Industrial Estate
WSNGN B18 ....88 F8
Hodge Hill Girls School
CBROM B36 ....91 G6
Hodge Hill School
CBROM B36 ....91 G6
The Holborn Shopping Centre
SEDG DY3 ....66 C4
Holbrook Park
Industrial Estate
COVN CV6 ....134 B5
Holbrook Primary School
COVN CV6 ....134 C4
Holiday Inn
GTB/HAM B43 ....70 D2
LGN/SDN/BHAMAIR B26 ...128 E2
RCOVN/BALC/EX CV7 ....135 M5
Holland House Infant School
CSCFLD/WYGN B72 ....73 G1
Holland Industrial Park
DARL/WED WS10 ....52 B5
Holliday Wharf
CBHAMW B1 ....6 D7
Hollies Business Park
CNCK/NC WS11 ....16 D4
The Hollies Clinic
LGLYGN/QTN B68 ....104 F1
Hollies Industrial Estate
BDMR/CCFT WV3 ....2 D8
Holloway Bank Trading Estate
DARL/WED WS10 ....68 D4
Holly Bush Medical Centre
RIDG/WDGT B32 ....105 H6
Holly Farm Business Park
KNWTH CV8 ....177 M6
Hollyfast Primary School
COVN CV6 ....133 J6
Hollyfield Primary School
MGN/WHC B75 ....73 K1
Holly Grove Primary School
BNTWD WS7 ....18 C4
Holly Hall Clinic
DUDN DY1 ....84 C6
Holly Hall (GM) School
DUDN DY1 ....84 D5
Hollyhedge Primary School
HHTH/SAND B71 ....69 J5
Holly Hill Infant School
RBRY B45 ....143 K3
Holly Lane Cemetery
SMTHWK B67 ....87 H8
Holly Lodge High School
SMTHWKW B67 ....87 H6
Holly Park Industrial Estate
ERDE/BCHGN B24 ....91 G3
Hollywalk Clinic
RLSN WS13 ....206 E5
Hollywood Primary School
ALE/KHTH/YWD B14 ......146 E4
Holte School
LOZ/NWT B19 ....89 H6
Holt Farm Primary School
RMSLY B62 ....104 C4
Holy Child School
EDG B15 ....106 F7
Holy Family RC J & I School
COVN CV6 ....133 M2
Holy Family RC Primary School
SMHTH B10 ....108 C6

Holy Name RC Primary School
GTB/HAM B43 ....70 C4
Holyoakes Field First School
REDW B97 ....202 B1
Holy Rosary RC
Primary School
WOLV WV1 ....50 E4
Holy Souls RC Primary School
ACGN B27 ....127 G2
Holy Trinity Catholic
Primary School
BILS/COS WV14 ....51 J8
Holy Trinity CE Primary School
BFLD/HDSWWD B20 ....89 G3
Holy Trinity CE Primary School
BRWNH WS8 ....26 E5
Holy Trinity CE Primary School
WBROM B70 ....87 H4
Holy Trinity RC School
SMHTH B10 ....108 A5
Holy Trinity School
KIDD DY10 ....138 D7
Honiley Court Hotel
KNWTH CV8 ....177 M8
Hoobrook Industrial Estate
KIDDW DY11 ....164 B2
Hood Street Industrial Estate
COV CV1 ....9 J4
Hoo Farm Industrial Estate
KIDDW DY11 ....164 C4
Hope Aldridge
Business Centre
NUNW/HART CV10 ....81 G7
Horeston Grange
Shopping Centre
NUN CV11 ....81 L8
Hornchurch Close
Industrial Estate
COV CV1 ....8 F8
Horrell Road Health Centre
LGN/SDN/BHAMAIR B26 ...109 L6
Horse Shoe Associated FC
SHLY B90 ....147 K7
Hospital of St Cross
RUGBYS/DCH CV22 ....186 F4
Hotel Clarine
LDYWD/EDGR B16 ....106 C4
Hotel Du Vin
CBHAMNW B3 ....6 E4
Hotel Ibis
CBHAMW B1 ....6 E8
COV CV1 ....9 G7
COVS CV3 ....155 K7
DIG/EDG B5 ....7 G7
SMHTH B10 ....107 M4
Howard Street
Industrial Estate
WBROM B70 ....68 D6
Howes Primary School
COVS CV3 ....155 H4
Howley Grange
Primary School
RMSLY B62 ....104 E8
HRS Business Park
STECH B33 ....109 M4
HRS Industrial Estate
STECH B33 ....110 A4
Hudson Industrial Estate
BKHL/PFLD WV2 ....50 D6
Hulbert Industrial Estate
DUDS DY2 ....84 F7
Hunt End Industrial Estate
REDW B97 ....202 A8
Hunters Hill School
BRGRVE B60 ....169 K8
Hunters Lane Industrial Estate
RUGBYN/HIL CV21 ....160 E8
Huntington CP School
HEDN WS12 ....12 B5
Huntingtree Primary School
HALE B63 ....121 J1
Hurley Primary School
ATHST CV9 ....77 H1
Hurst Business Park
BRLYHL DY5 ....102 D1
Hurstgreen Primary School
RMSLY B62 ....104 C5
Hurst Hill Primary School
BILS/COS WV14 ....66 E5
Hydesville Tower School
RUSH/SHEL WS4 ....5 J7
Hylands Hotel
COVS CV3 ....8 E5
Ikon Gallery
CBHAMW B1 ....6 C6
IMAX Cinema
DIG/EDG B5 ....7 K4
Imex Business Park
BKHL/PFLD WV2 ....50 A4
Imex Business Park
BORD B9 ....108 B3
Imex Business Park
SPARK B11 ....108 D7
Imex Business Park
STECH B33 ....91 H8
Imex Business Park
TPTN/OCK DY4 ....85 L2
Imex Industrial Estate
WSNGN B18 ....106 E1
Indian High Commission
KNWTH CV8 ....177 M8
Industrial Training Centre
TLHL/CAN CV4 ....153 J5
Industrial Weston Estate
SPARK B11 ....126 C1
Infant Welfare Clinic
GTB/HAM B43 ....70 B3
Innkeeper's Hotel
DOR/KN B93 ....176 B2
Innisfree House School
HLYWD B47 ....173 H1
Innkeeper's Lodge
BRGRVW B61 ....168 F4
Innkeeper's Lodge Hotel
KGSWFD DY6 ....83 C7
Innkeepers Lodge Hotel
LGN/SDN/BHAMAIR B26 ...127 M1
Innkeepers Lodge Hotel
RCOVN/BALC/EX CV7 ....131 C4
Innkeeper's Lodge Hotel
RIDG/WDGT B32 ....105 G4
The Innkeepers Lodge Hotel
LICH WS13 ....20 B1
The Innkeeper's Lodge Hotel
SCFLD/BOLD B75 ....55 L8
International Convention
Centre
CBHAMW B1 ....6 C6
International School &
Community College
STECH B33 ....110 A2
Ipsley CE Middle School
REDE B98 ....203 H7
Izons Lane Industrial Estate
WBROM B70 ....86 D7
Jack o'Watton Business Park
CSHL/WTROR B46 ....93 J3
Jack o'Watton Industrial Estate
CSHL/WTROR B46 ....93 H2

Jaguar Daimler
Heritage Centre
COVW CV5 ....132 C3
The James Gilbert
Rugby Football Museum
RUGBYN/HIL CV21 ....186 E2
James Watt Industrial Park
SMTHWK B66 ....88 A7
James Watt J & I School
SMTHWK B66 ....88 C6
Jane Lane Special School
WSLW WS2 ....52 D2
Janet Shaw Clinic
CHWD/FDBR/MGN B37 ......110 F5
Jas Industrial Park
OLDBY B69 ....104 C1
Jerome Primary School
CNCK/NC WS11 ....17 K8
Jerome Retail Park
WSL WS1 ....4 C3
Jervoise J & I School
SLYOAK B29 ....123 L4
Jessons CE F & M School
DUDN DY1 ....84 E1
Jewellery Quarter
WSNGN B18 ....6 C1
The Jewellery Quarter
Discovery Centre
WSNGN B18 ....88 F2
Jewish Cemetery
AST/WIT B6 ....71 L8
JFK Memorial
CBHAMNE B4 ....6 F3
John Black Day Hospital
CHWD/FDBR/MGN B37 ......110 F5
John Gulson Primary School
COV CV1 ....134 D1
John Shelton Primary School
COVN CV6 ....134 B1
John Willmott School
WALM/CURD B76 ....73 K1
John Wood CE Infant School
CNCK/NC WS11 ....16 B5
Joseph Cash Primary School
COVN CV6 ....134 A6
Joseph Chamberlain
Sixth Form College
BHTH/HG B12 ....107 K3
Joseph Leckie
Comprehensive School
WSL WS1 ....53 J8
Joseph Turner Primary School
TPTN/OCK DY4 ....67 M4
Josiah Mason College
ERDW/GRVHL B23 ....90 A4
Jubilee Business Park
HAG/WOL DY9 ....102 D3
Jubilee Park Primary School
TPTN/OCK DY4 ....67 M5
Jubilee Sports Centre
NUNW/HART CV10 ....98 E2
Junction 1 Retail Park
RUGBYN/HIL CV21 ....187 K6
Junction 2 Industrial Estate
OLDBY B69 ....86 D7
Junction 6 Industrial Park
AST/WIT B6 ....89 M3
Junction Industrial Estate
SMTHWK B66 ....87 K5
Jury's Inn
CBHAMW B1 ....6 C6
Karis Industrial Centre
LDYWD/EDGR B16 ....106 C4
Kates Hill Primary School
DUDS DY2 ....85 J3
Kelvin Way Trading Estate
WBROM B70 ....86 F2
Kenilworth Business Centre
KNWTH CV8 ....197 L2
Kenilworth Castle
KNWTH CV8 ....179 H6
Kenilworth Golf Club
KNWTH CV8 ....180 E7
Kenilworth RFC
KNWTH CV8 ....198 B1
Kenilworth School
KNWTH CV8 ....180 A4
Kenilworth Wardens
Cricket Club
KNWTH CV8 ....198 A2
Ken Marriott Leisure Centre
RUGBYS/DCH CV22 ....186 F4
Kent Close Primary School
HHTH/SAND B71 ....68 E6
Keresley Grange
Primary School
COVN CV6 ....133 M4
Keresley Health Centre
RCOVN/BALC/EX CV7 ......115 K6
Keresley Newland
Primary School
RCOVN/BALC/EX CV7 ......115 K6
Key Business Park
ERDE/BCHGN B24 ....91 G2
Key Industrial Park
WLNHL WV13 ....51 H2
Keyway Retail Park
WLNHL WV13 ....51 M5
Khalsa Industrial Estate
SMTHWK B66 ....106 B1
Kidderminster College
KIDD DY10 ....164 C6
Kidderminster General
Hospital
KIDDW DY11 ....138 A8
Kidderminster Golf Club
KIDD DY10 ....164 D1
Kidderminster Harriers FC
(Aggborough Stadium)
KIDD DY10 ....164 D1
Kidderminster Health Centre
KIDD DY10 ....138 C7
Kidderminster
Industrial Estate
KIDD DY10 ....164 C3
KIDD DY10 ....165 H8
Kidderminster Railway
Museum Trust
KIDD DY10 ....138 D8
Kineton Green Infant School
HIA/OLT B92 ....127 H4
King Charles I High School
KIDD DY10 ....138 E8
King Charles Primary School
WSLW WS2 ....52 D3
King David Primary School
MOS/BIL B13 ....125 K3
King Edward Business Park
NUN CV11 ....99 J3
King Edwards School (Boys)
EDG B15 ....124 E1
King Edwards VI Aston School
AST/WIT B6 ....89 K4
King Edwards VI Handsworth
School
HDSW B21 ....88 B4
King Edward VI Camp Hill
School for Boys
ALE/KHTH/YWD B14 ......125 H6

King Edward VI Camp Hill
School for Girls
ALE/KHTH/YWD B14 ....125 H5
King Edward VI College
NUN CV11 ....99 H1
King Edward VI College
STRBR DY8 ....101 L7
King Edward VI County School
LICHS WS14 ....21 G1
King Edward VI Five Ways
School
RIDG/WDGT B32 ....123 G5
King Edward VI Girls High School
EDG B15 ....124 E1
King Edward VI Leisure Centre
LICHS WS14 ....21 G1
Kingfield Industrial Estate
COVN CV6 ....134 C4
Kingfisher Business Park
REDE B98 ....202 C1
Kingfisher Industrial Estate
WBROM B70 ....86 C1
Kingfisher Primary School
CBROM B36 ....92 E5
Kingfisher Shopping Centre
REDW B97 ....202 C1
King George V Primary School
HHTH/SAND B71 ....87 J2
King Henry VIII School
COVW CV5 ....8 D8
Kingsbury Business Park
WALM/CURD B76 ....74 C7
Kingsbury J & I School
POL/KGSB/FAZ B78 ....60 D1
Kingsbury School
ERDE/BCHGN B24 ....90 D3
Kingsbury School
POL/KGSB/FAZ B78 ....60 A1
Kingsbury Water Park
WALM/CURD B76 ....59 M8
Kings Business Centre
NUN CV11 ....99 H1
Kings Business Park
KGSTG B44 ....71 G4
The Kings CE School
DUNHL/THL/PER WV6 ....34 K3
Kings Cinema
WBROM B70 ....87 H2
Kings Heath Boys School
MOS/BIL B13 ....125 L7
Kings Heath CC
ALE/KHTH/YWD B14 ....125 J7
Kings Heath J & I School
ALE/KHTH/YWD B14 ....125 J4
The Kings High School
for Girls
WWCK CV34 ....205 J6
Kings Hill Business Park
DARL/WED WS10 ....68 C4
Kings Hill Clinic
DARL/WED WS10 ....52 C8
Kings Hill JMI School
DARL/WED WS10 ....52 C8
Kingshurst City Technology
College
CHWD/FDBR/MGN B37 ....110 D4
Kingshurst Clinic
CHWD/FDBR/MGN B37 ....92 E8
Kingshurst J & I School
CHWD/FDBR/MGN B37 ....92 E7
Kingsland Primary School
KGSTG B44 ....71 K1
Kingsley College
REDE B98 ....203 G7
Kingsley Preparatory School
DOR/KN B93 ....175 K1
The Kingsley School
RLSN CV32 ....206 D4
Kingsmead Technology
College
HEDN WS12 ....17 G1
Kings Norton Boys School
BVILLE B30 ....145 J1
Kings Norton Business Centre
BVILLE B30 ....145 K1
Kings Norton Girls School
BVILLE B30 ....124 C8
Kings Norton Golf Club
ALVE B48 ....172 A4
Kings Norton High School
HWK/WKHTH B38 ....145 K5
Kings Norton Primary School
BVILLE B30 ....145 L2
Kingsrise Community
Primary School
KGSTG B44 ....71 M3
Kings Road Industrial Estate
YDLY B25 ....108 D7
Kingstanding Leisure Centre
KGSTG B44 ....71 M5
Kingstanding Special School
KGSTG B44 ....71 J4
Kingsthorne Primary School
KGSTG B44 ....71 L4
Kingston Court
Shopping Arcade
CNCK/NC WS11 ....16 C4
Kingston Industrial Estate
BORD B9 ....7 M7
Kingsway Community
Primary School
RLSS CV31 ....206 C7
The Kingswinford
Secondary School
KGSWFD DY6 ....83 H6
Kingswood School
SHLY B90 ....147 M3
Kitwell J & I School
RIDG/WDGT B32 ....122 E6
Klark Industrial Estate
KIDDW DY11 ....163 L5
Klaxon Industrial Estate
SPARK B11 ....126 D1
The Knibbs Shopping Centre
WWCK CV34 ....205 K6
Knightlow CE (Aided)
Primary School
RRUGBY CV23 ....183 K6
The Knoll School
KIDDW DY11 ....137 L6
Knowle CE Primary School
DOR/KN B93 ....150 A6
Knowle & Dorridge Cricket Club
DOR/KN B93 ....175 L1
Knowle FC
DOR/KN B93 ....150 A6
Knowle Village Cricket Club
DOR/KN B93 ....150 A6
Lady Katherine Leveson CE
Primary School
RCOVN/BALC/EX CV7 ....150 F8
Ladypool Primary School
SPARK B11 ....107 M7
Ladywood Arts &
Leisure Centre
LDYWD/EDGR B16 ....106 E3
Ladywood Middleway
Health Centre
CBHAMW B1 ....106 E2

Lakeside Industrial Estate
REDE B98 ....202 F2
Lakeside Industrial Park
POL/KGSB/FAZ B78 ....45 J4
Lakeside JMI School
WLNHL WV13 ....51 J2
Lakeside Medical Centre
DUNHL/THL/PER WV6 ....48 C1
Lakeside Primary School
TAM/AM/WIL B77 ....46 C3
Lakeside Trading Centre
REDE B98 ....202 E1
Lakey Lane Primary School
HLGN/YWD B28 ....126 E5
Lammas Field
WWCK CV34 ....205 G7
Lanchester School
CBROM B36 ....92 C4
Landywood County
Primary School
GTWY WS6 ....24 D5
Lane Green First School
CDSL WV8 ....34 F2
The Lane Medical Centre
BHTH/HG B12 ....107 M8
Lanesfield Primary School
ETTPK/GDPK/PENN WV4 ....66 E2
The Lanes Shopping Centre
SCFLD/BOLD B73 ....72 F6
Langley High School
LGLYGN/QTN B68 ....104 F1
Langley Infants School
HIA/OLT B92 ....127 H7
Langley Primary School
OLDBY B69 ....86 D8
Langley School
HIA/OLT B92 ....127 H6
Langley Special School
MGN/WHC B75 ....57 L7
Langley Swimming Centre
LGLYGN/QTN B68 ....104 F1
Lansdowne Health Centre
WSNGN B18 ....106 D1
Lansdowne Hotel
RLSN CV32 ....206 E4
Lapal Primary School
RMSLY B62 ....122 D1
Lark Hall Infants School
CRTAM B79 ....31 L5
Larkhill Industrial Estate
KIDD DY10 ....138 C6
Lasercare Clinics Birmingham
EDG B15 ....6 B9
Laurie Pike Health Centre
AST/WIT B6 ....89 H5
Lawford Heath
Industrial Estate
RRUGBY CV23 ....185 G6
Lawrence Sheriff School
RUGBYN/HIL CV21 ....186 F2
Lea Marston Hotel &
Leisure Complex
WALM/CURD B76 ....75 L4
Leamington CC
RLSN CV32 ....206 D3
Leamington Museum &
Art Gallery
RLSS CV31 ....206 D5
Leamore Industrial Estate
WSLW WS2 ....38 E6
Leamore Primary School
BLOX/PEL WS3 ....39 G6
Leasowes Community College
RMSLY B62 ....104 C7
Lea Street First School
KIDD DY10 ....138 D7
Leaverstock Industrial Estate
STETCH B33 ....110 A4
Lee Bank Business Centre
CBHAMW B1 ....6 E7
Legg Brothers Industrial Estate
ETTPK/GDPK/PENN WV4 ....50 D8
Leigh CE Primary School
TLHL/CAN CV4 ....153 H4
Leigh JI (NC) School
WASH/WDE B8 ....90 C7
Leighswood Junior School
ALDR WS9 ....40 F6
Leighswood School
ALDR WS9 ....40 E5
Lemar Industrial Estate
BVILLE B30 ....125 G4
Lennon Indoor Market
KGSTG B44 ....71 L2
Leoma Industrial Estate
RMSLY B62 ....104 B4
Leviss Industrial Estate
STETCH B33 ....109 H1
Lewisham Industrial Estate
SMTHWK B66 ....87 L6
Leyhill Health Centre
NFLD/LBR B31 ....123 J7
Ley Hill Primary School
NFLD/LBR B31 ....123 H8
Leyland School
BDWTH CV12 ....116 F2
Leys Industrial Estate
BRLYHL DY5 ....101 L2
Lichfield Business Centre
LICH WS13 ....21 H4
Lichfield Cathedral
LICH WS13 ....20 F5
Lichfield Cathedral School
(Bishops Palace)
LICH WS13 ....20 F5
Lichfield Cricket Club
LICH WS13 ....20 E7
Lichfield Magistrates Court
LICH WS13 ....20 F6
Lichfield Road Industrial Estate
CRTAM B79 ....31 K8
Lichfield RUFC
LICHS WS14 ....21 K8
Lichfield Trading Estate
CRTAM B79 ....31 K5
Lickey End First School
BRGRVE B60 ....169 G7
Lickey Hills Country Park
RBRY B45 ....169 L1
Lickey Hills Golf Club
RBRY B45 ....169 L1
Lickey Hills Primary School
RBRY B45 ....169 K3
Lickhill First School
STRPT DY13 ....188 B1
Lickhill Middle School
STRPT DY13 ....188 D1
Lifford Trading Estate
BVILLE B30 ....145 L1
Light Hall School
SHLY B90 ....147 M4
Light House Cinema
WOLV WV1 ....3 G4
Lightwoods Primary School
LGLYGN/QTN B68 ....105 H5
Lillington Primary School
RLSN CV32 ....206 F1
Limbrick Wood Primary School
TLHL/CAN CV4 ....153 K2

Linden Road Instruction
Swimming Pool
BVILLE B30 ....124 D6
Lindens Primary School
FOAKS/STRLY B74 ....55 K7
Lindley Lodge Industrial Estate
ALDR WS9 ....40 C7
Lindsworth North School
ERDW/GRVHL B23 ....72 E7
Lindsworth School
BVILLE B30 ....146 A2
Link One Industrial Park
WBROM B70 ....68 C7
Linkway Retail Park
CNCK/NC WS11 ....15 M7
Linkwood Industrial Estate
STRBR DY8 ....101 K7
Linthurst First School
BRGRVE B60 ....169 L7
Lion Industrial Park
BVILLE B30 ....40 E4
Lisle Court Medical Centre
RLSS CV31 ....206 E7
Little Aston CP School
FOAKS/STRLY B74 ....42 A7
Little Aston Golf Club
FOAKS/STRLY B74 ....55 M1
Little Barrow Hotel
LICH WS13 ....20 E5
Little Heath Industrial Estate
COVN CV6 ....134 E3
Little Heath Primary School
COVN CV6 ....134 D4
Little London JMI School
WLNHL WV13 ....51 L3
Little Sutton Primary School
MGN/WHC B75 ....57 H2
Littleton Business Park
HEDN WS12 ....12 A6
Living Museum
DUDN DY1 ....85 H2
Locarno Primary School
TPTN/OCK DY4 ....67 K7
The Lock Museum
WLNHL WS10 ....51 K4
Lode Heath School
SOLH B91 ....128 A7
Lodge Farm Campsite
RRUGBY CV23 ....185 M3
Lodge Farm Primary School
WSLW WS2 ....52 C1
Lodge Forge Trading Estate
CDYHTH B64 ....103 G6
Lodge Hill Cemetery
SLYOAK B29 ....123 M4
Lodge Hill Crematorium
SLYOAK B29 ....123 M3
Lodge Primary School
WBROM B70 ....86 F2
The Loft Theatre
RLSN CV31 ....206 D6
Long Acre Trading Estate
VAUX/NECH B7 ....89 M6
Longford Industrial Estate
CNCK/NC WS11 ....16 B7
Longford Medical Centre
COVN CV6 ....116 E8
Longford Park
Primary School
COVN CV6 ....134 E2
Longford Primary School
CNCK/NC WS11 ....16 A5
Long Knowle Primary School
WNSFLD WV11 ....37 G5
Long Lane Medical Centre
RMSLY B62 ....104 B4
Long Lane Trading Estate
RMSLY B62 ....104 B4
Long Lawford Primary School
RRUGBY CV23 ....159 L8
Longmoor Special School
SCFLD/BOLD B73 ....57 M1
Longwill Special School
NFLD/LBR B31 ....123 L8
Longwood Primary School
POL/KGSB/FAZ B78 ....45 G4
Lord Leycester Hospital
WWCK CV34 ....205 J7
Lord Leycester Hotel
WWCK CV34 ....205 J7
Lordswood Boys School
HRBN B17 ....105 L5
Lordswood Girls School
HRBN B17 ....105 M5
Lordswood Medical Practice
HRBN B17 ....105 M7
Lower Farm JMI School
BLOX/PEL WS3 ....39 G1
Lower Gornal Health Centre
SEDG DY3 ....83 M3
Low Hill Medical Centre
WOLVN WV10 ....36 C6
Loxdale Industrial Estate
BILS/COS WV14 ....67 J1
Loxdale Primary School
BILS/COS WV14 ....67 K1
Lozells Primary School
LOZ/NWT B19 ....89 H6
Lucy Baldwin Hospital
STRPT DY13 ....163 K8
Lugman Medical Centre
WSL WS1 ....4 C8
Lunt Roman Fort
KNWTH CV8 ....181 K2
Lutley Primary School
HALE B63 ....121 H4
Lye Business Centre
HALE B63 ....102 D6
Lye CC
HAG/WOL DY9 ....102 B8
Lye Town FC
HAG/WOL DY9 ....102 B8
Lye Valley Industrial Estate
HAG/WOL DY9 ....102 D7
Lyndon Green J & I School
LGN/SDN/BHAMAIR B26 ....109 K7
Lyndon School
HIA/OLT B92 ....127 L2
Lyne Hill Industrial Estate
PENK ST19 ....10 C6
Lyng Hall School
COVE CV2 ....135 G2
Lyng Primary School
WBROM B70 ....87 G4
Lythalls Lane Industrial Estate
COVN CV6 ....134 C1
Madinatul Uloom Alislamiya
KIDD DY10 ....165 H5
Magistrates Court
(Victoria Law Courts)
CBHAMW B4 ....7 G3
Magreal Industrial Estate
LDYWD/EDGR B16 ....106 D2
Maguire Industrial Estate
TLHL/CAN CV4 ....153 J5
Maidensbridge Primary School
KGSWFD DY6 ....82 F4
The Mailbox
CBHAMW B1 ....6 E6

Mainstream Forty Seven
Industrial Park
VAUX/NECH B7 ....90 A8
Mainstream Industrial Park
VAUX/NECH B7 ....108 A1
Malt Mill Lane Trading Estate
RMSLY B62 ....104 B5
Mander Shopping Centre
WOLV WV1 ....2 F5
Manders Industrial Estate
WOLVN WV10 ....3 M3
Maney Hill Primary School
CSCFLD/WYGN B72 ....73 H3
Manor CP School
POL/KGSB/FAZ B78 ....45 J8
Manor Farm Community
School
RUSH/SHEL WS4 ....39 M7
The Manor General Hospital
WSLW WS2 ....4 A4
Manor High School
(Foundation)
DARL/WED WS10 ....69 H2
Manor Hotel
RCOVN/BALC/EX CV7 ....131 H4
Manor House Hotel
RLSS CV31 ....206 D6
Manor Industrial Estate
WSLW WS2 ....4 B4
Manor Park Community School
NUN CV11 ....80 E8
Manor Park Primary School
AST/WIT B6 ....89 L5
Manor Park Primary School
COVS CV3 ....155 G6
Manor Primary School
BILS/COS WV14 ....66 F3
Manor Primary School
FOAKS/STRLY B74 ....55 L4
Manor Road Industrial Estate
ATHST CV9 ....63 J6
Manor Side Industrial Estate
REDE B98 ....195 J7
Manor Way Primary School
HALE B63 ....122 A2
Manse Business Centre
NUN CV11 ....99 J3
Mansfield Green Primary School
AST/WIT B6 ....89 J6
Mansfield Medical Centre
COVS CV3 ....155 L3
Maple Business Park
VAUX/NECH B7 ....89 M7
Mapledene J & I School
LGN/SDN/BHAMAIR B26 ....110 C2
Maple Hayes Dyslexia School
LICH WS13 ....20 B5
Maple Leaf Industrial Estate
WSLW WS2 ....52 F2
Mappleborough Green CE
J & I School
STUD B80 ....203 M3
Market Hall
BRGRVW B61 ....191 K3
Market Hall
COV CV1 ....8 E5
Market Hall
KIDD DY10 ....138 C2
Market Hall & Museum
WWCK CV34 ....205 H7
Marlborough J & I School
SMTH B10 ....108 C4
Marlfield Farm First School
REDE B98 ....194 F7
Marlow Estate
BLKHTH/ROWR B65 ....103 M4
The Marlpool First School
KIDDW DY11 ....138 A5
Marmion Junior School
CRTAM B79 ....31 L7
Marriott Forest of Arden Hotel
Golf & Country Club
RCOVN/BALC/EX CV7 ....112 E6
Marshalls Industrial Estate
BKHL/PFLD WV2 ....50 A6
Marshbrook J & I School
PENK ST19 ....10 C4
Marsh Hill Primary School
ERDW/GRVHL B23 ....89 M1
Marston Farm Hotel
WALM/CURD B76 ....75 K1
Marston Green Clinic
CHWD/FDBR/MGN B37 ....110 E6
Marston Green Infant School
CHWD/FDBR/MGN B37 ....110 D6
Marston Green Junior School
CHWD/FDBR/MGN B37 ....110 E6
Marston Road
Industrial Estate
BKHL/PFLD WV2 ....50 A6
Martindale Trading Estate
CNCK/NC WS11 ....16 E3
Martyr's Memorial
COV CV1 ....9 G7
Mary Ann Evans Hospice
NUNW/HART CV10 ....98 E3
Mary Elliot Special School
WSLW WS2 ....53 J1
Maryvale Catholic Primary School
KGSTG B44 ....71 K3
Maryvale Institute
KGSTG B44 ....71 K3
Matchborough First School
REDE B98 ....203 J4
Maternity Welfare Clinic
BDMR/CCFT WV3 ....49 H7
Matthew Boulton College of
Further & Higher Education
DIG/EDG B5 ....107 H5
Matthew Boulton Community
Primary School
HDSW B21 ....88 C6
Maxstoke Castle
CSHL/WTROR B46 ....94 C4
Maxstoke Park Golf Club
CSHL/WTROR B46 ....94 D7
Maybrook Industrial Estate
BRWNH WS8 ....26 D3
The Mayfair Centre
DIG/EDG B5 ....7 G6
Mayfield Preparatory School
WSL WS1 ....5 J5
Mayfield Special School
BFLD/HDSWWD B20 ....89 G5
Maypole Health Centre
ALE/KHTH/YWD B14 ....146 D2
Meadow Green
Primary School
HLYWD B47 ....172 G2
Meadow Mill Industrial Estate
KIDD DY10 ....138 C4
Meadows First School
BRGRVW B61 ....191 K2
Meadows Primary School
NFLD/LBR B31 ....144 D3
The Meadows Special School
TLHL/CAN CV4 ....153 J4
Meadow View JMI School
GTB/HAM B43 ....55 H8

Meadwood Industrial Estate
BILS/COS WV14 ....51 J8
Meeting House Lane Industrial Estate
BRLYHL DY5 ....101 M4
Memorial Clock
WSNGN B18 ....6 B2
Menzies Baron's Court Hotel
ALDR WS9 ....40 C3
Menzies High School
HHTH/SAND B71 ....69 G5
Menzies Leofric Hotel
COV CV1 ....8 F4
Mere Green Combined School
MGN/WHC B75 ....56 F3
Meriden CE Primary School
RCOVN/BALC/EX CV7 ....131 G3
Meriden Green Business Park
COVW CV5 ....131 M5
Merridale Primary School
BDMR/CCFT WV3 ....2 A7
Merry Hill Shopping Centre
BRLYHL DY5 ....102 D3
Merstone School
CHWD/FDBR/MGN B37 ....110 E4
Mesnes Green Industrial Estate
LICHS WS14 ....21 G6
Mesty Croft Primary School
DARL/WED WS10 ....68 G2
Metalloys Industrial Estate
WALM/CURD B76 ....73 M8
Michael Drayton Junior School
NUNW/HART CV10 ....79 L5
Middlemarch Business Park
KNWTH CV8 ....181 M4
Middlemarch Business Park
KNWTH CV8 ....182 A2
Middlemarch Middle School
NUNW/HART CV10 ....98 F4
Middlemore Business Park
ALDR WS9 ....40 C2
Middlemore Industrial Estate
HDSW B21 ....87 M4
Middleton Hall
POL/KGSB/FAZ B78 ....59 J4
Middleton Trading Estate
WLNHL WV13 ....51 J3
Middleway Industrial Estate
BHTH/HG B12 ....107 K6
Midland Air Museum
KNWTH CV8 ....181 M2
Midland House Dawley
Industrial Estate
KGSWFD DY6 ....83 H5
Midland Institute
CBHAMNW B3 ....6 E4
Midland Oak Industrial Estate
COVN CV6 ....134 C4
Midland Oak Trading Estate
COVN CV6 ....134 C4
Midlands Arts Centre Cinema
BHTH/HG B12 ....125 H1
Midlands Sports Centre for
the Disabled
RCOVN/BALC/EX CV7 ....153 G4
Midland Trading Estate
RUGBYN/HIL CV21 ....160 D7
Mid Warwickshire
Magistrates Court
RLSN CV32 ....206 D3
Milby F & M Schools
NUN CV11 ....81 K5
Mile Oak Business Park
POL/KGSB/FAZ B78 ....45 G3
Milking Bank Primary School
DUDN DY1 ....84 C3
Millard Industrial Estate
WBROM B70 ....86 E3
Millbuck Industrial Estate
WOLVN WV10 ....36 B6
Millennium Point
CBHAMNE B4 ....7 K4
Millfield CP School
BRWNH WS8 ....26 E6
Millfield Primary School
POL/KGSB/FAZ B78 ....45 J1
Millfields First School
BRGRVW B61 ....191 J5
Millfields Special School
HHTH/SAND B71 ....69 H5
Mill Lodge Primary School
SHLY B90 ....147 J3
Mill Park Industrial Estate
CNCK/NC WS11 ....16 E3
Milverton House
Preparatory School
NUN CV11 ....99 H4
Milverton Primary School
RLSN CV32 ....206 C1
Minster Hall Youth &
Community Centre
LICH WS13 ....20 F5
Minster House Clinic
KIDD DY10 ....138 C7
Minworth Industrial Park
WALM/CURD B76 ....73 M7
Minworth J & I School
WALM/CURD B76 ....74 B8
Mirah Day Hospital
NUN CV11 ....80 E7
Miras Business Estate
HEDN WS12 ....17 H2
Mitton Mill Industrial Estate
STRPT DY13 ....189 G1
Moat Farm J & I School
LGLYGN/QTN B68 ....105 G2
Moat Hall Primary School
GTWY WS6 ....24 D2
Moat House Primary School
COVE CV2 ....135 H4
Mobarak Health Centre
BHTH/HG B12 ....107 J8
Monarch Industrial Estate
SPARK B11 ....108 E8
Monkspath Business Park
SOLH B91 ....148 D5
Monkspath Primary School
SHLY B90 ....148 H4
Monkton Recreation Centre
PENK ST19 ....10 B4
Monmer Close
Industrial Estate
WLNHL WV13 ....51 J2
Monmore Business Park
BKHL/PFLD WV2 ....50 A4
Monmore Green
Greyhound Stadium
WOLV WV1 ....50 A4
Monmore Park
Industrial Estate
BKHL/PFLD WV2 ....50 A4
Montgomery Primary School
KIDD DY10 ....108 A6
Montgomery Street
Business Centre
SPARK B11 ....108 A6
Montville Hotel
REDW B97 ....202 B3
Monway Industrial Estate
DARL/WED WS10 ....68 G2

Moons Moat First School
REDE B98 ....195 C8
The Moore Group
Business Centre
WSL WS1 ....4 F7
Moorgate Primary School
CRTAM B79 ....31 L8
Moor Green FC
HLGN/YWD B28 ....126 C6
Moor Green J & I School
MOS/BIL B13 ....125 C4
Moor Green Sports Centre
MOS/BIL B13 ....125 G3
Moor Hall Golf Club
MGN/WHC B75 ....57 H4
Moor Hall Hotel
MGN/WHC B75 ....57 H4
Moor Hall Primary School
MGN/WHC B75 ....57 H3
Moorhill County Primary School
CNCK/NC WS11 ....12 C8
Moorhill Primary School
CNCK/NC WS11 ....16 C1
Moorlands Primary School
HHTH/SAND B71 ....68 F5
Moor Lane Trading Estate
AST/WIT B6 ....89 K1
Moor Street Industrial Estate
BRLYHL DY5 ....102 A3
Moreton Community School
WOLVN WV10 ....36 D4
Morley Road Shopping Centre
BNTWD WS7 ....18 F6
Moseley CC
HIA/OLT B92 ....127 C8
Moseley CE Primary School
MOS/BIL B13 ....125 K3
Moseley Golf Club
MOS/BIL B13 ....125 L5
Moseley Hall Hospital
MOS/BIL B13 ....125 J2
Moseley Park School &
Technology College
BILS/COS WV14 ....51 J5
Moseley Primary School
COVN CV6 ....8 A1
Moseley School
MOS/BIL B13 ....126 A3
Mossley Clinic
BLOX/PEL WS3 ....38 D4
Mossley Primary School
BLOX/PEL WS3 ....38 D3
Mount Carmel RC First School
REDW B97 ....201 K3
Mount Nod Primary School
COVW CV5 ....153 L2
Mount Pleasant
Primary School
BRLYHL DY5 ....102 C4
Mount School
BRGRVW B61 ....168 F8
Mount Street Business Centre
VAUX/NECH B7 ....90 A7
Mount Street Business Park
VAUX/NECH B7 ....90 B6
Moxley Industrial Centre
DARL/WED WS10 ....68 A1
Moxley Infant School
DARL/WED WS10 ....67 M1
Moxley Medical Centre
DARL/WED WS10 ....52 A7
Mucklow Hill Industrial Estate
RMSLY B62 ....104 A8
Mucklow Hill Trading Estate
RMSLY B62 ....104 A8
Municipal Art Gallery
WOLV WV1 ....2 F4
Munrow Sports Centre
EDG B15 ....124 D1
Museum of British Road
Transport
COV CV1 ....8 F3
The Museum of Cannock Chase
HEDN WS12 ....13 H7
Myton School
WWCK CV34 ....205 M7
Nailcote Hall Hotel
RCOVN/BALC/EX CV7 ....152 E6
The Nancy Doyle Clinic
BRGRVE B60 ....191 L3
Nansen J & I School
WASH/WDE B8 ....90 D8
Nathaniel Newton
Infant School
NUNW/HART CV10 ....79 M5
Nation Agricultural Centre
KNWTH CV8 ....198 E1
National Exhibition Centre
BHAMNEC B40 ....111 J8
National Indoor Arena
CBHAMW B1 ....6 B5
National Institute of
Conductive Education
MOS/BIL B13 ....125 H1
National Motorcycle Museum
HIA/OLT B92 ....129 L3
National Sea Life Centre
CBHAMW B1 ....6 B5
The Natural Health Centre
HWK/WKHTH B38 ....145 K3
Nature Centre
HHTH/SAND B71 ....70 A7
Nature Park
WALM/CURD B76 ....73 L8
Nature Reserve
KIDD DY10 ....167 G6
Nature Reserve
SEDG DY3 ....82 E2
Neachells Lane
Industrial Estate
WLNHL WV13 ....51 H1
Nechells Primary School
VAUX/NECH B7 ....90 A5
Neilston Street
Business Centre
RLSS CV31 ....206 E7
Nelson Mandela
Primary School
BHTH/HG B12 ....107 L8
Nelson Primary School
CBHAMW B1 ....6 A4
Neptune Industrial Estate
WLNHL WV13 ....51 M5
Netherbrook Primary School
DUDS DY2 ....103 H3
The Nethersole School
(CE Controlled Primary)
POL/KGSB/FAZ B78 ....47 M3
Nether Stowe County
High School
LICH WS13 ....20 F4
Netherton Business Park
DUDS DY2 ....103 H2
Netherton CE
DUDS DY2 ....102 F1
Netherton CE Primary School
DUDS DY2 ....84 F8
Network Park Industrial Estate
VAUX/NECH B7 ....108 A1

The New Art Gallery Walsall
WSLW WS2 ....4 D3
Newbold Comyn Golf Club
RLSN CV32 ....207 G4
Newbold Comyn
Leisure Centre
RLSS CV31 ....206 F5
Newbold Comyn Park
RLSN CV32 ....207 H5
Newbold FC
RUGBYN/HIL CV21 ....160 B7
Newbold Leisure Centre
RUGBYN/HIL CV21 ....160 B6
Newbold Riverside
Primary School
RUGBYN/HIL CV21 ....160 C7
Newbridge Preparatory School
DUNHL/THL/PER WV6 ....49 J1
New Cross Hospital
WNSFLD WV11 ....36 F8
New Cross Industrial Estate
WLNHL WV13 ....51 G2
New Cross Industrial Estate
WOLV WV1 ....50 B2
Newdigate Primary School
BDWTH CV12 ....116 A4
Newfield Park Primary School
HALE B63 ....103 L8
New Hall Hotel
WALM/CURD B76 ....73 J3
New Hall J & I School
MGN/WHC B75 ....57 M8
Newhampton Arts Centre
WOLV WV1 ....2 D3
New Inn Industrial Estate
COVN CV6 ....134 D3
New Invention CP School
SHHTH WV12 ....38 A6
Newman College of
Higher Education
RIDG/WDGT B32 ....123 G5
New Oscott J & I School
SCFLD/BOLD B73 ....72 A2
New Oxford Medical Centre
COV CV1 ....8 E3
New Palace Theatre
REDE B98 ....202 C2
Newshire Industrial Estate
SPARK B11 ....108 B7
Newton Industrial Estate
BORD B9 ....108 B3
Newton Health Centre
LOZ/NWT B19 ....89 H7
Newtown Primary School
WBROM B70 ....86 B2
Newtown Shopping Centre
LOZ/NWT B19 ....89 J7
Nicholas Chamberlaine School
BDWTH CV12 ....117 H2
Ninestiles School
ACGN B27 ....126 F4
Nonsuch Primary School
RIDG/WDGT B32 ....123 H3
Norfolk House School
EDG B15 ....106 B5
Norman Green Sports Centre
& Athletics Track
SOLH B91 ....148 E2
North Birmingham College
PBAR/PBCH B42 ....71 J4
North Bromsgrove High School
BRGRVE B60 ....191 L3
Northbrook Health Centre
SHLY B90 ....127 G8
Northbrook Sports Club
COVW CV5 ....133 G5
North East Worcestershire
College
BRGRVE B60 ....191 M2
REDW B97 ....202 C1
North East Worcestershire
Community Health Care
NHS Trust
REDW B97 ....202 C1
Northfield Manor
Primary School
SLYOAK B29 ....123 L6
Northfield Pool &
Fitness Centre
NFLD/LBR B31 ....144 D2
Northfield Road
Primary School
DUDS DY2 ....85 H8
Northcote Secondary School
WOLVN WV10 ....36 C2
Northlands Primary School
RUGBYN/HIL CV21 ....186 F1
North Leamington
Community College
RLSN CV32 ....206 C3
North Leamington School
RLSN CV32 ....206 D1
Northmoor Industrial Estate
BRLYHL DY5 ....102 B2
Northside Business Centre
WSNGN B18 ....88 C8
North Solihull Sports Centre
& Track
CHWD/FDBR/MGN B37 ....110 E2
North Walsall Primary School
WSLW WS2 ....53 J1
North Warwickshire Golf Club
RCOVN/BALC/EX CV7 ....130 D5
North Warwickshire &
Hinckley College
ATHST CV9 ....63 H5
NUN CV11 ....81 J7
North Worcestershire
Golf Club
NFLD/LBR B31 ....144 B2
Norton Canes
Business Park
CNCK/NC WS11 ....25 L1
Norton Canes
Greyhound Track
CNCK/NC WS11 ....25 M1
Norton Canes Primary School
CNCK/NC WS11 ....17 L7
Norton Canes School
CNCK/NC WS11 ....17 L6
Norwood Hotel
NFLD/LBR B31 ....144 F1
Novotel
CBHAMW B1 ....6 B6
COVN CV6 ....116 D7
LGN/SDN/BHAMAIR B26 ....129 C1
WOLV WV1 ....3 H5
Nuneaton Borough AFC
NUNW/HART CV10 ....98 D1
Nuneaton Co-operative
Sports Club
NUN CV11 ....98 F1
Nuneaton Indoor Market
NUN CV11 ....99 G1
Nuneaton Museum &
Art Gallery
NUN CV11 ....99 G2
Nuneaton Old Edwardians RFC
NUNW/HART CV10 ....81 G7

Nuneaton Private Hospital
NUNW/HART CV10 ....99 G4
Nuneaton RFC
NUN CV11 ....99 K1
Oak Cottage Primary School
SOLH B91 ....127 J7
Oakdale Trading Estate
KGSWFD DY6 ....83 H4
Oakeswell Health Centre
DARL/WED WS10 ....68 E2
Oakfield Junior School
ATHST CV9 ....63 J6
Oakham Primary School
OLDBY B69 ....85 M6
Oakhill First School
REDE B98 ....202 D3
Oakhill Primary School
TAM/AM/WIL B77 ....46 D3
Oak House Museum
WBROM B70 ....86 F3
The Oak Industrial Park
KGSWFD DY6 ....83 J4
Oakland Industrial Estate
HEDN WS12 ....16 F2
Oaklands Academy of
Theatre Dance
BNTWD WS7 ....19 H8
Oaklands Business Park
KIDDW DY11 ....164 C4
Oaklands Primary School
ACGN B27 ....127 G3
Oakleigh Trading Estate
BILS/COS WV14 ....66 F3
Oak Meadow Primary School
WNSFLD WV11 ....37 L6
Oakridge Golf Club
NUNW/HART CV10 ....96 F3
The Oaks Primary School
ALE/KHTH/YWD B14 ....146 B3
Oakstreet Industrial Estate
DUNHL B64 ....103 H4
Oak Street Industrial Estate
BRLYHL DY5 ....102 C4
Oakwood Special School
ALDR WS9 ....40 E2
Ocker Hill J & I School
TPTN/OCK DY4 ....68 A5
Odeon Cinema
CBHAM B2 ....7 G6
COV CV1 ....9 G5
CSCFLD/WYGN B72 ....72 F2
NUNW/HART CV10 ....98 E7
Offmore First School
KIDD DY11 ....138 F7
Ogley Hay Infant School
BRWNH WS8 ....26 D5
Oil Storage Depot
POL/KGSB/FAZ B78 ....60 C5
Oken's House & Doll Museum
WWCK CV34 ....205 J7
Oldbury Business Centre
LGLYGN/QTN B68 ....104 E3
Oldbury Green Retail Park
OLDBY B69 ....86 D5
Oldbury Health Centre
OLDBY B69 ....86 E5
Oldbury Leisure Centre
OLDBY B69 ....86 C7
Oldbury Road Industrial Estate
SMTHWK B66 ....87 H6
WBROM B70 ....86 D3
Oldbury United FC
BLKHTH/ROWR B65 ....104 C2
Old Bush Trading Estate
BRLYHL DY5 ....84 B8
BRLYHL DY5 ....102 A3
BRLYHL DY5 ....102 C2
Old Church CE Primary School
DARL/WED WS10 ....52 A7
The Olde Corner House Hotel
LICHS WS14 ....27 L3
Old Edwardians Sports Club
HIA/OLT B92 ....127 G8
Oldfield Trading Estate
CDYHTH B64 ....103 H5
Old Forge Business Centre
REDE B98 ....203 G5
Old Forge Trading Estate
HAG/WOL DY9 ....102 C7
Old Halesonians RFC
HAG/WOL DY9 ....120 D5
Old Hall Industrial Estate
BLOX/PEL WS3 ....39 G5
Oldhall Special School
WSLW WS2 ....38 C8
Old Hill CC
CDYHTH B64 ....103 K5
Old Hill Primary School
CDYHTH B64 ....103 K4
Oldington Trading Estate
KIDDW DY11 ....163 M4
Oldknow Junior School
SMHTH B10 ....108 C6
Old Leamingtonians RFC
RLSN CV32 ....198 C6
Old Limberlost Sports Club
BFLD/HDSWWD B20 ....88 E2
Old Mill Hotel
KNWTH CV8 ....181 J2
Old Park Industrial Estate
DARL/WED WS10 ....68 C1
Old Park Primary School
DARL/WED WS10 ....52 C8
Old Park Special School
DUDN DY1 ....84 D5
Old Rep Theatre
DIG/EDG B5 ....6 F7
The Old Square
Shopping Centre
WSL WS1 ....4 F4
Oldswinford CE
Primary School
STRBR DY8 ....119 L2
Old Swinford Hospital School
STRBR DY8 ....119 L1
Old Warwickian
Sports Ground
RWWCK/WEL CV35 ....204 E8
Olive Hill Primary School
RMSLY B62 ....104 B6
Olton Golf Club
SOLH B91 ....127 L6
Olympia Sports Centre
CNCK/NC WS11 ....16 C4
One Stop Medical Centre
COV CV1 ....8 E3
One Stop Retail Park
PBAR/PBCH B42 ....89 H2
Oratory RC Primary School
LDYWD/EDGR B16 ....106 D3
Orbital Retail Centre
CNCK/NC WS11 ....16 D7
Orchard Lane Clinic
WLNHL WV13 ....51 L2
Orchard Retail Park
COVS CV3 ....182 B1
The Orchard School
SMTHWK B66 ....87 J6
SMTHWK B67 ....87 K8

Orthodontists Surgery
ACGN B27 ....126 E2
Osborne Primary School
ERDW/GRVHL B23 ....72 E8
Ounsdale High School
WMBN WV5 ....64 D6
Ounsdale Sports Centre
WMBN WV5 ....64 D6
Our Lady of Compassion RC
Primary School
HIA/OLT B92 ....127 H6
Our Lady of Fatima RC
Primary School
HRBN B17 ....105 K6
Our Lady of Lourdes RC
Primary School
MOS/BIL B13 ....126 B8
Our Lady of the Assumption
RC Primary School
TLHL/CAN CV4 ....153 J4
Our Lady of the Wayside RC
Primary School
SHLY B90 ....148 A5
Our Lady & St Chad RC
Secondary School
WOLVN WV10 ....36 D5
Our Lady & St Kenelm RC
Primary School
HALE B63 ....121 K2
Our Lady & St Rose of Lima
RC Primary School
SLYOAK B29 ....123 M4
Our Lady & St Teresas RC
Combined School
RLSN CV32 ....199 H8
Our Ladys RC Primary School
STETCH B33 ....110 B3
The Oval Primary School
STETCH B33 ....109 K3
Owen Road Industrial Estate
WLNHL WV13 ....52 A4
Owen Road Trading Estate
WLNHL WV13 ....52 A4
Oxbarn Social & Sports Club
BDMR/CCFT WV3 ....49 K6
Oxford Street Industrial Park
BILS/COS WV14 ....51 K8
Oxley Park Golf Club
WOLVN WV10 ....36 A6
Packwood House
HOCK/TIA B94 ....175 L8
Paddox Primary School
RUGBYS/DCH CV22 ....187 H5
Paddys Wide Water
Industrial Estate
BRLYHL DY5 ....84 A8
Paganel J & I School
SLYOAK B29 ....123 L3
Paget Primary School
ERDE/BCHGN B24 ....91 G1
Palfrey Girls School
WSL WS1 ....4 E4
Palfrey Infant School
WSL WS1 ....4 D8
Palfrey Junior School
WSL WS1 ....4 D8
Pallasades Shopping Centre
CBHAM B2 ....6 F6
Palmers Cross Primary School
DUNHL/THL/PER WV6 ....35 H5
Paper Mill End Industrial Estate
PBAR/PBCH B42 ....71 H7
Park Attwood Clinic
BEWD DY12 ....137 H1
Park Farm Industrial Estate
REDE B98 ....203 G5
Park Farm Industrial Estate
REDE B98 ....203 J5
Parkfield Clinic
BKHL/PFLD WV2 ....50 B7
Parkfield High School
ETTPK/GDPK/PENN WV4 ....50 C8
Parkfield Primary School
ETTPK/GDPK/PENN WV4 ....50 C8
TAM/AM/WIL B77 ....46 A4
WASH/WDE B8 ....108 C2
Parkgate Primary School
COVN CV6 ....133 M2
Park Hall Hotel &
Conference Centre
ETTPK/GDPK/PENN WV4 ....66 A1
Park Hall Infant School
DSYBK/YTR WS5 ....54 A6
Park Hall Junior School
DSYBK/YTR WS5 ....54 A6
Park Hall School
CBROM B36 ....92 C4
Park Hill Junior School
KNWTH CV8 ....180 A7
Park Hill Primary School
COVW CV5 ....153 L1
Park Hill Primary School
DARL/WED WS10 ....69 G1
Park Hill Primary School
MOS/BIL B13 ....125 K1
Park Lane Industrial Estate
HHTH/SAND B71 ....87 L4
Park Lane Industrial Estate
KIDDW DY11 ....164 B1
Park Lane Primary School
NUNW/HART CV10 ....97 K2
Park Lane Trading Estate
OLDBY B69 ....86 E6
Park Lane Trading Estate
WLNHL WV13 ....51 H1
Park Medical Centre
SMHTH B10 ....108 C6
Parkrose Industrial Estate
SMTHWK B66 ....87 M5
Park School
CRTAM B79 ....31 L6
Parkside Business Park
COV CV1 ....9 G7
Parkside Industrial Estate
WOLV WV1 ....3 M7
Parkside Middle School
BRGRVW B61 ....191 K2
Park Street Industrial Estate
COVN CV6 ....134 C6
Park Trading Estate
WSNGN B18 ....88 E7
Park View School
WASH/WDE B8 ....90 C8
Parkway Industrial Centre
VAUX/NECH B7 ....7 L1
Pattison College
COVS CV3 ....155 L3
Pavilions Shopping Centre
CBHAMNE B4 ....7 H5
PDH Industrial Estate
DARL/WED WS10 ....68 A1
PDH Industrial Estate
WLNHL WV13 ....51 H2
Pearl Hyde Primary School
COVE CV2 ....135 L8

Peartree Industrial Park
DUDS DY2 ....84 E4
Pedmore CE Primary School
HAG/WOL DY9 ....119 M4
Pedmore Road
Industrial Estate
BRLYHL DY5 ....102 C1
The Peel Medical Centre
CRTAM B79 ....31 L8
Pegasus Primary School
CVALE B35 ....91 M7
Pelsall Clinic
BLOX/PEL WS3 ....39 L1
Pelsall Village School
BLOX/PEL WS3 ....39 K1
Pendeford Business Park
COVEN WV9 ....35 K2
Pendeford Health Centre
COVEN WV9 ....35 L3
Pendeford High School
WOLVN WV10 ....35 M3
Pendene Complimentary
Medical Centre
WOLV WV10 ....2 C4
Penderford Mill
Nature Reserve
COVEN WV9 ....35 J1
Penkridge Industrial Estate
PENK ST19 ....10 C6
Penkridge Leisure Centre
PENK ST19 ....10 F5
Penkridge Middle School
PENK ST19 ....10 D3
Pennfields Health Centre
BDMR/CCFT WV3 ....2 A1
Penn Fields School
BDMR/CCFT WV3 ....49 K5
Penn Golf Club
ETTPK/GDPK/PENN WV4 ....65 J1
Penn Hall Special School
ETTPK/GDPK/PENN WV4 ....65 J1
Penn Hospital
ETTPK/GDPK/PENN WV4 ....65 J1
Penn Industrial Estate
DUDS DY2 ....103 G4
Penn Manor Medical Centre
ETTPK/GDPK/PENN WV4 ....65 K1
Penn Road Retail Park
BKHL/PFLD WV2 ....2 D7
Pens Primary School
CSCFLD/WYGN B72 ....73 C7
Pens Meadow Special School
STRBR DY8 ....101 J2
The Pennsett School of
Technology
BRLYHL DY5 ....83 L7
Pensnett Trading Estate
KGSWFD DY6 ....83 K5
The Pennsett Trading Estate
KGSWFD DY6 ....83 L4
Percy Business Park
OLDBY B69 ....86 D6
Percy Shurmer Primary School
DIG/EDG B5 ....107 J6
Perry Barr Greyhound Stadium
PBAR/PBCH B42 ....89 G4
Perry Beeches J & I School
PBAR/PBCH B42 ....71 G6
Perry Common Primary School
ERDW/GRVHL B23 ....71 M6
Perryfields High School
LGLYGN/QTN B68 ....104 E5
Perryfields Primary School
LGLYGN/QTN B68 ....104 E5
Perry Hall Primary School
WNSFLD WV11 ....37 K7
Perry Street Industrial Estate
BILS/COS WV14 ....67 J2
Personal & Child Health Centre
BVILLE B30 ....124 E7
Perton Clinic
DUNHL/THL/PER WV6 ....48 C1
Perton First School
DUNHL/THL/PER WV6 ....34 C8
Perton Middle School
DUNHL/THL/PER WV6 ....48 C1
Perton Park Golf Club
DUNHL/THL/PER WV6 ....48 C2
Peterbrook Primary School
SHLY B90 ....147 M4
Peters Hill Primary School
BRLYHL DY5 ....102 A6
Pheasey Clinic
GTB/HAM B43 ....71 G2
Pheasey Park Farm
Primary School
GTB/HAM B43 ....71 G1
Phillips Street Industrial Estate
AST/WIT B6 ....89 J1
Phoenix Business Park
VAUX/NECH B7 ....89 L7
Phoenix Industrial Estate
BILS/COS WV14 ....67 K4
Phoenix International
Industrial Estate
WBROM B70 ....68 C8
Phoenix Road Industrial Estate
WLNHL WV13 ....51 K2
Phoenix Works Industrial Estate
DARL/WED WS10 ....52 C5
Piccadilly Cinema
SPARK B11 ....107 M8
Pickwick Picture Gallery
COVN CV6 ....133 J8
The Picture House
CNCK/NC WS11 ....16 C5
STRBR DY8 ....119 L1
WASH/WDE B8 ....90 E8
WLNHL WV13 ....51 H1
Pines Special School
CBROM B36 ....91 K5
Pinfold Industrial Estate
BLOX/PEL WS3 ....39 G5
Pinfold Street Primary School
DARL/WED WS10 ....52 A8
Pingles Leisure Centre
NUN CV11 ....99 H3
Pingles Stadium
NUN CV11 ....99 H2
Pitcheroak Golf Club
REDW B97 ....202 B3
Pitcheroak Special School
REDW B97 ....201 M1
Planetary Industrial Estate
WLNHL WV13 ....51 G1
Planet Ice Arena
DIG/EDG B5 ....7 H7
Plantsbrook School
CSCFLD/WYGN B72 ....73 G1
Playbox Theatre
KNWTH CV8 ....197 L1
Pleck Business Park
WSLW WS2 ....4 A8
Pleck Industrial Estate
WSLW WS2 ....4 A6
Plough & Harrow Hotel
LDYWD/EDGR B16 ....106 E4
Polesworth High School
POL/KGSB/FAZ B78 ....47 M5

Polesworth Nethersole
  Infant School
  POL/KGSB/FAZ B78 ....47 L3
Pool Hayes
  Comprehensive School
  SHHTH WV12 ....37 M8
Pool Hayes Primary School
  SHHTH WV11 ....37 M7
Pool Meadow Bus Station
  COV CV1 ....9 G4
Pool Road Business Centre
  NUNW/HART CV10 ....80 D8
Pool Road Industrial Estate
  NUNW/HART CV10 ....80 D8
Poplar Road Clinic
  ALE/KHTH/YWD B14 ....125 K4
Poplars Trading Estate
  STUD B80 ....203 H7
Poplar Trading Estate
  AST/WIT B6 ....71 K8
Portersfield Industrial Estate
  CDYHTH B64 ....103 G5
Portland Hotel
  LDYWD/EDGR B16 ....106 A4
Portway Road Industrial Estate
  OLDBY B69 ....86 C7
Posthouse Hotel
  EDG/EDG B5 ....6 F7
Potters Green Primary School
  COVE CV2 ....135 J3
Powke Lane Industrial Estate
  BLKHTH/ROWR B65 ....103 L3
The Precinct
  COV CV1 ....8 E4
Premier Business Centre
  HAG/WOL DY9 ....102 D8
Premier Business Park
  WSLW WS2 ....4 C5
Premier Lodge
  LDYWD/EDGR B16 ....6 B7
  MGN/WHC B75 ....57 K6
  RBRY B45 ....143 M5
  REDW B97 ....201 J2
Premier Partnership
  Industrial Estate
  KGSWFD DY6 ....101 L1
Premier Trading Estate
  VAUX/NECH B7 ....89 K8
President Kennedy
  Comprehensive School &
  Community College
  RCOVN/BALC/EX CV7 ....133 L1
Priestley Smith Special School
  ERDW/GRVHL B23 ....71 M7
Primrose Hill Primary School
  HWK/WKHTH B38 ....145 K5
Primrose Hill Trading Estate
  DUDS DY2 ....103 H1
Primrose Lane Health Centre
  WOLVN WV10 ....36 E5
Prince Albert Primary School
  AST/WIT B6 ....89 J5
Princefield First School
  PENK ST19 ....10 D1
Prince of Wales Centre
  CNCK/NC WS11 ....16 C4
Princes Drive Industrial Estate
  KNWTH CV8 ....179 L5
Princes End Industrial Park
  BILS/COS WV14 ....67 J4
Princes End Primary School
  TPTN/OCK DY4 ....67 J6
Princess of Wales Hospital
  BRGRVW B61 ....191 L1
Princethorpe J & I School
  SLYOAK B29 ....123 L3
Priors Field CP School
  KNWTH CV8 ....179 L6
Priory Clinic
  DUDN DY1 ....84 F2
The Priory
  (County Record Office)
  WWCK CV34 ....205 J4
Priory Courts
  CBHAMNW B3 ....7 G4
Priory Green Junior &
  Infants School
  COVEN WV9 ....35 L3
Priory House Industrial Estate
  WSNGN B18 ....88 F8
Priory Junior Mixed &
  Infants School
  BLOX/PEL WS3 ....38 F6
Priory New Way
  Industrial Estate
  AST/WIT B6 ....89 J8
Priory Primary School
  DUDN DY1 ....84 F2
The Priory School
  DARL/WED WS10 ....69 H3
Priory Theatre
  KNWTH CV8 ....179 L6
Private Medical Clinic
  BRGRVW B61 ....191 L2
Progress Business Centre
  CNCK/NC WS11 ....16 C6
Prospect Business Park
  CNCK/NC WS11 ....16 A6
Prospect Trading Estate
  CBHAMW B1 ....6 C4
Providence Industrial Estate
  HAG/WOL DY9 ....102 C7
Provost Williams CE
  Primary School
  KNWTH CV8 ....182 E4
Purley Chase Golf Club
  NUNW/HART CV10 ....78 E3
Pye Green Valley CP School
  HEDN WS12 ....12 E6
Pype Hayes Golf Club
  WALM/CURD B76 ....73 J7
Qualcast Road Industrial Estate
  WOLV WV1 ....3 L5
Quality Hotel
  BDMR/CCFT WV3 ....2 D9
  FOAKS/STRLY B74 ....57 G7
  PENK ST19 ....10 B4
  REDE B98 ....202 C4
  WSLW WS2 ....52 D3
Quarry Bank Primary School
  BRLYHL DY5 ....102 E4
Queen Alexandra College
  HRBN B17 ....105 L7
Queen Elizabeth Hospital
  EDG B15 ....106 C8
Queen Elizabeth Law Courts
  CBHAMNE B4 ....7 H1
Queen Elizabeth Lower School
  ATHST CV9 ....63 K6
Queen Elizabeth
  Psychiatric Hospital
  EDG B15 ....124 C1
Queen Elizabeth's
  Mercian School
  CRTAM B79 ....31 M7
Queen Elizabeth Upper School
  ATHST CV9 ....63 J5
Queen Marys Grammar School
  WSL WS1 ....5 K6

Queen Marys High School
  RUSH/SHEL WS4 ....5 H1
Queensbridge School
  MOS/BIL B13 ....125 J3
Queensbury Special School
  ERDE/BCHGN B24 ....90 D2
Queens CE Junior School
  NUN CV11 ....98 E1
Queens College
  EDG B15 ....106 D8
Queens Court Trading Estate
  WBROM B70 ....86 D2
Queens Croft School
  LICH WS13 ....20 E6
Queen Street Industrial Estate
  BNTWD WS7 ....18 D8
Queensway Trading Estate
  DIG/EDG B5 ....7 J4
Queensway Trading Estate
  RLSS CV31 ....206 C7
Queen Victoria Primary School
  SEDG DY3 ....66 B5
Quince Tree Special School
  TAM/AM/WIL B77 ....46 E1
Quinton Business Park
  RIDG/WDGT B32 ....104 E8
Quinton CE Primary School
  RIDG/WDGT B32 ....104 E7
Racecourse Road
  Industrial Estate
  DUNHL/THL/PER WV6 ....35 L8
Race Leys Primary School
  BDWTH CV12 ....116 F1
Racemeadow Primary School
  ATHST CV9 ....63 J4
Racing Club Warwick FC
  WWCK CV34 ....205 G8
Raddlebarn J & I School
  SLYOAK B29 ....124 D4
Radford Primary School
  COVN CV6 ....133 M8
Radford Semele CE
  Primary School
  RLSS CV31 ....207 J8
Radleys Primary School
  RUSH/SHEL WS4 ....40 A6
Radway Industrial Estate
  SHLY B90 ....148 C6
Rainbow Business Park
  WLNHL WV13 ....51 M2
Rake Gate Infant School
  WOLVN WV10 ....35 M4
Rake Gate Junior School
  WOLVN WV10 ....35 M4
Raleigh Industrial Estate
  HDSW B21 ....87 M4
Rathville School
  NFLD/LBR B31 ....144 F2
Ravens Bank First School
  REDE B98 ....195 H7
Ravensdale Primary School
  COVE CV2 ....156 A1
The Rawlett School
  CRTAM B79 ....31 L4
Rea Business Park
  VAUX/NECH B7 ....107 M1
Read Street Industrial Estate
  COV CV1 ....9 K4
Reaside Clinic
  RBRY B45 ....143 L4
Reaside Junior School
  RBRY B45 ....143 J4
Reddal Hill Primary School
  CDYHTH B64 ....103 J4
Red Deeps Special School
  NUNW/HART CV10 ....98 F5
Reddicap Trading Estate
  MGN/WHC B75 ....73 H1
Redditch County Court
  REDW B97 ....202 B1
Redditch Golf Club
  REDW B97 ....201 L5
Redditch Magistrates Court
  REDE B98 ....202 C1
Redditch United FC
  REDW B97 ....202 A1
Red Hall Primary School
  SEDG DY3 ....84 A2
Redhill I & I School
  YDLY B25 ....108 E6
Redhill Primary School
  CNCK/NC WS11 ....12 C8
Redhill Secondary School
  STRBR DY8 ....101 M8
Red Hill Street Clinic
  WOLV WV1 ....2 F1
Redhouse Industrial Estate
  ALDR WS9 ....40 B7
Redhouse Industrial Estate
  ALDR WS9 ....40 C7
Redhouse JMI School
  ALDR WS9 ....40 C7
Rednal Hill J & I School
  RBRY B45 ....143 M6
Red Rooster Industrial Estate
  ALDR WS9 ....40 C7
Redwood Business Park
  SMTHWK B66 ....87 G6
Reedswood Retail Park
  WSLW WS2 ....52 F1
Reflex Industrial Park
  WLNHL WV13 ....51 K2
Regency Business Centre
  RLSN CV32 ....206 D4
Regency Hotel
  SHLY B90 ....148 C6
Regent Health Centre
  RUGBYN/HIL CV21 ....186 E1
Regents Park
  Primary School
  SMTH B10 ....108 A5
Regent Special School
  OLDBY B69 ....85 L4
Regis Medical Centre
  BLKHTH/ROWR B65 ....104 A4
Reliance Trading Estate
  BILS/COS WV14 ....50 F8
Renaissance Solihull Hotel
  SOLH B91 ....148 F1
Retail Market Hall
  BDMR/CCFT WV3 ....2 E6
Retail Market Shops
  BKHL/PFLD WV2 ....2 E6
Reynolds Cross School
  HIA/OLT B92 ....127 H6
Richard Lee Primary School
  COVE CV2 ....156 B2
The Ridge Primary School
  STRBR DY8 ....101 G2
Ridgeway Primary School
  BNTWD WS7 ....18 B8
Ridgeway School
  WWCK CV34 ....205 K4
Ridgewood High School
  KINVER DY7 ....101 G7
Ridpool Primary School
  STETCH B33 ....109 M2
Rigby Hall Special School
  BRGRVE B60 ....192 A5

Riland Industrial Estate
  MGN/WHC B75 ....57 G8
Ringway Industrial Estate
  LICH WS13 ....21 G2
River Brook Medical Centre
  BVILLE B30 ....124 F5
Riverside Business Centre
  STRPT DY13 ....188 F2
Riverside Industrial Estate
  POL/KGSB/FAZ B78 ....45 M4
Riverside Industrial Estate
  REDE B98 ....203 G5
Riversley Park Clinic
  NUN CV11 ....99 G2
RMW Business Centre
  HAG/WOL DY9 ....102 D8
Robert Clinic
  BVILLE B30 ....124 C8
Roberts Primary School
  SEDG DY3 ....84 C1
Robin Hood Cemetery
  SHLY B90 ....126 F8
Robin Hood Golf Club
  HIA/OLT B92 ....127 G7
Robin Hood Primary School
  HLGN/YWD B28 ....126 F1
Robins Business Park
  TPTN/OCK DY4 ....68 C3
Rocklands Special School
  LICH WS13 ....21 G5
Rocky Lane Trading Estate
  VAUX/NECH B7 ....89 L7
Rokeby Infant School
  RUGBYS/DCH CV22 ....186 E5
Rokeby Junior School
  RUGBYS/DCH CV22 ....186 E5
Rollingmill Business Park
  WSLW WS2 ....4 B5
Roman Way First School
  REDE B98 ....203 H2
Roman Way Hotel
  CNCK/NC WS11 ....15 M6
Romney House
  Industrial Estate
  BILS/COS WV14 ....51 M6
Rood End Primary School
  LGLYGN/QTN B68 ....87 G7
Rookery Primary School
  HDSW B21 ....88 C4
Rosary RC Primary School
  WASH/WDE B8 ....108 C2
Rosedale CE Infant School
  SHHTH WV12 ....38 B4
Rose Theatre
  KIDD DY10 ....138 D5
Rosewood Special School
  DUDN DY1 ....84 C4
Rosslyn School
  HLGN/YWD B28 ....126 E8
Rotton Park Medical Centre
  LDYWD/EDGR B16 ....106 B2
Rotunda
  CBHAM B2 ....7 G6
Rough Hay Primary School
  DARL/WED WS10 ....52 A6
Roughwood (Nature Reserve)
  SHHTH WV12 ....38 C7
Round Oak School
  RLSN CV32 ....206 E2
Rounds Green Primary School
  OLDBY B69 ....86 C5
Rovex Business Park
  SPARK B11 ....108 D8
Rowley Hall Primary School
  BLKHTH/ROWR B65 ....104 A1
Rowley Regis Cemetery &
  Crematorium
  BLKHTH/ROWR B65 ....103 L3
Rowley Regis College
  BLKHTH/ROWR B65 ....103 M2
Rowley Regis Hospital
  BLKHTH/ROWR B65 ....103 M2
Rowleys Green
  Industrial Estate
  COVN CV6 ....134 C1
Royal Birmingham
  Society of Arts
  CBHAMNW B3 ....6 D2
Royal Brierley Trading Estate
  BRLYHL DY5 ....102 F3
The Royal Leamington Hotel
  RLSN CV32 ....206 E4
Royal Mail Depot
  WOLVN WV10 ....3 K4
Royal Orthopaedic Hospital
  NFLD/LBR B31 ....123 M8
Royal Priors Shopping Centre
  RLSN CV32 ....206 D5
The Royal Pump Rooms
  RLSS CV31 ....206 D5
Royal Spa Centre Cinema
  RLSN CV32 ....206 E5
Royal Theatre
  CDYHTH B64 ....103 J4
The Royal Wolverhampton
  Junior School
  BDMR/CCFT WV3 ....49 L6
The Royal Wolverhampton
  School
  BDMR/CCFT WV3 ....49 M6
Rubery Clinic
  RBRY B45 ....143 J6
The Rubicon Business Centre
  REDE B98 ....202 F3
Ruckleigh School
  SOLH B91 ....149 G1
Rufford Primary School
  HAG/WOL DY9 ....102 A8
Rugby Athletics Track
  RUGBYS/DCH CV22 ....186 F3
Rugby College
  RUGBYN/HIL CV21 ....187 H3
Rugby FC
  RUGBYS/DCH CV22 ....186 C3
Rugby Golf Club
  RUGBYN/HIL CV21 ....187 J1
Rugby High School for Girls
  RUGBYS/DCH CV22 ....186 B7
Rugby School
  RUGBYS/DCH CV22 ....186 H2
Rugby School Museum
  RUGBYN/HIL CV21 ....186 E2
Rugby School Sports Centre
  RUGBYS/DCH CV22 ....186 F3
Rugby Theatre
  RUGBYN/HIL CV21 ....186 E2
Rugby Welsh RFC
  RUGBYN/HIL CV21 ....186 D2
Rumer Hill Business Estate
  CNCK/NC WS11 ....16 C6
Rushall Jm School & Education
  Development Centre
  RUSH/SHEL WS4 ....39 L4
Russell Medical Centre
  DARL/WED WS10 ....68 D3
Russells Hall Hospital
  BRLYHL DY5 ....84 B6
Russells Hall Primary School
  DUDN DY1 ....84 C4

Ryders Green Primary School
  WBROM B70 ....86 E1
Ryders Hayes JMI School
  BLOX/PEL WS3 ....25 L8
Ryecroft Shopping Centre
  BNTWD WS7 ....18 D5
Rylands Sports Centre
  BORD B60 ....191 L4
Ryton Gardens
  KNWTH CV8 ....183 J4
Sacred Heart RC
  Primary School
  BFLD/HDSWWD B20 ....89 H4
Sacred Heart RC
  Primary School
  COVE CV2 ....155 L2
Sacred Heart RC
  Primary School
  TPTN/OCK DY4 ....85 K1
Saddlers Shopping Centre
  WSL WS1 ....4 E4
Sai Medical Centre
  WSLW WS2 ....4 B3
St Albans CE Primary School
  WNSFLD WV11 ....37 M5
St Albans CE School
  BHTH/HG B12 ....107 K6
St Albans RC Primary School
  ALE/KHTH/YWD B14 ....146 D1
St Alphege CE Infant School
  SOLH B91 ....149 G2
St Alphege CE Junior School
  SOLH B91 ....149 G3
St Ambrose Barlow RC
  Primary School
  HLGN/YWD B28 ....126 E7
St Ambrose RC Primary School
  KIDD DY10 ....138 D7
St Andrews CE Primary &
  Middle School
  RUGBYN/HIL CV21 ....187 H1
St Andrews CE Infant School
  COVW CV5 ....132 A3
St Andrews Industrial Estate
  BORD B9 ....108 A3
St Andrews Primary School
  BORD B9 ....107 M3
St Andrews RC
  Primary School
  HIA/OLT B92 ....127 L1
St Andrews RUFC
  RUGBYS/DCH CV22 ....187 H1
St Annes CE Middle School
  BEWD DY12 ....162 D3
St Annes Industrial Estate
  WLNHL WV13 ....51 M2
St Anne's RC JMI School
  FOAKS/STRLY B74 ....55 J5
St Annes RC Primary School
  BHTH/HG B12 ....7 L9
  CHWD/FDBR/MGN B37 ....110 E3
  COVS CV3 ....155 M7
  NUNW/HART CV10 ....89 H6
St Anthonys RC Primary School
  CHWD/FDBR/MGN B37 ....92 E8
  RLSS CV31 ....207 G6
  WOLVN WV10 ....36 B2
St Augustines Catholic
  High School
  REDW B97 ....202 B8
St Augustines Catholic
  Primary School
  HDSW B21 ....88 B3
St Augustines RC
  Primary School
  SOLH B91 ....148 E3
St Augustines RC
  Primary School
  COVN CV6 ....133 L6
  KNWTH CV8 ....179 J6
St Barnabas CE First School
  KIDDW DY11 ....137 M4
St Barnabas CE Primary School
  ERDE/BCHGN B24 ....90 F2
St Bartholomews CE
  Primary School
  COVS CV3 ....156 C6
  ETTPK/GDPK/PENN WV4 ....65 J2
St Bedes RC Middle School
  REDE B98 ....202 D2
St Benedict Biscop CE
  Primary School
  WMBN WV5 ....64 D2
St Benedicts Infant School
  SMHTH B10 ....108 D6
St Benedicts RC School
  ATHST CV9 ....63 K6
St Bernadettes RC JMI School
  BRWNH WS8 ....26 D5
St Bernadettes RC
  Primary School
  SMHTH B10 ....108 F5
  WMBN WV5 ....64 D7
St Bernards RC Primary School
  MOS/BIL B13 ....126 A4
St Brigids RC Primary School
  NFLD/LBR B31 ....144 D2
St Catherine of Siena RC School
  EDG B15 ....6 F9
St Chads CE (VC) Primary School
  LICH WS13 ....21 G5
St Chads Industrial Estate
  LOZ/NWT B19 ....89 J8
St Chad's RC Cathedral
  CBHAMNE B4 ....6 F2
St Chads RC Primary School
  LOZ/NWT B19 ....89 H8
  SEDG DY3 ....66 B8
St Christopher Primary School
  COVW CV5 ....154 B1
St Christophers RC
  Primary School
  CDSL WV8 ....34 C2
St Clares Primary School
  BFLD/HDSWWD B20 ....88 F4
St Clements CE Primary School
  VAUX/NECH B7 ....89 M6
St Columbas RC
  Primary School
  RBRY B45 ....144 B6
St Cuthberts RC
  Primary School
  WASH/WDE B8 ....109 G1
St Dunstans RC Primary School
  ALE/KHTH/YWD B14 ....125 J5
St Edmund Campion
  Lower School
  ERDE/BCHGN B24 ....73 G7
St Edmund Campion RC School
  ERDE/BCHGN B24 ....72 F7
St Edmund & John CE
  Primary School
  DUDS DY2 ....85 J1
St Edmunds Catholic School
  DUNHL/THL/PER WV6 ....49 H2
St Edmunds RC Primary School
  WSNGN B18 ....106 D1
St Edwards RC Primary School
  CSHL/WTROR B46 ....93 L8

St Edwards RC Primary School
  CSHL/WTROR B46 ....111 L2
  SLYOAK B29 ....124 F4
St Elizabeths C Primary School
  COVN CV6 ....134 C6
St Elizabeths RC
  Primary School
  CRTAM B79 ....31 L5
St Francis CE Primary School
  BVILLE B30 ....124 B7
St Francis of Assisi RC School
  ALDR WS9 ....41 G8
St Francis RC Combined School
  BDWTH CV12 ....116 F2
St Francis RC Primary School
  LOZ/NWT B19 ....88 F7
St Francis Xavier RC
  Primary School
  OLDBY B69 ....86 E5
St Gabriels RC Primary School
  TAM/AM/WIL B77 ....46 C4
St George & St Teresa RC
  Primary School
  DOR/KN B93 ....175 L1
St Georges CE First School
  KIDD DY10 ....138 D6
  REDE B98 ....202 D2
St Georges CE Primary School
  LDYWD/EDGR B16 ....106 D4
St Georges School Edgbaston
  EDG B15 ....106 F5
St Georges Sixth Form & CE
  Primary School
  LOZ/NWT B19 ....89 H8
St Gerards Orthopaedic
  Hospital
  CSHL/WTROR B46 ....93 L8
St Gerards RC Primary School
  CVALE B35 ....91 M1
St Giles CE Primary School
  WLNHL WV13 ....51 M3
St Giles Junior School
  RCOVN/BALC/EX CV7 ....116 D5
St Gregorys RC Primary School
  COVE CV2 ....156 C2
  SMTHKWK B67 ....105 K3
St Huberts RC
  Primary School
  LGLYGN/QTN B68 ....105 G4
St James CE Junior School
  SHLY B90 ....147 M3
St James CE Primary School
  HDSW B21 ....88 B4
  OLDBY B69 ....86 B8
  STRBR DY8 ....101 H6
St James Medical Centre
  COVS CV3 ....156 A8
  HDSW B21 ....88 B5
St James Primary School
  BRWNH WS8 ....26 D5
St James RC Primary School
  RBRY B45 ....143 L6
St John Bosco RC
  Primary School
  HHTH/SAND B71 ....68 F6
St John Fisher RC
  Primary School
  COVE CV2 ....135 H7
St John Fishers RC
  Primary School
  NFLD/LBR B31 ....144 F1
St John & St Monica RC
  Primary School
  MOS/BIL B13 ....125 J1
St Johns CE First School
  KIDDW DY11 ....137 H7
St Johns CE JMI School
  ALDR WS9 ....40 D7
St Johns CE Middle School
  BRGRVW B61 ....191 J3
  KIDDW DY11 ....137 M7
St Johns CE Primary School
  COVW CV5 ....154 A11
  DARL/WED WS10 ....68 D3I
  LDYWD/EDGR B16 ....106 E3I
  SEDG DY3 ....82 C3
  SPARK B11 ....126 A1
  WNSFLD WV11 ....37 L1
St John's Hospital
  COV CV1 ....8 F3
St John's Museum
  & Royal Warwickshire
  Regimental Museum
  WWCK CV34 ....205 K6
St Johns Primary School
  KNWTH CV8 ....197 K3
St Johns Retail Park
  BKHL/PFLD WV2 ....2 F7
St John the Baptist RC
  Primary School
  CBROM B36 ....92 A4
St John the Divine CE
  Primary School
  COVS CV3 ....156 A8
St John Vianney RC
  Primary School
  COVW CV5 ....153 M2
St John Wall RC School
  HDSW B21 ....88 B3
St Joseph & St Theresa RC
  Primary School
  BNTWD WS7 ....18 C2
St Josephs Catholic
  Primary School
  DARL/WED WS10 ....52 A6
St Josephs Catholic Primary School
  MGN/WHC B75 ....57 G6
  STRBR DY8 ....119 K3
St Josephs RC First School
  NUN CV11 ....99 G2
St Josephs RC Primary School
  BVILLE B30 ....124 C8
  DUDS DY2 ....85 J4
  HEDN WS12 ....17 G1
  LICHS WS14 ....21 G6
  VAUX/NECH B7 ....89 M7
St Josephs RC Primary School
  KNWTH CV8 ....179 M6
St Judes CE Primary School
  BDMR/CCFT WV3 ....3 K6
  ALE/KHTH/YWD B14 ....146 D3
St Kenelms CE First School
  RMSLY B62 ....142 E1
St Laurence CE J & I School
  CRTAM B79 ....32 A4
St Leonards CE Primary School
  CRTAM B79 ....144 F1
St Lukes CE Aided
  Primary School
  BKHL/PFLD WV2 ....49 M6
St Lukes CE First School
  REDW B97 ....202 B3
St Margaret Mary RC
  Primary School
  ERDW/GRVHL B23 ....72 A7
St Margarets CE Primary School
  GTB/HAM B43 ....70 C1

HIA/OLT B92 ....127 K3
KNWTH CV8 ....183 K1
St Margarets Hospital
DSYBK/YTR WS5 ....54 C5
St Maries Catholic
Infant School
RUGBYS/DCH CV22 ....186 E3
St Maries RC Junior School
RUGBYS/DCH CV22 ....186 D3
St Marks CE Primary School
BRLYHL DY5 ....84 A6
St Marks RC Primary School
PBAR/PBCH B42 ....70 D6
St Martin de Porres RC
Primary School
MOS/BIL B13 ....125 L2
St Martins CE Primary School
BILS/COS WV14 ....67 L3
TPTN/OCK DY4 ....67 M8
St Martins Industrial Estate
OLDBY B69 ....86 E7
St Martins Market
DIG/EDG B5 ....7 H7
St Martins School
SOLH B91 ....149 H2
St Mary & Johns RC
Primary School
BKHL/PFLD WV2 ....3 H9
St Mary Magdalene CE
Primary School
HHTH/SAND B71 ....69 H7
St Mary of the Angels RC
JMI School
ALDR WS9 ....40 F8
St Mary's Abbey (Remains)
RMSLY B62 ....122 B3
St Mary & St Benedict RC
Primary School
COV CV1 ....9 K2
St Mary & St John RC
Primary School
ERDE/BCHGN B24 ....90 C2
St Mary & St Margarets CE
Primary School
CBROM B36 ....91 M5
St Marys Catholic
Primary School
WWCK CV34 ....205 J5
St Marys CE First School
KIDDW DY11 ....138 C5
St Marys CE Primary School
BFLD/HDSWWD B20 ....88 F4
KGSWFD DY6 ....83 H5
SLYOAK B29 ....124 B4
St Mary's Guildhall
COV CV1 ....9 G5
St Mary's Priory
COV CV1 ....8 F4
St Marys RC Primary School
BRLYHL DY5 ....102 C3
CNCK/NC WS11 ....16 C5
DARL/WED WS10 ....106 A8
HRBN B17 ....68 D1
WOLVN WV10 ....36 C6
St Marys the Mount RC School
WSL WS1 ....5 J7
St Matthews Bloxam CE
School
RUGBYS/DCH CV22 ....186 C3
St Matthews CE Primary School
SMTHWK B66 ....87 M8
VAUX/NECH B7 ....7 M1
St Michaels CE First School
PENK ST19 ....10 C4
St Michaels CE High School
OLDBY B69 ....86 B8
St Michaels CE Primary School
BLOX/PEL WS3 ....39 K3
HDSW B21 ....88 F1
LICH WS13 ....21 G6
RIDG/WDGT B32 ....123 G5
St Michael's Hospital
WWCK CV34 ....205 H5
St Michaels RC Primary School
BDMR/CCFT WV3 ....49 H6
St Nicholas CE
Combined School
KNWTH CV8 ....179 L8
St Nicholas CE Vc First School
CDSL WV8 ....34 D1
St Nicholas Park Leisure Centre
WWCK CV34 ....205 L6
St Nicholas RC JMI School
SCFLD/BOLD B73 ....72 D3
St Nicolas CE Primary School
NUN CV11 ....81 K7
St Osburgs RC Primary School
COV CV1 ....8 C2
St Oswalds CE First School
KIDD DY10 ....138 E3
St Oswalds CE Primary School
RUGBYS/DCH CV22 ....186 B2
St Patrick CE Primary School
HOCK/TIA B94 ....174 A3
St Patricks Catholic
Primary School
CHWD/FDBR/MGN B37 ....111 G3
WSLW WS2 ....4 D1
St Patricks RC
Combined School
RLSS CV31 ....206 C8
St Patricks RC Primary School
COVE CV2 ....135 H4
WNSFLD WV11 ....37 G8
WSNGN B18 ....106 D1
St Pauls C E First School
COVEN WV9 ....22 C4
St Pauls Cemetery
COV CV6 ....134 A8
St Pauls CE Primary School
NUNW/HART CV10 ....98 A2
RLSN CV32 ....206 F4
TPTN/OCK DY4 ....67 K7
HWK/WKNTH B38 ....145 L4
St Pauls School
BHTH/HG B12 ....107 L8
St Pauls School for Girls
LDYWD/EDGR B16 ....106 C4
St Peter & Paul RC
Primary School
ERDE/BCHGN B24 ....91 G2
St Peter & St Paul RC
Primary School
COVE CV2 ....135 J6
LICH WS13 ....20 F4
St Peters CE Infant School
HRBN B17 ....123 K1
St Peters CE Junior School
HRBN B17 ....124 A1
St Peters CE Primary School
ALDR WS9 ....41 J1
HEDN WS12 ....17 H1
St Peters CJMI School
BLOX/PEL WS3 ....38 F3
St Peters Collegiate
Secondary School
DUNHL/THL/PER WV6 ....49 J2
St Peters RC First School
BRGRVE B60 ....191 J5

St Peters RC Primary School
RIDG/WDGT B32 ....123 G4
RLSN CV32 ....206 D5
St Peters RC School
SOLH B91 ....148 F3
St Philips Cathedral
CBHAMNW B1 ....6 F4
St Philips RC Primary School
SMTHWK B66 ....87 M7
St Philips RC Sixth Form
College
LDYWD/EDGR B16 ....106 D5
St Saviours CE Primary School
WASH/WDE B8 ....90 B8
St Stephens CE First School
REDE B98 ....194 D8
St Stephens CE Primary School
WOLVN WV10 ....3 L1
St Teresas RC Primary School
BFLD/HDSWWD B20 ....88 E3
ETTPK/GDPK/PENN WV4 ....50 C8
St Thomas Aquinas RC School
HWK/WKNTH B38 ....145 L1
St Thomas CE Primary School
EDG B15 ....6 E8
St Thomas More Catholic
School
WLNHL WV13 ....51 M5
St Thomas More RC
Primary School
CNCK/NC WS11 ....24 E1
COVS CV3 ....155 H8
LGN/SDN/BHAMAIR B26 ....109 H8
St Thomas More RC School
NUNW/HART CV10 ....98 E2
St Thomas of Canterbury RC
JMI School
BLOX/PEL WS3 ....39 K7
St Vincents RC Primary School
VAUX/NECH B7 ....107 M2
St Wilfrids RC Primary School
CBROM B36 ....91 K5
Salafi Independent School
SMHTH B10 ....108 B5
Salford Trading Estate
AST/WIT B6 ....90 A5
Salisbury Place
Industrial Estate
BDMR/CCFT WV3 ....2 C7
Salisbury Primary School
DARL/WED WS10 ....52 C6
Saltbrook Trading Estate
HALE B63 ....102 E6
Salters Meadow
Health Centre
BNTWD WS7 ....18 D6
Saltley Business Park
WASH/WDE B8 ....90 B7
Saltley Health Centre
WASH/WDE B8 ....90 C8
Saltley Industrial Centre
WASH/WDE B8 ....108 A2
Saltley Leisure Centre
BORD B9 ....108 E2
Saltley School
BORD B9 ....108 E2
Saltley Trading Estate
WASH/WDE B8 ....90 A8
The Samuel Johnson
Birthplace Museum
LICH WS13 ....20 F6
Sanders Industrial Estate
BRGRVW B61 ....191 J4
Sandown First School
DUNHL/THL/PER WV6 ....48 D1
Sandwell Borough FC
OLDBY B69 ....86 C6
Sandwell Business
Development Centre
OLDBY B69 ....87 G6
Sandwell Business Park
SMTHWK B66 ....87 G5
Sandwell Business &
Technology Centre
LGLYGN/QTN B68 ....104 D4
Sandwell College
DARL/WED WS10 ....68 E4
Sandwell College of
Further & Higher Education
WBROM B70 ....87 G2
Sandwell District General
Hospital
HHTH/SAND B71 ....69 H8
Sandwell Park Golf Club
HHTH/SAND B71 ....87 K3
Sandwell Park
Industrial Estate
HHTH/SAND B71 ....87 K4
Sandwell Valley
HHTH/SAND B71 ....69 L7
Sandyhill Industrial Estate
SHLY B90 ....147 L1
Sandy Lane Business Park
COV CV1 ....134 A8
Sandy Lane Industrial Estate
STRPT DY13 ....188 F4
Sapcote Business Centre
SMHTH B10 ....108 C7
Sapcote Industrial Estate
CDYHTH B64 ....103 K2
Sapcote Trading Centre
AST/WIT B6 ....89 L2
Sapcote Trading Centre
CDYHTH B64 ....103 K2
Sapcote Trading Estate
SMHTH B10 ....108 C7
Sarehole Mill
MOS/BIL B13 ....126 B5
Sarepfield Medical Centre
SMTHWKW B67 ....87 L8
Sargent Turner Trading Estate
HAG/WOL DY9 ....102 D7
Satellite Industrial Park
WLNHL WV13 ....51 G1
Saxon Hill Special School
LICHS WS14 ....21 G7
School of Jewellery (UCE)
CBHAMNW B1 ....6 C2
Scotch Orchard County
Primary School
LICH WS13 ....21 H4
Scott Arms Shopping Centre
GTB/HAM B43 ....70 C4
Sears Retail Park
SHLY B90 ....148 A4
Securehold Business Centre
REDE B98 ....202 F4
Sedgley Golf Centre
SEDG DY3 ....65 M7
Selly Manor Museum
BVILLE B30 ....124 D5
Selly Oak Health Centre
SLYOAK B29 ....124 C5
Selly Oak Hospital
SLYOAK B29 ....124 D4
Selly Oak Industrial Estate
SLYOAK B29 ....124 C4

Selly Oak School
SLYOAK B29 ....124 C5
Selly Park Technology
College for Girls for Girls
SLYOAK B29 ....124 C4
Seven Stars Industrial Estate
COVS CV3 ....155 L6
Severne Primary School
ACGN B27 ....127 G5
Severnside Business Park
STRPT DY13 ....188 E2
Severn Valley Railway
BEWD DY12 ....136 D3
BEWD DY12 ....163 J3
Shaftmoor Industrial Estate
HLGN/YWD B28 ....126 D3
Sharmans Cross
Junior School
SOLH B91 ....148 C1
Shaw Hill Primary School
WASH/WDE B8 ....90 B8
Shaw Park Business Village
WOLVN WV10 ....36 B7
The Sheila Godfrey Clinic
DOR/KN B93 ....175 K2
Sheldon CC
YDLY B25 ....109 H5
Sheldon Country Park
LGN/SDN/BHAMAIR B26 ....110 C7
Sheldon Heath
Community School
STECH B33 ....110 A5
Shelfield Clinic
RUSH/SHEL WS4 ....40 A3
Shelfield Sports &
Community College
RUSH/SHEL WS4 ....40 A3
Shell Corner Trading Estate
RMSLY B62 ....104 B5
Shelter Waterside
Industrial Estate
ETTPK/GDPK/PENN WV4 ....50 E8
Shenley Court School
NFLD/LBR B31 ....123 K6
Shenley Lane Community
Association Sports Centre
SLYOAK B29 ....123 L7
Shenstone Lodge Special School
LICHS WS14 ....42 E2
Shenstone Sports Club
LICHS WS14 ....28 E7
Shenstone Trading Estate
HALE B63 ....122 A1
Shepperton Business Park
NUN CV11 ....99 G4
Sherborne Wharf
LDYWD/EDGR B16 ....6 A6
Sherbourne Fields
Special School
COVN CV6 ....133 H8
Sherbourne Medical Centre
RLSN CV32 ....206 D4
Sheriden House Hotel
BFLD/HDSWWD B20 ....88 D2
Shireland Hall Primary School
SMTHWK B66 ....106 A2
Shireland Language College
SMTHWK B66 ....105 L2
Shire Oak School
BRWNH WS8 ....26 E8
Shires Gate Trading Estate
RLSS CV31 ....206 C4
Shires Industrial Estate
LICH WS13 ....20 E7
Shires Retail Park
RLSS CV31 ....206 B7
Shirestone Primary School
STECH B33 ....110 B3
Shirley Clinic
SHLY B90 ....147 M2
Shirley Heath Junior School
SHLY B90 ....148 A4
Shirley Park Sports Club &
Golf Club
SHLY B90 ....174 E1
Shirley Road Health Clinic
ACGN B27 ....126 F4
The Shopping Centre
RLSS CV31 ....206 F8
Short Heath Clinic
SHHTH WV12 ....38 B7
Short Heath Primary School
ERDW/GRVHL B23 ....72 B7
Shorth Heath Junior School
SHHTH WV12 ....38 B8
Showcase Cinemas
DUDN DY1 ....85 J2
Showcase Cinemas
ERDE/BCHGN B24 ....91 H3
Showcase Cinemas
RCOVN/BALC/EX CV7 ....135 M4
Showcase Cinemas
WSLW WS2 ....52 D4
Showell Road Industrial Estate
WOLVN WV10 ....36 B7
The Shrubbery School
WALM/CURD B76 ....73 K6
Shrubland Street Community
Primary School
RLSS CV31 ....206 E7
Shustoke CE Primary School
CSHL/WTROR B46 ....94 E3
Sidemoor First School
BRGRVW B61 ....191 J2
Sidney Stringer Community
Technology College
COV CV1 ....9 H3
Silhill FC
SOLH B91 ....148 C1
Silver Birches Business Park
BRGRVE B60 ....191 L7
Silver End Business Park
BRLYHL DY5 ....101 M5
Sion Mill Middle School
KIDD DY10 ....138 D3
Sir Frank Whittle
Business Centre
RUGBYN/HIL CV21 ....161 H8
Sir Robert Peel Hospital
POL/KGSB/FAZ B78 ....45 H3
Skydome Leisure Complex
COV CV1 ....8 D5
Sladefield Infant School
WASH/WDE B8 ....90 E8
The Sladen CE Middle School
KIDD DY10 ....138 D5
Slade CE Primary School
ERDW/GRVHL B23 ....90 A3
Sledmere Primary School
DUDS DY2 ....85 H7
Small Heath Business Park
SMHTH B10 ....108 C6
Small Heath Lower School
SMHTH B10 ....108 B6
Small Heath Trading Estate
SPARK B11 ....108 B5
Small Heath Upper School &
Sixth Form Centre
SMHTH B10 ....108 B5

Smestow Bridge
Industrial Estate
WMBN WV5 ....64 A7
Smestow Secondary School
BDMR/CCFT WV3 ....48 F4
Smethwick Medical Centre
SMTHWK B66 ....87 L7
Smethwick Swimming Centre
SMTHWK B67 ....105 K3
Smith's Wood School
CBROM B36 ....92 E7
Sneyd Community School
BKHL/PFLD WS3 ....38 C3
Snow Hill Clinic
BKHL/PFLD WV2 ....3 D6
Soho Health Centre
HDSW B21 ....88 D6
Soho House
WSNGN B18 ....88 E6
Solihull College
SOLH B91 ....148 E2
Solihull Hospital
SOLH B91 ....149 H1
Solihull Ice Rink
HIA/OLT B92 ....127 M2
Solihull Magistrates Court
SOLH B91 ....149 G2
Solihull Retail Park
SHLY B90 ....148 B4
Solihull School
SOLH B91 ....149 H1
Solihull Sixth Form College
SOLH B91 ....149 H3
Somerville Primary School
SMHTH B10 ....108 B5
South Birmingham College
HLGN/YWD B28 ....126 C5
South Birmingham
Mental Health NHS Trust
BVILLE B30 ....146 B2
South Bromsgrove
Community High School
Technical College
BRGRVE B60 ....191 K5
Southfield Primary School
COV CV1 ....9 K4
South Moons Moat
Industrial Estate
REDE B98 ....203 H1
Southside Business Centre
BHTH/HG B12 ....107 L8
South Staffordshire Golf Club
DUNHL/THL/PER WV6 ....35 G7
South Staffs Business Park
CNCK/NC WS11 ....24 A1
Sovereign Trading Estate
STRBR DY8 ....101 J8
Sowe Valley Primary School
COVS CV3 ....156 B5
Sparkbrook Health Centre
SPARK B11 ....107 M6
Sparkbrook Street
Industrial Estate
COV CV1 ....9 K3
Sparkhill Pool & Fitness Centre
SPARK B11 ....126 A1
Sparrowdale Special School
ATHST CV9 ....62 B1
Spartan Industrial Centre
WBROM B70 ....68 C7
Speedwell Trading Estate
YDLY B25 ....108 E7
Spennells First School
KIDD DY10 ....164 E3
Spines Clinic
WMBN WV5 ....64 D7
Spinners End Industrial Estate
CDYHTH B64 ....103 H4
Spon Gate Primary School
COV CV1 ....8 B7
Spon Lane Industrial Estate
SMTHWK B66 ....87 H5
Spon Lane Trading Estate
WBROM B70 ....87 G3
Springdale J & I School
ETTPK/GDPK/PENN WV4 ....49 G8
Springfield House School
DOR/KN B93 ....150 E8
Springfield Infant School
MOS/BIL B13 ....126 B3
Springfield Junior School
BLKHTH/ROWR B65 ....103 L1
Springfield Junior School
SPARK B11 ....126 B3
Springfield Primary School
BLKHTH/ROWR B65 ....85 L8
Spring Hill Industrial Estate
RCOVN/BALC/EX CV7 ....96 D5
Spring Hill Industrial Estate
WSNGN B18 ....106 D1
Springhill Medical Centre
BNTWD WS7 ....18 E6
Spring Hill Medical Centre
RCOVN/BALC/EX CV7 ....96 D6
Springhill Primary School
BNTWD WS7 ....18 F7
Spring Lane Industrial Estate
SHHTH WV12 ....52 A1
Spring Road Industrial Estate
ETTPK/GDPK/PENN WV4 ....66 C3
Springvale Business Park
BILS/COS WV14 ....66 F1
Springvale Industrial Park
BILS/COS WV14 ....66 F1
Springvale Primary School
CNCK/NC WS11 ....16 C5
Spring Vale Primary School
ETTPK/GDPK/PENN WV4 ....66 C5
Sprint Industrial Estate
WOLVN WV10 ....14 B7
Stafford Road Sports Club
BLOX/PEL WS3 ....38 F3
Staffordshire College of
Agriculture
PENK ST19 ....14 C1
Staffordshire Regiment
Museum, Whittington
LICHS WS14 ....30 A3
Stag Industrial Estate
BILS/COS WV14 ....67 L1
Stag Industrial Estate
COVN CV6 ....134 B5
Stambermill Industrial Estate
HAG/WOL DY9 ....102 A4
Stanhope Road Clinic
SMTHWKW B67 ....105 K2
Stanton Bridge
Primary School
COVN CV6 ....134 D7
Stanville Primary School
LGN/SDN/BHAMAIR B26 ....109 M6
Starbank Primary School
SMHTH B10 ....108 F5
Star City
VAUX/NECH B7 ....90 B5
Starcrest Industrial Estate
COVE CV2 ....102 C4
Star Industrial Park
COVE CV2 ....135 J8

Start Point Trading Estate
SPARK B11 ....126 B1
Station Road Industrial Estate
BLKHTH/ROWR B65 ....104 E3
Station Road Industrial Estate
CSHL/WTROR B46 ....93 K3
Station Road Industrial Estate
CSHL/WTROR B46 ....93 L5
Station Street West
Business Park
COVN CV6 ....134 C8
Status Business Centre
COVW CV5 ....8 B7
Stechford Cascades
STETCH B33 ....109 J2
Stechford Health Centre
STETCH B33 ....109 J3
Stechford Primary School
STETCH B33 ....109 H3
Stechford Retail Park
STETCH B33 ....109 J1
Stechford Trading Estate
STETCH B33 ....109 J1
Steetley Industrial Estate
TPTN/OCK DY4 ....67 G6
Stephens Industrial Estate
SPARK B11 ....126 D1
Stevens Dental Health Centre
STRBR DY8 ....119 K1
Stirchley Primary School
BVILLE B30 ....124 E7
Stirchley Trading Estate
BVILLE B30 ....124 F6
Stivichall Primary School
COVS CV3 ....154 E7
Stock Exchange
CBHAMNW B3 ....6 E4
Stockingford Clinic
NUNW/HART CV10 ....98 B2
Stockingford Primary &
Middle School
NUNW/HART CV10 ....98 B2
Stockland Clinic
ERDW/GRVHL B23 ....90 B1
Stockland Green Health Centre
ERDW/GRVHL B23 ....90 B1
Stockland Green School
ERDW/GRVHL B23 ....90 A1
Stoke Aldermoor
Medical Centre
COVS CV3 ....155 M5
Stoke Heath J & I School
COVE CV2 ....134 E7
Stoke Old Boys RFC
COVS CV3 ....156 B4
Stoke Park School and
Community Technology
College
COVE CV2 ....155 H4
Stoke Primary School
COVE CV2 ....155 L1
Stoke Row Industrial Estate
COVE CV2 ....155 L1
Stonebridge Golf Club
RCOVN/BALC/EX CV7 ....130 D4
Stonebridge Trading Estate
COVS CV3 ....181 M2
Stone CE First School
KIDD DY10 ....165 J3
Stone Cross Clinic
HHTH/SAND B71 ....69 J3
Stoneleigh Abbey
KNWTH CV8 ....198 D3
Stoneleigh Deer Park
Business Village
KNWTH CV8 ....199 H1
Stoneleigh Deer Park Golf Club
KNWTH CV8 ....181 J8
Stone Manor Hotel
KIDD DY10 ....165 J4
Stoneydelph Infants School
TAM/AM/WIL B77 ....46 E4
Stoneydelph Primary School
TAM/AM/WIL B77 ....46 E4
Stoney Lane Industrial Estate
KIDDW DY11 ....138 C5
Stourbridge CC
STRBR DY8 ....101 K8
Stourbridge Clinic
STRBR DY8 ....119 K1
Stourbridge College of
Technology & Art
STRBR DY8 ....119 L2
Stourbridge Crematorium
STRBR DY8 ....119 H1
Stourbridge FC
STRBR DY8 ....101 K7
Stourbridge Golf Club
STRBR DY8 ....119 L4
Stourbridge Industrial Estate
STRBR DY8 ....101 L7
Stourbridge Lawn Tennis &
Squash Club
KINVER DY7 ....118 F4
Stourbridge RFC
KINVER DY7 ....100 F7
Stourminster Special School
KIDD DY10 ....164 F1
Stourport Health Centre
STRPT DY13 ....188 E2
Stourport on Severn
First School
STRPT DY13 ....188 E1
Stourport on Severn High School
STRPT DY13 ....163 L8
Stourport Sports Centre
STRPT DY13 ....188 D3
Stourport Tennis Club
STRPT DY13 ....188 D1
Stourside Industrial Estate
KIDD DY10 ....138 C8
Stourvale Industrial Estate
HAG/WOL DY9 ....102 D7
Stourvale Trading Estate
HALE B63 ....103 J7
Stowe CE School
LICHS WS14 ....21 G5
Stowheath Industrial Estate &
New Enterprise Centre
WOLV WV1 ....50 B4
Stow Heath J & I School
WLNHL WV13 ....51 L1
Stowlawn Primary School
BILS/COS WV14 ....51 G5
Straits Primary School
SEDG DY3 ....65 M8
Stratford Road Clinic
SPARK B11 ....126 B3
The Streetley School
FOAKS/STRLY B74 ....55 J5
Streetly Cemetery
ALDR WS9 ....55 H5
Streetly Clinic
FOAKS/STRLY B74 ....55 J4
Streetly Hockey & Cricket Club
FOAKS/STRLY B74 ....55 J4

Streetly Methodist
Recreation Centre
FOAKS/STRLY B74 ....55 K3
Streetsbrook Infant School
SHLY B90 ....148 A1
Stuart Bathurst RC
High School
DARL/WED WS10 ....52 F8
Stuart Crystal
STRBR DY8 ....101 J4
Studley Cricket Club
STUD B80 ....203 J7
Summerfield Hospital
WSNGN B18 ....106 D1
Summerfield Primary School
WSNGN B18 ....106 C1
Summer Hill Industrial Park
CBHAMW B1 ....6 A3
The Summerhill Secondary
School
KGSWFD DY6 ....82 F8
Sundridge Primary School
KGSTG B44 ....71 J1
Sunfield School
HAG/WOL DY9 ....141 J1
Sunrise Business Park
STRBR DY8 ....101 J3
Sunshine Infant School
BLOX/PEL WS3 ....39 G5
Superintendent Public Baths
SLYOAK B29 ....124 D4
Sutton Arts Theatre
CSCFLD/WYGN B72 ....73 G1
Sutton Coldfield College
FOAKS/STRLY B74 ....57 G7
Sutton Coldfield Crematorium
MGN/WHC B75 ....57 L3
Sutton Coldfield Girls School
SCFLD/BOLD B73 ....72 F2
Sutton Coldfield Golf Club
FOAKS/STRLY B74 ....55 M4
Sutton Coldfield Hospital
SCFLD/BOLD B73 ....72 F1
Sutton Coldfield
Magistrates Court
FOAKS/STRLY B74 ....56 F7
Sutton Coldfield Town FC
CSCFLD/WYGN B72 ....73 G2
Sutton Coldfield Town Hall
SCFLD/BOLD B73 ....56 F7
Sutton Park First School
KIDDW DY11 ....163 M1
The Sutton Special School
DUDN DY1 ....84 D5
Sutton Town Sports Club
CSCFLD/WYGN B72 ....73 G1
Sutton United FC
MGN/WHC B75 ....57 J8
The Swallows
Industrial Estate
SHLY B90 ....148 B5
Swallows Rise Business Park
BRLYHL DY5 ....102 C2
Swan Centre
KIDD DY10 ....138 C7
Swan Corner Shopping Centre
BNTWD WS7 ....19 G2
Swan Lane Industrial Estate
WBROM B70 ....68 E8
Swan Medical Centre
YDLY B25 ....109 H6
Swanpool Medical Centre
TPTN/OCK DY4 ....67 L5
Swanshurst Girls School
MOS/BIL B13 ....125 M6
Swanswell Medical Centre
COV CV1 ....9 G2
Swift Valley Industrial Estate
RUGBYN/HIL CV21 ....160 D5
Swinfen Hall Hotel
LICHS WS14 ....29 J4
Sycamore Green
Primary School
DUDN DY1 ....66 D8
Sycamore House
Medical Centre
WSL WS1 ....5 K7
Sycamore Industrial &
Trading Estate
HDSW B21 ....88 B6
Sydenham Industrial Estate
RLSS CV31 ....206 F7
Sydenham Primary School
RLSS CV31 ....207 G7
Symphony Hall
CBHAMW B1 ....6 C5
Tachbrook Park
Industrial Estate
WWCK CV34 ....206 B8
Talbots Lane Trading Estate
BRLYHL DY5 ....102 C4
Talisman Theatre & Arts Centre
KNWTH CV8 ....197 K2
Tamar Medical Centre
DUNHL/THL/PER WV6 ....48 C1
Tamebridge Industrial Estate
PBAR/PBCH B42 ....89 J1
Tame Road Industrial Estate
AST/WIT B6 ....89 M4
Tame Valley Industrial Estate
TAM/AM/WIL B77 ....46 C6
Tame Valley Industrial Estate
TAM/AM/WIL B77 ....46 C8
Tame Valley Primary School
ERDE/BCHGN B24 ....91 H5
Tame Valley Small Business
Centre
TAM/AM/WIL B77 ....46 C7
Tame View Caravan Site
POL/KGSB/FAZ B78 ....59 M4
Tamworth Assembly Rooms
CRTAM B79 ....31 M8
Tamworth Business Centre
TAM/AM/WIL B77 ....46 F2
Tamworth Business Park
TAM/AM/WIL B77 ....46 F2
Tamworth Castle
CRTAM B79 ....45 M1
Tamworth FC (The Lamb)
TAM/AM/WIL B77 ....46 A2
Tamworth Leisure Island
(Snowdome Ski
& Peaks Leisure Centre)
TAM/AM/WIL B77 ....45 M2
Tamworth & Lichfield College
CRTAM B79 ....31 M7
Tamworth Municipal Golf Club
TAM/AM/WIL B77 ....47 G1
Tamworth RUFC
CRTAM B79 ....31 K6
Tamworth Sports Stadium
TAM/AM/WIL B77 ....46 D4
Tandon Medical Centre
SEDG DY3 ....66 C8
Tanks Glebe Farm
Industrial Estate
RUGBYN/HIL CV21 ....160 D5
Tansey Green Trading Estate
BRLYHL DY5 ....83 M5

Tardebigge CE First School
BRGRVE B60 ....192 F6
Teachers Centre
COV CV1 ....9 G7
Telford Infant School
RLSN CV32 ....199 G8
Telford Junior School
RLSN CV32 ....198 F8
Telsen Industrial Centre
AST/WIT B6 ....89 K7
Templar Industrial Park
TLHL/CAN CV4 ....153 L5
Templars Primary School
TLHL/CAN CV4 ....153 L5
Temple Meadow
Primary School
CDYHTH B64 ....103 K4
Ten Acres First School
REDE B98 ....203 K2
Tenlons Road Industrial Estate
NUNW/HART CV10 ....98 D3
Tenterfields Primary School
HALE B63 ....122 A1
Terrace Industrial Estate
RUGBYN/HIL CV21 ....186 F1
The Terrace School
RLSN CV32 ....206 C5
Terry Business Centre
REDE B98 ....202 D2
Tettenhall College
DUNHL/THL/PER WV6 ....49 H1
Tettenhall Wood
Special School
DUNHL/THL/PER WV6 ....48 F2
Theatre One
COV CV1 ....9 G3
Thinktank Museum
DIG/EDG B5 ....7 K4
Thomas Barnes CP School
POL/KGSB/FAZ B78 ....30 F6
Thornleigh Trading Estate
DUDS DY2 ....84 E6
Thorns Community College
BRLYHL DY5 ....102 B5
Thorns County Infant School
KNWTH CV8 ....197 L1
Thorns Primary School
BRLYHL DY5 ....102 C6
Thornton Junior School
WASH/WDE B8 ....90 F8
Three Crowns Special School
DSYBK/YTR WS5 ....54 D4
Three Spires Industrial Estate
COVN CV6 ....116 E7
Three Spires Shopping Centre
LICH WS13 ....20 F6
Three Spires Special School
COVW CV5 ....133 H7
Tidbury Green
Primary School
SHLY B90 ....173 J1
Tile Cross Trading Estate
STECH B33 ....110 B4
Tile Hill Wood
Comprehensive School
TLHL/CAN CV4 ....153 L4
Timberley Primary School
BKDE/SHDE B34 ....92 B7
Timbertree Primary School
CDYHTH B64 ....103 J6
Tindal Primary School
BHTH/HG B12 ....107 K8
Tipper Trading Estate
HAG/WOL DY9 ....102 E8
Tipton Green Junior School
TPTN/OCK DY4 ....85 K1
Tipton Sports Academy
TPTN/OCK DY4 ....67 M4
Tiverton J & I School
SLYOAK B29 ....124 D3
Tiverton Special School
COVN CV6 ....133 H8
Tividale Business Park
TPTN/OCK DY4 ....85 M2
Tividale Comprehensive School
OLDBY B69 ....86 A4
Tividale FC
OLDBY B69 ....85 M4
Tividale Hall Primary School
OLDBY B69 ....85 L4
Tividale Medical Centre
OLDBY B69 ....86 B5
Tividale Primary School
OLDBY B69 ....85 M3
Toffs Country House Hotel
RCOVN/BALC/EX CV7 ....132 H9
Tollgate Shopping Precinct
SMTHWKW B67 ....87 K7
Tolson Industrial Estate
POL/KGSB/FAZ B78 ....45 L5
Tolsons Mill Industrial Estate
POL/KGSB/FAZ B78 ....45 L5
Topcliffe Primary School
CVALE B35 ....91 L2
Touchwood Shopping Centre
SOLH B91 ....149 G1
Tower Hill Health Centre
PBAR/PBCH B42 ....70 E7
Tower Works Industrial Estate
BDMR/CCFT WV3 ....2 A7
Town Gate Retail Park
DUDN DY1 ....85 K3
Town Junior School
CSCFLD/WYGN B72 ....73 G1
Town Wharf Business Park
WSLW WS2 ....4 D4
T P Riley Community School
BLOX/PEL WS3 ....39 G1
Tractor Spares Industrial Estate
WLNHL WV13 ....51 H1
Trading Estate Parkview
HWK/WKHTH B38 ....145 K2
The Trafford Park
Industrial Estate
REDE B98 ....202 D2
Travel Inn
BRGRVE B60 ....191 M4
CBHAMW B1 ....6 D6
CNCK/NC WS11 ....16 M6
COVS CV3 ....156 F5
HAG/WOL DY9 ....120 D6
HOCK/TIA B94 ....174 F6
KGSWFD DY6 ....83 K6
NUNW/HART CV10 ....98 F7
POL/KGSB/FAZ B78 ....45 L1
RCOVN/BALC/EX CV7 ....151 L5
RRUGBY CV23 ....161 G4
SHLY B90 ....147 M2
SHLY B90 ....148 D8
VAUX/NECH B7 ....89 K8
WBROM B70 ....22 D8
WOLVN WV10 ....58 B8
WSLW WS2 ....52 C7
Travelodge
BRLYHL DY5 ....102 C1
CBHAMW B1 ....6 C7
LCN/SDN/BHAMAIR B26 .....109 J7
NUN CV11 ....81 L7
OLDBY B69 ....86 B6

SCFLD/BOLD B73 ....72 D4
STRPT DY13 ....189 L6
TAM/AM/WIL B77 ....47 G6
WNSFLD WV11 ....23 L6
Traveldage Birmingham
RIDG/WDGT B32 ....122 D6
Trent Valley Trading Estate
LICH WS13 ....21 G2
Trescott Primary School
RIDG/WDGT B32 ....144 B2
Trevor Street Industrial Estate
VAUX/NECH B7 ....90 A7
Tribune Trading Estate
RUGBYN/HIL CV21 ....160 E7
Trident Business Park
NUN CV11 ....99 H2
Trident Retail Park
BORD B9 ....7 M6
Trident Shopping Centre
DUDN DY1 ....85 G4
Trinity Business Park
HIA/OLT B92 ....129 H2
The Trinity Catholic
Technology College
RLSN CV32 ....206 B3
Trinity CE Primary School
KNWTH CV8 ....197 K3
Trinity High School &
6th Form College
REDE B98 ....202 D1
Trinity RC School
WWCK CV34 ....206 A7
Tripontium Business Centre
RRUGBY CV23 ....161 L1
Tromans Industrial Estate
DUDS DY2 ....103 H2
Truck Stop Business Park
SPARK B11 ....108 F7
Tudor Business Centre
REDE B98 ....202 C2
Tudor Grange School
SOLH B91 ....148 E3
Tudor Grange
Sports Centre & Pool
SOLH B91 ....148 F2
Tudor Industrial Estate
SPARK B11 ....108 F8
Tulip Inn Hotel
KNWTH CV8 ....198 L1
Turves Green Boys School
NFLD/LBR B31 ....144 E5
Turves Green Girls School
NFLD/LBR B31 ....144 E4
Turves Green Primary School
NFLD/LBR B31 ....144 E4
Tuttle Hill Industrial Estate
NUNW/HART CV10 ....80 C7
Twickenham Primary School
KGSTG B44 ....72 A4
Two Gates Primary School
TAM/AM/WIL B77 ....46 A5
Two Gates Industrial Estate
TAM/AM/WIL B77 ....46 B6
Two Woods Industrial Estate
BRLYHL DY5 ....102 C5
Two Woods Trading Estate
BRLYHL DY5 ....102 D4
Tyburn Industrial Estate
ERDE/BCHGN B24 ....91 H3
Tyseley Industrial Estate
SPARK B11 ....108 C8
Tyseley Locomotive Works Visitor
Centre
SPARK B11 ....108 D8
UCI Cinema
BRLYHL DY5 ....102 C3
CRTAM B79 ....46 A1
SHLY B90 ....148 C6
Uffculme Clinic
MOS/BIL B13 ....125 J3
Uffculme Special School
MOS/BIL B13 ....125 J4
UGC Cinema
DIG/EDG B5 ....7 G7
UGC Cinema
EDG B15 ....6 B8
Ulverley Primary School
HIA/OLT B92 ....127 M5
Underhill J & I School
WOLVN WV10 ....36 F4
Underhill Primary School
WOLVN WV10 ....36 F4
Union Business Park
WSLW WS2 ....4 D4
Unisant Trading Estate
CDYHTH B64 ....103 K3
University of Birmingham
EDG B15 ....106 E8
University of Birmingham
EDG B15 ....124 D2
University of Central England
PBAR/PBCH B42 ....89 H2
University of Warwick
TLHL/CAN CV4 ....179 M1
TLHL/CAN CV4 ....180 A1
University of Warwick
Sports Centre
TLHL/CAN CV4 ....154 A8
University of Wolverhampton
WOLV WV1 ....2 F3
University of Wolverhampton
Wulfrun Campus
DUNHL/THL/PER WV6 ....49 J2
Uplands Cemetery
SMTHWKW B67 ....105 J2
Uplands Junior School
BDMR/CCFT WV3 ....49 H5
Uplands Manor Primary School
SMTHWKW B67 ....105 J2
USAM Trading Estate
WOLVN WV10 ....36 B3
Vale Business Park
STRPT DY13 ....188 F2
Vale Industrial Estate
KIDDW DY11 ....164 A3
Valley Infant School
HIA/OLT B92 ....128 B2
Valley Park Campus
DUNHL/THL/PER WV6 ....35 K8
Vaughan Trading Estate
TPTN/OCK DY4 ....85 M2
Vauxhall Trading Estate
VAUX/NECH B7 ....107 M1
The Vaynor First School
REDW B97 ....202 A6
Vector Industrial Estate
HHTH/SAND B71 ....69 G7
Venkat Medical Centre
STETCH B33 ....110 C2
Ventura Park Shopping Centre
POL/KGSB/FAZ B78 ....45 K2
Ventura Retail Park
POL/KGSB/FAZ B78 ....45 L2
Vernon Trading Estate
RMSLY B62 ....104 A5
Victor Business Centre
REDE B98 ....202 D4
Victoria Business Centre
RLSS CV31 ....206 E6

Victoria Health Centre
SMTHWK B66 ....105 M1
Victoria Infant School
TPTN/OCK DY4 ....67 J8
Victoria Park Primary School
SMTHWK B66 ....87 M8
Victoria School
NFLD/LBR B31 ....123 L8
Villiers Primary School
BILS/COS WV14 ....51 H6
Villiers Trading Estate
BKHL/PFLD WV2 ....50 A6
Viva! Health & Leisure Club
SOLH B91 ....149 G6
Vulcan House Industrial Estate
SOLH B91 ....128 A7
Vulcan Industrial Estate
WSLW WS2 ....39 G7
Wainbody Wood
Special School
TLHL/CAN CV4 ....180 B3
Wake Green FC
SHLY B90 ....147 J5
Walhouse CE Junior School
CNCK/NC WS11 ....16 A4
Walkmill Business Park
CNCK/NC WS11 ....16 A8
Walkwood CE Middle School
REDW B97 ....202 A5
Wallbrook Primary School
BILS/COS WV14 ....67 J5
The Wallows Industrial Estate
BRLYHL DY5 ....84 B8
Wall Roman Site Museum
LICHS WS14 ....28 B5
Walmley CC
WALM/CURD B76 ....73 J6
Walmley Golf Club
CSCFLD/WYGN B72 ....73 G5
Walmley Junior School
WALM/CURD B76 ....73 L6
Walsall Business Park
ALDR WS9 ....40 F8
Walsall Business Park
ALDR WS9 ....54 C1
Walsall CC
WSL WS1 ....5 J8
Walsall College of Arts
& Technology
WSL WS1 ....4 E2
WSLW WS2 ....4 A5
Walsall FC (Bescot Stadium)
WSL WS1 ....53 H8
Walsall Gala Baths
WSL WS1 ....4 F3
Walsall Golf Club
DSYBK/YTR WS5 ....53 M7
Walsall Leather Museum
WSLW WS2 ....4 E1
Walsall Museum & Library
WSL WS1 ....5 G3
Walsall RFC
WSL WS1 ....53 K7
Walsall Wood Primary School
ALDR WS9 ....40 D1
Walsgrave CE Primary School
COVE CV2 ....135 L7
Walsgrave General Hospital
COVE CV2 ....135 L8
Walsgrave Health Centre
COVE CV2 ....135 K7
Walsgrave Retail Park
COVE CV2 ....135 M6
Walsgrave Triangle
Business Park
RCOVN/BALC/EX CV7 ....135 L4
Ward Arms Hotel
DUDN DY1 ....85 K3
Ward End Medical Centre
WASH/WDE B8 ....90 F8
Ward End Primary School
WASH/WDE B8 ....90 F7
Warley High School
LGLYGN/QTN B68 ....104 E3
Warley Infant School
LGLYGN/QTN B68 ....105 G5
Warley Magistrates Court
OLDBY B69 ....86 E6
Warley Woods Golf Club
SMTHWKW B67 ....105 J5
Warren Farm Primary School
KGSTG B44 ....71 M5
Warstones Primary School
ETTPK/GDPK/PENN WV4 ....49 J7
Wartell Bank Industrial Estate
KGSWFD DY6 ....83 H5
Warwick Arms Hotel
WWCK CV34 ....205 J7
Warwick Castle
WWCK CV34 ....205 J7
Warwick CC
WWCK CV34 ....205 H8
Warwick County &
Crown Courts
WWCK CV34 ....205 H7
Warwick Golf Club
WWCK CV34 ....205 H7
Warwick Hospital
WWCK CV34 ....205 J5
Warwick Preparatory School
WWCK CV34 ....205 L7
Warwick Race Course
WWCK CV34 ....205 G7
Warwick Road Trading Estate
SPARK B11 ....126 B1
Warwick School
WWCK CV34 ....205 L7
Warwickshire CCC
(Edgbaston)
DIG/EDG B5 ....107 H8
Warwickshire College
RLSN CV32 ....206 B5
The Warwickshire Golf Club
RWWCK/WEL CV35 ....197 J8
Warwickshire Nuffield Hospital
RLSN CV32 ....198 D1
Warwickshire Racquet &
Health Centre
COVS CV3 ....155 K6
Warwickshire Yeomanry
Museum
WWCK CV34 ....205 J7
Warwick Sports Club
WWCK CV34 ....205 H8
Warwick Technology Park
WWCK CV34 ....205 M8
Waseley Hills Country Park
BRGRVE B61 ....143 G5
Waseley Hills High School
RBRY B45 ....143 H6
Washington Street
Industrial Estate
DUDS DY2 ....103 H2
Washwood Heath
Technology College
WASH/WDE B8 ....91 G4
Waterfall Lane
Trading Estate
CDYHTH B64 ....103 L4

Waterfront Business Park
BRLYHL DY5 ....102 B1
Waterloo Industrial Estate
CBROM B36 ....92 F8
Watermill Primary School
SLYOAK B29 ....124 B2
Water Orton CC
CSHL/WTROR B46 ....92 F2
Water Orton Primary School
CSHL/WTROR B46 ....92 F3
Waterside Industrial Estate
BKHL/PFLD WV2 ....50 E7
BLKHTH/ROWR B65 ....103 K1
Watling Street
Business Park
BLOX/PEL WS3 ....25 L3
Watling Street JMI School
BRWIH WS8 ....26 C1
Wattville Primary School
HDSW B21 ....87 M5
Wattville Road
Industrial Estate
SMTHWK B66 ....87 M6
Waverley School
SMHTH B10 ....108 E5
WCC Sports Ground
WWCK CV34 ....205 M6
Webb Ellis Business Park
RUGBYN/HIL CV21 ....160 F9
Webheath First School
REDW B97 ....201 L3
Webnor Industrial Estate
BKHL/PFLD WV2 ....50 E7
Weddington Industrial Estate
NUNW/HART CV10 ....81 G8
Weddington Primary School
NUNW/HART CV10 ....81 H6
Wedgnock Industrial Estate
WWCK CV34 ....205 G5
Wednesbury Art Gallery
DARL/WED WS10 ....68 D3
Wednesbury Chiropody
Surgery
DARL/WED WS10 ....68 D2
Wednesbury Cricket Club
DARL/WED WS10 ....68 E1
Wednesbury Leisure Centre
DARL/WED WS10 ....68 C3
Wednesbury Medical Centre
DARL/WED WS10 ....68 C3
Wednesbury Oak Primary School
TPTN/OCK DY4 ....67 H4
Wednesbury Rugby Club
DARL/WED WS10 ....68 D3
Wednesbury Town Hall
DARL/WED WS10 ....68 D3
Wednesbury Trading Estate
DARL/WED WS10 ....68 D3
Wednesfield FC
WNSFLD WV11 ....37 G3
Wednesfield High School
WNSFLD WV11 ....37 J8
Wednesfield Village
Primary School
WNSFLD WV11 ....37 H8
Wednesfield Way
Industrial Estate
WNSFLD WV11 ....51 H1
Welfare Clinic
KNWTH CV8 ....197 L1
Welford Primary School
BFLD/HDSWWD B20 ....88 F5
Wellington Industrial Estate
TPTN/OCK DY4 ....67 C6
Welsh House Farm
Primary School
RIDG/WDGT B32 ....123 J3
Welsh RFC
HIA/OLT B92 ....129 G2
Wembrook Primary School
NUN CV11 ....99 G3
Weoley Castle Health Centre
SLYOAK B29 ....123 L4
Weoley Castle Ruins & Museum
SLYOAK B29 ....123 L3
Wergs Golf Club
CDSL WV8 ....34 E6
Westacre Infant School
BDMR/CCFT WV3 ....49 H5
West Bromwich Albion FC
(The Hawthorns)
HHTH/SAND B71 ....87 L4
West Bromwich Dartmouth
Cricket Club
HHTH/SAND B71 ....87 K4
West Bromwich Magistrates
Court
WBROM B70 ....87 G2
West Chadsmoor Clinic
CNCK/NC WS11 ....12 C7
West Croft Special School
& Sports College
WOLVN WV10 ....36 F4
West Cross Shopping Centre
SMTHWK B66 ....87 H6
Western Business Park
RMSLY B62 ....103 M6
Western Business Park
WSNGN B18 ....88 C7
Westfield First School
RUGBYS/DCH CV22 ....186 D3
Westfield Lodge College
RUGBYS/DCH CV22 ....186 D4
Westfield Primary School
WMBN WV5 ....64 G6
West Gate
WWCK CV34 ....205 H7
Westgate Primary School
WWCK CV34 ....205 H8
Westgate Trading Estate
ALDR WS9 ....40 C7
West Heath Hospital
HWK/WKHTH B38 ....145 L4
West Heath J & I School
NFLD/LBR B31 ....145 G4
West Hill Primary School
HEDN WS12 ....12 C7
West House School
EDG B15 ....107 G5
The Westley Hotel
ACGN B27 ....126 F2
Westmead Hotel
ALVE B48 ....170 F1
West Midland Safari &
Leisure Park
BEWD DY12 ....163 J1
West Midlands Hospital
HALE B63 ....103 H8
Westminster Industrial Estate
DUDS DY2 ....103 H3
Westminster Primary School
BFLD/HDSWWD B20 ....89 G4
Westminster School
TPTN/OCK DY4 ....67 L7
Weston Hall Hotel
BDWTH CV12 ....117 M2
West Orchards
Shopping Centre
COV CV1 ....8 E4

West Park Hospital
WOLV WV1 ....2 C4
West Park Primary School
WOLV WV1 ....2 C2
West Side Business Centre
TLHL/CAN CV4 ....153 K5
Westwood Business Park
AST/WIT B6 ....89 M3
TLHL/CAN CV4 ....153 K7
Wharton Park Golf Club
BEWD DY12 ....162 B4
Wharton Street
Industrial Estate
VAUX/NECH B7 ....90 B5
Wheatsheaf Studio Theatre
COVE CV2 ....134 F8
Wheelers Lane J & i School
ALE/KHTH/YWD B14 ....125 K6
Wheelers Lane Technology
College
ALE/KHTH/YWD B14 ....125 K6
Wheeler Street
Shopping Centre
LOZ/NWT B19 ....89 G7
Whetstone Field
Primary School
ALDR WS9 ....54 F1
Whitacre Road Industrial Estate
NUN CV11 ....99 J1
Whitecrest Primary School
GTB/HAM B43 ....70 E3
Whitefriars Friary
COV CV1 ....9 J6
Whitehall Industrial Park
TPTN/OCK DY4 ....68 C8
Whitehall Infant School
WSL WS1 ....4 F9
Whitehall Junior School
WSL WS1 ....5 H9
Whiteheath Clinic
OLDBY B69 ....86 B8
Whitehouse Common
Primary School
MGN/WHC B75 ....57 H6
Whitesmore School
CHWD/FDBR/MGN B37 ...110 D4
Whitestone Clinic
NUN CV11 ....99 L5
Whitestone County
Infant School
NUN CV11 ....99 L5
Whitgreave J & I School
WOLVN WV10 ....36 C5
Whitgreave Primary School
WOLVN WV10 ....22 F6
Whitley Abbey
Community School
COVS CV3 ....155 K7
Whitley Abbey Primary School
COVS CV3 ....155 K7
Whitmore Medical Centre
WOLV WV1 ....2 E2
Whitmore Park J & I School
COVN CV6 ....133 L4
Whitmore Reans
Health Centre
DUNHL/THL/PER WV6 ....2 B1
Whittington Heath Golf Club
LICHS WS14 ....29 M3
Whittington Primary School
LICHS WS14 ....30 C1
Whitworth Industrial Park
BORD B9 ....108 A3
Whoberley Clinic
COVW CV5 ....154 A1
Whoberley Hall
Primary School
COVW CV5 ....154 A2
Wholesale Markets
DIG/EDG B5 ....7 H7
Widney Junior School
SOLH B91 ....148 D4

Wightwick Hall Special School
DUNHL/THL/PER WV6 ......48 C3
Wilden All Saints CE
First School
STRPT DY13 ....164 A8
Wilden Industrial Estate
STRPT DY13 ....164 A7
Wilden Village Cricket Club
STRPT DY13 ....164 B8
Wilkes Green J & I School
HDSW B21 ....88 C4
Wilkinson Primary School
BILS/COS WV14 ....67 K2
Willenhall Industrial Estate
WLNHL WV13 ....52 A2
Willenhall Lane
Industrial Estate
WLNHL WV13 ....38 E5
Willenhall Leisure Centre
WLNHL WV13 ....51 M4
Willenhall Town FC
WLNHL WV13 ....51 K2
Willenhall Trading Estate
WLNHL WV13 ....51 K4
Willenhall Wood
Primary School
COVS CV3 ....156 B7
William Baxter Special School
HEDN WS12 ....12 E7
William Cowper Primary School
LOZ/NWT B19 ....89 J7
William Hanke Industrial Estate
BRLYHL DY5 ....102 C4
William Macgregor
Primary School
TAM/AM/WIL B77 ....46 B2
Willingsworth High School
TPTN/OCK DY4 ....67 M3
Willows Primary School
WSL WS1 ....20 F3
Wilnecote Health Centre
TAM/AM/WIL B77 ....46 D6
Wilnecote Junior School
TAM/AM/WIL B77 ....46 D6
Wilnecote School
TAM/AM/WIL B77 ....46 D7
Wilson Stuart Special School
ERDW/GRVHL B23 ....72 A7
Wiltell Road Industrial Estate
LICH WS13 ....20 F6
The Windmill CE Middle School
STRPT DY13 ....188 C4
Windmill Hill (look out)
RBRY B45 ....143 G5
Windmill Industrial Estate
COVW CV5 ....132 D6
Windmill Village Golf &
Leisure Club
COVW CV5 ....132 D6
Windmill Works Industrial Park
DUDS DY2 ....84 F6
Windsor High School
HALE B63 ....121 K1
Windsor Industrial Estate
VAUX/NECH B7 ....89 L8
Winward Way
Industrial Estate
CBROM B36 ....92 D5
Windy Arbor Primary School
CHWD/FDBR/MGN B37 ...111 H2
Winster Grove
Industrial Centre
KGSTG B44 ....71 H3
KGSTG B44 ....71 J3
Winterfold House School
KIDD DY10 ....165 L5
Winyates Health Centre
REDE B98 ....203 J2
Wishaw CC
WALM/CURD B76 ....74 E3
Witherley CE Primary School
ATHST CV9 ....63 M6

Witherley United FC
ATHST CV9 ....63 L5
Withymoor Primary School
BRLYHL DY5 ....102 B4
Withy Road
Industrial Estate
BILS/COS WV14 ....67 G2
Witton Industrial Estate
AST/WIT B6 ....89 L3
Witton Park
Industrial Estate
AST/WIT B6 ....89 L4
Woden Primary School
WOLVN WV10 ....3 J1
Wodensborough Community
Technology College
DARL/WED WS10 ....68 F3
Wodensfield Primary School
WNSFLD WV11 ....36 F7
Wolgarston School
PENK ST19 ....10 E5
Wollescote Business Park
HAG/WOL DY9 ....102 D8
Wollescote Primary School
HAG/WOL DY9 ....120 D1
Wolston Business Park
KNWTH CV8 ....183 L1
Wolverhampton CC
DUNHL/THL/PER WV6 ......35 G7
Wolverhampton Central Baths
WOLV WV1 ....2 D4
Wolverhampton College
(Bilston Campus)
WOLV WV1 ....50 F6
Wolverhampton Girls
High School
DUNHL/THL/PER WV6 ......49 K2
Wolverhampton
Grammar School
BDMR/CCFT WV3 ....49 K3
Wolverhampton Healthcare
NHS Trust
WOLV WV1 ....50 F1
The Wolverhampton
Nuffield Hospital
DUNHL/THL/PER WV6 ......49 G1
Wolverhampton Racecourse
DUNHL/THL/PER WV6 ......35 L7
Wolverhampton University
WOLVN WV10 ....36 A7
Wolverhampton Wanderers FC
(Molineux Stadium)
WOLV WV1 ....2 E2
Wolverley High School
KIDDW DY11 ....138 B1
Wolverley Sebright
First School
KIDDW DY11 ....138 B2
Wombourne Cricket Tennis
& Bowling Club
WMBN WV5 ....64 E6
Wombrook Business Centre
WMBN WV5 ....64 C6
Wombrook Industrial Estate
WMBN WV5 ....64 C7
Woodbourne Priory Hospital
HRBN B17 ....106 A4
Woodcock Hill
Primary School
NFLD/LBR B31 ....123 J6
Woodcock Sports Centre
CBHAMNE B4 ....7 K2
Woodcross Clinic
BILS/COS WV14 ....66 E3
Wood End Health Centre
COVE CV2 ....135 G4
Wood End Primary School
COVE CV2 ....135 H4
Wood End Primary School
POL/KGSB/FAZ B78 ....60 F4
Wood End Primary School
WNSFLD WV11 ....37 G6

Woodfield J&ischool
BDMR/CCFT WV3 ....49 K7
Woodfield Middle School
REDE B98 ....202 E3
Woodgate Business Park
RIDG/WDGT B32 ....122 F5
Woodgate Primary School
RIDG/WDGT B32 ....122 F4
Woodgate Valley
RIDG/WDGT B32 ....123 G1
Woodgate Valley
Health Centre
RIDG/WDGT B32 ....123 G3
Wood Green High School
College of Sport
DARL/WED WS10 ....52 F8
Wood Green Junior School
DARL/WED WS10 ....68 D1
Woodhouse High School &
Community Sports Centre
TAM/AM/WIL B77 ....46 D1
Woodhouse J & I School
RIDG/WDGT B32 ....105 J7
Woodlands Cemetery
CSHL/WTROR B46 ....93 G8
Woodlands Infant School
SHLY B90 ....147 M5
Woodlands Primary School
SHHTH WV12 ....38 B7
Woodlands Primary School
TAM/AM/WIL B77 ....46 C1
The Woodlands School
TLHL/CAN CV4 ....153 H2
Woodloes J & I School
WWCK CV34 ....205 J4
Woodrow First School
REDE B98 ....202 F6
The Woodrush High School
HLYWD B47 ....146 E7
Woodrush RFC
HWK/WKHTH B38 ....171 M1
The Woodsbank Industrial Estate
DARL/WED WS10 ....68 B1
The Woodsbank Trading Estate
DARL/WED WS10 ....68 B1
The Woodsetton Special School
SEDG DY3 ....66 D6
Woodside Business Park
RUGBYN/HIL CV21 ....160 E8
Woodside Industrial Estate
BRLYHL DY5 ....84 D8
Woodside Medical Centre
TLHL/CAN CV4 ....153 K3
Woodstock Girls School
BHTH/HG B12 ....125 L1
Woodthorpe Primary School
ALE/KHTH/YWD B14 ....125 J8
Woodview Primary School
EDG B5 ....107 G5
Woodway Park
Community School
COVE CV2 ....135 K3
Worcester Street Surgery
STRBR DY8 ....101 L8
Wordsley Green Health Centre
STRBR DY8 ....101 H3
Wordsley Green
Shopping Centre
STRBR DY8 ....101 H3
Wordsley Hospital
STRBR DY8 ....101 J2
Works Trading Estate
SMTHWK B66 ....87 L6
Worlds End J & I School
RIDG/WDGT B32 ....105 J8
The Worsley School
STRBR DY8 ....101 K2
Wren's Nest National
Nature Reserve
DUDN DY1 ....84 F1
Wrens Nest Primary School
DUDN DY1 ....84 E1

Wribbenhall First School
BEWD DY12 ....137 G8
Wribbenhall Middle School
BEWD DY12 ....163 G2
Wrottesley Hall
CDSL WV8 ....34 A5
Wulfrun Shopping Centre
WOLV WV1 ....2 E5
Wulfrun Trading Estate
DUNHL/THL/PER WV6 ......36 A8
Wychall Farm Primary School
NFLD/LBR B31 ....145 G3
Wyken Croft Primary School
COVE CV2 ....135 J8
Wyken Medical Centre
COVE CV2 ....134 F7
Wylde Green Primary School
SCFLD/BOLD B73 ....72 F6
Wyley Brook Retail Park
CNCK/NC WS11 ....16 B7
Wyndcliffe Primary School
BORD B9 ....108 B4
Wyndley Leisure Centre
SCFLD/BOLD B73 ....56 E8
Wyndley Swimming Baths
SCFLD/BOLD B73 ....72 E1
Wynford Industrial
Trading Estate
ACGN B27 ....109 G8
Wynford Road
Industrial Estate
ACGN B27 ....109 G8
Wyre Forest Golf Club
STRPT DY13 ....163 K5
Wythall Health Centre
HLYWD B47 ....146 E6
Yardley Cemetery
LGN/SDN/BHAMAIR B26 .109 H8
Yardley Green Health Centre
BORD B9 ....108 D4
Yardley Green Medical Centre
SMHTH B10 ....108 A5
Yardley J & I School
LGN/SDN/BHAMAIR B26 .109 H6
Yardley Medical Centre
YDLY B25 ....108 F6
Yardleys School
SPARK B11 ....126 C2
Yardleys Secondary School
SPARK B11 ....126 D1
Yardley Wood Health Centre
ALE/KHTH/YWD B14 ....126 A8
Yardley Wood Primary School
ALE/KHTH/YWD B14 ....147 H1
Yarnfield Primary School
SPARK B11 ....126 E2
Yenton Infant School
ERDE/BCHGN B24 ....72 F7
Yenton Junior School
ERDE/BCHGN B24 ....72 F8
Yew Tree Community
Junior School
AST/WIT B6 ....89 L4
Yew Tree Medical Centre
DSYBK/YTR WS5 ....69 M1
Yew Tree Primary School
SOLH B91 ....128 C8
York House Medical Centre
STRPT DY13 ....188 D2
York Mead Primary School
HLGN/YWD B28 ....126 C3
Yorks Wood Primary School
CHWD/FDBR/MGN B37 ....92 D8
Zip Theatre
WOLV WV1 ....2 D2

Acknowledgements

The Post Office is a registered trademark of Post Office Ltd. in the UK and other countries.

Schools address data provided by Education Direct.

Petrol station information supplied by Johnsons

One-way street data provided by © Tele Atlas N.V. *Tele Atlas*

Garden centre information provided by:

Garden Centre Association   Britains best garden centres

Wyevale Garden Centres

 **Street by Street**

QUESTIONNAIRE

Dear Atlas User

Your comments, opinions and recommendations are very important to us. So please help us to improve our street atlases by taking a few minutes to complete this simple questionnaire.

You do NOT need a stamp (unless posted outside the UK). If you do not want to remove this page from your street atlas, then photocopy it or write your answers on a plain sheet of paper.

Send to: The Editor, AA Street by Street, FREEPOST SCE 4598, Basingstoke RG21 4GY

ABOUT THE ATLAS...

Which city/town/county did you buy?

Are there any features of the atlas or mapping that you find particularly useful?

Is there anything we could have done better?

Why did you choose an AA Street by Street atlas?

Did it meet your expectations?

Exceeded ☐ **Met all** ☐ **Met most** ☐ **Fell below** ☐

Please give your reasons

continued overleaf

Where did you buy it?

For what purpose? (please tick all applicable)

To use in your own local area ☐   **To use on business or at work** ☐

Visiting a strange place ☐   **In the car** ☐   **On foot** ☐

Other (please state)

LOCAL KNOWLEDGE...

Local knowledge is invaluable. Whilst every attempt has been made to make the information contained in this atlas as accurate as possible, should you notice any inaccuracies, please detail them below (if necessary, use a blank piece of paper) or e-mail us at *streetbystreet@theAA.com*

ABOUT YOU...

Name (Mr/Mrs/Ms)

Address

                                             Postcode

Daytime tel no

E-mail address

Which age group are you in?

Under 25 ☐   **25-34** ☐   **35-44** ☐   **45-54** ☐   **55-64** ☐   **65+** ☐

Are you an AA member?   **YES** ☐   **NO** ☐

Do you have Internet access?   **YES** ☐   **NO** ☐

Thank you for taking the time to complete this questionnaire. Please send it to us as soon as possible, and remember, you do not need a stamp (unless posted outside the UK).

MX035z

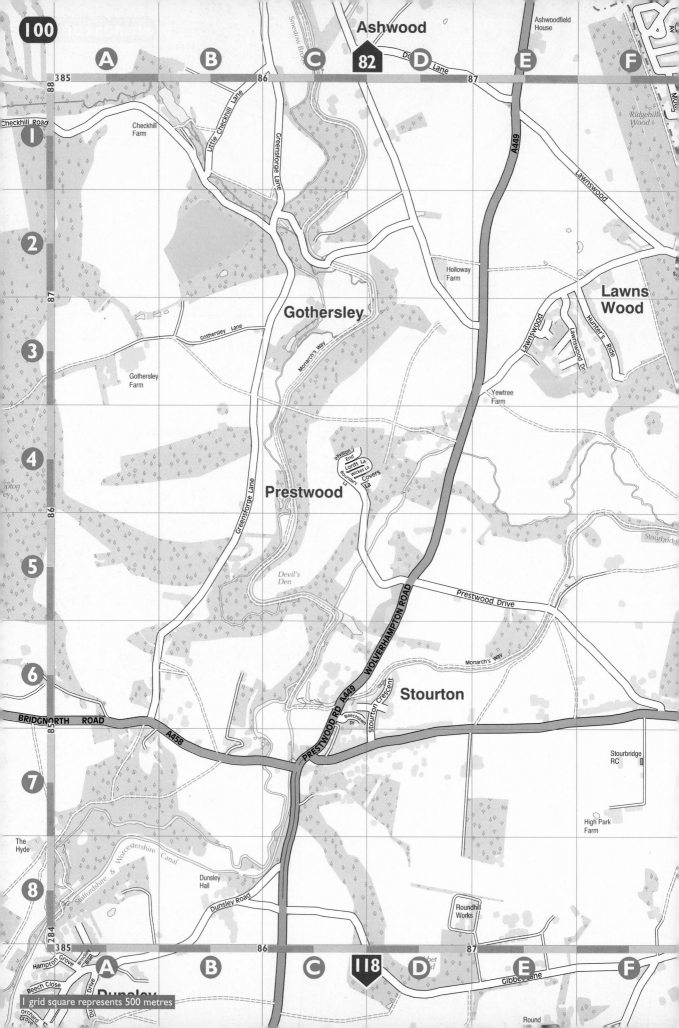

A B C **78** D E F

NUNEATON ROAD B4114

B4112

Ansley

St Law Rd
Surg

Monwode House Farm

Ballard's Green

Bourne Brook

Hood Lane Farm

Brook House Farm

Arley Wood

Ansley La

Arley Hall Farm

Herbert Fowler Junior School

Church

Church Lane

Old Arley

Arley House Farm

Oakridge Golf Club

Golf Course

Hill Top

Elm Cv
Oak Av
Ash Cv
Beech Cv

Arley Sports Centre

Woodside

Meadow Cft
Rowland Ct

Rectory Road
Bournebrook Vw

Devitts Green

Station Road

Spring Hill

Spinney Cl

Colliers Way

Arley Industrial Estate

Frederick Road

Arley Industrial Estate

Spring Hill Industrial Estate

Hollick Cft
Mullein Way
Morgan Close
Ryder Av
Daffern Avenue
Firtree Lane
George Street
Charles Street
Ransome Road
Gun Hill
Sycamore Crescent
Herth Av

New Arley

St Michael's Close
Lichfield Close
Fourfields Way

Gun Hill Infant School

PO

TAMWORTH ROAD B4098

95

Stonehouse Lane

Spring Hill

Gun Hill

Spring Hill Medical Centre

Lamp Lane

Slowley Hall

Tipper's Hill Lane

Fillongley Lodge

Tamworth

Tipper's Hill

The Uplands

PARK LANE

B4102

Wood End

bury Lane

Mill Lane
Hall Lane

TAMWORTH ROAD B4098

A B C **114** D WOOD END ROAD E Wood End Lane F

Fillongley Hall

Berryfields

Castle Hills

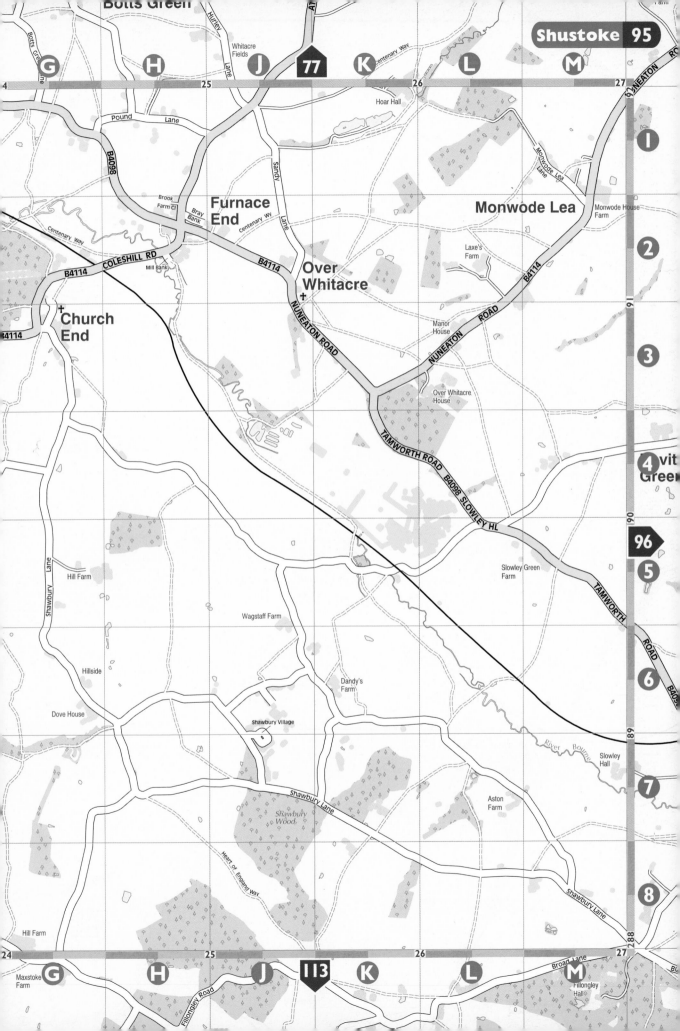

G **H** **J** 75 **K** **L** **M**

8 19 20 21

Marsh Lane
Road
Newlands Farm
Avenue
Works
Canton Lane
Works

Hams Hall National Distribution Park

River Tame
LANE B4118
Coleshill Road
Faraday
Avenue

2

Salisbury Dr
Overton Drive
George Road
Edward Rd
Maud Rd
Industrial Estate
Jack o' Watton Business Park
Edison Road
Hams Hall International Freight Terminal

COLESHILL ROAD
WATTON LANE
Gypsy Lane
Park Dr
Turnpike
Coleshill Road
Gorsey Lane
Roman Way
Industrial Estate
Coleshill Industrial Estate
River Cole

3

Blaise Lane
Chattle Hill
Chattle Hill
Imperial Rise
Brutus Dr
Caesar Way
Stn Road Industrial Est
Coleshill Industrial Estate
Station Road
River Blythe

4

Junction 8
Gilson
Grimstock Country House Hotel
Augustus Cl
Centurion
Julius Dr
Temple
Trajan Hl
Station Rd Ind Estate

LICHFIELD ROAD A446
GILSON ROAD
GILSON ROAD B4117
LICHFIELD ROAD
High Meadow Infant School
Norton Road
Rose Road
James Rd
Davis

94 ► Blyth Bridge

5

Gilson Drive
Coleshill Hall Farm
Cole End
Old Mill Rd
High Brink Road
Ravenswood
Works
Council Building
Chestnut Cl
Orchard Av
St Paul's Wk
Church Hill
BLYTHE ROAD

6

M6 (Toll)
STONEBRIDGE ROAD
A446
South Dr
Park Road
Parkfield Rd
Coleshill Leisure Centre
HIGH STREET
Cemetery
COLESHILL
B4114

7

M6
Woodlands Cemetery
BIRMINGHAM RD B4114
Police Station
Digby Rd
Clinton Rd
Coleshill CE Primary School
Hudson Av
Town Hall
Council Building Coleshill Clinic
Maxstoke Lane
St Gerards Orthopaedic Hospital
B4117
St Edwards RC Primary School

8

B4114 BIRMINGHAM ROAD
STONEBRIDGE ROAD
Wingfield Rd
Montfort Rd
Green La
Castle Drive
Green La
Wall
Springfields
Brendan Close
Blythe Special School

A452
Clopton Crs
Solihull
River Cole
Hall Wk
The
Southfields Farm

1 grid square represents 500 metres

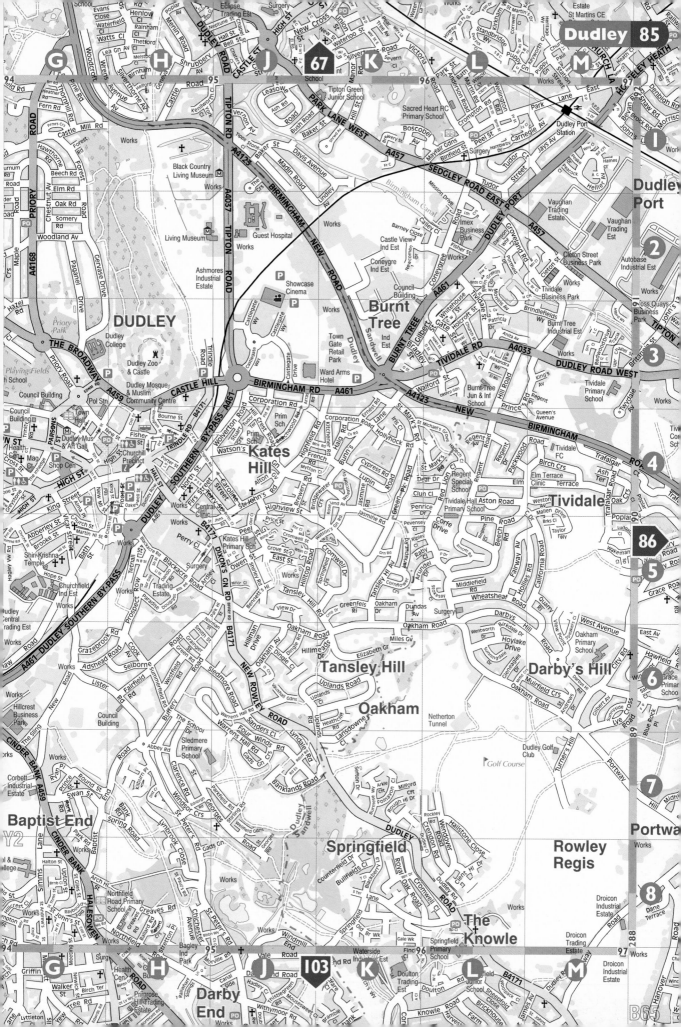

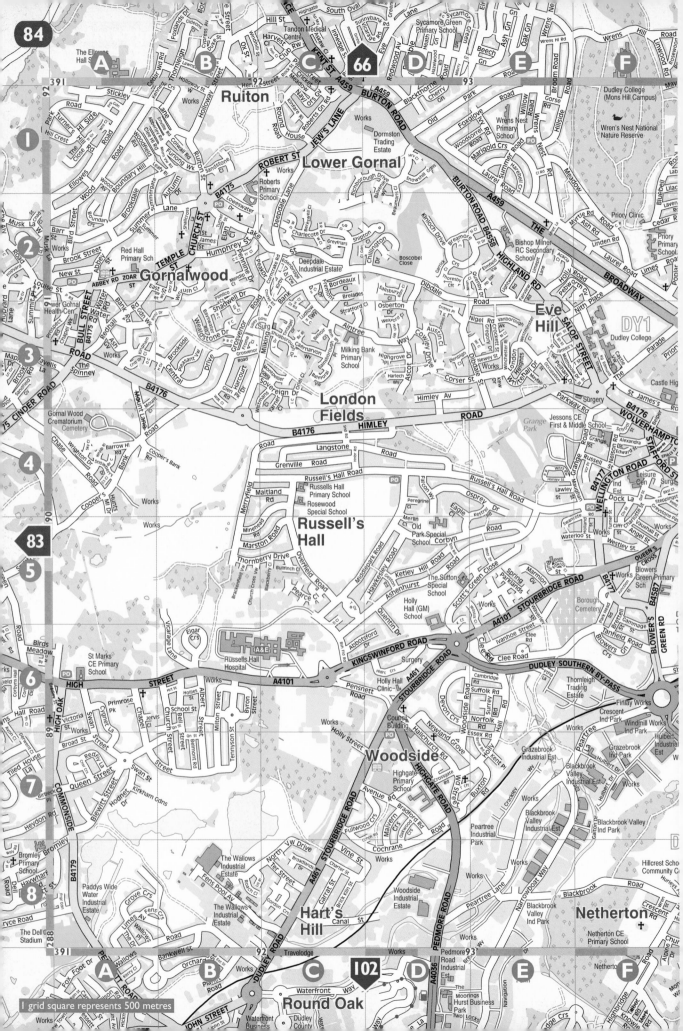

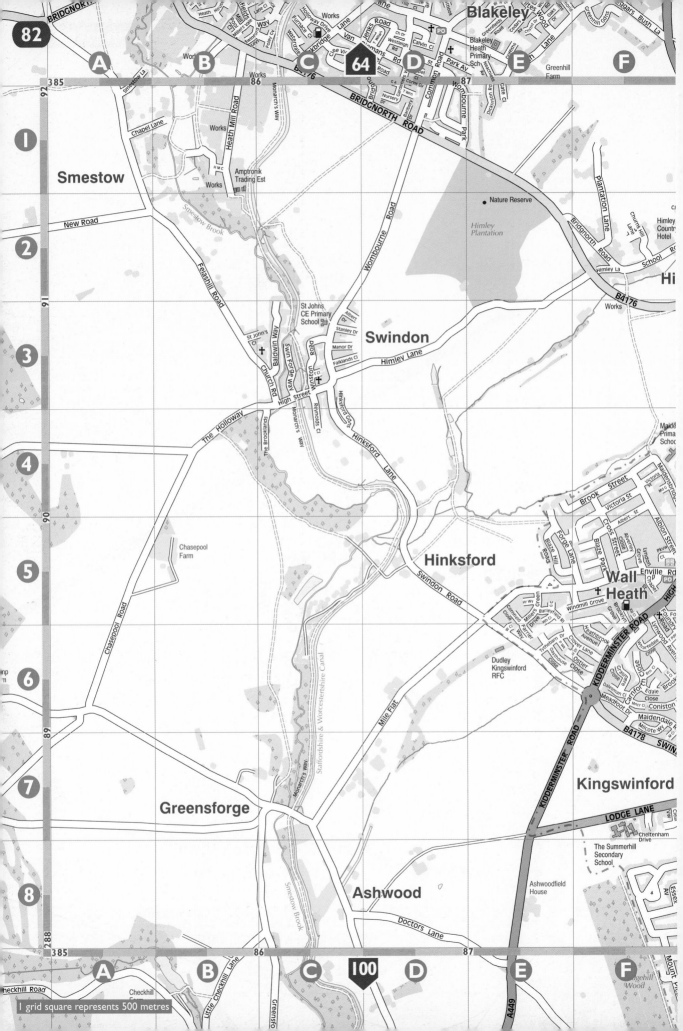